Graphis Inc. is committed to celebrating exceptional work in Design, Advertising, Photography, & Art/Illustration internationally.

Published by **Graphis** | Publisher & Creative Director: **B. Martin Pedersen**

Chief Visionary Officer: **Patti Judd** | Design Director: **Hee Ra Kim** | Senior Designer: **Hie Won Sohn** | Associate Editor: **Colleen Boyd**

Interns: **Lindsay Gregson, Shaylah Lloyd, Elizabeth Rost, Yuanduo Wang** | Account/Production: **Bianca Barnes**

Published by:
Graphis Inc.
389 Fifth Avenue, Suite 1105
New York, NY 10016
Phone: 212-532-9387
www.graphis.com
help@graphis.com

ISBN 13: 978-1-954632-14-1

We extend our heartfelt thanks to the international contributors who have made it possible to publish a wide spectrum of the best work in Design, Advertising, Photography, and Art/Illustration. Anyone is welcome to submit work at www.graphis.com.

Printed in China

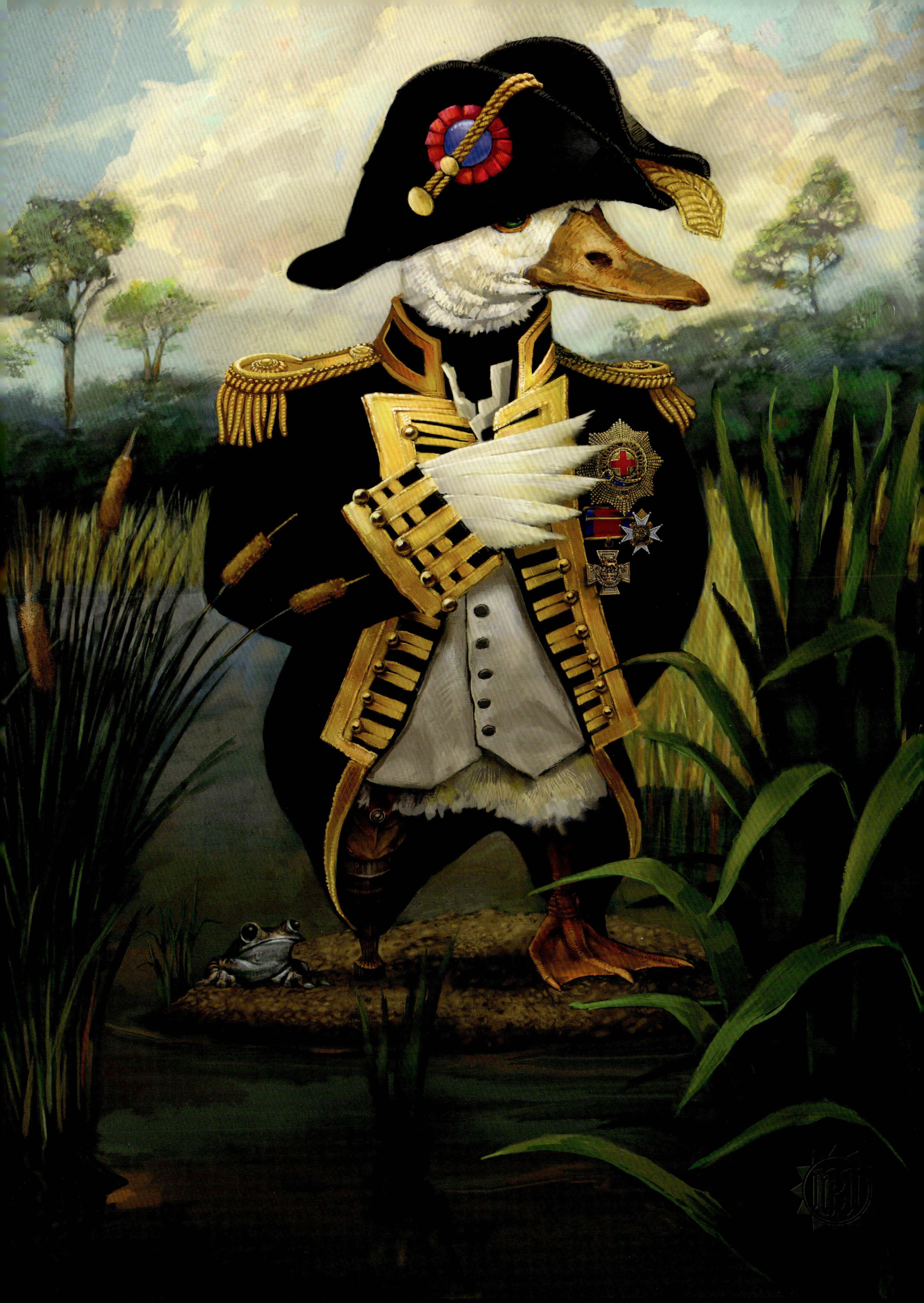

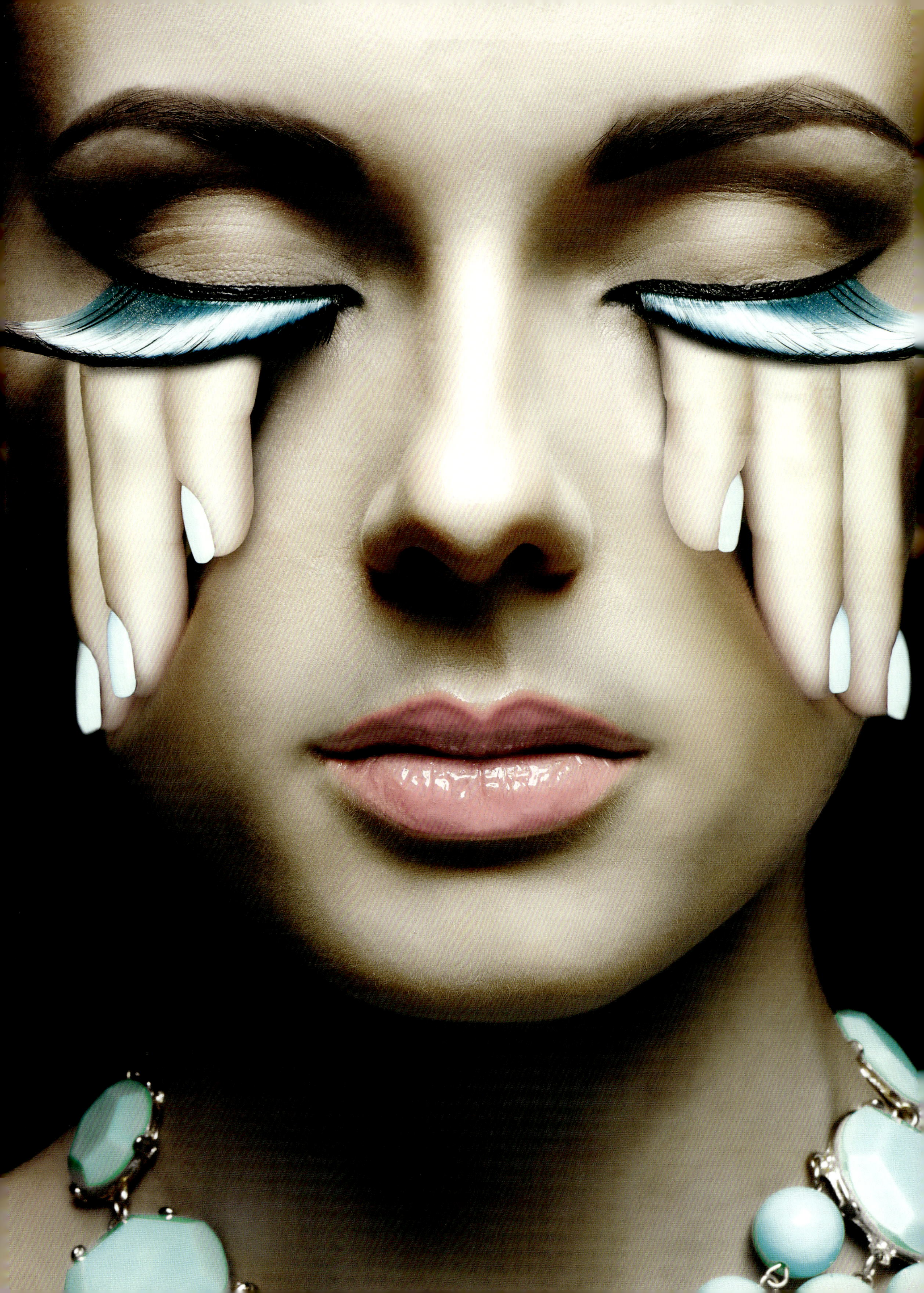

Contents

Page 3: *"Strange Ducks,"* designed by Mark Braught Studios
Page 4: *"Intertwined,"* designed by Carmit Design Studio

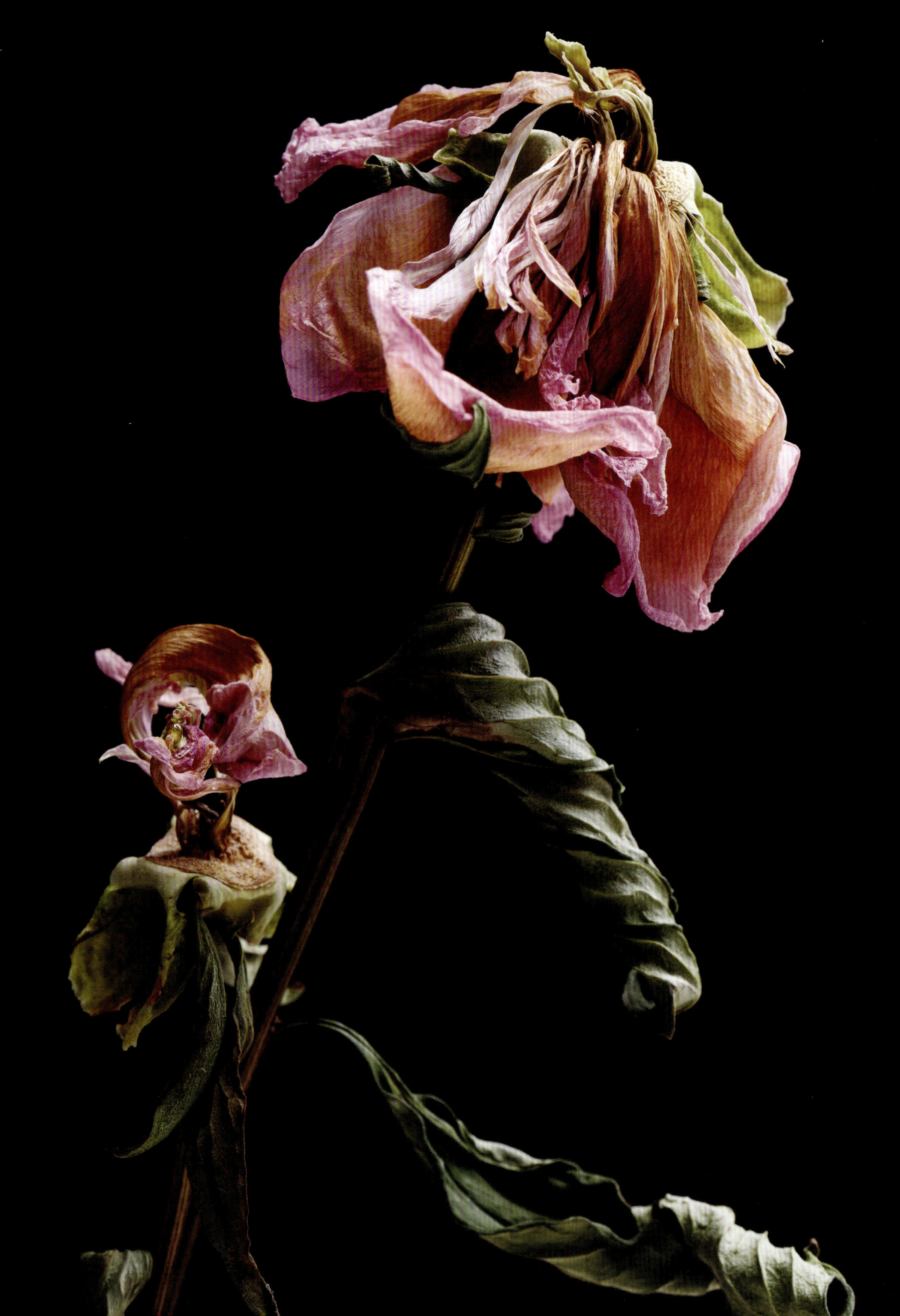

AMERICAS

Virgil Abloh
American Fashion Designer
1980-2021

Christopher Alexander
British-American Architect & Design Theorist
1936-2022

Marshall Arisman
American Illustrator & Art Professor
1938-2022

James Bama
American Artist & Book Cover Illustrator
1926-2022

Ashley Brian
American Illustrator & Author
1923-2022

Augusto Cicaré
Argentine Inventor, Engineer, & Aviation Designer
1937-2022

Chuck Close
American Artist
1940-2021

Charles Csuri
American Artist
1922-2022

Cathy Daley
Canadian Visual Artist & Educator
1955-2022

Janet Doub Erickson
American Graphic Artist & Writer
1924-2021

Bob Gill *
American Graphic Designer & Illustrator
1931-2021

Stan Gomberg
American Cartoonist & Graphic Designer
1927-2022

Alan Heller
American Housewares Designer
1940-2021

Adé Hogue
American Graphic Designer & Art Director
1989-2021

Louis "Bud" Jacobs
American Graphic Artist & Teacher
1933-2022

Radhika Khanna
Indian-American Fashion Designer, Entrepreneur, & Author
1974-2022

Carmen Herrera
Cuban-American Artist
1915-2022

Lance Hosey
American Architect & Sustainable Design Advocate
1965-2021

Hung Liu
Chinese-American Artist
1948-2021

Chris Madden
American Home Furnishings Designer
1948-2022

Ardina Moore
American Quapaw-Osage Fashion Designer
1930-2022

Gyo Obata
Japanese-American Architect & Co-founder of HOK
1923-2022

Jerry Pinkney
American Illustrator
1939-2021

Clark Richert
American Geometric Designer & Artist
1941-2021

Bill Robinson
American Industrial Designer
1926-2022

Richard Rogers
American Architect
1933- 2022

Bill Sadler
Canadian Racecar & Aircraft Designer
1931-2022

Adolfo Faustino Sardiña
Cuban-American Fashion Designer
1923-2021

Ilona Royce Smithkin
Polish-American Artist
1920-2021

Keith Taylor
American Cartoonist & Graphic Designer
1949-2021

Henriette Valium
Canadian Comic Book Artist & Painter
1959-2021

Tony Walton
American Film & Theater Designer
1935-2022

Frankie Welch
American Fashion Designer
1924-2021

Eberhard Zeidler
German-Canadian Architect
1926-2022

EUROPE & AFRICA

Elizabeth Blackadder
Scottish Painter & Printmaker
1913-2021

Ricardo Bofill
Spanish Architect
1940-2022

Oriol Bohigas
Catalan Architect
1925-2021

Calvi
French Cartoonist, Caricaturist, & Illustrator
1938-2022

Federica Cavenati
Italian Fashion Designer
1993-2021

Clive Collins
British Cartoonist & Illustrator
1942-2022

Riccardo Dalisi
Italian Architect & Designer
1931-2022

Pauline Deltour
French Industrial Designer
1983-2021

Guy de Rougemont
French Painter & Furniture Designer
1935-2021

Johanna Ekström
Swedish Author & Artist
1970-2022

Colin Forbes *
British Graphic Designer
1928-2022

Ezio Frigerio
Italian Costume Designer & Art Director
1930-2022

Christian Gasc
French Costume Designer
1945-2022

Robert Gillmor
British Wildlife Artist & Illustrator
1936-2022

Michel Goma
French Fashion Designer & Director of Balenciaga
1932-2022

Shirley Hughes
British Illustrator
1928-2022

Ian Kennedy
British Comic Book Artist
1932-2022

Clive Lee
British Design Engineer
1939-2021

Owen Luder
British Architect
1928-2021

Fedor Madurov
Russian Sculptor & Graphic Artist
1942-2022

Henry Mavrodin
Romanian Painter, Designer, & Essayist
1937-2022

Niall McCullough
Irish Architect & Author
1958-2021

Jean-Claude Mézières
French Comic Book Artist & Illustrator
1938-2022

Antonio Miró
Spanish Fashion Designer
1947-2022

Thierry Mugler
French Fashion Designer
1948-2021

Hermann Nitsch
Austrian Artist
1938-2022

Lyubov Panchenko
Ukrainian Visual Artist & Fashion Designer
1938-2022

Michel Quarez
Syrian-French Painter & Poster Artist
1938-2021

Richard Rogers
Italian-British Architect
1933-2021

Thomas Ryan
Irish Artist & Designer
1929-2021

Tony Walton
British Set & Costume Designer
1934-2022

Rolf Zehetbauer
German Production Designer
1929-2022

ASIA & OCEANIA

Yevgeny Aryeh
Israeli Theater Director, Playwright, & Set Designer
1947-2022

Kambiz Derambakhsh
Iranian Graphic Designer
1942-2021

Hiroshi Hirata
Japanese Artist
1937-2021

Issey Miyake
Japanese Fashion Designer
1938-2022

Baruch Nachshon
Israeli Artist
1939-2021

Akhtar Rasool
Indian Graphic Designer
1980-2021

Barbara Sansoni
Sri Lankan Artist, Designer, & Writer
1928-2022

Mirian Shvelidze
Georgian Stage Designer & Painter
1947-2022

Hossein Valamanesh
Iranian-Australian Artist
1949-2022

Emi Wada
Japanese Costume Designer
1937-2021

* Bob Gill passed away last year, and Alan Fletcher passed away in 2006; along with Colin Forbes, all three started Fletcher, Forbes and Gill, which was the originator of Pentagram

Opposite page: *"After the bloom,"* photographed by Beth Galton

THE AMERICAS

A+D Architecture and Design Museum
www.aplusd.org
900 E. 4th St.
Los Angeles, CA
United States
Tel +1 424 221 9818

Alfredo Guati Rojo National Watercolor Museum
www.acuarela.org.mx
C. Salvador Novo 88, Santa Catarina
Coyoacán, 04010 Ciudad de México, CDMX
Mexico
Tel +52 55 5554 1801

Aspen Art Museum
www.aspenartmuseum.org
637 E. Hyman Ave.
Aspen, CO 81611
United States
Tel +1 970 925 8050

CAM Raleigh
www.camraleigh.org
409 W. Martin St.
Raleigh, NC 27603
United States
Tel +1 919 261 5920

Carnegie Museum of Art
www.cmoa.org
4400 Forbes Ave
Pittsburgh, PA 15213
United States
Tel +1 412 622 3131

Cleveland Museum of Art
www.clevelandart.org
11150 East Blvd.
Cleveland, OH 44106
United States
Tel +1 216 421 7350

Clyfford Still Museum
www.clyffordstillmuseum.org
1250 Bannock St.
Denver, CO 80204
United States
Tel +1 720 354 4880

Cranbrook Art Museum
www.cranbrookartmuseum.org
39221 Woodward Ave. Box 801
Bloomfield Hills, MI 48303
United States
Tel +1 248 645 3323

David and Alfred Smart Museum of Art
www.smartmuseum.uchicago.edu
5550 S. Greenwood Ave.
Chicago, IL 60637
United States
Tel +1 773 702 0200

Design Exchange
www.elevate.ca/book-your-event
234 Bay St.
Toronto, ON M5K 1B2
Canada
Tel +1 647 643 4585

Diablo Rosso
www.diablorosso.com
Avenida Central and Parque de Santa Ana
Rep. of Panama
Panama
Tel +507 212 0832

Eli and Edythe Broad Art Museum
www.broadmuseum.msu.edu
547 E. Circle Drive
East Lansing, MI 48824
United States
Tel +1 517 884 4800

Hamilton Wood Type and Printing Museum
www.woodtype.org
1816 10th St.
Two Rivers, WI 54241
United States
Tel +1 920 794 6272

Hammer Museum
www.hammer.ucla.edu
10899 Wilshire Blvd.
Los Angeles, CA 90024
United States
Tel +1 310 443 7000

Harvard Art Museum
www.harvardartmuseums.org
32 Quincy St.
Cambridge, MA 02138
United States
Tel +1 617 495 9400

High Museum of Art
www.high.org
1280 Peachtree St. NE.
Atlanta, GA 30309
United States
Tel +1 404 733 4400

Katonah Museum of Art
www.katonahmuseum.org
134 Jay St.
Katonah, NY 10536
United States
Tel +1 914 232 9555

MacKenzie Art Gallery
www.mckenziefineart.com
55 Orchard St.
New York, NY 10002
United States
Tel +1 212 989 5467

Madsonian Museum of Industrial Design
www.madsonian.org
45 Bridge St.
Waitsfield, VT 05673
United States
Tel +1 802 496 6611

MALBA, Fundación Constantini, Buenos Aires
www.malba.org.ar
Av. Figueroa Alcorta 3415
C1425CLA Buenos Aires
Argentina
Tel +54 11 4808 6500

Morris Museum
www.morrismuseum.org
6 Normandy Heights Road
Morristown, NJ 07960
United States
Tel +1 973 971 3700

Museo de Arte Contemporanea da Universidade, Sao Paulo
www.mac.usp.br/mac
Av. Pedro Álvares Cabral, 1301 - Vila Mariana
São Paulo - SP, 04094-050
Brazil
Tel +55 11 2648 0254

Museo de Arte de El Salvador
www.museomarte.org
Colonia San Benito,
Final Avenida la Revolución
San Salvador
El Salvador
Tel +503 2243 6099

Museo de Arte Popular
www.map.cdmx.gob.mx
Revillagigedo 11,
Colonia Centro, Centro,
Cuauhtémoc
06050 Ciudad de México, CDMX
Mexico
Tel +52 55 5510 2201

Museo de la Estampa
www.museonacionaldelaestampa.inba.gob.mx
Av. Hidalgo 39, Centro Histórico de la Cdad. de México, Guerrero, Cuauhtémoc
06050 Ciudad de México, CDMX
Mexico
Tel +52 55 8647 5220

Museum of Craft and Design
www.madmuseum.org
2 Columbus Circle
New York, NY 10019
United States
Tel +1 212 299 7777

Museum of Design Atlanta
www.museumofdesign.org
1315 Peachtree St. NE.
Atlanta, GA 30309
United States
Tel +1 404 979 6455

Muskegon Museum of Art
www.muskegonartmuseum.org
296 W. Webster Ave.
Muskegon, MI 49440
United States
Tel +1 231 720 2570

National Academy of Design
www.nationalacademy.org
15 Gramercy Park S.
New York, NY 10003
United States
Tel +1 212 369 4880

National Building Museum
www.nbm.org
401 F St. NW.
Washington, D.C. 20001
United States
Tel +1 202 272 2448

Norman Rockwell Museum
www.nrm.org
9 Glendale Road
Stockbridge, MA 01262
United States
Tel +1 413 298 4100

Philbrook Museum of Art
www.philbrook.org
2727 S. Rockford Road
Tulsa, OK 74114
United States
Tel +1 918 748 5300

Poster House
www.posterhouse.org
119 W. 23rd St.
New York, NY 10011
United States
Tel +1 917 722 2439

The Branch Museum of Architecture and Design
www.branchmuseum.org
2501 Monument Ave.
Richmond, VA 23220
United States
Tel +1 804 655 6055

EUROPE AND AFRICA

ARoS Aarhus Kunstmuseum
www.aros.dk/da
Aros Allé 2
8000 Aarhus
Denmark
Tel +45 87 30 66 00

Astrup Fearnley Museum of Modern Art
www.afmuseet.no
Strandpromenaden 2
0252 Oslo
Norway
Tel +47 22 93 60 60

Designmuseum Denmark
www.designmuseum.dk
Bredgade 68
1260 København
Denmark
Tel +45 33 18 56 56

Die Neue Sammlung
www.dnstdm.de
Barer Str. 40
80333 München
Germany
Tel +49 89 272 725 560

Everard Read
www.everard-read.co.za
6 Jellicoe Ave.
Rosebank, Johannesburg, 2196
South Africa
Tel +27 11 788 4805

Fondation Galeries Lafayette
www.lafayetteanticipations.com
9 Rue du Plâtre
75004 Paris
France
Tel +33 1 42 74 95 59

Fundació Miró Mallorca
www.miromallorca.com
C/ de Saridakis, 29
07015 Palma, Illes Balears
Spain
Tel +34 971 70 14 20

Guggenheim Museum Bilbao
www.guggenheim-bilbao.eus
Avenida Abandoibarra, 2
48009 Bilbao
Spain
Tel +34 944 35 90 00

Iziko South African National Gallery
www.iziko.org.za/museums/south-african-national-gallery
Government Ave.
Gardens, Cape Town, 8001
South Africa
Tel +27 21 481 3970

Kunsthaus Graz
www.museum-joanneum.at/kunsthaus-graz
Lendkai 1
8020 Graz
Austria
Tel +43 316 8017 9200

Mode Museum
www.momu.be
Nationalestraat 28
2000 Antwerp
Belgium
Tel +32 0 3 470 2770

Moderna Museet
www.modernamuseet.se/stockholm
Exercisplan 4
111 49 Stockholm
Sweden
Tel +46 8 520 235 00

Musée Salvatore Ferragamo
www.ferragamo.com/museo
Piazza di Santa Trinita
5R, 50123 Firenze Florence
Italy
Tel +39 055 356 2846

Museu del Disseny de Barcelona
www.ajuntament.barcelona.cat/museudeldisseny
Plaça de les Glòries Catalanes
37, 08018 Barcelona
Spain
Tel +34 932 56 68 00

Museum of Contemporary Art
www.msub.org.rs
Ušće 10
Beograd
Serbia
Tel +381 11 3115713

Museum of Design in Plastics
www.modip.ac.uk
Arts University Bournemouth
Wallisdown, Poole BH12 5HH
United Kingdom
Tel +44 0 1202 363727

Museum of Modern Art of Algiers
www.mama-dz.com
25 Rue Larbi Ben M'hidi
Alger Ctre 16002
Algeria
Tel +213 21 71 72 52

MUZA - Museum of Fine Arts
www.muza.mt
Auberge D'Italie
Merchants St., Valletta
Malta
Tel +356 2122 0006

Nationalmuseum
www.nationalmuseum.se/en
Södra Blasieholmshamnen 2
Stockholm
Sweden
Tel +46 8 519 543 00

National Museum of Contemporary Art Athens
www.emst.gr
Kallirrois Ave. and Amvr. Frantzi St.
Athens, 11743
Greece
Tel +30 211 101 9000

Palais Galliera
www.palaisgalliera.paris.fr
10 Av. Pierre 1er de Serbie
75116 Paris
France
Tel +33 1 56 52 86 00

Red Dot Design Museum
www.museum.red-dot.sg
11 Marina Blvd.
018940
Singapore
Tel +65 6514 0111

Southern Guild
www.southernguild.co.za
Silo 5, V&A Waterfront
Cape Town
South Africa
Tel +27 21 461 2856

Street Art Museum Amsterdam
www.streetartmuseumamsterdam.com
Immanuel Kanthof 1
1064 VR Amsterdam
The Netherlands
answers@streetartmuseumamsterdam.com

Triennale di Milano
www.triennale.org
Viale Emilio Alemagna
6, 20121 Milano MI
Italy
Tel +39 02 724341

Turner Contemporary
www.turnercontemporary.org
Rendezvous
Margate CT9 1HG
United Kingdom
Tel +44 1843 233 000

Vitra Design Museum
www.design-museum.de/de/informationen.html
Charles-Eames-Straße 2
79576 Weil am Rhein
Germany
Tel +49 7621 702 3200

WHATIFTHEWORLD
www.whatiftheworld.com
First Floor, 16 Buiten St.
Cape Town City Centre, Cape Town, 8000
South Africa
Tel +27 21 569 0680

ASIA AND OCEANIA

Bangkok Art and Culture Centre
www.bacc.or.th
939 Rama I Rd, Wang Mai
Pathum Wan, Bangkok 10330
Thailand
Tel +66 2 214 6630

Bihar Museum
www.biharmuseum.org
J45C+69Q, Jawaharlal Nehru Marg
Bailey Rd, Patna, Bihar 800001
India
Tel +91 0612 223 5732

Design Museum Holon
www.dmh.org.il
Pinkhas Eilon St. 8
Holon, 5845400
Israel
Tel +972 73 215 1515

Heide Museum of Modern Art
www.heide.com.au
7 Templestowe Road
Bulleen VIC 3105
Australia
Tel +61 3 9850 1500

Hong Kong Museum of Art
www.hk.art.museum/zh_TW/web/ma/home.html
10 Salisbury Road
Tsim Sha Tsui
Hong Kong
Tel +852 2721 0116

Louvre Abu Dhabi
www.louvreabudhabi.ae
Saadiyat
Abu Dhabi
United Arab Emirates
Tel +971 600 565 566

M+
www.mplus.org.hk
38 Museum Drive
West Kowloon Cultural District
Hong Kong
Tel +852 2200 0217

Museum MACAN
www.museummacan.org
AKR Tower, Jl. Perjuangan No.5, RT.11/RW.10, Kb. Jeruk,
Kec. Kb. Jeruk
Kota Jakarta Barat, Daerah Khusus Ibukota Jakarta 11530
Indonesia
Tel +62 21 2212 1888

Museum of Old and New Art
www.mona.net.au
655 Main Road
Berriedale TAS 7011
Australia
Tel +61 3 6277 9900

Museum SAN
www.museumsan.org/museum-san
260 Okeubaelli 2-gil, Jijeong-myeon
Wonju-si, Gangwon-do
South Korea
Tel +82 33 730 9000

Pintô Art Museum
www.pintoart.org/museum
1 Sierra Madre St., Grand Heights Subdivision
Antipolo, 1870 Rizal
Philippines
Tel +63 2 8697 1015

Shepparton Art Museum
www.sheppartonartmuseum.com.au
530 Wyndham St.
Shepparton VIC 3630
Australia
Tel +61 3 4804 5000

Sifang Art Museum
www.sifang.art
Jiangsu, Zhen Pukou District, No. 9
Seventh Road, 210000 Nanjing
China
Tel +86 25 5865 6360

Tel Aviv Museum of Art
www.tamuseum.org.il
The Golda Meir Cultural and Art Center
Sderot Sha'ul HaMelech 27, Tel Aviv-Yafo
Israel
Tel +972 3 607 7020

Tokyo Metropolitan Art Museum
www.tobikan.jp
8-36 Uenokoen, Taito City
Tokyo 110-0007
Japan
Tel +81 3 3823 6921

WA Museum Boola Bardip
www.visit.museum.wa.gov.au/boolabardip
Perth Cultural Centre
Perth WA 6000
Australia
Tel +61 1300 134 081

ADDITIONAL MUSEUMS:

If you are a museum that collects posters and are not listed above, please contact us for inclusion in our next Annual at help@graphis.com.

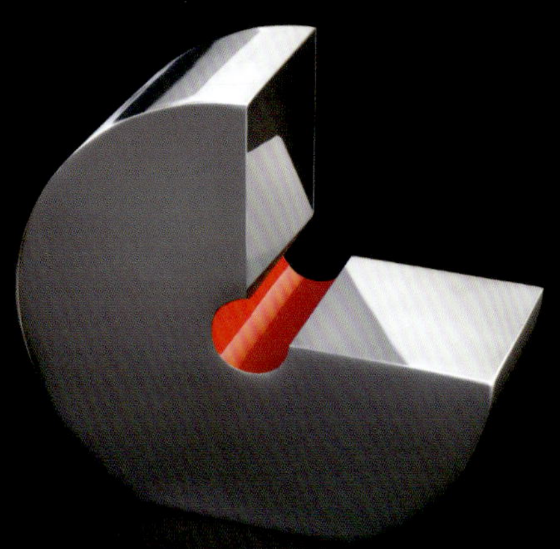

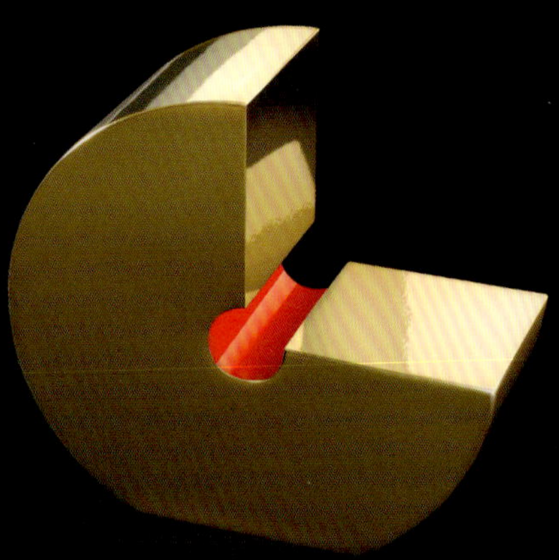

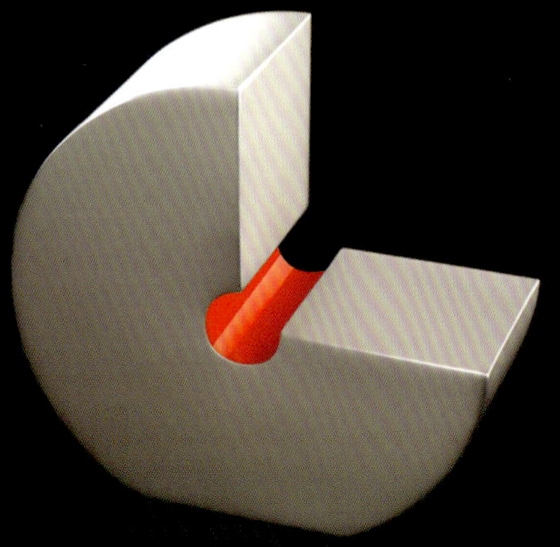

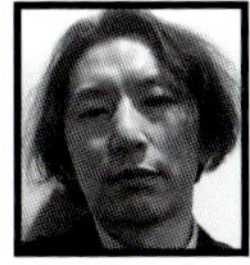

Masahiro Aoyagi | Art Director & Graphic Designer | Toppan Inc.
Biography: Masahiro Aoyagi is a Japanese art director and graphic designer. Since 1998, he has worked for the creative department of Toppan Inc. He has worked on the art direction of corporate calendars and various other tools related to corporate branding, specializing in value-added printing and expression in printed materials using special processing. He is a member of the Japan Graphic Designers Association (JAGDA). He has won various Graphis awards, including three platinum awards, one gold award, and one silver award. He has also won photography awards from the Gregor International Calendar Awards, and gold, silver, and bronze awards from BtoB Advertising. He is the winner of the All Japan Catalogue and Poster Competition, the Benny Award at the Premier Print Awards, and the Prime Minister's Award at the All Japan Calendar Competition.
Commentary: Thank you for the honor of judging the Graphis Design Annual 2023 competition. It was a good experience to see work from other categories that I would not normally be exposed to, which was very stimulating and influential. I usually judge the designs I like based on my own tastes, from the superficial layout design to the beauty of the photographs and typography, but being on this jury was very valuable, since I could learn about the thoughts, approaches, and results of each designer's work. Through seeing the excellent concepts and high quality of these designs, I feel that this expereince will change my attitude toward design in the future.

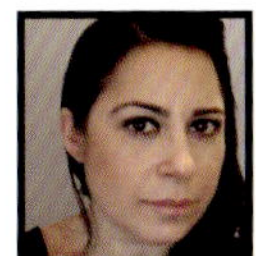

Jennifer Bernstein | Principal, Creative Director, & Educator | Level Group
Biography: Jennifer Bernstein has been a practicing designer and educator for over 20 years. She is the principal and creative director of her own NYC-based firm, Level Group, that specializes in branding and design across different media. Since 1998, Level Group has worked for clients such as Deutsche Bank, the Smithsonian, P.S.1/MoMA, and the Sotheby's auction house. Her work has been recognized by 50 Books | 50 Covers, *Core77*, Graphis, and *Communication Arts*, and has been exhibited at the Cooper-Hewitt National Design Museum. Jennifer has also taught extensively at all levels of undergraduate and graduate design education, including 12 years at the University of the Arts in Philadelphia and four years as part of the Pratt Graduate Communications Design MFA program. In 2014, she joined Rutgers University-Newark, where she is a tenured associate professor in graphic design. Jennifer received her B.A. from Brown University and her M.F.A. in graphic design from the Yale School of Art.
Commentary: Being a judge for this year's Design Annual competition was an honor and a responsibility I took very seriously. The work that stood out to me the most were concepts whose aesthetic matched the intended audience and message. I was impressed by strategically-driven design that felt effortless, but where no decision was arbitrary. It was exciting to see the range of excellent design from both large firms and single practitioner studios.

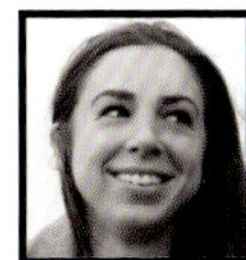

Lauren Chepiga | Senior Designer | PepsiCo Design & Innovation
Biography: Lauren Chepiga is a New York-based senior designer for brand and customer experience at PepsiCo Design and Innovation. She attended the School of Visual Arts from 2010 to 2014, and graduated with her B.F.A. in graphic design. She then worked in a variety of internships, freelance positions, and full-time positions for companies such as Conde Nast, BBH New York, Hearst Magazines, and Showtime Networks Inc. before landing her current position. When it comes to design, Lauren has a multidisciplinary approach, and is guided by a strong emphasis on research, exploration, experimentation, and collaboration, with experience in leading the creative process from ideation to execution across brand initiatives for campaigns, partnerships, activations, experiences, identities, systems, and spaces for nonprofit and corporate clients.
Commentary: It has been an honor to judge the Design 2023 competition, and I am amazed by the amount of talent out there.

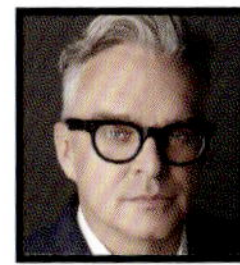

Brian Collins | Chief Creative Officer | COLLINS
Biography: Brian Collins is the chief creative officer of COLLINS, an independent strategy and experience design company in San Francisco and New York City. In their work, they aim to mix imagination, craft, and technology to build brands that can't be ignored. They were named by *Forbes* as one of the companies reshaping the future of brand building. The firm has won every major creative award. Their work has been featured in *The New York Times*, *Businessweek*, *Creativity*, *Fortune*, NBC News, MSNBC, ABC News, and *Fast Company*, which named Brian an "American Master of Design." Prior to the founding of COLLINS, Brian was chief creative officer of the brand and innovation division of Ogilvy. COLLINS has been on Working Not Working's annual list of companies "Creative People Want to Work For Next," along with Pixar, Tesla, Disney, Nike, and NASA. COLLINS was the first design company to appear on the AdAge A-List, and won their "Design Agency of the Year" award for three consecutive years, from 2019 to 2021. In July 2021, DesignWeek awarded the firm "Best of Show" for their creative partnership with Twitch.
Commentary: What a delight. This year's work inspired a deep, rewarding sense of reassurance of the relentless constancy of talent and the crucial, ongoing legacy and leadership of Graphis. One after another, design competitions around the world have been hijacked by mediocrity and an explosion of people who now conflate fame with mastery. However, what jumps out, as always, is extraordinary, with the independent and small design companies still pioneering, still leading the way, still showing everyone how it's done. And this annual is filled with extraordinary work. Go, everyone.

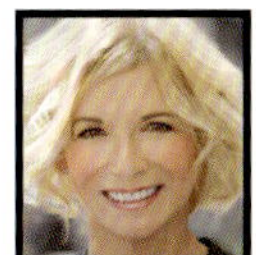

Lynda Decker | President & Creative Director | Decker Design
Biography: Lynda Decker is a multidisciplinary designer whose work encompasses brand strategy and identity, interactive communication, publications, information graphics, and design criticism. A native New Yorker, Lynda studied at Syracuse University and the School of Visual Arts, and holds multiple graduate degrees in design. She was fortunate to land her dream job after college working at *U&lc* for the typographic design legend, Herb Lubalin, and was mentored by Herb's partner, Tony DiSpigna. Her love of typography has never waned. Before founding Decker Design in 1996, she spent ten years in advertising at McCaffrey and McCall, Backer Spielvogel, Bates and Wells, and Rich Greene where she won every major advertising award. Under her leadership, Decker Design continues to receive recognition from its peers. Decker Design's clients vary and include many Fortune 100 corporations and international law firms.
Commentary: I never cease to be amazed by how branding reflects the moment. I imagine that most of the work was created during the pandemic—a time of uncertainty and crisis for many. I felt like many of the entries played it safe and stayed within expected visual tropes for their categories. Healthcare startups featured cartoon rubber people, and bright colors juxtaposed with pale pinks. Alcohol labels were elaborate typographic souffles of wood type, lines, and curves. Lippincott's work, and especially Brendan Murphy, stood above the rest. They rarely slipped into cliché. Turner Duckworth's work for Pennington Biomedical demonstrated the value of a clear consistent voice in crafting a brand.

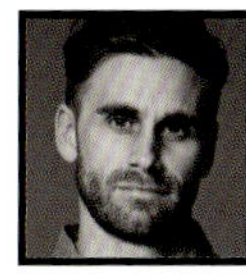

Thorsten Kulp | Founder & Art Director | Toben
Biography: Thorsten Kulp is the art director at Toben. His design approach is multidisciplinary, with a strong interest in visual design innovation and design for engaging experiences. In his 15 years as an art director, he has worked for numerous cultural clients, as well as corporate clients that connect with their audiences in a cultural context. In 2010 his creative vision led him to co-found Toben, a creative studio that empowers brands through strategy and design. Thorsten's work has been displayed in many industry publications and group exhibitions. He has been invited to judge industry awards and speak at industry events such as "Semipermanent."
Commentary: The strongest category, bar none, was the packaging category. On average, they had a really high standard.

Special care was taken to insure that they did not judge their own work.

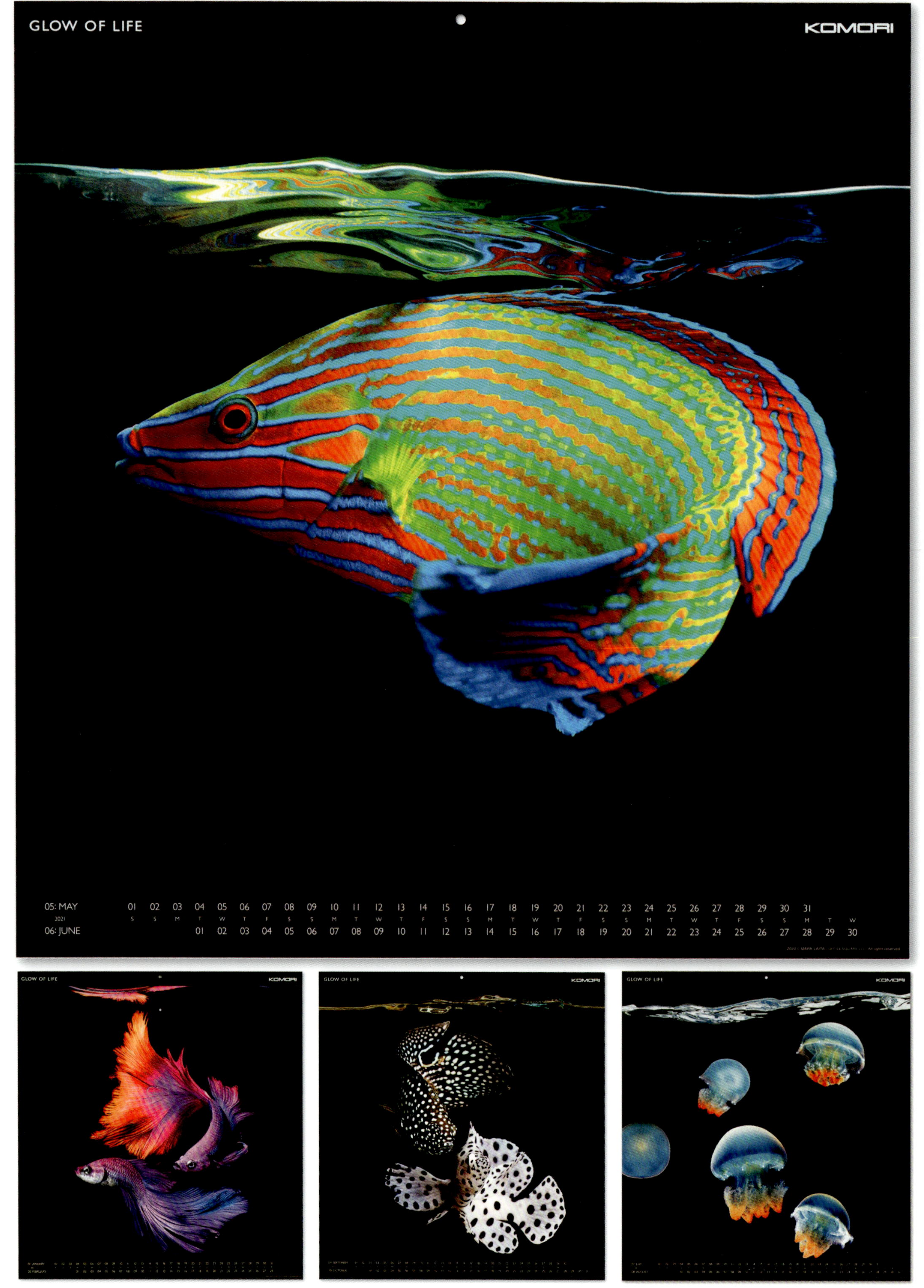

Title: GLOW OF LIFE | **Client:** Komori Corporation

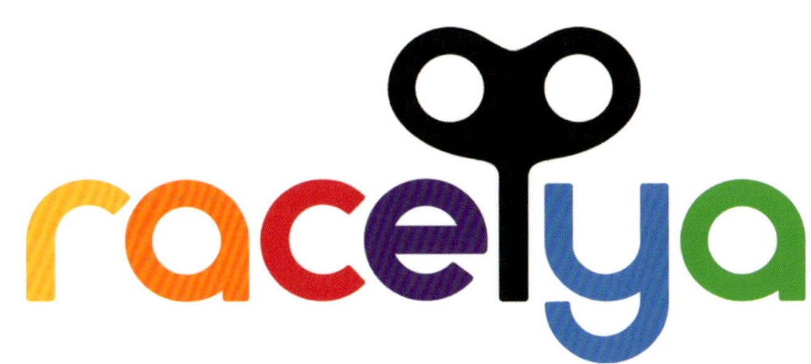

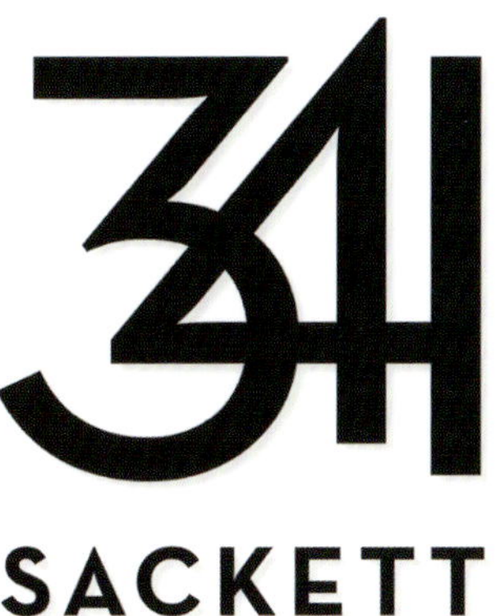

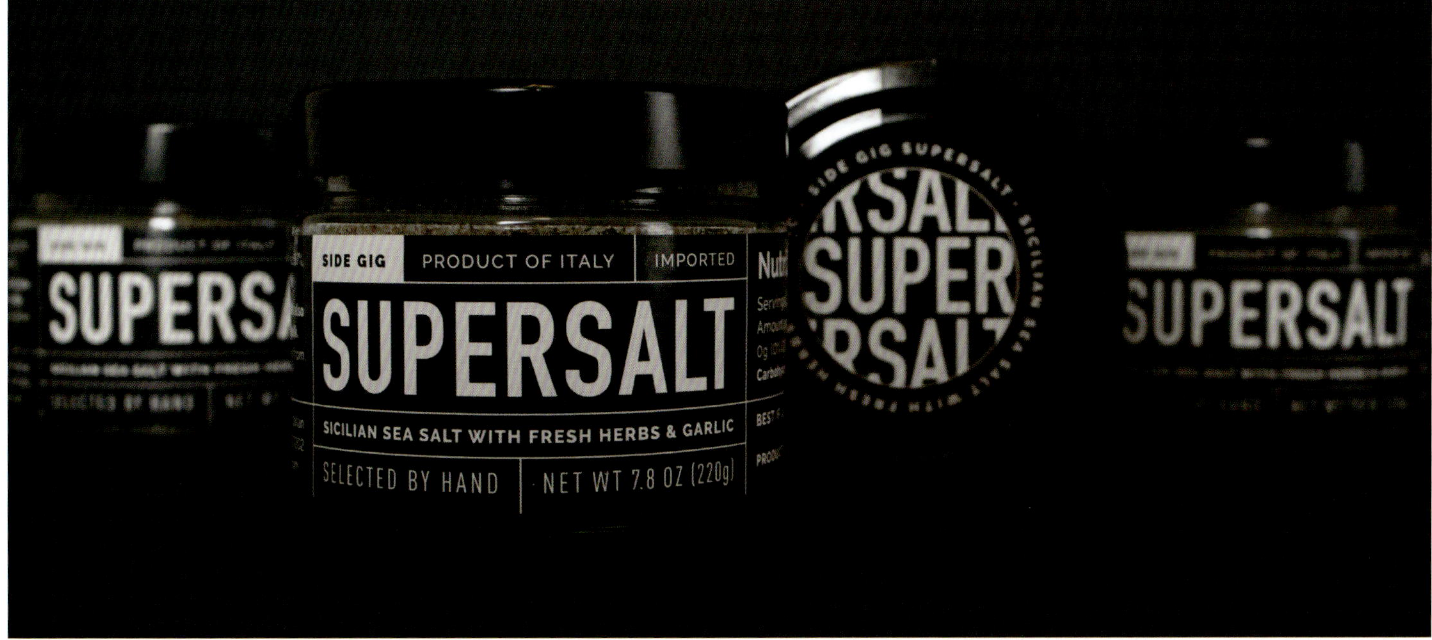

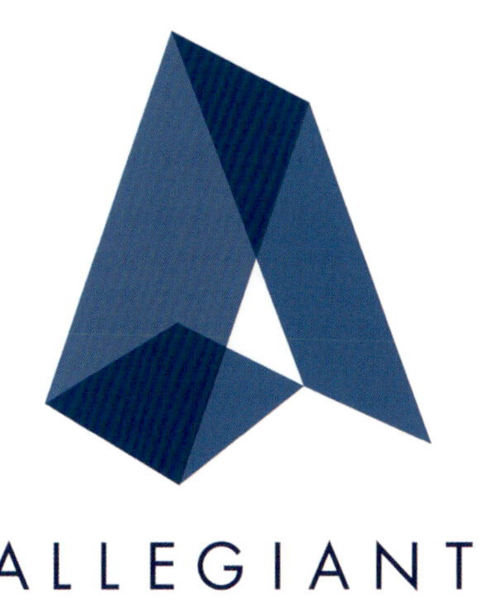

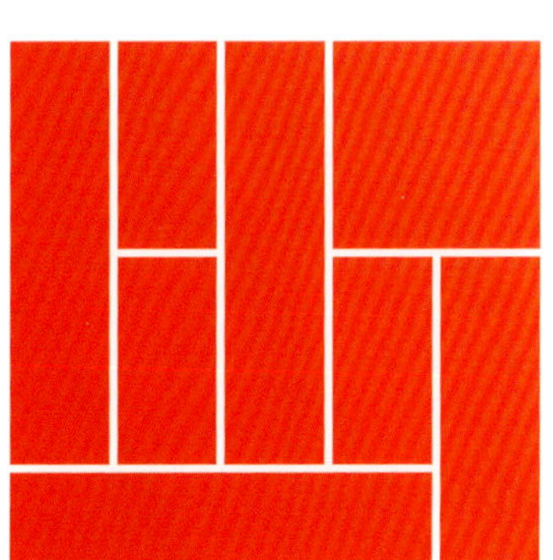

Titles: RaceYa, 341 Sackett Branding, Side Gig SuperSalt Packaging, Allegiant, Lily Auchincloss Foundation Identity
Clients: RaceYa, 341 Sackett, LLC, Side Gig SuperSalt, Allegiant Real Estate Capital, Lily Auchincloss Foundation

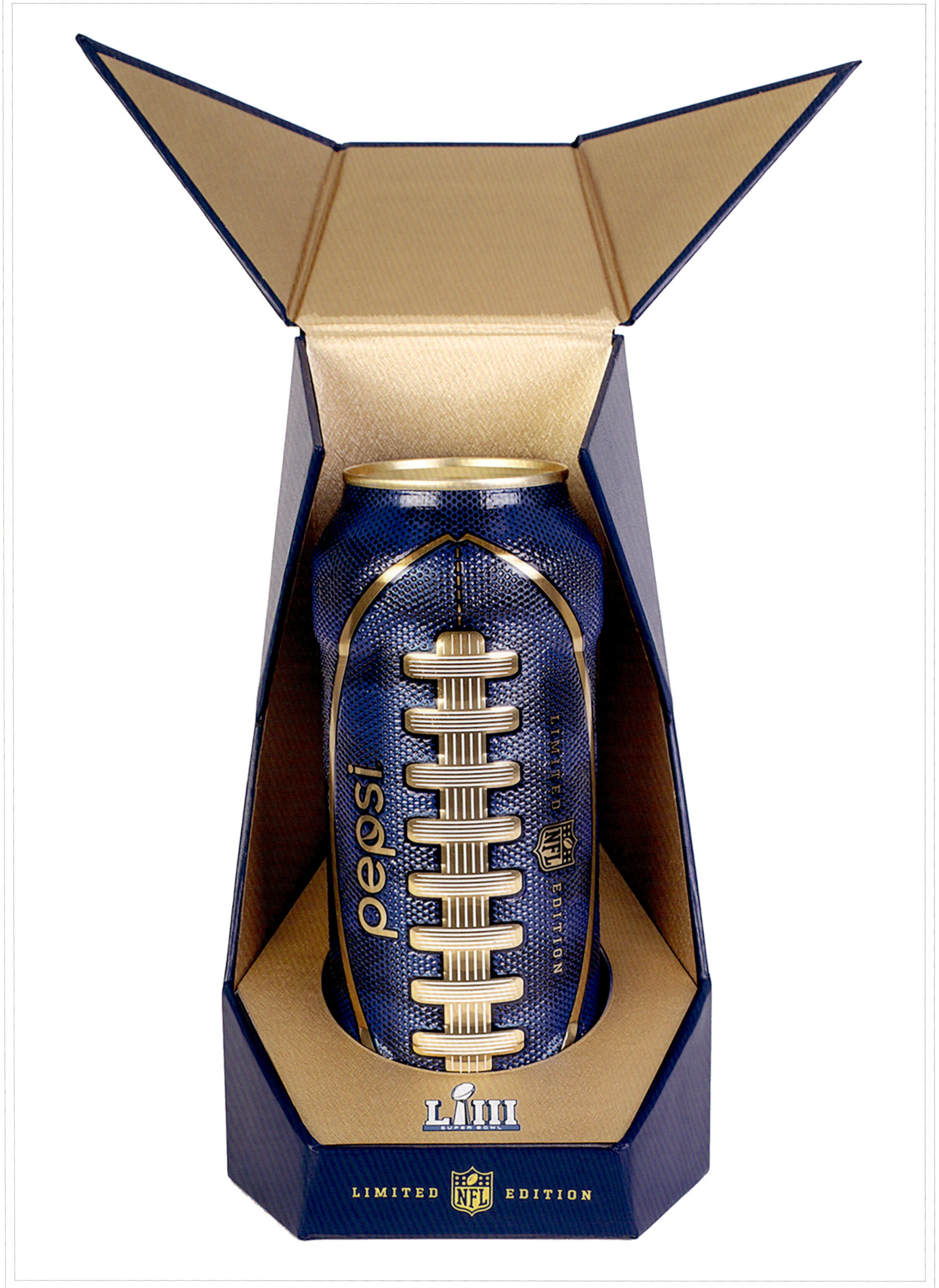

Title: Pepsi NFL Laces Can | **Client:** PepsiCo Design & Innovation

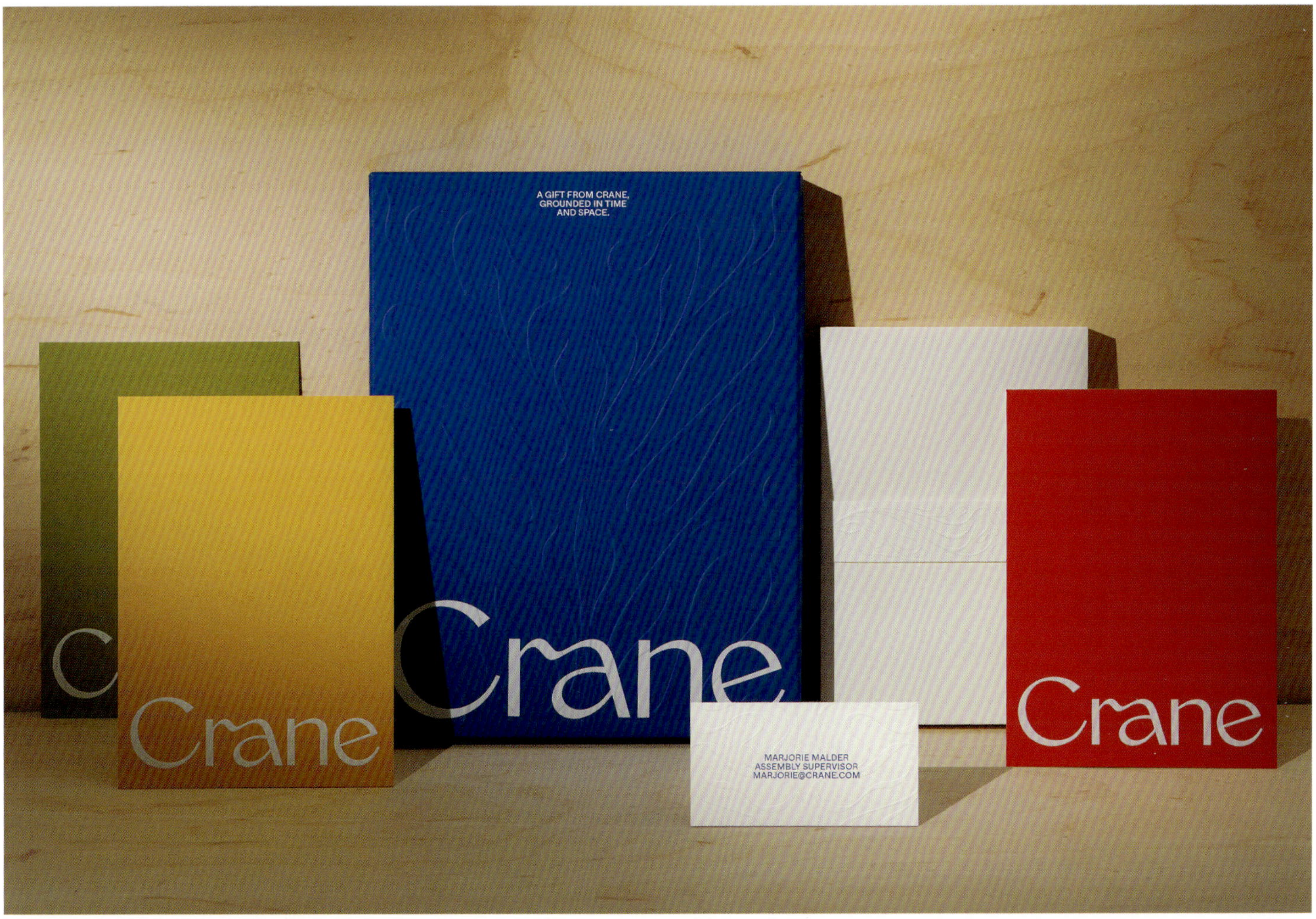

A GIFT FROM CRANE,
GROUNDED IN TIME
AND SPACE.

Crane

MARJORIE MALDER
ASSEMBLY SUPERVISOR
MARJORIE@CRANE.COM

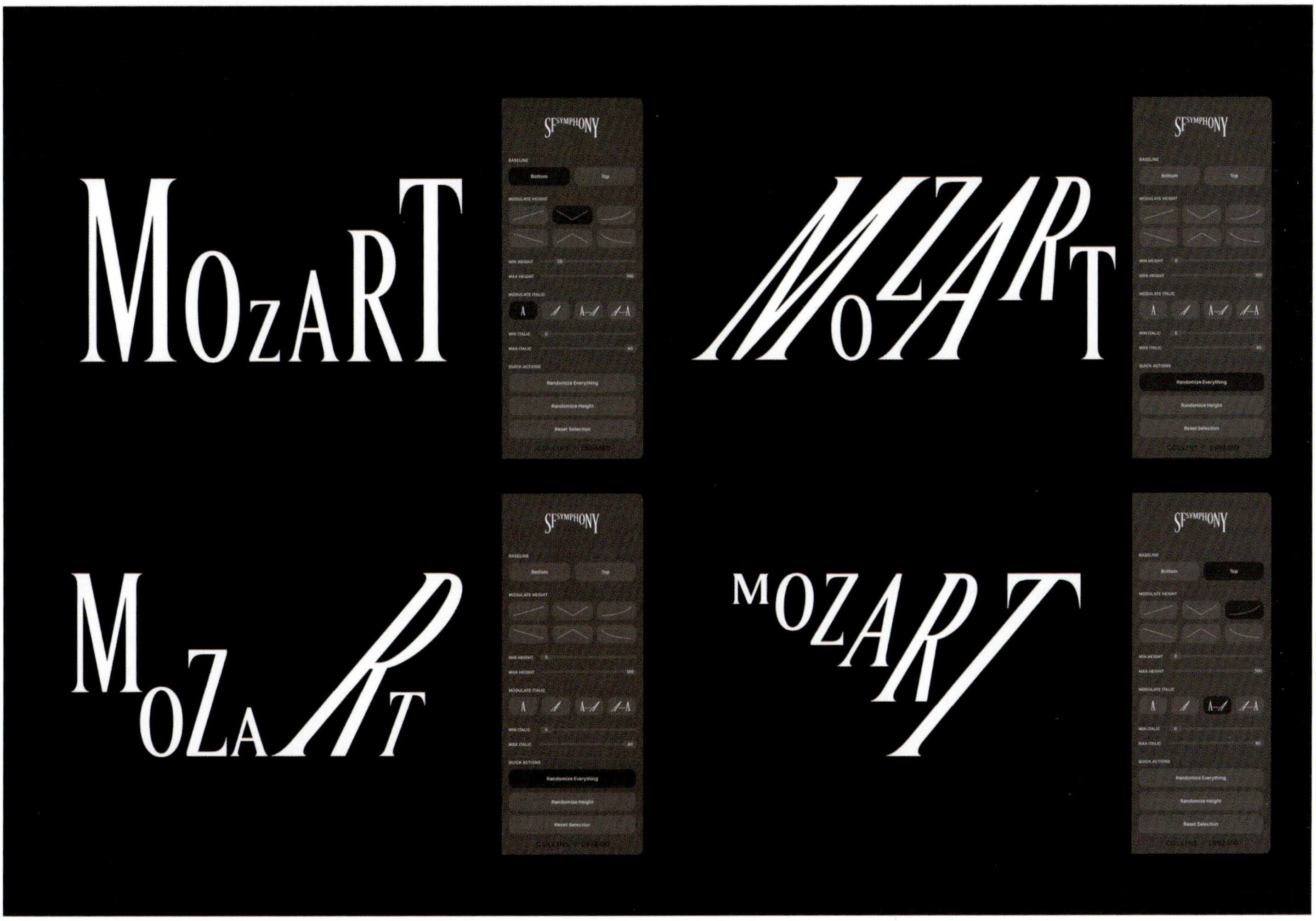

MOZART

Titles: Crane Paper Company Brand Identity, San Francisco Symphony Brand Identity | **Clients:** Crane Paper Company, San Francisco Symphony

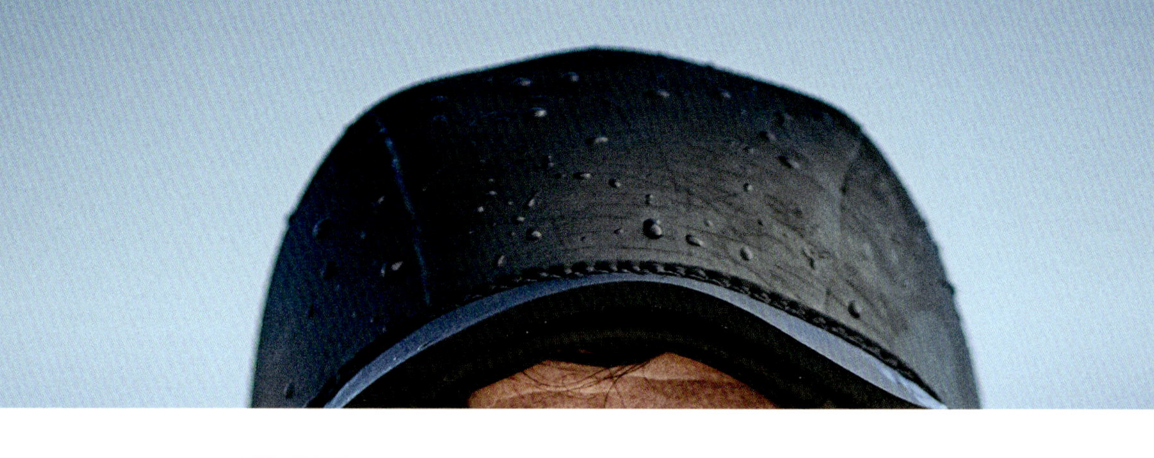
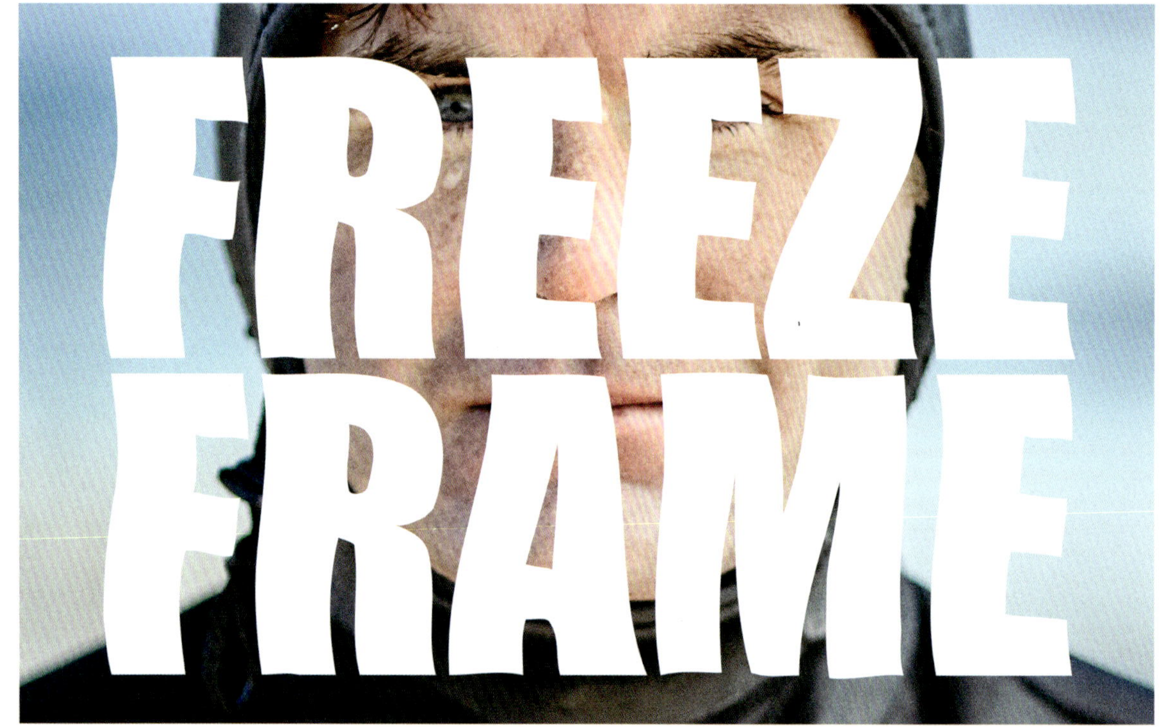

Title: Montauk Winter Surfers Photography Exhibition | **Client:** Montauk Winter Surfers Photography Exhibition

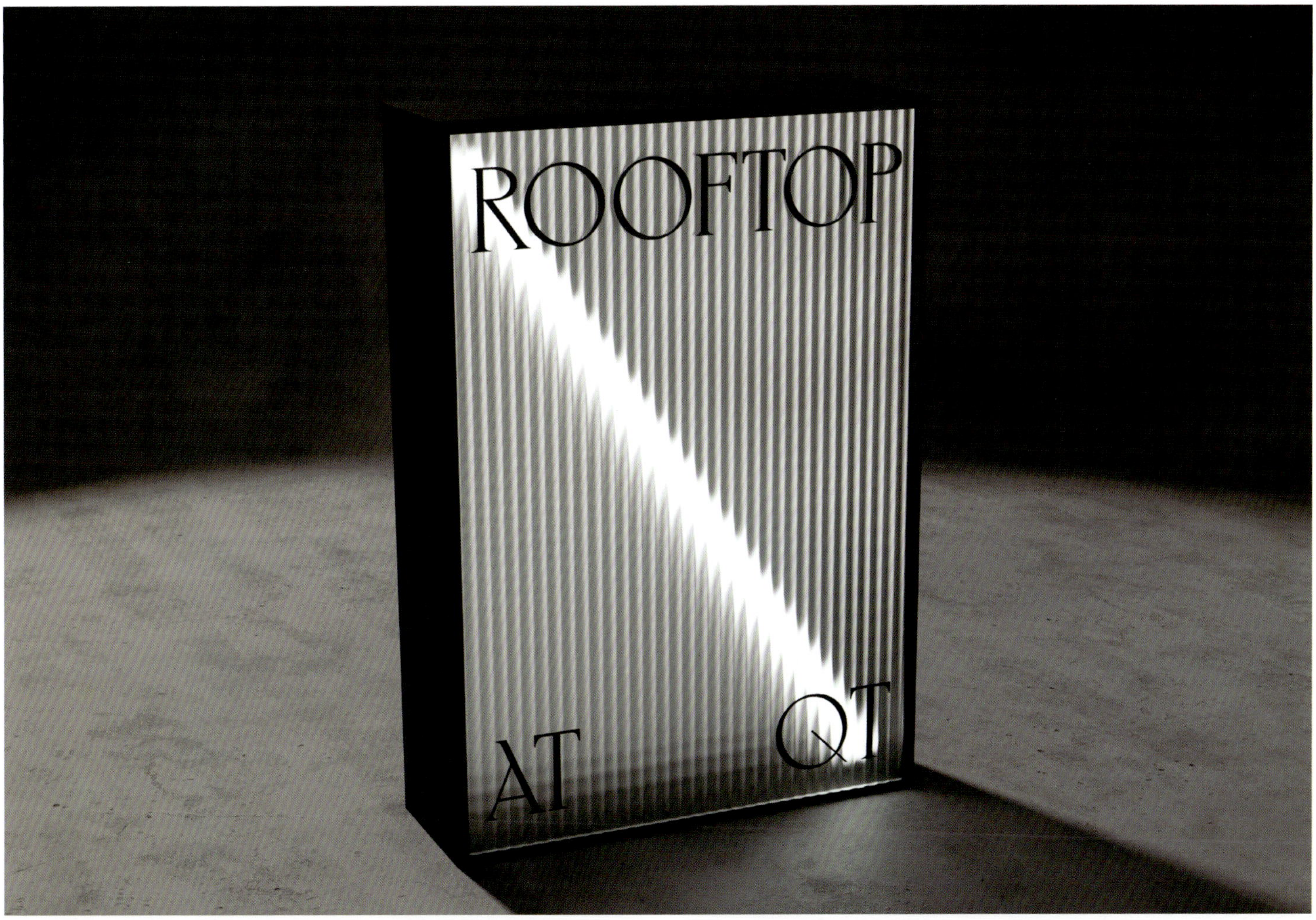

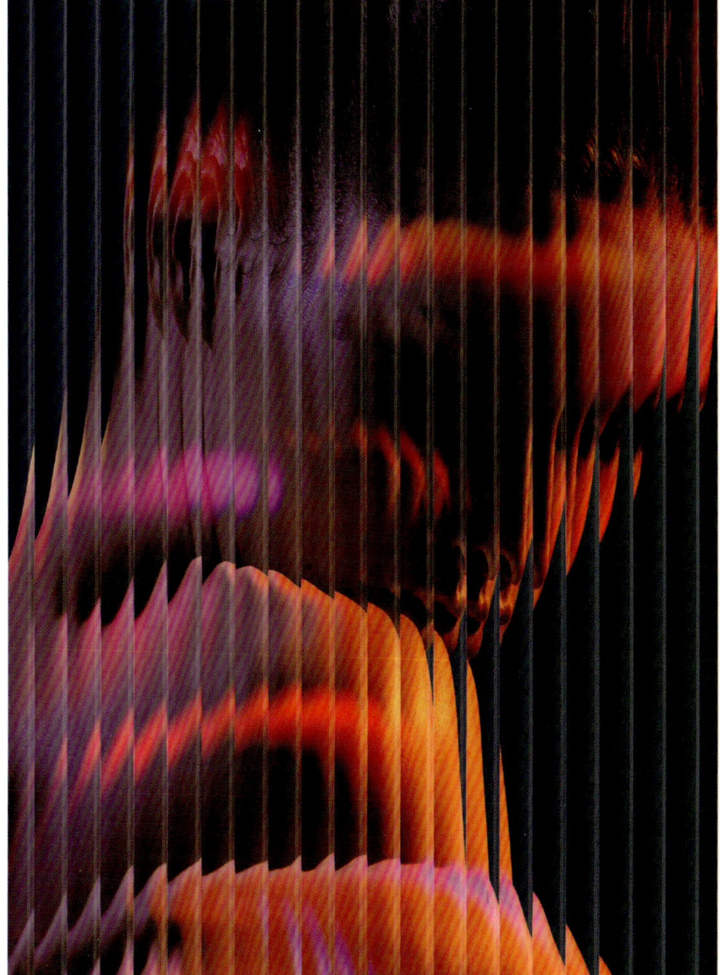

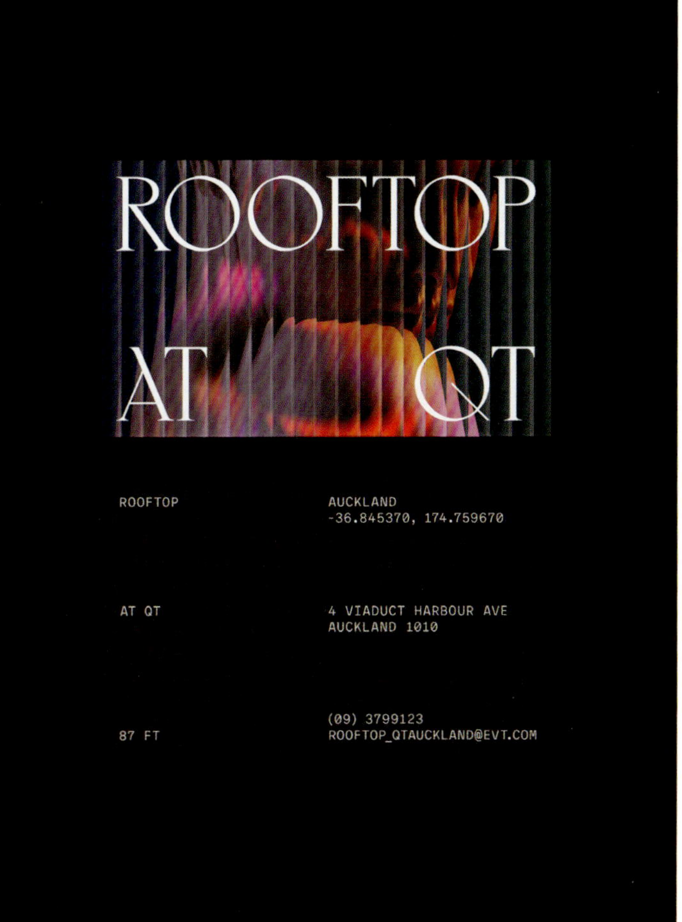

Title: Rooftop at QT | **Client:** QT Hotels & Resorts

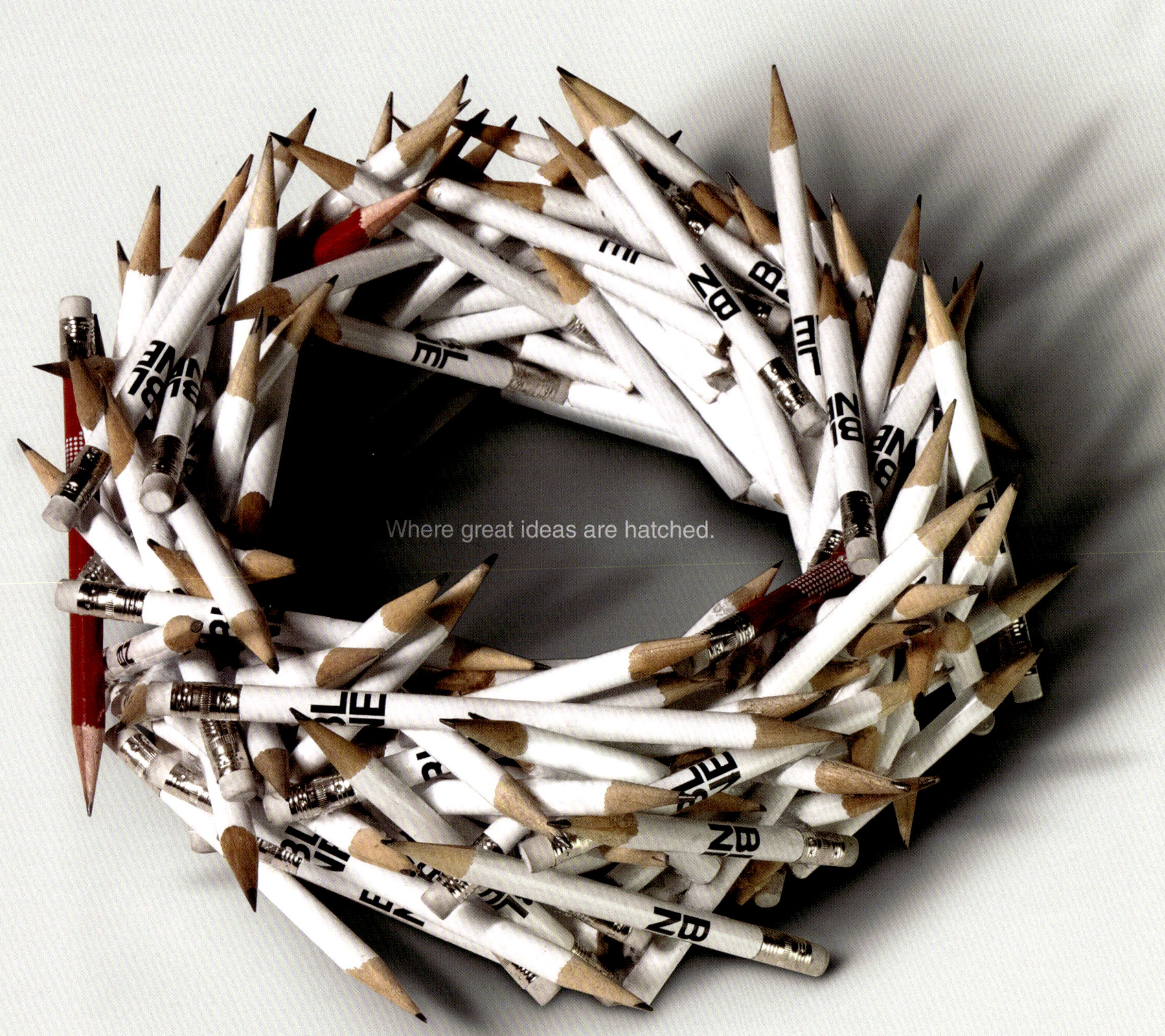
Where great ideas are hatched.

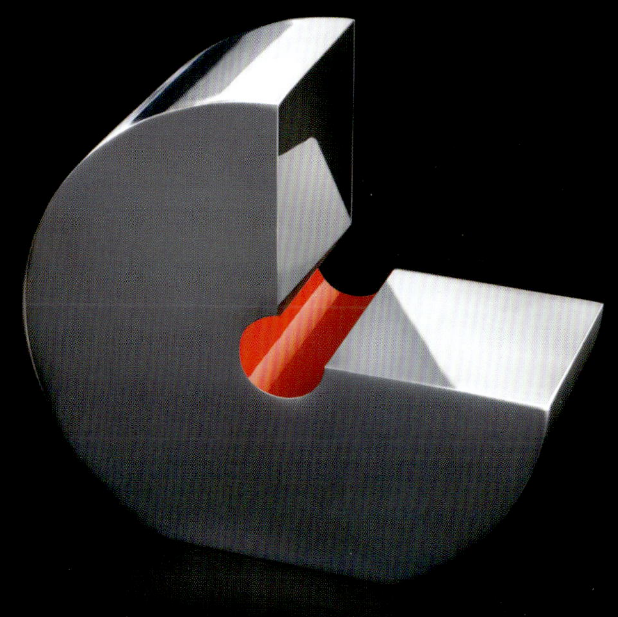

Opposite page: *"BL Nest Poster,"* designed by Bailey Lauerman.

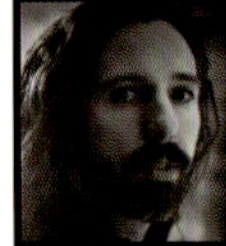
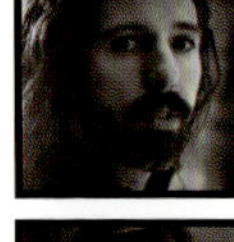

Trevitt McCandliss, Nancy Campbell | McCandliss & Campbell/Wainscot Media | Founders, Creative Directors, & Educators
Page: 22 | www.mccandlissandcampbell.com

Biography: McCandliss and Campbell is an art direction and design team that combines innovative typography and conceptually-driven fashion photography to create award-winning editorial designs. They have received more than 300 design and photography awards from Graphis, the Society of Publication Designers, the Type Directors Club, *Print*, *HOW*, *Communication Arts*, *Creative Quarterly*, and more. They are creative directors for *Earnshaw's*, a children's fashion magazine, *Footwear Plus*, a fashion magazine covering the footwear industry, and *MR*, a fashion magazine covering the menswear industry. McCandliss and Campbell have presented their work at conferences in the United States and Europe. They have served on juries for the Society of Publication Designers, Graphis, and Communication Arts. The duo have taught master classes to an international roster of professional art directors and designers. Trevitt served as the vice president of the Society of Publication Designers. McCandliss and Campbell teach typography and editorial design at Kean University.

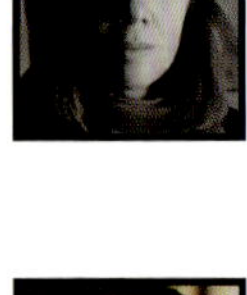

Ivan Bell | Stranger & Stranger | Designer | Pages: 23, 24 | www.strangerandstranger.com

Biography: For over the past twenty-one years, Ivan Bell has worked alongside Kevin Shaw, the founder of Stranger & Stranger, in building a specialist, award-winning alcoholic beverage packaging design consultancy. Stranger & Stranger is now one of the leading firms in the field with studios in London, New York, and San Francisco, and advises everyone from huge corporations all the way down to one-man startups. Stranger & Stranger labels up and over a billion bottles and cans every year, and it has helped create brands worth hundreds of millions of dollars.

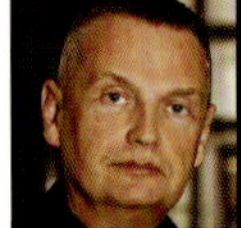

PepsiCo Design & Innovation | Page: 25 | design.pepsico.com

Biography: PepsiCo products are enjoyed by consumers more than one billion times a day, in more than 200 countries and territories around the world. PepsiCo generated more than $67 billion in net revenue in 2019, driven by a complementary food and beverage portfolio that includes Frito-Lay, Gatorade, Pepsi-Cola, Quaker, and Tropicana. PepsiCo's product portfolio includes a wide range of enjoyable foods and beverages, including 23 brands that generate more than $1 billion each in estimated annual retail sales.

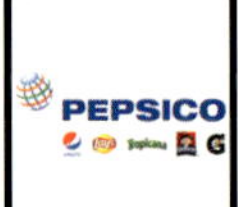

Vishal Vora | Sol Benito | Founder & Designer | Page: 26 | www.solbenito.com

Biography: Sol Benito is an award-winning packaging design studio based in Mumbai, India, and is headed by founder and designer Vishal Vora. He studied graphic design at the I.S. College of Fine Arts, and has over 20 years of multidisciplinary and multi-sector experience in design direction, management, and implementation in India and overseas. Having worked for various markets in Europe, America, and the GCC, Vishal has a keen eye for quality design and profound experience. He applies graphic principles to produce innovative designs for any type of media. He would describe his approach to design as emotional, intuitive, and inspirational. His inclination lies towards branding, packaging design, product design, and exhibition design.

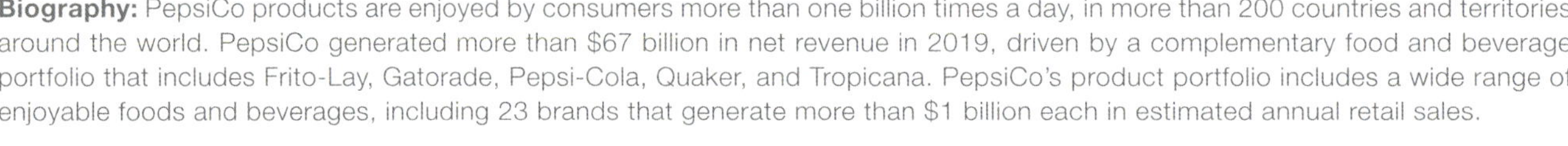

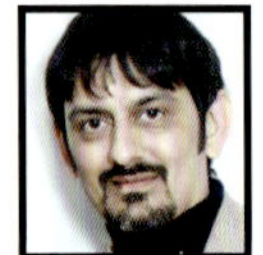

ARSONAL | Page: 27 | www.arsonal.com

Biography: ARSONAL is a collaborative agency of creative professionals who share a passion for design and advertising. The agency was formed by Brad Johnson and Ethan Archer in 2007. Operating as co-creative directors, they and their team have created some of the most eye-catching campaigns in their field. ARSONAL has been recognized as a leader in the industry, garnering numerous awards along the way, including over 50 CLIO Key Art Awards, over 100 Promax/BDA Awards, and the title of Graphis Design Master.

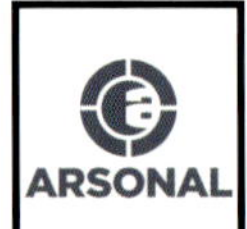
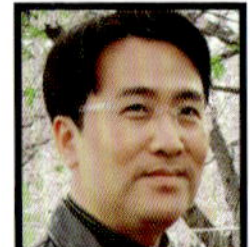

Hoon-Dong Chung | Dankook University | Designer & Associate Professor | Pages: 28, 30 | www.dankook.ac.kr

Biography: Hoon-Dong Chung was born in 1970 in South Korea. Currently, he is an associate professor at Dankook University and invited artist at the Grand Art Exhibition of Korea. His Ph. D. in Design is deeply associated with 3D Typography. His works have been showcased in international exhibitions and received more than 200 awards including Graphis, the German Design Award, the Design Award of the Federal Republic of Germany, the Red Dot Design Award, the iF Design Award, the Good Design Award, some Creativity Design Awards, some HOW Design Awards, and much more. He also received a Commendation from the President of Korea at the Korea Design Award which is known as "Korea's highest honor in Design". Furthermore, his works are in the collections of the Design Museum Munich, the Museum für Kunst und Gewerbe Hamburg, the Museum für Gestaltung, the Musée de la Publicité, the National Museum Poznan, the Poster Museum at Wilanów, the Chicago Athenaeum Museum of Architecture and Design, the Dansk Plakat Museum, the Ogaki Poster Museum, and more.

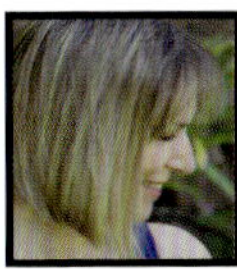

Carmit Haller | Carmit Design Studio | Founder & Designer | Pages: 29, 33 | www.carmitdesign.com
Biography: Carmit Haller is the owner of Carmit Design Studio. For the past 20 years, she has worked as a lead graphic designer in the fields of consumer market, high-tech startups, and luxury real estate. Her passion lies in poster design and typography. Haller addresses cultural, social, and political topics with a strong and thought-provoking view. Haller is the recipient of worldwide prestigious awards from ogranizations such as Graphis and Rockport Publishing. She has been a member of the American Institute of Graphic Arts (AIGA) since 2007 and an AIGA mentor since 2020. She currently resides in San Francisco, California.

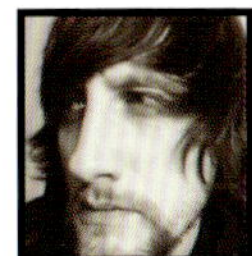

Michael Hughes | Mike Hughes Creative Direction + Design | Creative Director & Designer
Page: 31 | www.hughescreativework.com
Biography: Mike Hughes is a multi-award-winning creative director, art director, and designer with over 25 years of experience. He has lent his creative talents to brands such as Adidas, Converse, MINI, and Fiat to name a few. He is the co-founder/executive creative director of the fashion and design magazine *ROTOR*, which he designs and conducts high profile interviews for. He is also an avid writer and musician who has penned screenplays and leads his own band, Mount Deed. Though he is from the United States, he currently resides in Montreal, Canada.

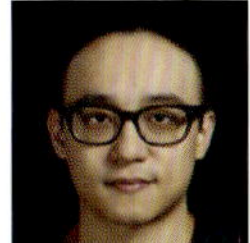

Jim Ma | Bailey Lauerman | Graphic Designer | Page: 32 | www.baileylauerman.com
Biography: Jim joined Bailey Lauerman after graduating from the University of Nebraska-Kearney with a degree in design and visual communications. He is a passionate designer and craftsman. In six years at the agency, Jim's design work continues to garner national attention for clients like Bosch, Disney, 559 Inc., and AAF Nebraska. He's developed a reputation for building brand identities, including full product line packaging systems for Phillips 66 and Kendall Motor Oil. Jim's fierce curiosity and desire to keep learning new things drives him, as he tackles every new project in front of him.

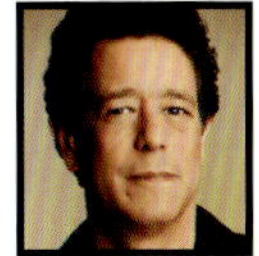

Antonio Alcalá | Studio A | Founder & Co-Owner | Page: 34 | www.studioa.com
Biography: Antonio Alcalá is the founder and co-owner of Studio A, a design practice working with museums and art institutions. He also art directs and designs postage stamps for the United States Postal Service, and teaches/lectures at schools such as the Corcoran School of Art & Design, SVA, Pratt, and MICA. Alcalá's work and contributions to the field of graphic design were recognized with his selection as a 2008 the American Institute of Graphic Arts (AIGA) fellow. His designs are represented in the AIGA Design Archives, the National Postal Museum, and the permanent collection of graphic design at the Library of Congress. Alcalá graduated from Yale University with a B.A. in history, and from the Yale School of Art with an M.F.A in graphic design. He lives with his wife in Alexandria, Virginia.

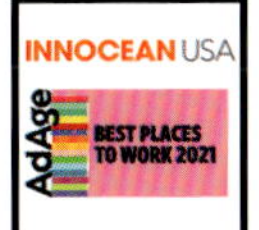

INNOCEAN USA | Page: 219 | www.innoceanusa.com
Biography: INNOCEAN USA is an award-winning, independent, full-service advertising agency that leverages their unbridled curiosity and unorthodox thinking to go beyond simply creating ads and to create culture. For more than a decade, INNOCEAN USA has merged innovative technology with cutting-edge digital, social, and experiential advertising to connect brands to people. They are doing this with their current clients, including Hyundai Motor America, Genesis Motor America, Kia Motors America, Hankook Tire, Wienerschnitzel, UC Davis Health, LG, Signature Kitchen Suite, TaylorMade Golf, Pacific Life, City of Hope, Toshiba Business Systems, Gravity Interactive, Los Angeles Angels of Anaheim, DC Comics, Hyundai Cradle, GreenBox POS, and UMASS Global.

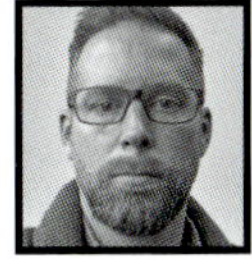

Clinton Carlson | Clinton Carlson Design | Designer & Associate Professor | Page: 219 | www.clintoncarlson.com
Biography: Clinton Carlson is a designer, educator, and researcher. He designs brand systems, interfaces, and information, teaches typography, brand identity, and interaction design, and researches how design can activate and empower communities in large and small-scale systems. His original plan was to become a cowboy or a second baseman on a baseball team, but he ended up being a professor that smokes brisket and plays Strat-O-Matic baseball. He's happy with that.

It was exciting to see the range of excellent design from both large firms and single studios.

Jennifer Bernstein, *Principal, Creative Director, & Educator, Level Group*

Visit our Credits & Commentary section in the back of the book to read the full assignments, approaches, and results from this year's Platinum Winners.

TREVETT MCCANDLISS, NANCY CAMPBELL EDITORIAL

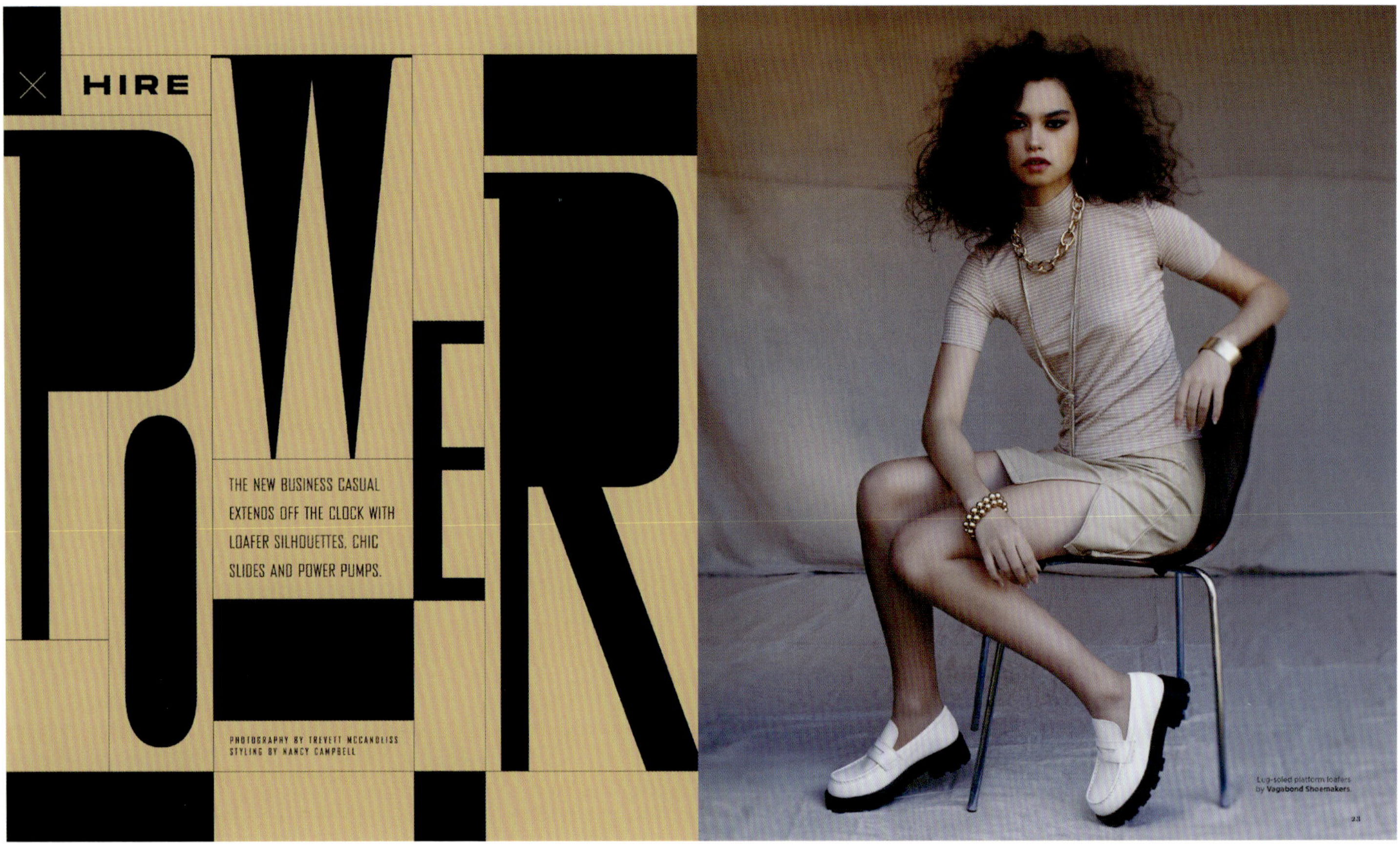

HIRE

POWER

THE NEW BUSINESS CASUAL EXTENDS OFF THE CLOCK WITH LOAFER SILHOUETTES, CHIC SLIDES AND POWER PUMPS.

PHOTOGRAPHY BY TREVETT MCCANDLISS
STYLING BY NANCY CAMPBELL

Lug-soled platform loafers by Vagabond Shoemakers.

23

P237: Credit & Commentary **Title:** Hire Power | **Client:** Footwear Plus Magazine | **Design Firm:** Wainscot Media

TREVETT MCCANDLISS, NANCY CAMPBELL EDITORIAL 

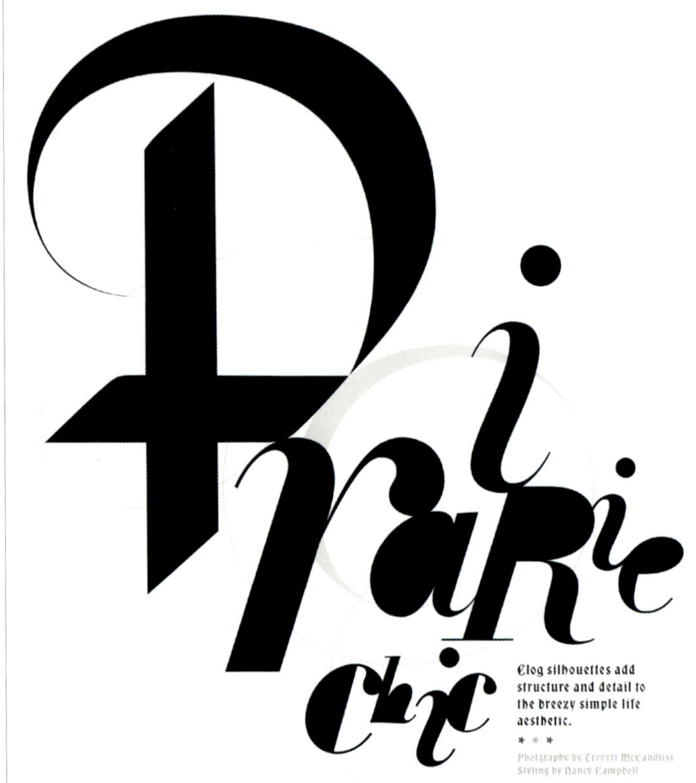

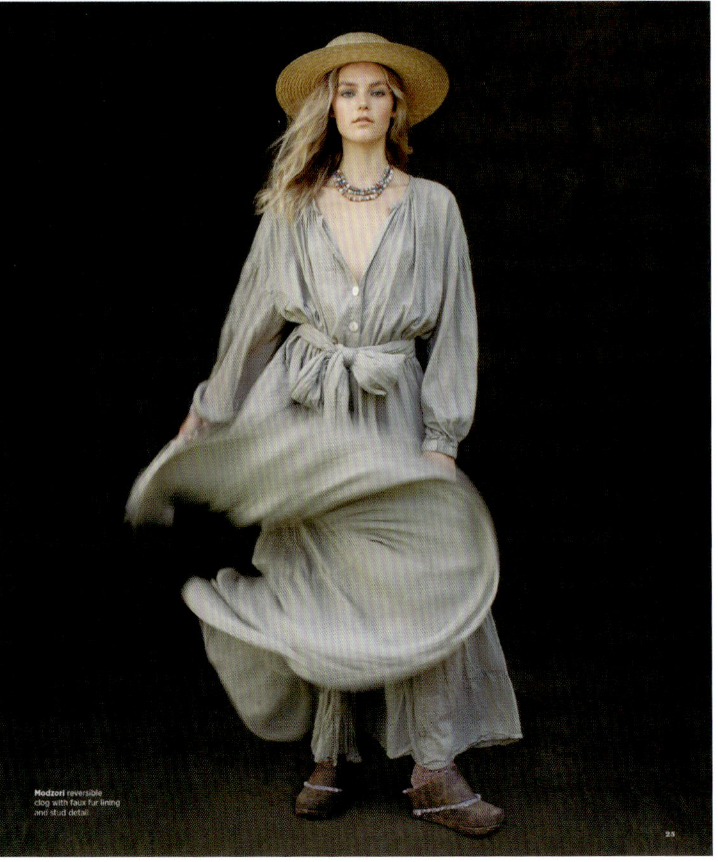

P237: Credit & Commentary **Title:** Prairie Chic | **Client:** Footwear Plus Magazine | **Design Firm:** Wainscot Media

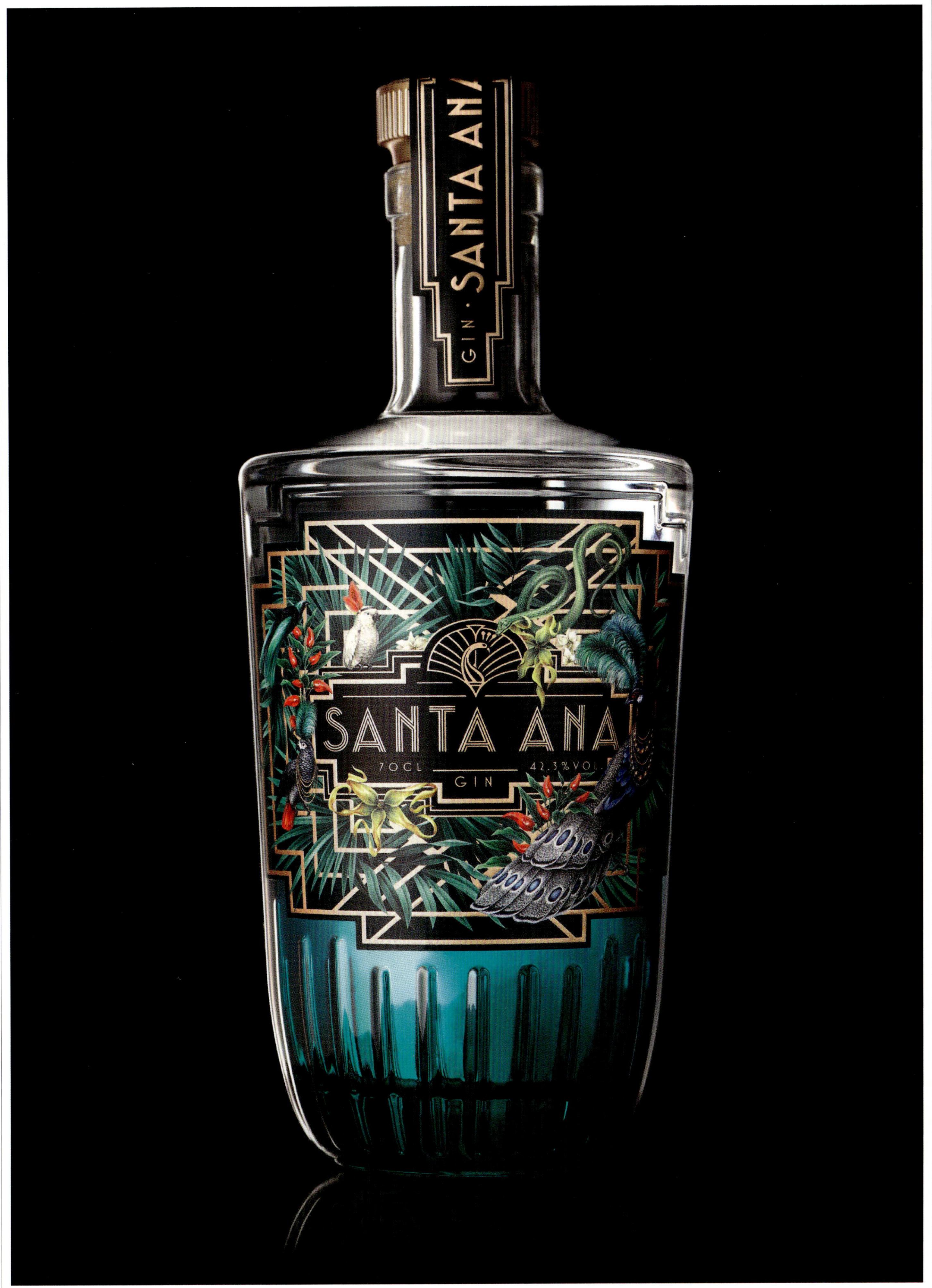

P237: Credit & Commentary **Title:** Santa Ana Gin | **Client:** Kanlaon Ltd. (Bleeding Heart Rum) | **Design Firm:** Stranger & Stranger

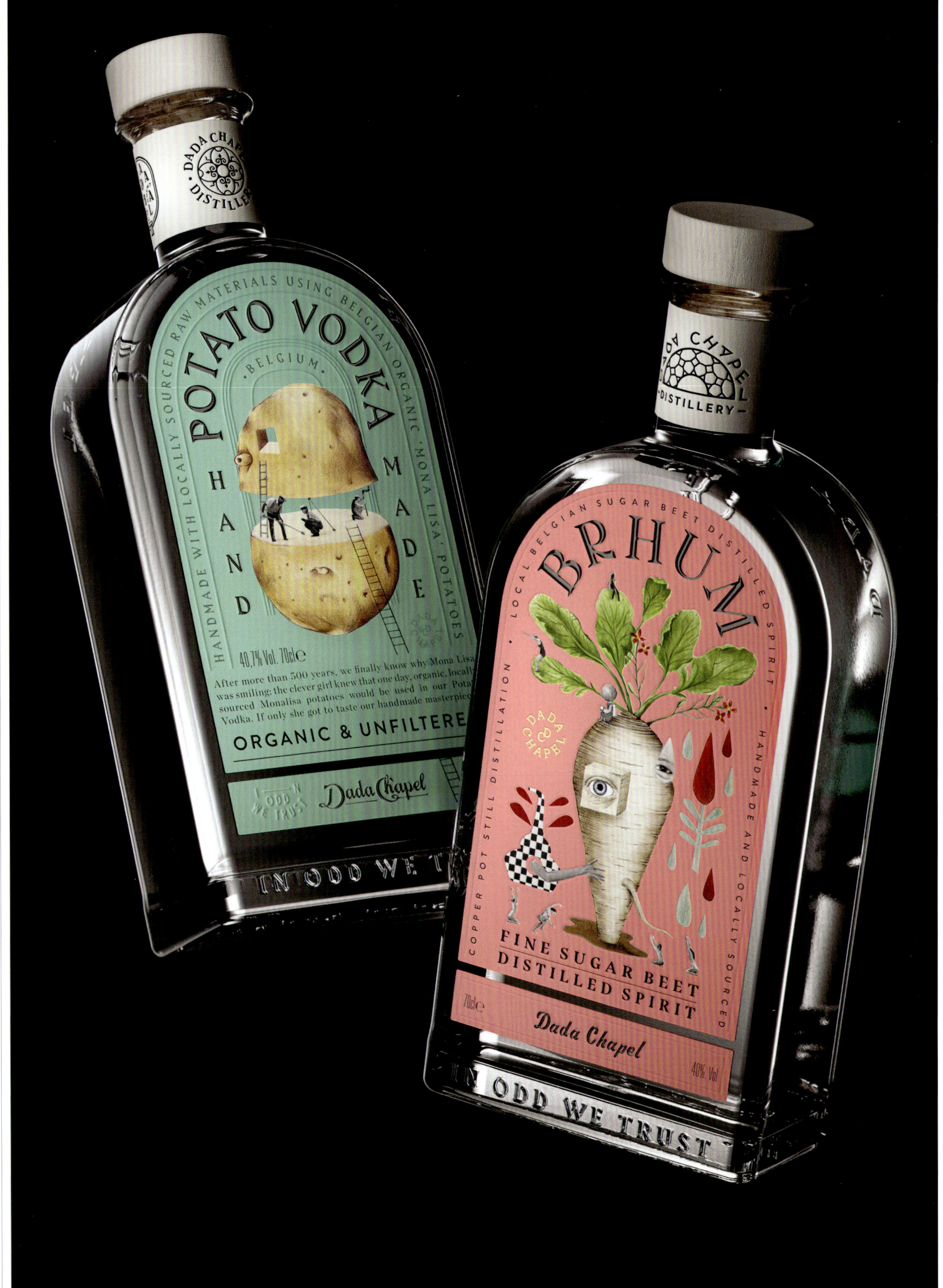

 Title: Dada Chapel | **Client:** Hotel Vanden Meersche NV | **Design Firm:** Stranger & Stranger

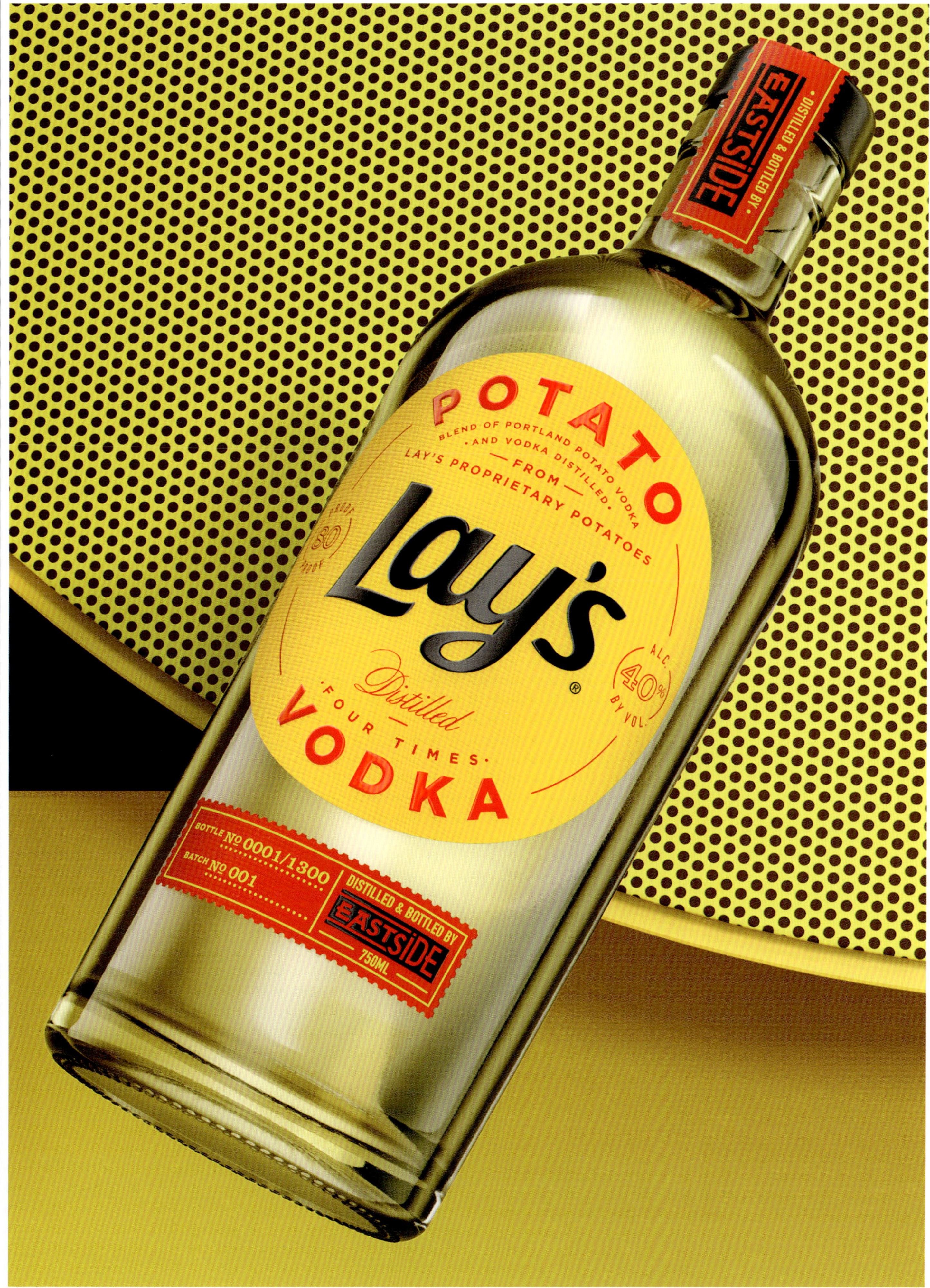
DISTILLED & BOTTLED BY
EASTSIDE
POTATO
BLEND OF PORTLAND POTATO VODKA
AND VODKA DISTILLED
FROM
LAY'S PROPRIETARY POTATOES
80 PROOF
Lay's
ALC. 40% BY VOL.
Distilled
FOUR TIMES
VODKA
BOTTLE Nº 0001/1300
BATCH Nº 001
DISTILLED & BOTTLED BY
EASTSIDE
750ML

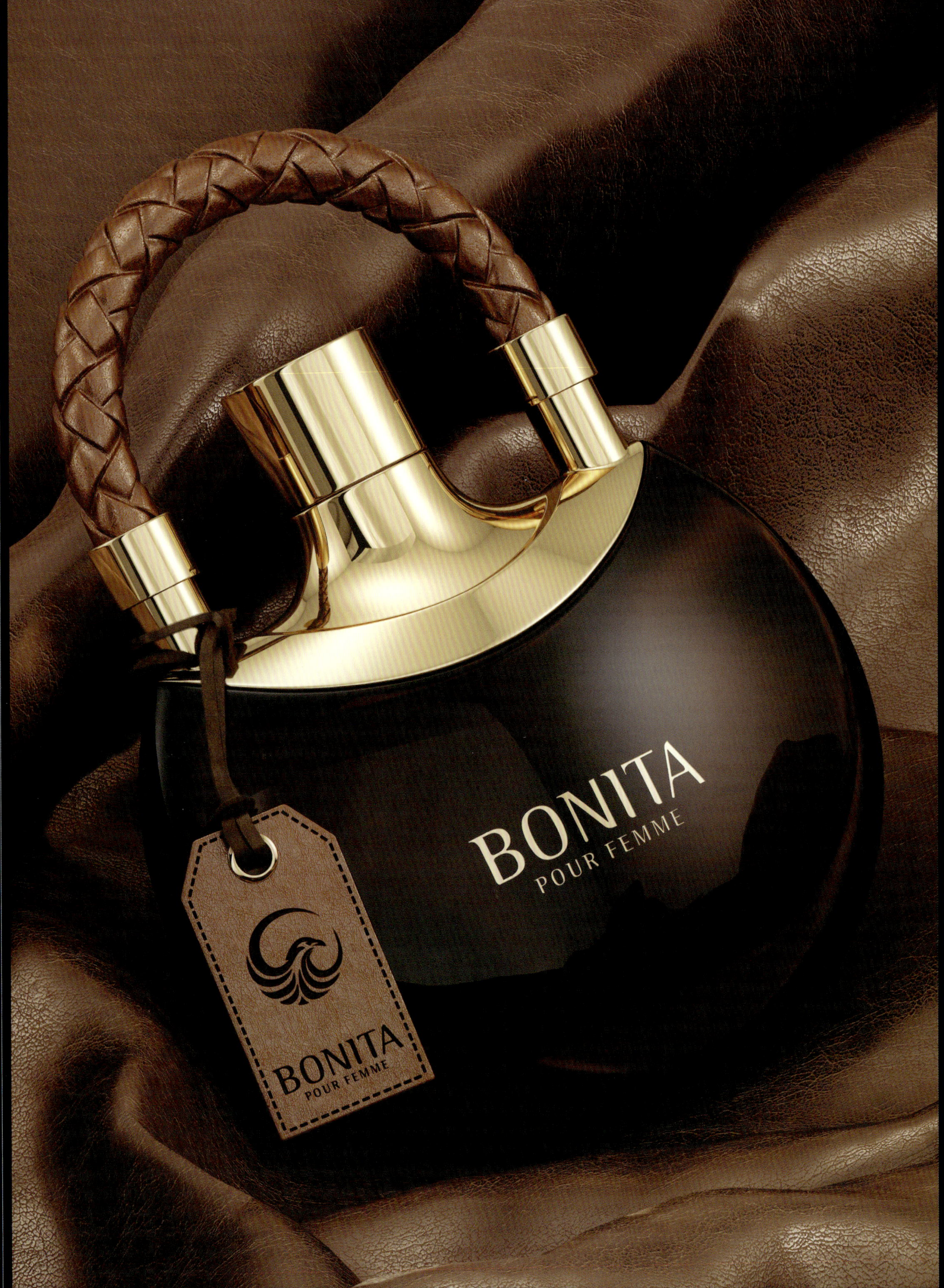

P237: Credit & Commentary

Title: Bonita | Client: Elite Brands | Design Firm: Sol Benito

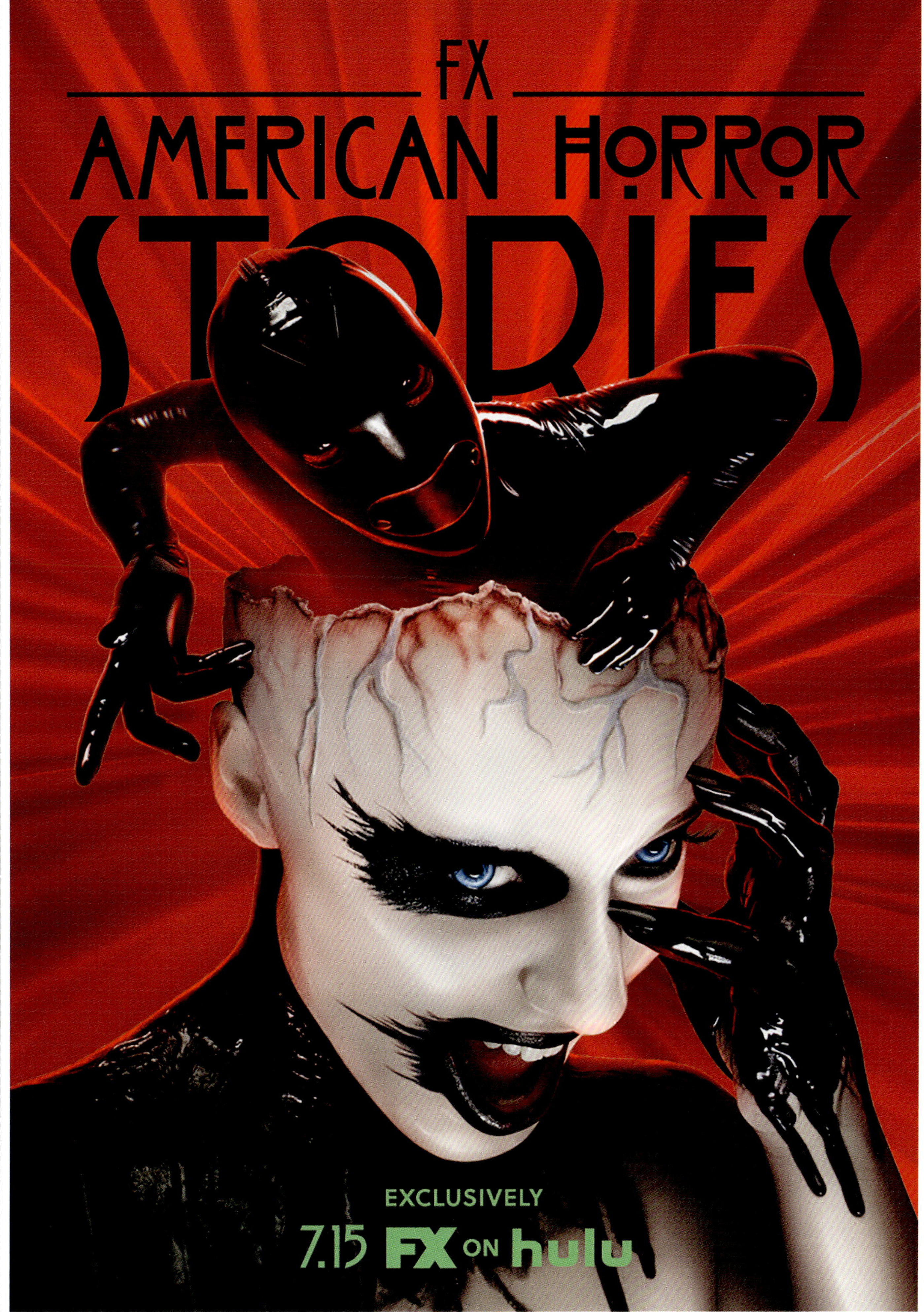

Title: AMERICAN HORROR STORIES | **Client:** FX | **Design Firm:** ARSONAL

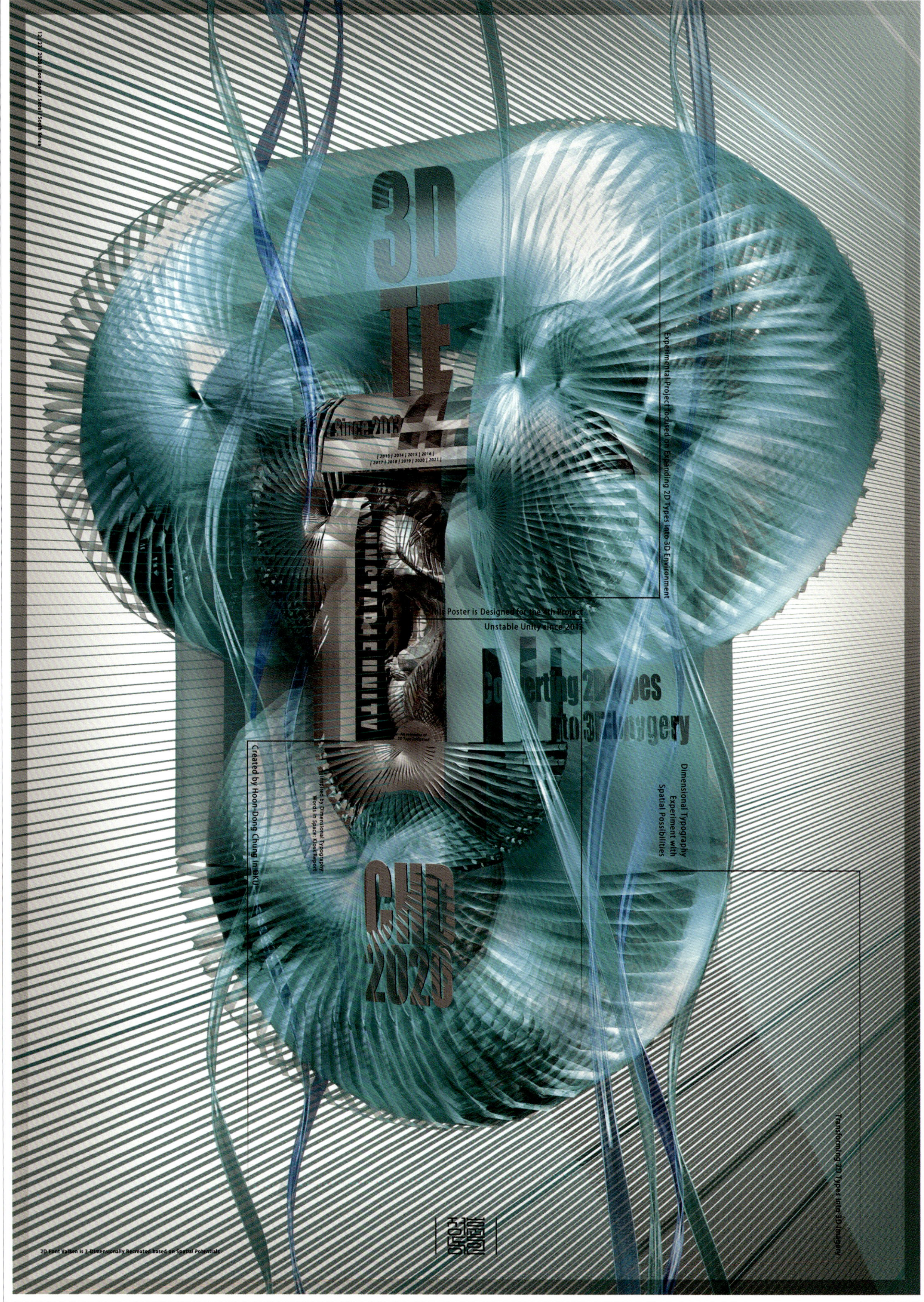

P237: Credit & Commentary Title: 3D Type Exhibition | Client: Self-initiated | Design Firm: Dankook University

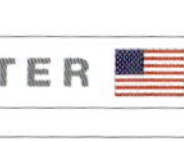

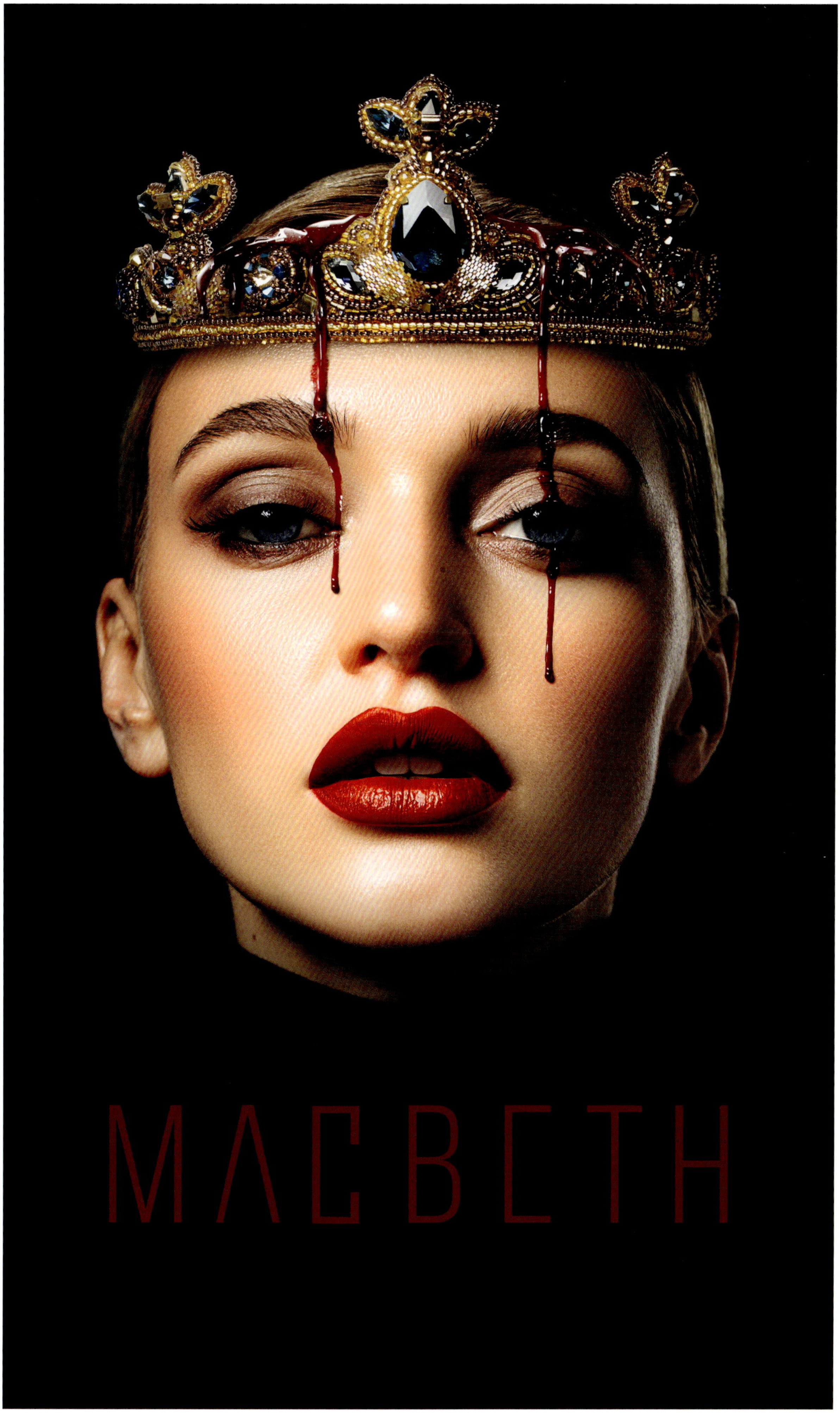

P237: Credit & Commentary **Title:** Macbeth | **Client:** Self-initiated | **Design Firm:** Carmit Design Studio

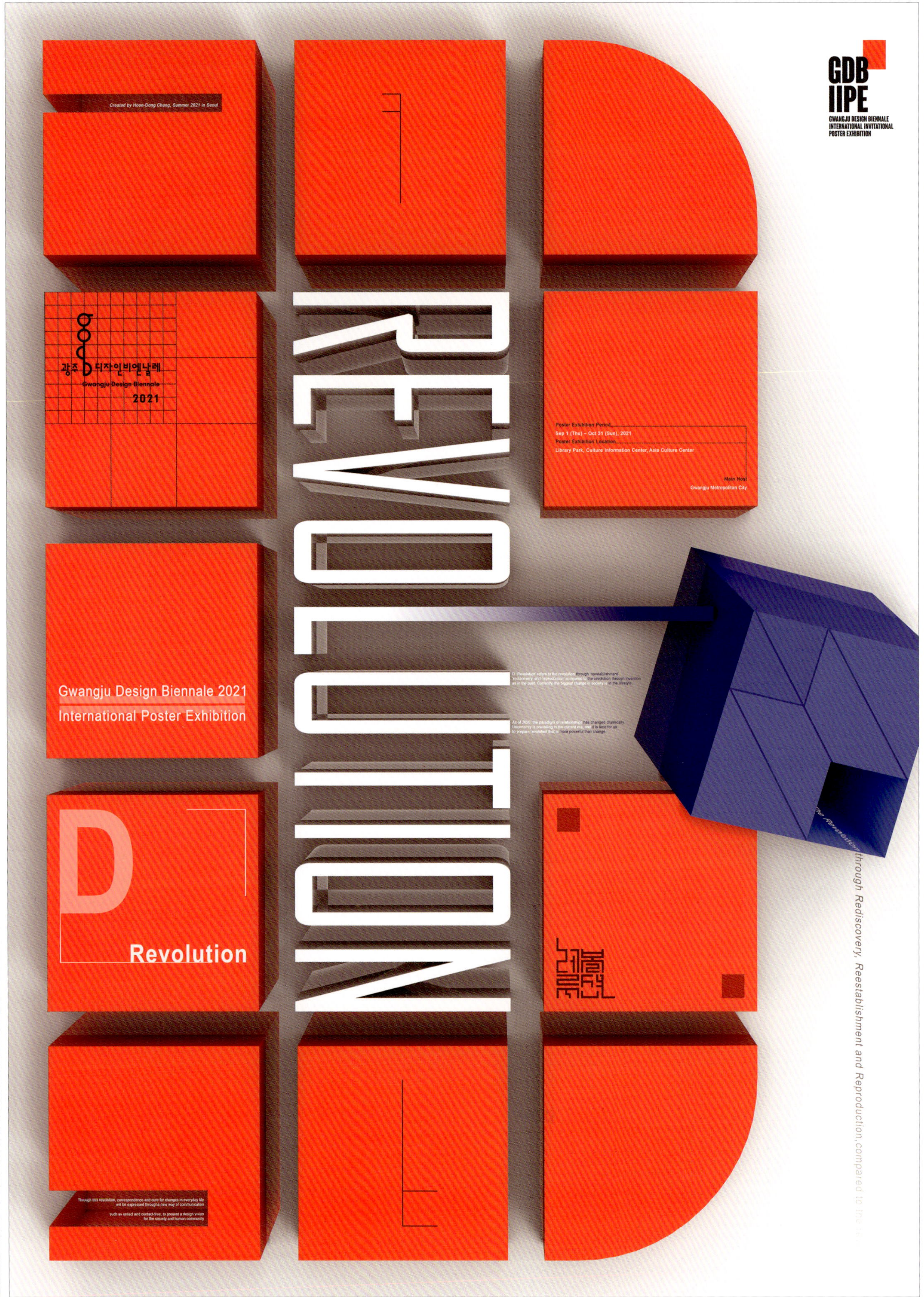

 Title: D Revolution | Client: Gwangju Design Biennale 2021 | Design Firm: Dankook University

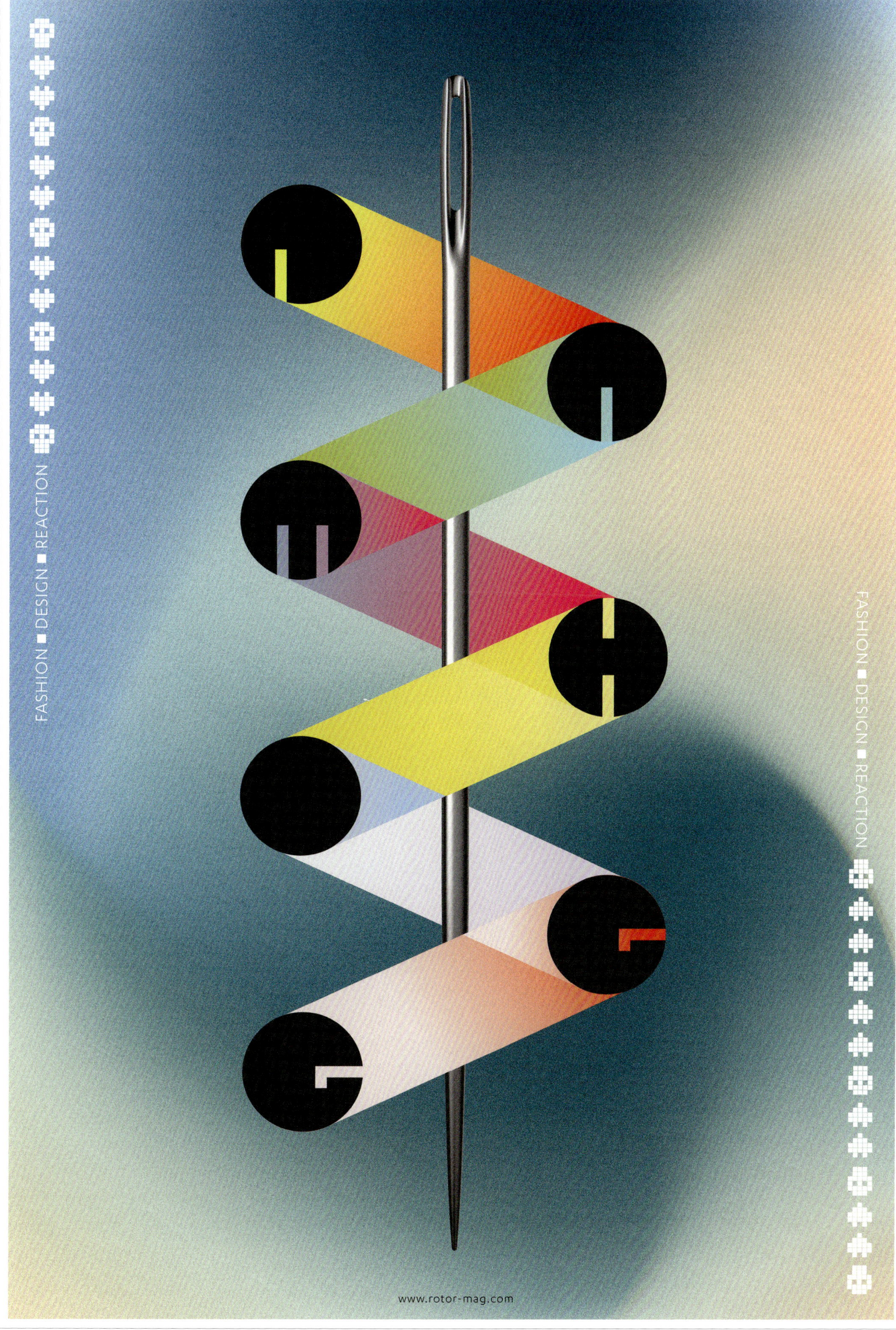

P237: Credit & Commentary **Title:** Pam Hogg Poster | **Client:** ROTOR Magazine | **Design Firm:** Mike Hughes Creative Direction + Design

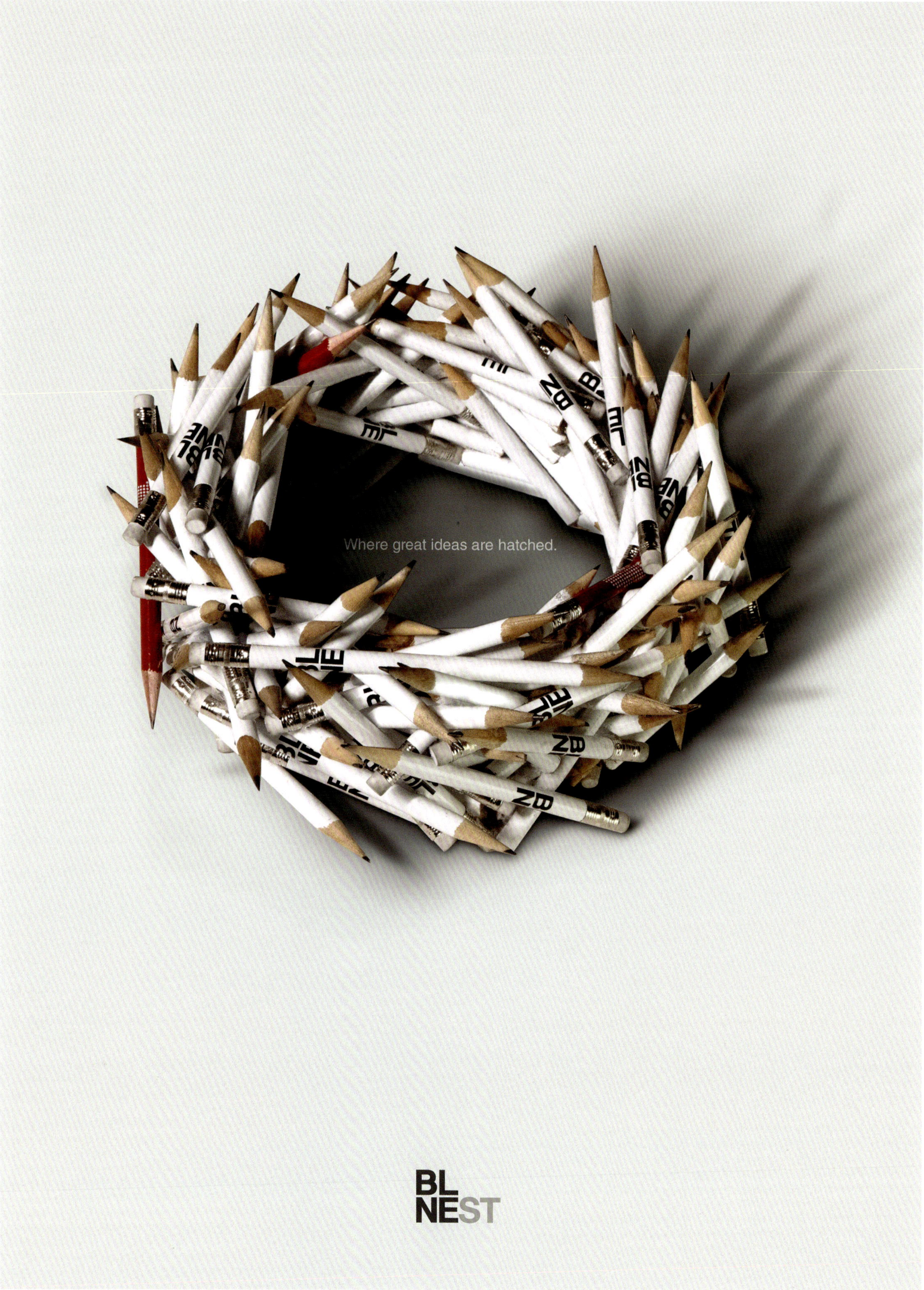

Where great ideas are hatched.

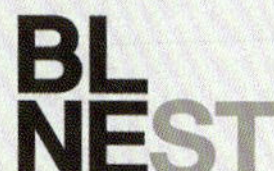

P237: Credit & Commentary **Title:** BL Nest Poster | **Client:** Nebraska College of Journalism | **Design Firm:** Bailey Lauerman

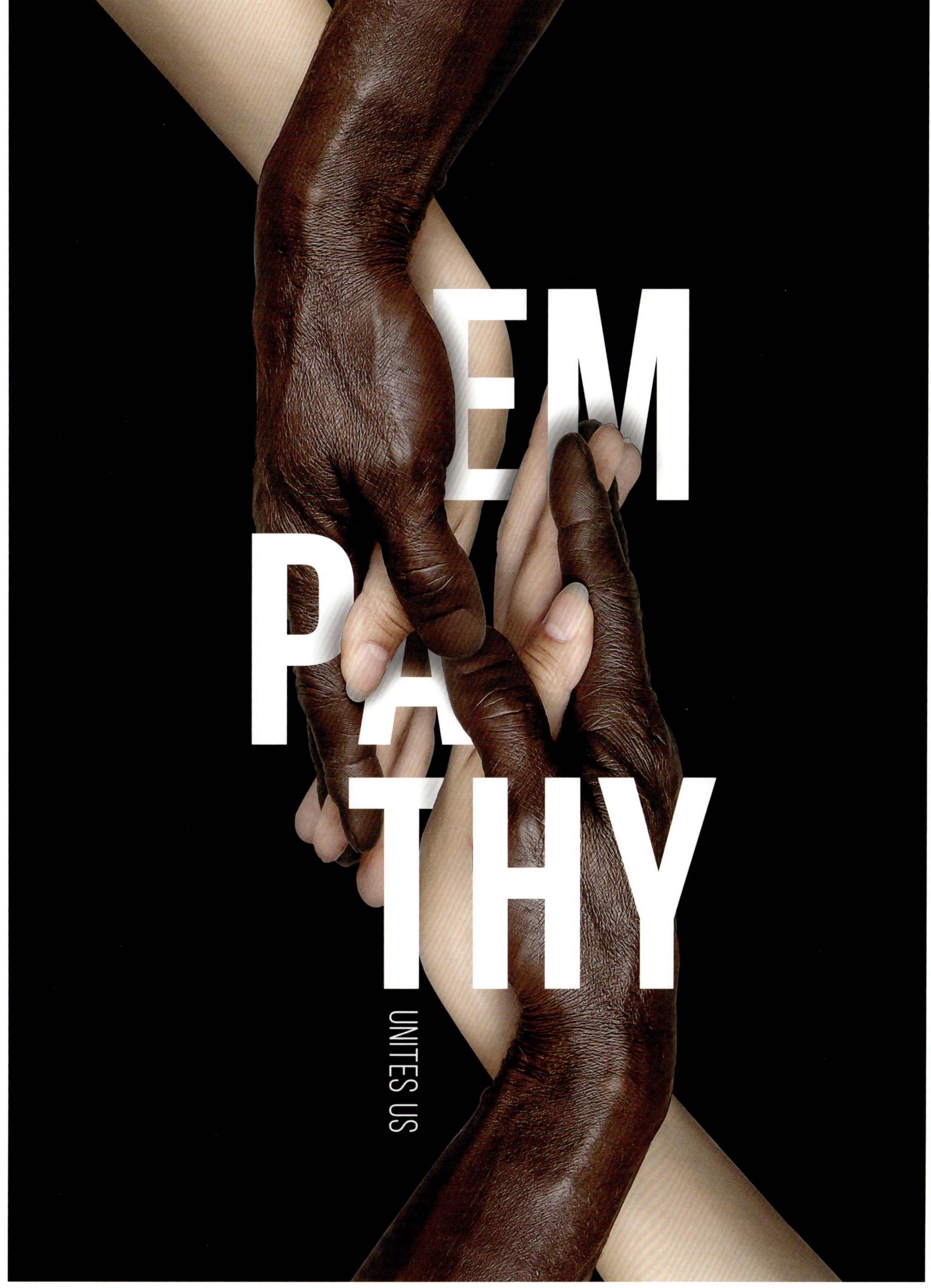

 Title: What Unites Us | **Client:** What Unites Us 3 Exhibition | **Design Firm:** Carmit Design Studio

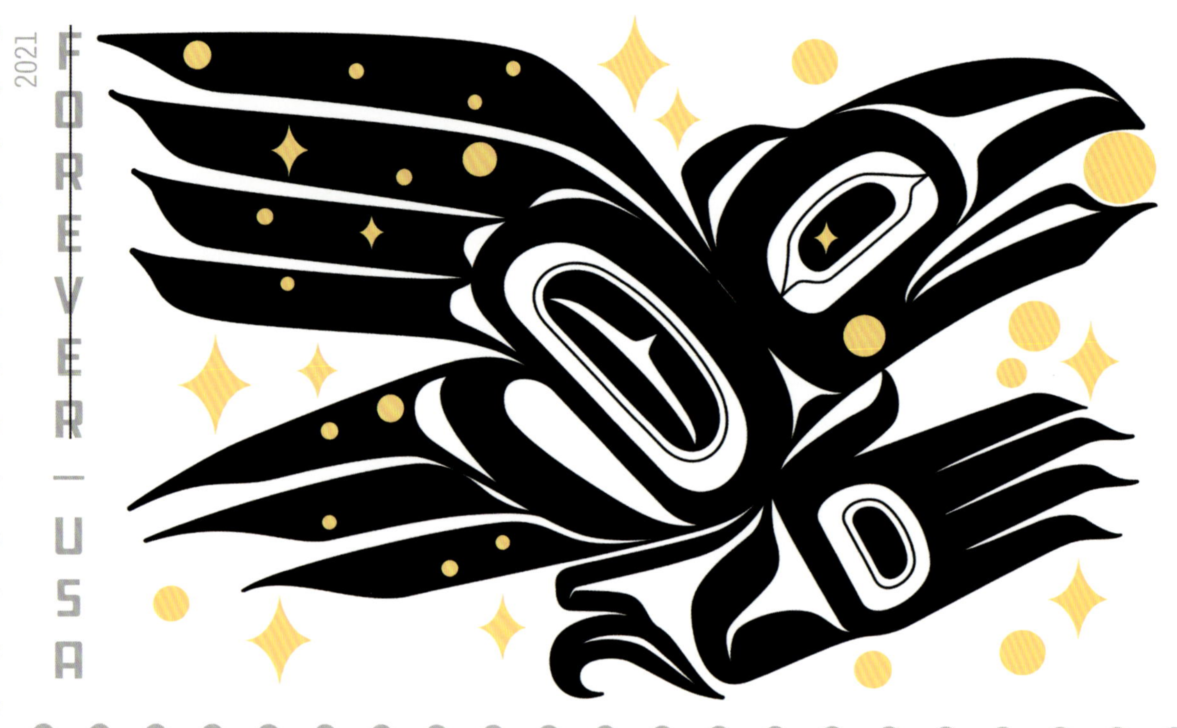

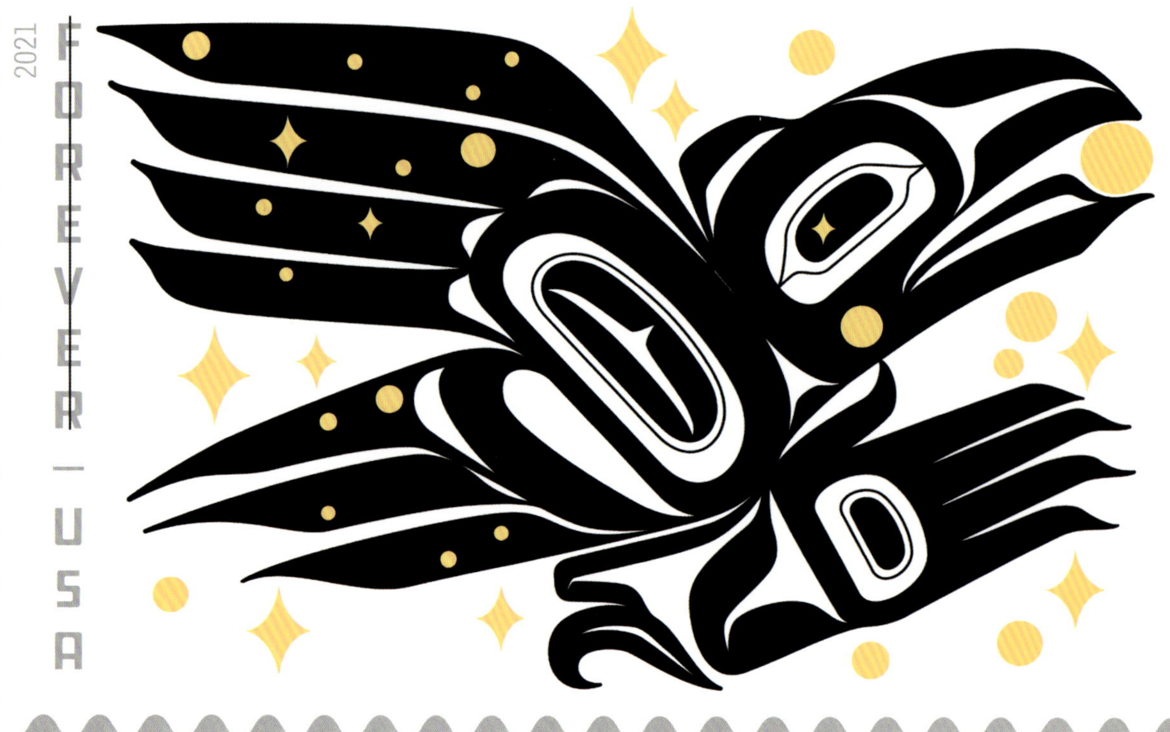

Title: Raven Story | **Client:** U.S. Postal Service | **Design Firm:** Studio A

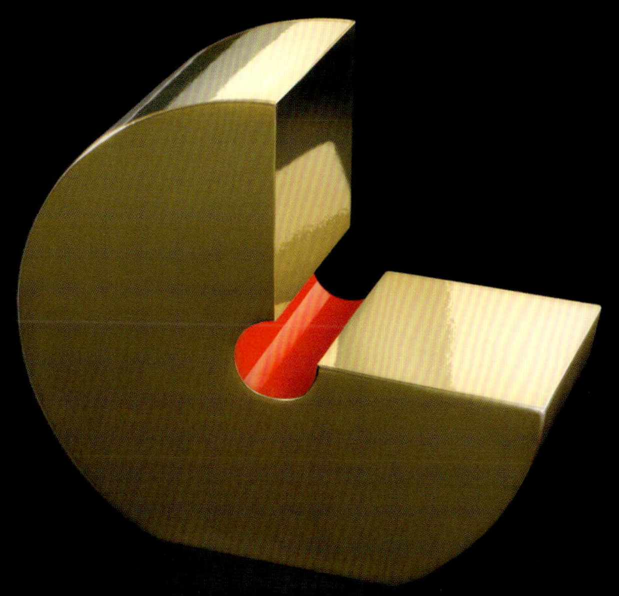

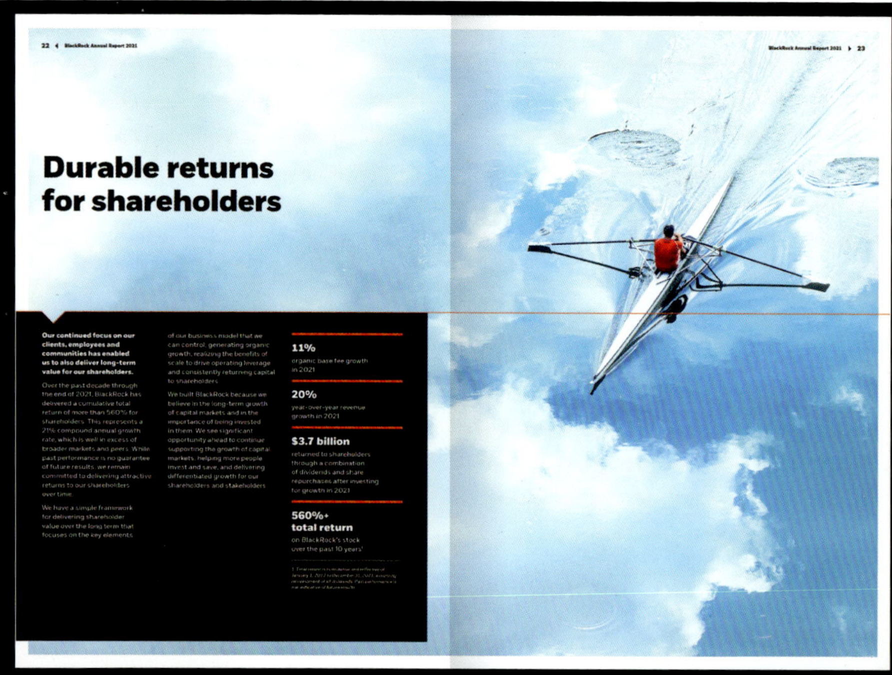

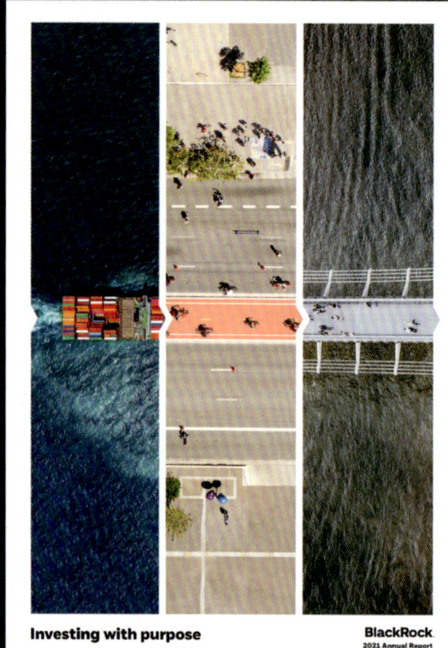

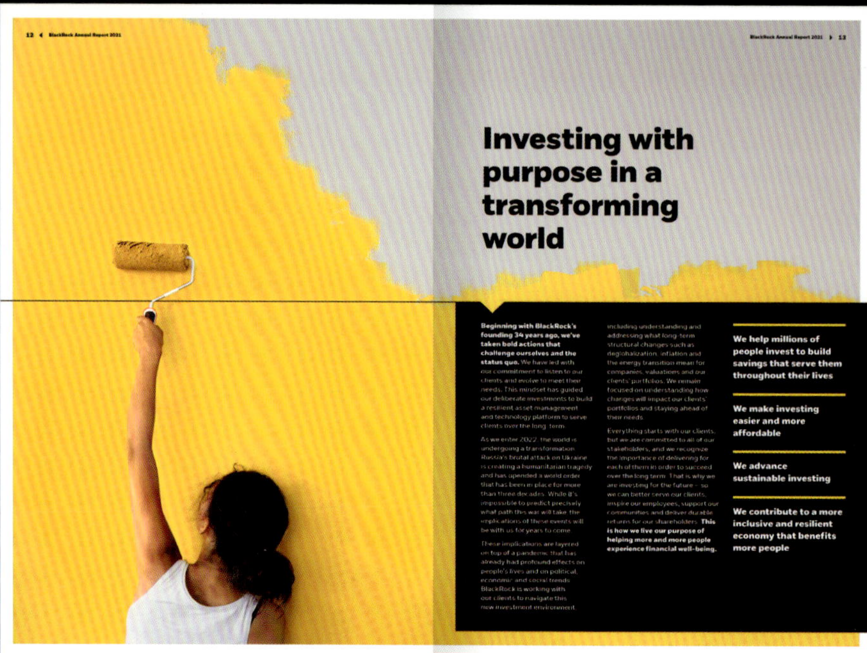

P238: Credit & Commentary

Title: BlackRock AR | **Client:** BlackRock | **Design Firm:** Addison

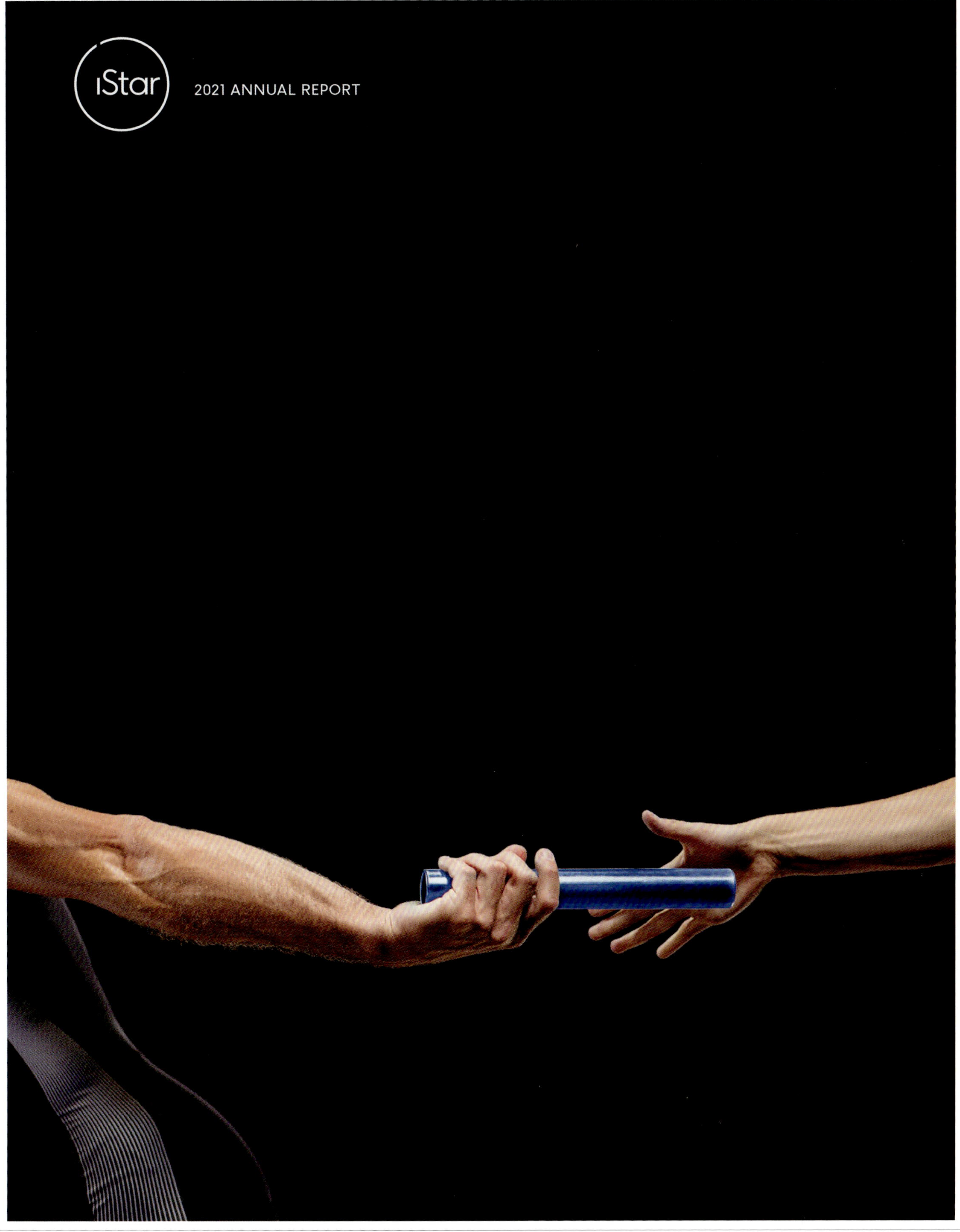

P238: Credit & Commentary **Title:** iStar AR | **Client:** iStar | **Design Firm:** Addison

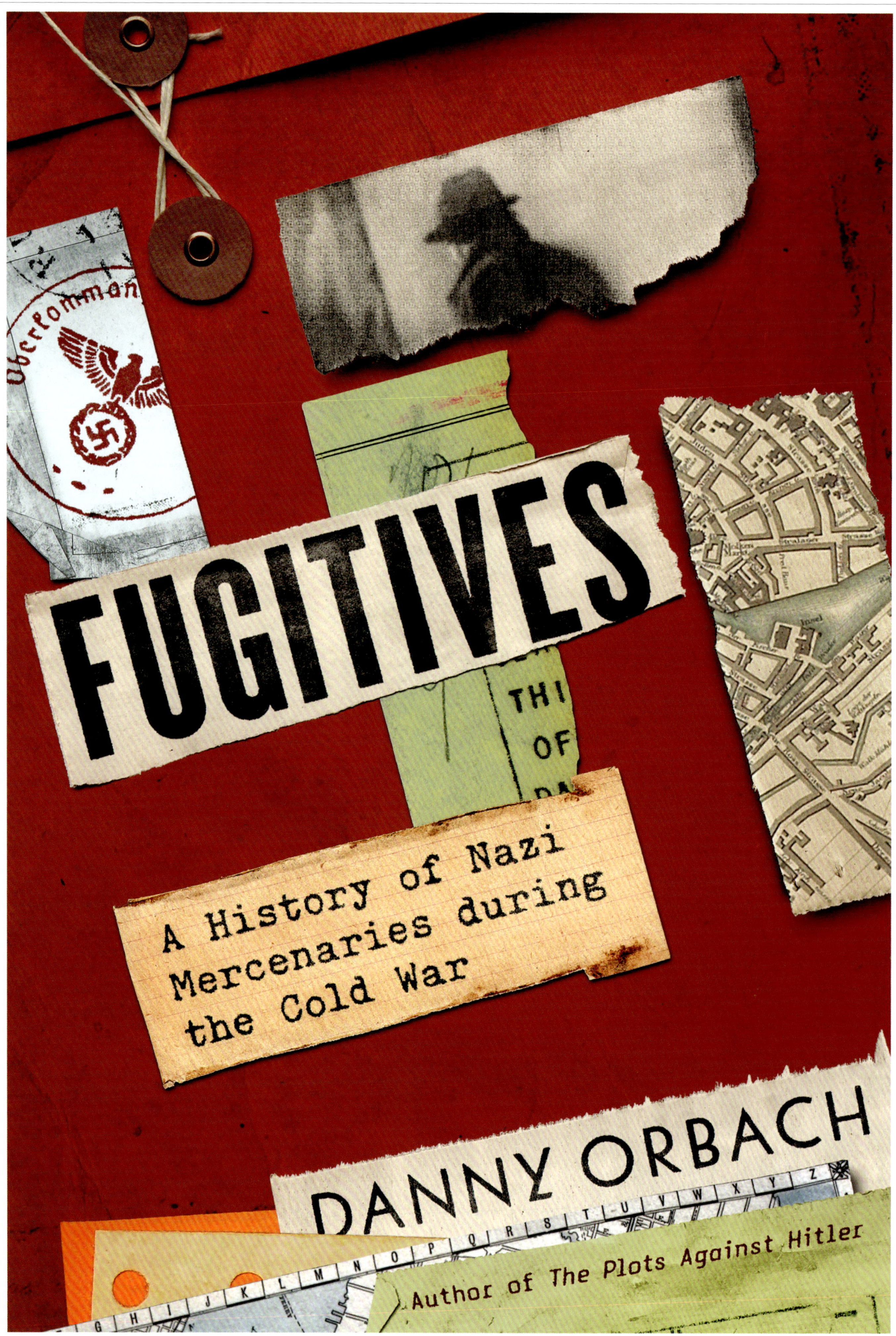

Title: Fugitives | **Client:** Pegasus Books | **Design Firm:** Faceout Studio

An Iris Grey Mystery

"I can't wait to see where Iris Grey's next artistic commission takes us."
-PAIGE SHELTON
NEW YORK TIMES BESTSELLING AUTHOR

MURDER at the CASTLE

M. B. SHAW

#1 New York Times Bestselling Author

 Title: Murder at the Castle | **Client:** Pegasus Books | **Design Firm:** Faceout Studio

Title: Witch Hunt | **Client:** Hammer Museum | **Design Firm:** Still Room

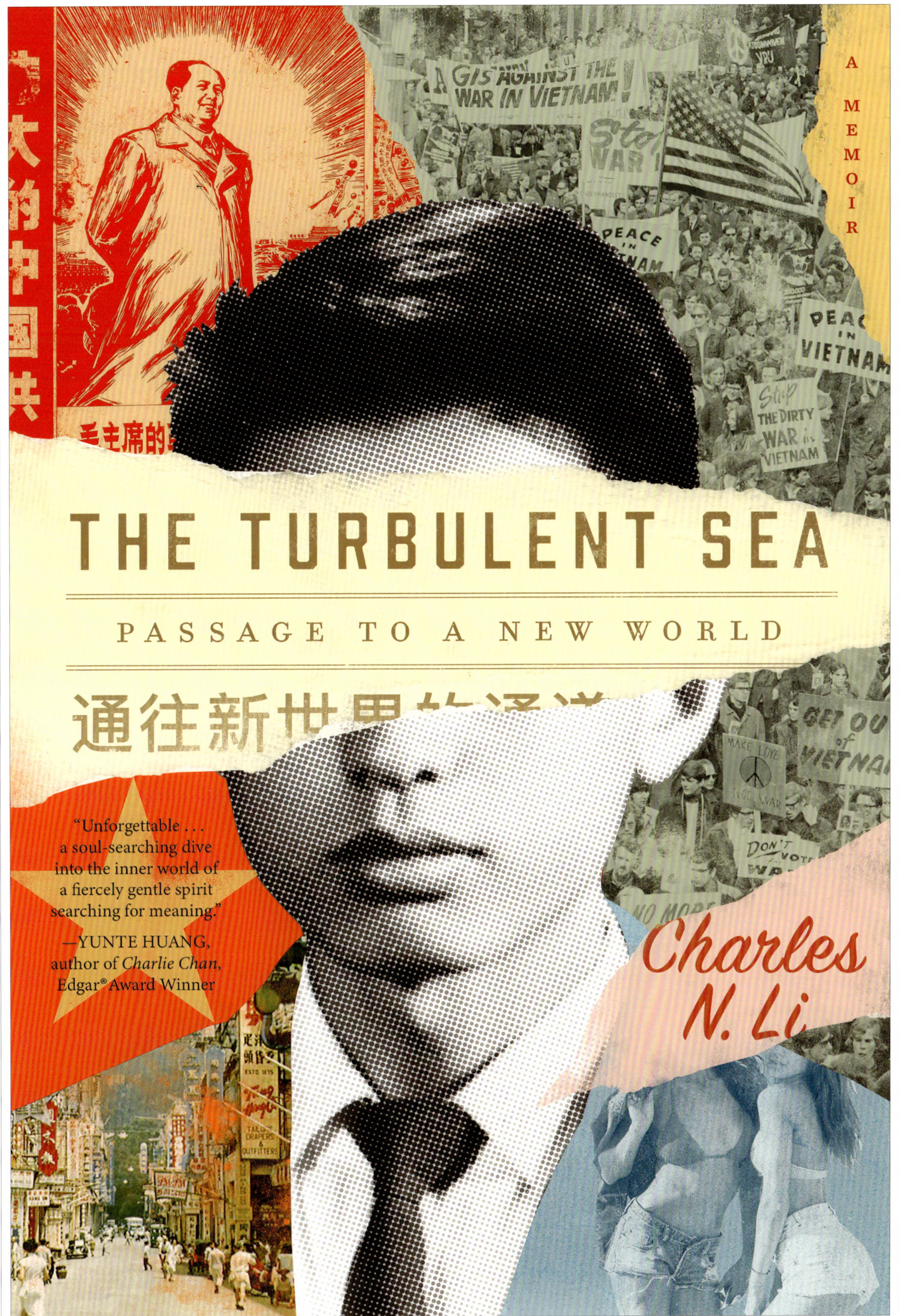

 Title: The Turbulent Sea | **Client:** Regan Arts | **Design Firm:** Richard Ljoenes Design LLC

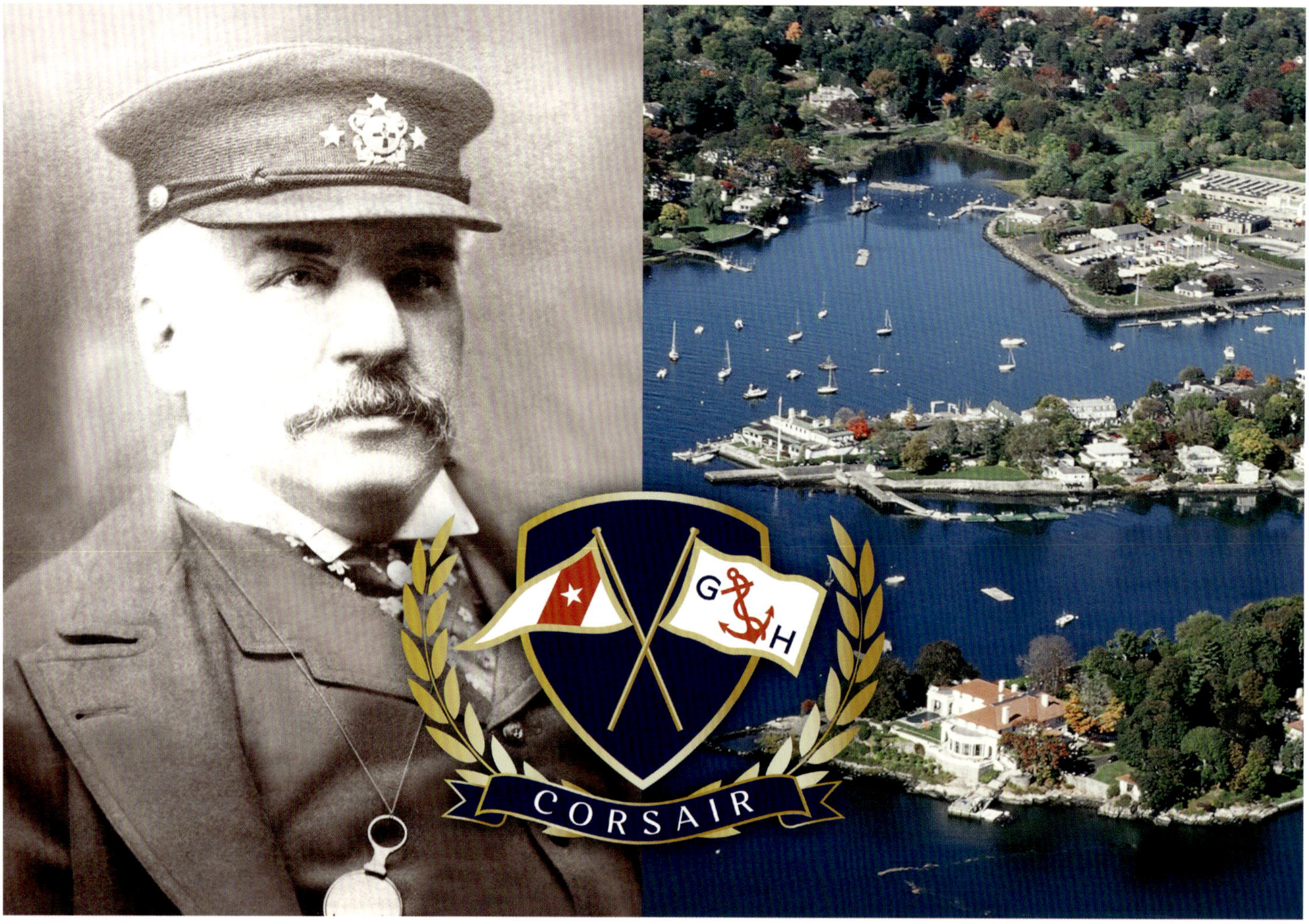

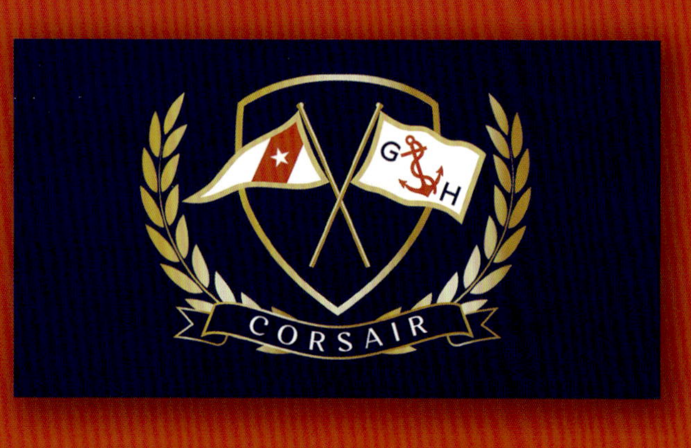

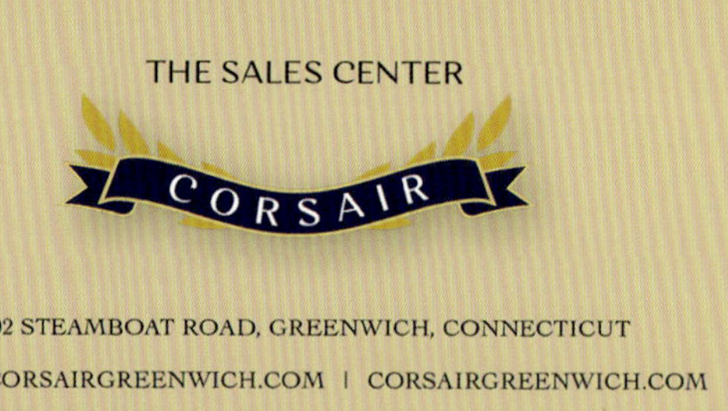

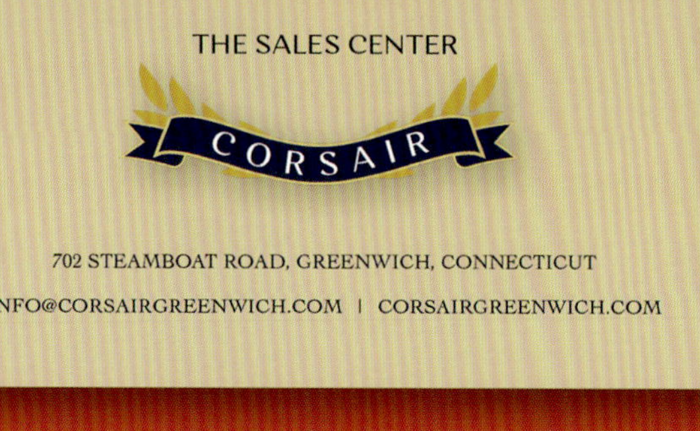

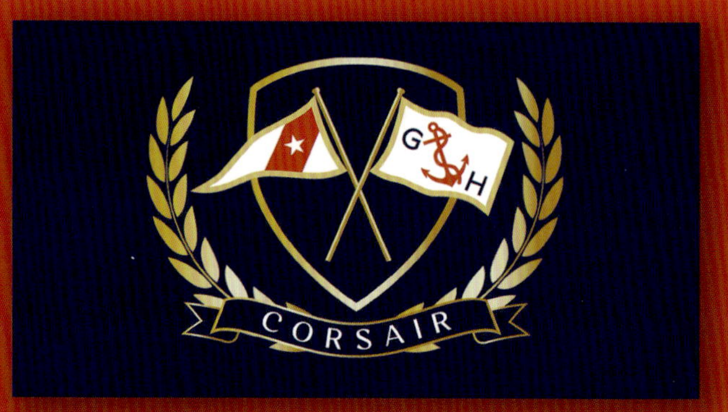

Title: The Corsair Branding | **Client:** National Resources | **Design Firm:** Mermaid, Inc.

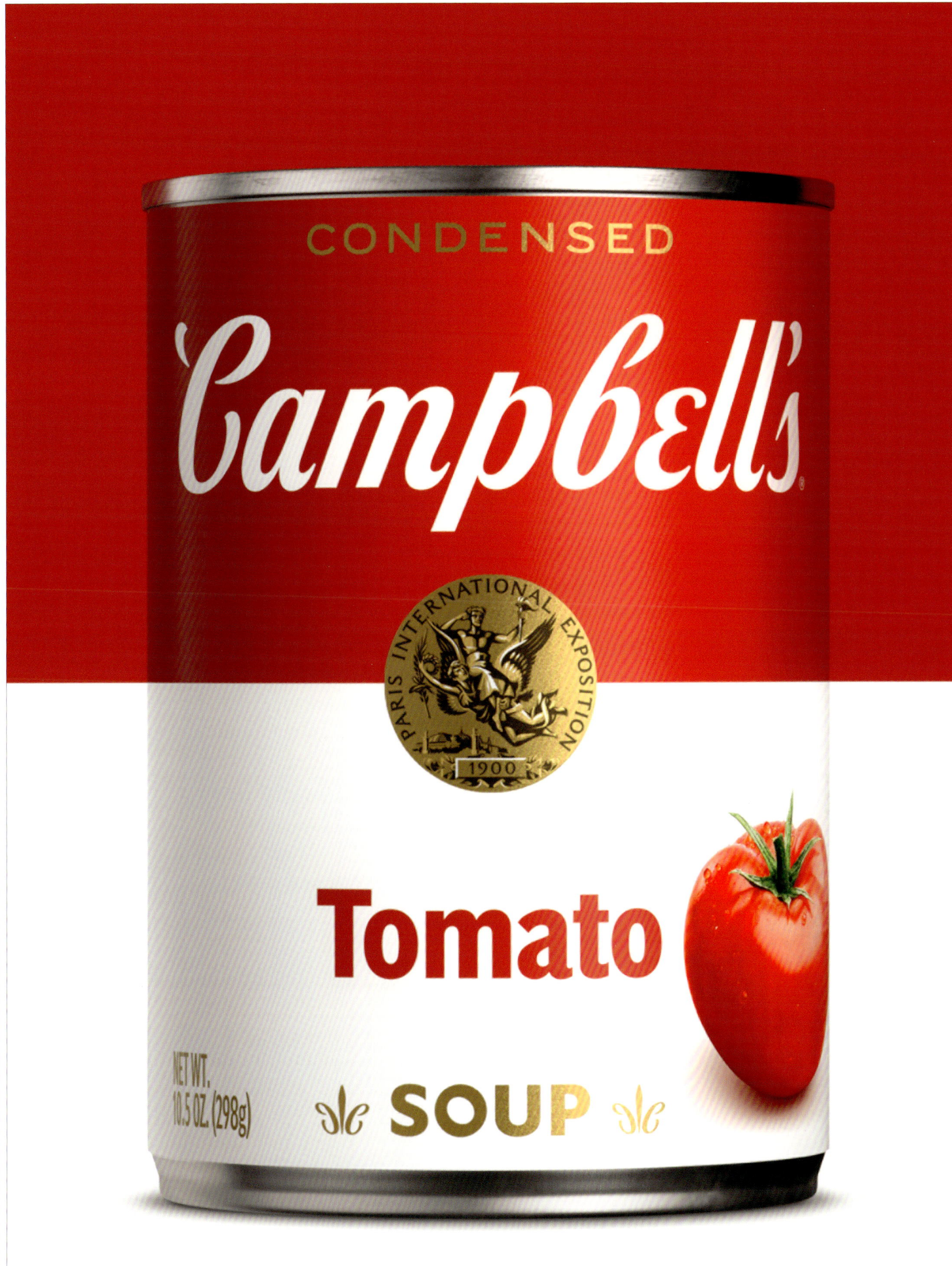

Title: Campbell's Red & White Condensed Soup Visual Identity | **Client:** Campbell's | **Design Firm:** Turner Duckworth: London, San Francisco & New York

P238: Credit & Commentary | Image 1 of 7

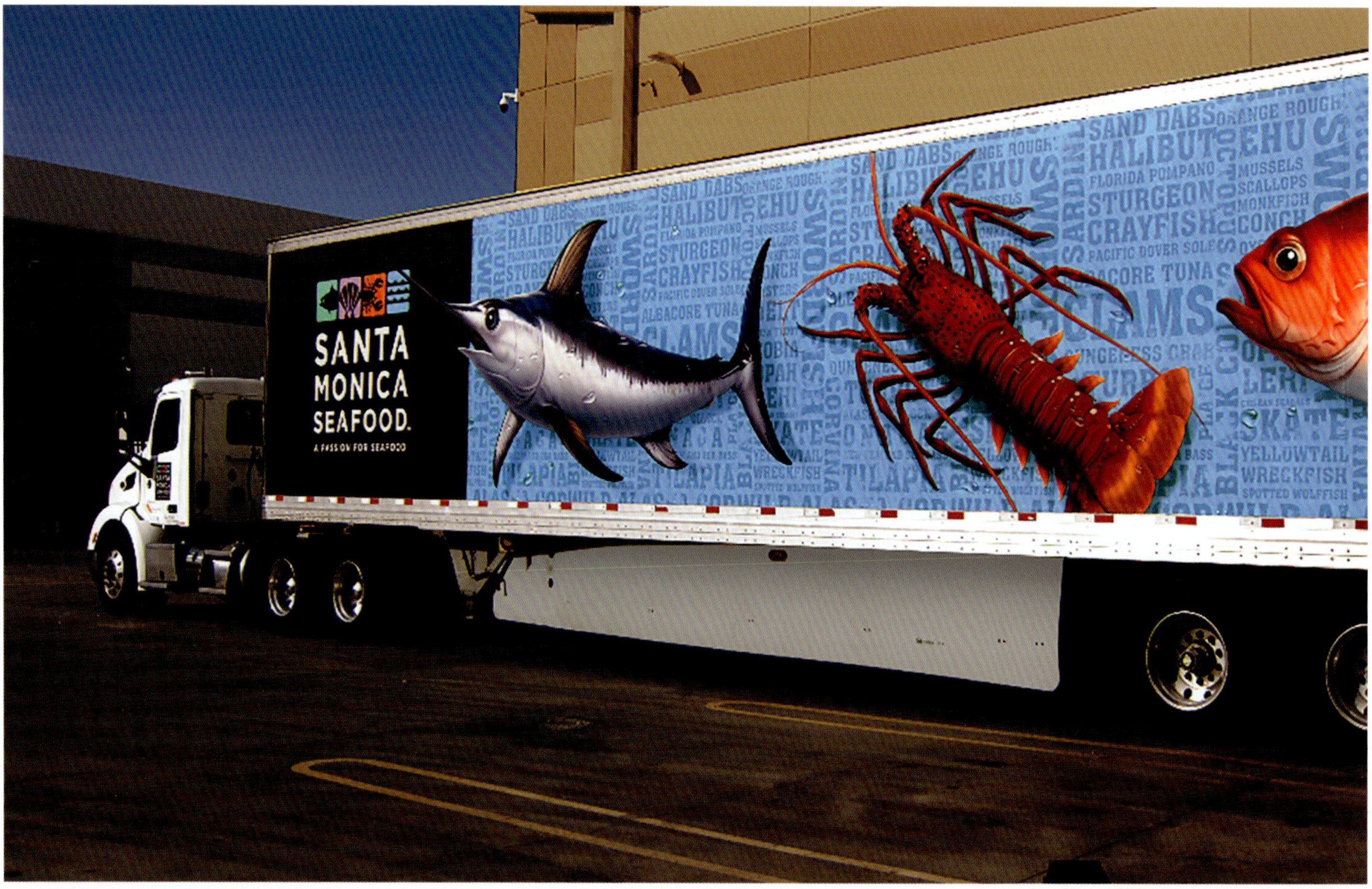

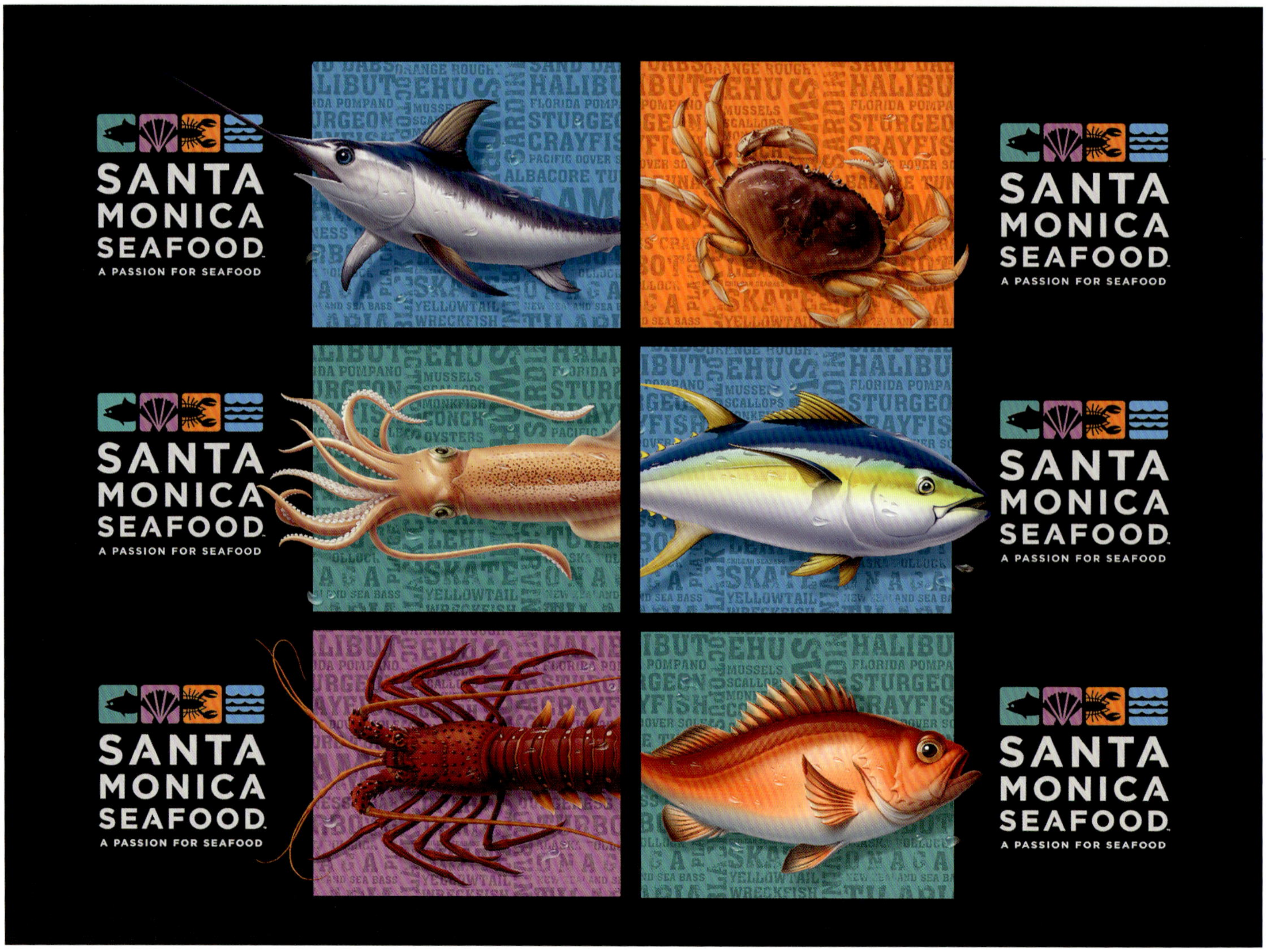

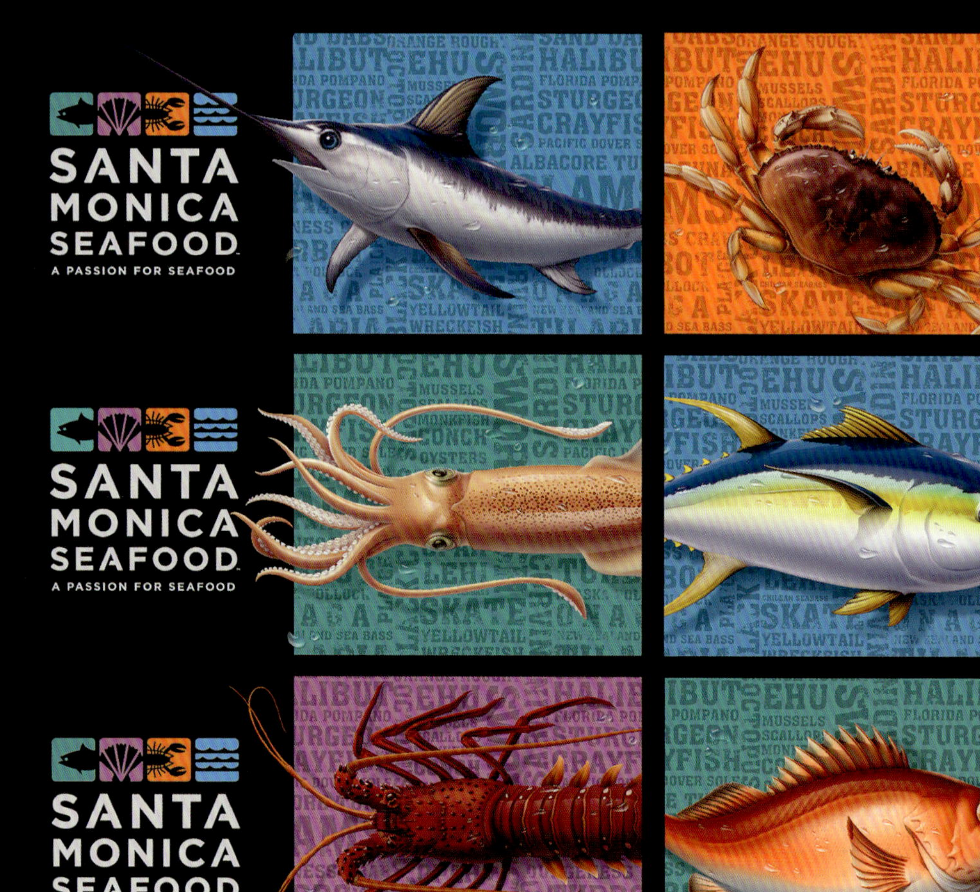

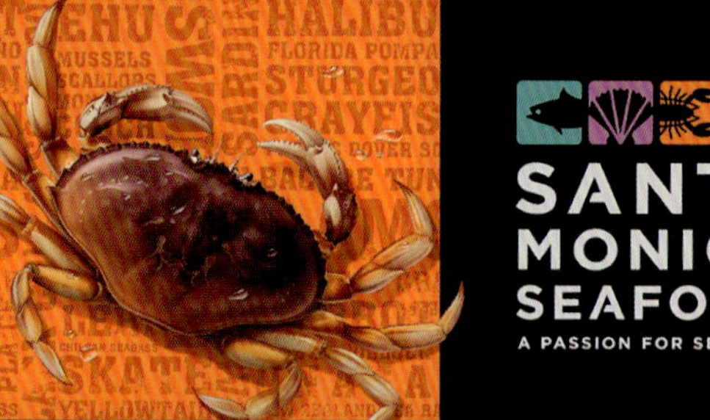

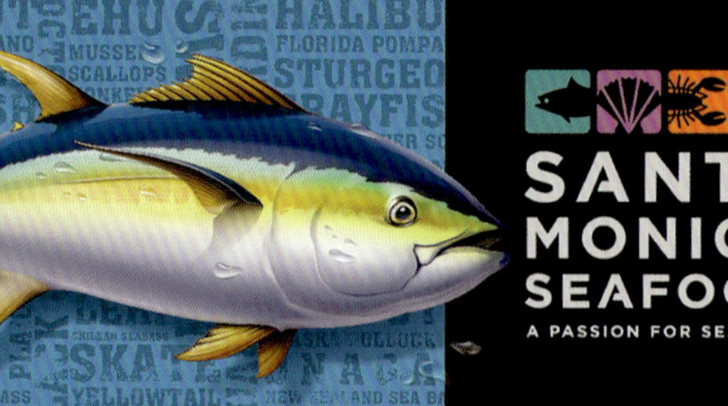

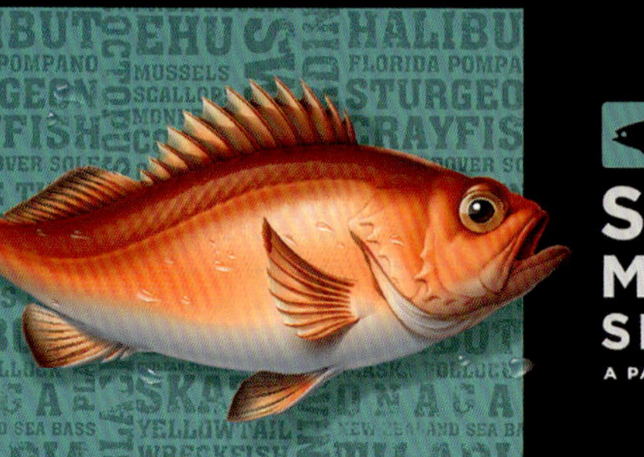

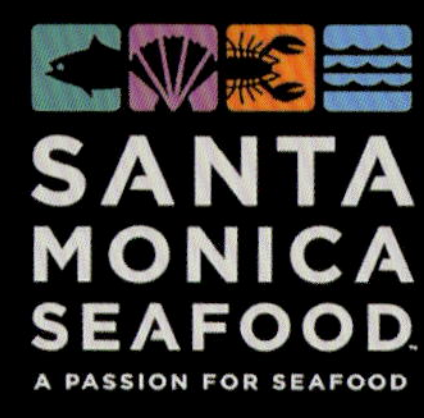

Title: Santa Monica Seafood Brand Identity | **Client:** Santa Monica Seafood | **Design Firm:** PH Studio

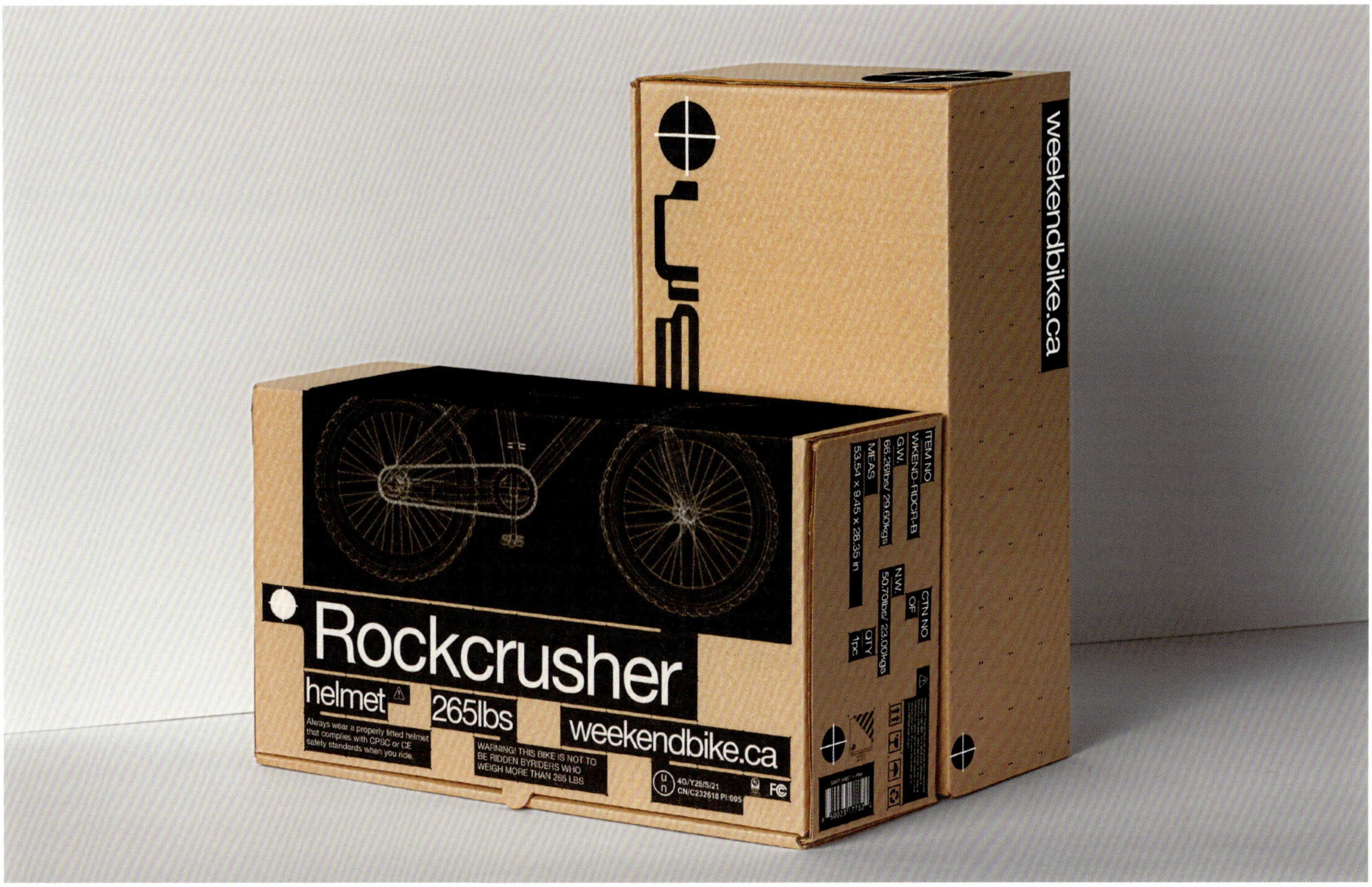

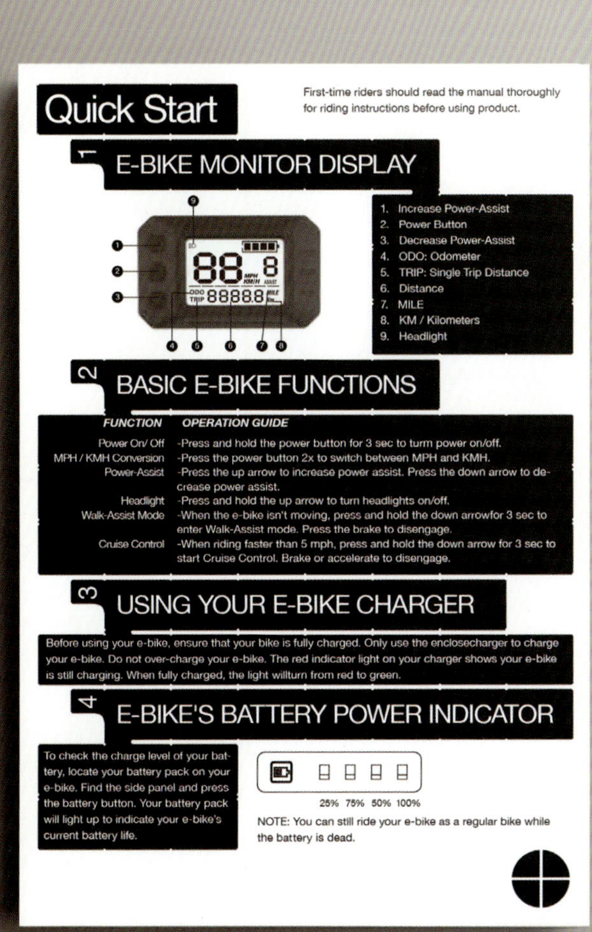

Quick Start

First-time riders should read the manual thoroughly for riding instructions before using product.

1 E-BIKE MONITOR DISPLAY

1. Increase Power-Assist
2. Power Button
3. Decrease Power-Assist
4. ODO: Odometer
5. TRIP: Single Trip Distance
6. Distance
7. MILE
8. KM / Kilometers
9. Headlight

2 BASIC E-BIKE FUNCTIONS

FUNCTION	OPERATION GUIDE
Power On/ Off	-Press and hold the power button for 3 sec to turm power on/off.
MPH / KMH Conversion	-Press the power button 2x to switch between MPH and KMH.
Power-Assist	-Press the up arrow to increase power assist. Press the down arrow to decrease power assist.
Headlight	-Press and hold the up arrow to turn headlights on/off.
Walk-Assist Mode	-When the e-bike isn't moving, press and hold the down arrowfor 3 sec to enter Walk-Assist mode. Press the brake to disengage.
Cruise Control	-When riding faster than 5 mph, press and hold the down arrow for 3 sec to start Cruise Control. Brake or accelerate to disengage.

3 USING YOUR E-BIKE CHARGER

Before using your e-bike, ensure that your bike is fully charged. Only use the enclosecharger to charge your e-bike. Do not over-charge your e-bike. The red indicator light on your charger shows your e-bike is still charging. When fully charged, the light willturn from red to green.

4 E-BIKE'S BATTERY POWER INDICATOR

To check the charge level of your battery, locate your battery pack on your e-bike. Find the side panel and press the battery button. Your battery pack will light up to indicate your e-bike's current battery life.

25% 75% 50% 100%

NOTE: You can still ride your e-bike as a regular bike while the battery is dead.

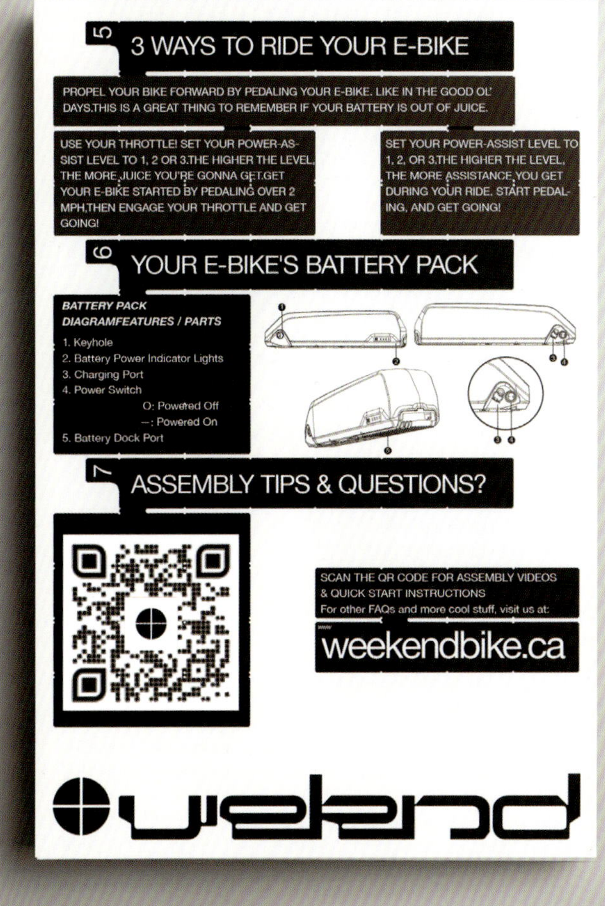

5 3 WAYS TO RIDE YOUR E-BIKE

PROPEL YOUR BIKE FORWARD BY PEDALING YOUR E-BIKE. LIKE IN THE GOOD OL' DAYS.THIS IS A GREAT THING TO REMEMBER IF YOUR BATTERY IS OUT OF JUICE.

USE YOUR THROTTLE! SET YOUR POWER-ASSIST LEVEL TO 1, 2 OR 3.THE HIGHER THE LEVEL, THE MORE JUICE YOU'RE GONNA GET.GET YOUR E-BIKE STARTED BY PEDALING OVER 2 MPH,THEN ENGAGE YOUR THROTTLE AND GET GOING!

SET YOUR POWER-ASSIST LEVEL TO 1, 2, OR 3.THE HIGHER THE LEVEL, THE MORE ASSISTANCE YOU GET DURING YOUR RIDE. START PEDALING, AND GET GOING!

6 YOUR E-BIKE'S BATTERY PACK

BATTERY PACK DIAGRAMFEATURES / PARTS

1. Keyhole
2. Battery Power Indicator Lights
3. Charging Port
4. Power Switch
   O: Powered Off
   —: Powered On
5. Battery Dock Port

7 ASSEMBLY TIPS & QUESTIONS?

SCAN THE QR CODE FOR ASSEMBLY VIDEOS & QUICK START INSTRUCTIONS
For other FAQs and more cool stuff, visit us at:

www weekendbike.ca

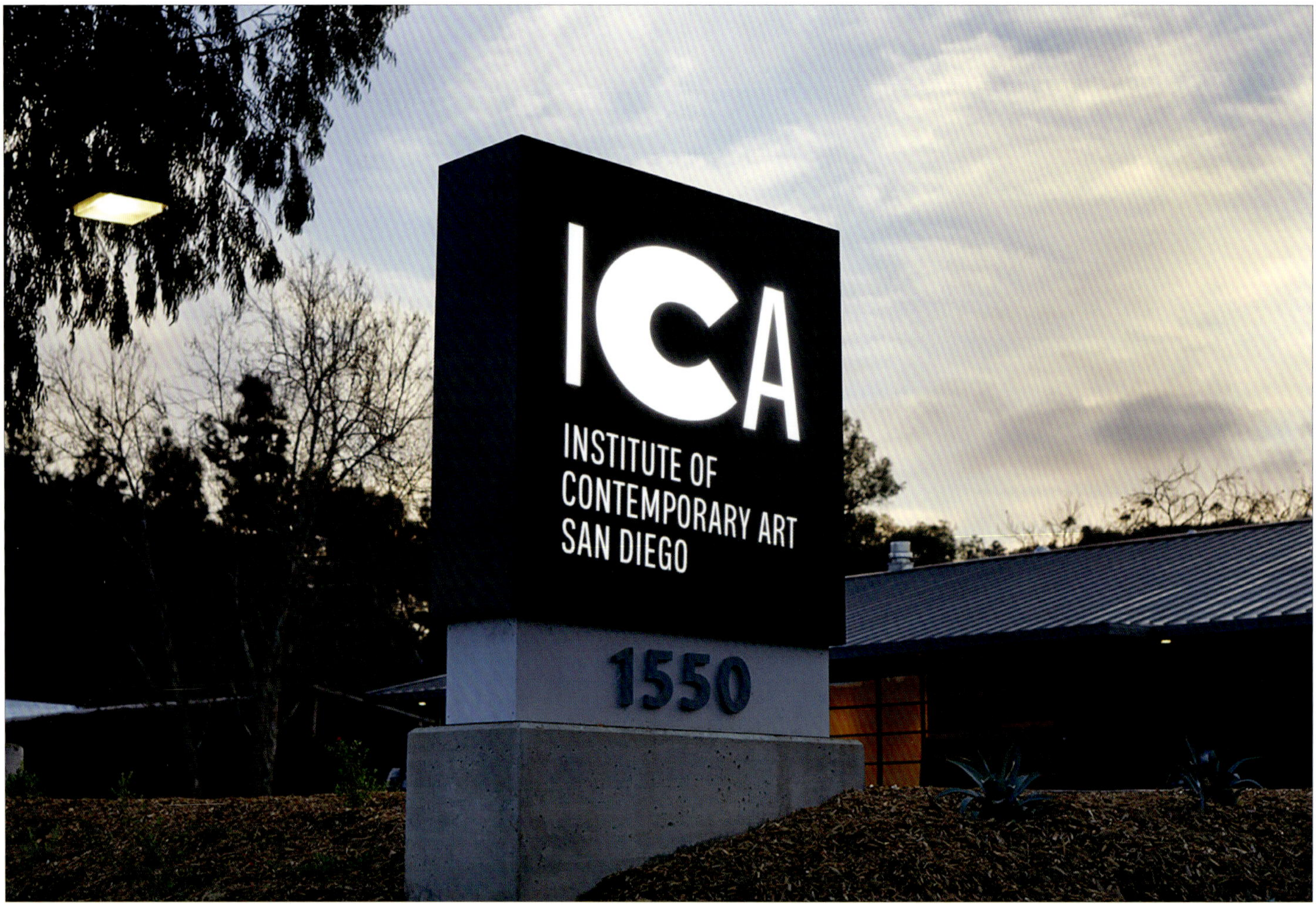

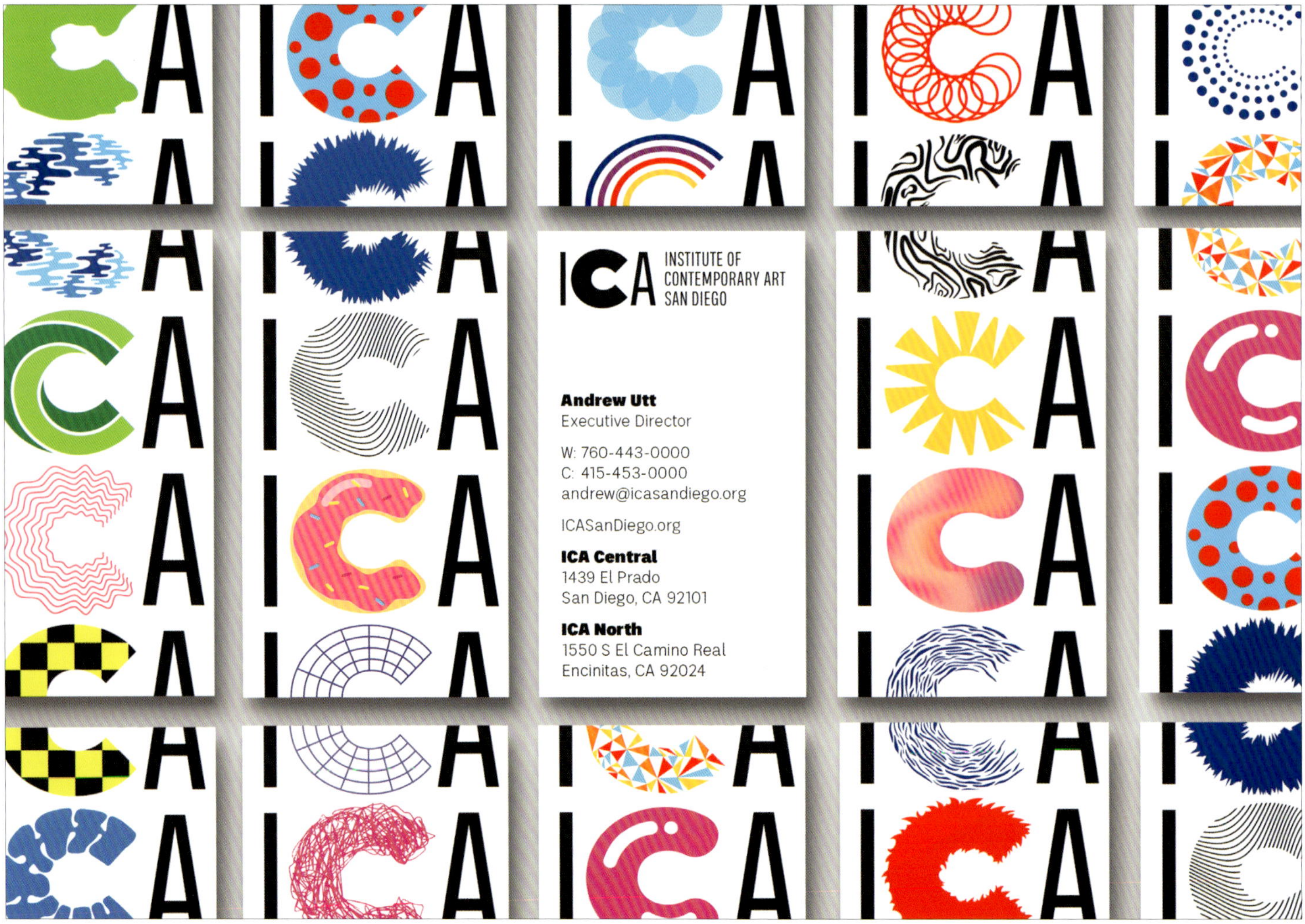

 Title: ICA Brand Identity | **Client:** Institute of Contemporary Art, San Diego | **Design Firm:** MiresBall Images 1, 2 of 7

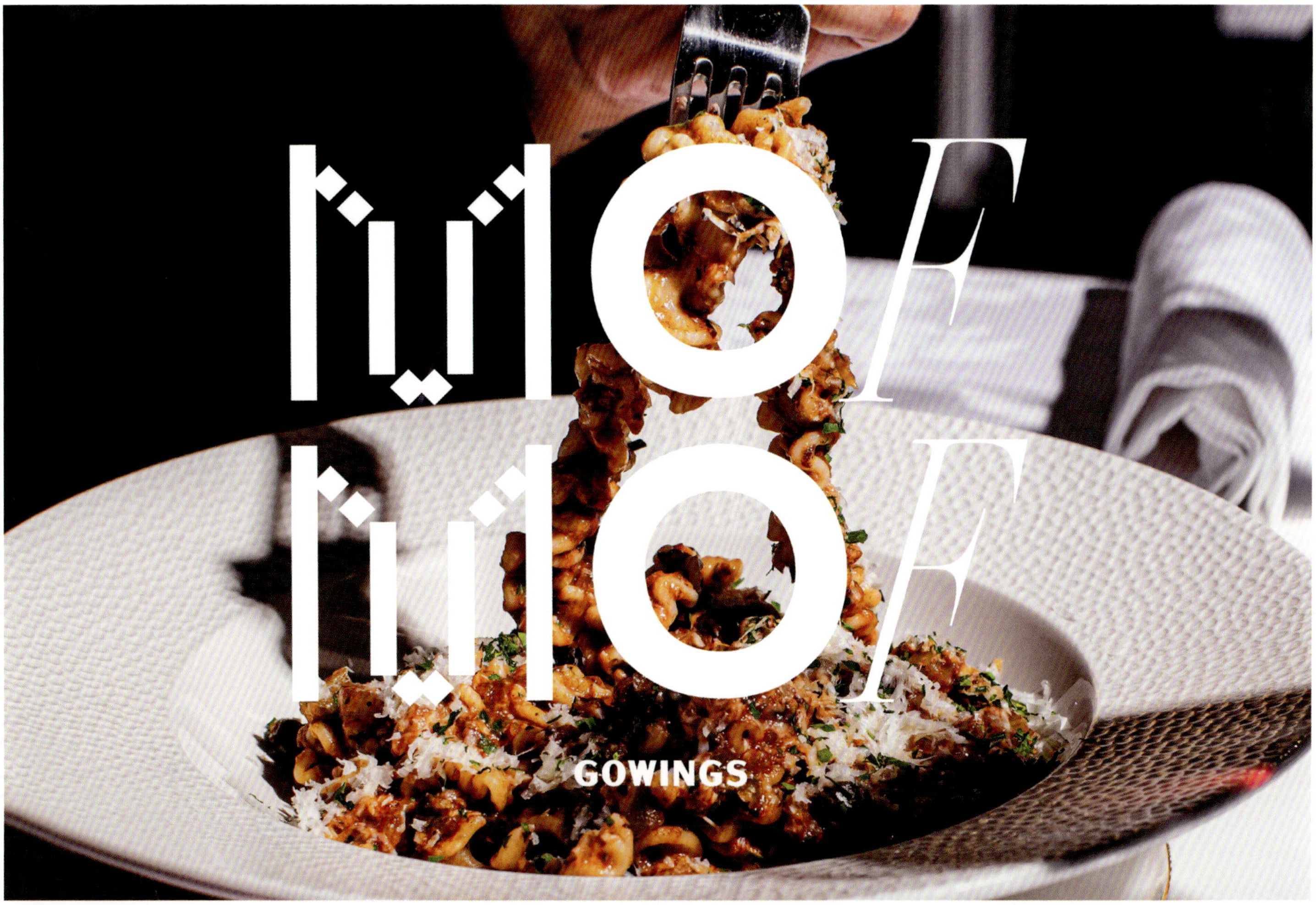

GOWINGS

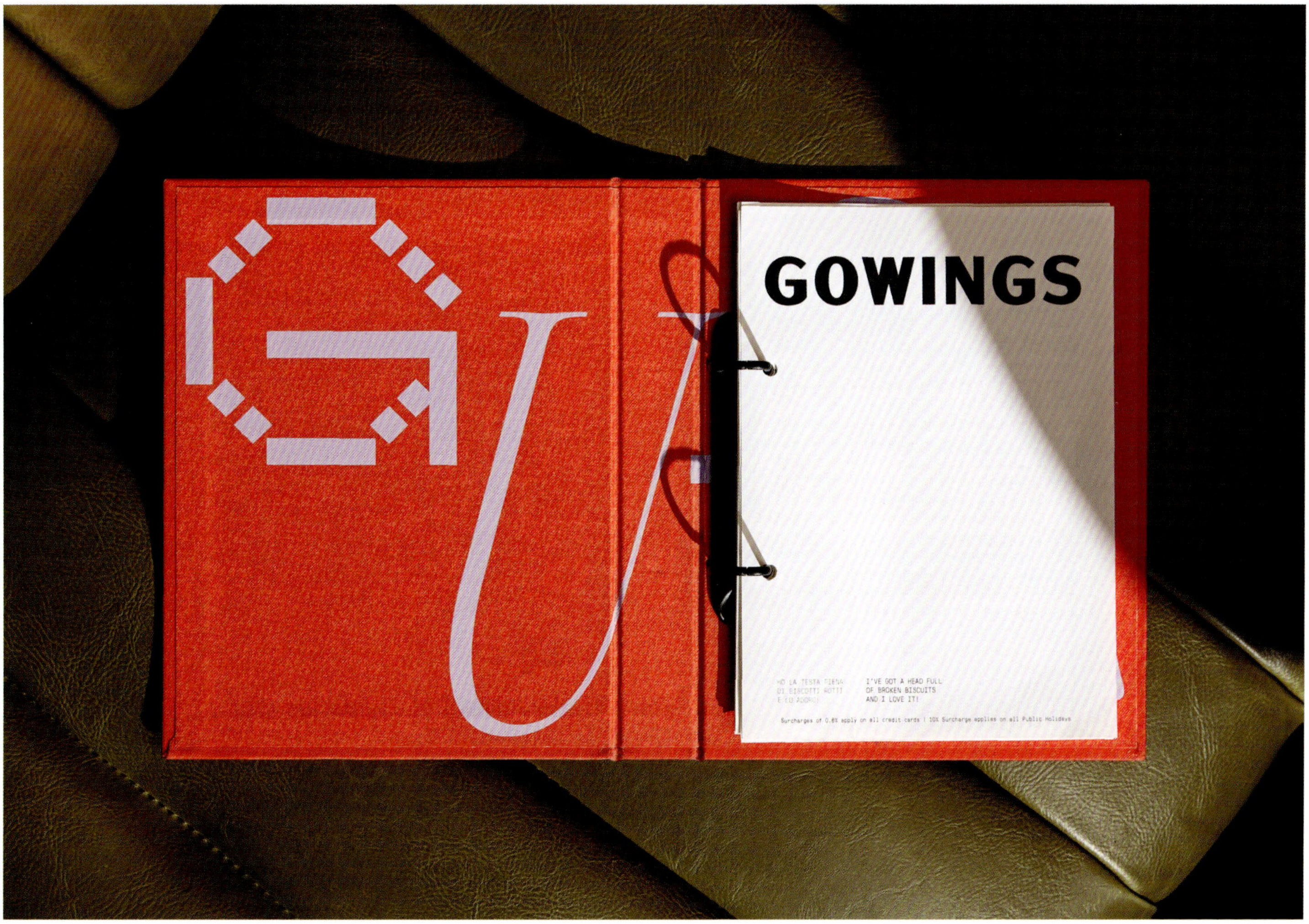

GOWINGS

Title: Gowings Restaurant | Client: Events & Hospitality | Design Firm: Toben

Images 1, 2 of 7

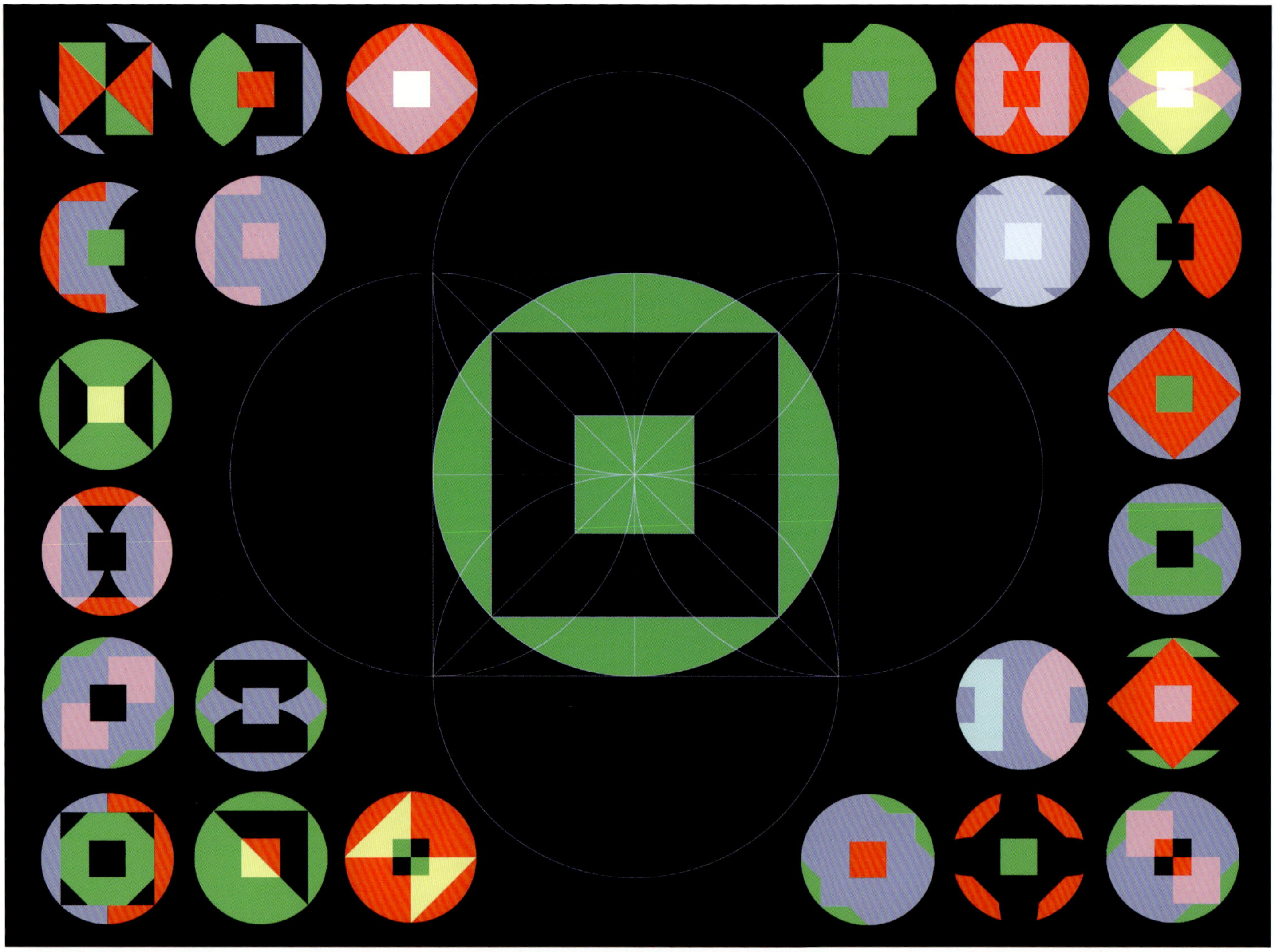

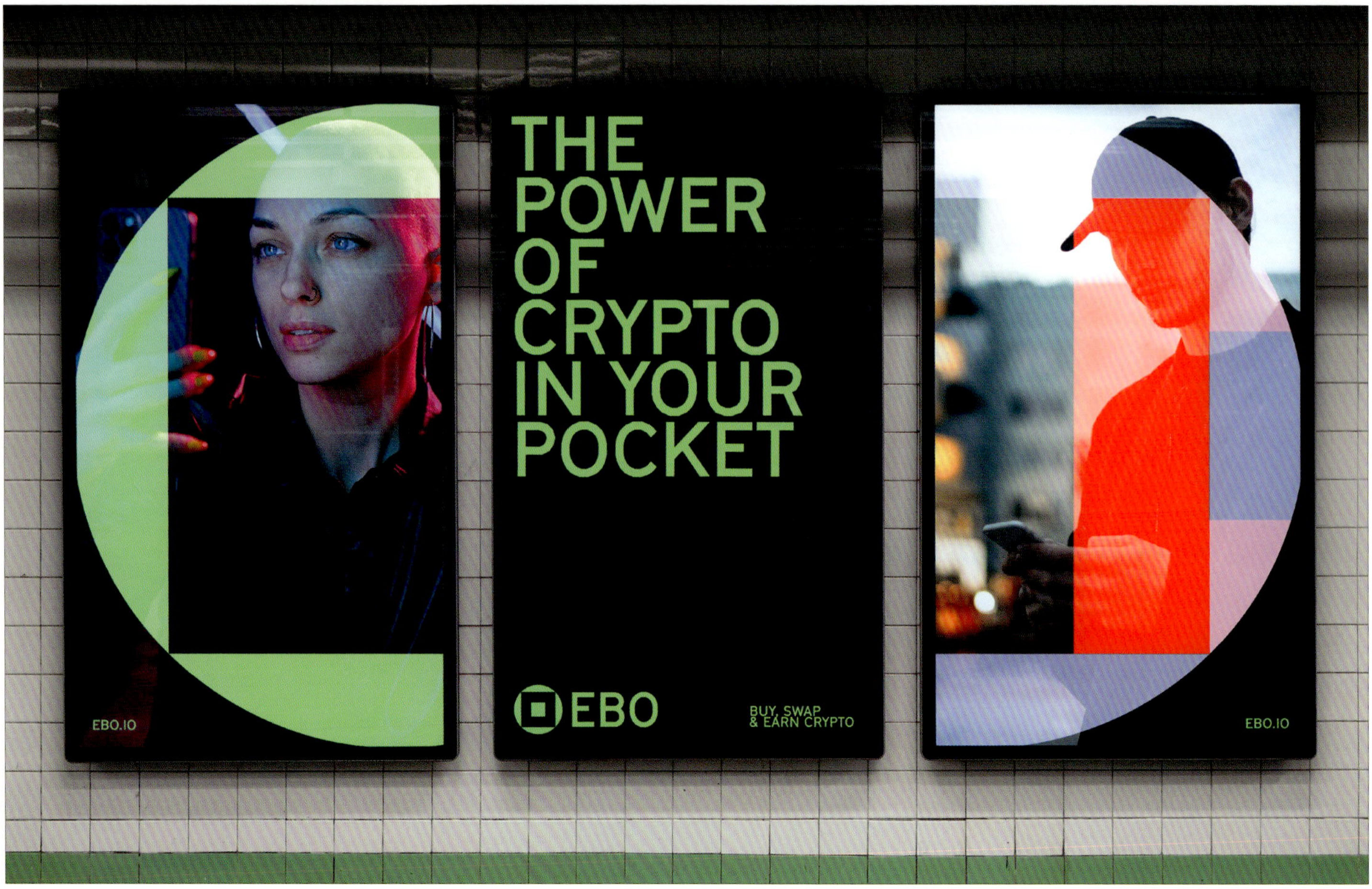

Title: EBO - Open Finance | **Client:** EBO Corp | **Design Firm:** Onrepeat Studio

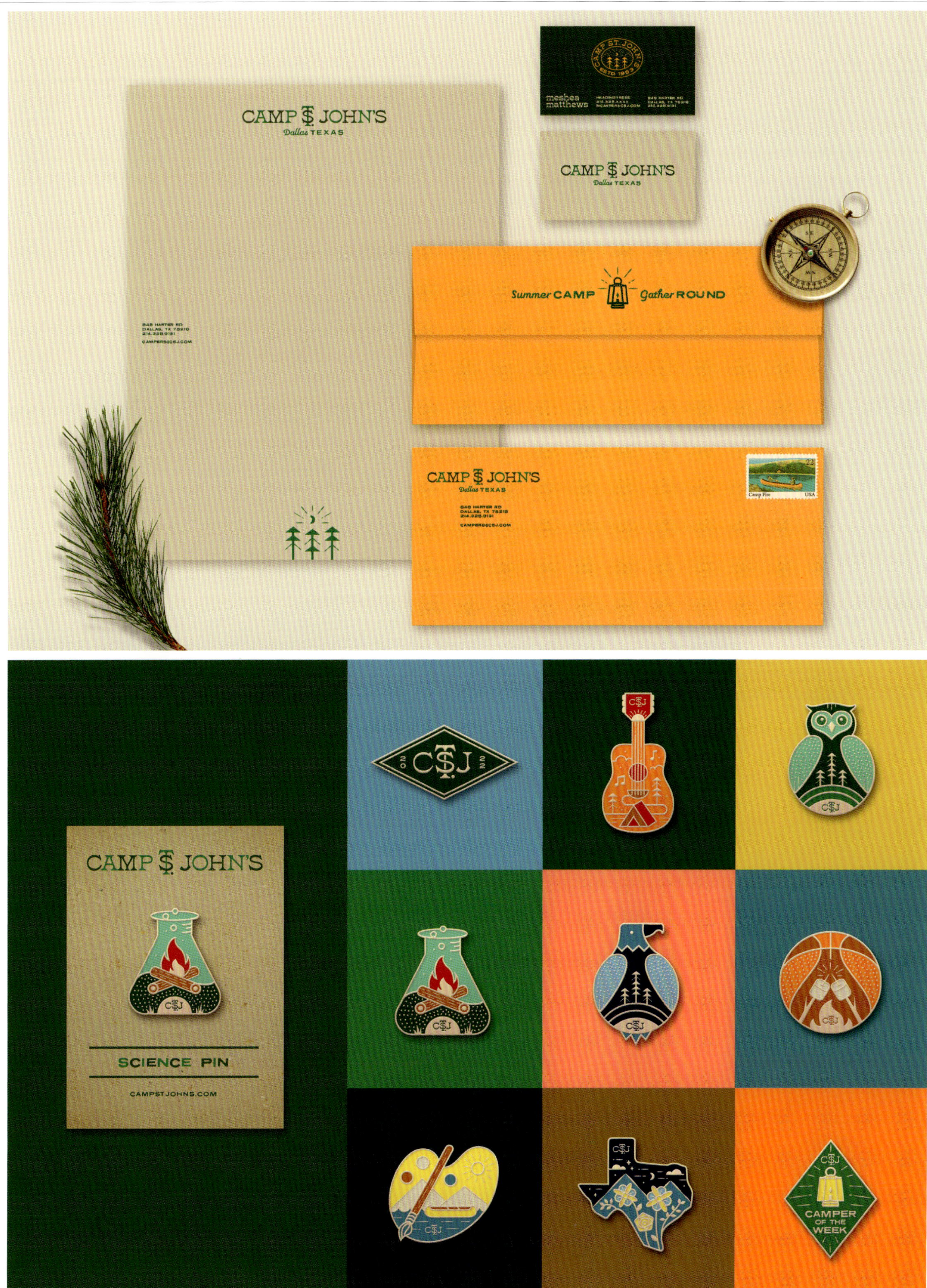

P239: Credit & Commentary Title: Camp St. John's Identity | Client: St. John's Episcopal School | Design Firm: *TraceElement Images 1, 2 of 7

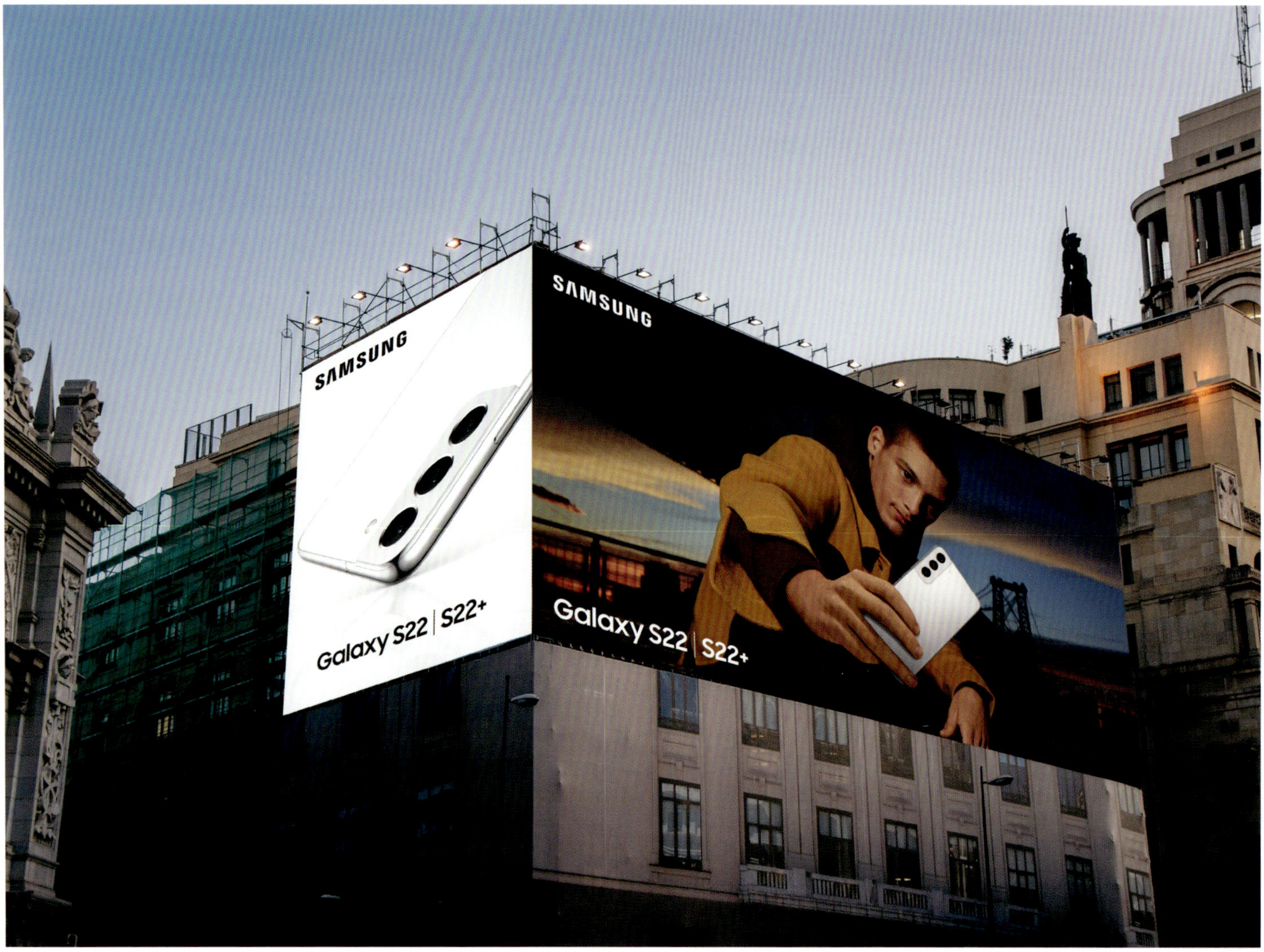

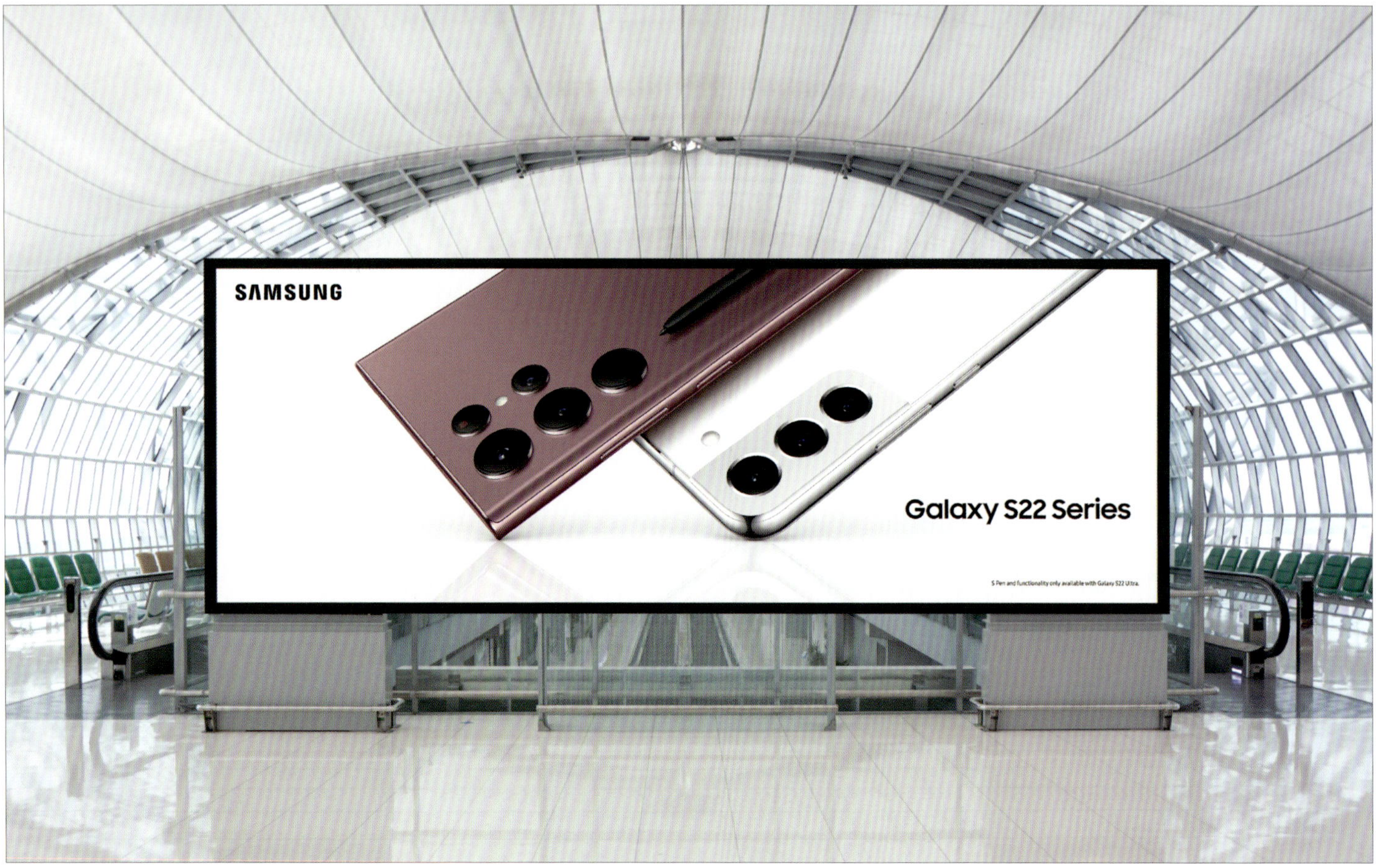

Title: Galaxy S22 Launch Campaign 2022 | **Client:** Samsung | **Design Firm:** Turner Duckworth: London, San Francisco & New York
P239: Credit & Commentary | Images 1, 2 of 7

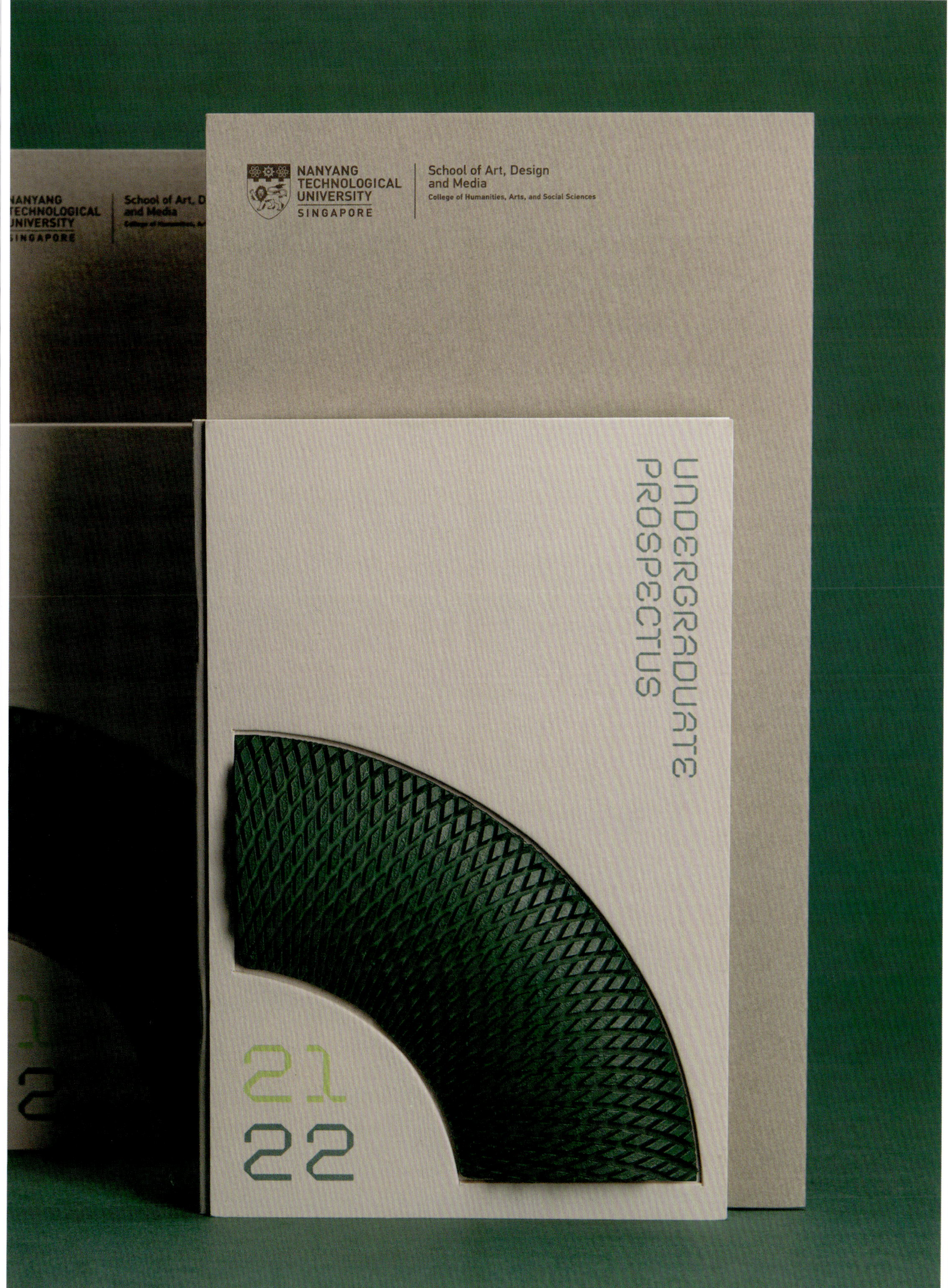

Title: ADM Prospectus 21/22 | **Client:** Nanyang Technological University: School of Art, Design and Media | **Design Firm:** FACTORY
P239: Credit & Commentary | Image 1 of 7

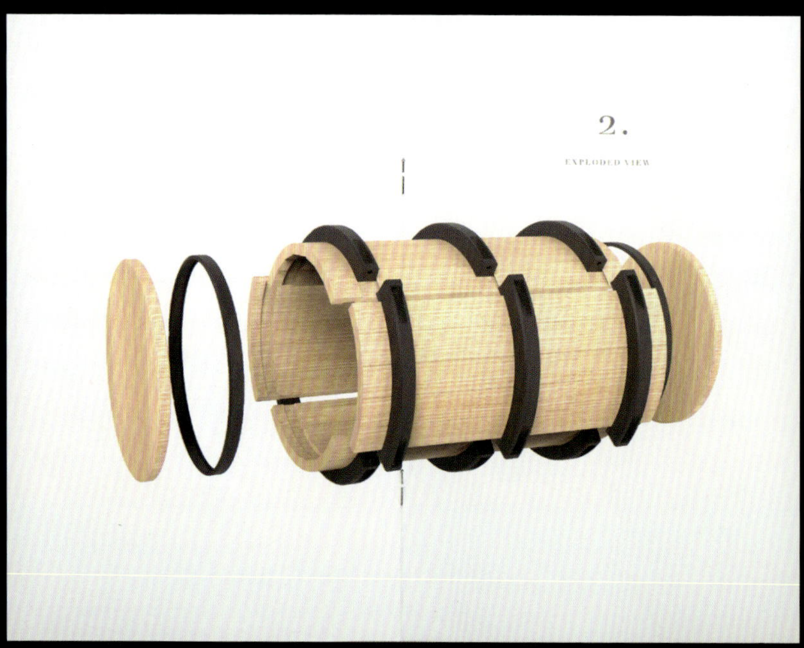

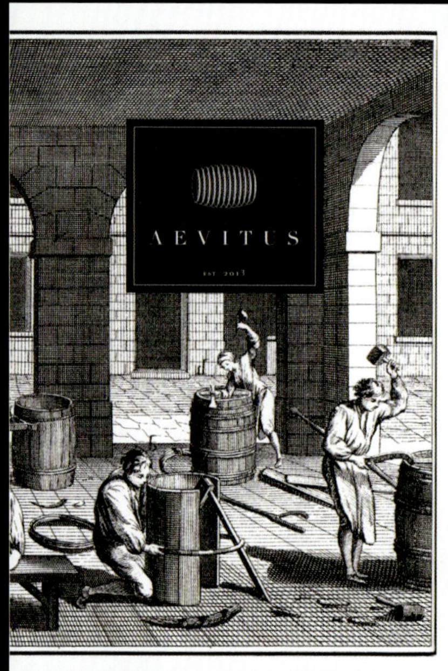

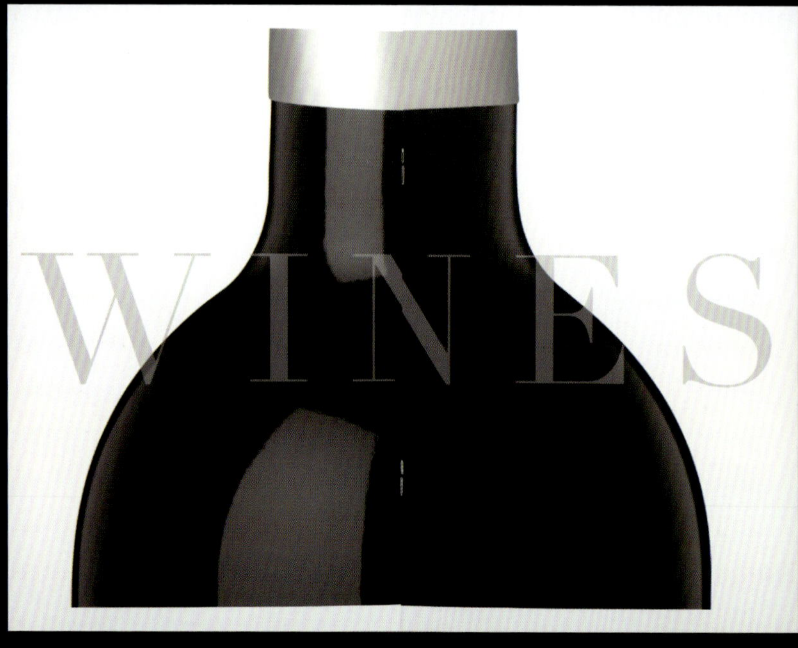

Title: Aevtius Brochure | **Client:** Aevtius | **Design Firm:** Vanderbyl Design

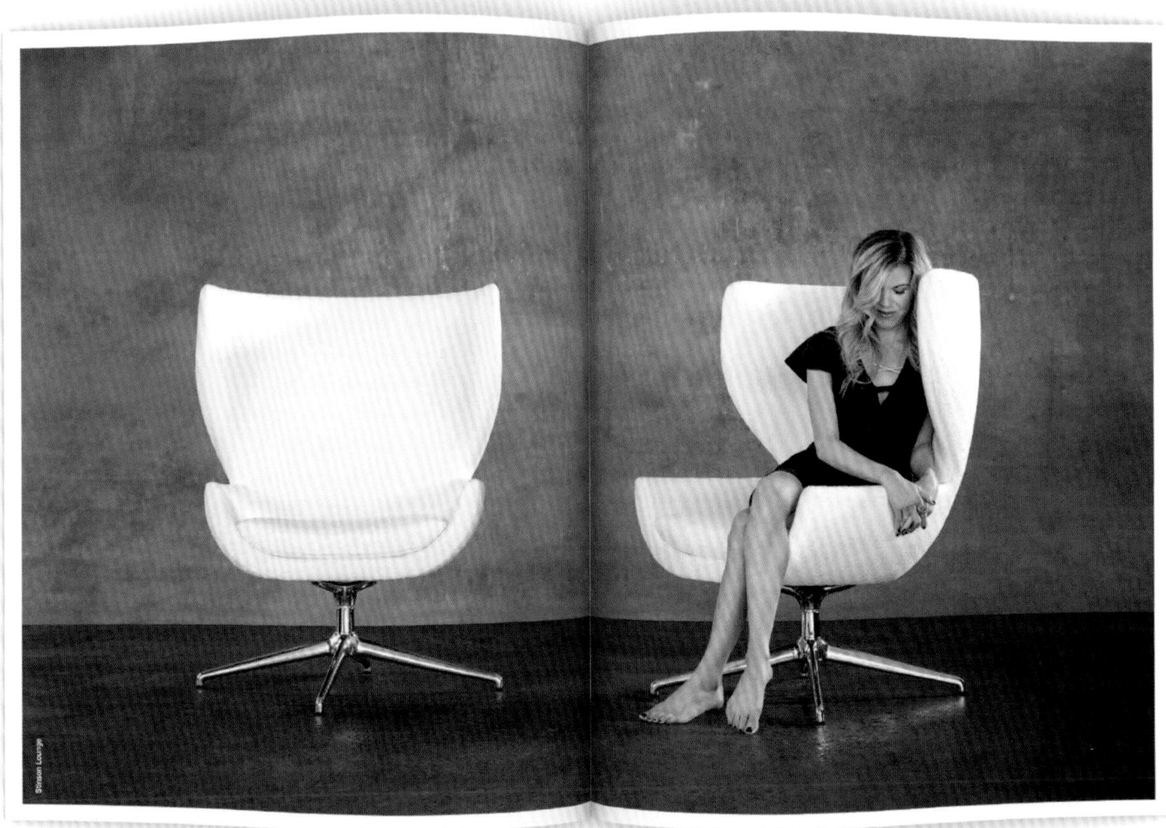

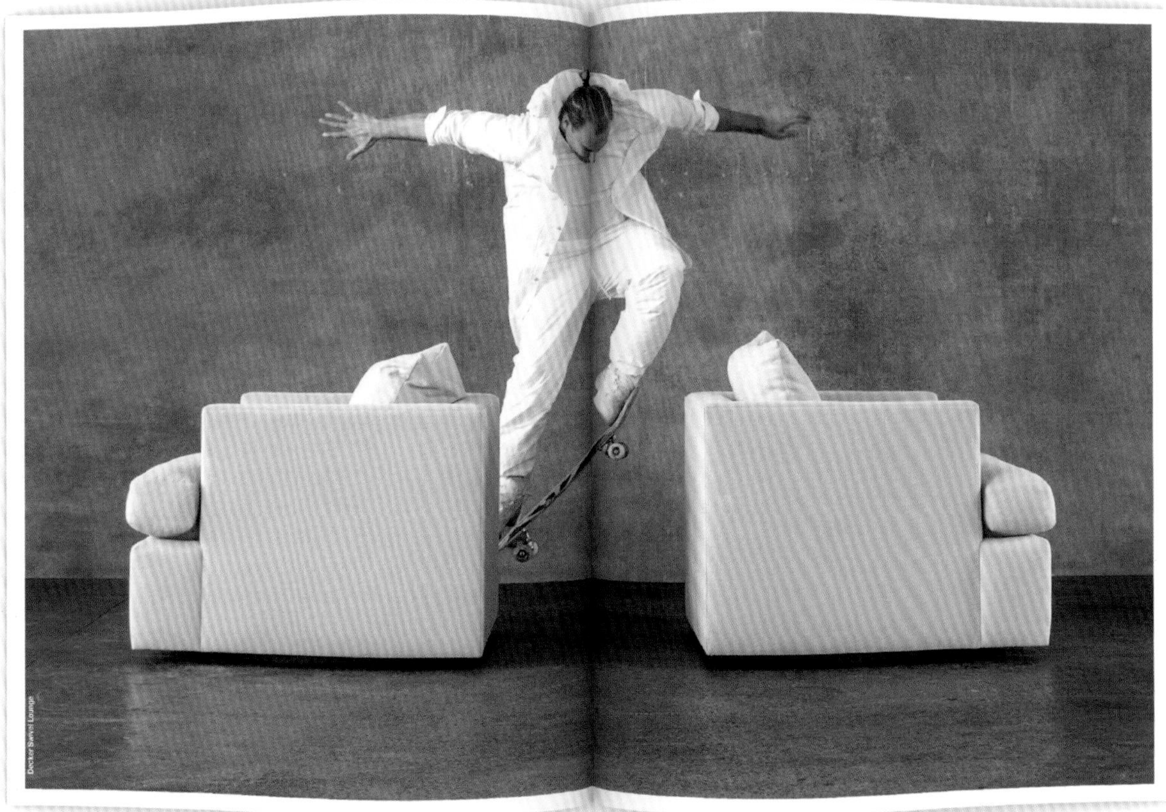

Title: Evan Spencer Brochure | **Client:** Evan Spencer | **Design Firm:** Vanderbyl Design

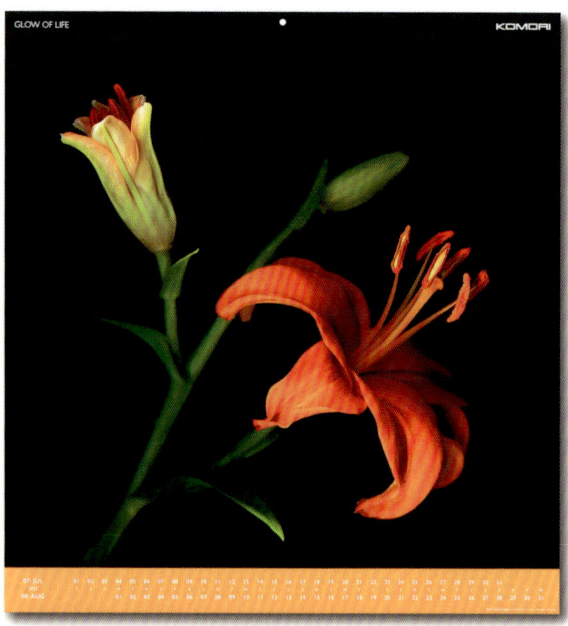

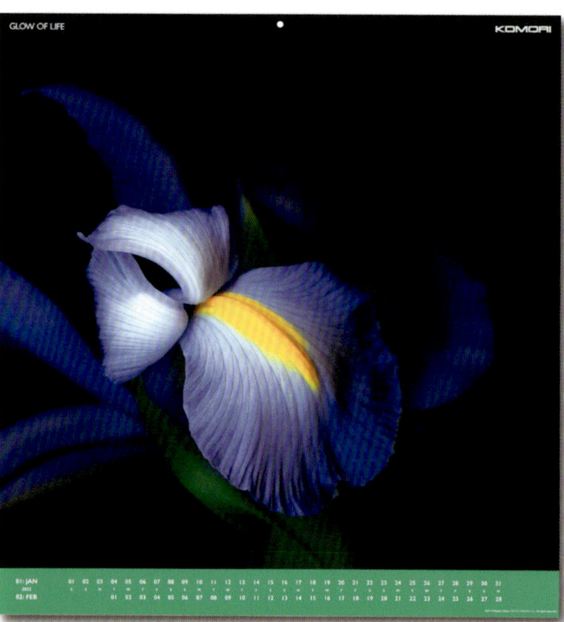

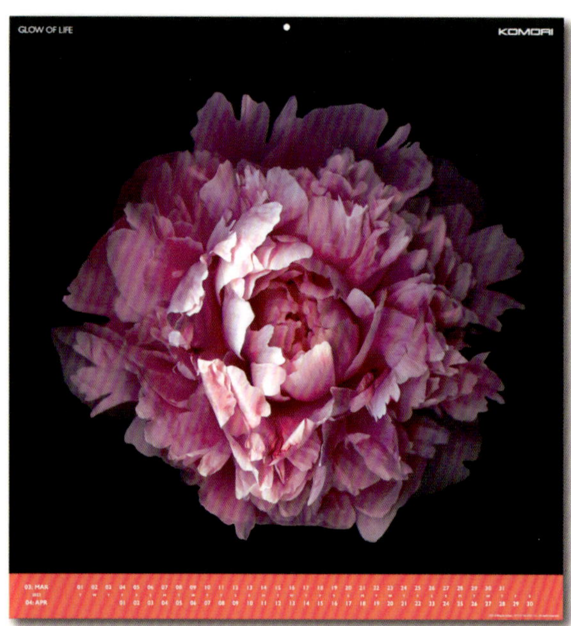

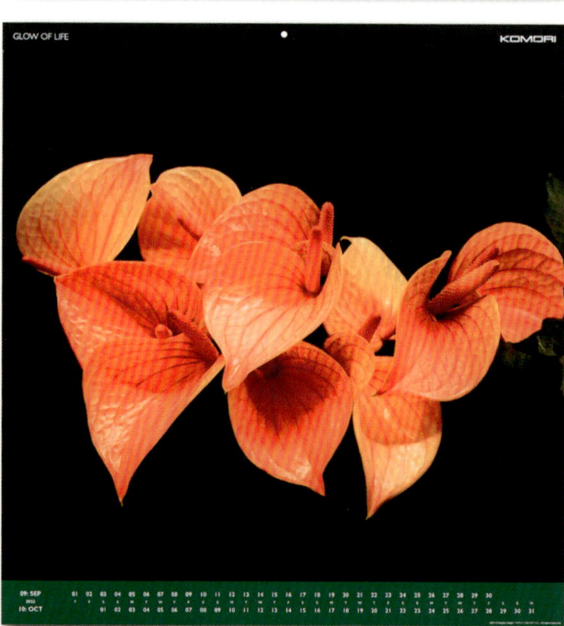

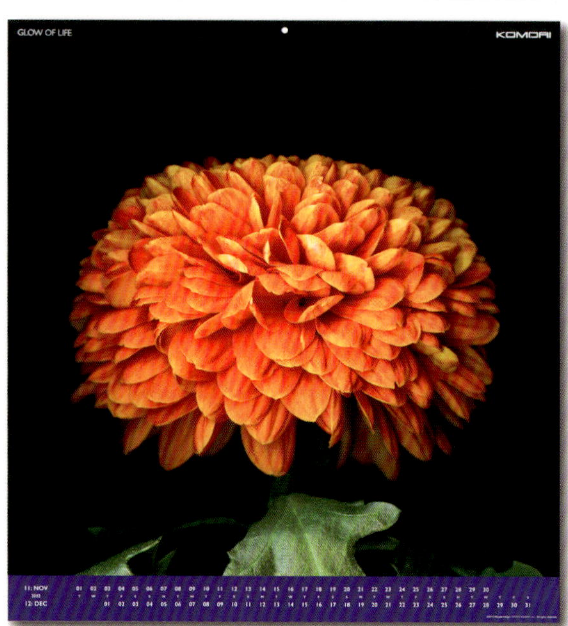

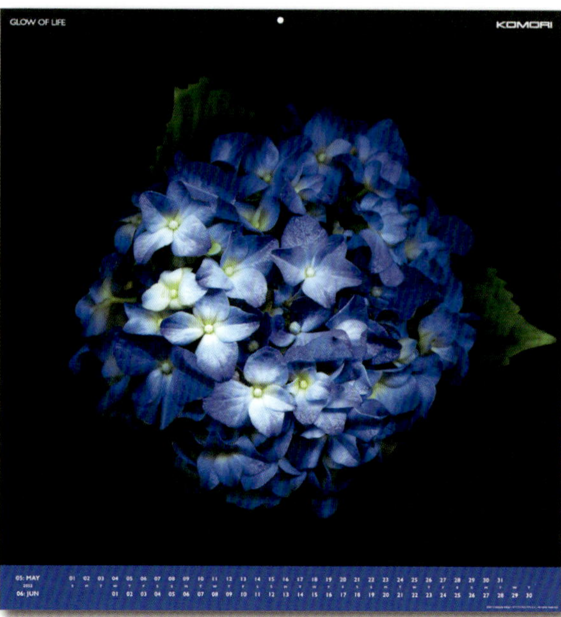

P239: Credit & Commentary

Title: GLOW OF LIFE | **Client:** Komori Corporation | **Design Firm:** Toppan Inc.

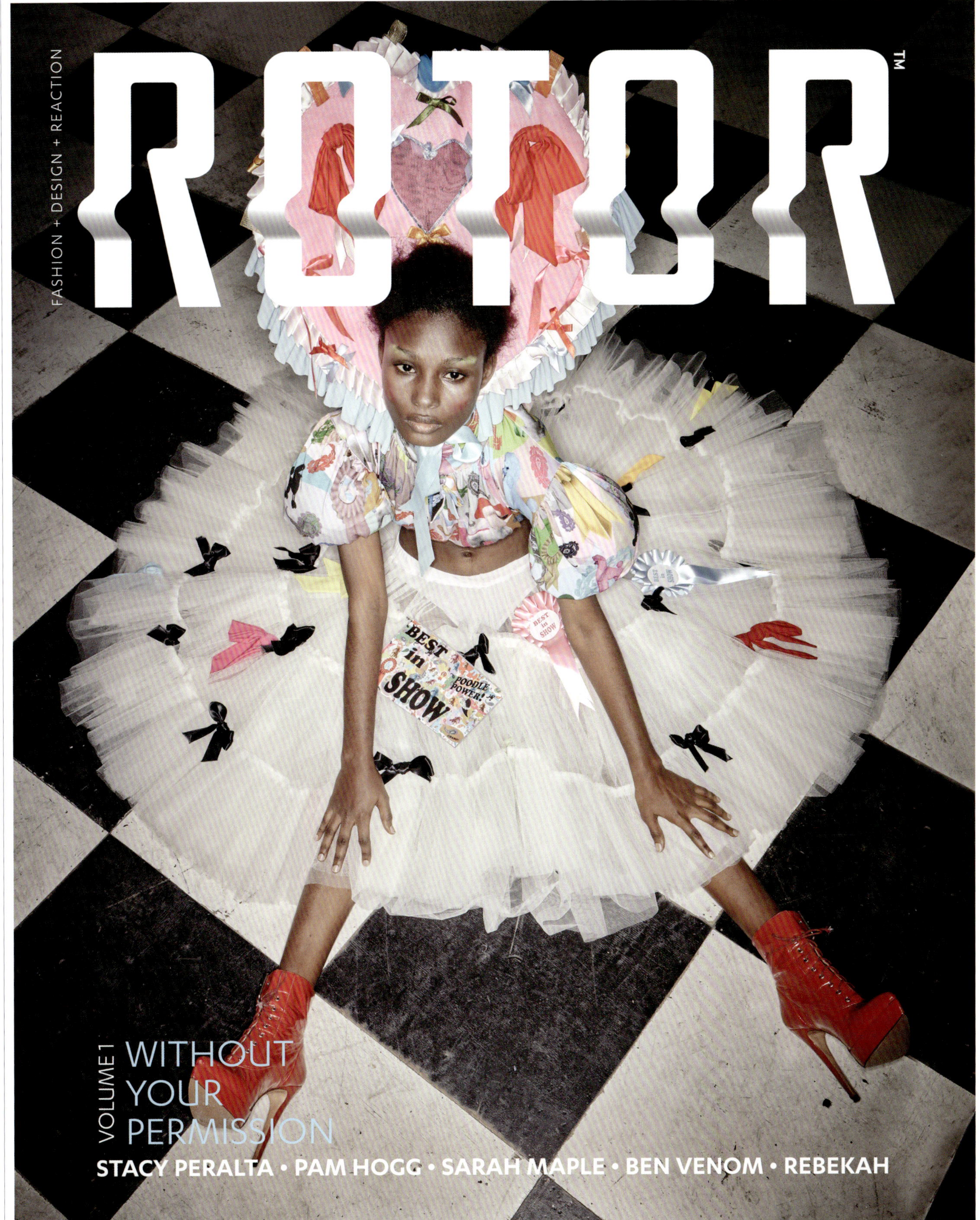

P239: Credit & Commentary **Title:** ROTOR Magazine Cover | **Client:** ROTOR Magazine | **Design Firm:** Mike Hughes Creative Direction + Design

TREVETT MCCANDLISS, NANCY CAMPBELL EDITORIAL

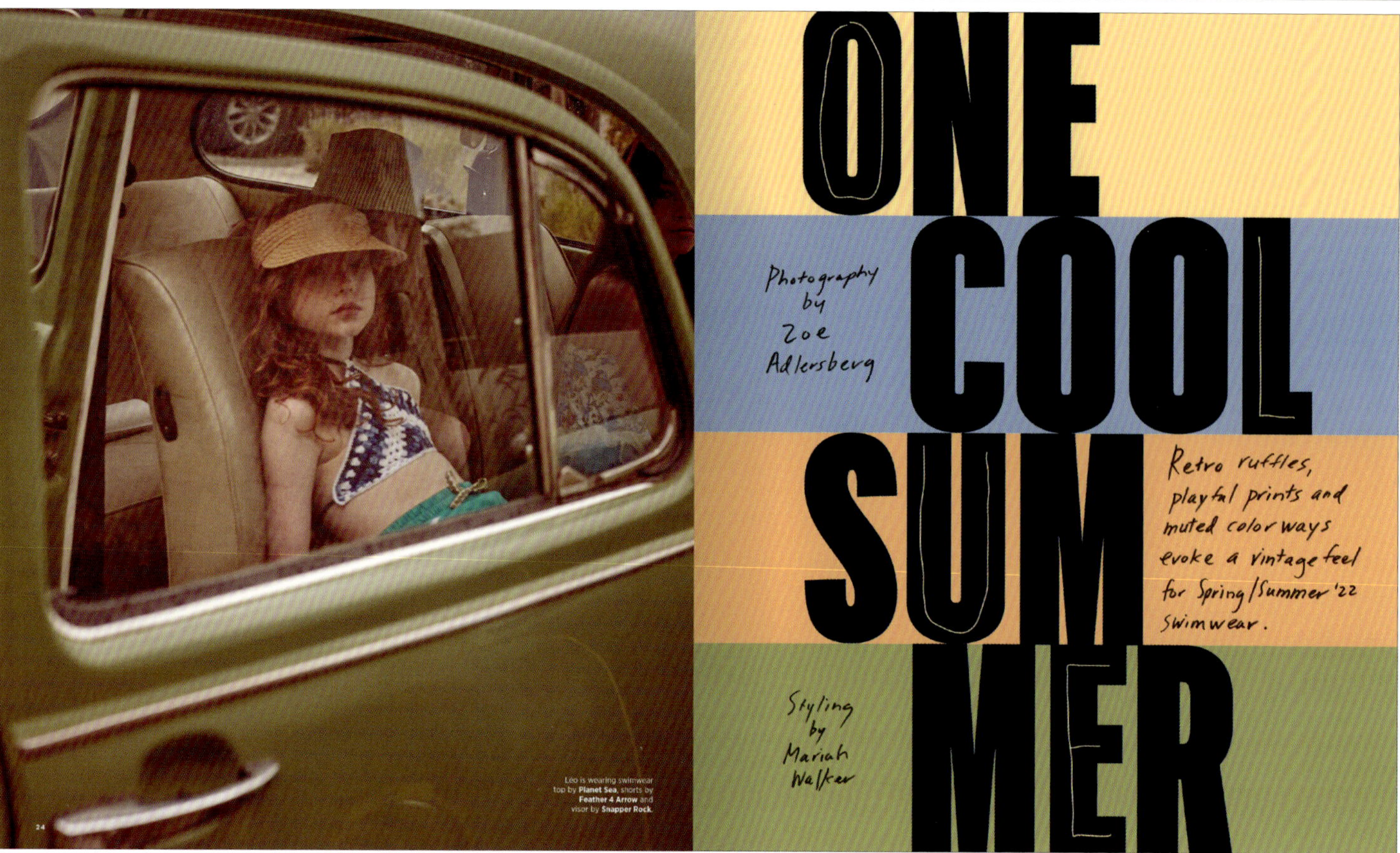

P239: Credit & Commentary **Title:** One Cool Summer | **Client:** Earnshaw's Magazine | **Design Firm:** Wainscot Media

TREVETT MCCANDLISS, NANCY CAMPBELL EDITORIAL

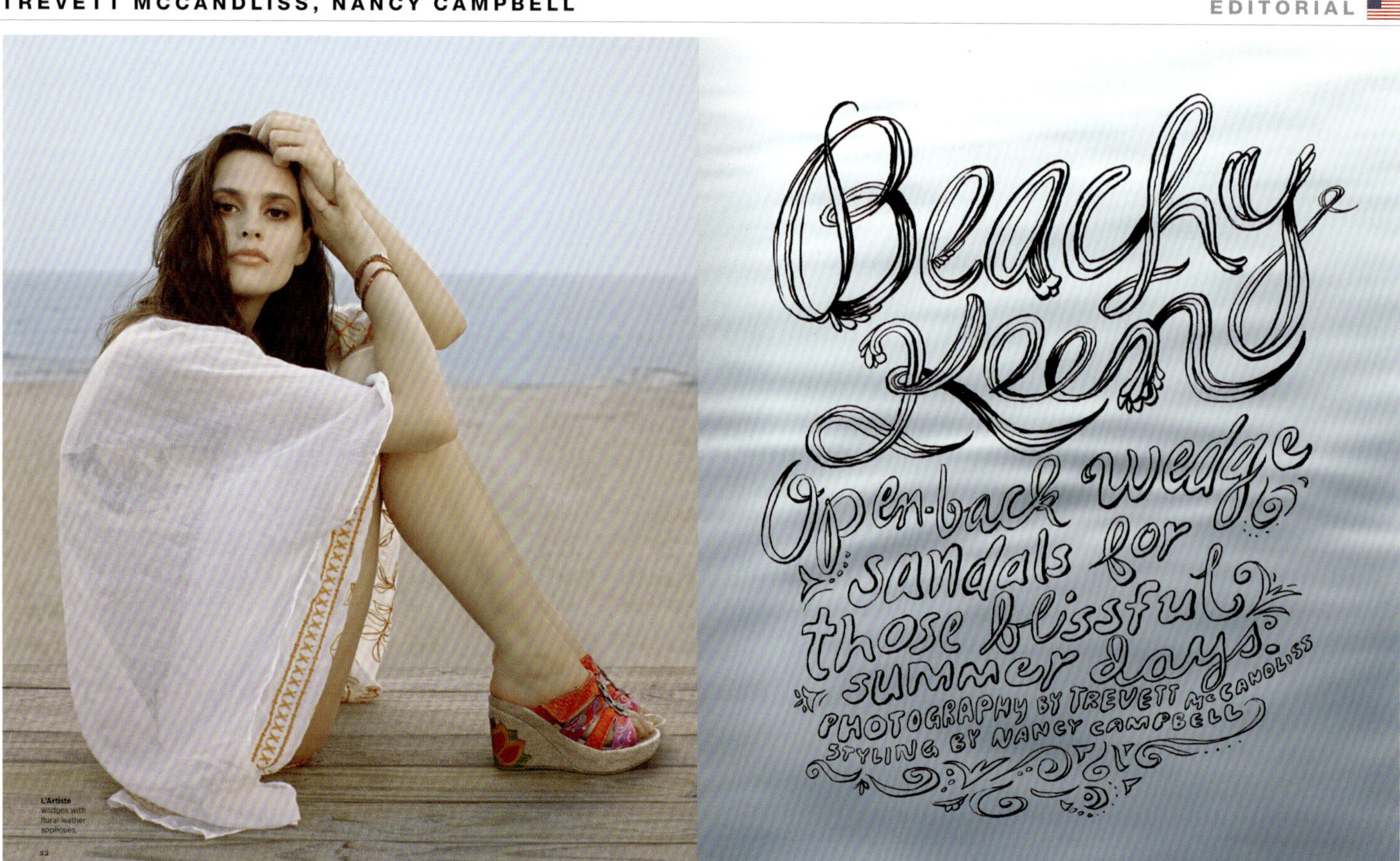

P240: Credit & Commentary **Title:** Beachy Keen | **Client:** Footwear Plus Magazine | **Design Firm:** Wainscot Media

TREVETT MCCANDLISS, NANCY CAMPBELL

EDITORIAL

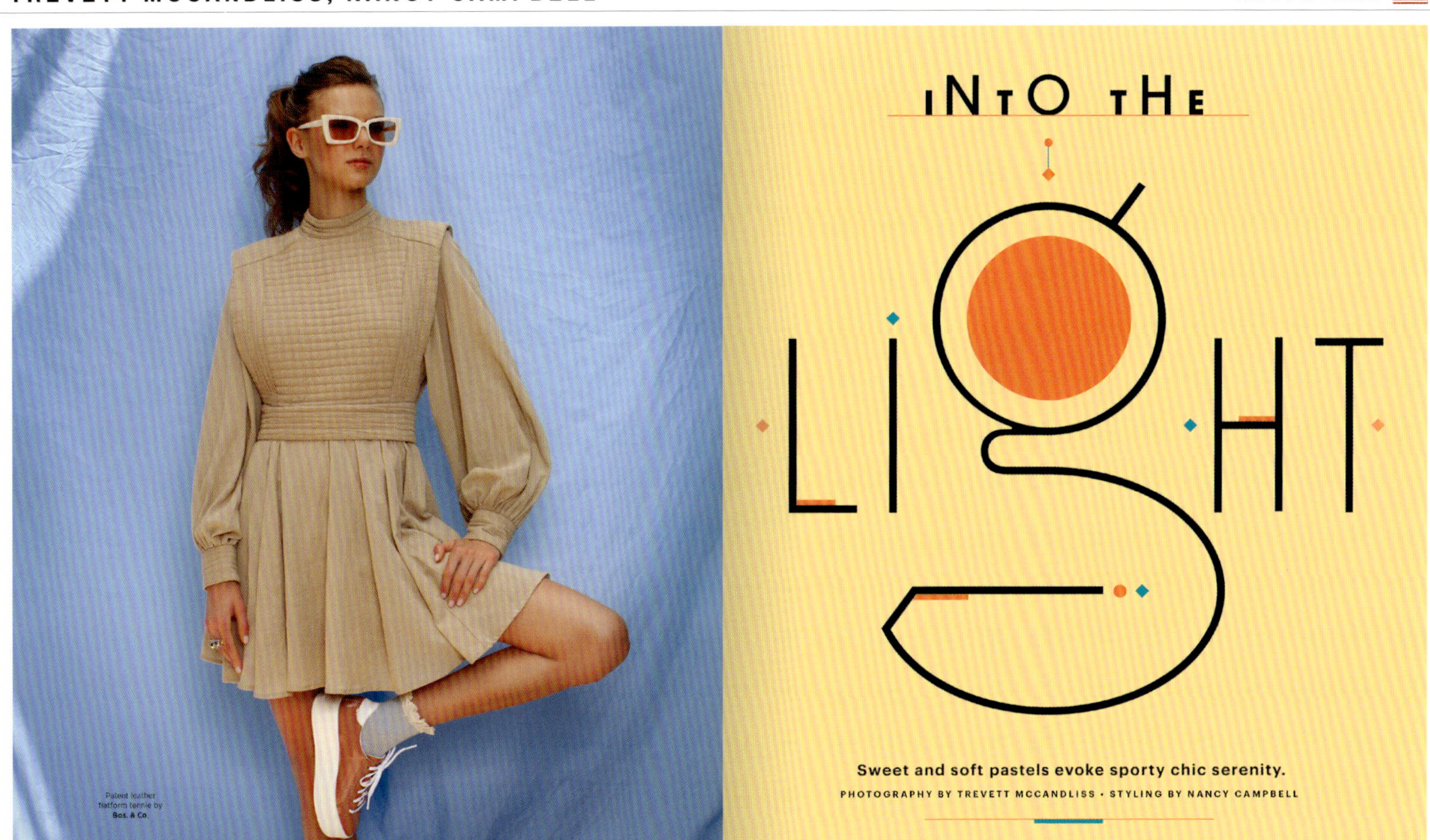

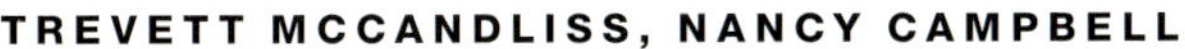

P240: Credit & Commentary **Title:** Into the Light | **Client:** Footwear Plus Magazine | **Design Firm:** Wainscot Media

TREVETT MCCANDLISS, NANCY CAMPBELL

EDITORIAL

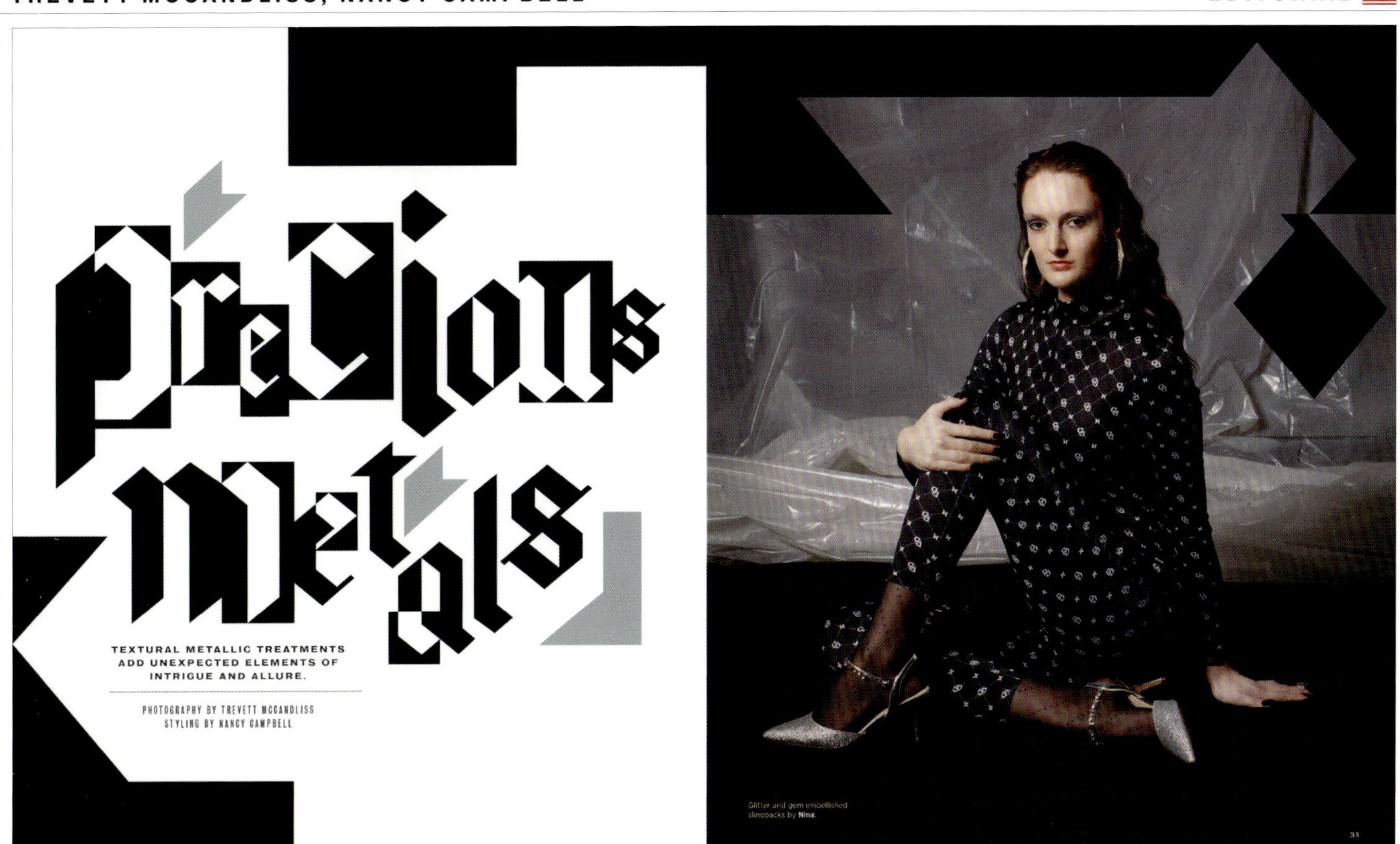

P240: Credit & Commentary **Title:** Precious Metals | **Client:** Footwear Plus Magazine | **Design Firm:** Wainscot Media

TREVETT MCCANDLISS, NANCY CAMPBELL

EDITORIAL

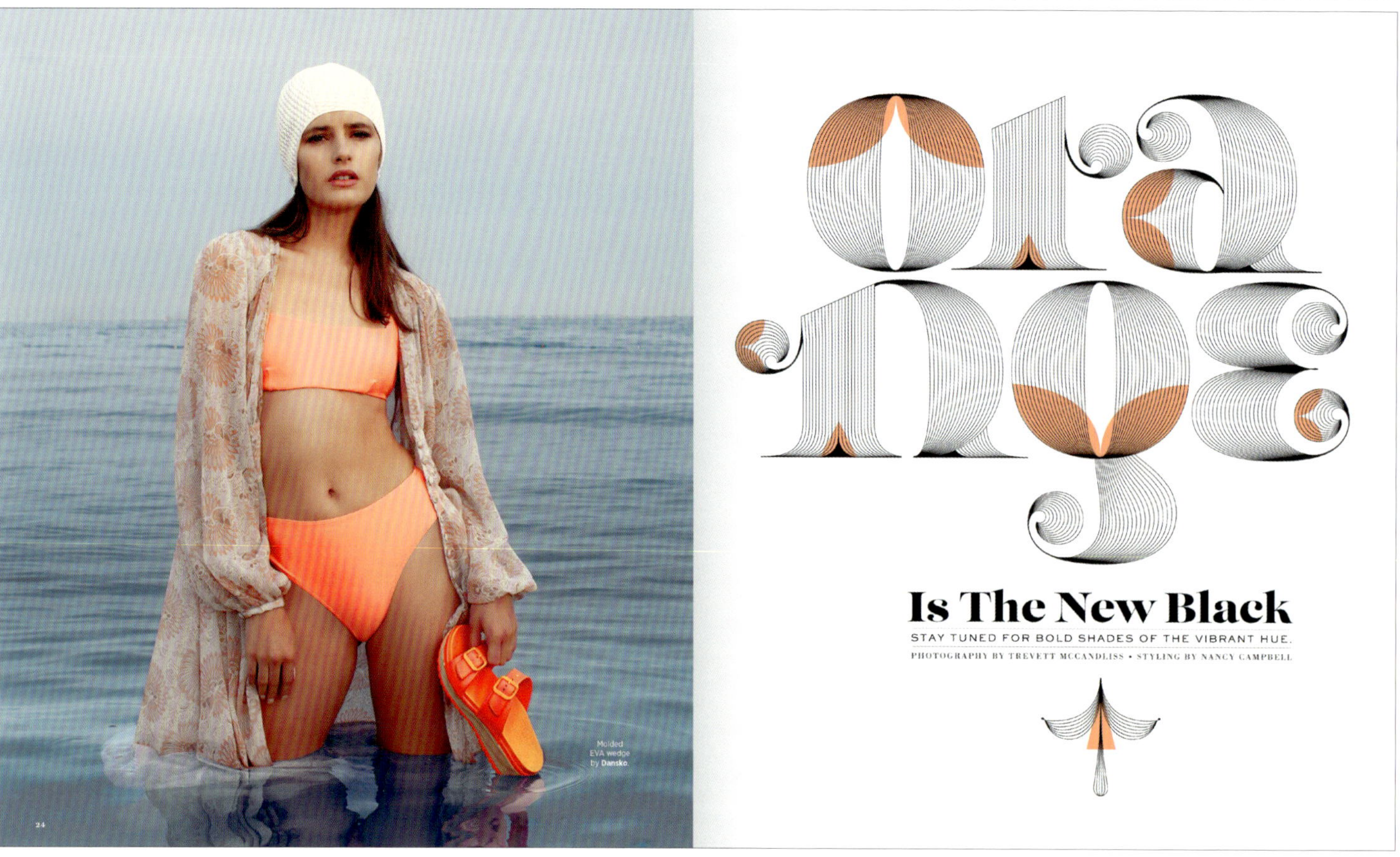

P240: Credit & Commentary **Title:** Orange Crush | **Client:** Footwear Plus Magazine | **Design Firm:** Wainscot Media

TREVETT MCCANDLISS, NANCY CAMPBELL

EDITORIAL

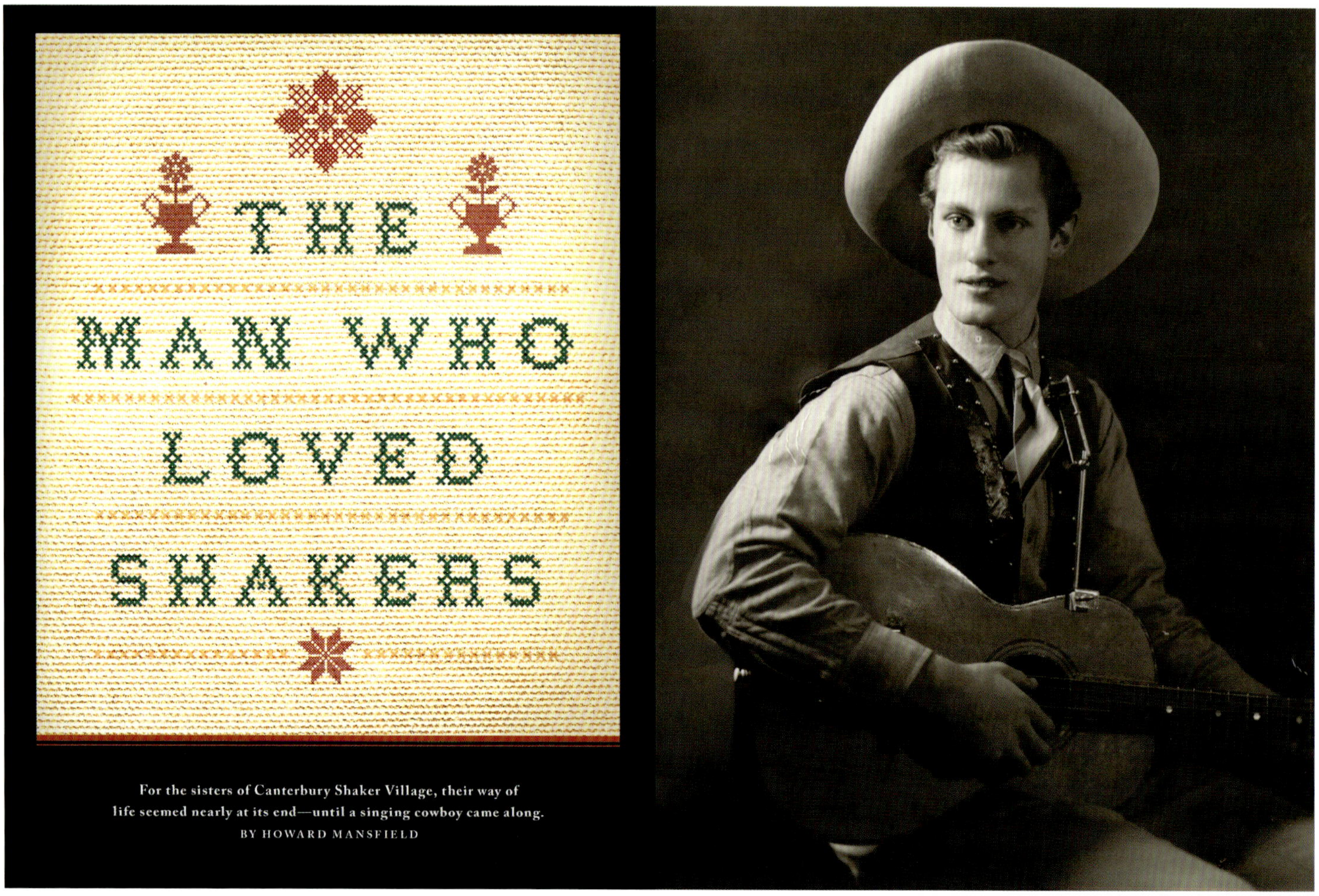

THE MAN WHO LOVED SHAKERS

For the sisters of Canterbury Shaker Village, their way of life seemed nearly at its end—until a singing cowboy came along.

BY HOWARD MANSFIELD

P240: Credit & Commentary **Title:** The Man Who Loved Shakers | **Client:** Yankee Magazine | **Design Firm:** Yankee Publishing Inc.

TREVETT MCCANDLISS, NANCY CAMPBELL

EDITORIAL

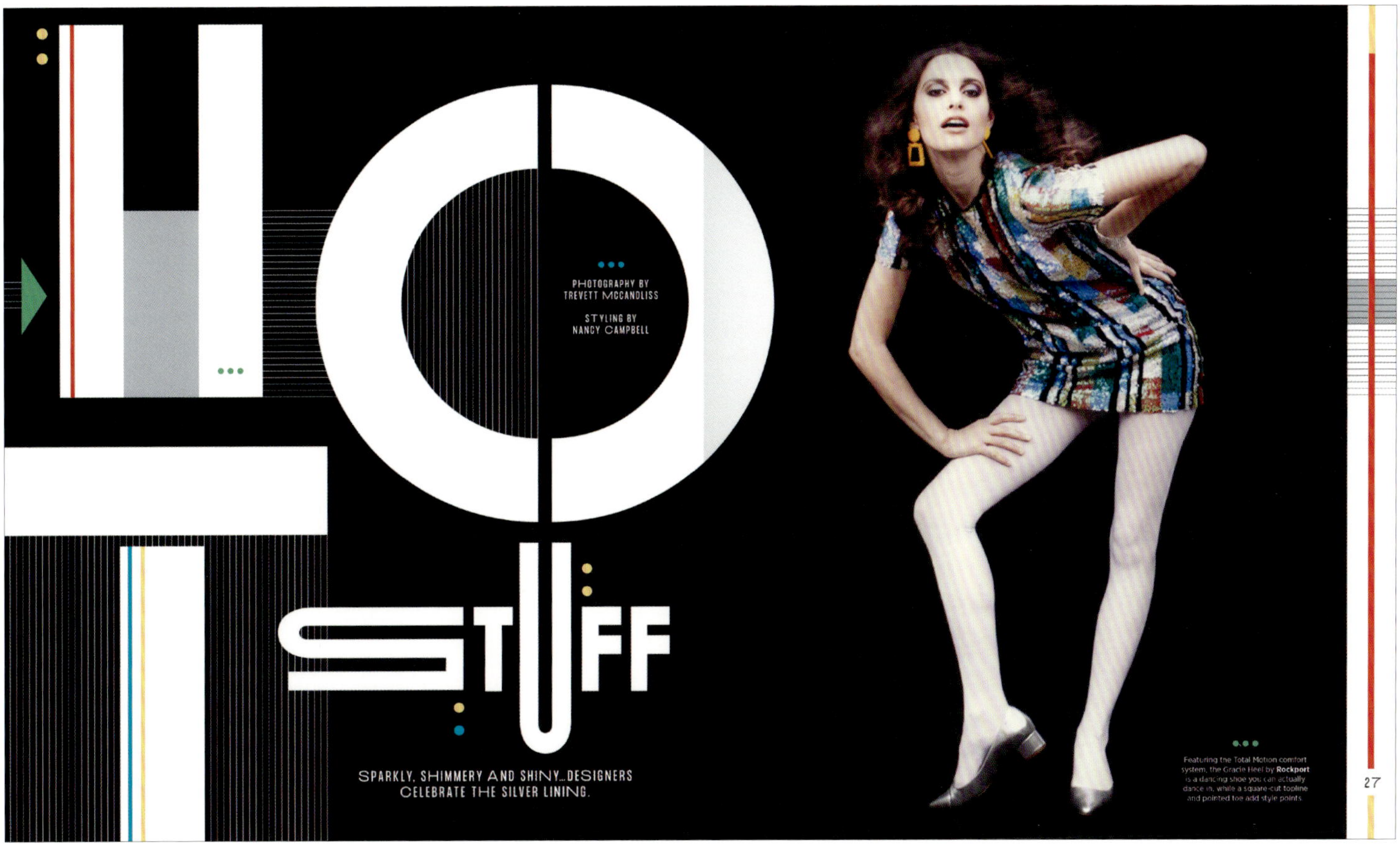

HOT

PHOTOGRAPHY BY
TREVETT MCCANDLISS

STYLING BY
NANCY CAMPBELL

STUFF

SPARKLY, SHIMMERY AND SHINY...DESIGNERS
CELEBRATE THE SILVER LINING.

Featuring the Total Motion comfort system, the Gracie Heel by **Rockport** is a dancing shoe you can actually dance in, while a square-cut topline and pointed toe add style points.

27

P240: Credit & Commentary

Title: Hot Stuff | **Client:** Footwear Plus Magazine | **Design Firm:** Wainscot Media

TREVETT MCCANDLISS, NANCY CAMPBELL

EDITORIAL

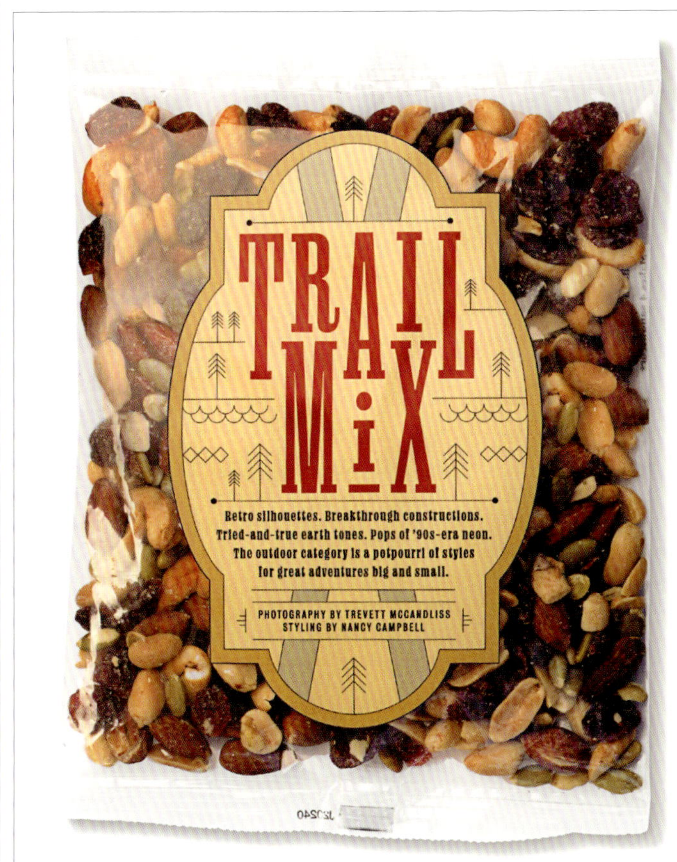

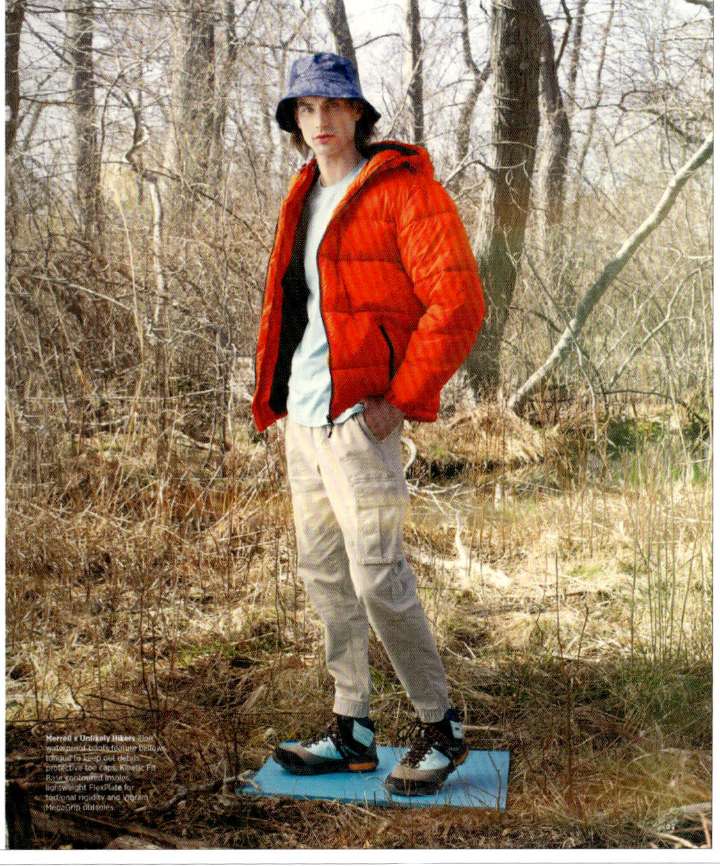

P240: Credit & Commentary

Title: Trail Mix | **Client:** Footwear Plus Magazine | **Design Firm:** Wainscot Media

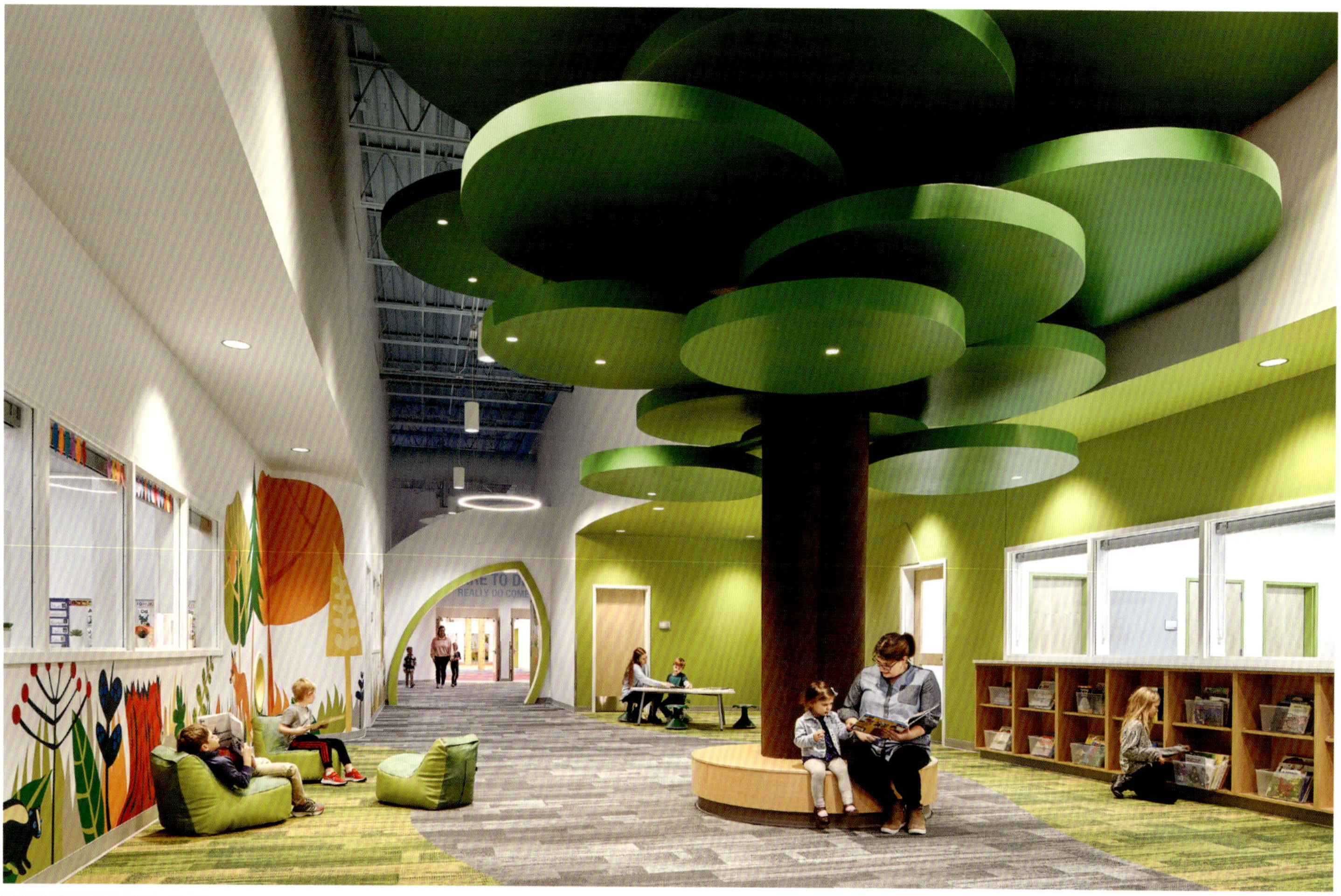

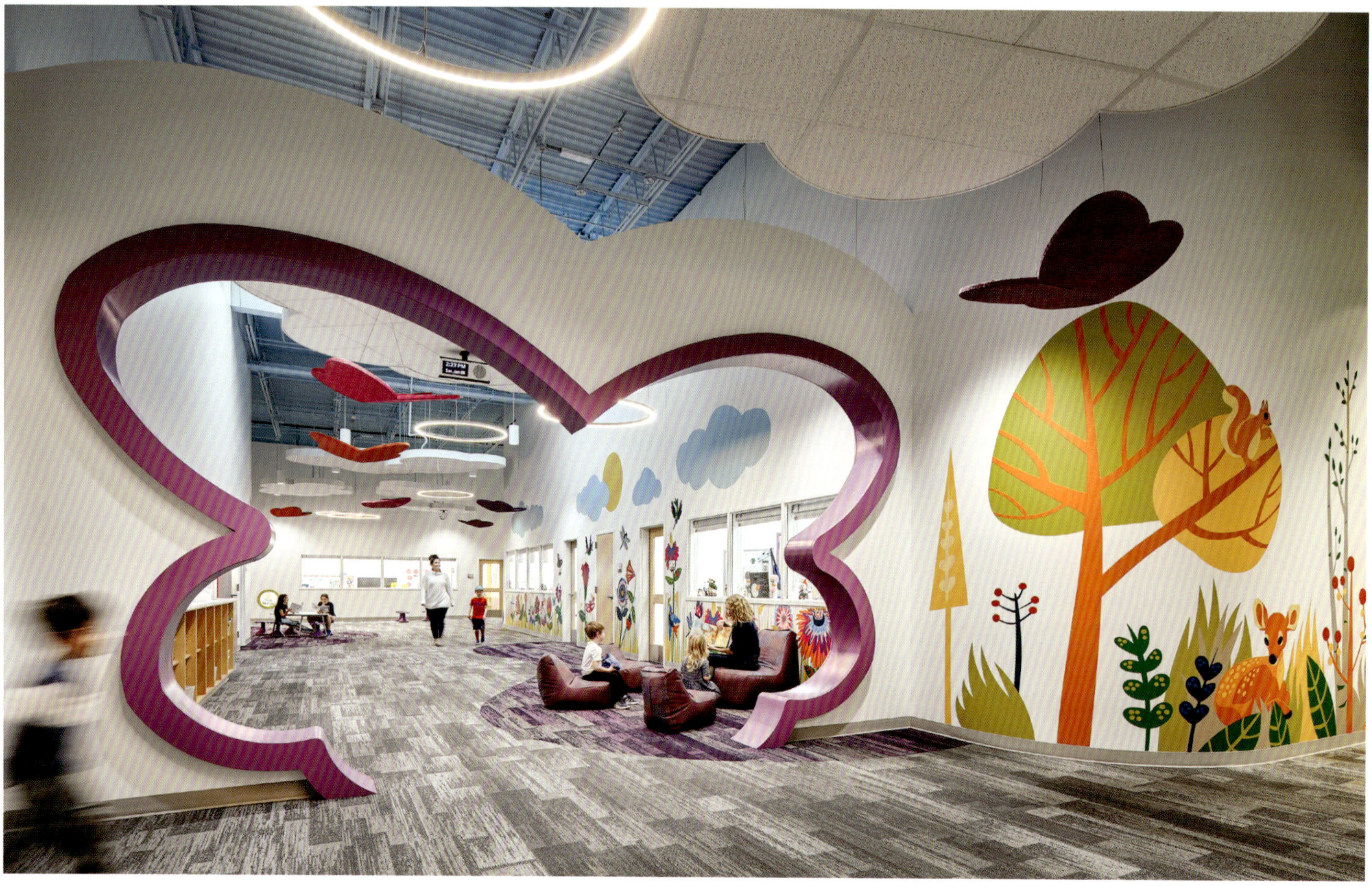

Title: North Kansas City Early Education Center | **Client:** North Kansas City School | **Design Firm:** DLR Group
P240: Credit & Commentary | Images 1, 2 of 7

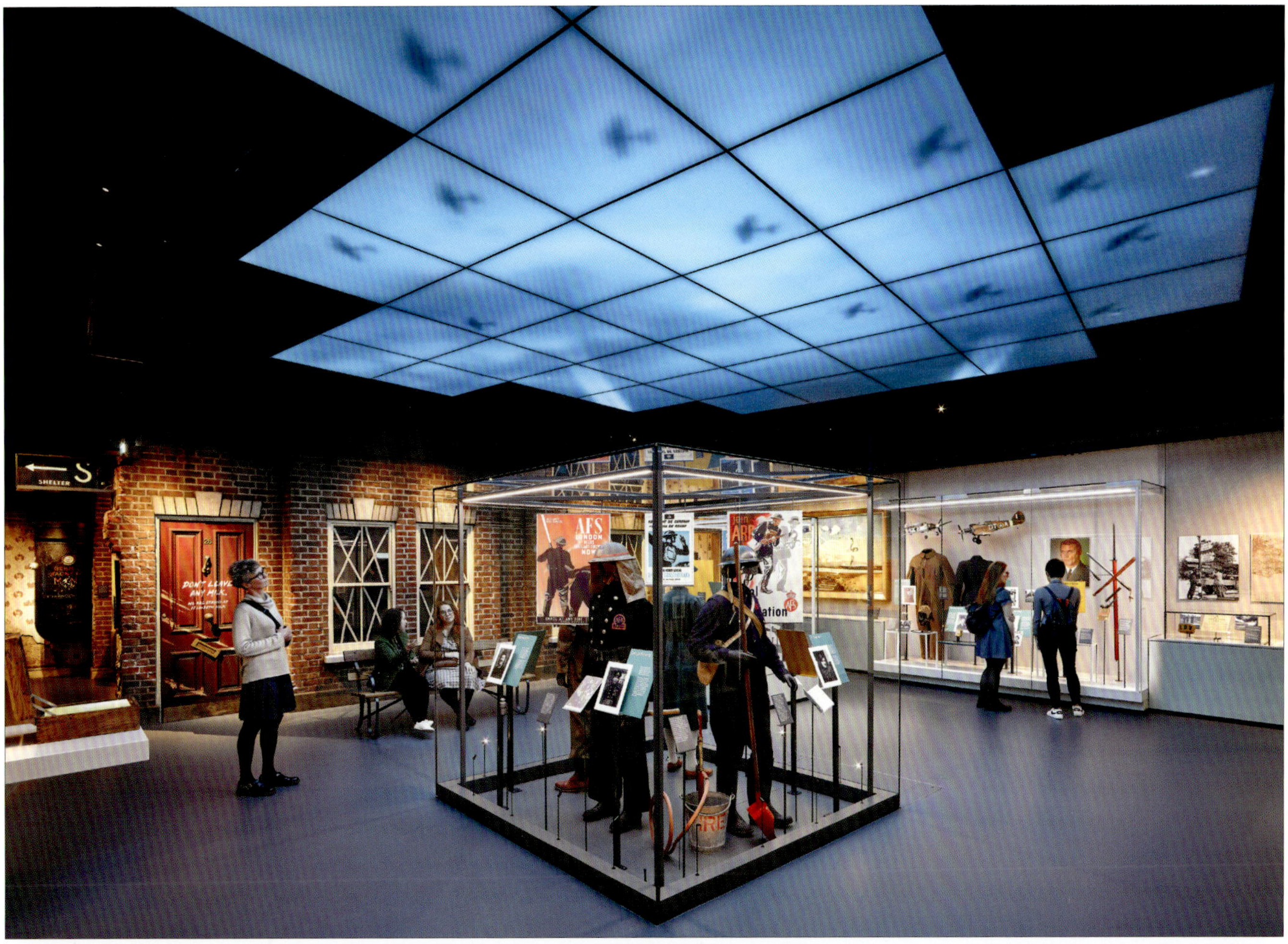

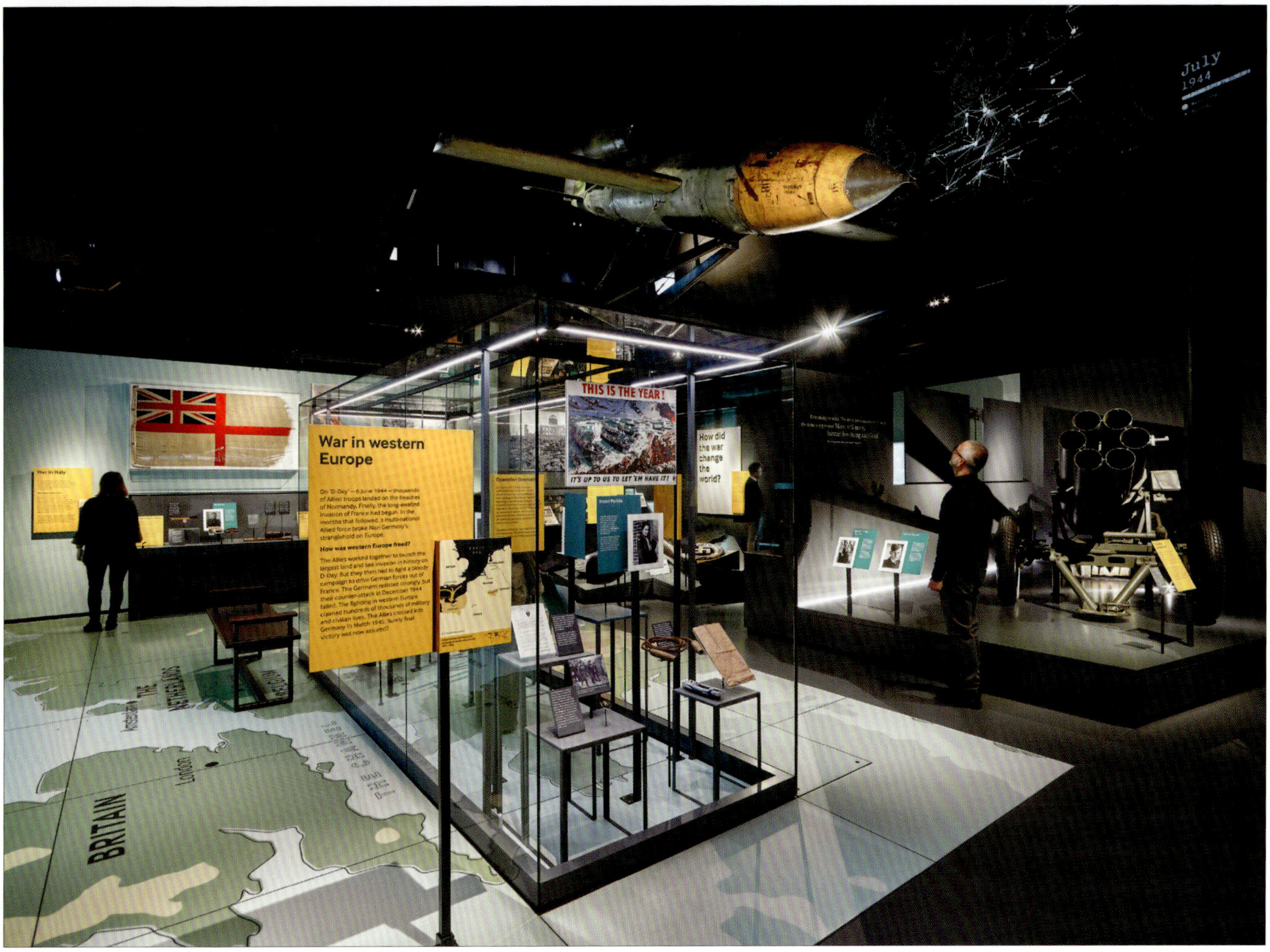

Title: Second World War Galleries | **Client:** Imperial War Museum | **Design Firm:** Ralph Appelbaum Associates
P240: Credit & Commentary | Images 1, 2 of 7

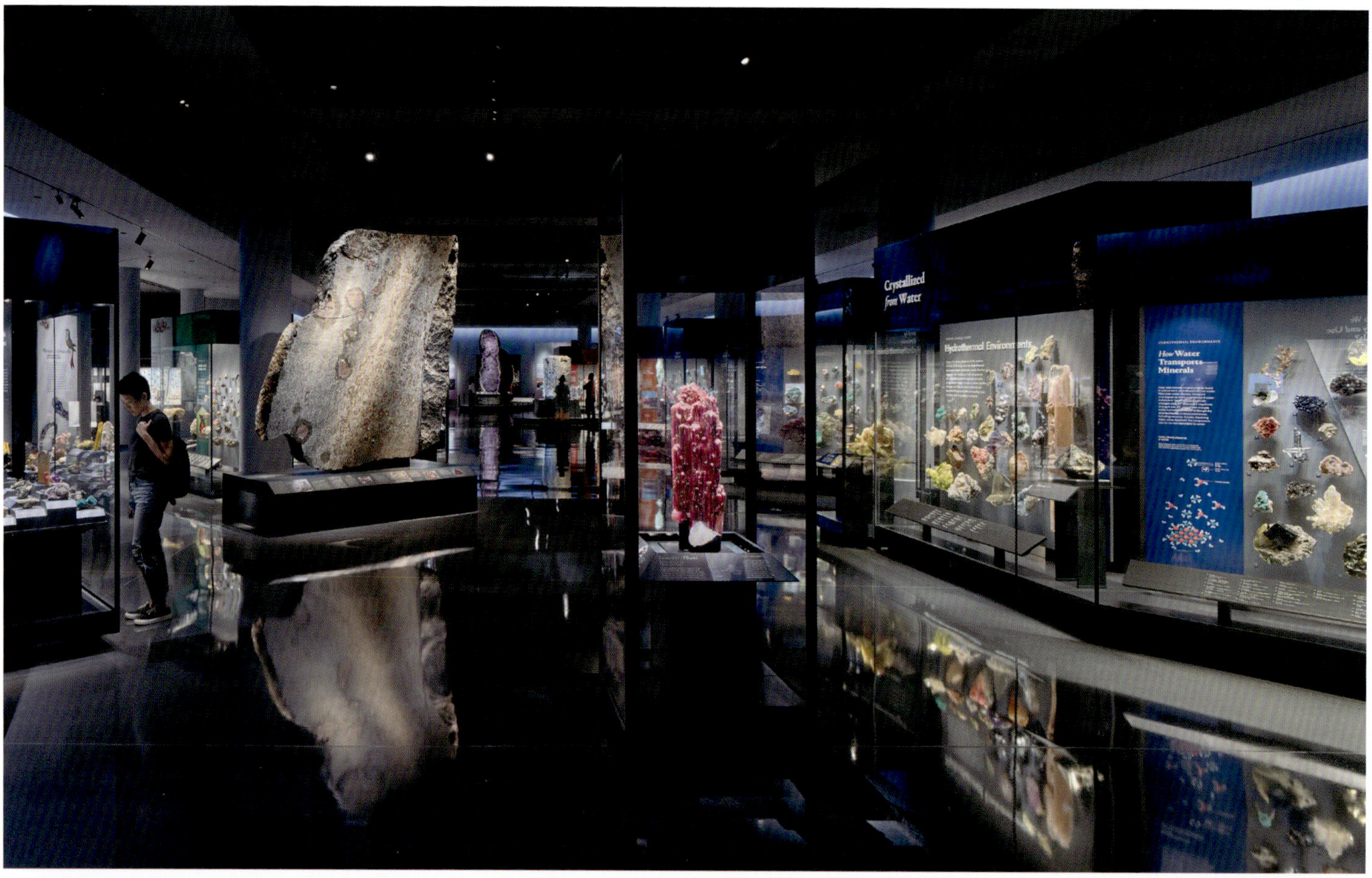

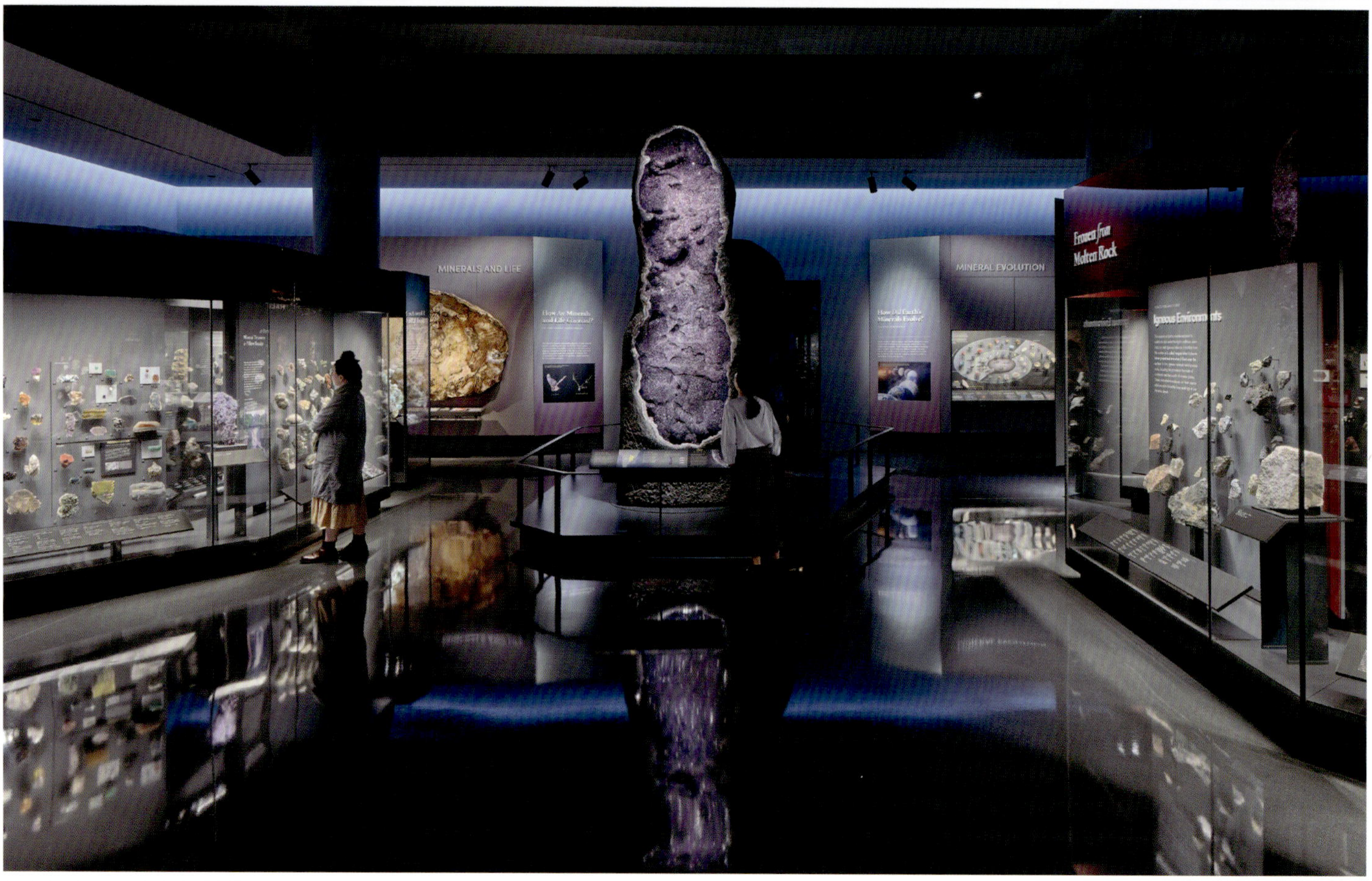

Title: The Allison and Roberto Mignone Halls of Gems and Minerals | **Client:** American Museum of Natural History
Design Firm: Ralph Appelbaum Associates | **P240:** Credit & Commentary | Images 1, 2 of 7

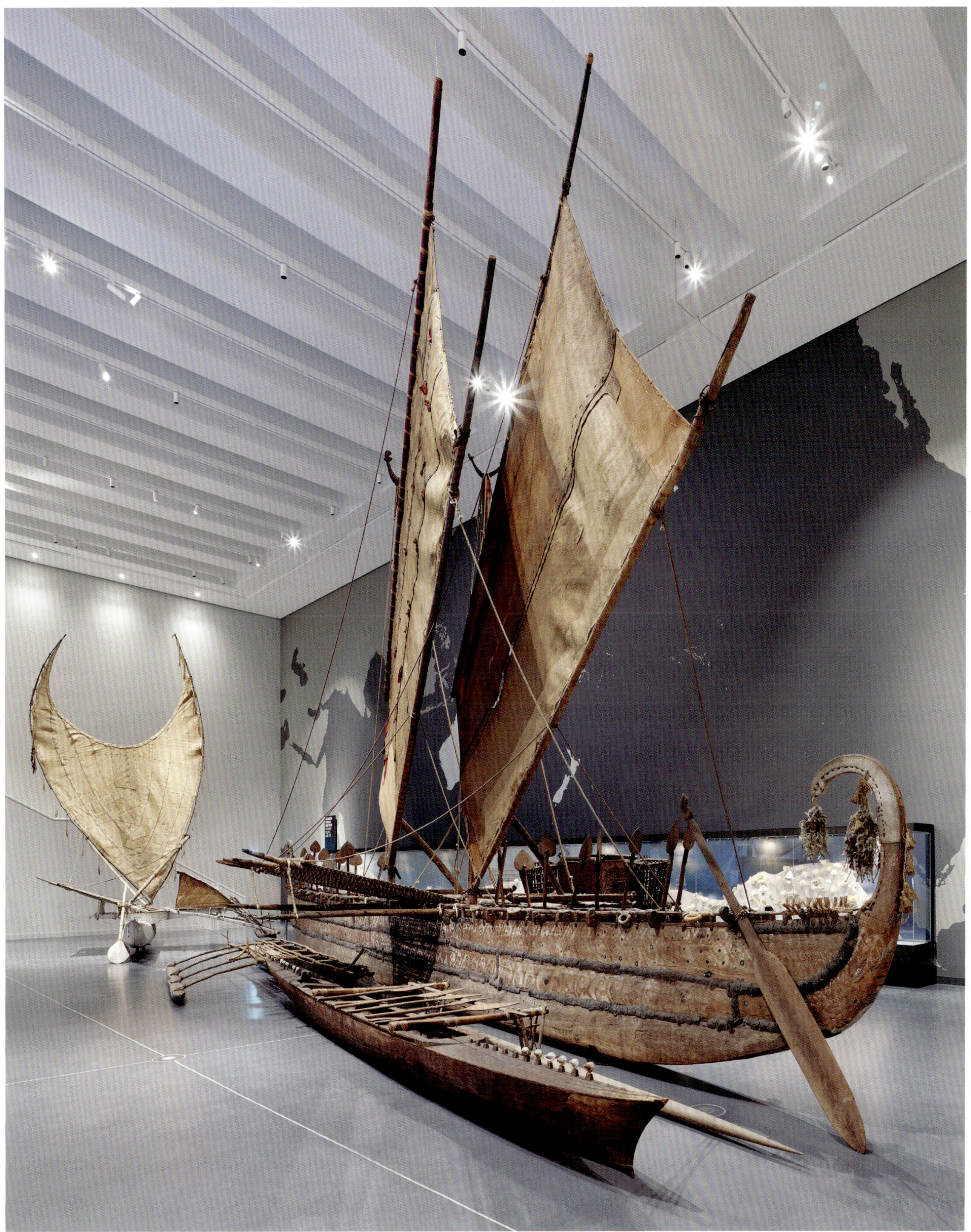

Title: State Ethnological Museum and Museum of Asian Art at the Humboldt Forum | **Client:** Humboldt Forum
Design Firm: Ralph Appelbaum Associates | **P241:** Credit & Commentary | Image 1 of 7

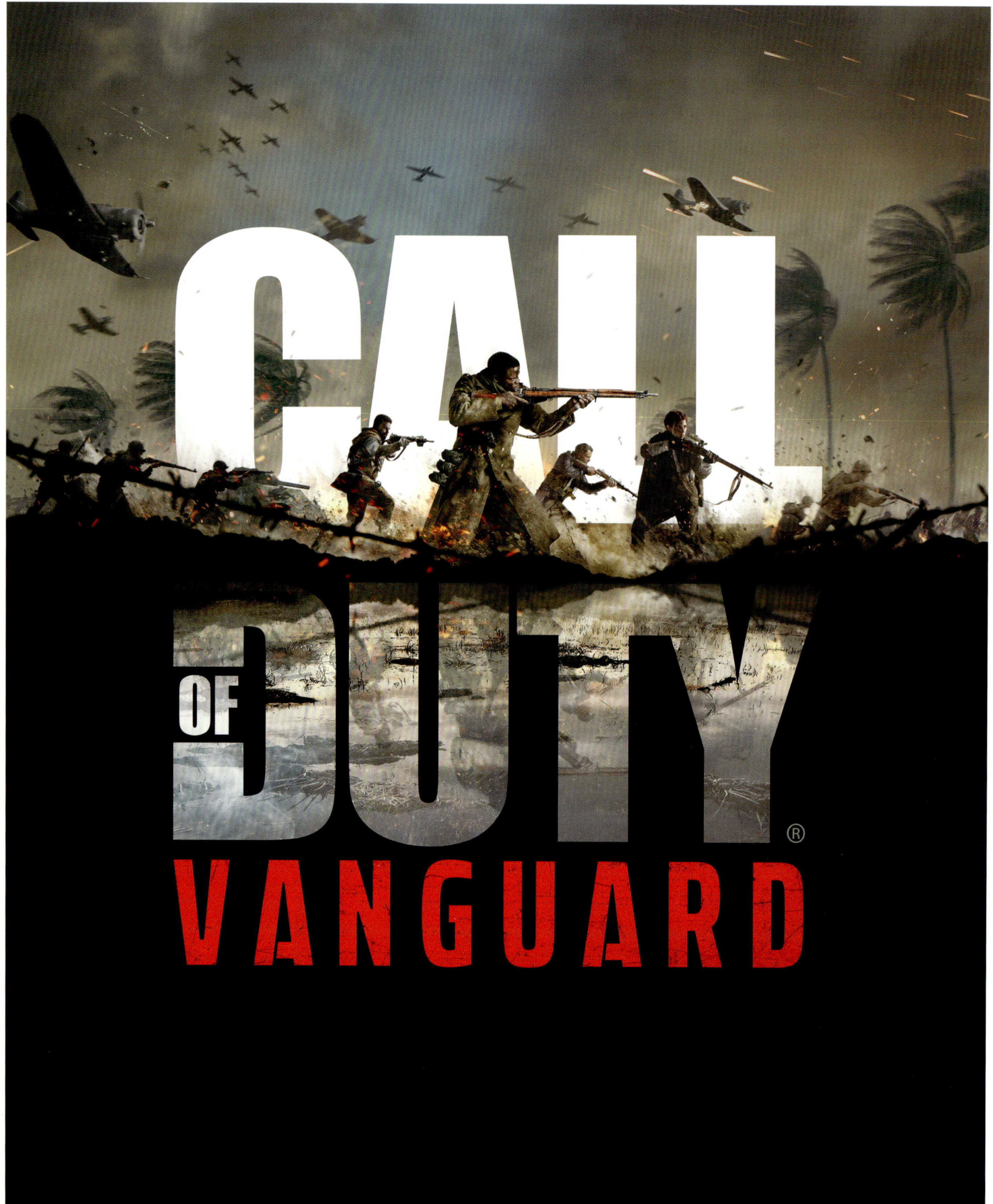

P241: Credit & Commentary **Title:** Call of Duty: Vanguard Key Art | **Clients:** Activision, Sledgehammer | **Design Firm:** PETROL Advertising

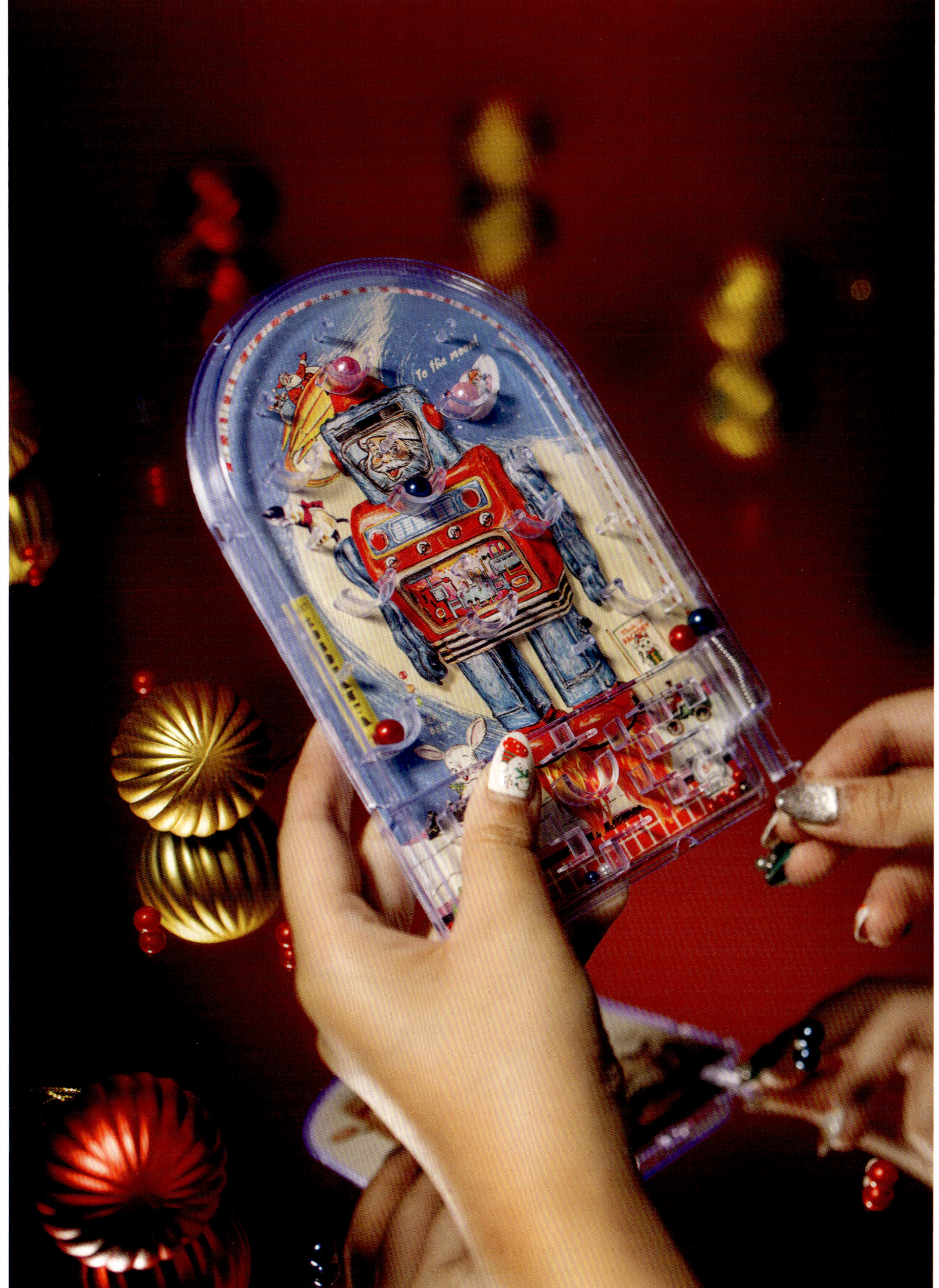

P241: Credit & Commentary

Title: Write a Christmas Card 2021 | **Client:** Self-initiated | **Design Firm:** FACTORY

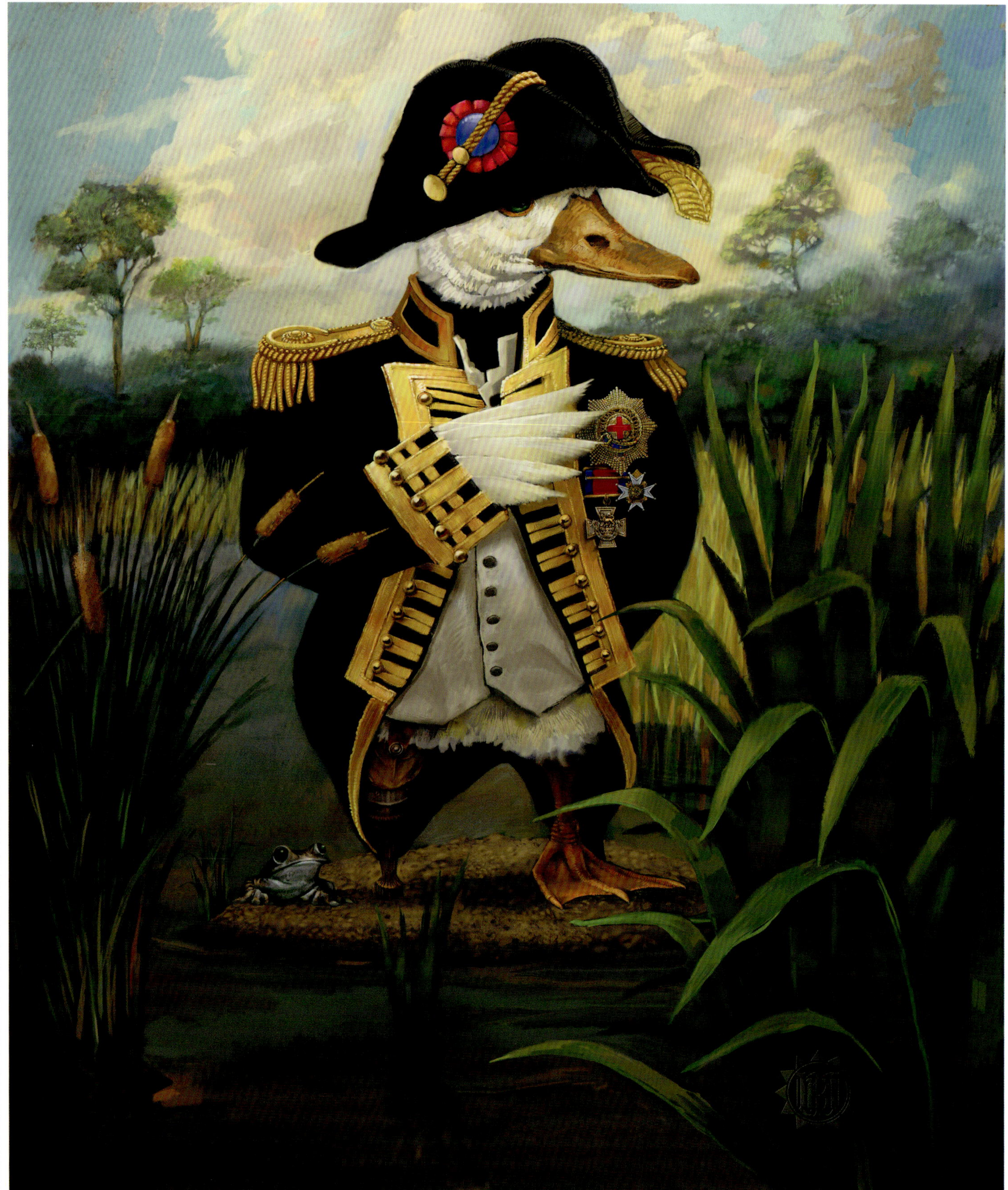

P241: Credit & Commentary Title: Strange Ducks | Client: Strange Duck Brewery | Design Firm: Mark Braught Studios Image 1 of 3

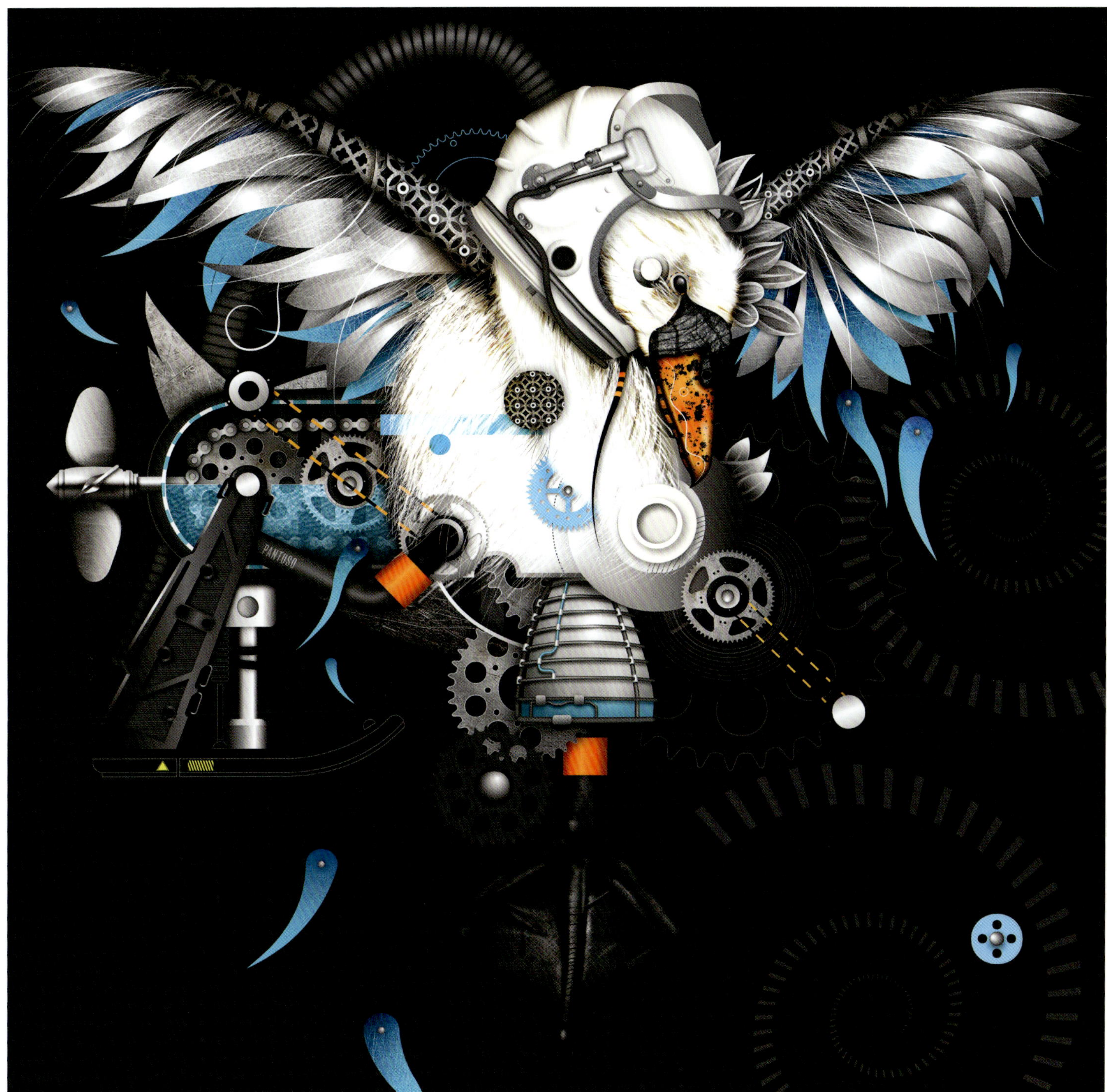

P241: Credit & Commentary **Title:** Serpentine Swan | **Client:** LAGO Innovation Fund | **Design Firm:** Michael Pantuso Design

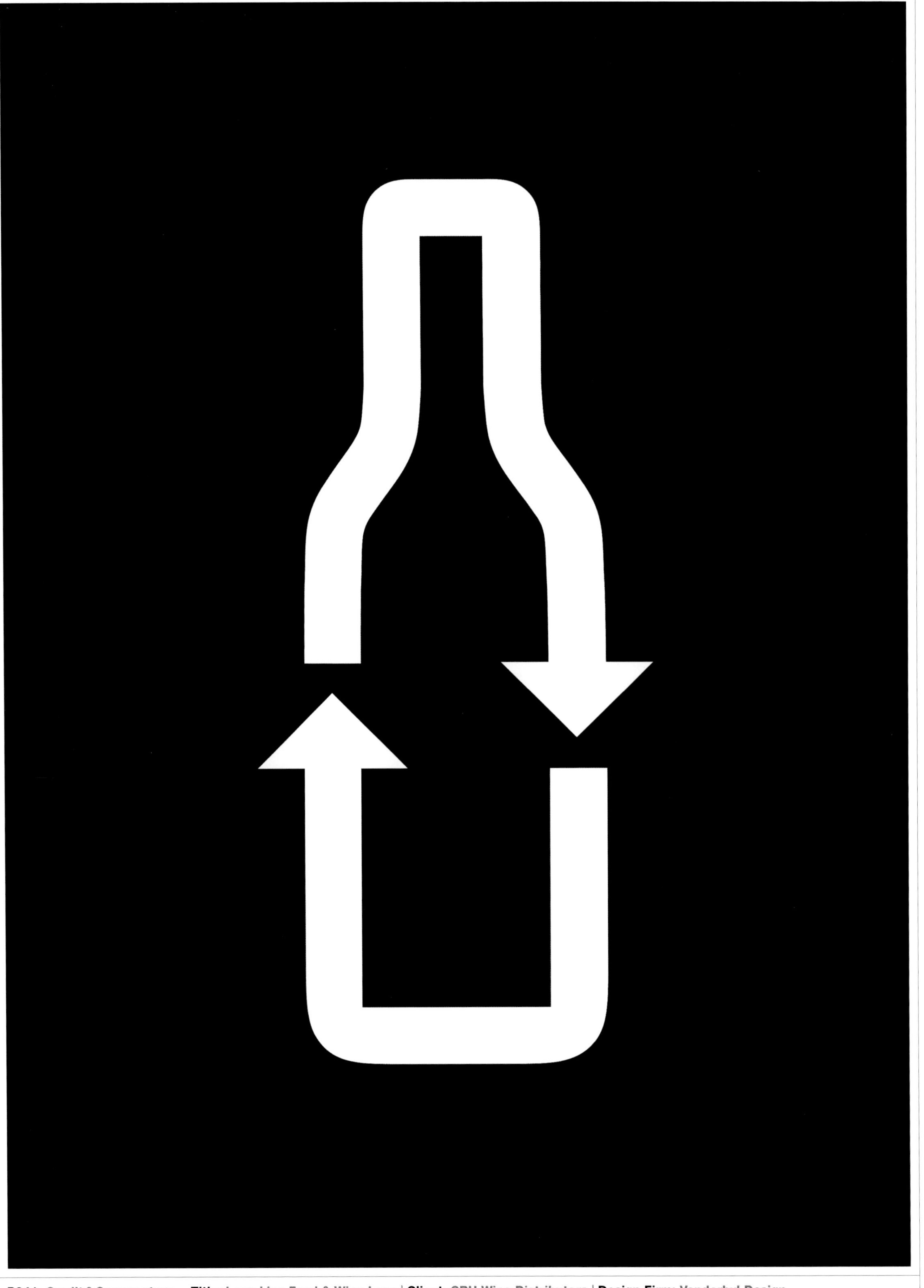

P241: Credit & Commentary **Title:** Loop Line Food & Wine Logo | **Client:** CRU Wine Distributors | **Design Firm:** Vanderbyl Design

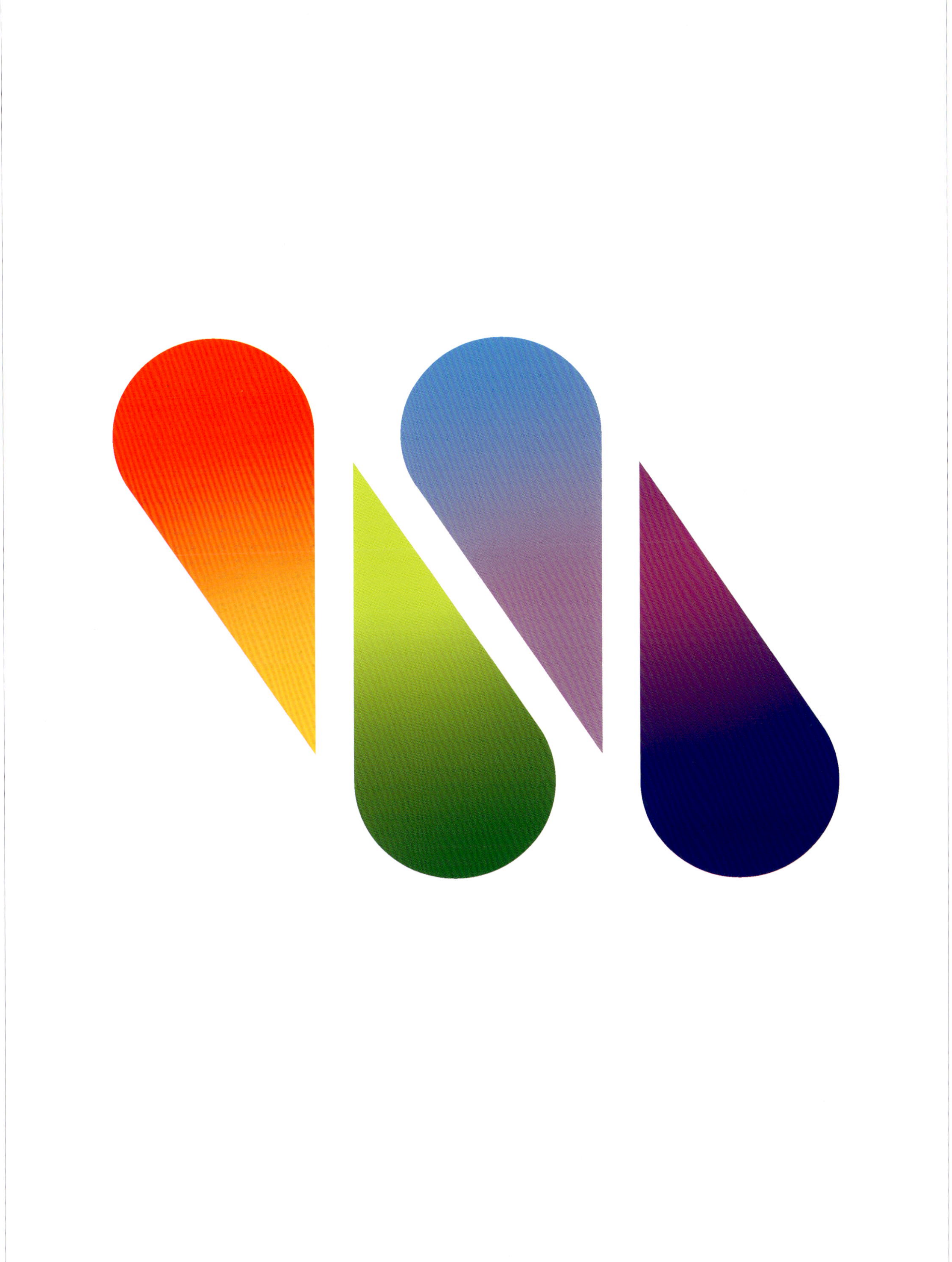

Title: NuTech Paint Identity | Client: NuTech Paint | Design Firm: SML Design

MICHAEL SCHWAB

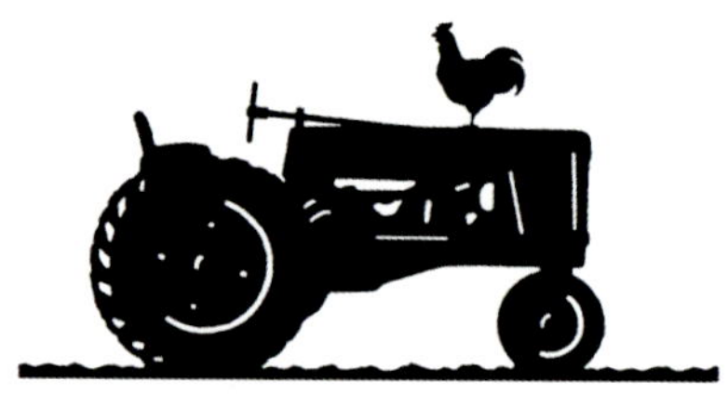

MOUNTAIN GIRLS FARM

RED LODGE, MONTANA

P241: Credit & Commentary **Title:** Mountain Girls Farm Logo | **Clients:** Jane Kleinman, Nancy Minion | **Design Firm:** Michael Schwab Studio

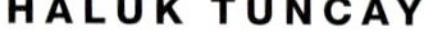

HALUK TUNCAY

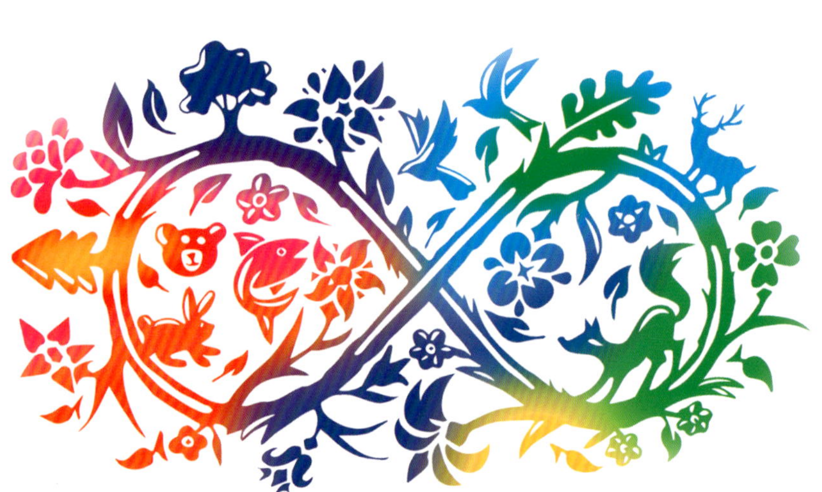

P241: Credit & Commentary **Title:** Biodiversity | **Client:** TEMA Foundation | **Design Firm:** H. Tuncay Design

MICHAEL SCHWAB

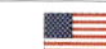

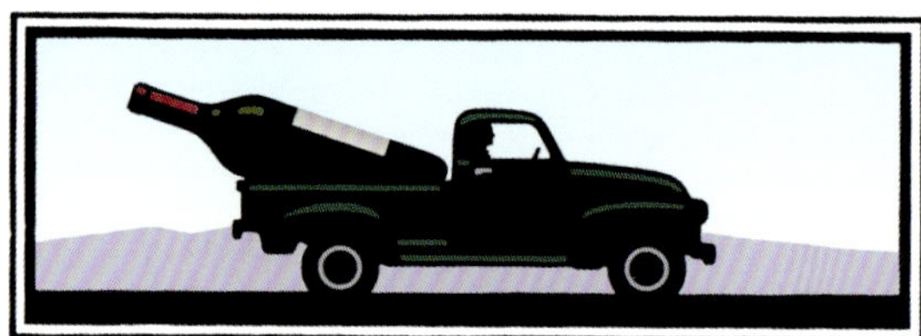

VINTAGE WINE FUND

WORLD CLASS WINES - DELIVERED

P241: Credit & Commentary **Title:** Vintage Wine Fund | **Client:** Lawrence D. Dutra | **Design Firm:** Michael Schwab Studio

MICHAEL VANDERBYL

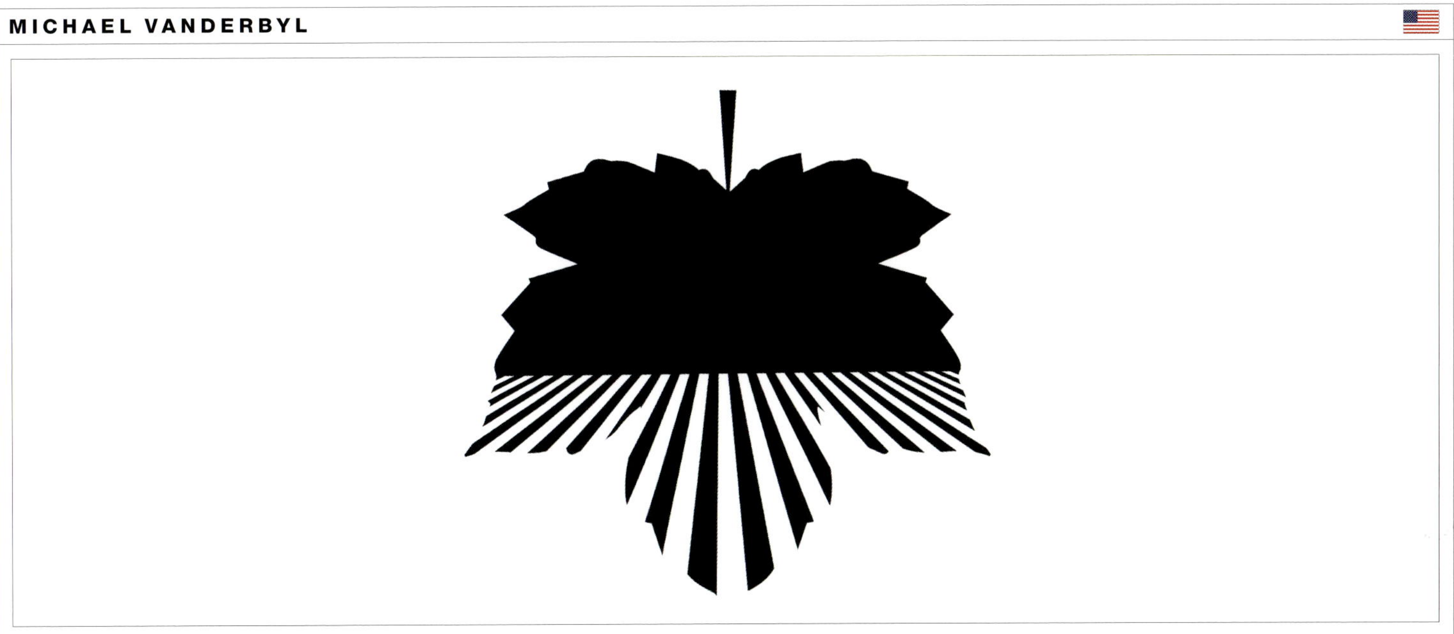

P241: Credit & Commentary **Title:** Gary's Wine & Marketplace Logo | **Client:** Gary's Wine & Marketplace | **Design Firm:** Vanderbyl Design

ANNIE CHEN

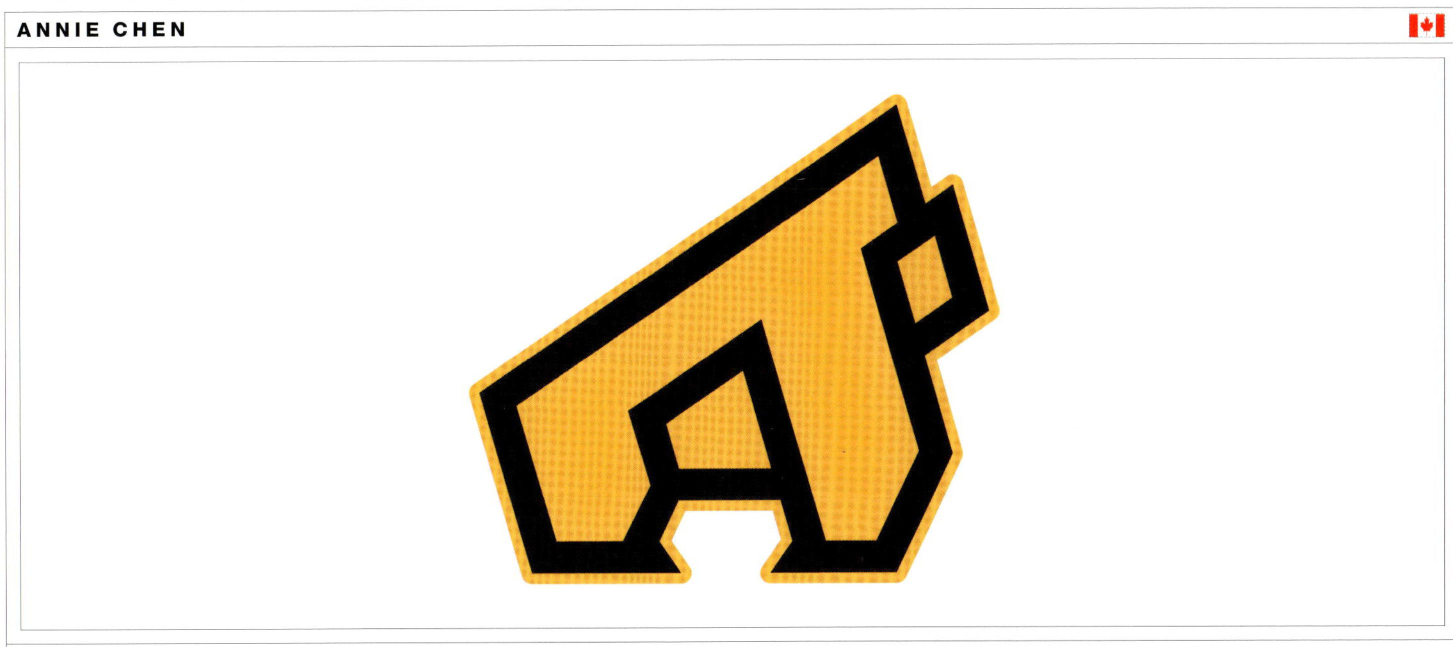

P241: Credit & Commentary **Title:** DK | **Client:** Sigma Intégrale | **Design Firm:** Annie Chen Design

ROGER ARCHBOLD

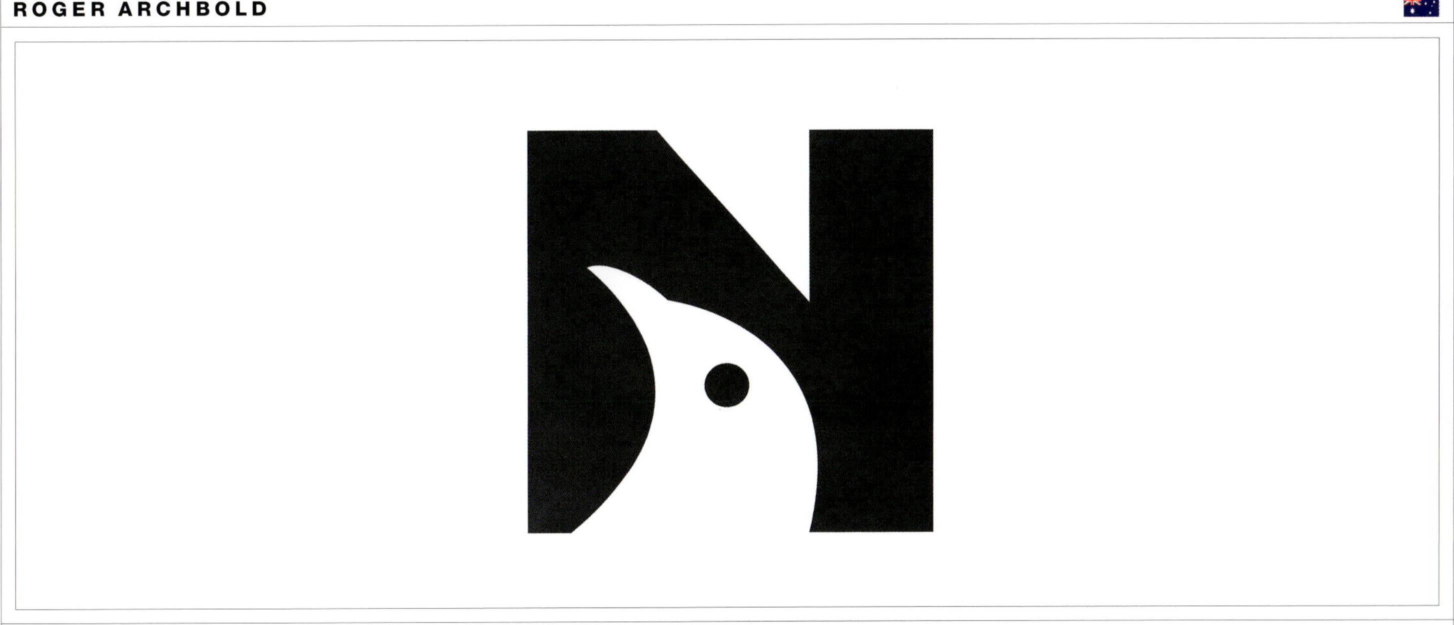

P241: Credit & Commentary **Title:** Nalini Scarfe Logo | **Client:** Nalini Scarfe | **Design Firm:** Roger Archbold

RESOURCE BRANDING

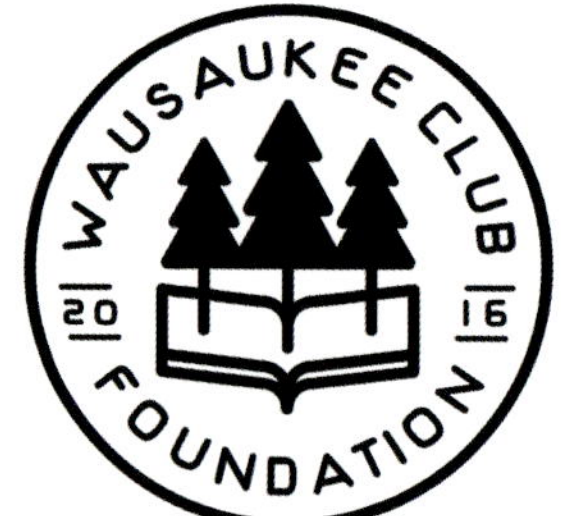

P242: Credit & Comm. **Title:** Wausaukee Club Foundation Logomark | **Client:** The Wausaukee Club | **Design Firm:** Resource Branding Image 1 of 2

DERWYN GOODALL

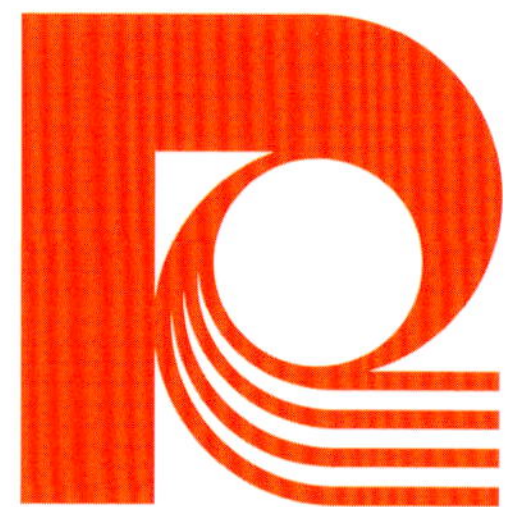

P242: Credit & Commentary **Title:** Revival Analytics Logo | **Client:** Revival Analytics | **Design Firm:** Goodall Integrated Design

NATE DYER

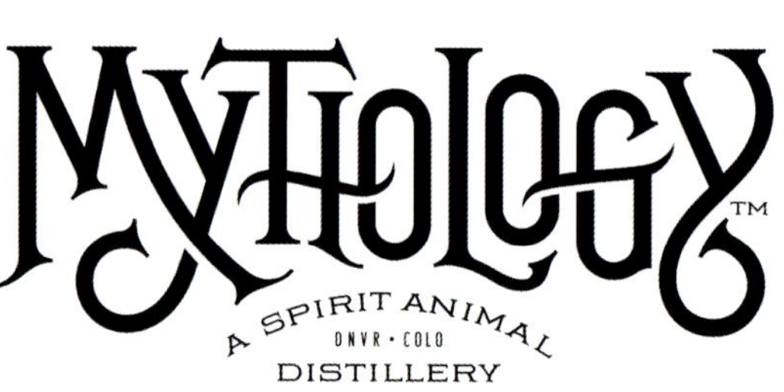

P242: Credit & Commentary **Title:** Mythology Distillery | **Client:** Mythology Distillery | **Design Firm:** Moxie Sozo

NATE DYER

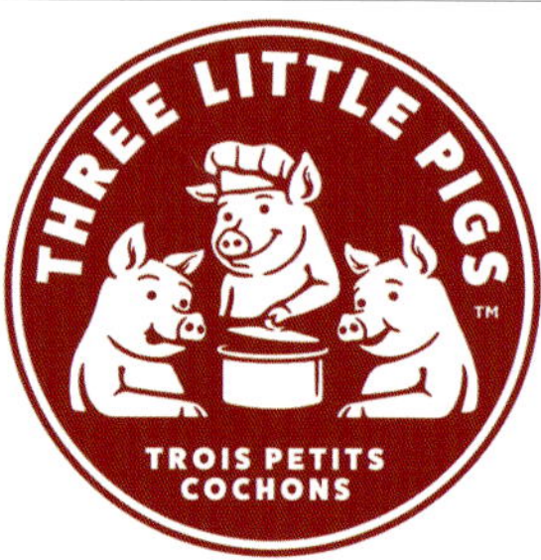

P242: Credit & Commentary **Title:** Three Little Pigs | **Client:** Three Little Pigs | **Design Firm:** Moxie Sozo

YOSHINORI SHIMOUSA

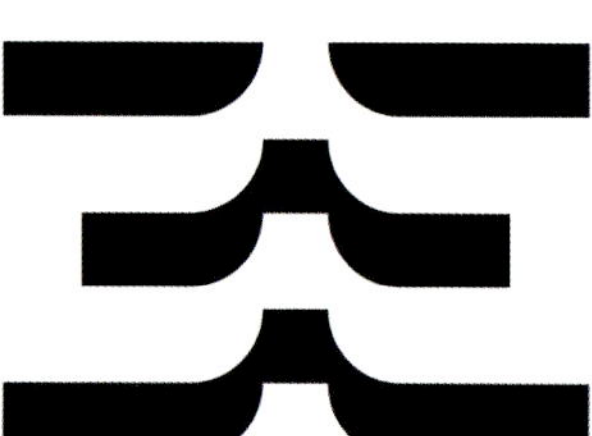

P242: Credit & Commentary **Title:** The Logo of Tenkodo Inc. | **Client:** Tenkodo Inc. | **Design Firm:** USADesign

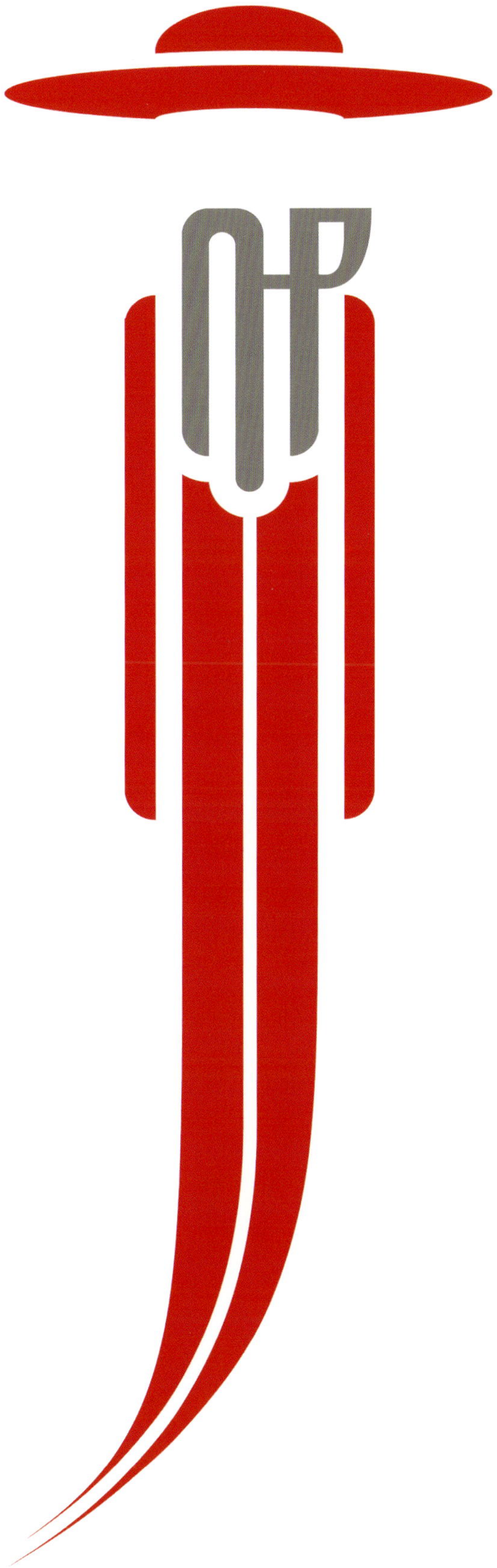

P242: Credit & Commentary Title: St. Jerome | Client: Museum of Croatian Archaeological Monuments | Design Firm: Stjepko Rošin

STEWART JUNG

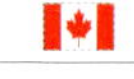

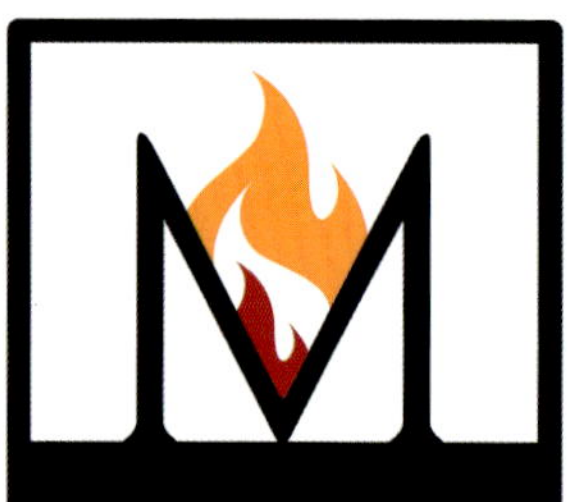

P242: Credit & Commentary **Title:** Maxwell Fireplaces Logo | **Client:** Maxwell Fireplaces | **Design Firm:** AG Creative Group

ISLAM HASSAN

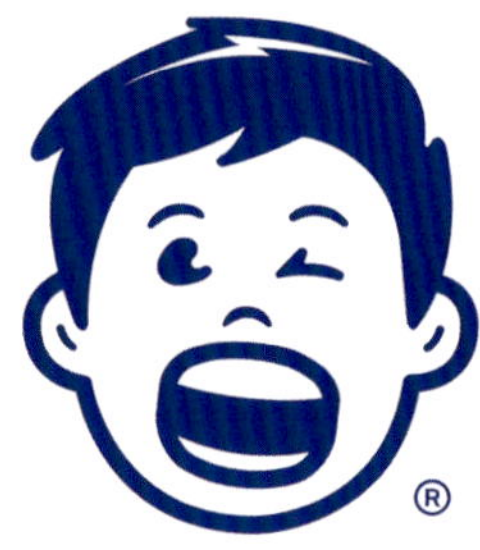

P242: Credit & Commentary **Title:** Encore Burgers Logo | **Client:** Encore Burgers | **Design Firm:** Islam Hassan

HEART HAUS AT CVS HEALTH

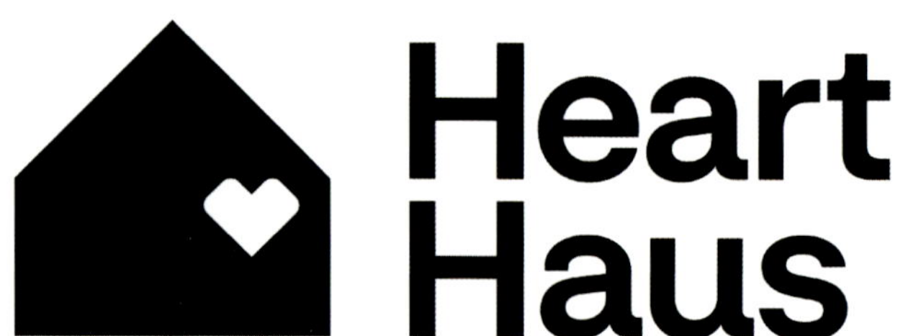

P242: Credit & Commentary **Title:** Heart Haus Logo | **Client:** Self-initiated | **Design Firm:** Heart Haus at CVS Health Image 1 of 3

JASON JAMES

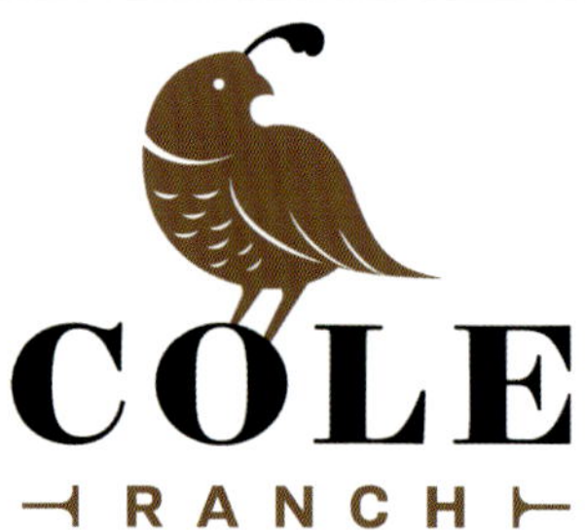

P242: Credit & Commentary **Title:** Cole Ranch Logo | **Client:** Cole Ranch | **Design Firm:** Spire Agency

SCOTT RAY

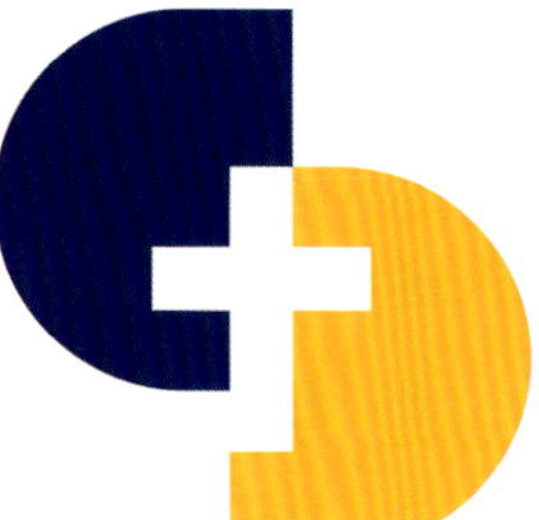

P243: Credit & Comm. **Title:** Sound Christian Academy Logo | **Client:** Sound Christian Academy | **Design Firm:** Peterson Ray & Company

SHARON LLOYD MCLAUGHLIN

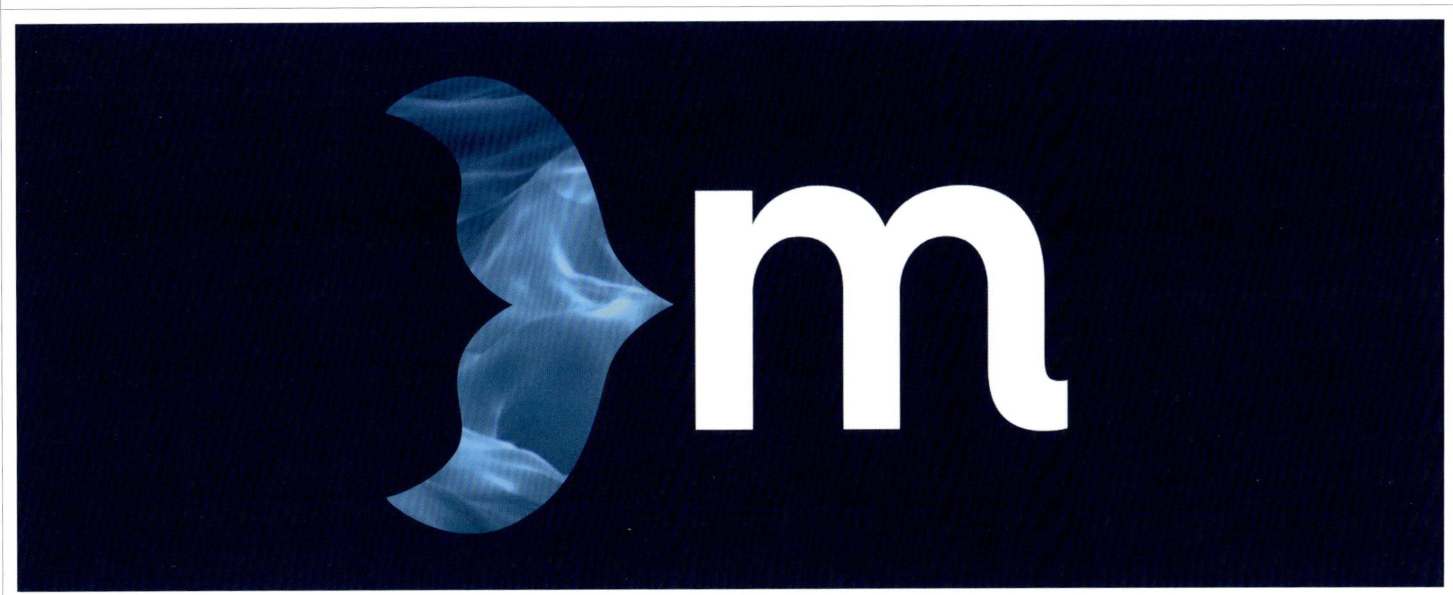

P243: Credit & Commentary **Title:** Mermaid, Inc. Logomark | **Client:** Self-initiated | **Design Firm:** Mermaid, Inc.

HAAS DESIGN

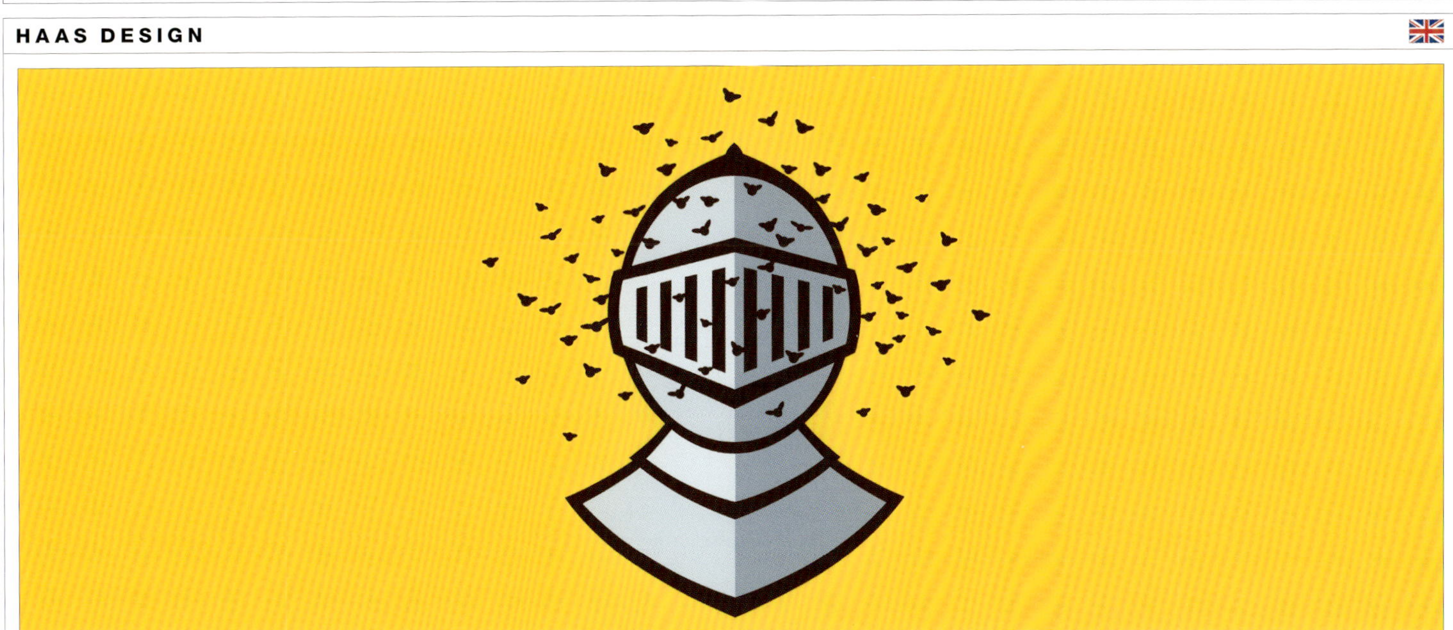

P243: Credit & Comm. **Title:** Borthwick Mains Farm Apiary | **Clients:** John Young, Borthwick Mains Farm Apiary | **Design Firm:** Haas Design

SHARON LLOYD MCLAUGHLIN

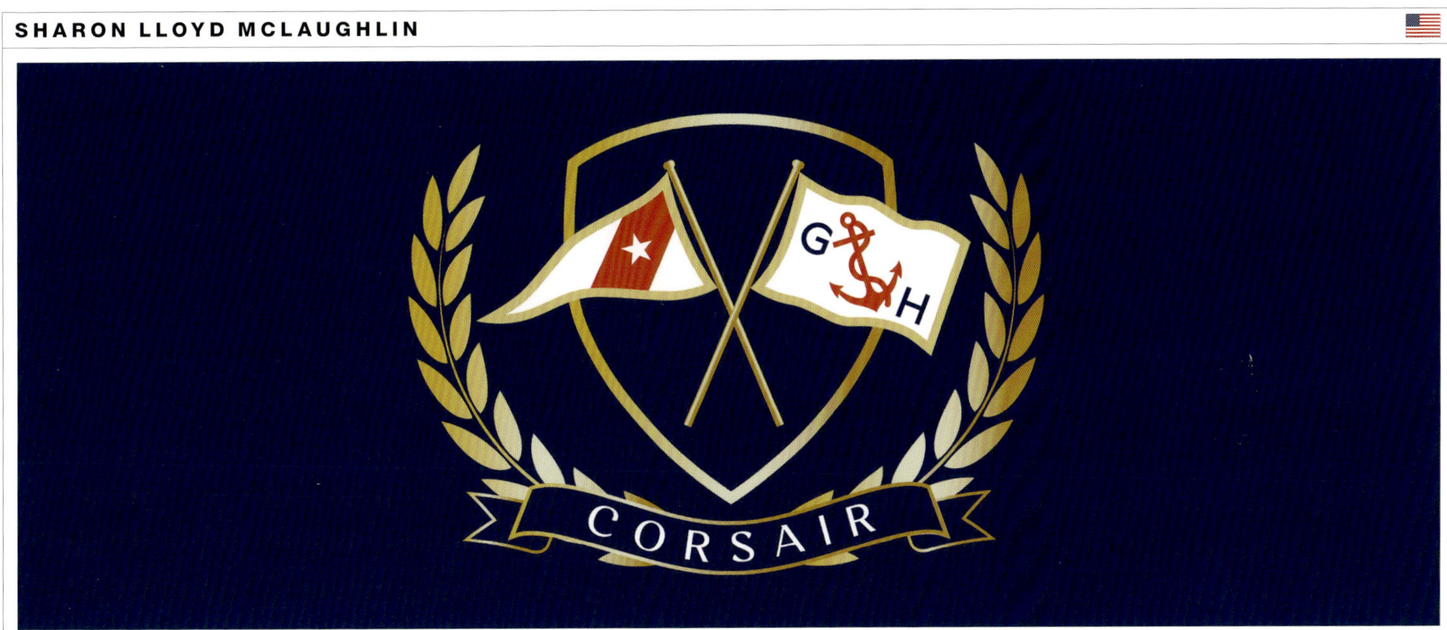

P243: Credit & Commentary **Title:** The Corsair Logo | **Client:** National Resources | **Design Firm:** Mermaid, Inc.

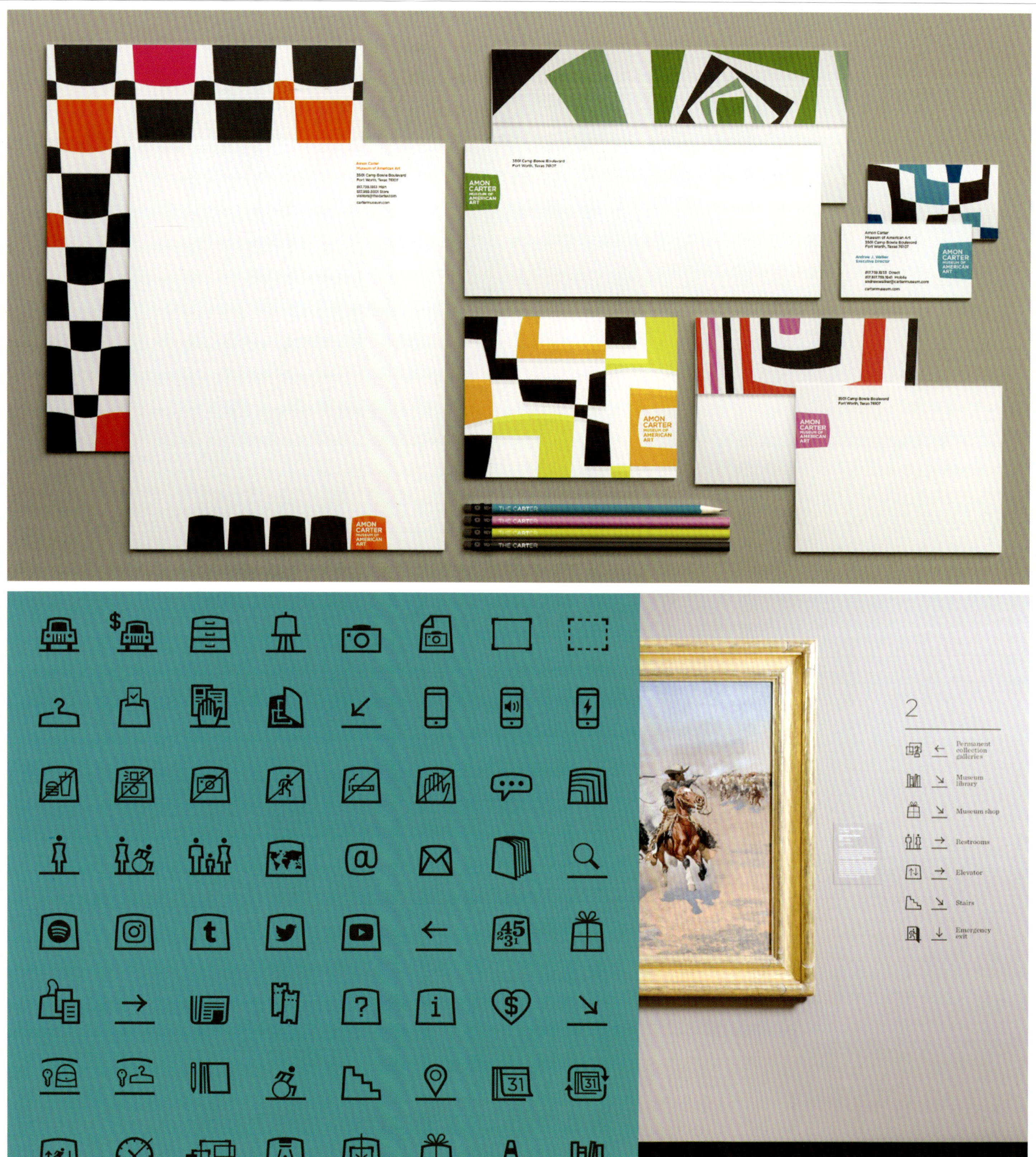

Title: The Amon Carter Museum of American Art Brand Identity | **Client:** The Amon Carter Museum of American Art | **Design Firm:** *TraceElement
P243: Credit & Commentary | Images 1, 2 of 7

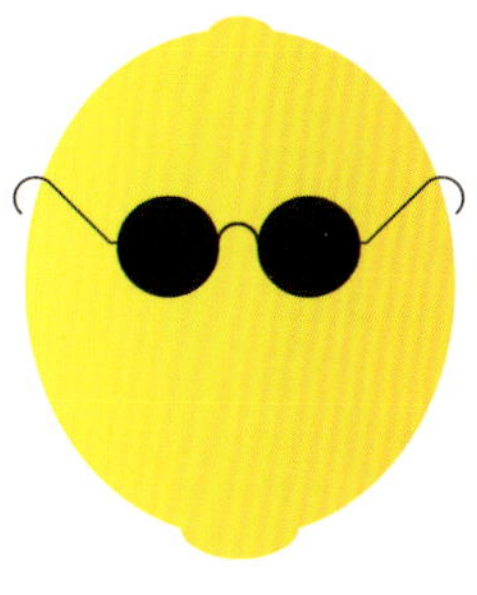

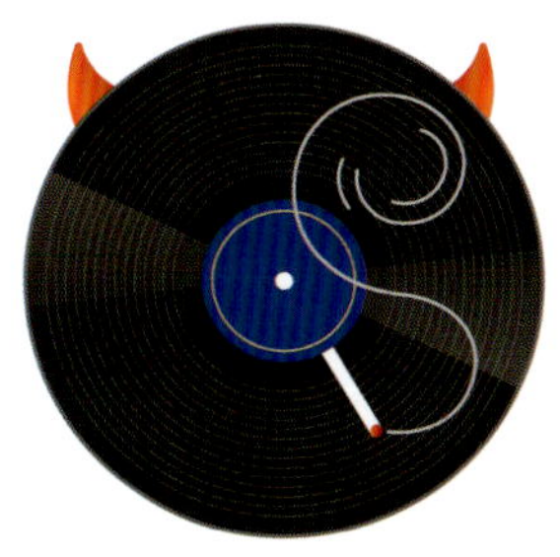

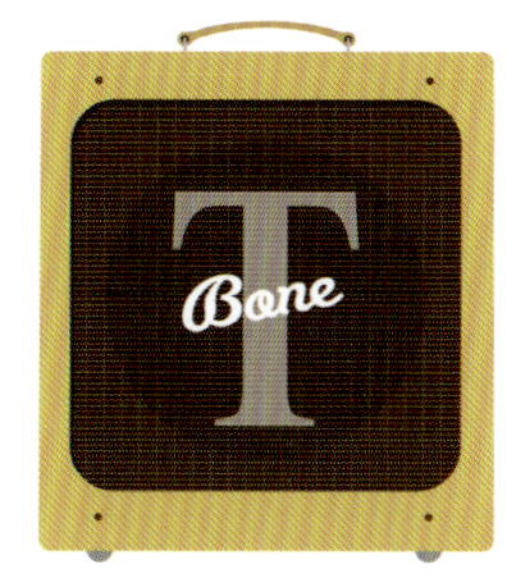

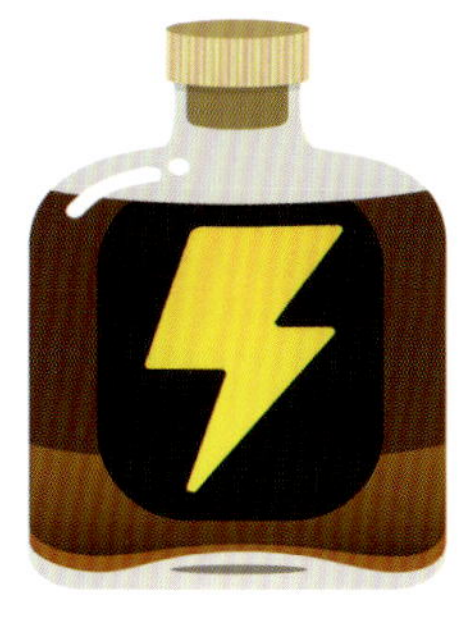

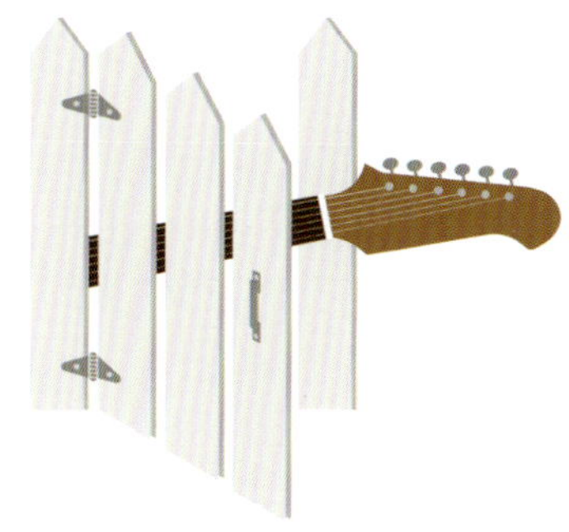

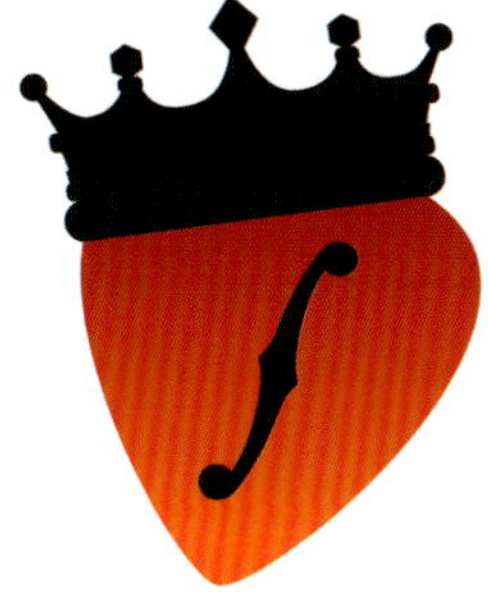

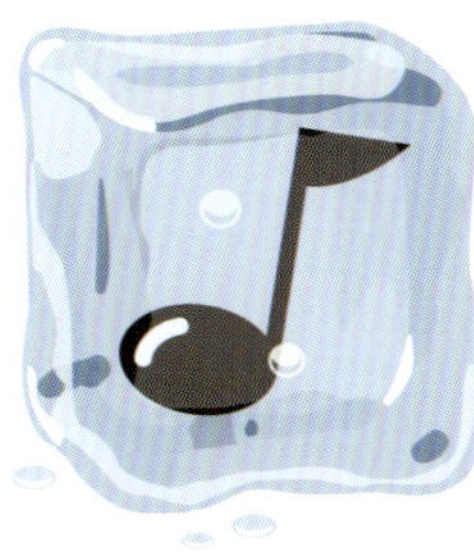

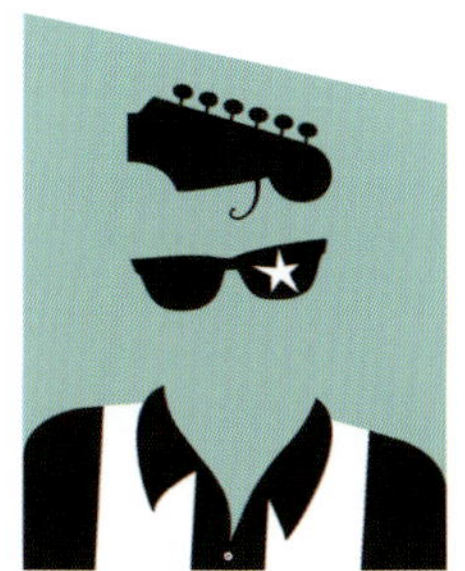

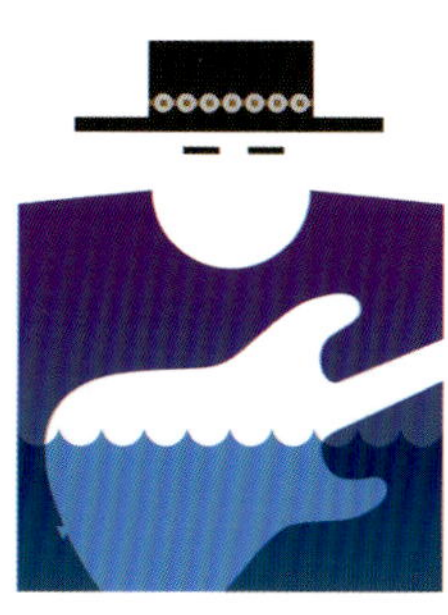

 Title: The Trinity River Blues Project | **Client:** The Trinity River Blues Society | **Design Firm:** May & Co.

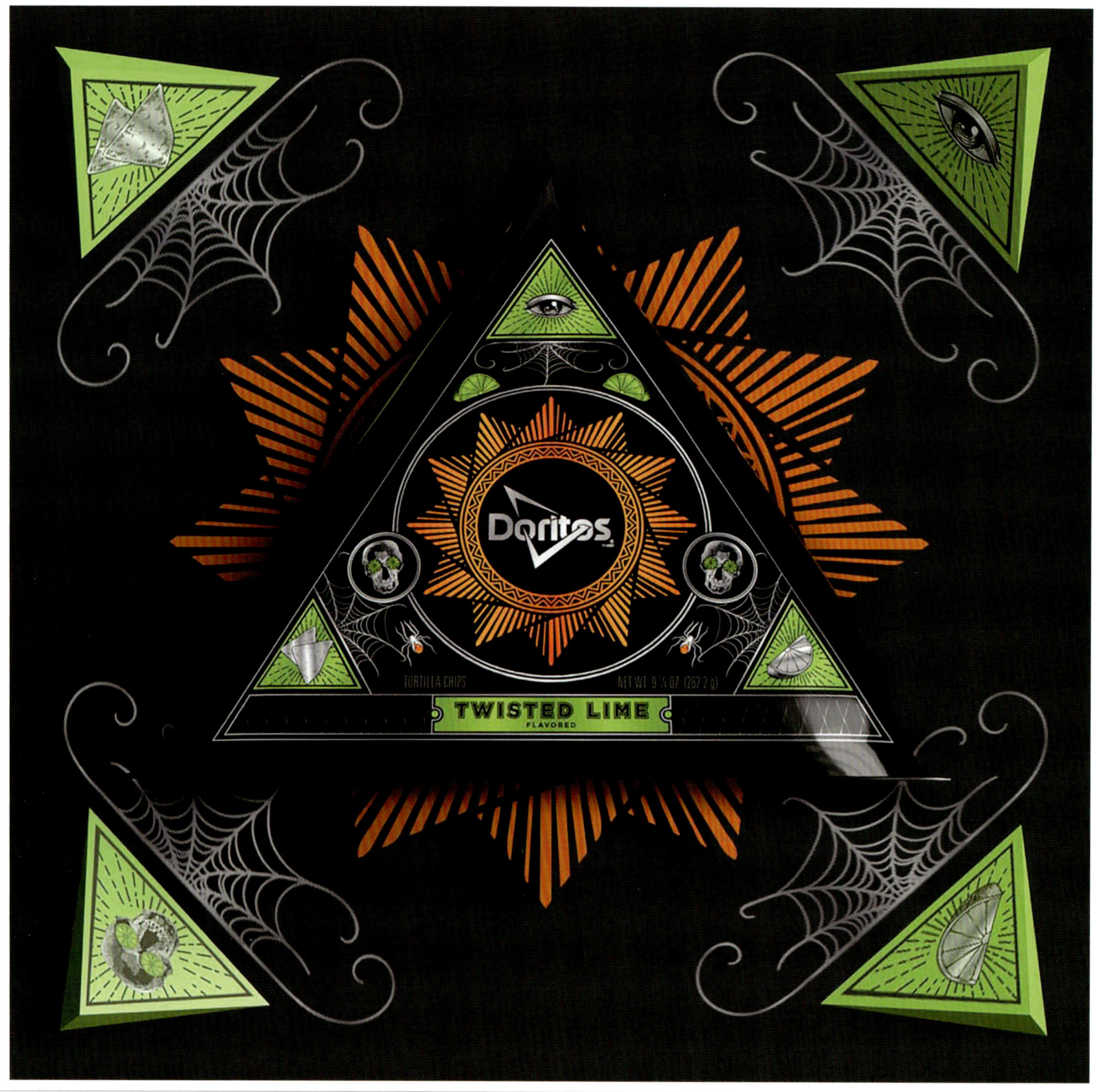

P243: Credit & Commentary **Title:** Doritos Twisted Lime Halloween | **Client:** Self-initiated | **Design Firm:** PepsiCo Design & Innovation Image 1 of 2

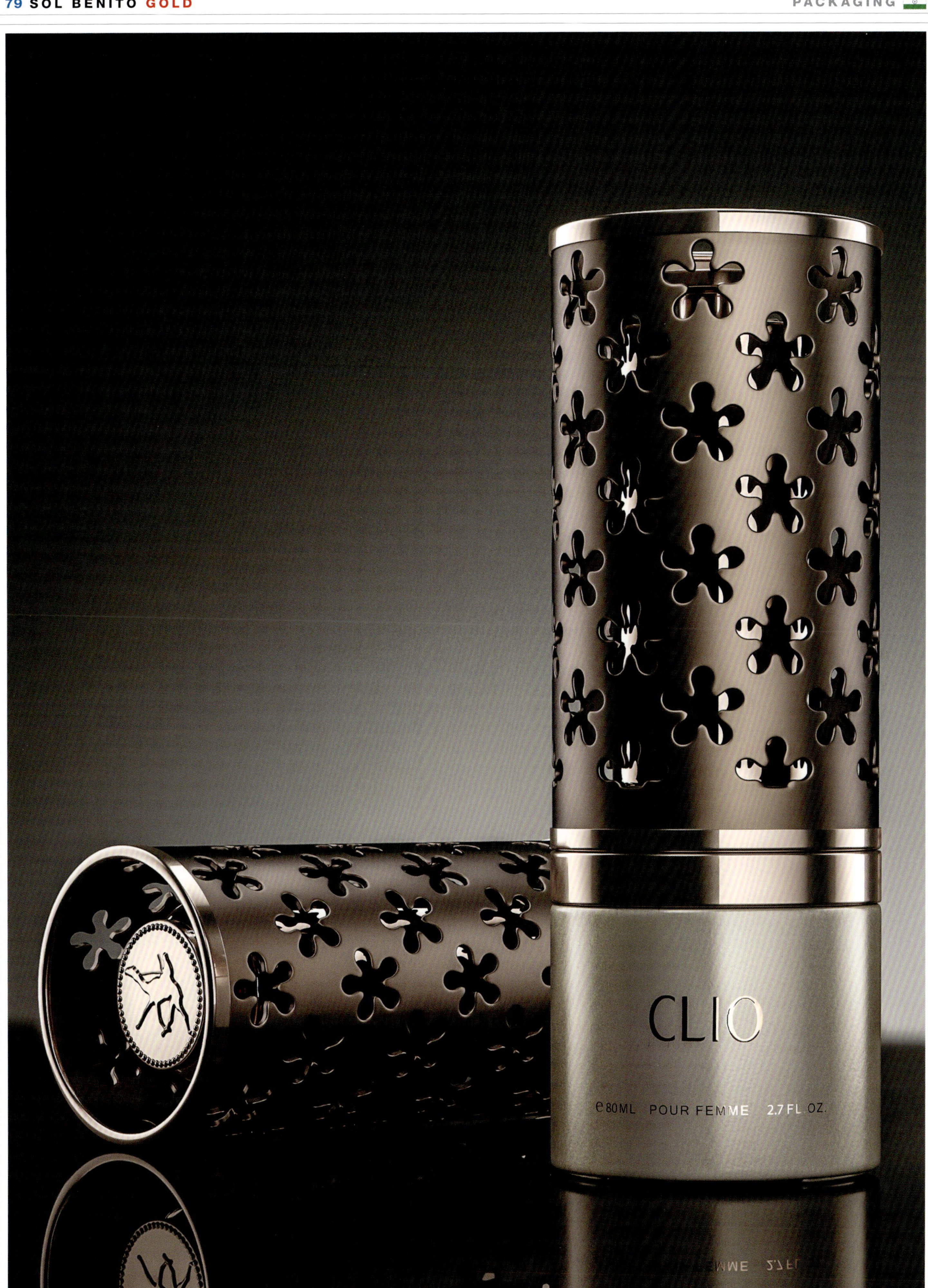

P243: Credit & Commentary

Title: Clio | Client: Emper | Design Firm: Sol Benito

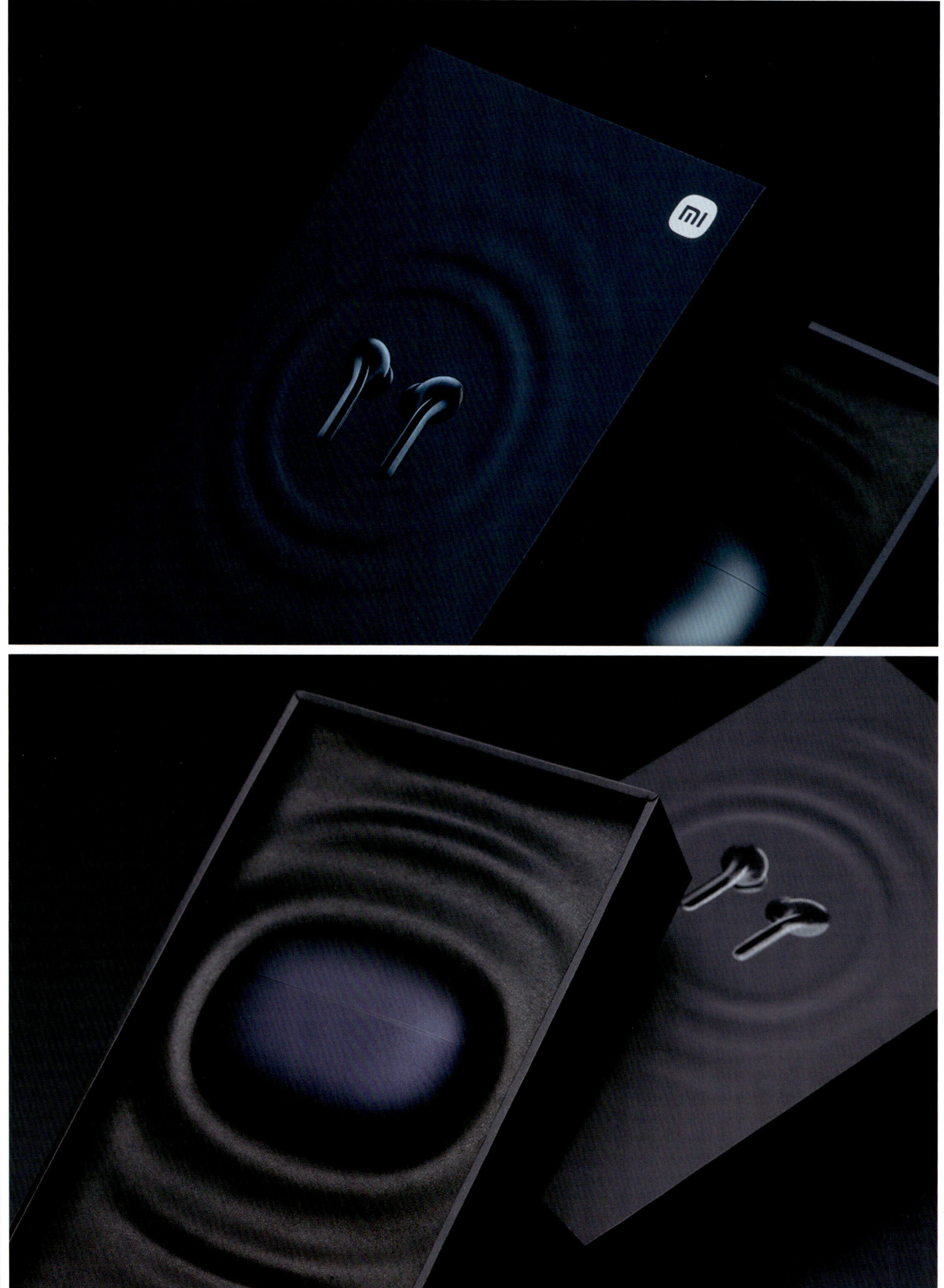

P243: Credit & Commentary

Title: Mi Buds 3T Pro | Client: Self-initiated | Design Firm: Xiaomi

Images 1, 2 of 7

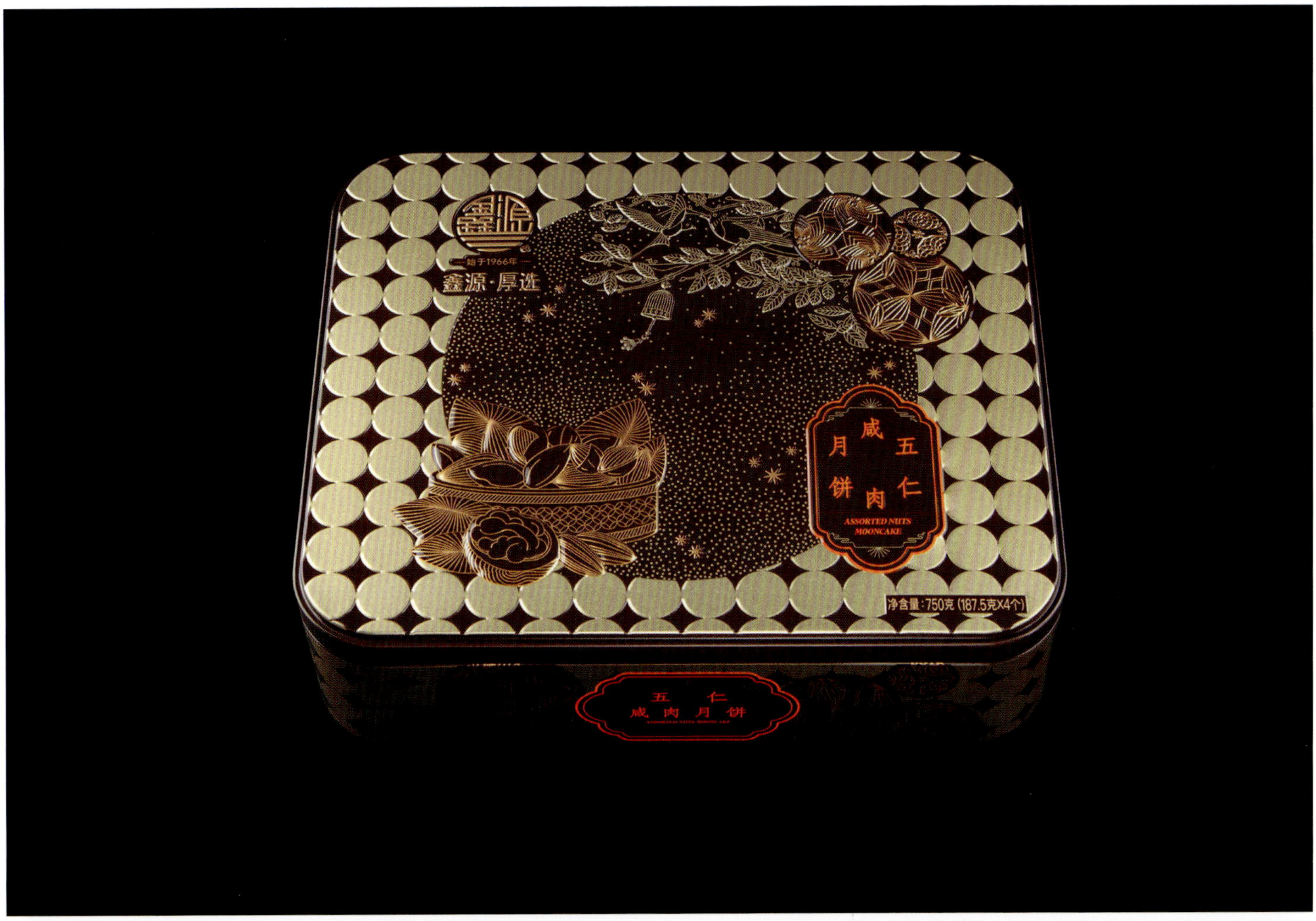

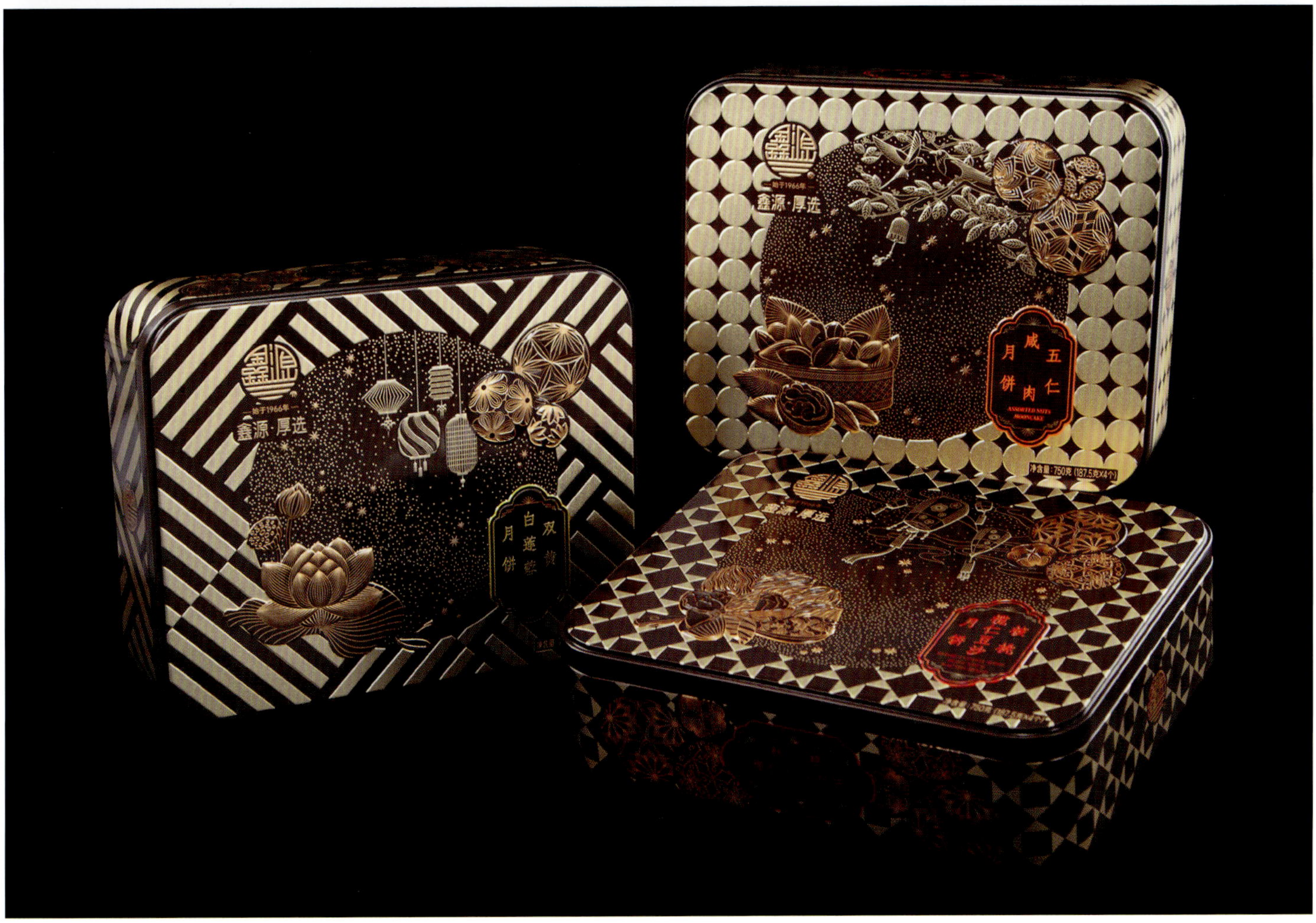

Title: Gold Label Mooncake | **Client:** Xiang Yuen | **Design Firm:** Box Brand Design Limited

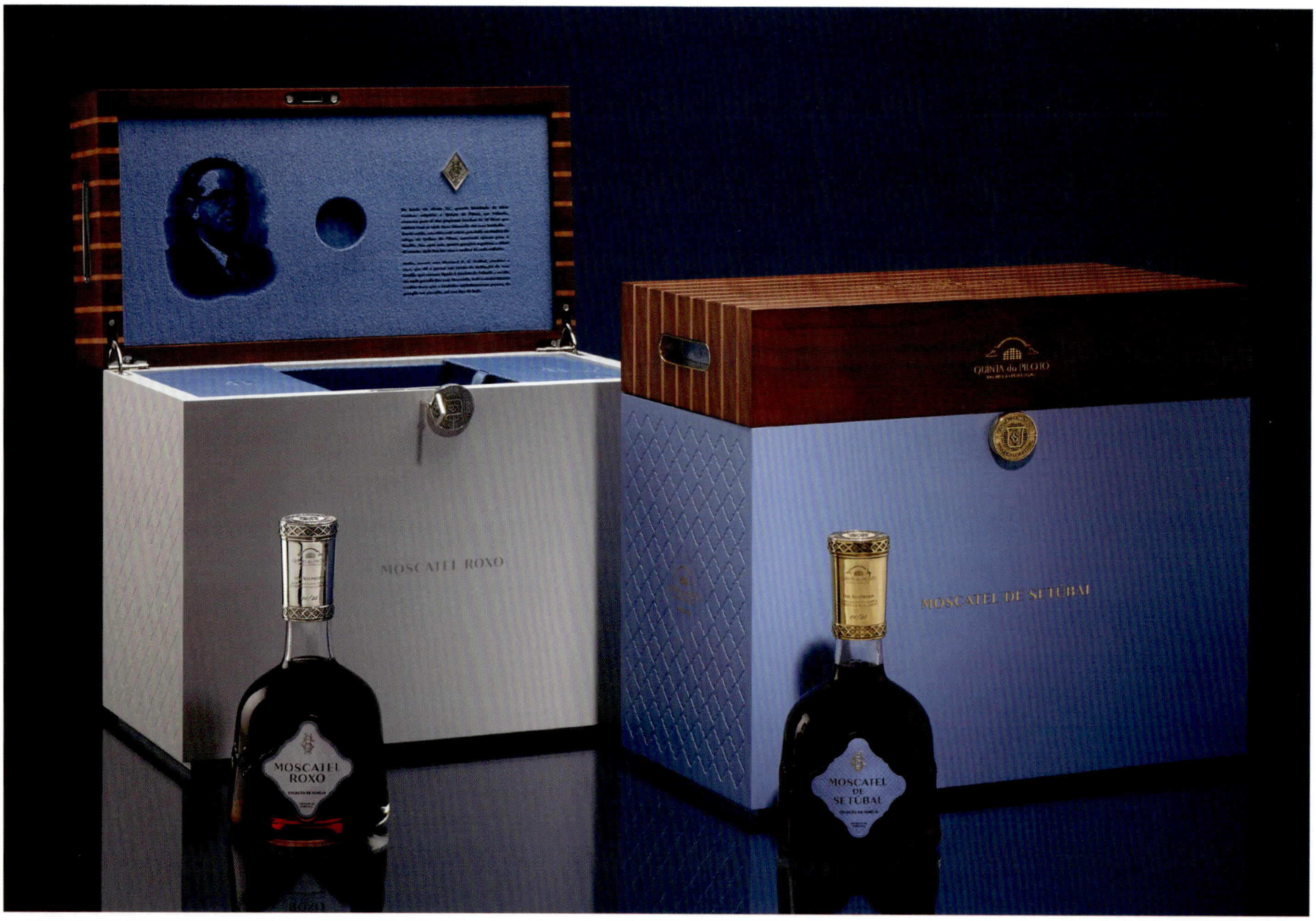

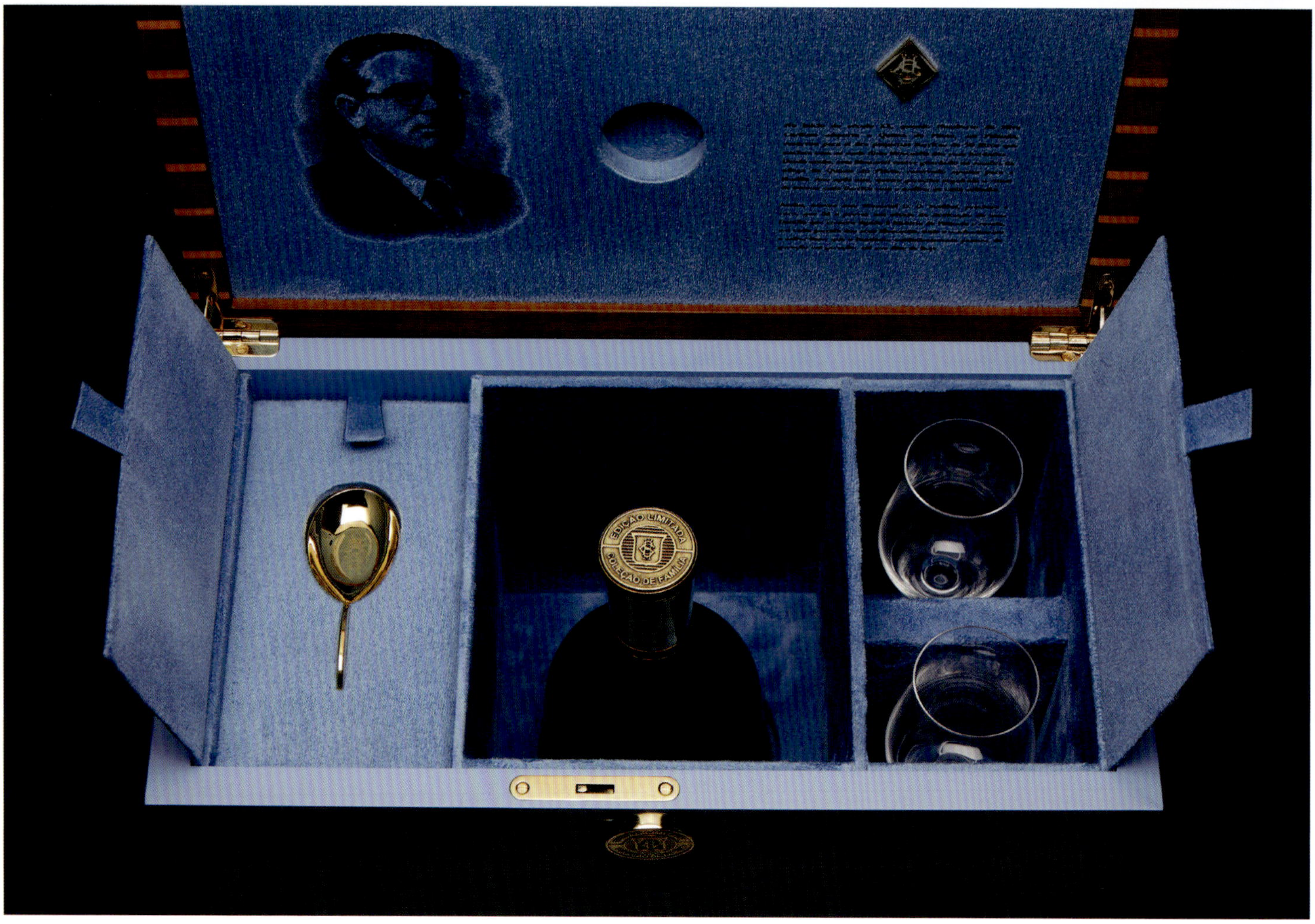

Title: Quinta do Piloto's Moscatéis | **Client:** Quinta do Piloto | **Design Firm:** Omdesign

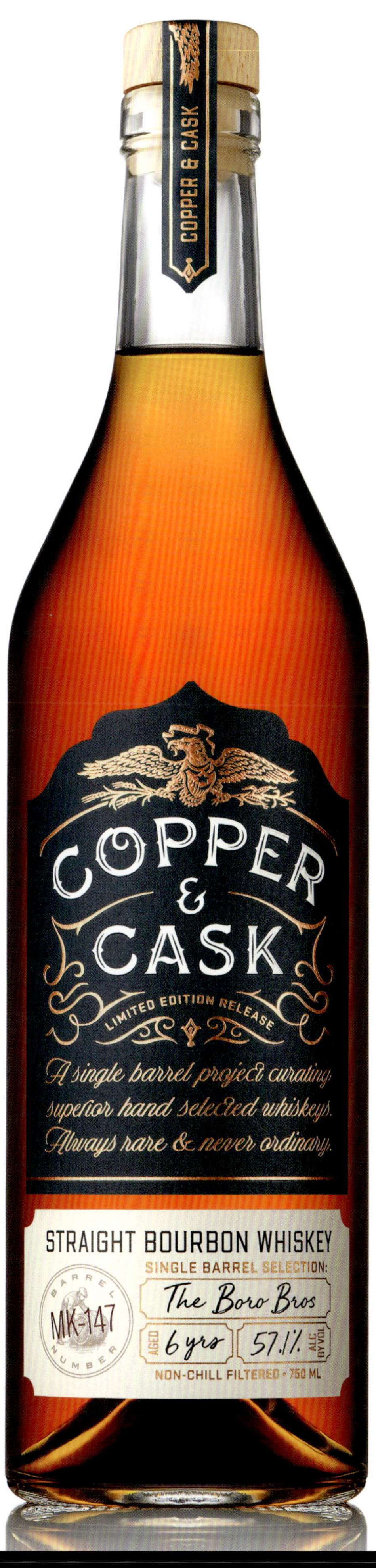

 Title: Copper & Cask Whiskey | **Client:** Latitude Beverage Co. | **Design Firm:** Pavement

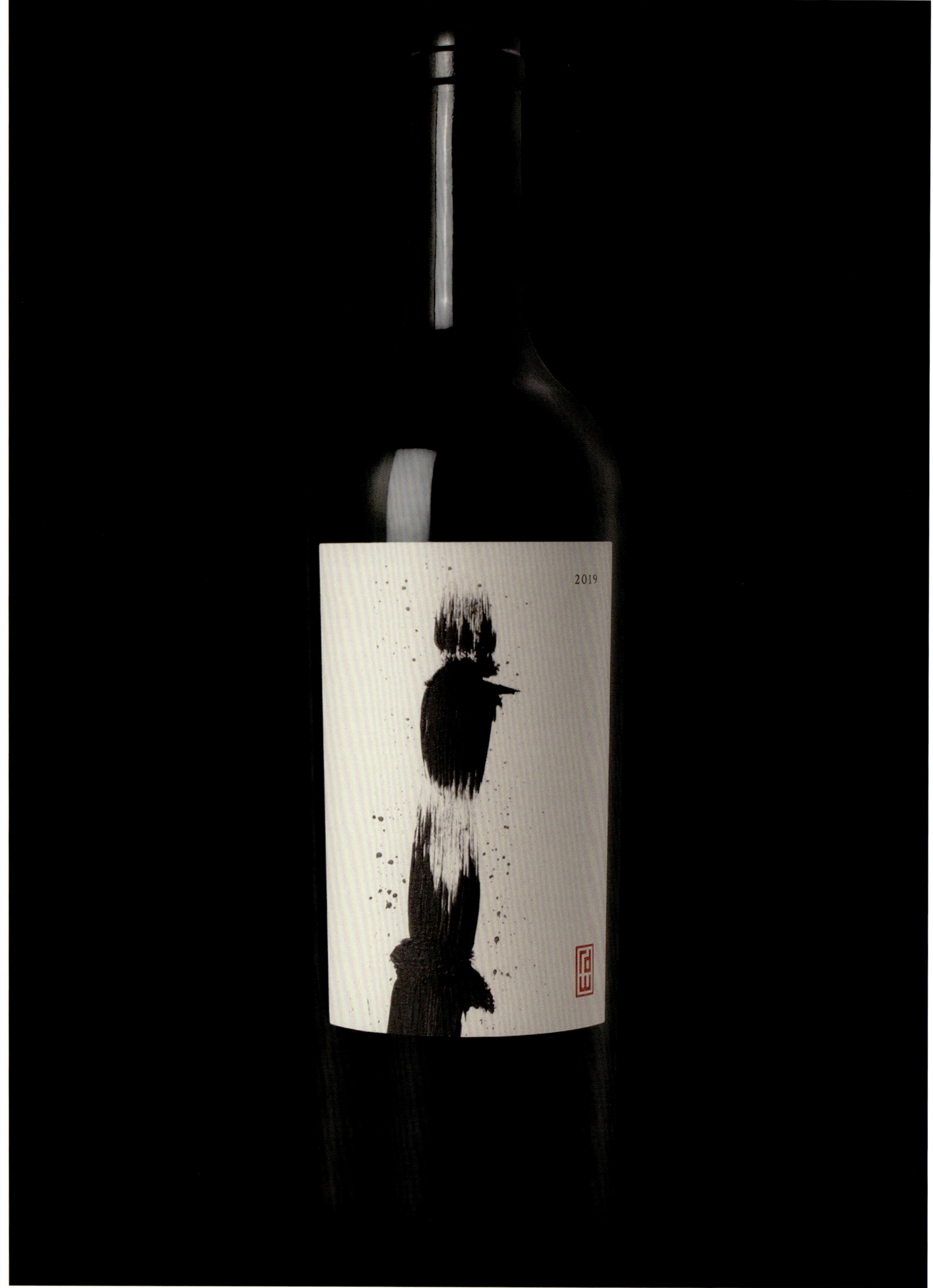

P244: Credit & Commentary **Title:** Hundred Knot Khoai Wines | **Client:** RD Winery | **Design Firm:** CF Napa Brand Design

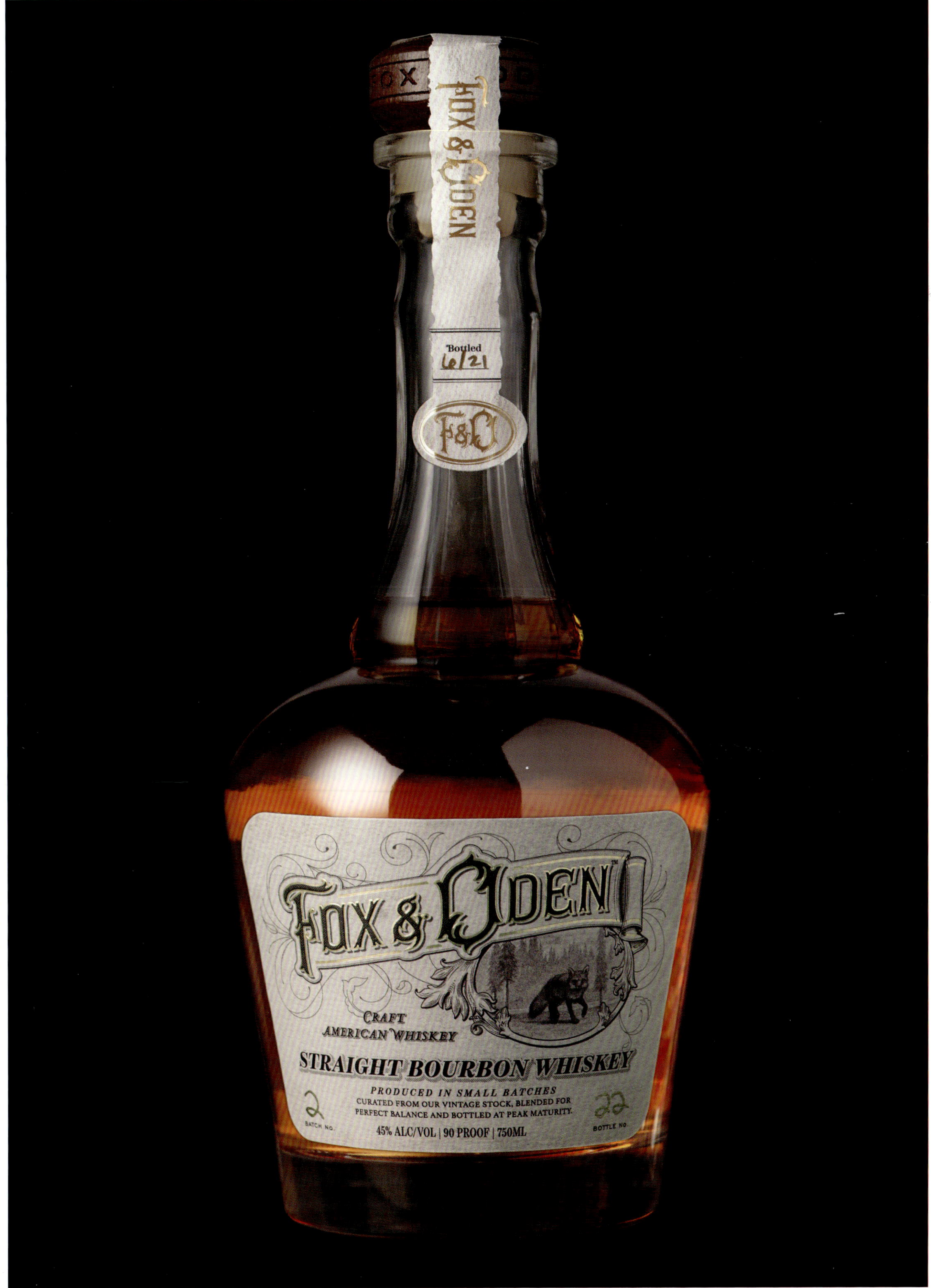

Title: Fox & Oden | **Client:** Fox & Oden | **Design Firm:** CF Napa Brand Design

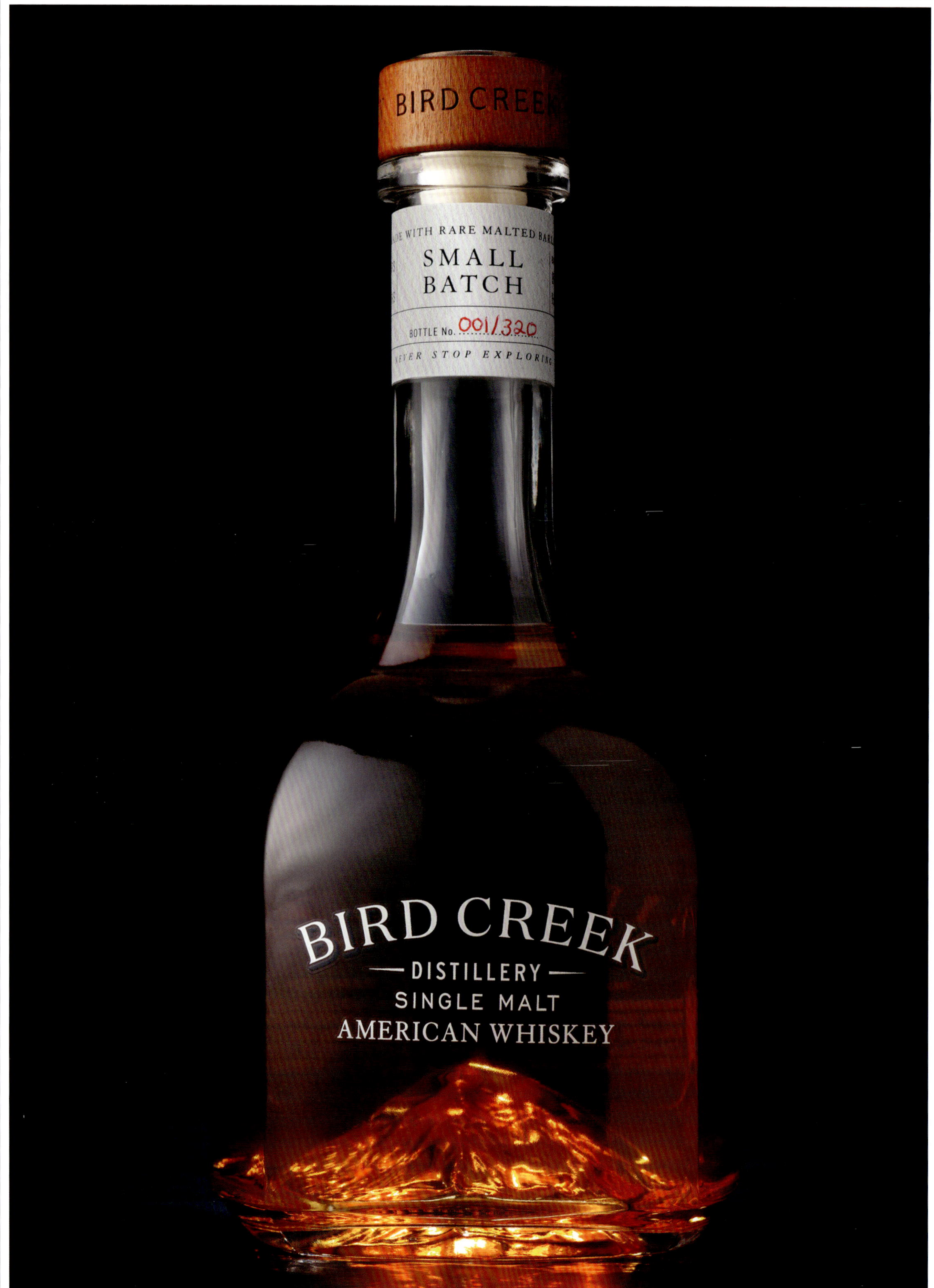

P244: Credit & Commentary **Title:** Bird Creek Distillery | **Client:** Bird Creek Distillery | **Design Firm:** CF Napa Brand Design

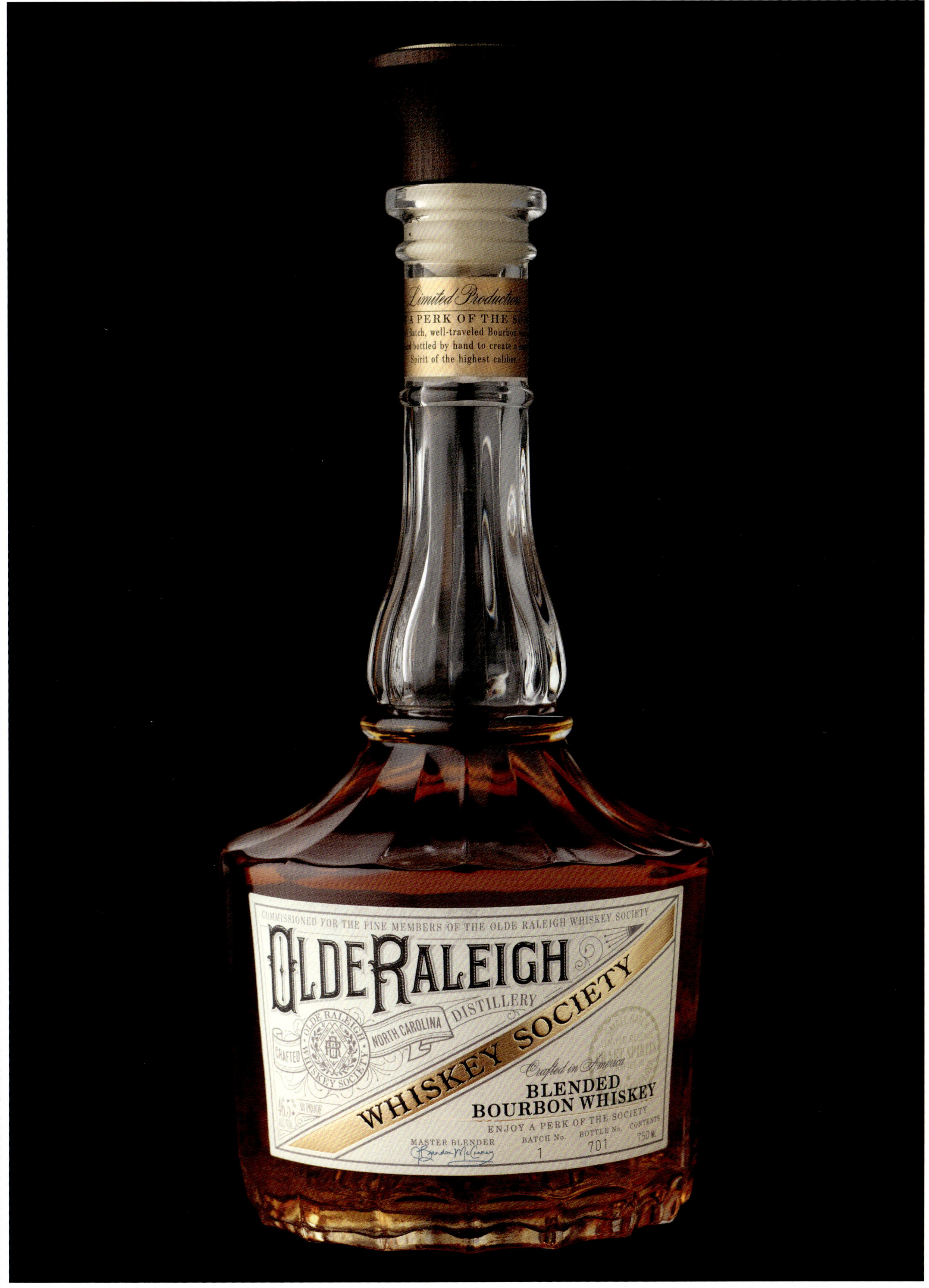

P244: Credit & Commentary Title: Olde Raleigh Distillery | Client: Olde Raleigh Distillery | Design Firm: CF Napa Brand Design

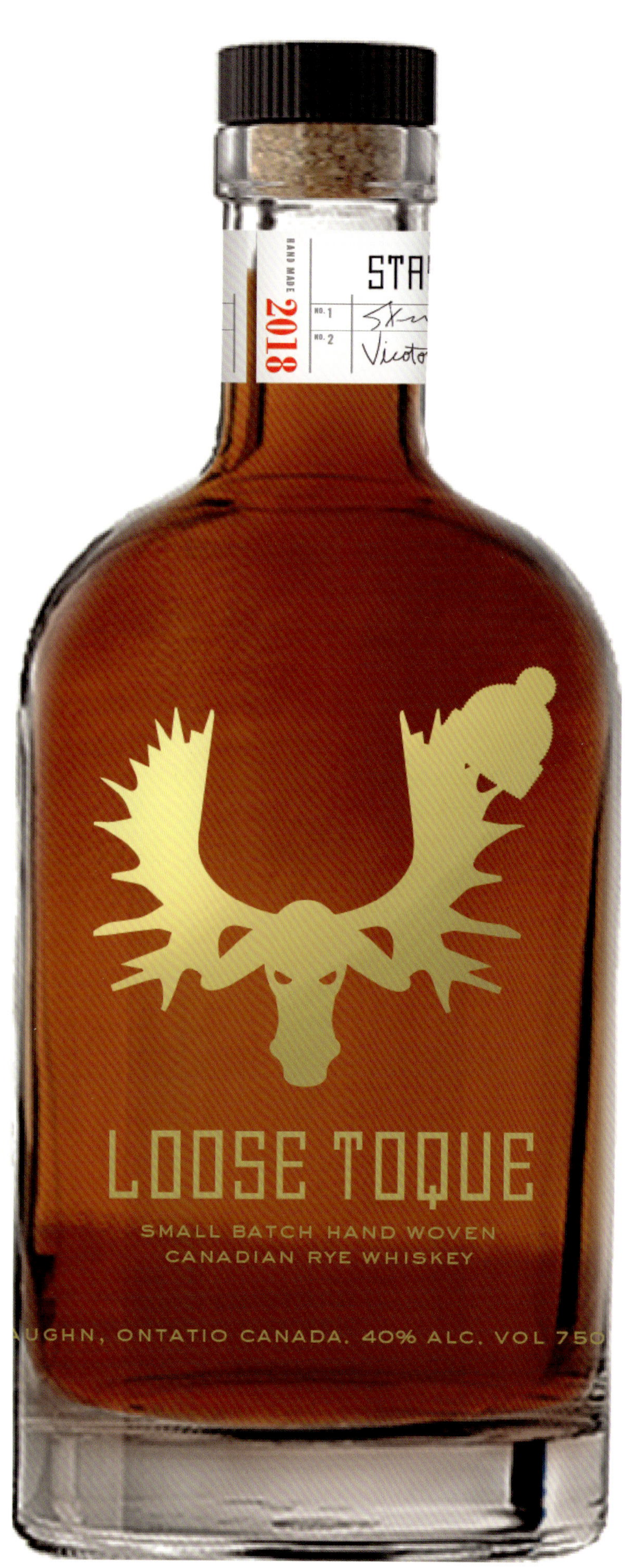

P244: Credit & Commentary **Title:** Loose Toque Whiskey Bottle Packaging | **Client:** Loose Toque | **Design Firm:** Vanderbyl Design

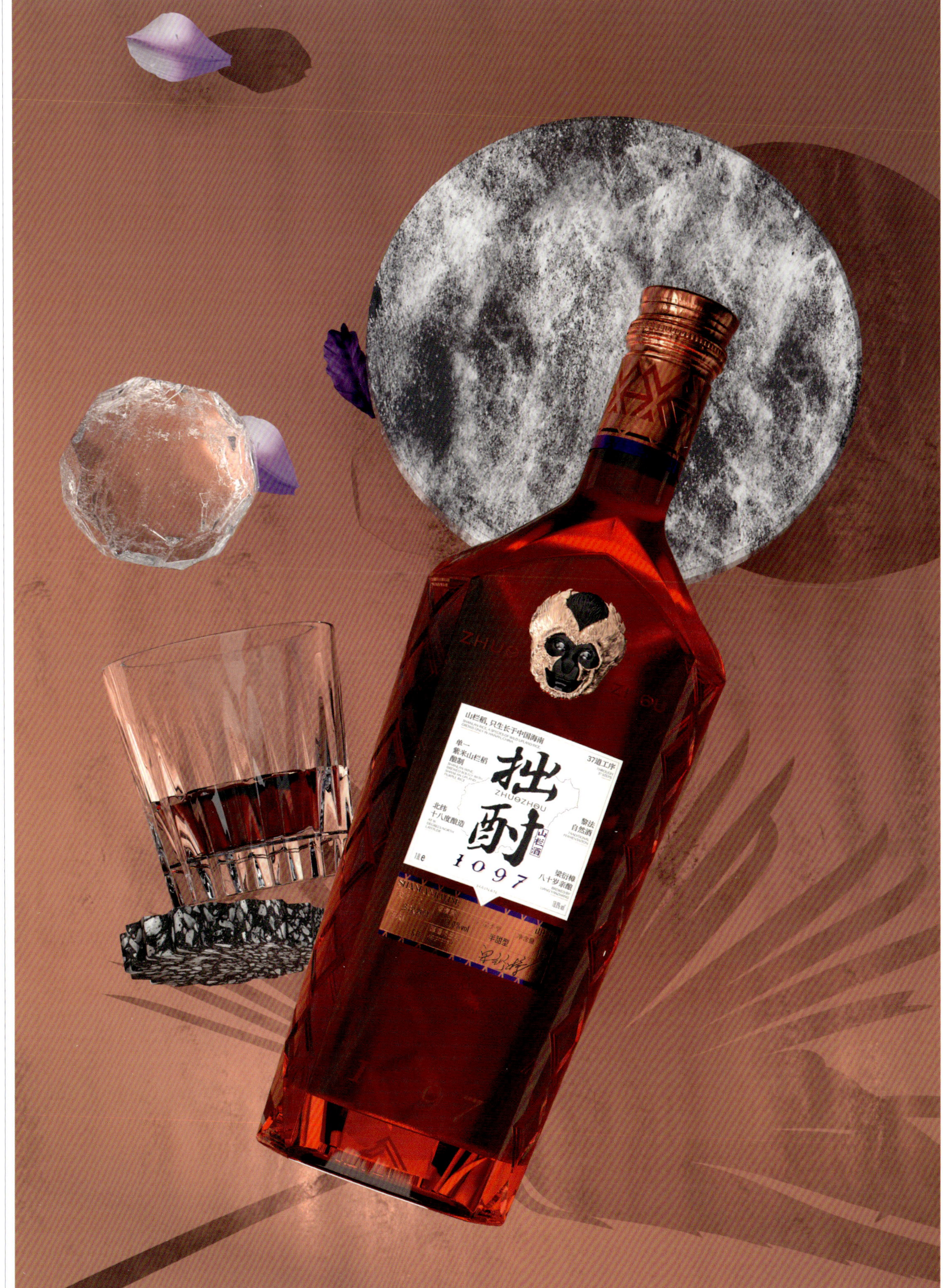

P244: Credit & Commentary Title: ZHUOZHOU (Shanlan Rice Wine) Package | Client: ZHUOZHOU | Design Firm: Grantz Jansword Image 1 of 5

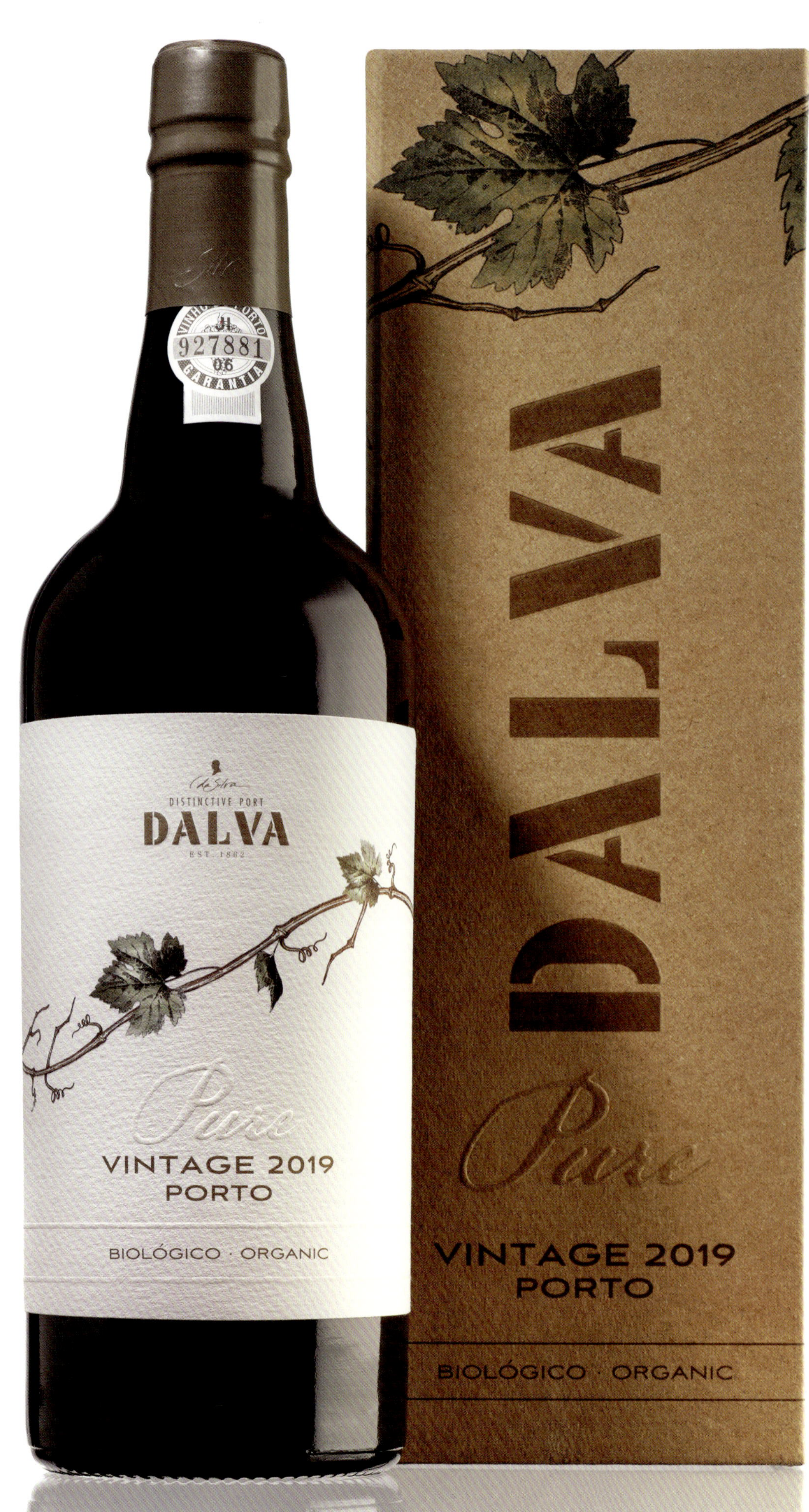

P244: Credit & Commentary

Title: Dalva Pure Vintage | **Client:** C. da Silva | **Design Firm:** Omdesign

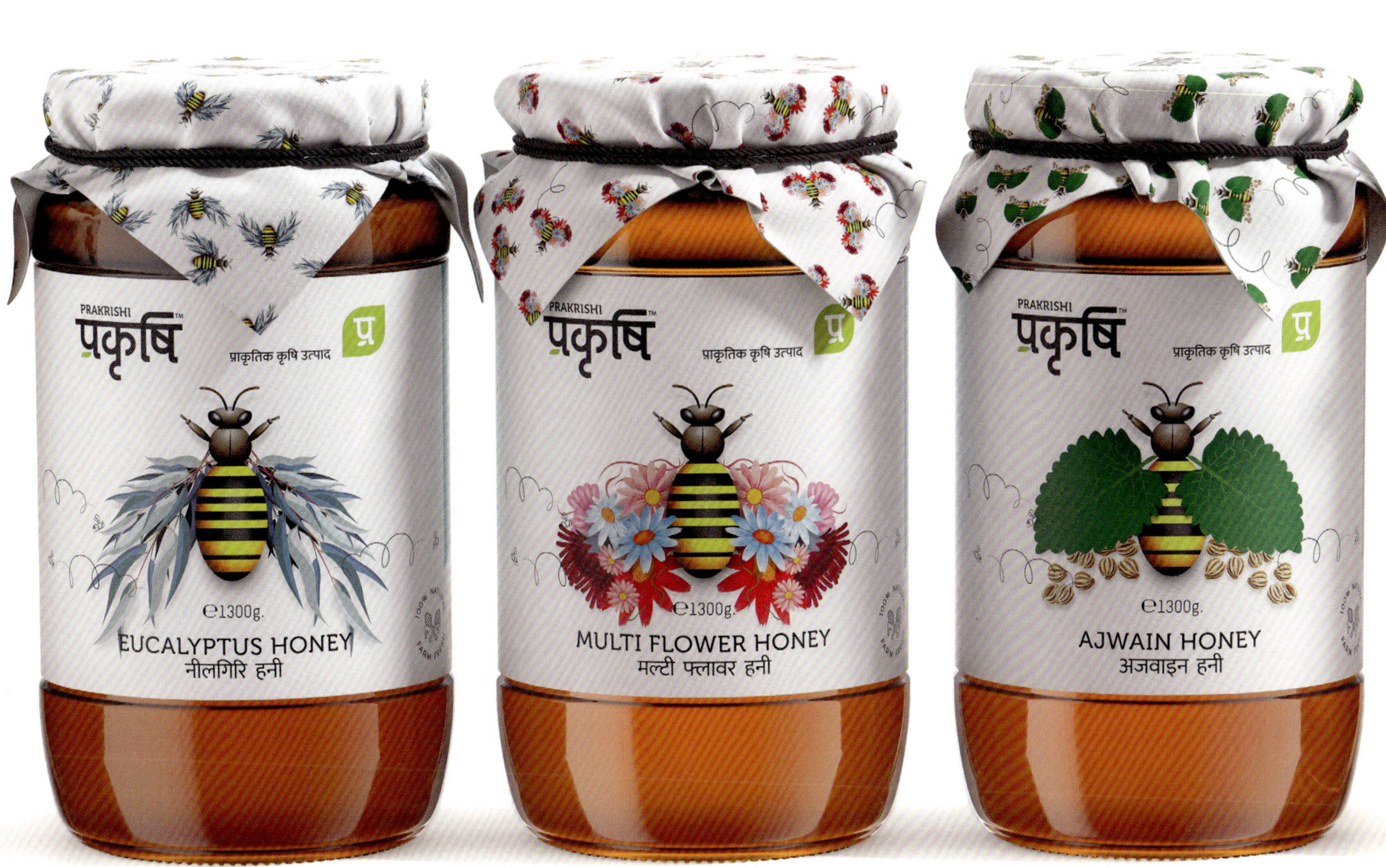

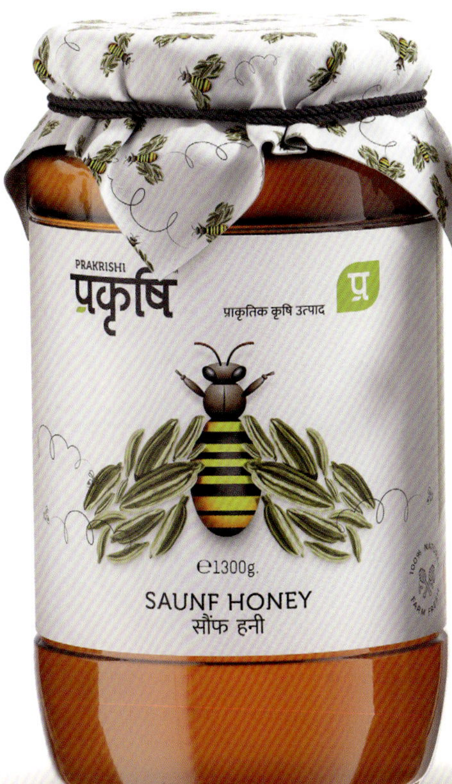

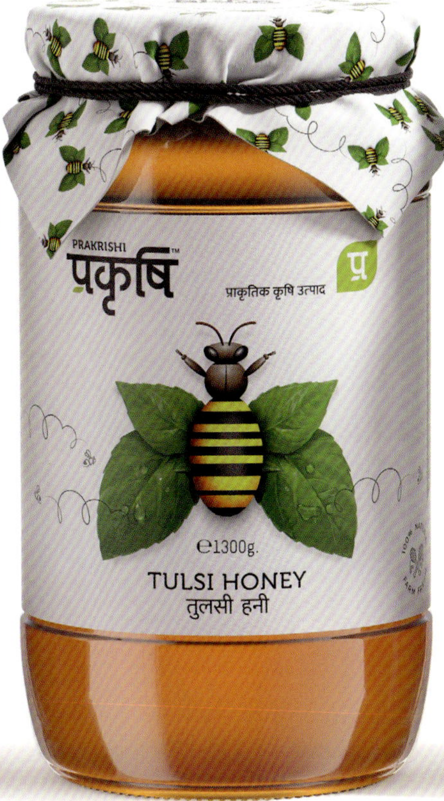

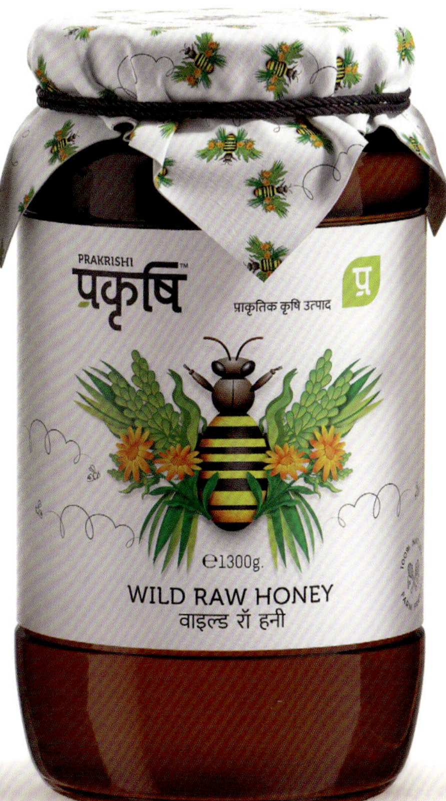

P245: Credit & Commentary

Title: Prakrishi Honey | **Client:** Prakrishi Organic | **Design Firm:** Sol Benito

JEFF BARFOOT

PACKAGING 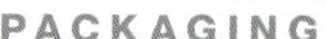

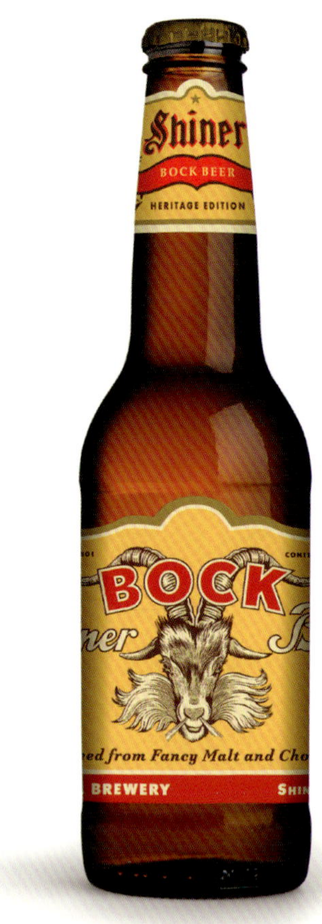

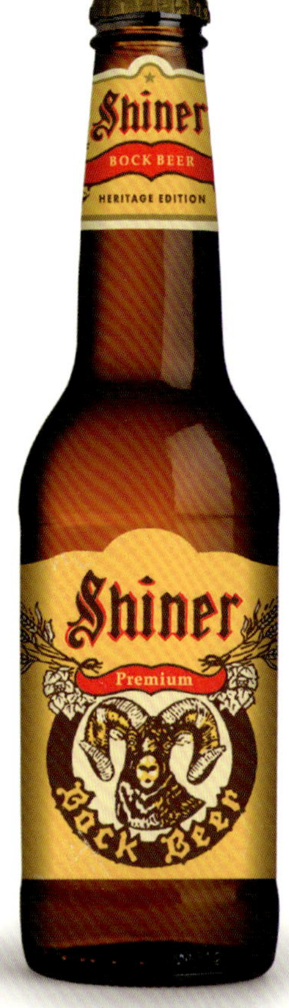

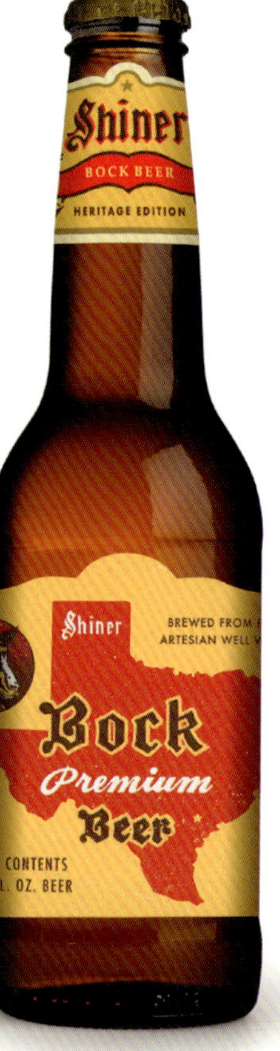

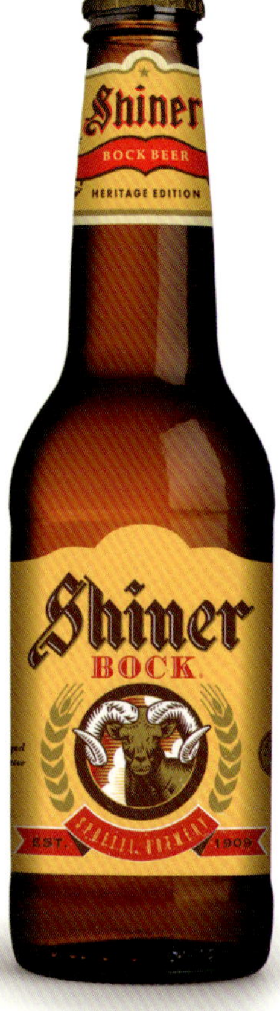

P245: Credit & Commentary **Title:** Shiner Heritage | **Clients:** Shiner Beer, Gambrinus Company | **Design Firm:** *TraceElement Image 1 of 4

MICHAEL HESTER

PACKAGING

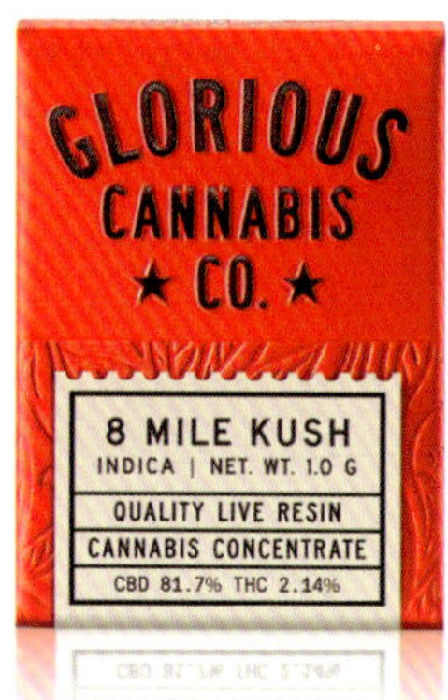

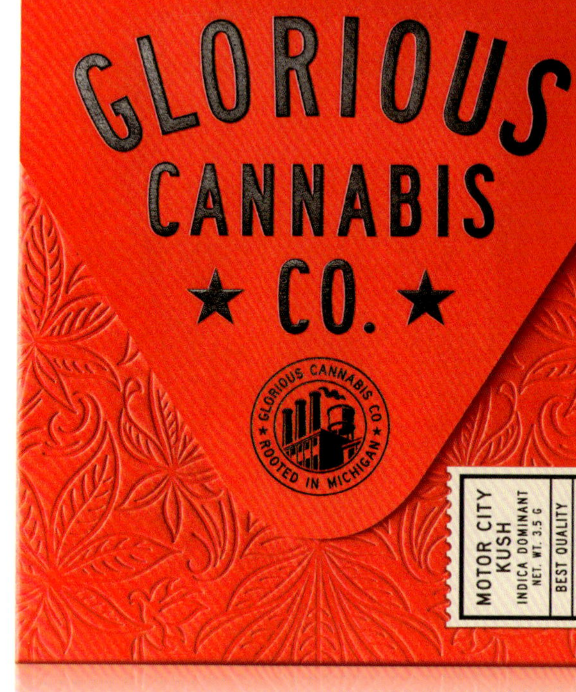

P245: Credit & Commentary **Title:** Glorious Cannabis Co. | **Client:** Glorious Cannabis Co. | **Design Firm:** Pavement Image 1 of 6

JEFF BARFOOT

PACKAGING

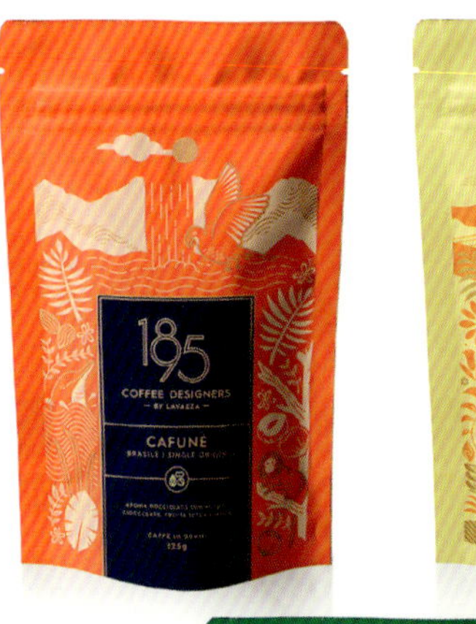

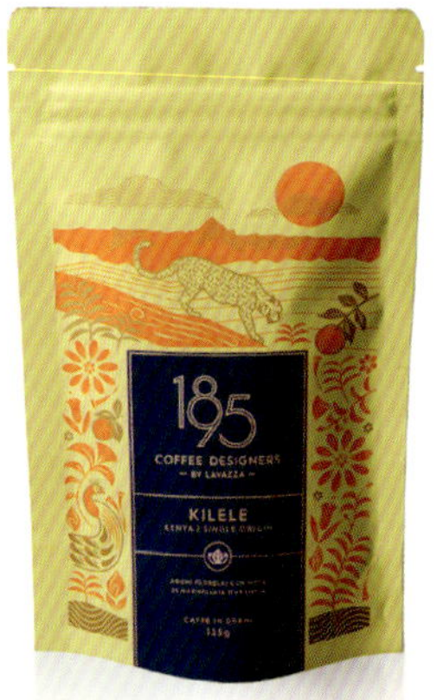

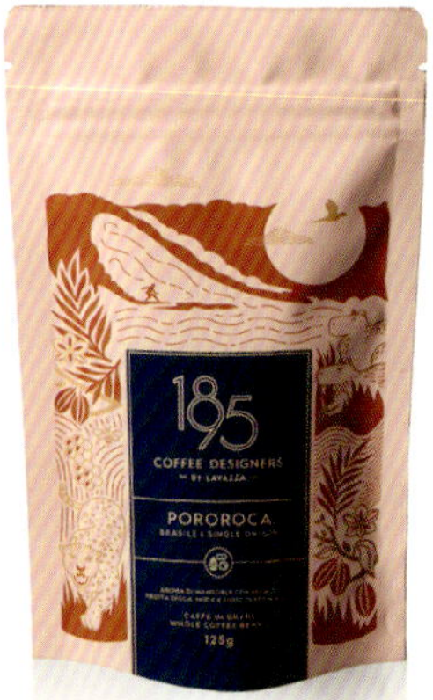

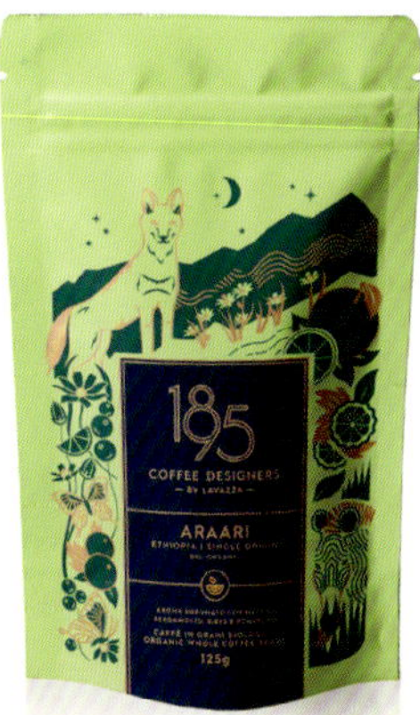

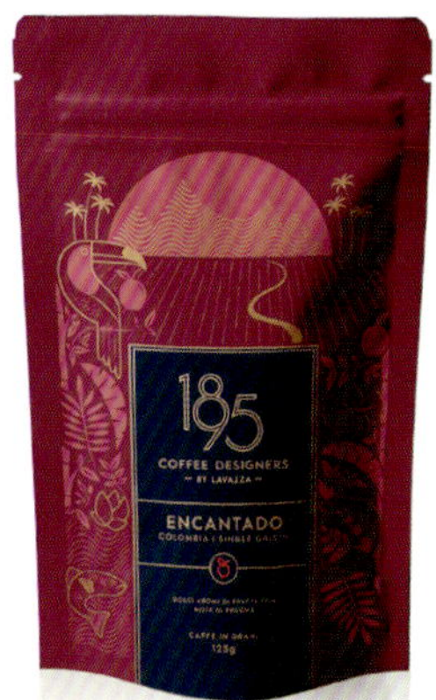

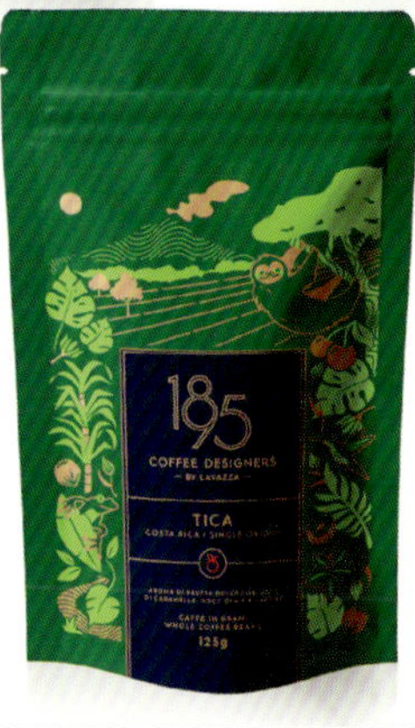

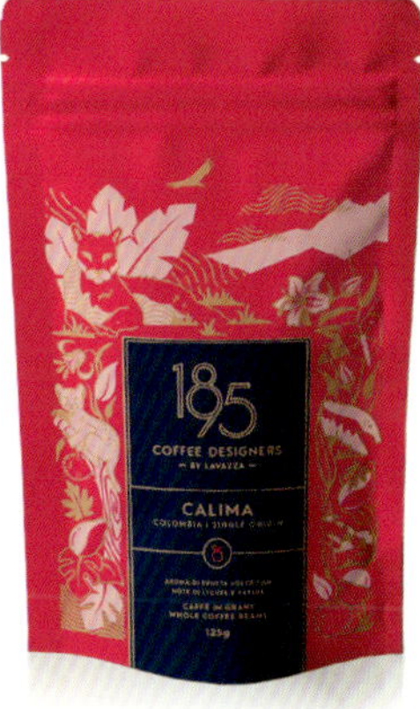

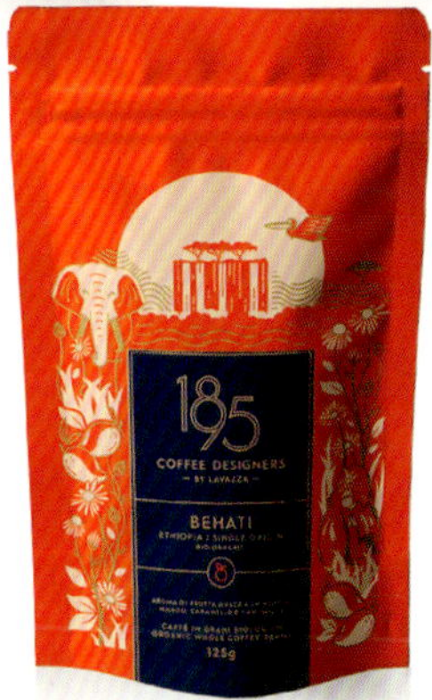

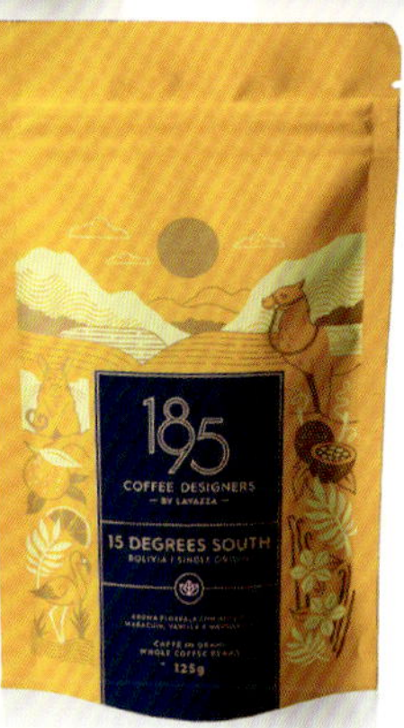

P245: Credit & Commentary **Title:** 1895 Single Origin Coffee | **Client:** Lavazza | **Design Firm:** *TraceElement Image 1 of 3

BRIAN CASSCLES

PACKAGING

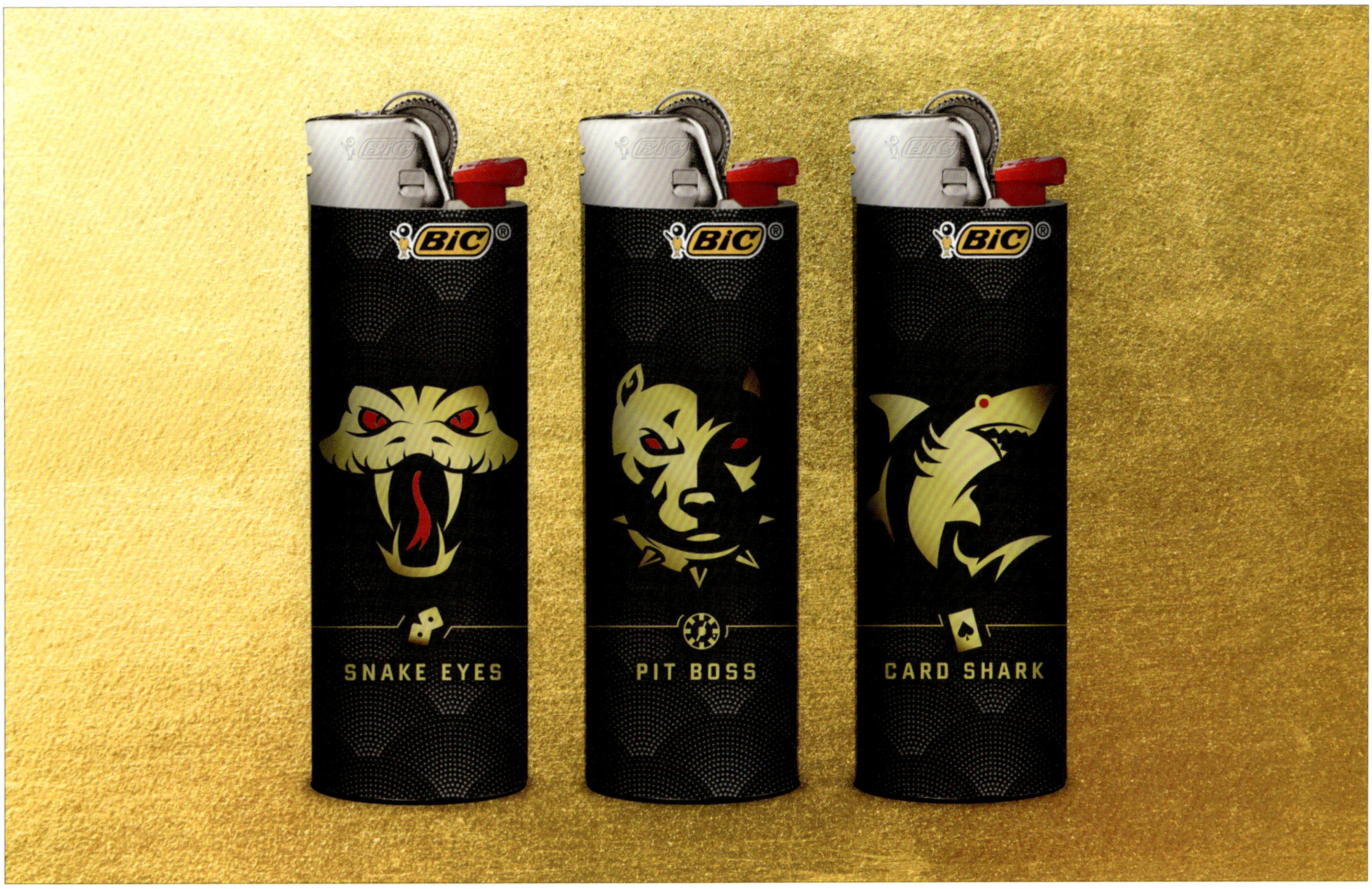

P245: Credit & Commentary **Title:** BIC Gambling Series | **Client:** BIC | **Design Firm:** Wallace Church & Co.

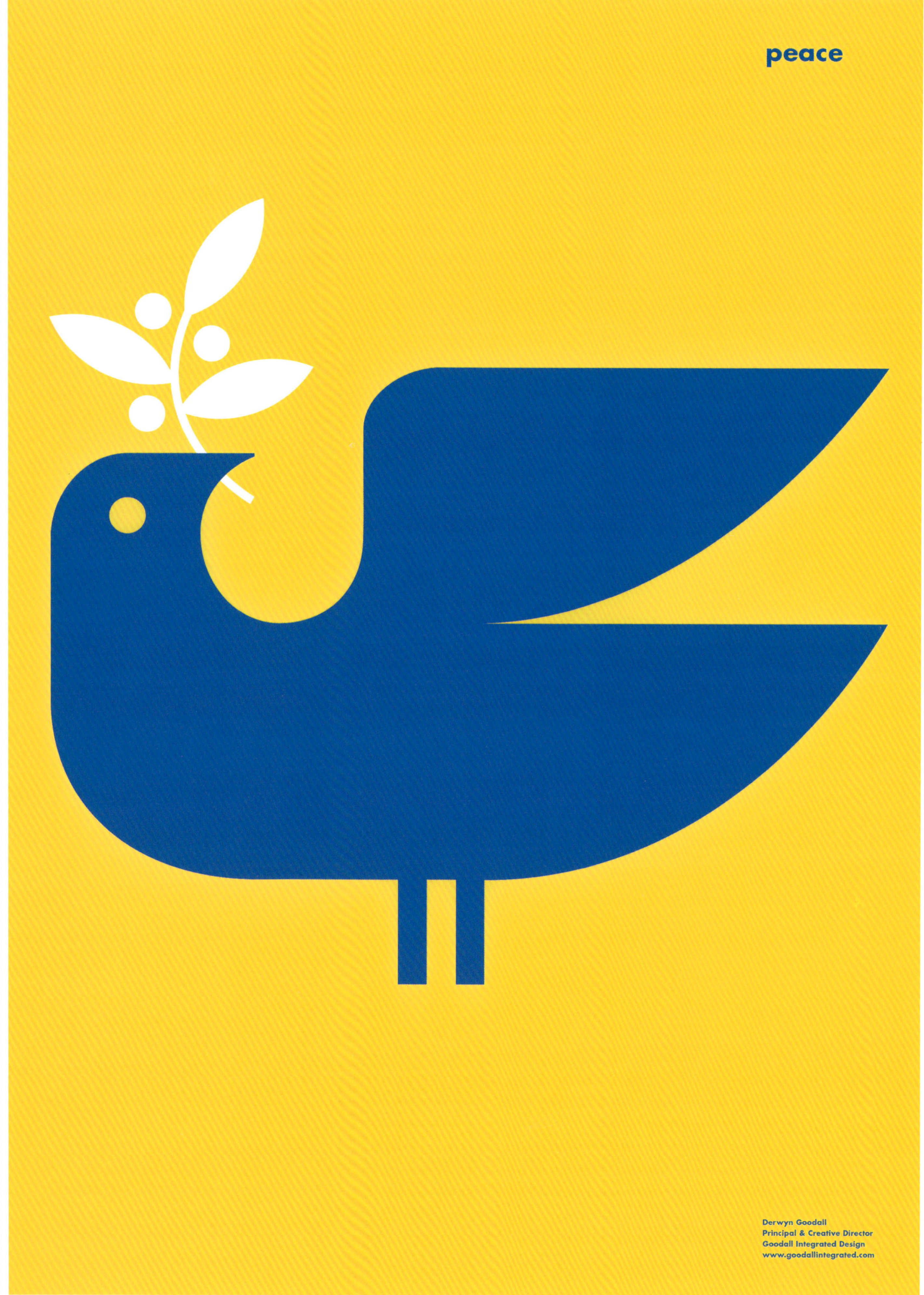

P245: Credit & Commentary

Title: Peace | **Client:** Self-initiated | **Design Firm:** Goodall Integrated Design

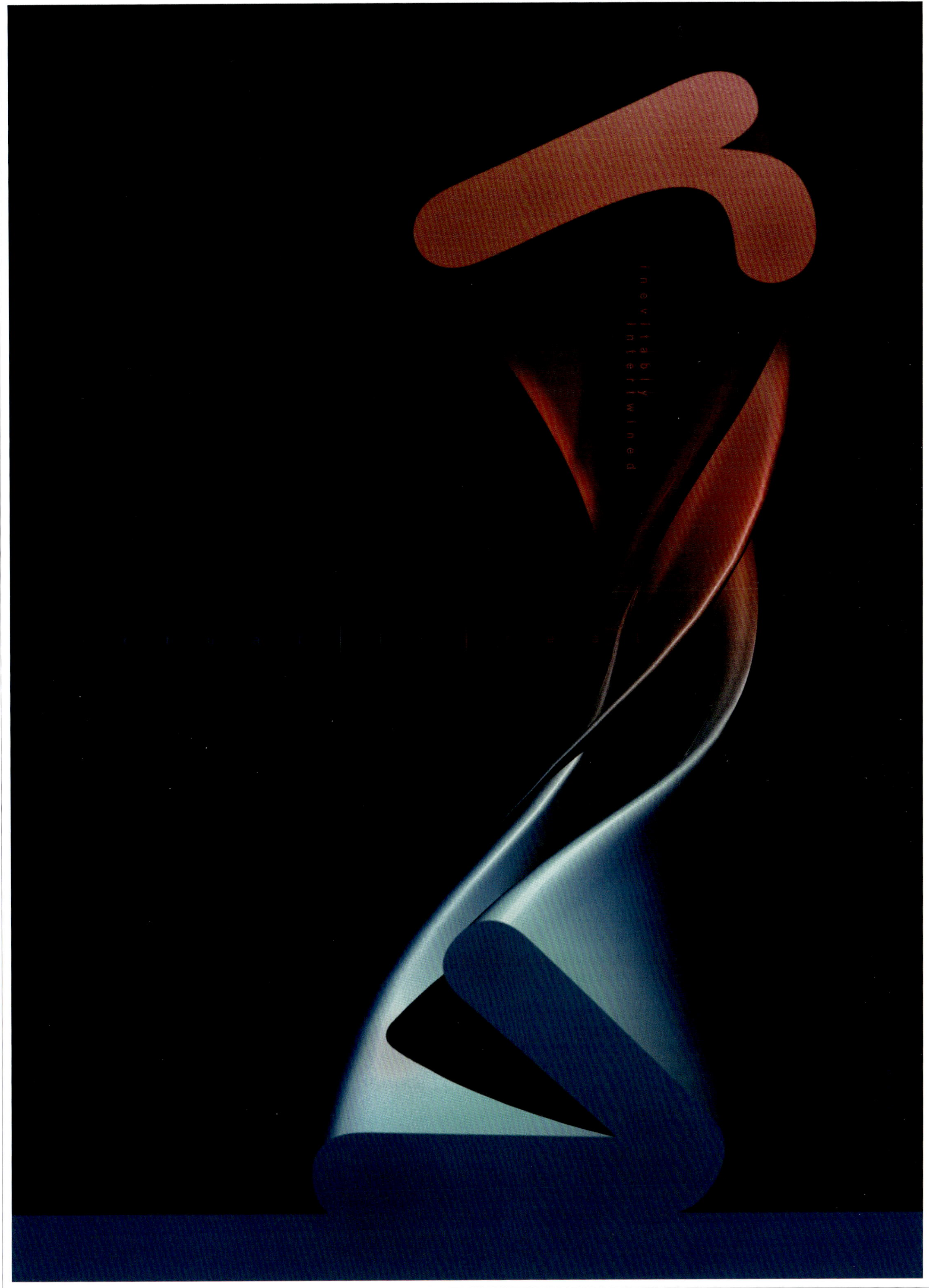

P245: Credit & Commentary

Title: Virtual is Real | **Client:** Self-initiated | **Design Firm:** Dankook University

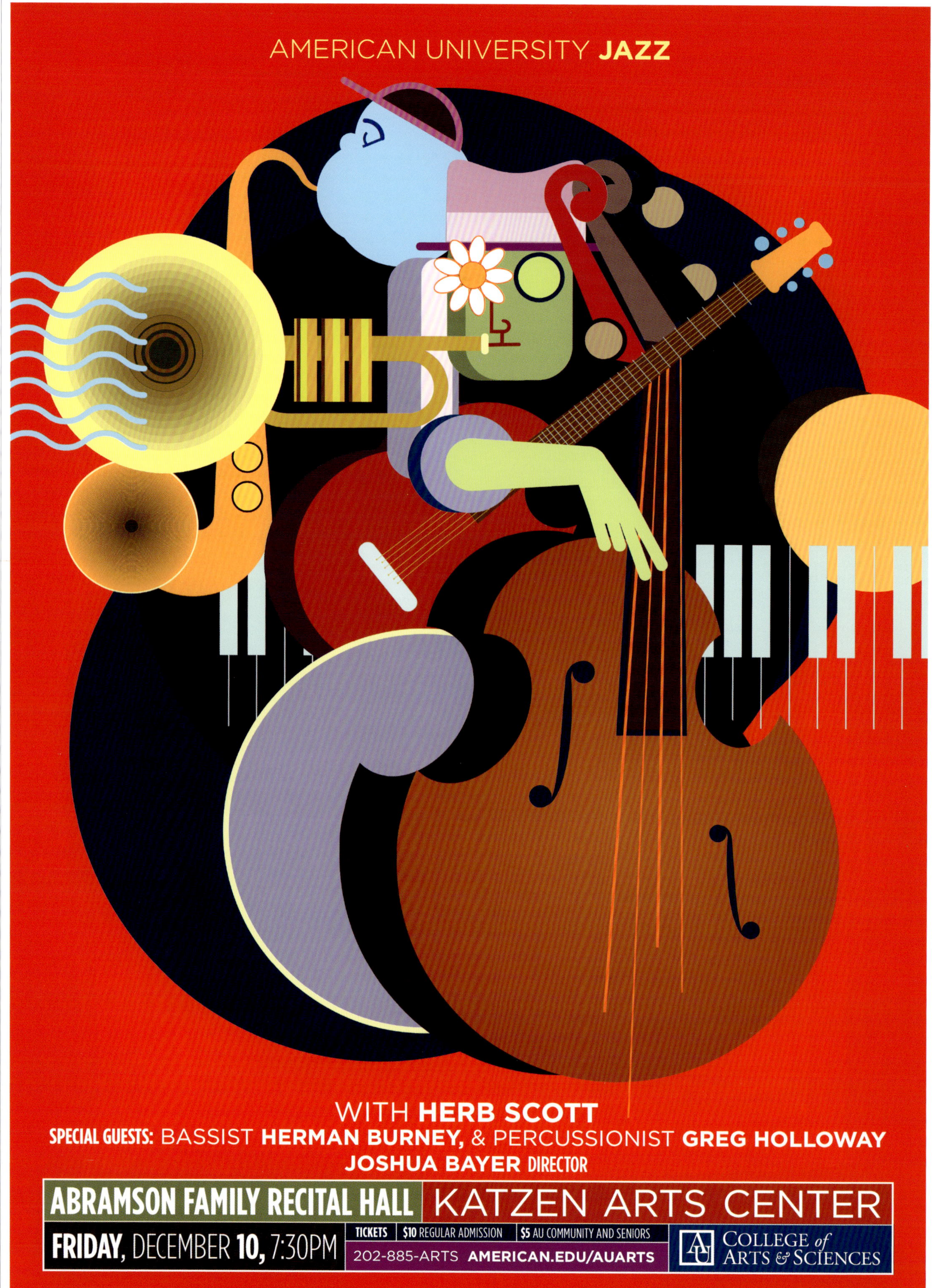

P245: Credit & Comm. **Title:** AU Jazz with Herb Scott | **Client:** American University Department of Performing Arts | **Design Firm:** Chemi Montes

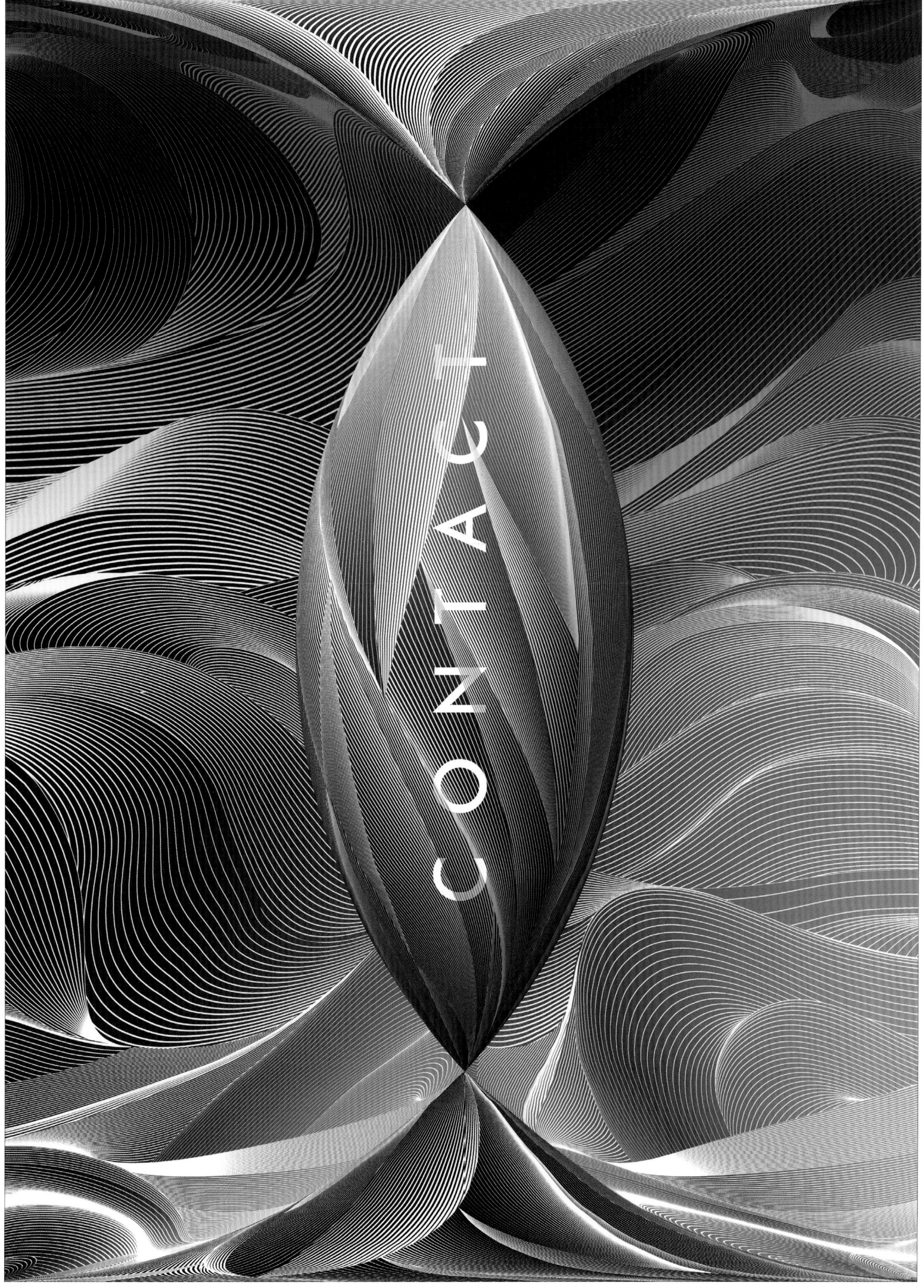

P245: Credit & Commentary

Title: Contact | **Client:** Osaka Poster Fest | **Design Firm:** Tsushima Design

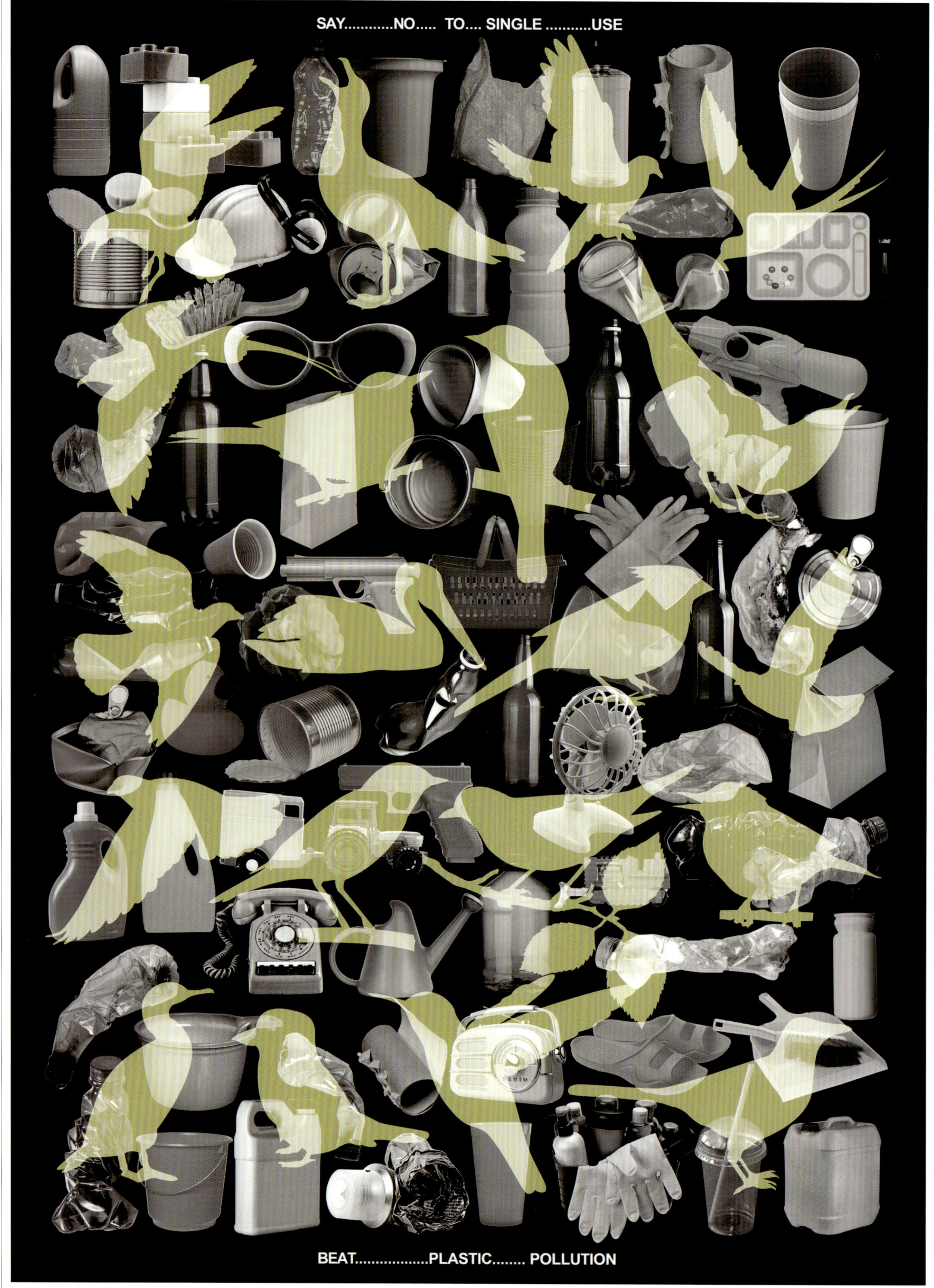

 Title: SAY NO TO SINGLE USE | **Client:** Ministry of Environment | **Design Firm:** Namseoul University

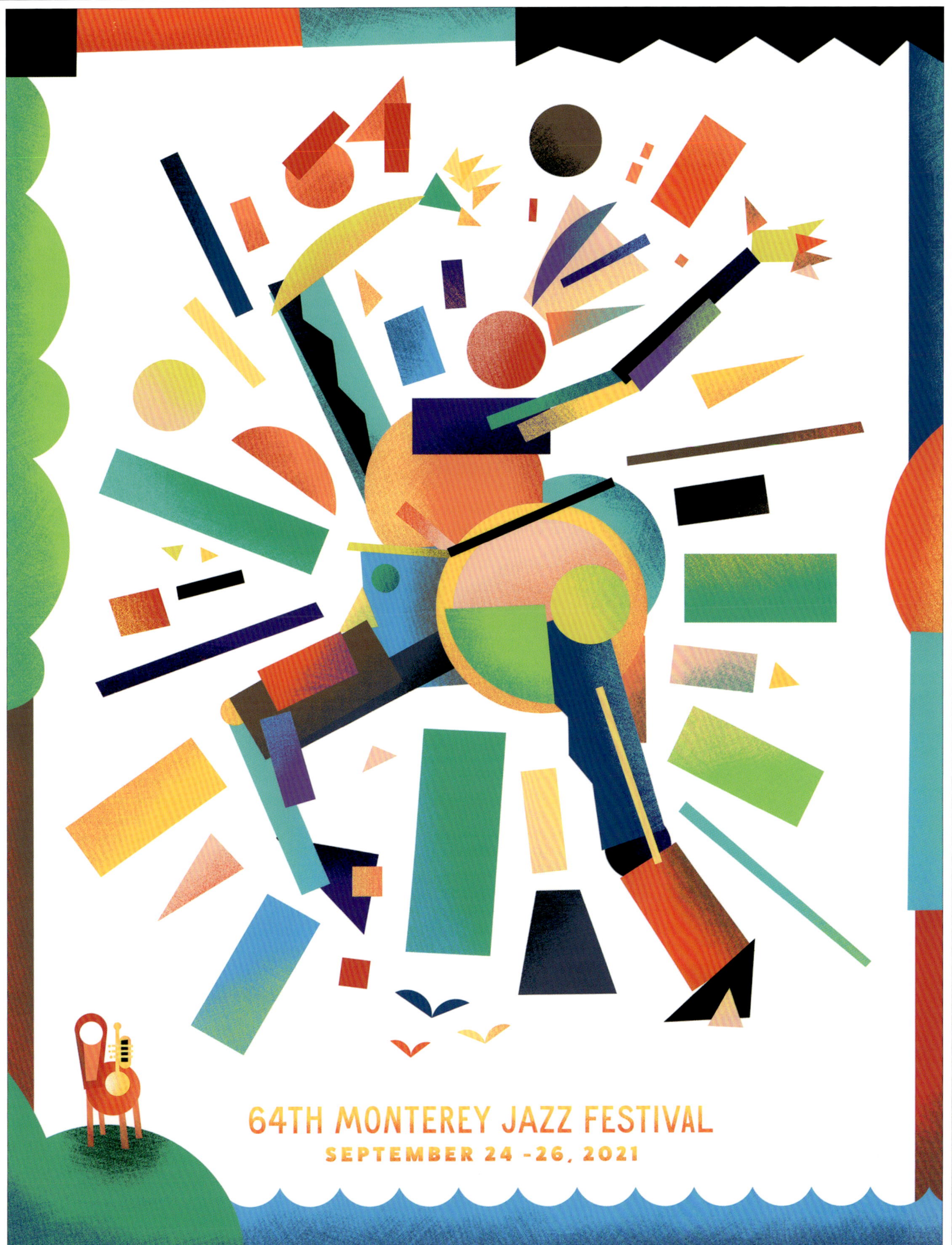

Title: 64th Monterey Jazz Festival Poster Series | **Client:** Monterey Jazz Festival | **Design Firm:** *TraceElement
P245: Credit & Commentary | Image 1 of 4

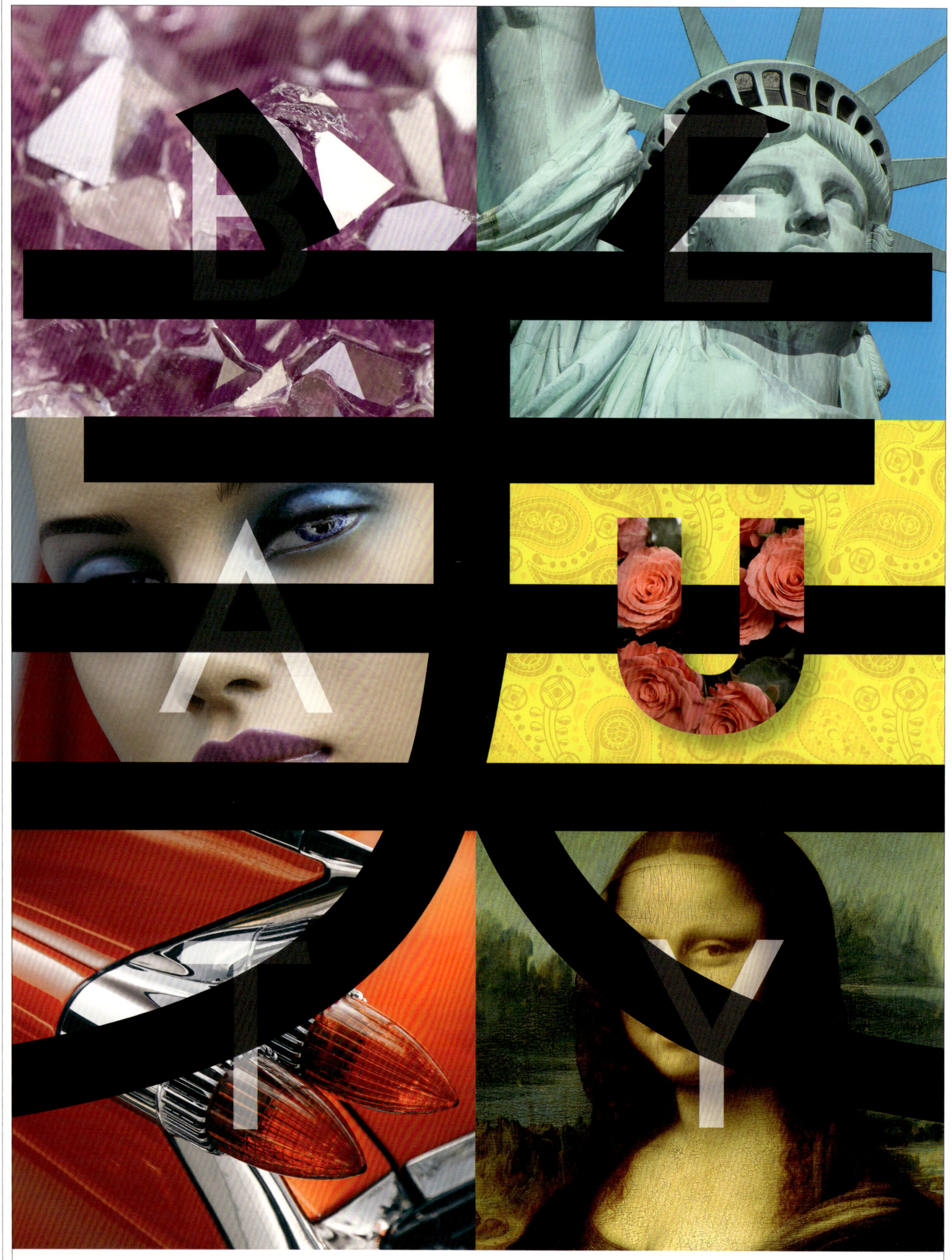

P246: Credit & Commentary **Title:** Beauty | **Client:** Wenzhou-Kean University | **Design Firm:** Randy Clark

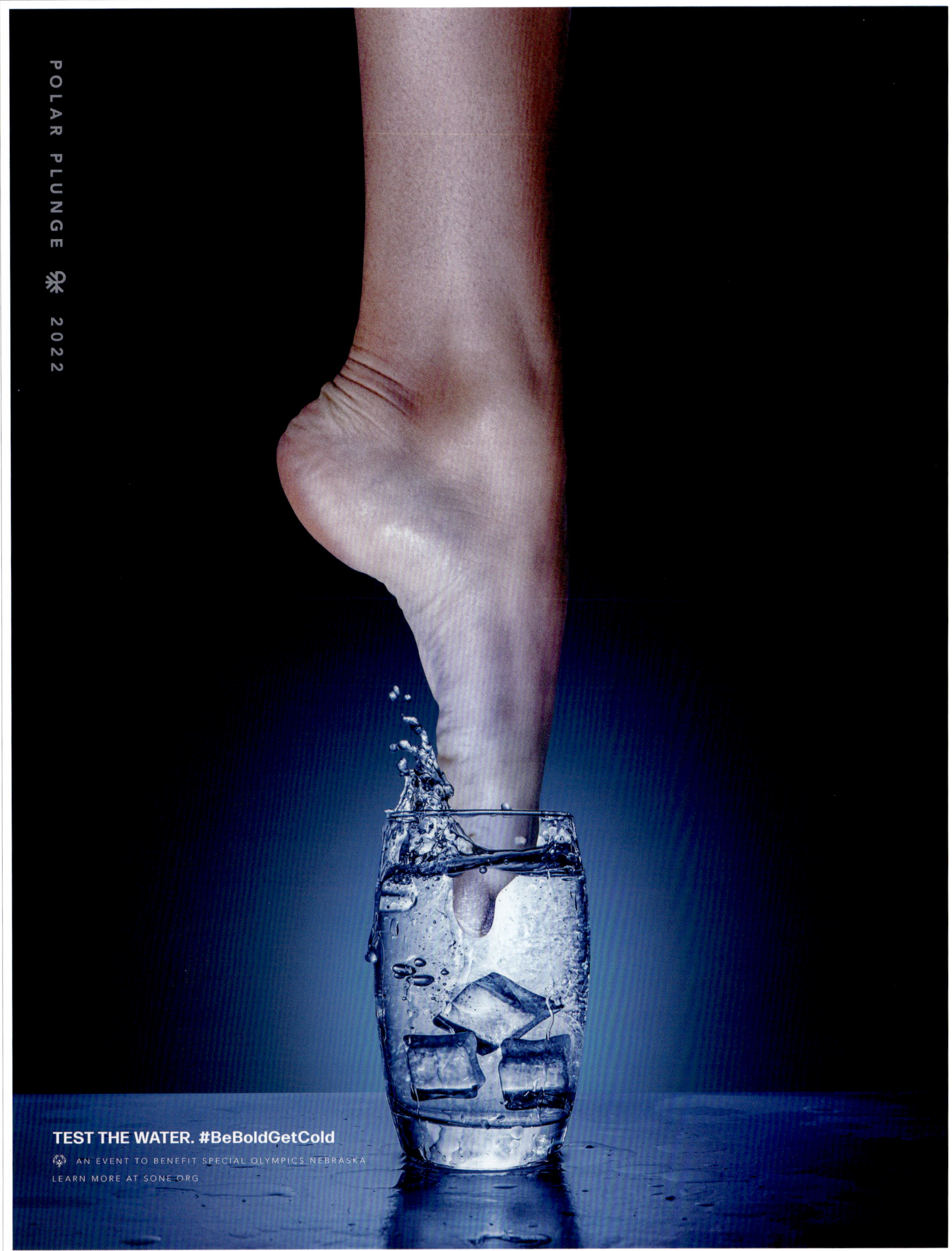

P246: Credit & Commentary **Title:** Test The Water | **Client:** Special Olympics Nebraska | **Design Firm:** Bailey Lauerman

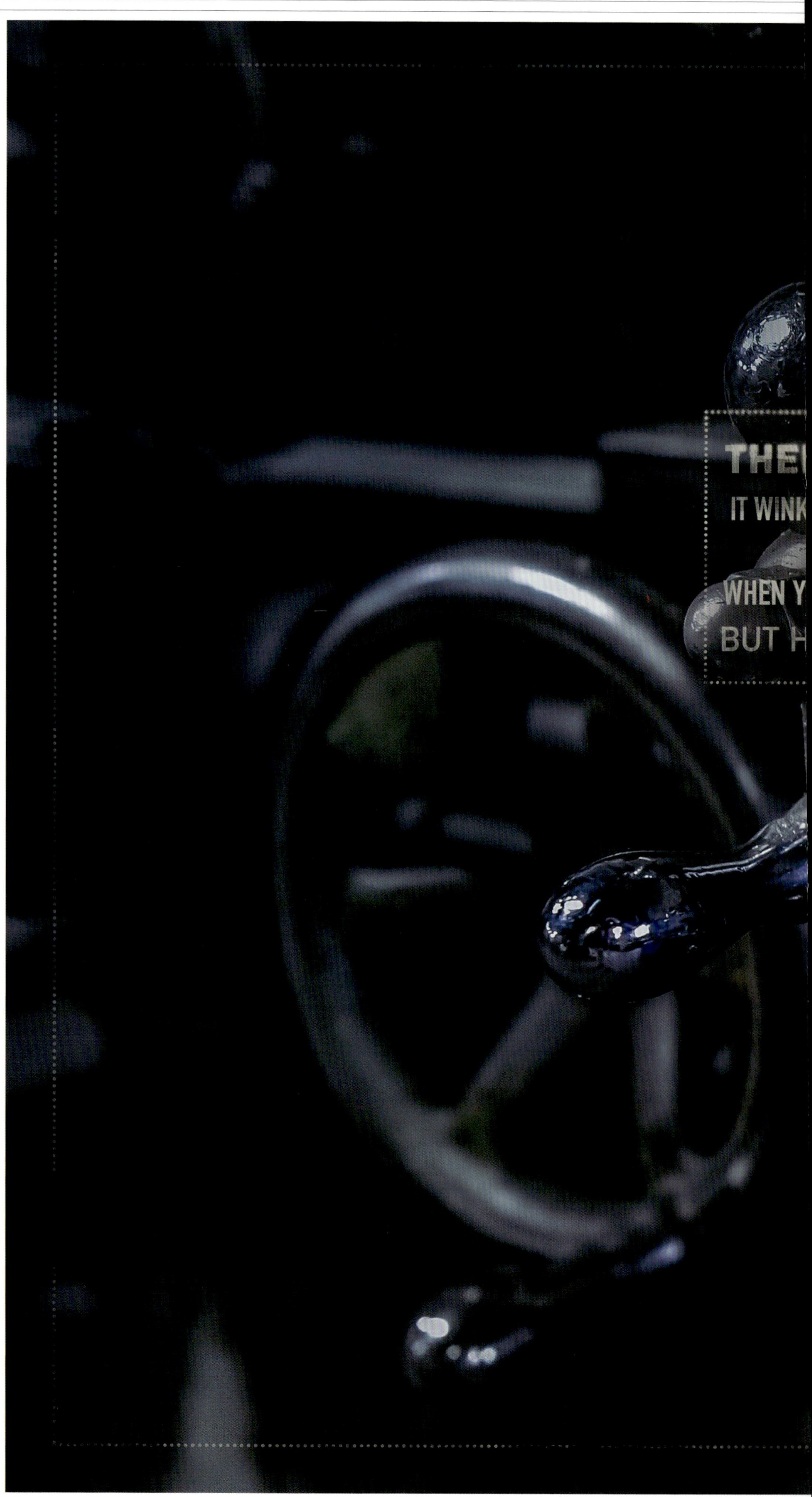

P246: Credit & Commentary

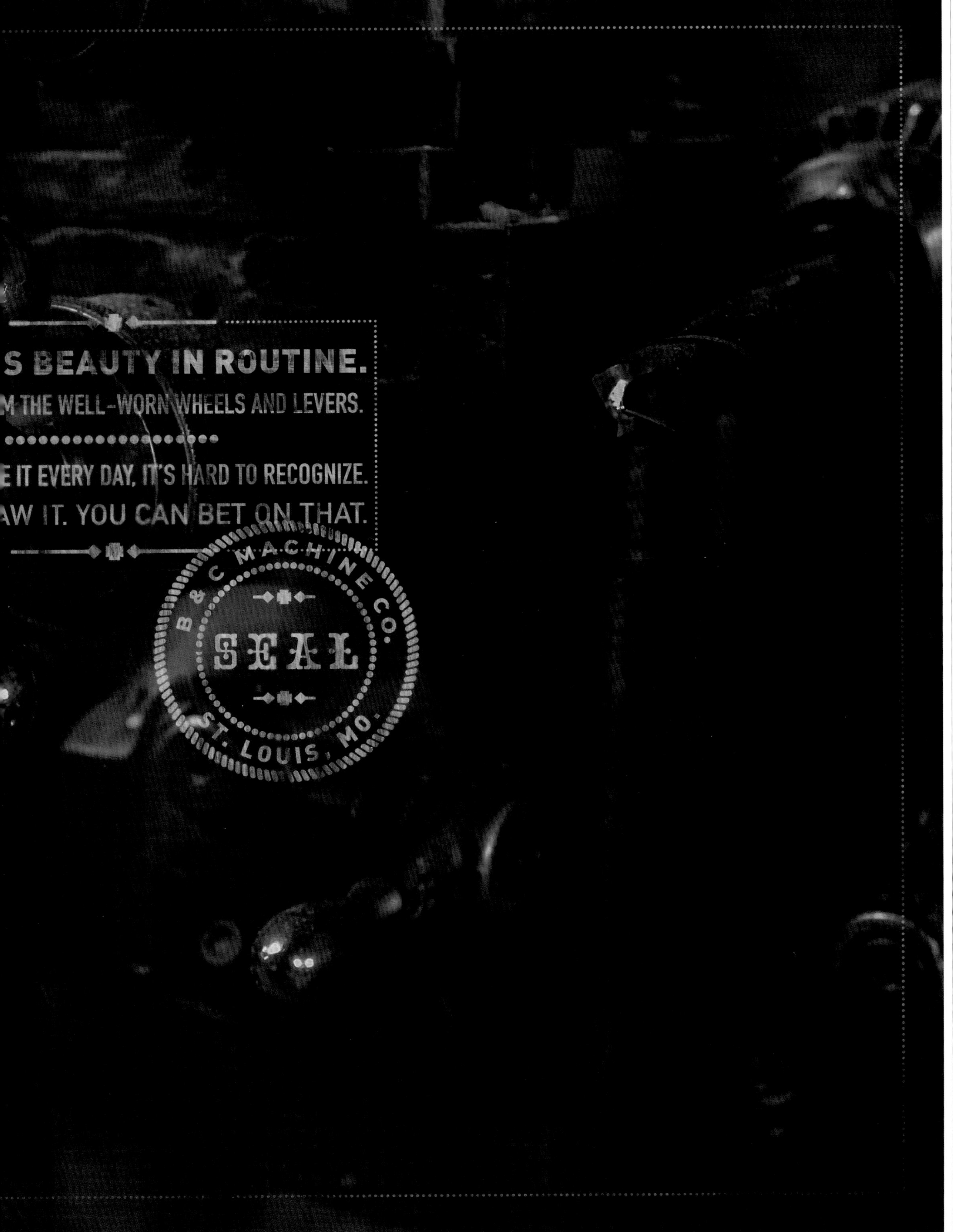

Title: Made in STL | **Client:** B&C Machine Co. | **Design Firm:** Rodgers Townsend

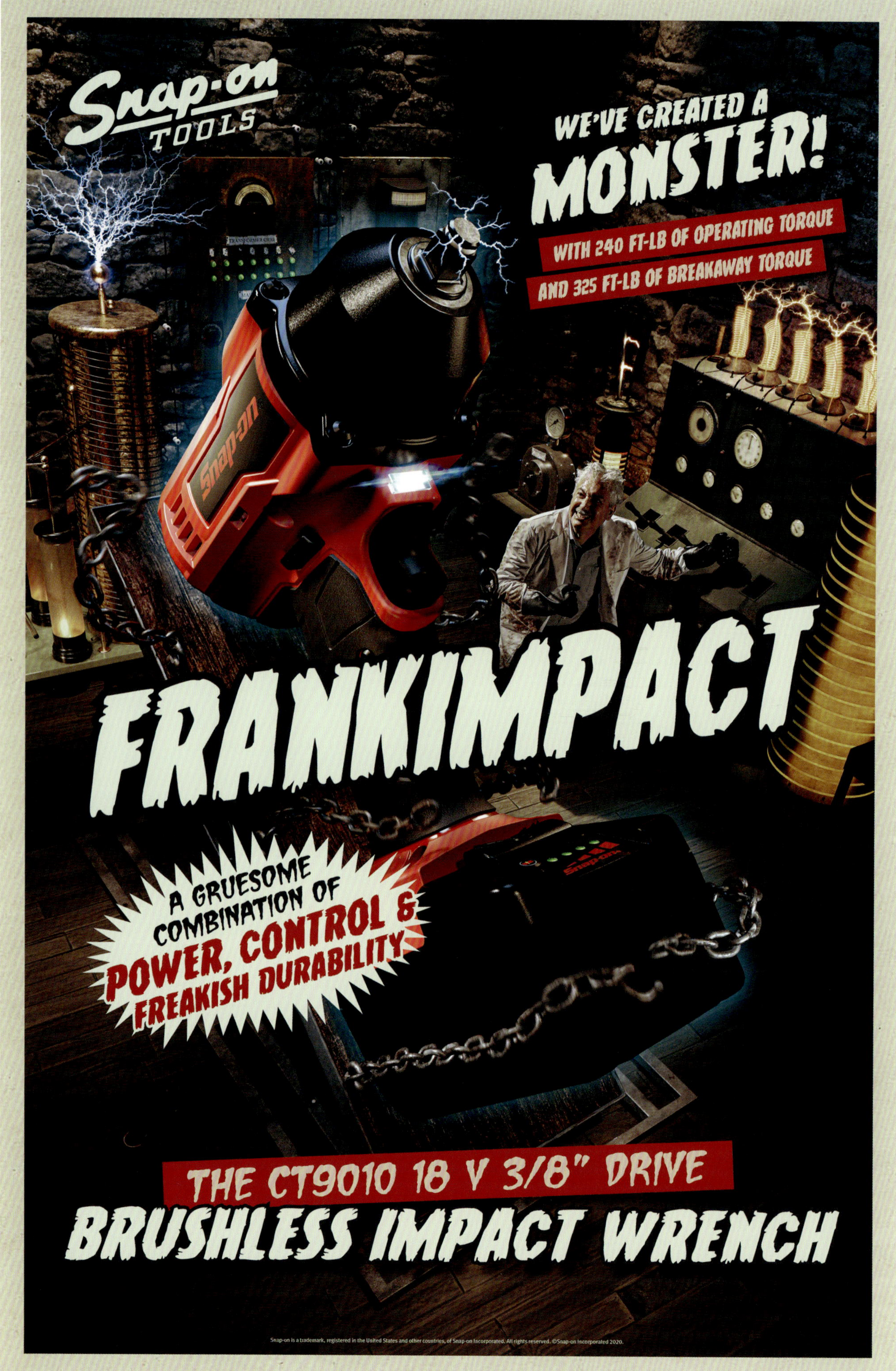

 Title: Frankimpact | **Client:** Snap-on Tools | **Design Firm:** Traction Factory

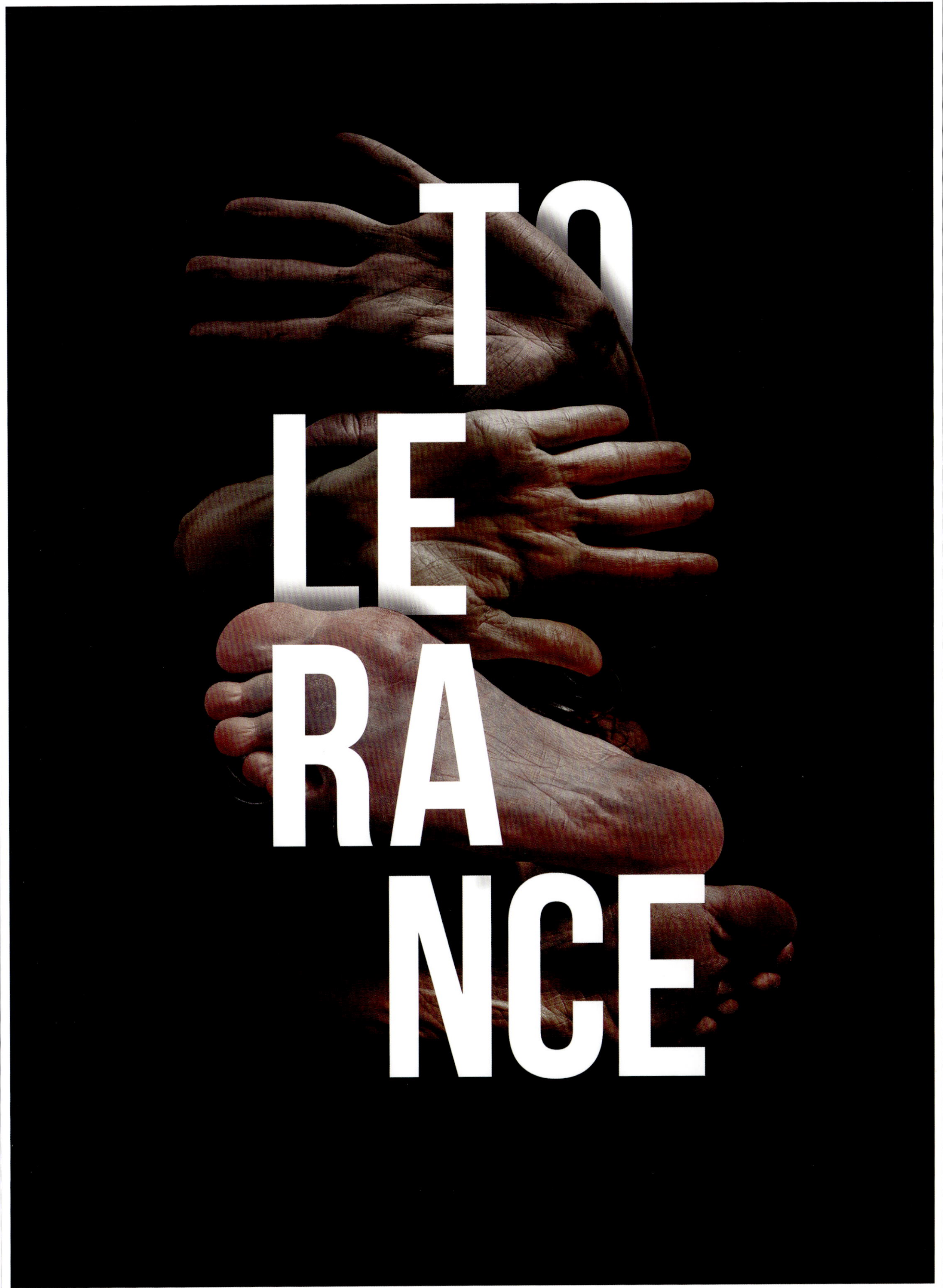

Title: Tolerance | **Clients:** Tolerance—6th International Poster Exhibition, Graphic Stories 2022 | **Design Firm:** Carmit Design Studio
P246: Credit & Commentary

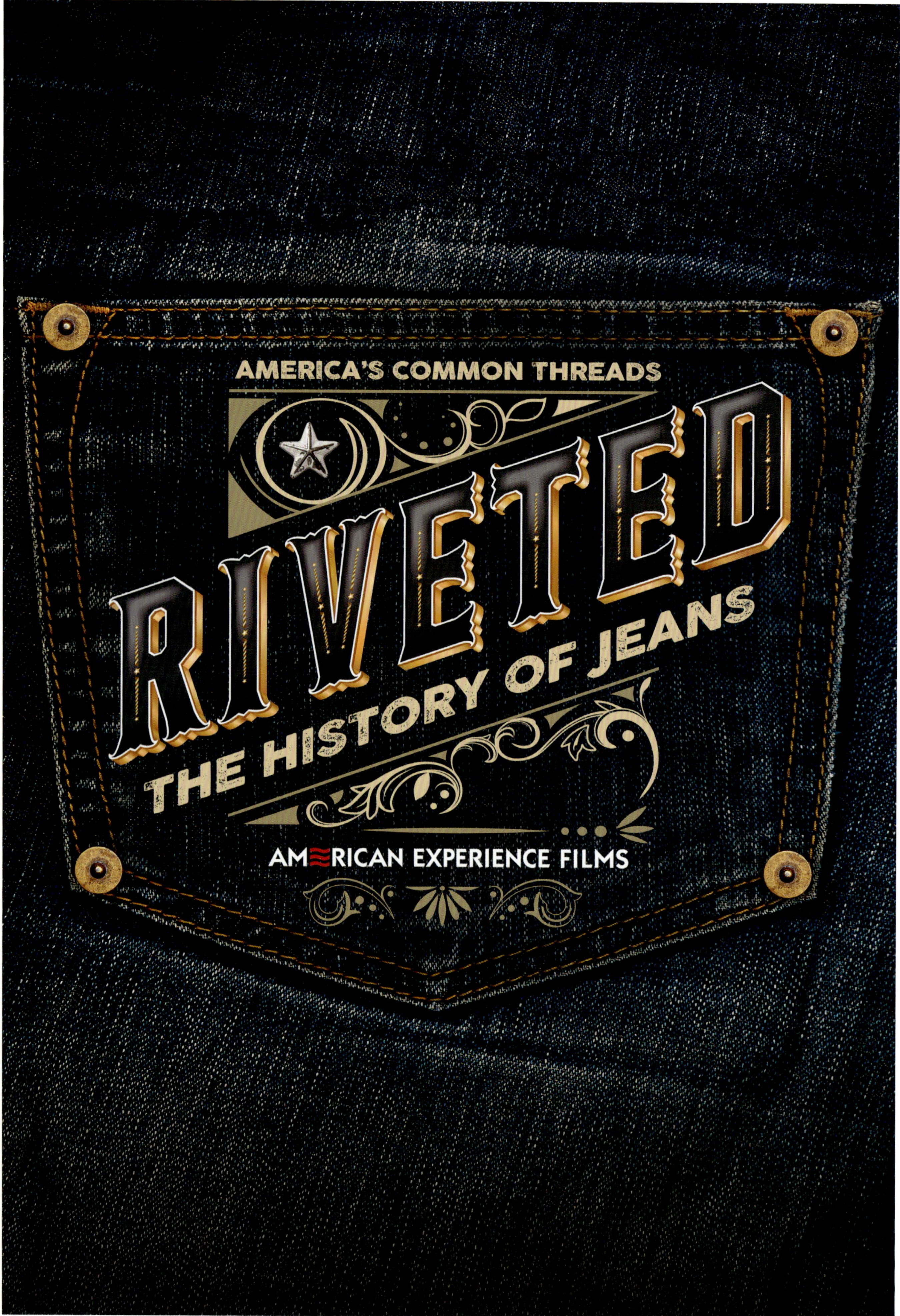

Title: Riveted - The History of Jeans | **Clients:** Chika Offurum, American Experience Films | **Design Firm:** SJI Associates
P246: Credit & Commentary

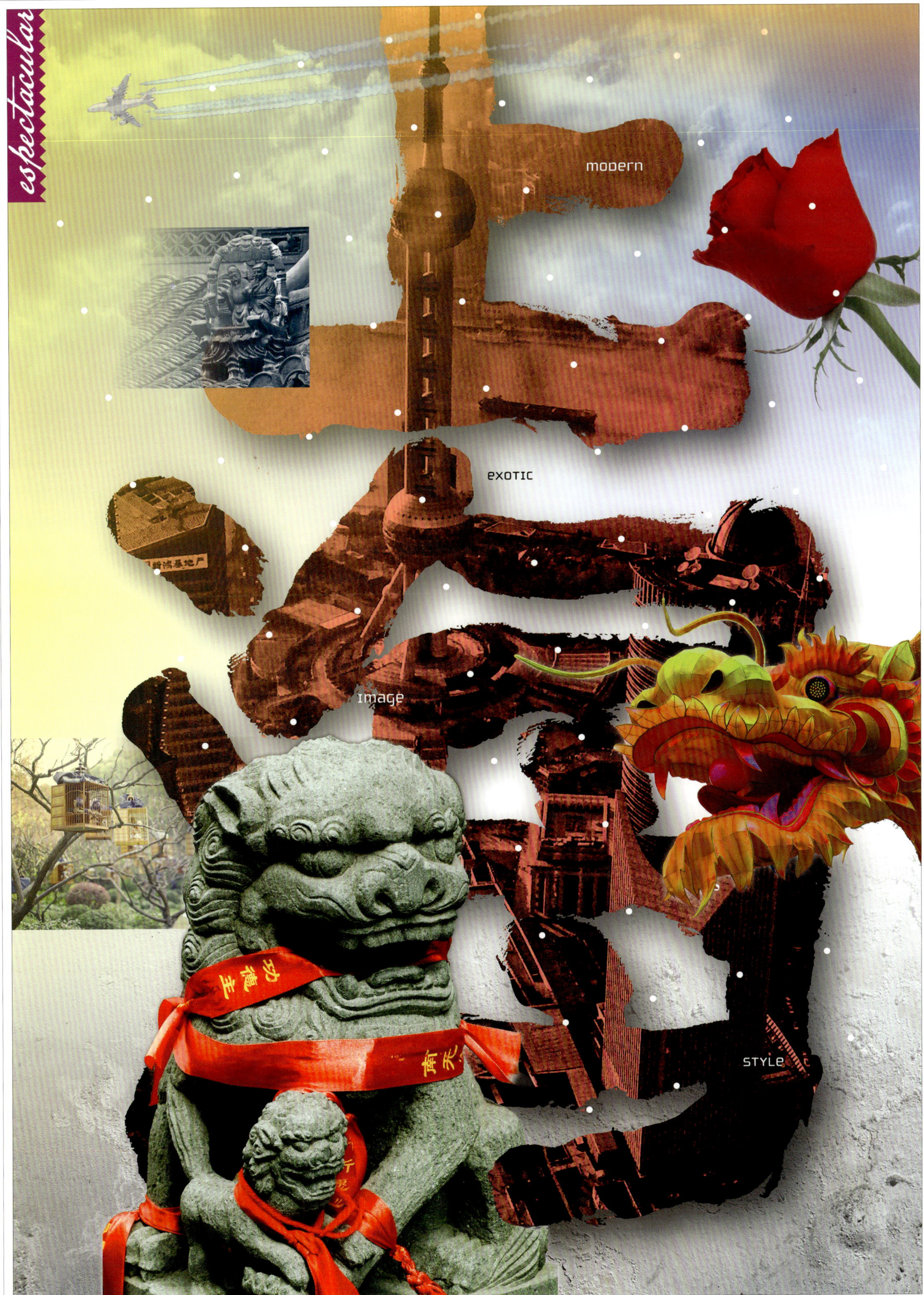

P246: Credit & Commentary **Title:** Espectacular | **Clients:** 10 x 10 Exhibition, China Art Museum | **Design Firm:** Randy Clark

SARA KLIMOSKA
ANAMARIA MARINCA
ALICE ENGLERT
FÉLIX MARITAUD
with CARLOTO COTTA
and NOOMI RAPACE

YOU WON'T BE ALONE

OFFICIAL SELECTION 2022
sundance
film festival

IT'S A WICKED THING THIS WORLD

FOCUS FEATURES PRESENTS IN ASSOCIATION WITH SCREEN AUSTRALIA FILM VICTORIA HEAD GEAR FILMS
A CAUSEWAY FILMS PRODUCTION IN ASSOCIATION WITH BALKANIC MEDIA "YOU WON'T BE ALONE" SARA KLIMOSKA ANAMARIA MARINCA
ALICE ENGLERT FELIX MARITAUD WITH CARLOTO COTTA AND NOOMI RAPACE SOUND DESIGNER EMMA BORTIGNON COMPOSER MARK BRADSHAW EDITOR LUCA CAPPELLI
PRODUCTION DESIGNER BETHANY RYAN DIRECTOR OF PHOTOGRAPHY MATTHEW CHUANG ACS CO-PRODUCER JONATHAN ENGLISH EXECUTIVE PRODUCERS STEPHEN KELLIHER PHIL HUNT COMPTON ROSS NOOMI RAPACE
CAUSEWAY FILMS VICTORIA FILM VICTORIA PRODUCED BY KRISTINA CEYTON AND SAMANTHA JENNINGS WRITTEN AND DIRECTED BY GORAN STOLEVSKI FOCUS FEATURES

ONLY IN THEATERS
THIS SPRING

P246: Credit & Commentary

Title: YOU WON'T BE ALONE | **Client:** Focus Features | **Design Firm:** ARSONAL

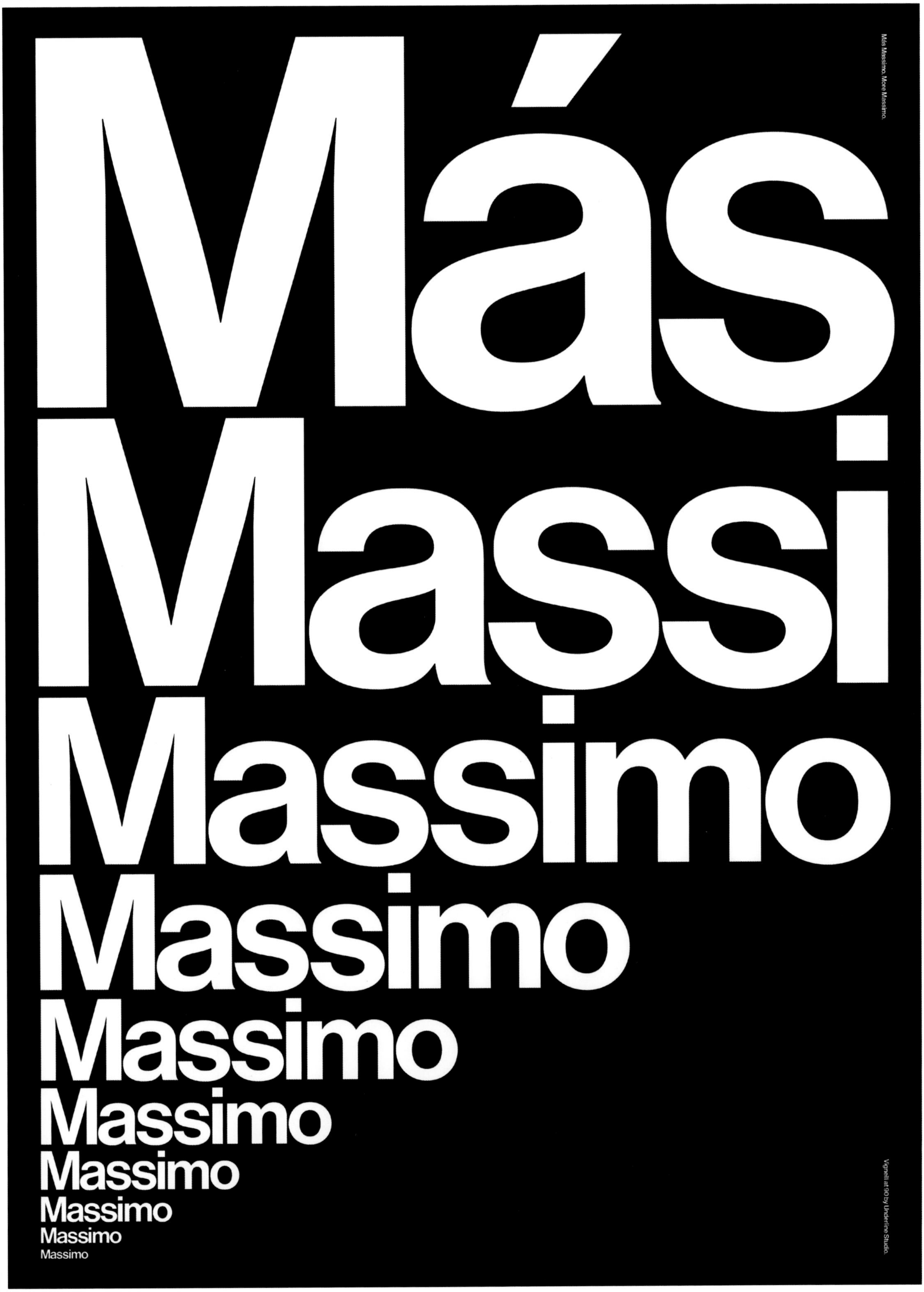

Más
Massi
Massimo
Massimo
Massimo
Massimo
Massimo
Massimo
Massimo
Massimo

Más Massimo. More Massimo.

Vignelli at 90 by Underline Studio.

P246: Credit & Commentary

Title: Vignelli 90 Poster | **Client:** Vignelli 90 | **Design Firm:** Underline Studio

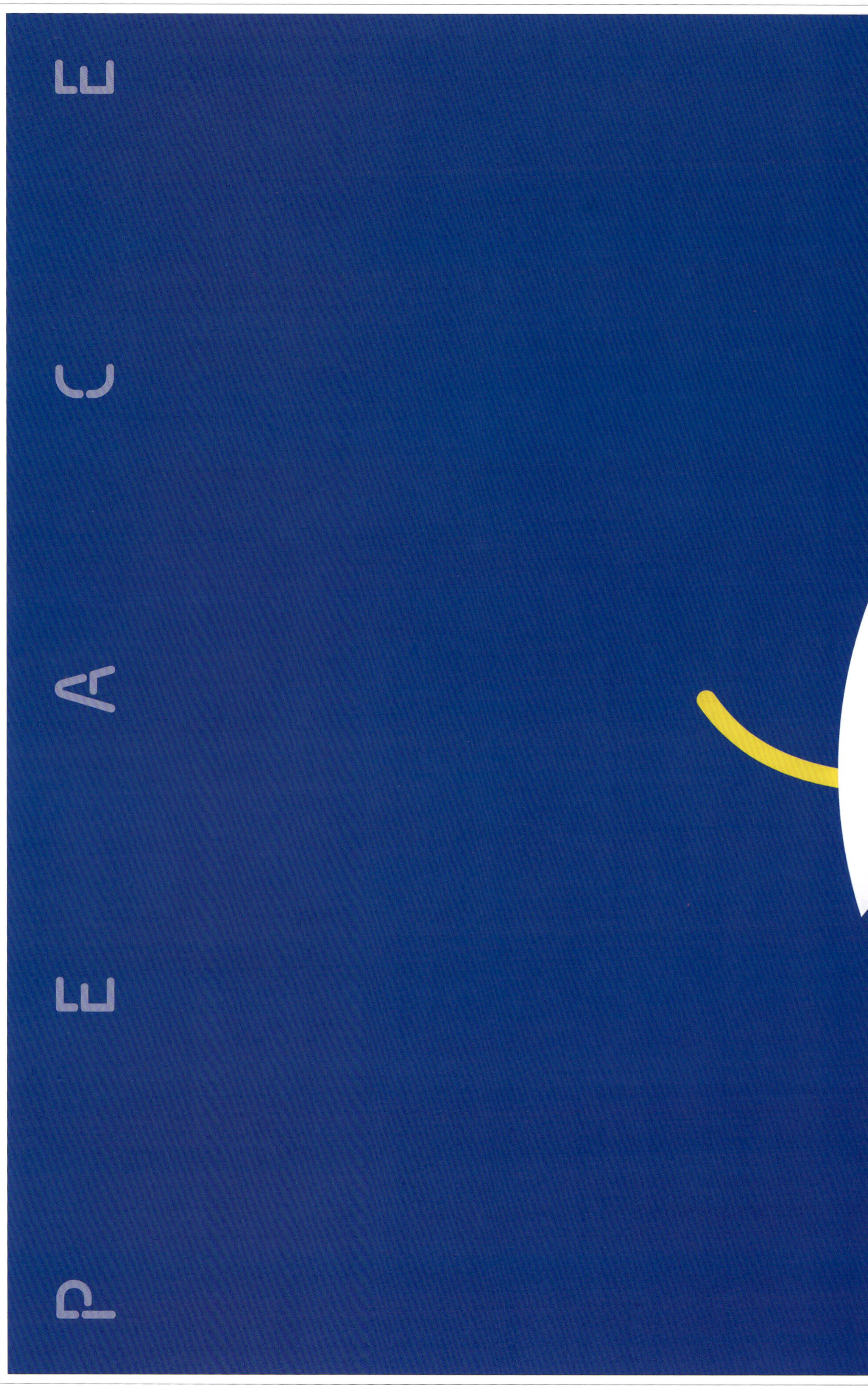

P246: Credit & Commentary

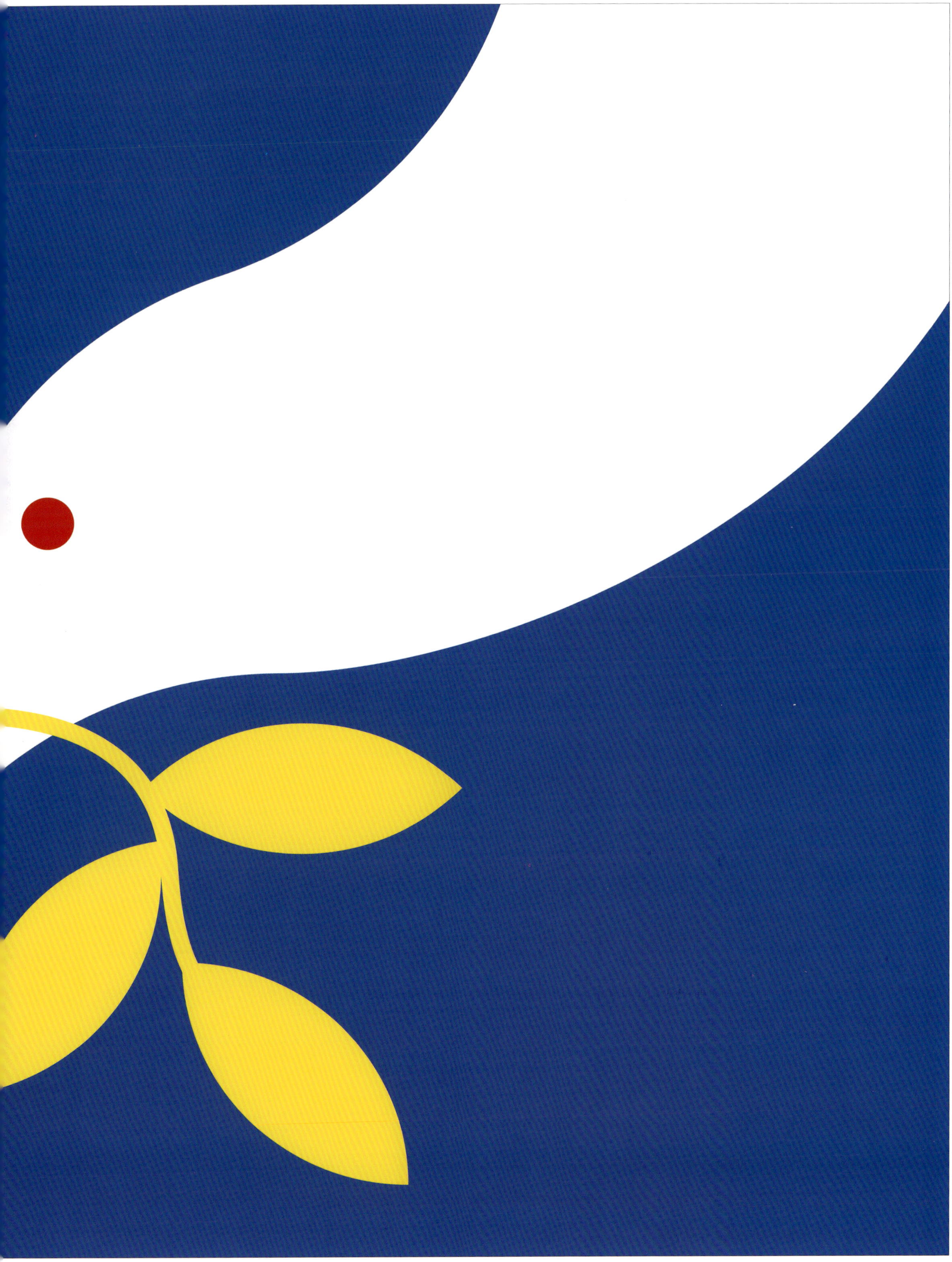

Title: Ukraine Dove | Client: Self-initiated | Design Firm: Randy Clark

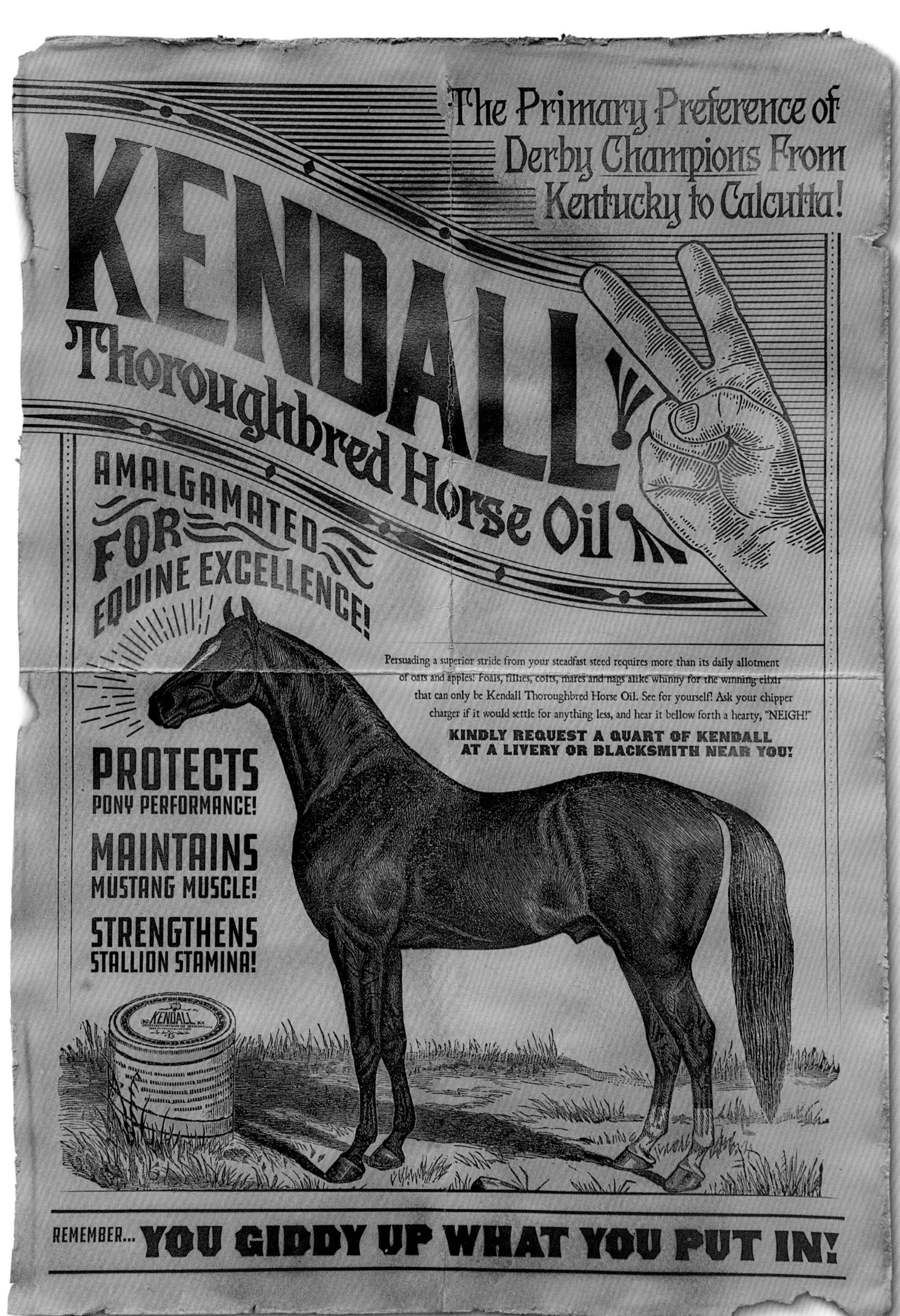

P246: Credit & Commentary **Title:** Thoroughbred Horse Oil—April Fool's Poster | **Client:** Kendall Motor Oil | **Design Firm:** Bailey Lauerman

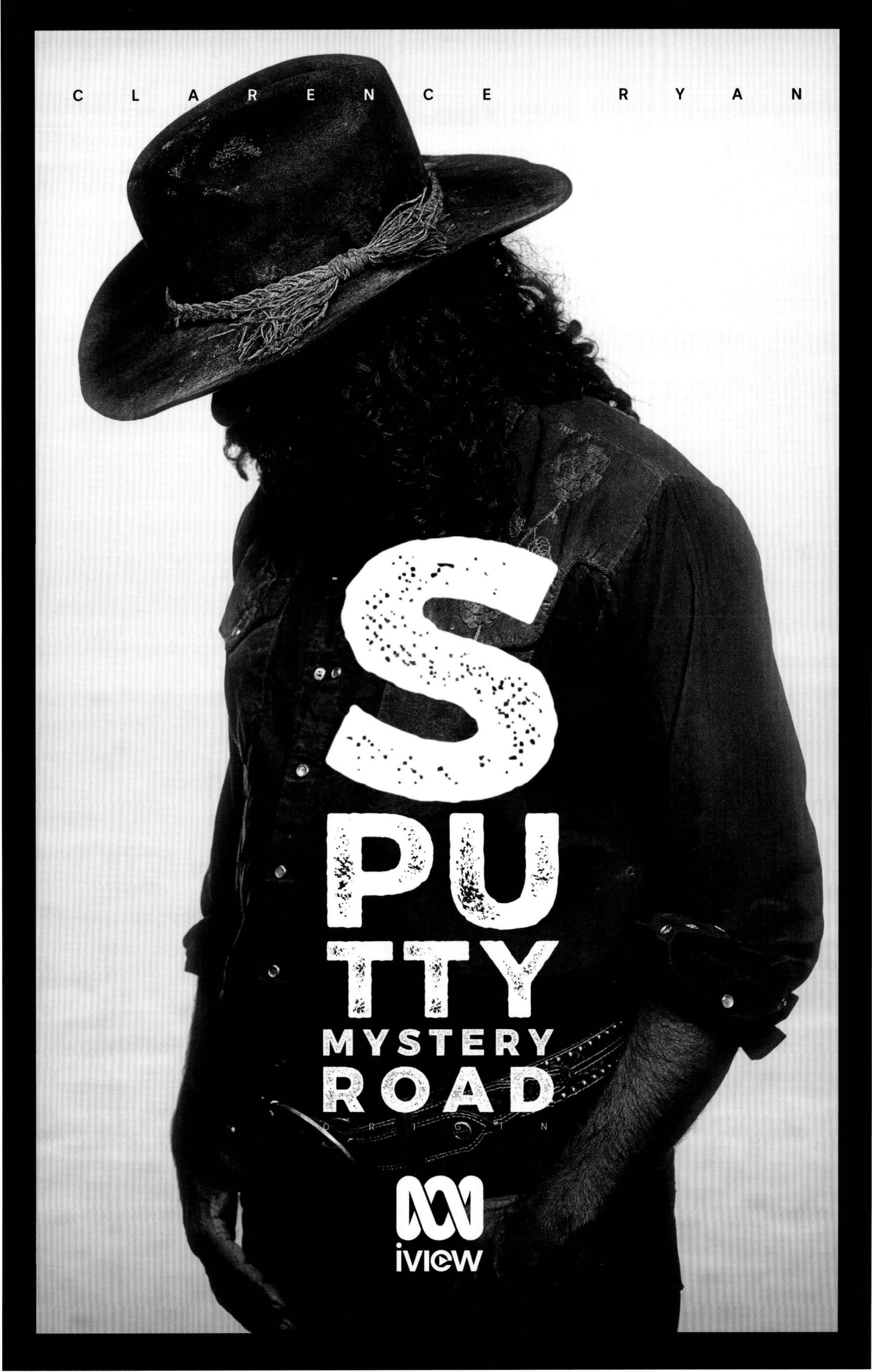

 Title: Mystery Road: Origin | **Client:** Bunya Productions | **Design Firm:** ABC Made

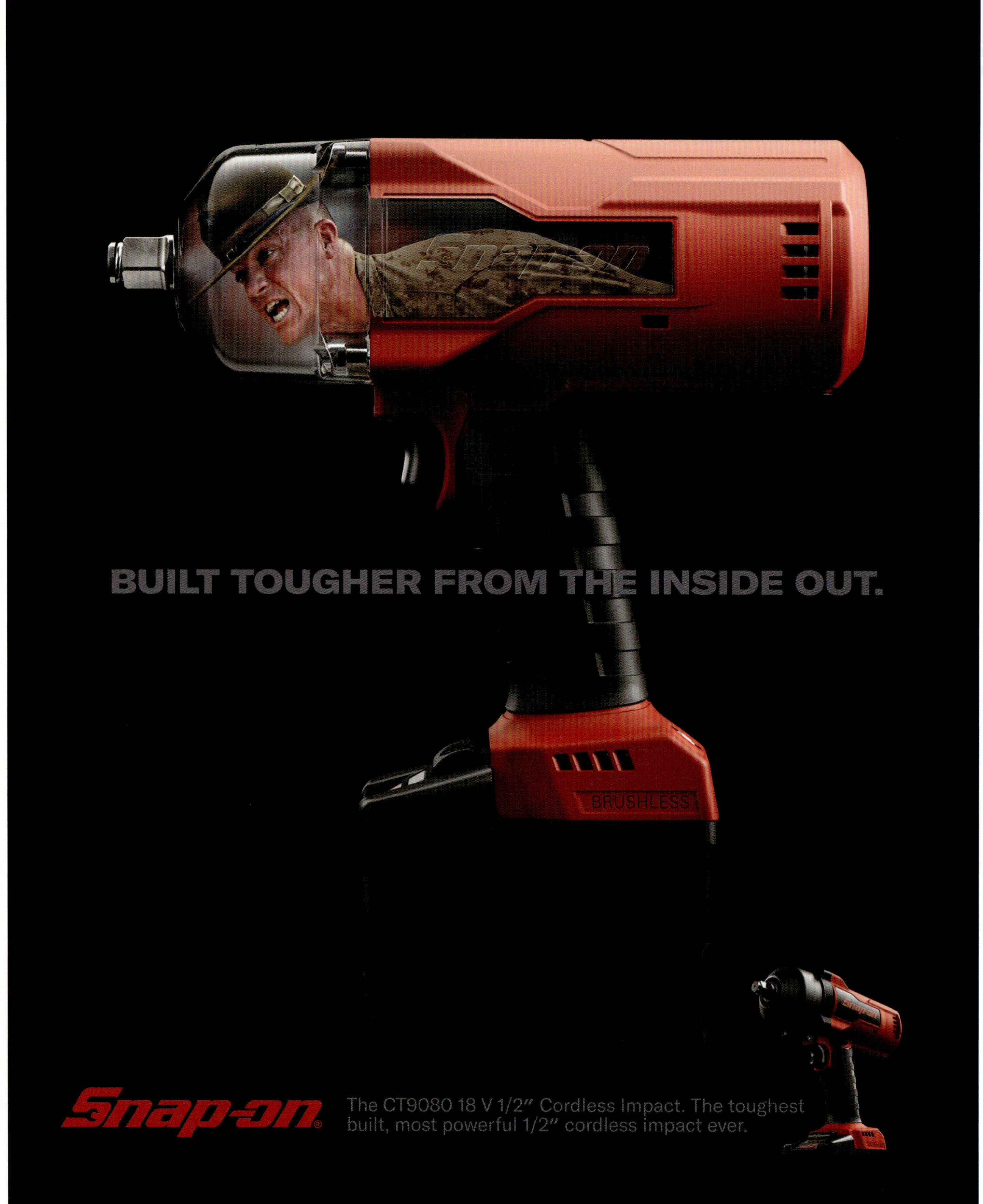

P246: Credit & Commentary

Title: CT9080 Product Launch | **Client:** Snap-on Tools | **Design Firm:** Traction Factory

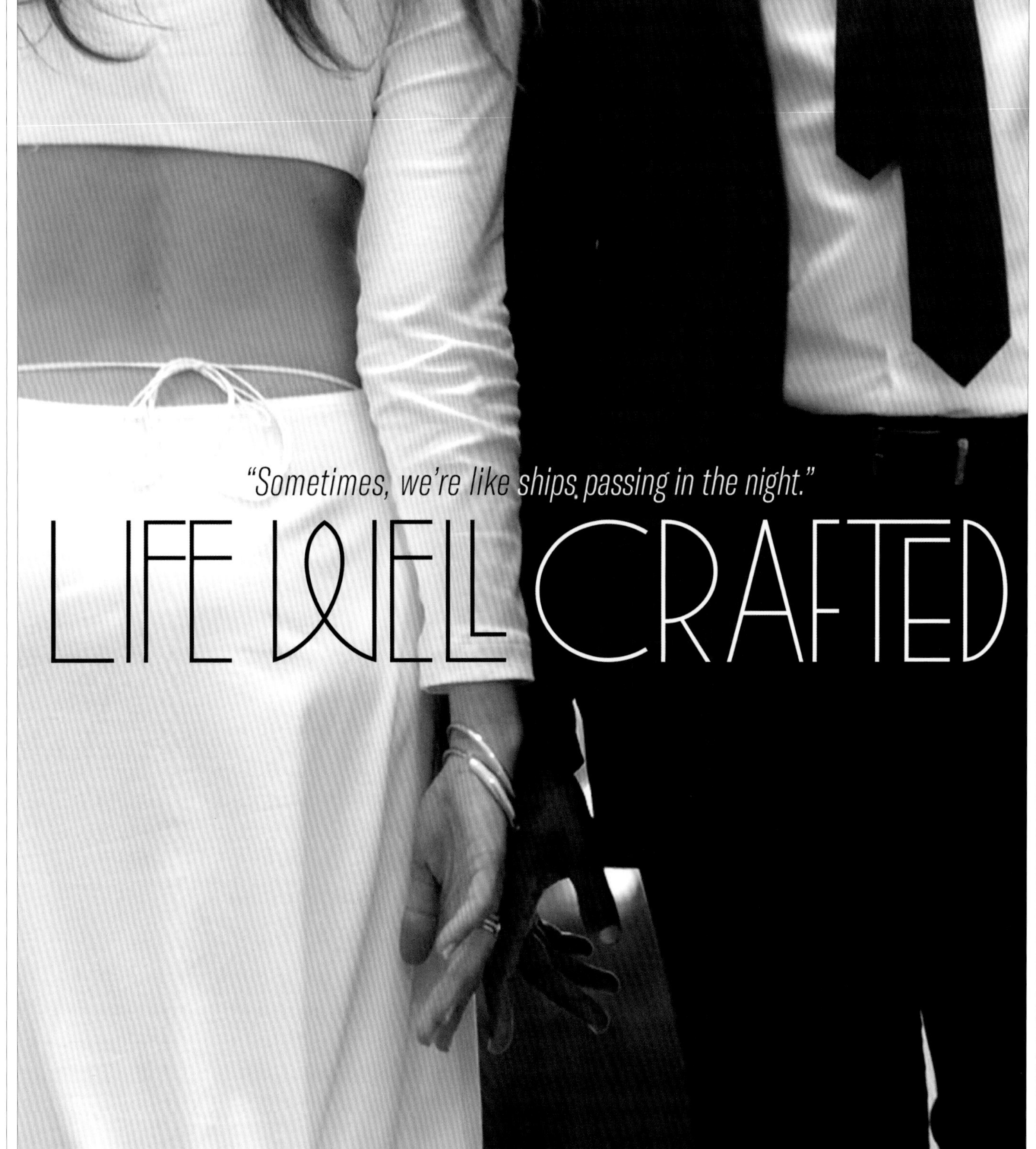

 Title: Life Well-Crafted | **Client:** House of Rohl | **Design Firm:** Rodgers Townsend

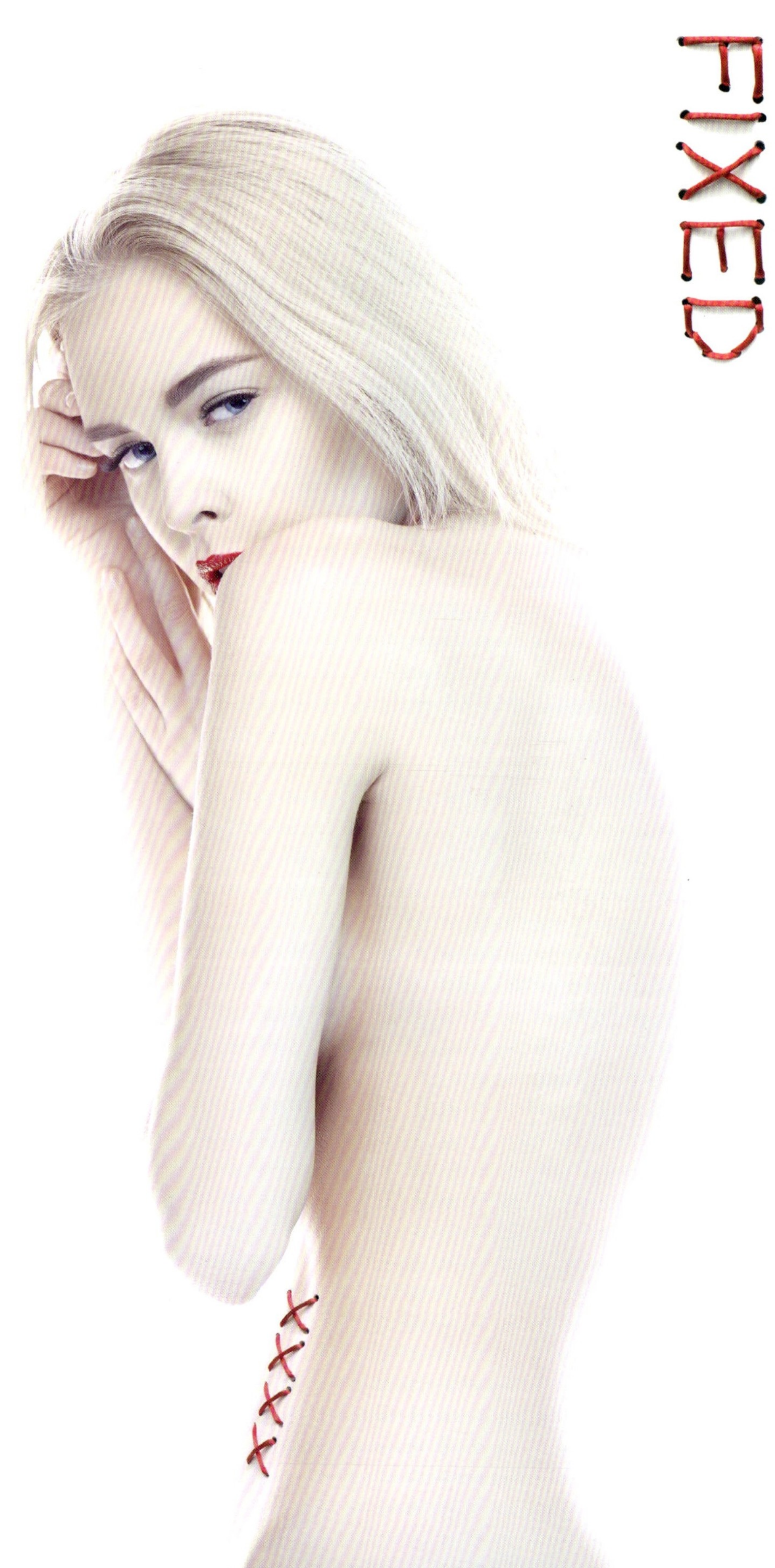
FIXED

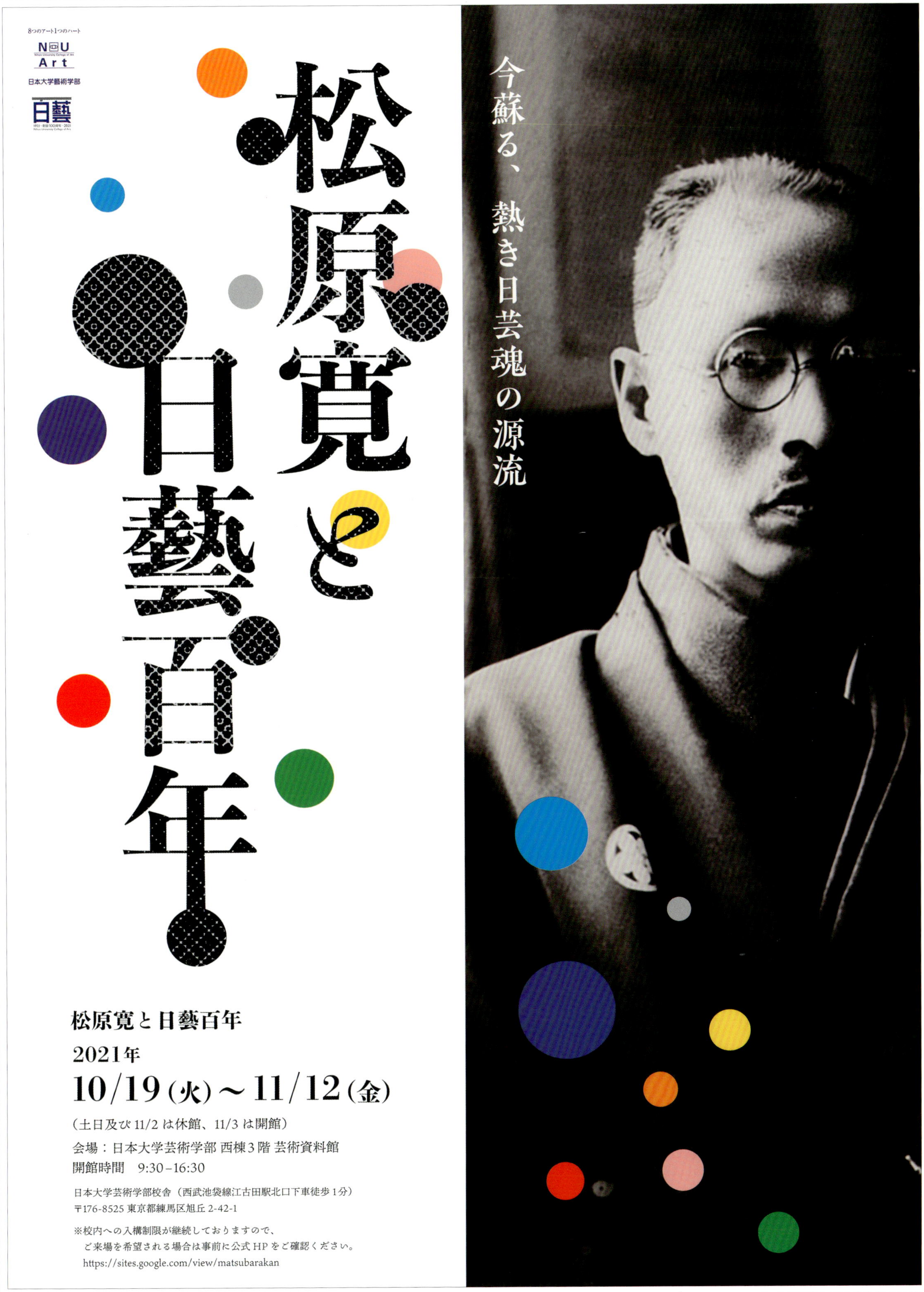

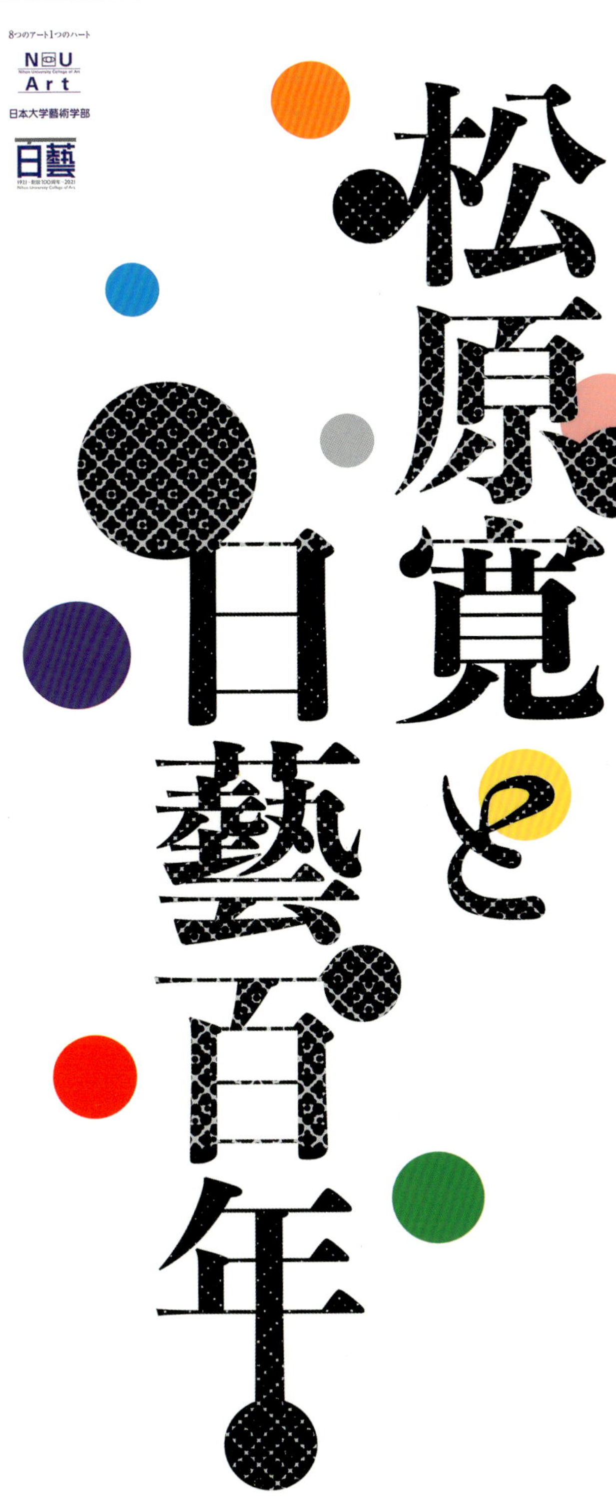

今蘇る、熱き日芸魂の源流

松原寛と日藝百年

2021年

10/19(火)～11/12(金)

(土日及び 11/2 は休館、11/3 は開館)

会場：日本大学芸術学部 西棟3階 芸術資料館

開館時間　9:30–16:30

日本大学芸術学部校舎（西武池袋線江古田駅北口下車徒歩1分）

〒176-8525 東京都練馬区旭丘 2-42-1

※校内への入構制限が継続しておりますので、
ご来場を希望される場合は事前に公式HPをご確認ください。
https://sites.google.com/view/matsubarakan

P247: Credit & Comm. **Title:** Kan Matsubara and 100 Years of Nichigei | **Client:** Nihon University College of Art | **Design Firm:** Noriyuki Kasai

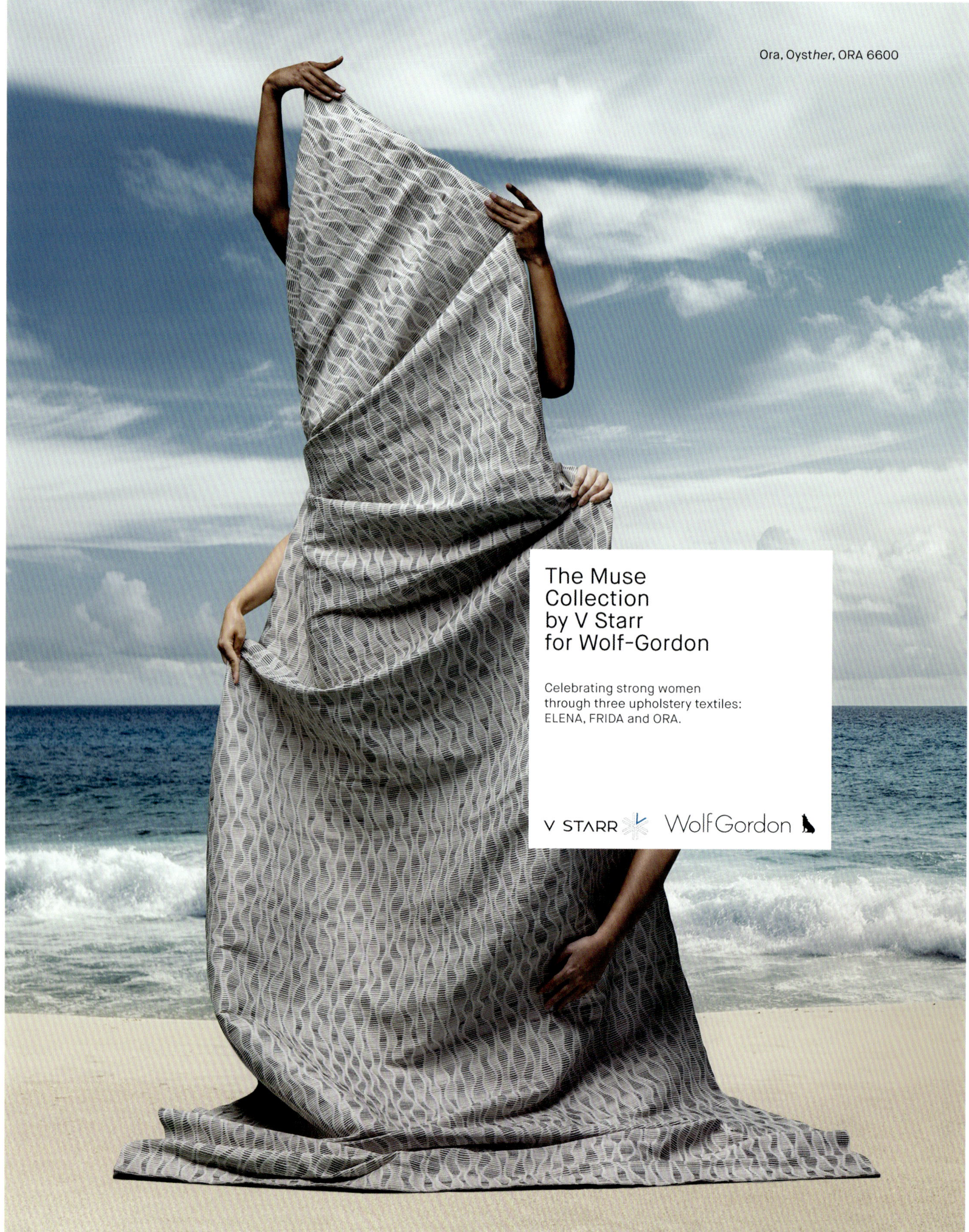

 Title: The Muse Collection by V Starr for Wolf-Gordon | **Client:** Wolf-Gordon | **Design Firm:** Ahoy Studios

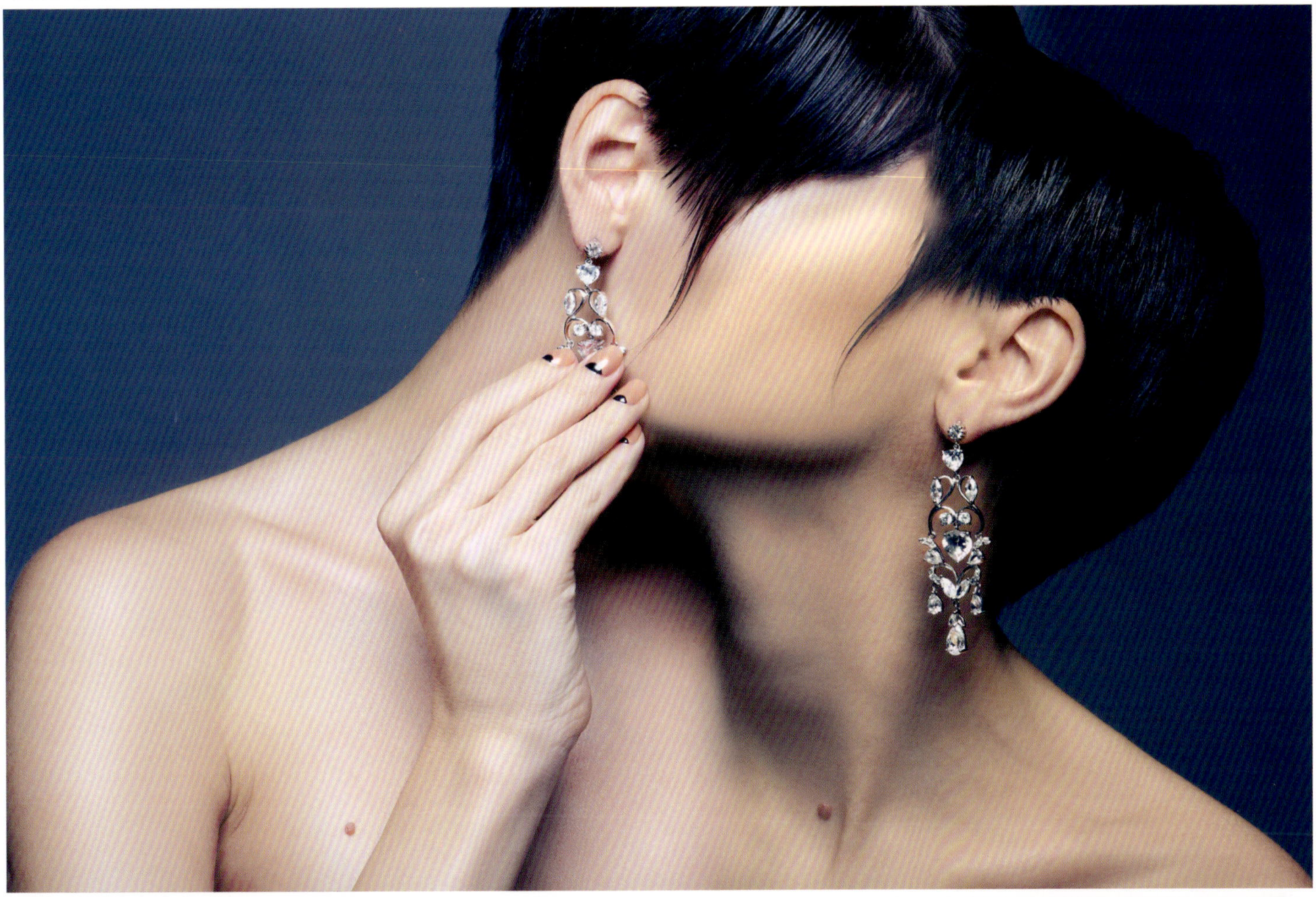

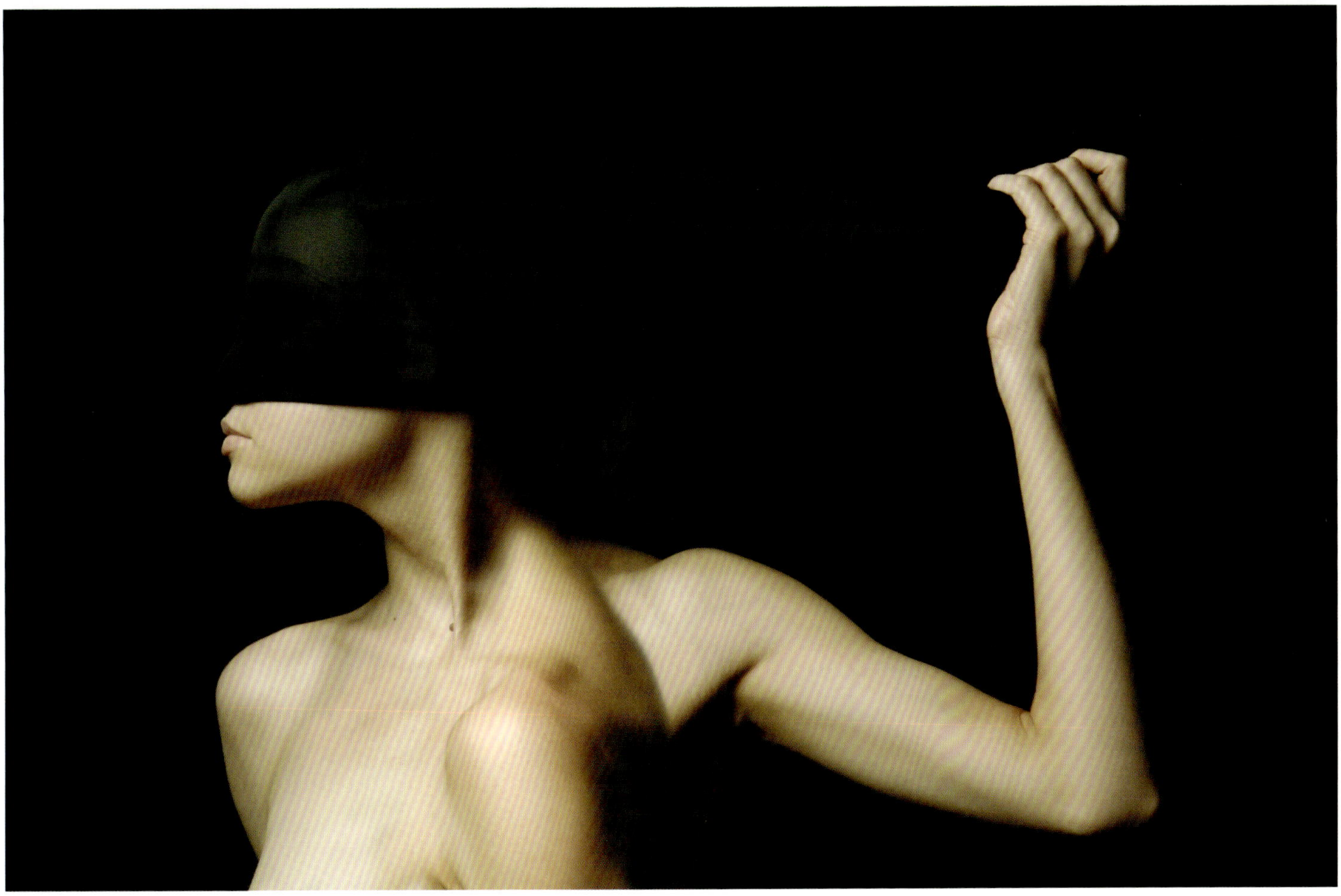

P247: Credit & Commentary

Title: Intertwined | **Client:** Self-initiated | **Design Firm:** Carmit Design Studio

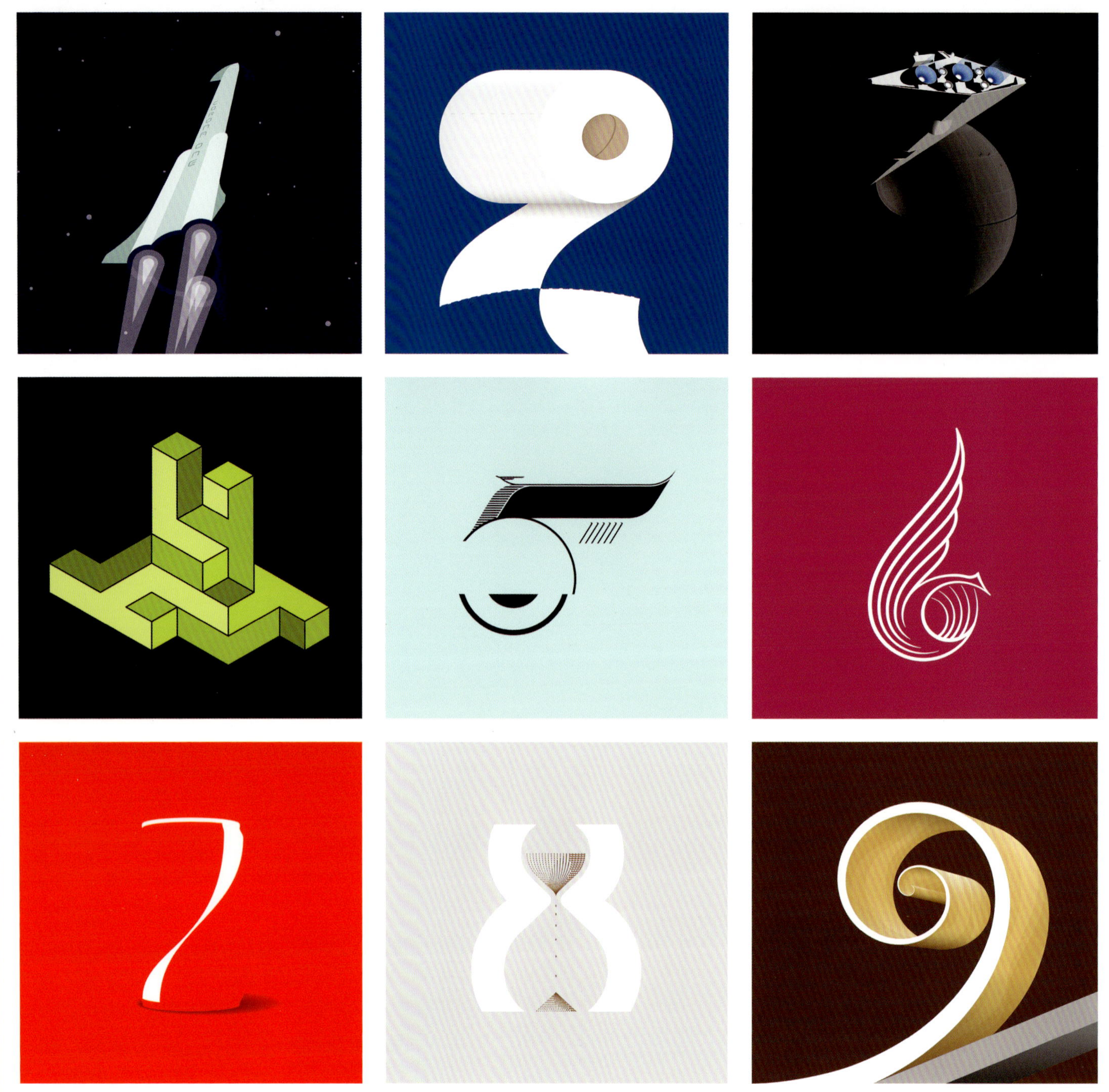

THE CORONA NUMBERS

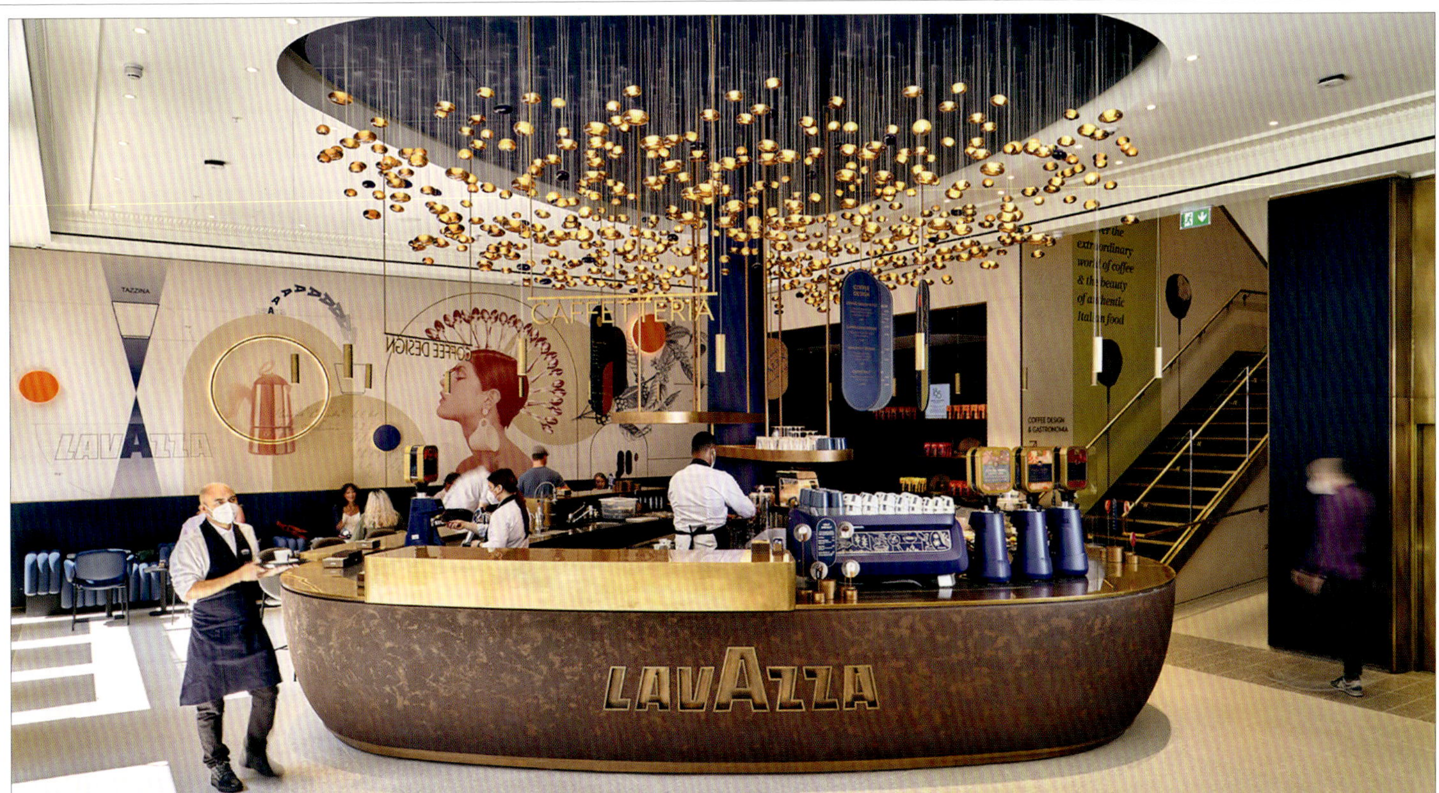

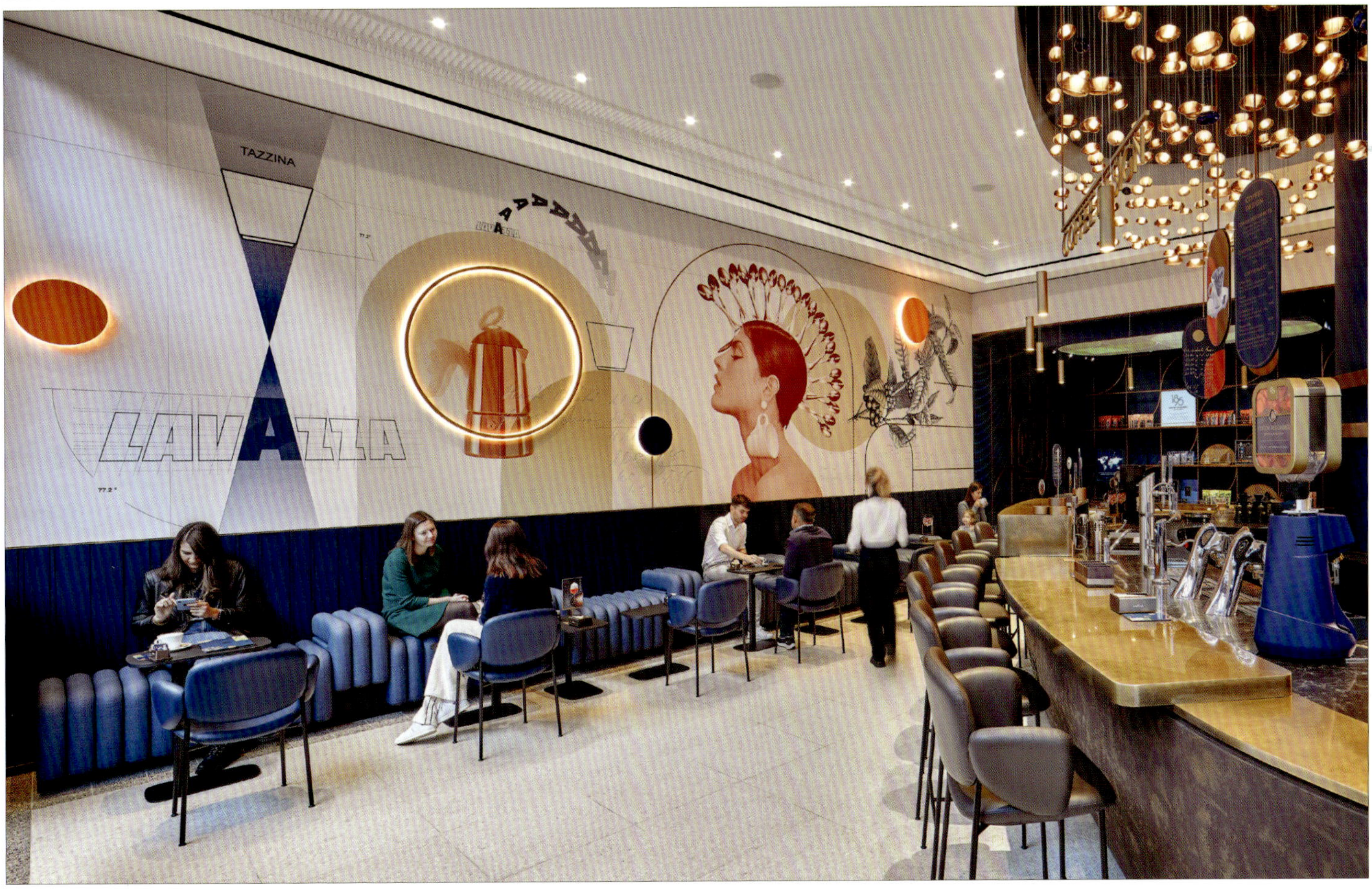

P247: Credit & Comm. **Title:** Lavazza Flagship Store London | **Client:** Lavazza Coffee | **Design Firm:** Ralph Appelbaum Associates Images 1, 2 of 6

U.S. POSTAL SERVICE

STAMPS

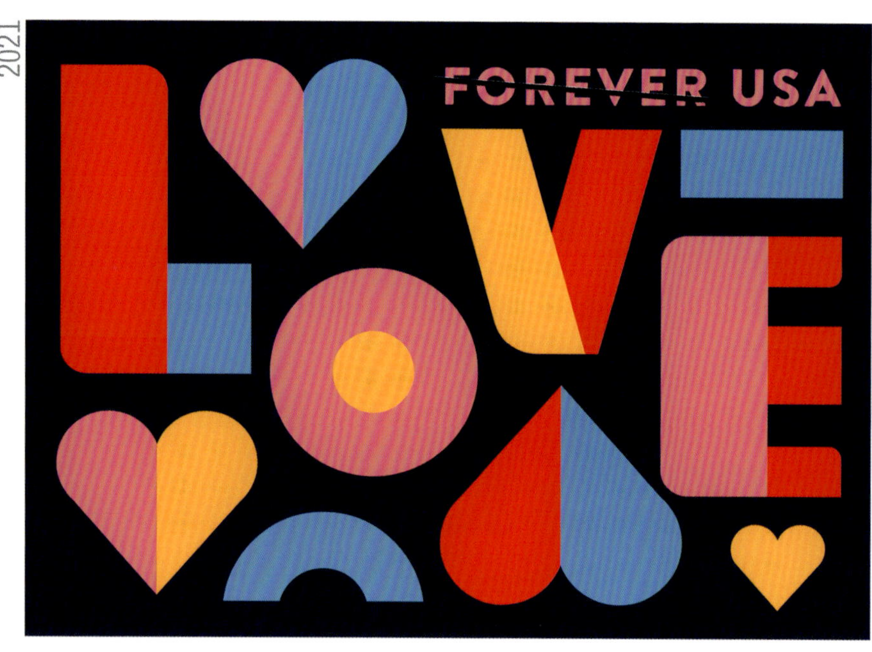

P247: Credit & Commentary

Title: Love 2021 | **Client:** U.S. Postal Service | **Design Firm:** Bailey Sullivan

U.S. POSTAL SERVICE

STAMPS

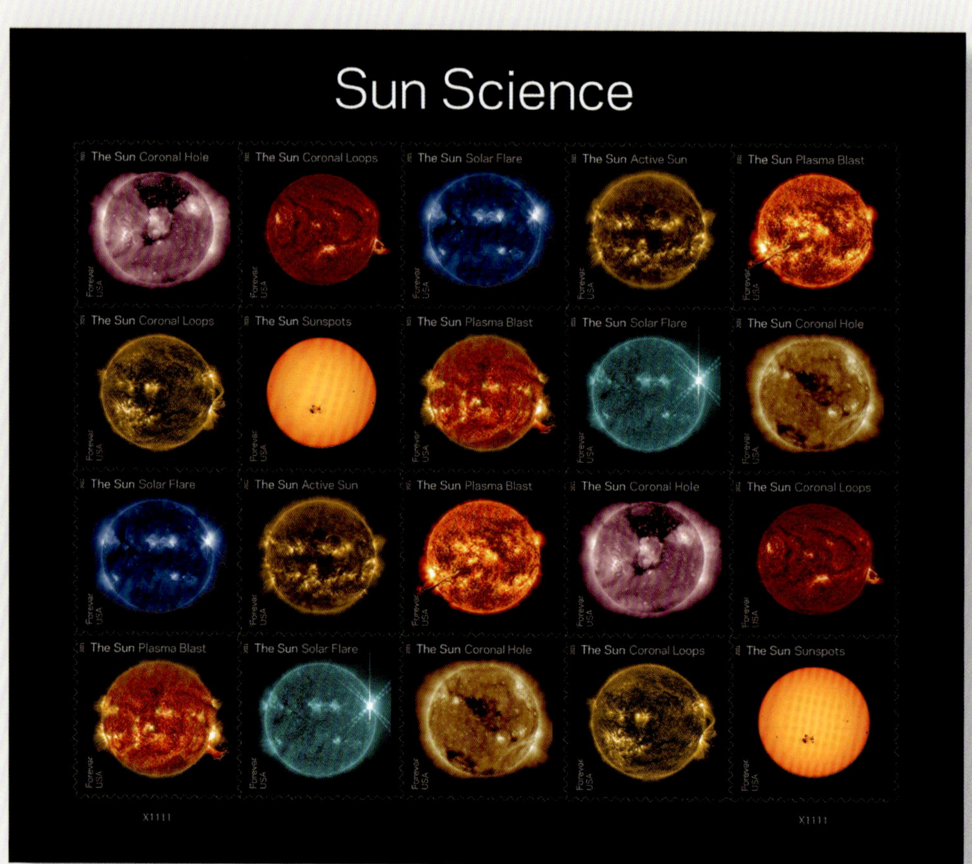

P247: Credit & Commentary

Title: Sun Science | **Client:** U.S. Postal Service | **Design Firm:** Studio A

HERITAGE BREEDS

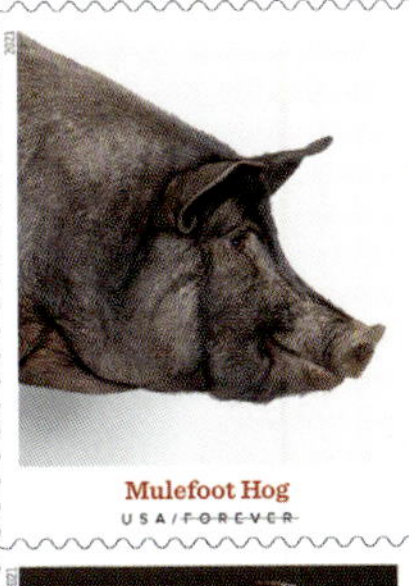
Mulefoot Hog

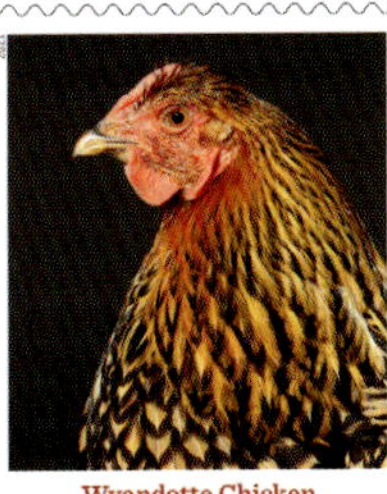
Wyandotte Chicken

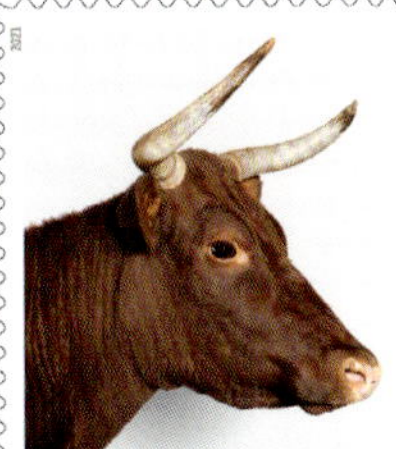
Milking Devon Cow

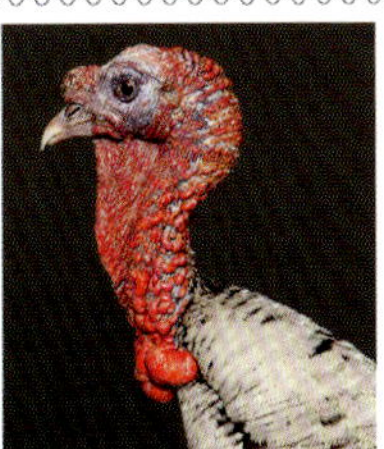
Narragansett Turkey

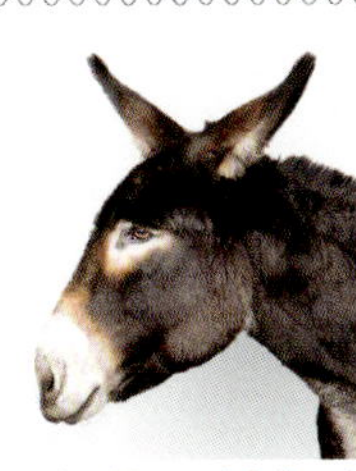
American Mammoth Jackstock

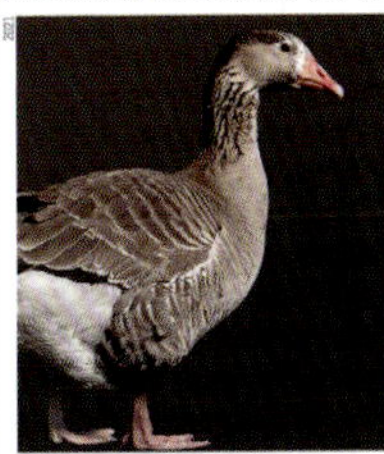
Cotton Patch Goose

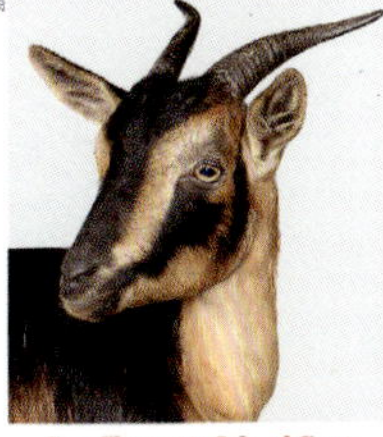
San Clemente Island Goat

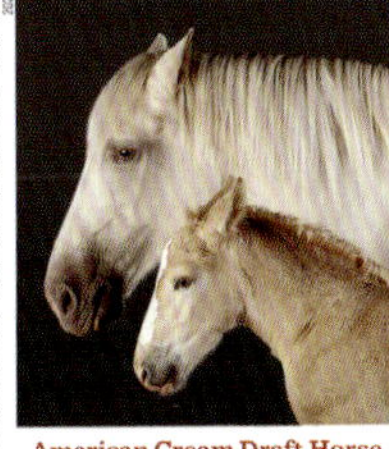
American Cream Draft Horse

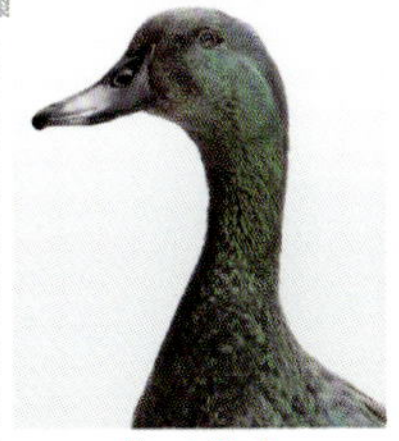
Cayuga Duck

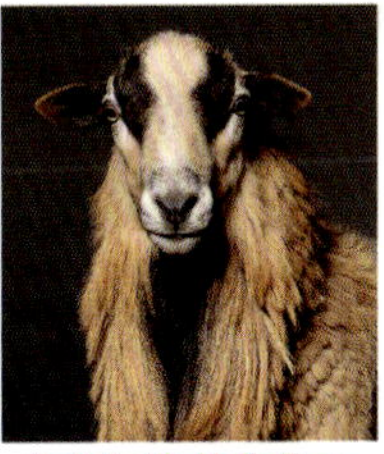
Barbados Blackbelly Sheep

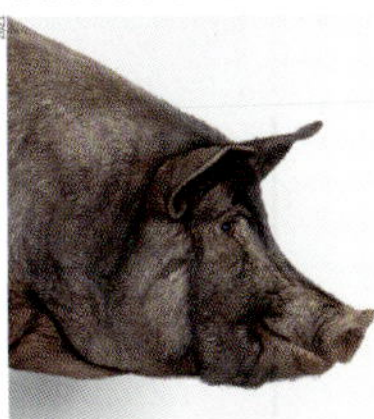
Mulefoot Hog

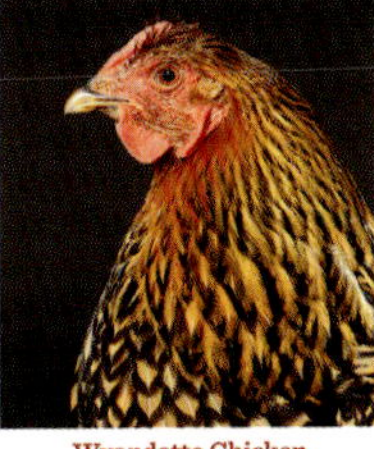
Wyandotte Chicken

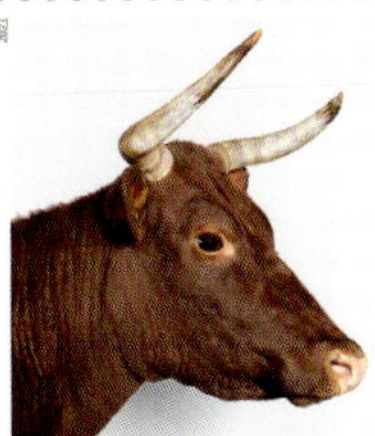
Milking Devon Cow

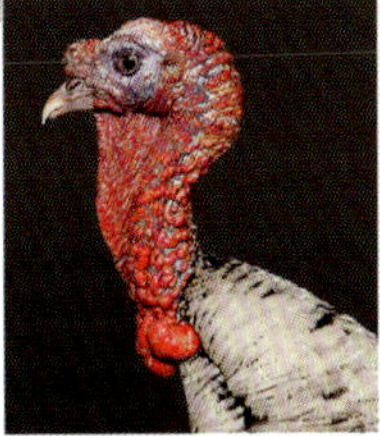
Narragansett Turkey

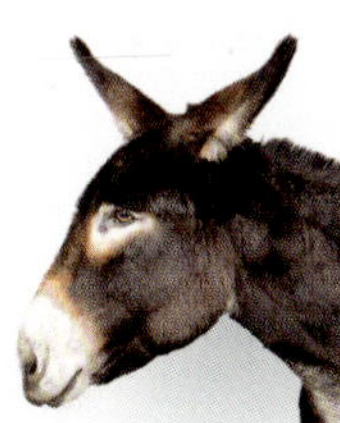
American Mammoth Jackstock

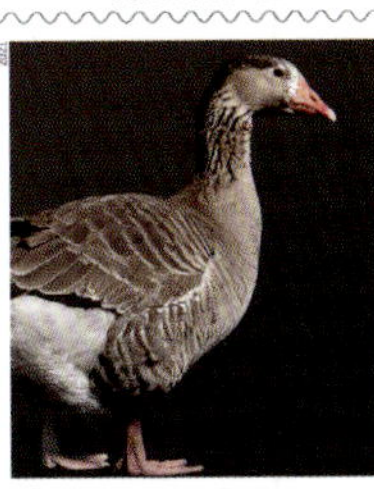
Cotton Patch Goose

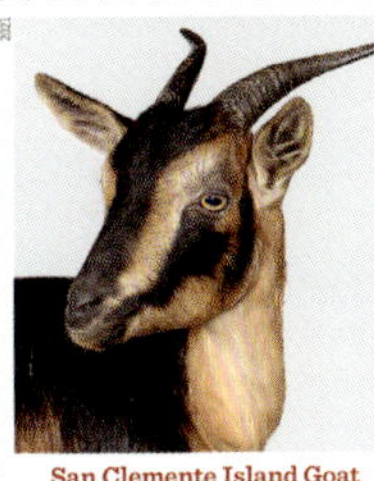
San Clemente Island Goat

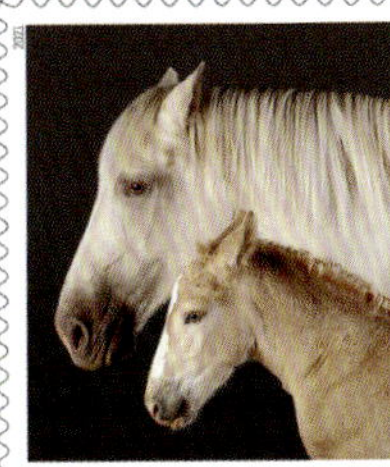
American Cream Draft Horse

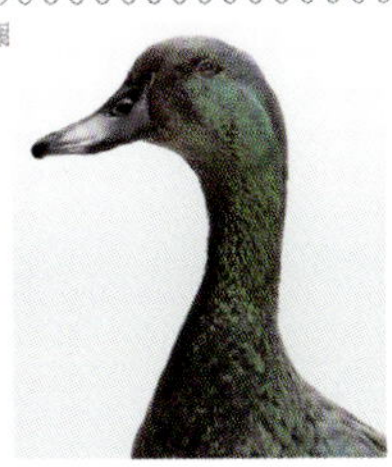
Cayuga Duck

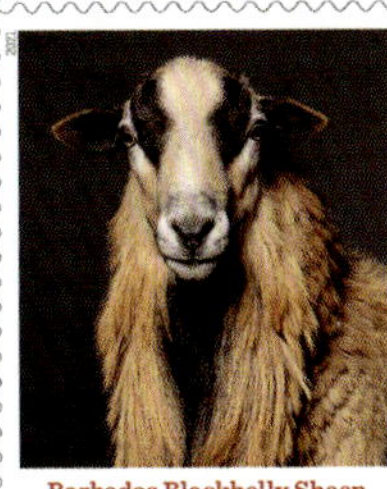
Barbados Blackbelly Sheep

X1111 X1111

Title: Heritage Breeds | **Client:** U.S. Postal Service | **Design Firm:** Journey Group

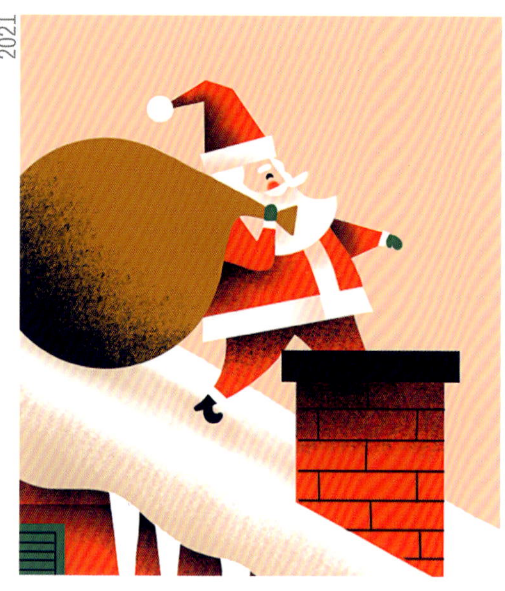

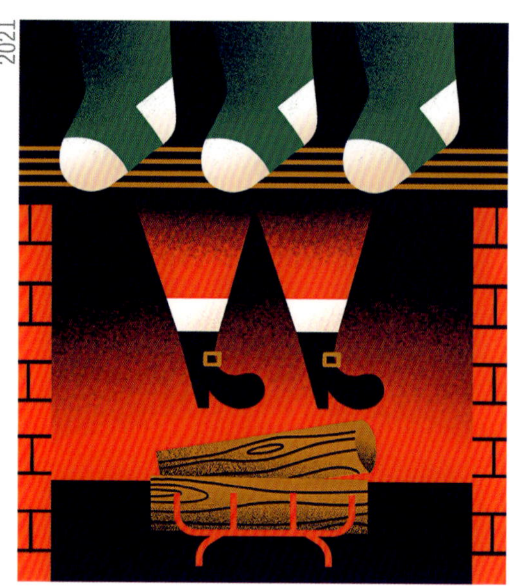

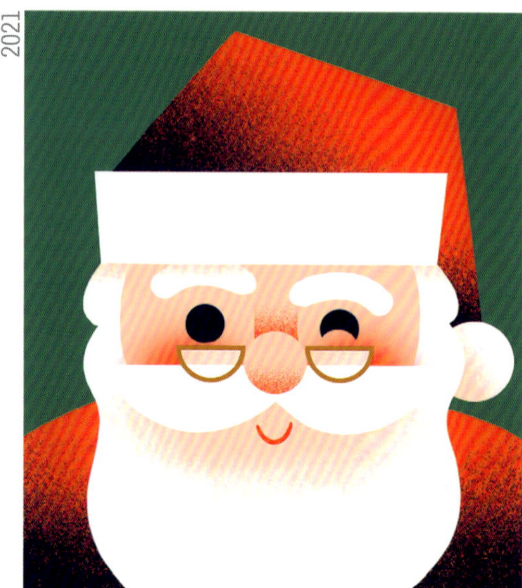

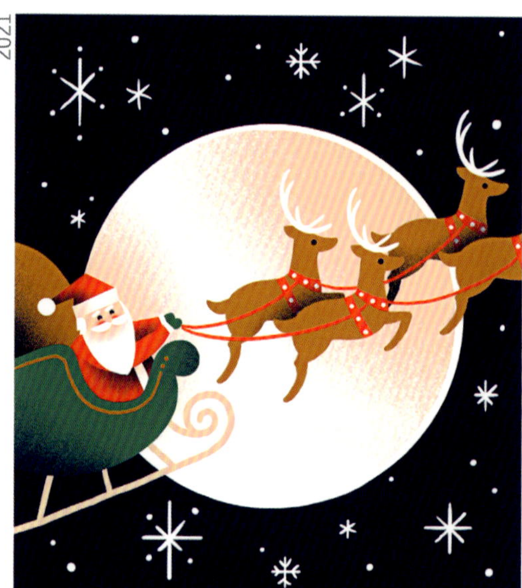

P247: Credit & Commentary **Title:** A Visit from St. Nick | **Client:** U.S. Postal Service | **Design Firm:** Greg Breeding

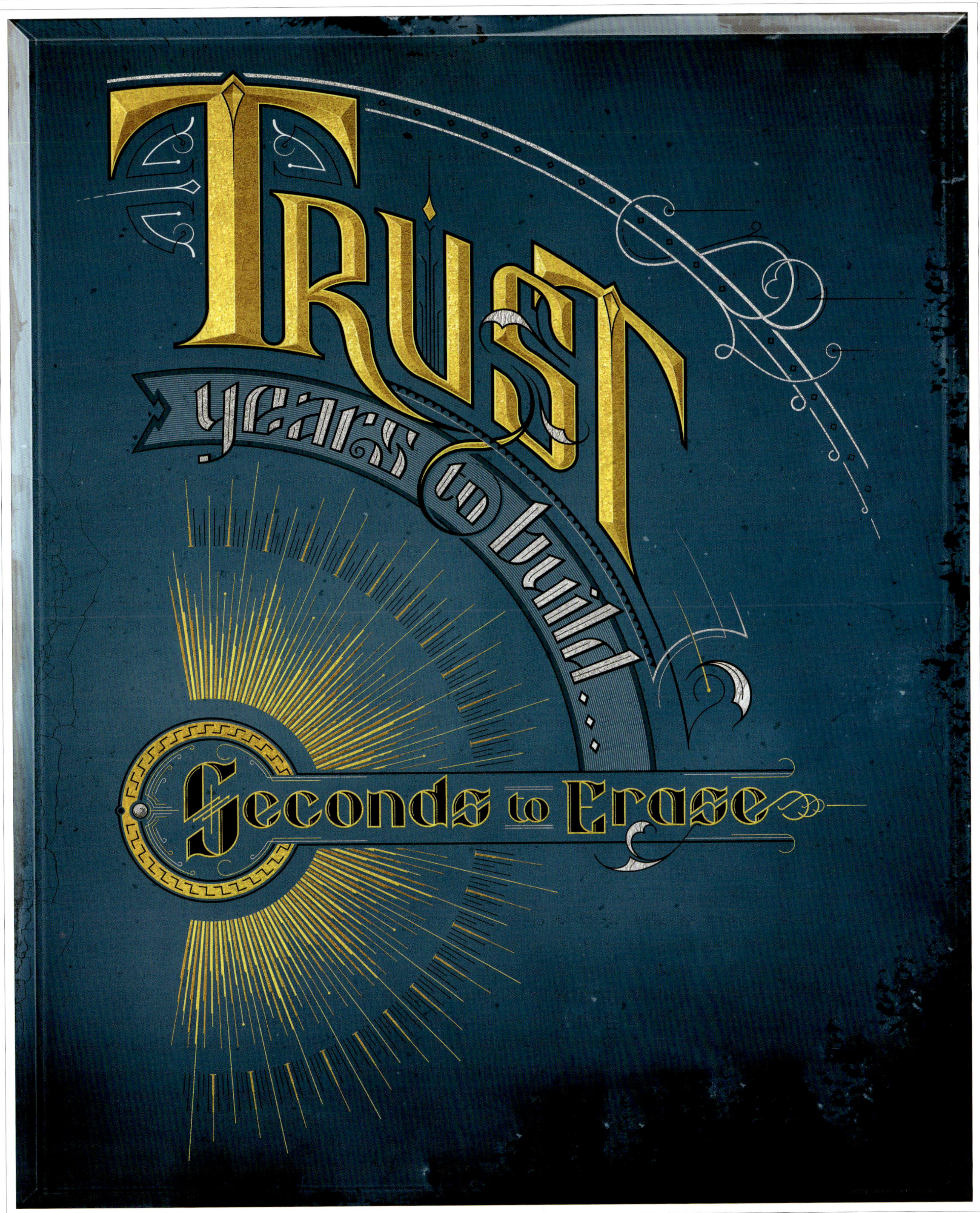

P247: Credit & Commentary

Title: Trust | **Client:** Self-initiated | **Design Firm:** UP-Ideas

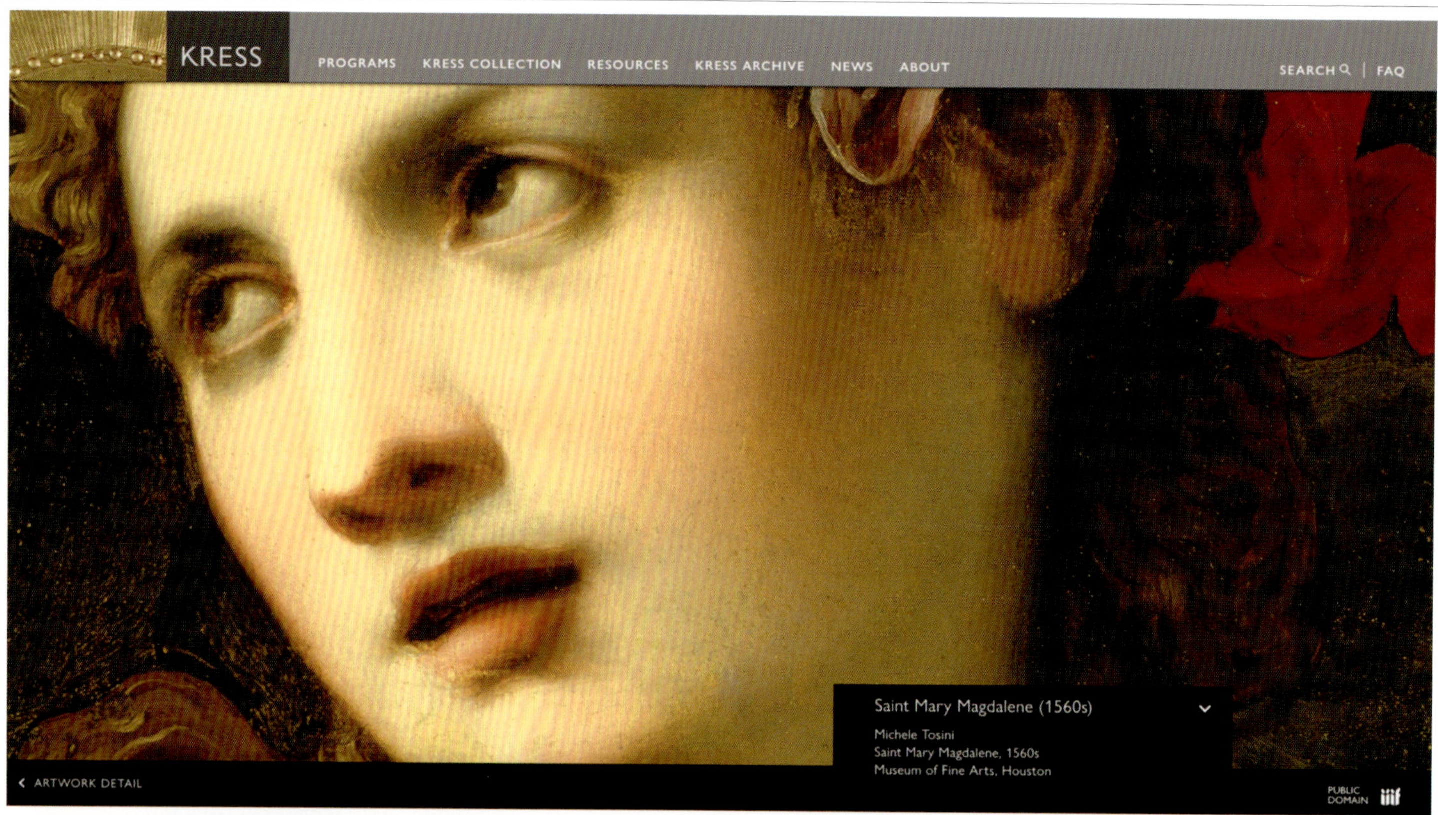

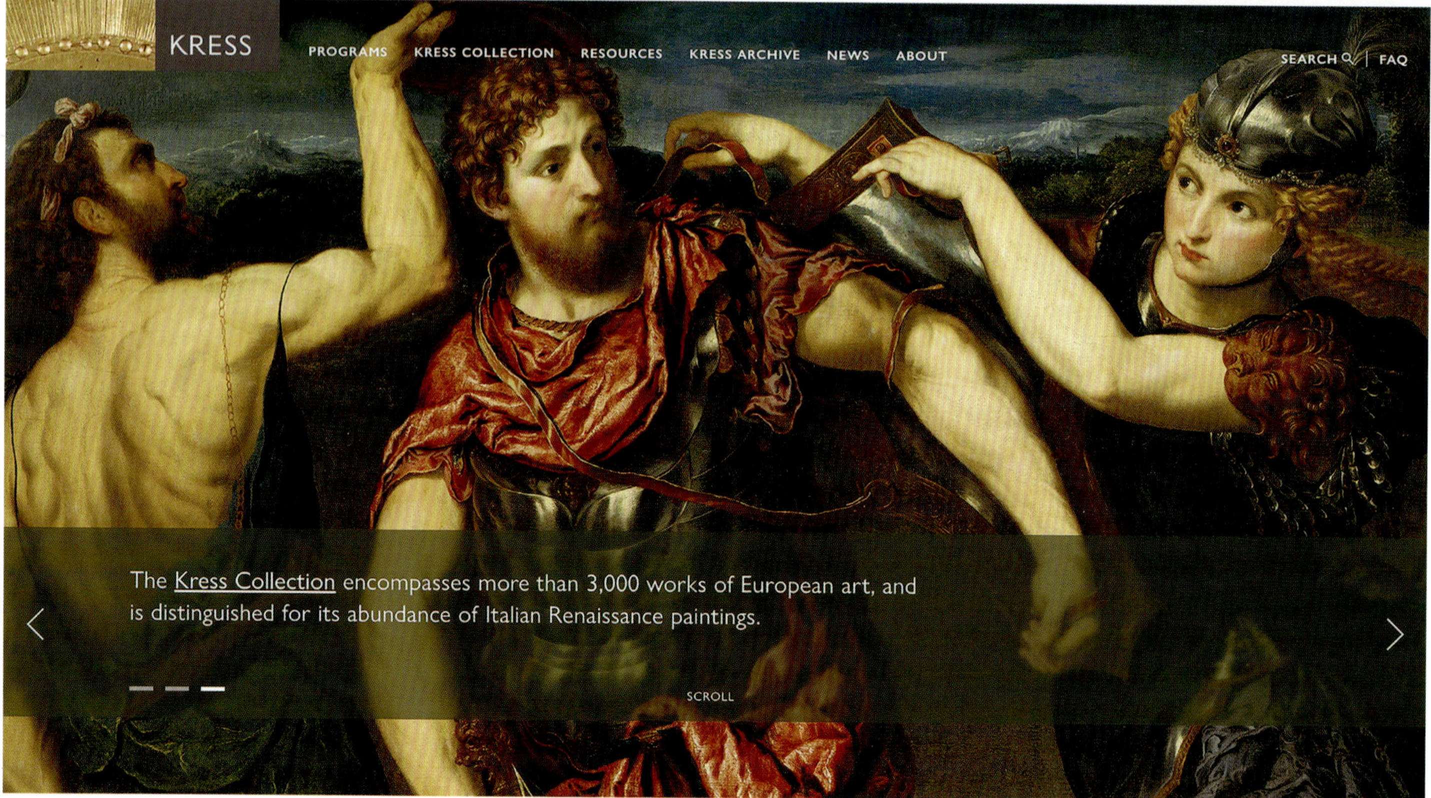

P247: Credit & Commentary **Title:** Kress Foundation Website | **Client:** Samuel H. Kress Foundation | **Design Firm:** C&G Partners Images 1, 2 of 7

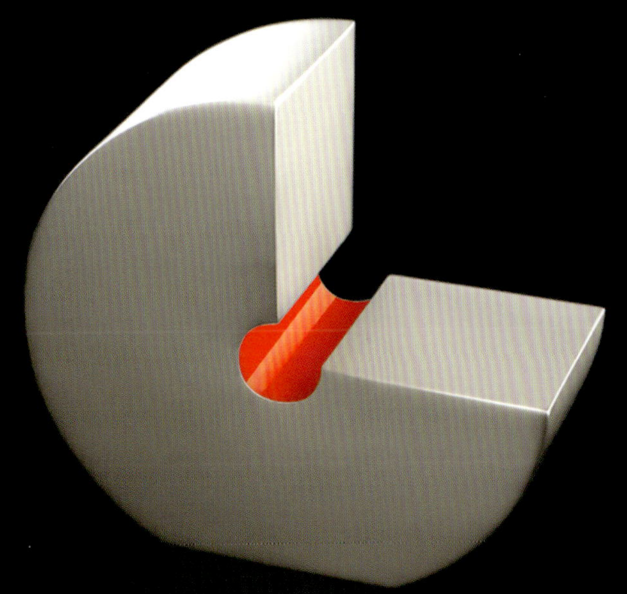

JESSICA NATASHA

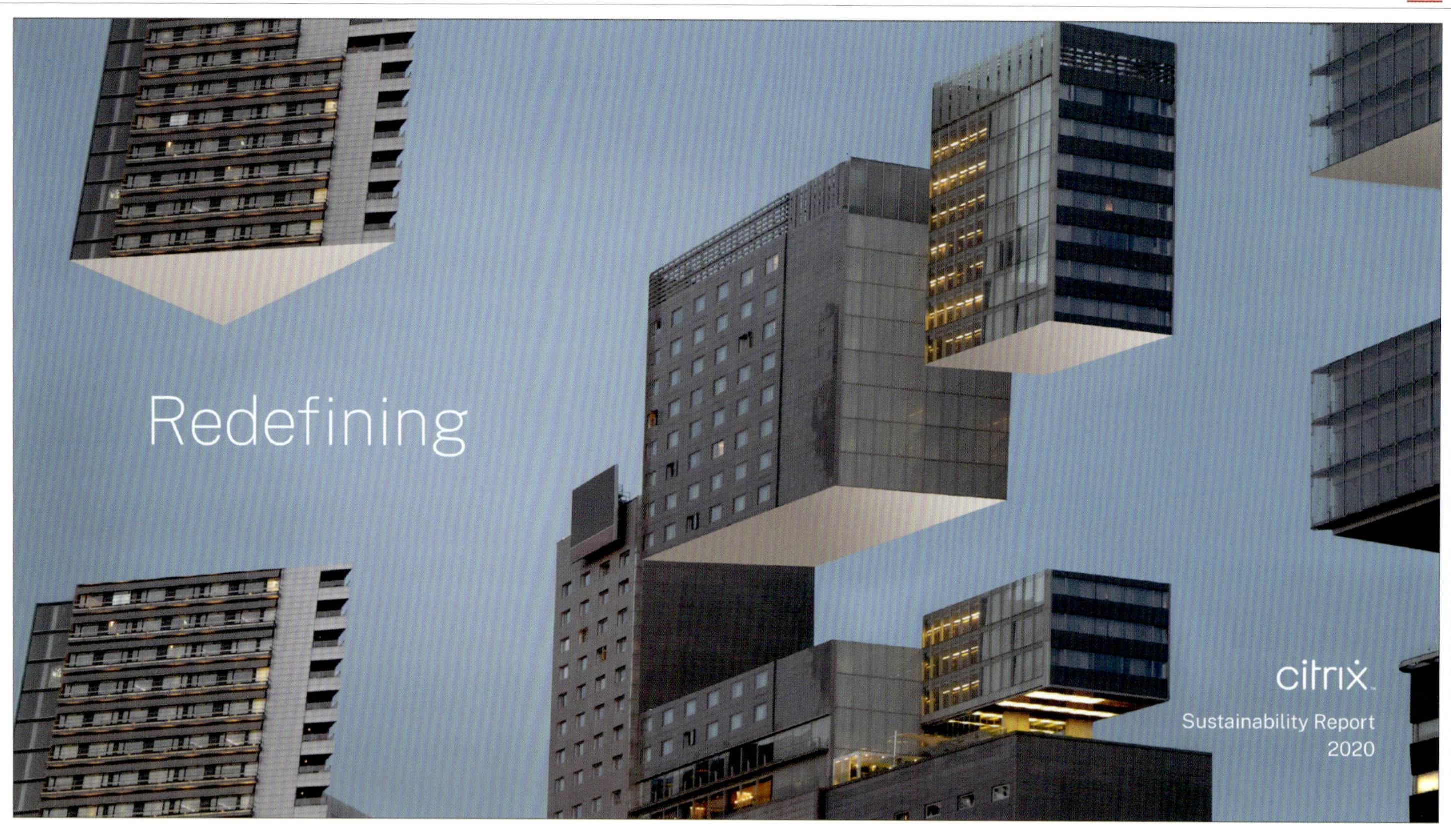

Title: Citrix CSR | **Client:** Citrix | **Design Firm:** Addison

JAMES TAYLOR

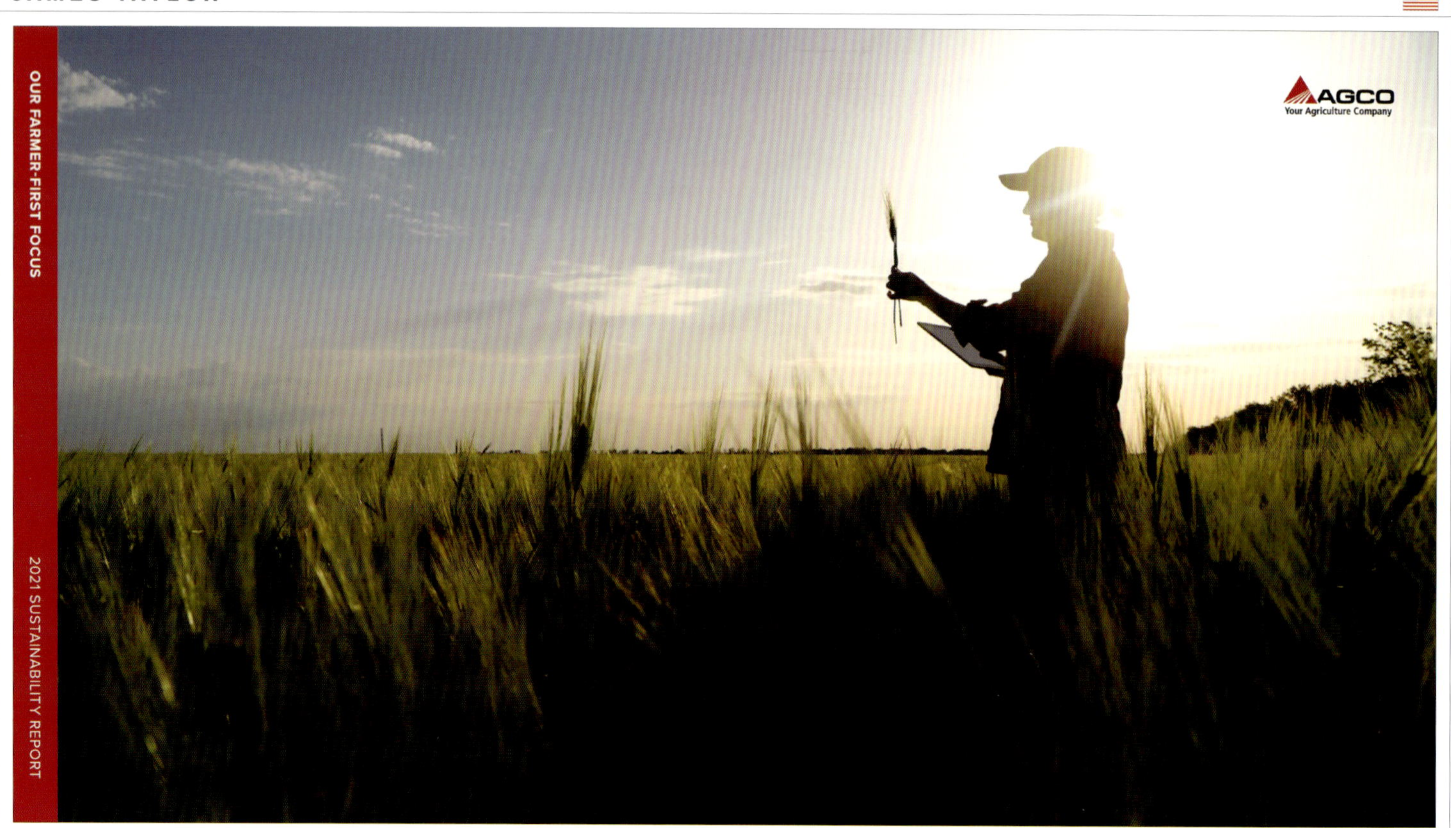

Title: AGCO AR / Sustainability Report | **Client:** AGCO | **Design Firm:** Addison

KIN YUEN

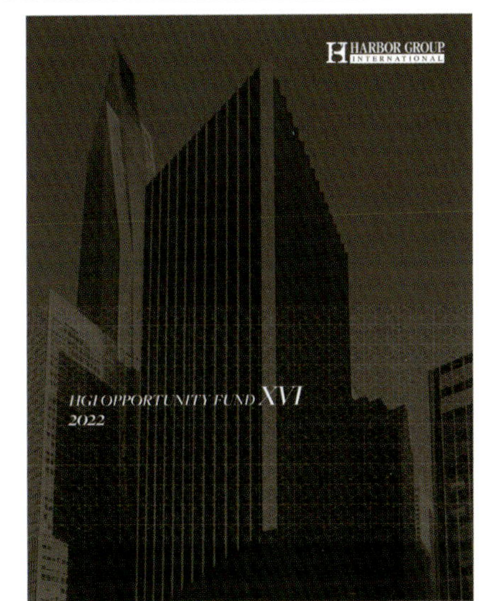

Title: Harbor Group International Fund Book
Client: Harbor Group International
Design Firm: Addison

KIN YUEN

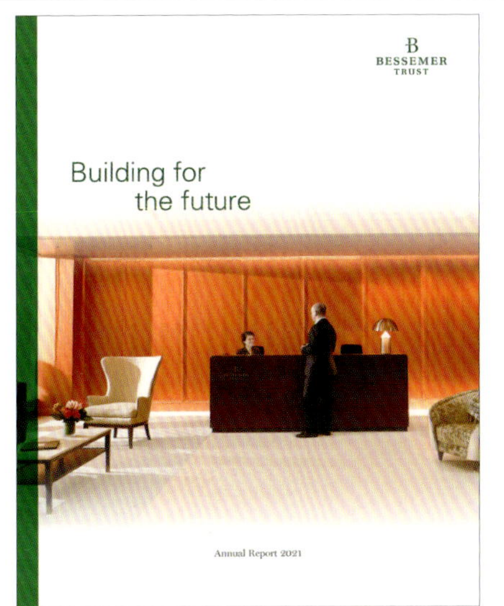

Title: Bessemer Trust AR 2021
Client: Bessemer Trust
Design Firm: Addison

GRANT CURRIE

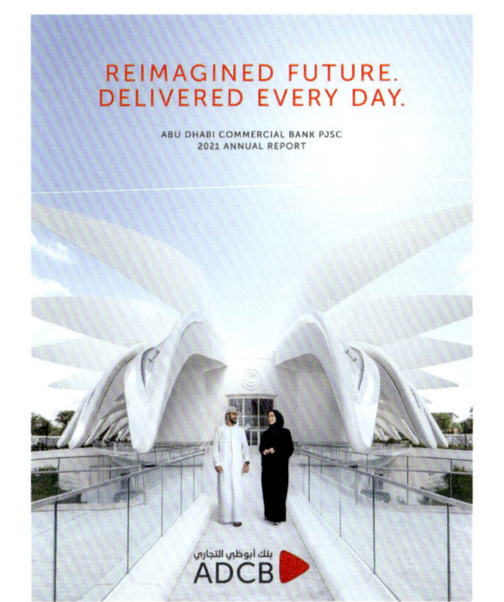

Title: ADCB AR
Client: ADCB
Design Firm: Addison

STUDIO 5 DESIGNS INC. (MANILA)

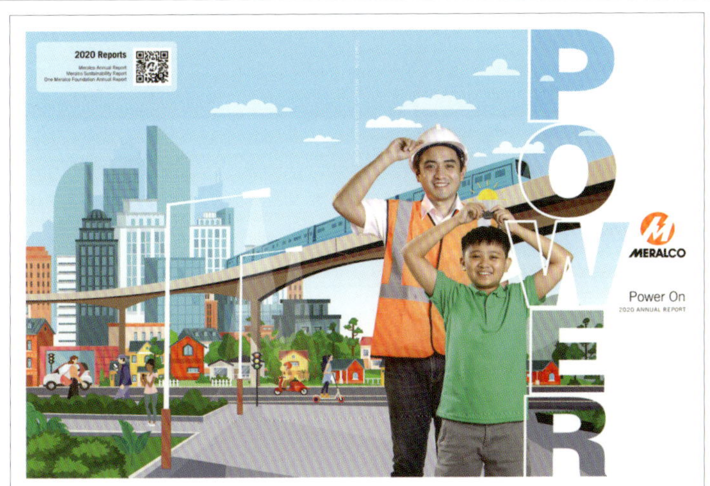

Title: MERALCO 2020 Annual Reports: Power, Life, Hope
Client: Meralco Company | **Design Firm:** Studio 5 Designs Inc. (Manila)

JOHN MONEY

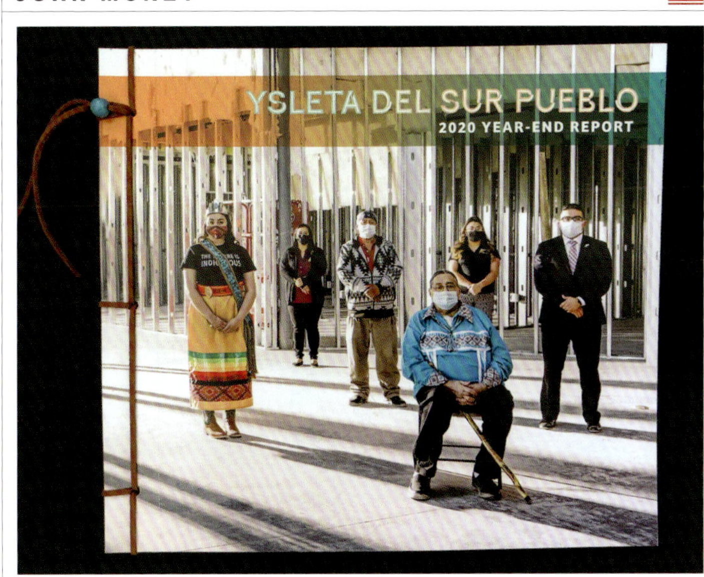

Title: Ysleta Del Sur Pueblo 2020 Year-End Report | **Clients:** Ysleta del Sur Pueblo, Helix Solutions | **Design Firm:** Anne M. Giangiulio Design

ANNA CELINE KAARLING KHAN

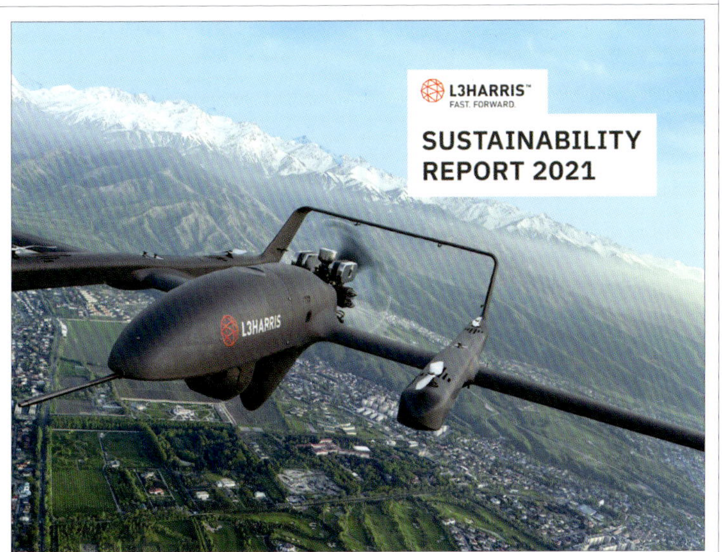

Title: L3Harris CSR | **Client:** L3Harris | **Design Firm:** Addison

MICHAEL ARNDT

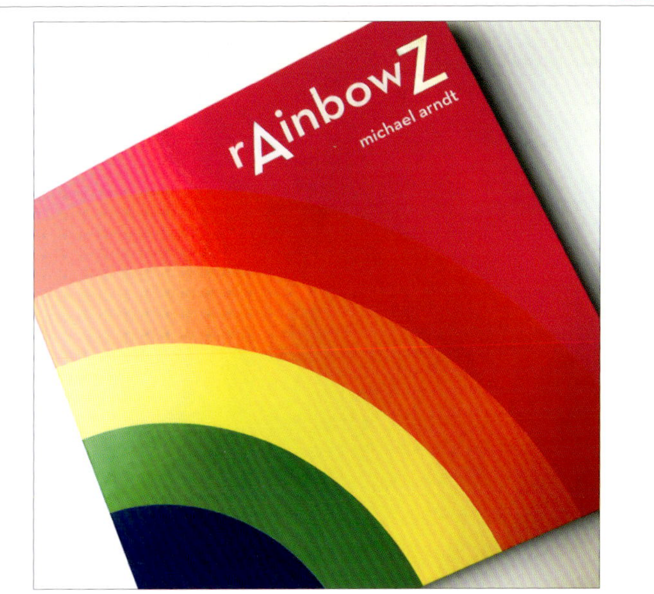

Title: rAinbowZ | **Client:** Andrews McMeel Publishing | **Design Firm:** M Books

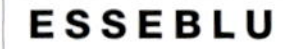

ESSEBLU

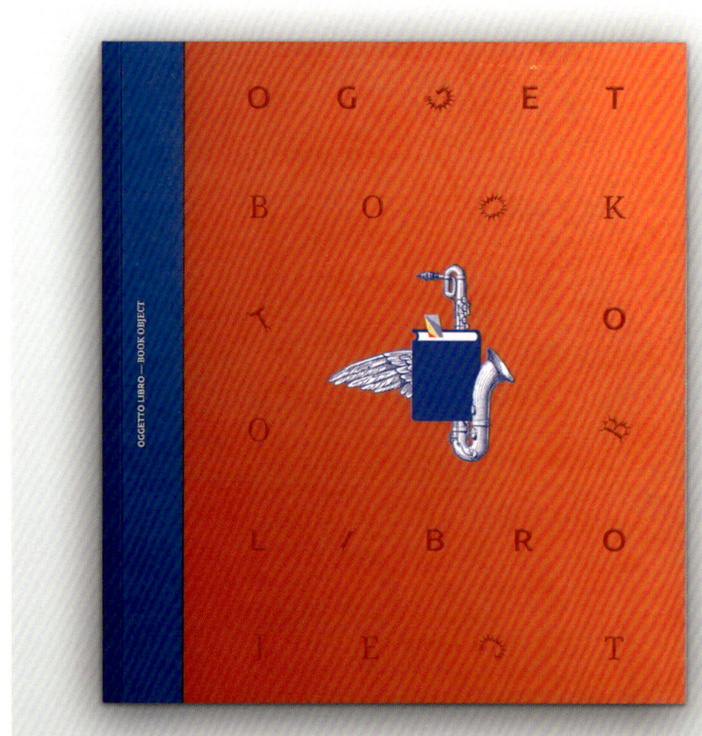

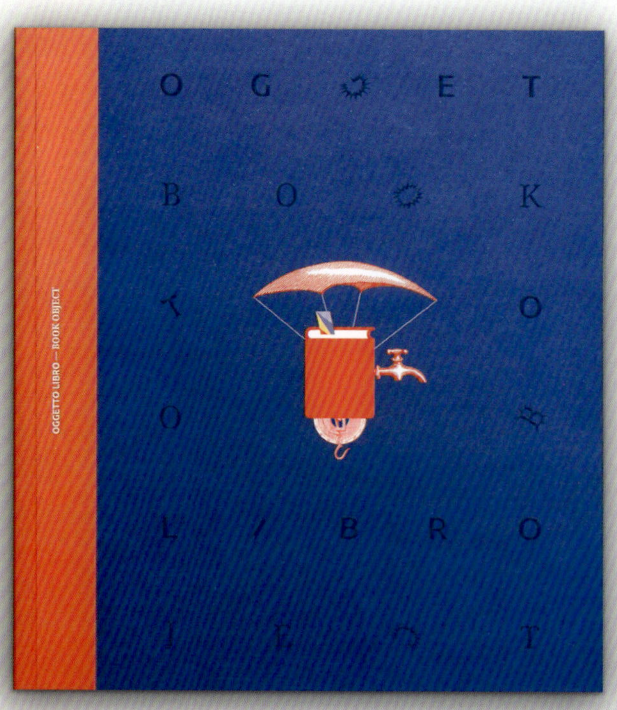

Title: Oggetto Libro (Catalogo) / Book Object (Catalogue) | **Client:** SBLU_spazioalbello | **Design Firm:** Esseblu

CRISTINA RODRIGUES STUDIO

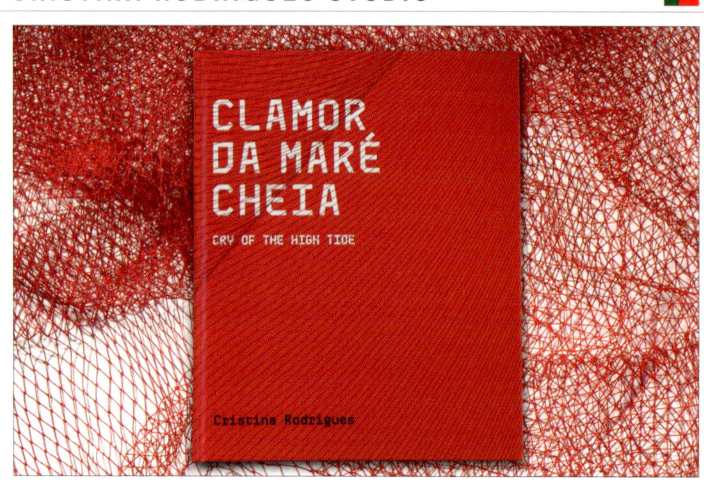

Title: CRY OF THE HIGH TIDE Book, Exhibition of Cristina Rodriges
Client: Cristina Rodriges | **Design Firm:** Duas Faces Design

ROBERT FINKEL

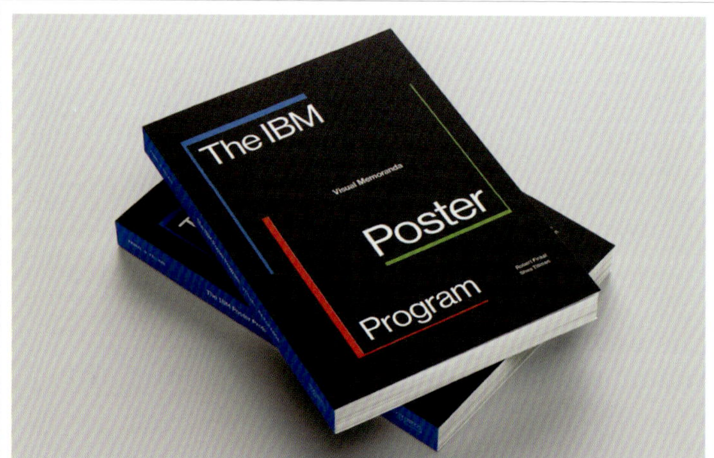

Title: The IBM Poster Program: Visual Memoranda
Client: Lund Humphries | **Design Firm:** Robert Finkel

BOYANG XIA

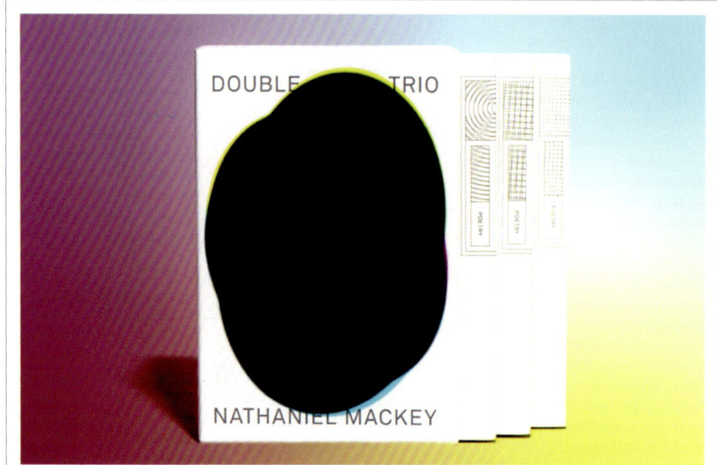

Title: Double Trio | **Client:** New Directions Publishing
Design Firm: Boyang Xia

PEDRO LEÃO NETO, OLÍVIA MARQUES DA SILVA

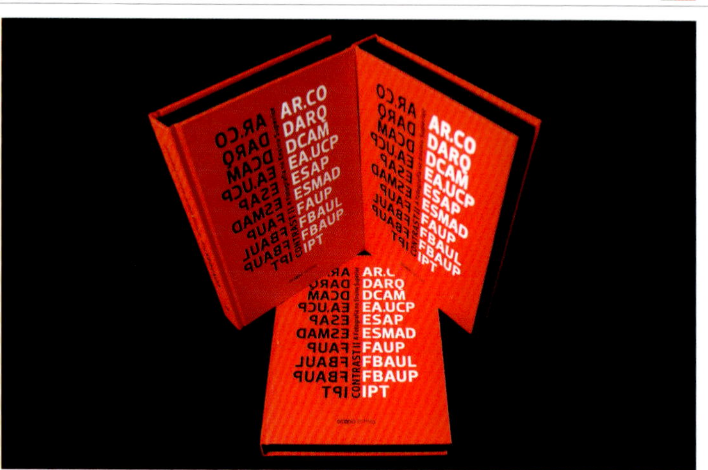

Title: CONTRAST II - A Fotografia no Ensino Superior
Client: Cityscopio – Scopio Editions | **Design Firm:** Né S. Design

JAN ŠABACH

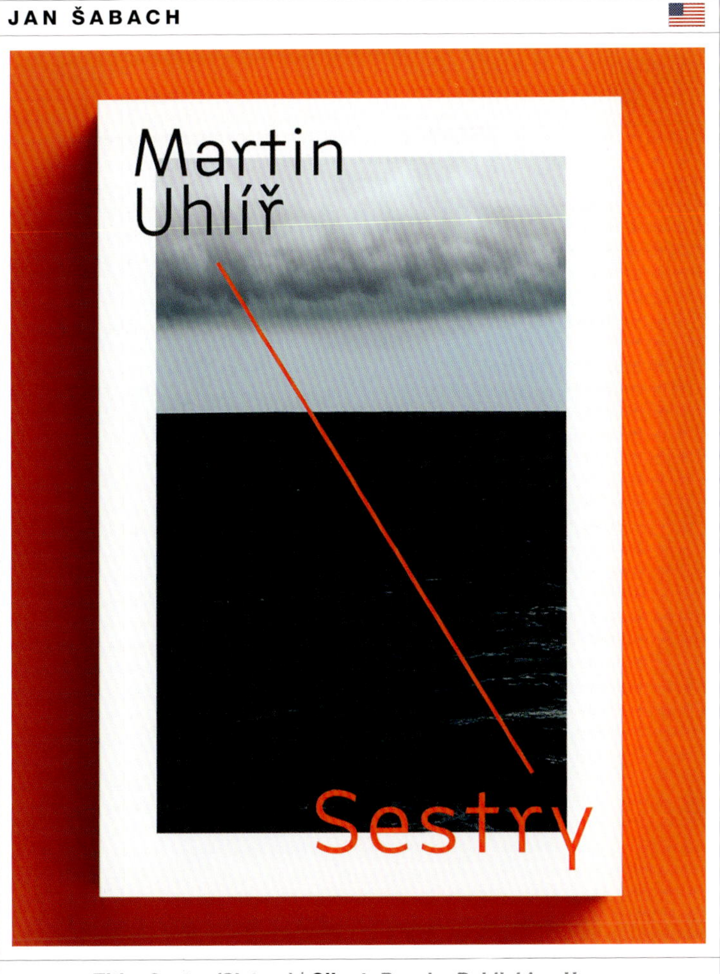

Title: Sestry (Sisters) | **Client:** Paseka Publishing House
Design Firm: Code Switch

NEIL GONZALEZ

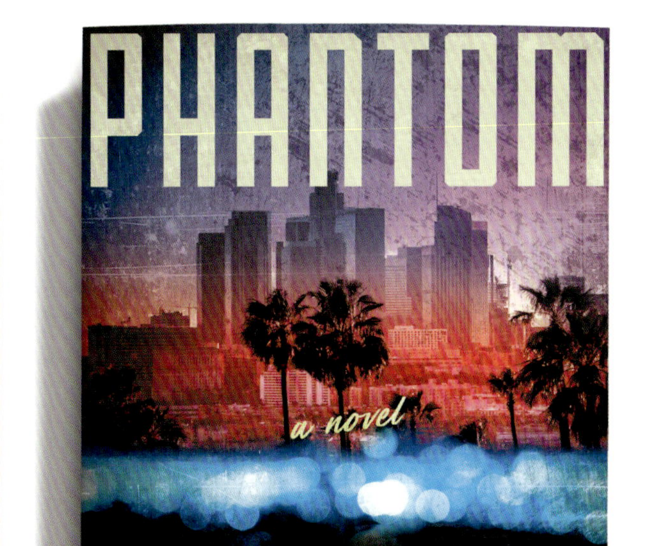

Title: Phantom Money | **Client:** S. Alexander O'Keefe
Design Firm: Greenleaf Book Group

CAMERON STEIN

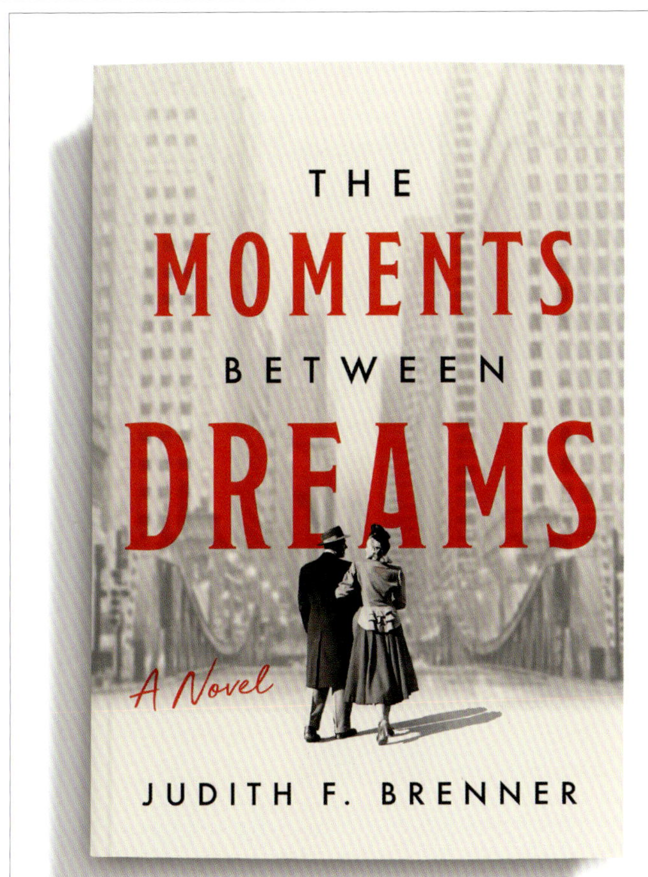

Title: The Moments Between Dreams | **Client:** Judith F. Brenner
Design Firm: Greenleaf Book Group

JEFF MILLER

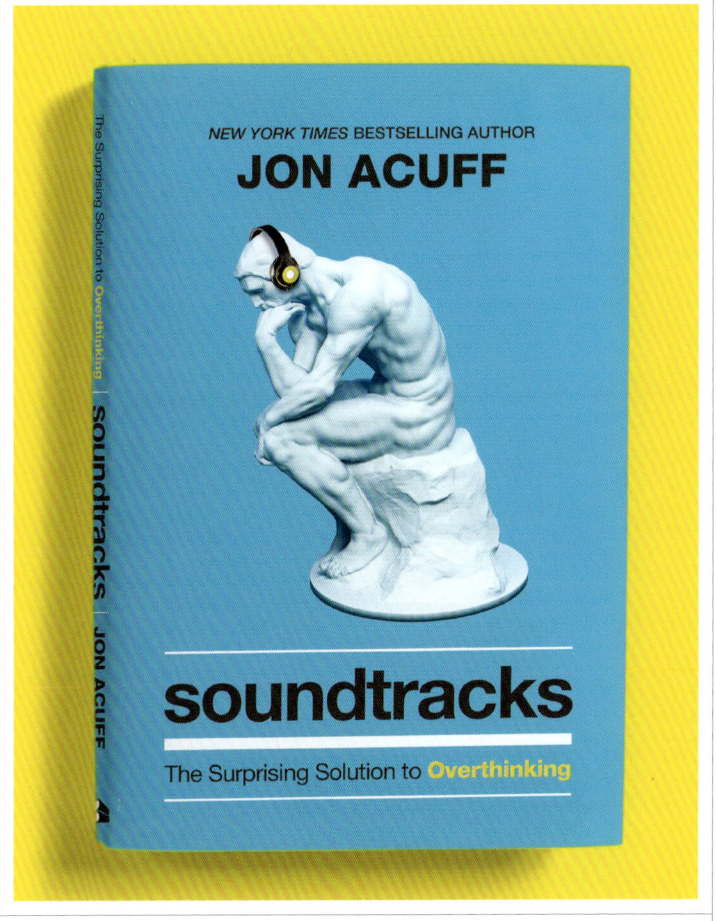

Title: Soundtracks | **Client:** Baker Books
Design Firm: Faceout Studio

LISA S. JOHNSON

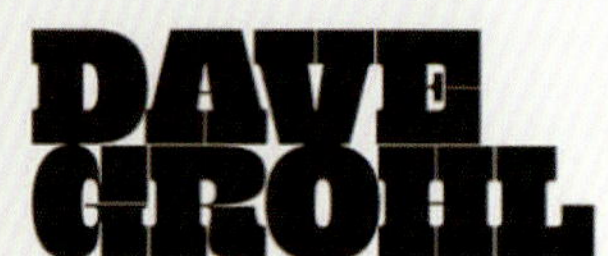

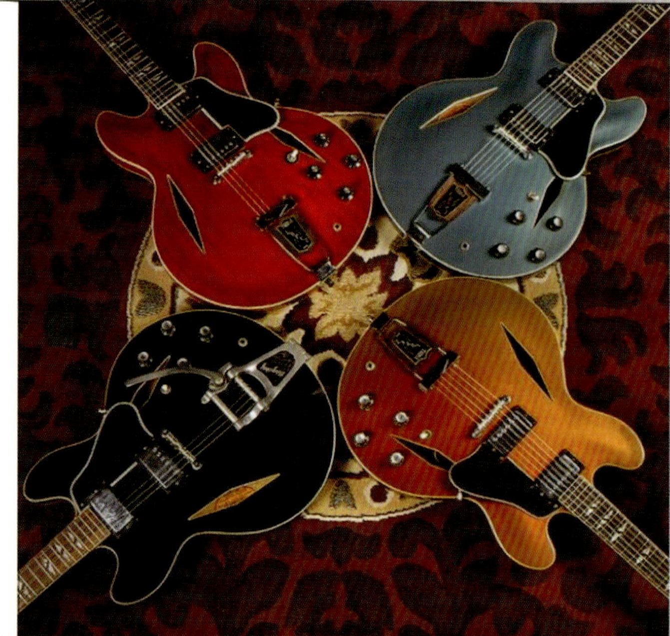

Title: Immortal Axes | **Client:** Rock Stars Worldwide | **Design Firms:** Nick Steinhardt, 23in

ANNA JORDAN

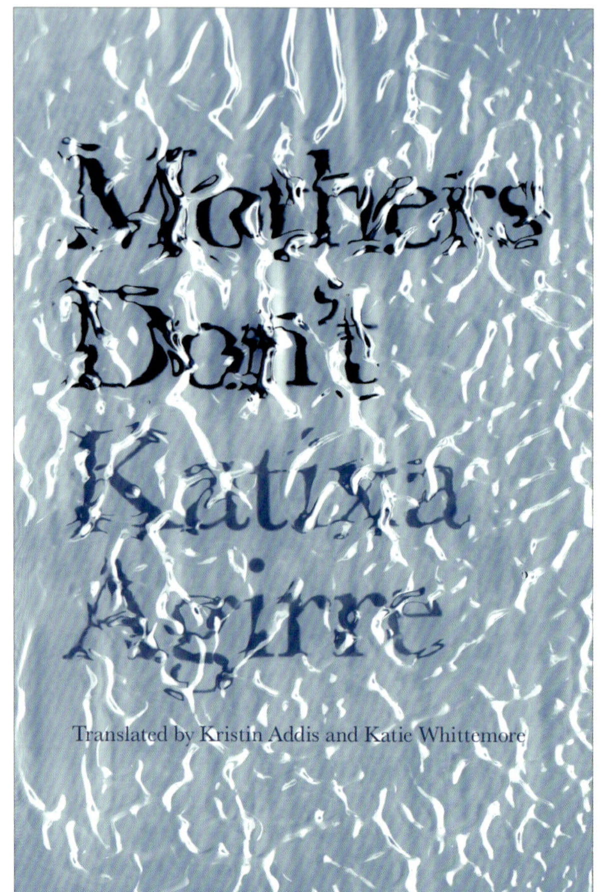

Title: Mothers Don't | **Client:** Open Letter Books
Design Firm: Anna Jordan

HANNAH GASKAMP

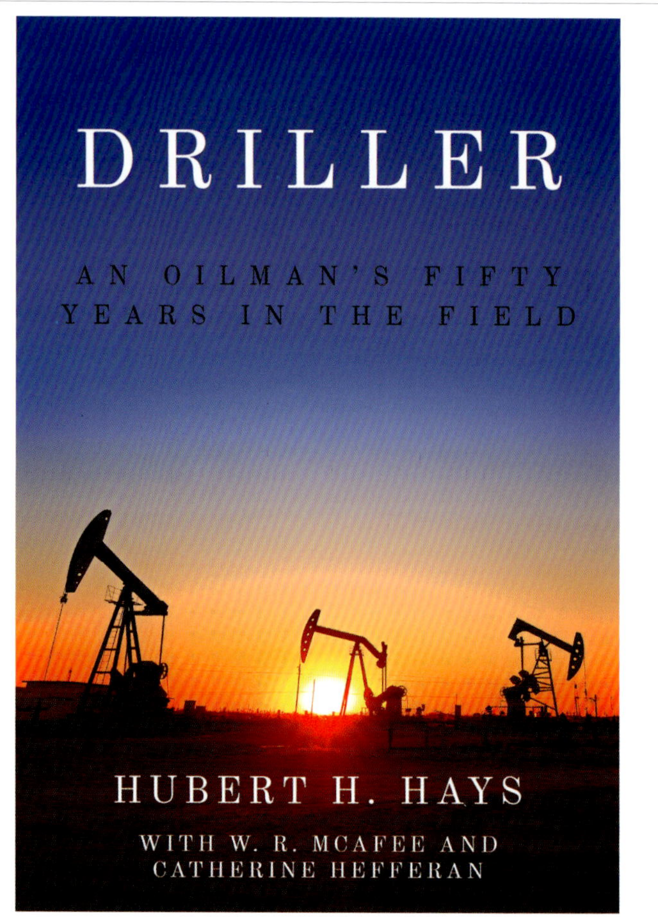

Title: Driller | **Client:** Self-initiated
Design Firm: Texas Tech University Press

ANNA JORDAN

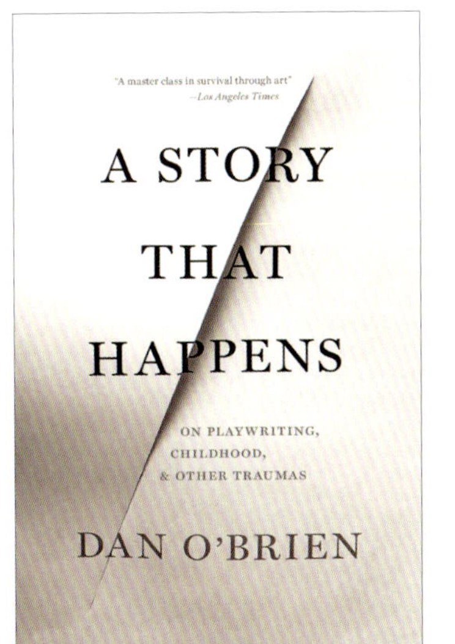

Title: A Story That Happens: On Playwriting, Childhood, and Other Traumas | **Client:** Dalkey Archive Press | **Design Firm:** Anna Jordan

JEFF MILLER, PAUL NIELSEN

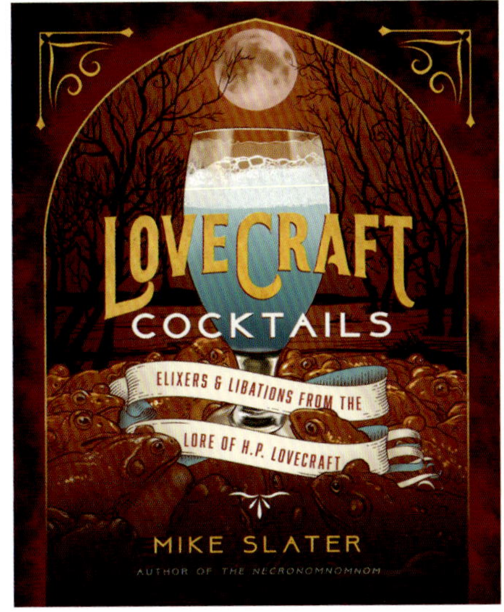

Title: Lovecraft Cocktails: Elixirs & Libations from the Lore of H. P. Lovecraft | **Client:** Countryman Press | **Design Firm:** Faceout Studio

AMANDA HUDSON

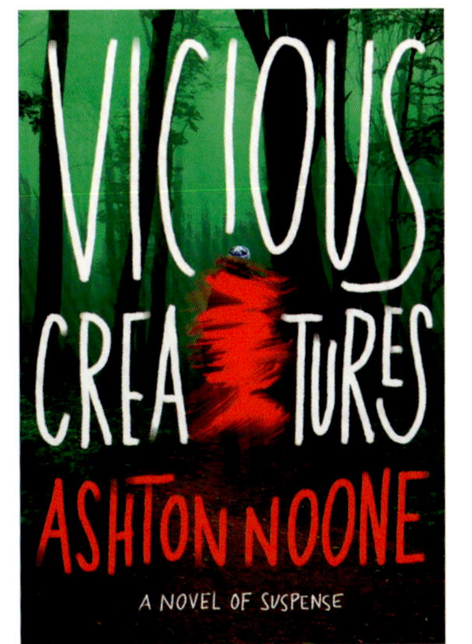

Title: Vicious Creatures
Client: Scarlet Publishing
Design Firm: Faceout Studio

HANNAH GASKAMP

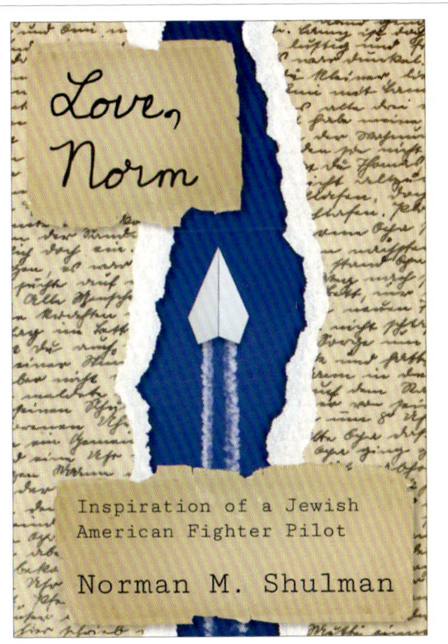

Title: Love, Norm | **Client:** Self-initiated
Design Firm: Texas Tech University Press

TIM GREEN

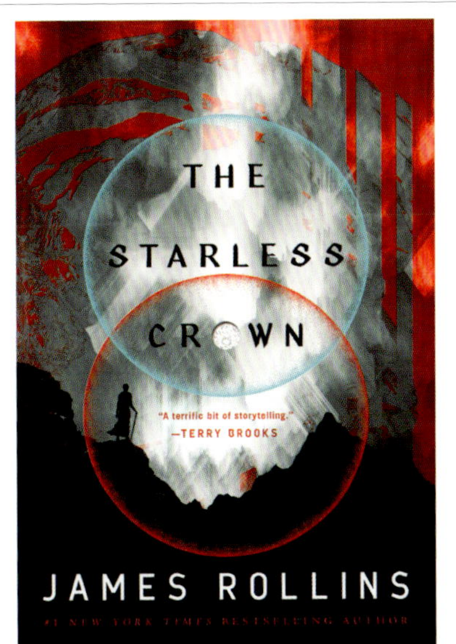

Title: The Starless Crown | **Client:** Tor Books
Design Firm: Faceout Studio

ALBAN FISCHER

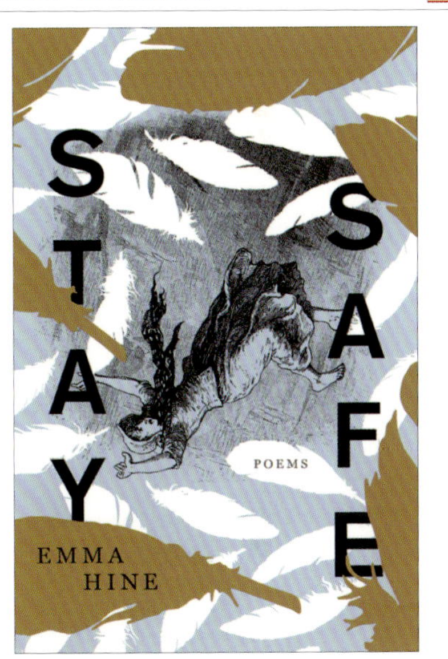

Title: Stay Safe | **Client:** Sarabande Books
Design Firm: Alban Fischer Design

RICHARD LJOENES DESIGN LLC

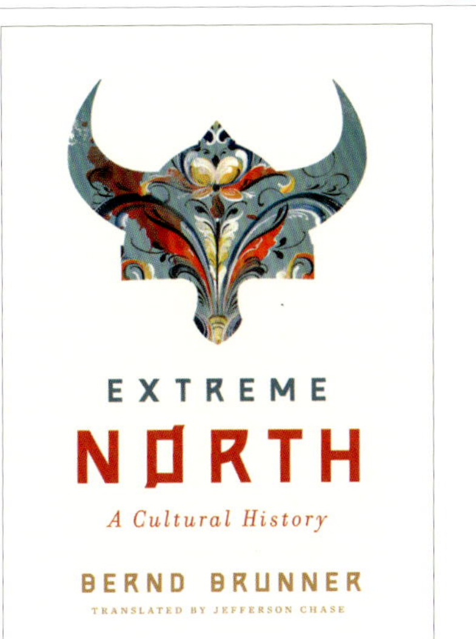

Title: Extreme North
Client: W. W. Norton
Design Firm: Richard Ljoenes Design LLC

HANNAH GASKAMP

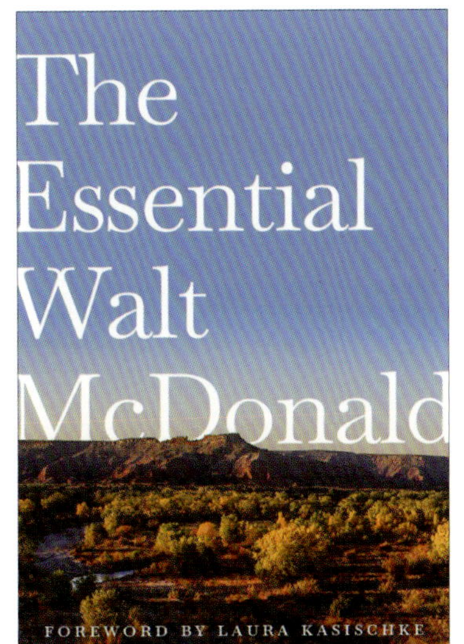

Title: The Essential Walt McDonald
Client: Self-initiated
Design Firm: Texas Tech University Press

RICHARD LJOENES DESIGN LLC

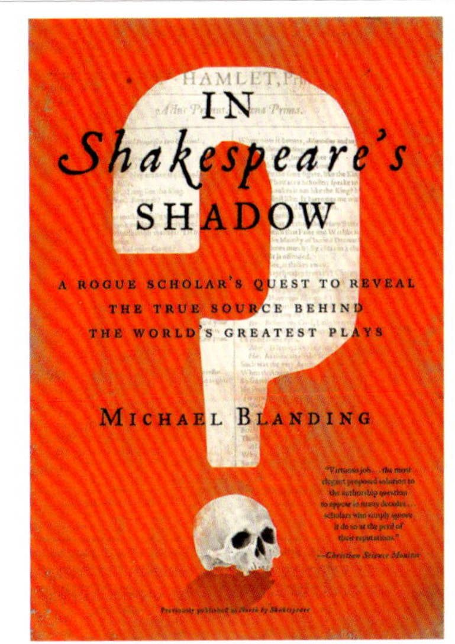

Title: In Shakespeare's Shadow
Client: Hachette Books
Design Firm: Richard Ljoenes Design LLC

JORGE ARAÚJO, ANA MOTA

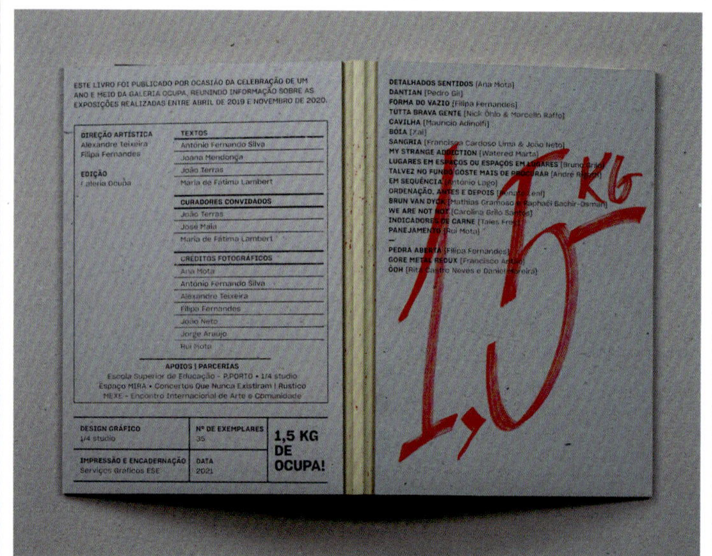

Title: 1.5 Kg de Ocupa! | **Client:** Galeria Ocupa!
Design Firm: 1/4 Studio

UNDERLINE STUDIO

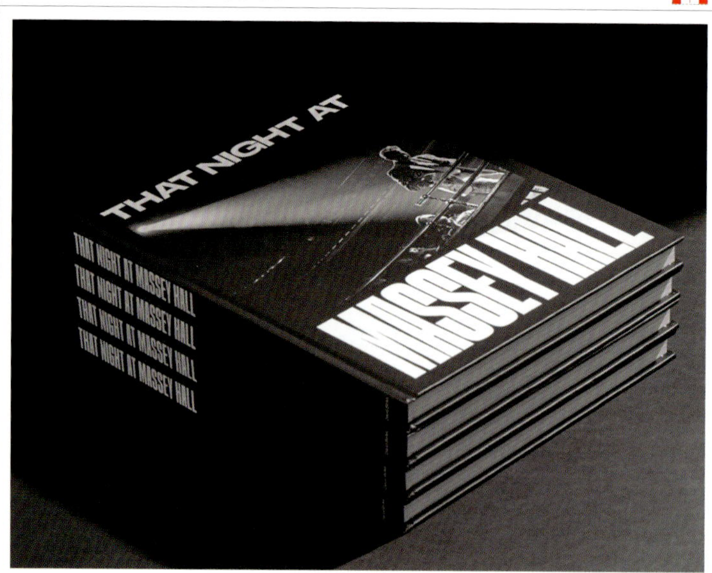

Title: That Night at Massey Hall | **Client:** David Binks
Design Firm: Underline Studio

MICHAEL ARNDT

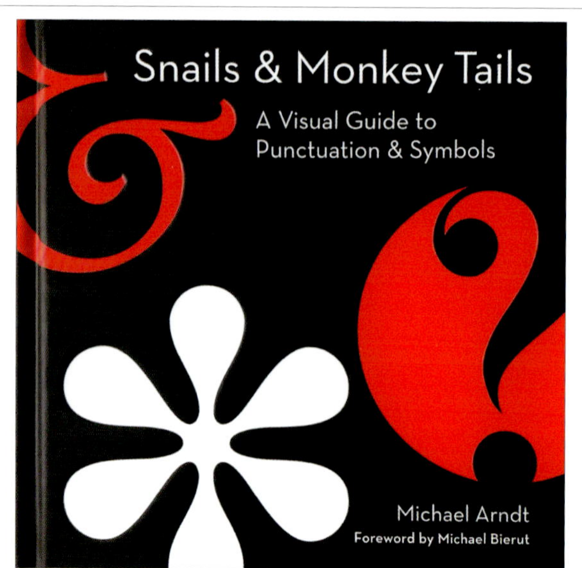

Title: Snails & Monkey Tails: A Visual Guide to Punctuation & Symbols
Client: Harper Design | **Design Firm:** M Books

HONG KA LOK

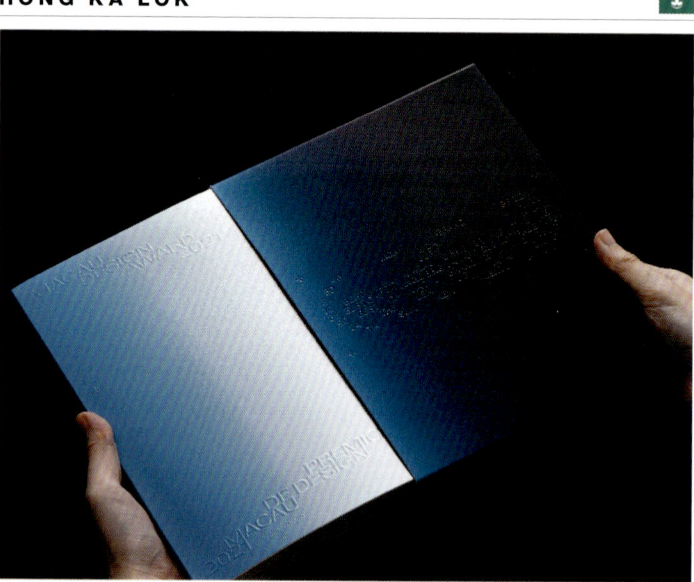

Title: Macau Design Award 2021 | **Client:** Macau Designers Association
Design Firm: Loksophy Design Ltd.

JESSICA FLEISCHMANN

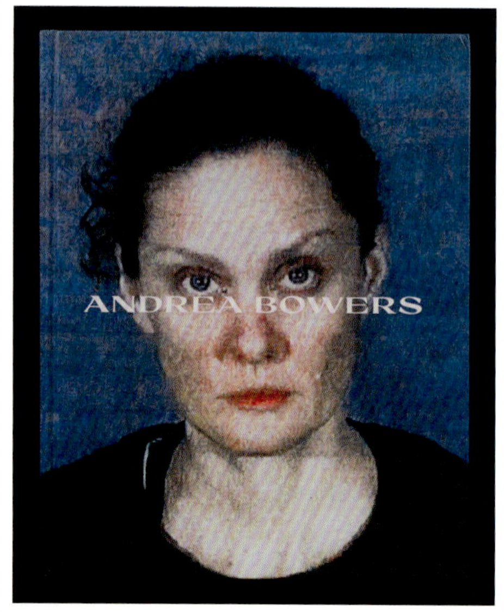

Title: Andrea Bowers | **Client:** MCA Chicago
Design Firm: Still Room

TIM GREEN, PAUL NIELSEN

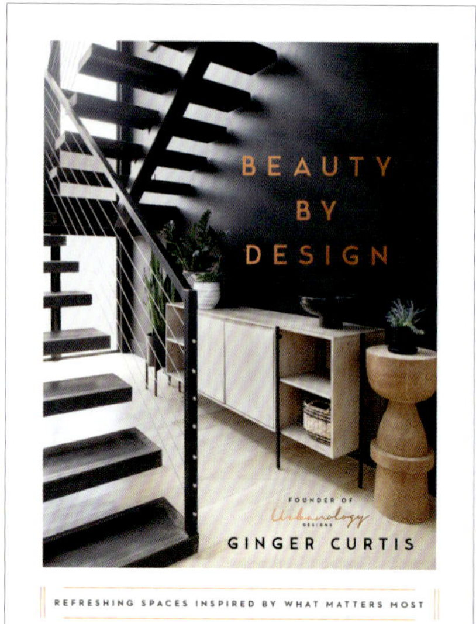

Title: Beauty By Design | **Client:** Ten Peaks Press
Design Firm: Faceout Studio

RANDY CLARK

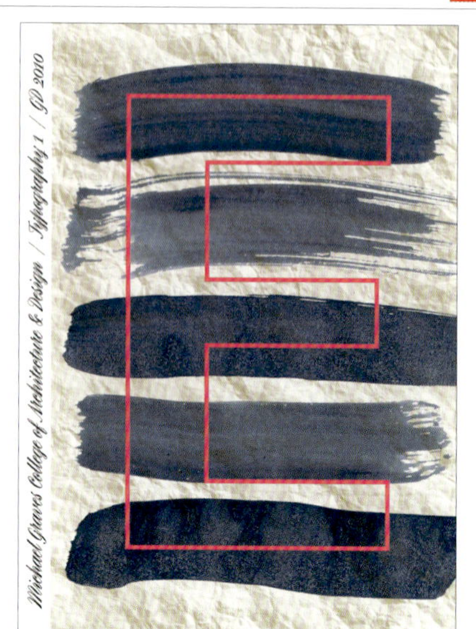

Title: Stripe E | **Client:** Wenzhou-Kean University
Design Firm: Randy Clark

MOLLY VON BORSTEL

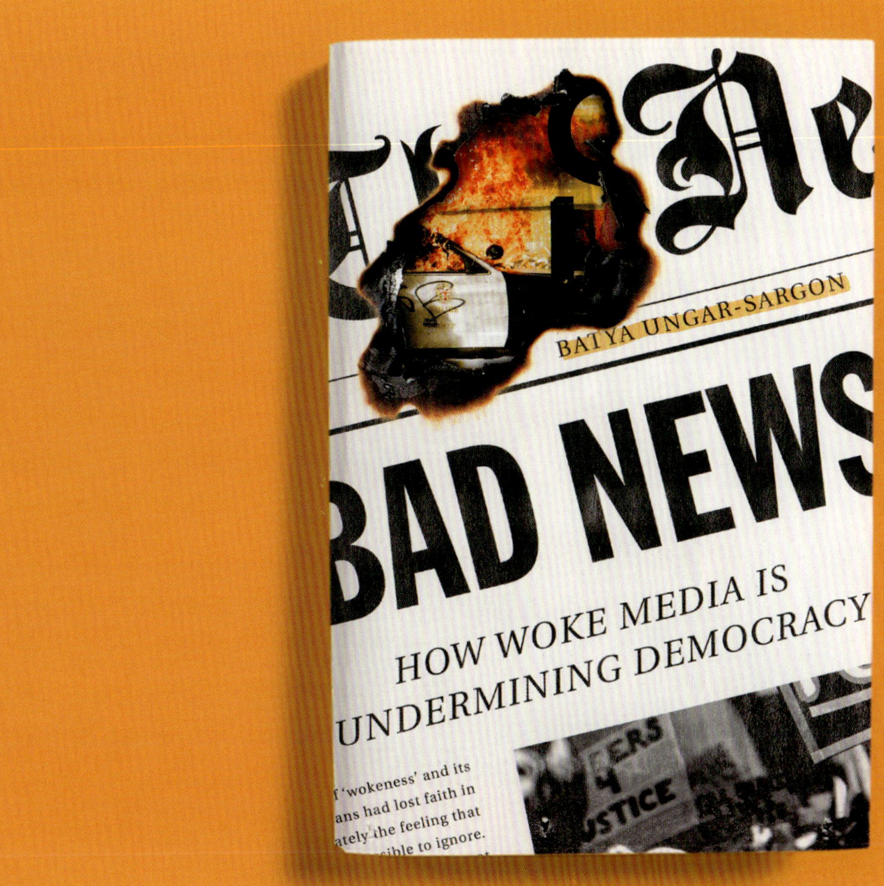

Title: Bad News | **Client:** Encounter Books | **Design Firm:** Faceout Studio

ALEX KALMAN, DEBBIE MILLMAN

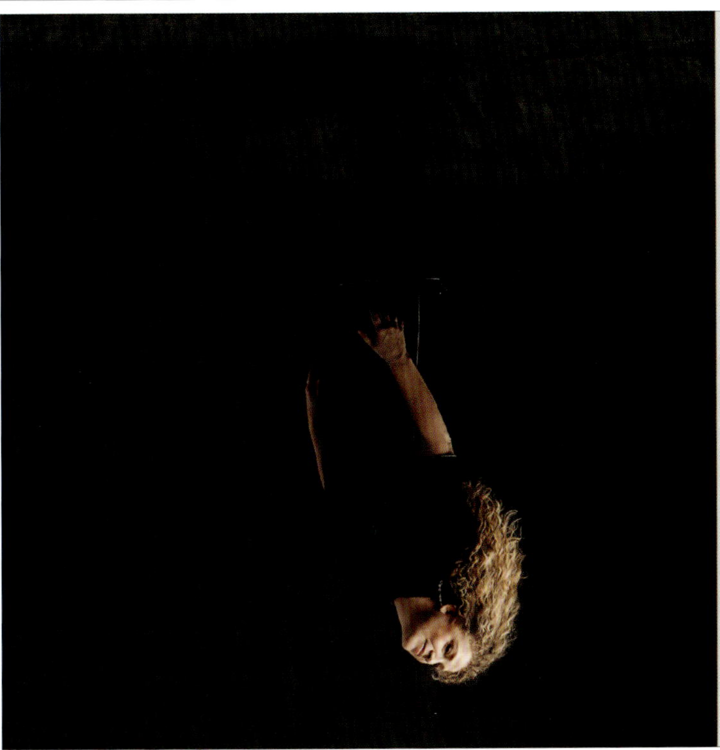

April 19, 2013

EMILY

Chances are you've seen Emily Oberman's design work.

Oberman has crafted work for *This American Life*, *Sex and the City*, and *Lucky* magazine. She's created campaigns for MTV, VH1, and HBO, and for the past two decades she's designed the title sequences for *Saturday Night Live*. Emily started her career working for the legendary designer Tibor Kalman at M&Co. and went on to co-found the firm Number 17, which closed in 2010 after a seventeen-year run. In 2012, shortly before we conducted this interview, Oberman became a partner at Pentagram, the global mega-design firm, working alongside Paula Scher and Michael Bierut.

OBERMAN

Title: Why Design Matters: Conversations with the World's Most Creative People | **Client:** Harper Collins | **Design Firm:** What Studio

NEXUS DESIGNS

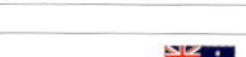

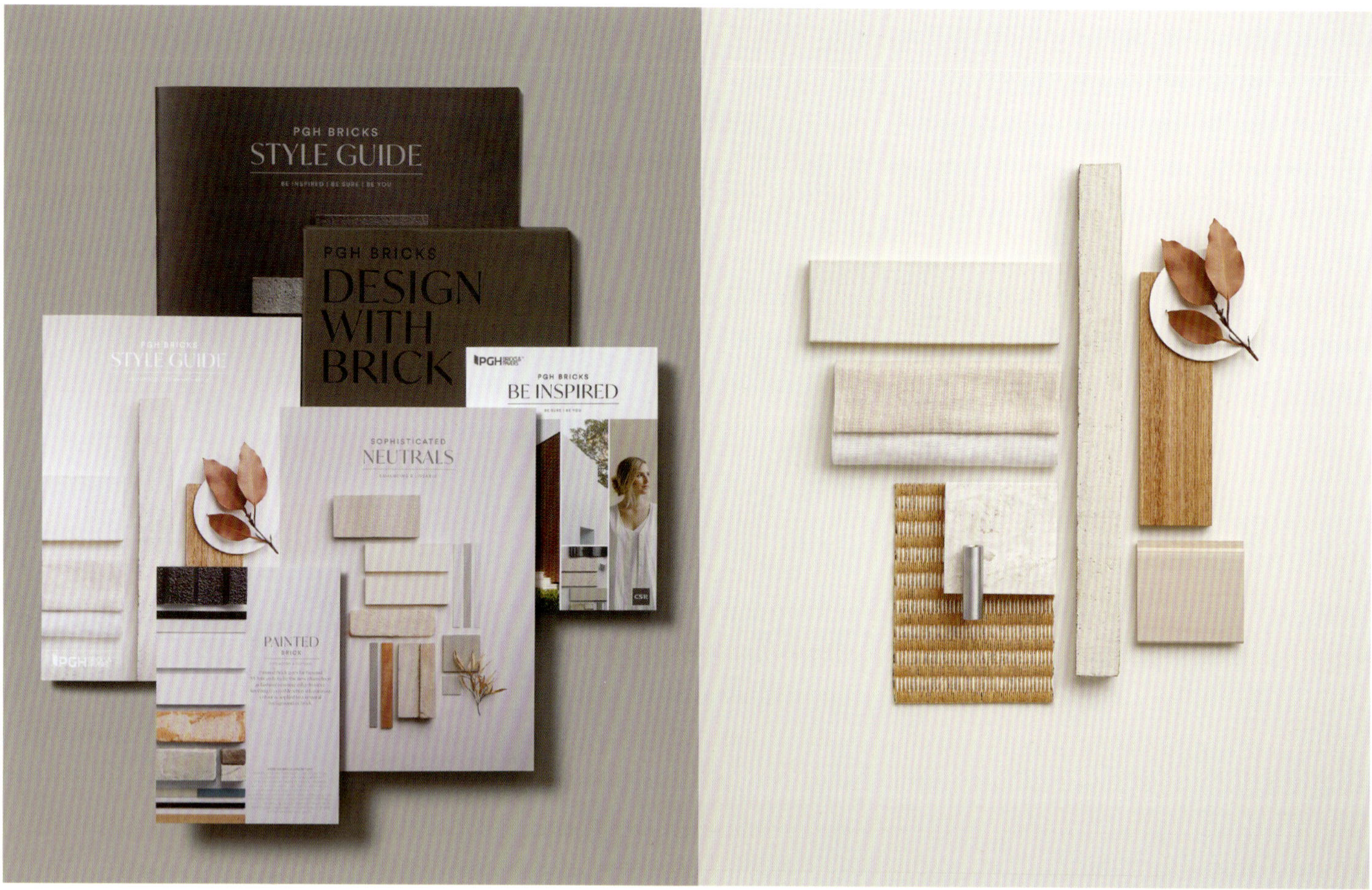

Title: PGH Style Guide Campaign | Client: PGH Bricks & Pavers | Design Firm: Nexus Designs

LOREN SCHOTT

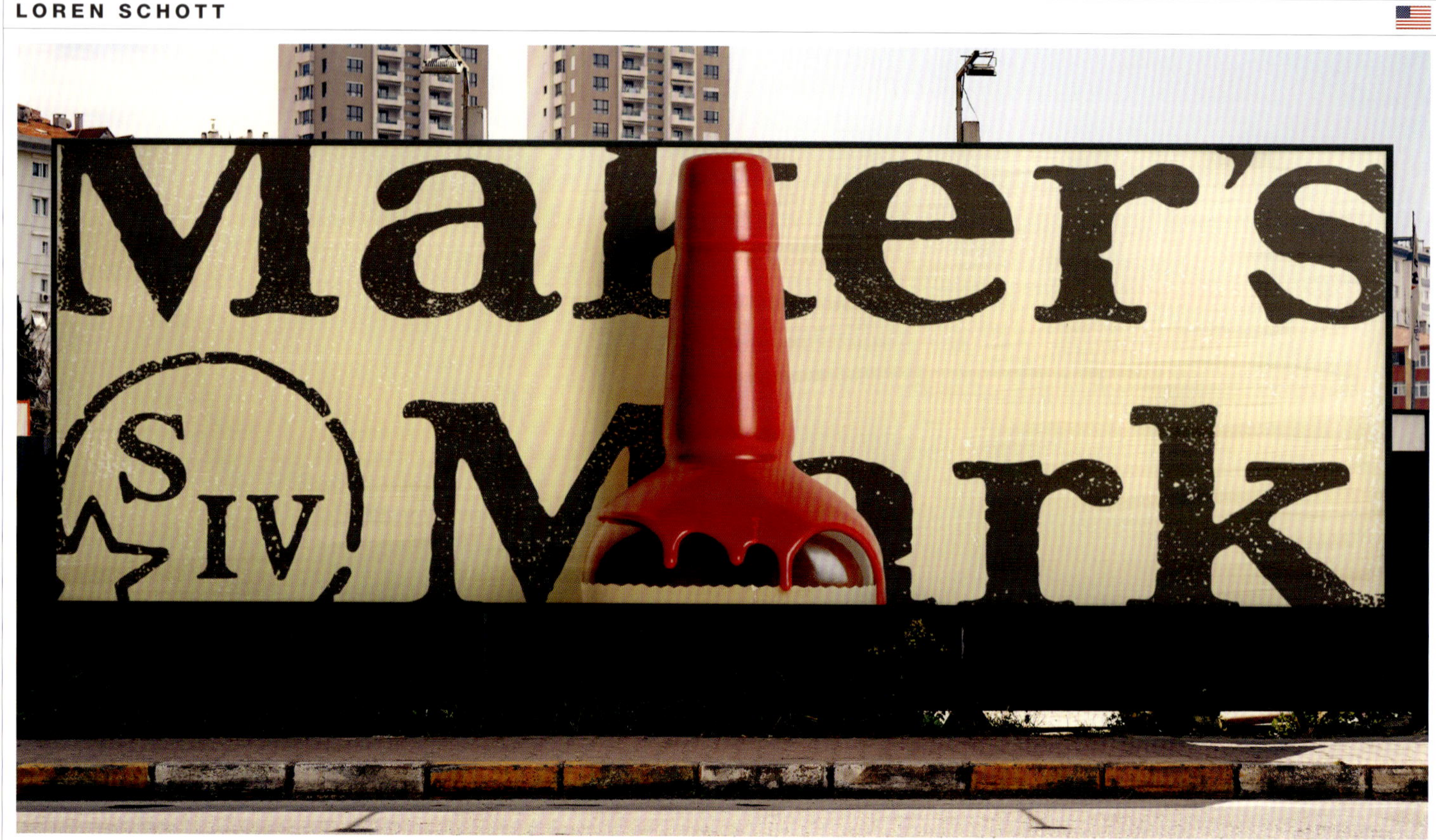

Title: Maker's Mark Visual Identity | Client: Maker's Mark | Design Firm: Turner Duckworth: London, San Francisco & New York

LAFAYETTE AMERICAN

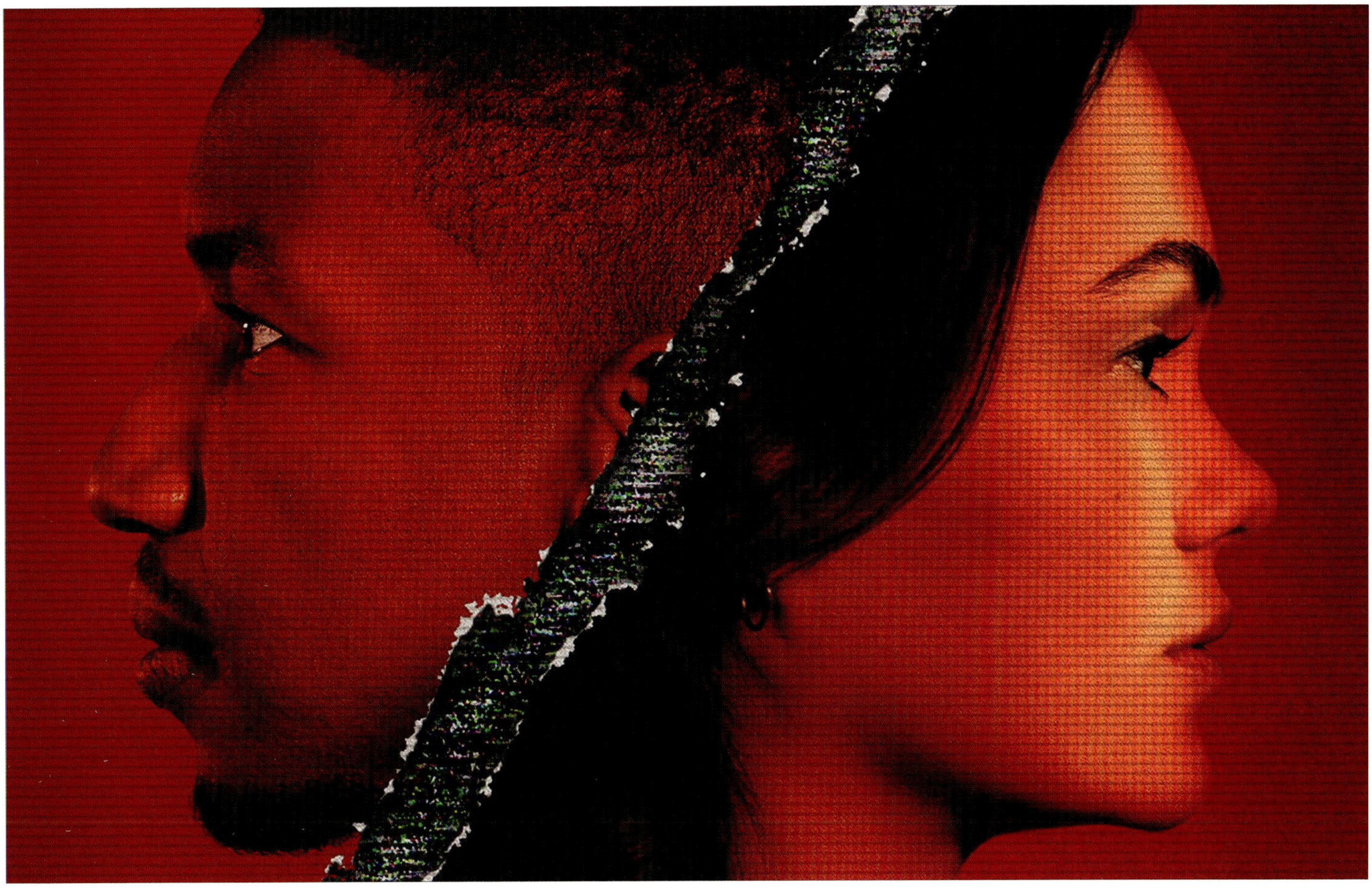

Title: Archive 81 | **Client:** Netflix | **Design Firm:** Lafayette American

BRENDÁN MURPHY

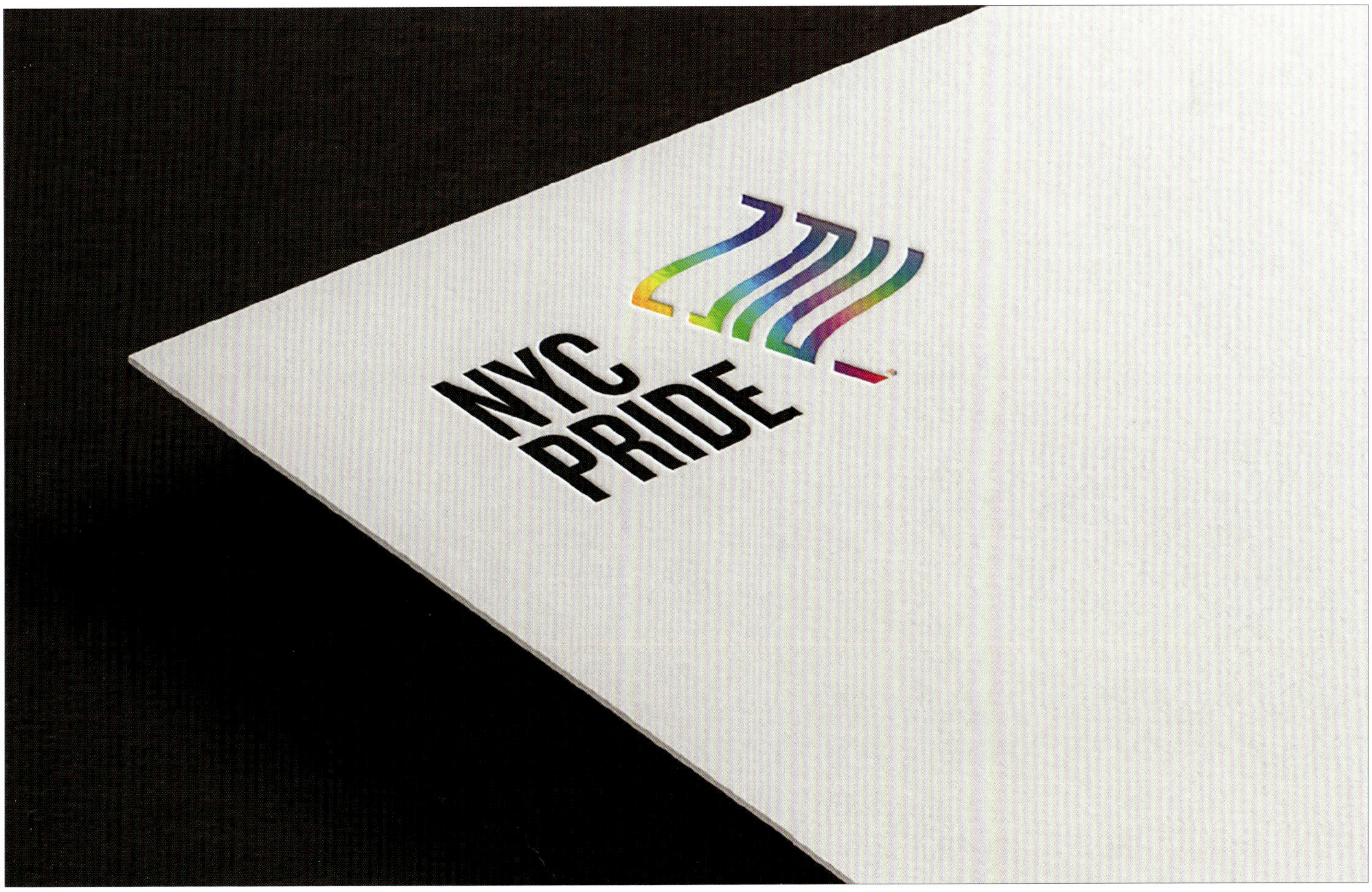

Title: Celebrating Pride with an Inclusive Brand Identity | **Client:** Heritage of Pride | **Design Firm:** Lippincott

LAFAYETTE AMERICAN

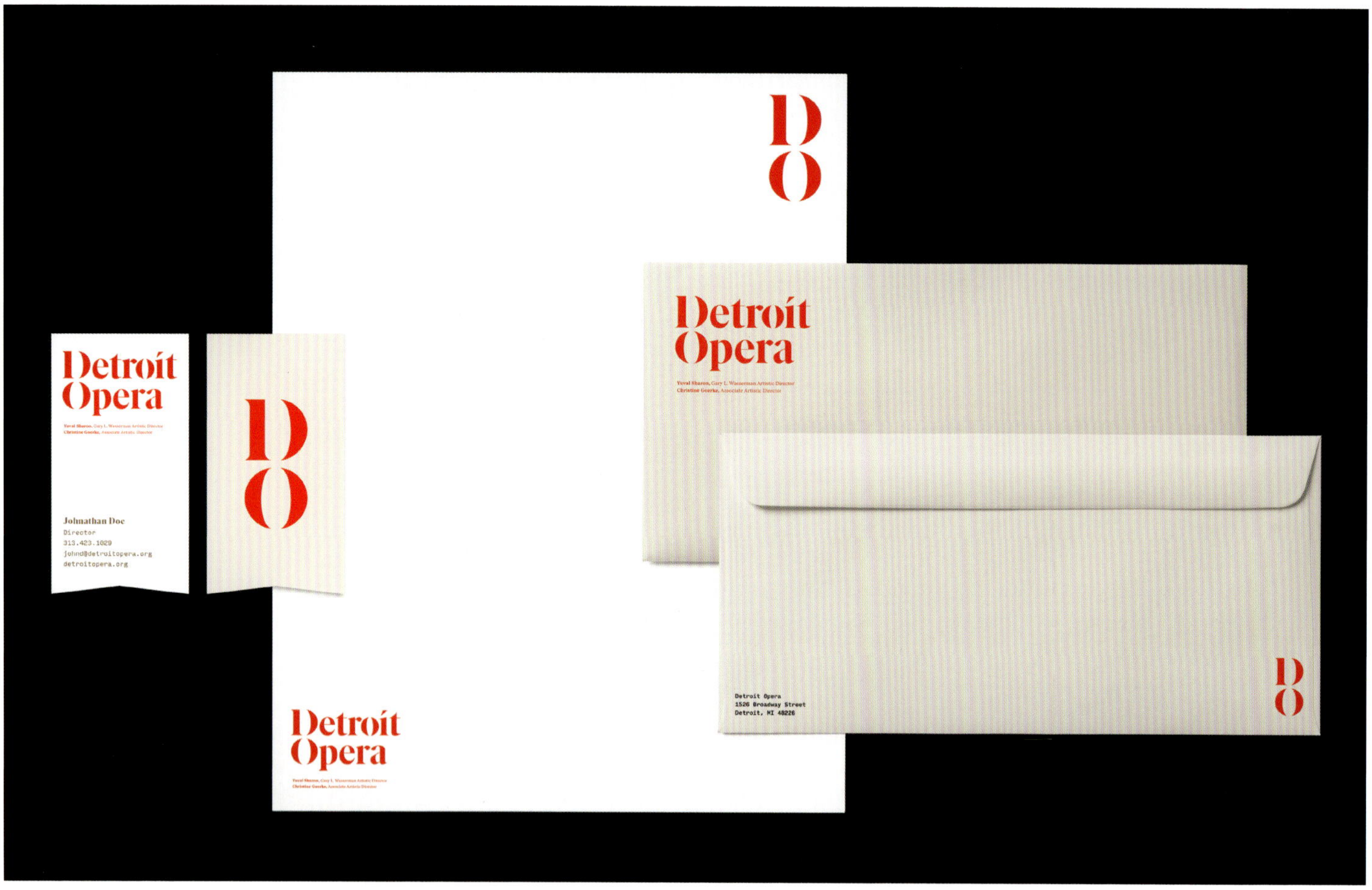

Title: Detroit Opera | **Client:** Detroit Opera | **Design Firm:** Lafayette American

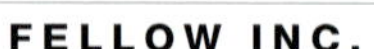

FELLOW INC.

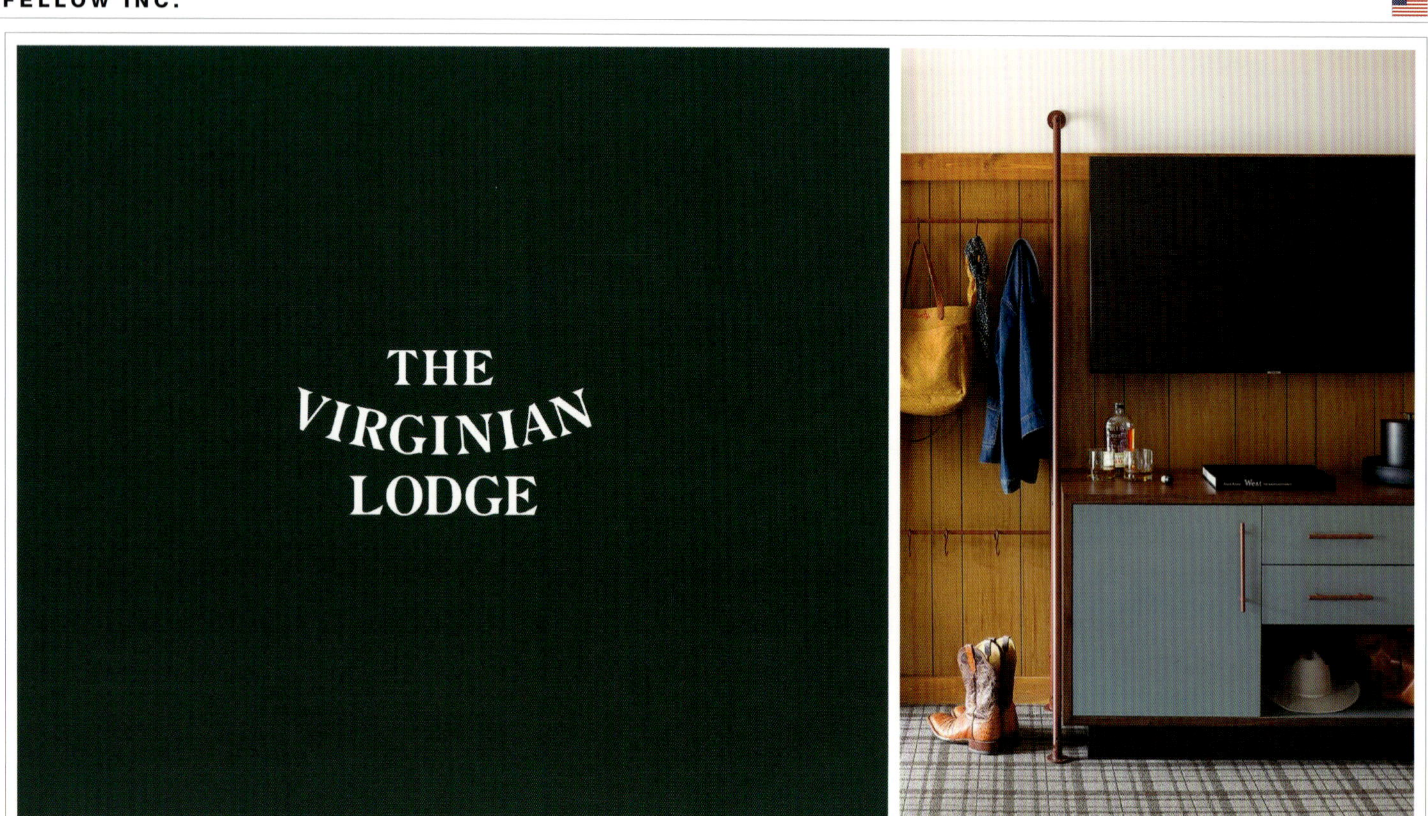

Title: The Virginian Lodge Brand Refresh | **Client:** Outbound | **Design Firm:** Fellow Inc.

ANDREA CASTELLETTI

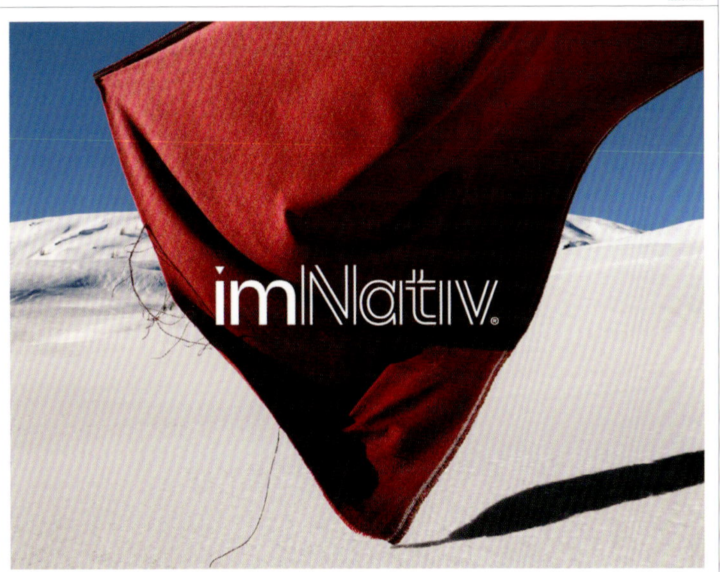

Title: imNativ. Born for Nature. | **Client:** Aurim
Design Firm: Andrea Castelletti Studio

COASTLINES

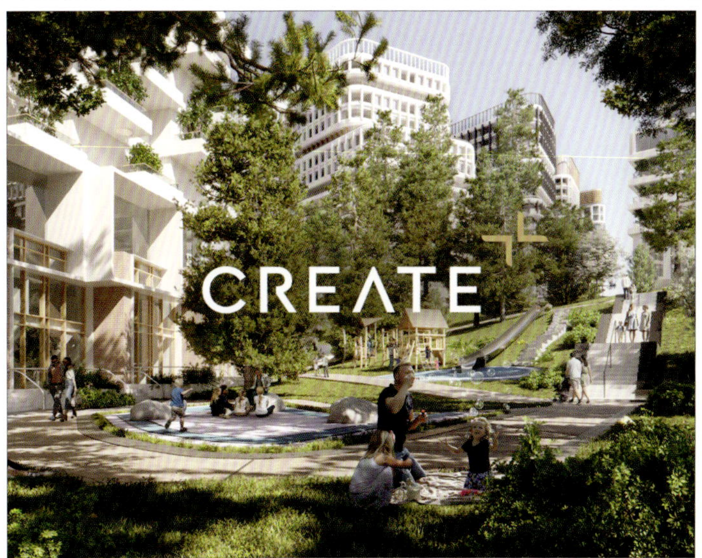

Title: Create Properties Rebrand | **Client:** Create Properties
Design Firm: Coastlines Creative Group

JANG WON LEE

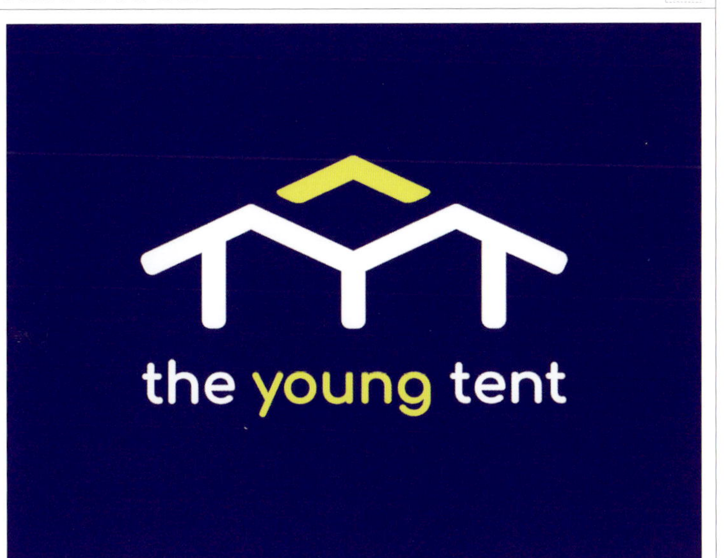

Title: The Young Tent: Brand Identity Design | **Client:** The Young Tent
Design Firm: Jang Won Lee

NATASHA MOZZ

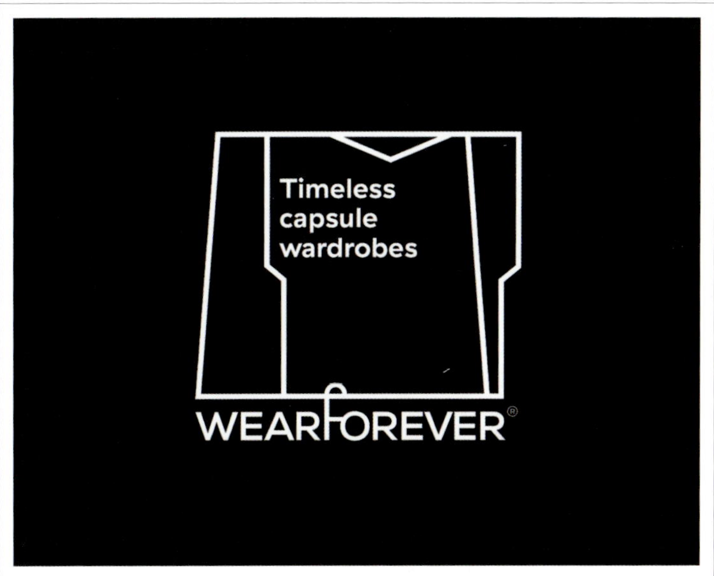

Title: WearForever Brand Identity | **Client:** WearForever
Design Firm: Natasha Mozz

UNIVISUAL

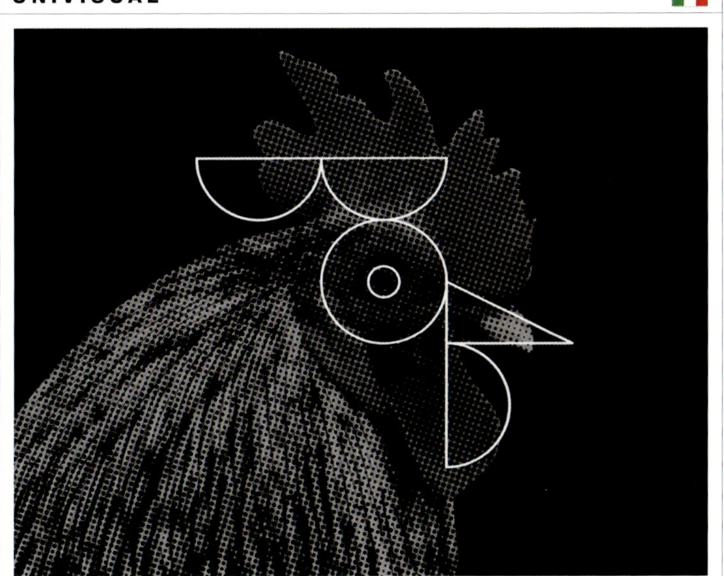

Title: The Awakening of Communication
Client: MAX GALLI Comminication | **Design Firm:** Univisual

CONJURE

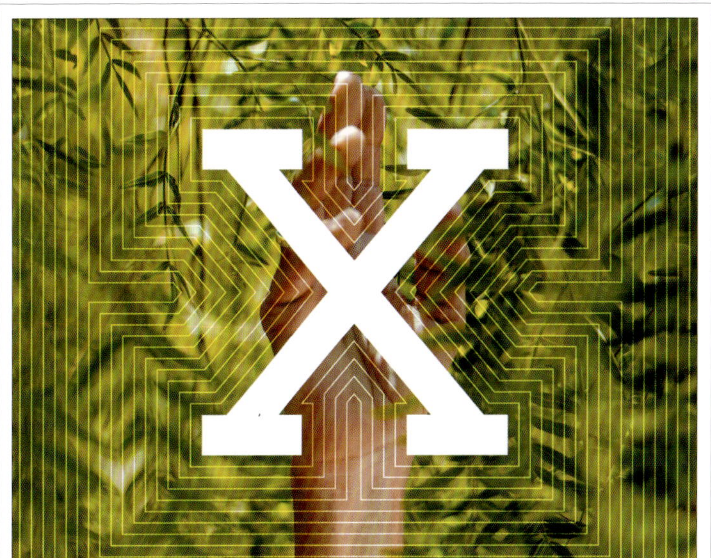

Title: X Campaign | **Client:** U.S. Steel
Design Firm: Conjure

NATE KILLAM

Title: Encompass Brush | **Client:** Ryca
Design Firm: Cue

GOODS & SERVICES

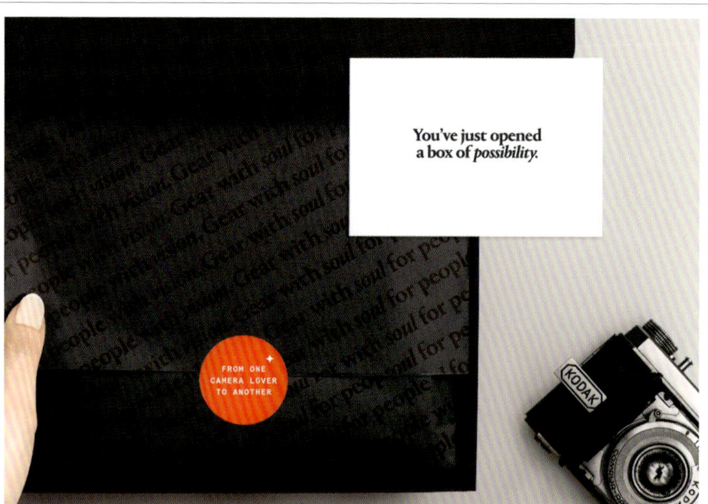

Title: KEH Camera | **Client:** KEH Camera
Design Firm: Goods & Services

MICHAEL D'ESOPO

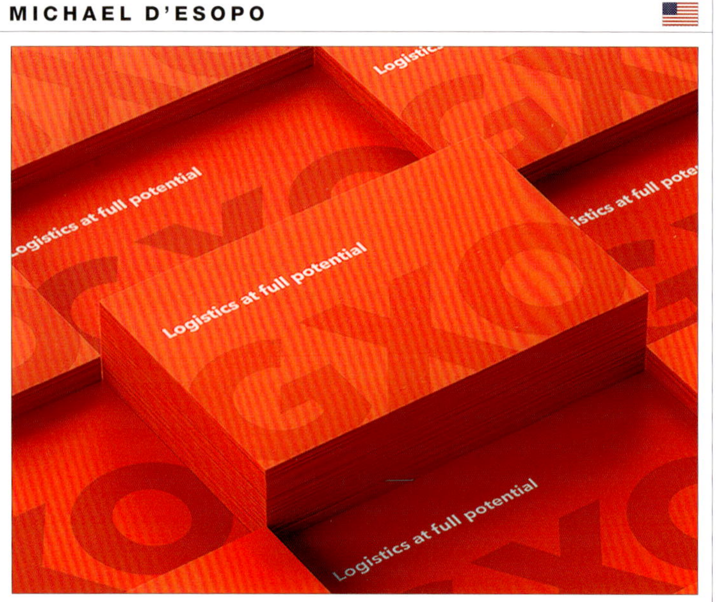

Title: Launching a Global Leader in Logistics | **Client:** GXO
Design Firm: Lippincott

RYO SHIMIZU

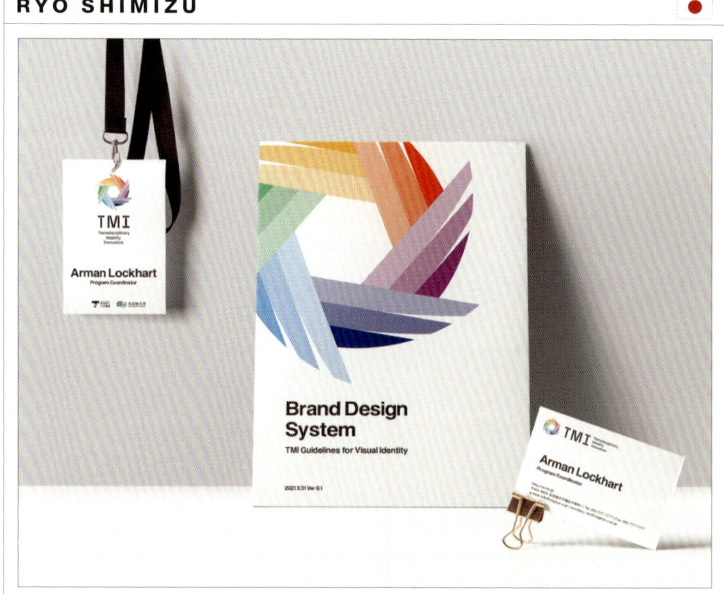

Title: TMI | **Client:** TMI-Nagoya University
Design Firm: Balloon Inc.

HEART HAUS AT CVS HEALTH

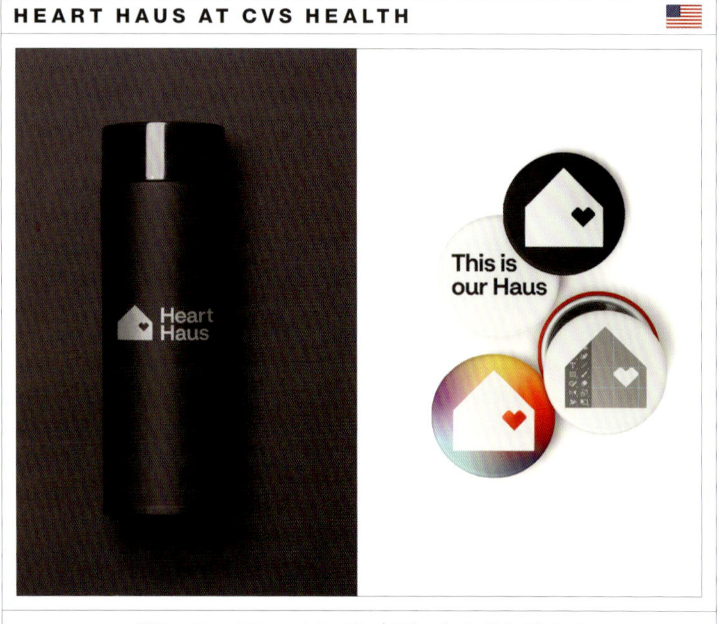

Title: Heart Haus Identity | **Client:** Self-initiated
Design Firm: Heart Haus at CVS Health

SHARON LLOYD MCLAUGHLIN

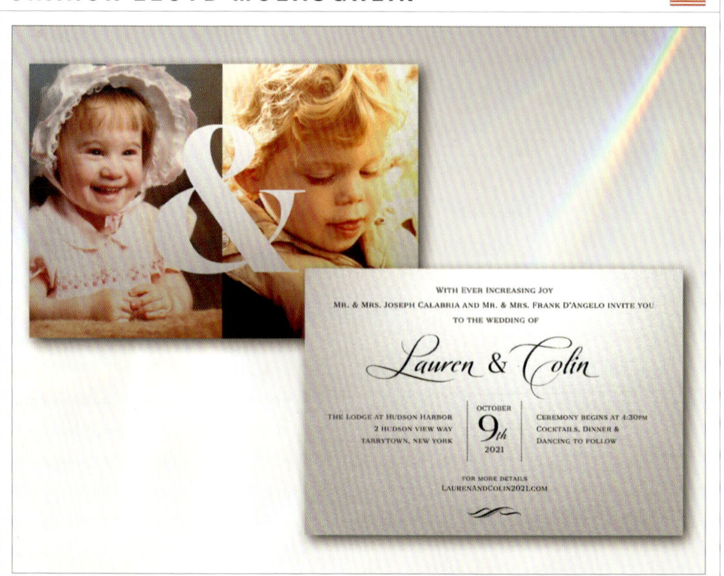

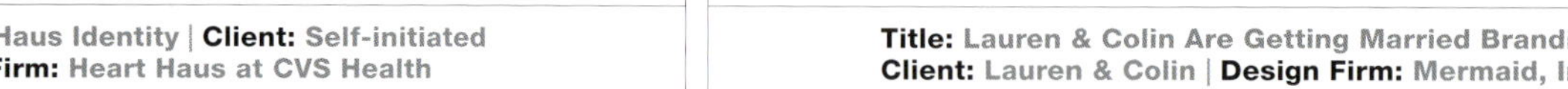

Title: Lauren & Colin Are Getting Married Branding
Client: Lauren & Colin | **Design Firm:** Mermaid, Inc.

HONG KA LOK

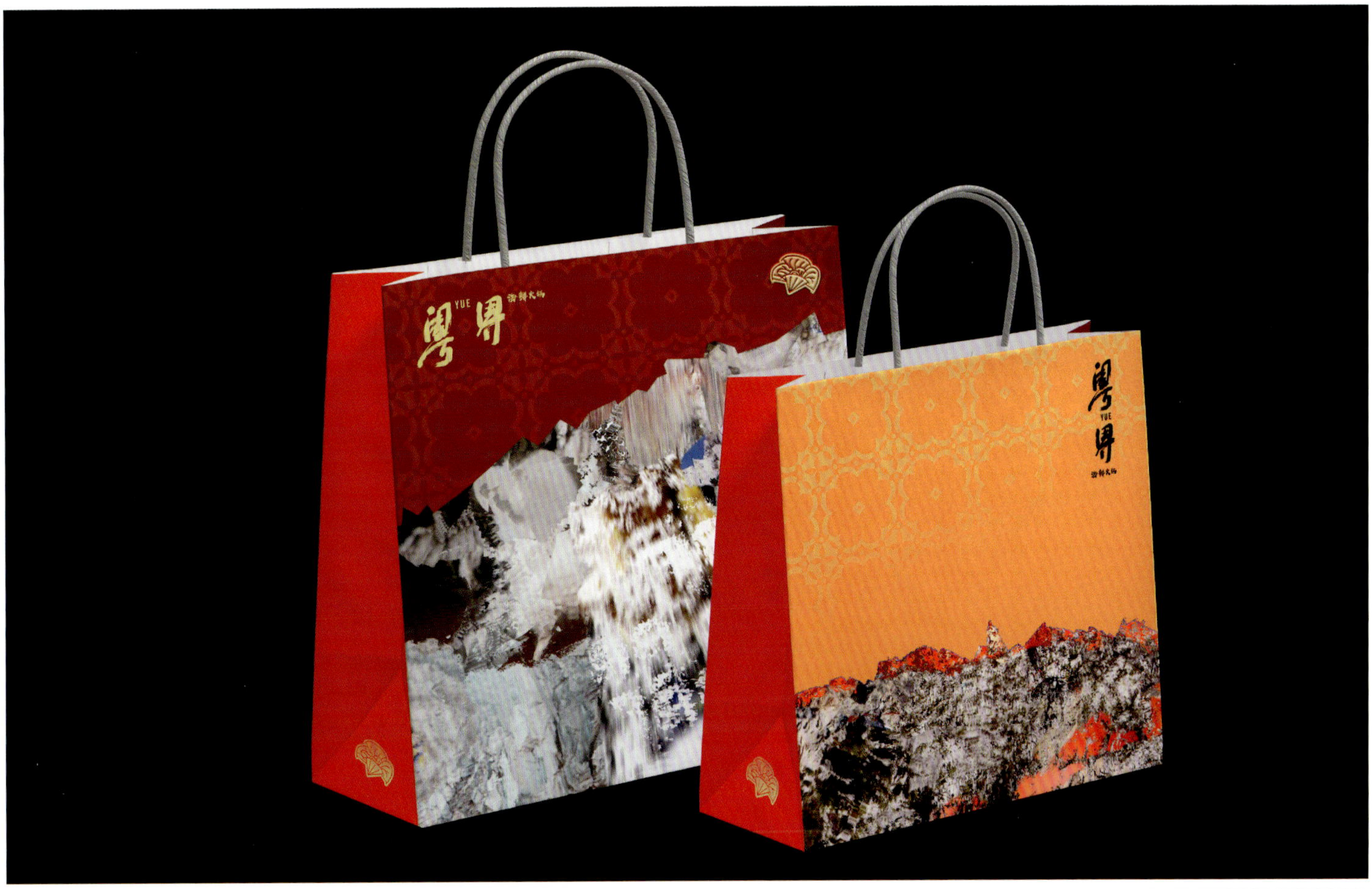

Title: Yue | Client: Yue - Beijing | Design Firm: Loksophy Design Ltd.

JEFF BARFOOT

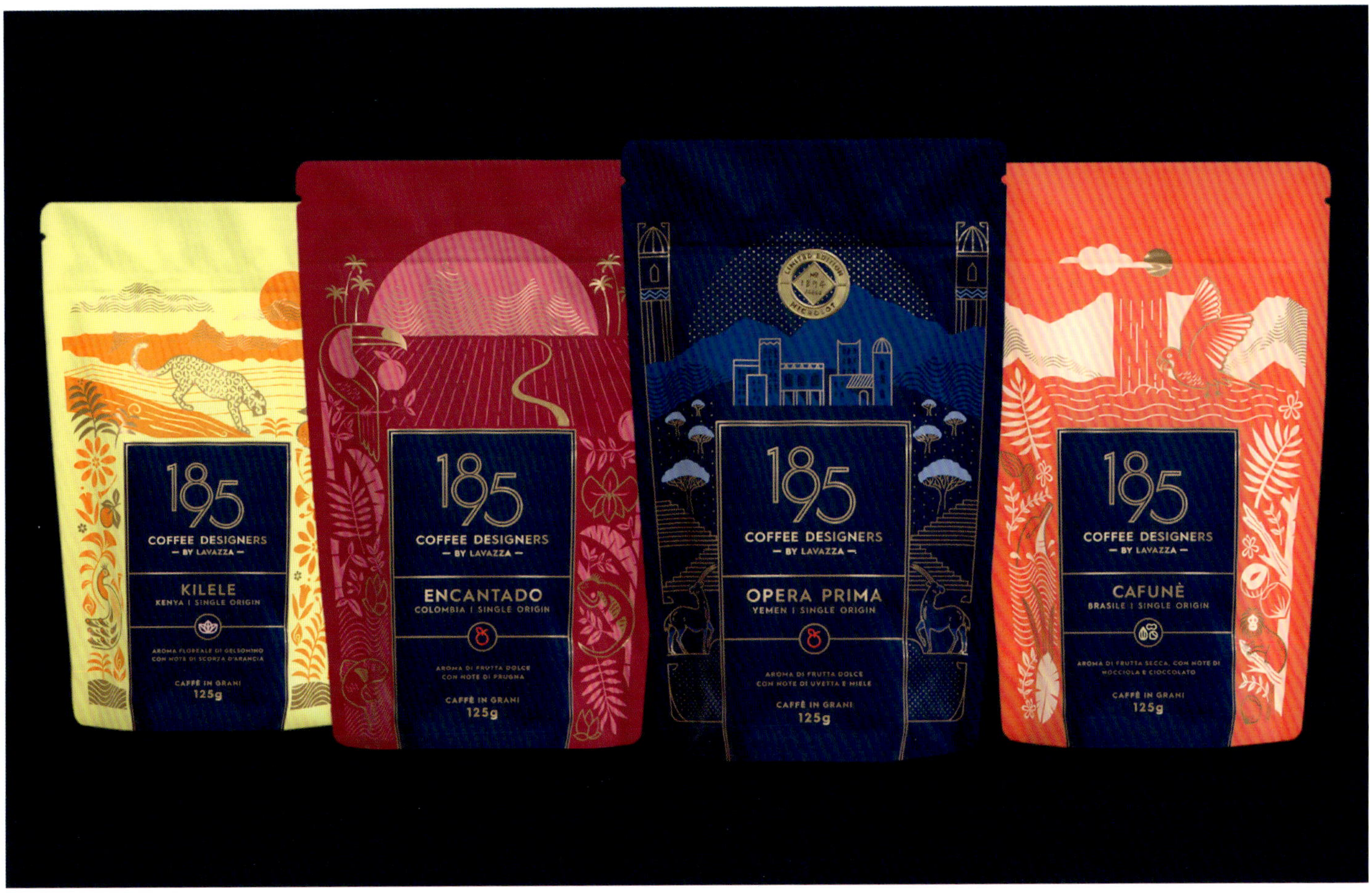

Title: 1895 by Lavazza Identity | Client: Lavazza | Design Firm: *TraceElement

SIREN SF

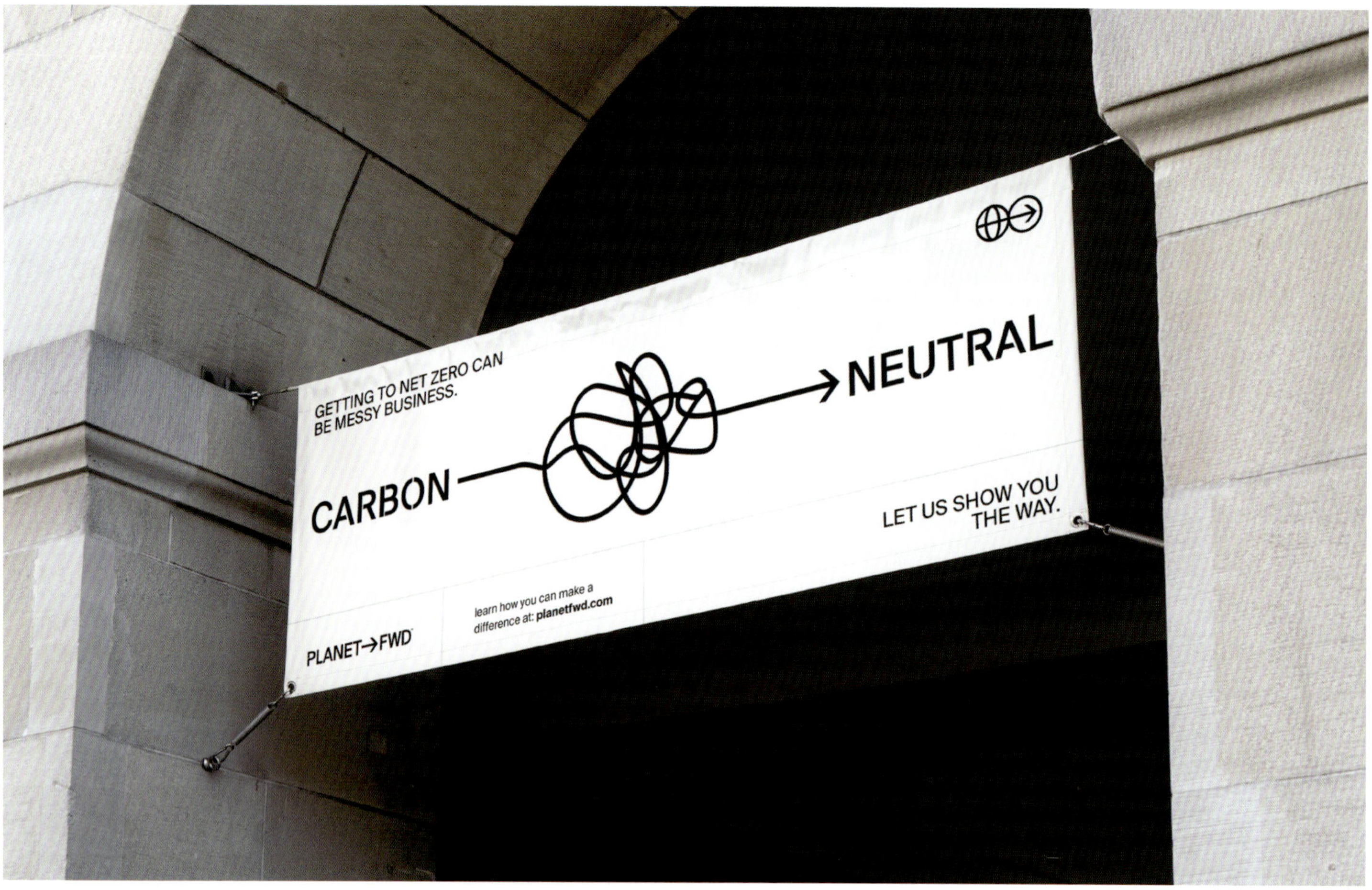

Title: Planet FWD Brand | **Client:** Planet FWD | **Design Firm:** SIREN SF

COMPASS DESIGN STUDIO

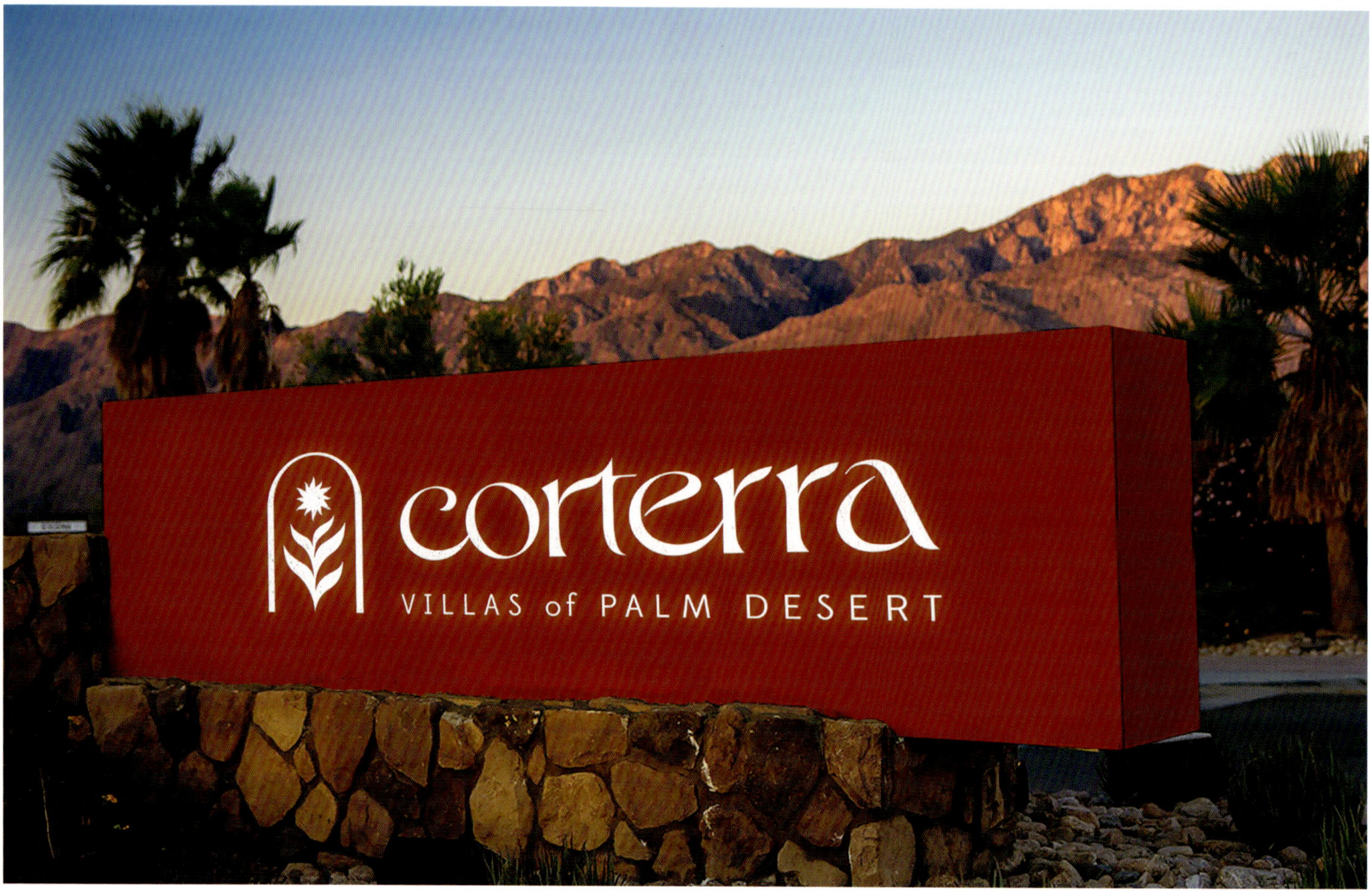

Title: Corterra Property Branding | **Client:** Corterra | **Design Firm:** Compass

SUZY SIMMONS, GABY QUINTANA

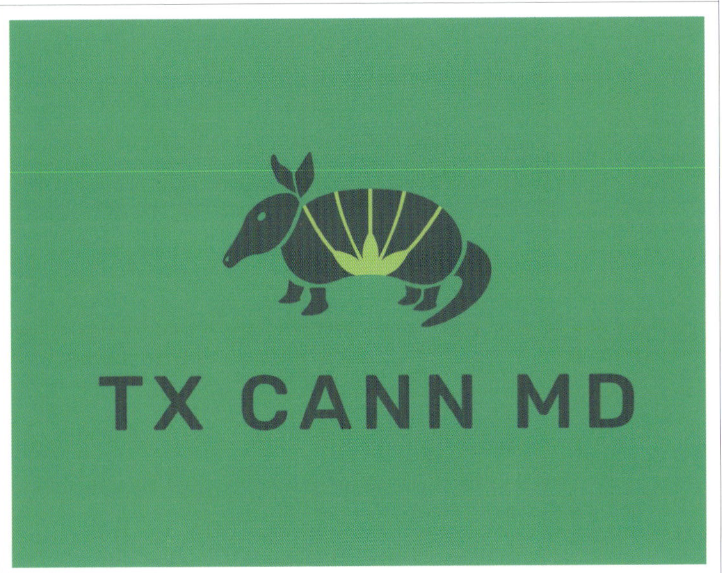

Title: TX Cann MD Brand Identity | **Client:** TX Cann MD
Design Firm: Test Monki

D. GONSALVES, D. AL-SALEH, N. VON OERTZEN

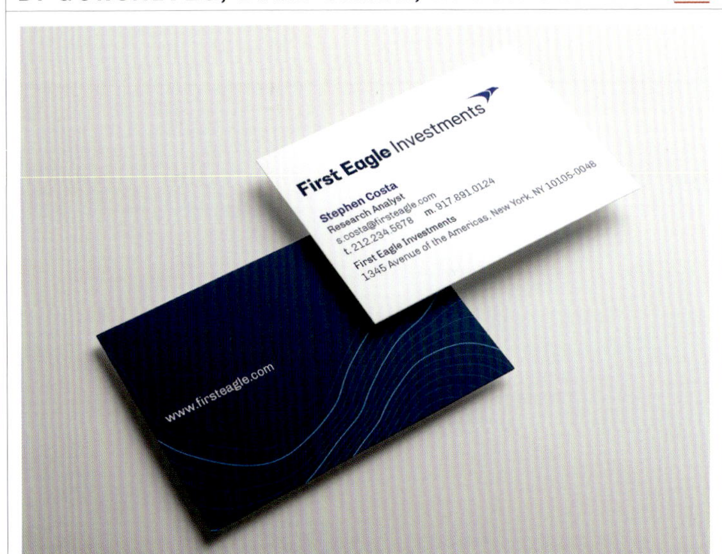

Title: First Eagle Investments | **Client:** First Eagle Investments
Design Firm: Sequel Studio

SHARON LLOYD MCLAUGHLIN

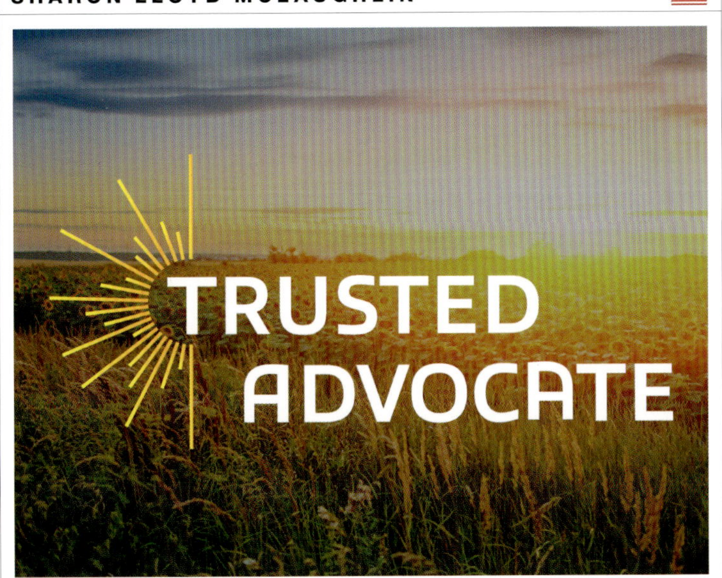

Title: Trusted Advocate Branding | **Client:** Trusted Advocate
Design Firm: Mermaid, Inc.

UNIVISUAL

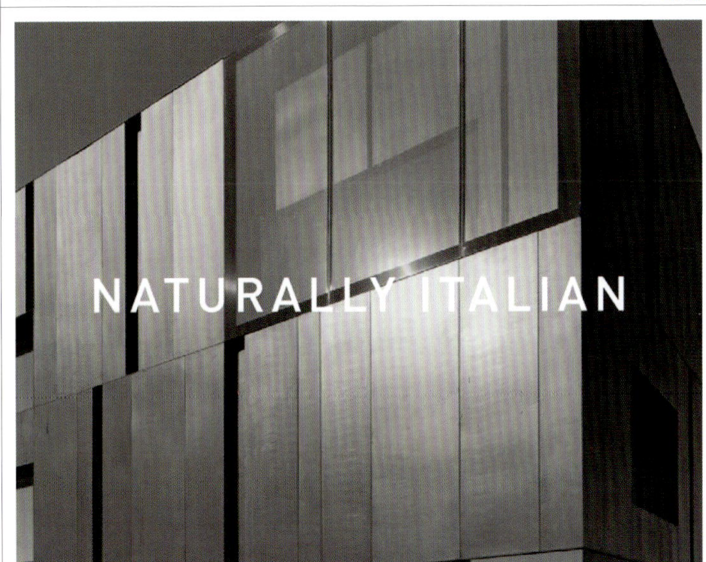

Title: Naturally Italian | **Client:** Lapitec Group
Design Firm: Univisual

GRAHAM HARVEY

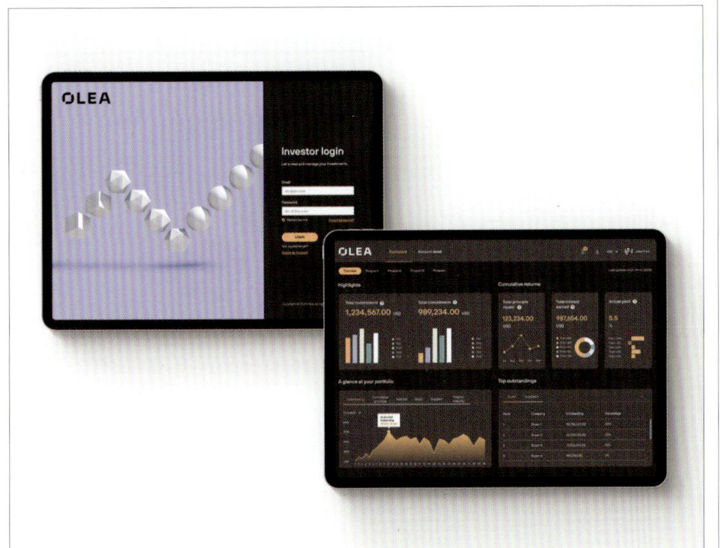

Title: Creating a Fintech Brand that Empowers Sustainable Trade
Client: Olea | **Design Firm:** Lippincott

COSTA POPOLIZIO

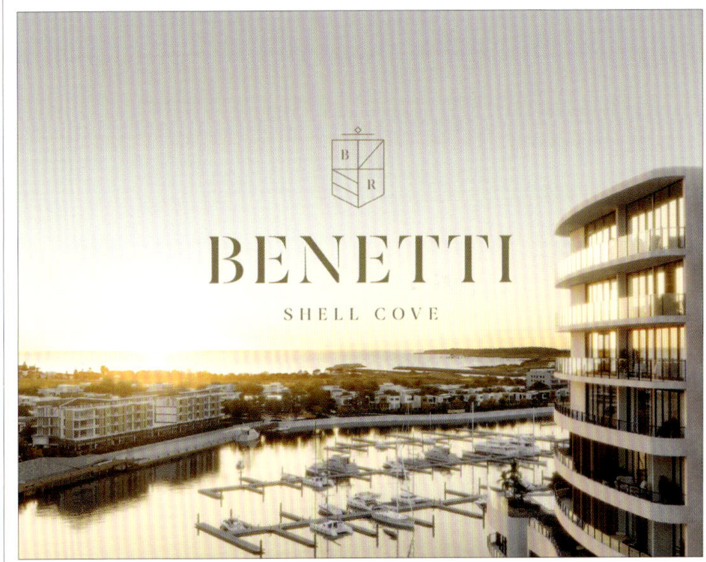

Title: Benetti Shell Cove Residential Branding
Client: Colliers and Oscars Hotels | **Design Firm:** The Property Agency

JEFF BARFOOT

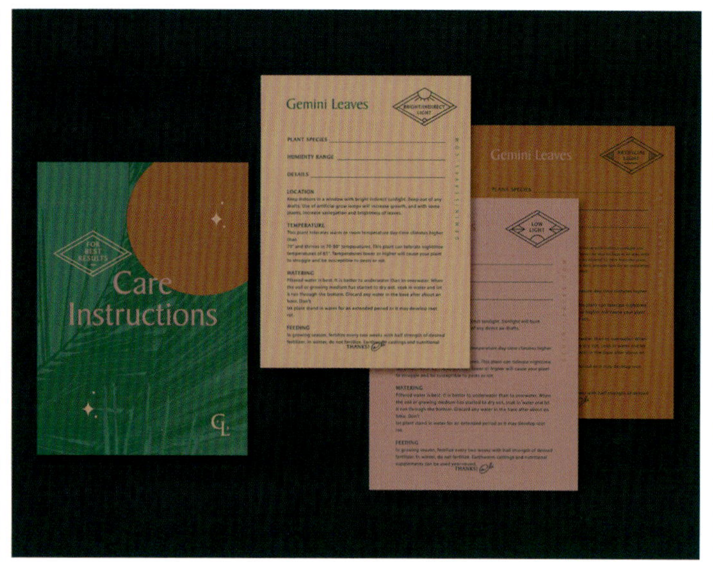

Title: Gemini Leaves Identity | **Client:** Gemini Leaves
Design Firm: *TraceElement

QIXIN WU

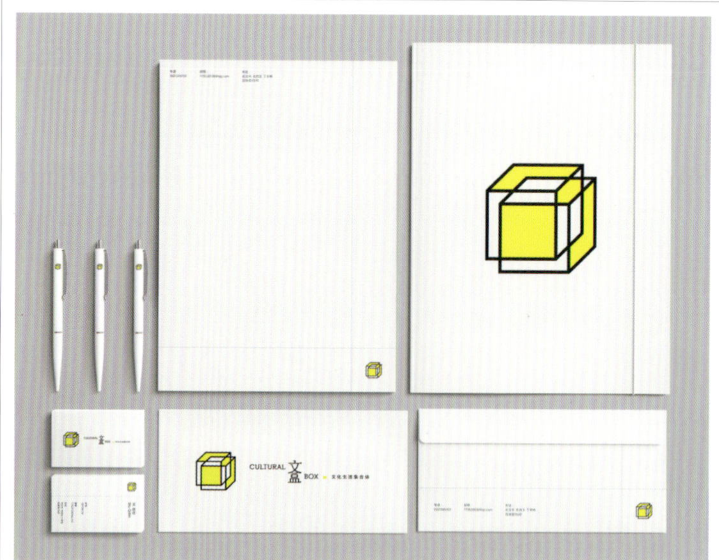

Title: CULTURAL BOX | **Client:** Cultural Box
Design Firm: Polygon

RYO SHIMIZU

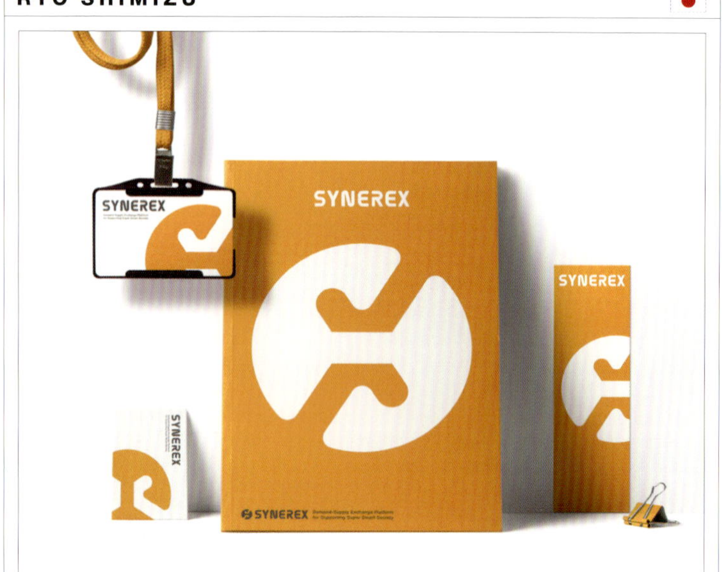

Title: Synerex | **Client:** Nagoya University - Synerex Project
Design Firm: Balloon Inc.

SUZY SIMMONS, GABY QUINTANA

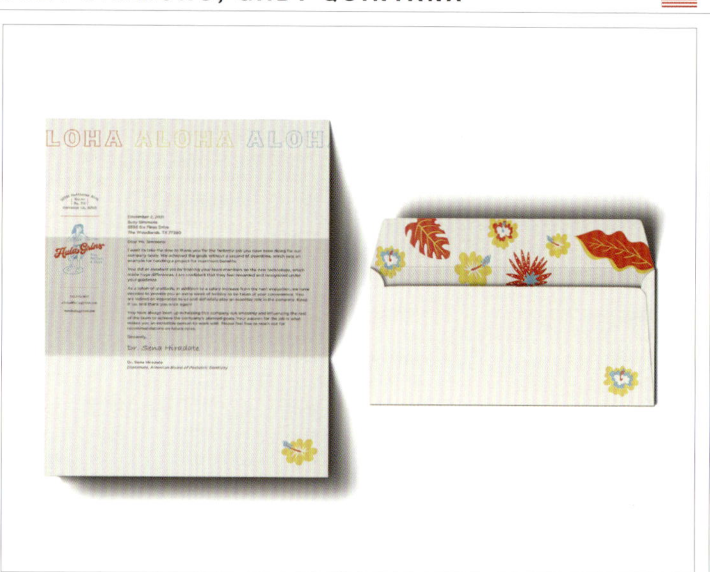

Title: HulaGrins Brand Identity | **Client:** HulaGrins Pediatric Dentistry
Design Firm: Test Monki

JEFF BARFOOT

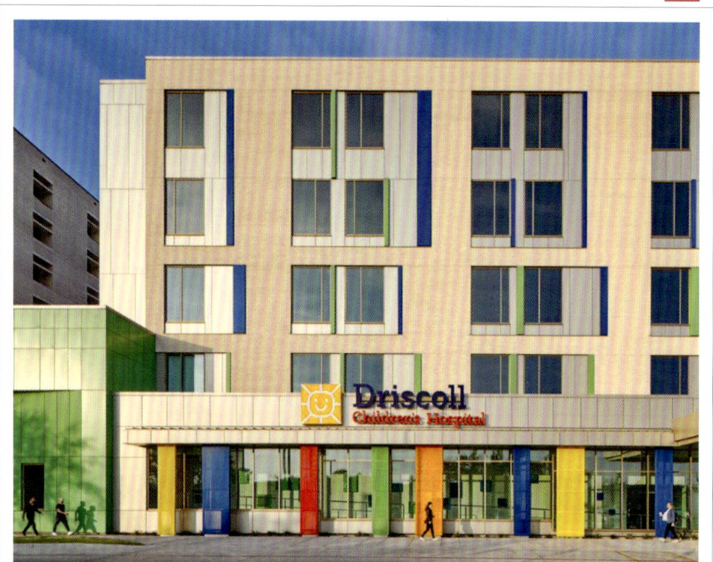

Title: Driscoll Children's Hospital Brand Identity
Client: Driscoll Children's Hospital | **Design Firm:** *TraceElement

MATCHSTIC

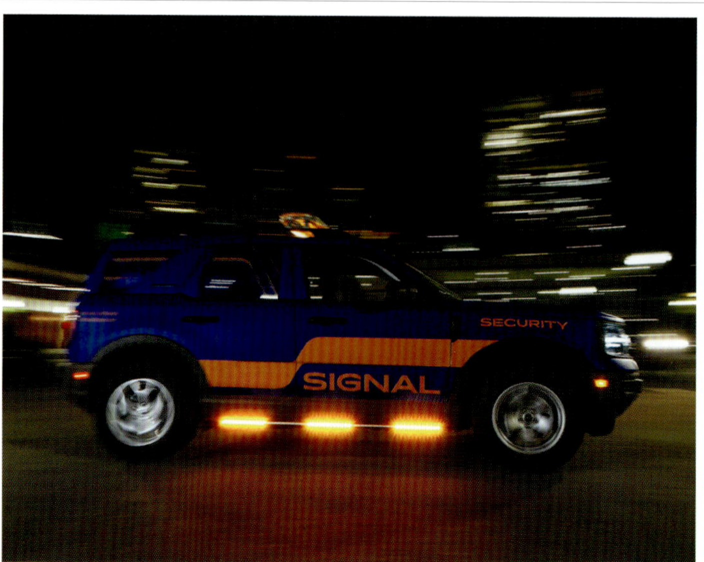

Title: Signal Rebrand | **Client:** Signal Security
Design Firm: Matchstic

PIERRE DELEBOIS

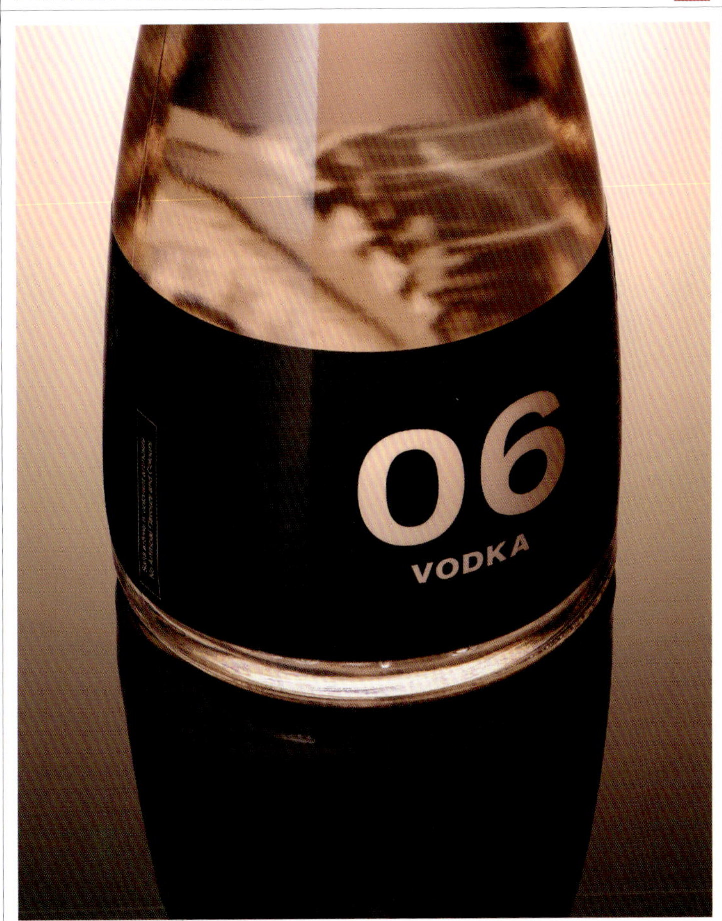

Title: Comte de Grasse 06 Vodka | **Client:** Comte de Grasse
Design Firm: Force MAJEURE

RESOURCE BRANDING

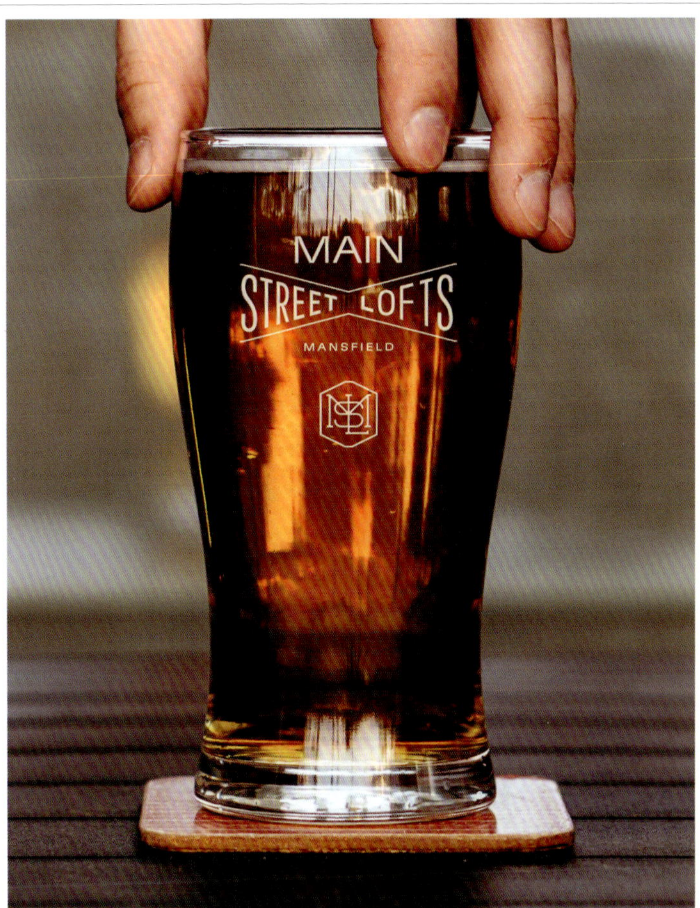

Title: Main Street Lofts Brand Identity | **Client:** Realty Capital Partners
Design Firm: Resource Branding

HONG KA LOK

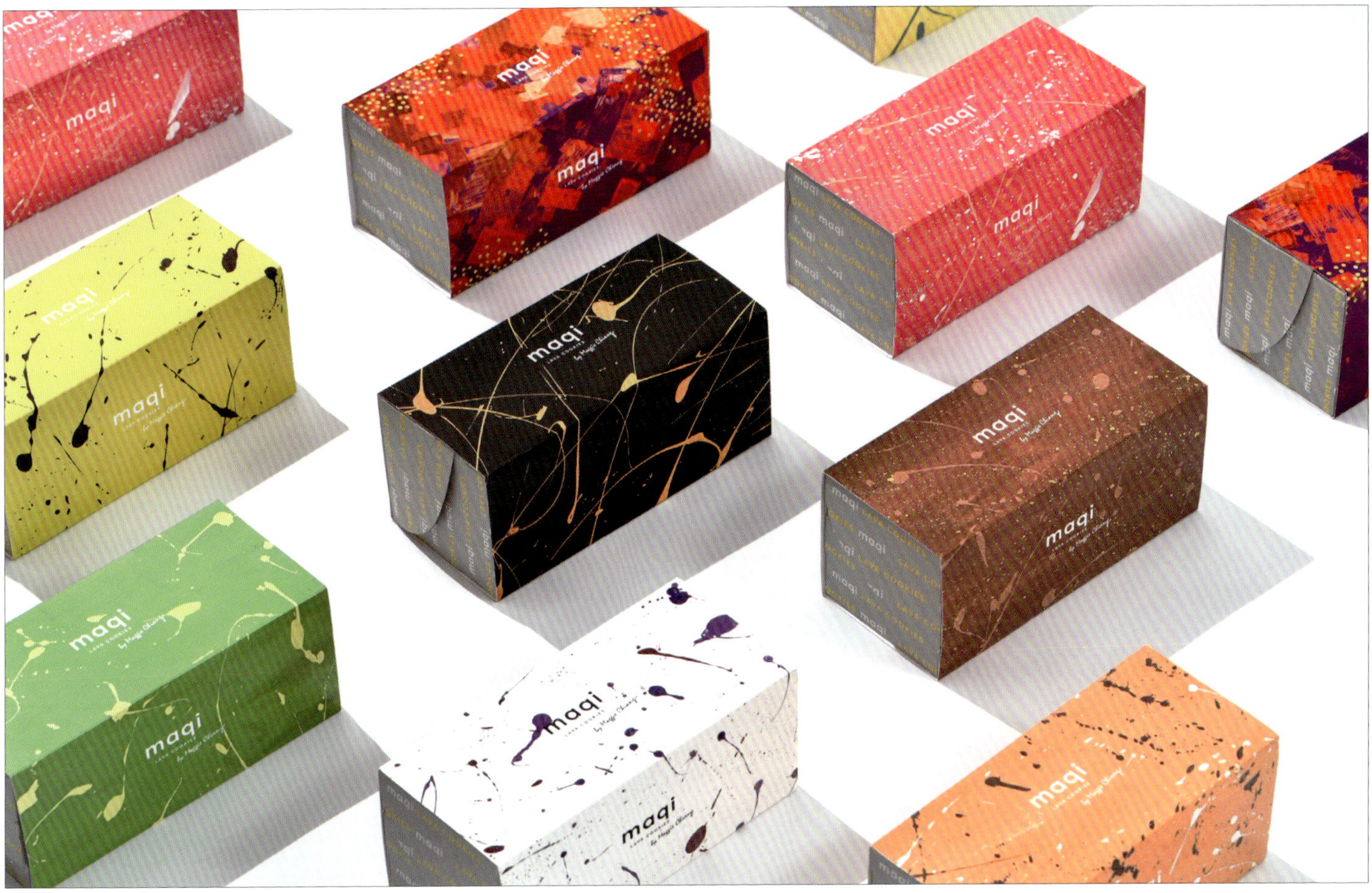

Title: Maqi - Lava Cookies | **Client:** Maqi - Lava Cookies | **Design Firm:** Loksophy Design Ltd.

MATT ERICKSON

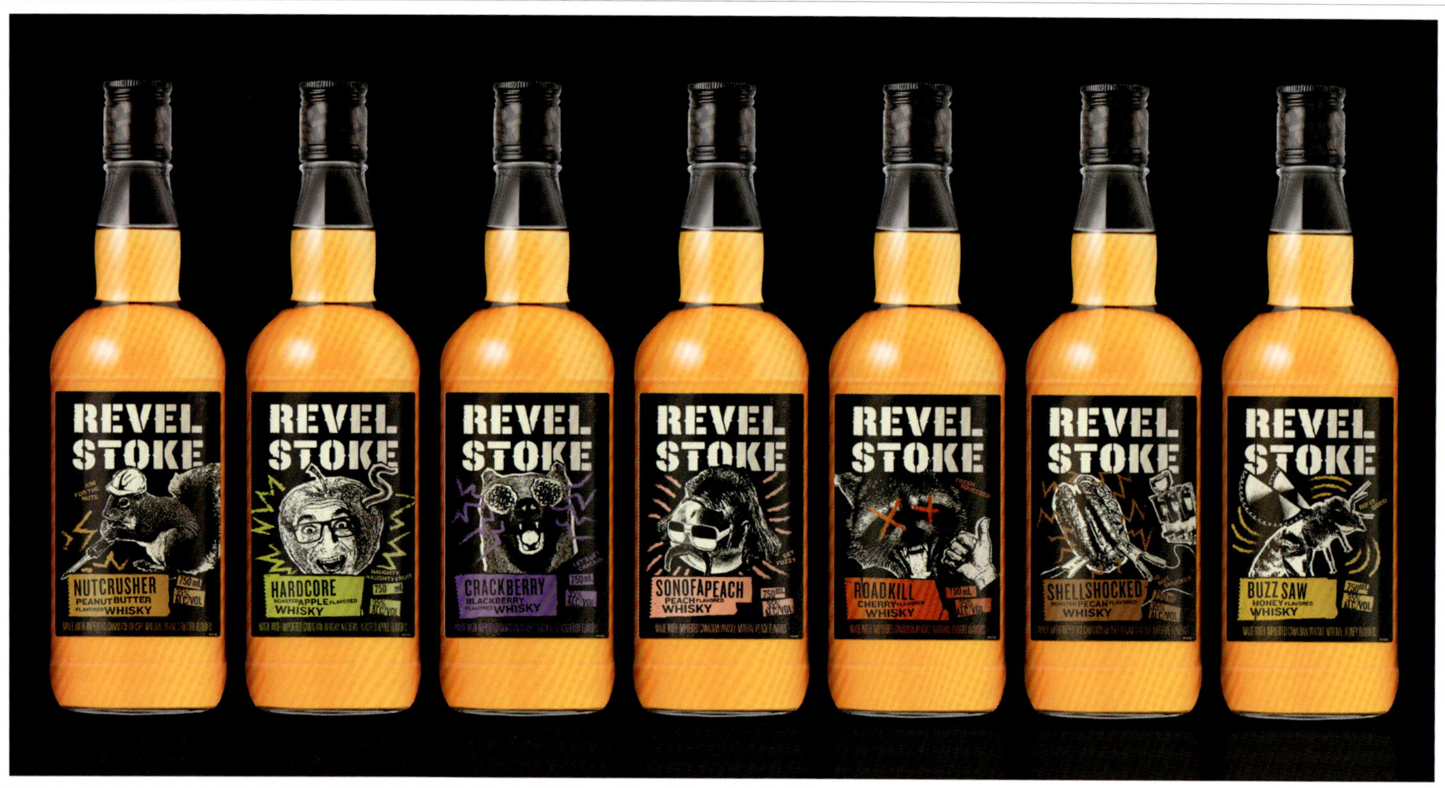

Title: Revel Stoke Whisky | **Client:** Phillips Distilling Co. | **Design Firm:** Cue

DEREK SPRINGSTON

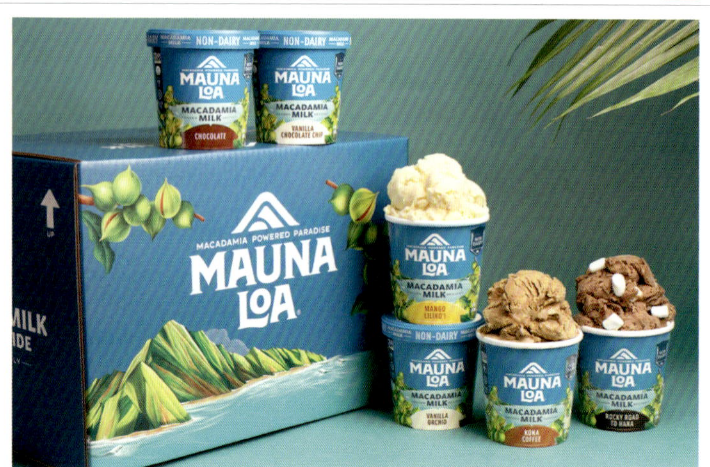

Title: Mauna Loa | **Client:** Mauna Loa
Design Firm: Moxie Sozo

BRENDÁN MURPHY

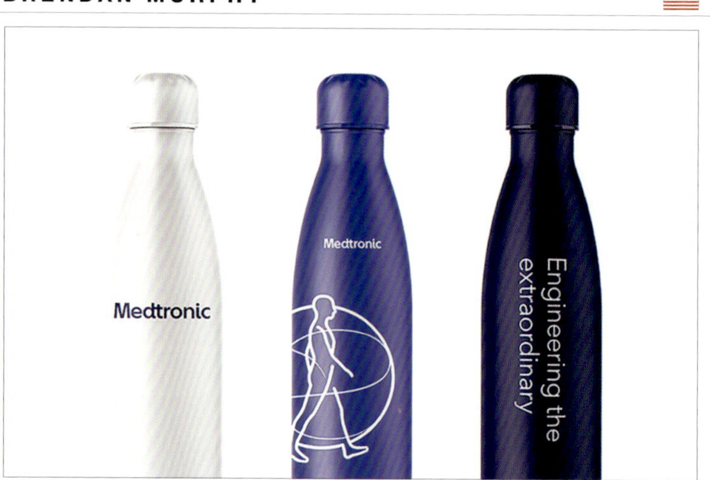

Title: Amplifying How a Brand Engineers the Extraordinary
Client: Medtronic | **Design Firm:** Lippincott

ROBERTO NÚÑEZ

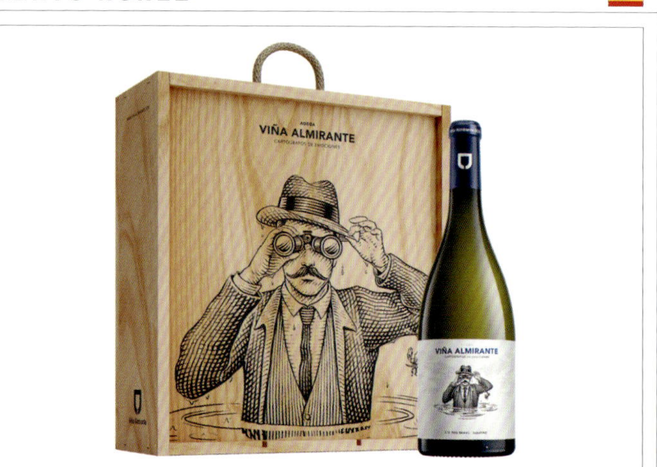

Title: Viña Almirante Branding | **Client:** Viña Almirante
Design Firm: Roberto Núñez Studio

CHARLES BLOOM

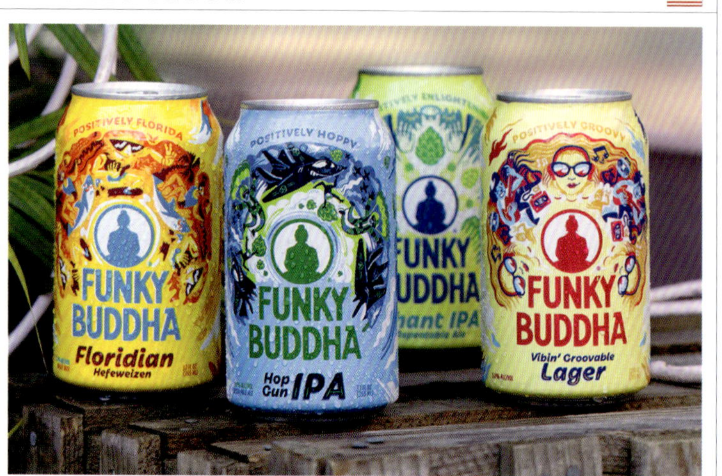

Title: Funky Buddha | **Client:** Funky Buddha
Design Firm: Moxie Sozo

ZILI MA

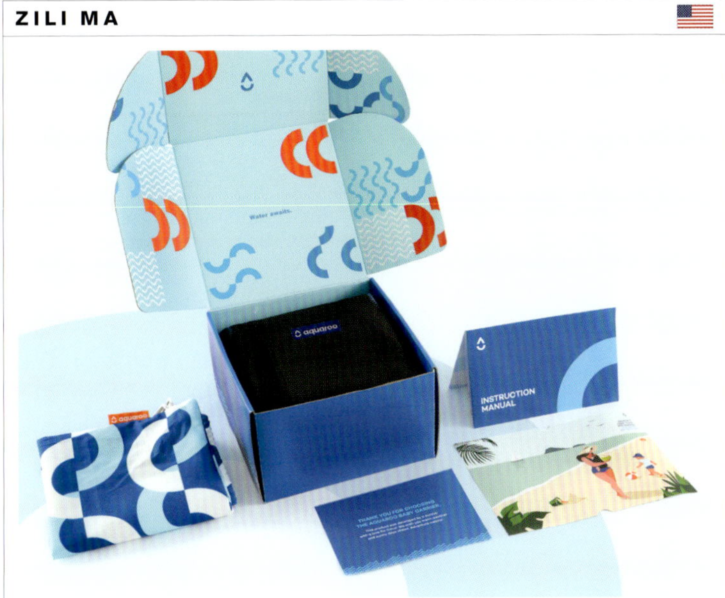

Title: Aquaroo Brand System | **Client:** Aquaroo
Design Firm: Noise 13

TIM LOO

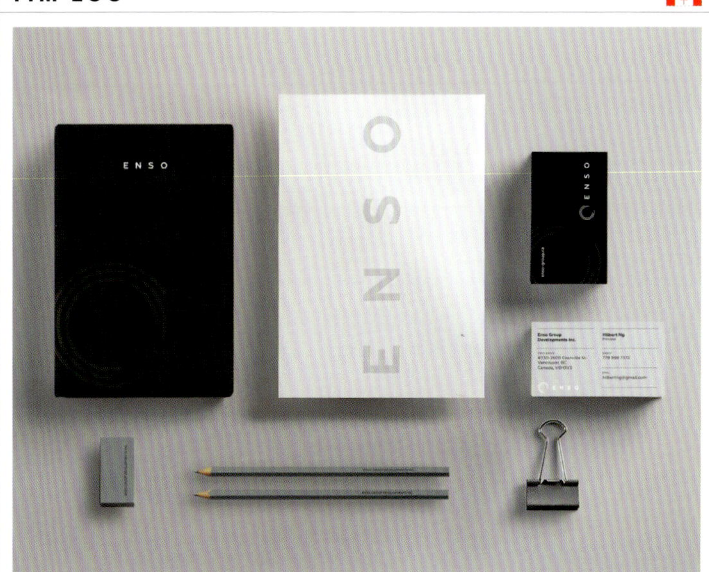

Title: Enso Group Branding | **Client:** Enso Group
Design Firm: Coastlines Creative Group

DORIS PALMEROS

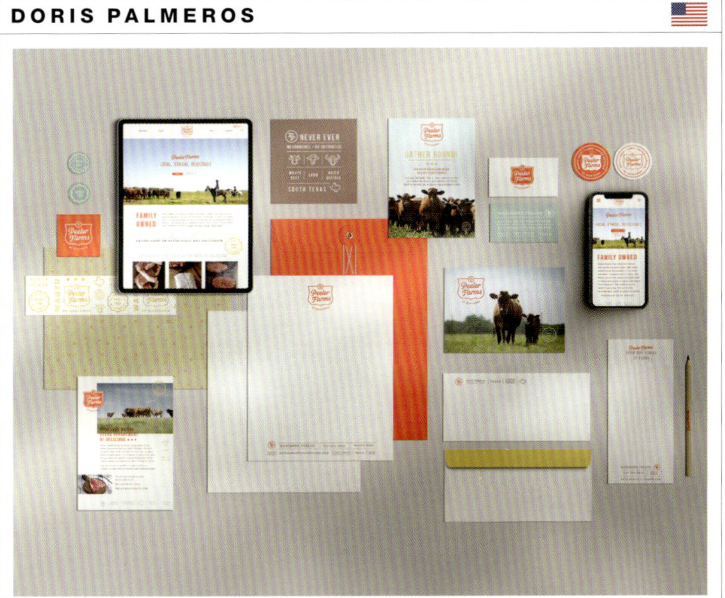

Title: Peeler Farms Branding | **Client:** Peeler Farms
Design Firm: Doris Palmeros Studio

BUNTIN

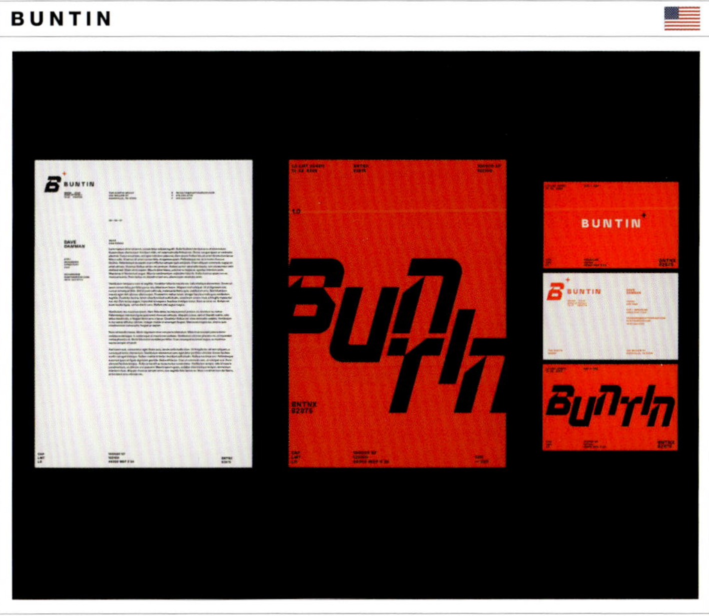

Title: REBRANDING | **Client:** Self-initiated
Design Firm: BUNTIN

FELLOW INC.

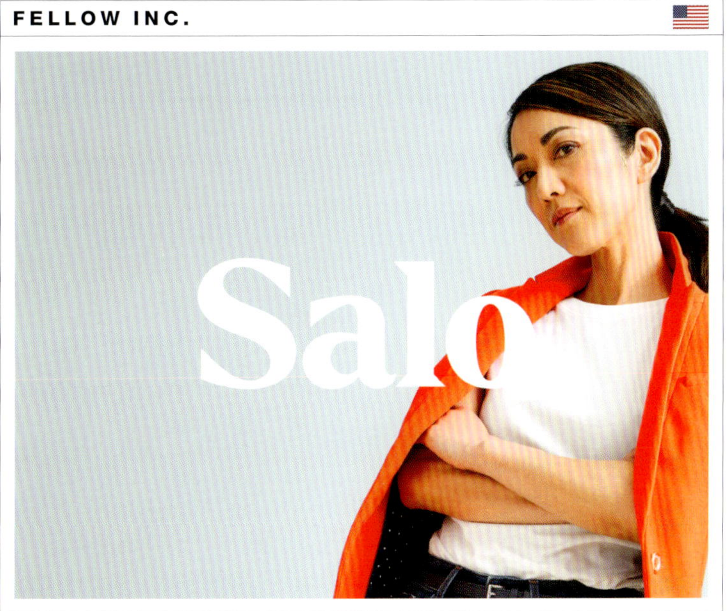

Title: Sale Rebranding | **Client:** Salo
Design Firm: Fellow Inc.

RESOURCE BRANDING

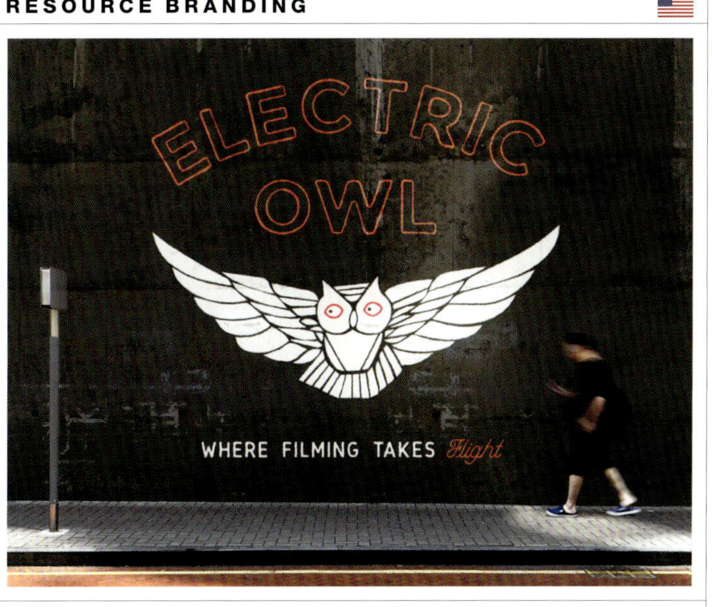

Title: Electric Owl Studios Brand Identity | **Client:** Electric Owl Studios
Design Firm: Resource Branding

PAOLO CATALLA

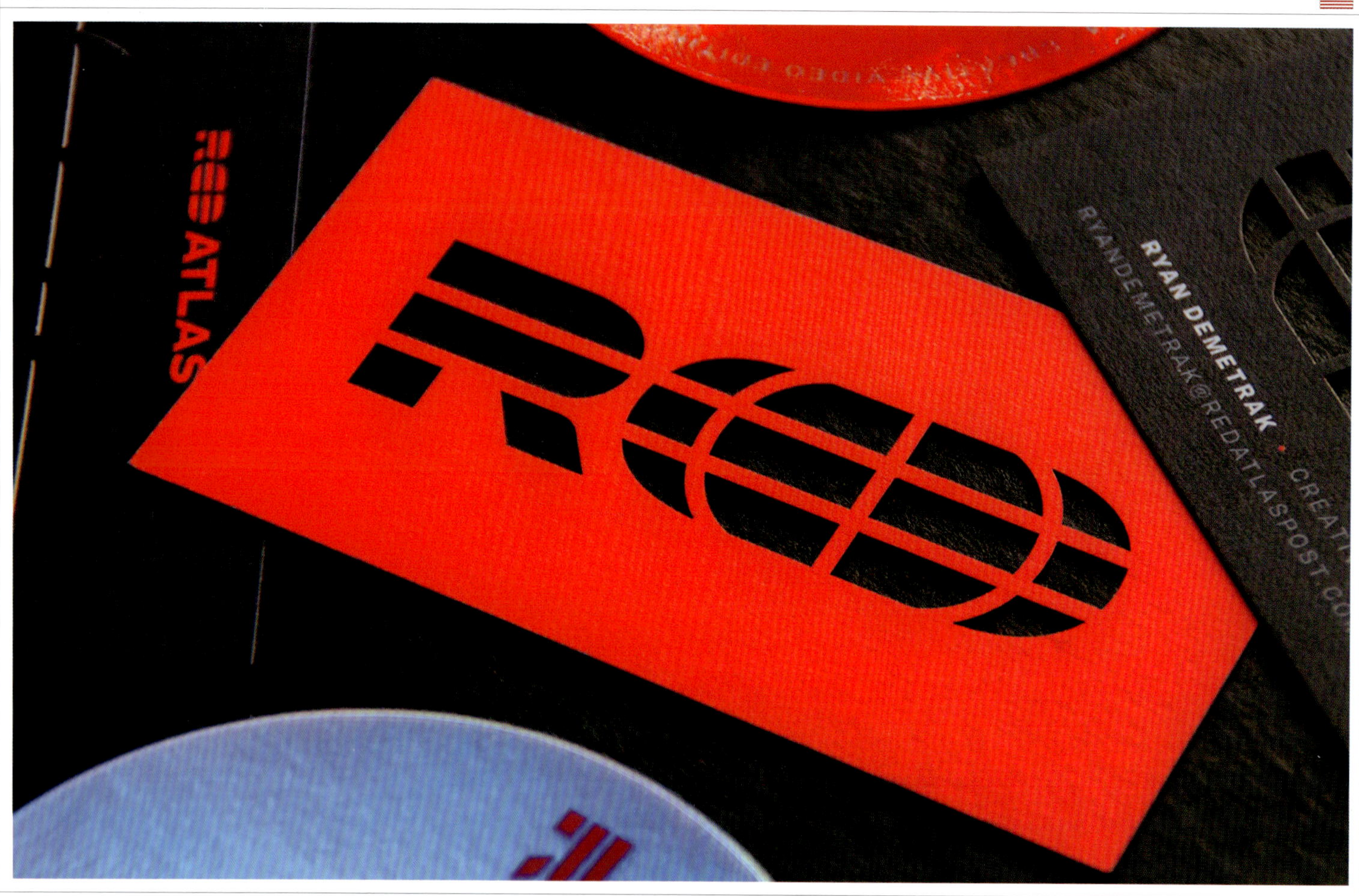

Title: Red Atlas Branding | **Client:** Red Atlas | **Design Firm:** Paolo Catalla

MATCHSTIC

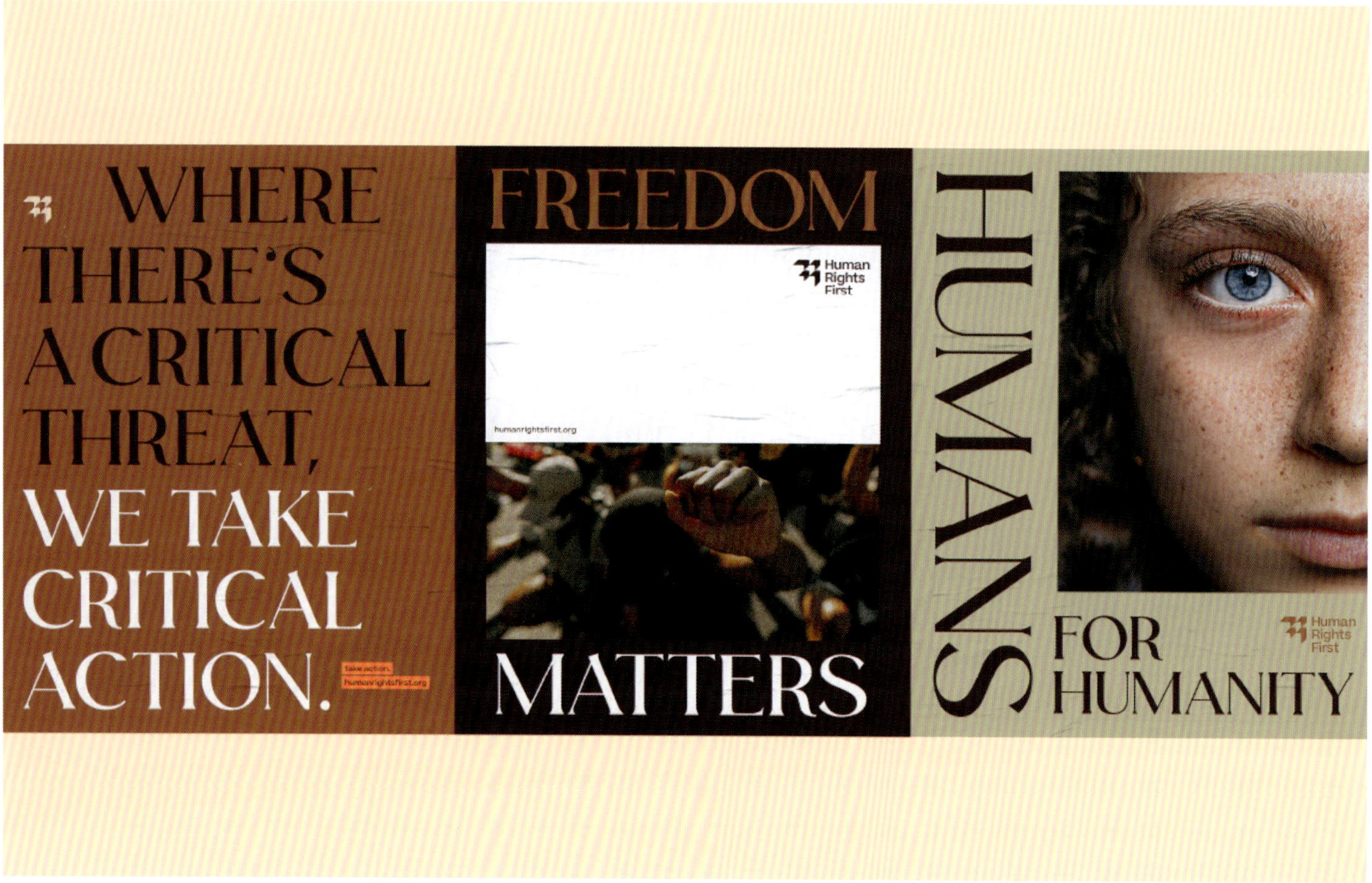

WHERE THERE'S A CRITICAL THREAT, WE TAKE CRITICAL ACTION.
FREEDOM
Human Rights First
humanrightsfirst.org
MATTERS
HUMANS
FOR HUMANITY
Human Rights First

Title: Human Rights First Rebrand | **Client:** Human Rights First | **Design Firm:** Matchstic

RICHARD PATTERSON

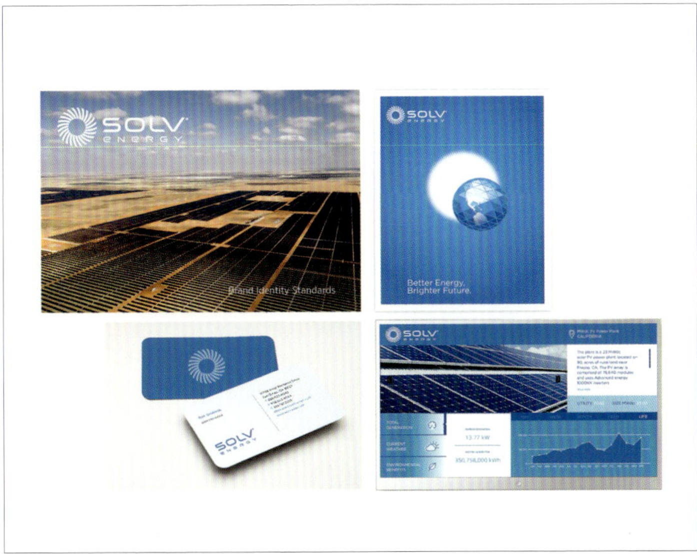

Title: SOLV Energy Brand Identity | **Client:** SOLV Energy
Design Firm: PH Studio

&BARR

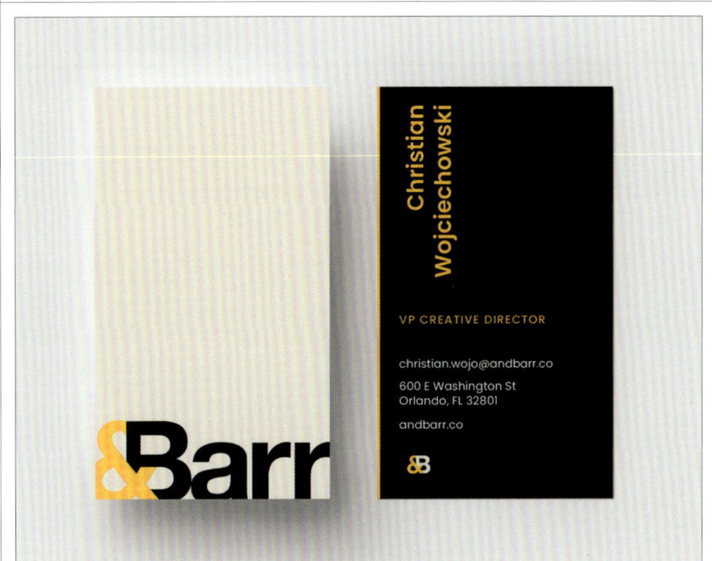

Title: &Barr Business Card Redesign | **Client:** Self-inititated
Design Firm: &Barr

COMPASS DESIGN STUDIO

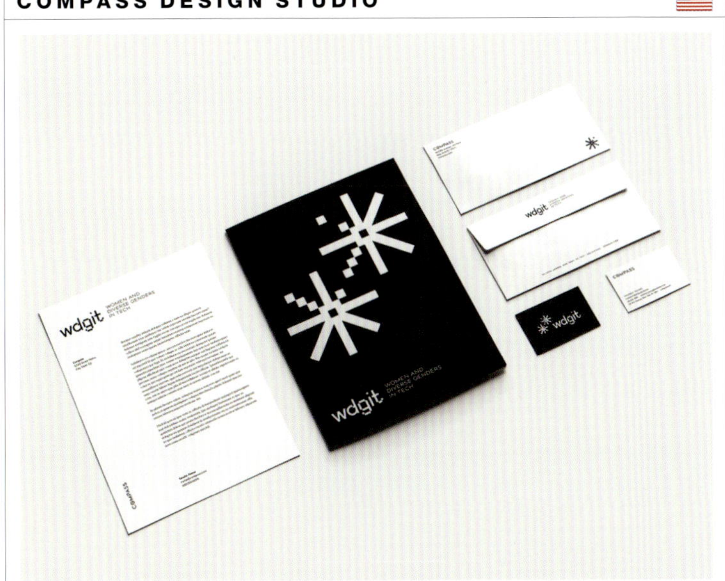

Title: WDGIT - Women and Diverse Genders in Tech
Client: Self-initiated | **Design Firm:** Compass

C. MILLER, D. AL-SALEH, D. GONSALVES

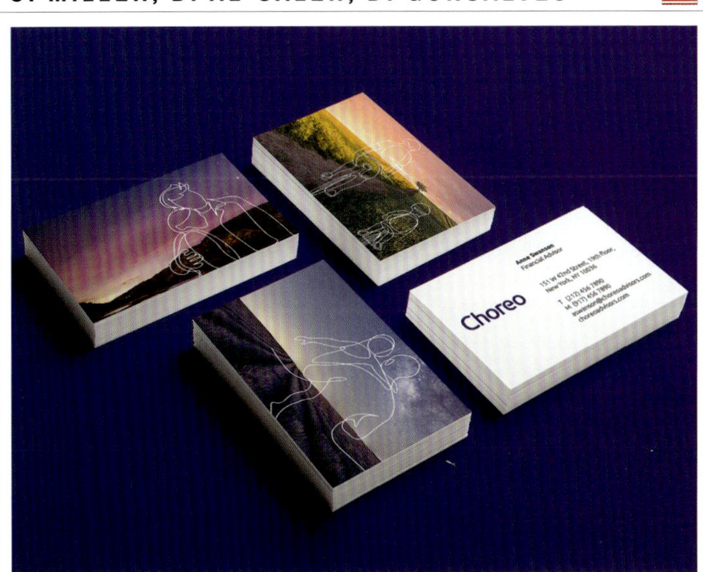

Title: Choreo | **Client:** Choreo Advisors
Design Firm: Sequel Studio

ERICA HOLEMAN

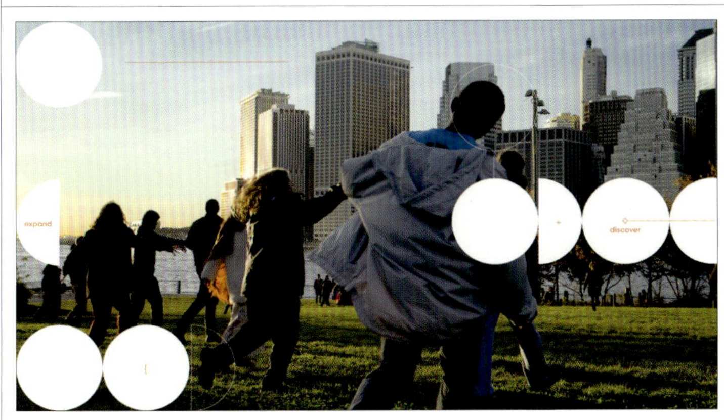

Title: Experience Design Certificate Program: Identity System
Client: Odyssey Works | **Design Firm:** Erica Holeman

CONJURE

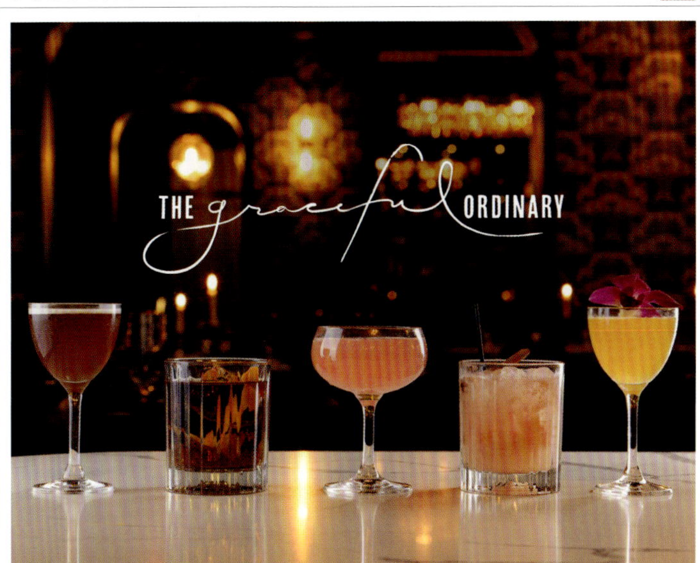

Title: The Graceful Ordinary Branding
Client: The Graceful Ordinary | **Design Firm:** Conjure

COMPASS DESIGN STUDIO

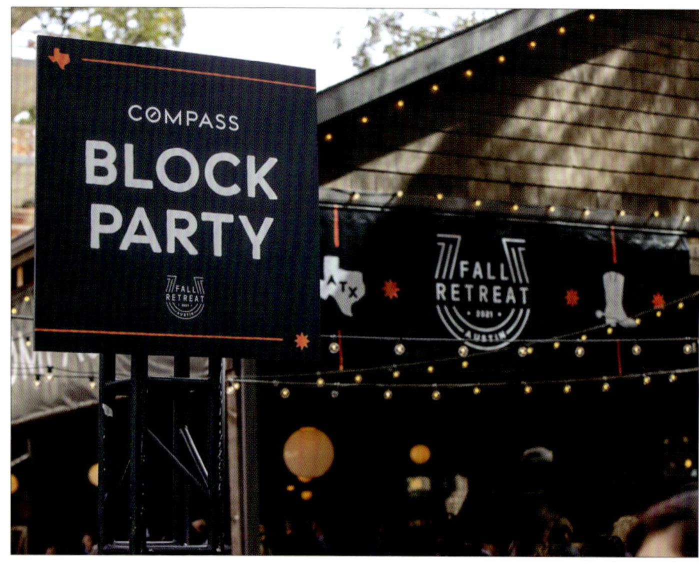

Title: Compass Fall REtreat 2021 Austin | **Client:** Self-initiated
Design Firm: Compass

UNIVISUAL

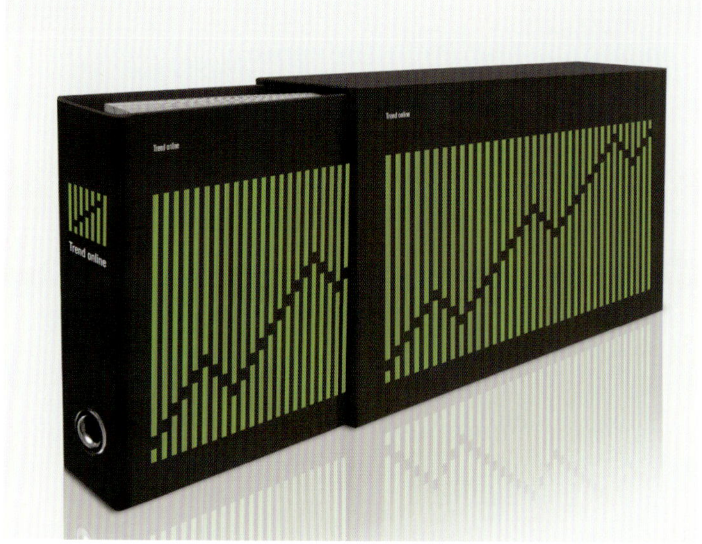

Title: The Financial Publishing Brand | **Client:** LeFonti Group
Design Firm: Univisual

DYLAN STUART

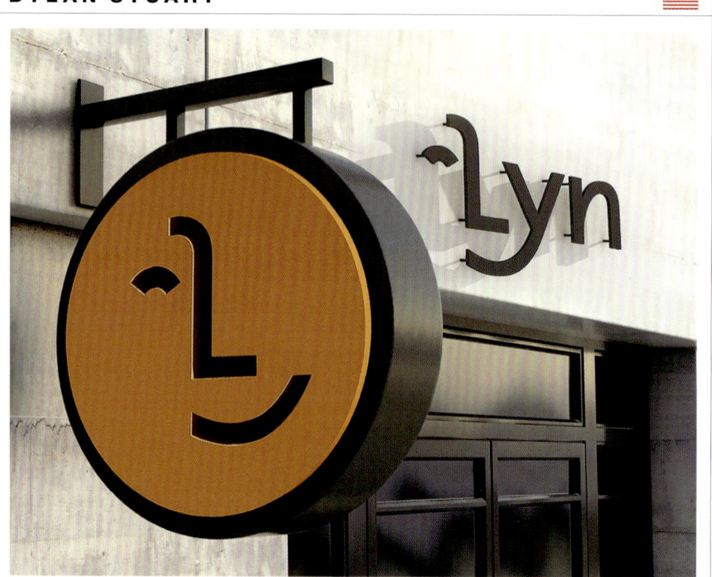

Title: Creating a People-First Healthcare Brand | **Client:** Lyn Health
Design Firm: Lippincott

UNIVISUAL

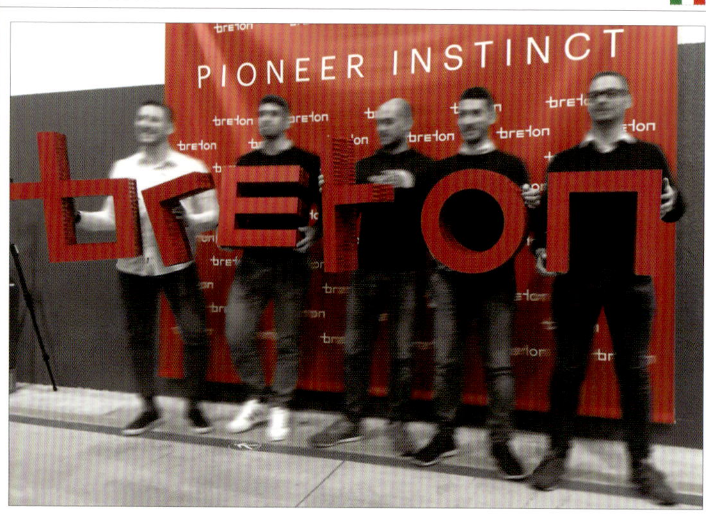

Title: The Rational Identity | **Client:** Breton Industry
Design Firm: Univisual

JOHN BALL, DAVID ALDERMAN

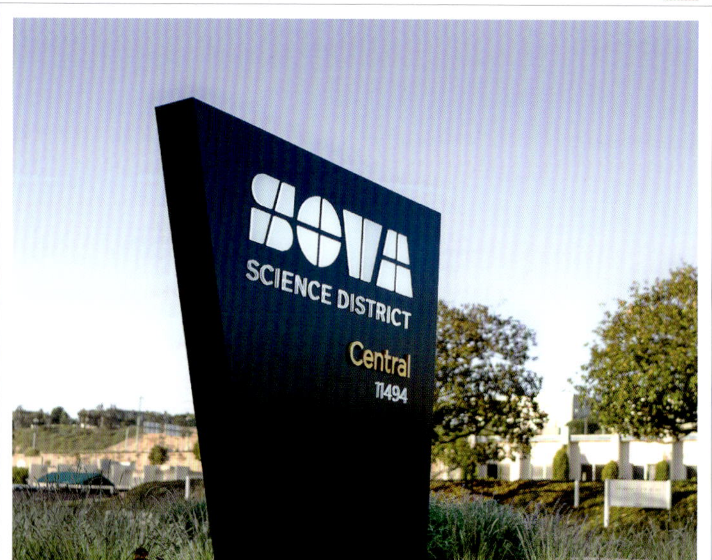

Title: SOVA Science District | **Client:** Longfellow Real Estate Partners
Design Firm: MiresBall

IDEON.AI

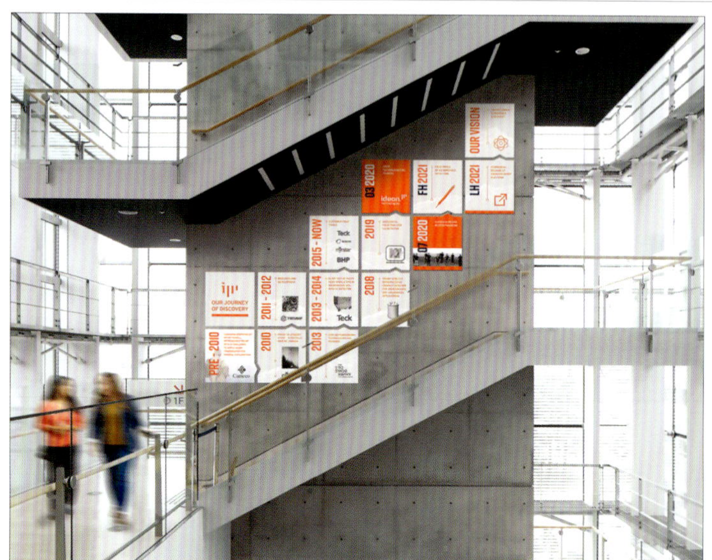

Title: Ideon Rebrand | **Client:** Ideon
Design Firm: Coastlines Creative Group

HONG KA LOK

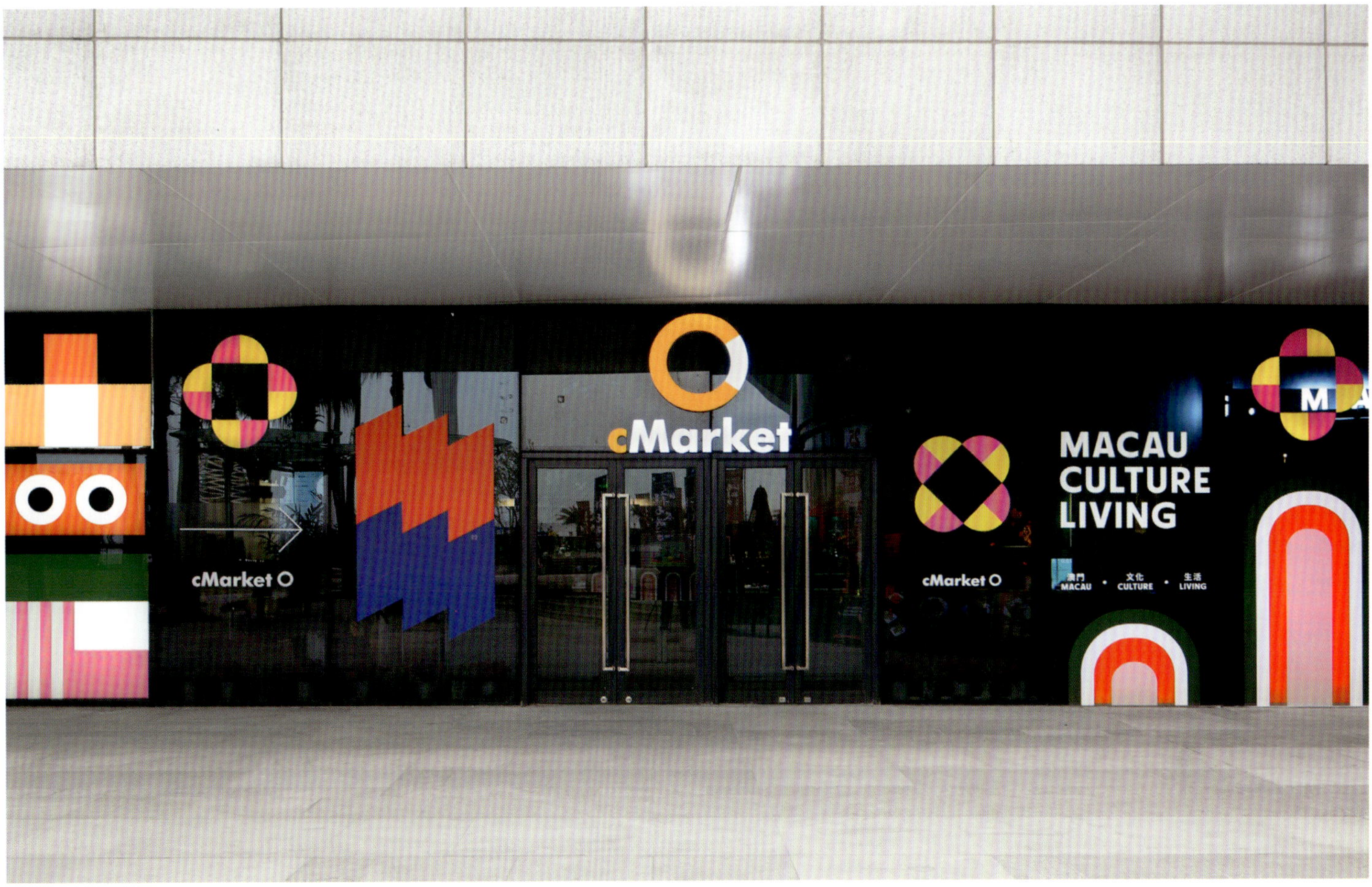

Title: cMarket | **Client:** cCentre | **Design Firm:** Loksophy Design Ltd.

COMPASS DESIGN STUDIO

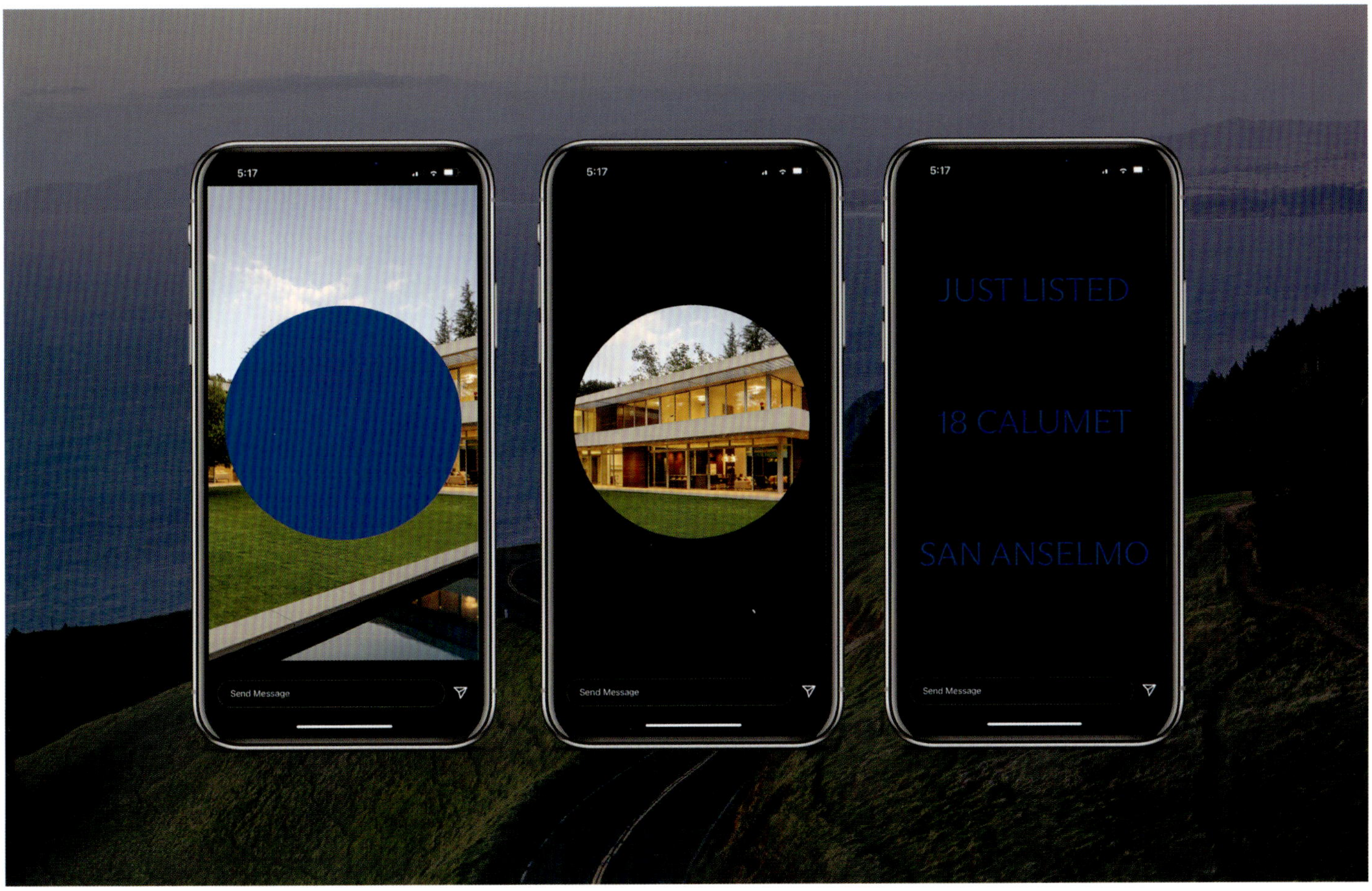

Title: Eric Gelman Agent Rebrand | **Client:** Eric Gelman | **Design Firm:** Compass

JOAO OLIVEIRA

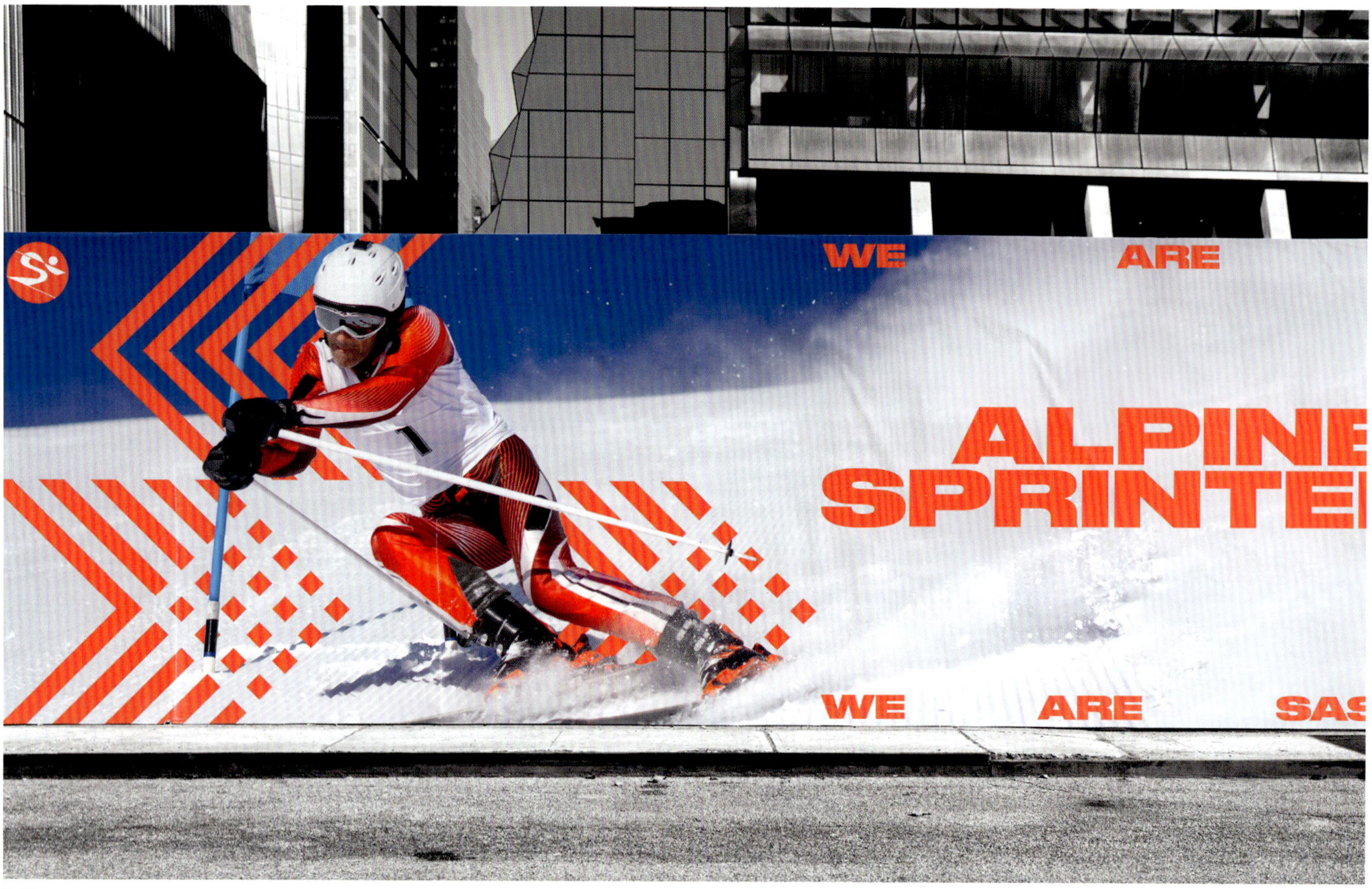

Title: Saslong | Client: Funivie Saslong S.p.a. | Design Firm: Onrepeat Studio

SIREN SF

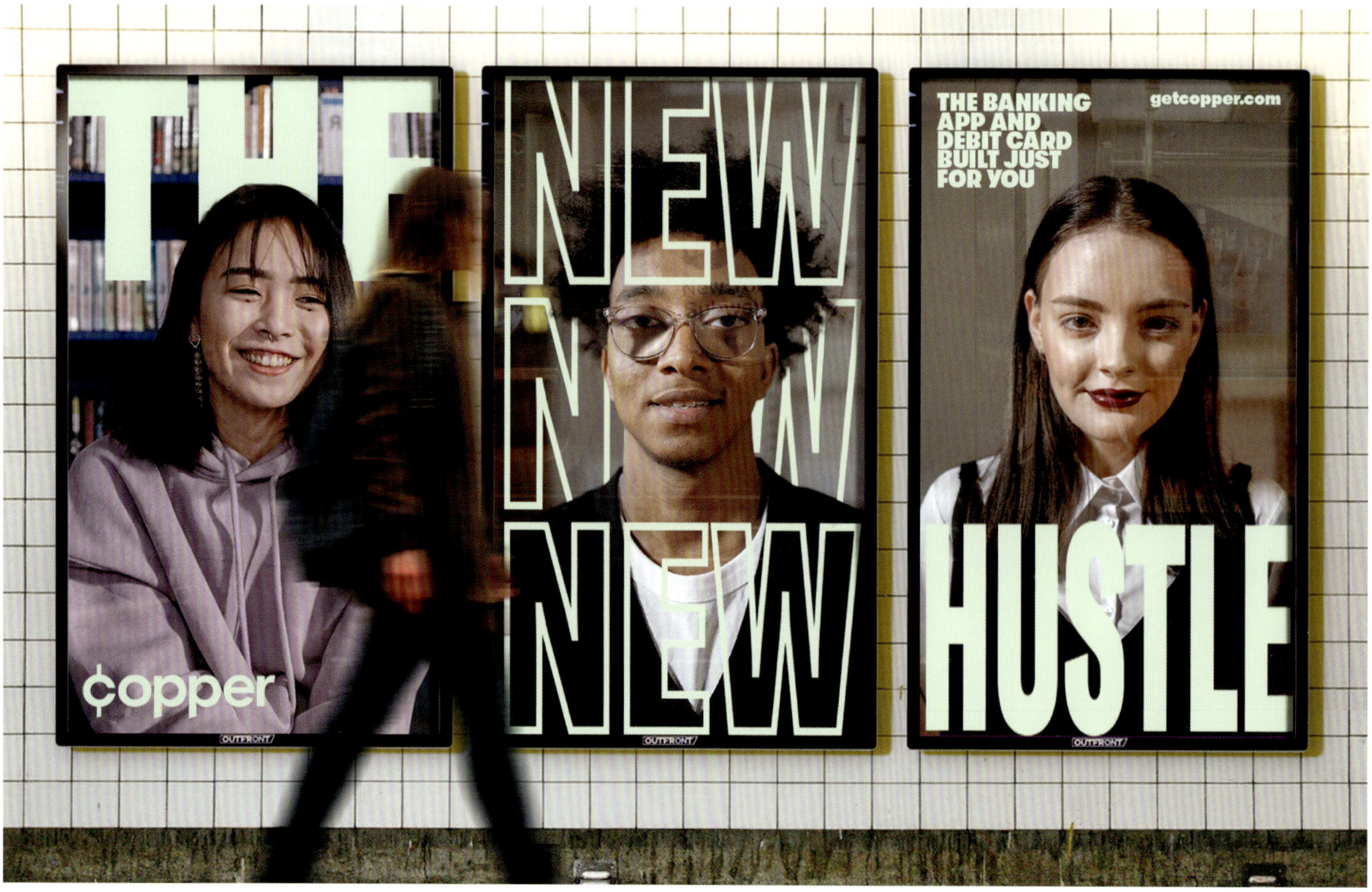

Title: Copper Banking Brand Identity | Client: Copper Banking | Design Firm: SIREN SF

CINTHIA WEN

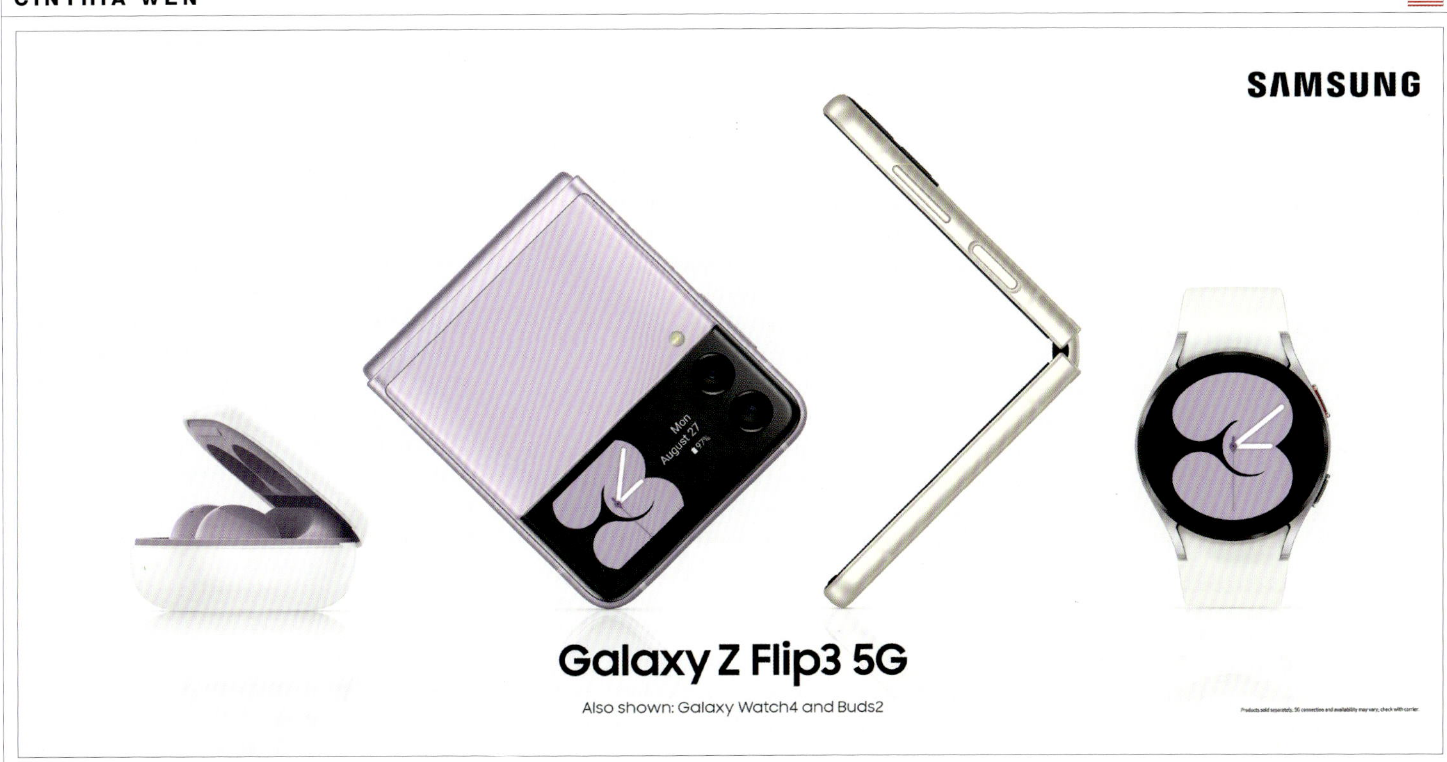

Title: Galaxy Flip Ecosystem Launch Poster | **Client:** Samsung | **Design Firm:** Turner Duckworth: London, San Francisco & New York

BRANDON TUSHKOWSKI

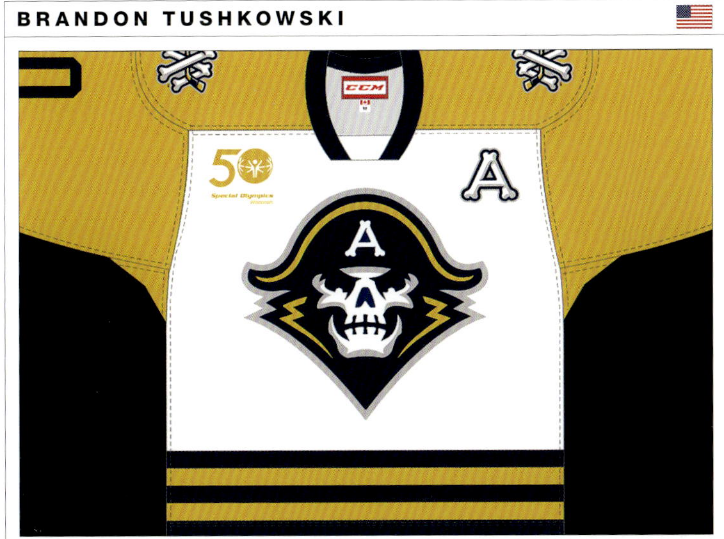

Title: Special Olympics Wisconsin Program | **Client:** Milwaukee Admirals
Design Firm: Traction Factory

NICOLE JORDAN

Title: Dollar Shave Club Visual Identity | **Client:** Dollar Shave Club
Design Firm: Turner Duckworth: London, San Francisco & New York

CONJURE

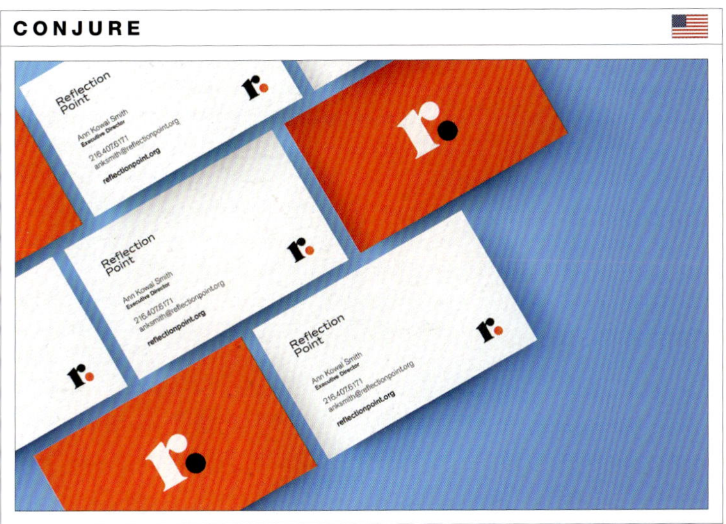

Title: Reflection Point Rebranding | **Client:** Books at Work
Design Firm: Conjure

COLEY PORTER BELL, OAK STREET HEALTH

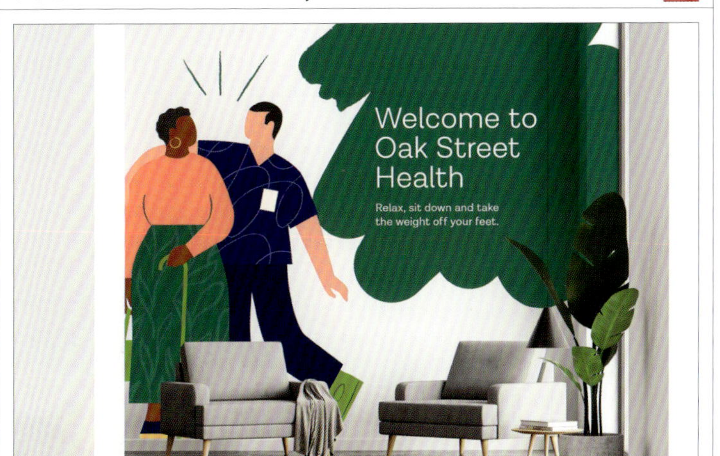

Title: Oak Street Health Branding | **Client:** Oak Street Health
Design Firm: Coley Porter Bell

VSA PARTNERS

Title: VSA Partners: Spacial | Client: Innovatus Capital Partners
Design Firm: VSA Partners

PETER LADD, DON CLELAND

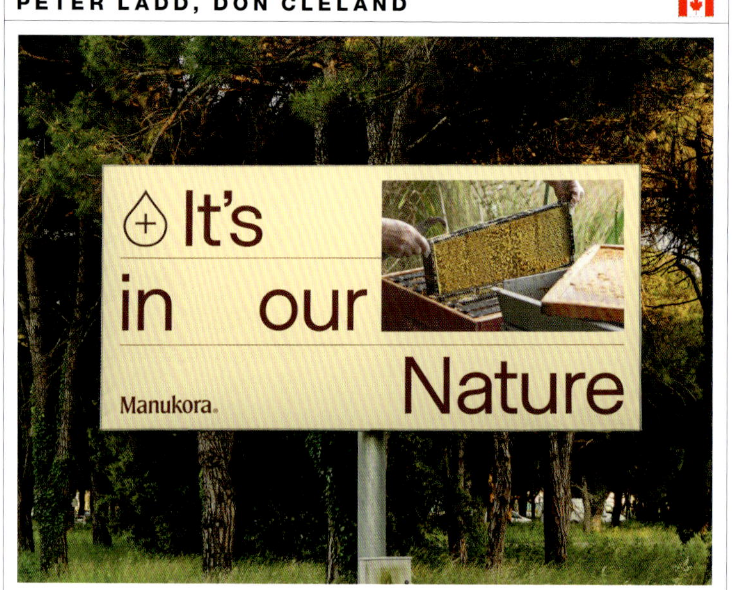

Title: Manukora Legacy | Client: Manukora
Design Firm: Pendo

JACY EMBRAY

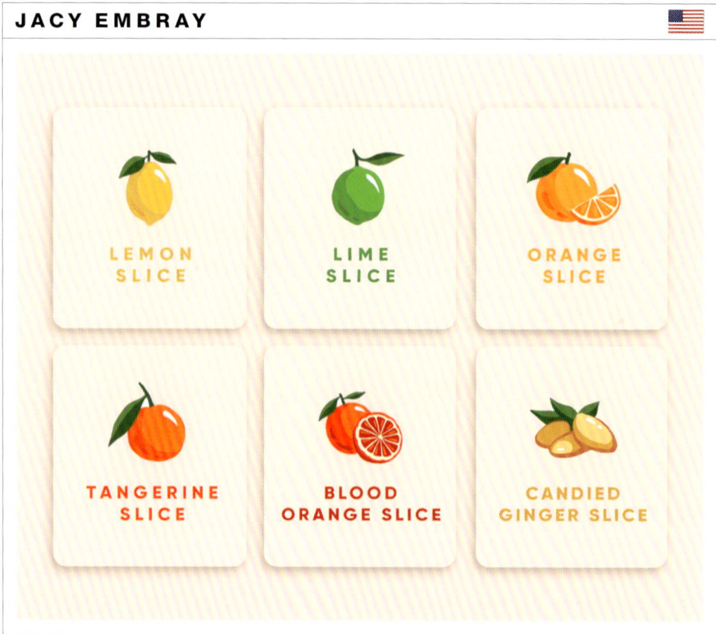

Title: Garniche | Client: Sugar Foods | Design Firm: Creative Energy

KATELYN MCVEY

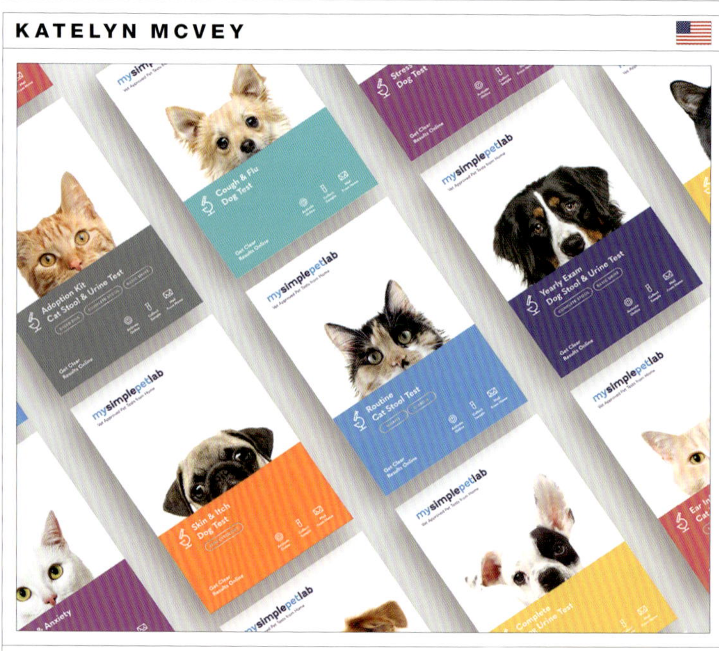

Title: MySimplePetLab | Client: MySimplePetLab | Design Firm: Cue

PETER LADD, DON CLELAND

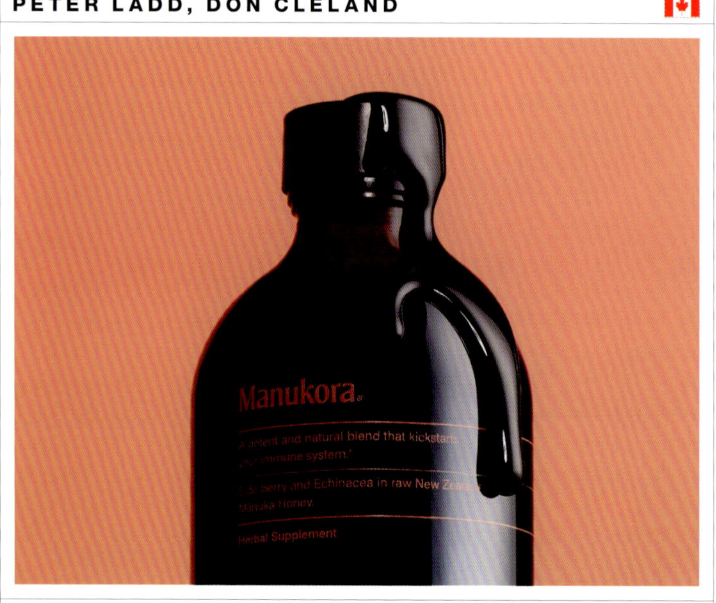

Title: Manukora Botanicals
Client: Manukora | Design Firm: Pendo

RESOURCE BRANDING

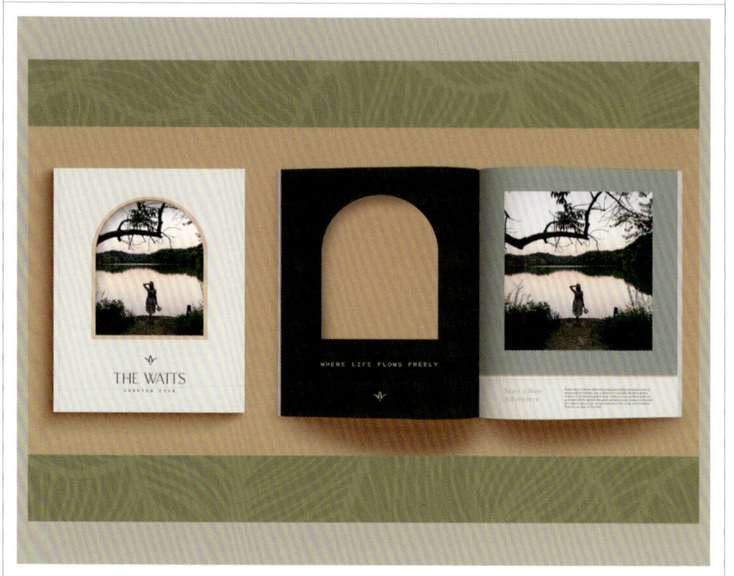

Title: The Watts at Hampton Cove Brand Identity
Client: Daniel Corporation | Design Firm: Resource Branding

BRAND BAR COMMUNICATIONS

Title: Can You See the Music? | **Client:** Franz Liszt Chamber Orchestra (LFKZ) | **Design Firm:** Brand Bar Communications

MATCHSTIC

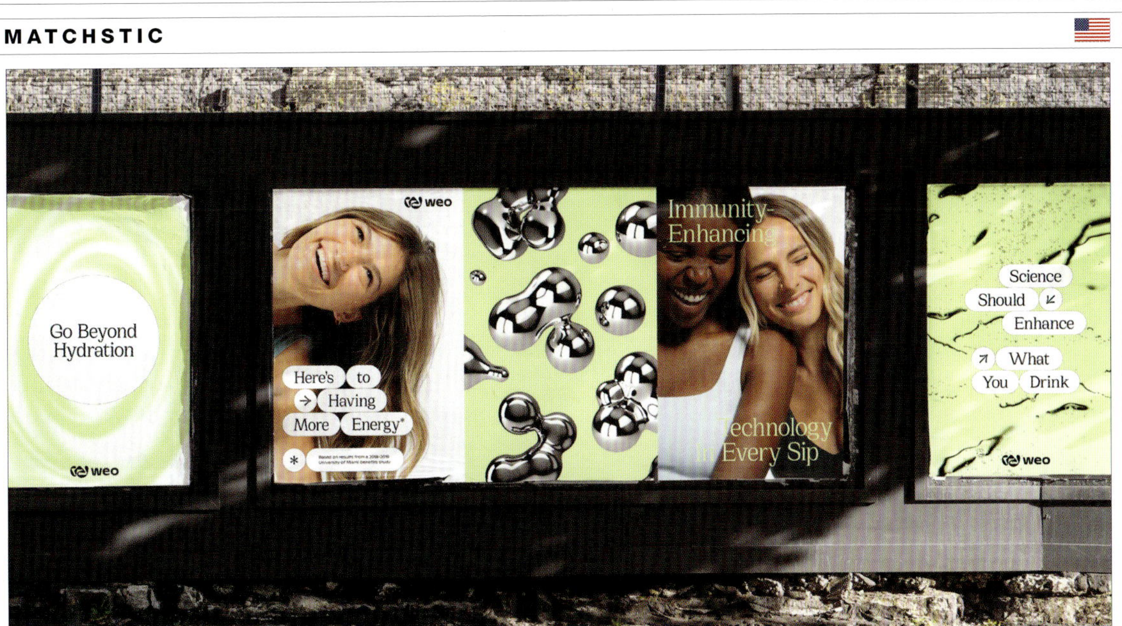

Title: Weo Brand Identity | **Client:** Weo | **Design Firm:** Matchstic

PAULO MARCELO

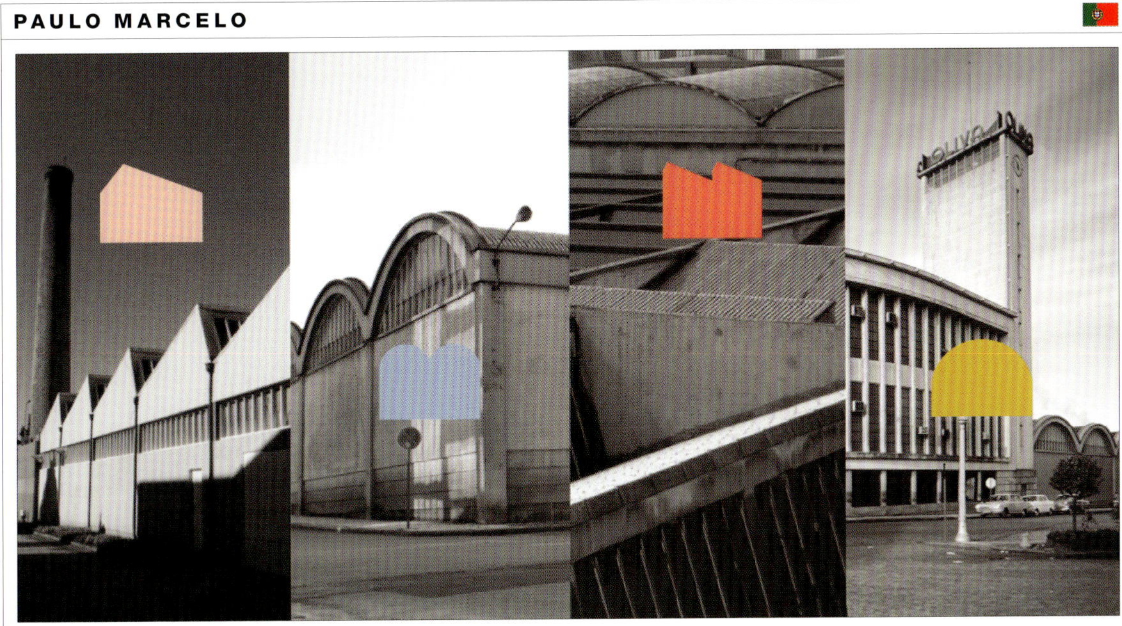

Title: Centro de Memórias da Indústria | **Client:** Município de S. João da Madeira | **Design Firm:** PMDesign

MICHAEL VANDERBYL

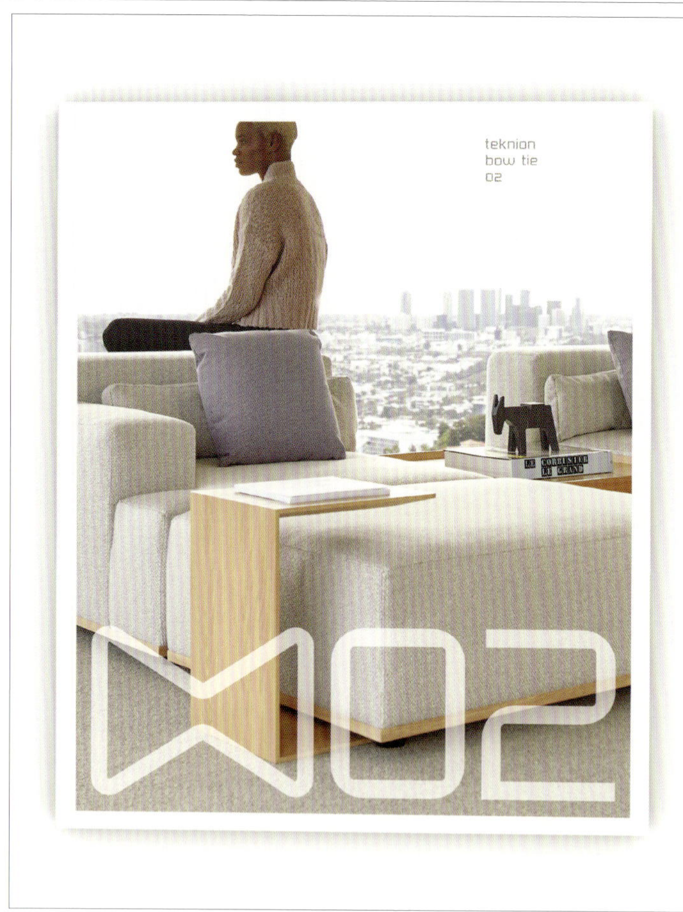

Title: Teknion Bow Tie Brochure | **Client:** Teknion
Design Firm: Vanderbyl Design

MICHAEL VANDERBYL

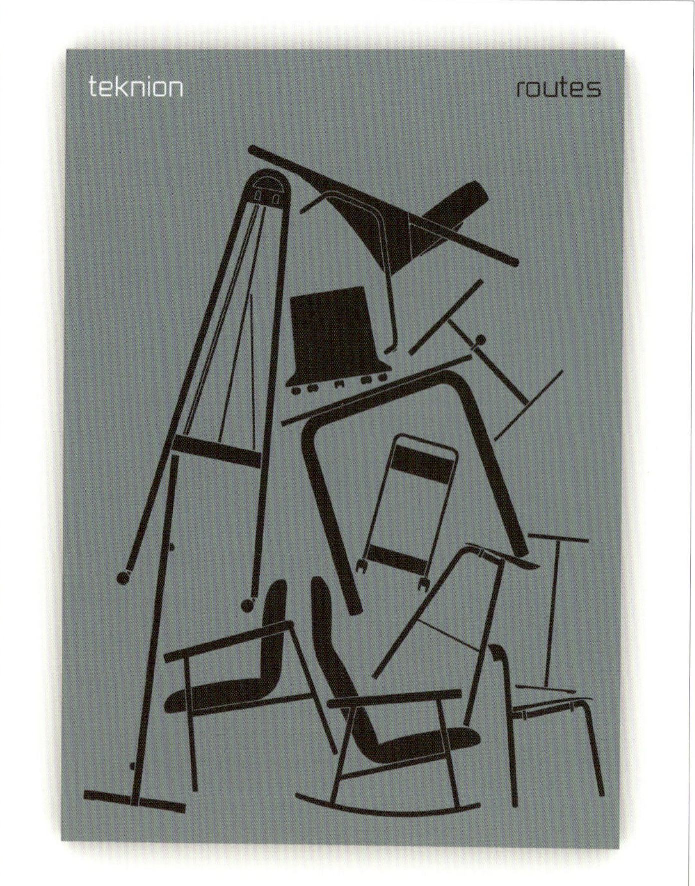

Title: Teknion Routes Brochure | **Client:** Teknion
Design Firm: Vanderbyl Design

WENDY LOWDEN

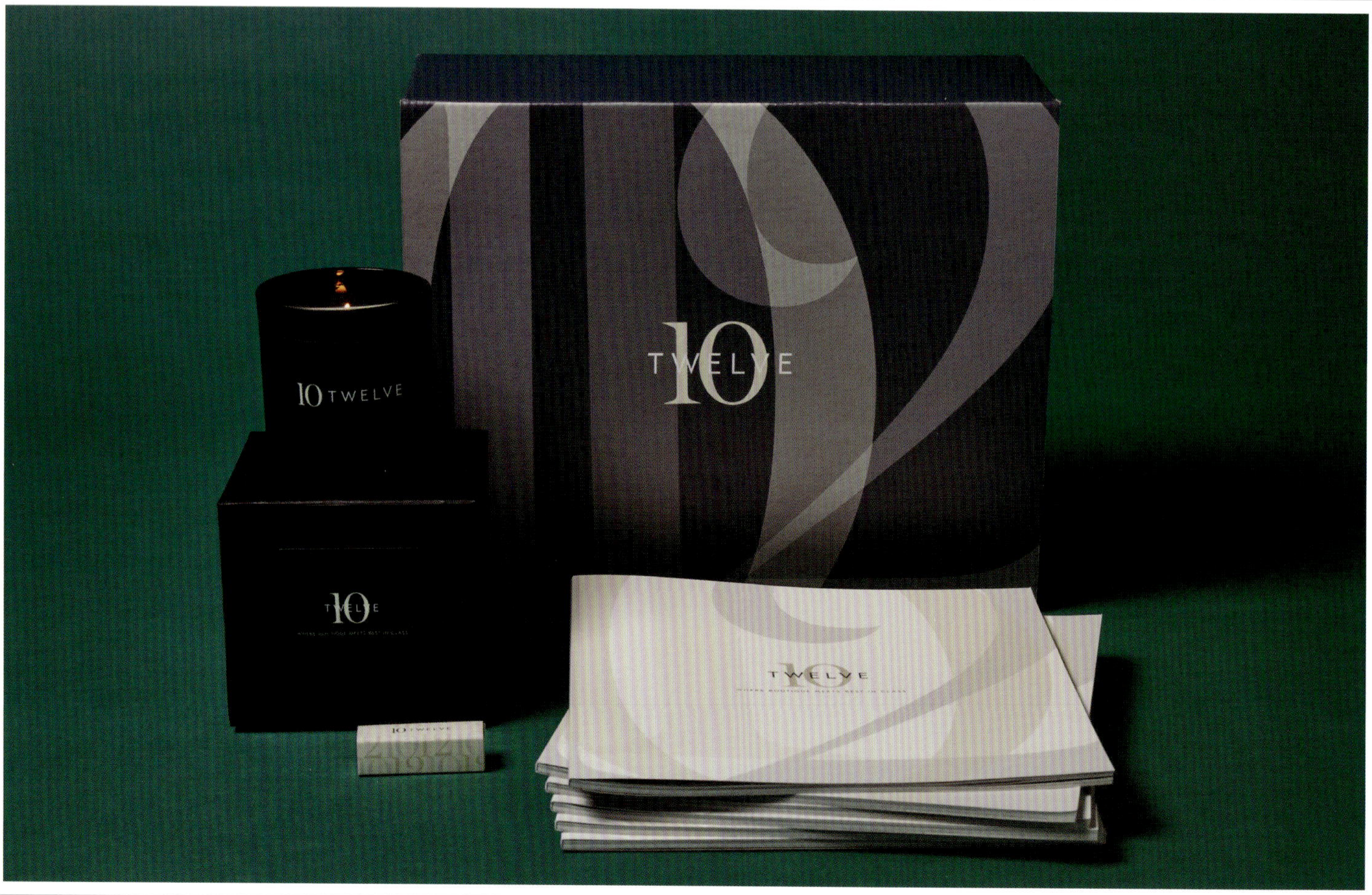

Title: 10twelve | **Client:** Jones Lang LaSalle | **Design Firm:** House of Current

WENDY LOWDEN

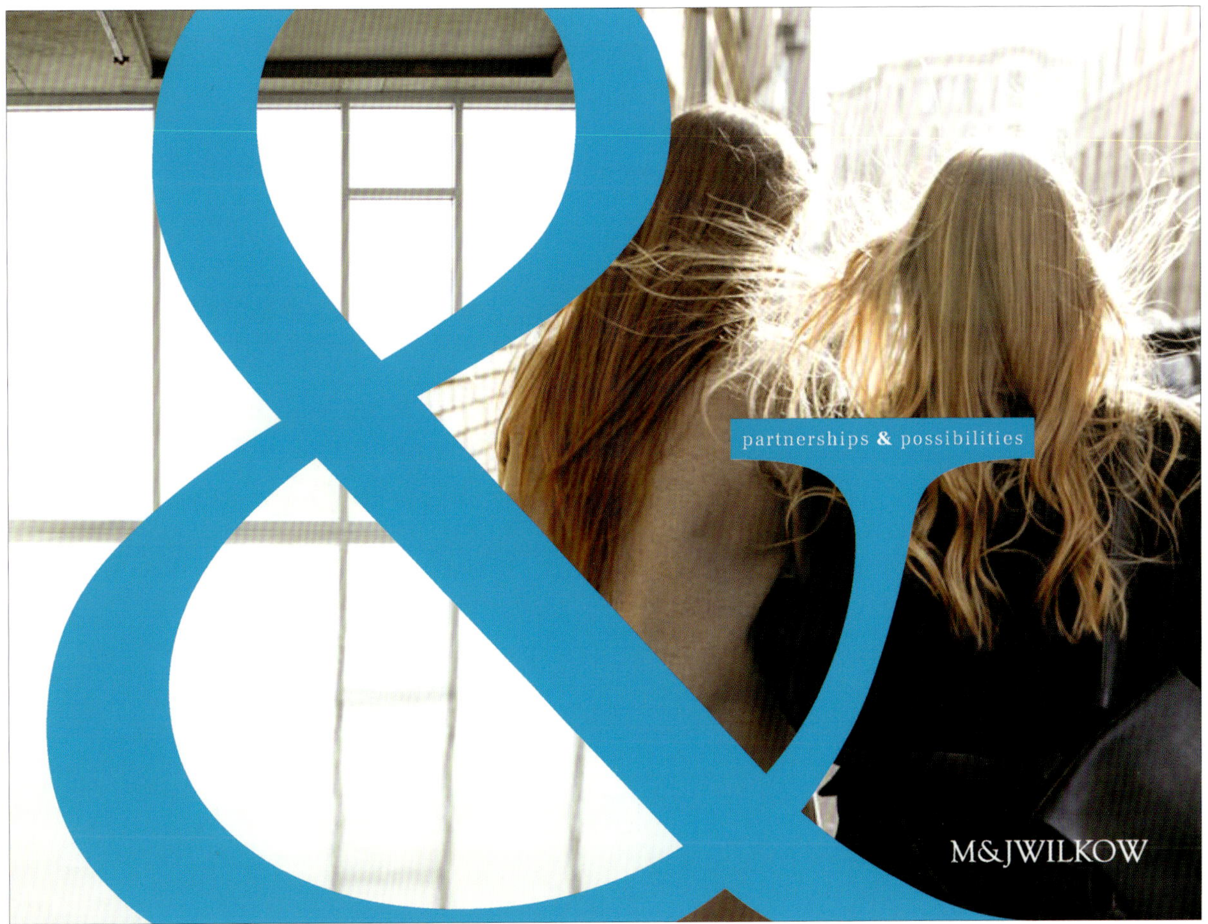

Title: 3rd Party Brochure | **Client:** M&J Wilkow | **Design Firm:** House of Current

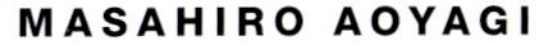

MASAHIRO AOYAGI

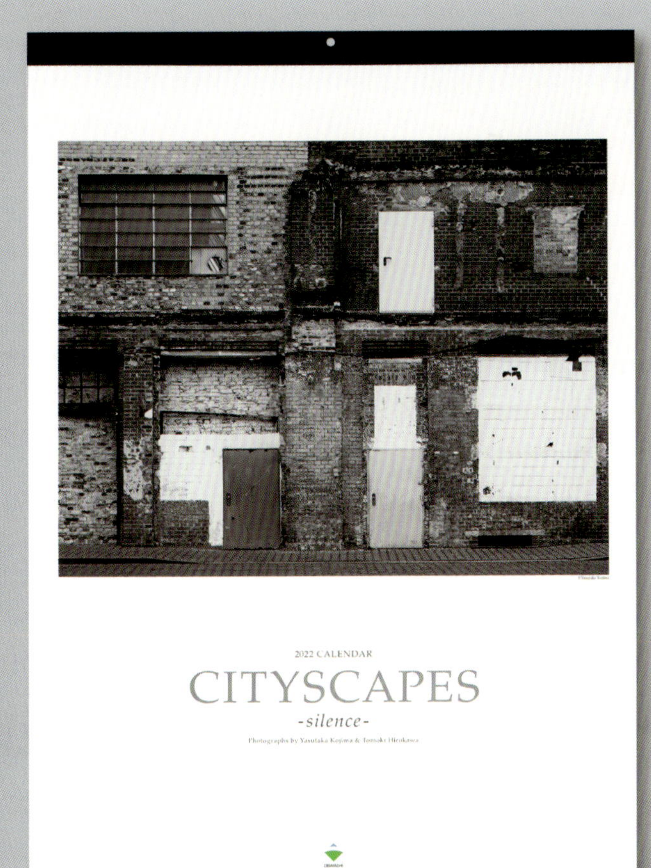

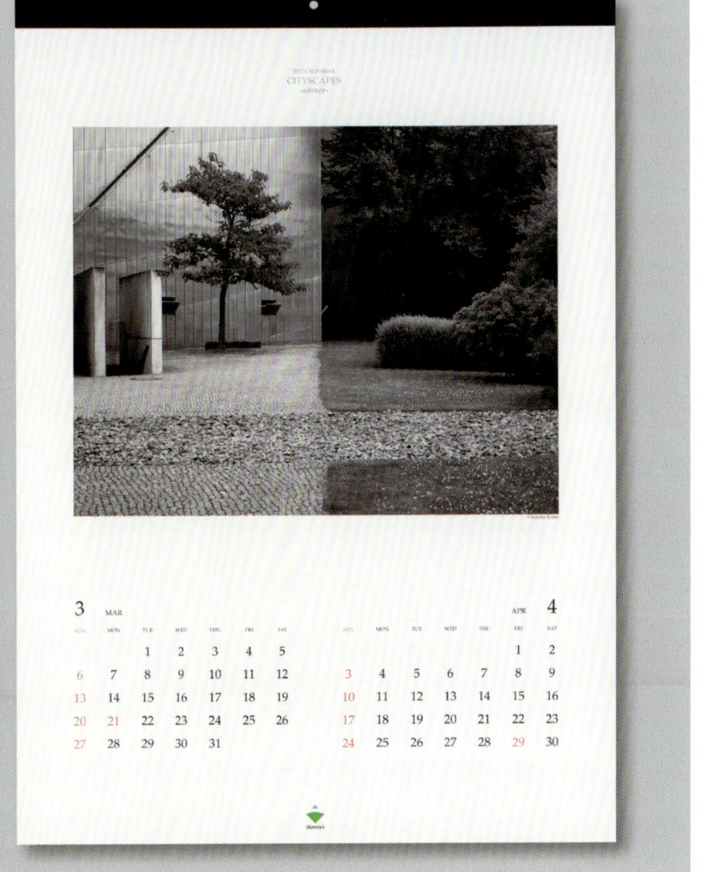

Title: CITYSCAPES -silence- | **Client:** Obayashi Corporation | **Design Firm:** Toppan Inc.

MASAHIRO AOYAGI

Title: PLANET OF LIFE | **Client:** Mitsubishi Electric Corporation | **Design Firm:** Toppan Inc.

MASAHIRO AOYAGI

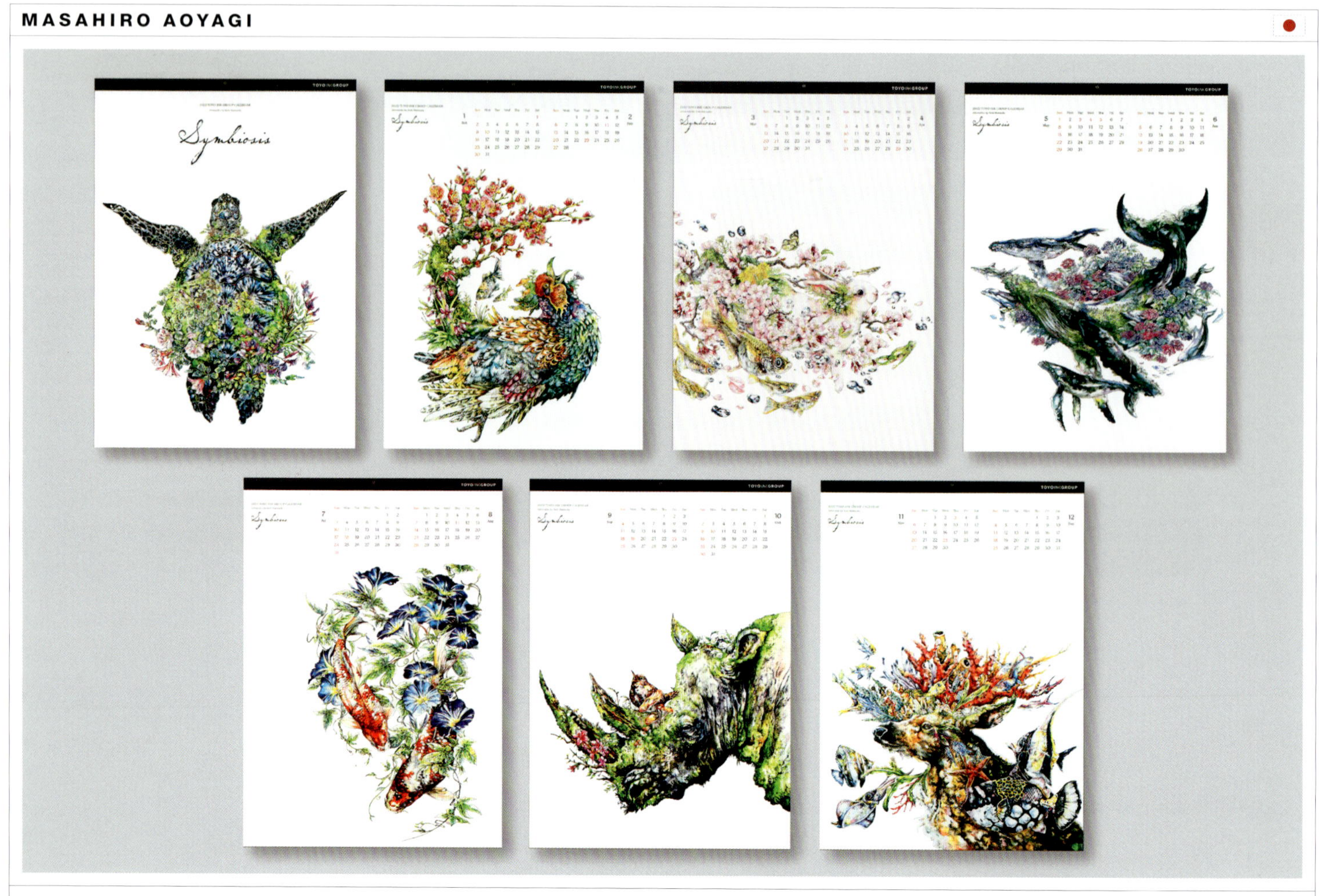

Title: 2022 TOYO INK GROUP CALENDAR SYMBIOSIS | **Client:** Toyo Ink SC Holdings Co., Ltd. | **Design Firm:** Toppan Inc.

KYLE R. THOMPSON

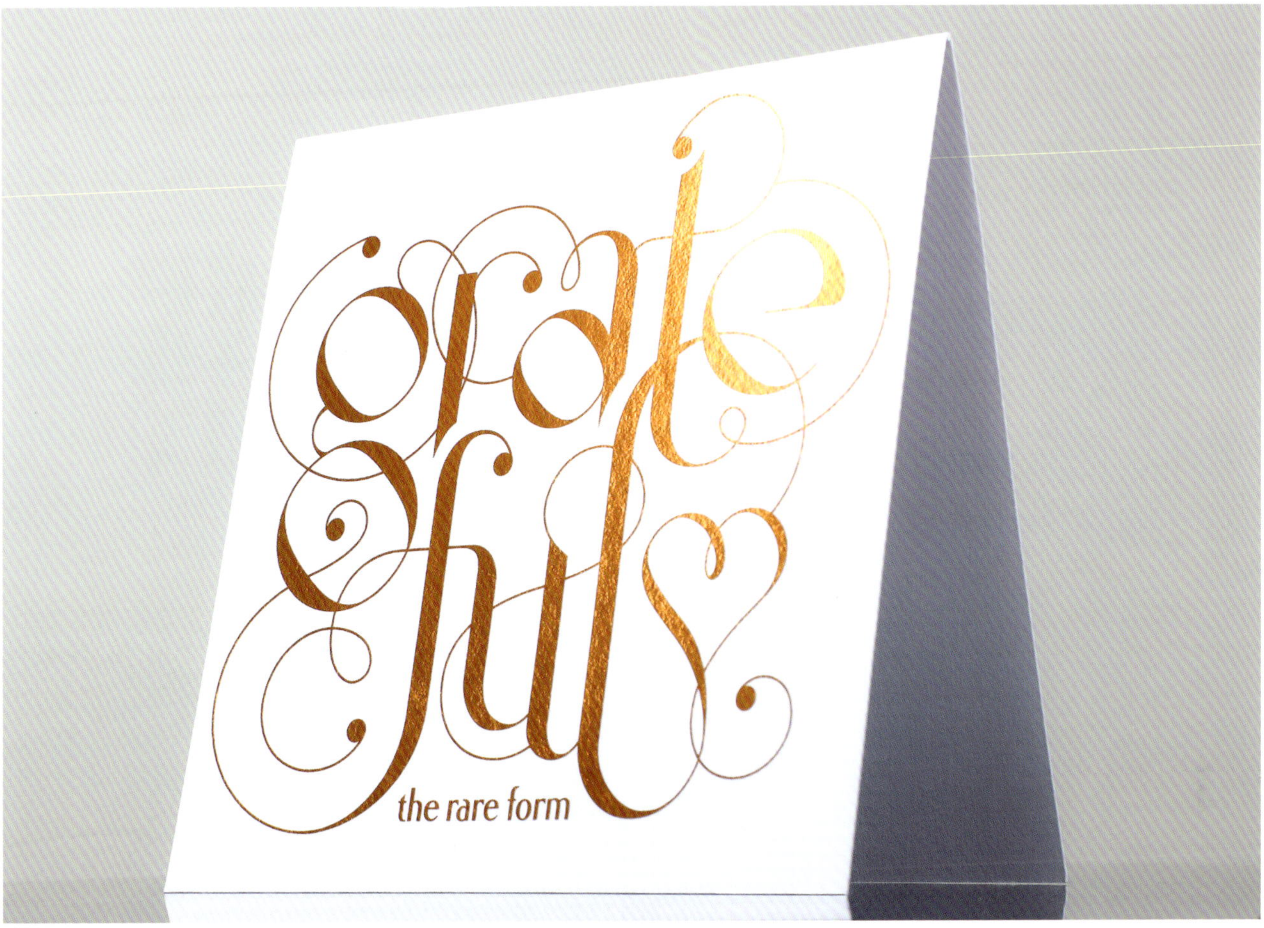

Title: Grateful — Typography Card | **Client:** Self-initiated | **Design Firm:** The Rare Form

LEGIS DESIGN

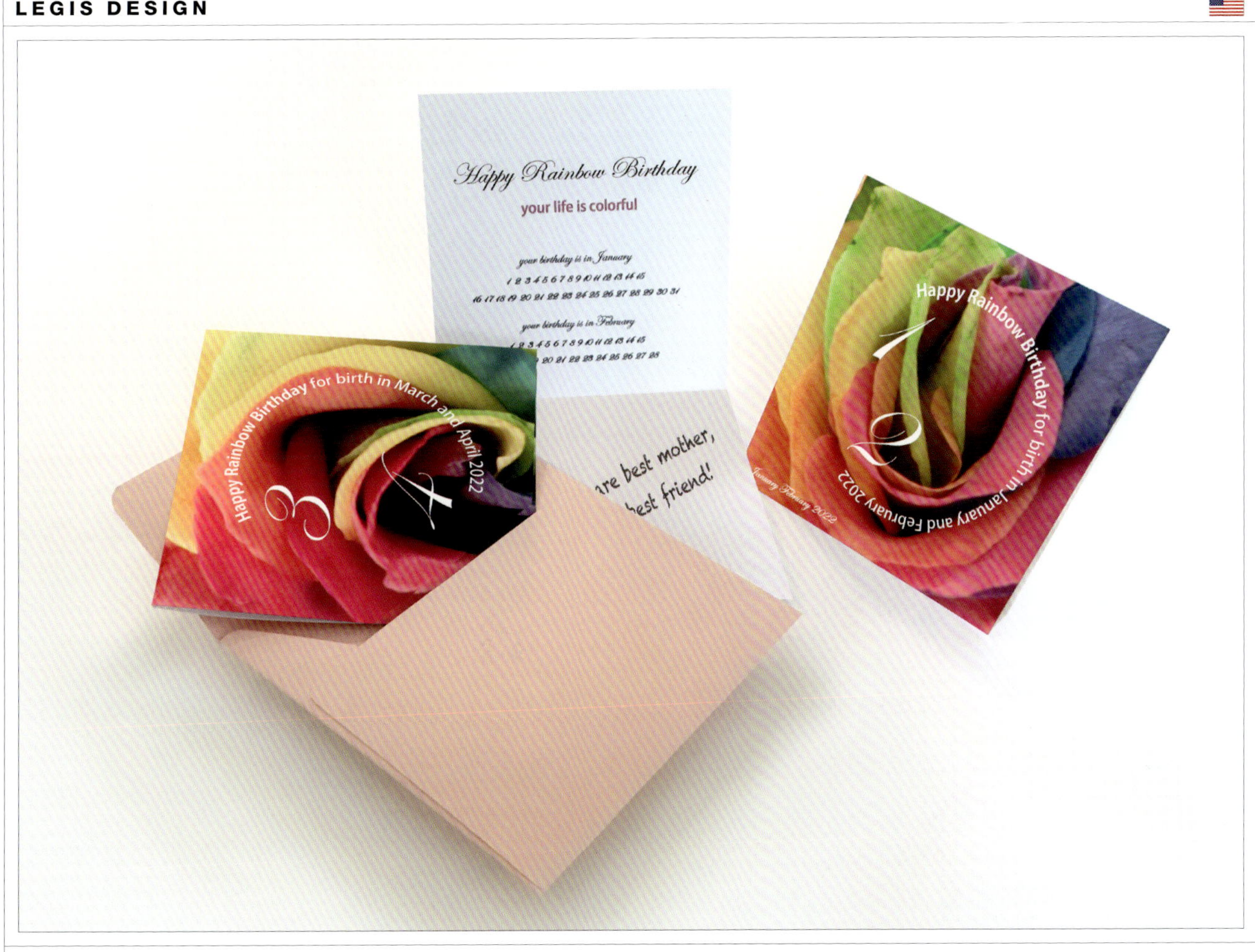

Title: Happy Rainbow Birthday Card | **Client:** Self-initiated | **Design Firm:** Legis Design

ANNA-LEA JENKINS-FERRELLE

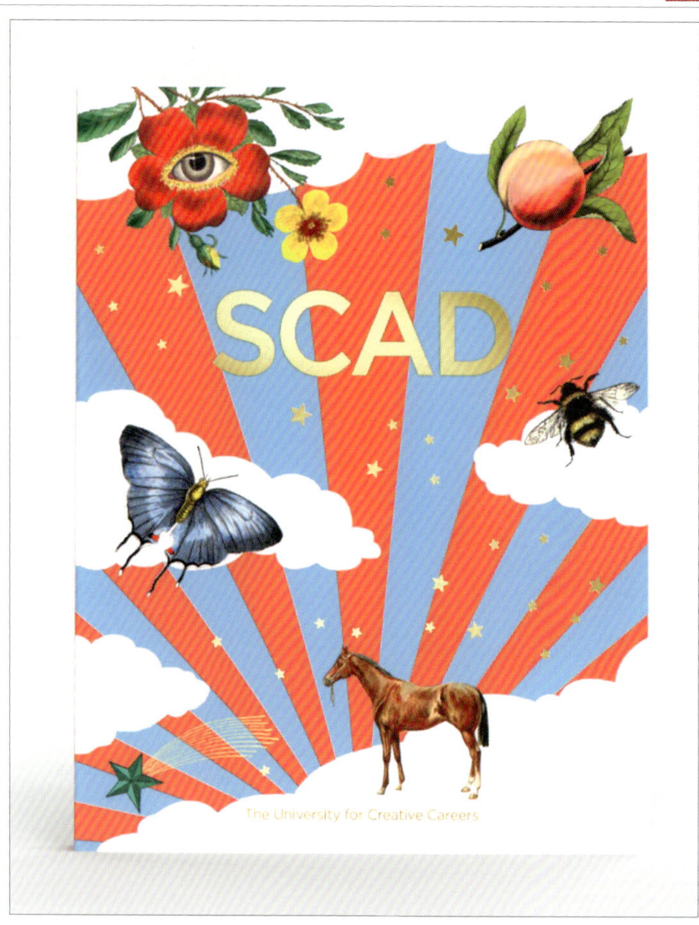

Title: SCAD Recruitment / Course Catalog | **Client:** Self-initiated
Design Firm: Savannah College of Art and Design

JENNIFER BERNSTEIN, REBECCA JAMPOL

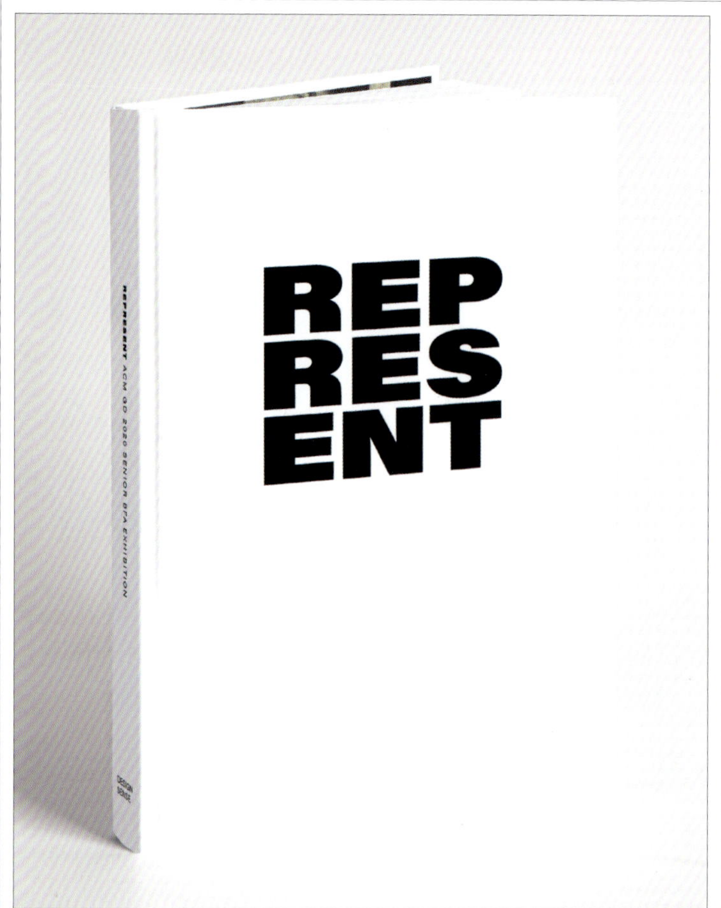

Title: REPRESENT: ACM Graphic Design 2020 BFA Printed Exhibition
Client: Rutgers University-Newark | **Design Firm:** REPRESENT Designers

KAREN WATKINS

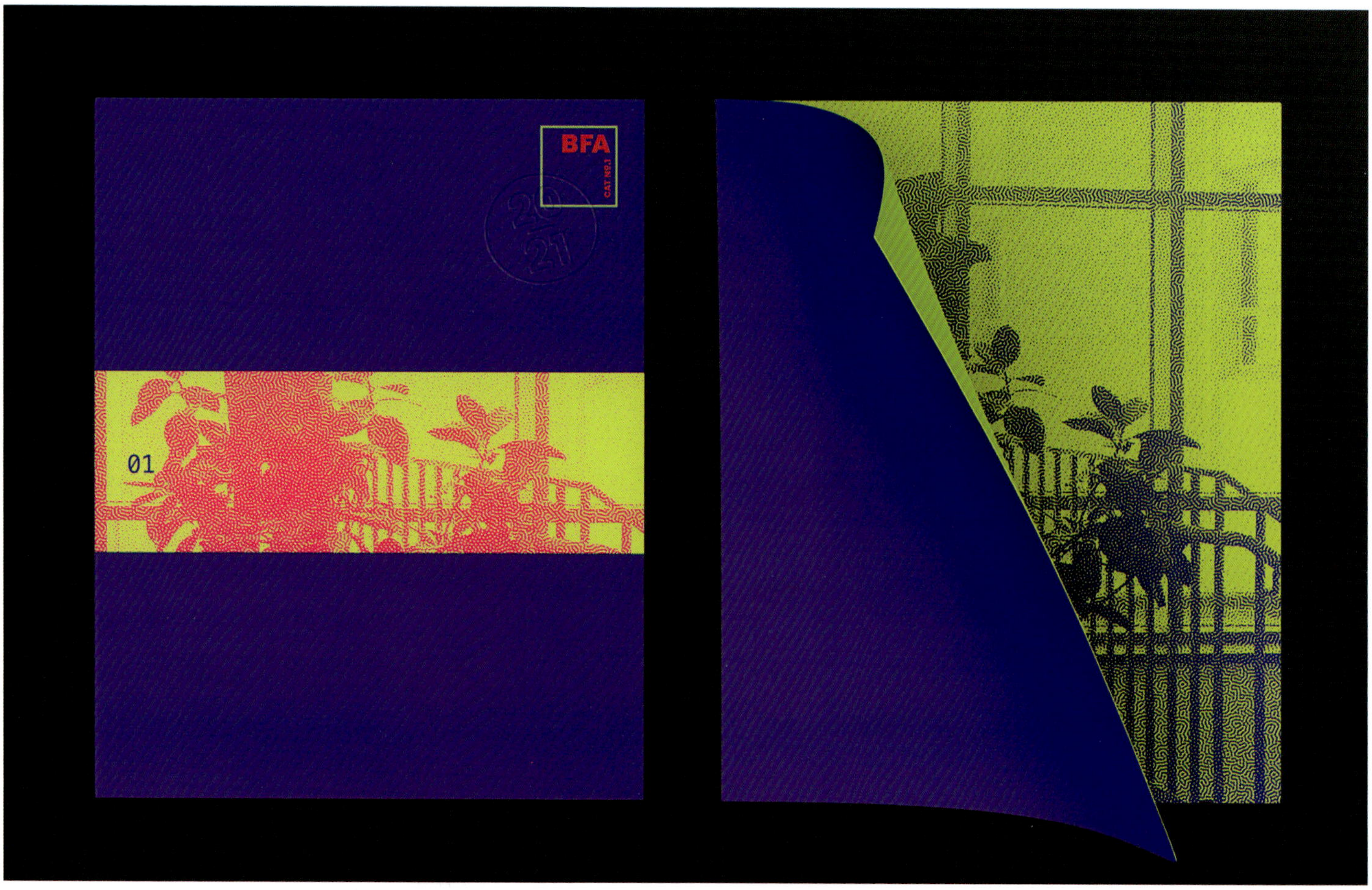

Title: West Chester University 2021 BFA Catalog | **Client:** West Chester University | **Design Firm:** Karen Watkins Design

ANDREW LAWRENCE

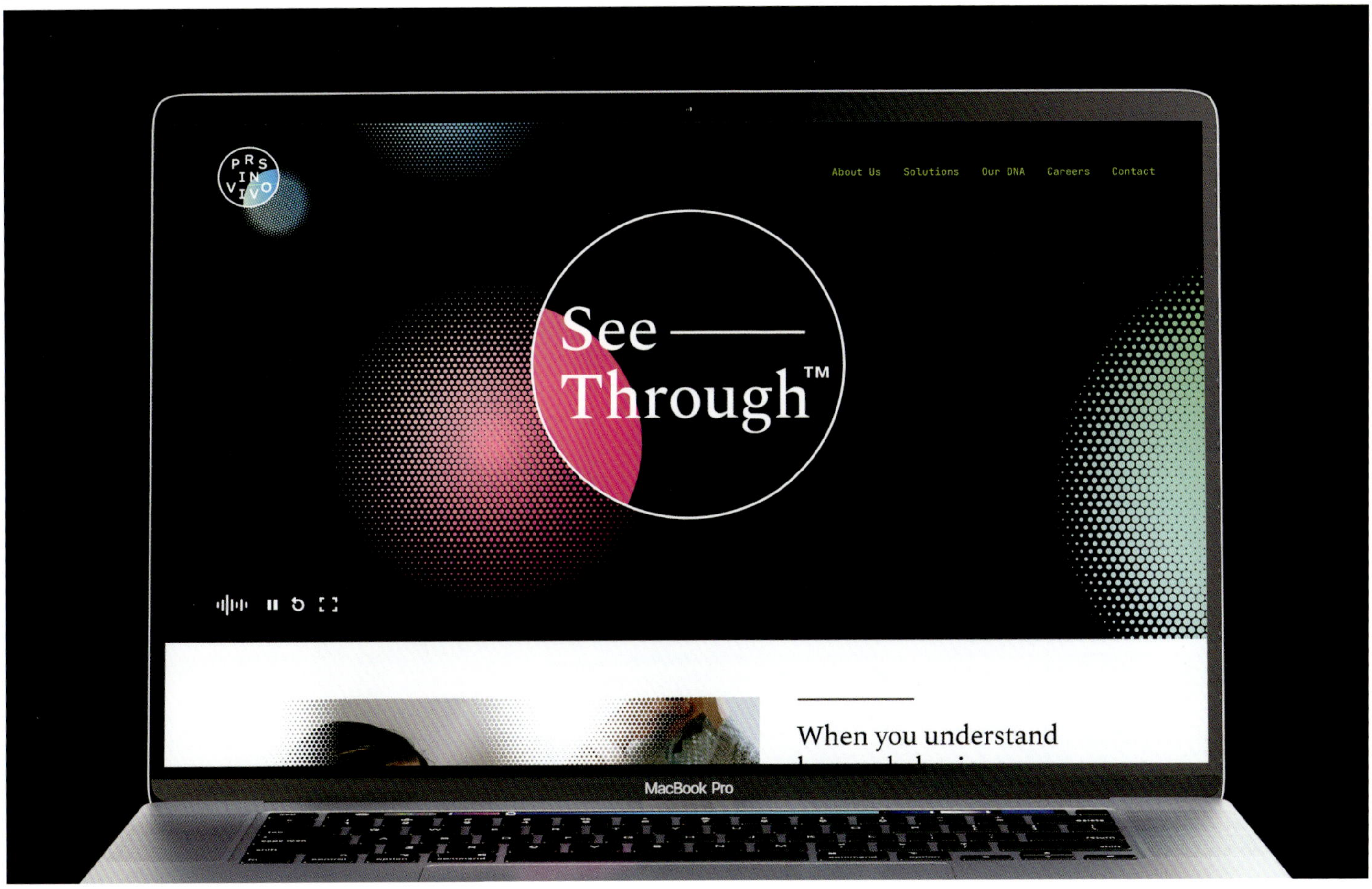

Title: PRS IN VIVO | **Client:** PRS IN VIVO | **Design Firm:** Elmwood

TEIGA, STUDIO.

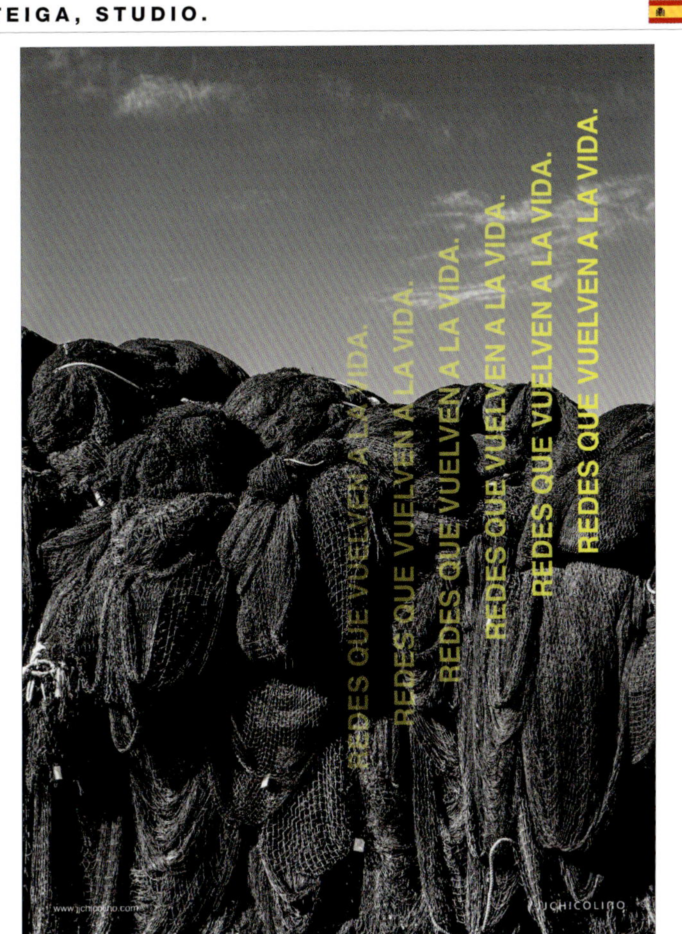

Title: Poster J.J. Chicolino | **Client:** J.J. Chicolino
Design Firm: Teiga, Studio.

NORIYUKI KASAI

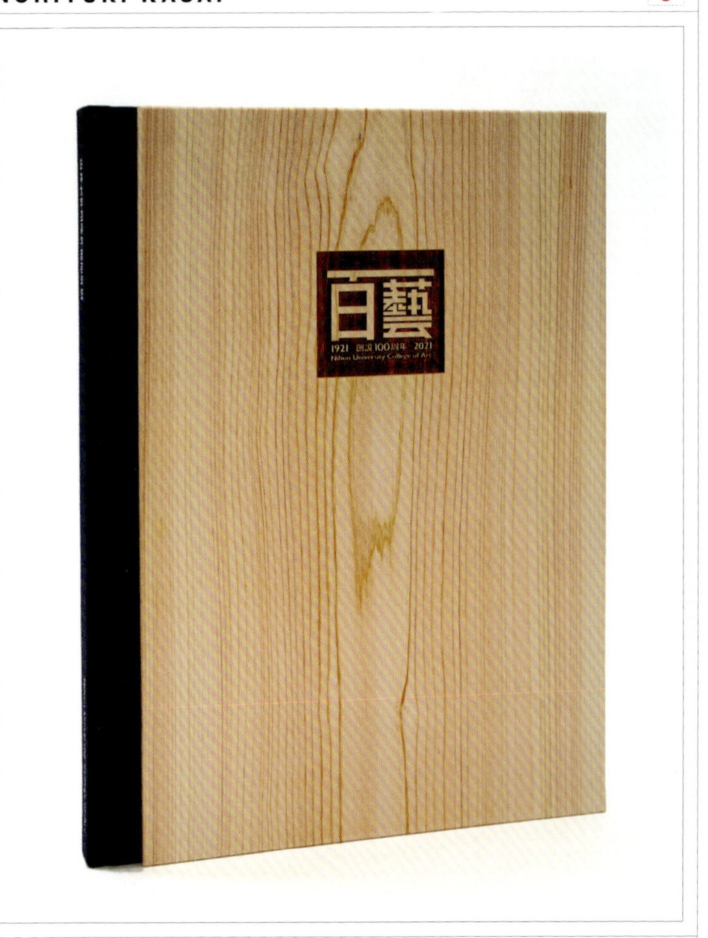

Title: Nihon University College of Art 100 Yearbook
Client: Nihon University College of Art | **Design Firm:** Noriyuki Kasai

TREVETT MCCANDLISS, NANCY CAMPBELL

a SHORE THING

Designers draw upon nature for organic hues, sweet prints and fabrics that move effortlessly in the salty air.

Photography by Trevett McCandliss & Thomas Viglietta

Arianna is wearing a dress by **Abel & Lula**.

19

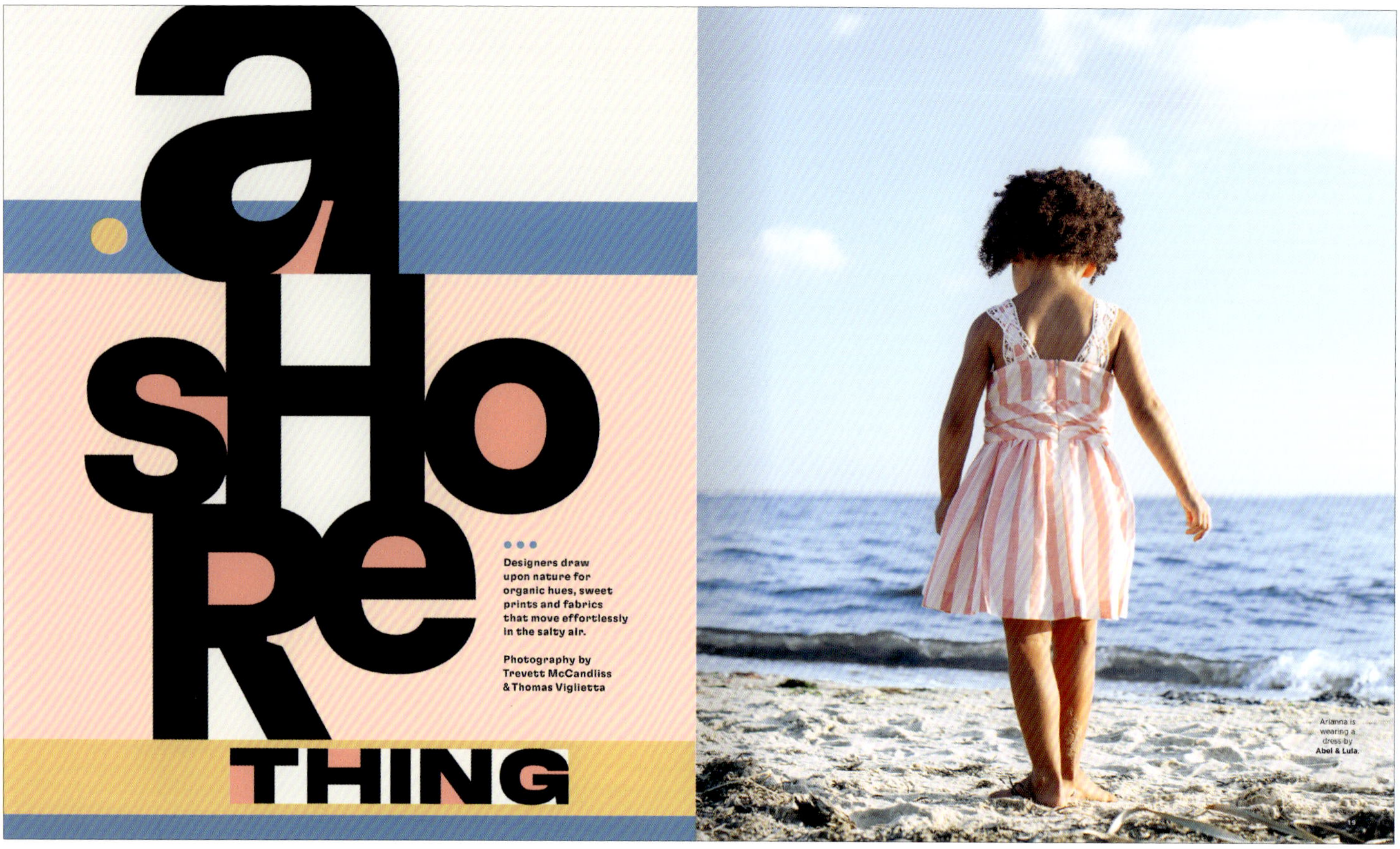

Title: A Shore Thing | **Client:** Earnshaw's Magazine | **Design Firm:** Wainscot Media

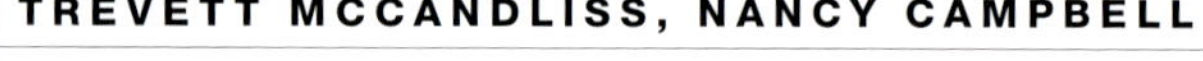

TREVETT MCCANDLISS, NANCY CAMPBELL

CULTURE CLUB

DYNAMIC AND DARING, THE FALL COLLECTIONS STEP OUT WITH HIGH-OCTANE COLOR, FUNKY PRINTS AND KINETIC MATERIALS ALL DESIGNED TO MOVE.

PHOTOGRAPHY BY ZOE ADLERSBERG
STYLING BY MARIAH WALKER

Victoria is wearing a T-shirt and pants by **Molo**, sweater by **Nono** and a vintage hat. *Opposite page:* Wyatt is wearing a bodysuit by **We Love Colors**, overalls and sweatshirt by **The Animal Observatory**, socks by **Puma**, shoes by **Cape Clogs**.

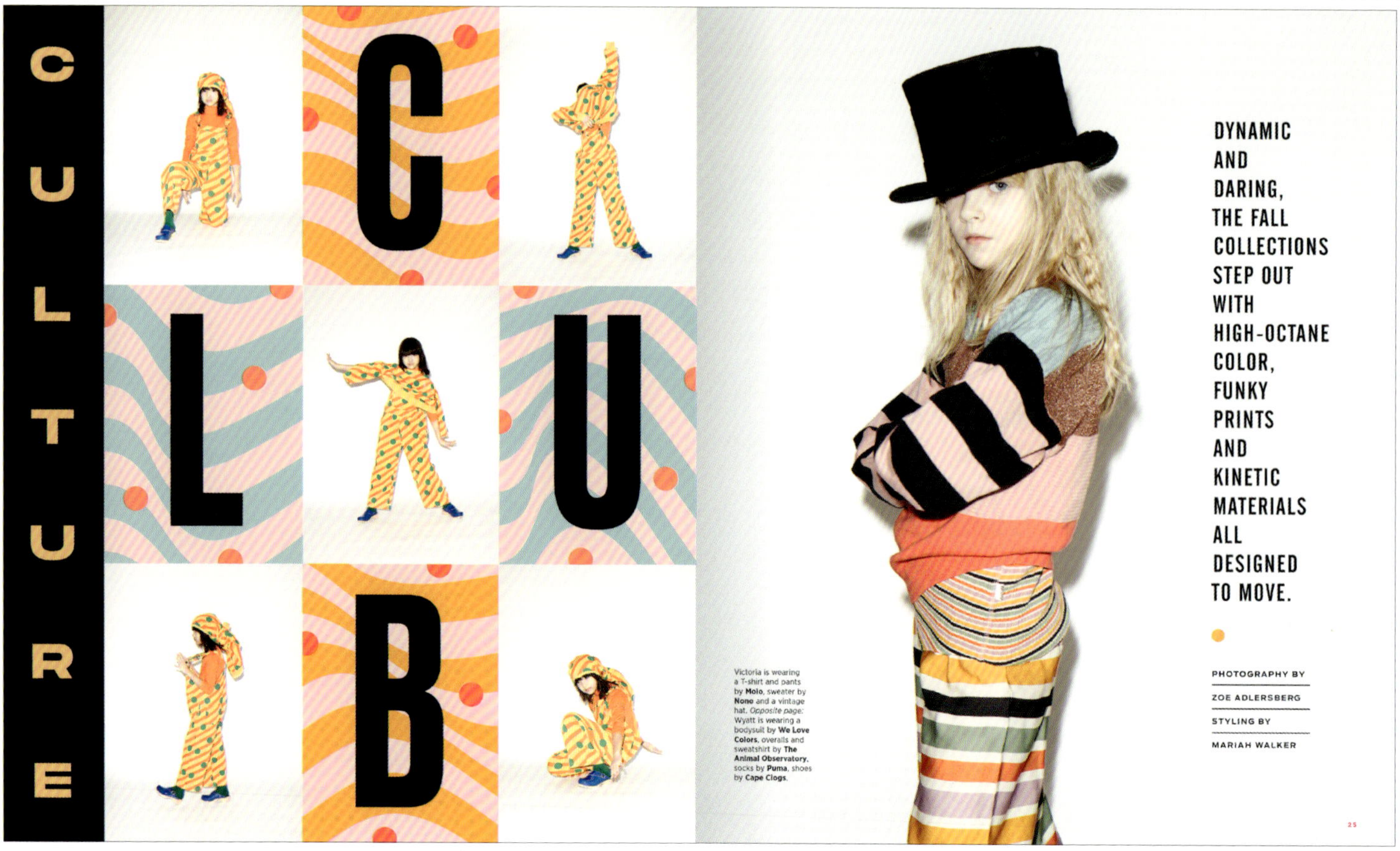

Title: Culture Club | **Client:** Earnshaw's Magazine | **Design Firm:** Wainscot Media

TREVETT MCCANDLISS, NANCY CAMPBELL

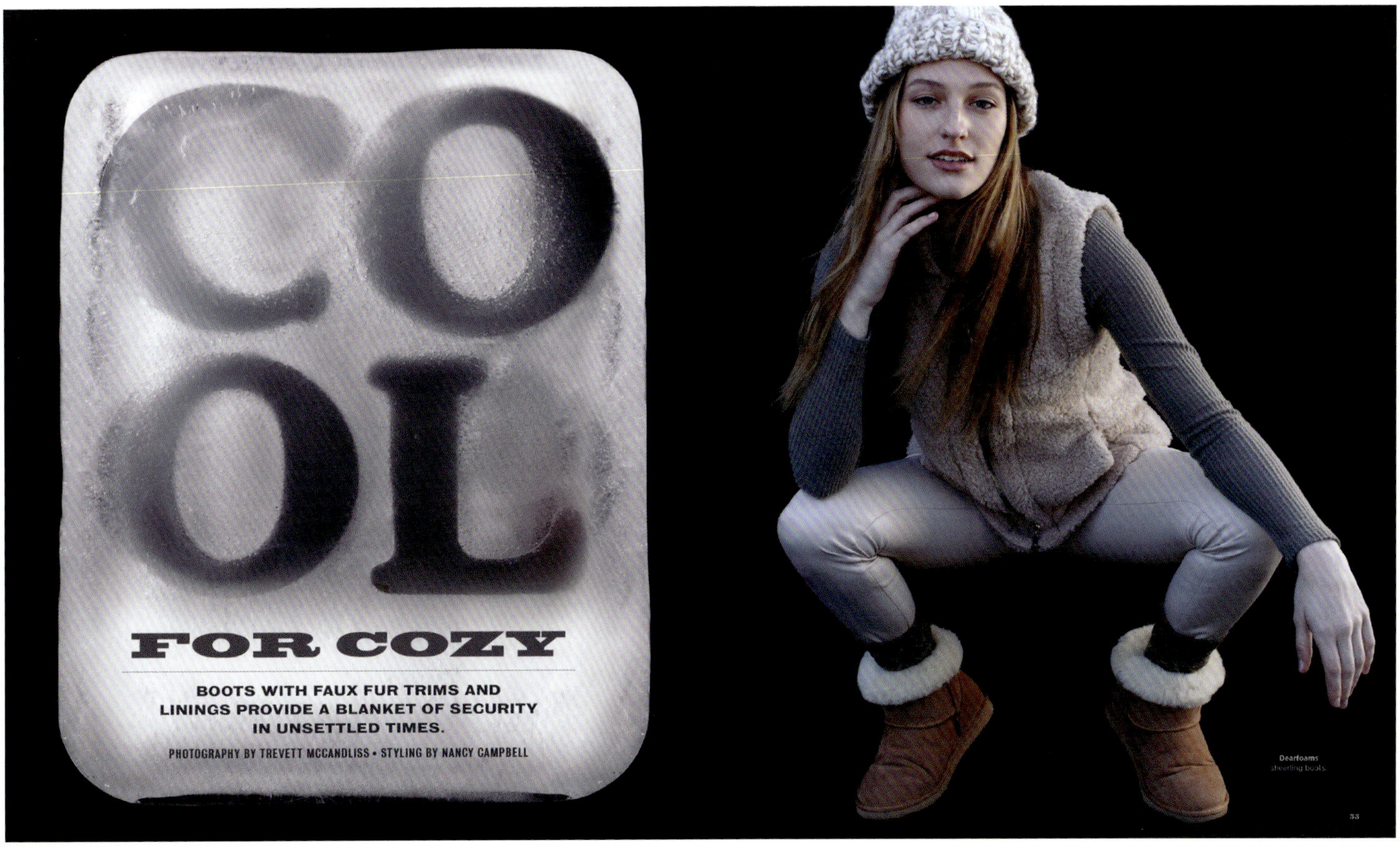

COOL

FOR COZY

BOOTS WITH FAUX FUR TRIMS AND LININGS PROVIDE A BLANKET OF SECURITY IN UNSETTLED TIMES.

PHOTOGRAPHY BY TREVETT MCCANDLISS • STYLING BY NANCY CAMPBELL

Title: Cool for Cozy | **Client:** Footwear Plus Magazine | **Design Firm:** Wainscot Media

GRACE CHUANG, LEON DISCHE BECKER, ALEXA GARCIA, CHRISTINA AGAPAKIS

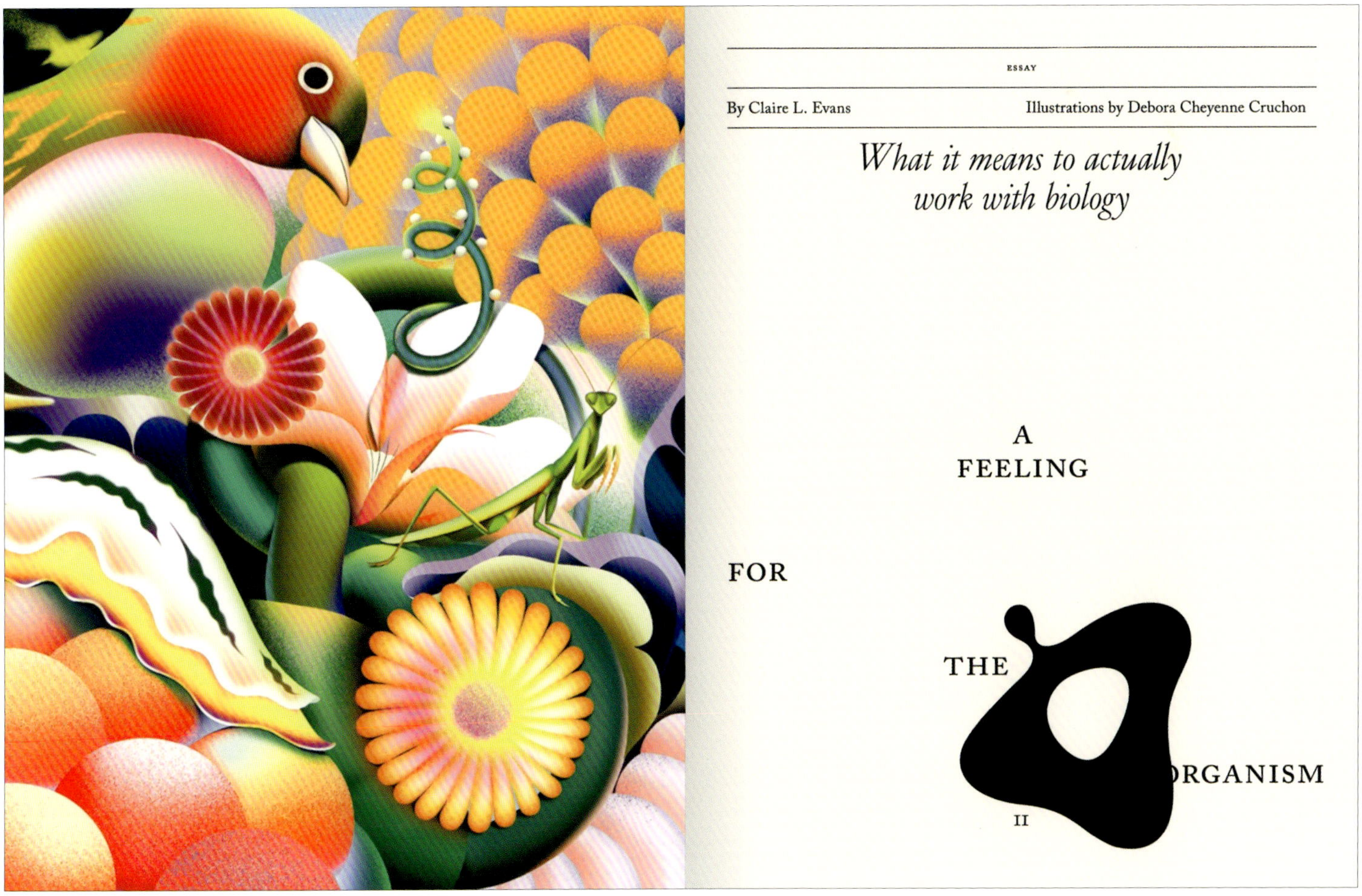

ESSAY

By Claire L. Evans Illustrations by Debora Cheyenne Cruchon

What it means to actually work with biology

A FEELING FOR THE ORGANISM

II

Title: Grow | **Client:** Self-initiated | **Design Firm:** Ginkgo Bioworks

JENNIFER BARLOW

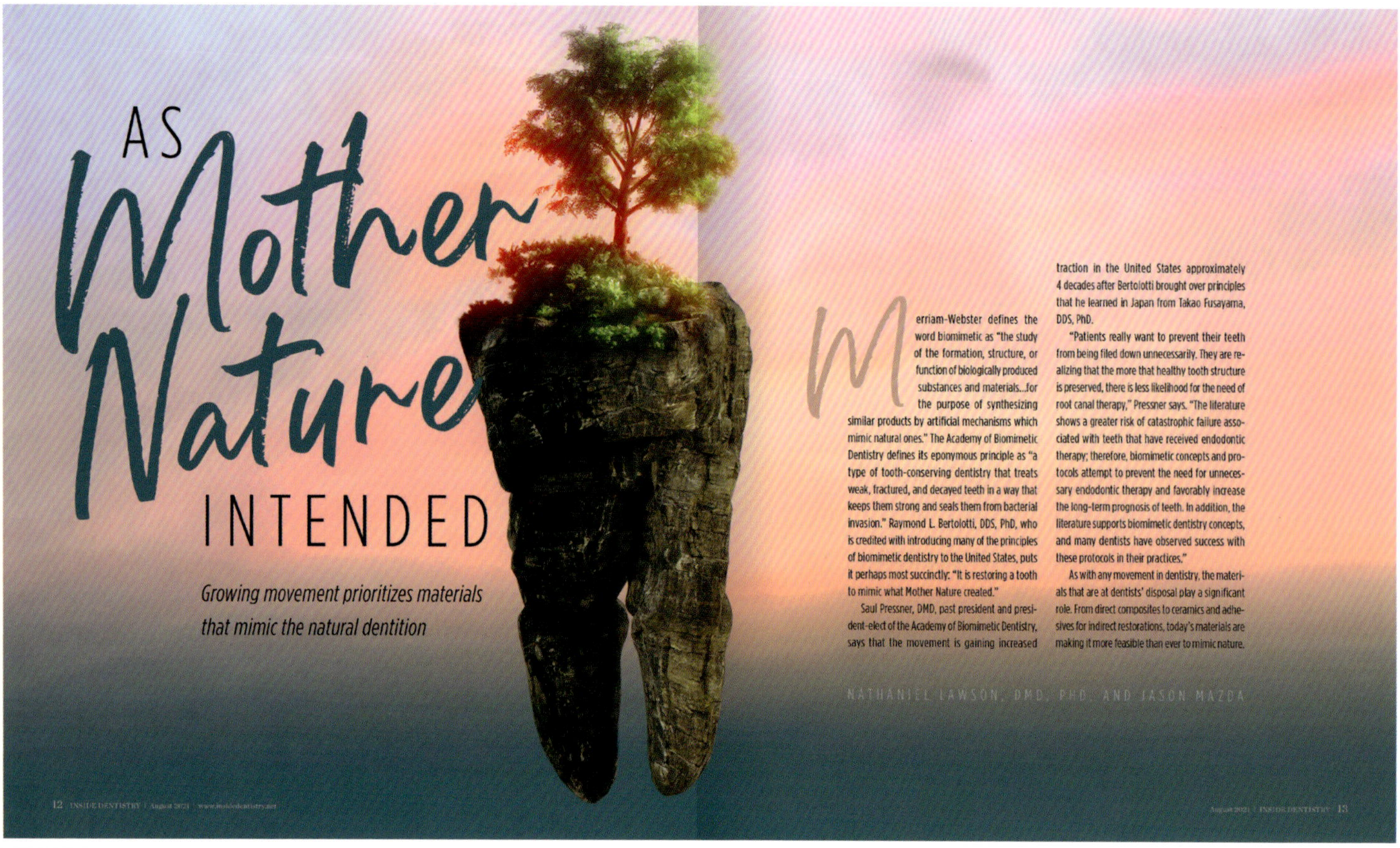

AS Mother Nature INTENDED

Growing movement prioritizes materials that mimic the natural dentition

Merriam-Webster defines the word biomimetic as "the study of the formation, structure, or function of biologically produced substances and materials…for the purpose of synthesizing similar products by artificial mechanisms which mimic natural ones." The Academy of Biomimetic Dentistry defines its eponymous principle as "a type of tooth-conserving dentistry that treats weak, fractured, and decayed teeth in a way that keeps them strong and seals them from bacterial invasion." Raymond L. Bertolotti, DDS, PhD, who is credited with introducing many of the principles of biomimetic dentistry to the United States, puts it perhaps most succinctly: "It is restoring a tooth to mimic what Mother Nature created."

Saul Pressner, DMD, past president and president-elect of the Academy of Biomimetic Dentistry, says that the movement is gaining increased traction in the United States approximately 4 decades after Bertolotti brought over principles that he learned in Japan from Takao Fusayama, DDS, PhD.

"Patients really want to prevent their teeth from being filed down unnecessarily. They are realizing that the more that healthy tooth structure is preserved, there is less likelihood for the need of root canal therapy," Pressner says. "The literature shows a greater risk of catastrophic failure associated with teeth that have received endodontic therapy; therefore, biomimetic concepts and protocols attempt to prevent the need for unnecessary endodontic therapy and favorably increase the long-term prognosis of teeth. In addition, the literature supports biomimetic dentistry concepts, and many dentists have observed success with these protocols in their practices."

As with any movement in dentistry, the materials that are at dentists' disposal play a significant role. From direct composites to ceramics and adhesives for indirect restorations, today's materials are making it more feasible than ever to mimic nature.

NATHANIEL LAWSON, DMD, PHD, AND JASON MAZDA

Title: As Mother Nature Intended | **Client:** Inside Dentistry | **Design Firm:** Aegis Dental Network

TREVETT MCCANDLISS, NANCY CAMPBELL

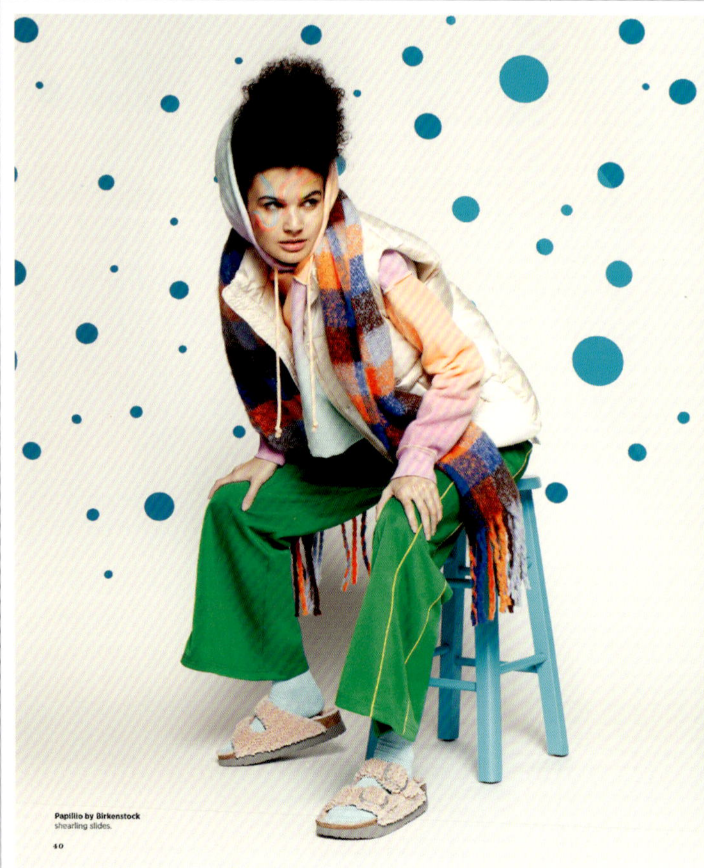

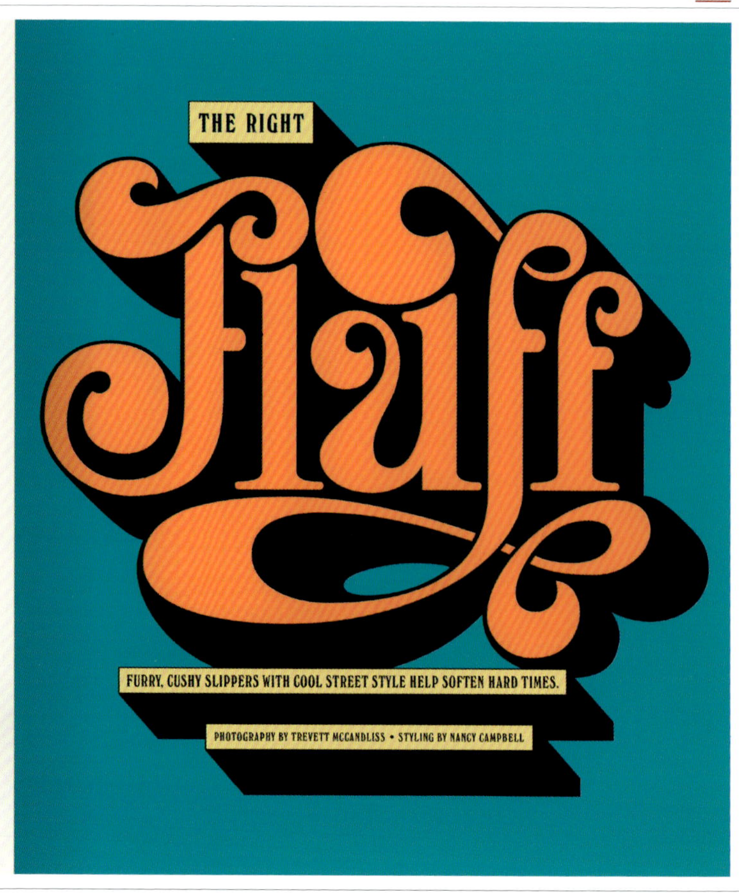

Title: The Right Fluff | **Client:** Footwear Plus Magazine | **Design Firm:** Wainscot Media

DREXEL UNIVERSITY THOMAS R. KLINE SCHOOL OF LAW

LEX

THE MAGAZINE OF DREXEL UNIVERSITY THOMAS R. KLINE SCHOOL OF LAW

2021

- Pasquale on Robots
- Horwitz on Balkin
- St. Katharine and the Drexel Family Legacy
- Benforado on Kids
- Cohen on the Court

Yesterday & Tomorrow

Title: Lex 2021 – The Magazine of Drexel Univ. Thomas R. Kline School of Law
Client: Drexel Univ. Thomas R. Kline School of Law | **Design Firm:** Ahoy Studios

WENDY LOWDEN

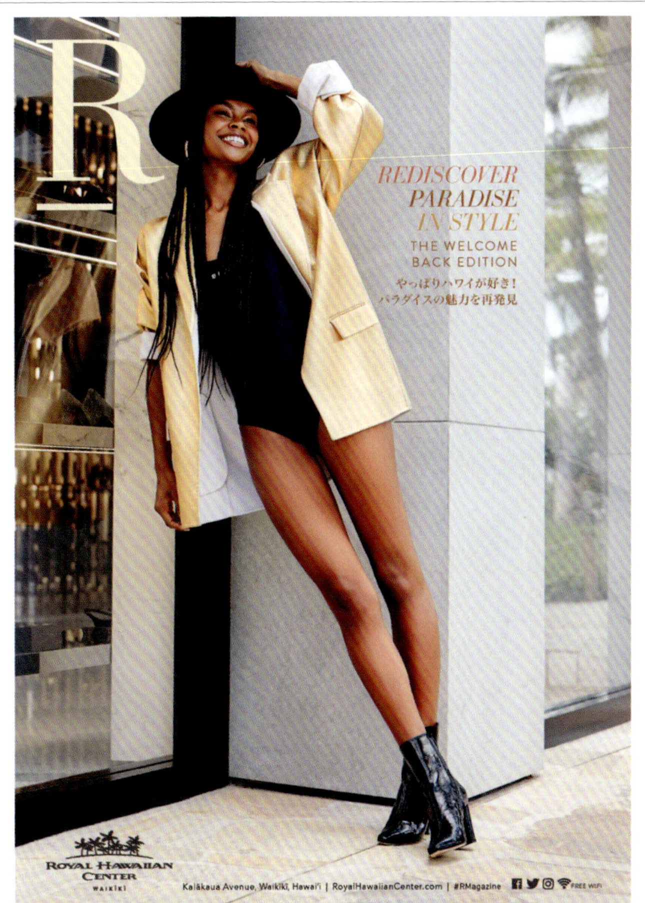

Title: R Magazine Fall 2021 | **Client:** Royal Hawaiian Center
Design Firm: House of Current

ARIEL FREANER

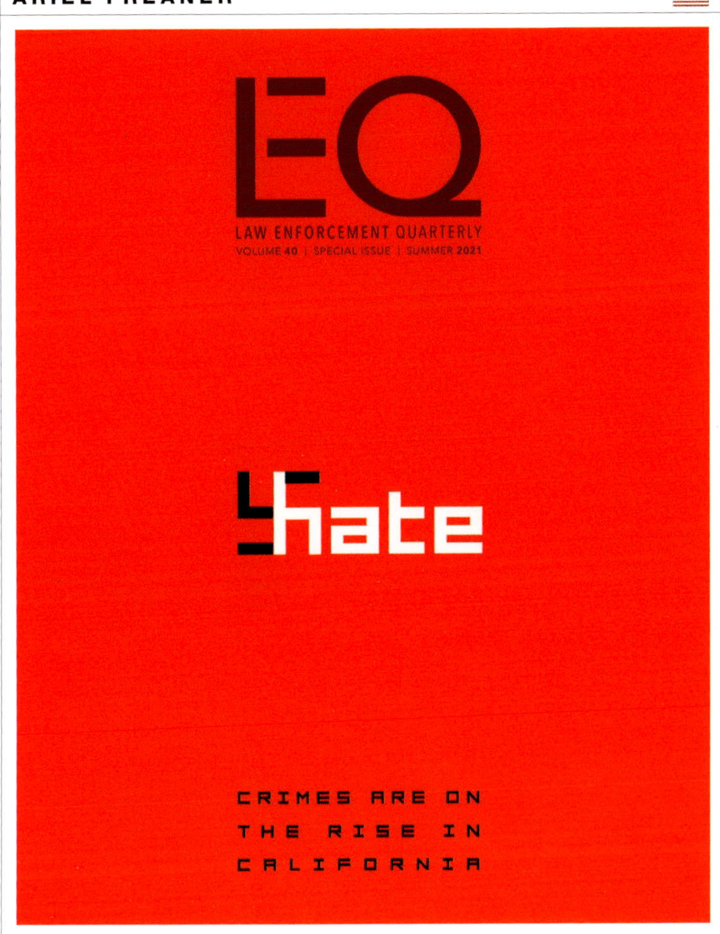

Title: LEQ Magazine Cover HATE | **Client:** San Diego County District Attorneys Office | **Design Firm:** Freaner Creative & Design

YIJIA XIE

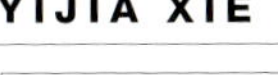

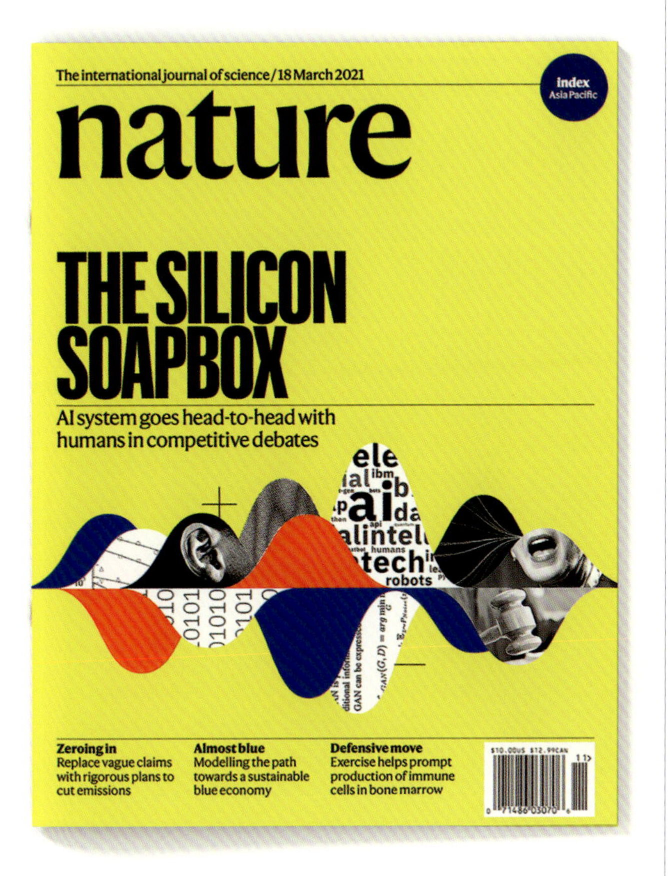

Title: Project Debater / Nature Cover Design
Client: Nature | **Design Firm:** IBM Research

HUNDREDWEIGHT

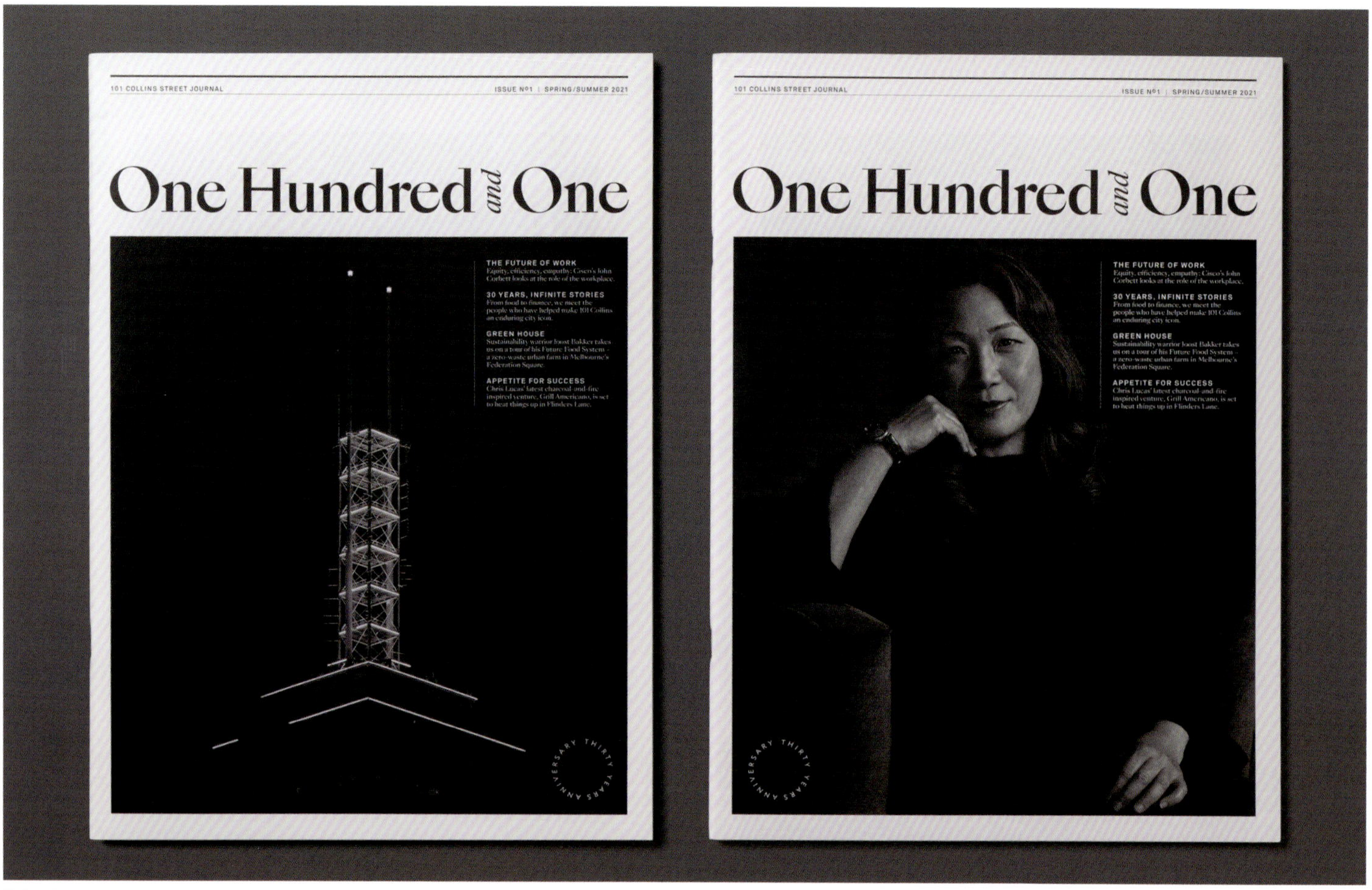

Title: One Hundred and One | **Clients:** AXA Investment Managers, Amy Elliot, Tanya Lambert | **Design Firm:** Hundredweight

COMPASS DESIGN STUDIO

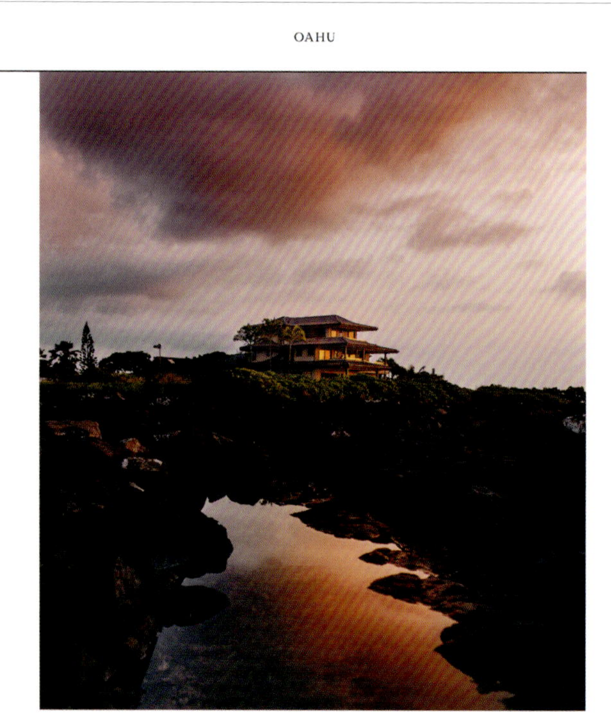

Title: 2021 Modern Luxury Compass Hawaii Takeover
Client: Self-inititated | **Design Firm:** Compass

DANIEL FRUMHOFF

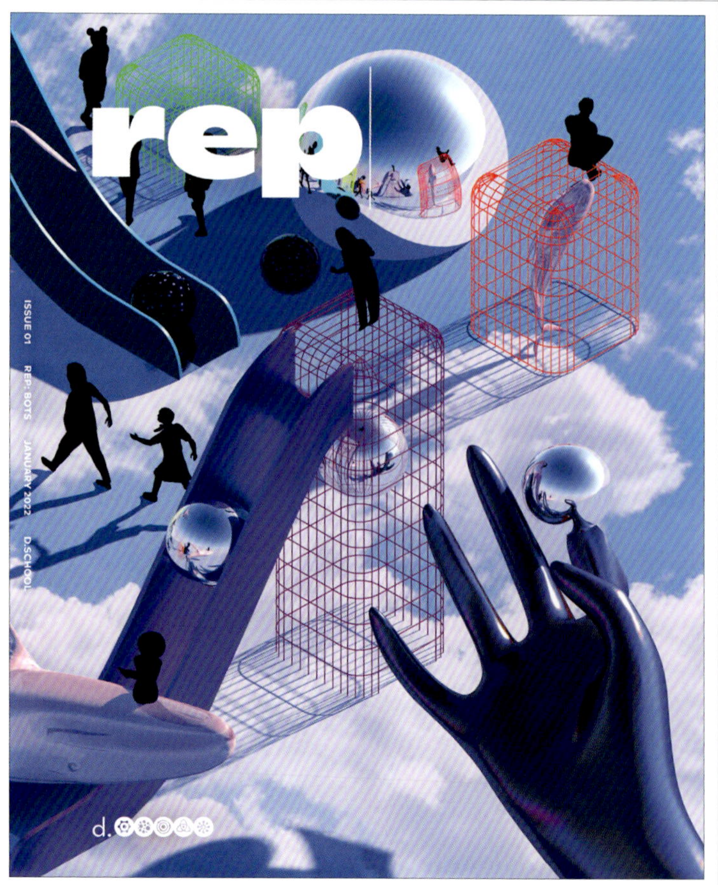

Title: Rep | Magazine | **Client:** Stanford D.School
Design Firm: Daniel Frumhoff Design

COURTNEY WINDHAM, MARGARET FLETCHER

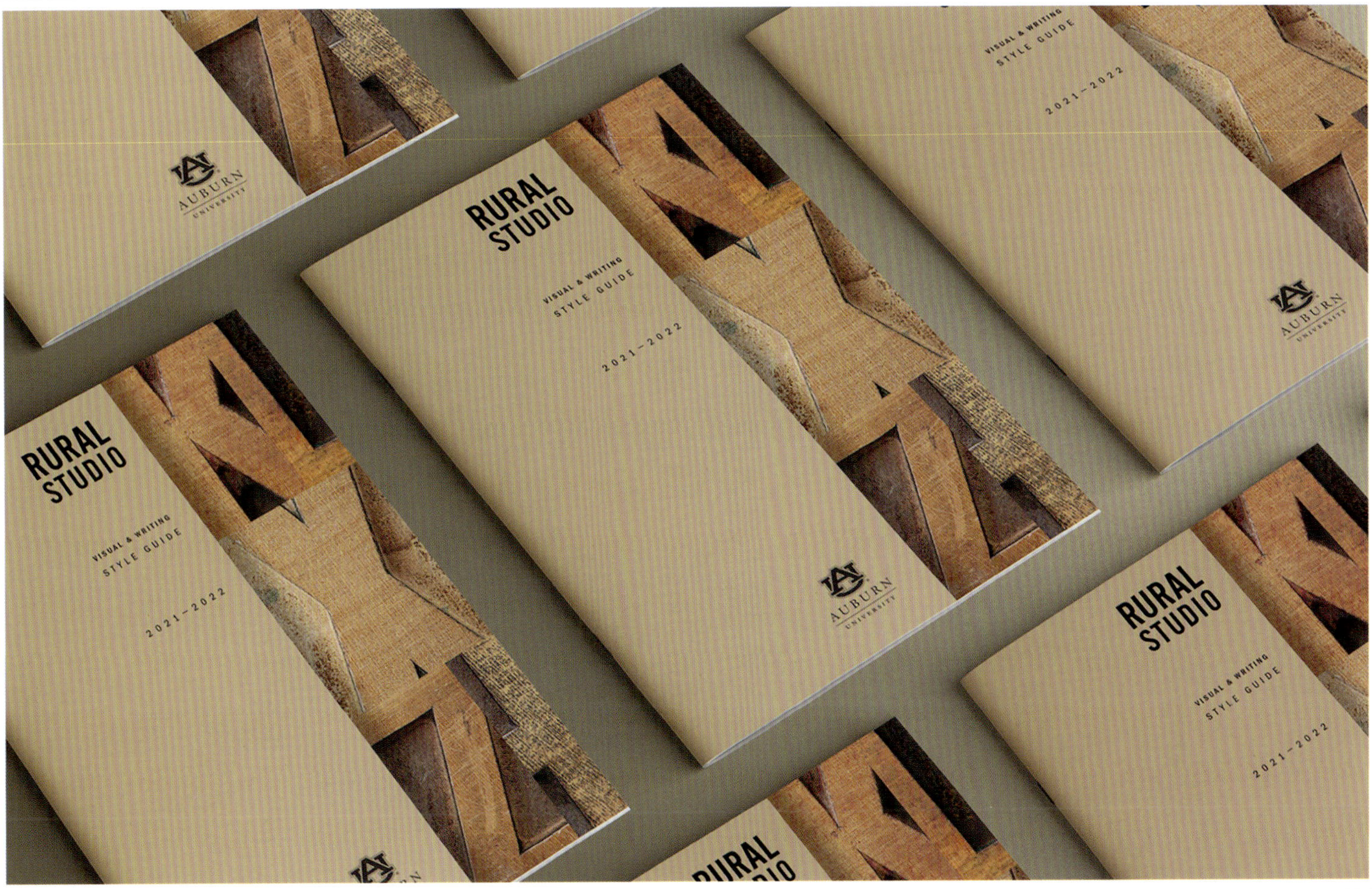

Title: Auburn University Rural Studio Style Guide | Client: Auburn University Rural Studio | Design Firms: Courtney Windham, Margaret Fletcher

ARTHOUSE DESIGN

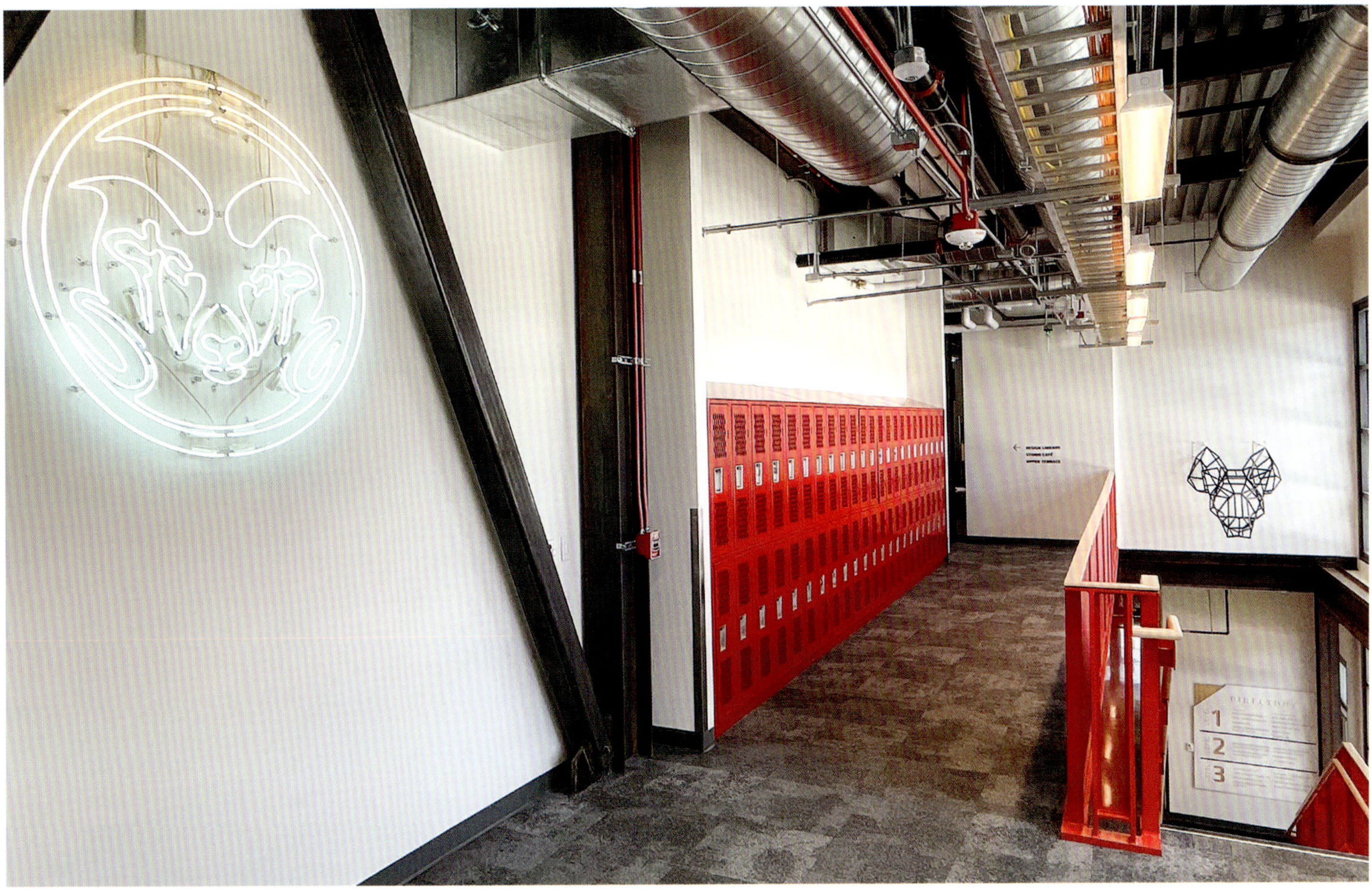

Title: CSU Nancy Richardson Design Center | Client: Colorado State University (CSU) | Design Firm: ArtHouse Design

UNDERLINE STUDIO

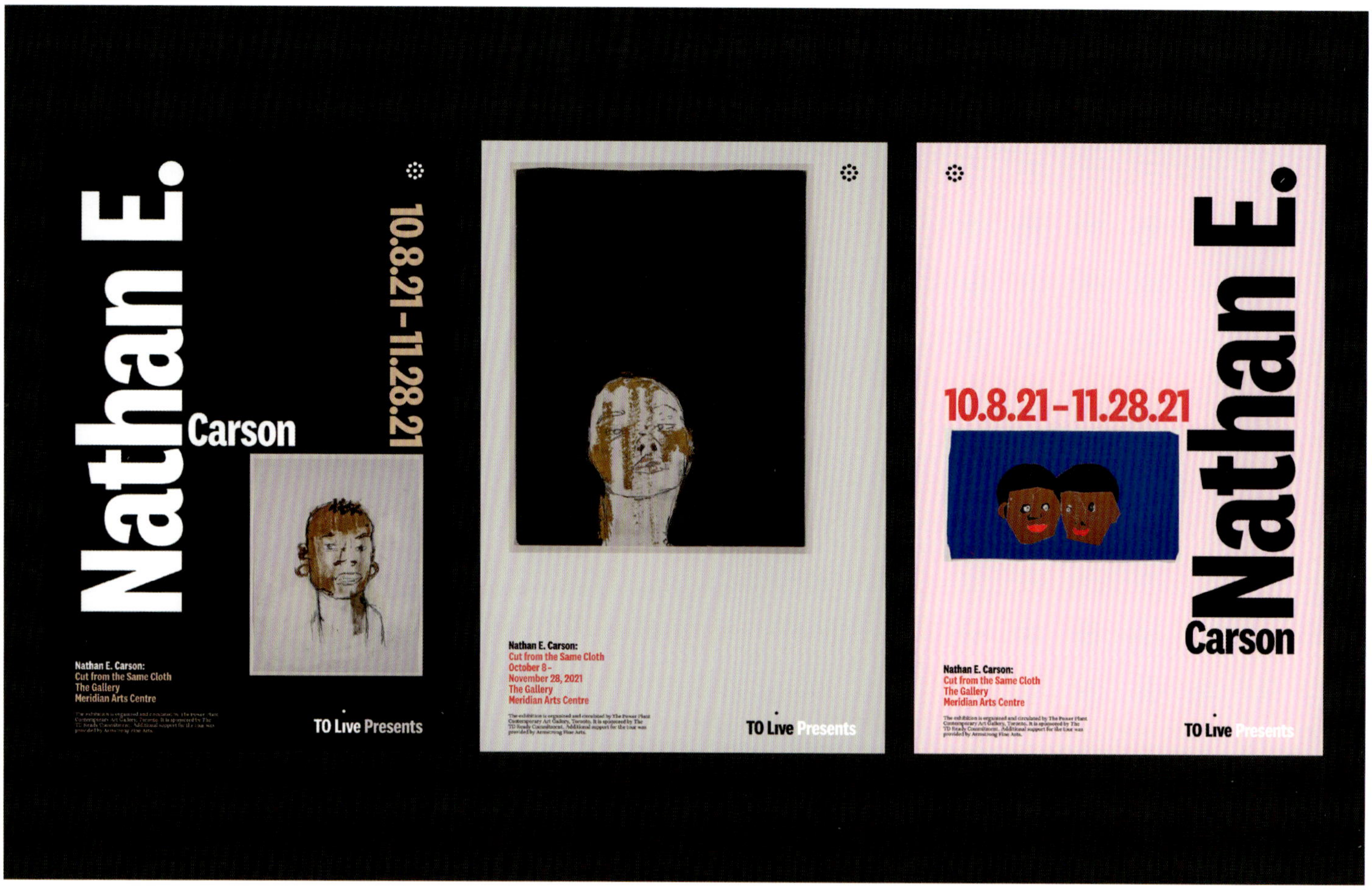

Title: TO Live Rebrand | Client: TO Live | Design Firm: Underline Studio

RANDY CLARK

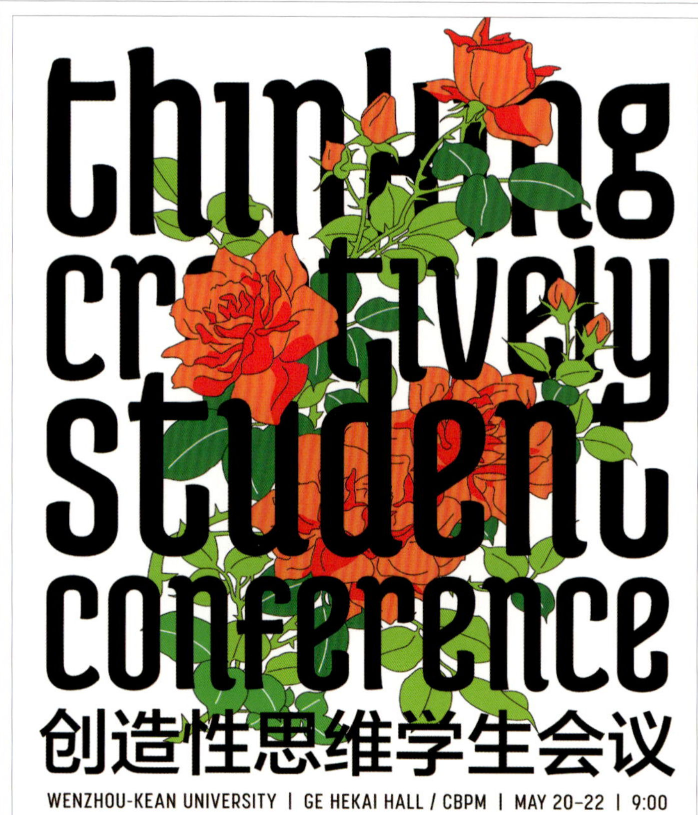

Title: Rose | **Client:** Wenzhou-Kean University
Design Firm: Randy Clark

RANDY CLARK

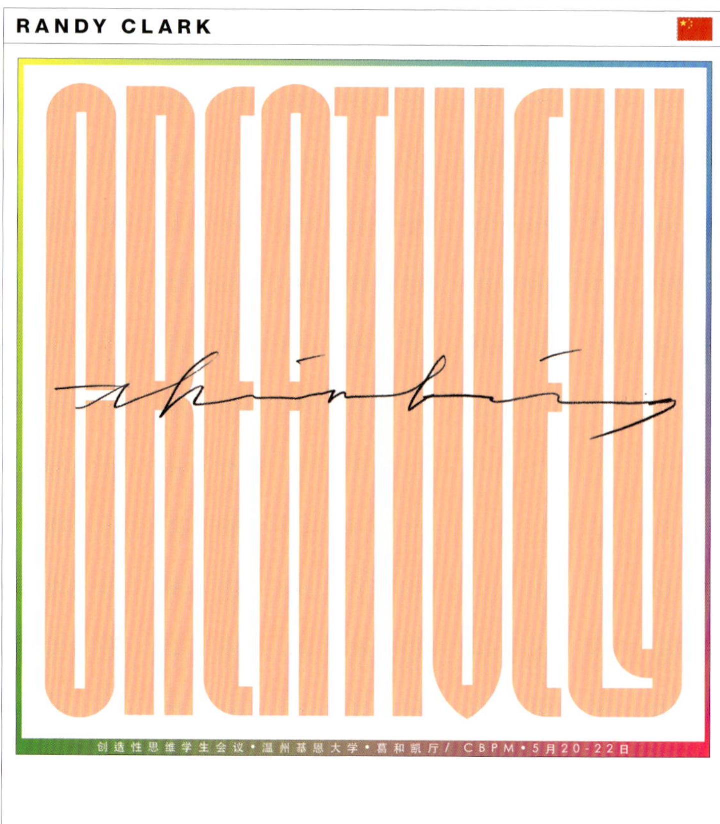

Title: Tall Type | **Client:** Wenzhou-Kean University
Design Firm: Randy Clark

ENTRO DESIGN TEAM

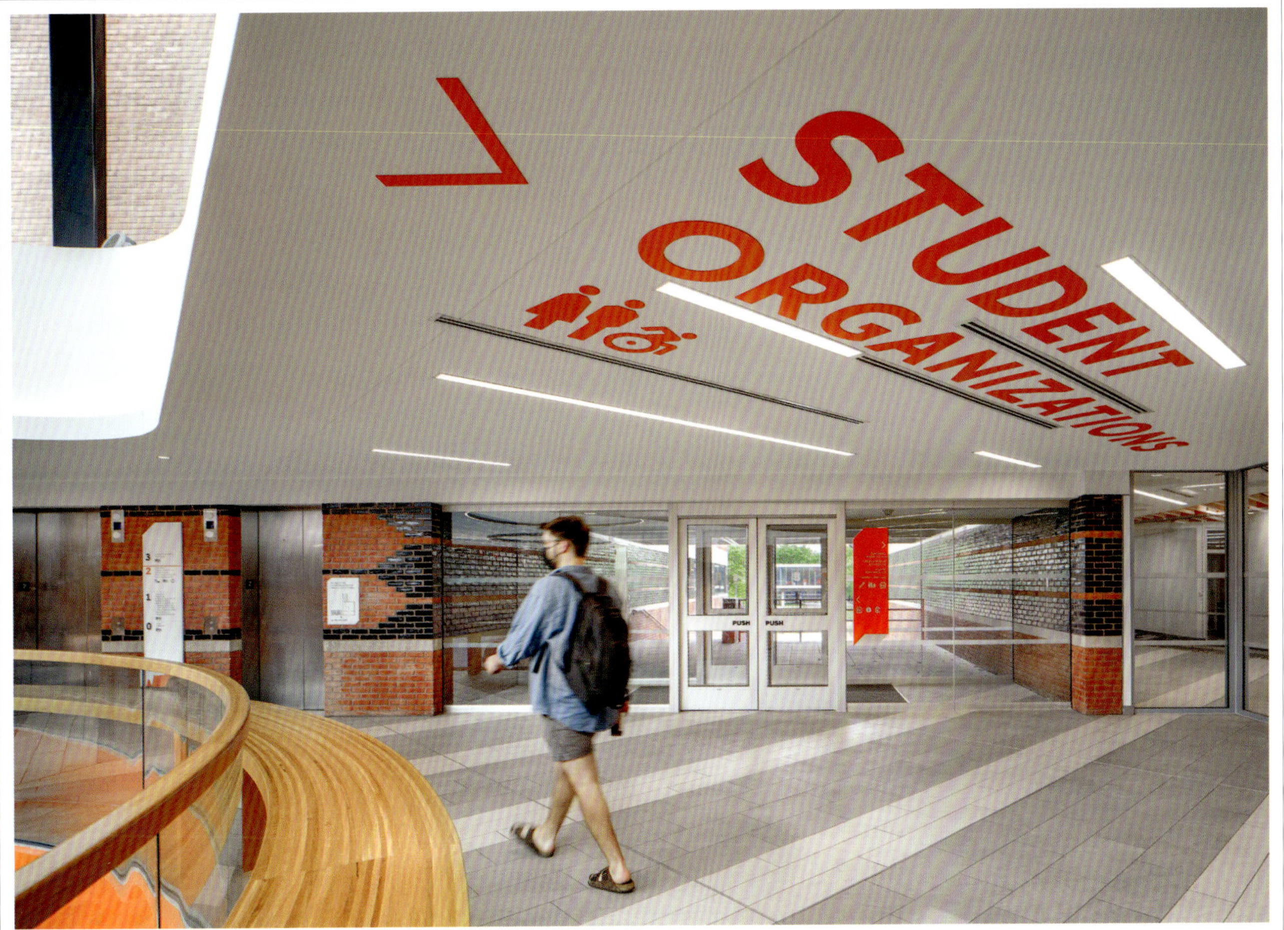

Title: Schine Student Center Wayfinding | **Client:** Syracuse University | **Design Firm:** Entro

ENTRO DESIGN TEAM

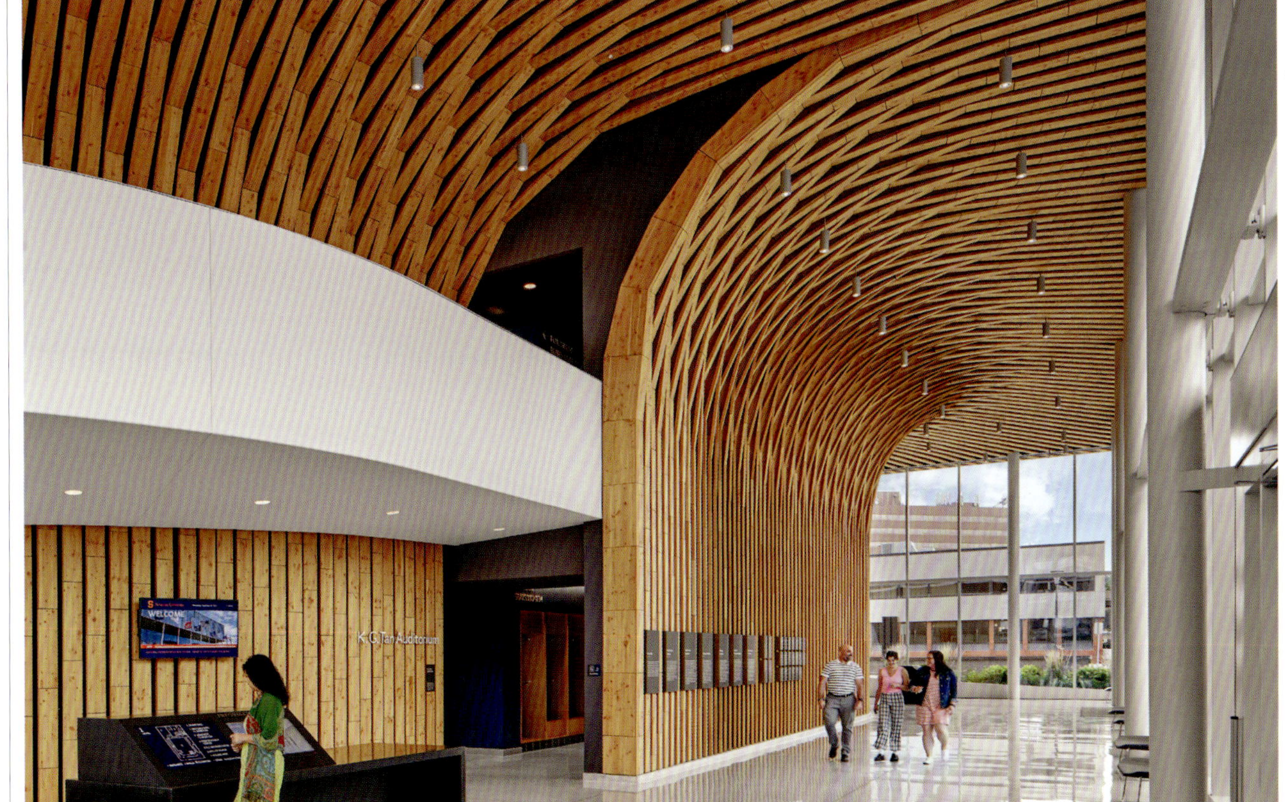

Title: National Veterans Resource Center Wayfinding, Donor Recognition, and Exhibit | **Client:** Syracuse University | **Design Firm:** Entro

JONATHAN ALGER

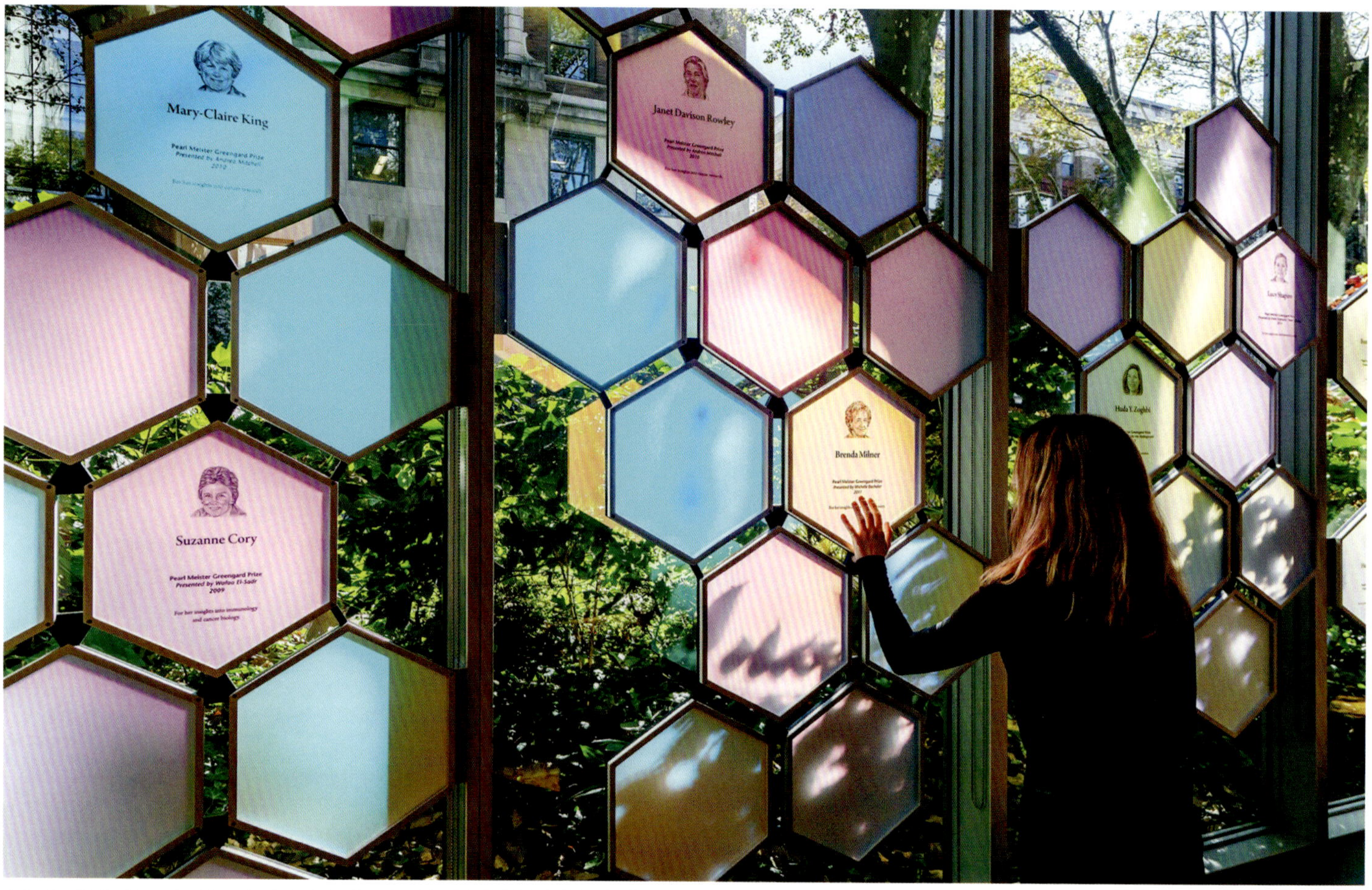

Title: Pearl Meister Greengard Prize Wall | **Client:** Rockefeller University | **Design Firm:** C&G Partners

ENTRO DESIGN TEAM

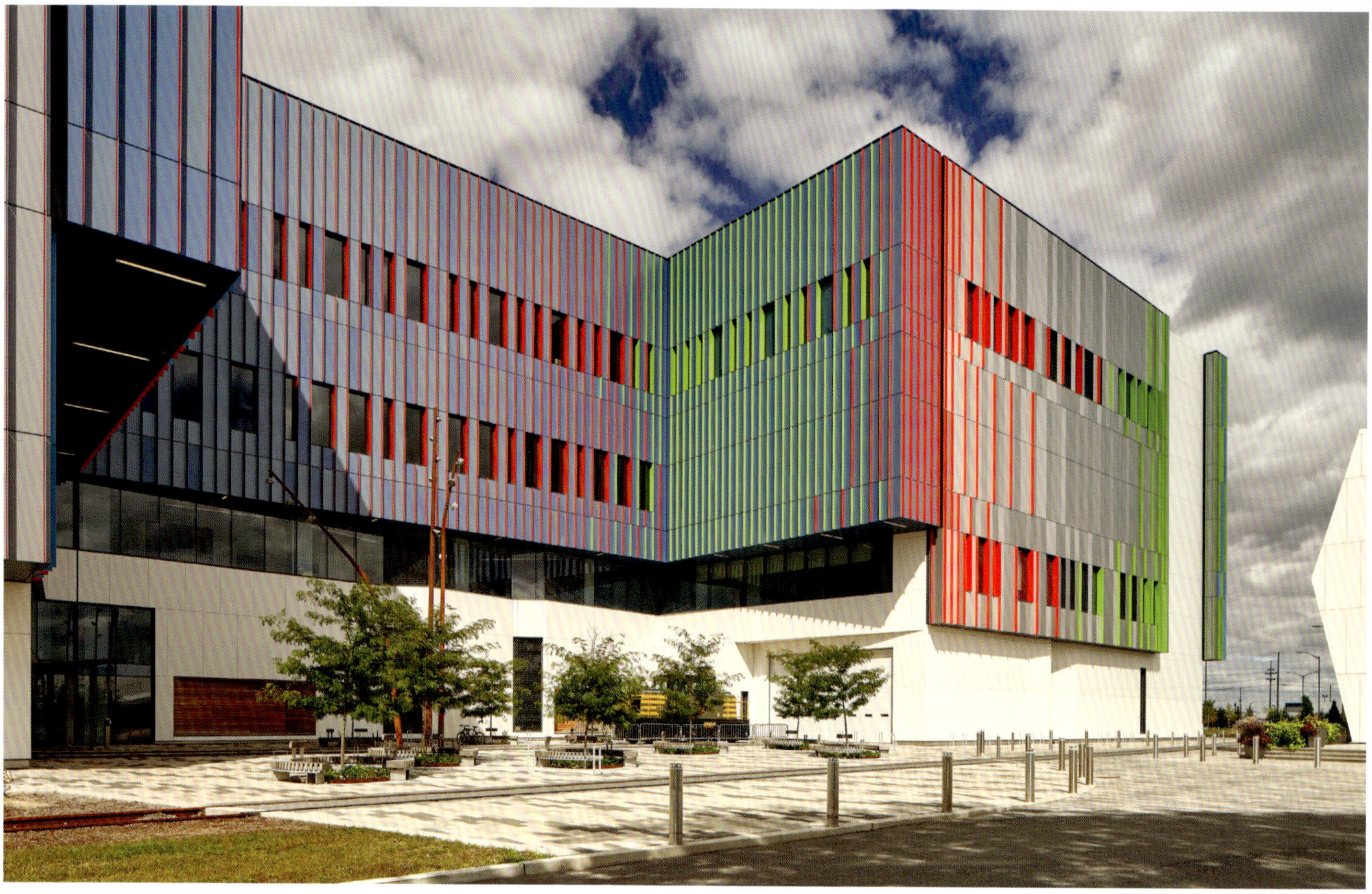

Title: Ingenium Centre Signage and Wayfinding | **Client:** Ingenium Centre | **Design Firm:** Entro

ENTRO

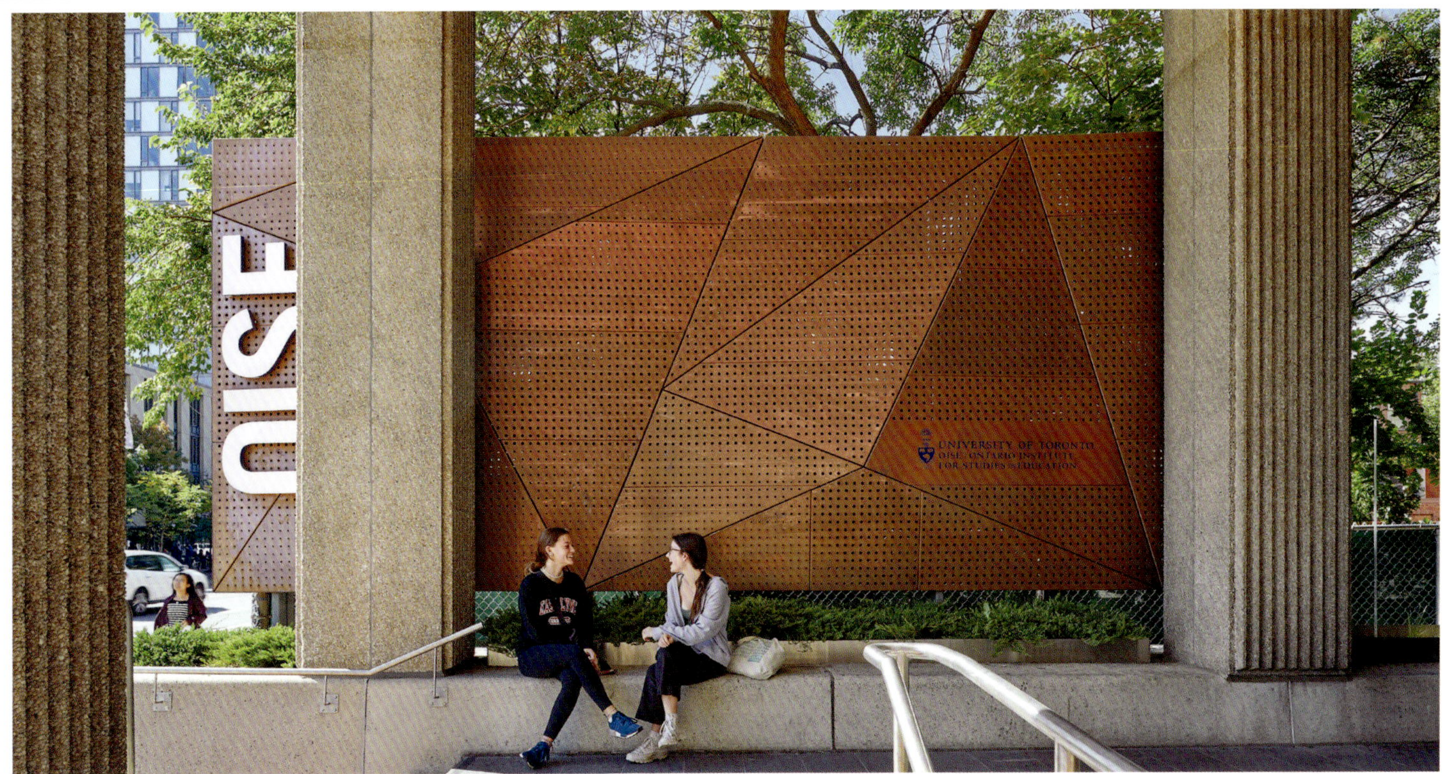

Title: Signage and Wayfinding at U of T OISE | **Client:** University of Toronto Ontario Institute for Studies in Education (OISE) | **Design Firm:** Entro

MONYEE CHAU

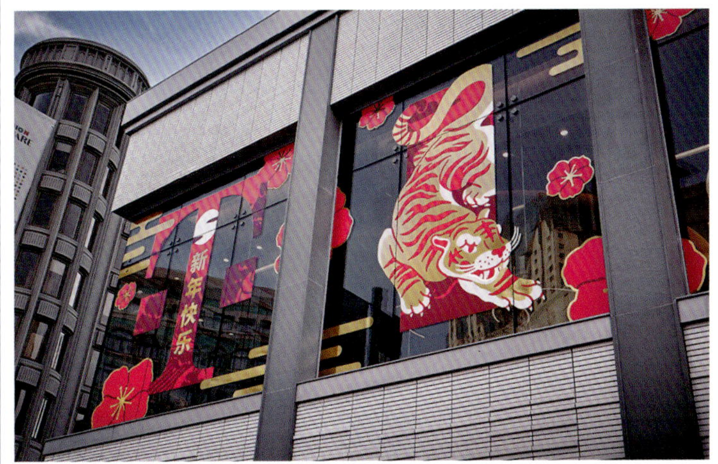

Title: T-Mobile Year of the Tiger | **Client:** T-Mobile
Design Firm: WONGDOODY

TEIGA, STUDIO.

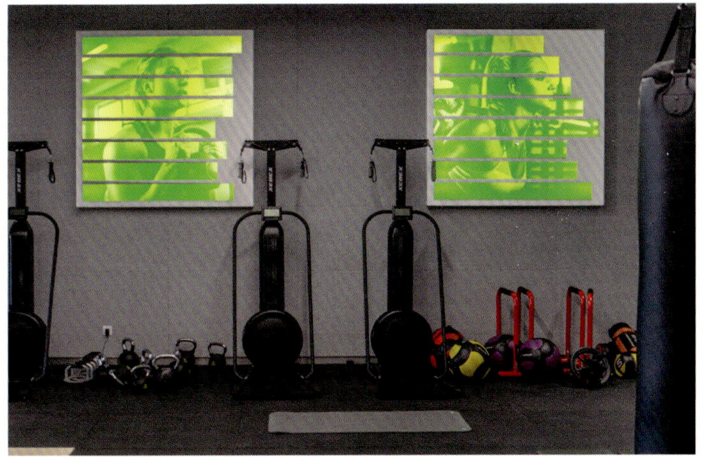

Title: Meufit | **Client:** Meufit
Design Firm: Teiga, Studio.

ASTERISK

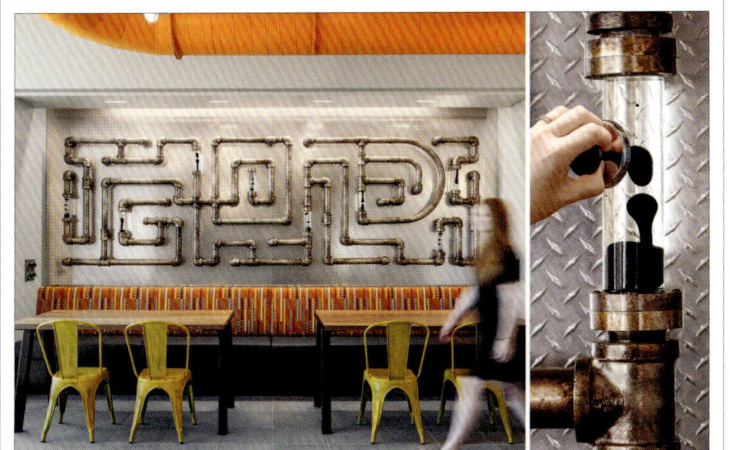

Title: Oracle Global Headquarters
Client: Oracle | **Design Firm:** Asterisk

ENTRO DESIGN TEAM

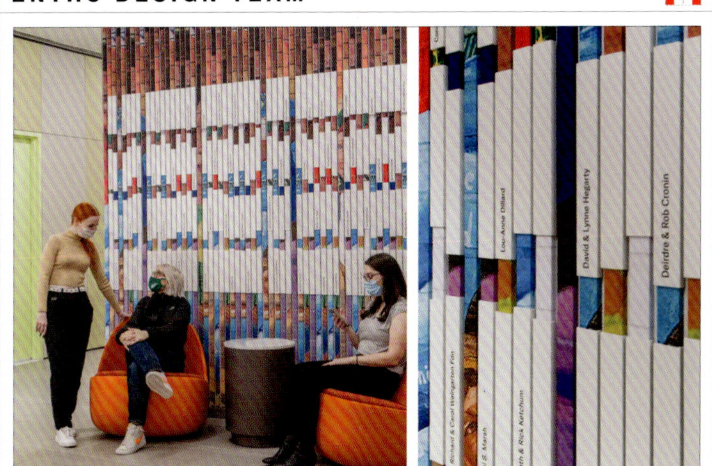

Title: Covenant House New York Wayfinding and Donor Recognition
Client: Covenant House | **Design Firm:** Entro

HONG KA LOK

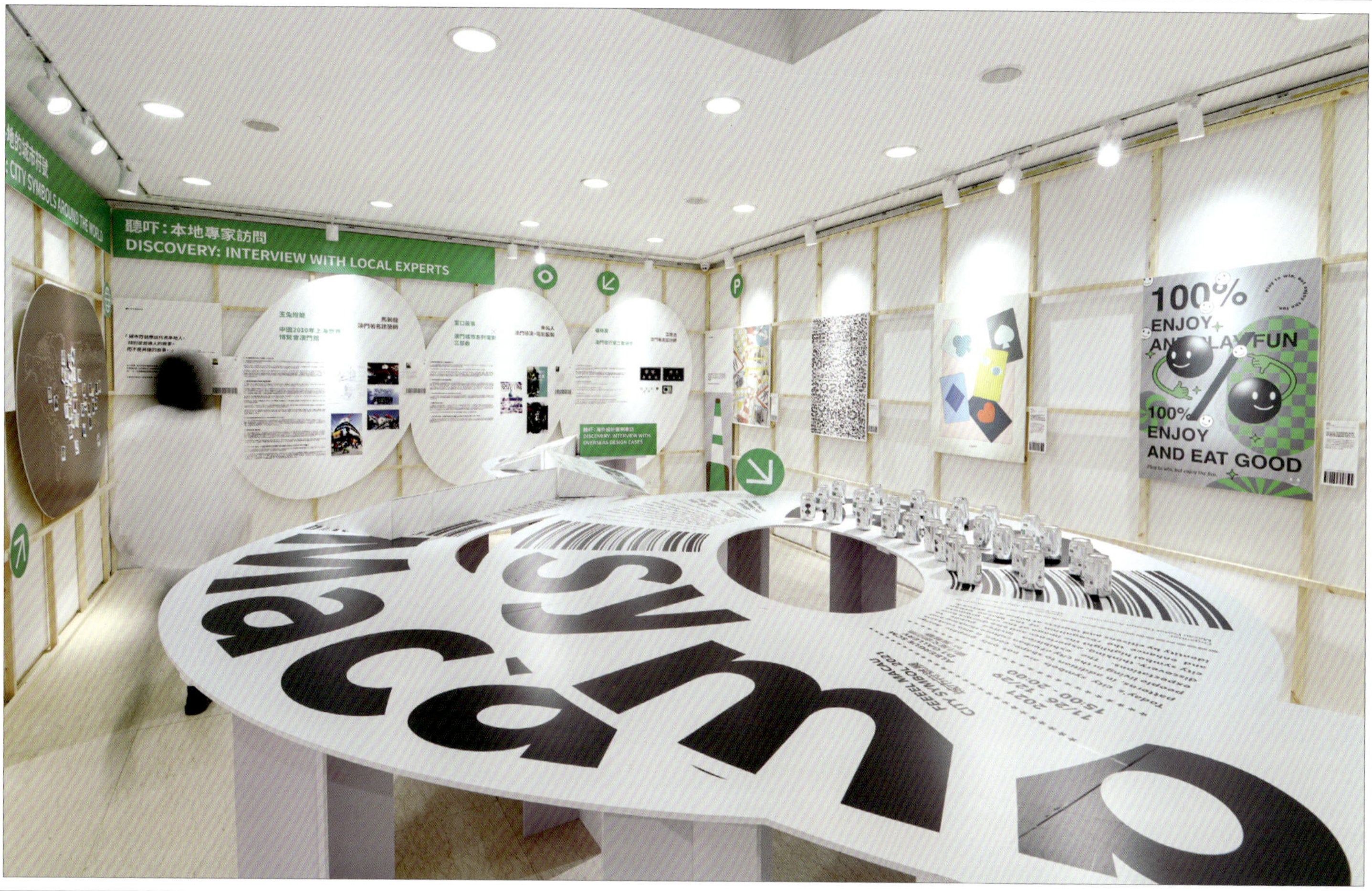

Title: FEEEEL MACAU 2021 | **Client:** Macau Poster Design Association | **Design Firm:** Loksophy Design Ltd.

JONATHAN ALGER

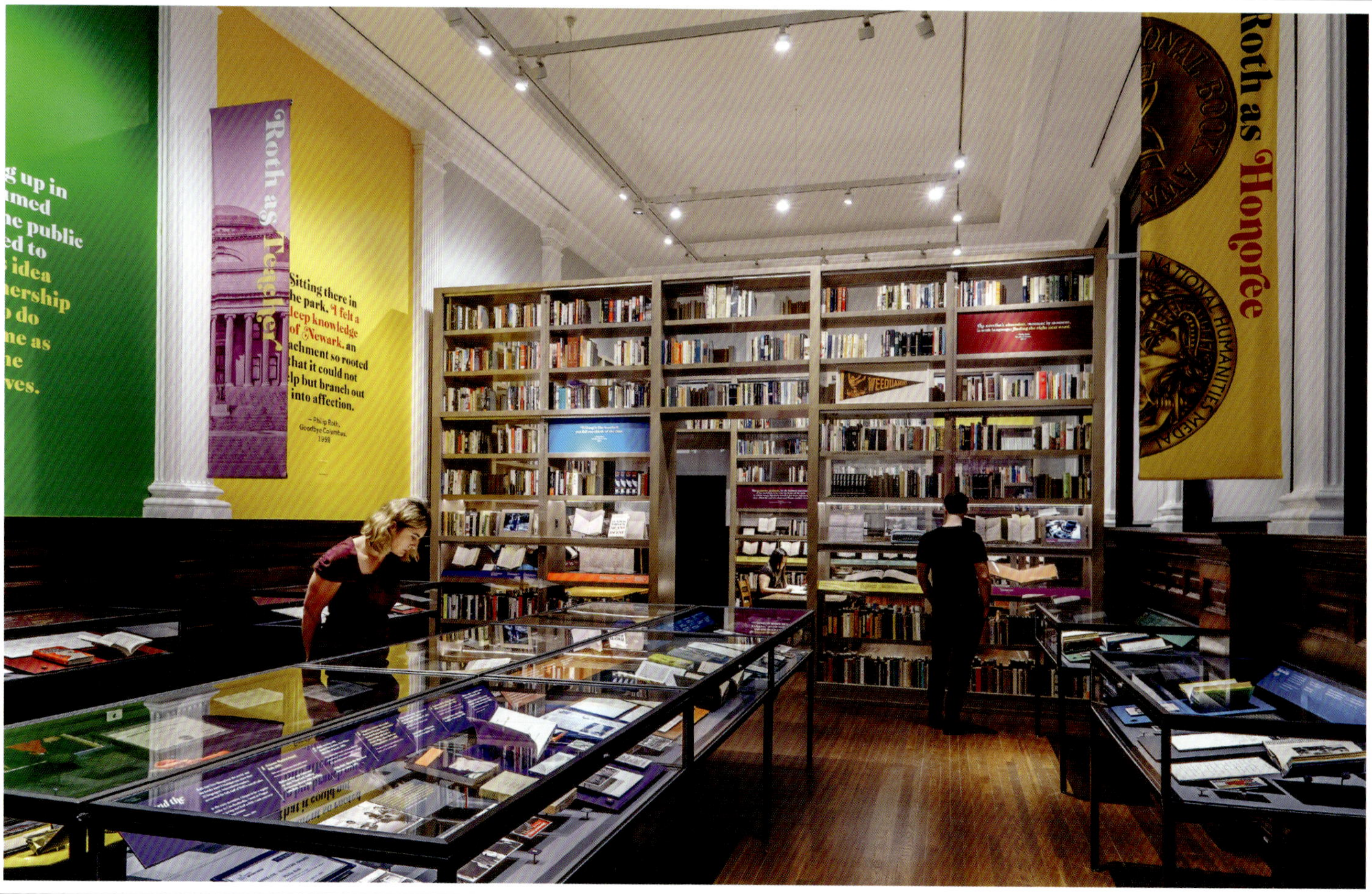

Title: Philip Roth Personal Library | **Client:** Newark Public Library | **Design Firm:** C&G Partners

RALPH APPELBAUM ASSOCIATES

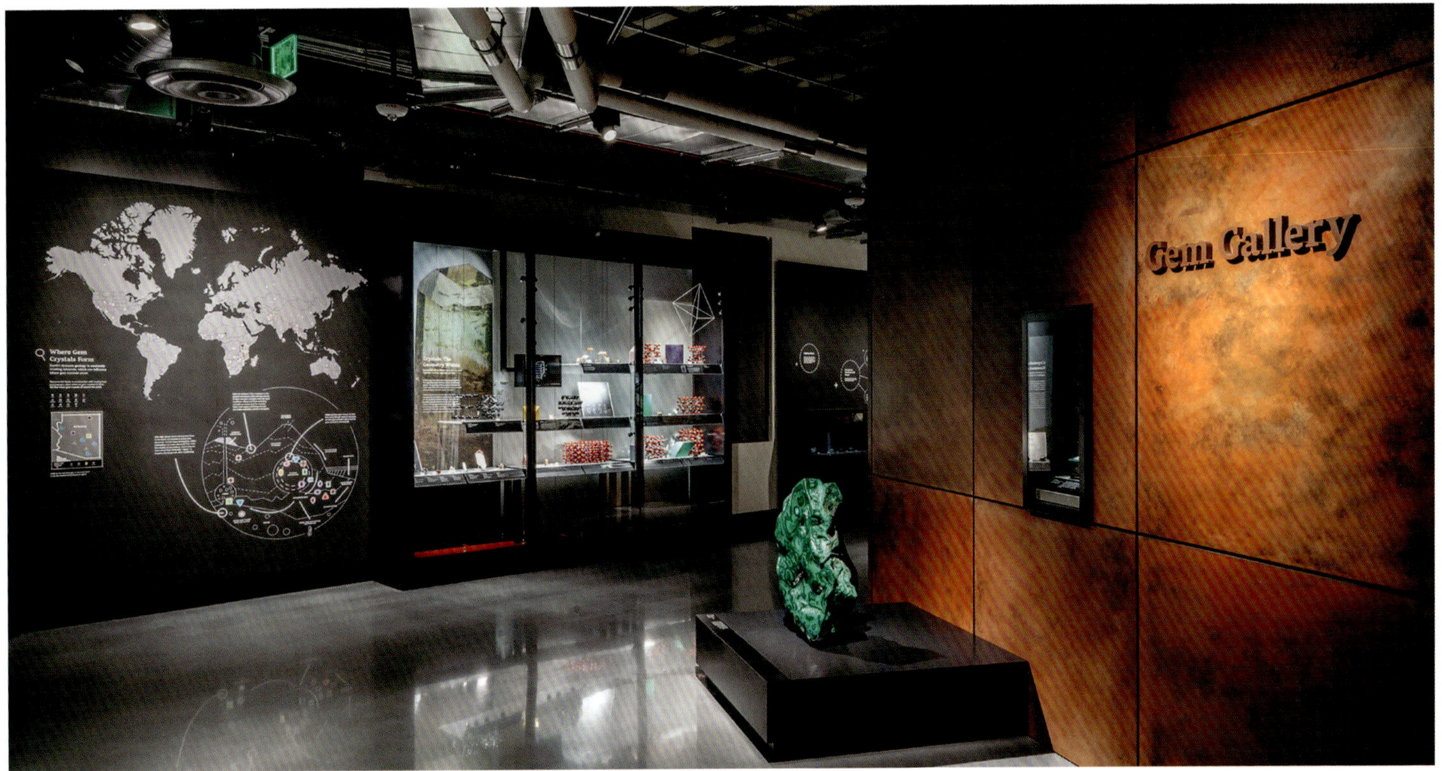

Title: Univ. of Arizona Alfie Norville Gem & Mineral Museum at the Historic Pima County Courthouse | **Client:** Pima County | **Design Firm:** Ralph Appelbaum Associates

TETSURO MINORIKAWA

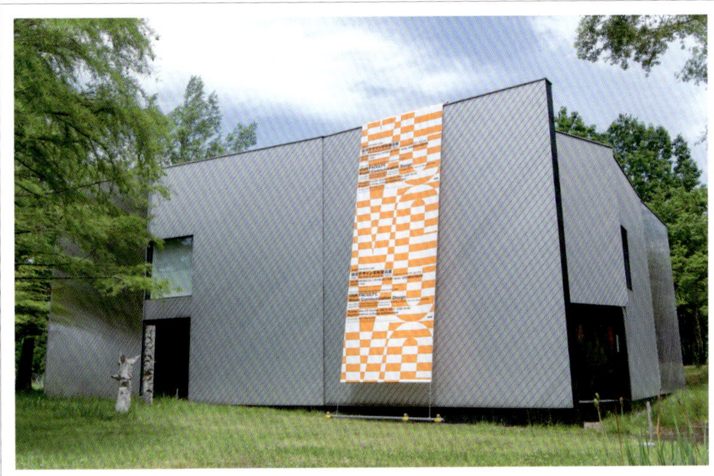

Title: Exhibition Project: Gallery MàRoù, Nagaoka Institute of Design Exhibition Hall | **Client:** Nagaoka Institute of Design | **Design Firm:** Tetsuro Minorikawa

GOODS & SERVICES

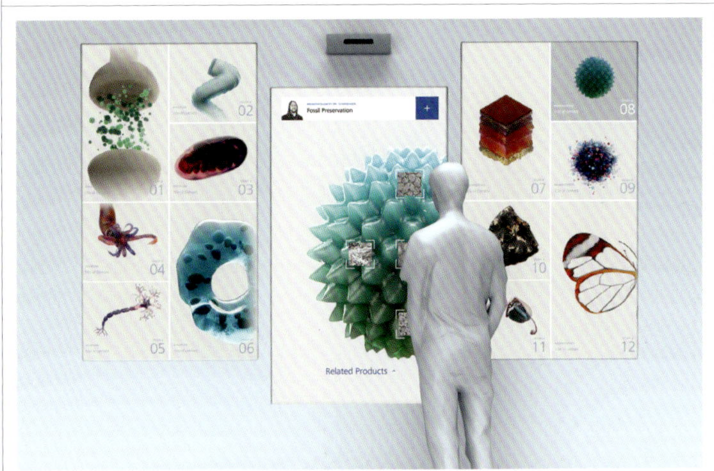

Title: Vision ID | **Client:** ZEISS
Design Firm: Goods & Services

SIENA SCARFF

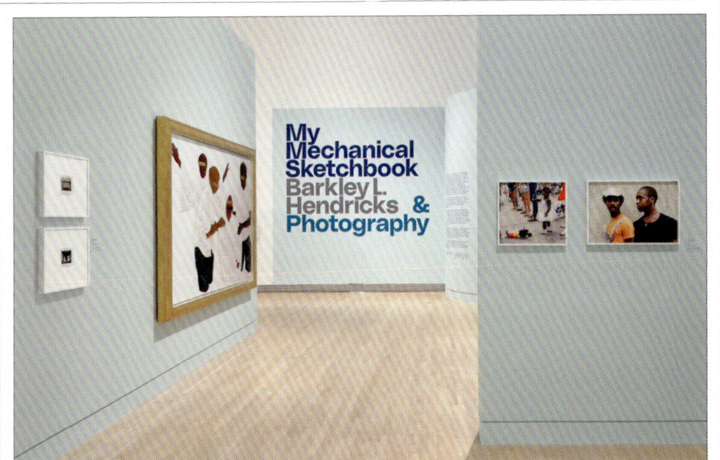

Title: "My Mechanical Sketchbook"—Barkley L. Hendricks & Photography
Client: The Rose Art Museum | **Design Firm:** Siena Scarff Design

KEVIN JONES

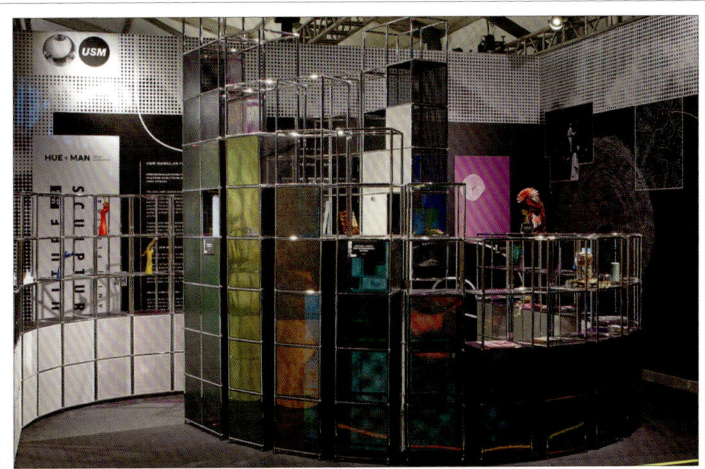

Title: People of Color: Hue+Man Exhibition
Clients: Art Basil, USM Modular Furniture | **Design Firm:** Joba Studio

OMDESIGN

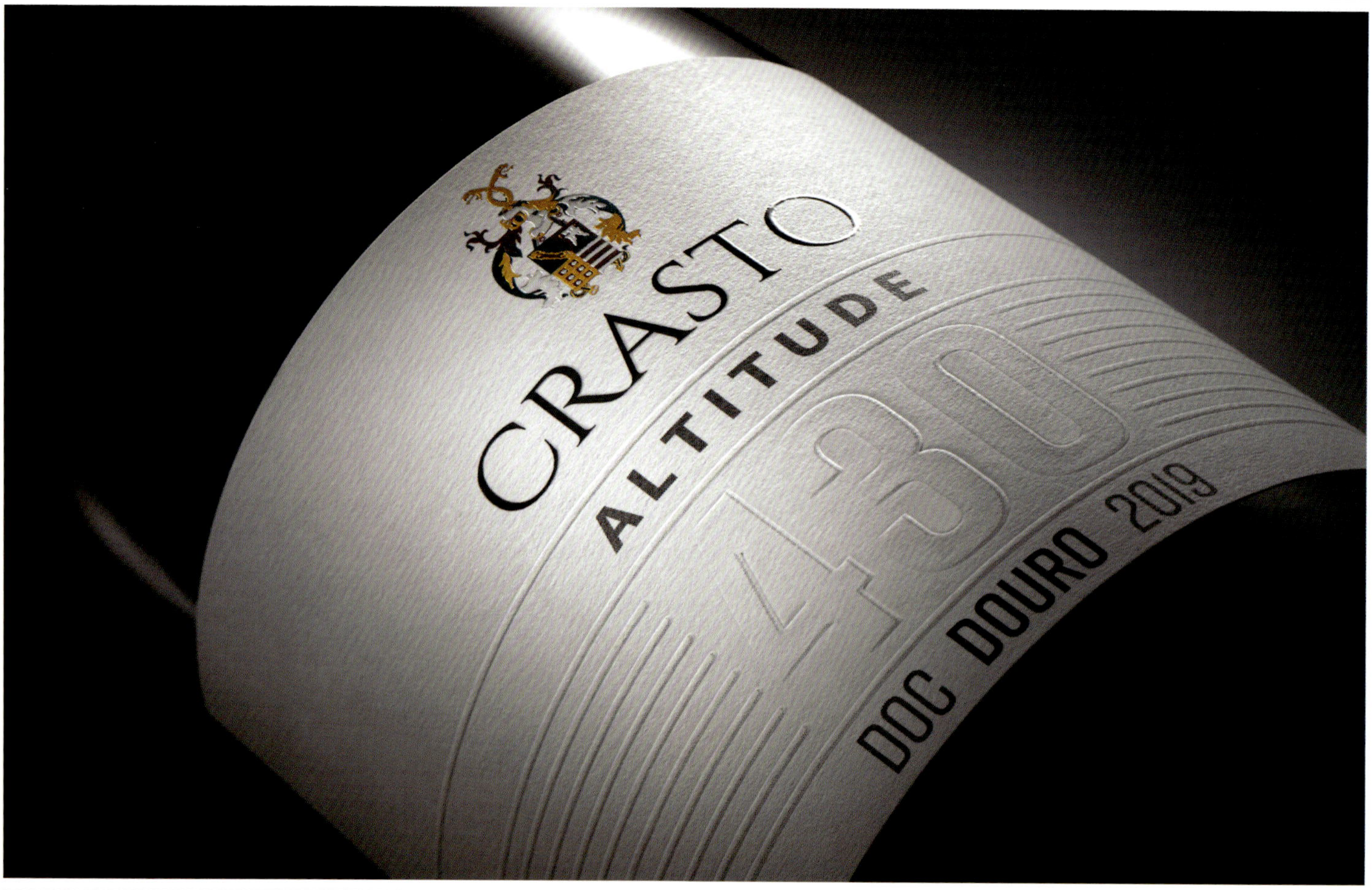

Title: Crasto Altitude 430 | Client: Quinta do Crasto | Design Firm: Omdesign

MICHAEL VANDERBYL

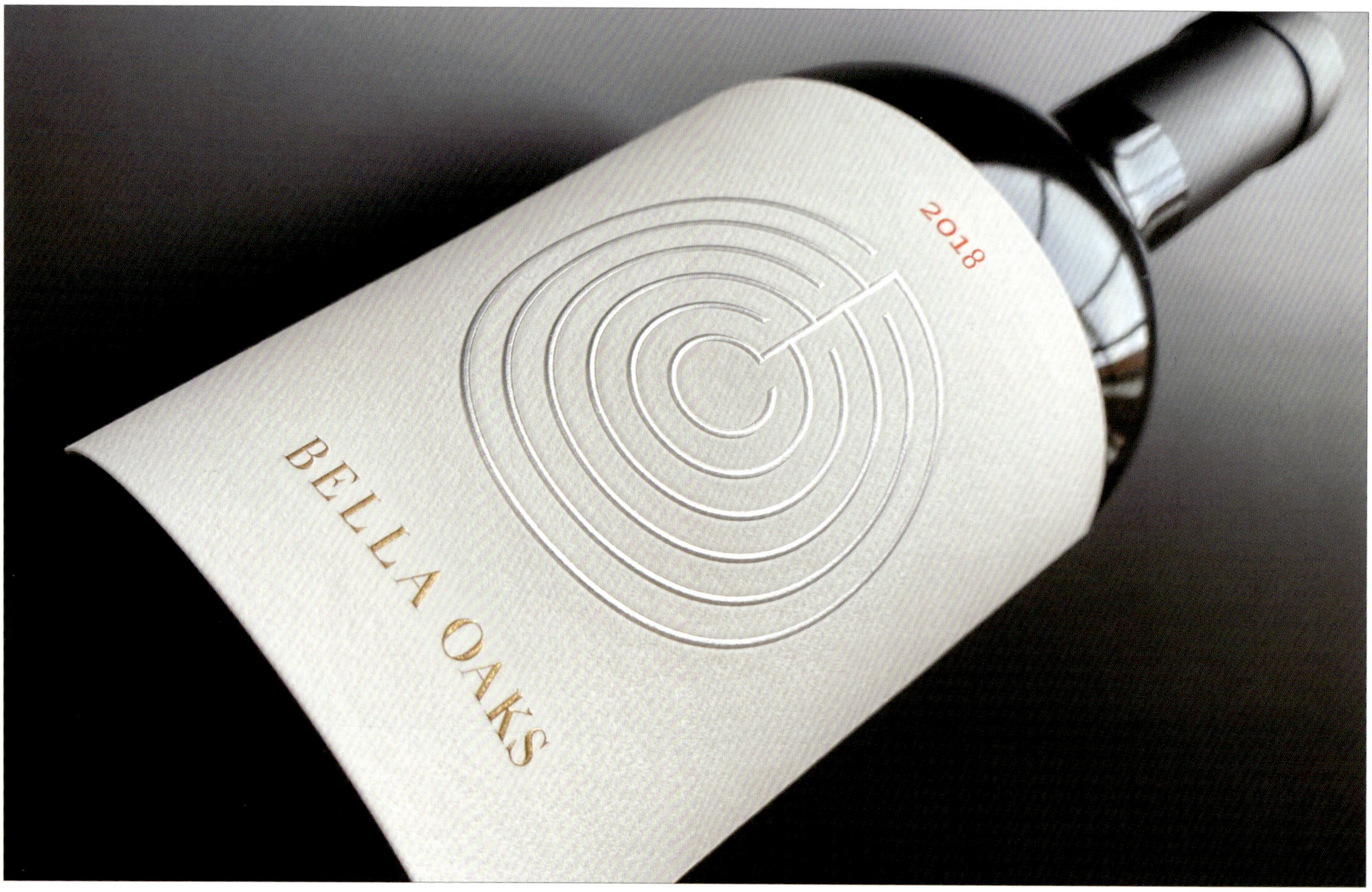

Title: Bella Oaks Wine Label | Client: Bella Oaks Vineyard | Design Firm: Vanderbyl Design

OMDESIGN

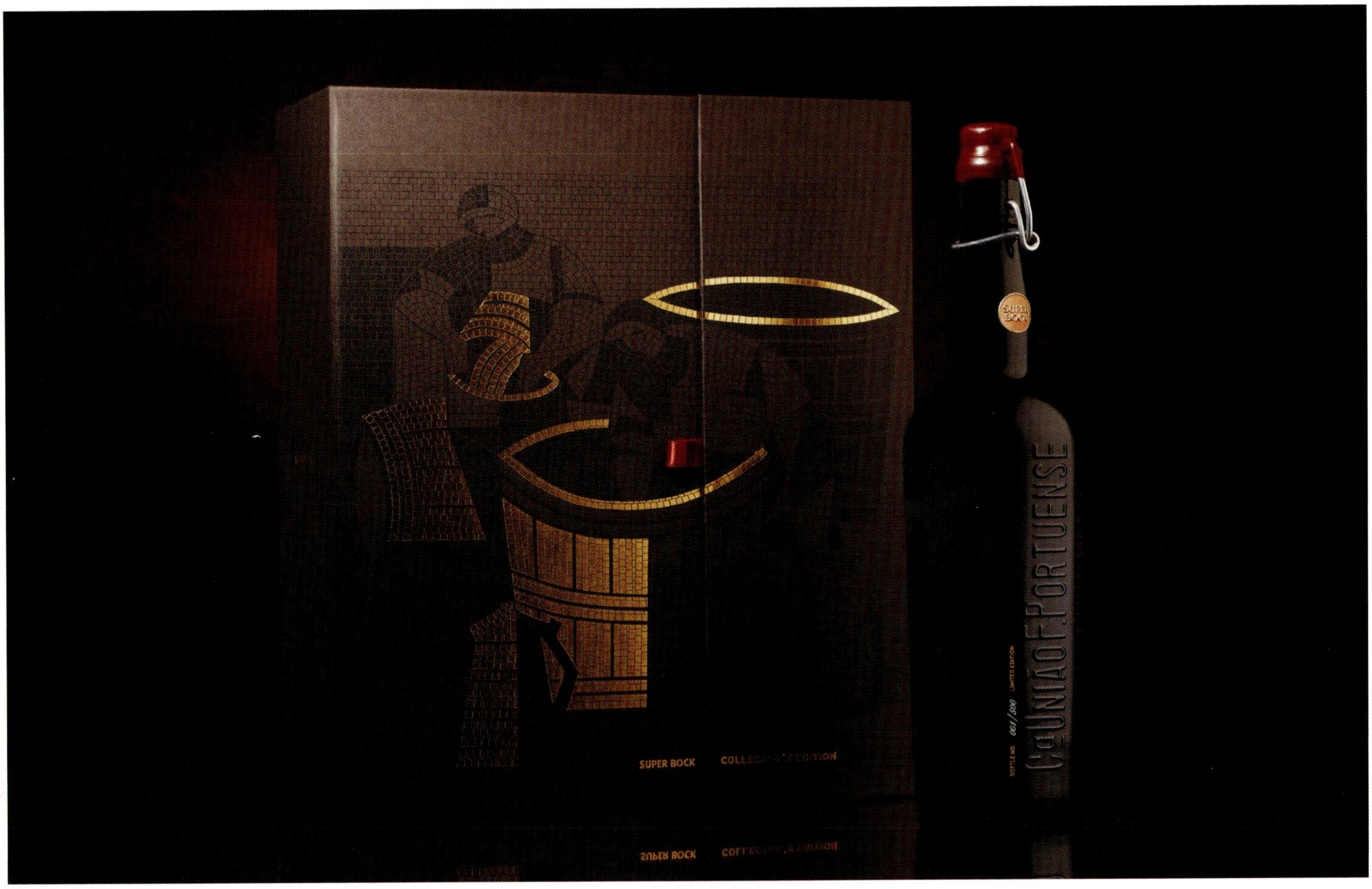

Title: Super Bock Collector's Edition | **Client:** Super Bock Group | **Design Firm:** Omdesign

MICHAEL VANDERBYL

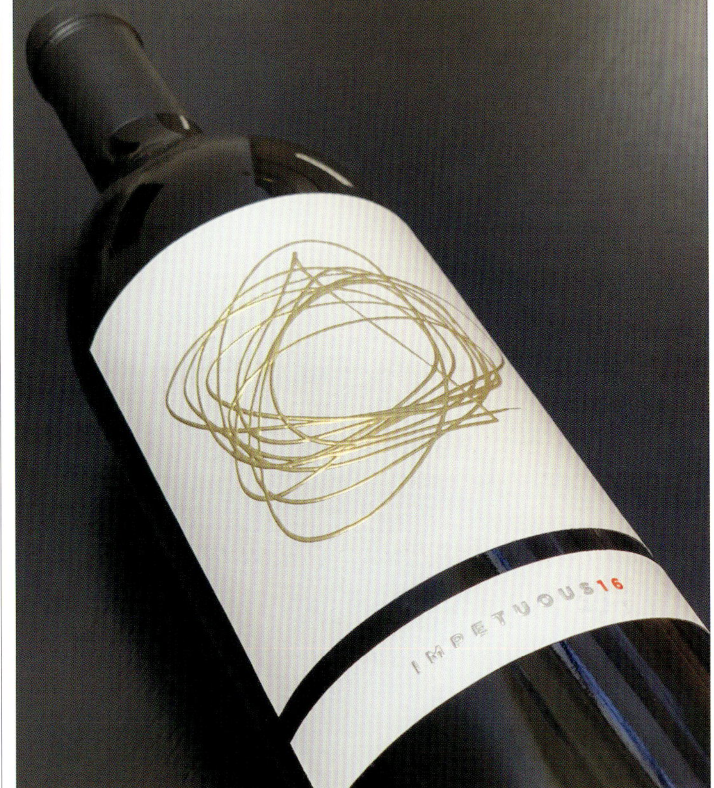

Title: Impetuous Wine Label | **Client:** Checkerboard Vineyards
Design Firm: Vanderbyl Design

MICHAEL VANDERBYL

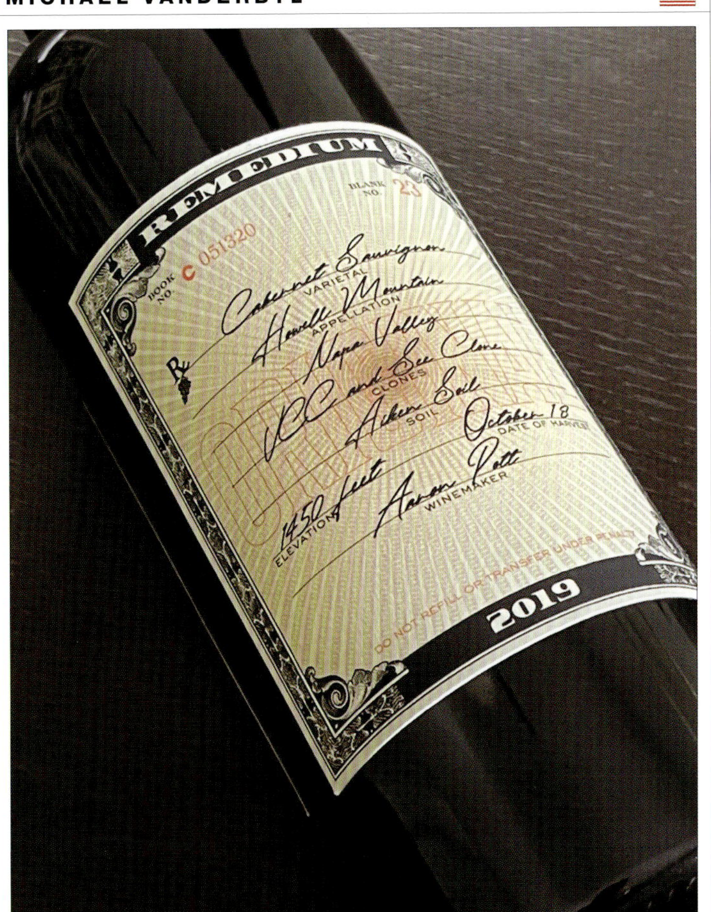

Title: Remedium Wine Label | **Client:** Remedium Wine
Design Firm: Vanderbyl Design

HATCH DESIGN

Title: Moonshot | Client: Planet FWD | Design Firm: Hatch Design

CAROLYN GIBBS

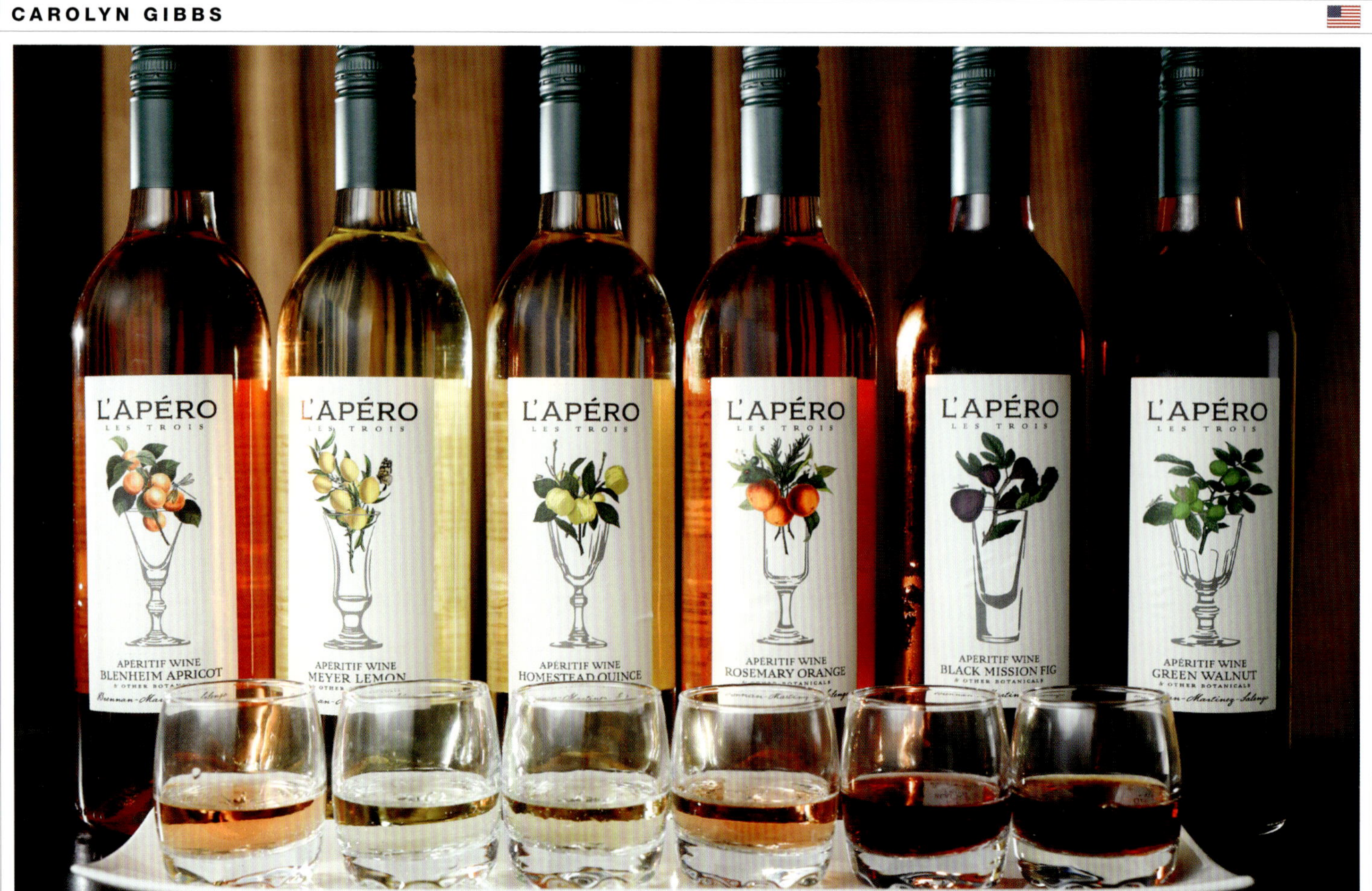

Title: L'Apero les Trois Label Series | Client: L'Apero les Trois | Design Firm: Carolyn Gibbs Design

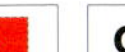

OMDESIGN

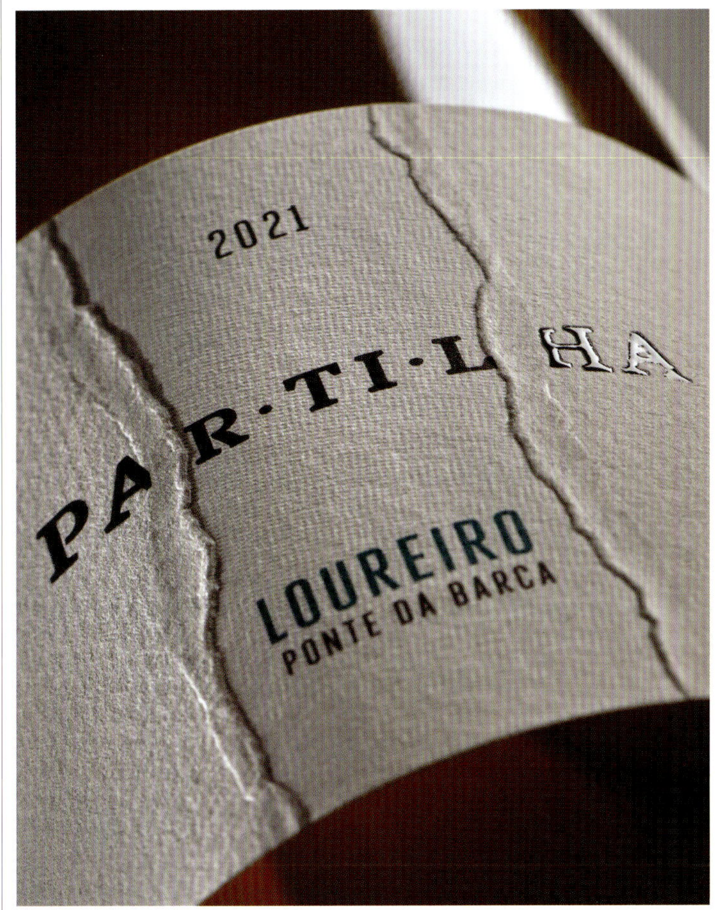

Title: Partilha | **Client:** Quinta do Outeiro
Design Firm: Omdesign

OMDESIGN

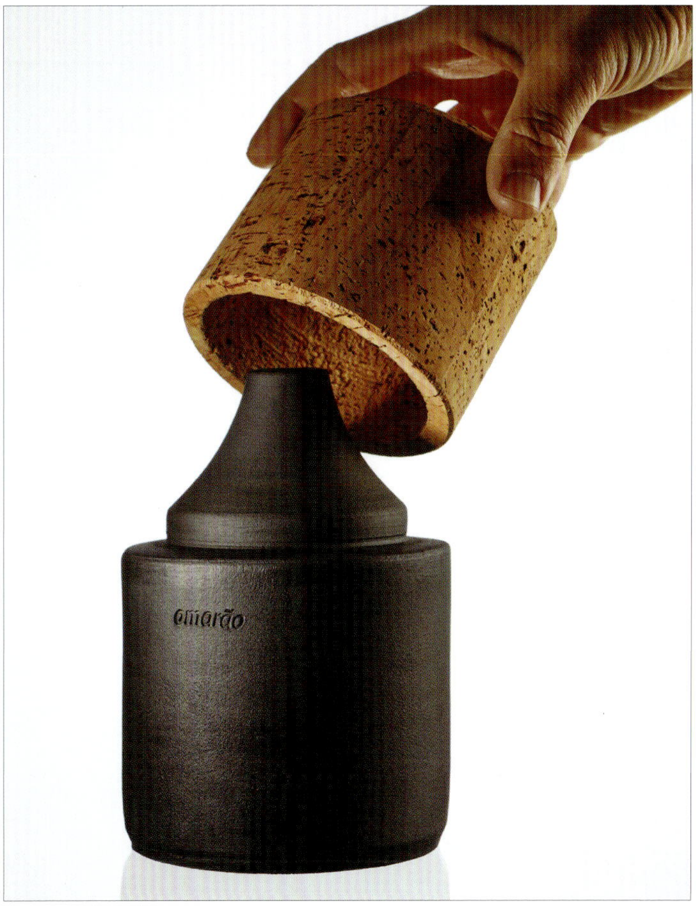

Title: OMarão Packaging – “Beyond the Mountains of Marão, Command Those Who Are There!” | **Client:** Self-initiated | **Design Firm:** Omdesign

HATCH DESIGN

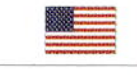

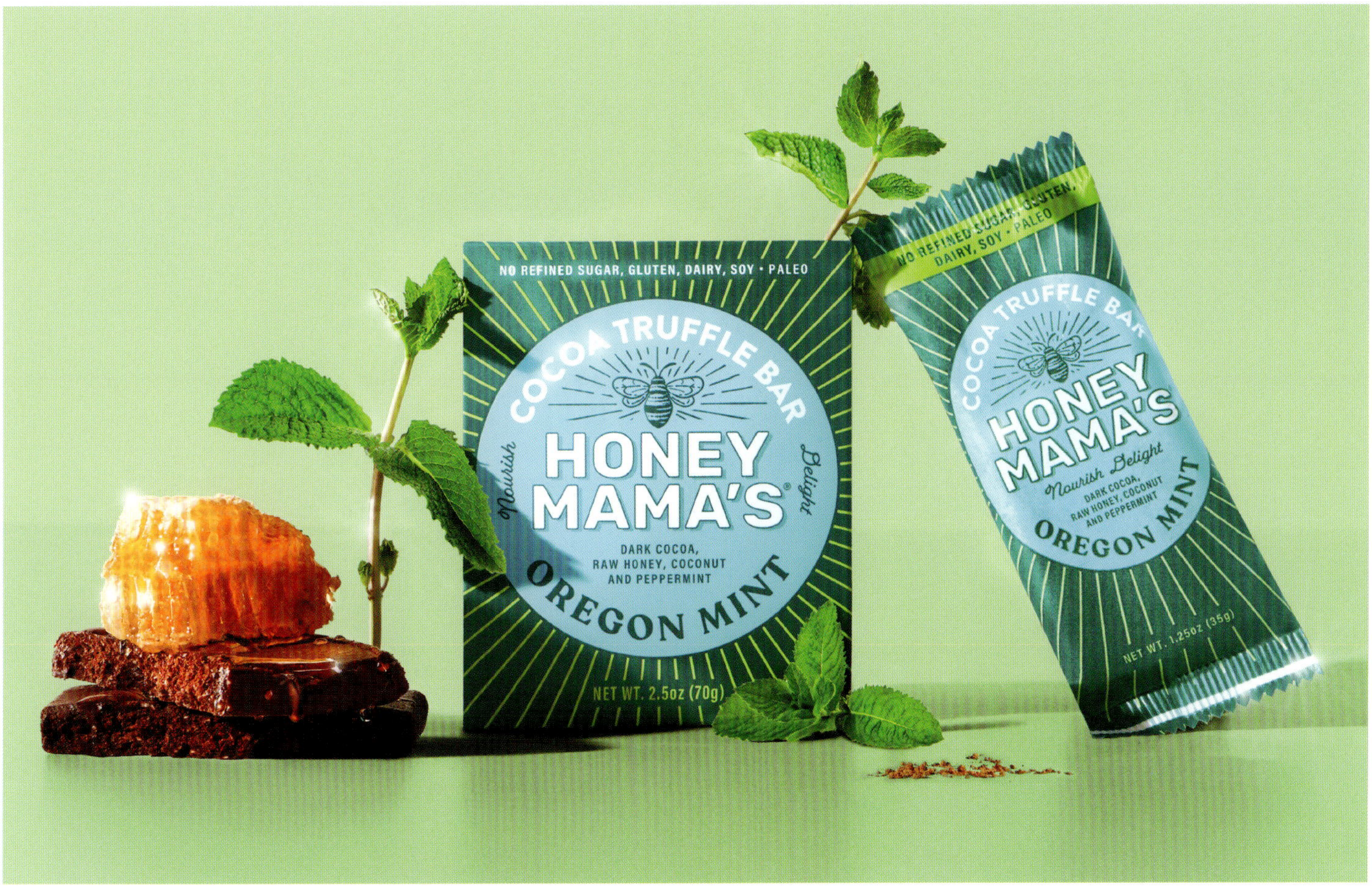

Title: Honey Mama’s | **Client:** Honey Mama’s | **Design Firm:** Hatch Design

PEPSICO DESIGN & INNOVATION

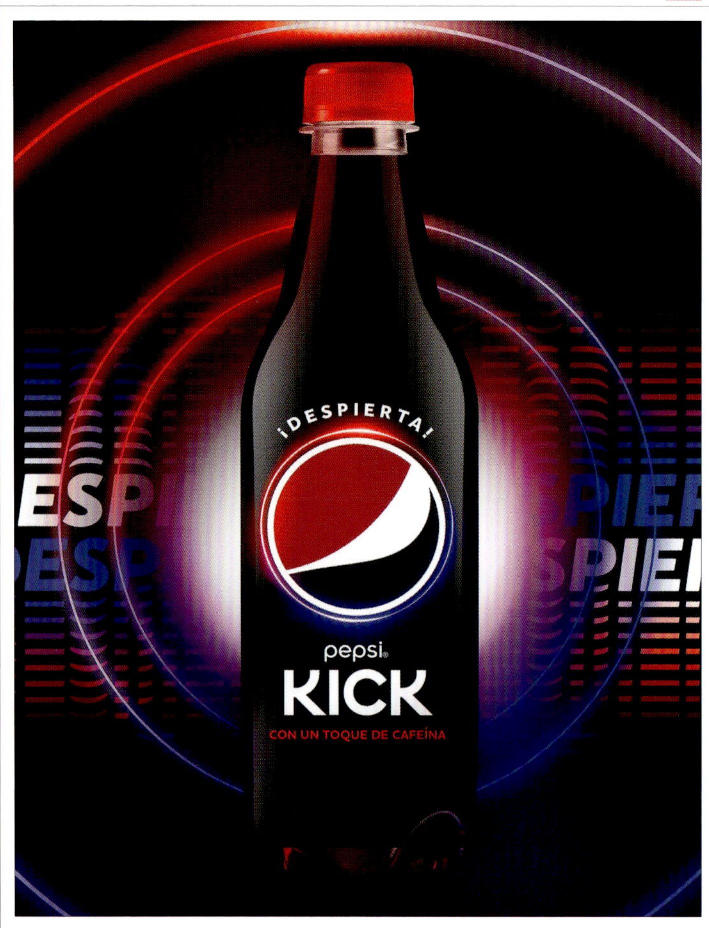

Title: Pepsi Kick Redesign – Mexico 2021 | **Client:** Self-initiated
Design Firm: PepsiCo Design & Innovation

PEPSICO DESIGN & INNOVATION

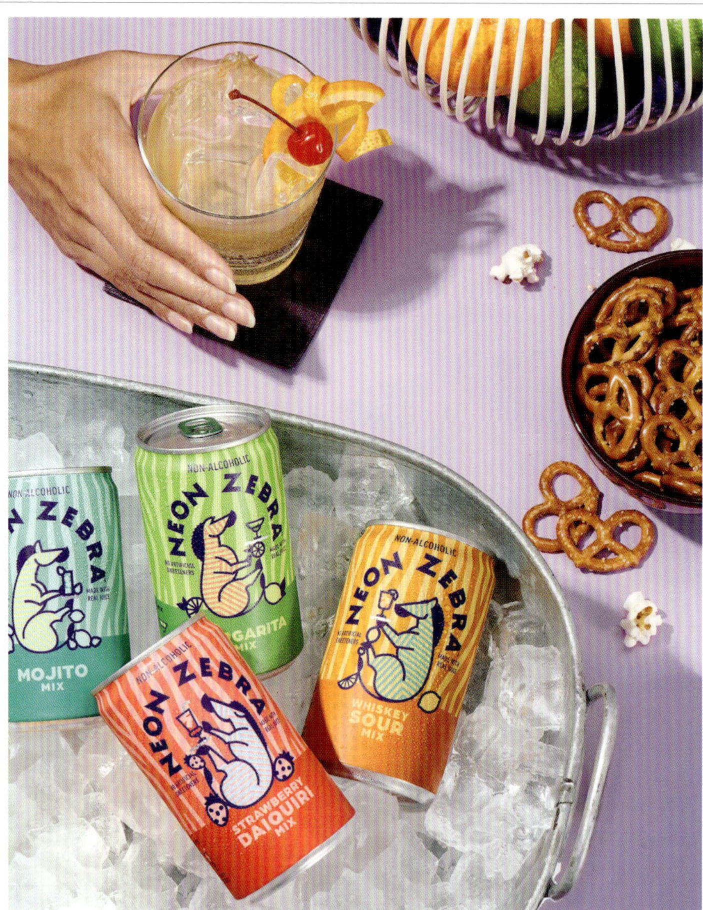

Title: Neon Zebra Brand Launch | **Client:** Self-initiated
Design Firm: PepsiCo Design & Innovation

PEPSICO DESIGN & INNOVATION

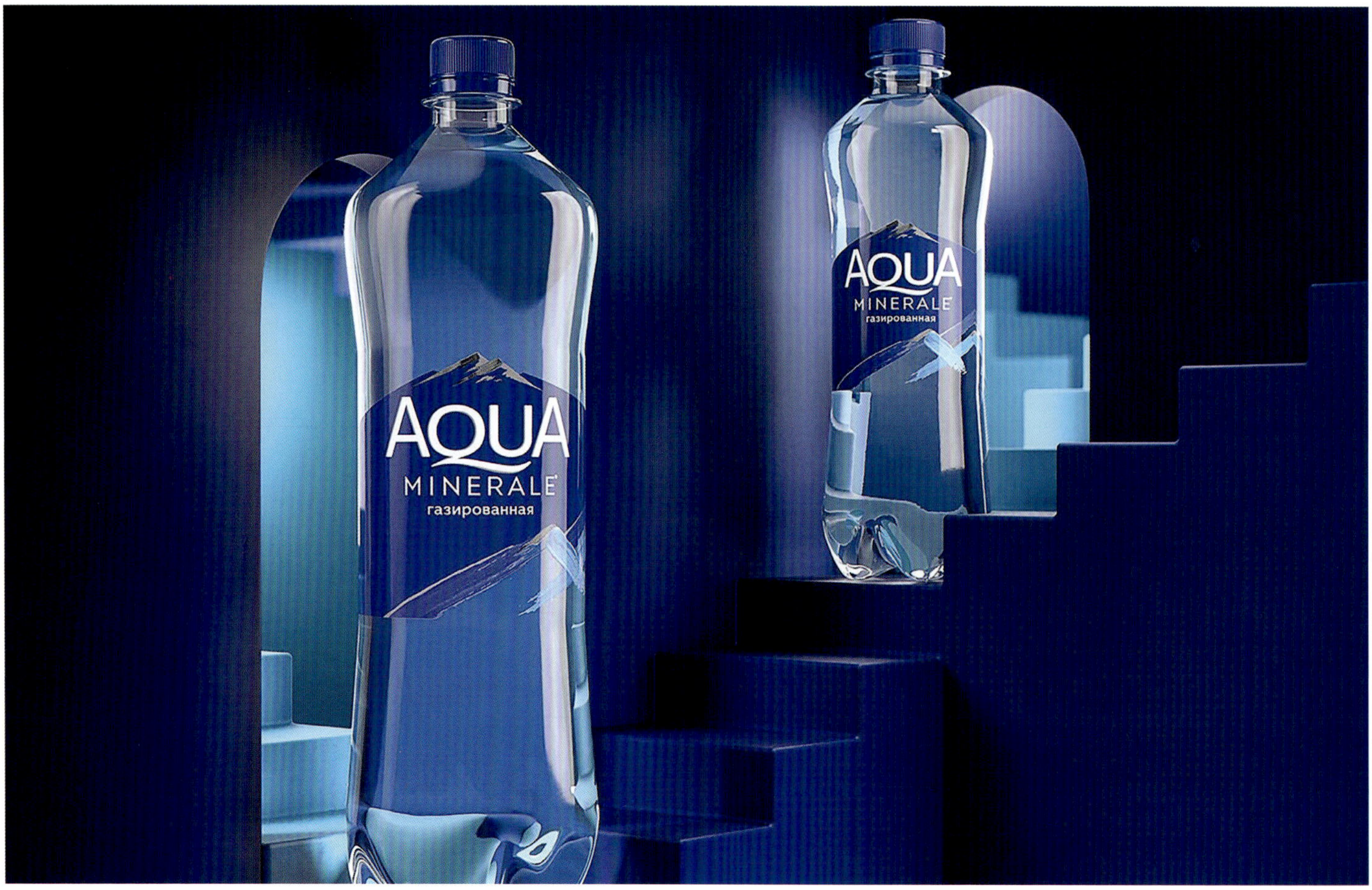

Title: Aqua Minerale Redesign | **Client:** Self-initiated | **Design Firm:** PepsiCo Design & Innovation

CRAIG BARNES

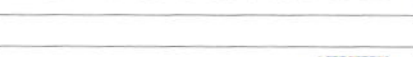

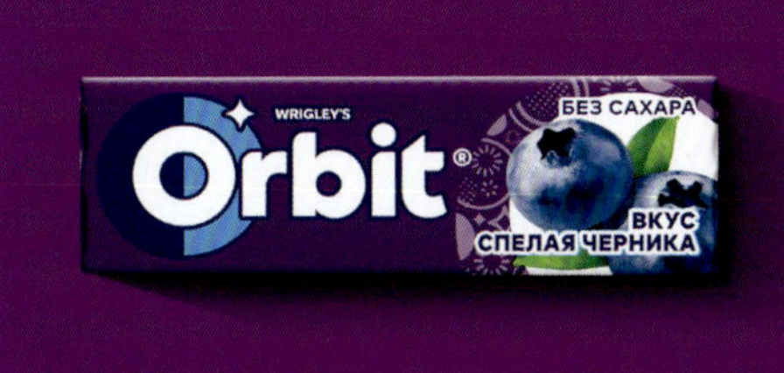

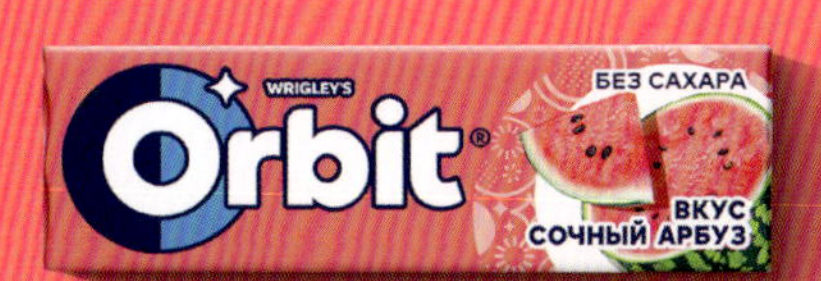

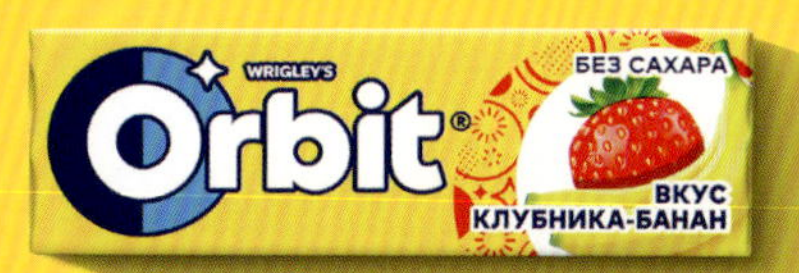

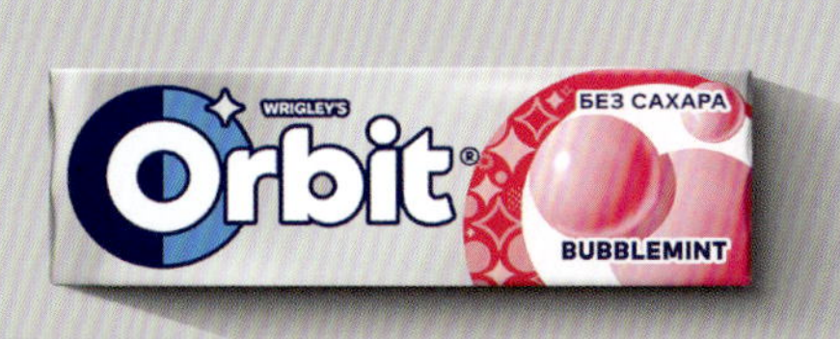

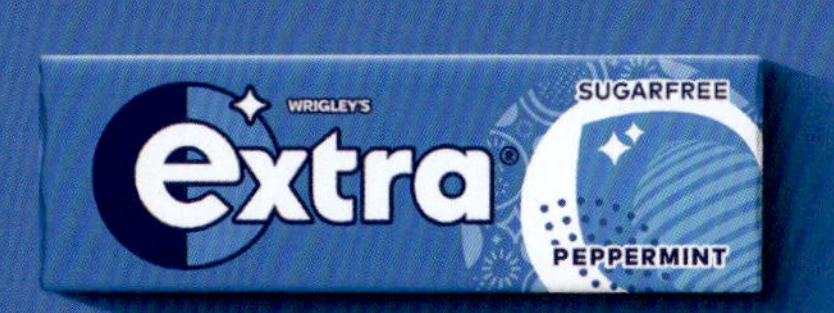

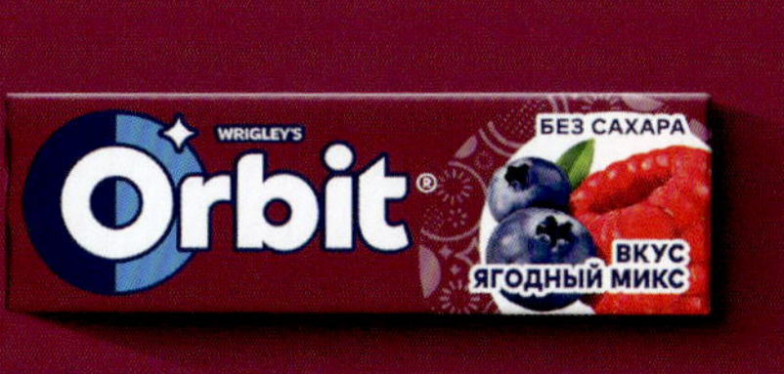

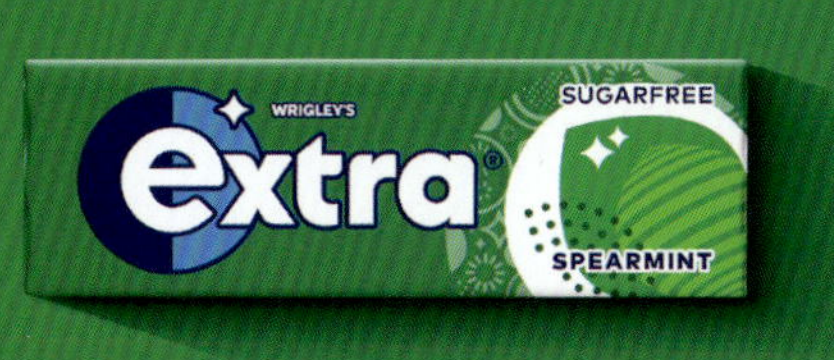

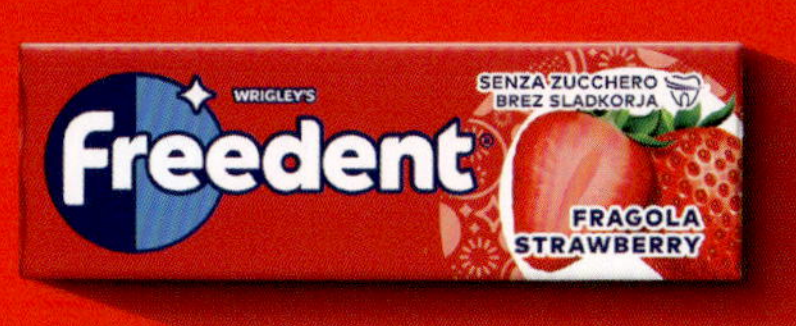

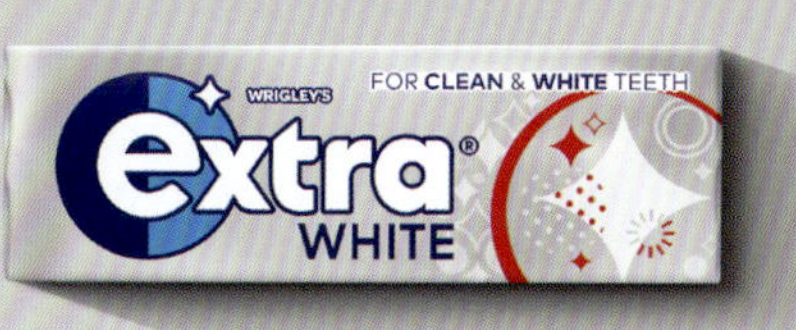

Title: Extra Rebrand | **Client:** Mars Wrigley | **Design Firm:** Elmwood

PEPSICO DESIGN & INNOVATION

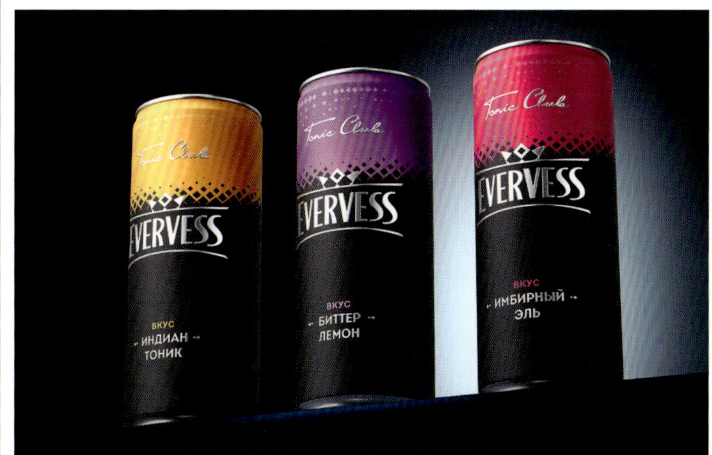

Title: Evervess Redesign | **Client:** Self-initiated
Design Firm: PepsiCo Design & Innovation

JEFF BARFOOT

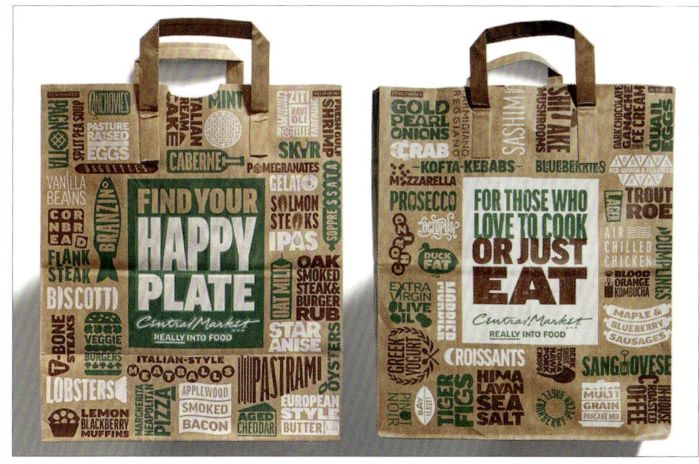

Title: Central Market Brand Bag | **Client:** Central Market
Design Firms: *TraceElement, Plot Twist Creativity

MAYUMI KATO

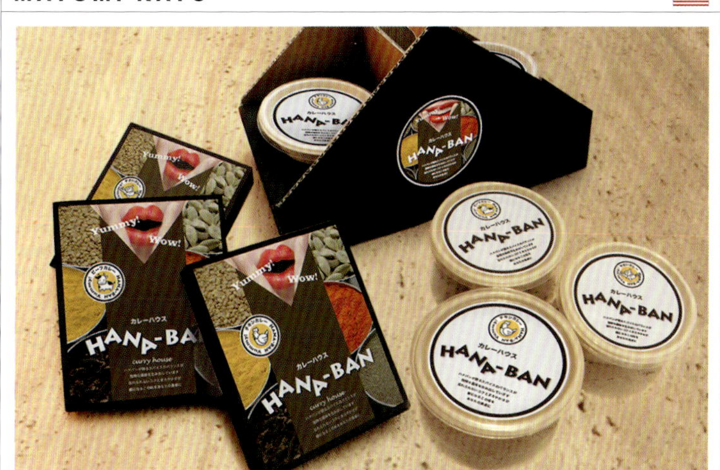

Title: Logo and Packaging Design for Curry House HANA-BAN
Client: Curry House HANA-BAN | **Design Firm:** Legis Design

PEPSICO DESIGN & INNOVATION

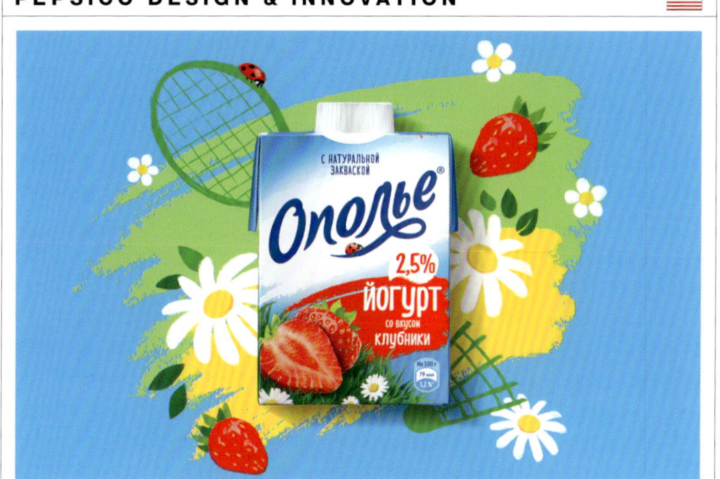

Title: Opolie | **Client:** Self-initiated
Design Firm: PepsiCo Design & Innovation

PETROL ADVERTISING

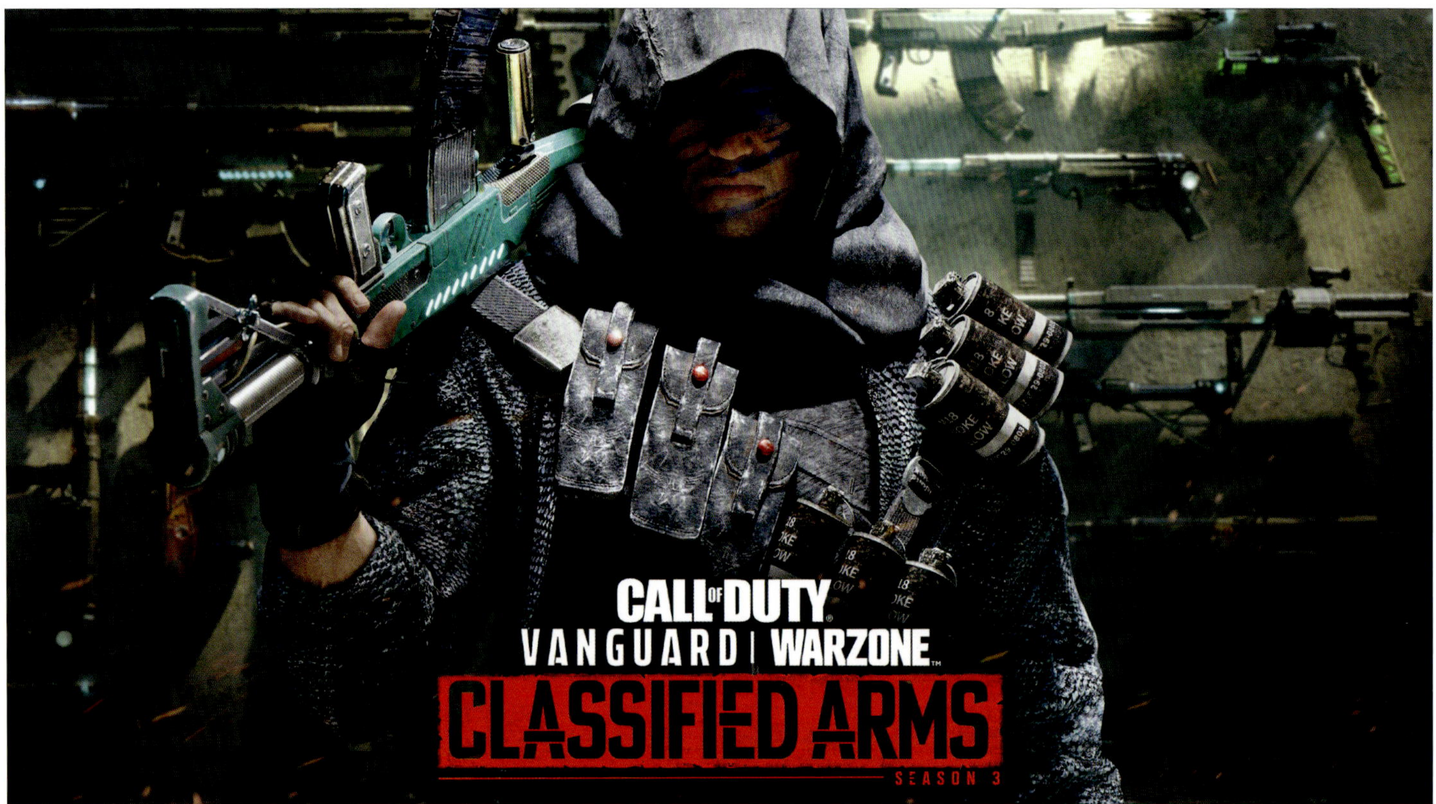

Title: Call of Duty: Vanguard x Warzone Key Art | **Clients:** Activision, Sledgehammer | **Design Firm:** PETROL Advertising

JEFF BARFOOT

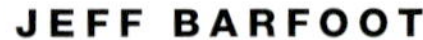

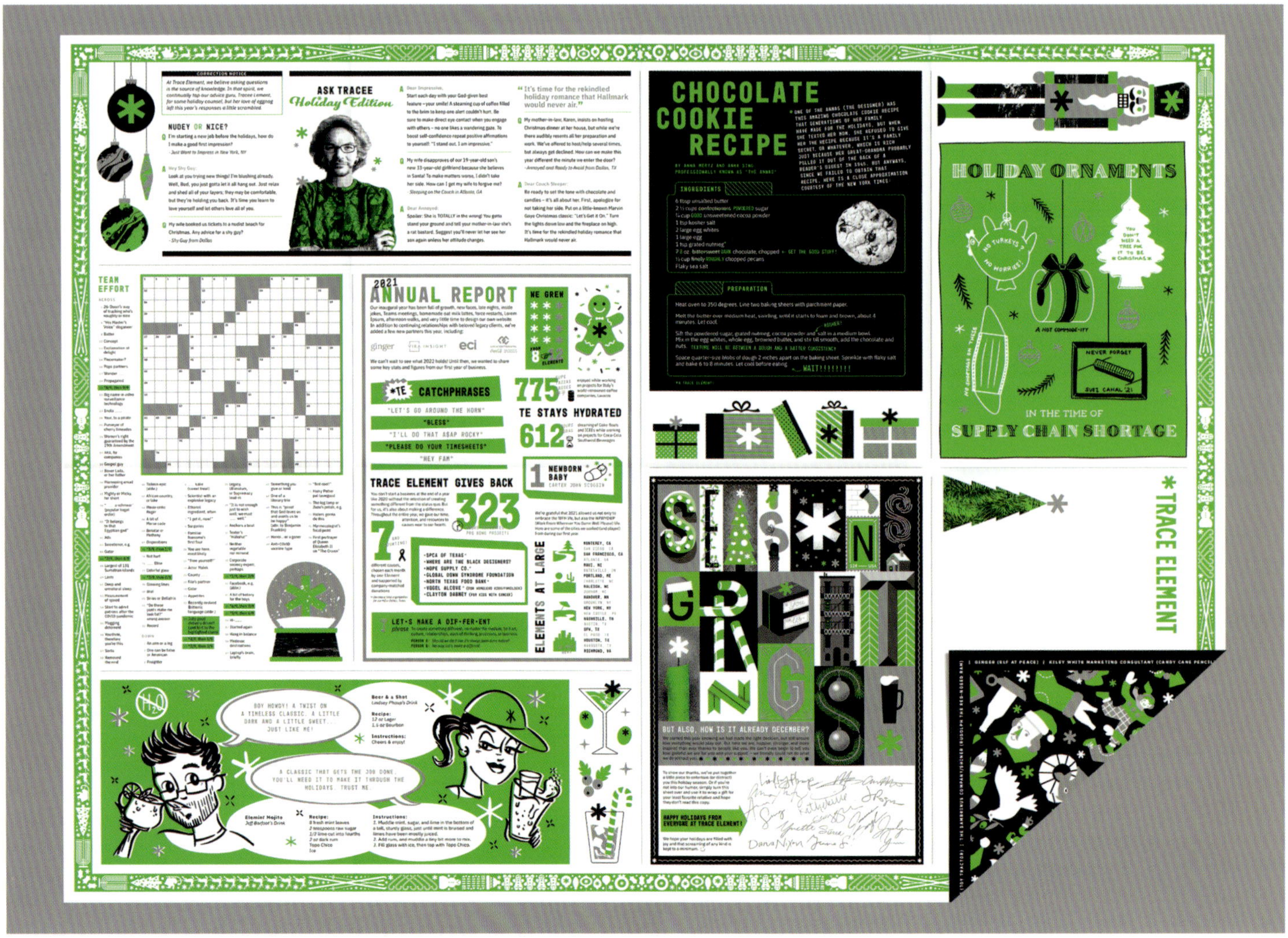

Title: *TraceElement 2021 Holiday Card | **Client:** Self-initiated | **Design Firm:** *TraceElement

NEETA VERMA

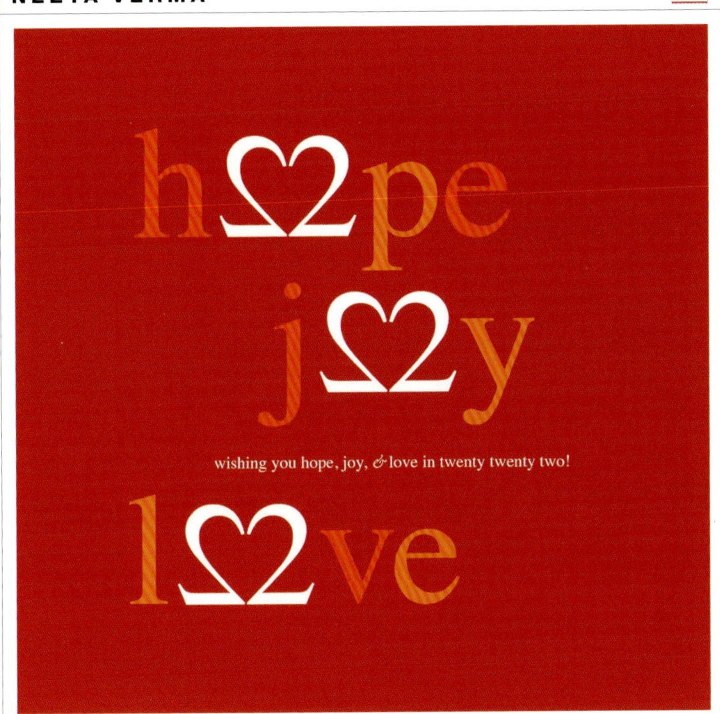

Title: New Year Card | **Client:** Self-initiated
Design Firm: DesigNV [Design + Envy]

MICHAEL PANTUSO

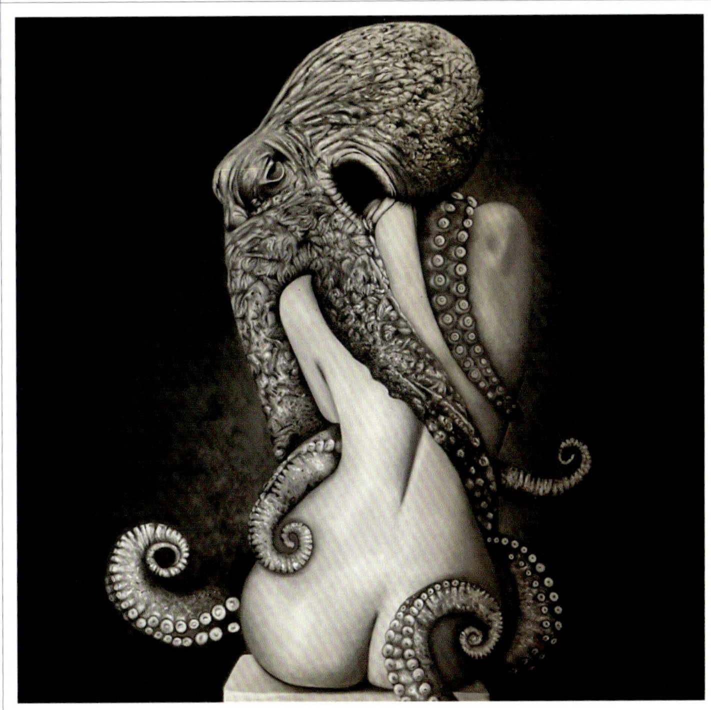

Title: Nude With Octopus | **Client:** Gallery and Exhibition
Design Firm: Michael Pantuso Design

THE REFINERY

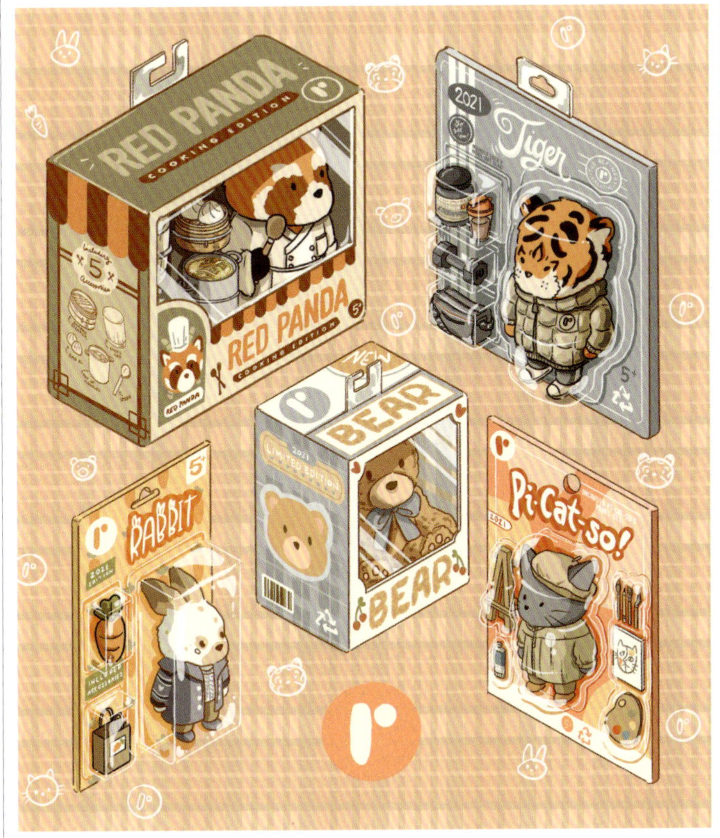

Title: Stocking Stuffers | **Client:** Self-initiated
Design Firm: The Refinery

PAUL ROGERS, BRIAN REA

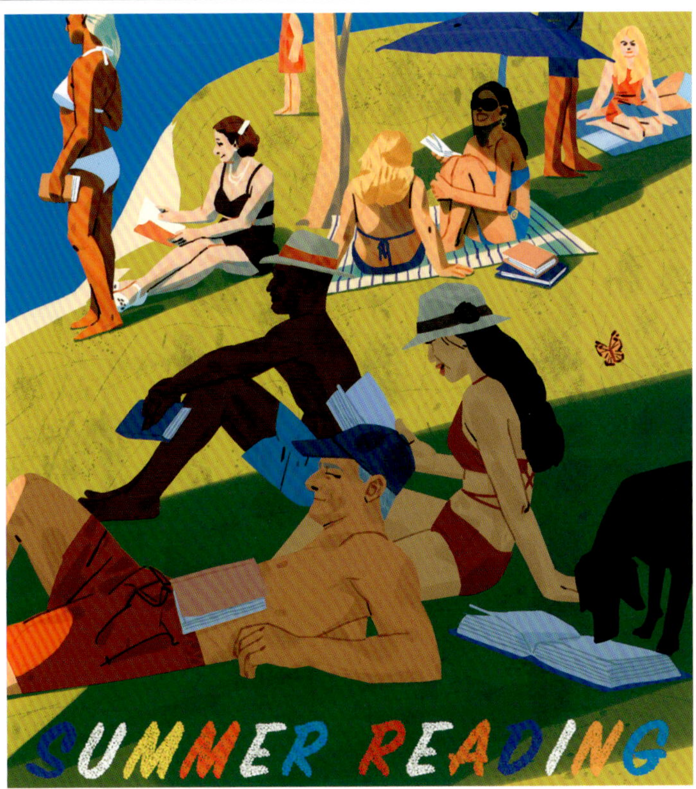

Title: Summer Reading, Book Review, NYT, 2022 | **Client:** Self-initiated
Design Firm: HyunJung Yi

JEFF BARFOOT

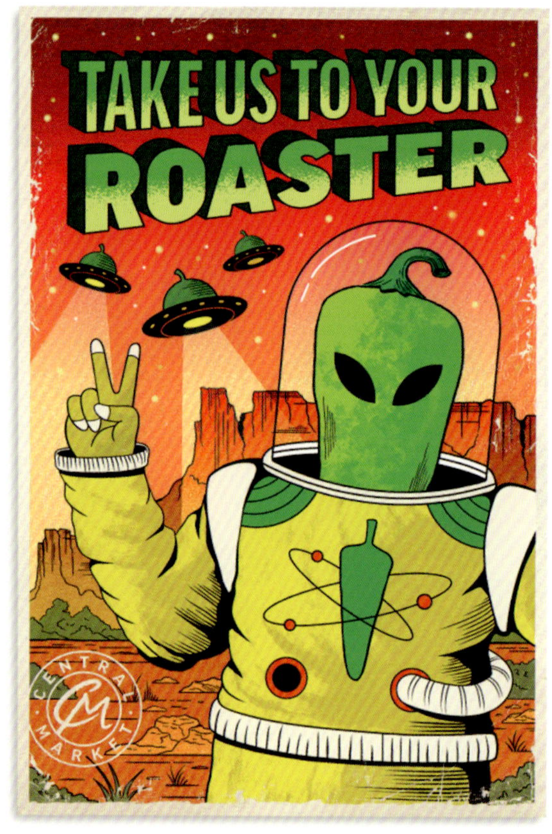

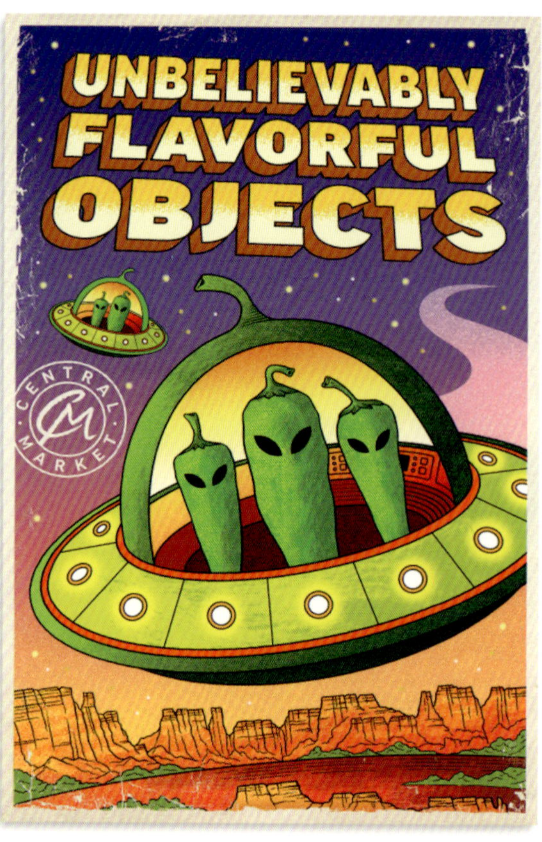

Title: Central Market Hatch 2021 | **Client:** Central Market | **Design Firms:** *TraceElement, Plot Twist Creativity

FEIXUE MEI

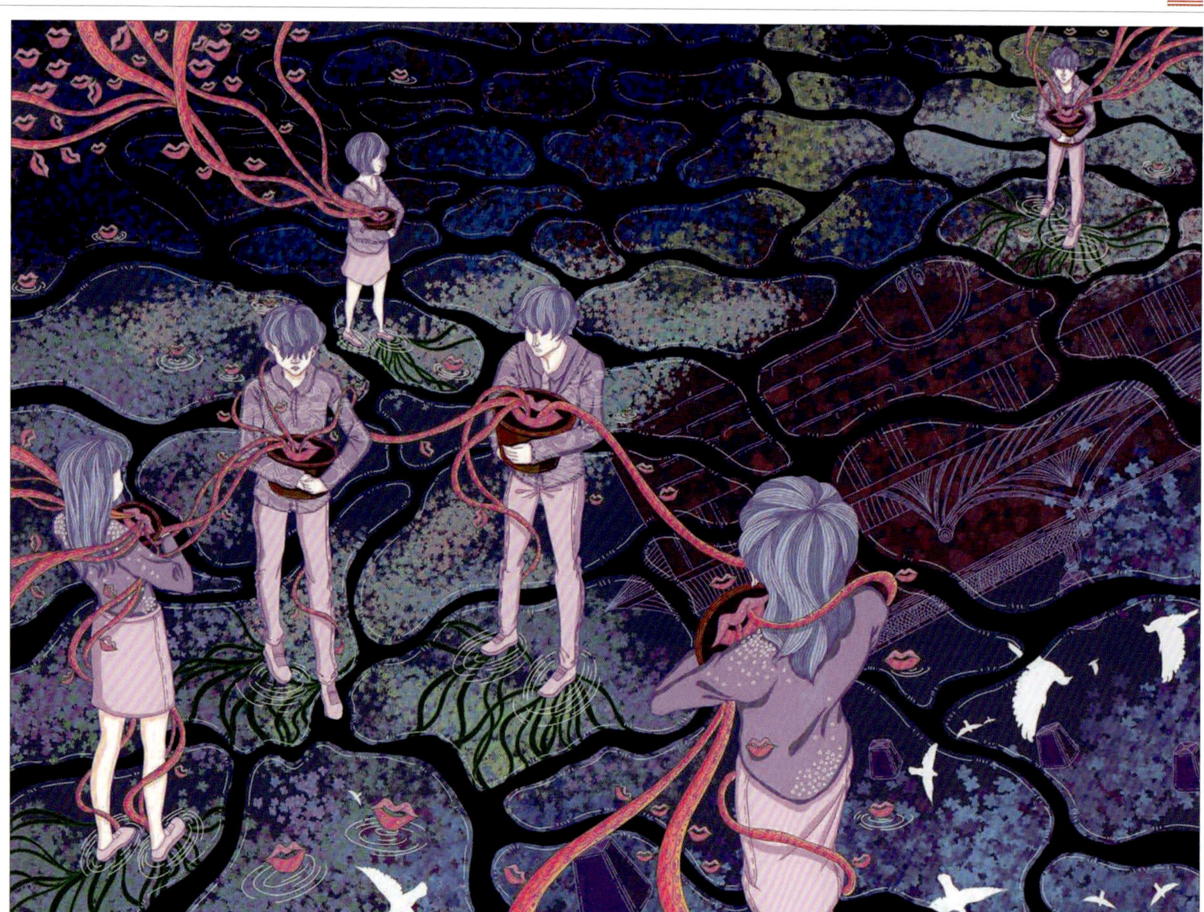

Title: The Crowd | **Client:** Self-initiated | **Design Firm:** Feixue Mei

ADAM CICCO

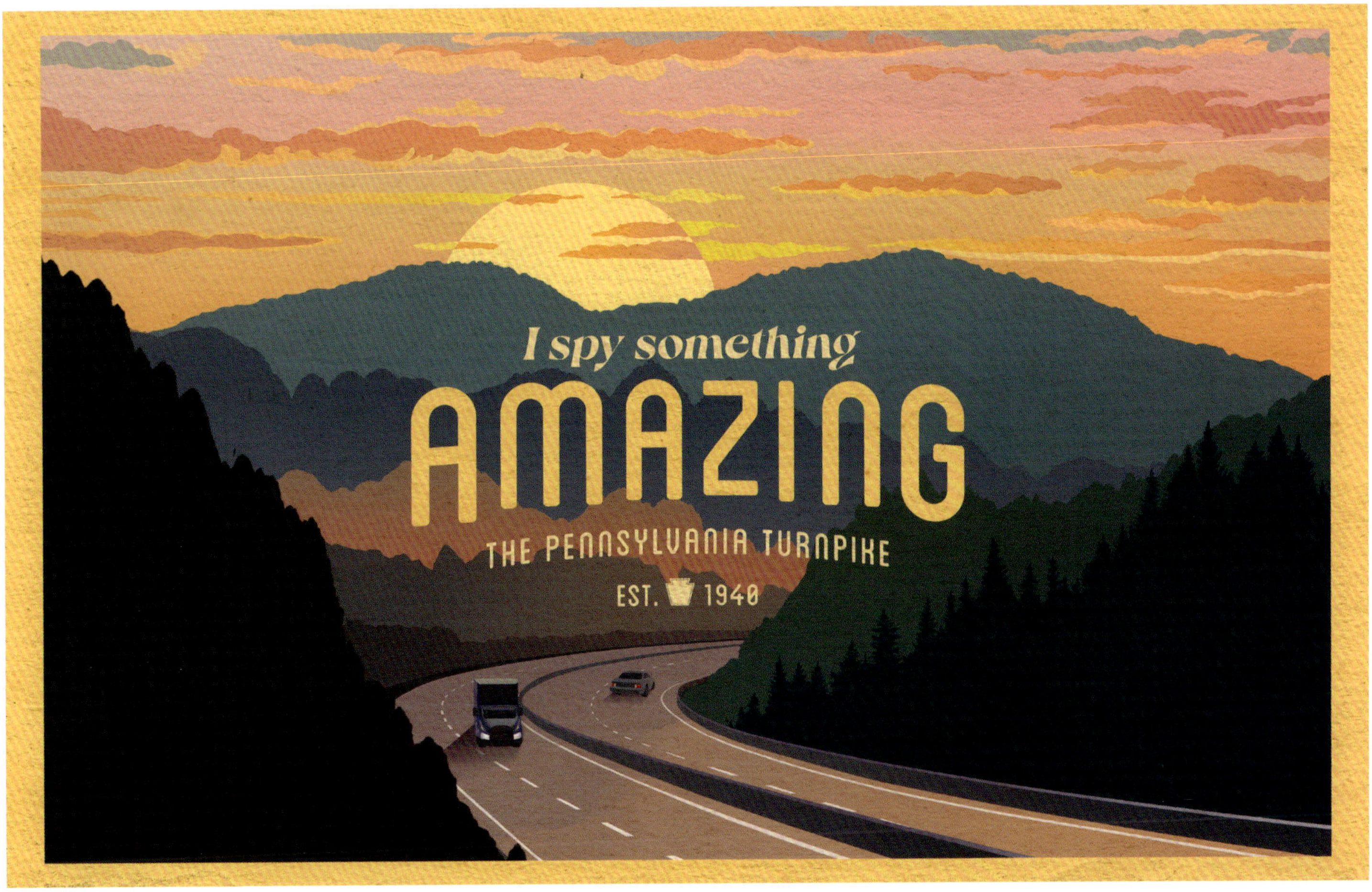

Title: The Road to Adventure | **Client:** The Pennsylvania Turnpike Commission | **Design Firm:** 9Rooftops

JEFF BARFOOT

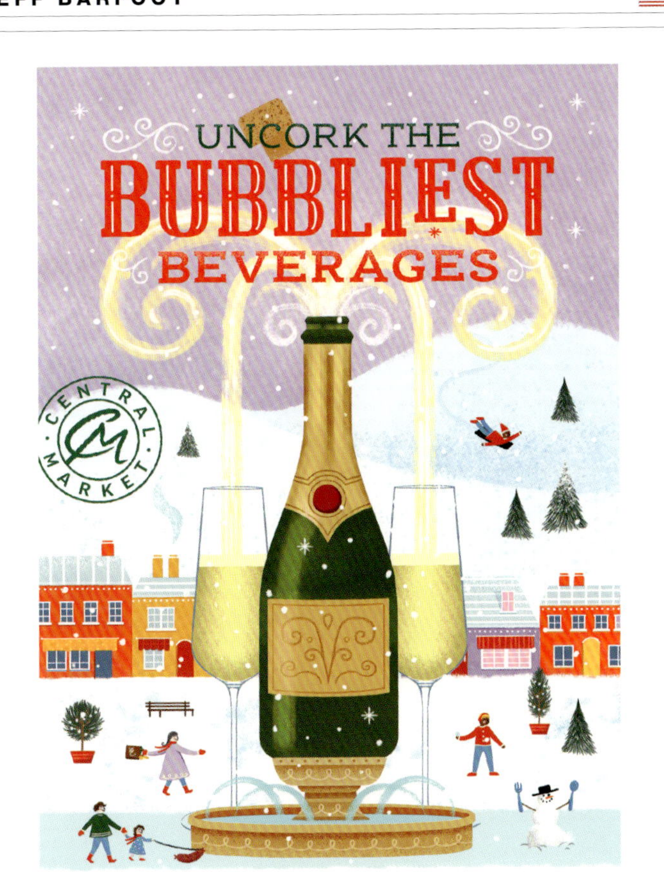

Title: Central Market Christmas | **Client:** Central Market
Design Firms: *TraceElement, Plot Twist Creativity

JIMBO PHILLIPS

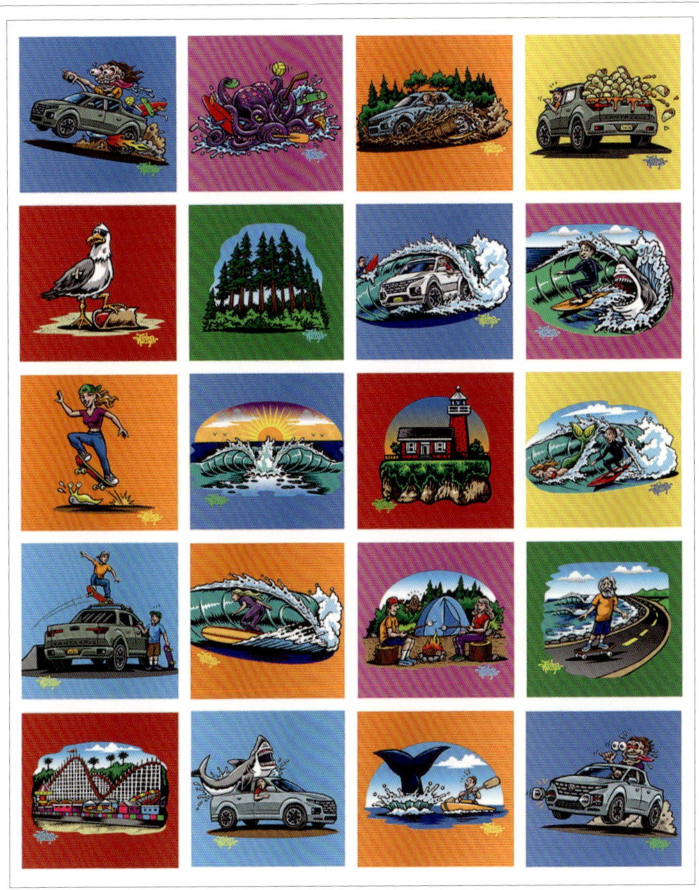

Title: Journey Through Santa Cruz | **Client:** Hyundai Motor America
Design Firm: INNOCEAN USA

JEFF BARFOOT

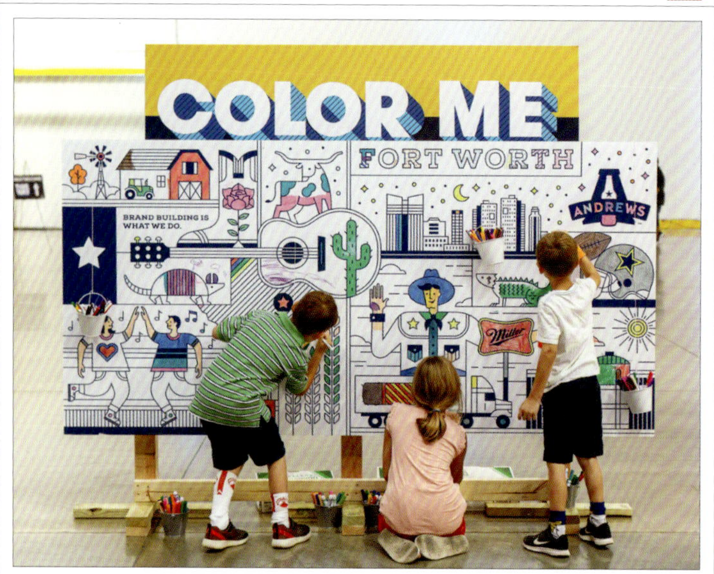

Title: Andrew's Distributing Coloring Walls
Client: Andrews Distributing | **Design Firm:** *TraceElement

JEFF BARFOOT

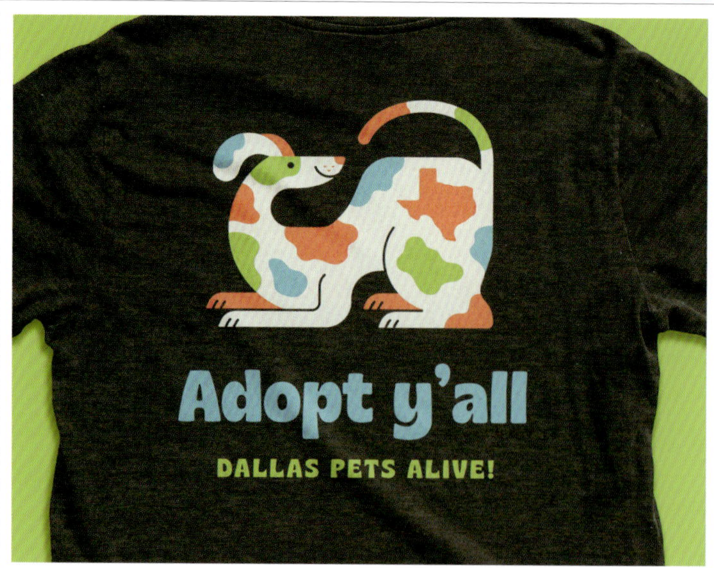

Title: Dallas Pets Alive! Apparel Series
Client: Dallas Pets Alive! | **Design Firm:** *TraceElement

ARIEL FREANER

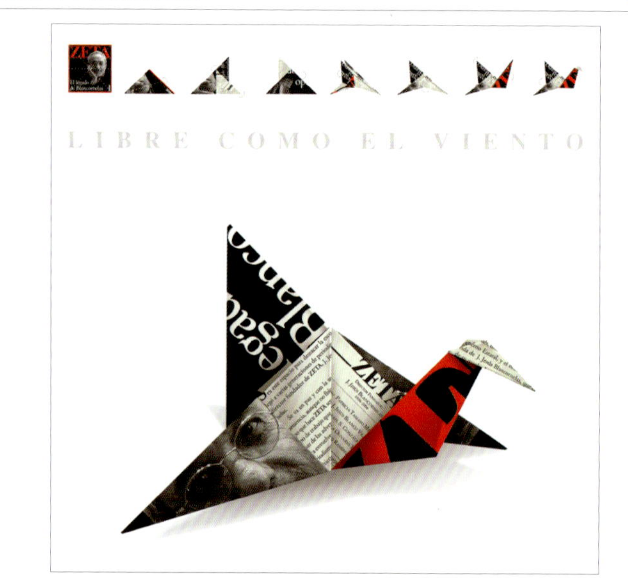

Title: ZETA Free As The Wind
Client: ZETA | **Design Firm:** Freaner Creative & Design

SCOTT RAY

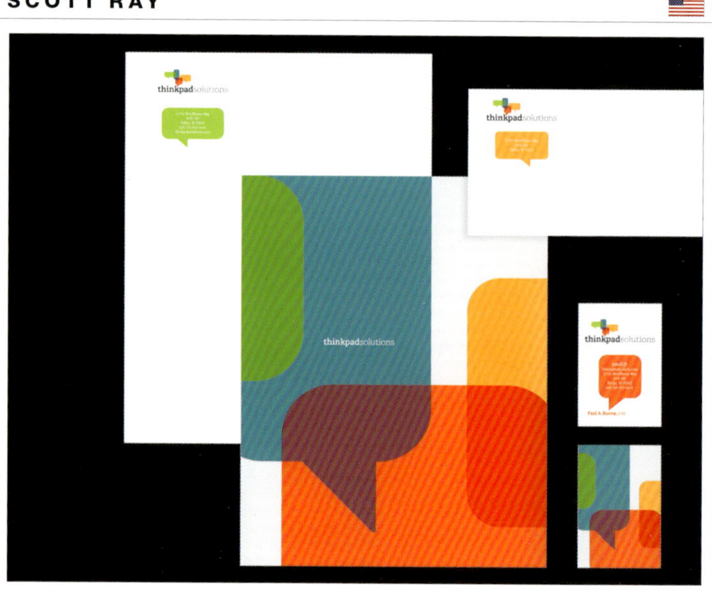

Title: Thinkpad Solutions Letterhead/Stationery
Client: Thinkpad Solutions | **Design Firm:** Peterson Ray & Company

BRAND BAR COMMUNICATIONS

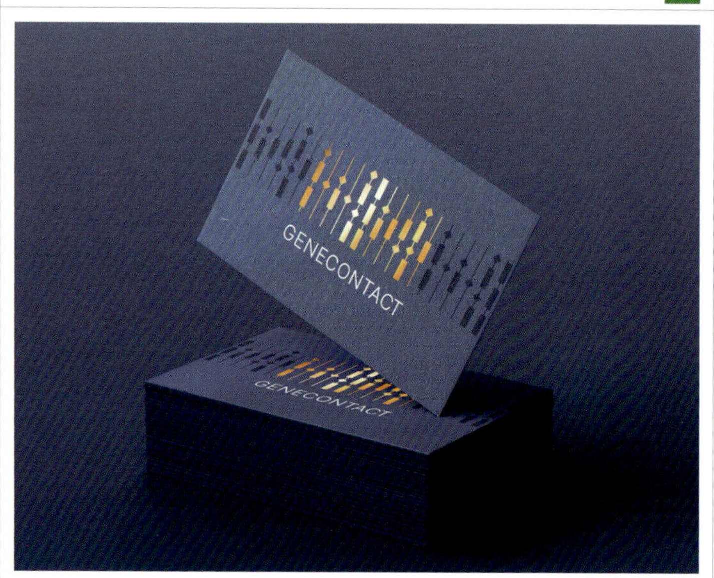

Title: It Is in Your Genes | **Client:** Genecontact
Design Firm: Brand Bar Communications

MICHAEL VANDERBYL

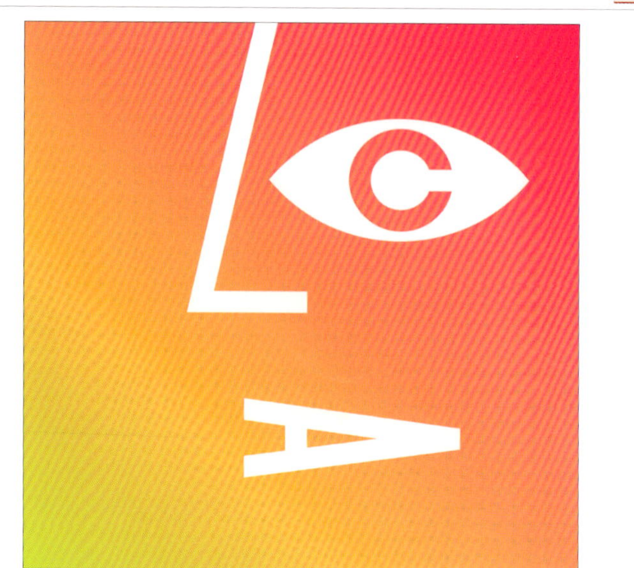

Title: City Center Live Art Logo | **Client:** City Center Bishop Ranch
Design Firm: Vanderbyl Design

NATE DYER

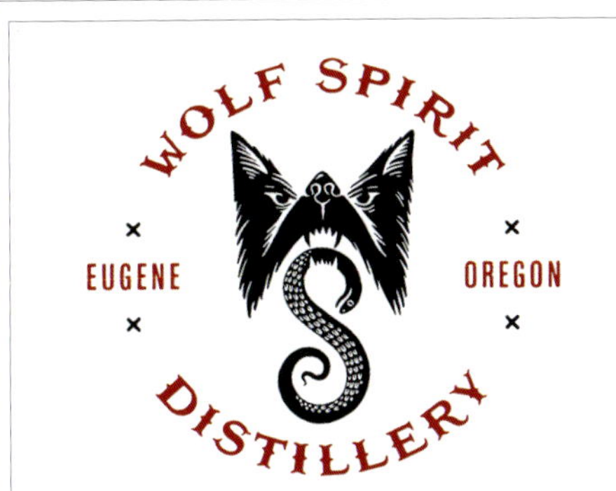

Title: Wolf Spirit Distillery
Client: Wolf Spirit Distillery
Design Firm: Moxie Sozo

MICHAEL VANDERBYL

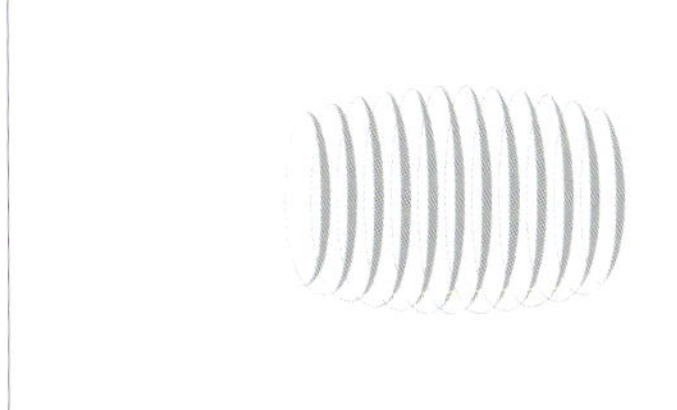

AEVITUS

Title: Aevtius Logo
Client: Aevtius
Design Firm: Vanderbyl Design

MICHAEL SCHWAB

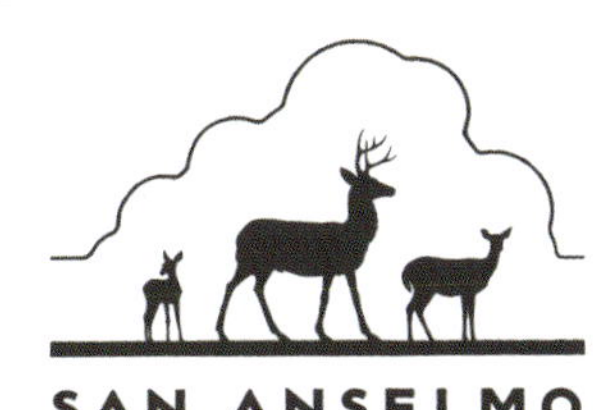

SAN ANSELMO
COMMUNITY
FOUNDATION

Title: San Anselmo Cmty. Fdn. Logo
Client: San Anselmo Cmty. Fdn.
Design Firm: Michael Schwab Studio

ALEX RHODES

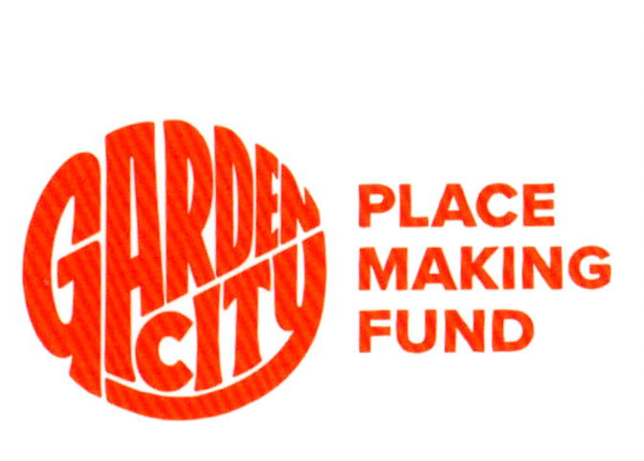

Title: Garden City Placemaking Fund
Client: Surel's Place
Design Firm: Rhodes Creative

&BARR

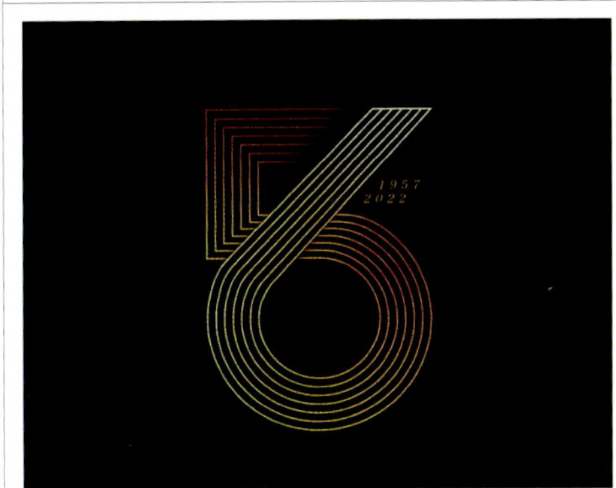

Title: &Barr 65th Anniversary Logo
Client: Self-initiated
Design Firm: &Barr

SHANTANU SUMAN

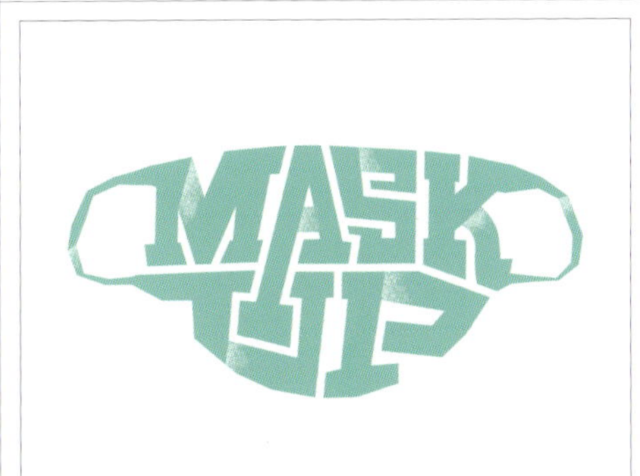

Title: Mask Up Identity | **Client:** United Way of Delaware, Henry and Randolph Counties
Design Firm: Open Door Design Studio

MICHAEL VANDERBYL

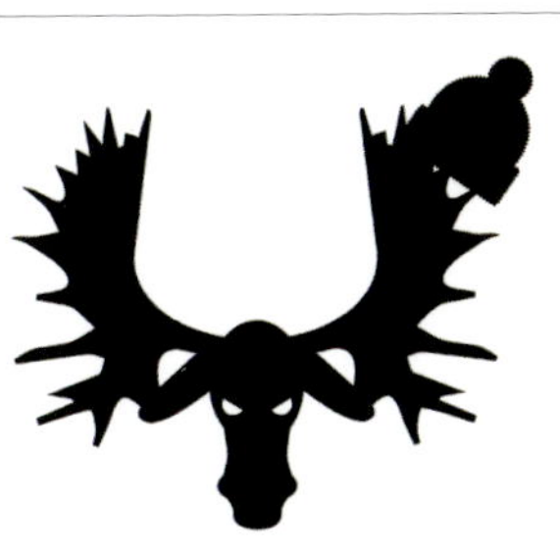

LOOSE TOQUE

Title: Loose Toque Logo
Client: Loose Toque
Design Firm: Vanderbyl Design

LEVEL GROUP

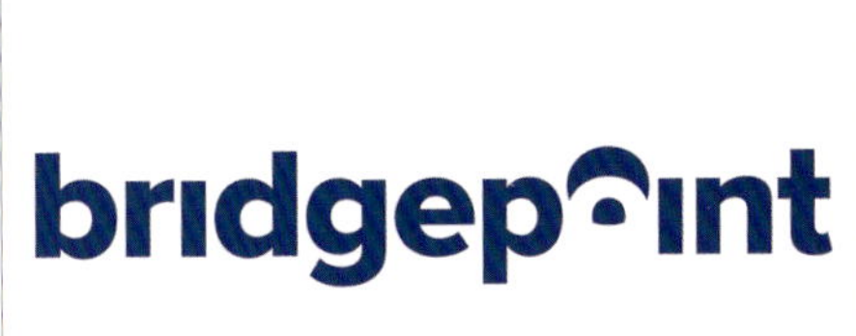

Title: Bridgepoint Logo
Client: Bridge Point Capital
Design Firm: Level Group

ANTON TIELEMANS

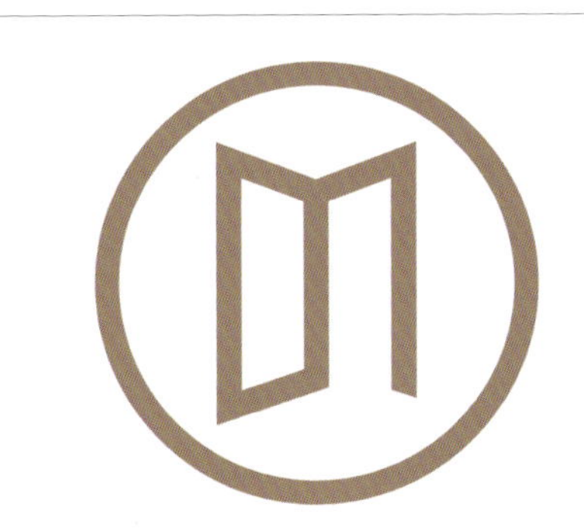

Title: My Home Real Estate Services Logo
Client: My Home Real Estate Services
Design Firm: Tielemans Design

&BARR 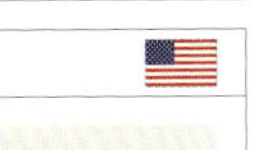

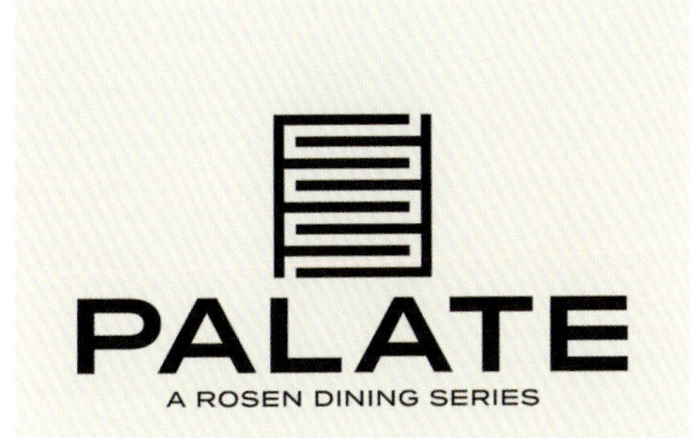

Title: Palate Dining Series
Client: Rosen Hotels & Resorts
Design Firm: &Barr

ANNIE CHEN 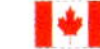

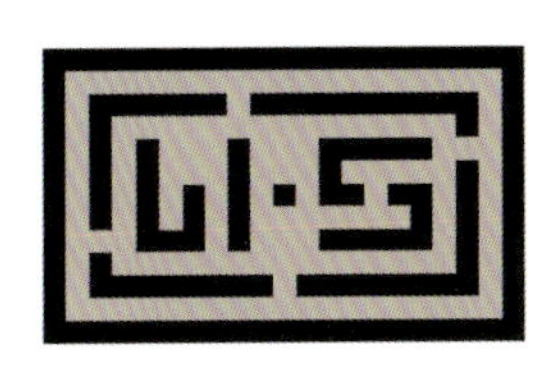

WENDY + SAM

Title: Wendy + Sam
Client: Wendy + Sam
Design Firm: Annie Chen Design

ANNIE CHEN 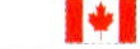

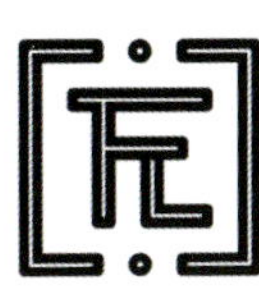

FERMENT
LAB

Title: Ferment Lab
Client: The Ferment Lab
Design Firm: Annie Chen Design

GREEN ASPHALT TEAM

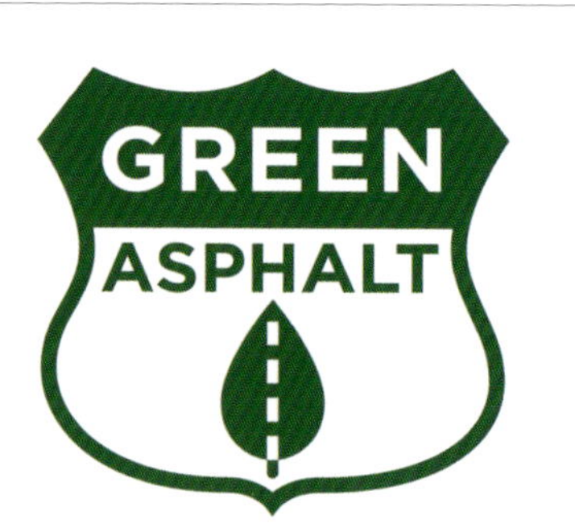

Title: Green Asphalt Brand Mark
Client: Green Asphalt Co.
Design Firm: Romeo and Company International

VANESSA RYAN

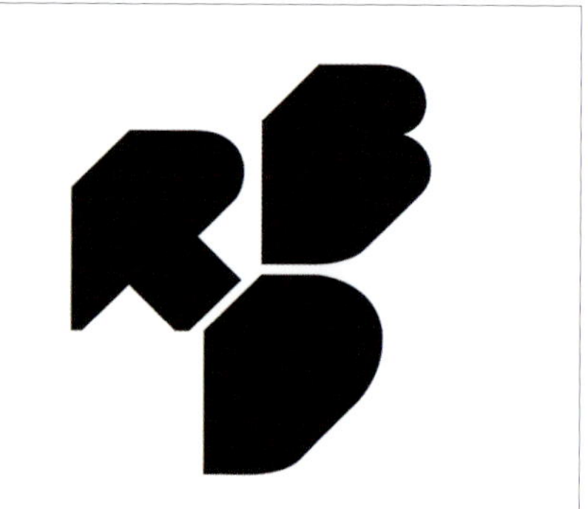

Title: RBD Identity
Client: Renovate Build Design
Design Firm: SML Design

STEWART JUNG

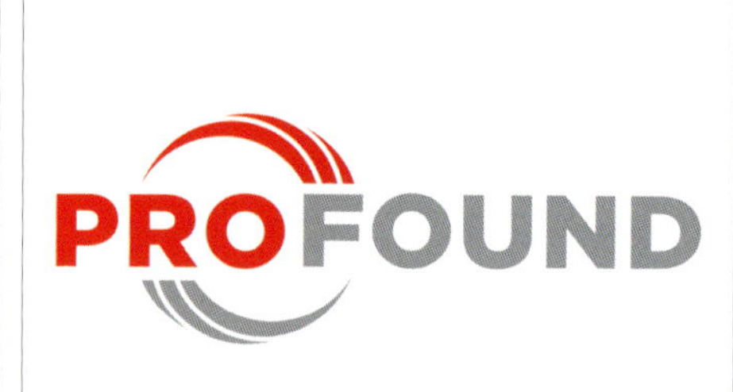

Title: Profound Talent Logo
Client: Profound Talent
Design Firm: AG Creative Group

HANNAH GASKAMP

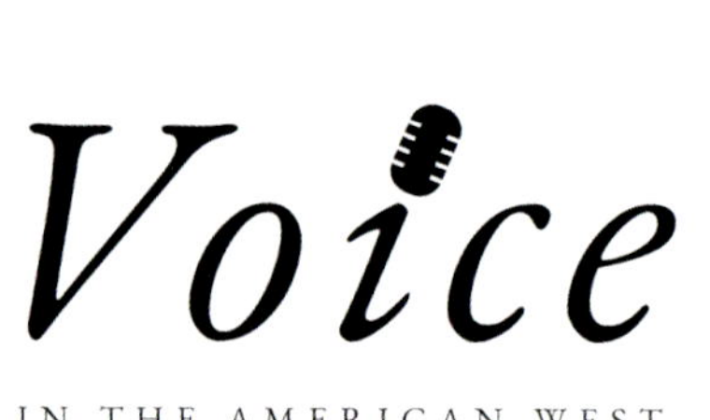

Title: Voice in the American West
Client: Self-initiated
Design Firm: Texas Tech University Press

DERWYN GOODALL

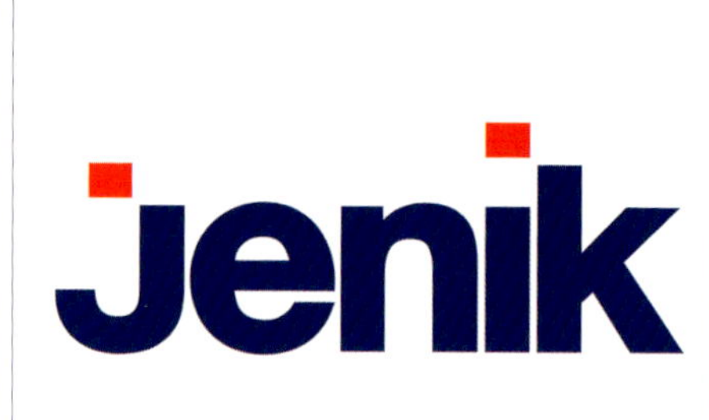

Title: Jenik Art Consultants Identity
Client: Jenik Art Consultants
Design Firm: Goodall Integrated Design

NATE DYER

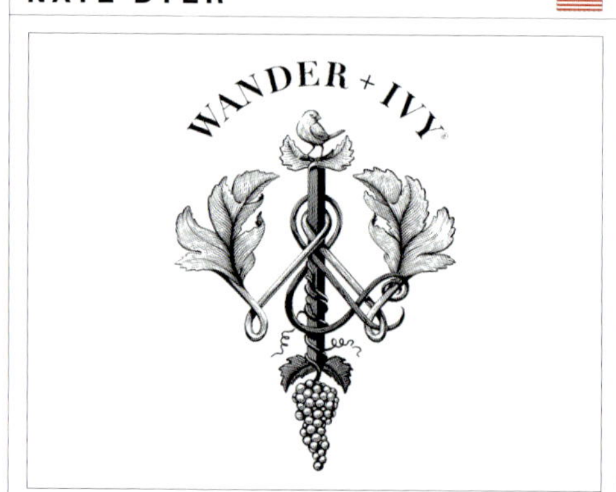

Title: Wander + Ivy
Client: Wander + Ivy
Design Firm: Moxie Sozo

EL PASO, GALERÍA DE COMUNICACIÓN

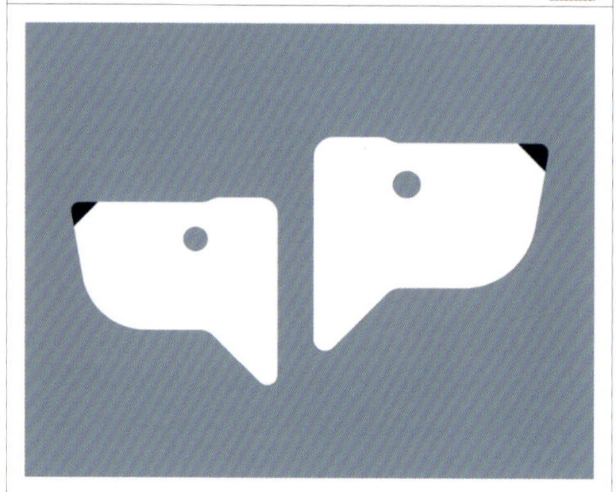

Title: TalkingVets
Client: IDEAVET
Design Firm: El Paso, Galería de Comunicación

KEVIN JONES

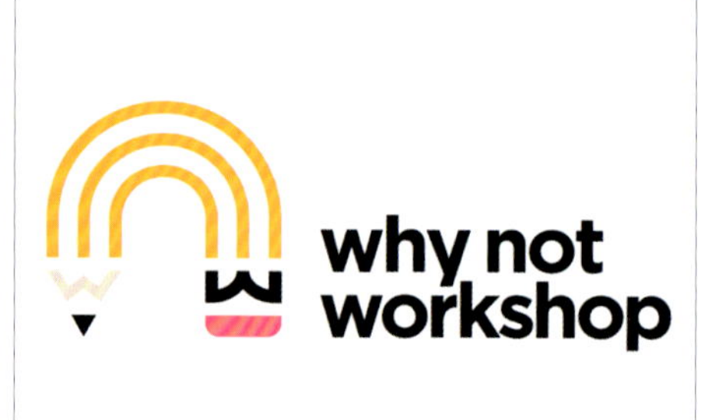

Title: Why Not Workshop
Client: Why Not Workshop
Design Firm: Joba Studio

DERWYN GOODALL

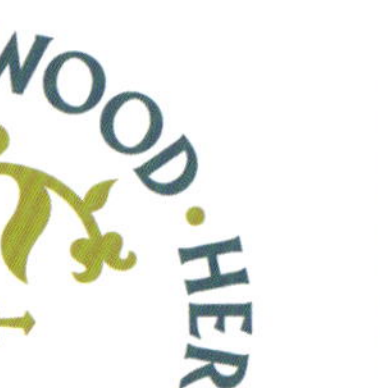

Title: Taddlewood Heritage Association Identity
Client: Taddlewood Heritage Association
Design Firm: Goodall Integrated Design

HYUNGJOO A. KIM

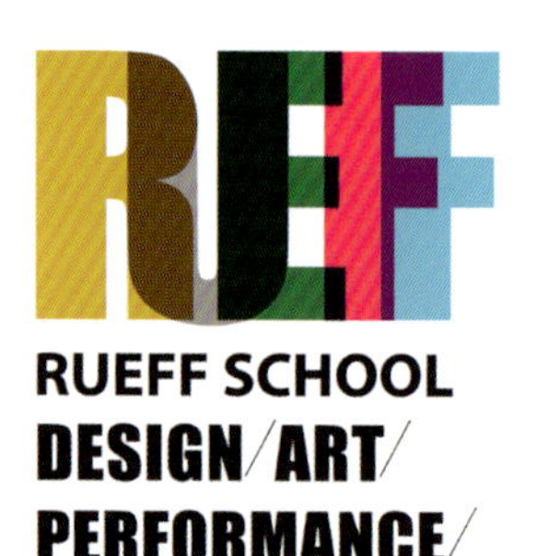

Title: RUEFF School of Design, Art, & Performance
Client: Patti & Rusty Rueff School of Design, Art, & Performance | **Design Firm:** HyungjooKimDesignLab

SHARON LLOYD MCLAUGHLIN

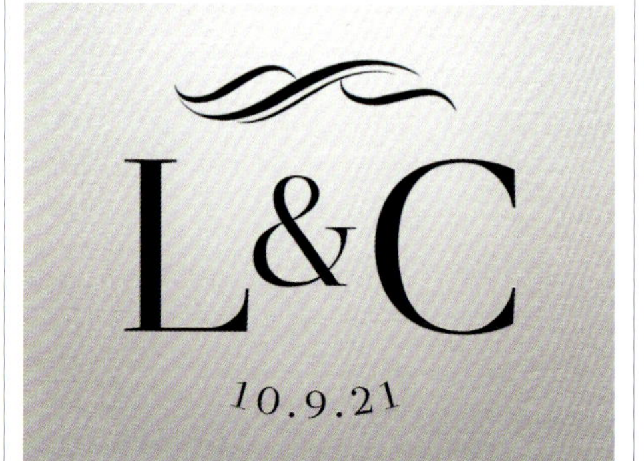

Title: Lauren & Colin Are Getting Married Logo
Client: Lauren & Colin
Design Firm: Mermaid, Inc.

LEVEL GROUP

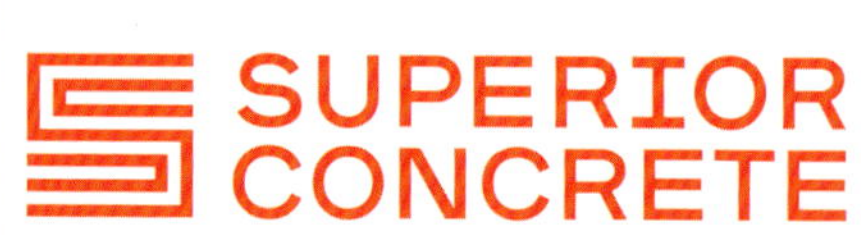

Title: Superior Concrete Logo
Client: Superior Concrete
Design Firm: Level Group

LEGACY79

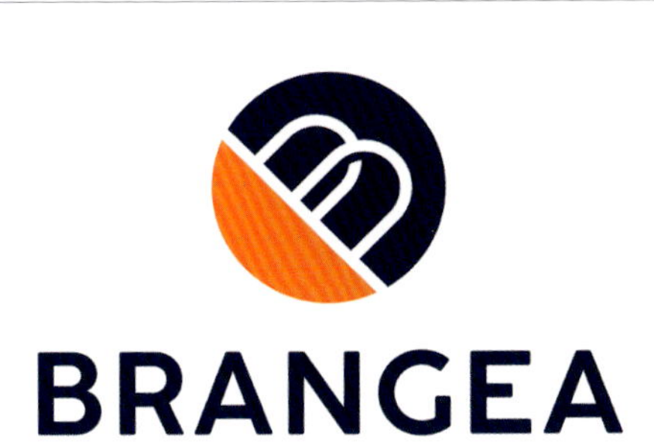

Title: Brangea Logo
Client: Brangea
Design Firm: Legacy79

EL PASO, GALERÍA DE COMUNICACIÓN

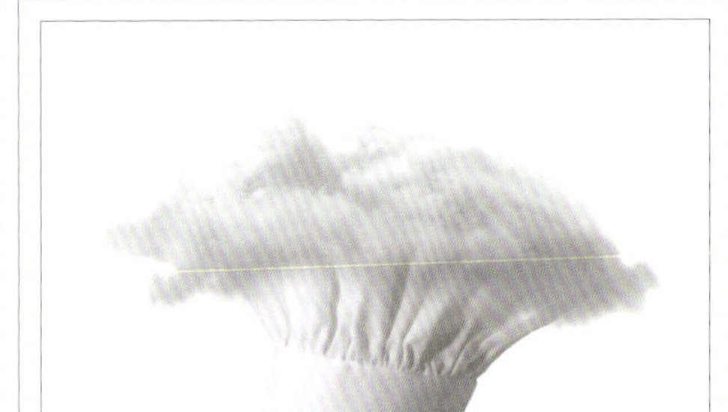

Title: Andrés López, Chef
Client: Andrés López
Design Firm: El Paso, Galería de Comunicación

JOHN BALL, DAVID ALDERMAN

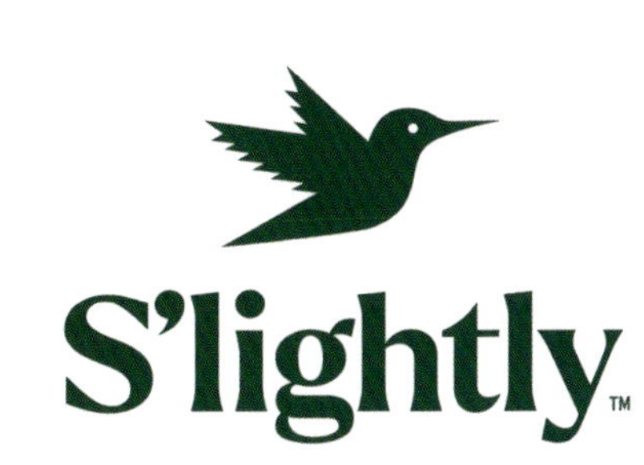

Title: S'lightly Identity
Client: S'lightly
Design Firm: MiresBall

LEVEL GROUP

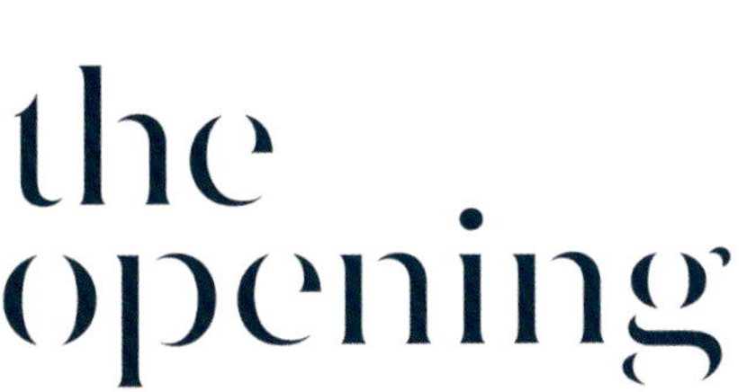

Title: The Opening Logo
Client: The Opening
Design Firm: Level Group

SCOTT RAY

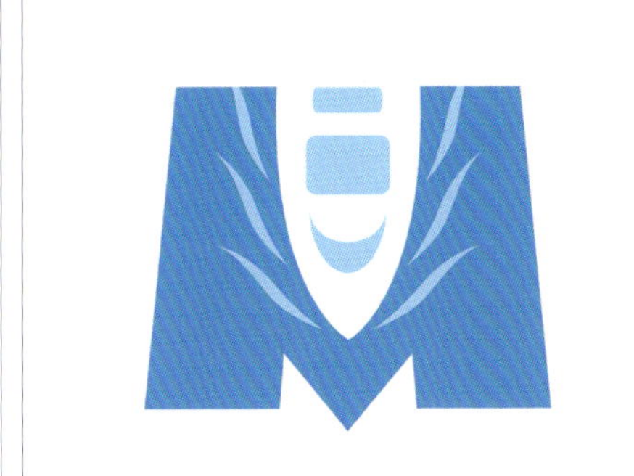

Title: Lake Murray Marina Logo
Client: Lake Murray Marina
Design Firm: Peterson Ray & Company

SHARON LLOYD MCLAUGHLIN

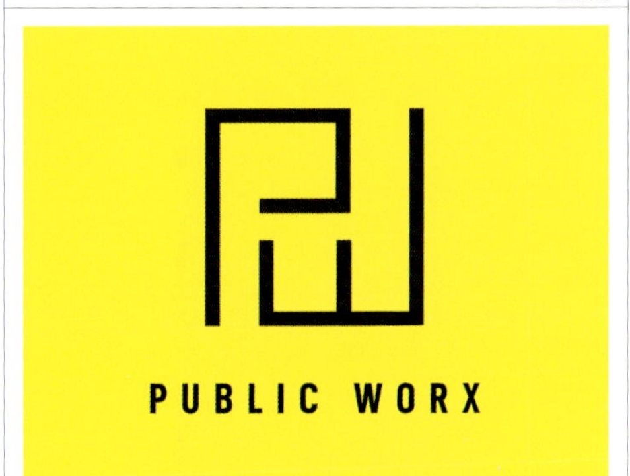

Title: Public WorX Logo
Client: Public WorX
Design Firm: Mermaid, Inc.

ANNIE CHEN

Title: Project Meteor
Client: Sigma Intégrale
Design Firm: Annie Chen Design

GRAHAM CLIFFORD

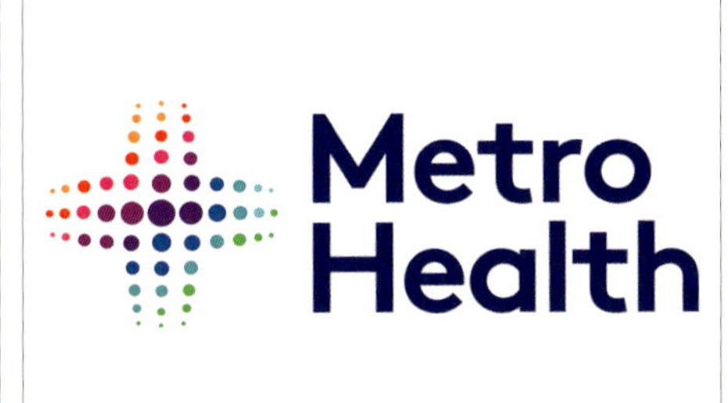

Title: Community Cross
Client: MetroHealth
Design Firm: DeVito/Verdi

ANTON TIELEMANS

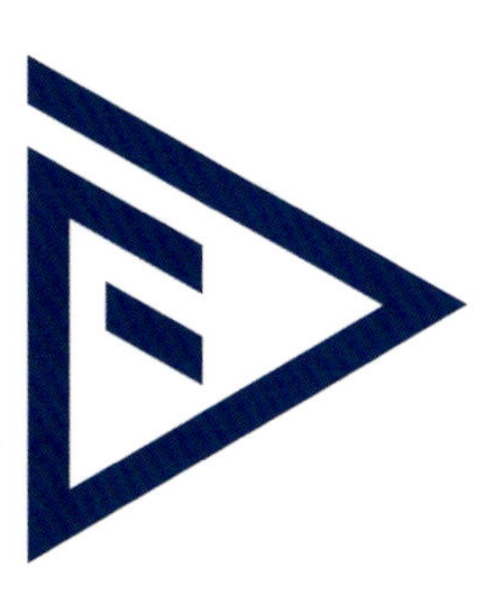

Title: Dana Finkelstein LPGA Golfer
Client: Dana Finkelstein
Design Firm: Tielemans Design

KELLY HOLOHAN, BRYAN SATALINO

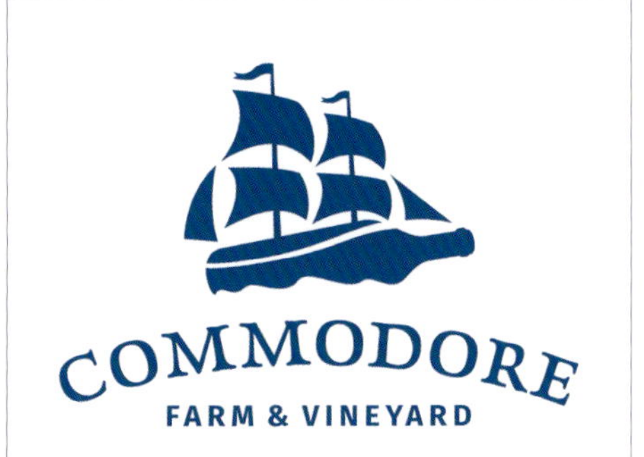

Title: Commodore Farm & Vineyard
Client: Commodore Farm & Vineyard
Design Firm: Holohan Design

JIM MA

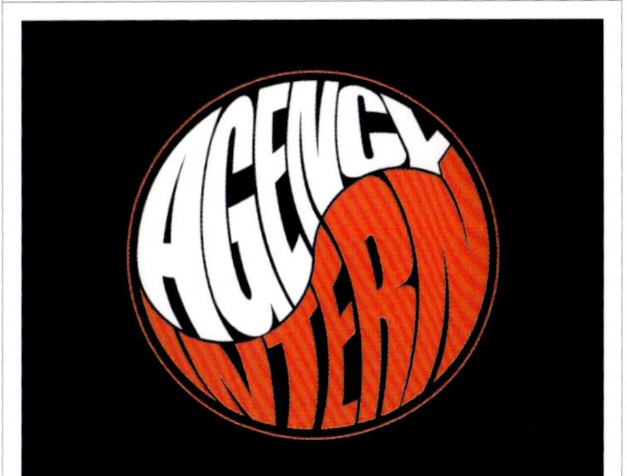

Title: BL Ying-Yang
Client: Self-initiated
Design Firm: Bailey Lauerman

DERWYN GOODALL

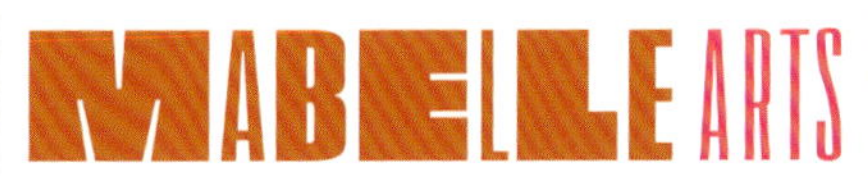

Title: Mabelle Arts Logo
Client: Mabelle Arts
Design Firm: Goodall Integrated Design

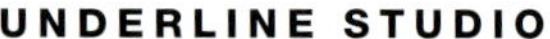

UNDERLINE STUDIO

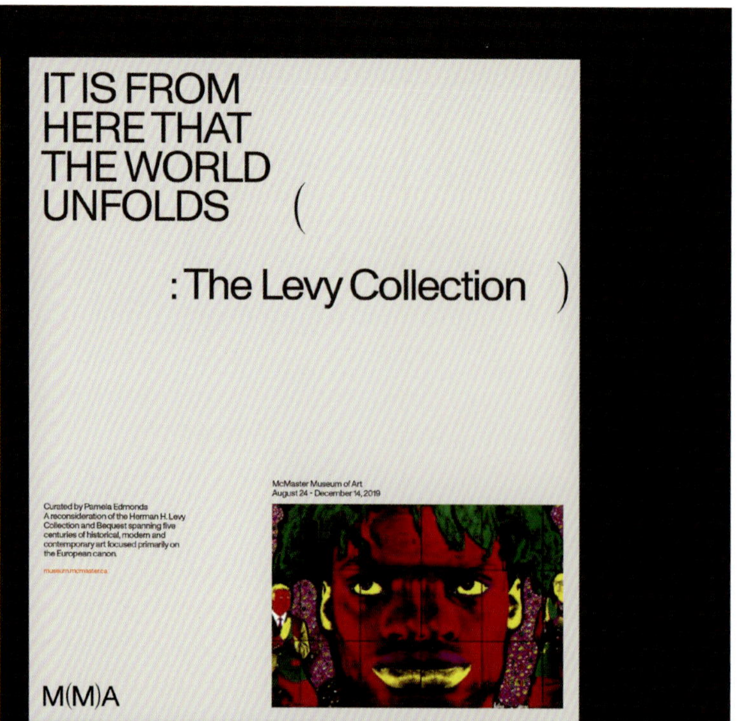

Title: McMaster Museum of Art Identity | **Client:** McMaster Museum of Art | **Design Firm:** Underline Studio

JACY EMBRAY

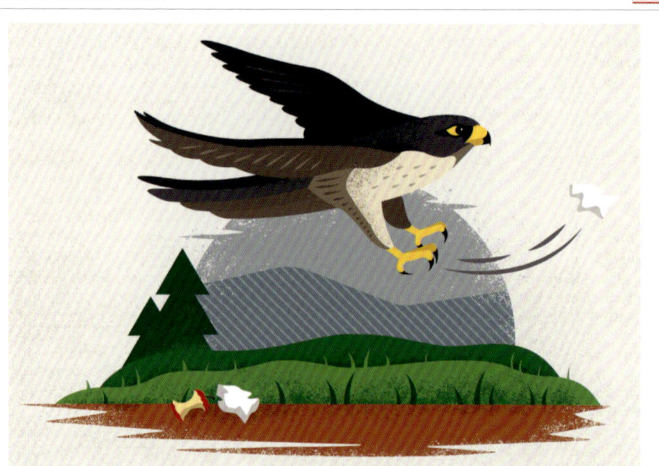

Title: Keep The Mountain Clean | **Client:** Beech Mountain Resort
Design Firm: Creative Energy

LEANNE BALEN

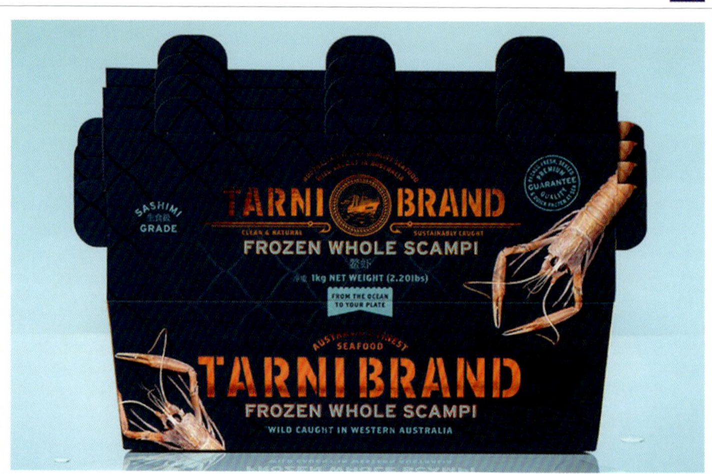

Title: Tarni Brand | **Client:** Shark Bay Seafoods Pty Ltd.
Design Firm: Dessein

ALEX FLORES

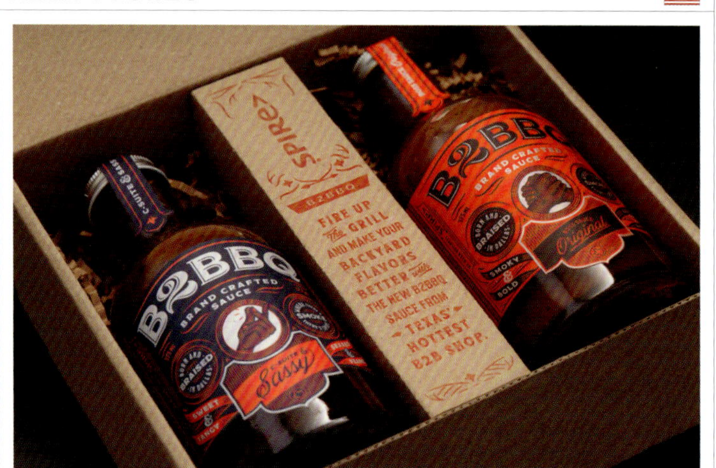

Title: Spire B2BBQ | **Client:** Self-initiated
Design Firm: Spire Agency

OUR MAN IN HAVANA

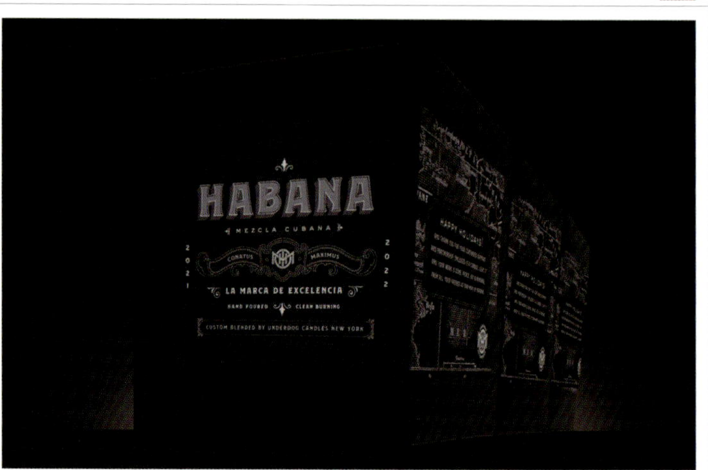

Title: OMIH Habana Candles | **Client:** Self-initiated
Design Firm: Our Man In Havana

HARCUS DESIGN

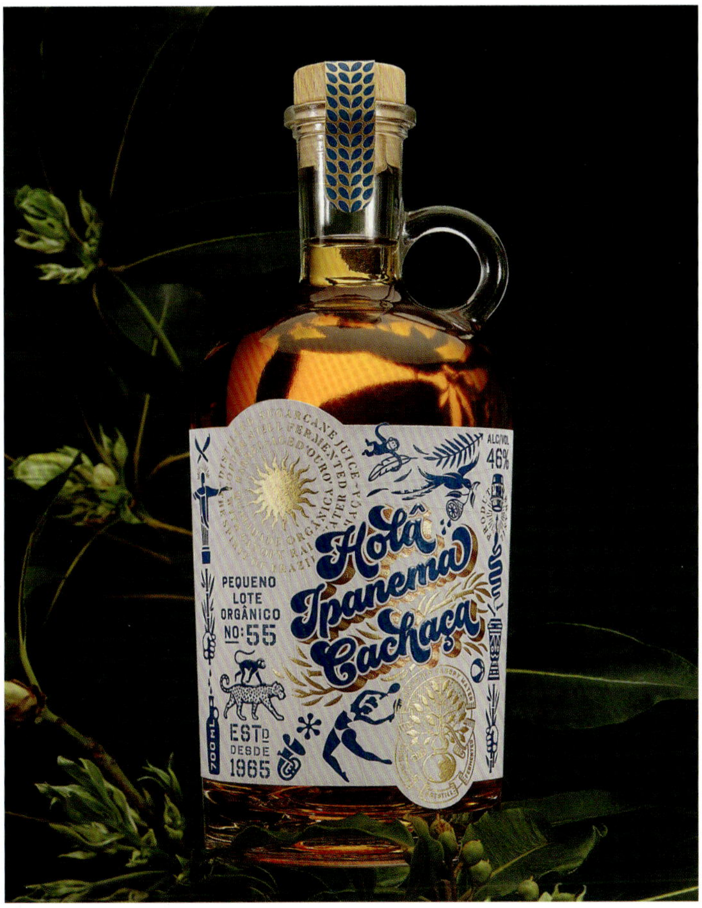

Title: Hola Ipanema Cachaça | **Client:** Spicers
Design Firm: Harcus Design

STRANGER & STRANGER

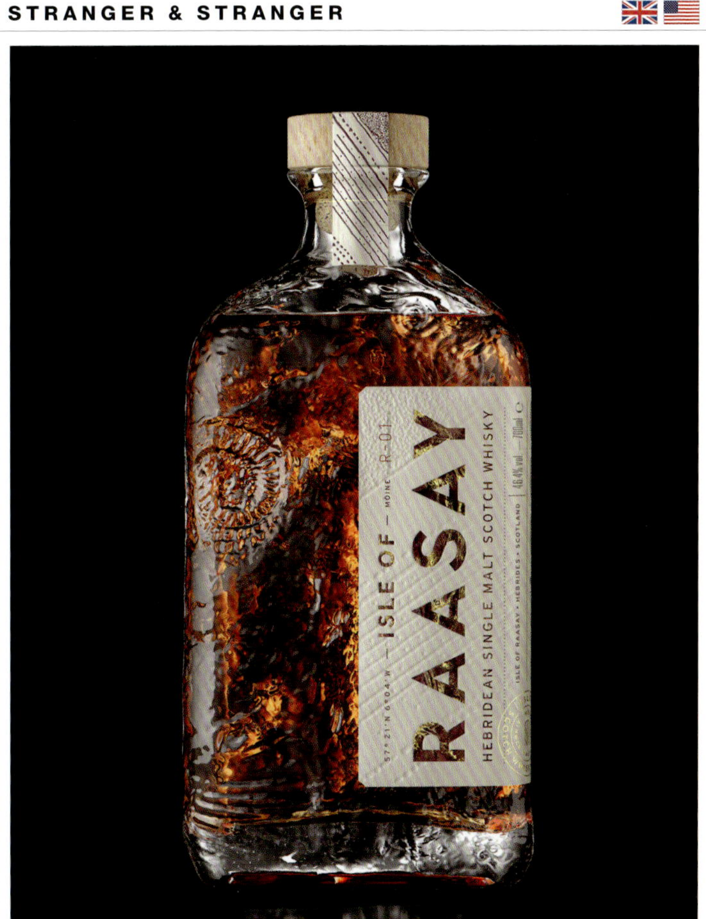

Title: Isle of Raasay Scotch Whisky | **Client:** R&B Distillers Ltd.
Design Firm: Stranger & Stranger

HATCH DESIGN

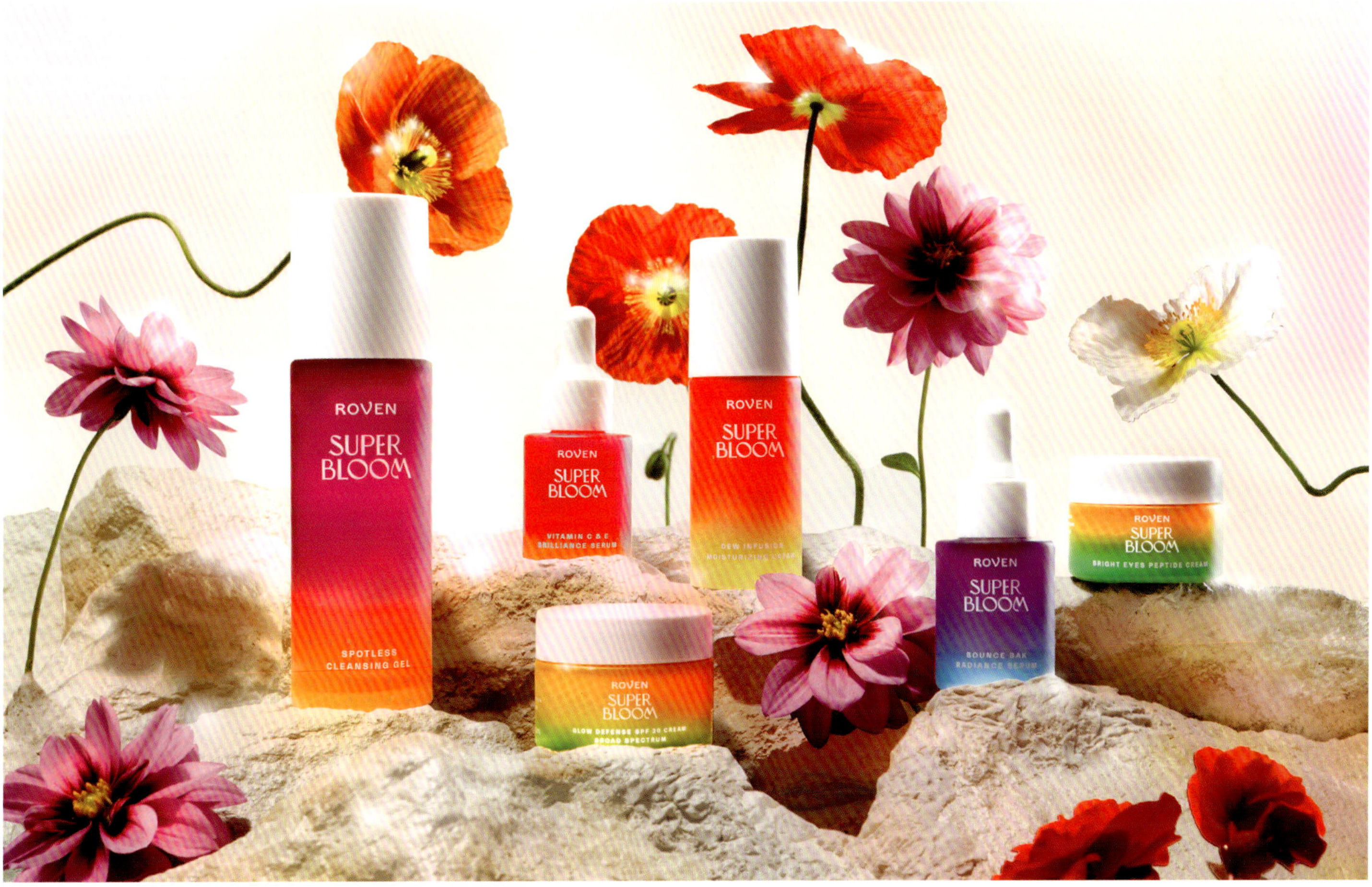

Title: Superbloom | **Client:** Grove Collaborative | **Design Firm:** Hatch Design

STRANGER & STRANGER

Title: Kástra Elión Vodka | **Client:** CMC Wine & Spirits
Design Firm: Stranger & Stranger

STRANGER & STRANGER

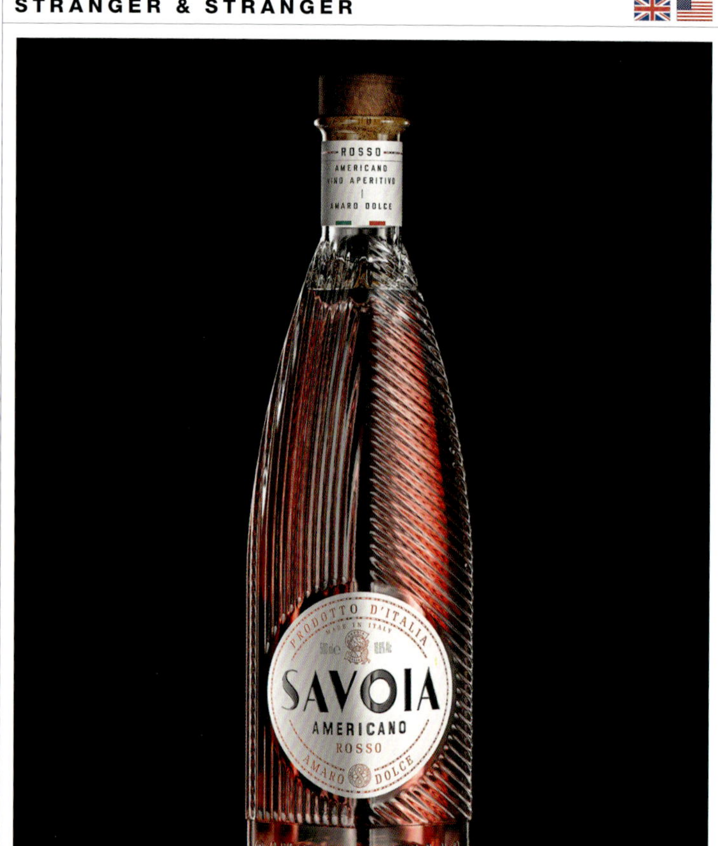

Title: Savoia Americano | **Client:** Giuseppe Gallo
Design Firm: Stranger & Stranger

STRANGER & STRANGER

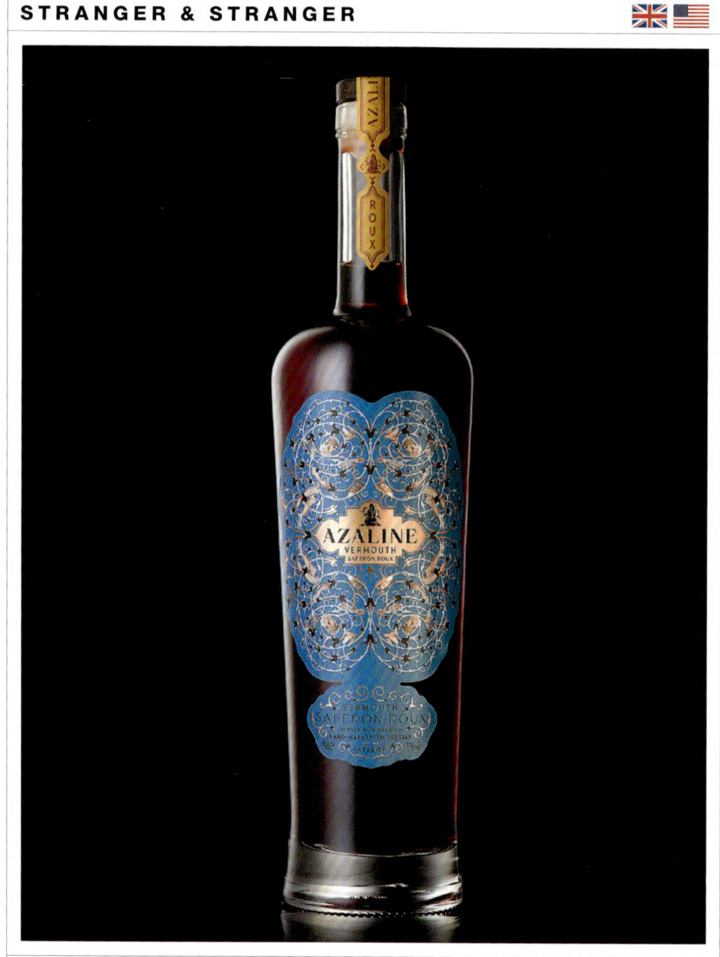

Title: Azaline Vermouth | **Client:** Kanlaon Ltd. (Bleeding Heart Rum)
Design Firm: Stranger & Stranger

PIERRE DELEBOIS

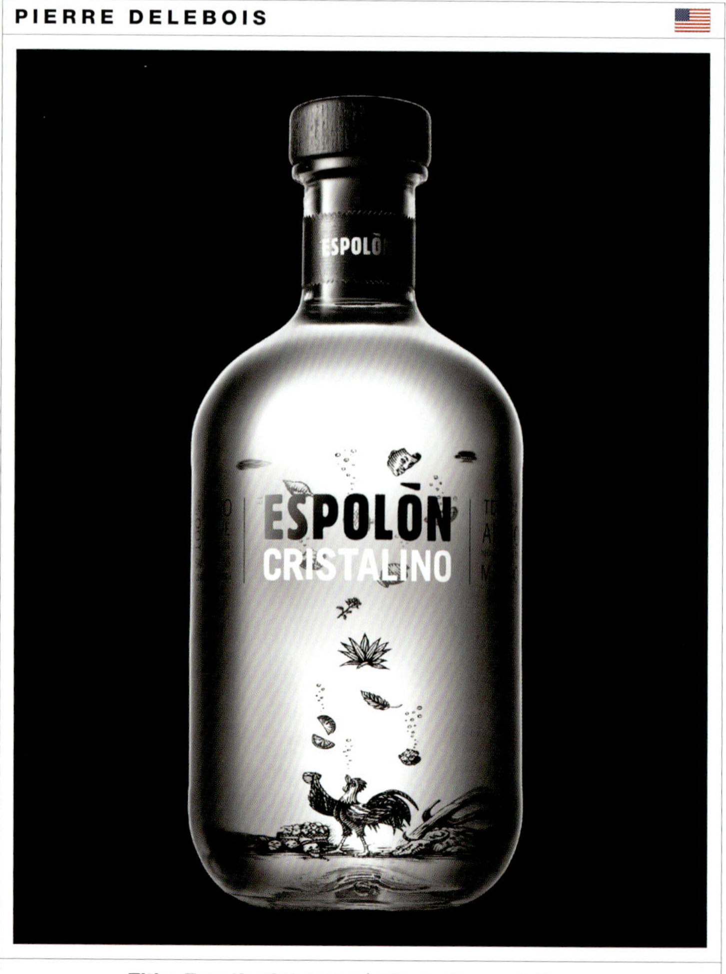

Title: Espolòn Cristalino | **Client:** Campari Group
Design Firm: Force MAJEURE

PEPSICO DESIGN & INNOVATION

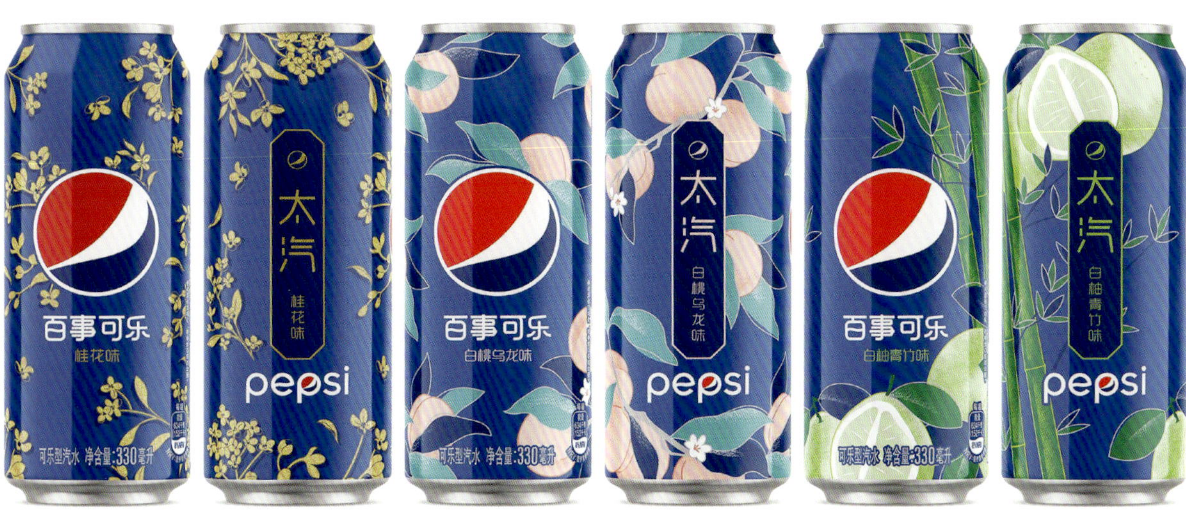

Title: Pepsi Cola China Series - Bamboo & Pomelo Flavor | **Client:** Self-initiated | **Design Firm:** PepsiCo Design & Innovation

JOHN ERESMAN, MARK ROWE

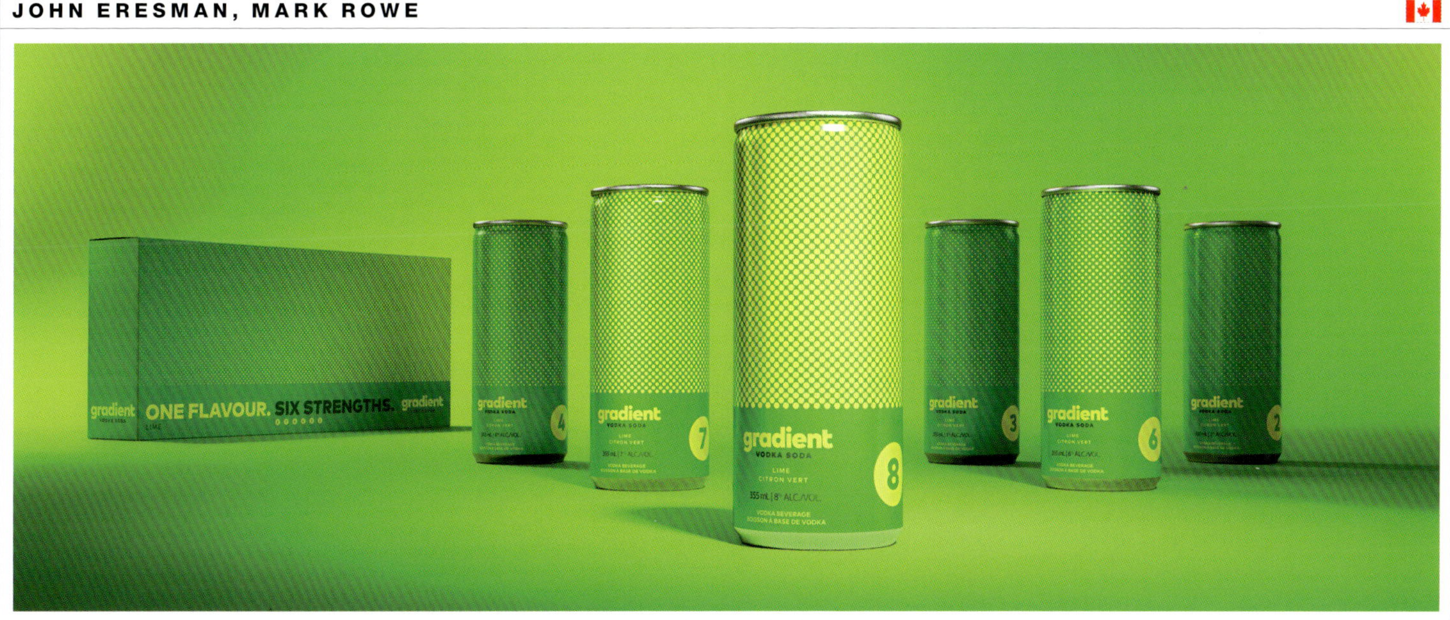

Title: Gradient Vodka Soda | **Client:** Gradient Vodka Soda | **Design Firm:** Trill

NAOMIE ROSS, MICHAEL BAGNARDI, KAREN SONG

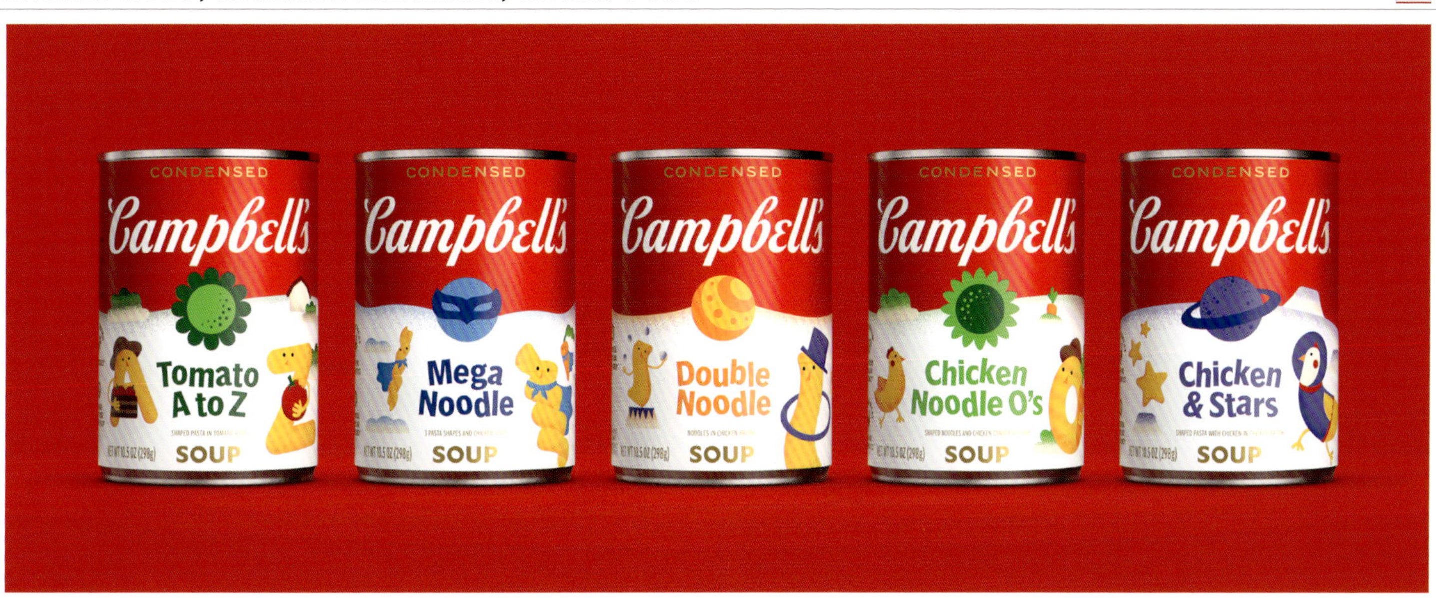

Title: Campbell's Red & White Condensed Soup Packaging | **Client:** Campbell's | **Design Firm:** Turner Duckworth: London, San Francisco & New York

OMDESIGN

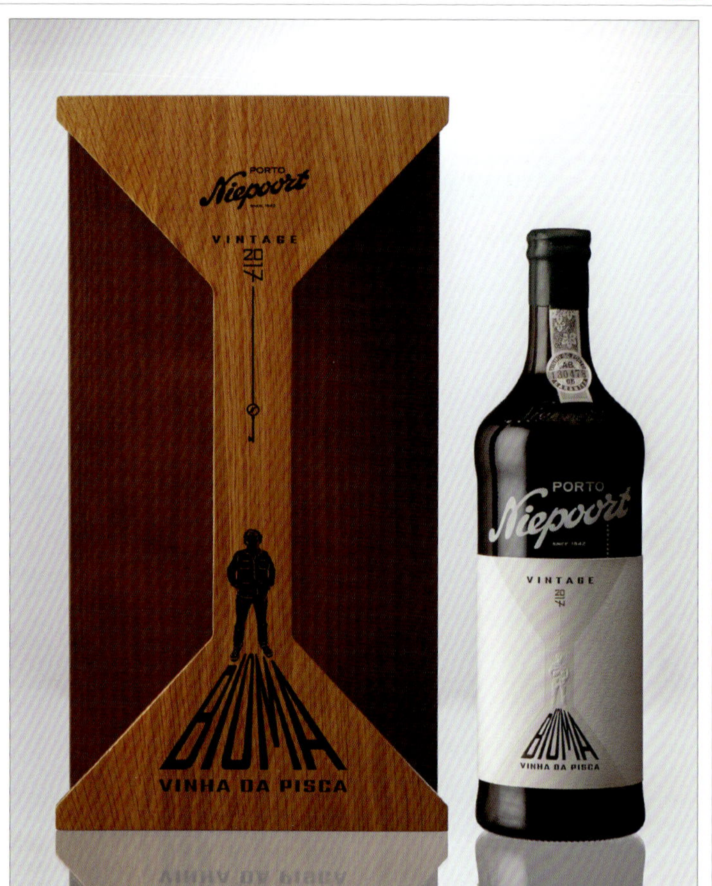

Title: Niepoort Bioma – "A Vintage with the Knife in Teeth"
Client: Niepoort | **Design Firm:** Omdesign

PIERRE DELEBOIS

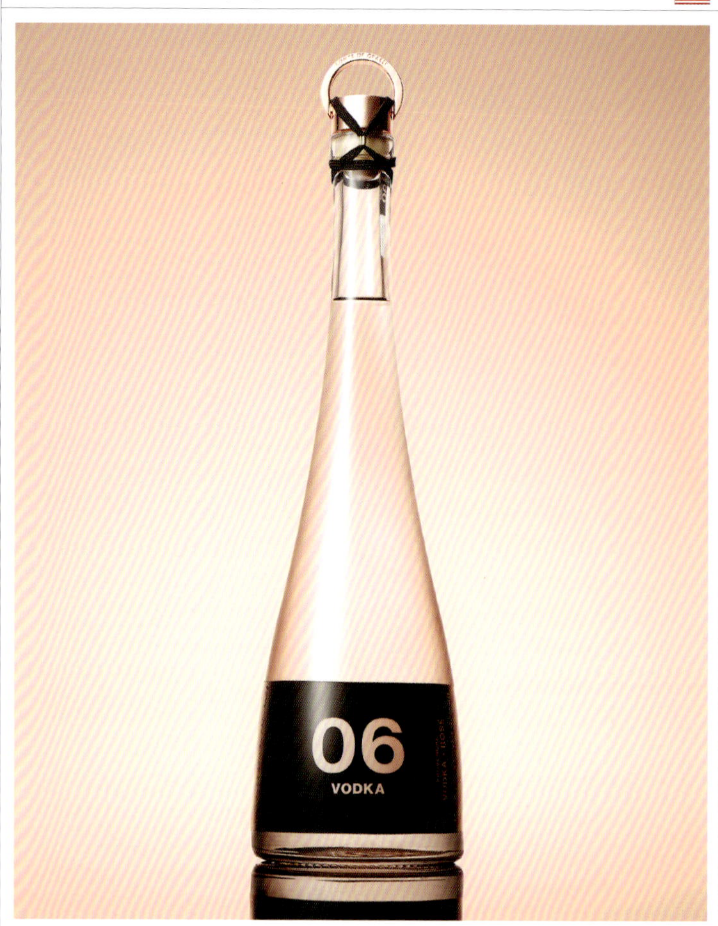

Title: Comte de Grasse 06 Vodka | **Client:** Comte de Grasse
Design Firm: Force MAJEURE

STRANGER & STRANGER

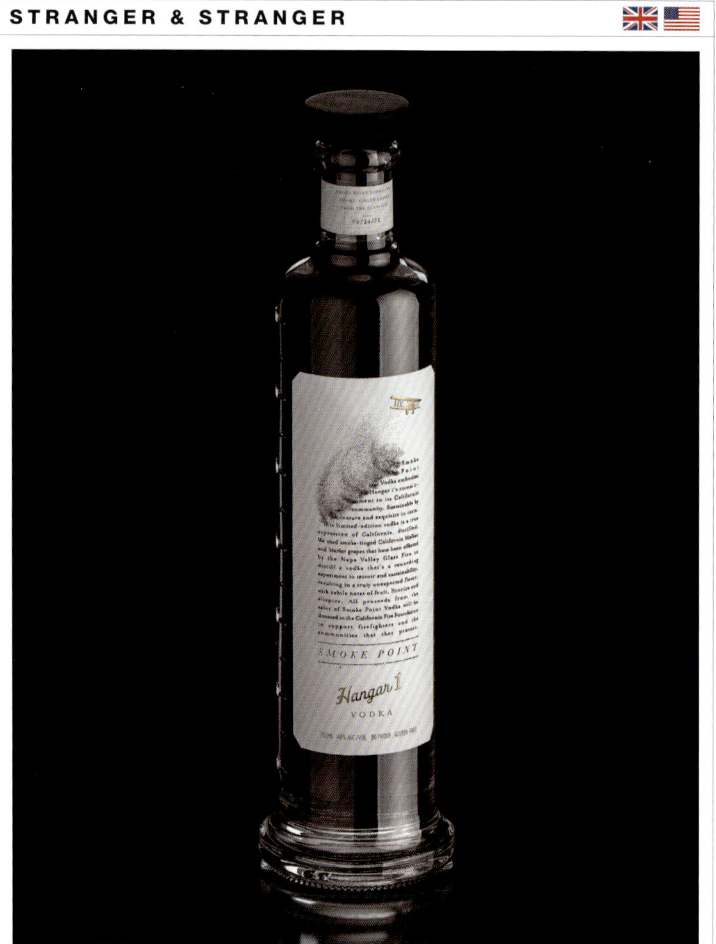

Title: Hangar 1 Vodka Smoke Point | **Client:** Proximo Spirits Inc.
Design Firm: Stranger & Stranger

HAJIME TSUSHIMA

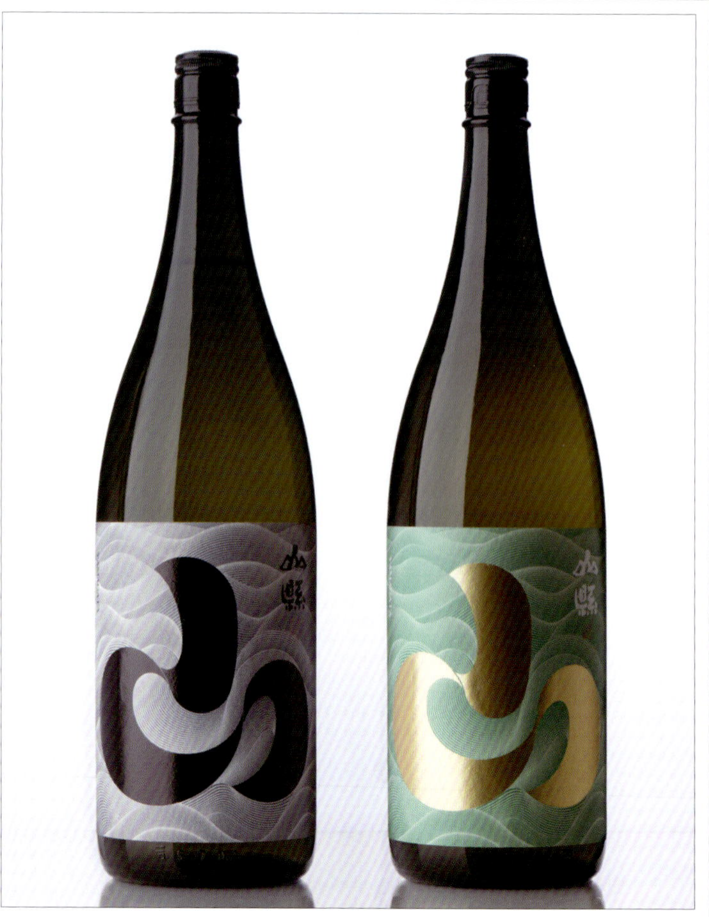

Title: YAMAGATA | **Client:** Sake-Show Yamada
Design Firm: Tsushima Design

LU CHEN, LEI ZHAO, ZHIZHUANG SONG

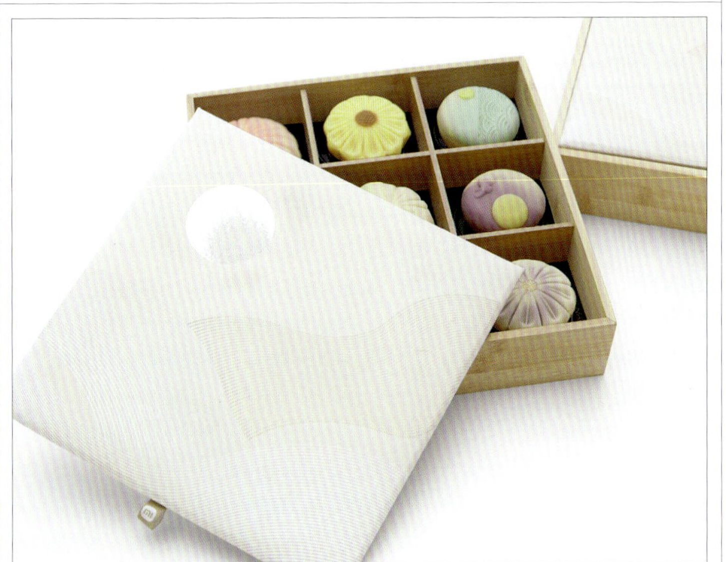

Title: XIAOMI Mid-Autumn Mooncake | **Client:** Self-initiated
Design Firm: Xiaomi

PEPSICO DESIGN & INNOVATION

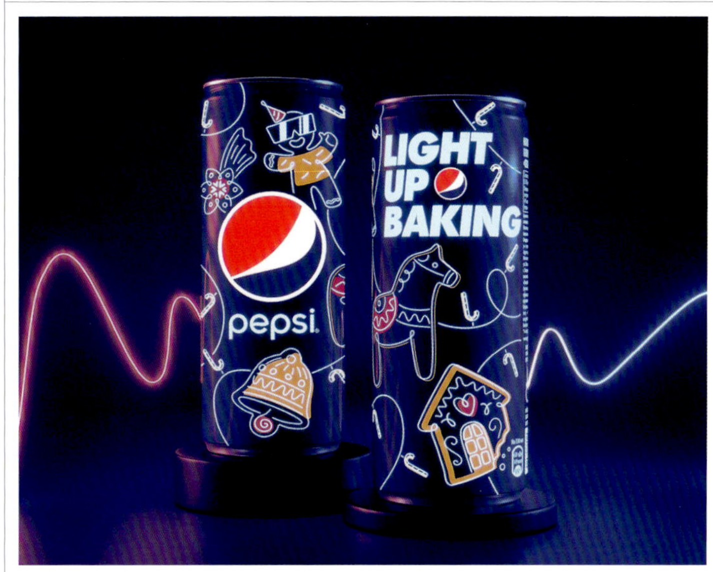

Title: Pepsi New Year 2022 LTO | **Client:** Self-initiated
Design Firm: PepsiCo Design & Innovation

BRENDAN CALLAHAN

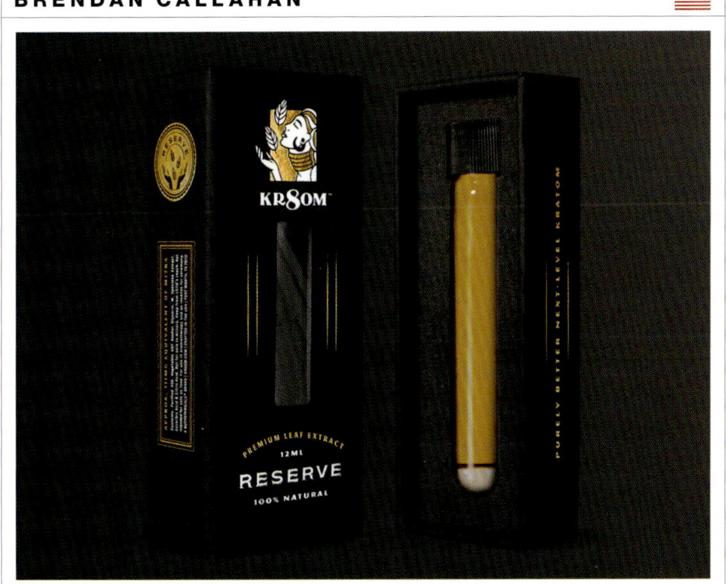

Title: Kr8om Reserve | **Client:** Kr8om
Design Firm: Spire Agency

JOEY LO

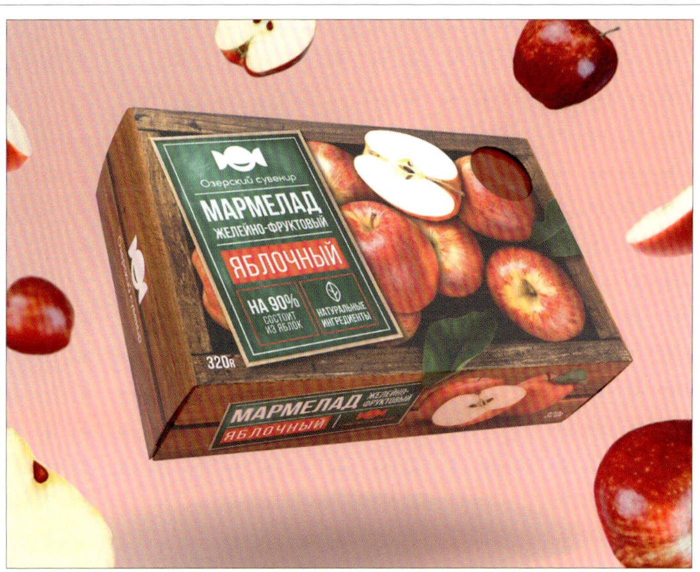

Title: Marmalade Packaging | **Client:** KDV Group
Design Firm: Box Brand Design Limited

PEPSICO DESIGN & INNOVATION

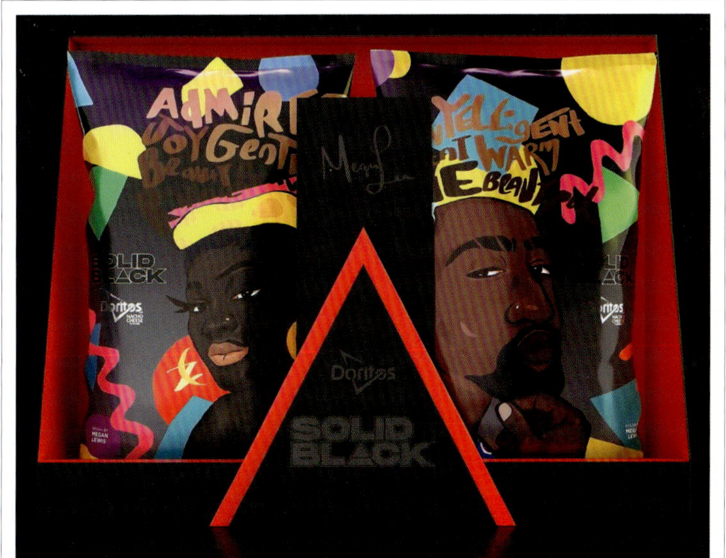

Title: Doritos Solid Black | **Client:** Self-initiated
Design Firm: PepsiCo Design & Innovation

LEANNE BALEN

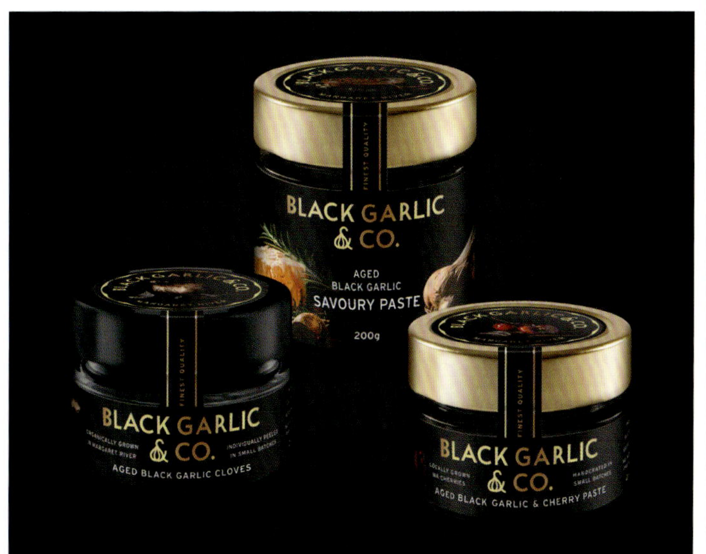

Title: Black Garlic & Co. | **Client:** Black Garlic & Co.
Design Firm: Dessein

SOL BENITO

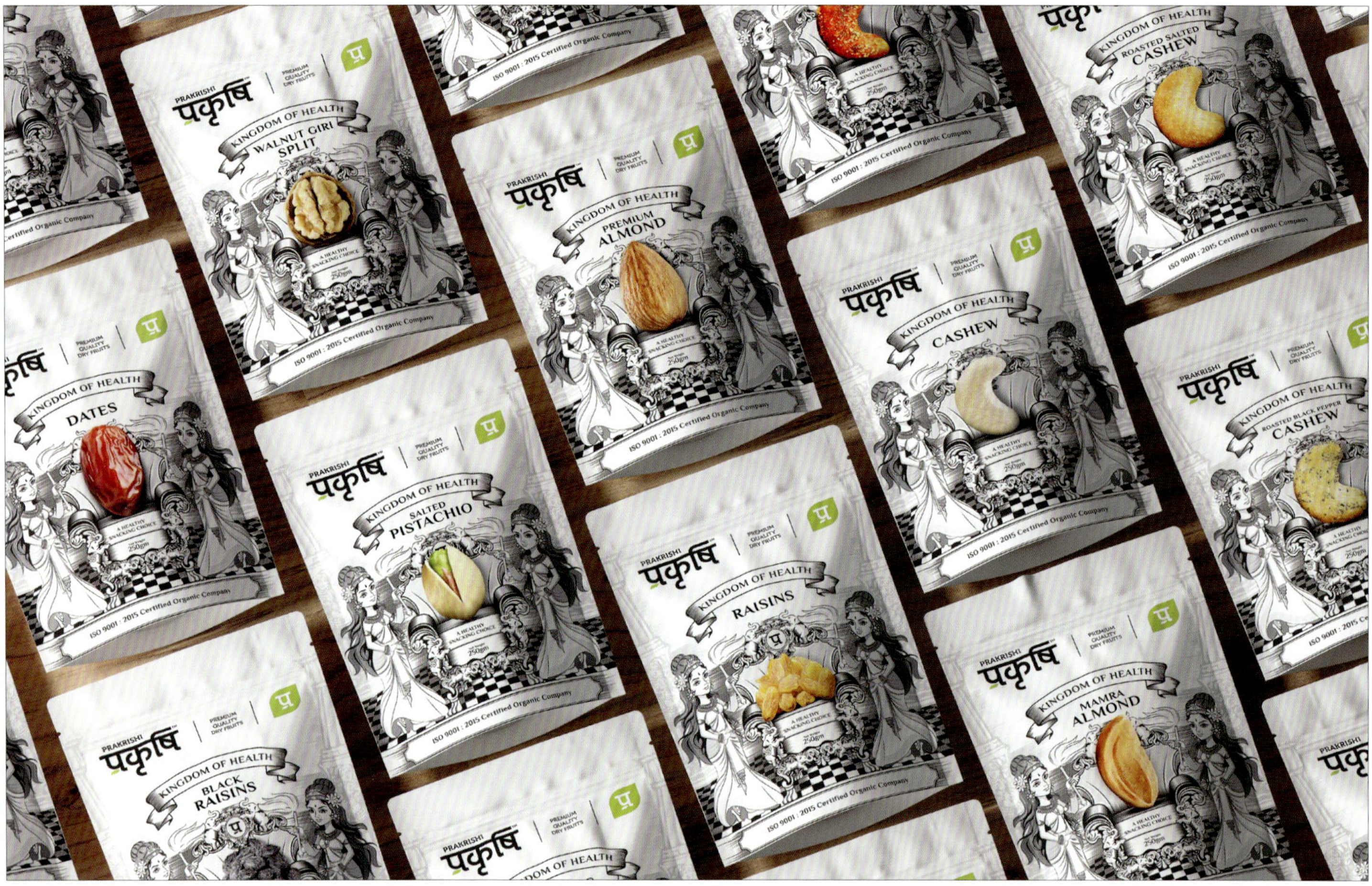

Title: Prakrishi Dryfruits | Client: Prakrishi Organic | Design Firm: Sol Benito

PEPSICO DESIGN & INNOVATION

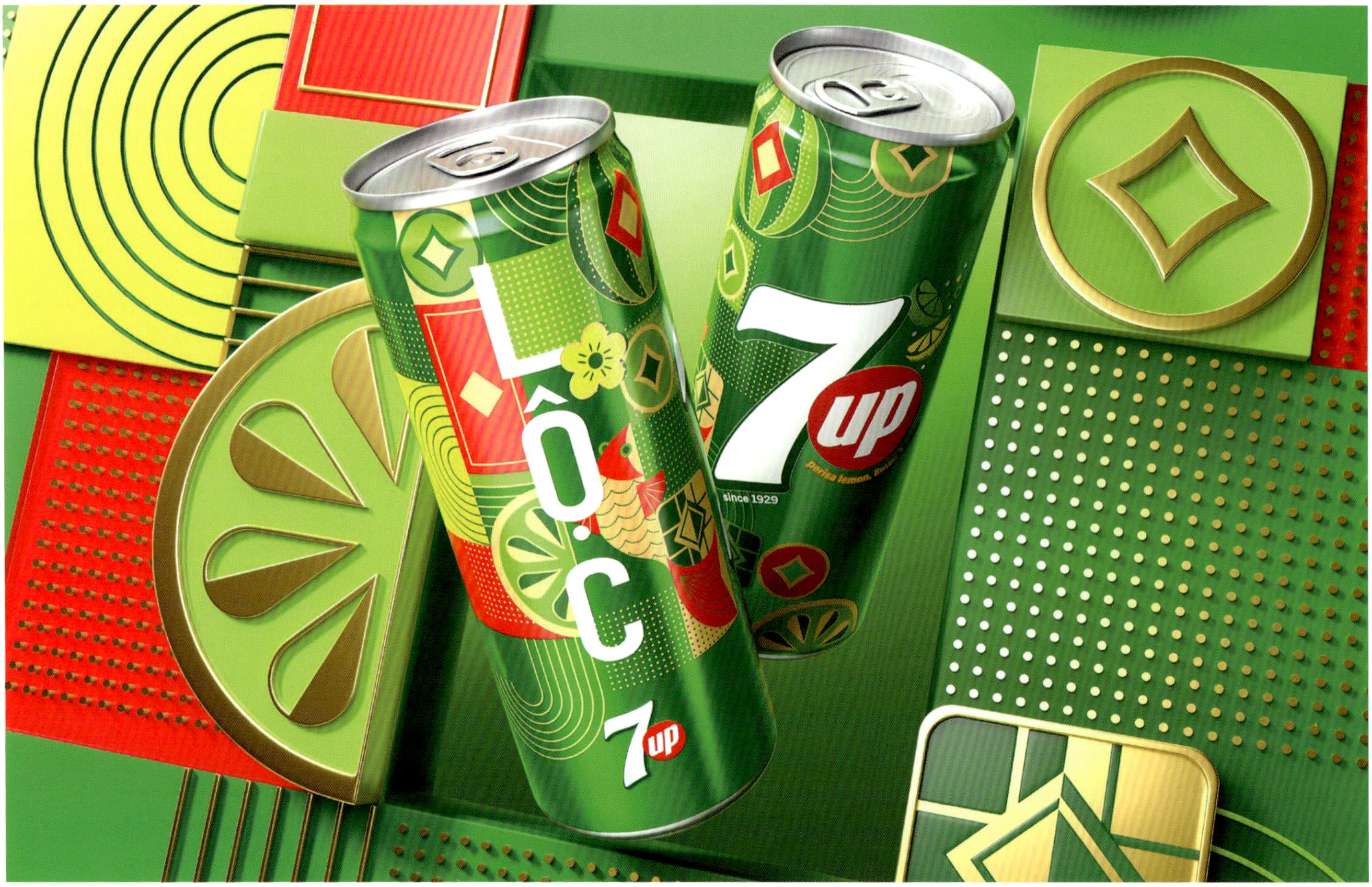

Title: Vietnam Tet 2022 LTO | Client: Self-initiated | Design Firm: PepsiCo Design & Innovation

OMDESIGN

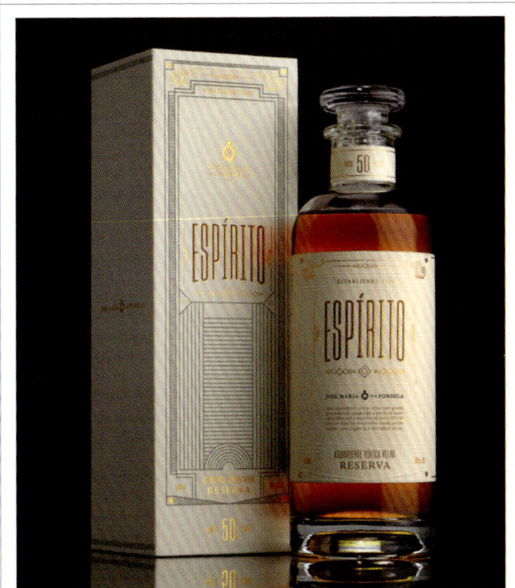

Title: Aguardente Espírito
Client: José Maria da Fonseca
Design Firm: Omdesign

ALEX RHODES

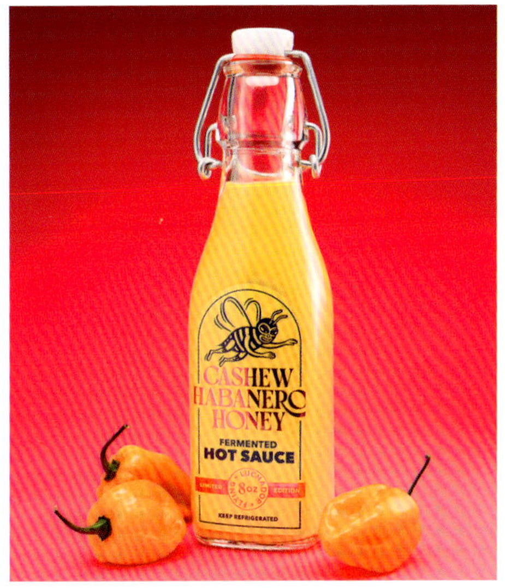

Title: Hot Sauce
Client: Vintage 86
Design Firm: Rhodes Creative

CF NAPA BRAND DESIGN

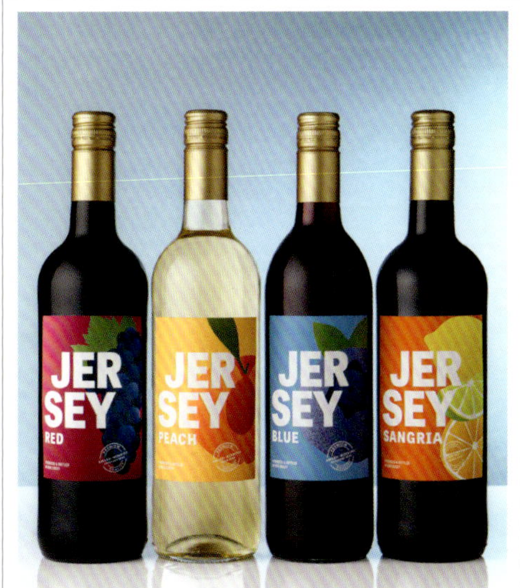

Title: Jersey Wine Collection
Client: William Heritage Winery
Design Firm: CF Napa Brand Design

CF NAPA BRAND DESIGN

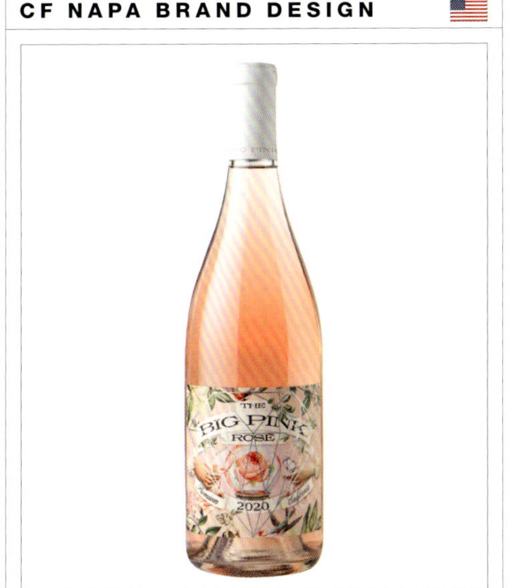

Title: The Big Pink Rosé
Client: West Coast Wine Group
Design Firm: CF Napa Brand Design

OMDESIGN

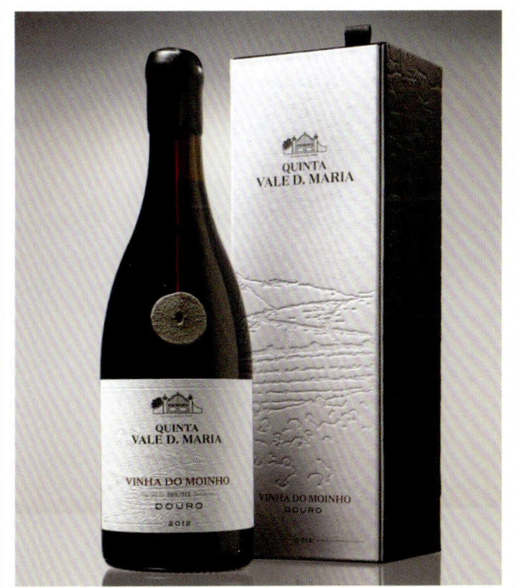

Title: Quinta Vale D. Maria Vinha do Moinho
Client: Aveleda
Design Firm: Omdesign

ADAM CARTWRIGHT

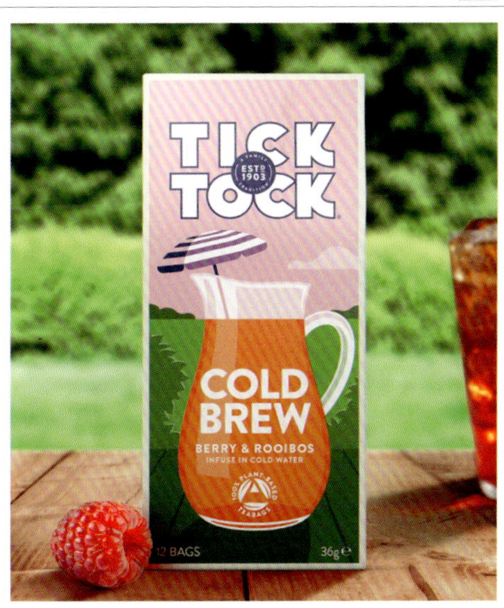

Title: Tick Tock Tea Cold Brew | **Client:** Tick Tock Teas Ltd. | **Design Firm:** Turner Duckworth: London, San Francisco & New York

KATELYN MCVEY

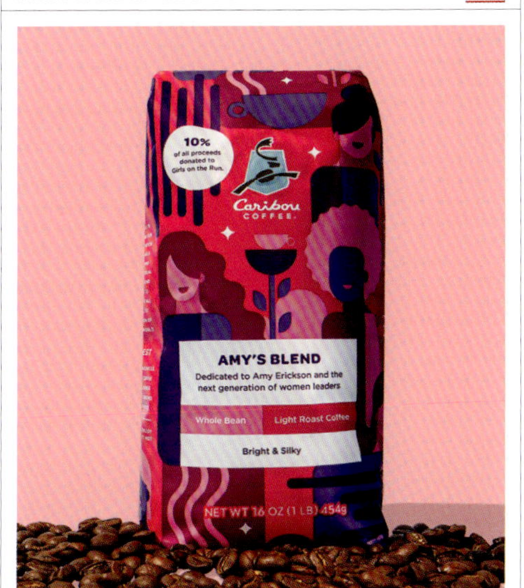

Title: Amy's Blend
Client: Caribou Coffee
Design Firm: Cue

NATE PHELPS

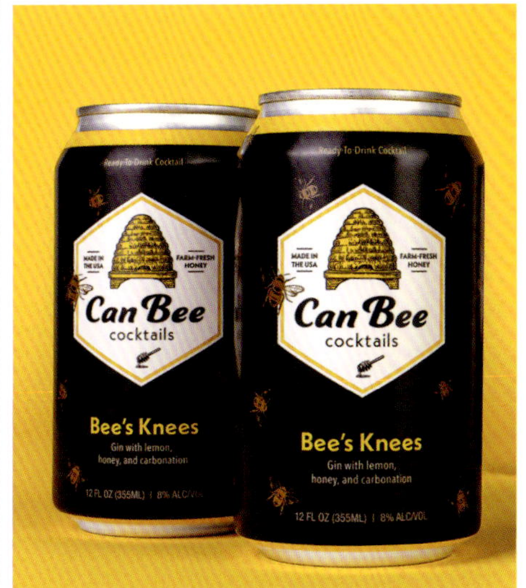

Title: CanBee Cocktails
Client: Black Button Distilling
Design Firm: Partners + Napier

PEPSICO DESIGN & INNOVATION

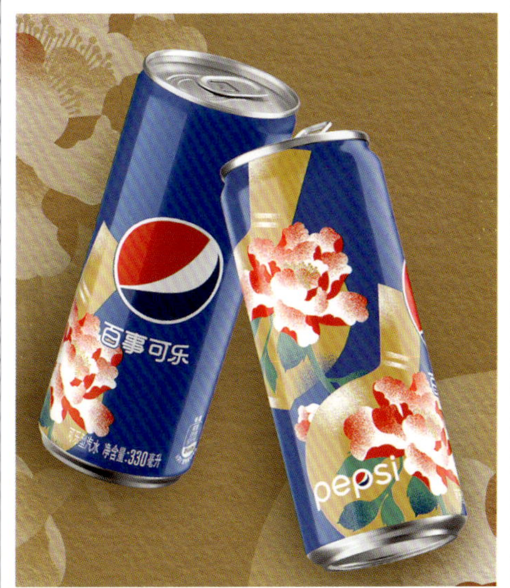

Title: Pepsi Culture Cans x People's Daily
Client: Self-initiated
Design Firm: PepsiCo Design & Innovation

DIANA LUISTRO

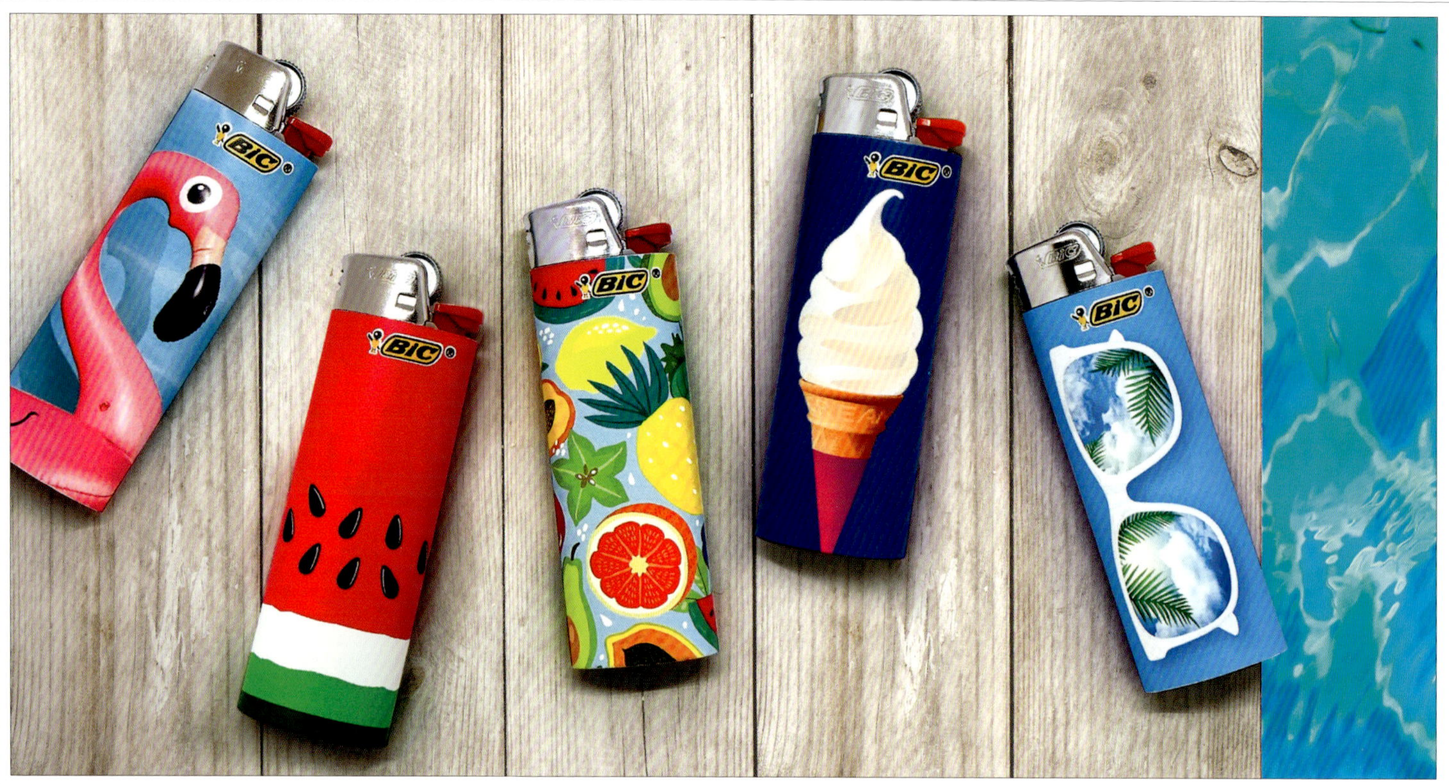

Title: BIC Vacation Series | **Client:** BIC | **Design Firm:** Wallace Church & Co.

MATT SHAPIRO

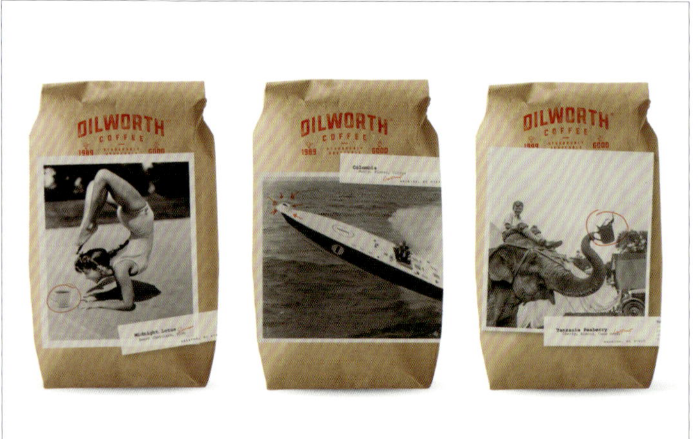

Title: Dilworth Coffee | **Client:** Dilworth Coffee
Design Firm: The Republik

MICHAEL HESTER

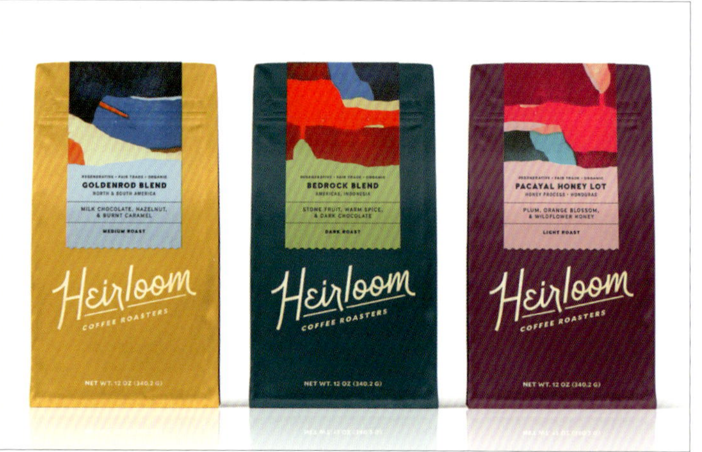

Title: Heirloom Coffee Roaster | **Client:** America's Best Coffee Roasters
Design Firm: Pavement

DUFT WATTERSON

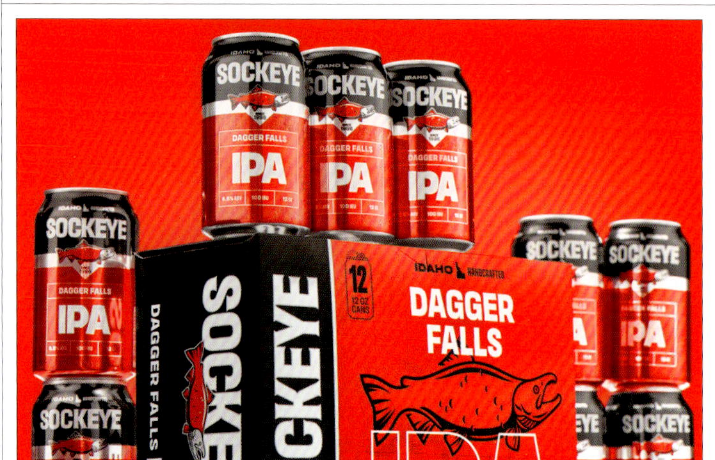

Title: Sockeye Packaging | **Client:** Sockeye Brewing
Design Firm: Duft Watterson

JOEY LO

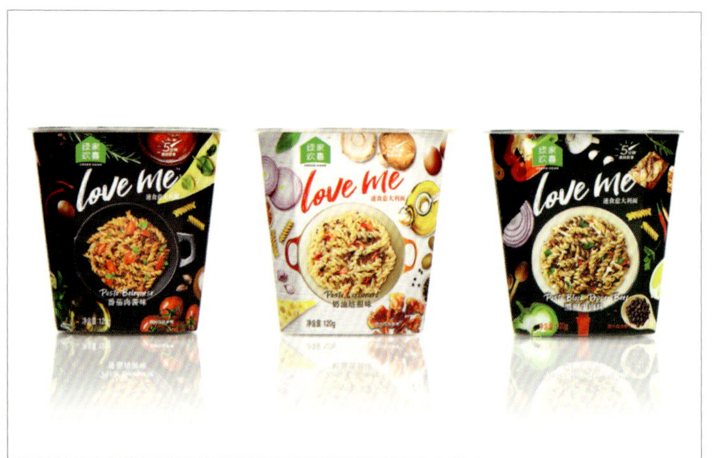

Title: Love Me | **Client:** Green Home
Design Firm: Box Brand Design Limited

MATT LURCOCK

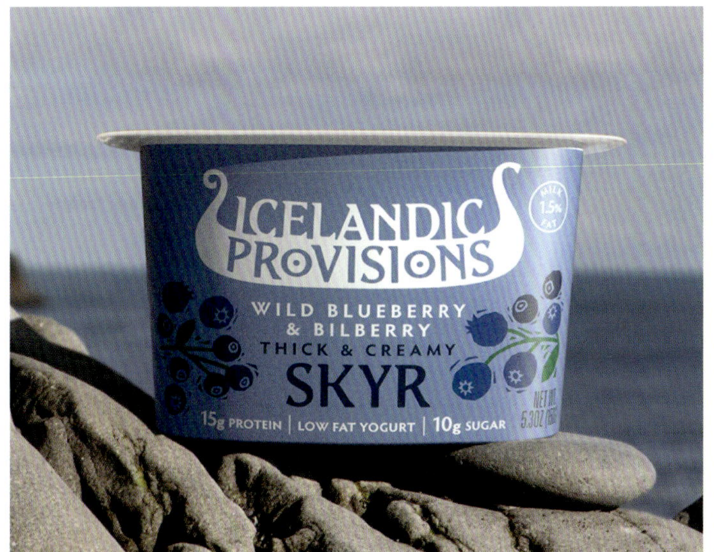

Title: Icelandic Provisions | **Client:** Icelandic Provisions
Design Firm: Turner Duckworth: London, San Francisco & New York

JEREMY SCHWARTZ

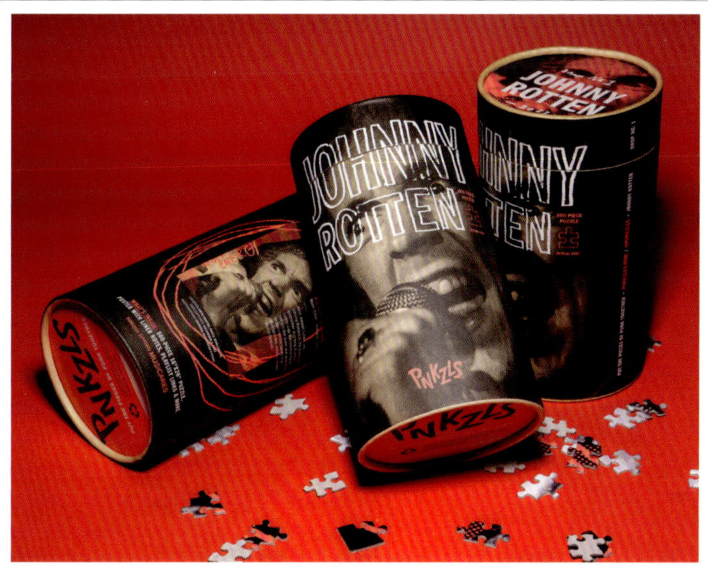

Title: Johnny Rotten Puzzle Experience Packaging | **Client:** Punkzles
Design Firm: Truth Collective

KYLE R. THOMPSON

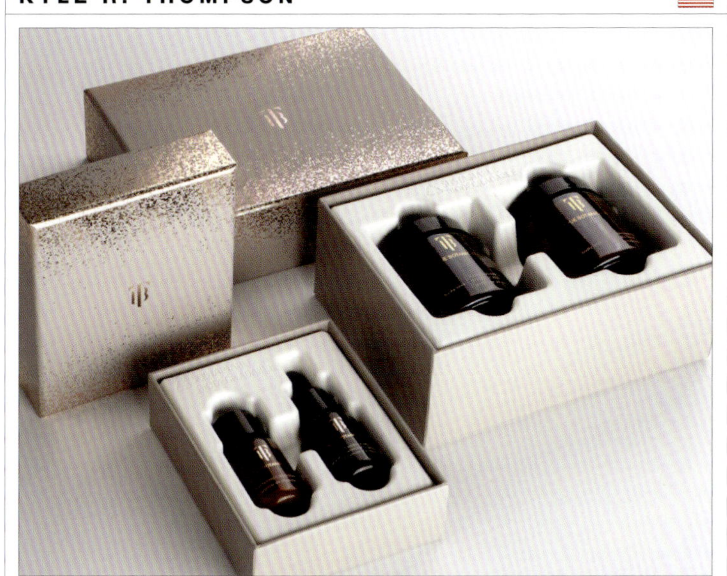

Title: True Botanicals Skincare — Sustainable Gift Sets Packaging
Client: True Botanicals | **Design Firm:** The Rare Form

JOEY LO

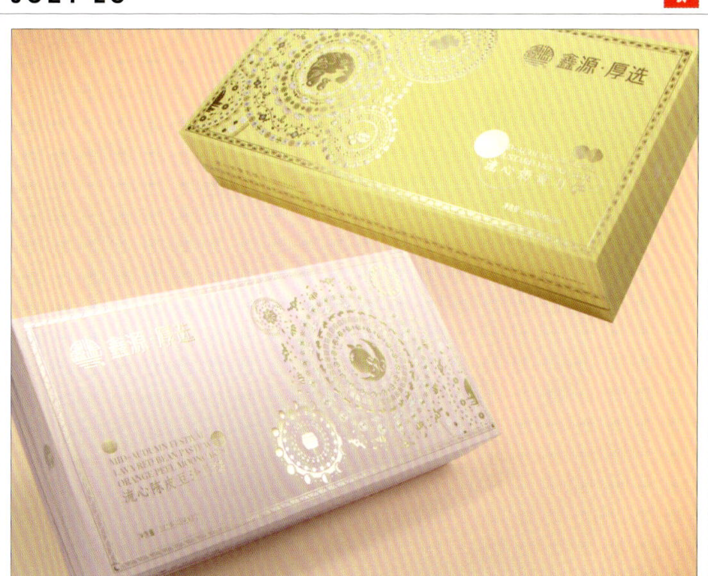

Title: XY Lava Mooncake | **Client:** XinYuan
Design Firm: Box Brand Design Limited

MARK ROWE

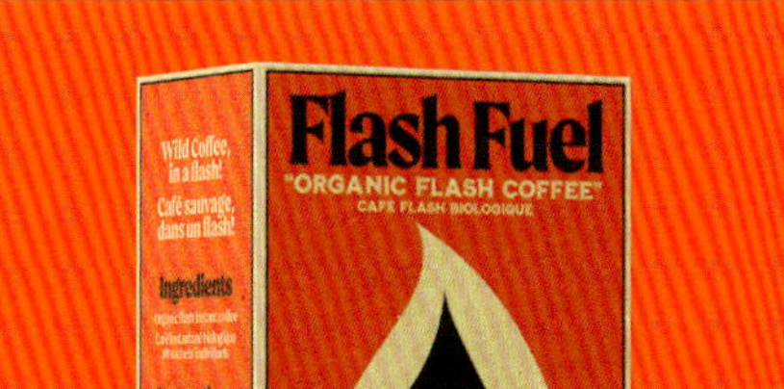

Title: Flash Fuel | **Client:** Calgary Heritage Roasting Co. | **Design Firm:** Trill

OMDESIGN

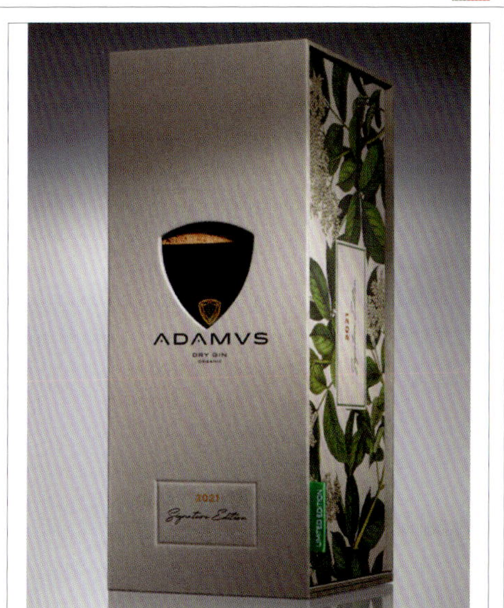

Title: Adamus Signature Edition 2021
Client: Destilaria Levira | **Design Firm:** Omdesign

KATELYN MCVEY

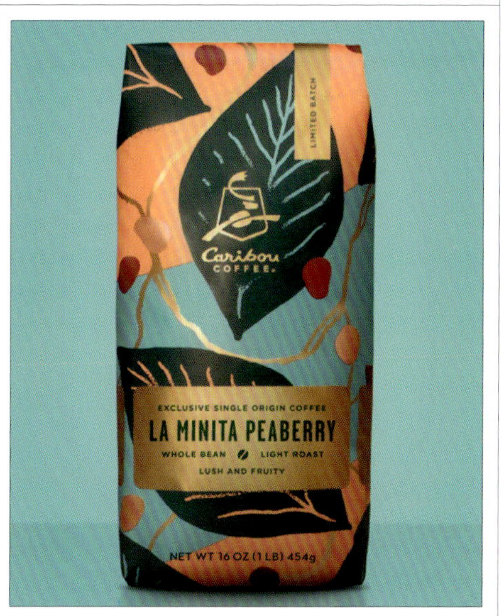

Title: La Minita Peaberry
Client: Caribou Coffee | **Design Firm:** Cue

UNDERLINE STUDIO

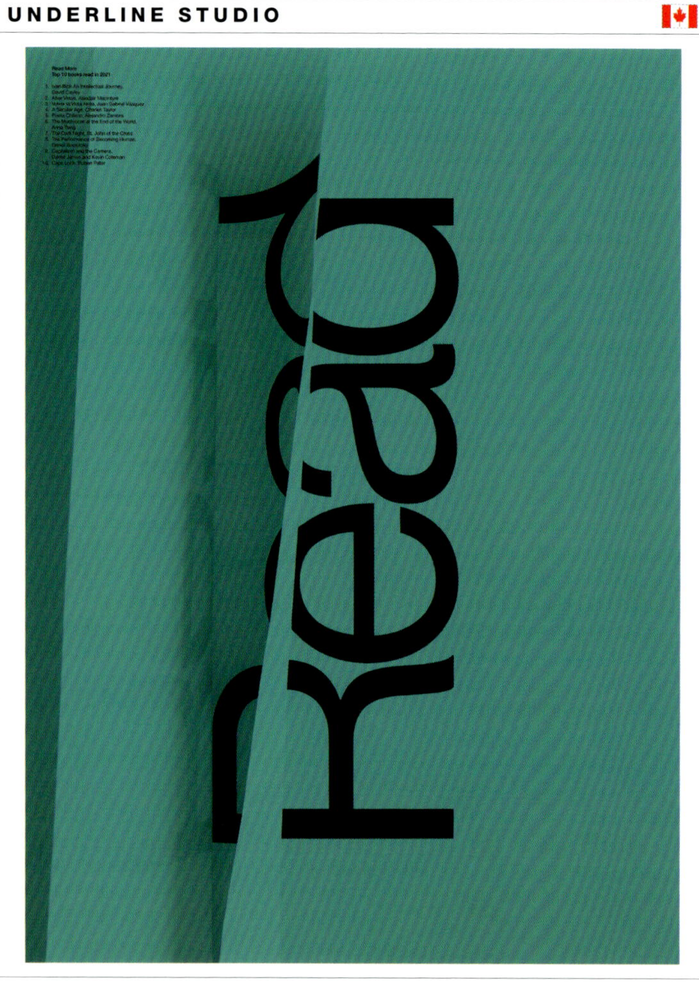

Title: Read More 2021 | **Client:** Self-initiated | **Design Firm:** Underline Studio

TEIGA, STUDIO.

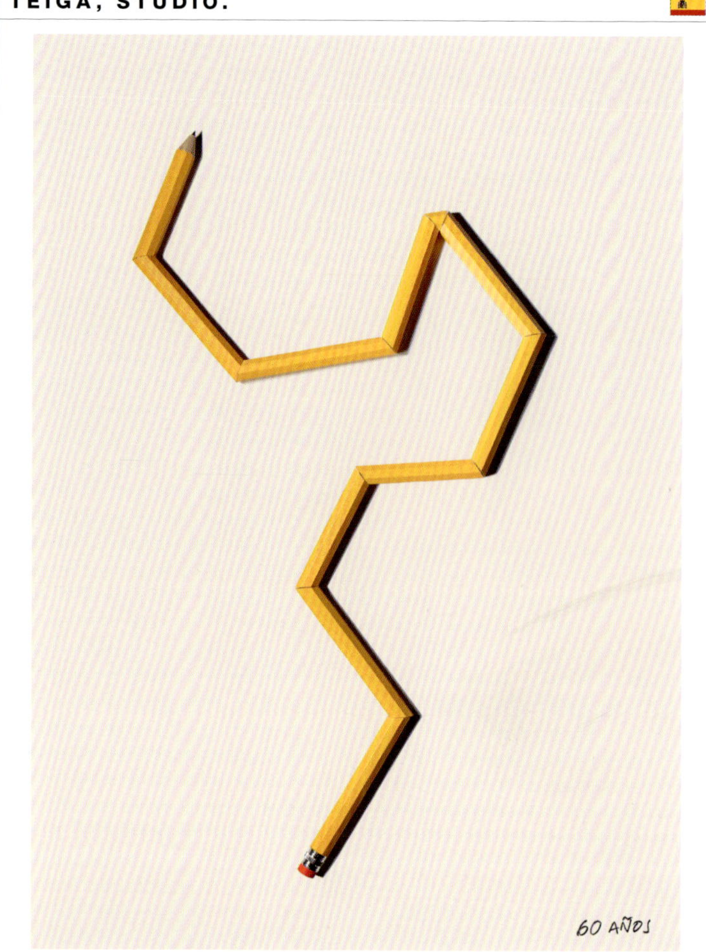

Title: 60 Years ADG FAD | **Client:** ADG FAD | **Design Firm:** Teiga, Studio.

ARSONAL

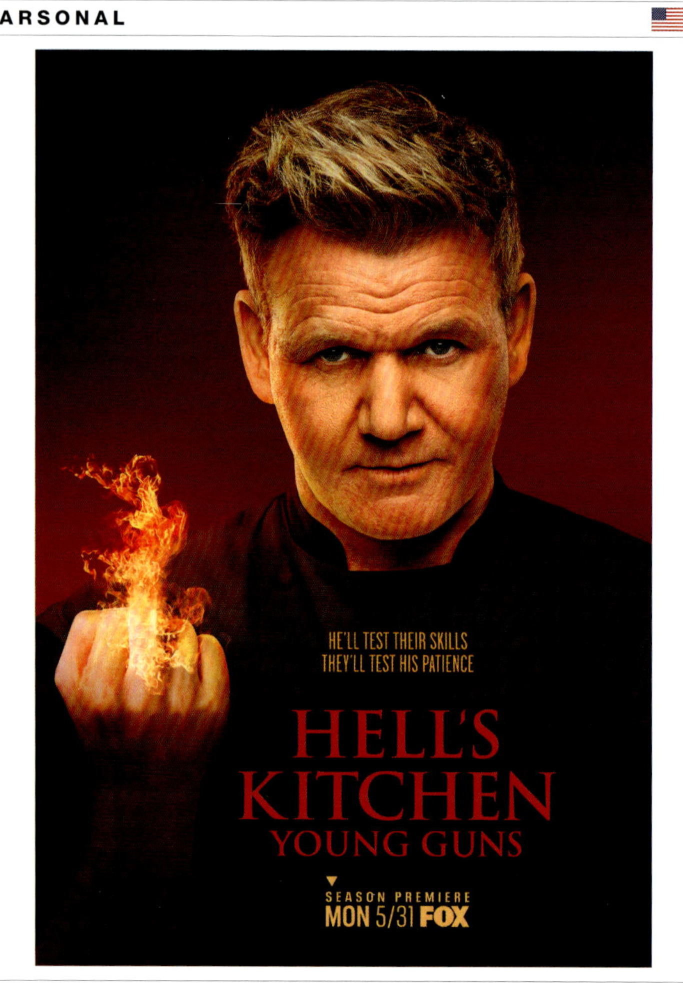

Title: HELL'S KITCHEN YOUNG GUNS | **Client:** FOX | **Design Firm:** ARSONAL

JORGE ARAÚJO, ANA MOTA

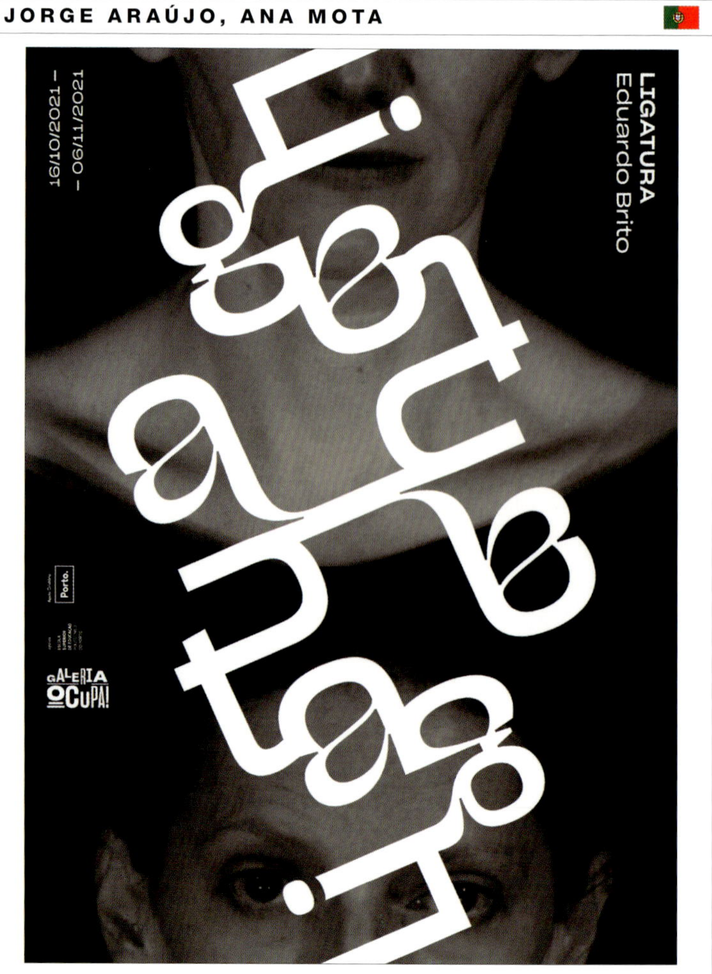

Title: Ligatura | **Client:** Galeria Ocupa! | **Design Firm:** 1/4 Studio

MICHAEL BRALEY

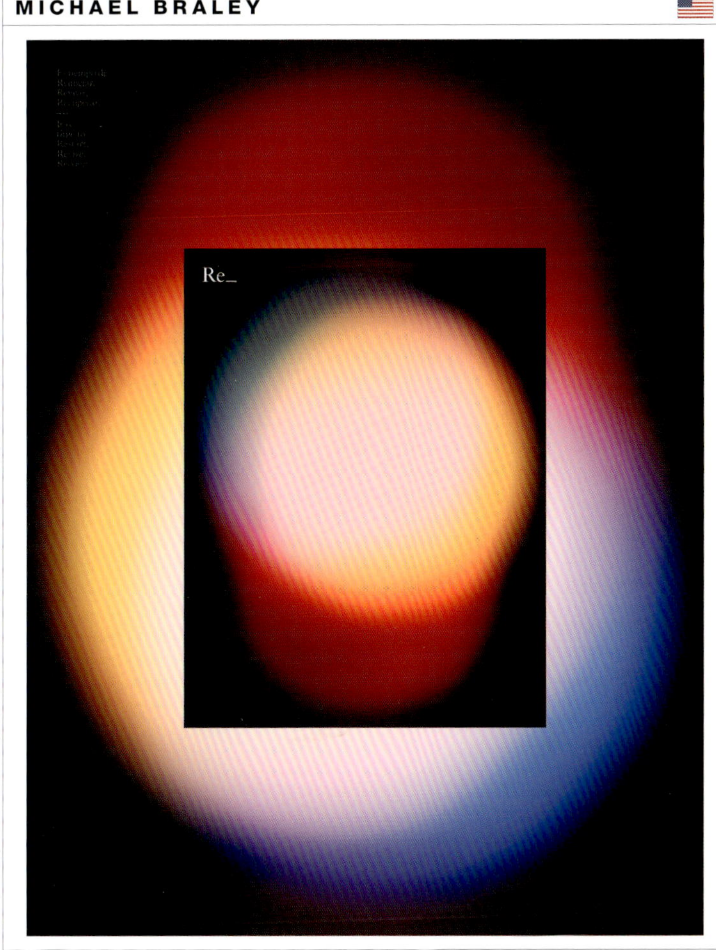

Title: Re_: Restart, Revive, Recover | **Client:** Self-initiated
Design Firm: Braley Design

UNDERLINE STUDIO

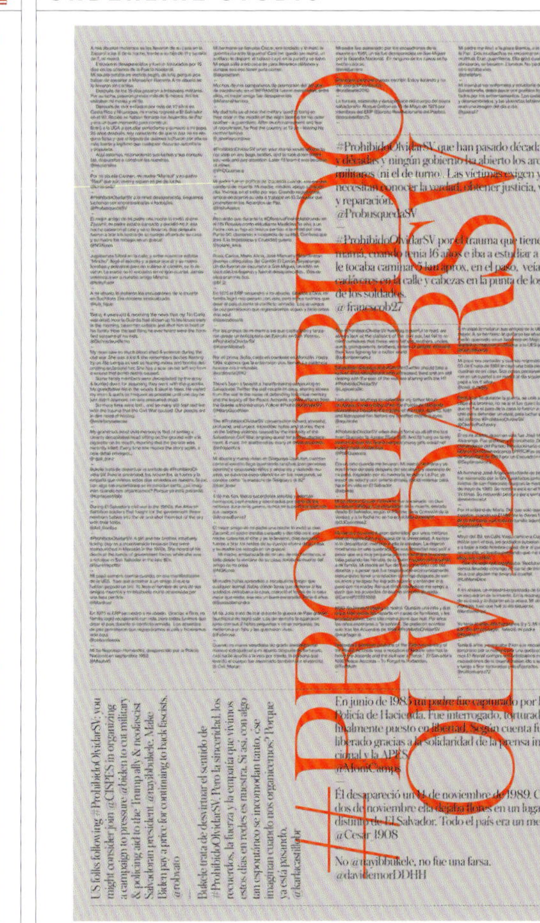

Title: Prohibido Olvidar Poster | **Client:** Self-initiated
Design Firm: Underline Studio

MICHAEL BRALEY

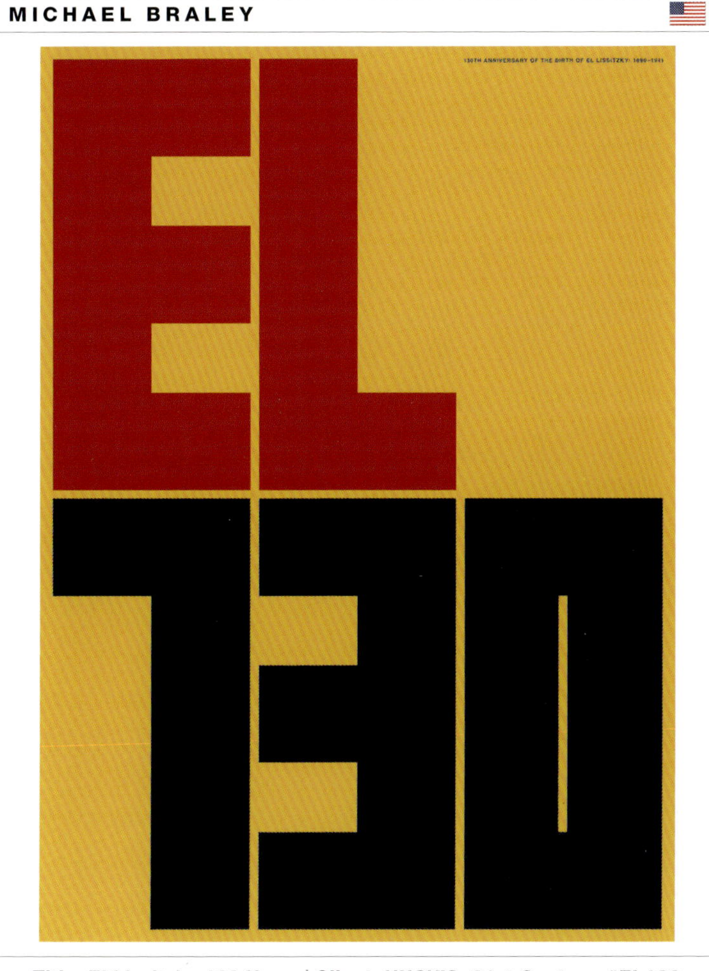

Title: El Lissitzky 130 Years | **Client:** UNOVIS. 21st Century. #EL130
Design Firm: Braley Design

ROGER SAWHILL

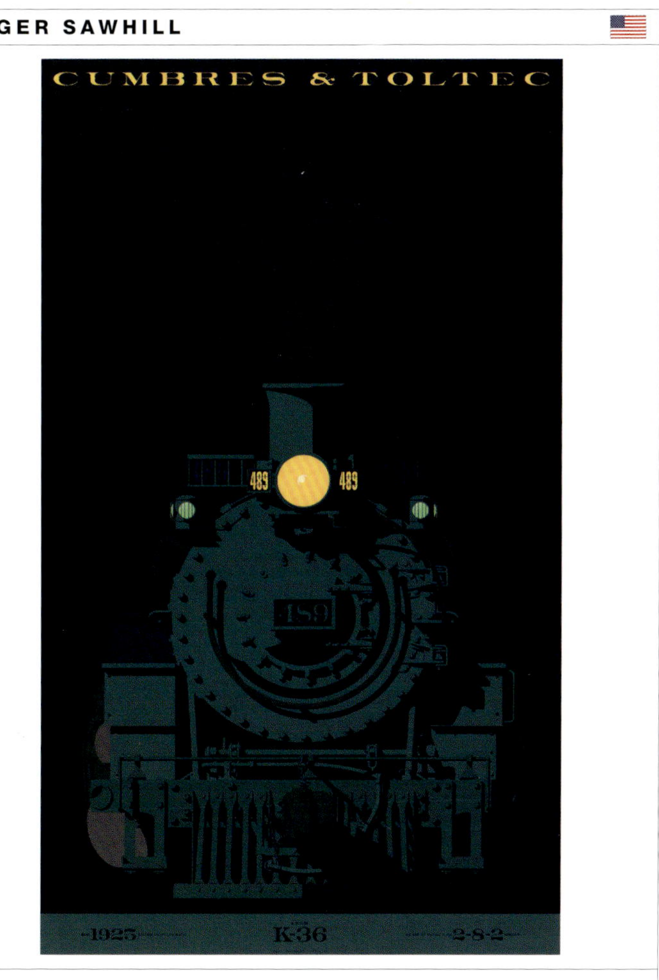

Title: Engine 489 | **Client:** Self-initiated
Design Firm: UP-Ideas

ARSONAL

Title: Ragdoll S1 Key Art
Client: AMC+
Design Firm: ARSONAL

CARTER WEITZ

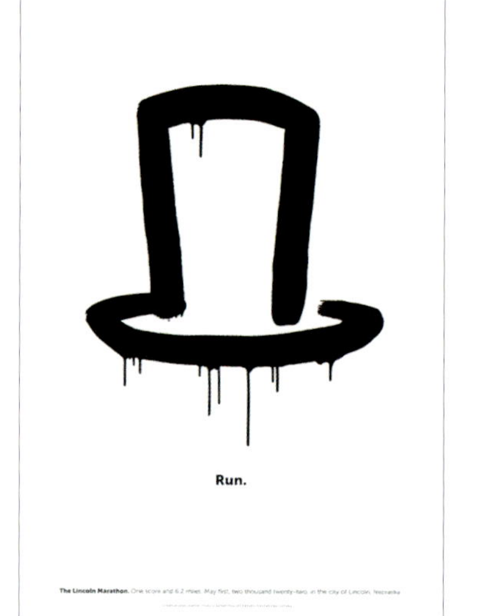

Title: Run
Client: Lincoln Track Club
Design Firm: Bailey Lauerman

B. RAE, P. RAE, A. MUNDAY

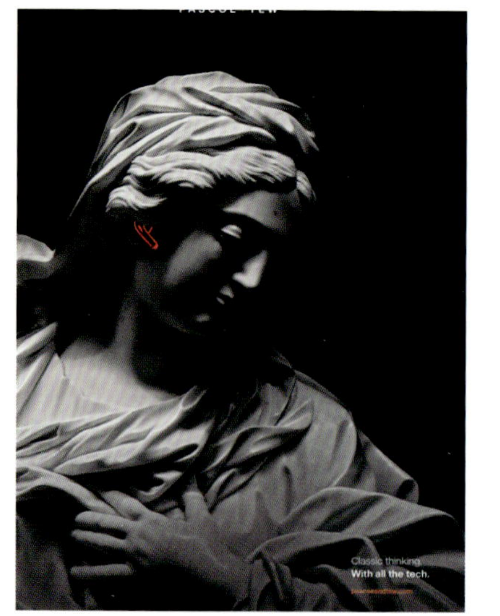

Title: Executive Search. Made Human.
Client: Pascoe and Tew
Design Firm: Curious

JOHN SPOSATO

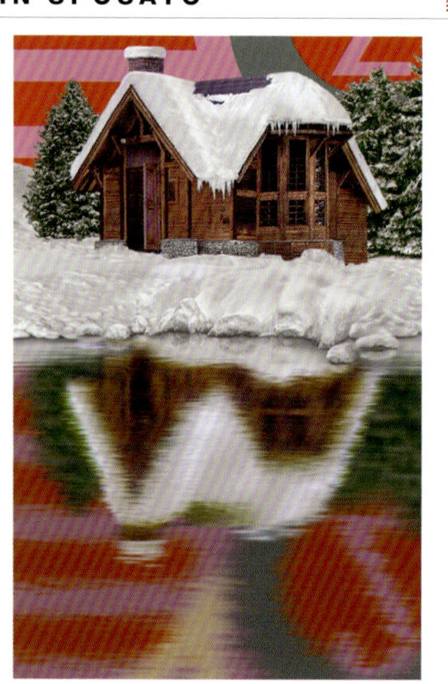

Title: Winter '22
Client: Self-initiated
Design Firm: John Sposato Design & Illustration

RENE V. STEINER

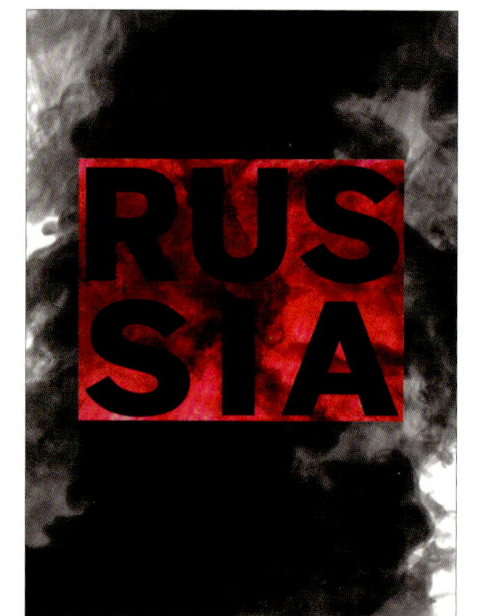

Title: Fog of War
Client: Self-initiated
Design Firm: Steiner Graphics

DOUGLAS MAY

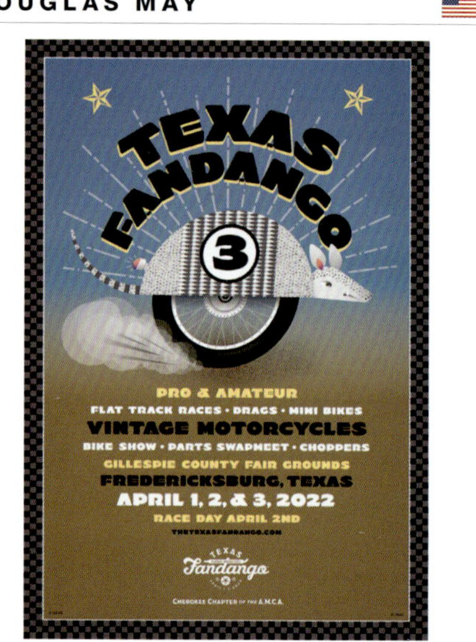

Title: Texas Fandango 3
Client: Texas Fandango
Design Firm: May & Co.

WARREN EAKINS

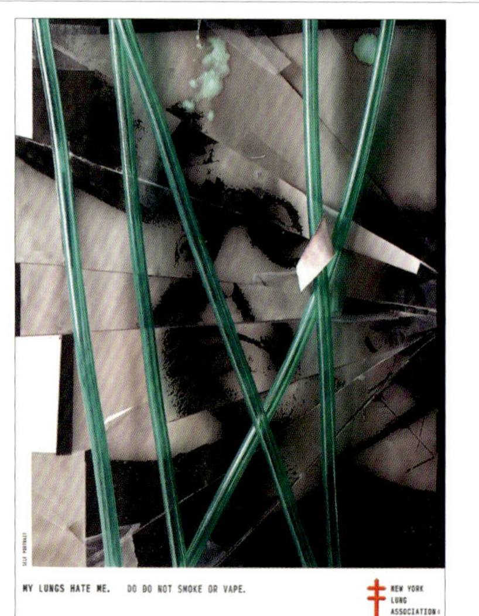

Title: My Lungs Hate Me No.1
Client: ROTS WORLDWIDE
Design Firm: Warren Eakins Inc.

KEN VILLENEUVE

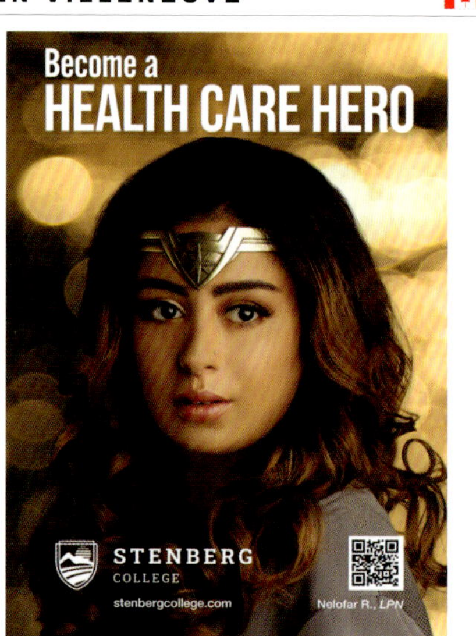

Title: Become a Health Care Hero.
Client: Stenberg College
Design Firm: Good Communication Marketing

JEFF BARFOOT

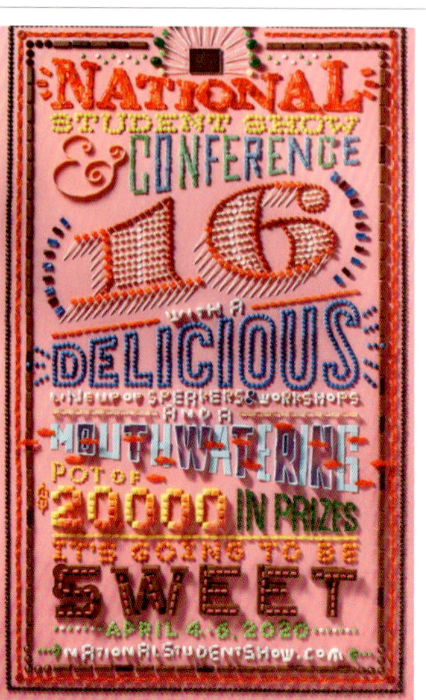

Title: The National Student Show & Conference 16 Poster | Client: The Dallas Society of Visual Comms Fdn. | Design Firm: *TraceElement

L. BEAUCHEMIN, M. WATSON, D. JASPERSE

Title: Seek New Cinema Poster
Client: Seattle Intl. Film Festival
Design Firm: WONGDOODY

HYUNGJOO A. KIM

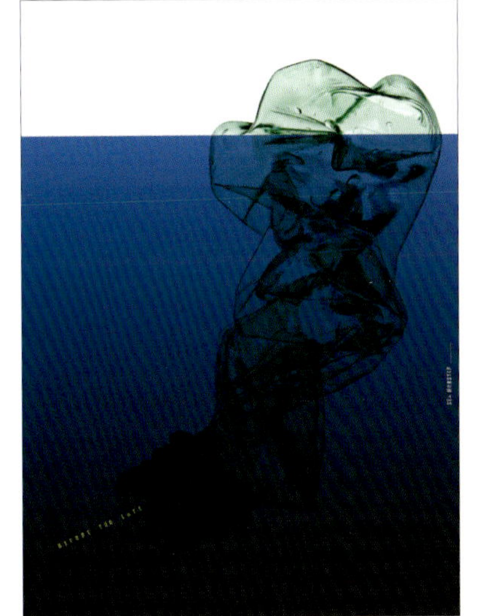

Title: SEA MONSTER
Client: Self-initiated
Design Firm: HyungjooKimDesignLab

SJI ASSOCIATES

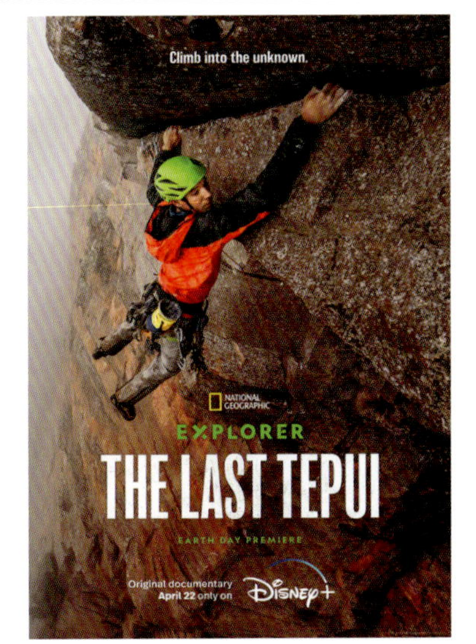

Title: Explorer — The Last Tepui
Client: National Geographic
Design Firm: SJI Associates

ARSONAL

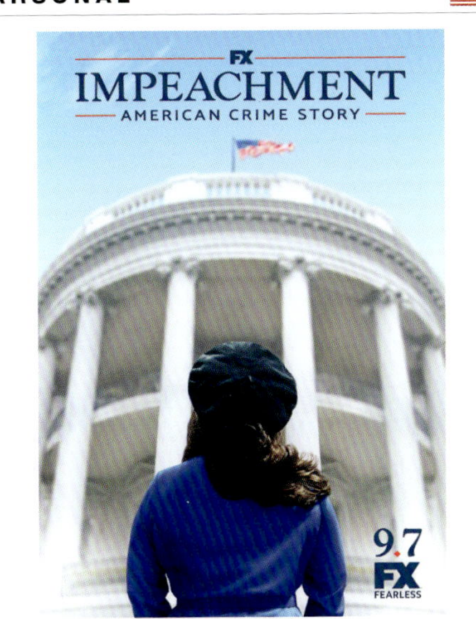

Title: AMERICAN CRIME STORY: IMPEACHMENT
Client: FX
Design Firm: ARSONAL

ELLIE PETERS

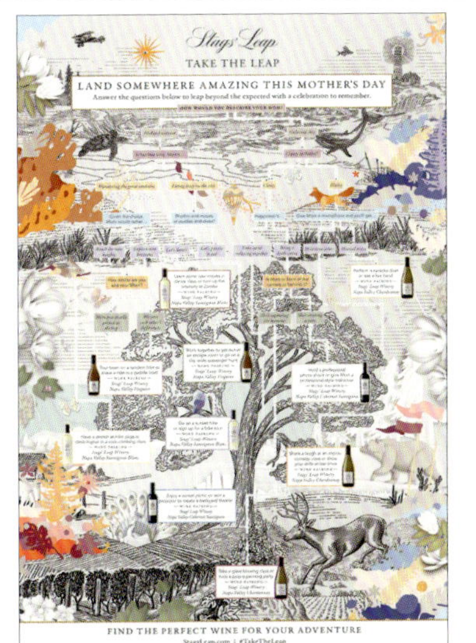

Title: Stags Leap Winery Decision Tree
Client: Treasury Wine Estates
Design Firms: Partners + Napier, Annex88

DAVID ILLIG

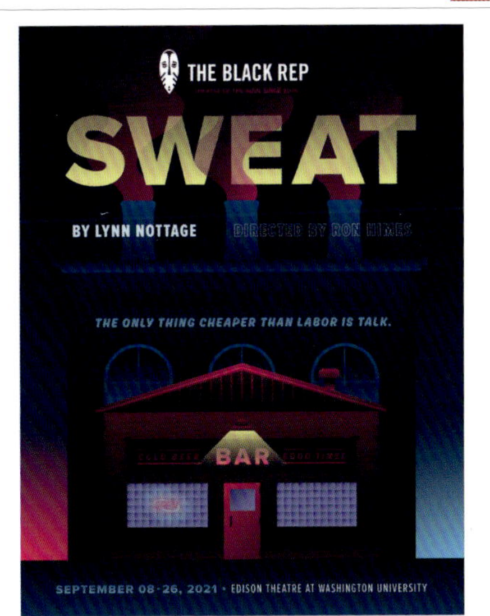

Title: Perspectives of Resilience
Client: The Black Rep
Design Firm: Rodgers Townsend

CARTER WEITZ

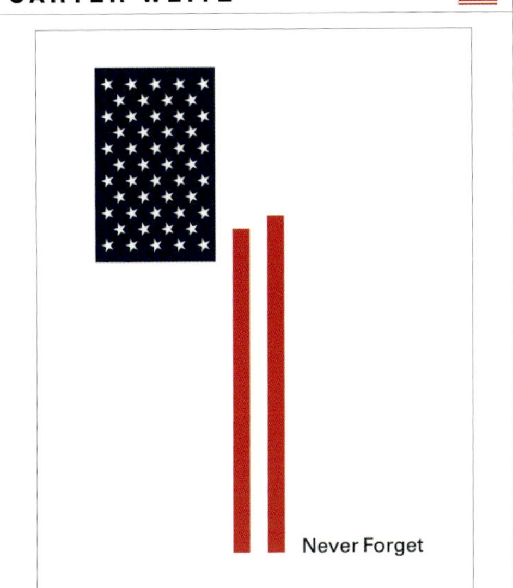

Title: Never Forget
Client: Self-initiated
Design Firm: Bailey Lauerman

WU QIXIN

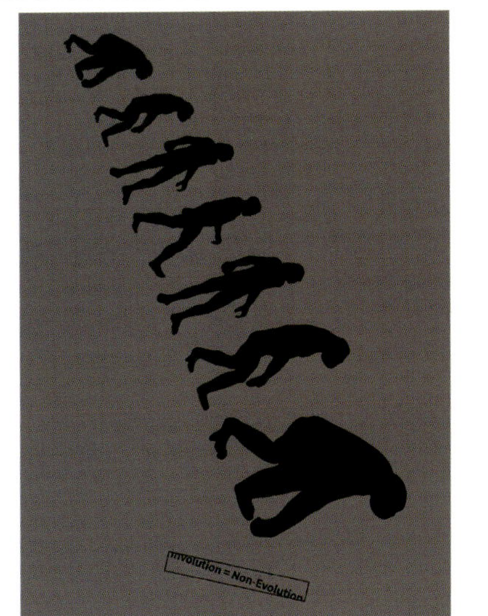

Title: Involution
Client: Human Beings
Design Firm: Polygon

BERLIN BURKHART

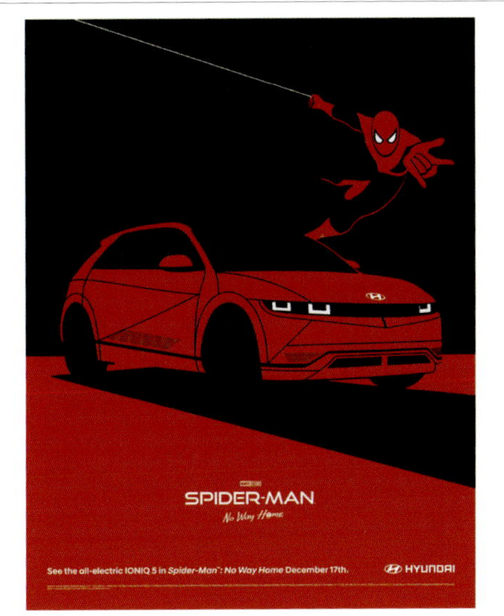

Title: Spider-Man: No Way Home Fan Art Series
Client: Hyundai Motor America
Design Firm: INNOCEAN USA

HAJIME TSUSHIMA

Title: LOVE | **Client:** Kaohsiung Creators Association
Design Firm: Tsushima Design

HAJIME TSUSHIMA

Title: METAVERSE | **Client:** Korea Institute of Cultural Product & Design
Design Firm: Tsushima Design

CHUGUO COMMUNICATION

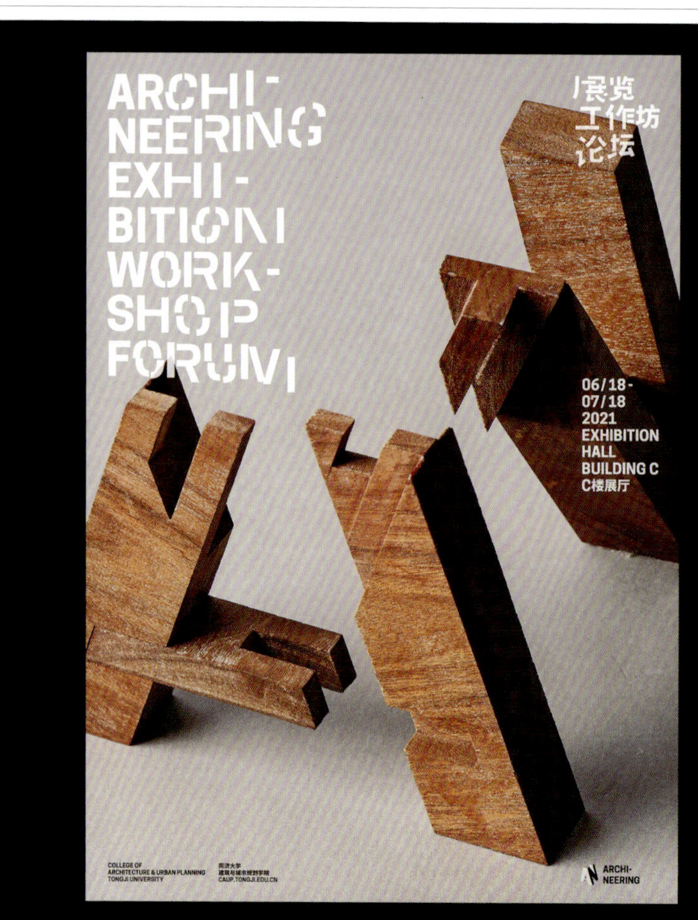

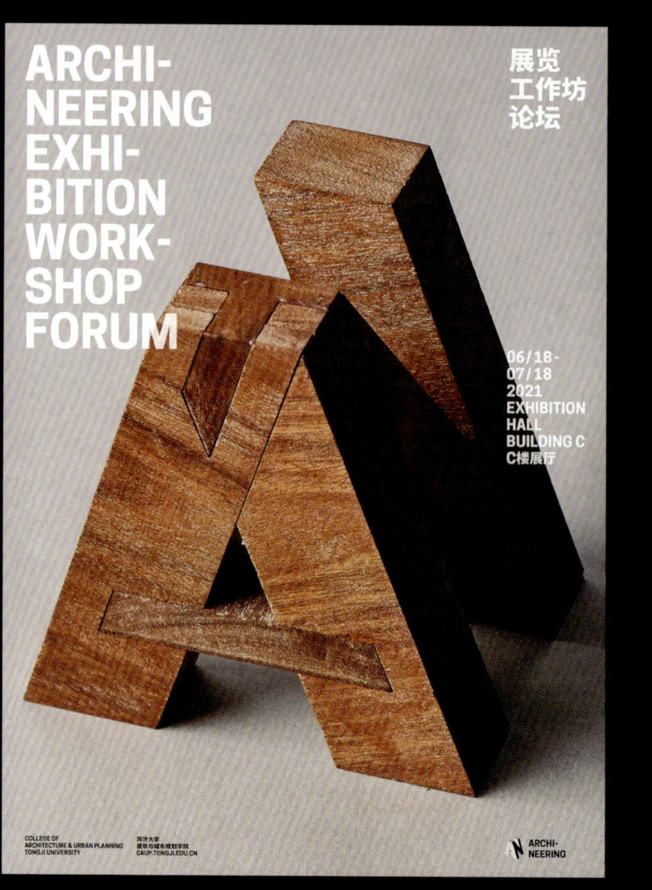

Title: Archi-Neering | **Client:** Tongji University | **Design Firm:** T9 Brand

ARSONAL

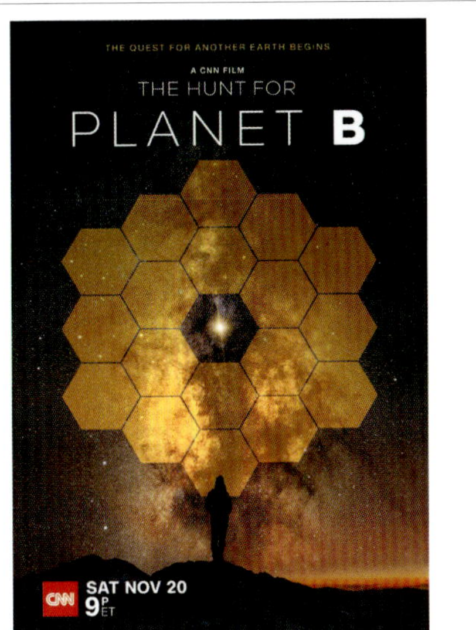

Title: The Hunt for Planet B
Client: CNN
Design Firm: ARSONAL

JOHN SPOSATO

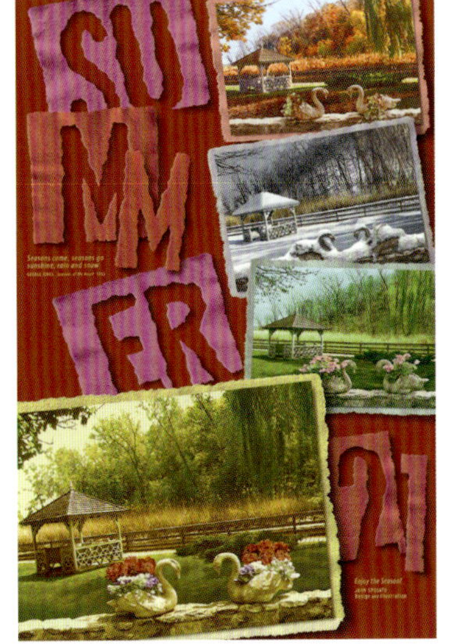

Title: Summer '21
Client: Self-initiated
Design Firm: John Sposato Design & Illustration

SJI ASSOCIATES

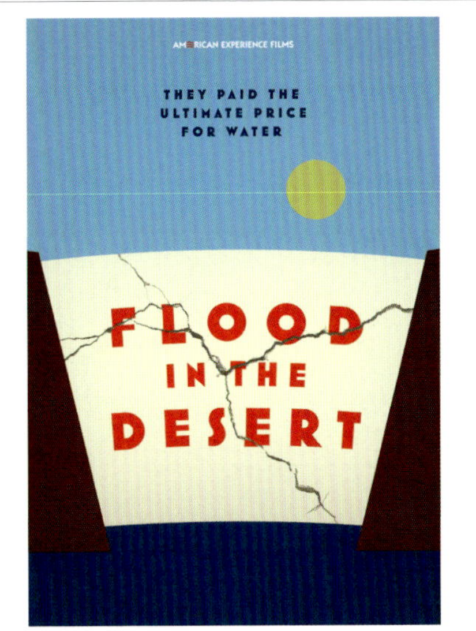

Title: Flood In The Desert Documentary Film Poster | **Clients:** Chika Offurum, American Experience Films | **Design Firm:** SJI Associates

KEITH KITZ

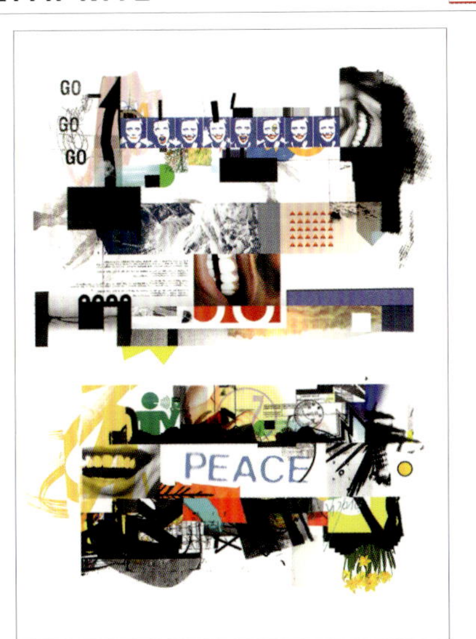

Title: 봄 Peace | **Client:** Visual Information Design Association of Korea
Design Firm: Keith Kitz Design

ARSONAL

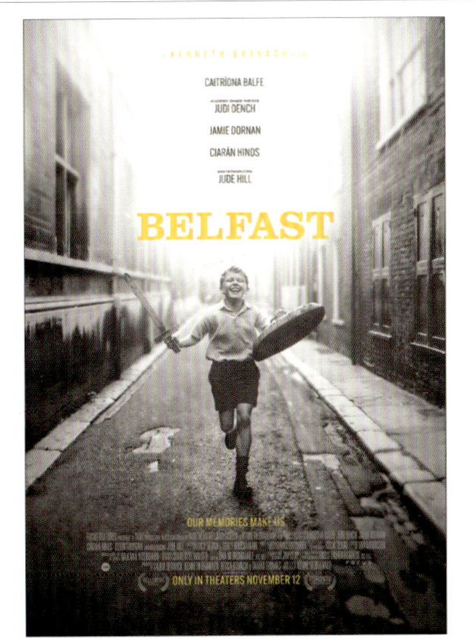

Title: BELFAST
Client: Focus Features
Design Firm: ARSONAL

ARSONAL

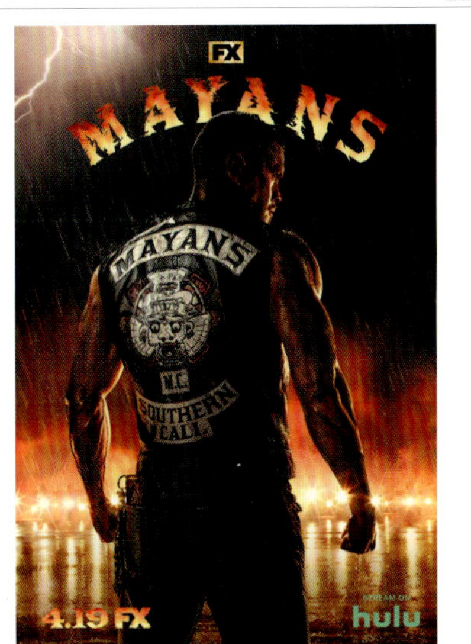

Title: Mayans S4
Client: FX
Design Firm: ARSONAL

ARSONAL

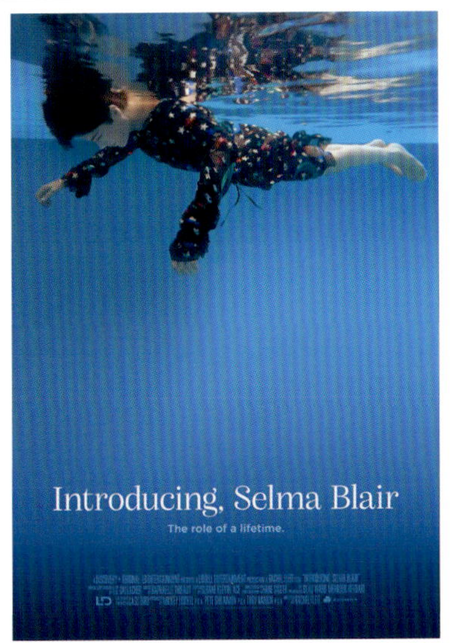

Title: INTRODUCING, SELMA BLAIR
Client: LD Entertainment
Design Firm: ARSONAL

KEITH KITZ

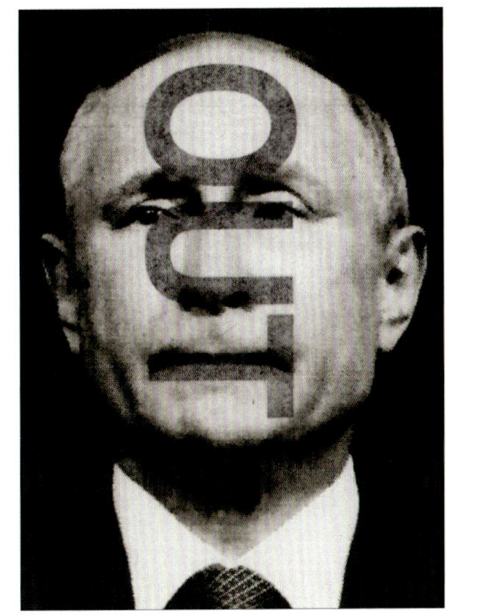

Title: PUT OUT | **Client:** The 4th Block Graphic Designers Association
Design Firm: Keith Kitz Design

DERWYN GOODALL

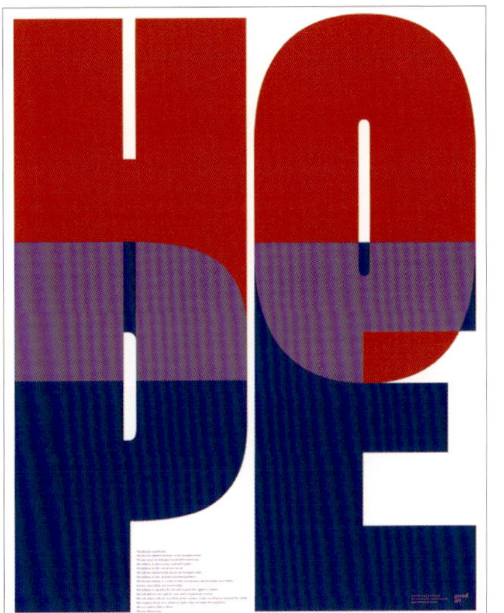

Title: The Purple Manifesto Project
Client: John Van Dyke
Design Firm: Goodall Integrated Design

MICHAEL BRALEY

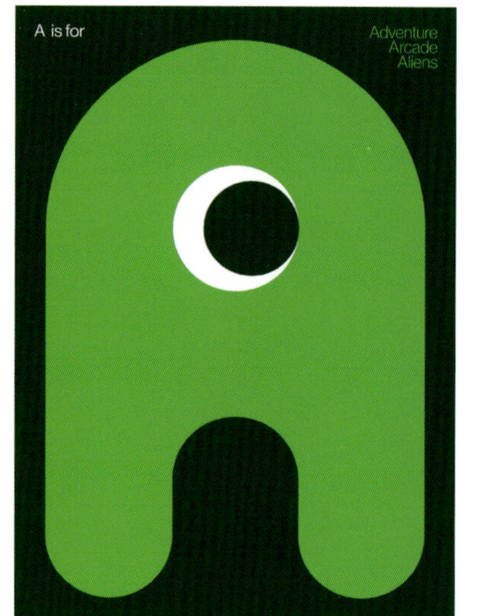

Title: A is for Adventure Arcade Aliens
Client: Poster Stellars
Design Firm: Braley Design

OSBORNE ROSS

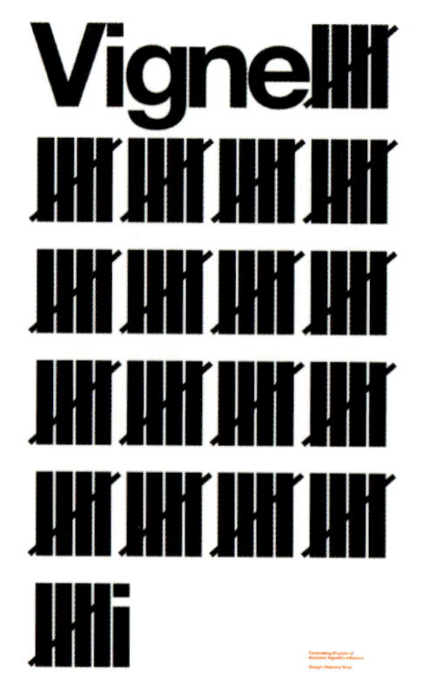

Title: Vignelli 90 Poster
Client: Vignelli 90
Design Firm: Osborne Ross

DAN MCMANUS

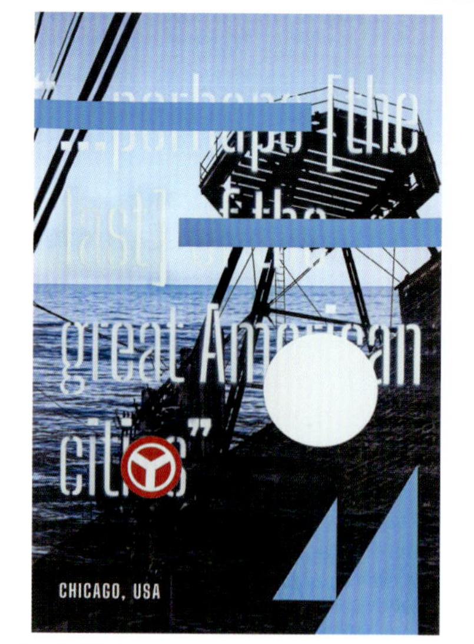

Title: "WHAT DOES CHICAGO MEAN TO YOU?"
Client: The Chicago Graphic Design Club
Design Firm: The Narrative

NIKKEISHA, INC.

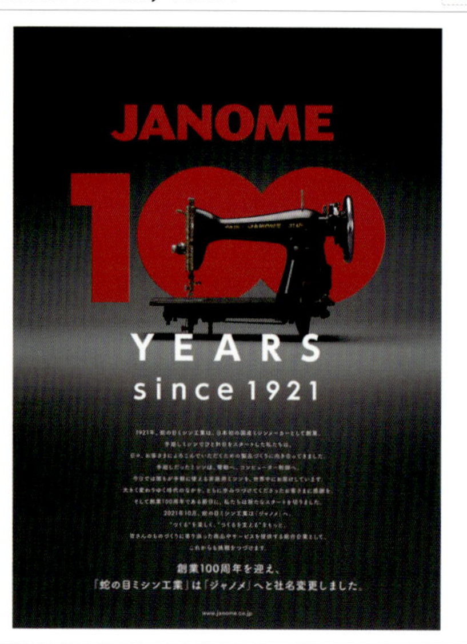

Title: The 100th Anniversary of JANOME
Client: JANOME Corporation
Design Firm: Nikkeisha, Inc.

WU QIXIN

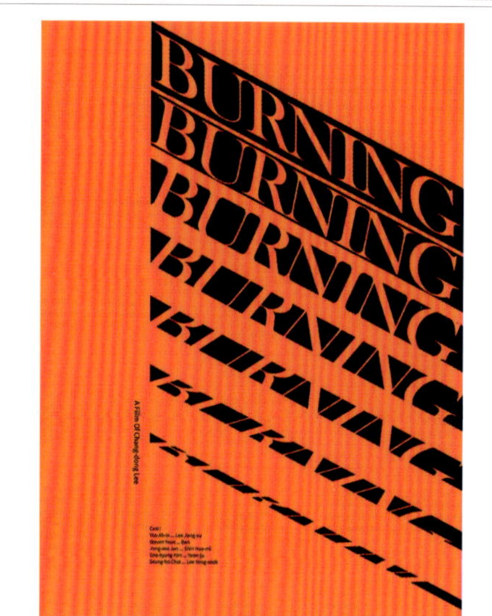

Title: Burning
Client: Burning
Design Firm: Cul-Box

RANDY CLARK

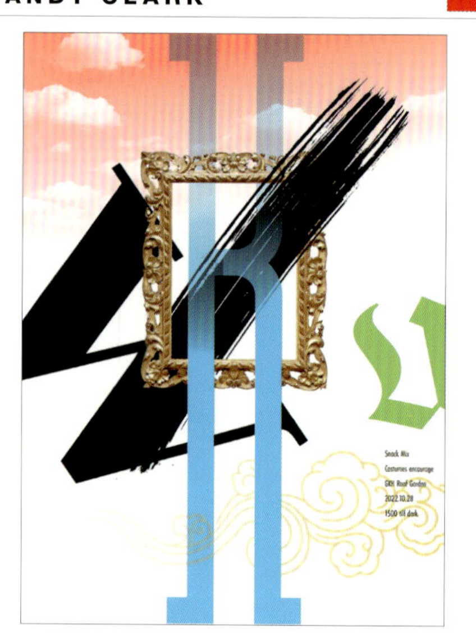

Title: W Frame
Client: Wenzhou-Kean University
Design Firm: Randy Clark

ARSONAL

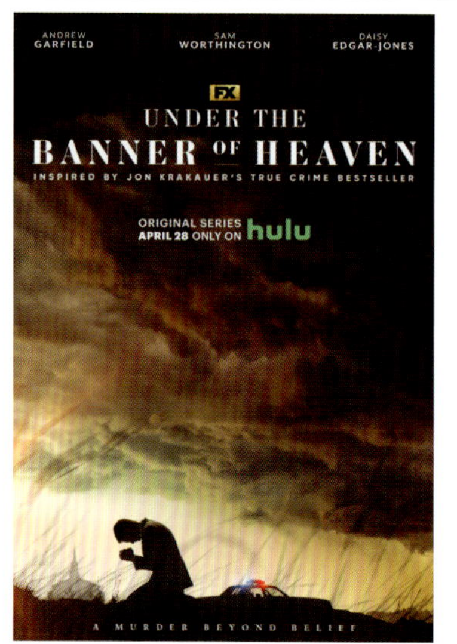

Title: Under The Banner of Heaven
Client: FX
Design Firm: ARSONAL

SJI ASSOCIATES

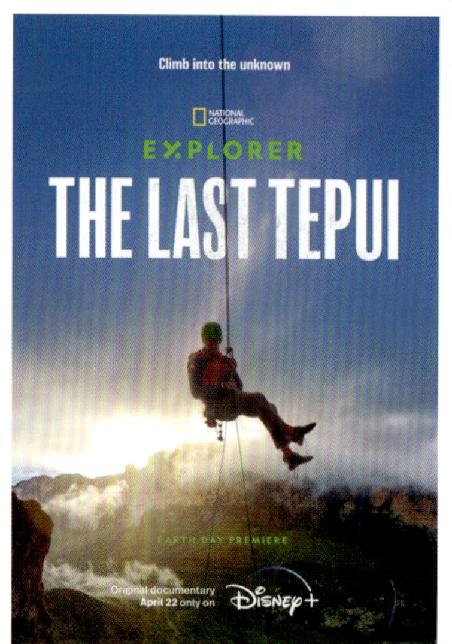

Title: Explorer – The Last Tepui | Alternative Poster | **Client:** National Geographic
Design Firm: SJI Associates

NORIYUKI KASAI

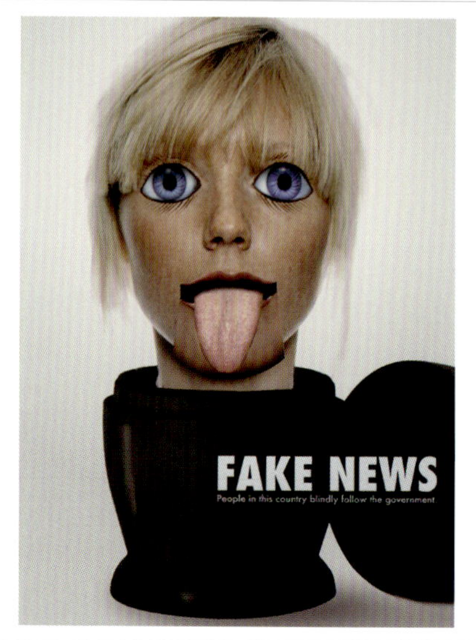

Title: FAKE NEWS
Client: Graphic Communication Laboratory
Design Firm: Noriyuki Kasai

JEFF BARFOOT

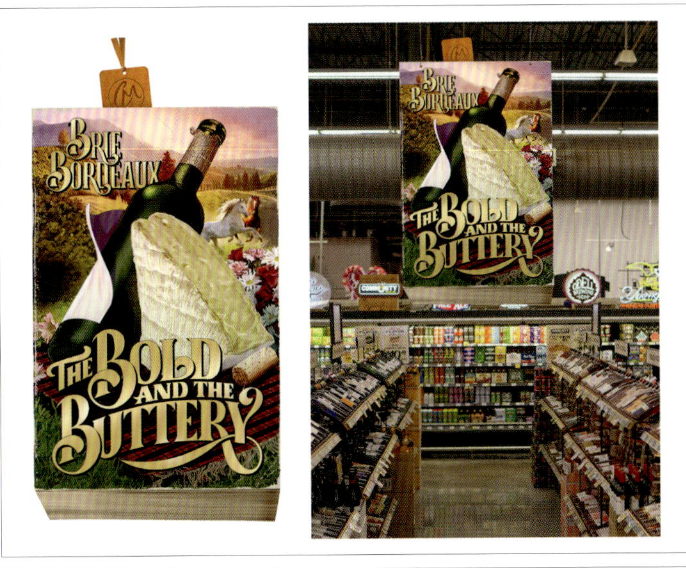

Title: Central Market Valentine's Day 2022 | **Client:** Central Market
Design Firms: *TraceElement, Plot Twist Creativity

SEAN FADEN

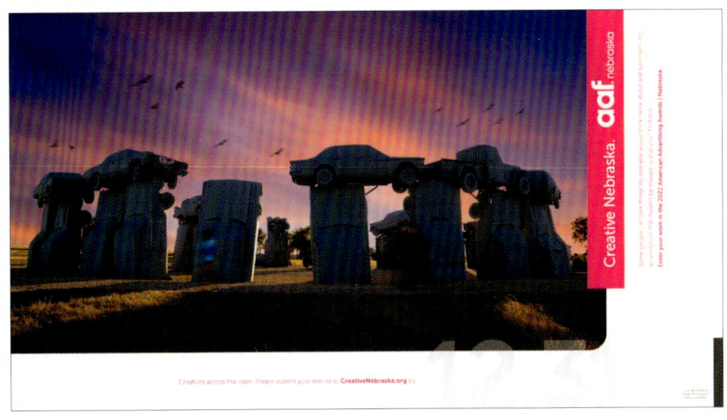

Title: Creative Nebraska | **Client:** AAF Nebraska
Design Firm: Bailey Lauerman

CAROLYN GIBBS

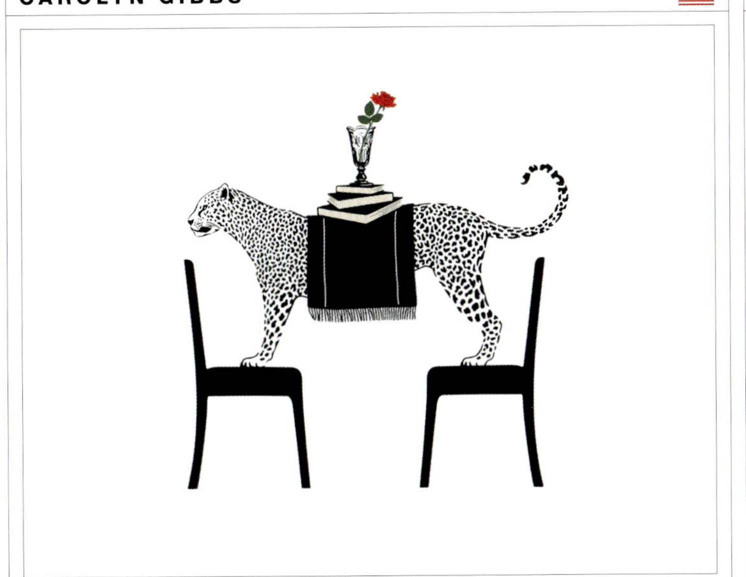

Title: Modern Leopard | **Client:** Self-initiated
Design Firm: Carolyn Gibbs Design

CARTER WEITZ

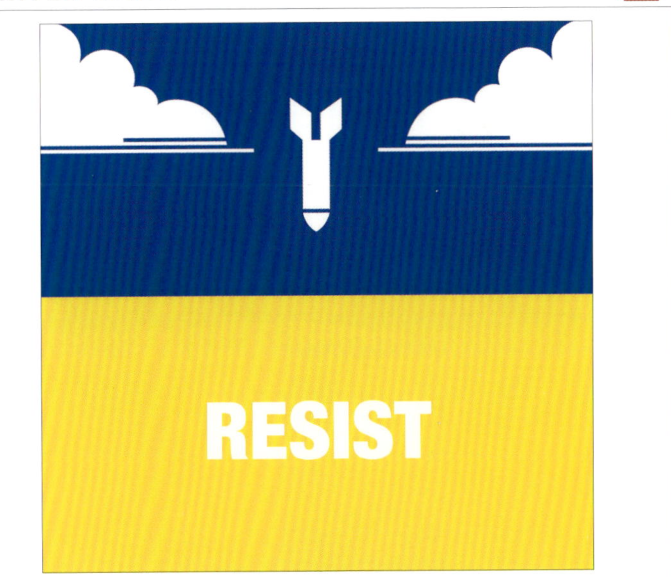

Title: Resist | **Client:** Self-initiated
Design Firm: Bailey Lauerman

DERWYN GOODALL

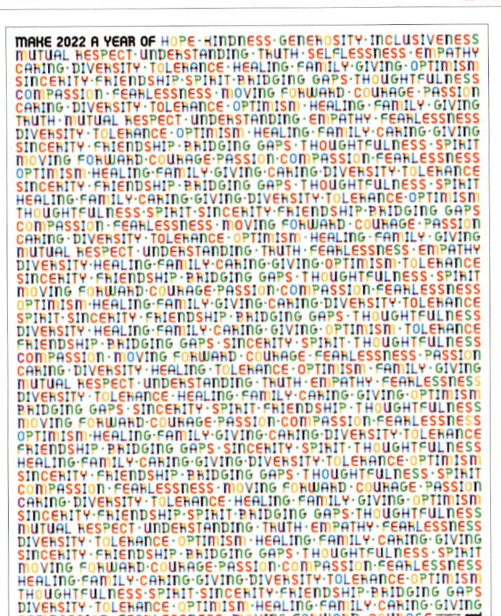

Title: Make 2022...
Client: Self-initiated
Design Firm: Goodall Integrated Design

KIMBERLY ELAM

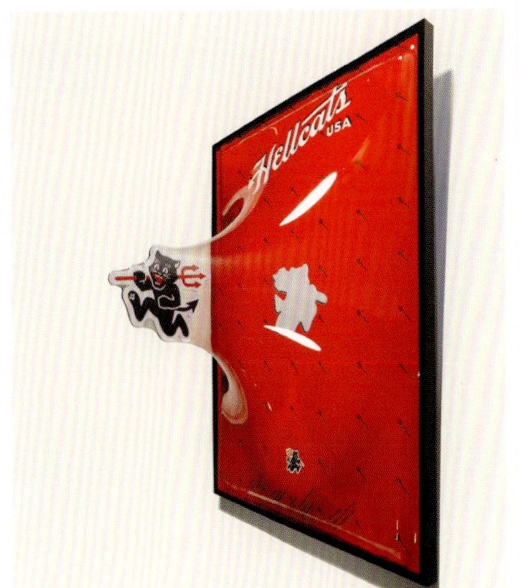

Title: Hellcats USA Vacuum Form Poster
Client: Ringling College of Art & Design
Design Firm: Kimberly Elam Design

LUCA PONTARELLI

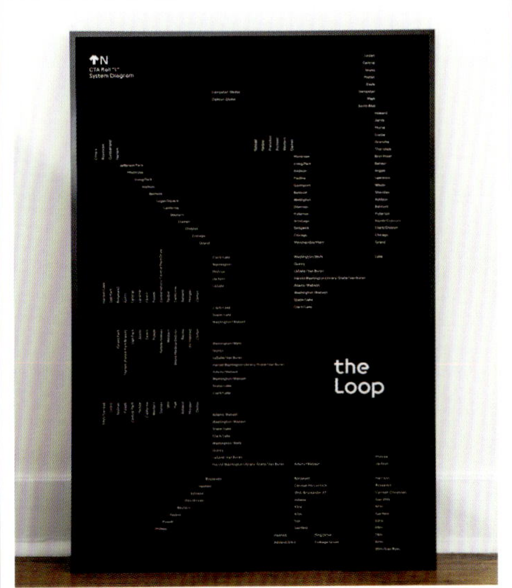

Title: Geometria
Client: Self-initiated
Design Firm: Luca Pontarelli

CINTHIA WEN

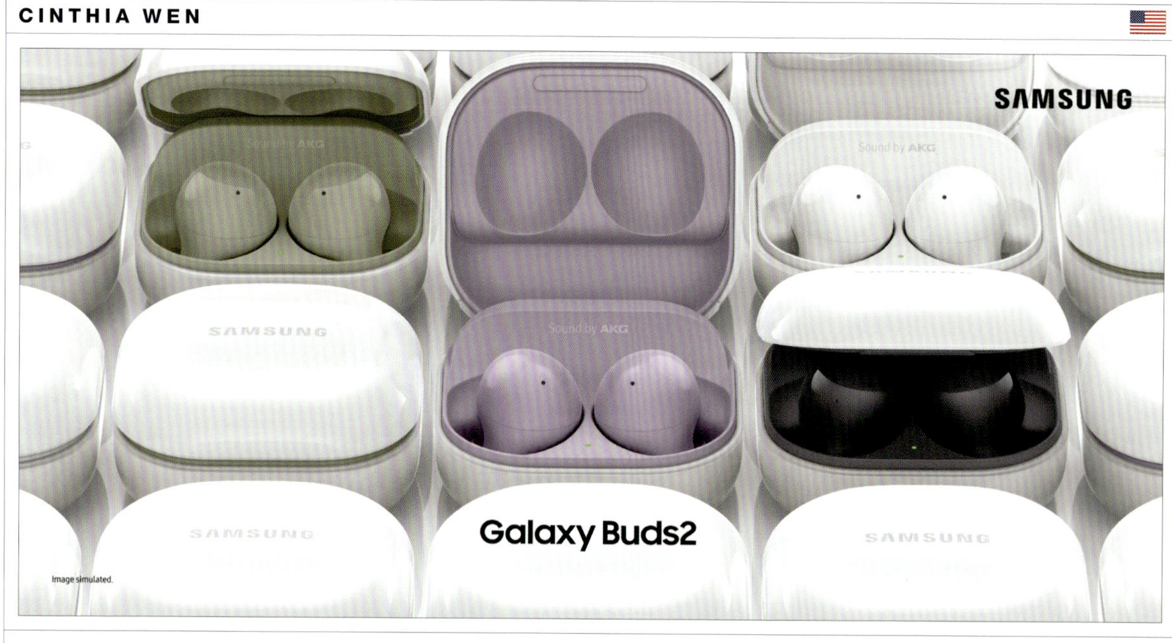

Title: Galaxy Buds2 Launch Poster | **Client:** Samsung | **Design Firm:** Turner Duckworth: London, S. F. & N. Y.

CINTHIA WEN

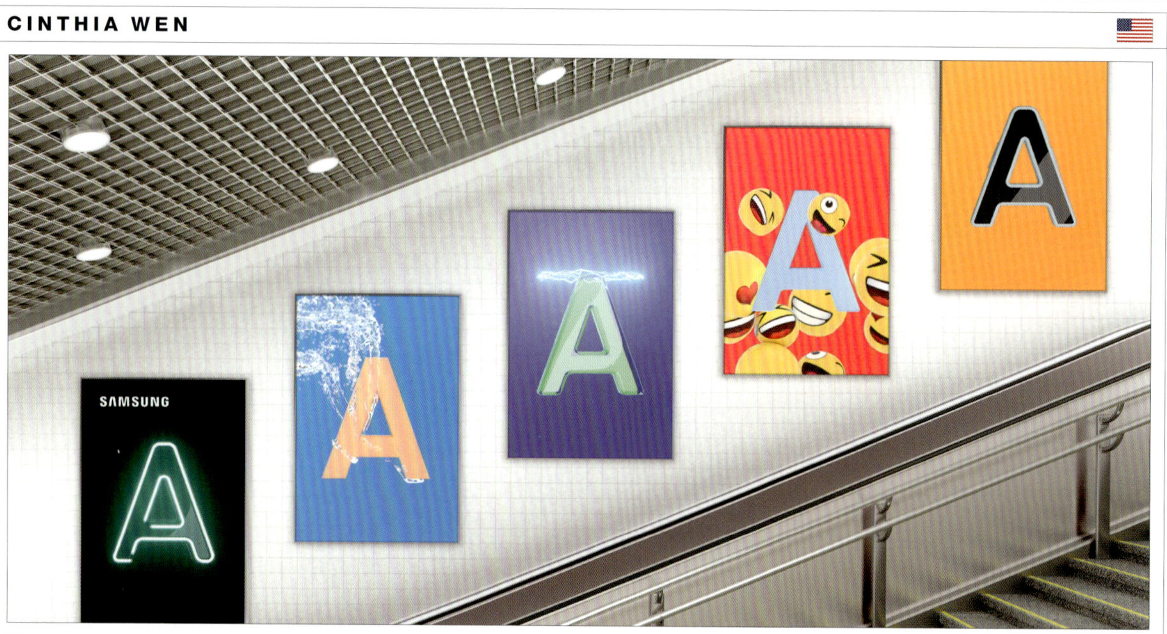

Title: Galaxy A Event Invite Poster Series 2022 | **Client:** Samsung | **Design Firm:** Turner Duckworth: London, S. F. & N. Y.

JOHN OLSON, GIANMARIA SCHONLIEB, KARIN ONSAGER BIRCH

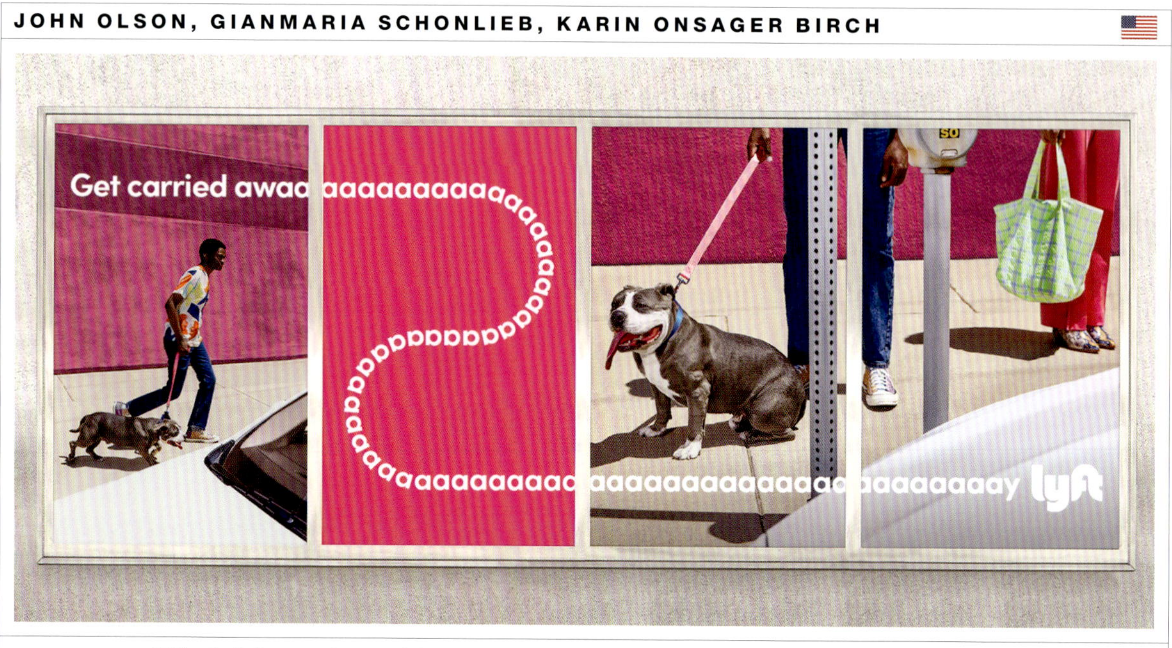

Title: Lyft Posters Design | **Client:** Self-initiated | **Design Firm:** Lyft Internal Creative Team

JOVANEY HOLLINGSWORTH

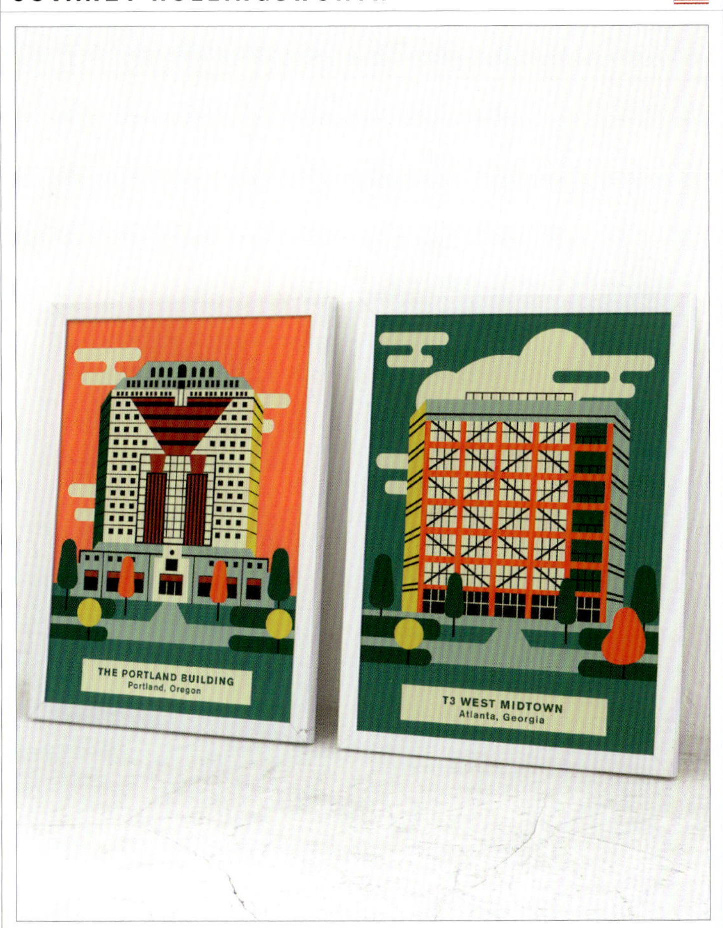

Title: DLR Group - Lincoln Office Posters
Client: Self-initiated | **Design Firm:** DLR Group

OSBORNE ROSS

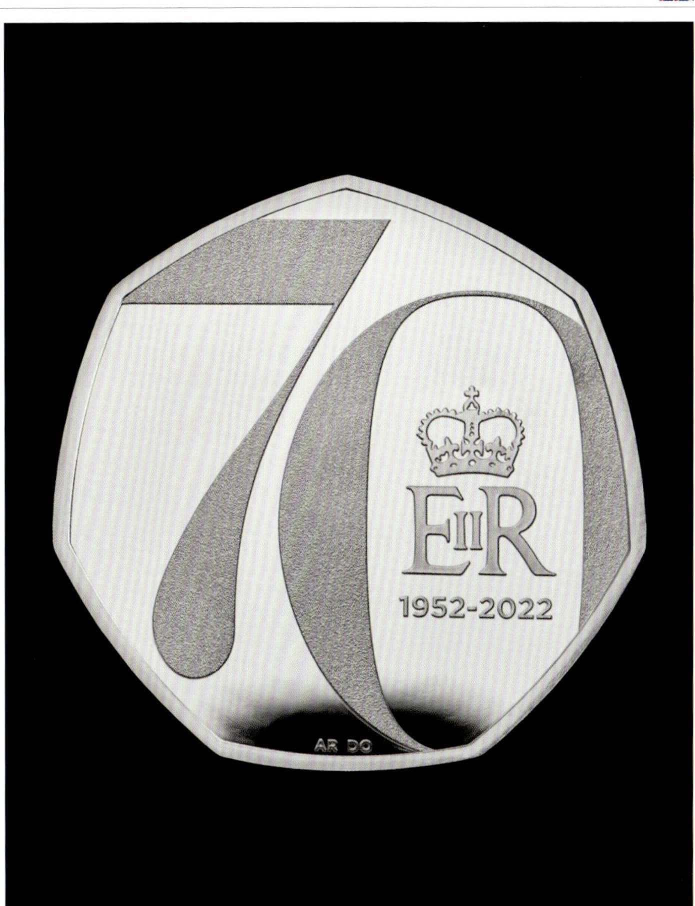

Title: Her Majesty The Queen's Platinum Jubilee Coin
Client: Royal Mint | **Design Firm:** Osborne Ross

SUI XIN

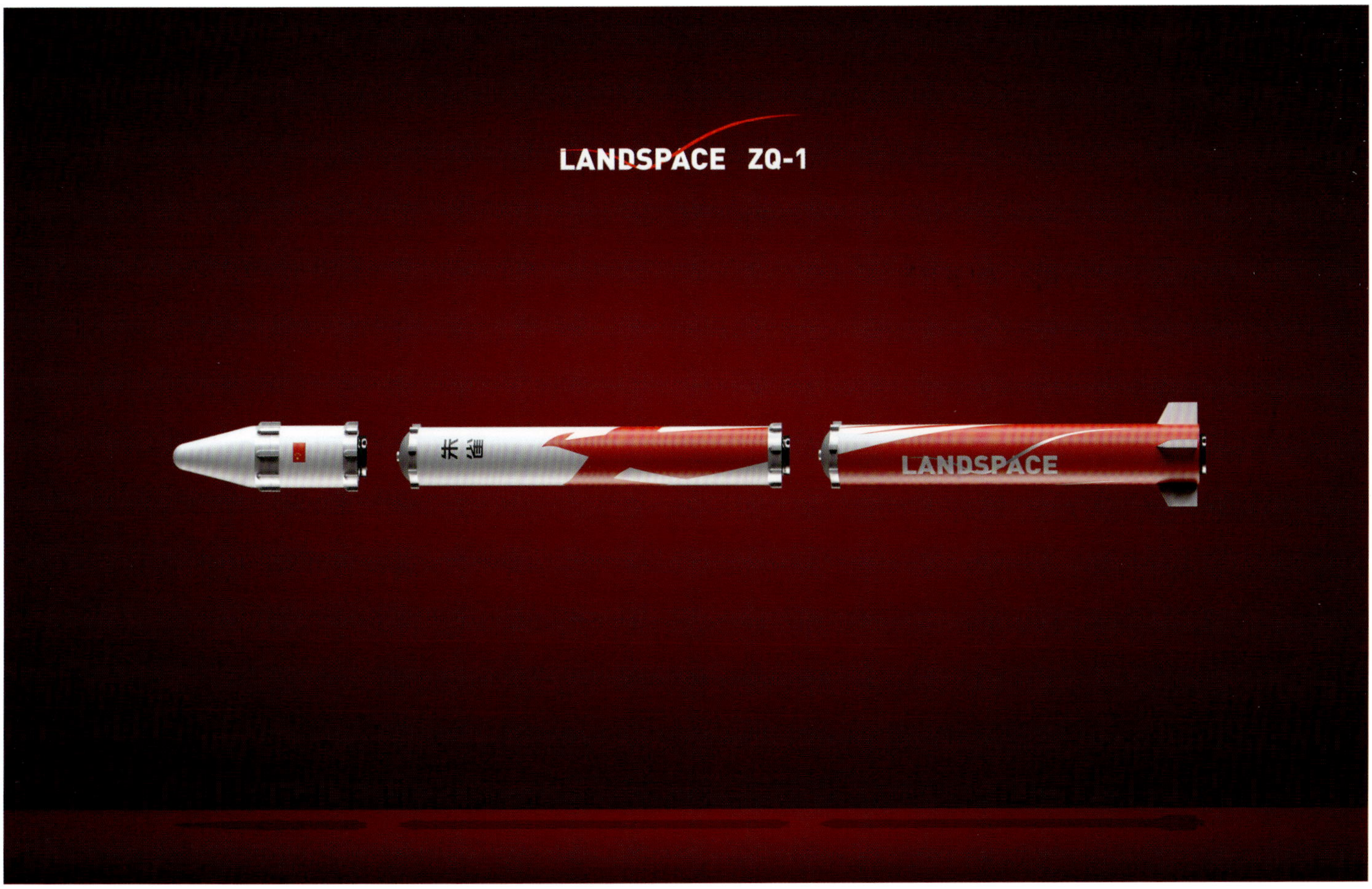

Title: Livery Design of ZQ Series Rocket | **Client:** Land Space Technology Corporation Ltd. | **Design Firm:** Dalian Cones Papa Technology Co., Ltd.

TODD HOUSER

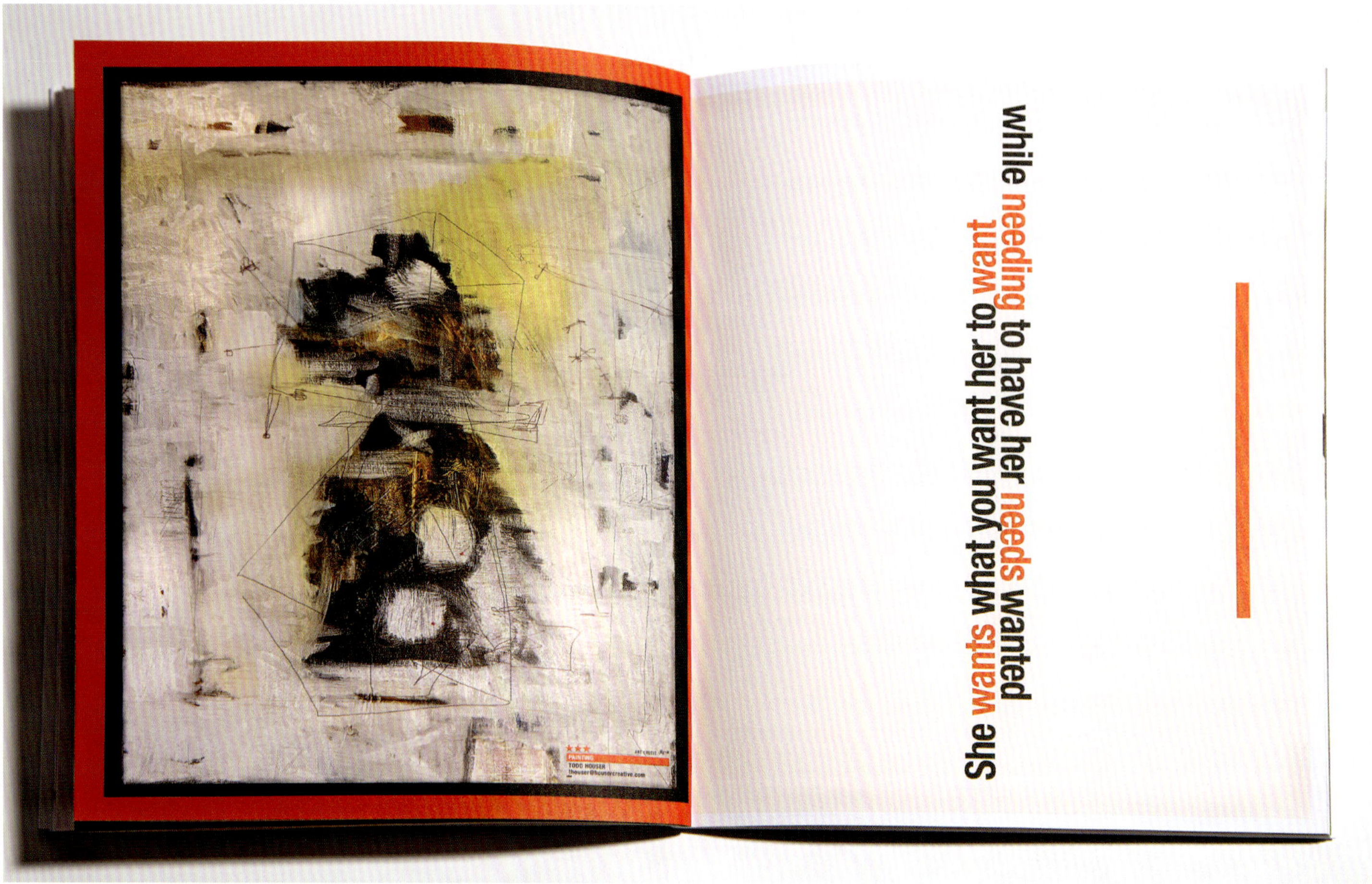

Title: She* | Client: Self-initiated | Design Firm: Rex C

TEIGA, STUDIO.

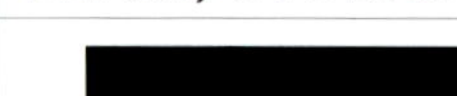

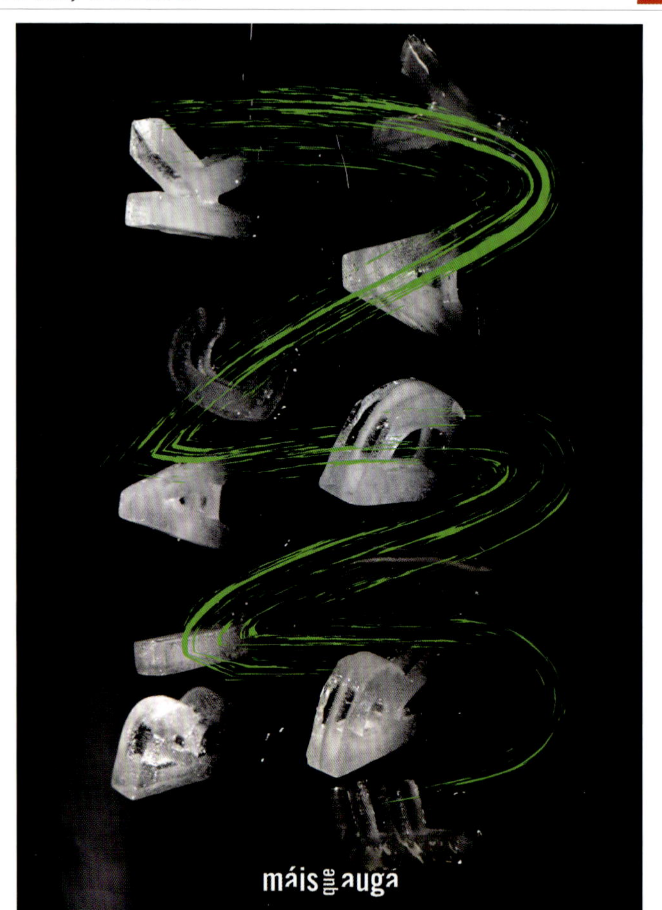

Title: Black Friday MQA | Client: Mais que Auga
Design Firm: Teiga, Studio.

LEGIS DESIGN

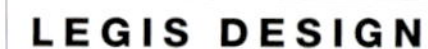

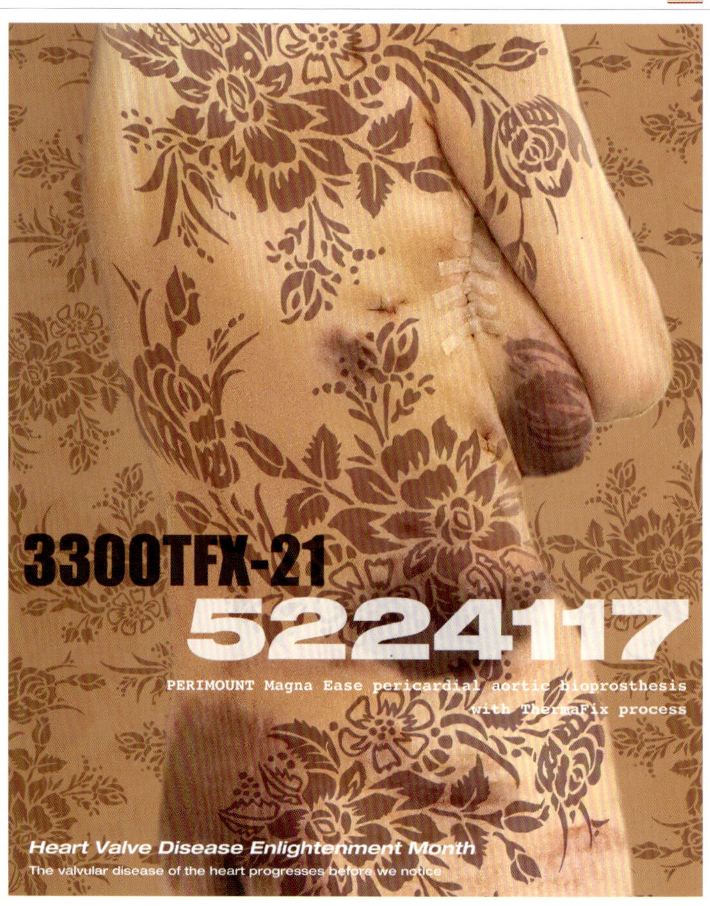

Title: Prevention of Valvular Disease of the Heart | Client: Self-initiated
Design Firm: Legis Design

LAFAYETTE AMERICAN

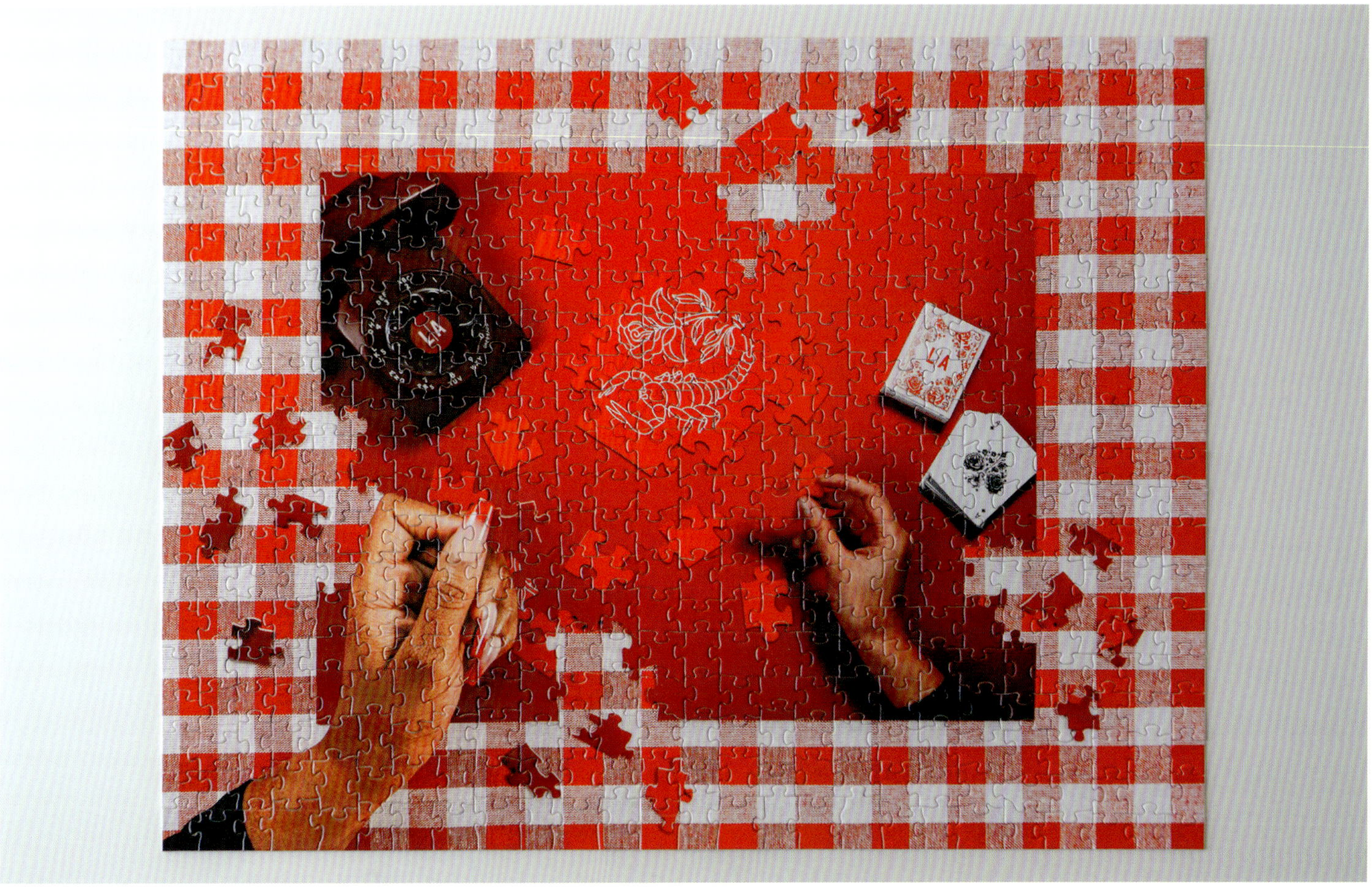

Title: Lafayette American Puzzle | **Client:** Self-initiated | **Design Firm:** Lafayette American

SEAN FADEN

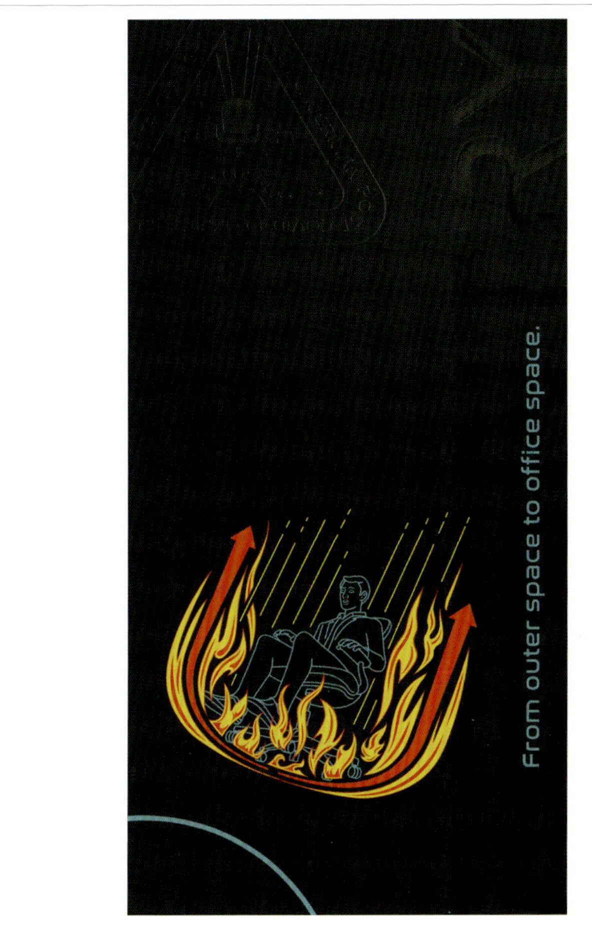

Title: Re-Entry | **Client:** Self-initiated
Design Firm: Bailey Lauerman

TEIGA, STUDIO.

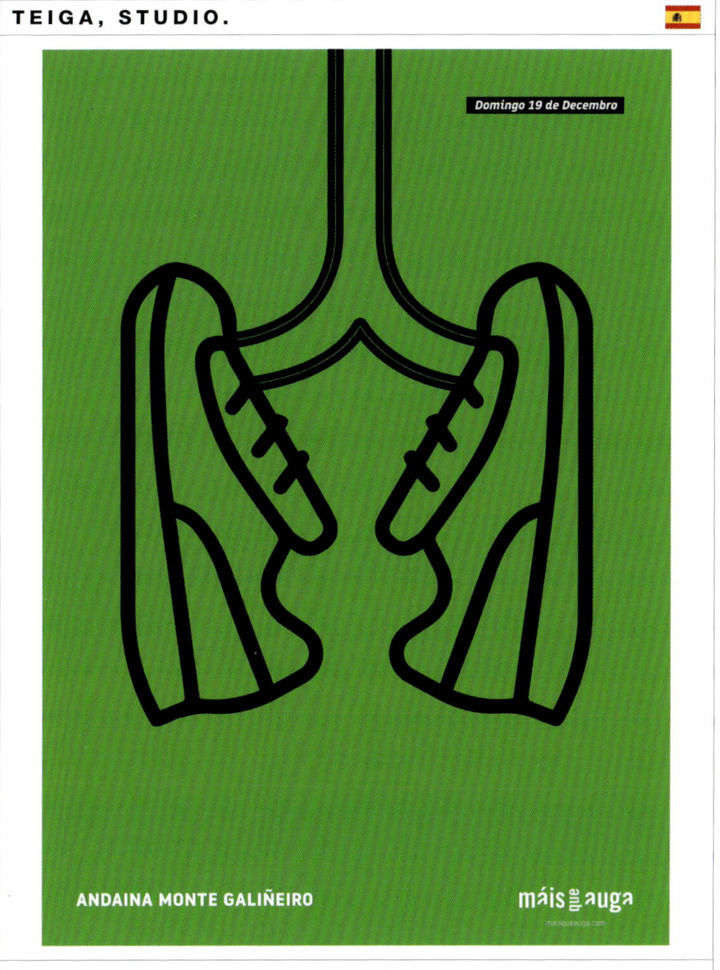

Title: Poster Mais Que Auga | **Client:** Mais que Auga
Design Firm: Teiga, Studio.

ALEX FLORES

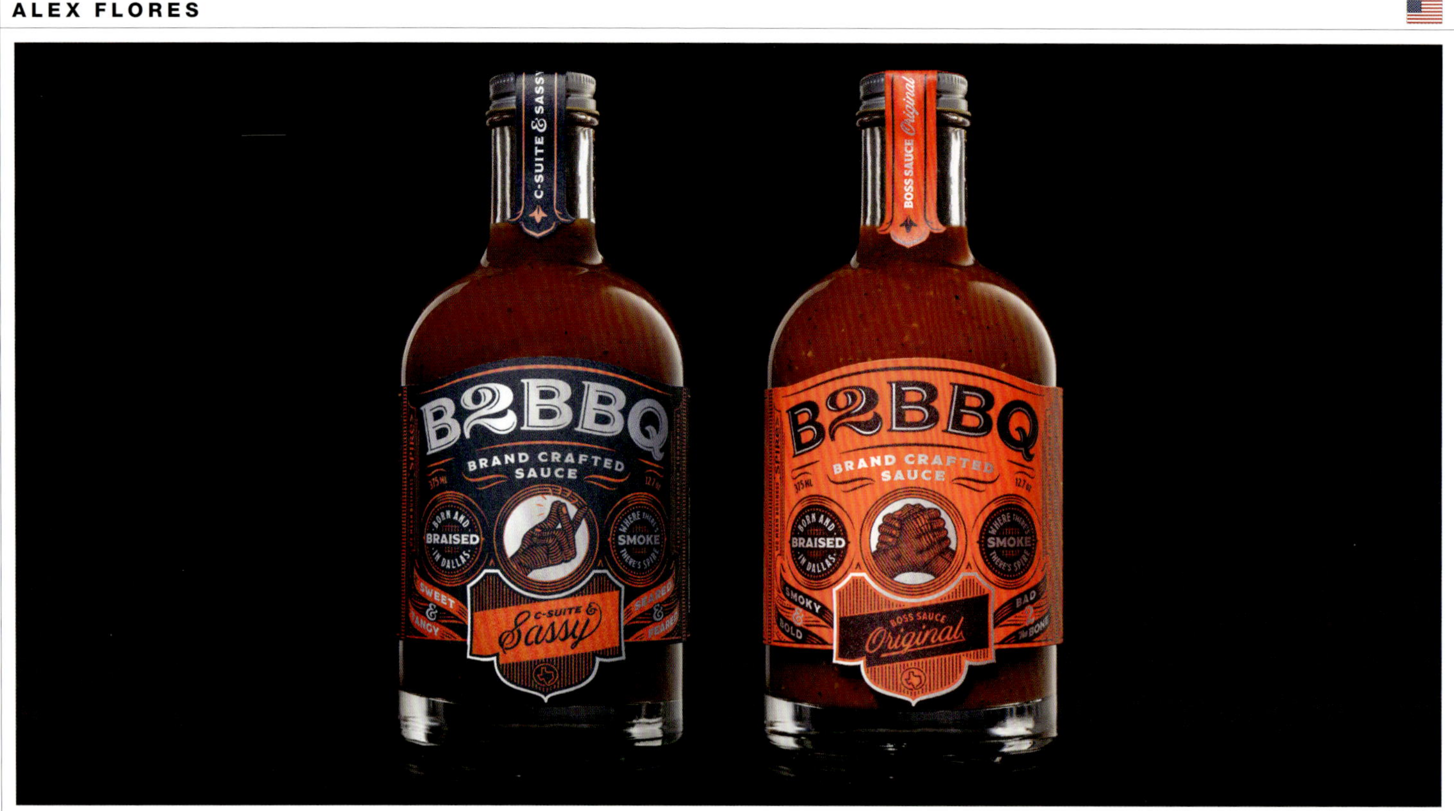

Title: Spire B2BBQ | **Client:** Self-initiated | **Design Firm:** Spire Agency

JAN ŠABACH

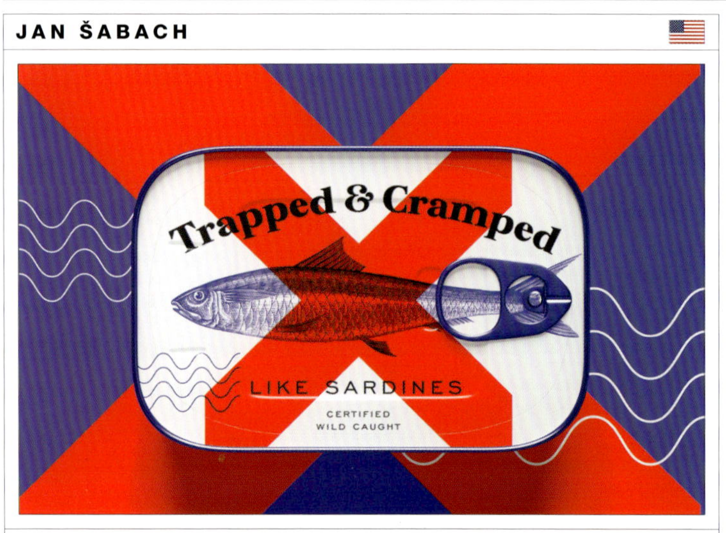

Title: Covid Feelings Packaged | **Client:** Self-initiated
Design Firm: Code Switch

LEGACY79

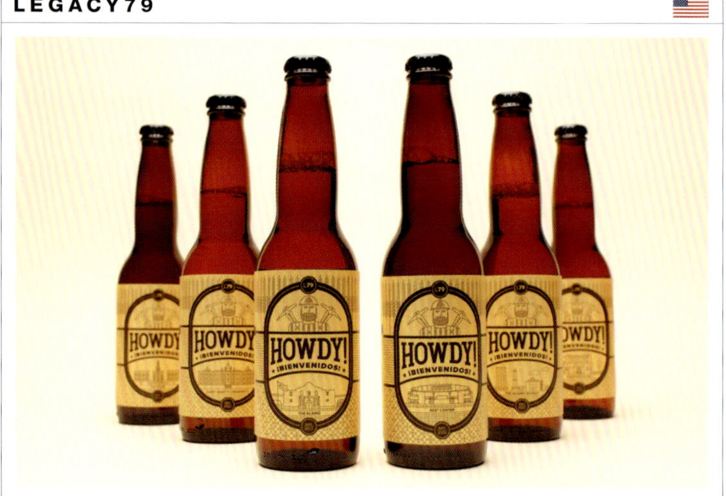

Title: Howdy, Legacy79 Brew | **Client:** Self-initiated
Design Firm: Legacy79

INNOCEAN USA

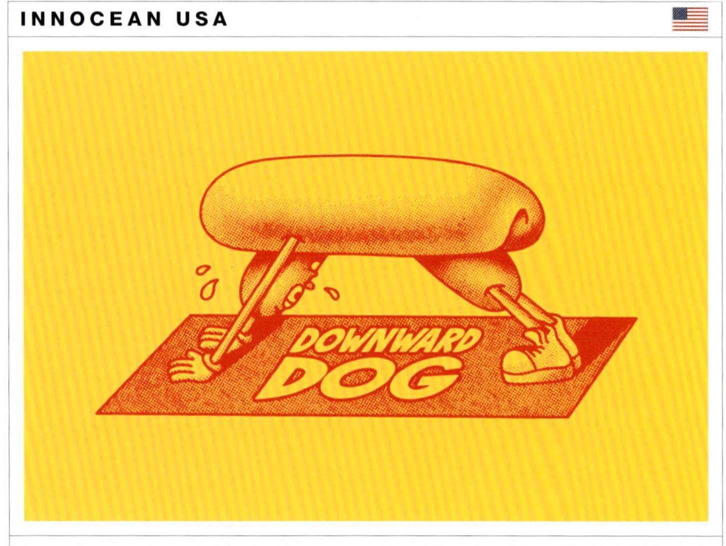

Title: Wienerisms | **Client:** Wienerschnitzel | **Design Firm:** INNOCEAN USA

MICHAEL HESTER

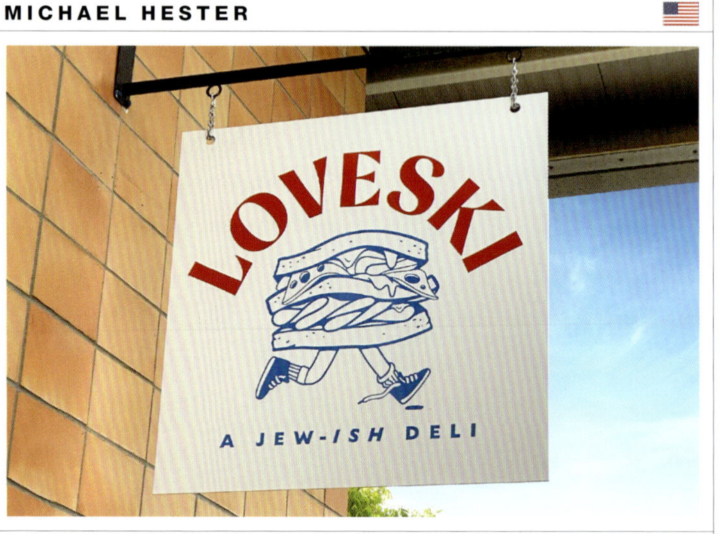

Title: Loveski Deli | **Client:** Loveski Deli | **Design Firm:** Pavement

CALDAS NAYA

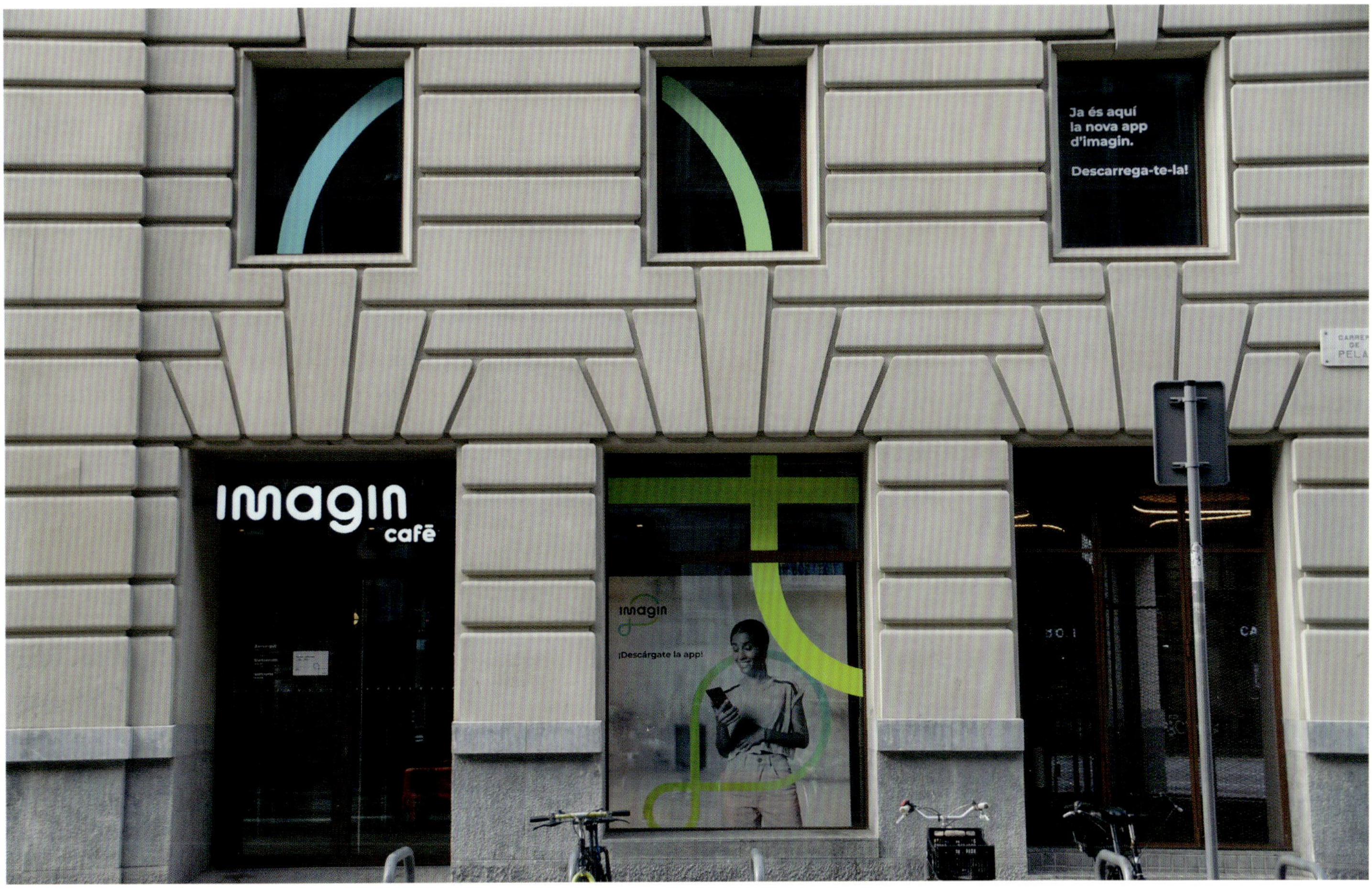

Title: Imagin Café Retail Project | **Clients:** Imagin, CaixaBank, Manel García Puig, David Urbano | **Design Firm:** Caldas Naya

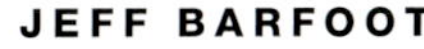

JEFF BARFOOT

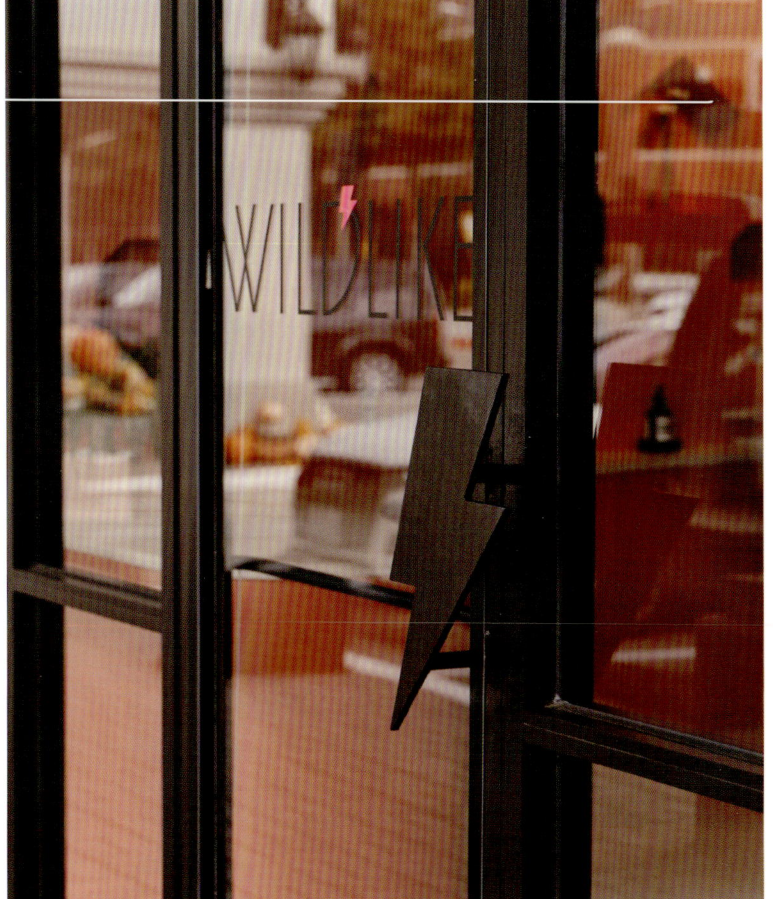

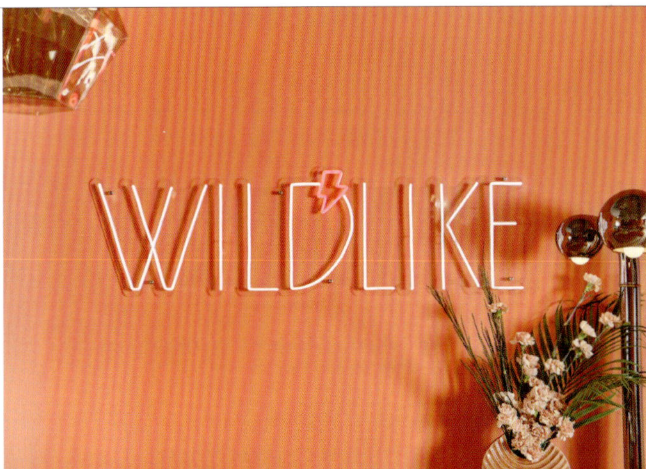

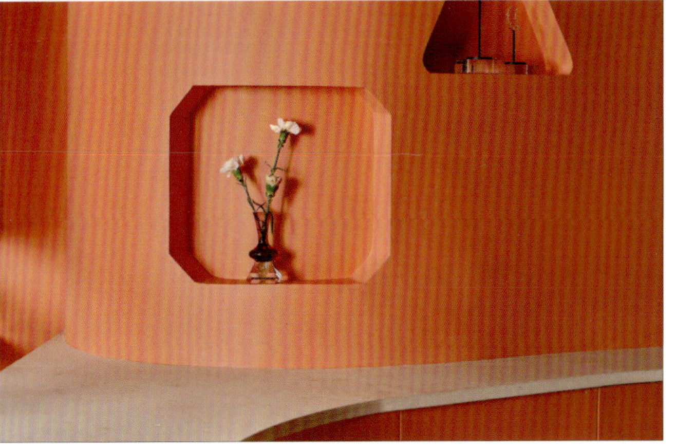

Title: Wildlike Identity | **Client:** Wildlike | **Design Firm:** *TraceElement

RES EICHENBERGER

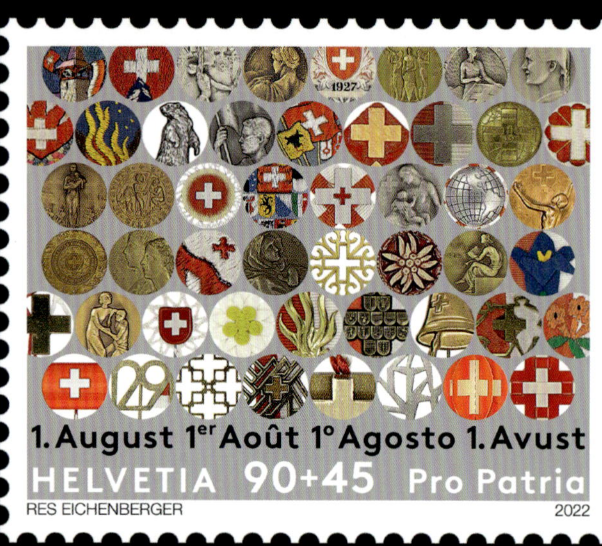

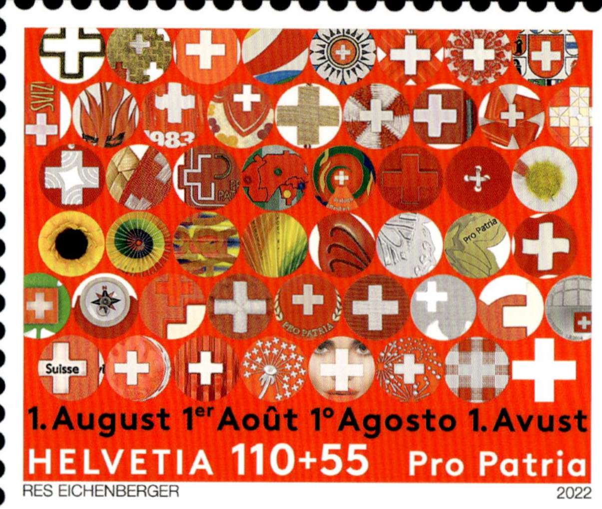

Title: Pro Patria Stamps | **Client:** Swiss Post | **Design Firm:** Res Eichenberger Design

U.S. POSTAL SERVICE

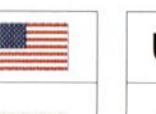

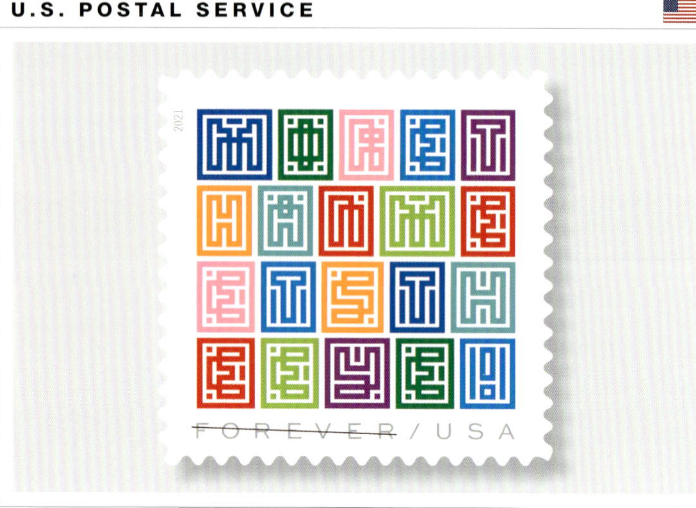

Title: Mystery Message | **Client:** U.S. Postal Service
Design Firm: Studio A

U.S. POSTAL SERVICE

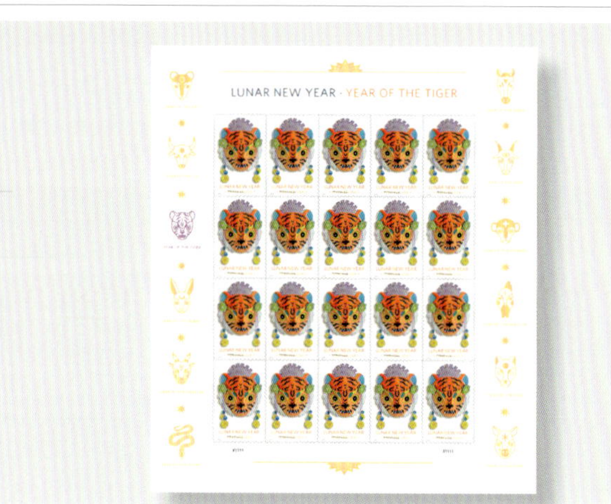

Title: Lunar New Year • Year of the Tiger | **Client:** U.S. Postal Service
Design Firm: Studio A

U.S. POSTAL SERVICE

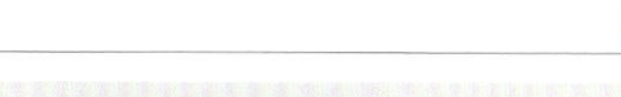

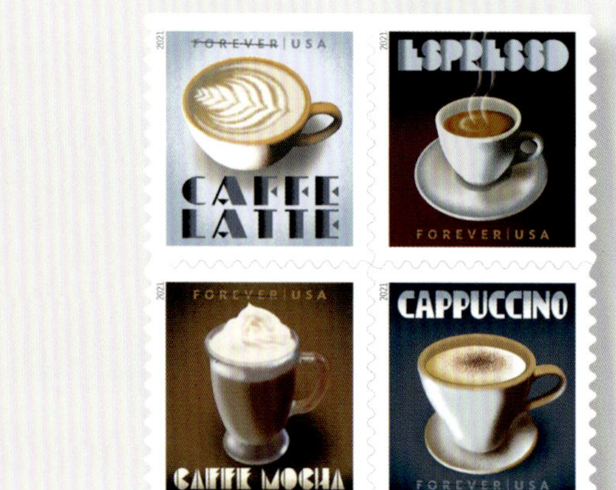

Title: Espresso Drinks | **Client:** U.S. Postal Service
Design Firm: Journey Group

U.S. POSTAL SERVICE

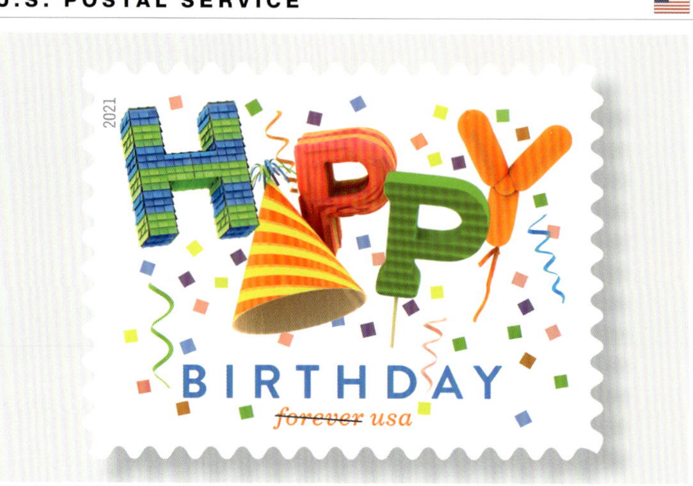

Title: Happy Birthday | **Client:** U.S. Postal Service
Design Firm: Catalone Design

U.S. POSTAL SERVICE

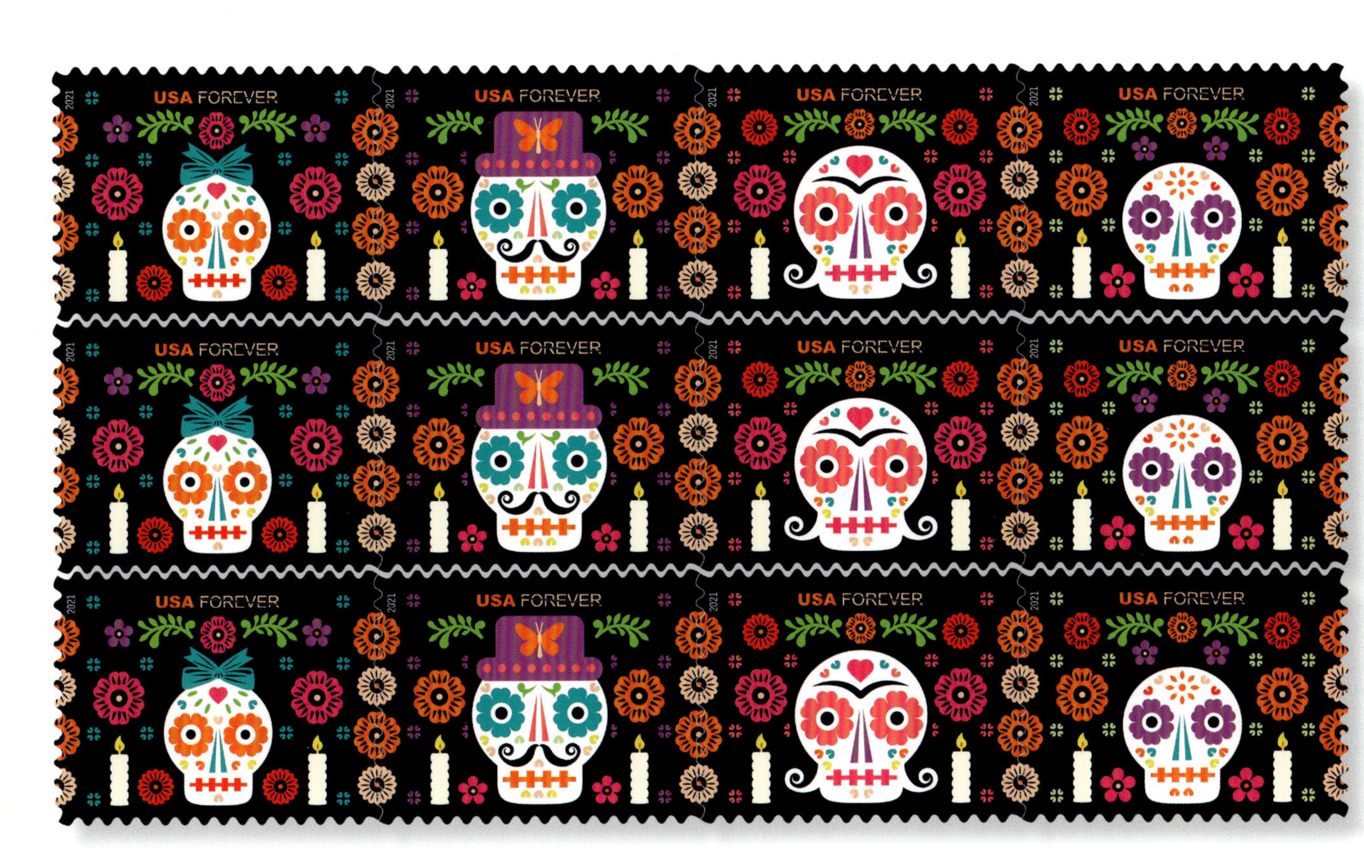

Title: Day of the Dead | **Client:** U.S. Postal Service | **Design Firm:** Studio A

YU CHEN

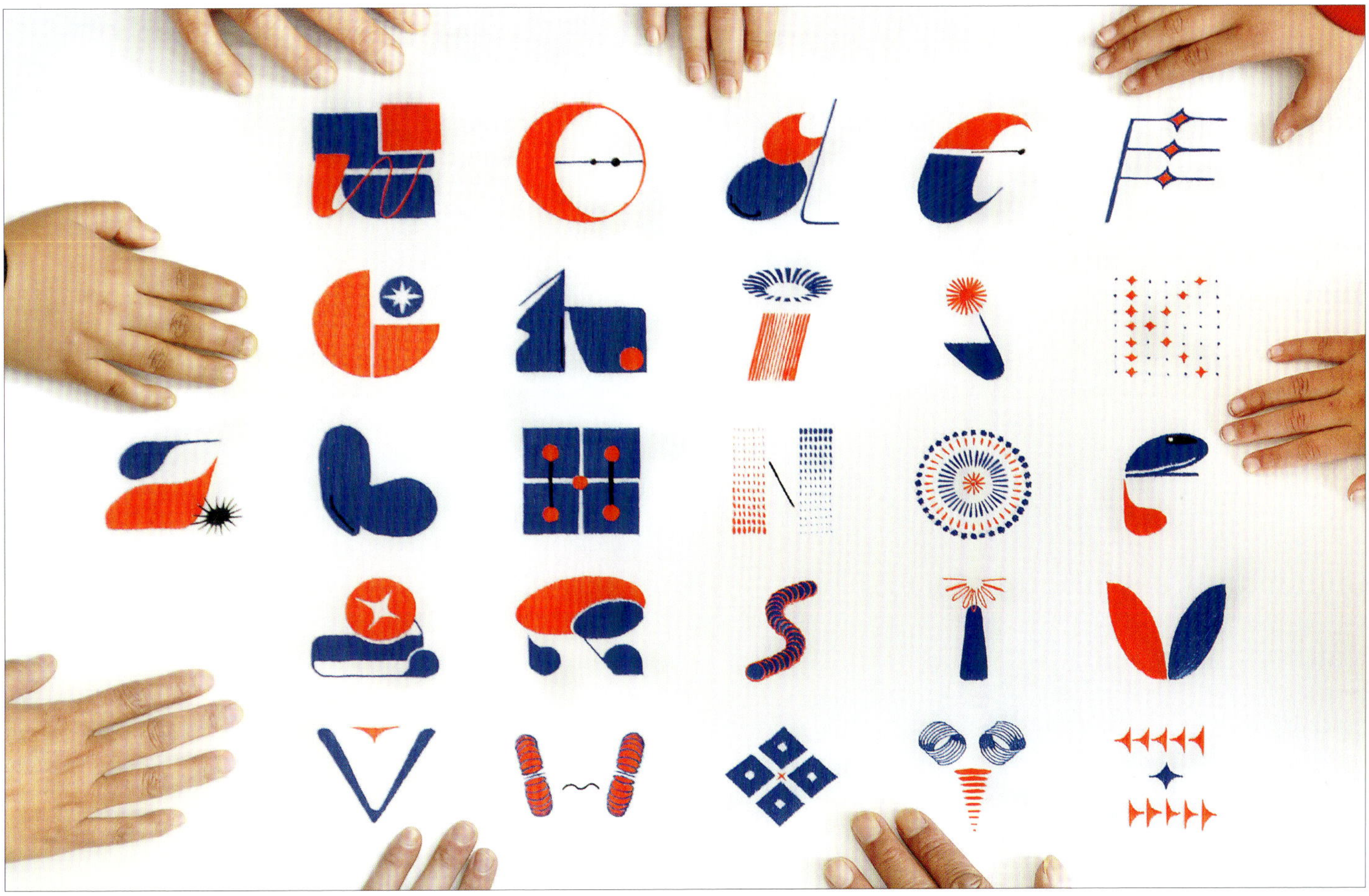

Title: Let Parents Stay (Han Embroidery Typeface) | **Client:** Hubei Han Embroidery Association | **Design Firm:** Yu Chen Design

NAOMIE ROSS, MICHAEL BAGNARDI, KAREN SONG

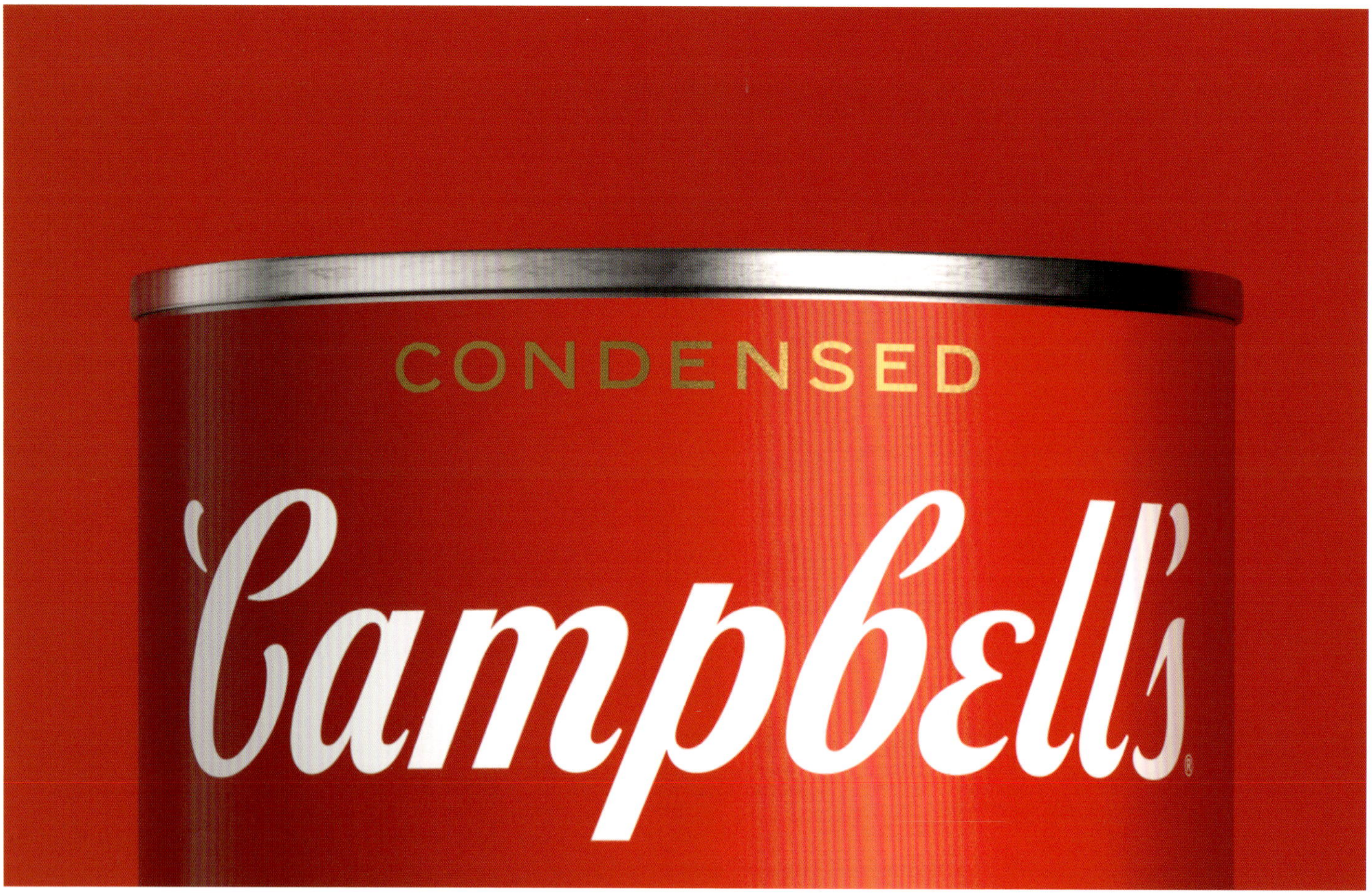

Title: Campbell's Red & White Condensed Soup Logo | **Client:** Campbell's | **Design Firm:** Turner Duckworth: London, San Francisco & New York

NAOMIE ROSS, MICHAEL BAGNARDI, KAREN SONG

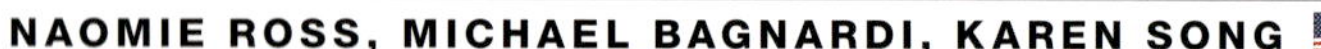

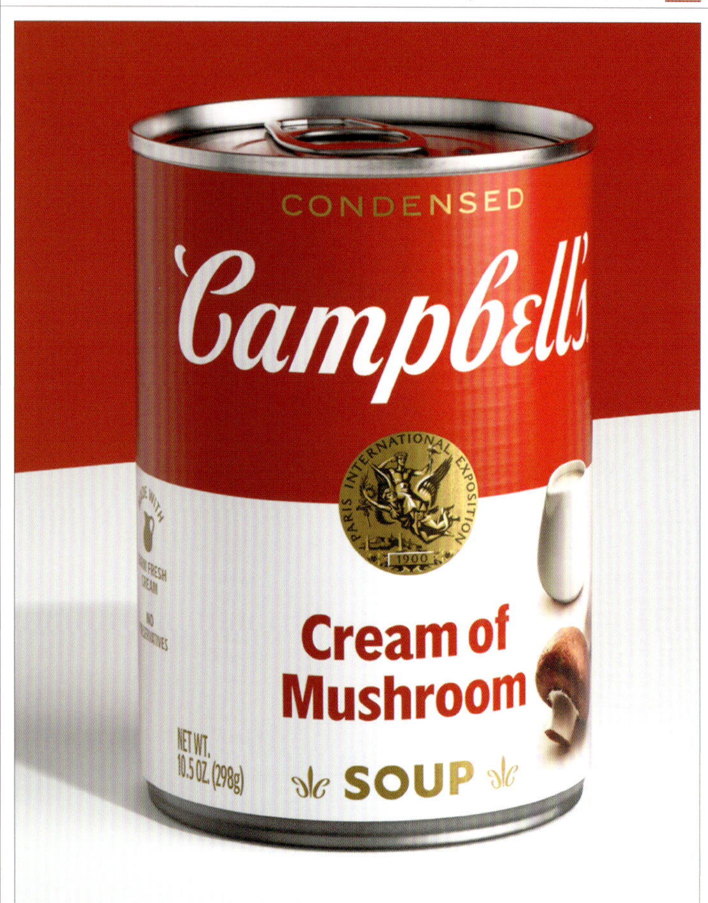

Title: Campbell's Red & White Condensed Soup Type | **Client:** Campbell's
Design Firm: Turner Duckworth: London, San Francisco & New York

BRENDA MCMANUS, NED DREW

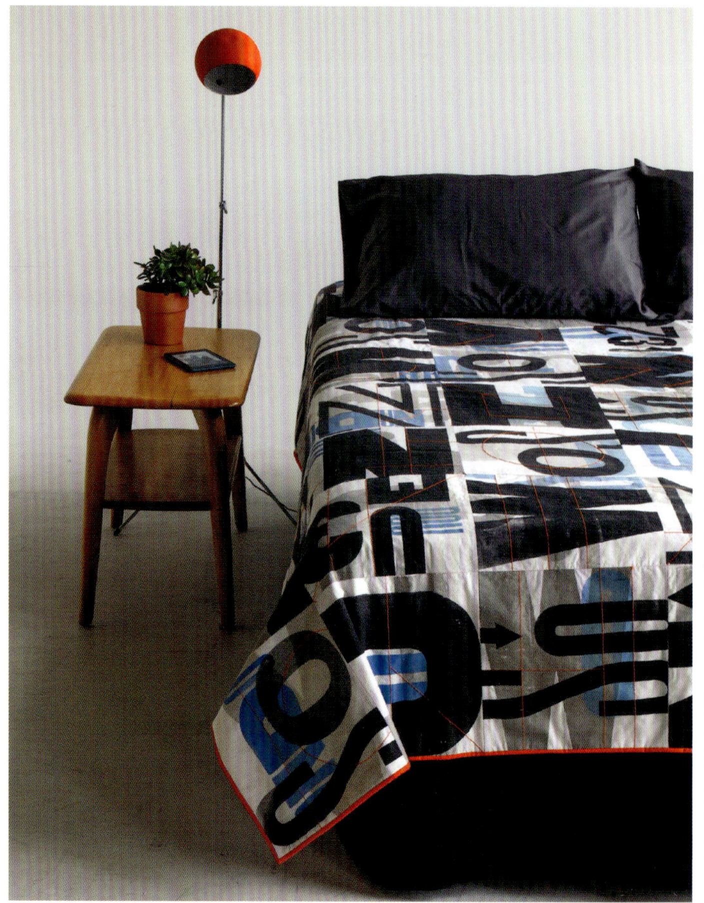

Title: The Letterpress Quilt Project | **Client:** Self-initiated
Design Firm: BRED

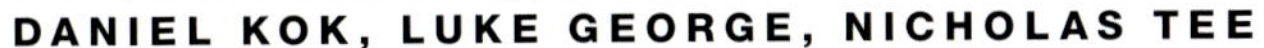

DANIEL KOK, LUKE GEORGE, NICHOLAS TEE

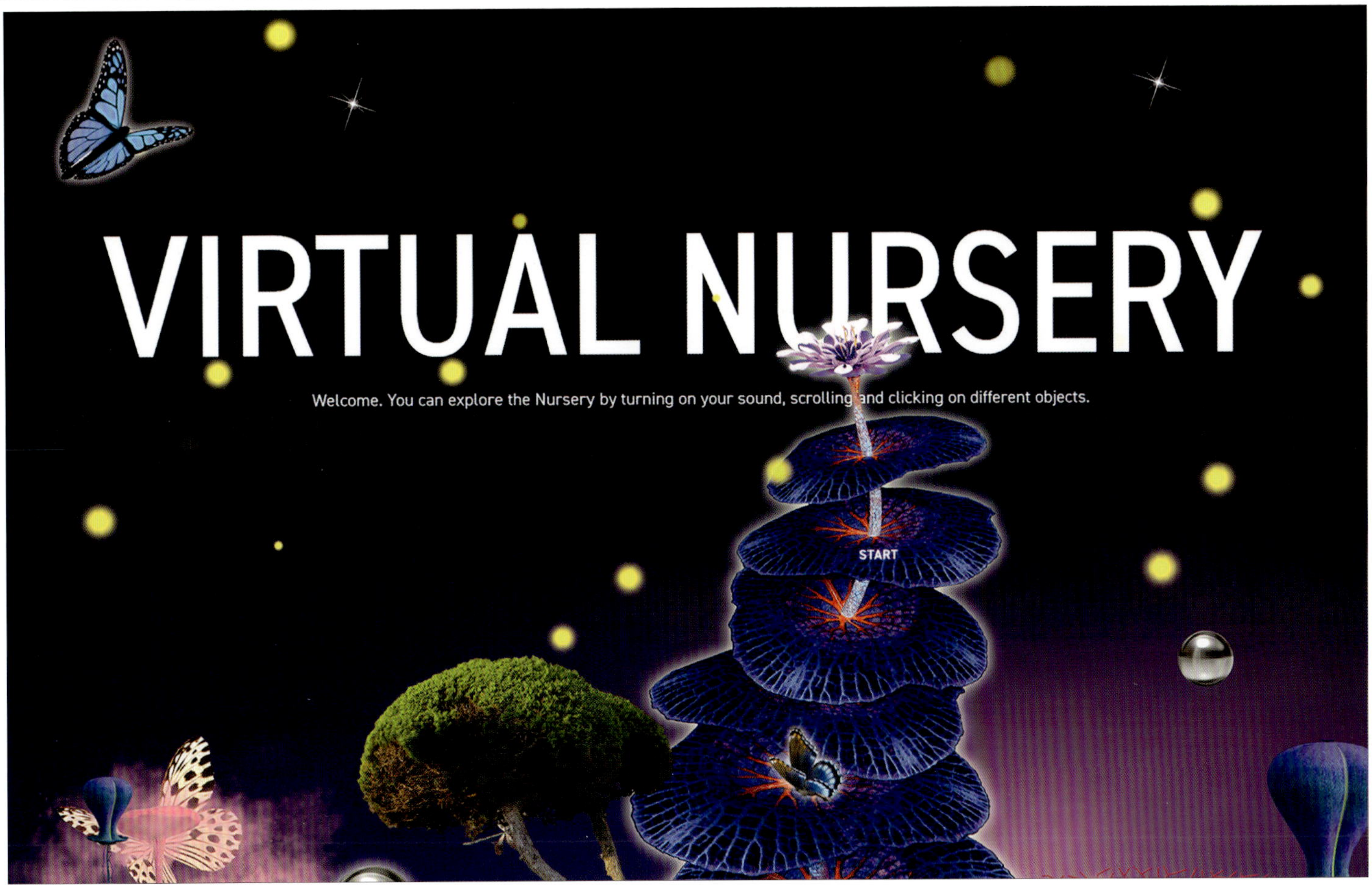

Title: Virtual Nursery, Hundreds + Thousands (Multi-City) | **Clients:** Daniel Kok, Luke George | **Design Firm:** FACTORY

ROBERTO NÚÑEZ

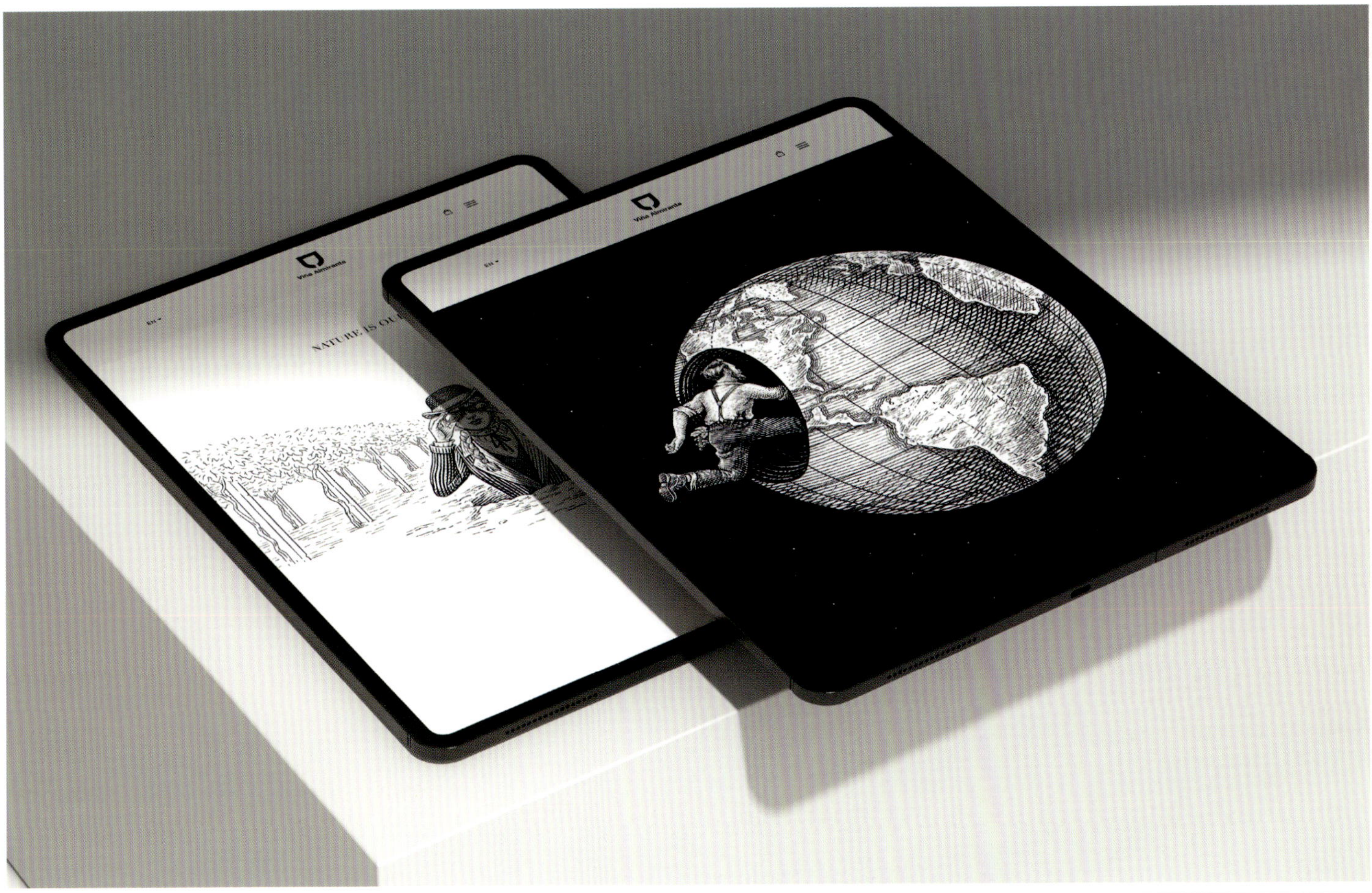

Title: Viña Almirante. Website. | **Client:** Viña Almirante | **Design Firm:** Roberto Núñez Studio

DANCE NUCLEUS, THE NATIONAL ARTS COUNCIL

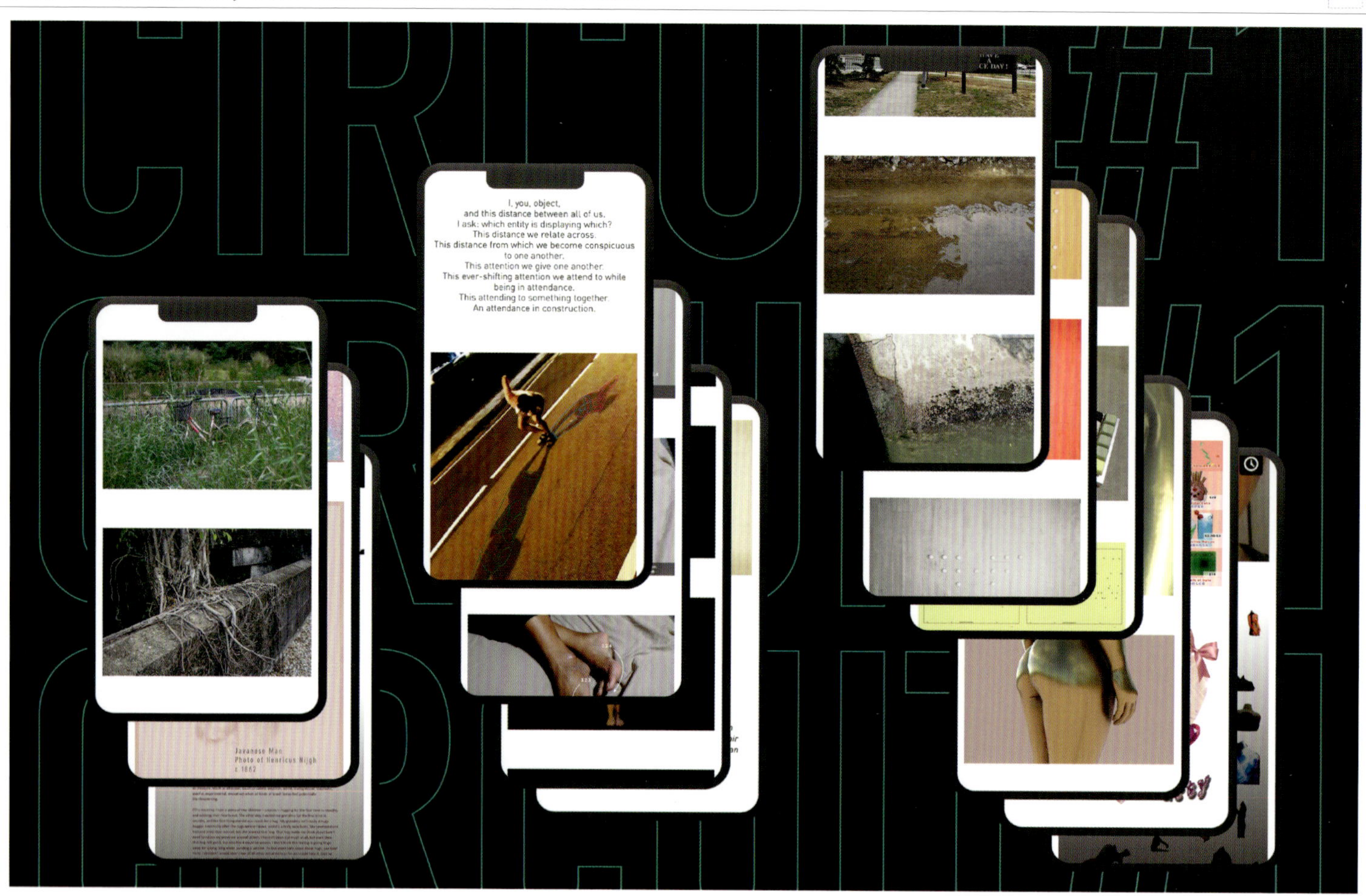

Title: Circuit #1 | **Client:** Dance Nucleus | **Design Firm:** FACTORY

SHARON LLOYD MCLAUGHLIN

Title: Mermaid, Inc. Fluid Creativity Website | **Client:** Self-initiated | **Design Firm:** Mermaid, Inc.

RACHEL PIGOTT

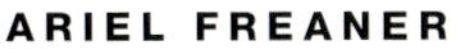

Title: AGCO Website | **Client:** AGCO | **Design Firm:** Addison

ARIEL FREANER

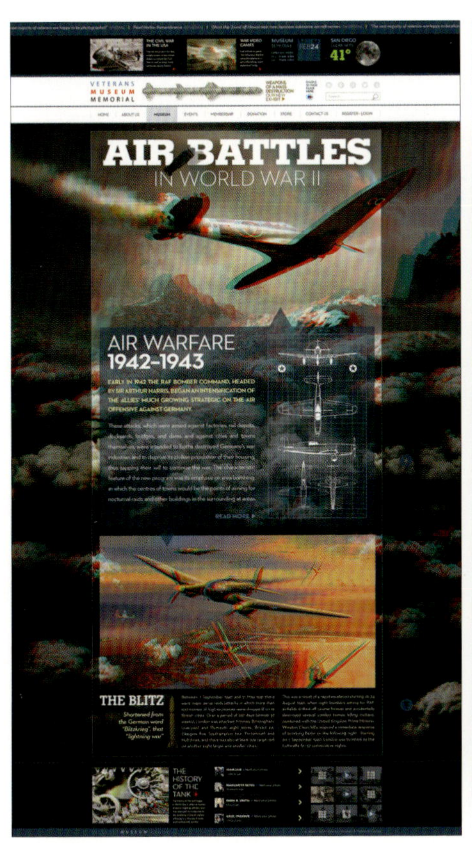

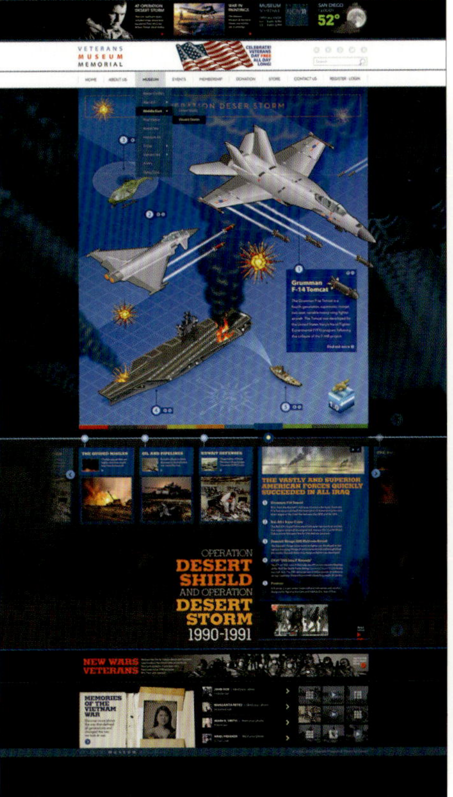

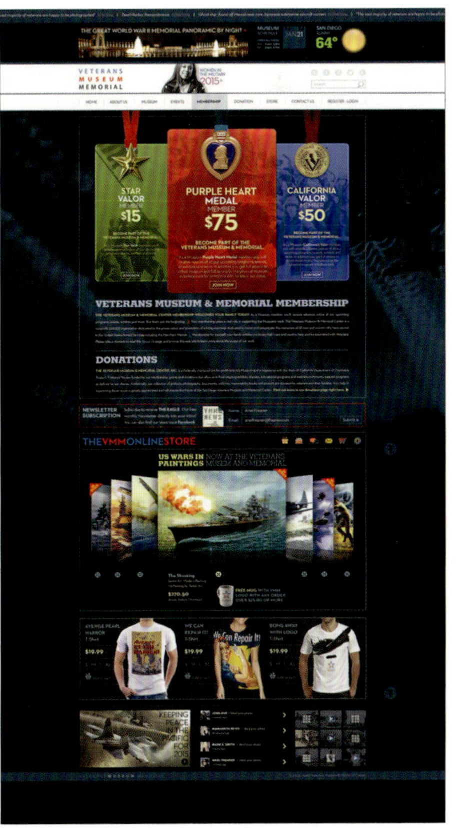

Title: Veterans Museum Website Design | **Client:** Veterans Memorial Museum | **Design Firm:** Freaner Creative & Design

LORI MARTIN

ANIMATION

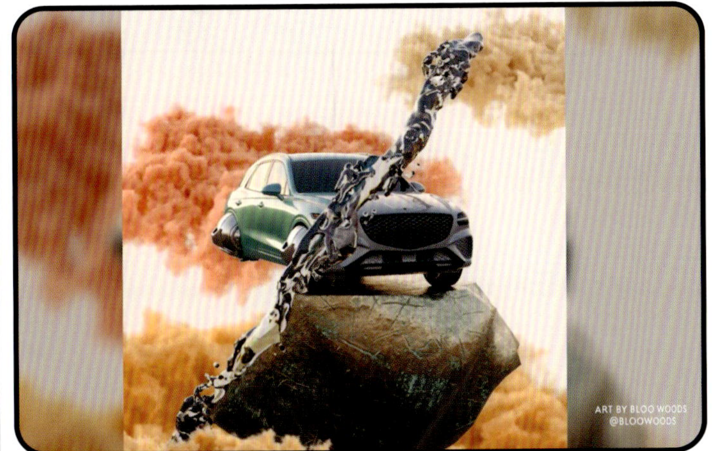

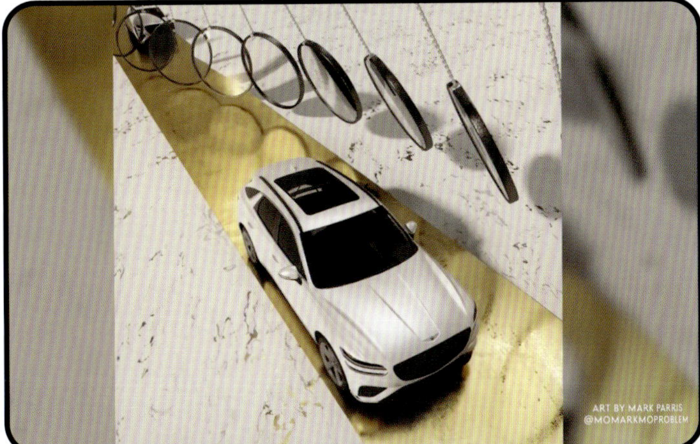

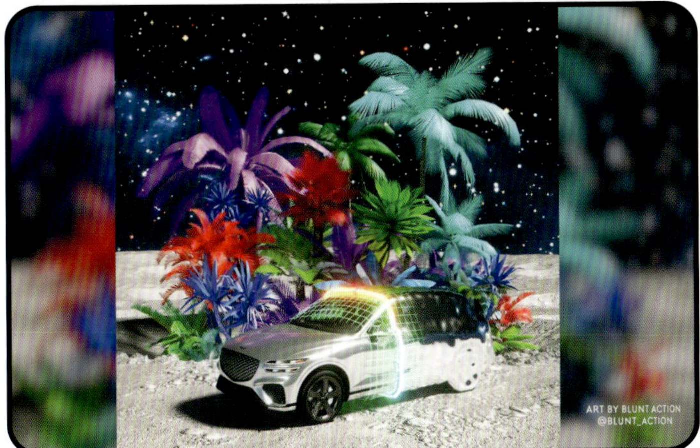

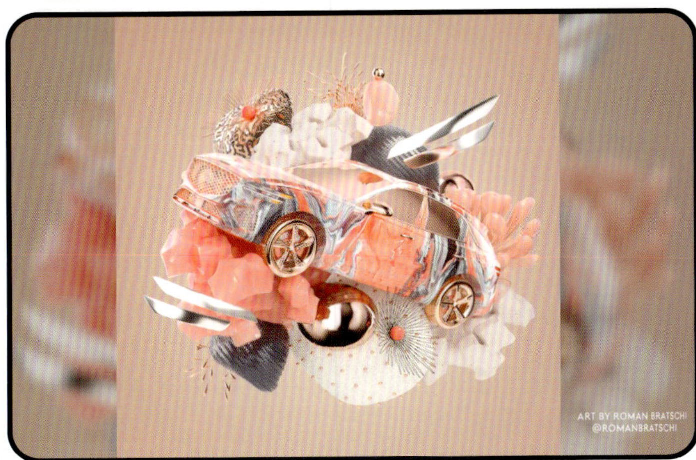

Title: Genesis GV70 "Want Wins" Artist Series
Client: Genesis Motor America
Design Firm: INNOCEAN USA
P256: Credit & Commentary

CLINTON CARLSON

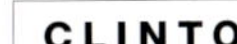

LOGO

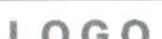

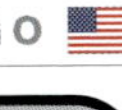

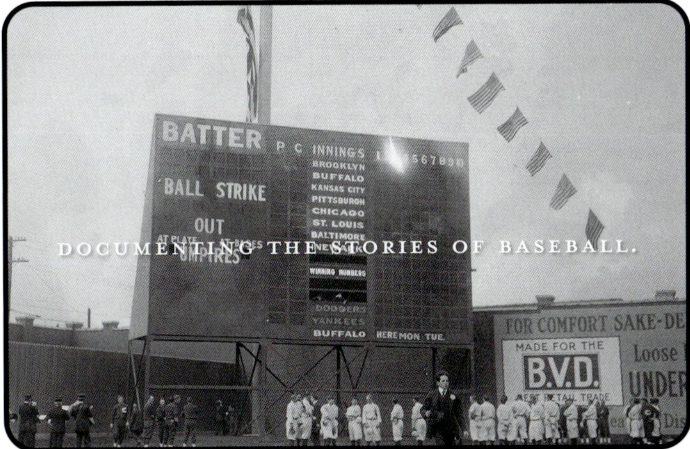

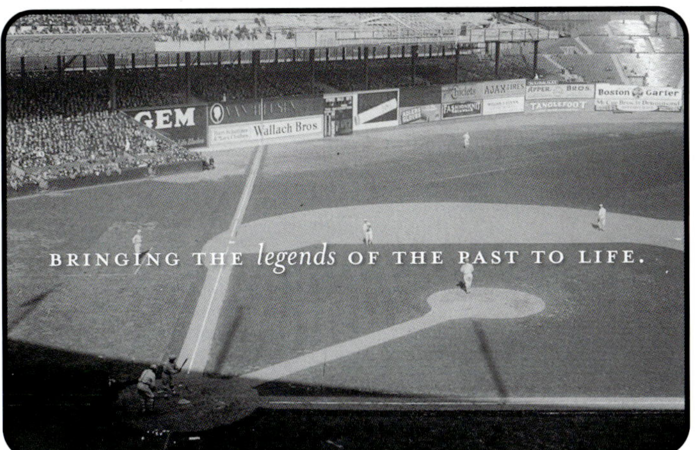

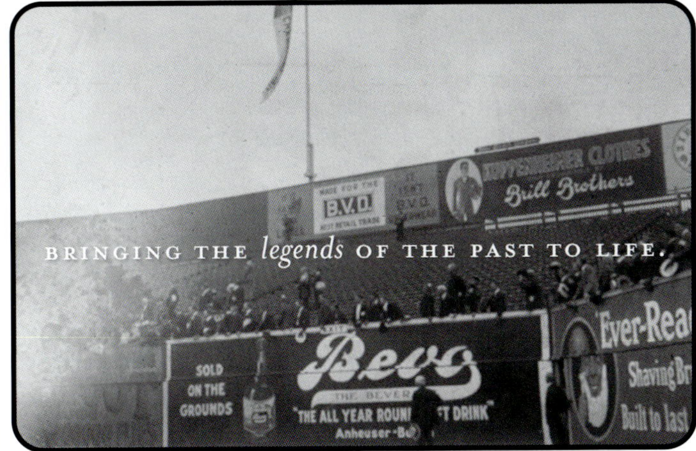

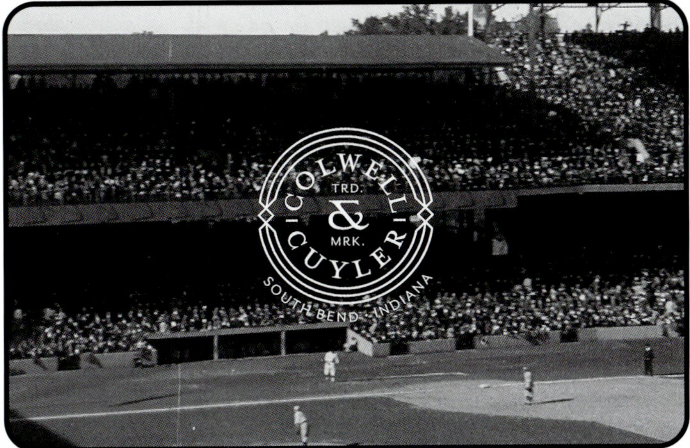

Title: Colwell & Cuyler Brand Identity
Client: Colwell & Cuyler
Design Firms: Clinton Carlson Design, University of Notre Dame
P256: Credit & Commentary

JENNIFER STERLING

ANIMATION 

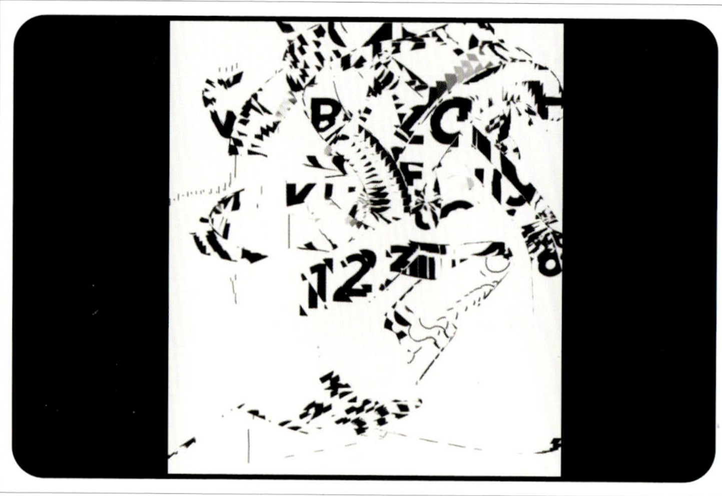

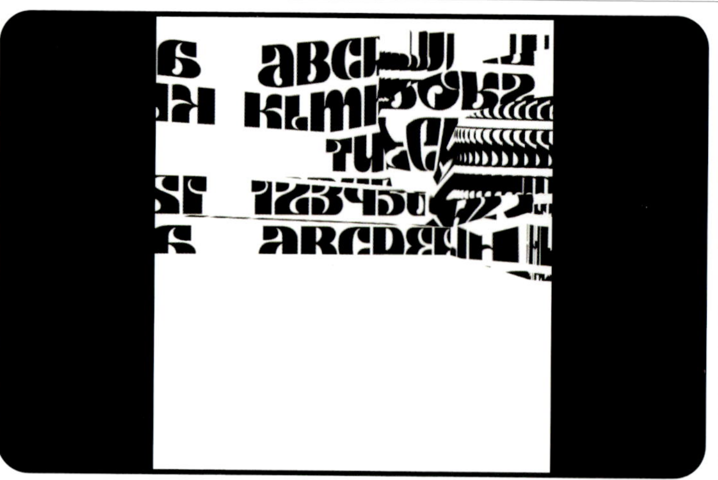

Title: Font Fabric Typographic Series
Client: Font Fabric
Design Firm: Jennifer Sterling Design
P257: Credit & Commentary

ARIEL FREANER

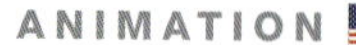

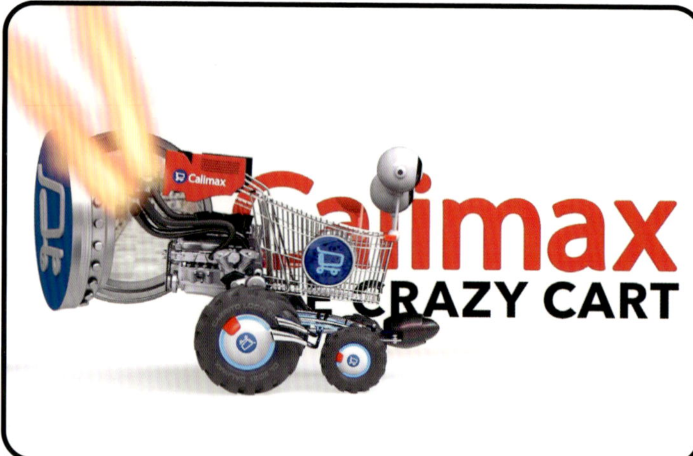

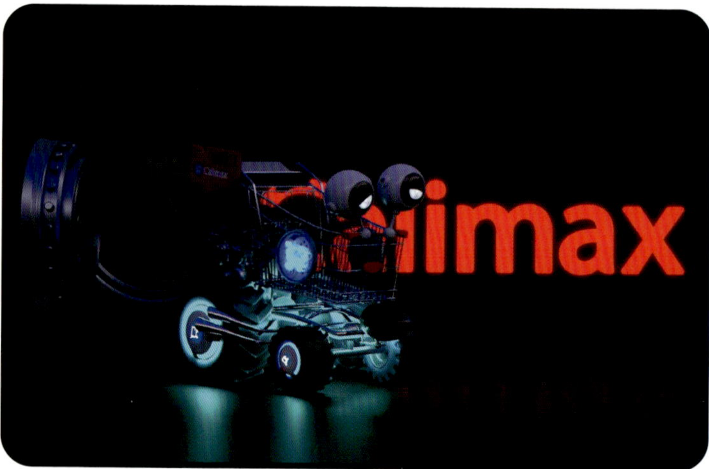

Title: Calimax Crazy Cart - Calimax Carrito Loco
Client: Calimax
Design Firm: Freaner Creative & Design
P257: Credit & Commentary

HAJIME TSUSHIMA

EXHIBIT

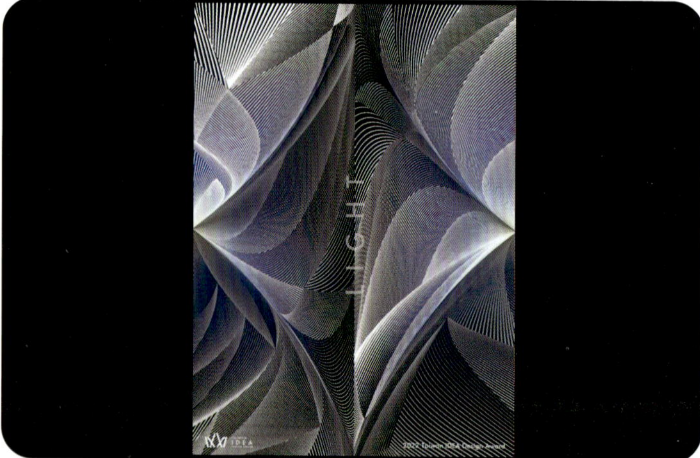

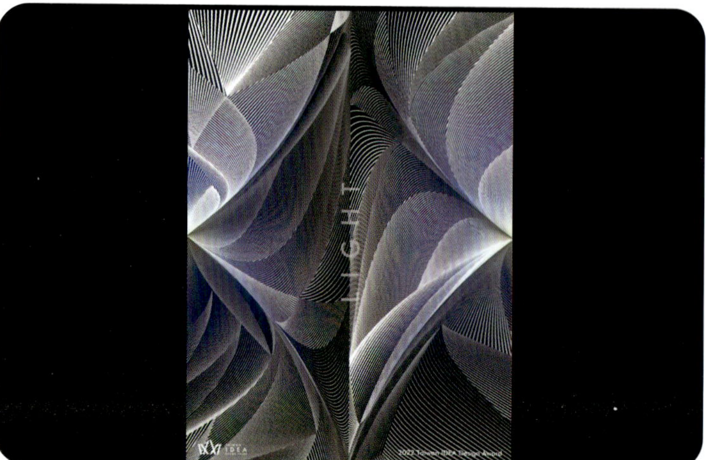

Title: LIGHT
Client: Taichung Advertising Association
Design Firm: Tsushima Design
P257: Credit & Commentary

HAJIME TSUSHIMA

EXHIBIT 

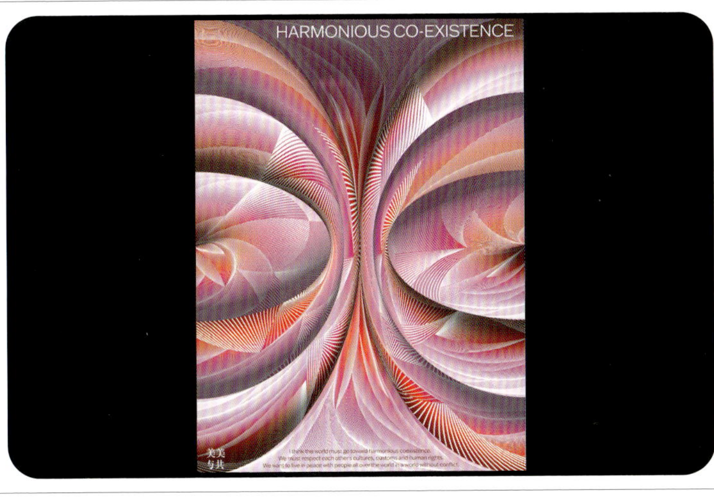

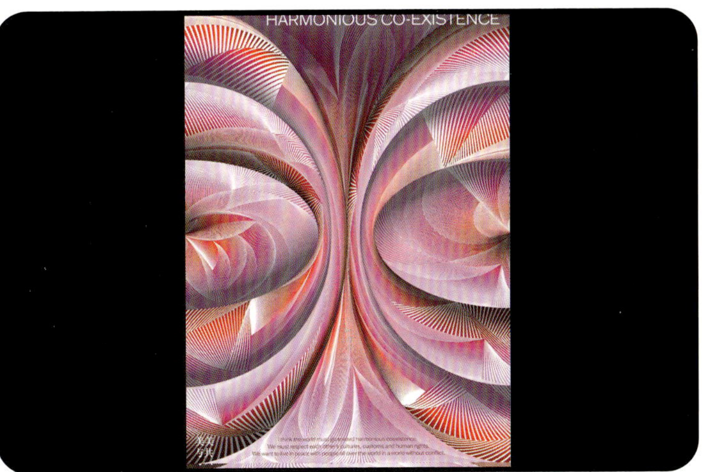

Title: Harmonious Co-Existence
Client: Organizing Committee of "Harmonious Co-Existence" 2022
Design Firm: Tsushima Design
P257: Credit & Commentary

HAJIME TSUSHIMA

EXHIBIT 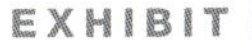

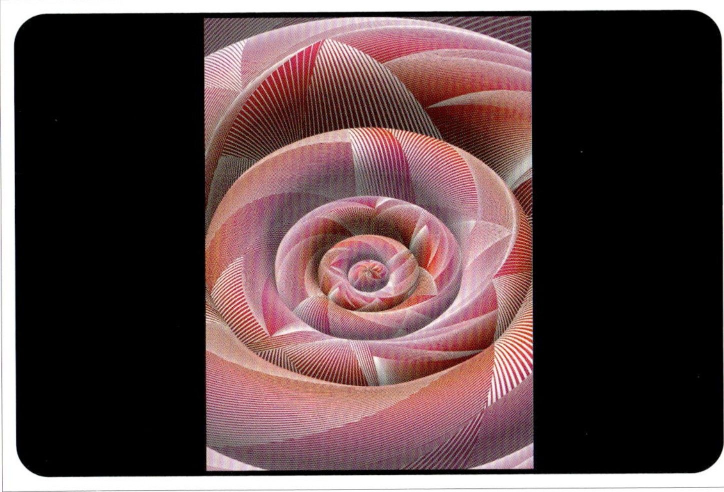

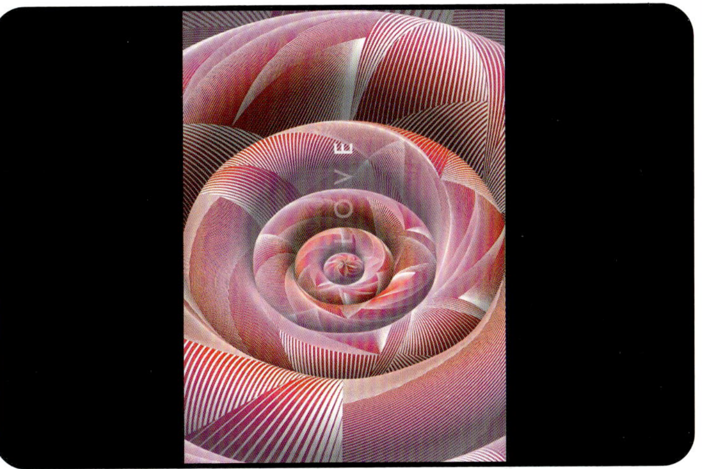

Title: LOVE
Client: Kaohsiung Creators Association
Design Firm: Tsushima Design
P257: Credit & Commentary

PAOLO CATALLA

FILM TITLES

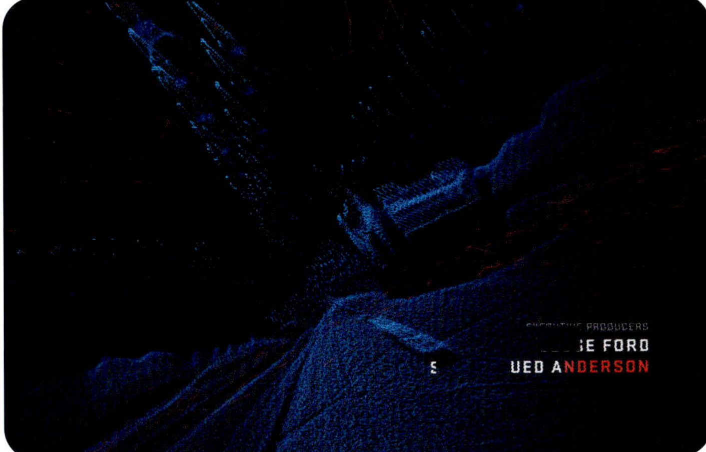

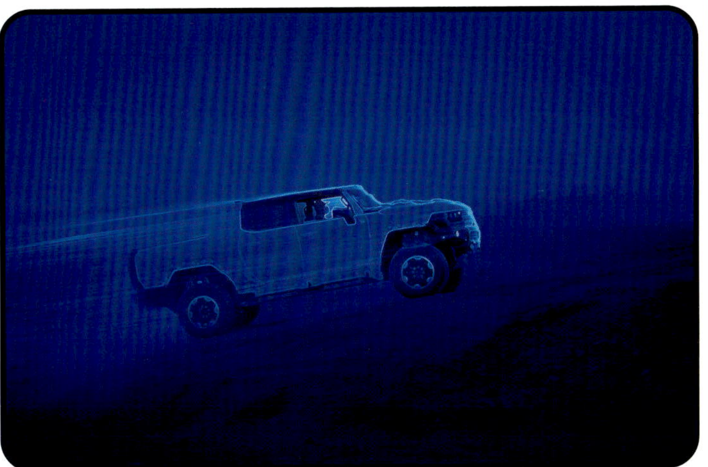

Title: Revolution Title Sequence
Client: General Motors
Design Firm: Paolo Catalla
P257: Credit & Commentary

JENNIFER STERLING

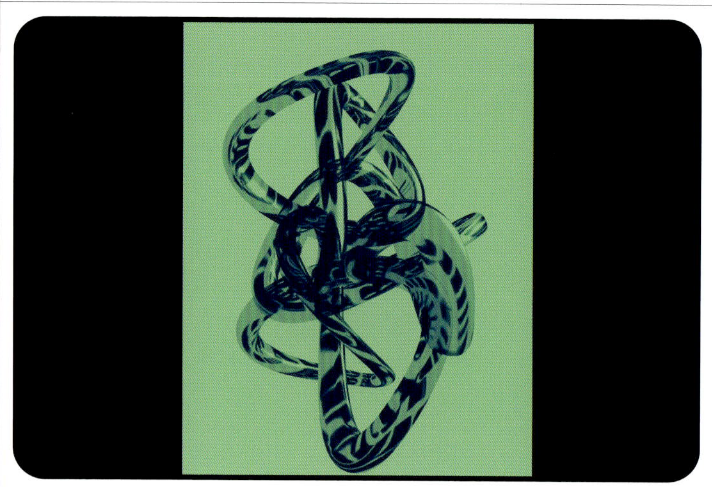

Title: Font Fabric Typographic Campaign
Client: Font Fabric
Design Firm: Jennifer Sterling Design

BARNEY GOLDBERG

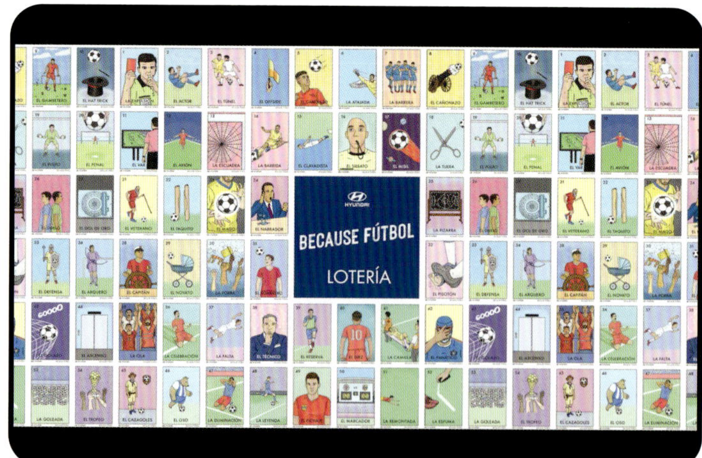

Title: Hyundai Sábado Futbolero 'Because Futbol' Loteria Cards
Client: Hyundai Motor America
Design Firm: INNOCEAN USA

JENNIFER STERLING

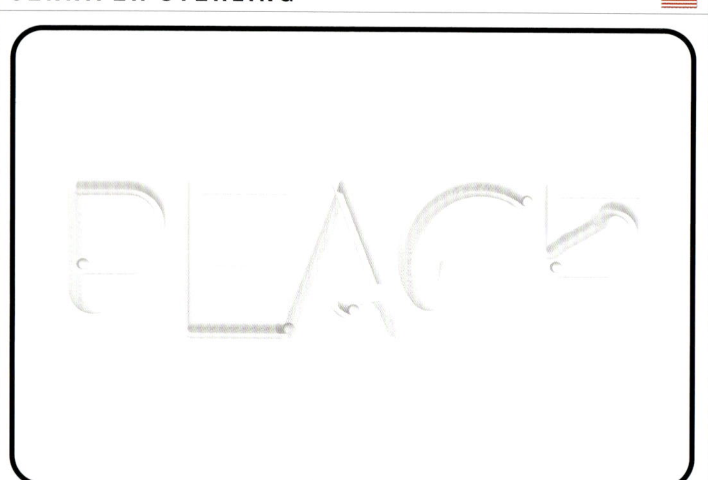

Title: Peace
Client: Self-initiated
Design Firm: Jennifer Sterling Design

ATSUSHI ISHIGURO

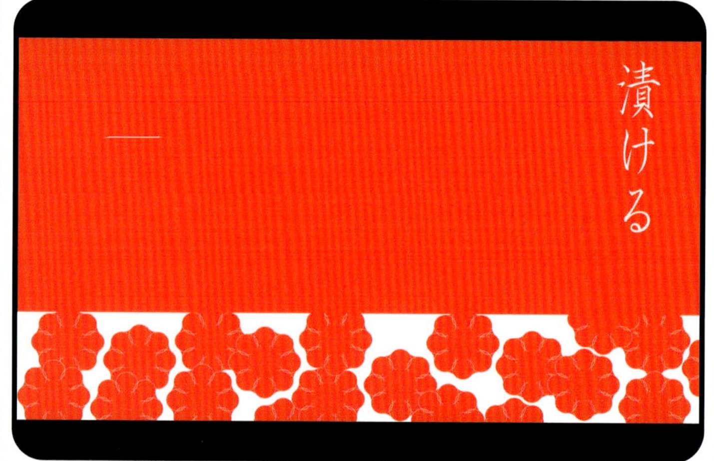

Title: SAKE MIYOSHI FLOWER
Client: Abunotsuru
Design Firm: OUWN

PAOLO CATALLA

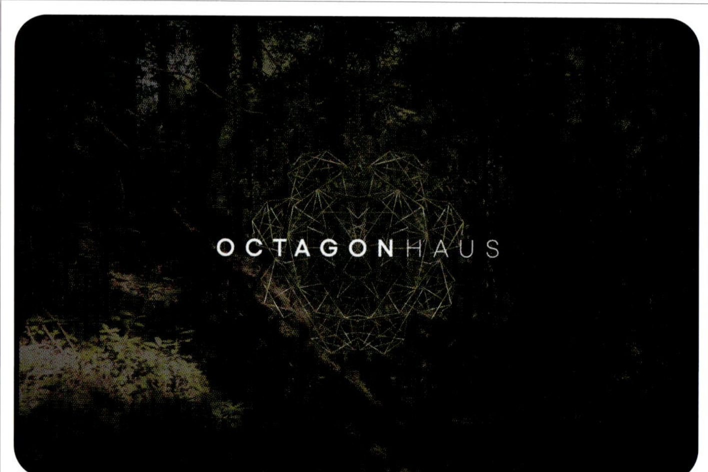

Title: Octagon Haus Brand Animation
Client: Octagon Haus
Design Firm: Paolo Catalla

SONALI MESTRI

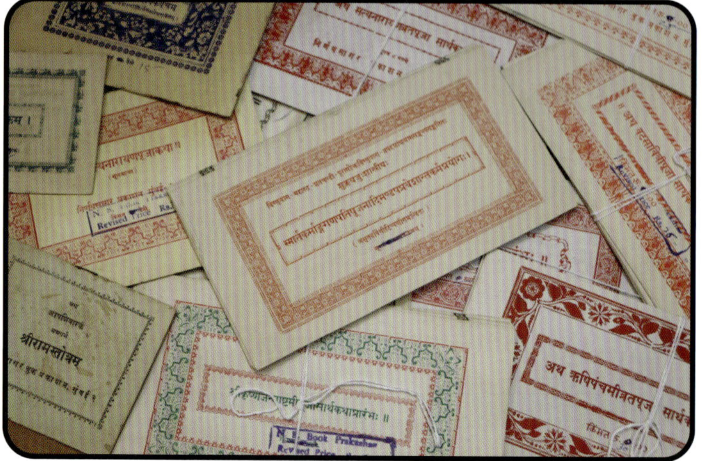

Title: 'AksharaSadhana' Letterpress Printing in Devanagari Script - Documentary Film
Client: Self-initiated
Design Firm: Sir J.J. Institute of Applied Art

YU CHEN

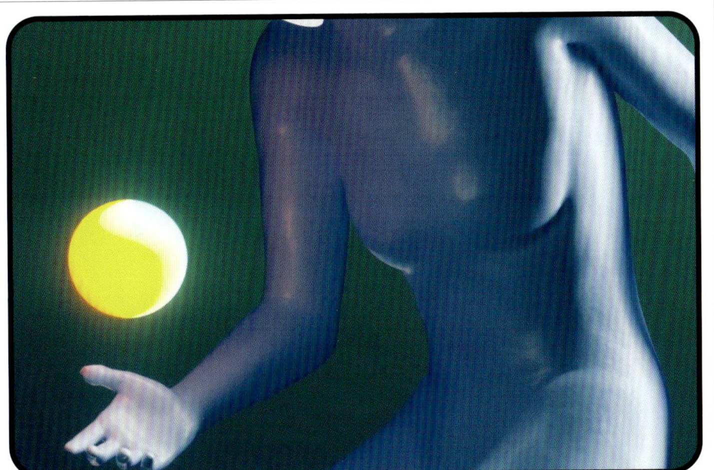

Title: School of the Art Institute of Chicago - ArtBash 2022
Client: Self-initiated
Design Firm: School of the Art Institute of Chicago

WORLD HEALTH ORGANIZATION AFRICA

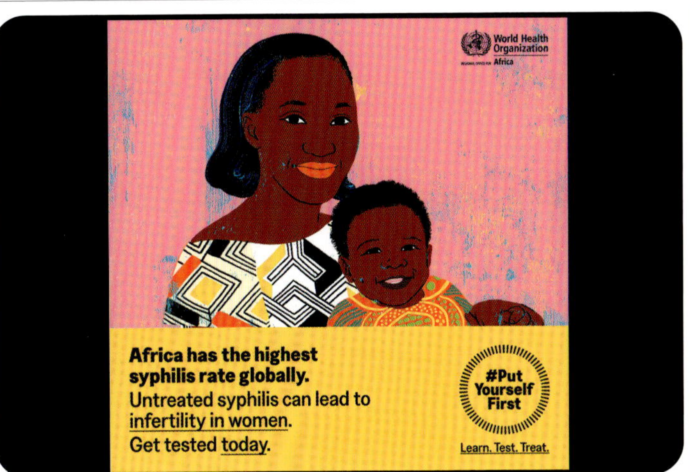

Title: World Health Organization Africa – Put Yourself First
Client: World Health Organization Africa
Design Firm: Ahoy Studios

JONATHAN ALGER, AMY SIEGEL

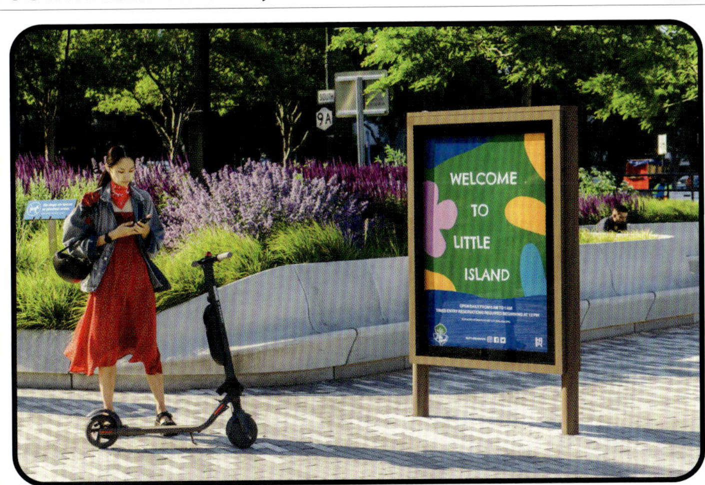

Title: Signage & Graphics for a Floating Park
Client: Little Island
Design Firm: C&G Partners

JONATHAN ALGER

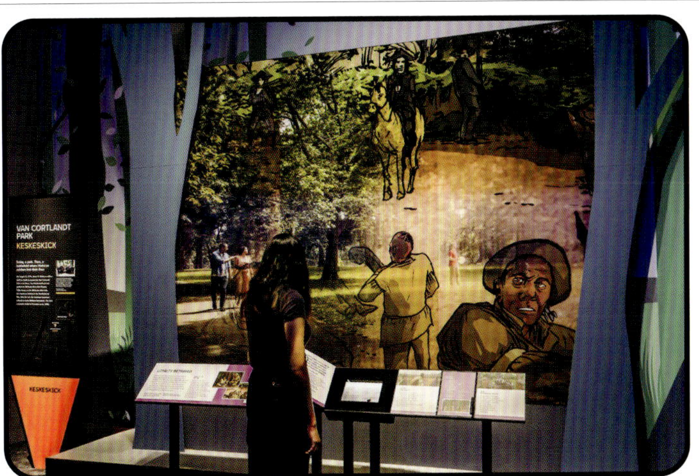

Title: Native New York
Client: Smithsonian Institution's National Museum of the American Indian
Design Firm: C&G Partners

JEFF SCIORTINO

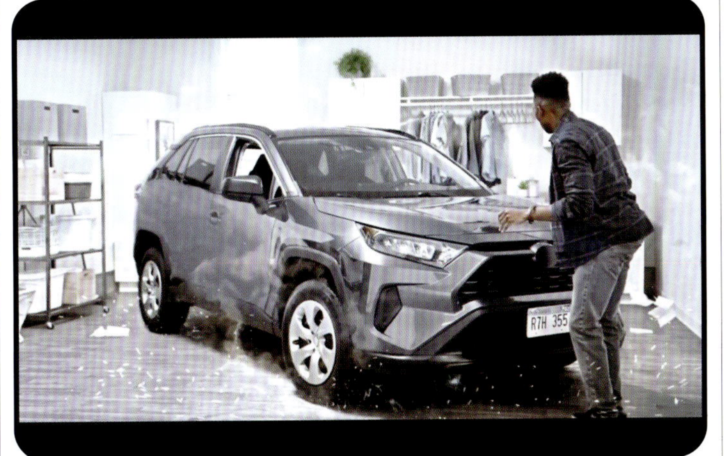

Title: Next-Level Recycling
Client: U.S. Steel
Design Firm: Conjure

LAUREN BEAUCHEMIN, LAUREN JONES (+5)

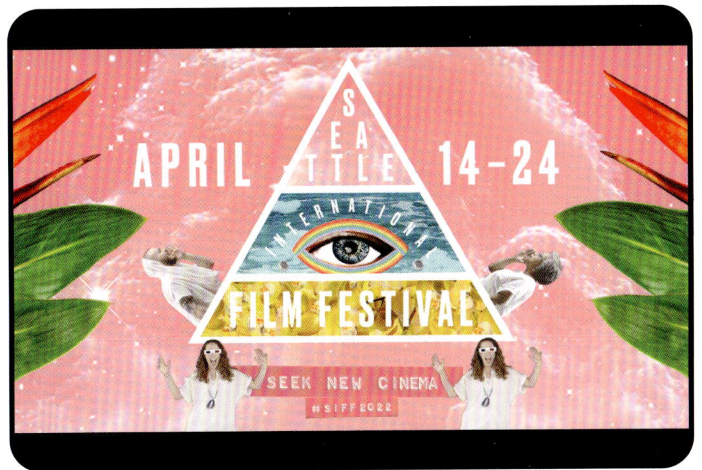

Title: Seek New Cinema Festival Trailer
Client: Seattle International Film Festival
Design Firm: WONGDOODY

JENNIFER STERLING DESIGN

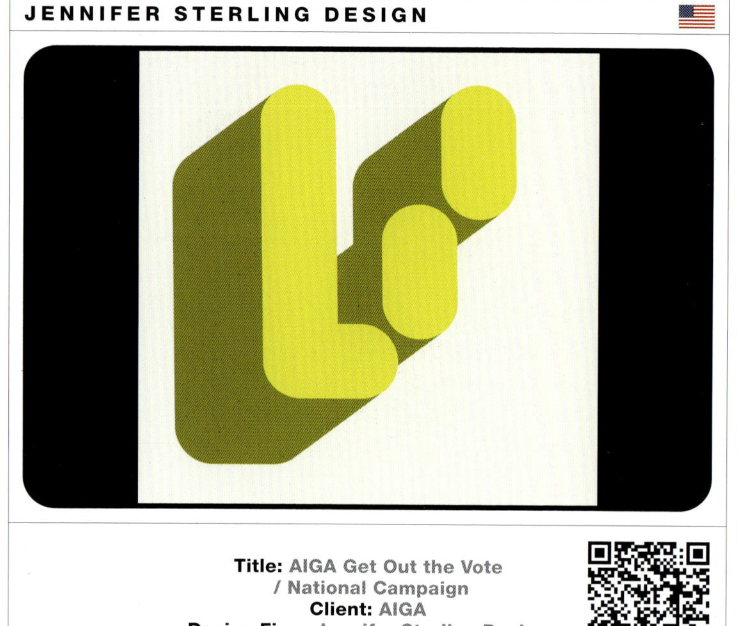

Title: AIGA Get Out the Vote / National Campaign
Client: AIGA
Design Firm: Jennifer Sterling Design

JENNIFER STERLING DESIGN

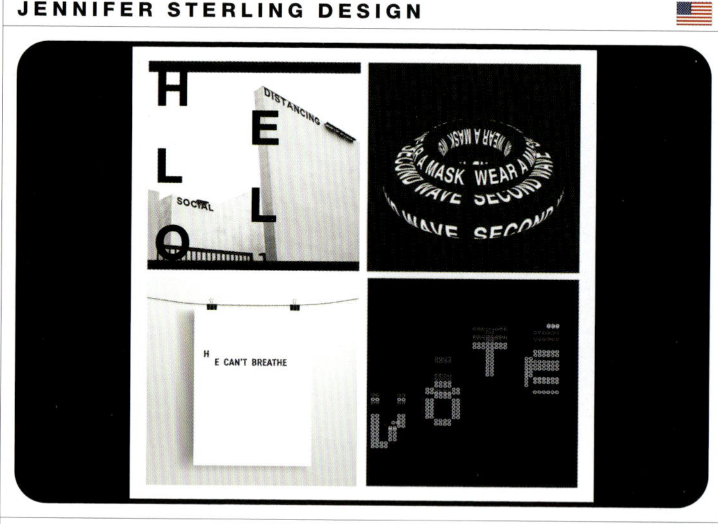

Title: 2020 in 4 Images
Client: Self-initiated
Design Firm: Jennifer Sterling Design

Thank you for the good experience of seeing works from various categories that I would not normally have the chance to see, which was very stimulating and influential. **Masahiro Aoyagi,** *Art Director & Graphic Designer, Toppan Inc.*

One after one, design competitions around the world have been hijacked by mediocrity and an explosion of people who now conflate fame with mastery.

However, what jumps out, as always, is extraordinary with the independent and small design companies still pioneering, still leading the way, still showing how it's done. **Brian Collins,** *Designer, Creative Director, & Educator, COLLINS*

Graphis Honorable Mentions

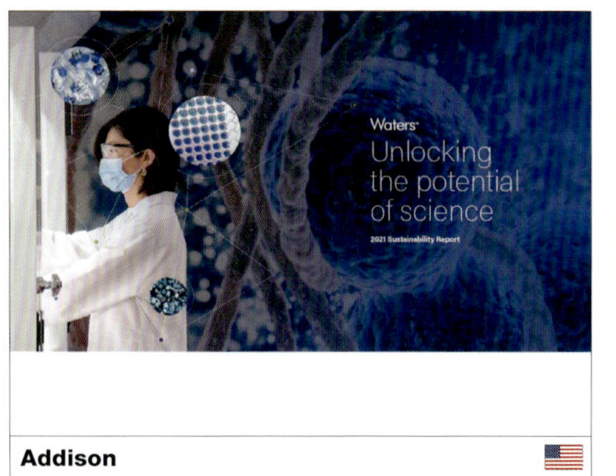

Addison

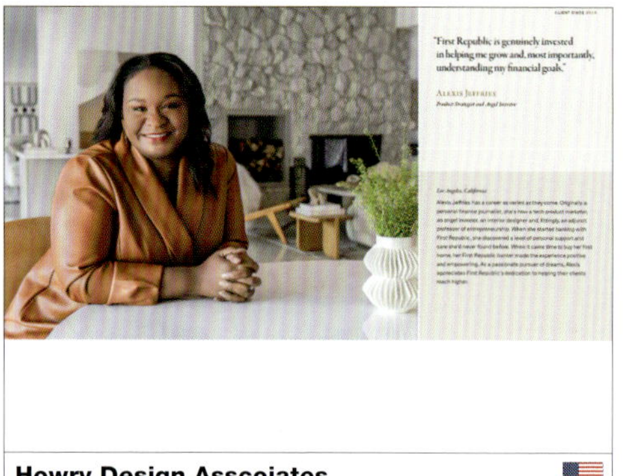

Howry Design Asscoiates

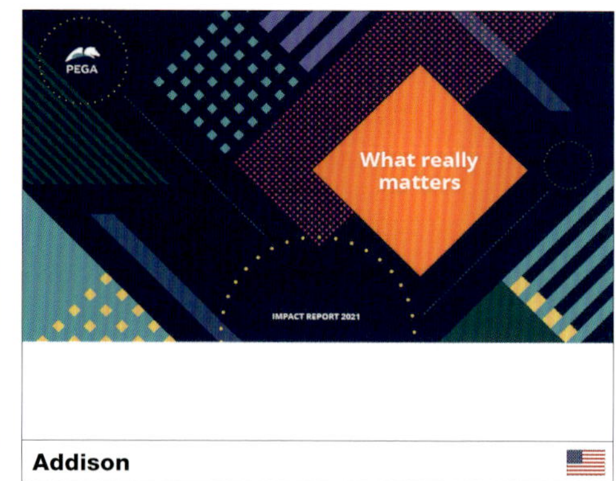

Addison

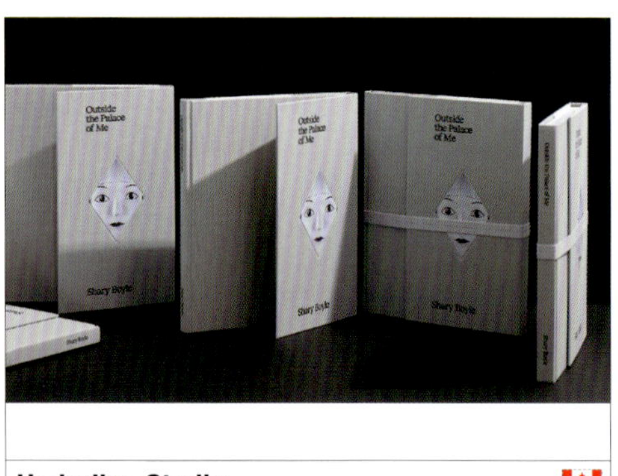

Underline Studio

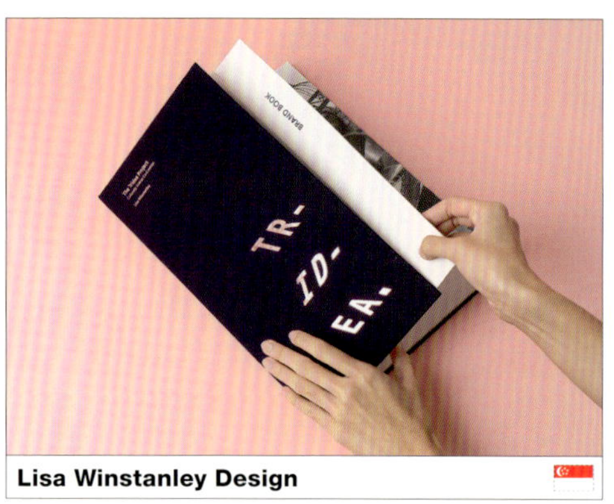

Lisa Winstanley Design

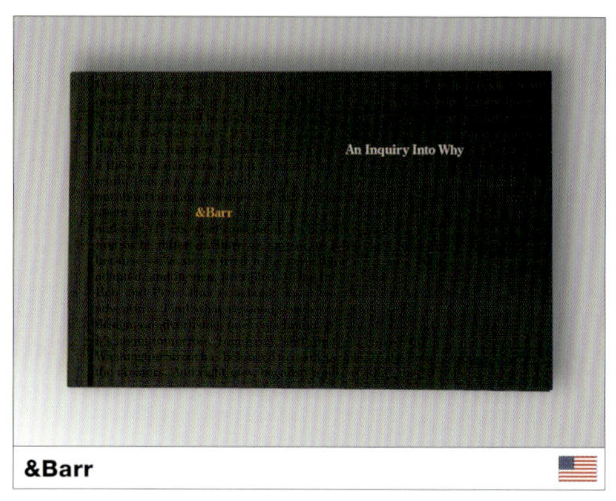

&Barr

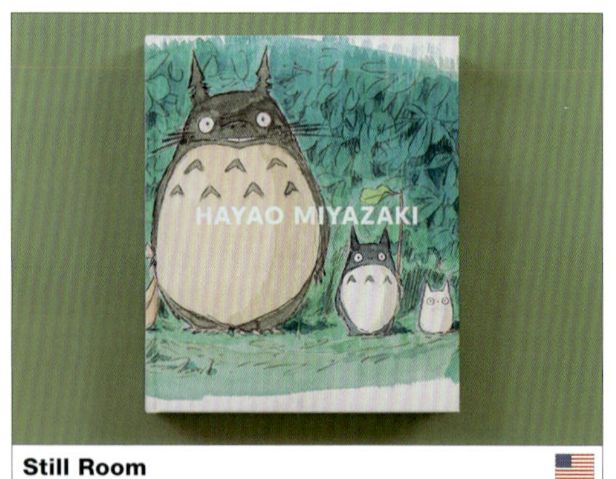

Still Room

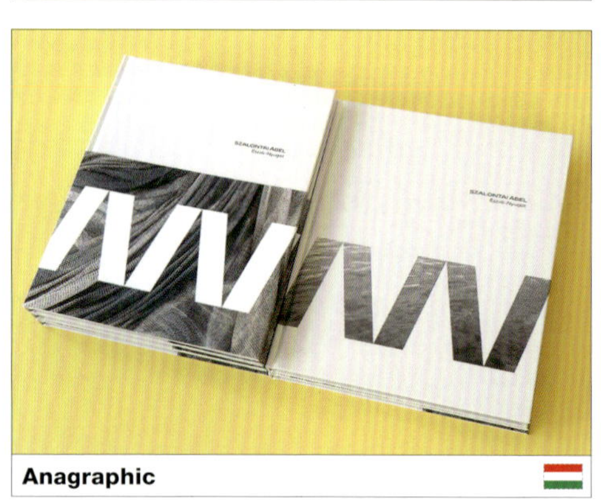

Anagraphic

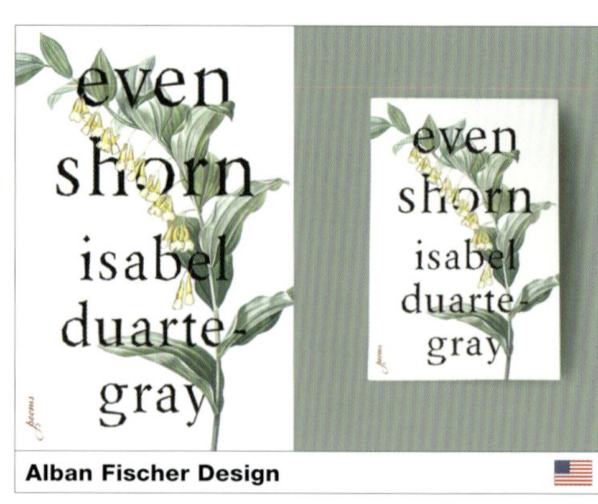

Alban Fischer Design

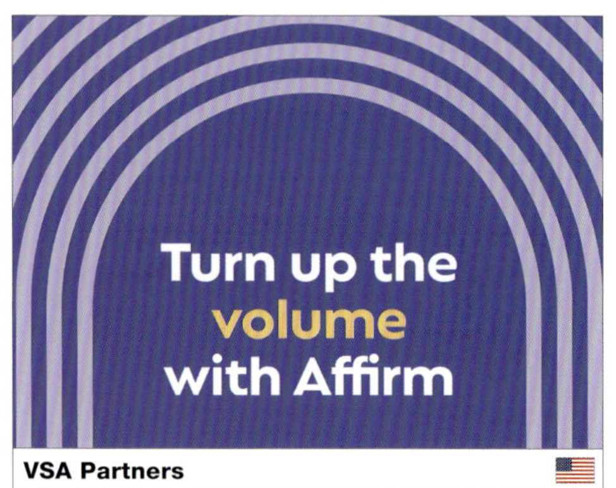

VSA Partners

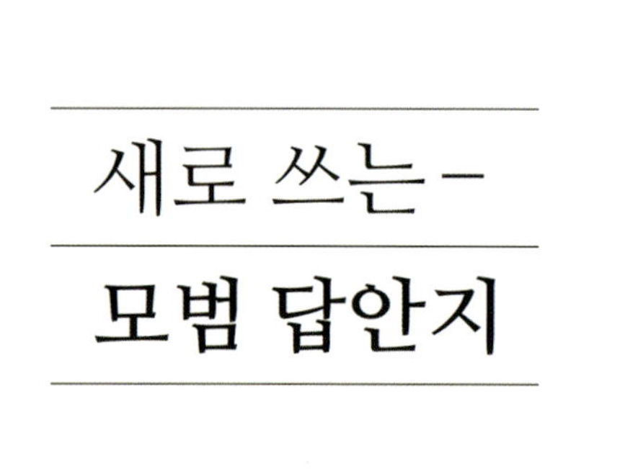

Jang Won Lee

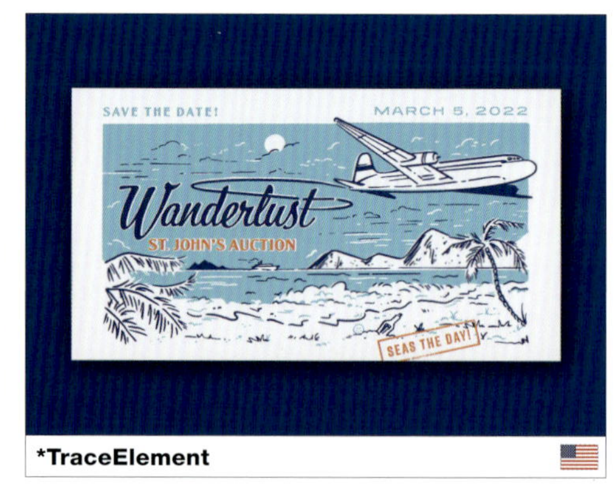

*TraceElement

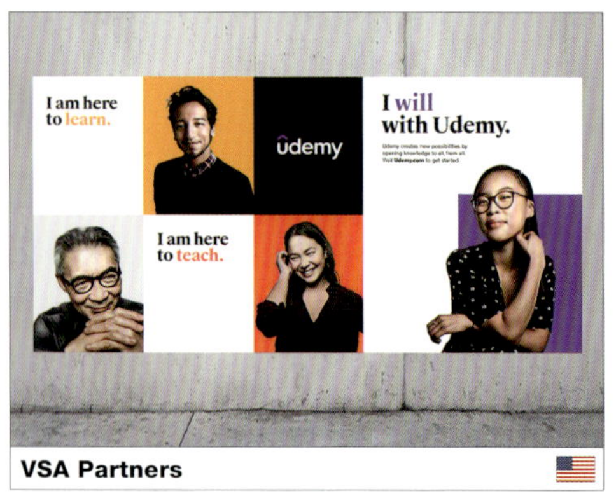

VSA Partners

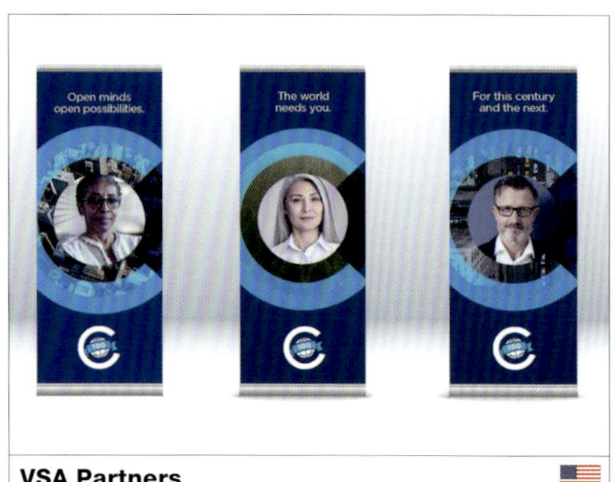

VSA Partners

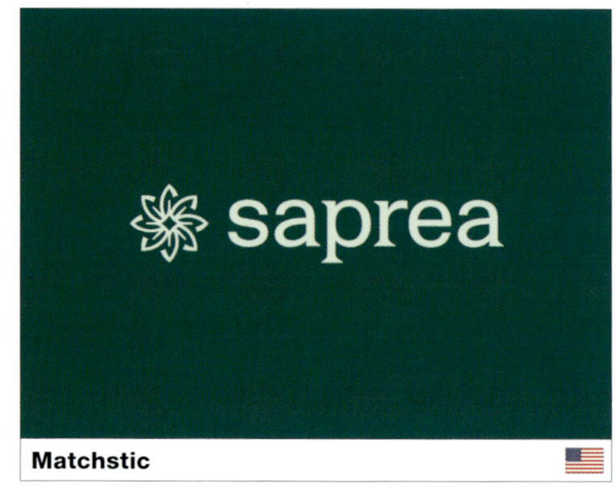

Matchstic

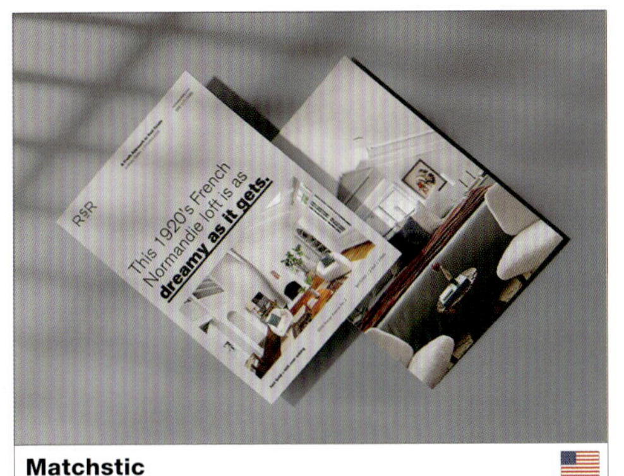

Matchstic

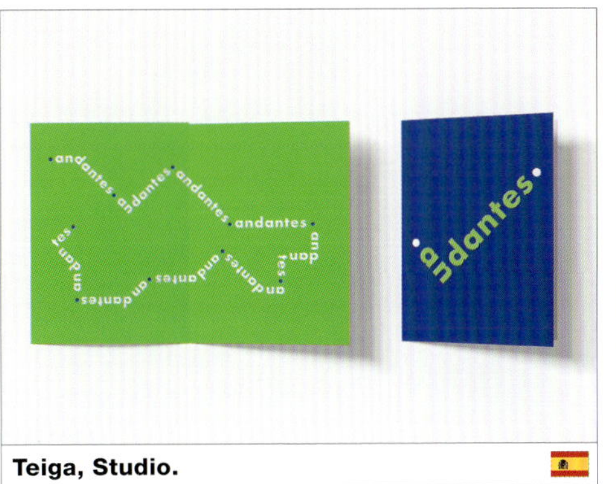

Teiga, Studio.

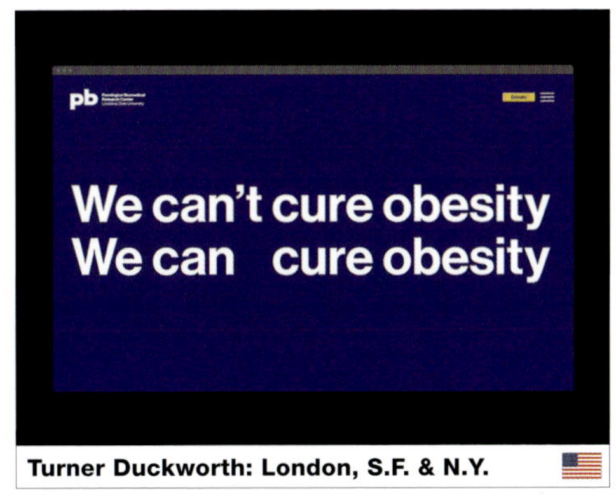

Turner Duckworth: London, S.F. & N.Y.

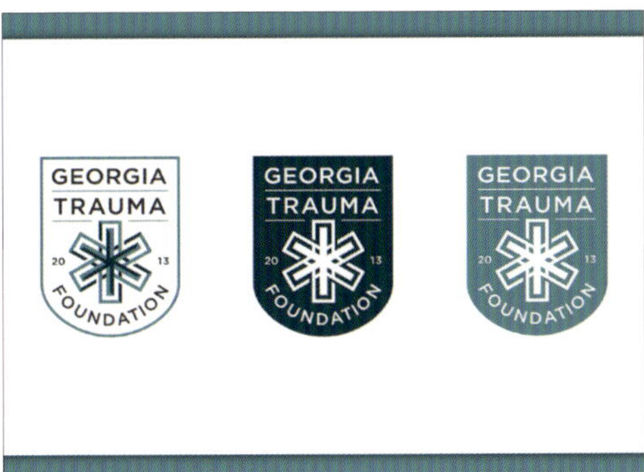

Resource Branding

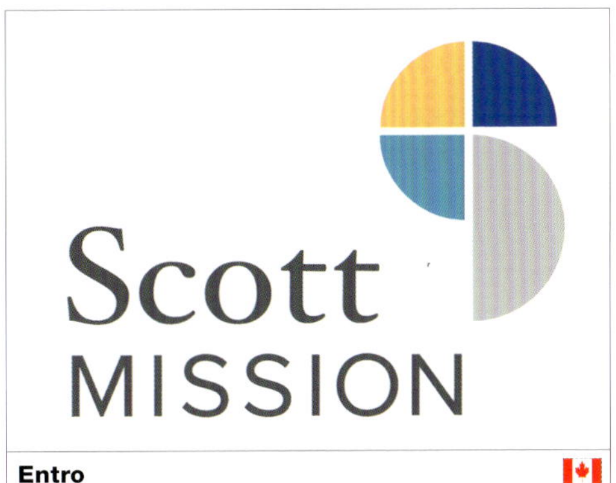

Entro

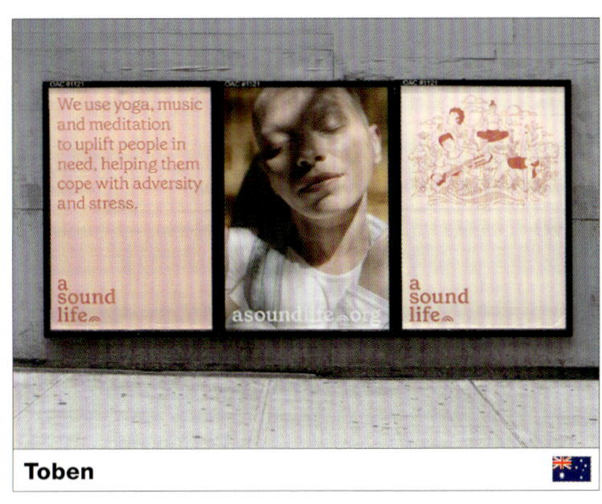

Toben

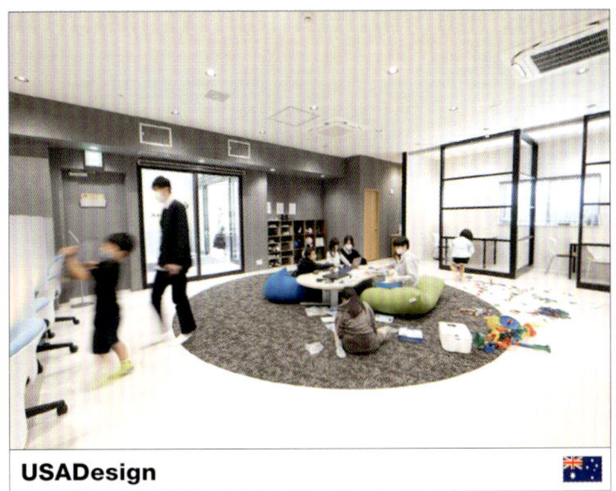

USADesign

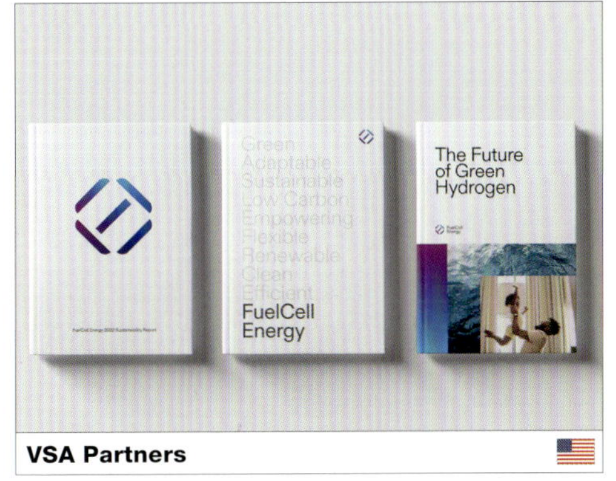

VSA Partners

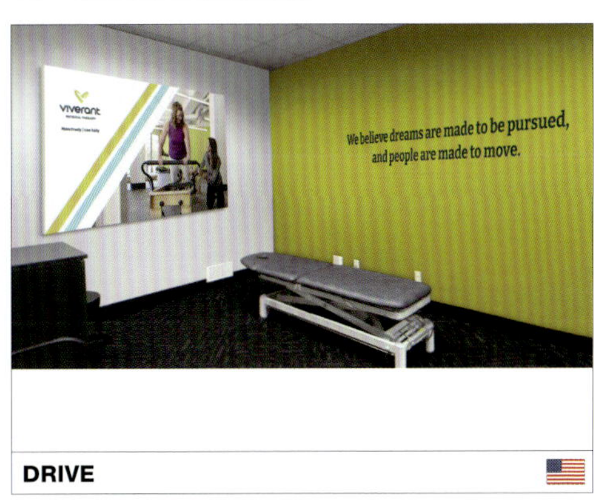

DRIVE

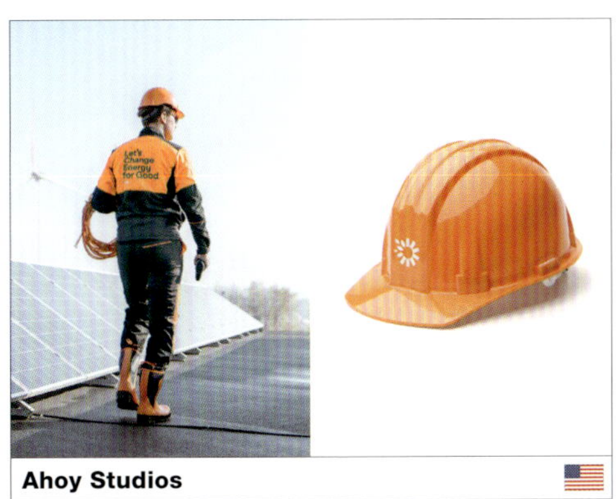

Ahoy Studios

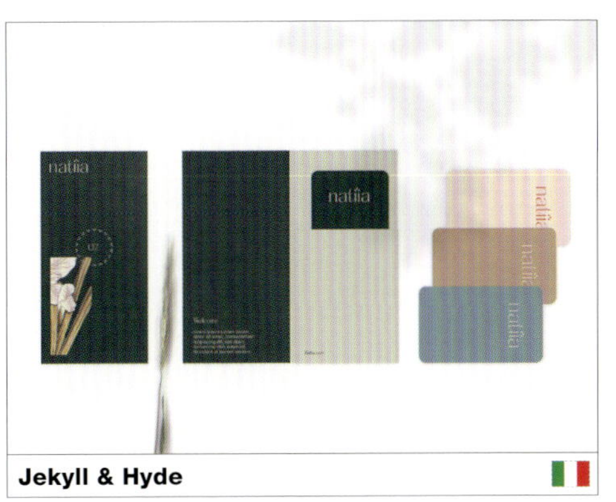

Jekyll & Hyde

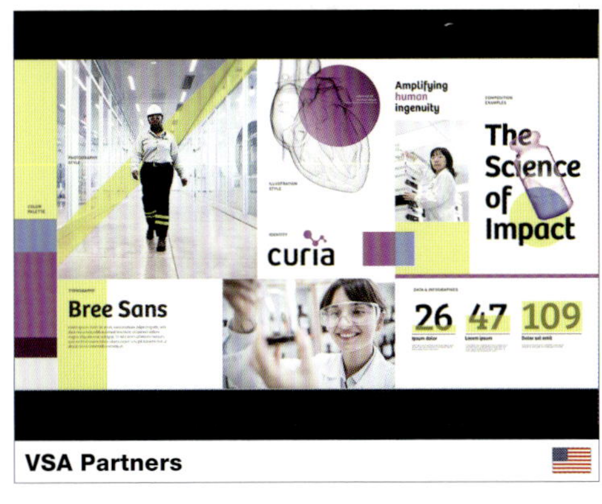

VSA Partners

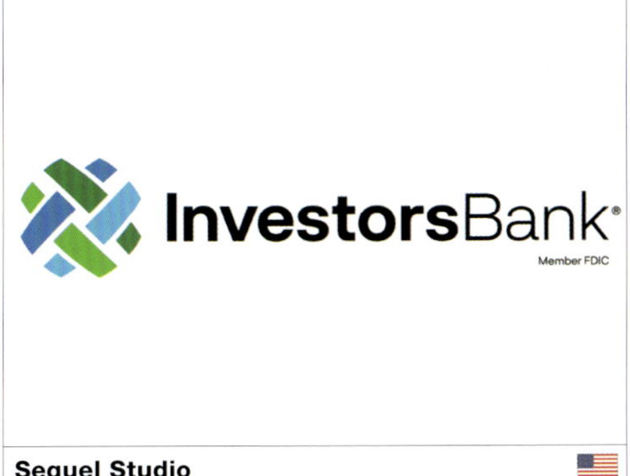

Sequel Studio

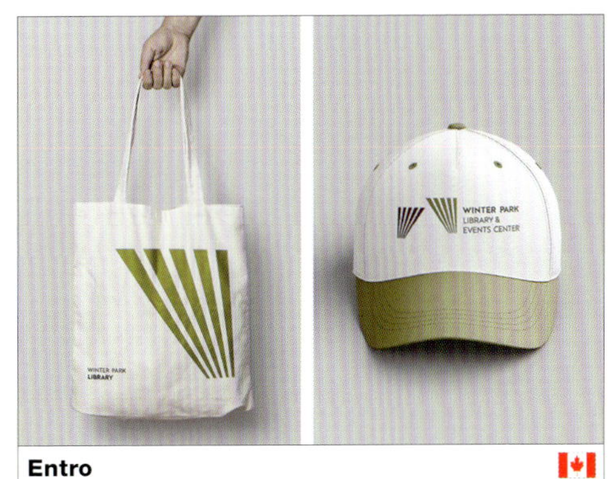

Entro

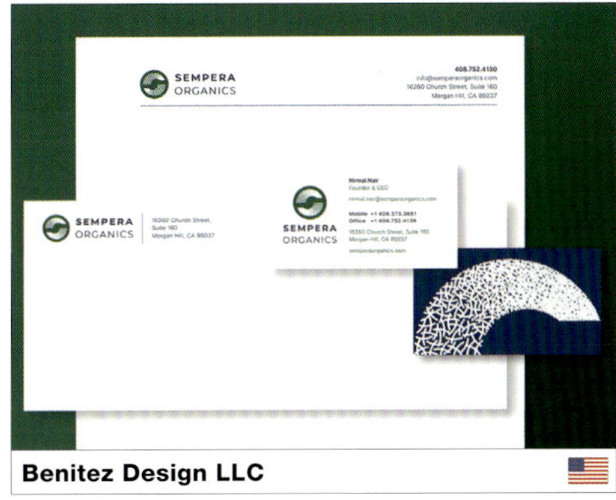

Benitez Design LLC

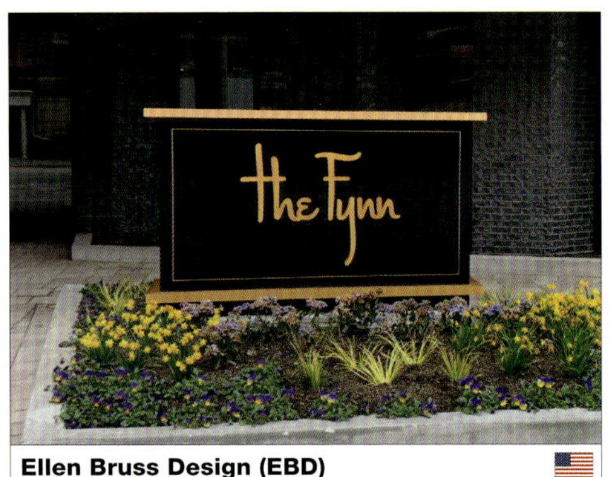

Ellen Bruss Design (EBD)

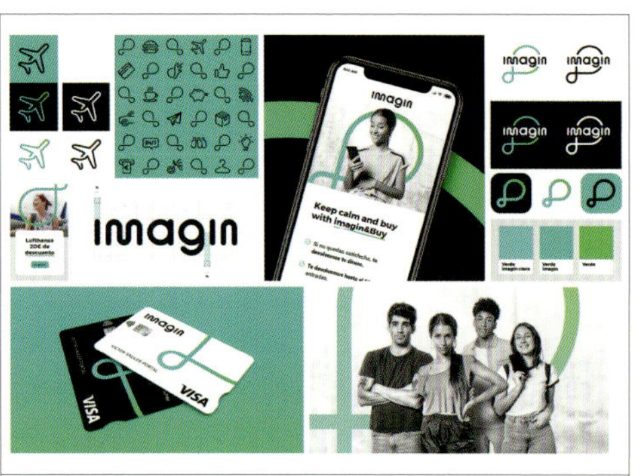

Caldas Naya

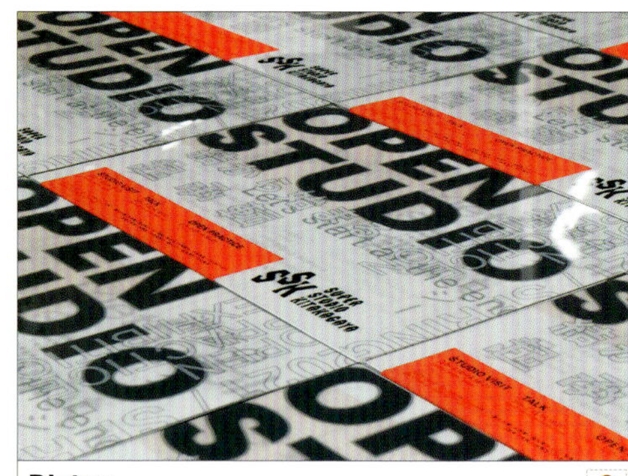

Diotop

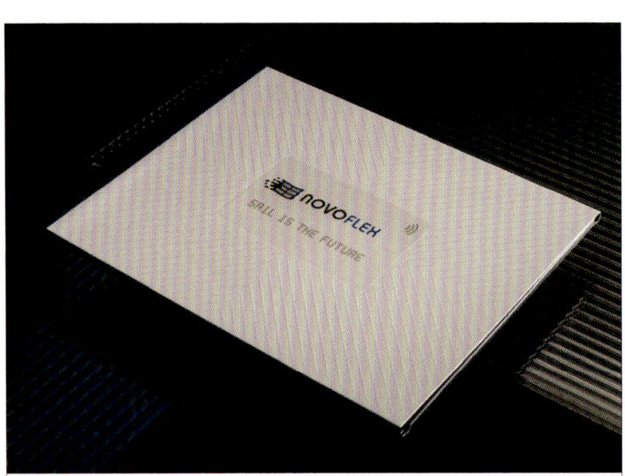

FACTORY

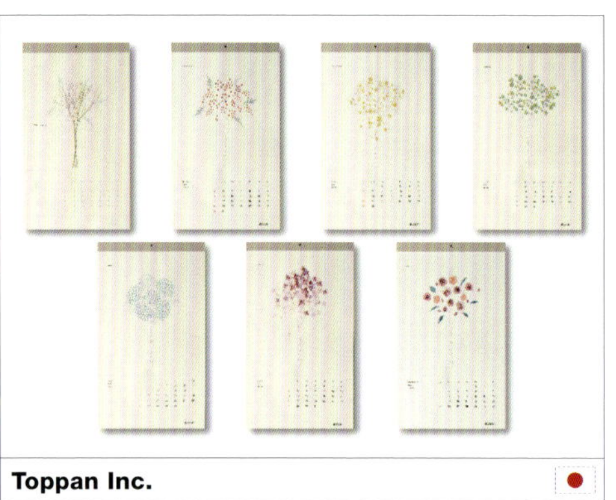
Toppan Inc.

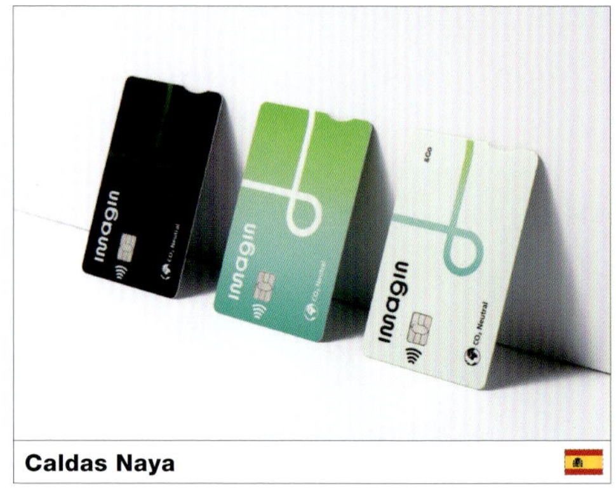

Caldas Naya

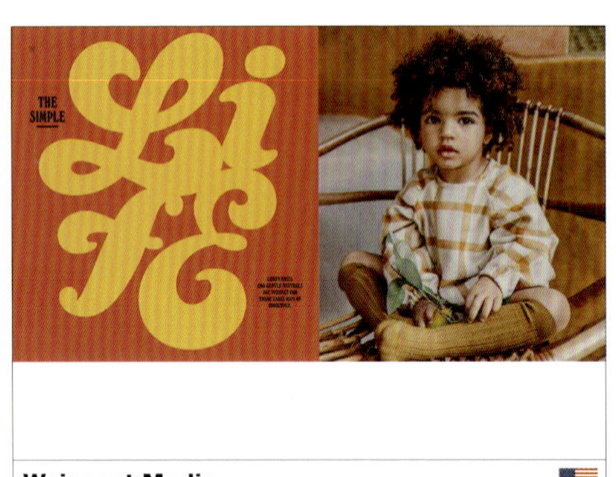

Wainscot Media

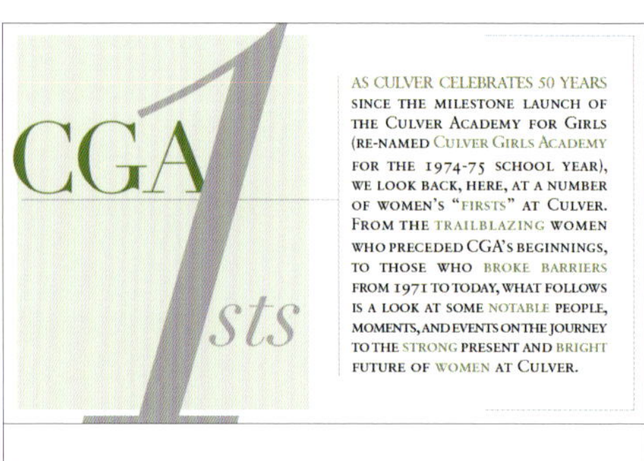

Scott Adams Design Associates

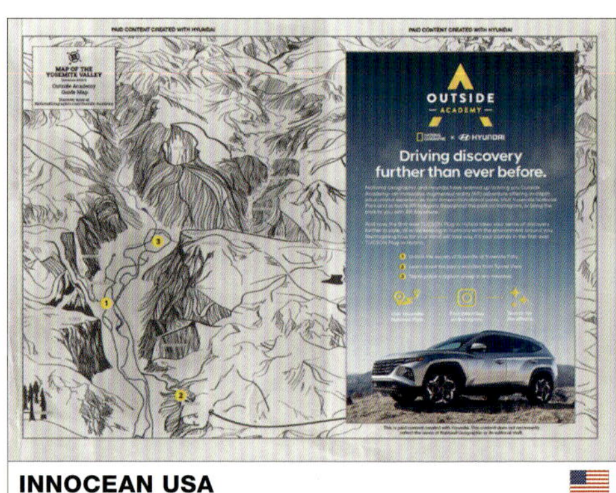

INNOCEAN USA

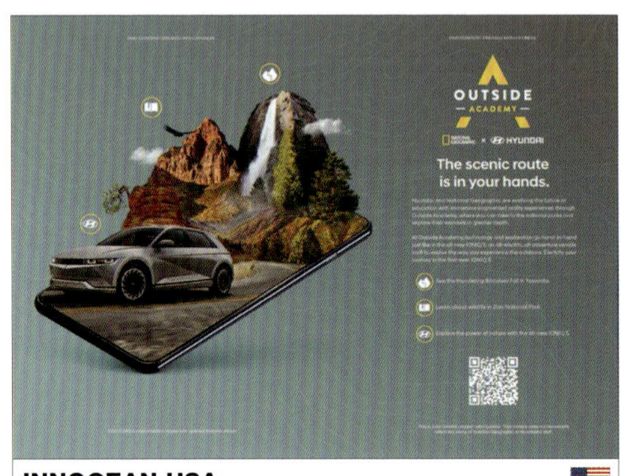

INNOCEAN USA

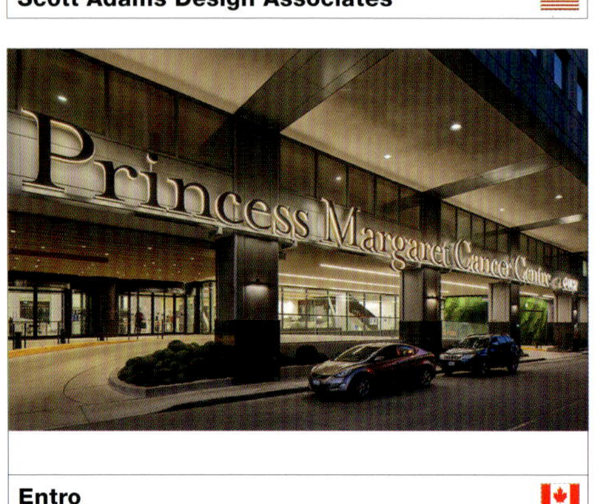

Entro

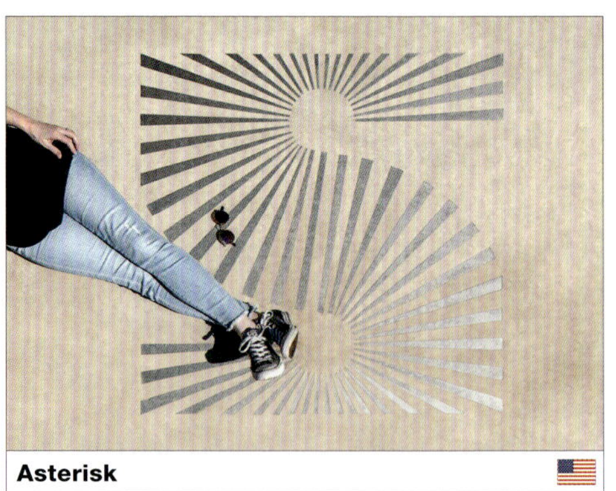
Asterisk

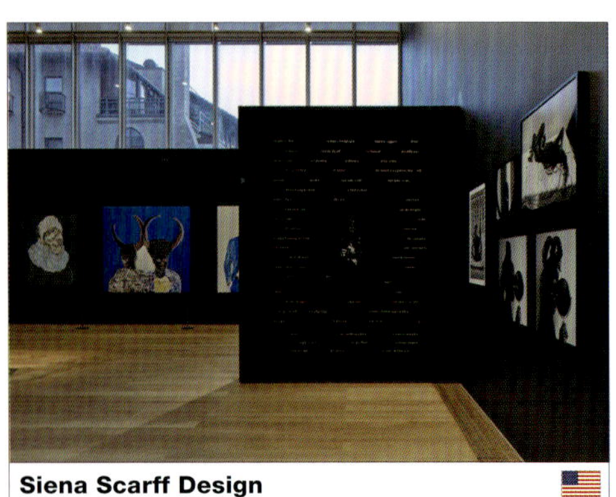
Siena Scarff Design

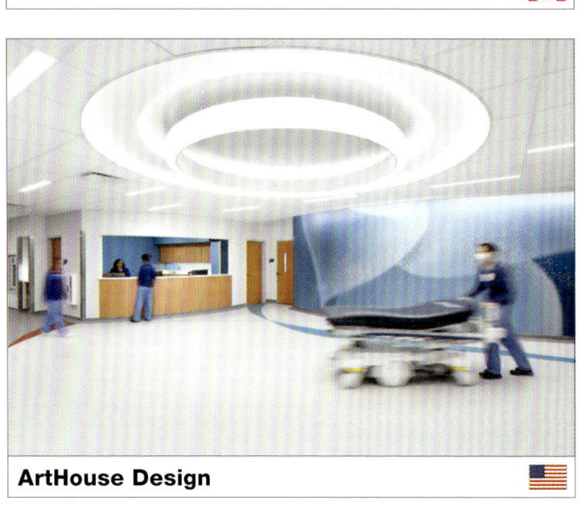
ArtHouse Design

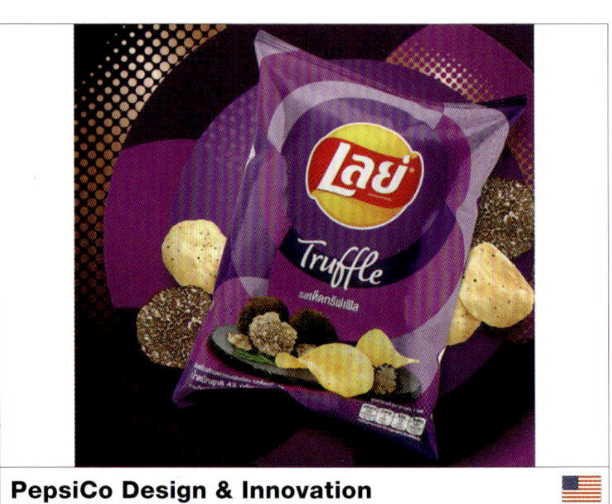

PepsiCo Design & Innovation

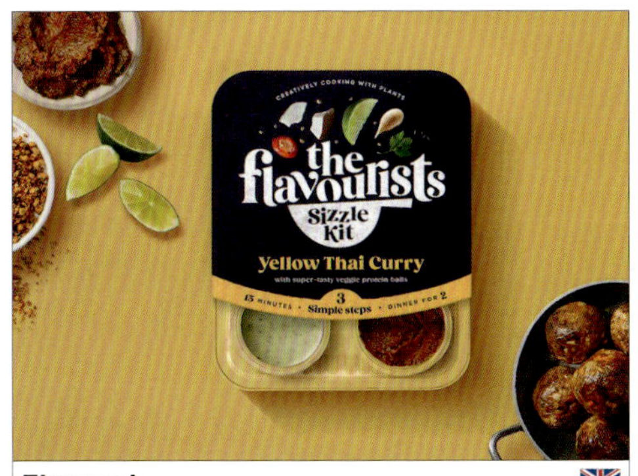

Elmwood

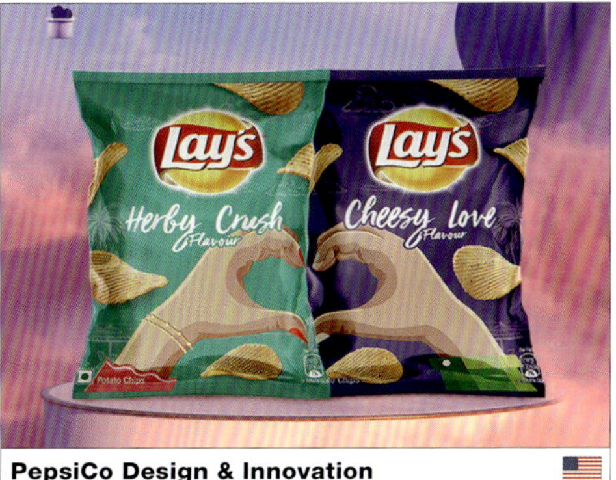

PepsiCo Design & Innovation

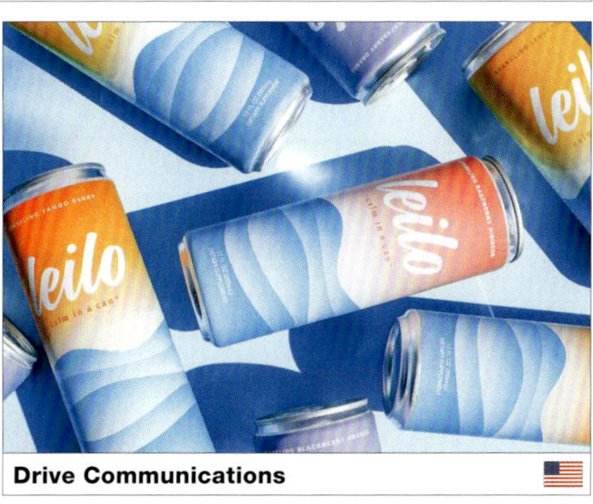

Drive Communications

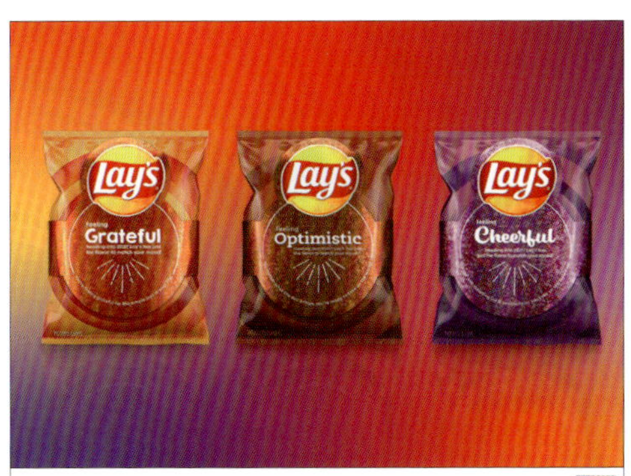

PepsiCo Design & Innovation

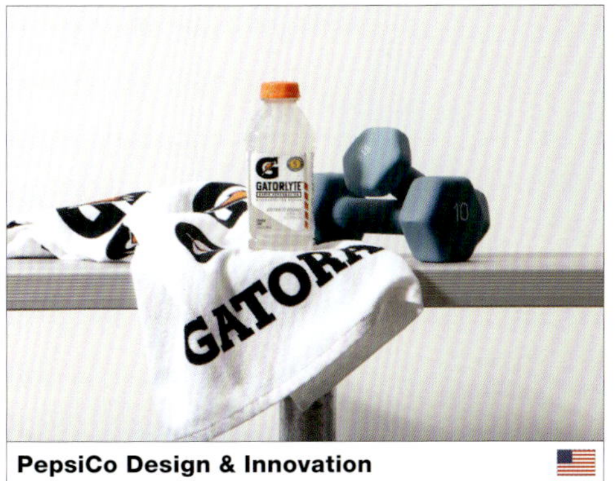

PepsiCo Design & Innovation

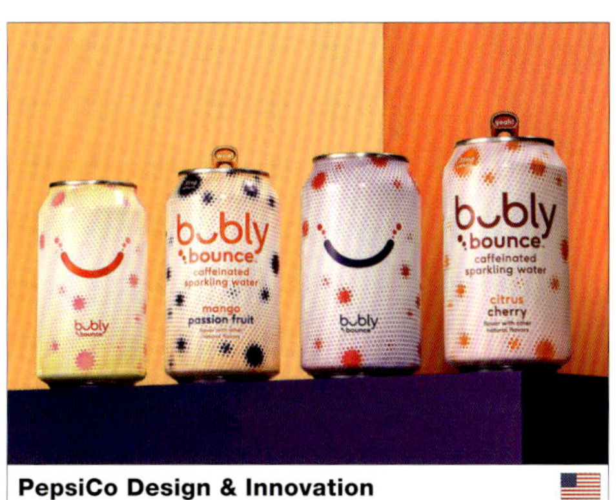

PepsiCo Design & Innovation

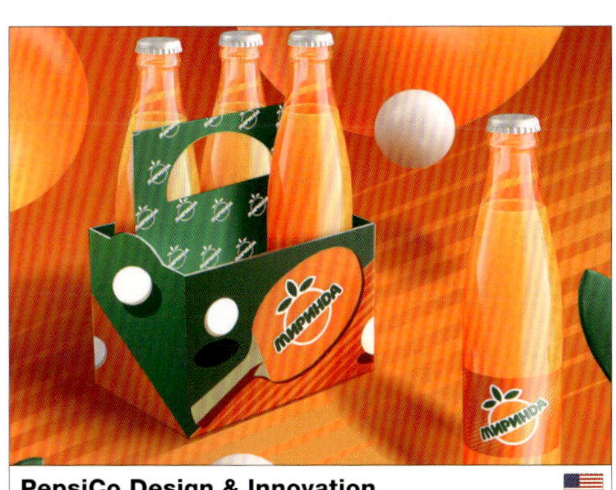

PepsiCo Design & Innovation

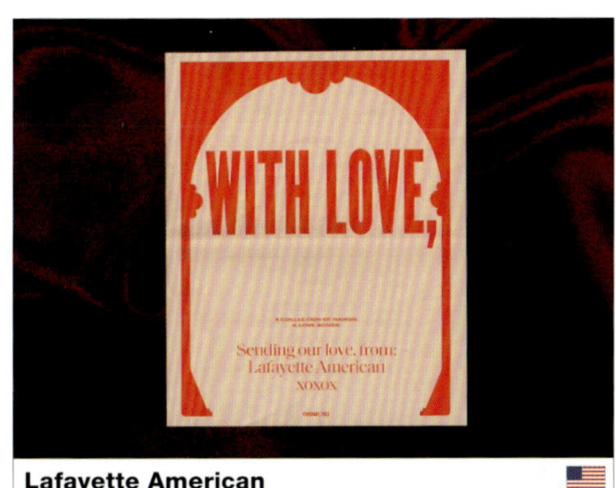

Lafayette American

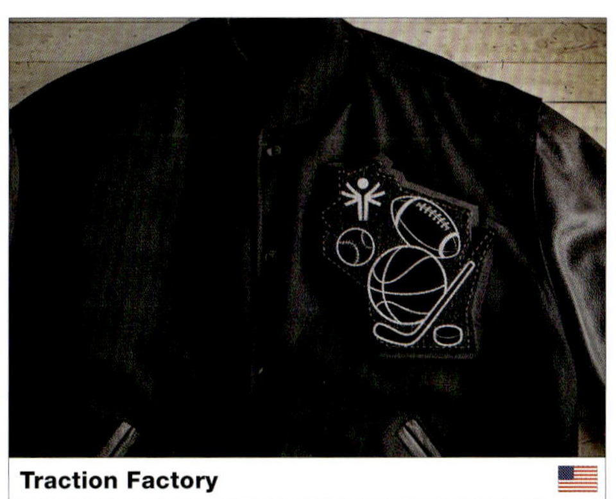

Traction Factory

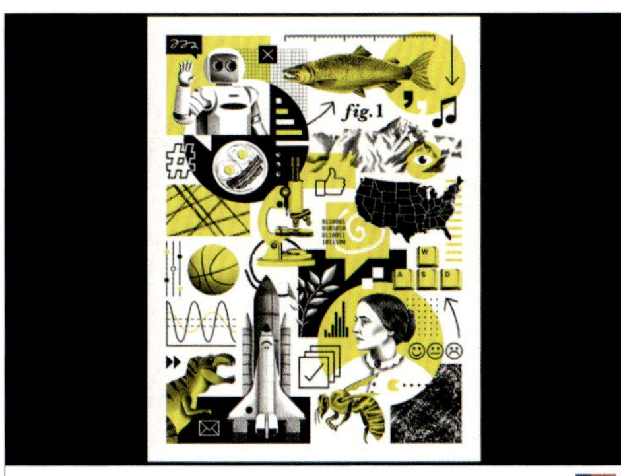

*TraceElement

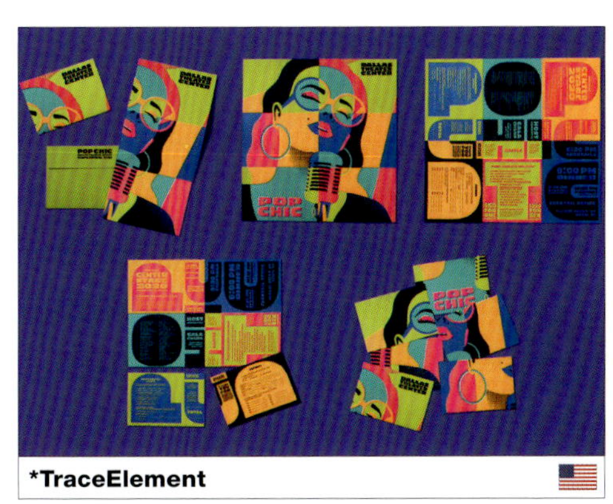

*TraceElement

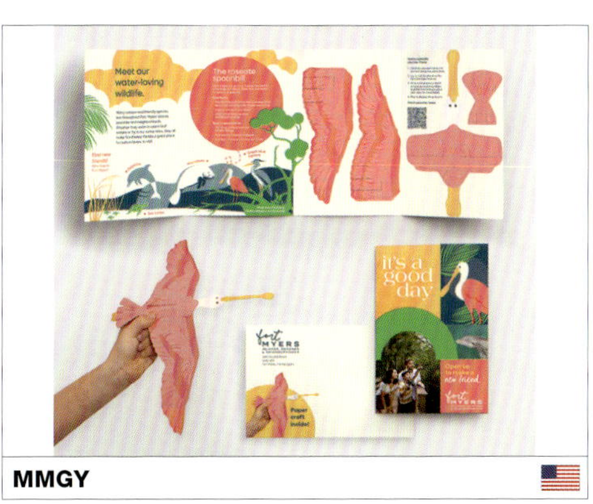

MMGY

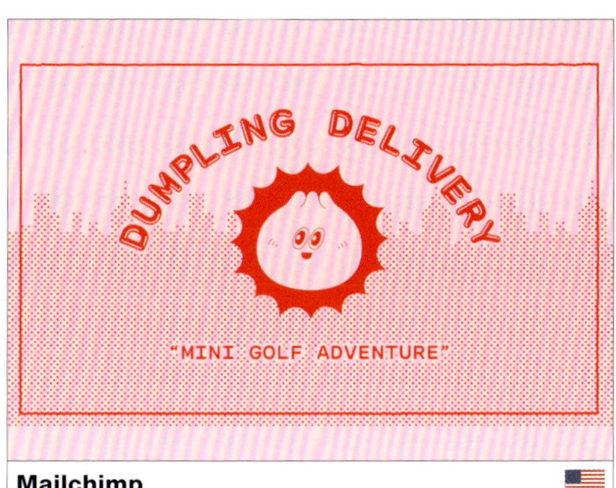

Mailchimp

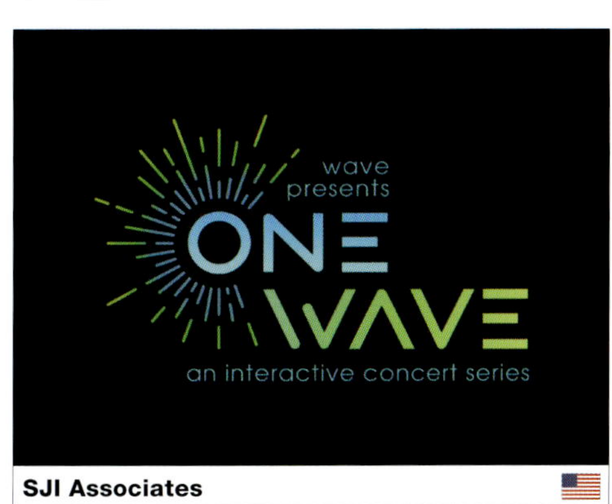

SJI Associates

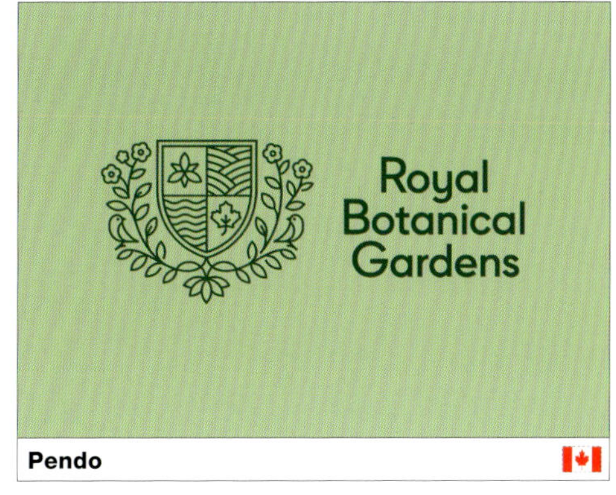

Pendo

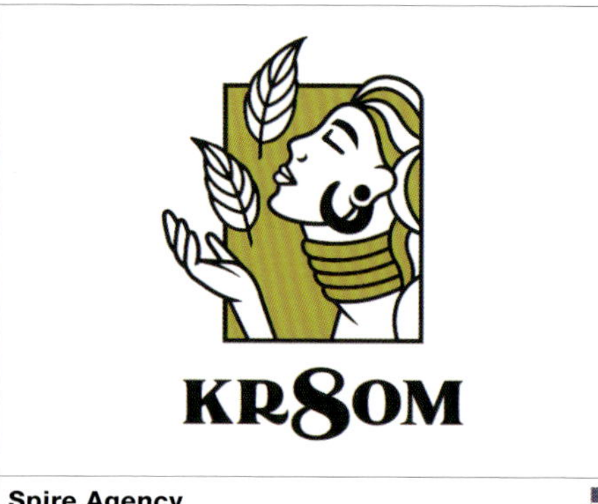

Spire Agency

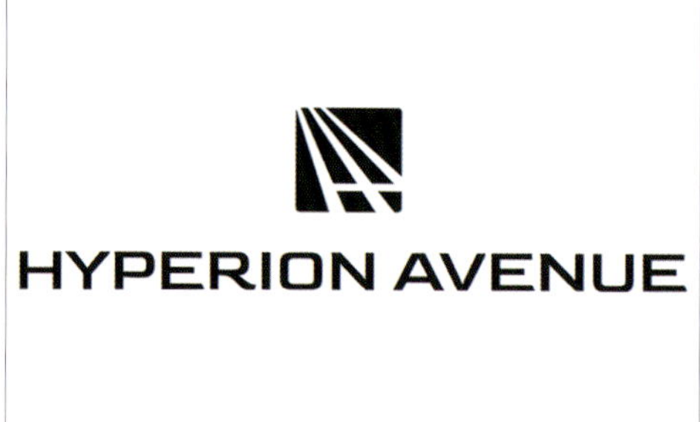

SJI Associates

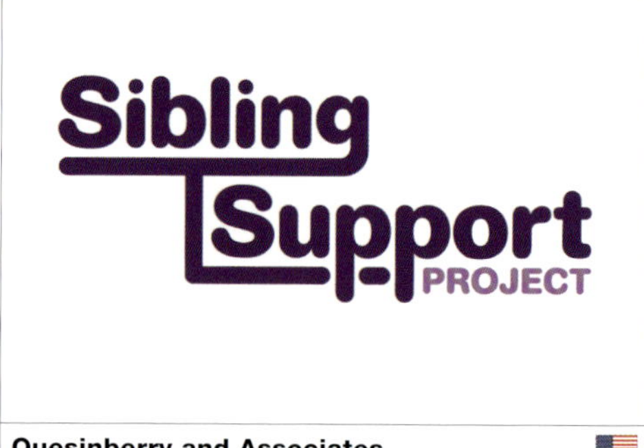

Quesinberry and Associates

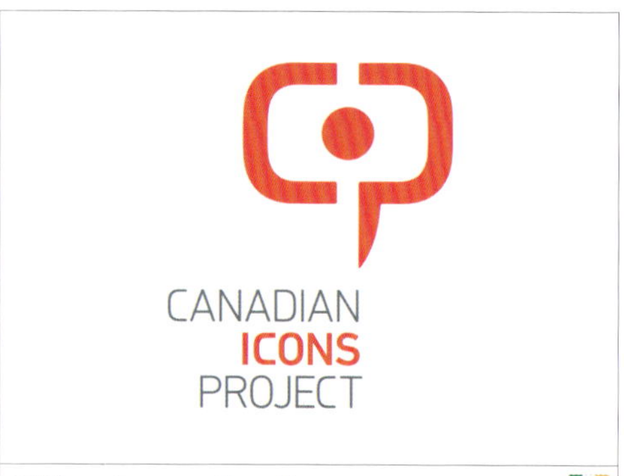

O'Shaughnessy Creative

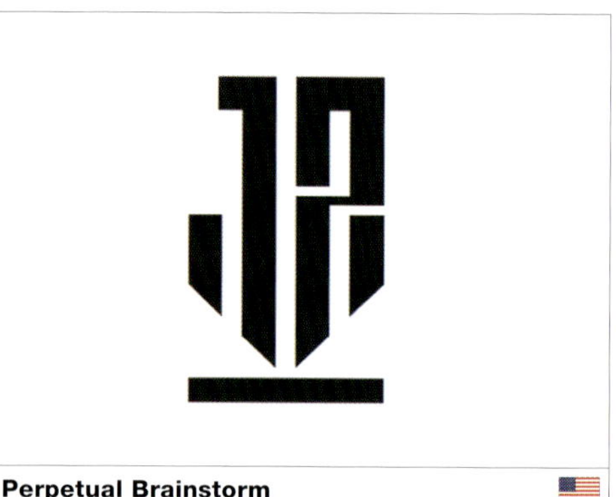

Perpetual Brainstorm

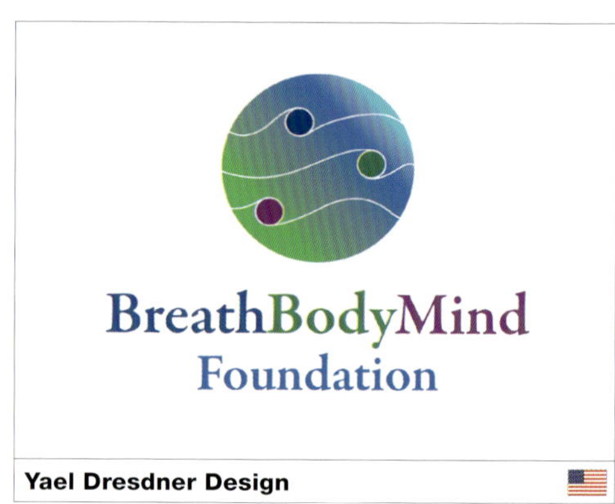

Yael Dresdner Design

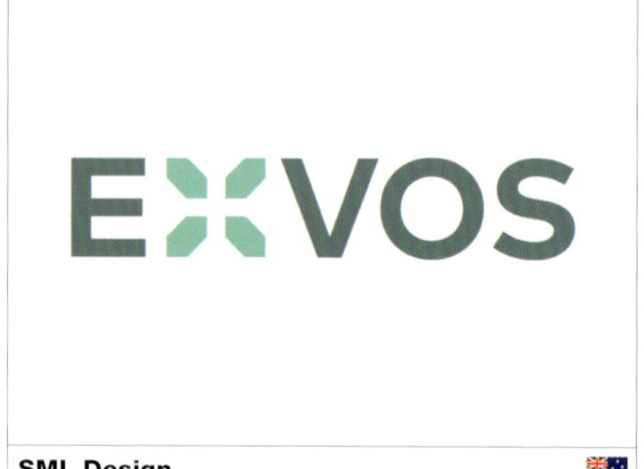

SML Design

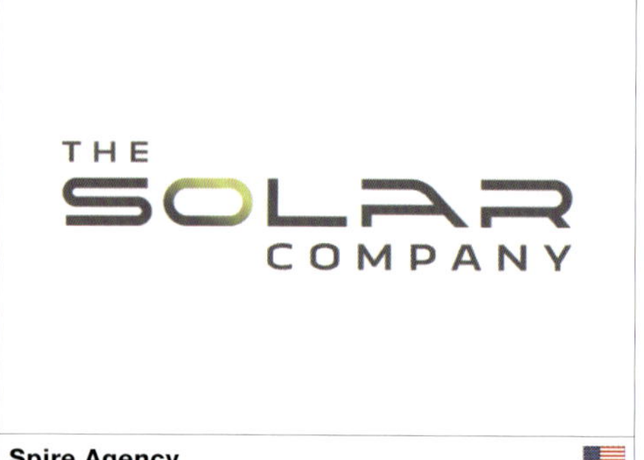

Spire Agency

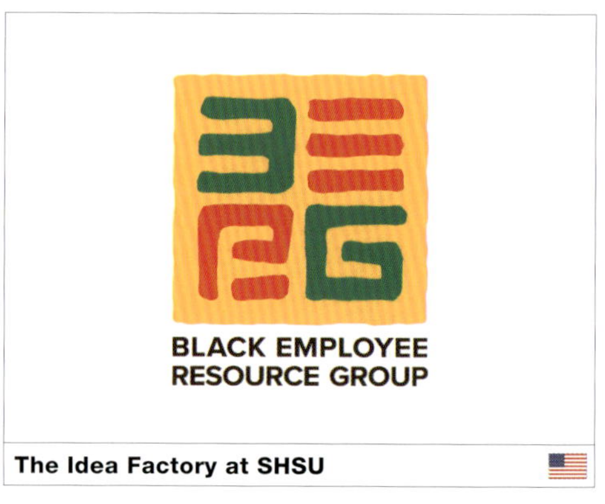

The Idea Factory at SHSU

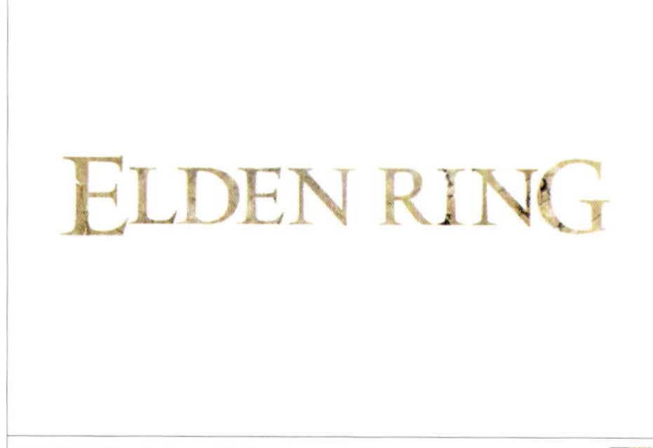

PETROL Advertising

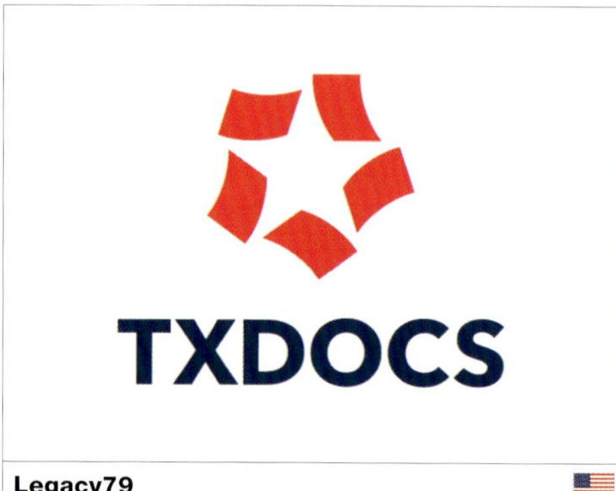

Legacy79

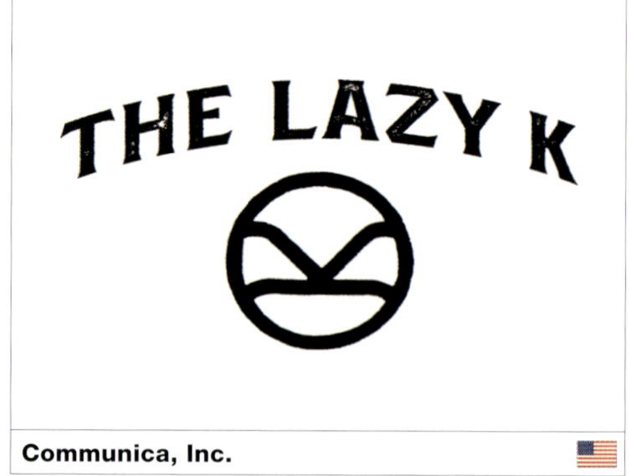

Communica, Inc.

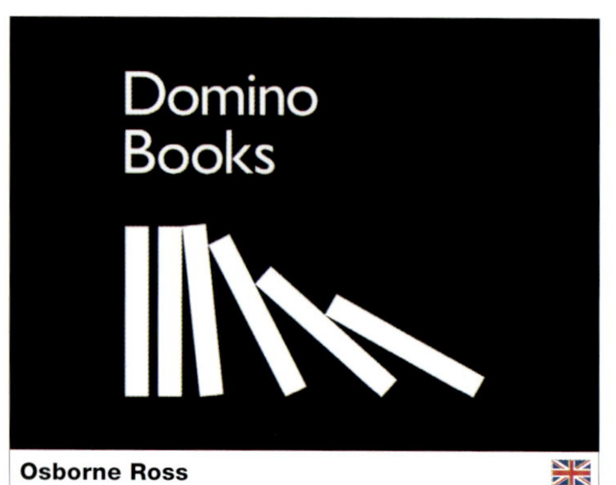

Osborne Ross

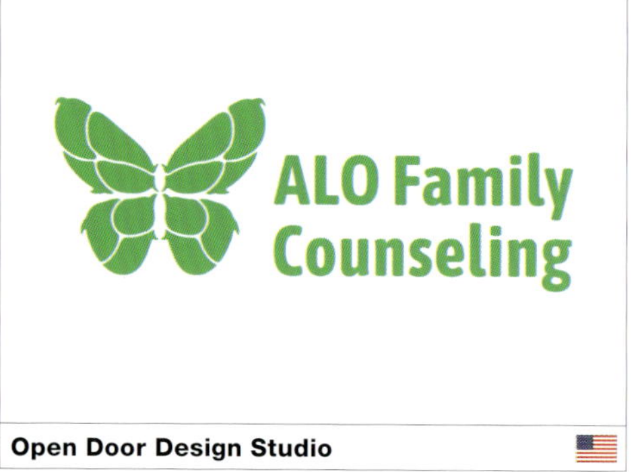

Open Door Design Studio

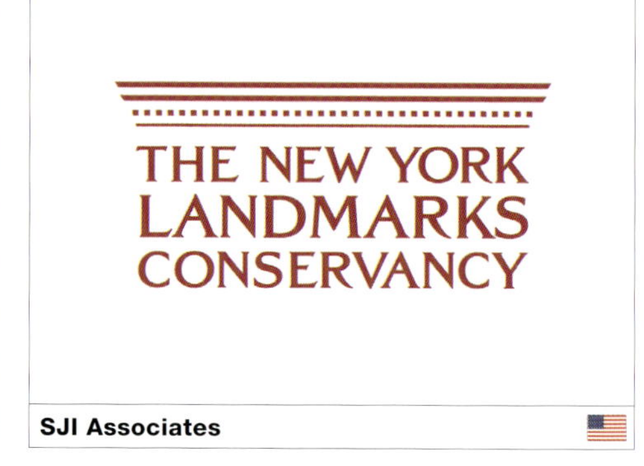

SJI Associates

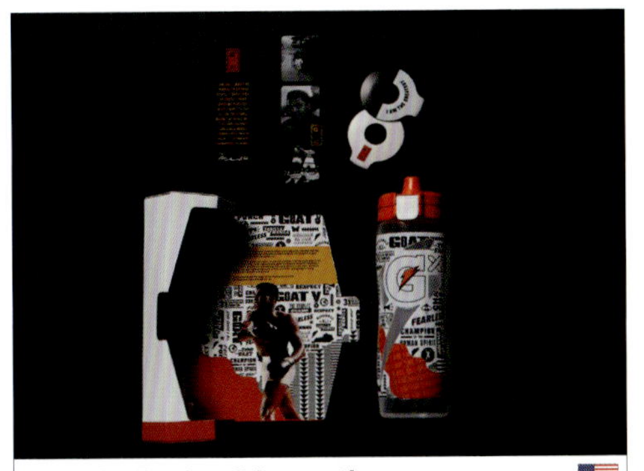

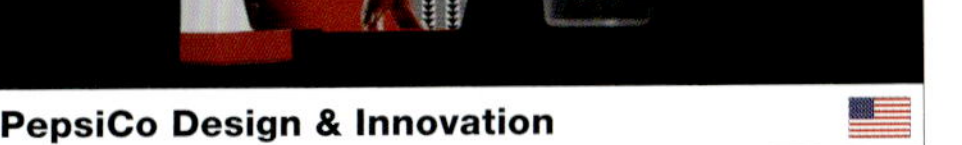

PepsiCo Design & Innovation

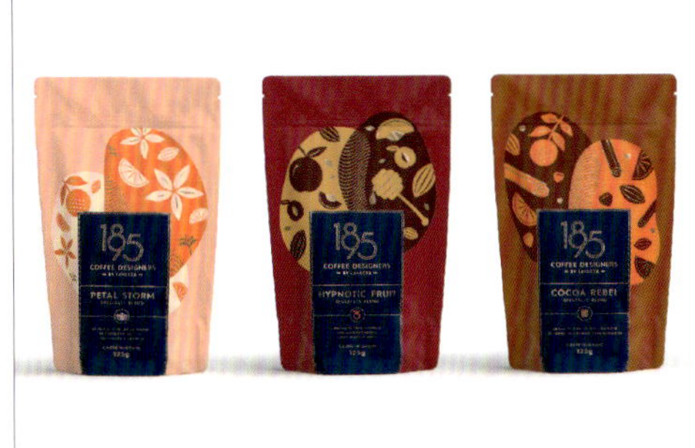

*TraceElement

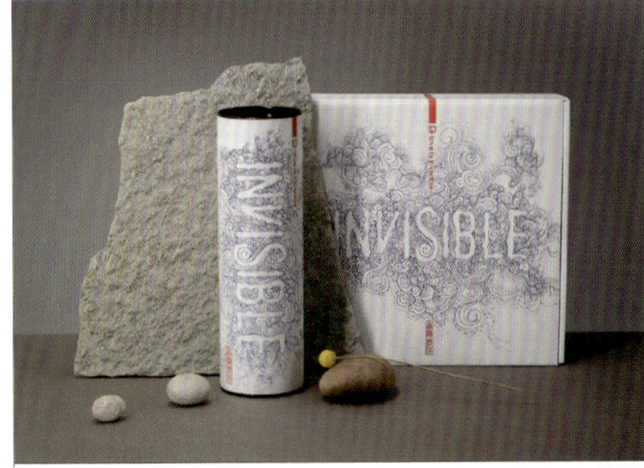

TSDDesign Inc.

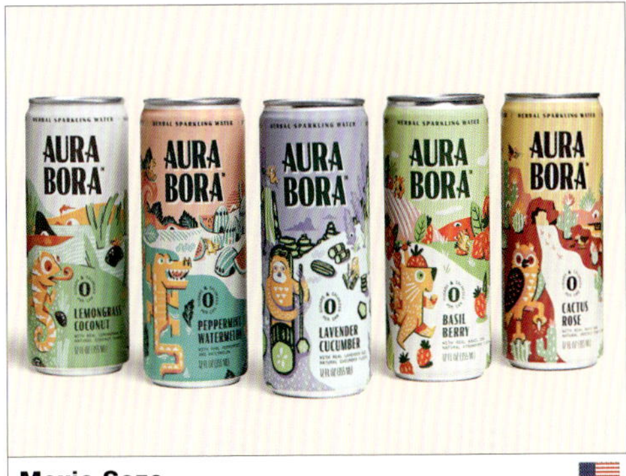

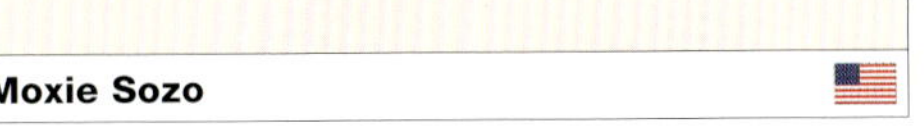

Moxie Sozo

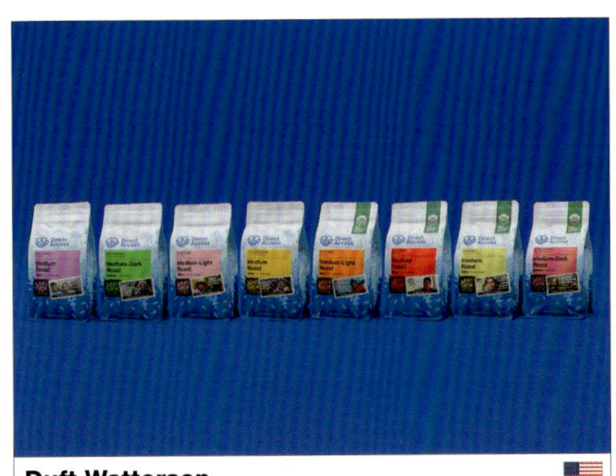

Duft Watterson

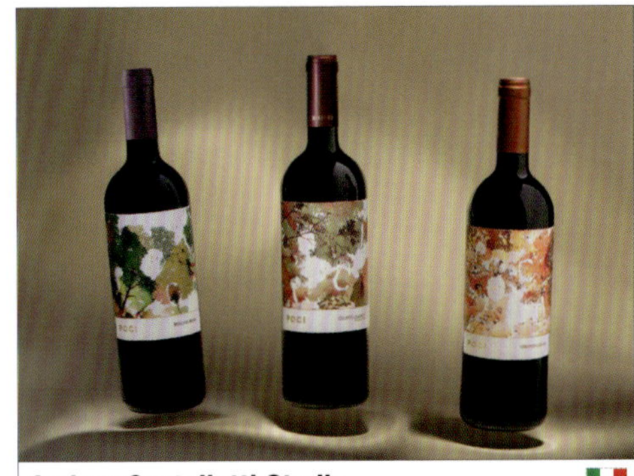

Andrea Castelletti Studio

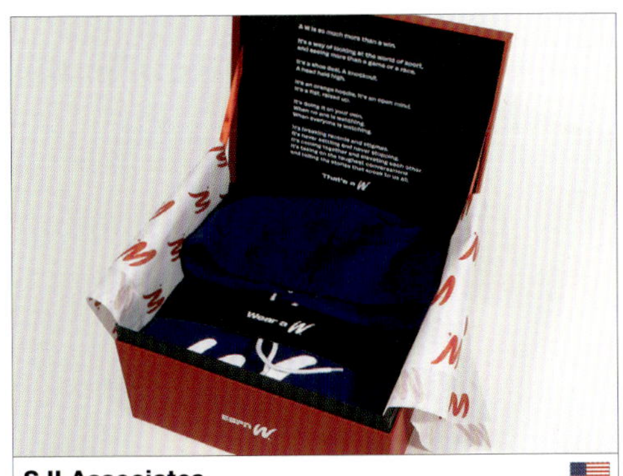

SJI Associates

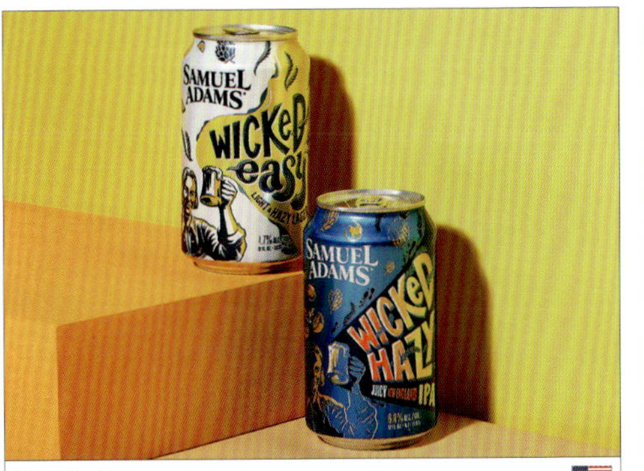

Moxie Sozo

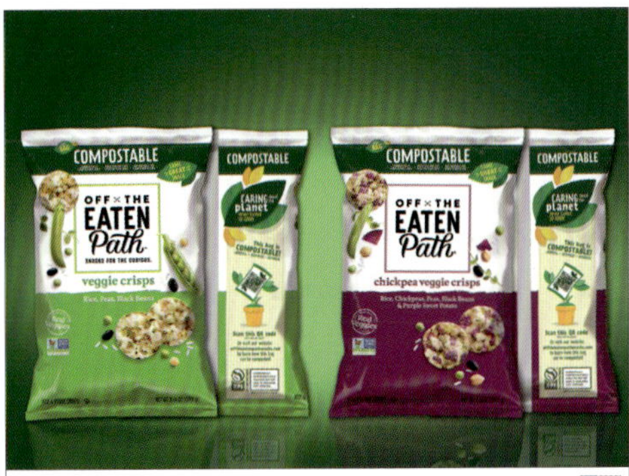

PepsiCo Design & Innovation

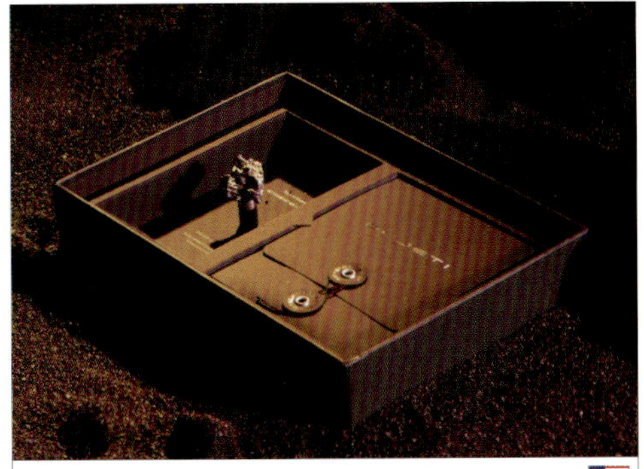

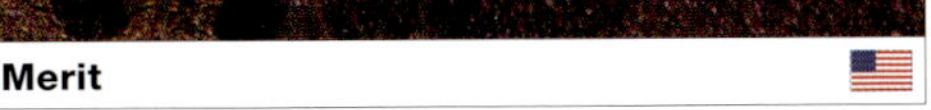

Merit

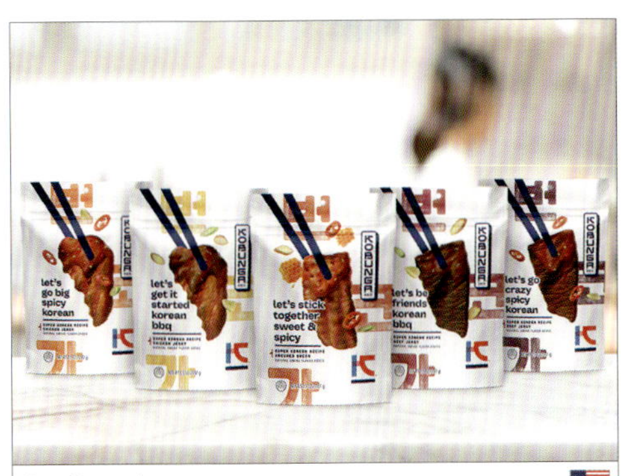

BexBrands

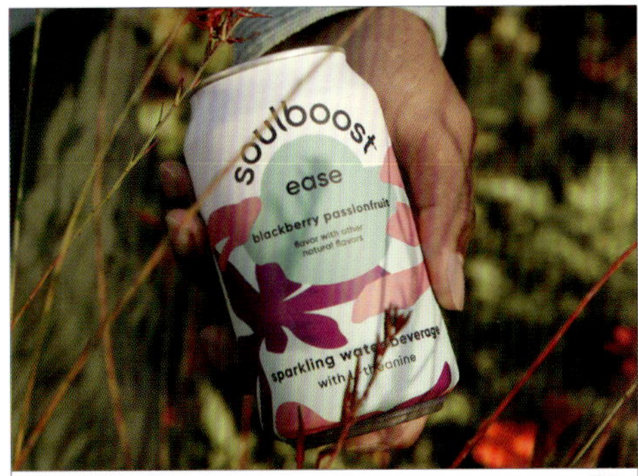

PepsiCo Design & Innovation

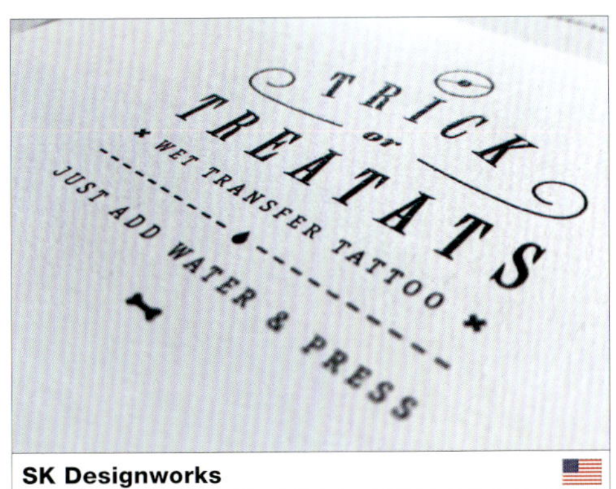

SK Designworks

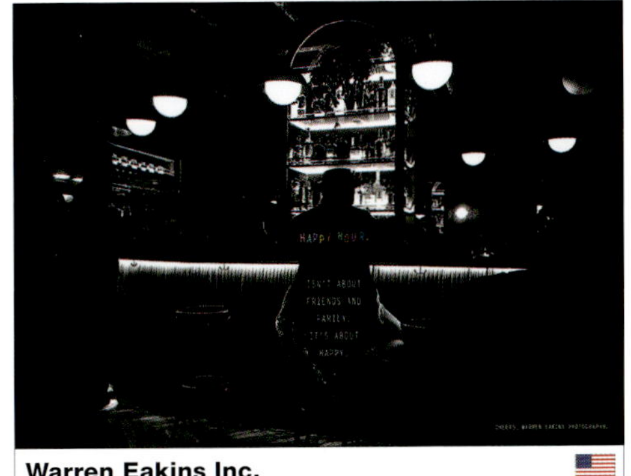

Warren Eakins Inc.

The Republik

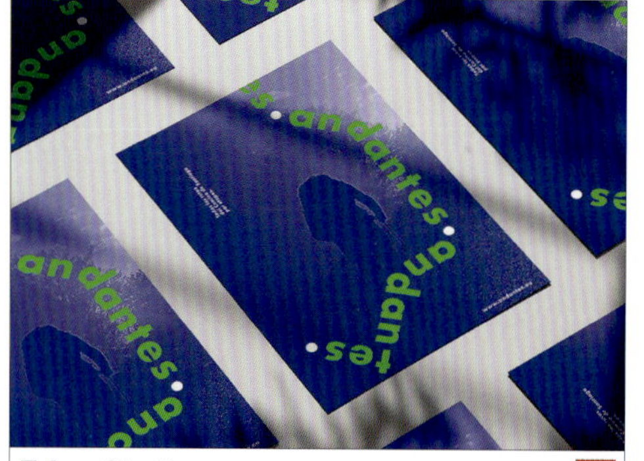

Teiga, Studio.

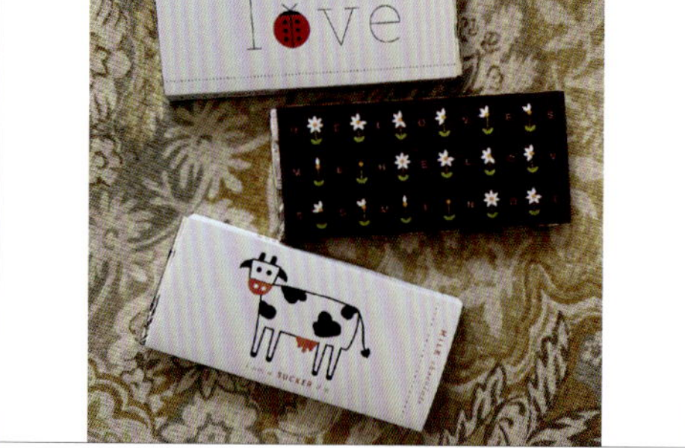

SK Designworks

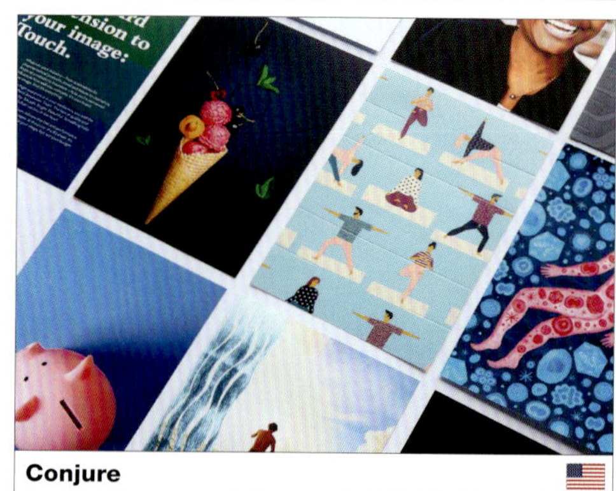

Conjure

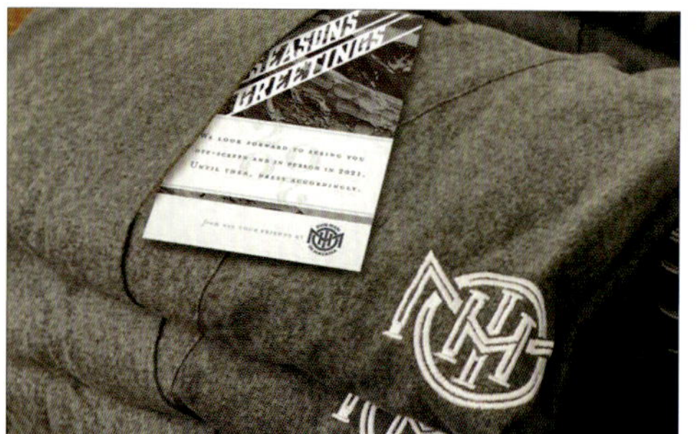

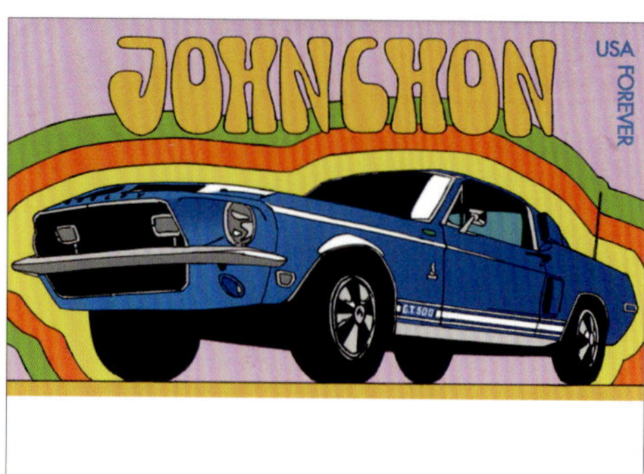

HyunJung Yi

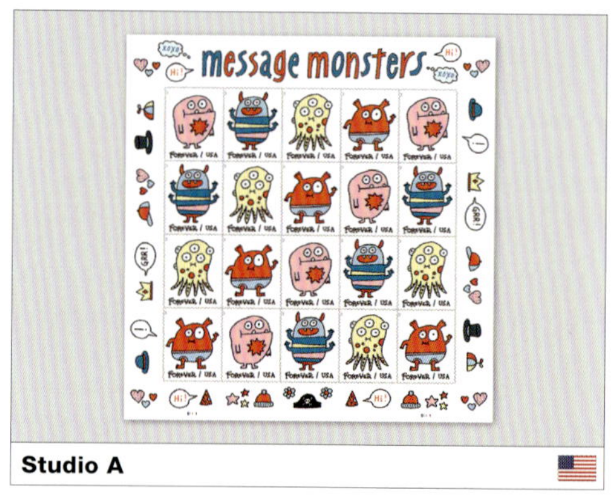

Studio A

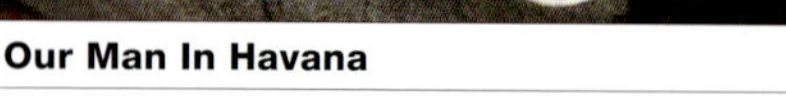

Our Man In Havana

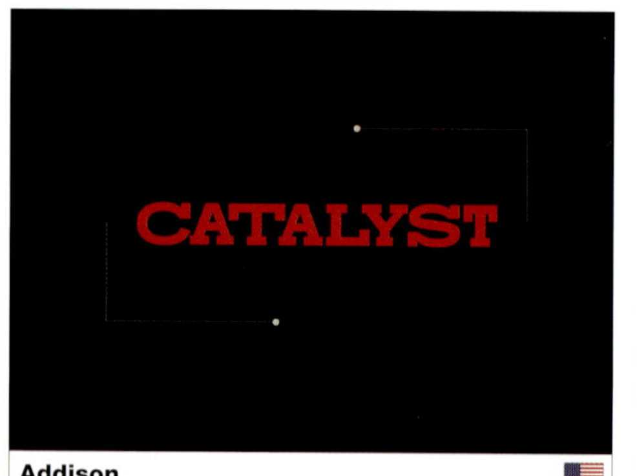

Addison

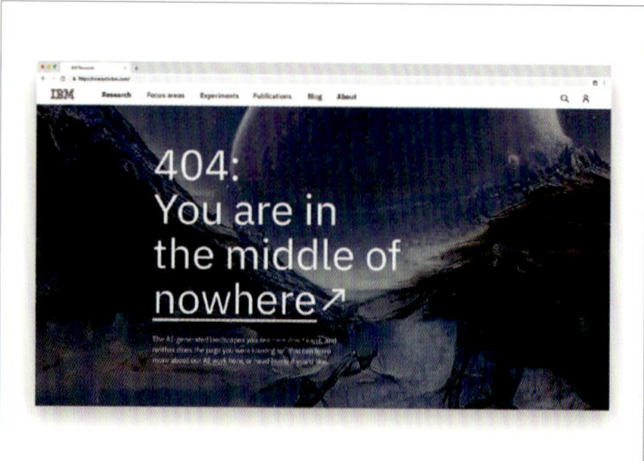

Goods & Services

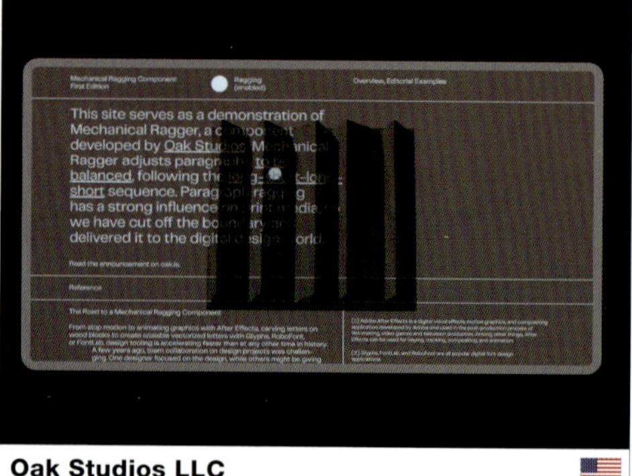

Oak Studios LLC

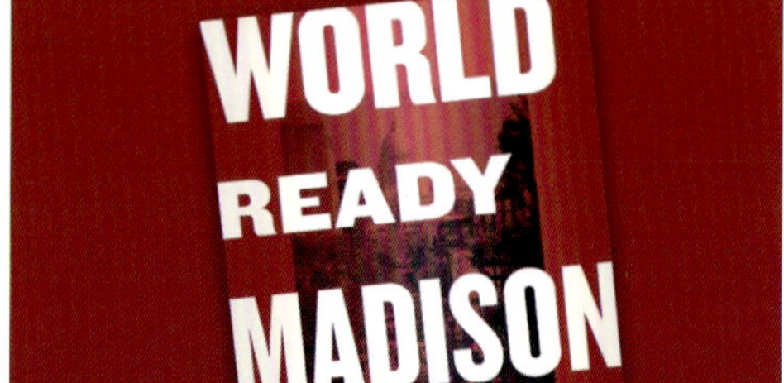

Traction Factory

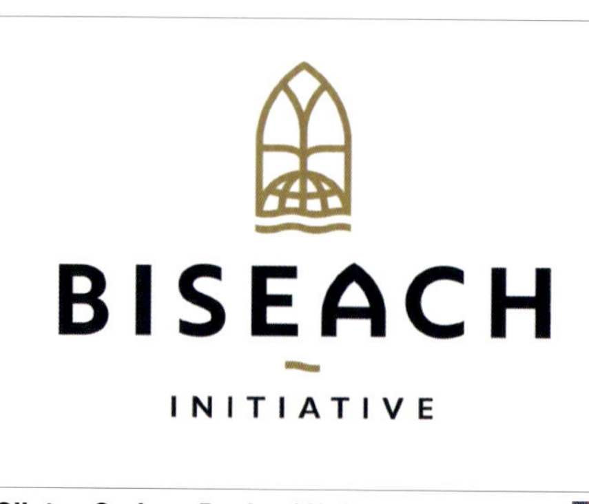

Clinton Carlson Design | Univ. of Notre Dame

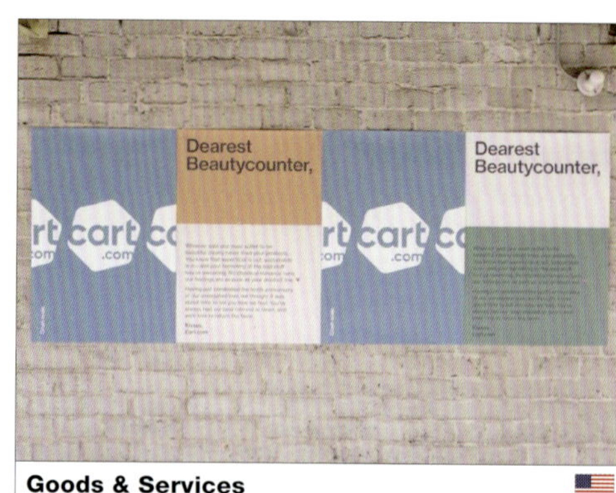

Goods & Services

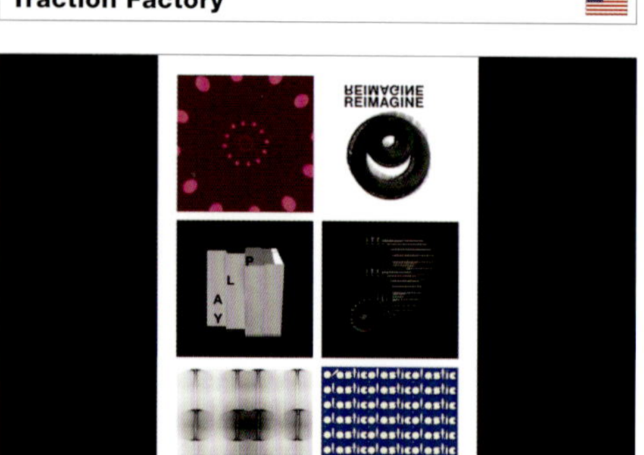

Jennifer Sterling Design

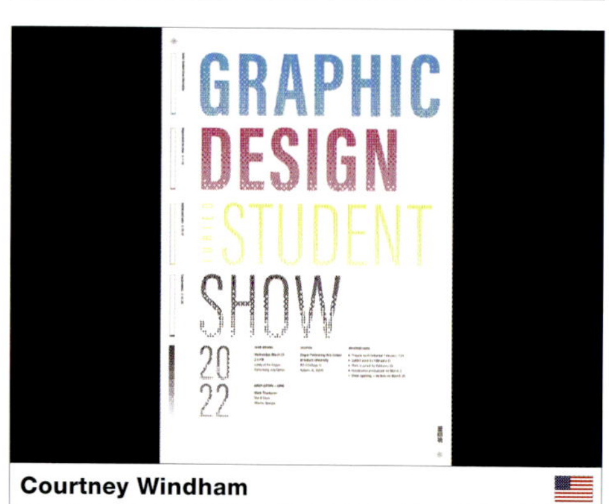

Courtney Windham

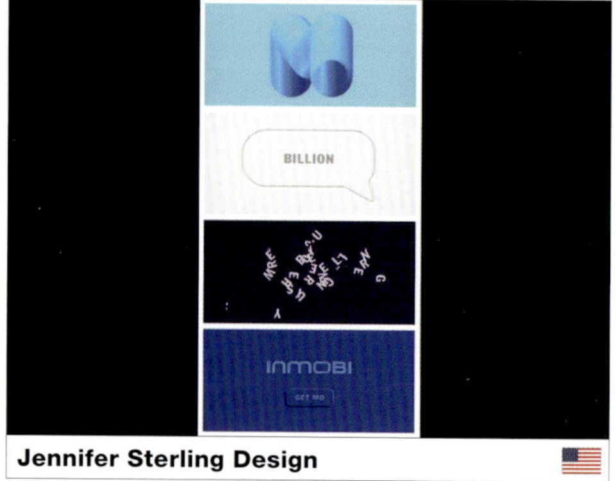

Jennifer Sterling Design

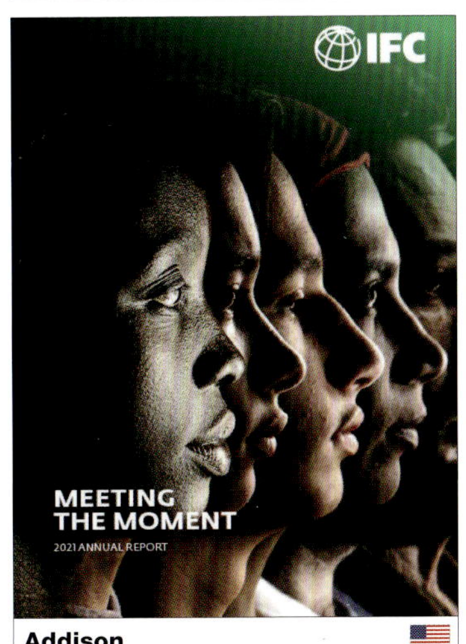

Addison

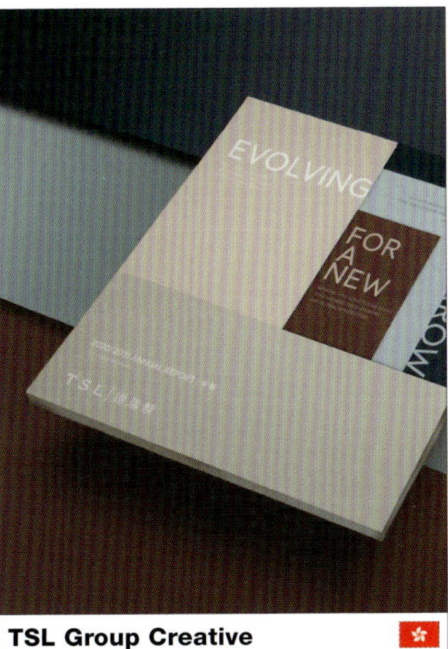

TSL Group Creative

Anna Jordan

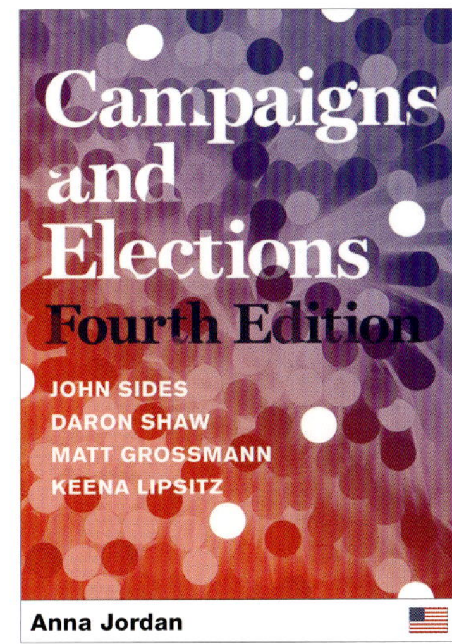

Anna Jordan

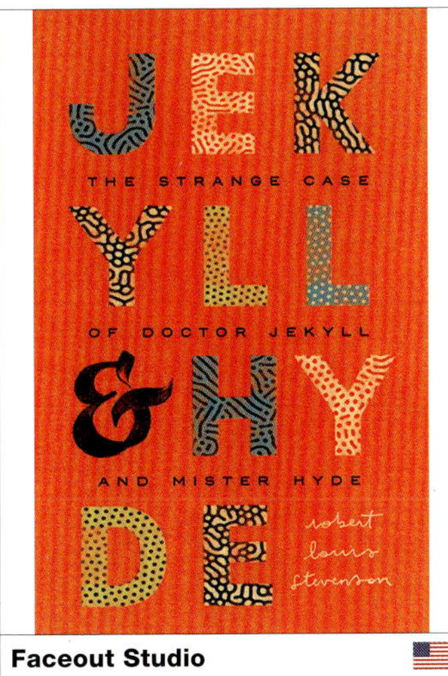

Faceout Studio

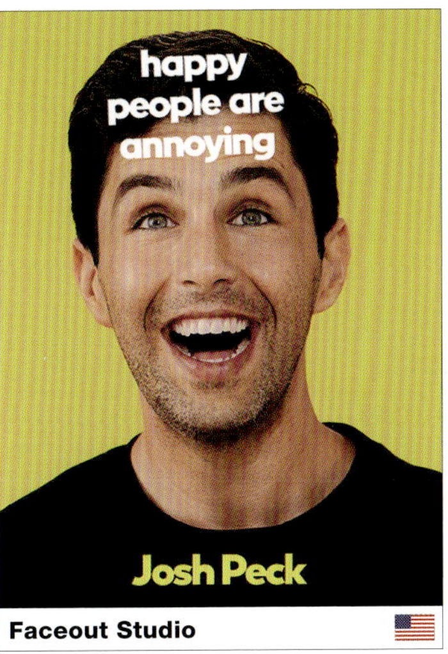

Faceout Studio

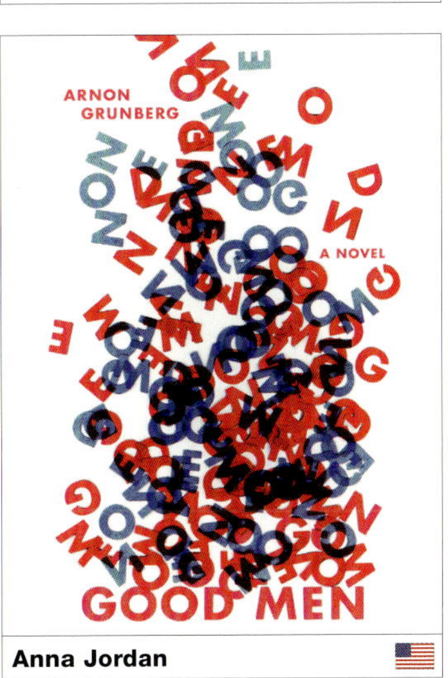

Anna Jordan

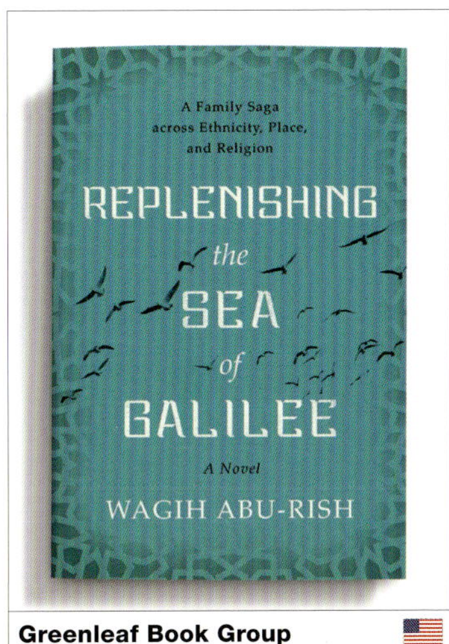

Greenleaf Book Group

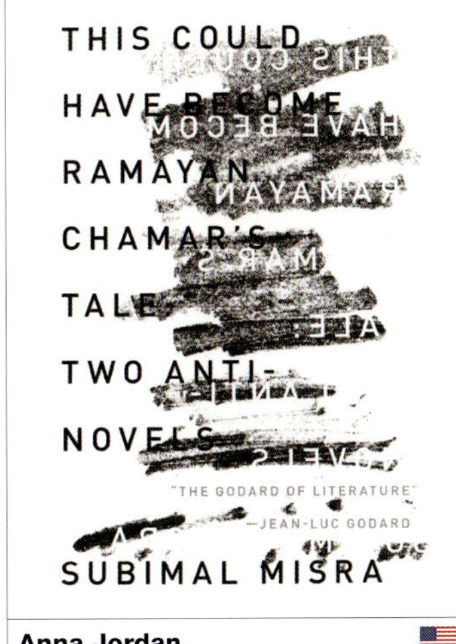

Anna Jordan

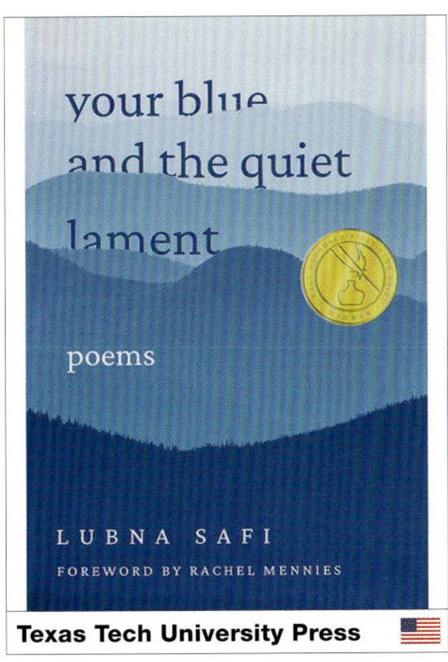

Texas Tech University Press

Wonderfull Design

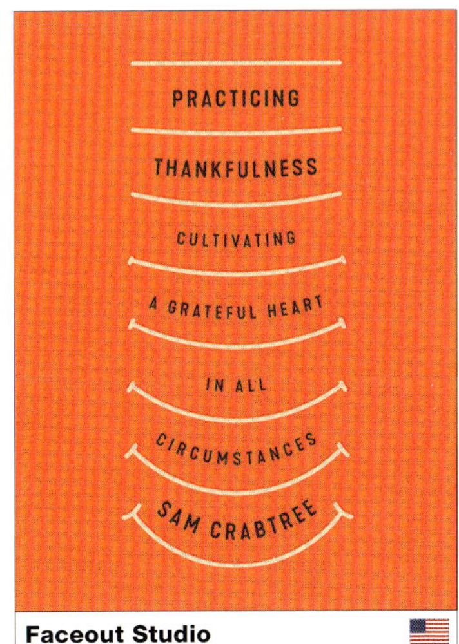

Faceout Studio

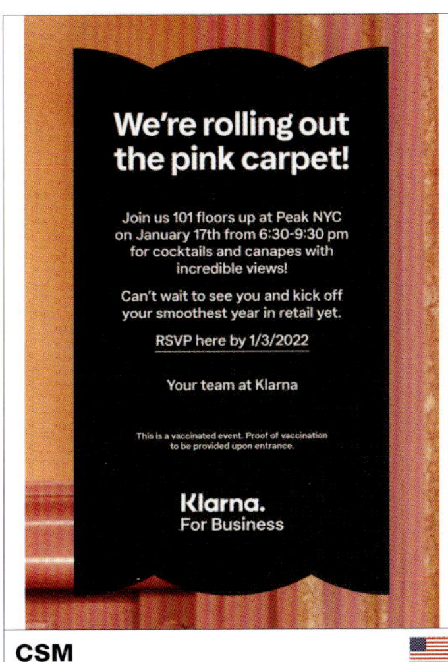

CSM

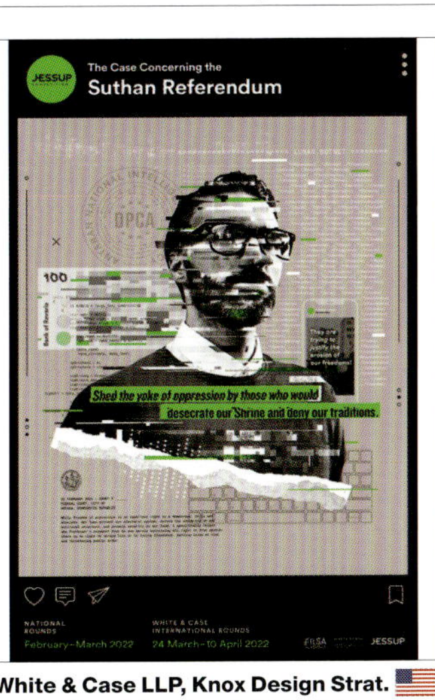

White & Case LLP, Knox Design Strat.

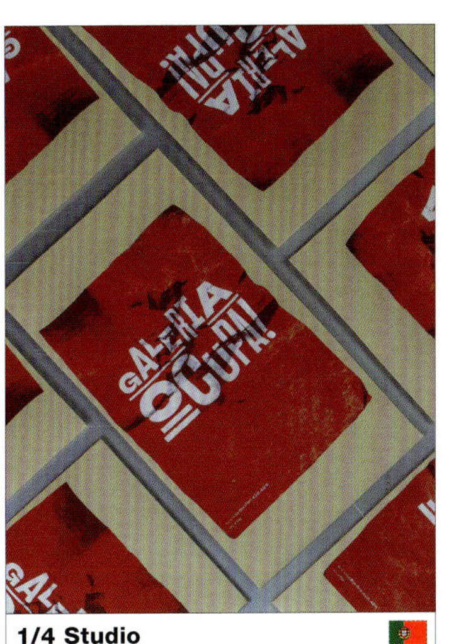
1/4 Studio

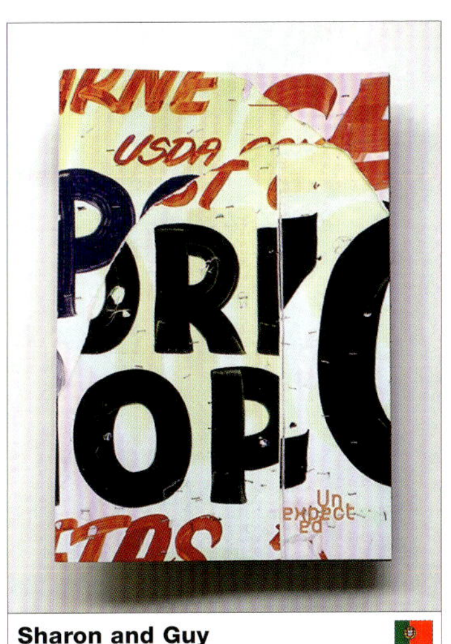
Sharon and Guy

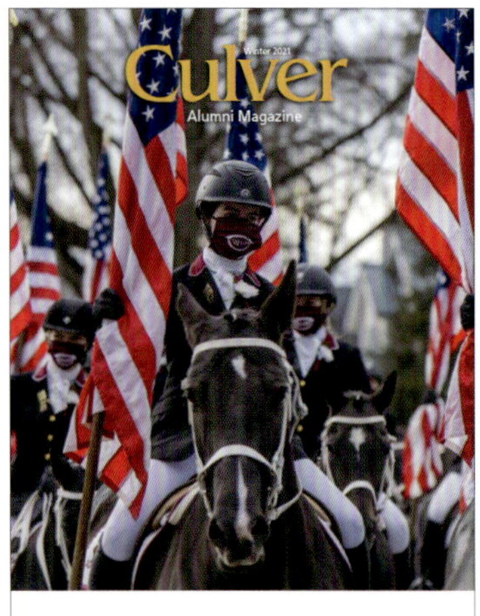

SJI Associates

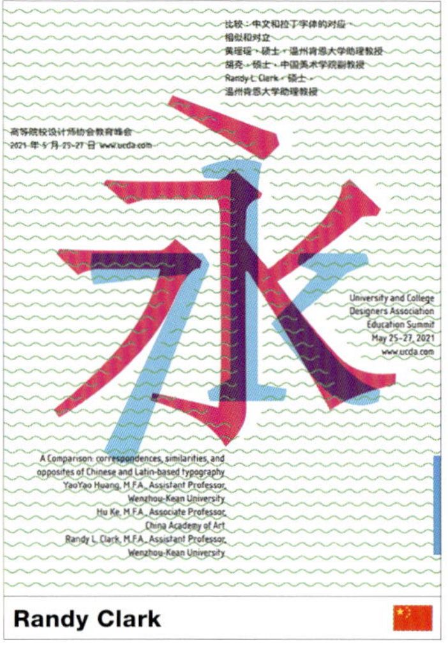

Randy Clark

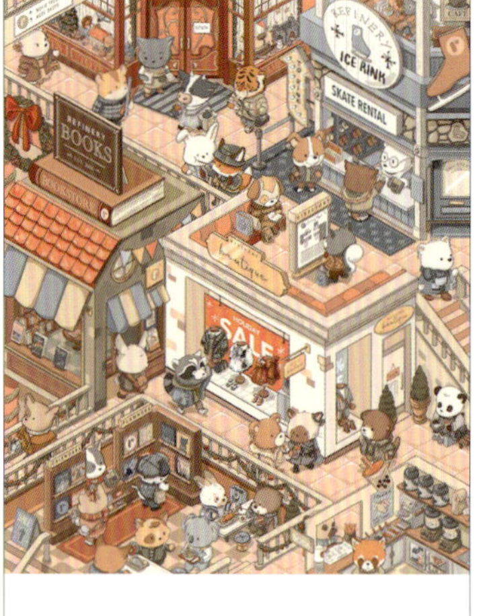

The Refinery

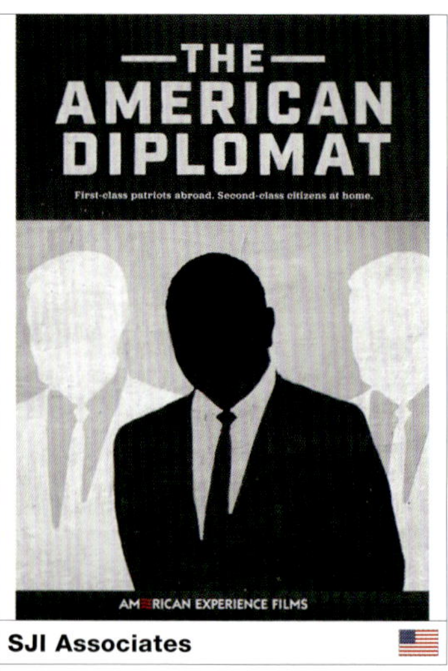

SJI Associates

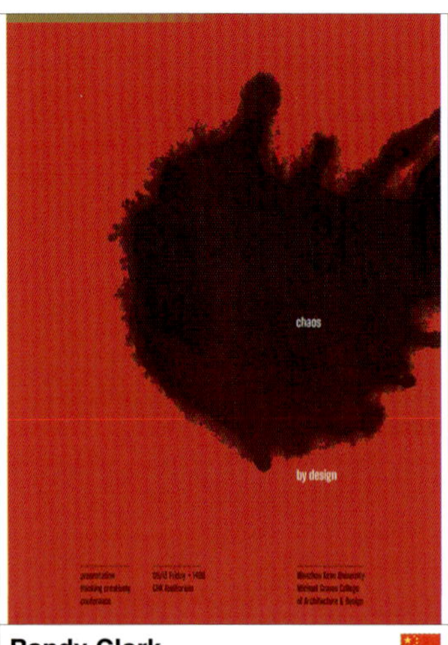

Randy Clark

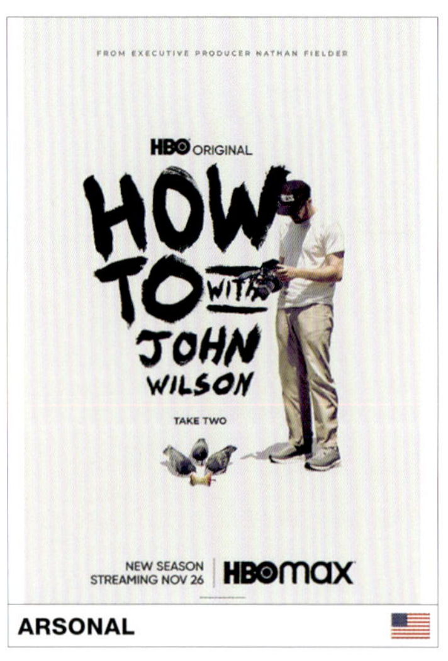

ARSONAL

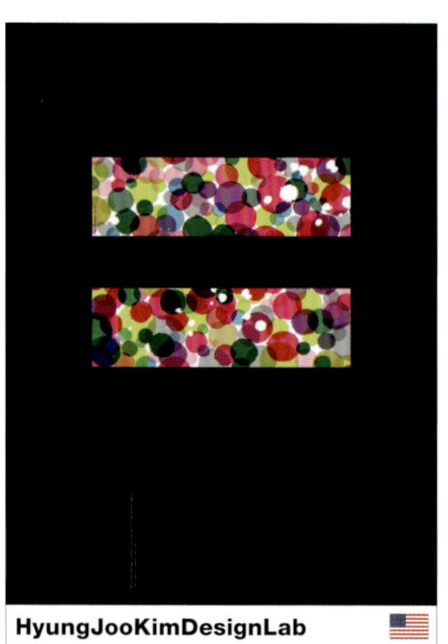

HyungJooKimDesignLab

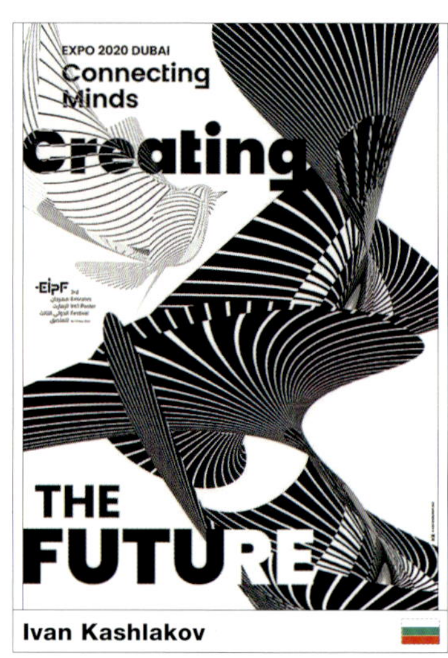

Ivan Kashlakov

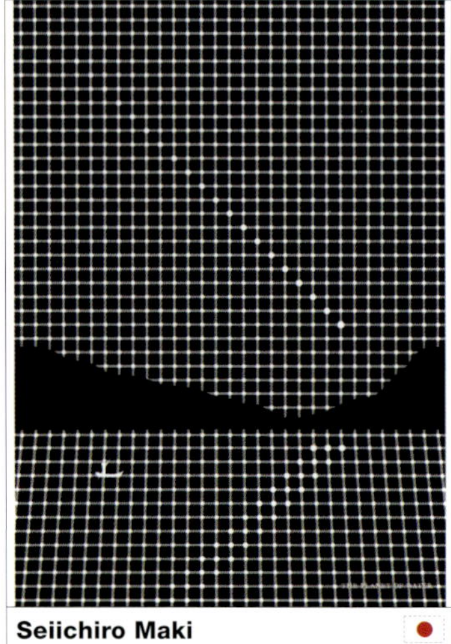

Seiichiro Maki

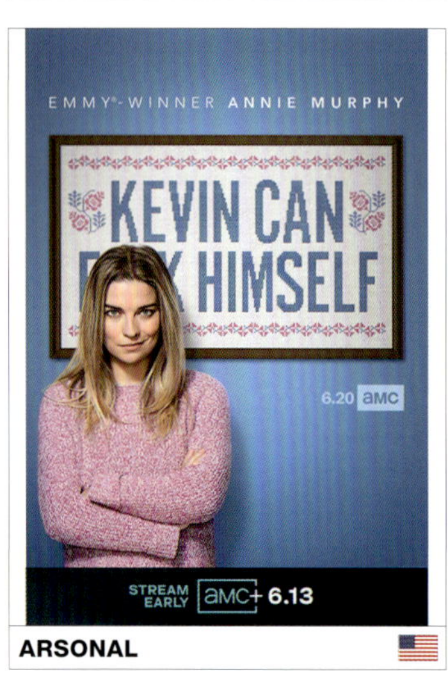

ARSONAL

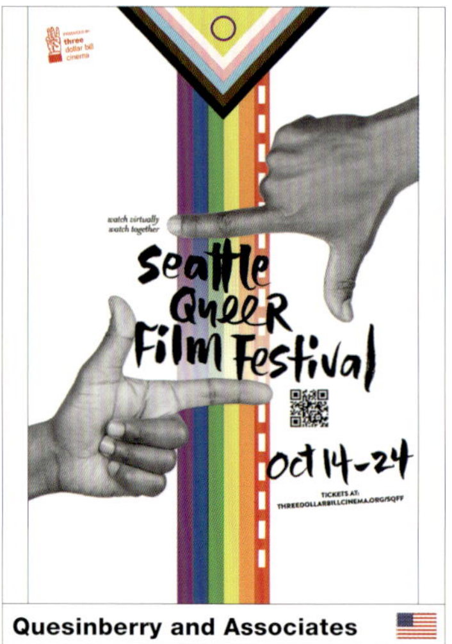

Quesinberry and Associates

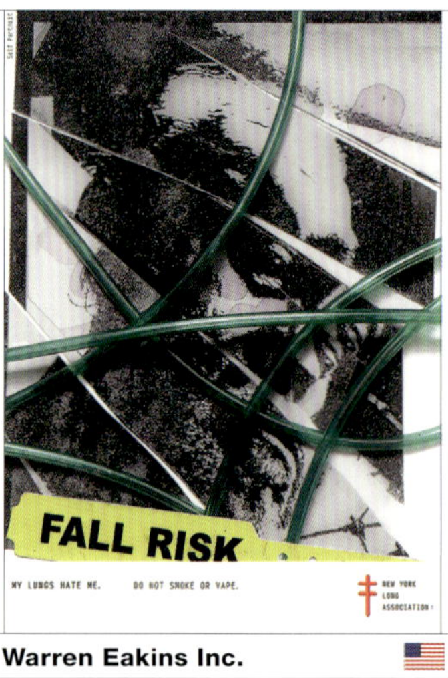

Warren Eakins Inc.

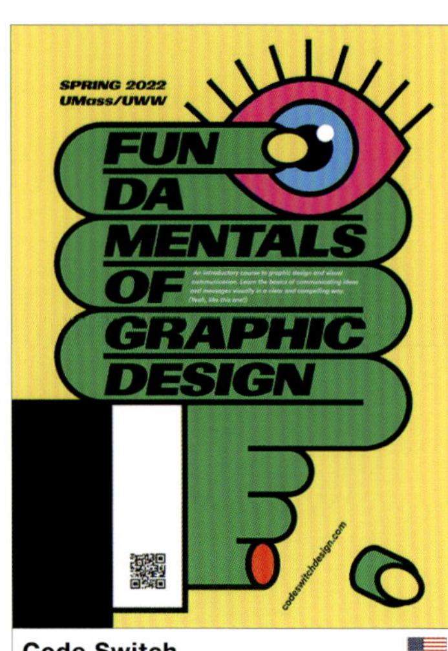

Code Switch

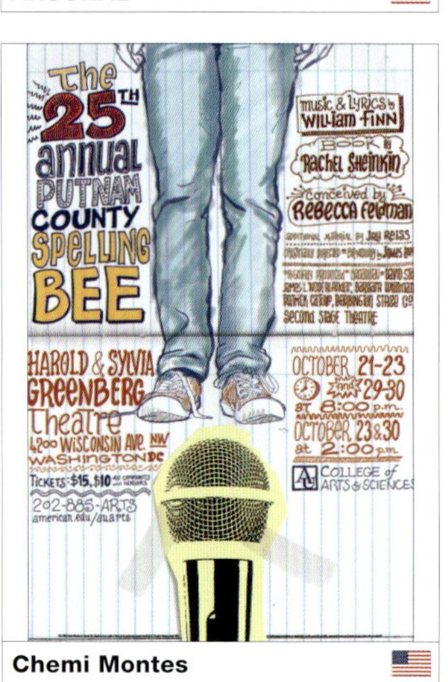

Chemi Montes

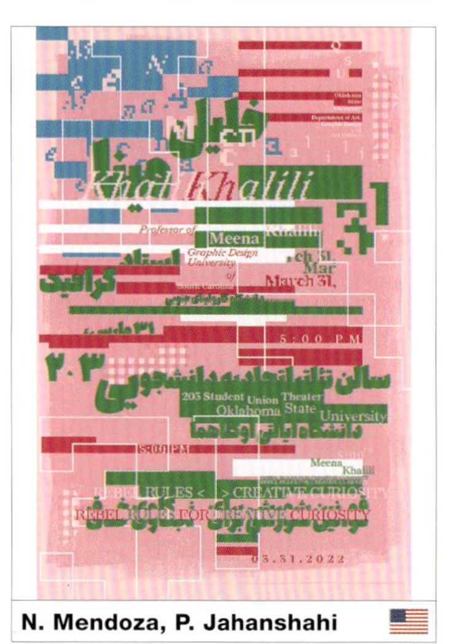

N. Mendoza, P. Jahanshahi

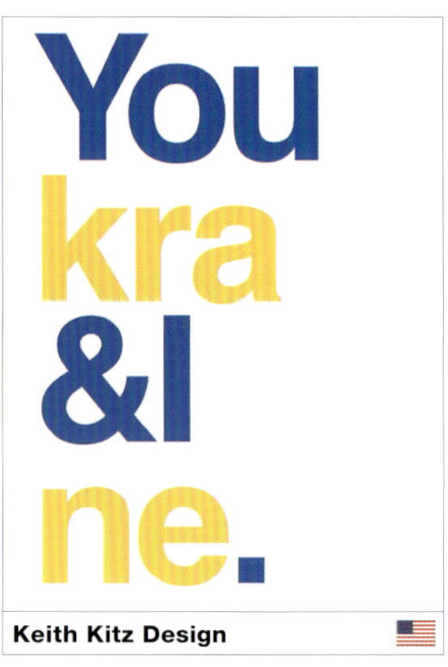

Keith Kitz Design

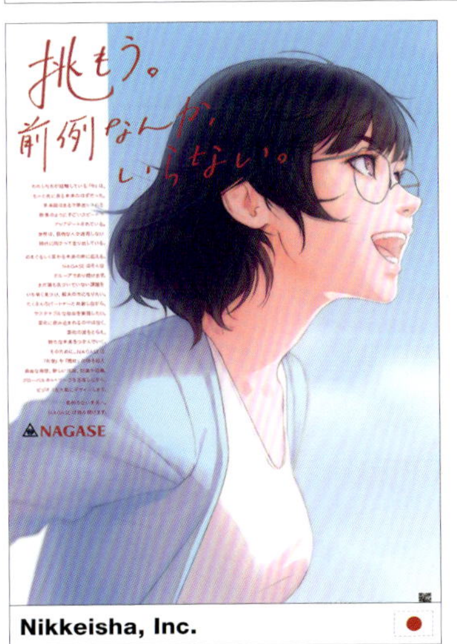

Nikkeisha, Inc.

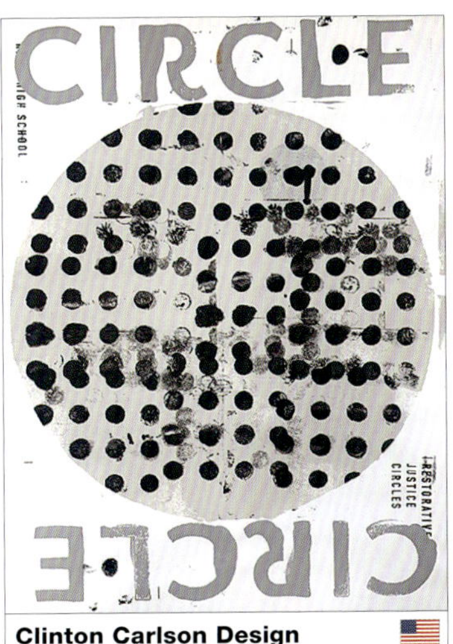

Clinton Carlson Design

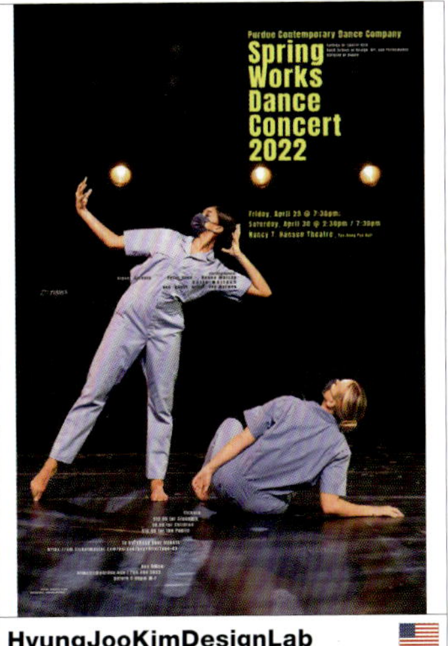

HyungJooKimDesignLab

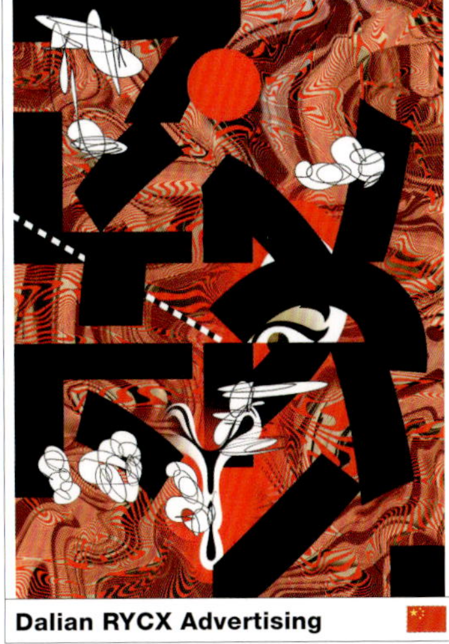
Dalian RYCX Advertising

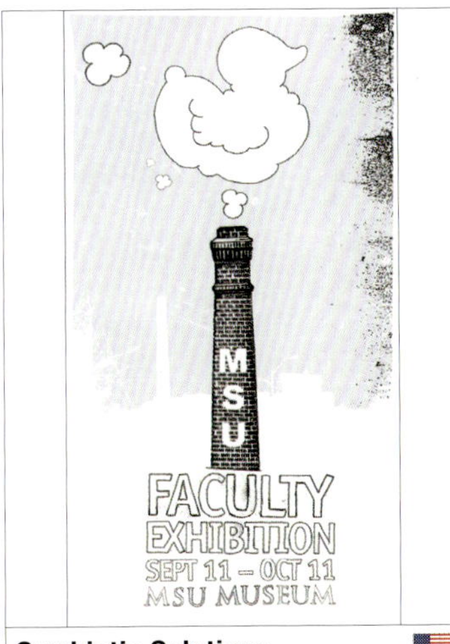

Symbiotic Solutions

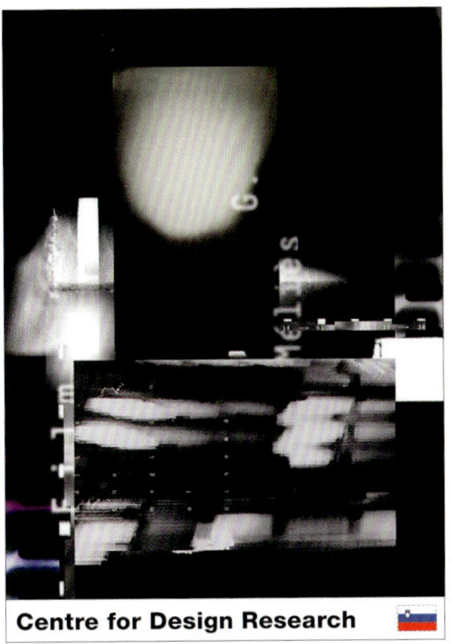
Centre for Design Research

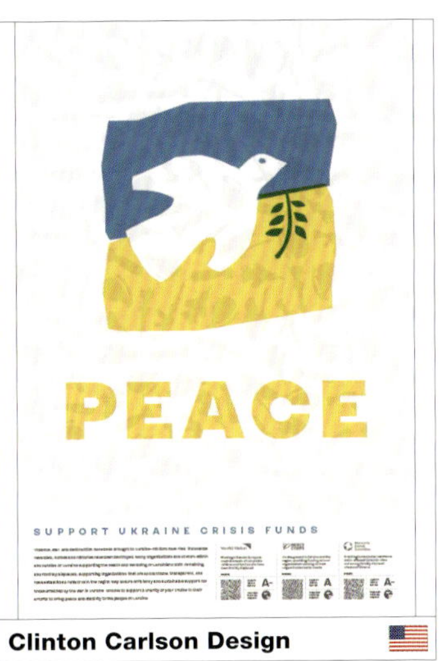

Clinton Carlson Design

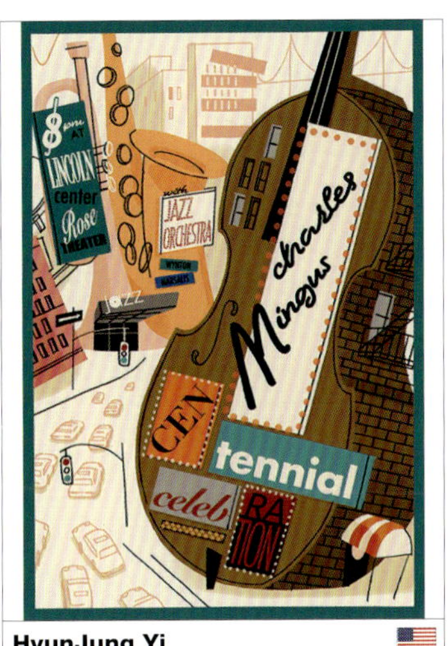

HyunJung Yi

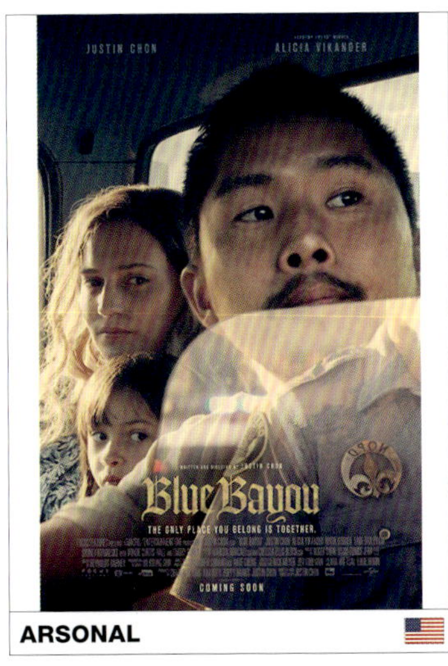

ARSONAL

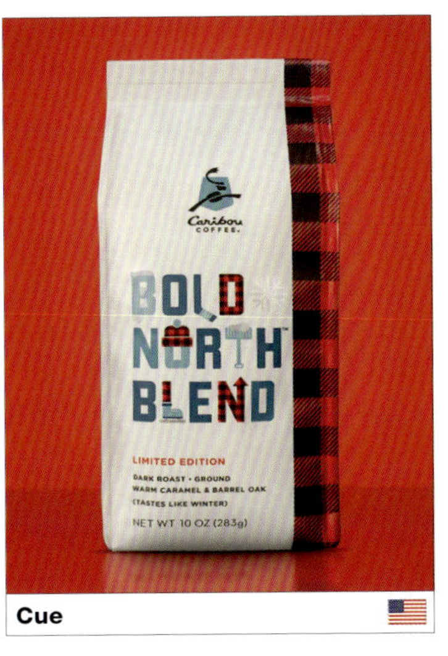

Cue

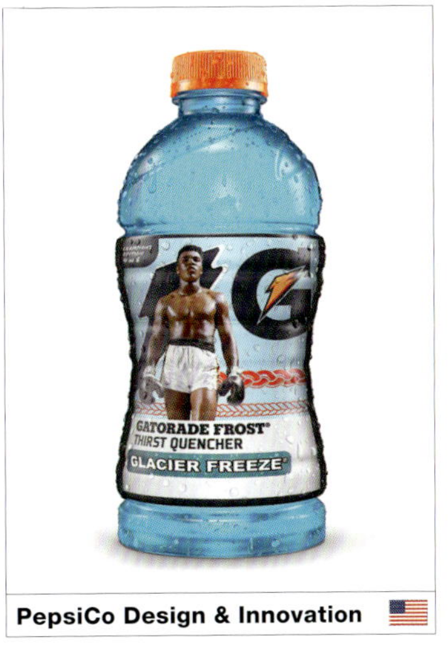

PepsiCo Design & Innovation

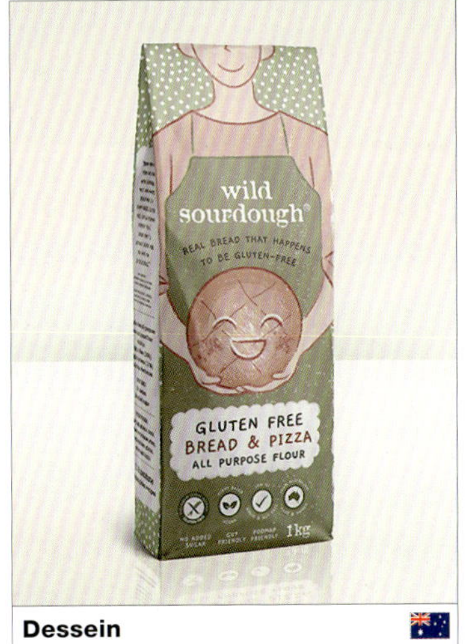

Dessein

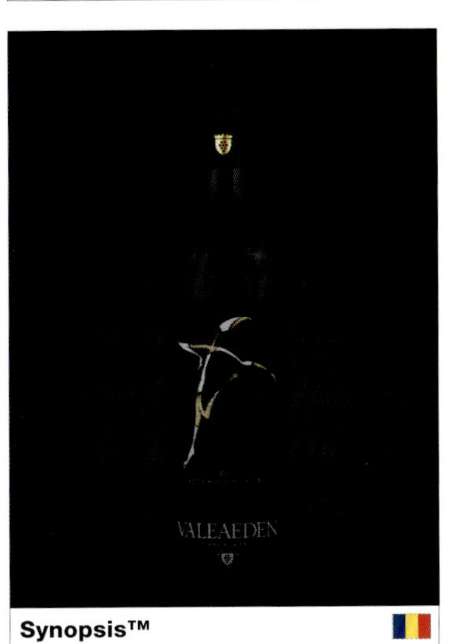

Synopsis™

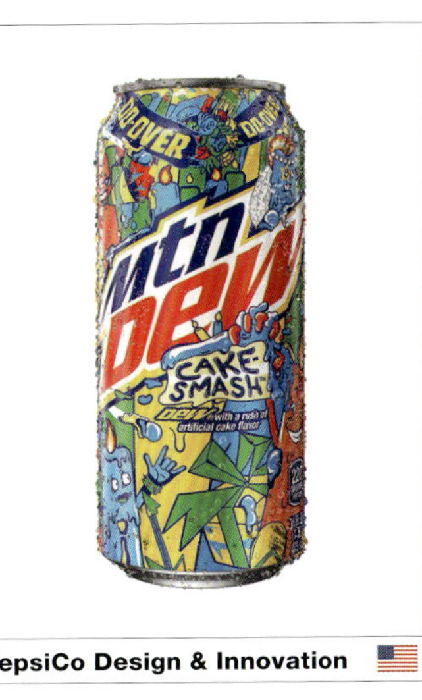

PepsiCo Design & Innovation

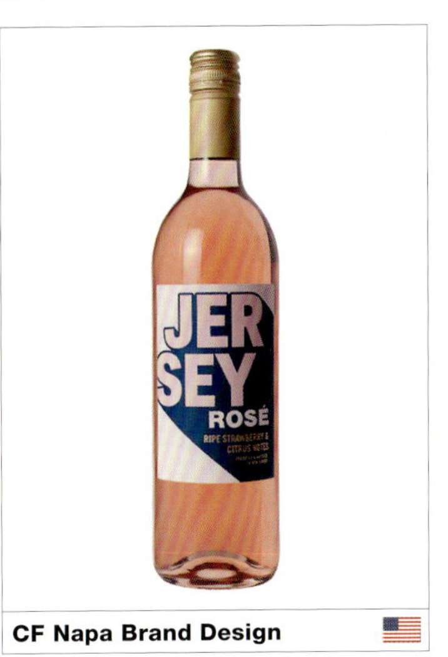

CF Napa Brand Design

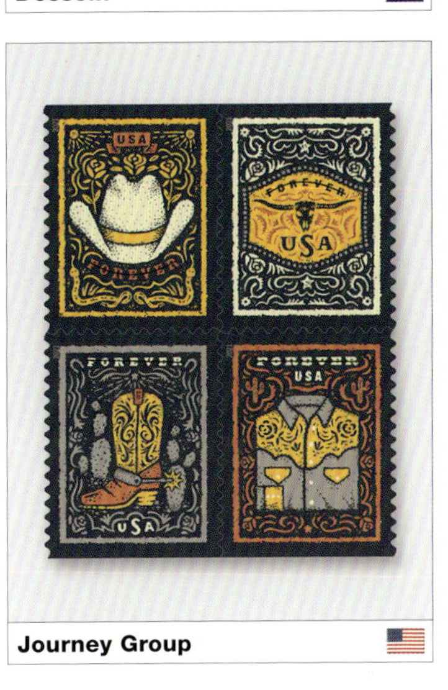

Journey Group

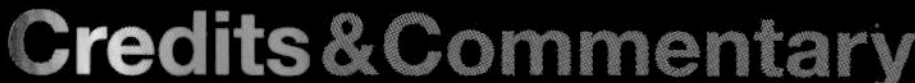
Credits & Commentary

PLATINUM WINNERS:

22 HIRE POWER | Design Firm: Wainscot Media
Designers: Trevett McCandliss, Nancy Campbell | Client: Footwear Plus Magazine
Editor-in-Chief: Greg Dutter | Photographer: Trevett McCandliss
Hair & Makeup: Clelia Bergonzoli | Main Contributors: Trevett McCandliss, Nancy Campbell
Assignment: Create a spread for a story that features back-to-the-office footwear.
Approach: We created a custom type solution to compliment the photo.
Results: It was very well-received!

22 PRAIRIE CHIC | Design Firm: Wainscot Media
Designers: Trevett McCandliss, Nancy Campbell | Client: Footwear Plus Magazine
Editor-in-Chief: Greg Dutter | Photographer: Trevett McCandliss
Model: Linnea Turner from Supreme Model Mgmt. | Hair & Makeup: Clelia Bergonzoli, Ray Brown Pro | Main Contributors: Trevett McCandliss, Nancy Campbell
Assignment: This is a spread to a story featuring prairie-inspired footwear.
Approach: We used a modified Bodoni style typeface to create our opening design.
Results: Everyone enjoyed the story!

23 SANTA ANA GIN | Design Firm: Stranger & Stranger
Designer: Stranger & Stranger | Client: Kanlaon Ltd. (Bleeding Heart Rum)
Main Contributor: Stranger & Stranger
Assignment: Distilled using botanicals from the Philippines, Santa Ana transports you to the dancehalls of the 1920s and the legendary Santa Ana Cabaret in Manila.

24 DADA CHAPEL | Design Firm: Stranger & Stranger | Designer: Stranger & Stranger
Client: Hotel Vanden Meersche NV | Main Contributor: Stranger & Stranger
Assignment: Branding and spirits packaging for a Belgium distillery like no other. Everything is dada. Nothing is dada. In Odd We Trust.

25 LAY'S POTATO VODKA | Design Firm: PepsiCo Design & Innovation
Designer: PepsiCo Design & Innovation | Client: Self-initiated
Main Contributor: PepsiCo Design & Innovation
Assignment: Lay's® is a beloved American brand and the undeniable salty snack category leader. But the brand wanted to expand consumers' perceptions when considering Lay's. We wondered if we could take an iconic brand and push it into new territories and break through to a consumer whose attention has become progressively harder to obtain. Inspired by the popularity and buzzworthiness of 'unexpected' brand collaborations, the Lay's team had a lightbulb moment – Lay's has the best potatoes that make the best potato chips, but what else can be made with them? The challenge was set, but matters were complicated as we found ourselves trying to accomplish this goal during the holiday season.
Approach: What if Lay's took its potatoes and transformed them into something unexpected? Just like that, Lay's Vodka was born. Lay's moved swiftly to forge a partnership with Portland-based Eastside Distilling to develop its very own small batch, premium potato vodka. An offering this noteworthy needed a packaging aesthetic to match the craft spirits inside, so with millennial consumers in mind, the design team took a sophisticated design approach. The label is beautifully foiled with Lay's signature yellow, showcasing the iconic logo embossed in black. The brand's red accent color touts the use of Lay's proprietary potatoes along with Eastside Distilling's Portland Potato Vodka. A red-notched label on the lower portion of the bottle indicates Eastside as the distiller and highlights the small-batch statistics, reminding consumers they own a bottle out of a run of just 1,300. The design team also developed an exclusive influencer kit, complete with a beautifully branded golden-hued cocktail shaker. Lay's leaned into Drop Culture to deliver its new vodka to the marketplace in a way that would generate maximum excitement. The team developed a custom-designed microsite for Eastside Distilling to digitally merchandise its vodka and enable direct-to-consumer sales. No detail was spared – all elements denoted the high-quality ingredients and products Lay's is made famous for. These details also ensured that Lay's vodka perfectly aligned with Gifting Culture, making it a 'must-have' item of the holiday season.
Results: Lay's teased its pending launch with consumers on its social media channels. In addition to social posts and PR outreach, the brand seeded 40 bottles with influencers – the luxe packaging was a hit in their unboxing videos and the vodka received rave reviews. To keep the momentum, Lay's then inspired consumers with easy-to-prepare cocktail recipes via social media. Lay's Potato Vodka landed 115 media placements and 1.6+ billion earned media impressions. Lay's was the lead or featured brand in 94% of the coverage, and 90% of coverage included 2+ brand messages. 88% of coverage included branded assets. Lay's Potato Vodka successfully shook up the perception of the Lay's brand and delivered a new extension that brought unexpected joy to consumers.

26 BONITA | Design Firm: Sol Benito | Designer: Vishal Vora
Client: Elite Brands | Digital Artist: Ramdhun | Main Contributor: Sol Benito
Assignment: Create a feminine perfume product and packaging for GCC market.
Approach: Conceptualized from the visual narratives of woman's obsession and desire, representation for Fashion, Class and Luxury was translated into the concept along with the name "BONITA". The key objective of the brief was to synthesize Feminity and fascination, thus we took inspiration from Hobo hand bag as a basic concept to tell the story of woman's obsession and desire. This product concept was further enhanced by using right set of material, finish and production technique. The color palette was kept minimal with Brown and Gold as prominent.

27 AMERICAN HORROR STORIES | Design Firm: ARSONAL
Designers: ARSONAL, FX Networks | Client: FX Networks | Creative Directors: Stephanie Gibbons, President (FX Networks),Todd Heughens, SVP (FX Networks), ARSONAL
Art Director: Michael Brittain, VP (FX Networks) | Design Manager: Laura Handy (FX Networks)
Photographer: Frank Ockenfels | Main Contributors: ARSONAL, FX Networks
Assignment: American Horror Stories is an anthology series spin-off of American Horror Story that features a different horror story each episode. Since the first two episodes harken back to the house and rubber man possession from season one of AHS, the client wanted the art to as well. The goal was also to show the rubber man's possession of the girl in a way that would read as creepy instead of silly.
Approach: To show the possession, we explored various ways of combining the girl in a possessed state with the rubber man emerging out of her and/or intertwining with her. To reflect back to the season one art, we brought the slick, shiny, red latex elements into the background, and also applied those same techniques to the possessed girl giving her mannequin, plastic-like skin.
Results: This campaign mirrored the same bold palette and iconography of the Season 1 American Horror Story poster and was equally provocative.

28 3D TYPE EXHIBITION | Design Firm: Dankook University
Designer: Hoon-Dong Chung | Client: Self-initiated | Main Contributor: Hoon-Dong Chung
Assignment: This poster is for an experimental project 'Unstable Unity' with the letter 'T' in conceptual aspects. The project has continuously focused on expanding 2D types into 3D environment.
Approach: I was transforming 2D types into 3D imagery and expanding the possibilities in dimensional typography.
Results: The latest work.

29 MACBETH | Design Firm: Carmit Design Studio | Designer: Carmit Makler Haller
Client: Self-initiated | Photographers: iStock Photo, CoffeeAndMilk
Digital Artists: Carmit Makler Haller, Jorge Gamboa, Mal de Ojo
Main Contributor: Carmit Makler Haller
Assignment: My take on the play is that Lady Macbeth becomes the lead heroine as much as Macbeth is. She is equal in crime. She's the one who comes up with a perfect plan, seducing and manipulating Macbeth to do the deed and kill the king. She's blood thirsty and very certain when handed the crown.
Approach: The portrait is of a beautiful, alluring woman. She expresses power through seduction that will convince her husband to murder King Duncan. Adding the blood on her crown and eyes represents the act of murder and the guilt she carries. The blood may be misleading: is it from the crown, or are those tears of regret, yet to come further along the play? The Apex and Arms of the typeface were altered in order to enhance the feminine/masculine feel in the play.

30 D REVOLUTION | Design Firm: Dankook University | Designer: Hoon-Dong Chung
Client: Gwangju Design Biennale 2021 | Main Contributor: Hoon-Dong Chung
Assignment: This poster is for the Gwangju Design Biennale 2021 in Korea.
Approach: In terms of 3D Typography, I try to convey 'D Revolution' which is the main theme of the biennale.
Results: This got good reviews in the design field.

31 PAM HOGG POSTER | Design Firm: Mike Hughes Creative Direction + Design
Designer: Mike Hughes | Client: ROTOR Magazine | Main Contributor: Mike Hughes
Assignment: Reflect fashion by Pam Hogg through typography and design. She has a bright, playful feel to her work, but she also has a punk rock edge.
Approach: The design derived its concept from fashion through measuring and sewing. The letter forms were kept very simple and meant to represent buttons. The corrugated/accordion fold was a design based off of foldable wood measuring devices. The needle was added to ground the concept in sewing and fashion.
Results: The results were made into a poster and the design made it into the fashion section of the magazine featuring exclusive content from Pam Hogg for ROTOR magazine. It's the opening design introducing her work.

32 BL NEST POSTER | Design Firm: Bailey Lauerman | Designer: Jim Ma
Client: Nebraska College of Journalism | Creative Director: Sean Faden
Chief Marketing Officer: Carter Weitz | Copywriter: Joey Googe | Photographer: Sean Faden
Photo Retouching: Gayle Adams | Main Contributor: Jim Ma
Assignment: Create a space at the University of Nebraska College of Mass Communication and Journalism for students to use for collaborating on group projects.
Approach: We named the space, provided furniture and decorated the walls with rotating examples of work—including this poster—for creative inspiration.
Results: The University of Nebraska appreciated of our efforts to help provide a rich and relevant learning environment for students and has since collaborated on other projects including scholarship competitions and additional learning space.

33 WHAT UNITES US | Design Firm: Carmit Design Studio
Designer: Carmit Makler Haller | Client: What Unites Us 3 Exhibition
Photographer: Adobe Stock | Main Contributor: Carmit Makler Haller
Assignment: An entry done for "What Unites Us 3 Online Poster Exhibition." Our diversity in color and race are united by our empathy.
Approach: Four hands, displaying difference races, are trying to touch each other in a gesture conveying empathy.

34 RAVEN STORY | Design Firm: Studio A | Designer: Antonio Alcalá
Client: United States Postal Service | Artist: Rico Worl | Art Director: Antonio Alcalá
Main Contributor: U.S. Postal Service
Assignment: The assignment was to design a stamp for the USPS to honor the living culture and heritage of Indigenous peoples in an area of the U.S. The art director found an artist who is passionate about representing his hometown, his tribe, and his family through art and design.
Approach: Merging traditional artwork with modern design touches, this stamp represents a story of great significance to the Indigenous peoples of the northern Northwest Coast, which ranges from Southeast Alaska through coastal British Columbia and south into Washington state. Inspired by the traditional story of Raven freeing the sun, the moon, and the stars, the artist of Tlingit/Athabascan decent depicts Raven just as he escapes from his human family and begins to transform back into his bird form. A five-fingered hand connected to Raven suggests the human form he is leaving behind. To create the stamp art, the artist used

formline, the traditional design style of the Indigenous people of the northern Northwest Coast. Formline relies on a stylized vocabulary of ovoids and related shapes, continuous lines of varying thicknesses, and ambiguous, even abstract patterns that often suggest both human and animal features to convey a sense of transformation and the oneness of all life. The artist first sketched his design with a pencil before completing the image digitally. Bright stars were illuminated with gold foil during printing for dramatic effect.
Results: The stamp has been widely praised for its beauty and the story it shares with the American public. After just seven months 88% of the stamps have sold.

GOLD WINNERS:
36 BLACKROCK AR | Design Firm: Addison | Designer: Nick Schmitz
Client: BlackRock | Executive Creative Director: Richard Colbourne
Production Manager: Joe Kester | Printer: Sandy Alexander
Senior Account Director: Lauren DeAngelis | Main Contributor: Nick Schmitz
Assignment: We were tasked to design this annual report as an extension of BlackRock's brand and as a way to convey their focus on "Investing with Purpose".
Approach: Using stakeholder examples demonstrating BlackRock's purpose, Addison approached this annual report with the idea of bold simplicity—utilizing hits of BlackRock's bright color palette to help direct the reader's eye, callouts and sidebars to showcase impact, and large typography to instill confidence.
Results: The work resulted in a piece with a strong declarative voice that echoed the brand perfectly and complemented their executive and corporate messaging. The client was thrilled with the results.

37 ISTAR AR | Design Firm: Addison | Designer: Adriana Soh Young Ji
Client: iStar | Senior Design Director: Rachel Pigott
Executive Creative Director: Richard Colbourne | Art Buyer: Anne Crosson
Account Manager: Julio Soler | Main Contributor: Adriana Soh Young Ji
Assignment: iStar annual reports are designed as an ongoing series, the overarching goal of which is to report year-on-year against the strategy laid out by the CEO.
Approach: A sports metaphor was established three years ago, and the challenge was to make it creative and different from year to year. The cover represents both teamwork and the passing of a milestone in the race to transform commercial real estate forever with a fundamentally more efficient capital solution. The imagery throughout the book always shows an athlete ahead of all competition, with no one else in sight. Simple data points tell the story in the clearest and most succinct way. The report is integrated into the corporate website and promoted on the home page.
Results: Short but powerful, this report stylishly delivers on the project goal.

38 FUGITIVES | Design Firm: Faceout Studio | Designer: Tim Green | Client: Pegasus Books
Image Sources: Photo illustration using several images from Shutterstock and Getty Images
Main Contributor: Tim Green
Assignment: Book cover design.
Approach: This book tells the story of the hunt for Nazi fugitives after WW2 and into the Cold War. To capture the time period and subject matter, I decided to create a twist on the look of a spy dossier, with pieces of information and photos. The scraps of paper, newspaper clippings, maps and photos are spread out against a file folder, with the cover text integrated into these materials. The arrangement of dossier materials creates the shape of a Nazi swastika—a delightful second read that underscores the idea of Nazis in hiding.

39 MURDER AT THE CASTLE | Design Firm: Faceout Studio | Designer: Amanda Hudson
Client: Pegasus Books | Illustrator: Additional Illustrated Elements - Amanda Hudson
Image Source: Getty | Main Contributor: Amanda Hudson
Assignment: Book cover design.
Approach: The client wanted something fun, modern and mysterious. A quirky yet clever illustrated approach seemed to fit the bill. The result is a fresh look for a somewhat classic genre of English murder mysteries.

40 WITCH HUNT | Design Firm: Still Room | Designer: Jessica Fleischmann
Client: Hammer Museum | Writers: Connie Butler, Anne Ellegood
Publisher: DelMonico | Proofreader: Jane Bobko | Project Manager: Claire Dilworth
Printer: Conti Tipocolor | PrePress: Echelon Color | Editor: Domenick Ammirati
Director of Project Management: Melanie Crader | Main Contributor: Jessica Fleischmann
Assignment: Exhibition catalog for "Witch Hunt," a major museum show featuring works by 16 non-male international artists, presented simultaneously at two museums — the Hammer Museum and ICA LA. This catalog needed to present the artists with design that could stand up to their work without overwhelming, providing consistency throughout yet also differentiating each artist's work.
Approach: The book begins and ends with an iconic image from each artist, all framed by bright yellow, after a cover that features a witchy puff of smoke from a performance. The system of containers then moves on to a section for each artist, each with its own bold color background to frame the works, printed on coated paper. Each artist section starts with a brief introduction, followed by a set of images. The book's "front matter", curatorial, and institutional texts are grouped together in a section that is ½ inch narrower than the rest of the book, on uncoated paper, nestled in between the artists' projects. The color-blocked sections are visible on the page edges, allowing the reader to easily navigate through the book. The typeface is Lelo, one of the few contemporary sans serif fonts by a female type designer, Katharina Köhler. Overall, the book's structure references the symmetry of the body, as well as the vibrance and strength of these artists.
Results: 2,000 copies were printed, and are sold at bookstores and museum shops in both the US and Europe. The book is celebrated as a dynamic accompaniment to this bold and progressive exhibition.

41 THE TURBULENT SEA | Design Firm: Richard Ljoenes Design LLC
Designer: Richard Ljoenes | Client: Regan Arts | Writer: Charles N. Li
Publishers: Judith Regan, Regan Arts | Art Director: Richard Ljoenes
Photographer: Main portrait courtesy of author, propaganda poster and Hong Kong street scene by Alamy, Women by Shutterstock, Vietnam war protest via Wikimedia Commons
Main Contributor: Richard Ljoenes Design LLC
Assignment: Design a cover for Charles N. Li's memoir. "The Turbulent Sea" recounts Li's escape to America and the shocking, cruel racism he not only endured but observed nationwide. Growing steadily more involved in the antiwar movement, Li, having suffered in Mao's China, becomes a dissident among his cohorts for holding the view that Mao was the diametrical opposite of a revolutionary hero. Yet, for his pacifist and law-abiding protest activities, Li is persecuted by the American law enforcement and immigration authorities. Li's intellectual and psychological journey at Bowdoin College, Stanford University and the University of California, Berkeley, is triumphant as he finds a group of talented friends who provide, at last, an opportunity for the love and care that eluded him for so long.
Approach: A collage became the right medium to convey the culture shock Li went through arriving in America, featuring both elements from Mao's China, Hong Kong, anti-war protests in Berkeley, and the sexual revolution. The torn paper over his eyes also helped convey the identity crisis he experienced.
Results: The client was very pleased, and the book has performed well.

42 THE CORSAIR BRANDING | Design Firm: Mermaid, Inc.
Designer: Sharon Lloyd McLaughlin | Client: National Resources
Marketing Manager: Lauren Calabria | Creative Director: Sharon Lloyd McLaughlin
Developer: Bart McLaughlin | Main Contributor: Sharon Lloyd McLaughlin
Assignment: This boutique condominium building, located on Greenwich Harbor, was inspired by the luxurious flagship yacht The Corsair, owned by J.P. Morgan. We were commissioned to create a timeless brand that connects the ultra-luxury craftsmanship of its namesake yacht with today's modern amenities.
Approach: These limited edition residences were built with attention to detail, and with natural materials that would be passed down & cherished by future generations. With this top-of-mind, we created the Corsair Crest, combining a modern nautical feel with historical ties to its famous namesake yacht. As part of the brand story, we showcased storied artifacts & images connected to the yacht and to J.P. Morgan - blending the historical with innovative modern detail to showcase a luxurious waterfront lifestyle for those few lucky enough to live there.
Results: This unique branding has captured the luxurious feeling of its namesake flagship yacht, enabling it to stand out in a crowded market.

43 CAMPBELL'S RED & WHITE CONDENSED SOUP VISUAL IDENTITY
Design Firm: Turner Duckworth: London, San Francisco & New York
Designers: Naomie Ross, Michael Bagnardi, Karen Song | Client: Campbell's
Typographer: Ian Brignell | Design Director: Drew Stocker | Illustrator: Filip Yip
Production: Craig Snelgrove, Jeff Ennslen | Photographer: Hone Studio
Implementation Director: Jeff Jones | Account Director: Kate Wierman | Other: Fakery
Executive Creative Service: Andy Baron | Director of Client Services: Bailey James
Main Contributors: Naomie Ross, Michael Bagnardi, Karen Song
Assignment: Campbell's Soup is an American icon of design and culture alike. Our assignment was to bridge the widening gap between historic brand love and decreasing space for Campbell's in consumers' shopping carts, and to reverse a steady decline in sales. Building on the insight that Campbell's is often used as a meal starter, a cooking-focused positioning of "start something good" was introduced, and we designed packaging and a broader visual identity centered around this. The Campbell's soup that you're picturing in your mind was largely missing from the shelf before this assignment. Over the years, 97% of the portfolio had adopted common CPG codes at the expense of the brand: swooshes, ribbons, etc. We needed to reintroduce Campbell's as a champion of design, while ensuring easy portfolio navigation by consumers. We also needed to find ways to use design off-pack to bring people back to the proverbial aisle.
Approach: We rebuilt the portfolio from the foundation of the classic red and white label architecture, and re-drew and lovingly contemporized assets made famous over the past 124 years. We united a huge portfolio while still retaining navigability and designed a system that inspires confidence and creativity both in the kitchen, and in the community. The new design is intended to make the statement that this is not just another product — this is Campbell's Soup. The redesign considered every aspect. We redrew the script, giving it a soup-dipped feel by separating the characters. We brought esteem back into the medallion with a crisp new illustration and updated, finessed typography. We added wit to the Fleur de Lys, creating it from the C in Campbell's. Shifting focus from bowls of soup, we carefully shot real-food ingredients. We added charm and organization to claims. Off-pack, we introduced a vibrant, food-inspired secondary color palette. Finally, a new illustration style uses the full palette to tell simple, heartfelt brand stories.
Results: The new packaging started hitting shelves June 2021 and the larger visual identity was launched in conjunction with soup season.

44 SANTA MONICA SEAFOOD BRAND IDENTITY | Design Firm: PH Studio
Designers: Richard Patterson, Amy Hershman | Client: Santa Monica Seafood
Illustrator: Cherie Sinnen | Main Contributor: Richard Patterson
Assignment: Founded in 1939, Santa Monica Seafood is the largest distributor of seafood on the west coast. The redesign included a new brand identity, truck fleet graphics, frozen seafood packaging, and sauce/marinade labels. Because the truck graphics had traditionally been an important face of the company we paid special attention to bringing those to life.
Approach: Our goal was to update the nearly 30 year-old brand identity system while keeping certain equity elements. Their current system utilized graphic illustrations of various seafood species in a dark blue, tone-on tone execution. Wanting to give a nod to that look we developed pictograms with sans serif typography for the primary brand. We developed a system of color backgrounds with a stressed typographic treatment with some of the many different seafood species offered. Utilizing the brand colors along with six seafood illustrations, the truck graphics could be rotated on each side to create variations on the different truck types.

Results: SMS was very pleased with the overall look and received a lot of positive feedback from customers and people from areas they serve.

45 WEEKEND BIKE BRANDING | Design Firm: Xuecheng Xiong
Designer: Xuecheng Xiong | Client: Weekend Bike CA | Main Contributor: Xuecheng Xiong
Assignment: Weekend Bike CA is a Vancouver-based bike shop. The visual identity includes type design, logo design, package design, business card, product graphics, and web design in the e-commerce environment to satisfy the need of a start-up. The visual identity system design, which embodies a technical aesthetic and reflects aspects of modernity, appeals to younger audiences, while it thoroughly aligns with the product and the mission of the company.
Approach: The project started with conducting research on everything related to the product, the biking culture, and the unique language of modernism and technology. The logotype design drew inspiration from the shapes of diverse bike parts. And the visual system took influence from a variety of machine labels and the ways that they create the visual hierarchy of specifications and information.

46 ICA BRAND IDENTITY | Design Firm: MiresBall
Designers: David Alderman, Joanne Yahn | Client: Institute of Contemporary Art, San Diego
Creative Director: John Ball | Main Contributors: John Ball, David Alderman, Joanne Yahn
Assignment: With a courageous mission to present experimental art that questions everything—and an equally ambitious goal to bring art to everyone—the Institute of Contemporary Art, San Diego (ICA) needed a flexible, functional identity system that would create instant recognition and invite people into the experience.
Approach: A bold C emphasizes "contemporary", creating a memorable mark at even the smallest sizes. For more expressive applications, stylized alternate Cs enable the brand to highlight an ever-changing dynamic. Used in headlines, the C invites people to "see" something different.
Results: The new identity toolkit enables a range of uses, helping the ICA create more impact in more places.

47 GOWINGS RESTAURANT | Design Firm: Toben | Designers: Thorsten Kulp, Geoff Courtman
Client: Events & Hospitality | Creative Director: Katja Hartung | Main Contributor: Toben
Assignment: In contrast to its rich heritage, Gowings had begun to settle into a traditional 'bar and grill' aesthetic, attracting a customer base of male bankers and professionals from Sydney's inner city. The aim for the identity refresh was to position Gowings as a "must visit" culinary destination, broadening its appeal, and engaging a more diverse clientele. Steered by one of Australia's most admired chefs Sean Connolly, Gowings looked to bring Sydney-siders a fresh culinary experience of simple yet indulgent Italian cuisine inspired by New York's "Little Italy". Toben were tasked to create an identity for the restaurant that paid homage to the rich history of the Gowings Building, but also stepped into unexpected creative territory; to breath a new perspective into the space and dining experience.
Approach: Housed within the old Gowings building and department store, Gowings Bar and Grill has a storied past. With such a rich history, it was important to find the perfect balance between the past and the future, combining historical touch points and contemporary motifs in an engaging manner. Toben looked to develop and execute an identity that combined Gowings' heritage with the unique charisma of head chef Sean Connolly and his goldmine of "Seanisms" translated into Italian to embody the cheek and charm of New York's "Little Italy".
Results: Toben delivered a brand identity that combines the past and the future, and deftly balances exuberance and refinement. The custom logo mark was inspired by key aspects found in previous Gowings department store and facade logos, and crafted to occupy the contemporary space of the new identity and restaurant. Contrasting but complimentary typographic combinations inspired by historical Gowings touch points are given life and zest through head chef Sean Connolly's idiosyncratic 'Seanisms', and a dynamic and expressive colour palette expels the outdated bar and grill tones. All in all, the many facets of Gowings come together to form a vibrant, unexpected and distinct identity, shifting the restaurant into a more contemporary, inclusive and welcoming space for visitors.

48 EBO - OPEN FINANCE | Design Firm: Onrepeat Studio
Designer: Joao Oliveira | Client: EBO Corp | Main Contributor: Joao Oliveira
Assignment: EBO is part of a positive change towards open finance, a platform that aims to empower people with the advantages of open finance. Open finance drops the cost of using 'banking' services to almost nothing. As long as a person has a smartphone or computer, they can use Ethereum-based open finance with EBO's suite of tools. Our goal was to develop a brand aligned with EBO's values of openness and empowerment and the concept of digital tokens, while achieving an exciting, expressive and engaging visual tone that makes it stands out.
Approach: We partnered closely with EBO to develop their strategy, copywriting and brand identity, built upon the "blockchain" concept, where different blocks generate more complex blocks, which can be combined, mixed and remixed, in chains or individually, illustrating the ideas of transactions: an open and dynamic system built on generative mechanics, never static, always dynamic. This generative design system allows the visual identity to feature an endless range of assets for any application. The motion system is connected to the concept of transactions, with two or more shapes (EBO blocks) intersecting to create a new, more complex, structure, in a quick succession.
Results: The brand identity was extremelly well received by the client, going further than the initial briefing by being not just a static brand but a generative, expressive and dynamic brand, developed as a foundation and framework for future expansions of EBO, made for the future.

49 CAMP ST. JOHN'S IDENTITY | Design Firm: *TraceElement | Designer: Dana Nixon
Client: St. John's Episcopal School | Chief Creative Officer: Jeff Barfoot
Account Manager: Katherine Scoggin | Main Contributor: Jeff Barfoot
Assignment: St. John's Episcopal School is a private school for pre-K to eighth grade in Dallas, Texas. They were revamping their summer program and wanted a new identity for it. They wanted to bring the overnight camp feel to the campus. Each year the students will be part of a new "crew" and each week there will be new programs and learning themes. We were tasked with creating an identity that would make students feel like they have been a part of history.
Approach: The new look needed to feel modern yet established. The identity we created features heritage elements executed in a playful yet vintage style to uphold their 1953 founding year. The color palette is inspired by elements found in nature, but brightened to appeal to a young camper.
Results: The client was thrilled with the final identity and felt that it provided them with an identity that evoked that vintage feel while still feeling very "St. John's."

50 GALAXY S22 LAUNCH CAMPAIGN 2022 | Design Firm: Turner Duckworth: London, San Francisco & New York | Designers: Jack Powell, Eli Walters | Client: Samsung
Design Directors: Glenn Chan, Akira Yasuda, Alice Koswara | Creative Director: Carolyn Ashburn
Senior Designers: Nathan Nickel, Thom Pastrano, Derek Price | Account Director: Gabi Lovelace
Others: Mallari Batlaw, Sara Scanlan | Main Contributor: Cinthia Wen, Head of Creative
Assignment: In February 2022, Samsung unveiled the Galaxy S22 Series devices. We were asked to develop a cohesive visual identity that highlighted the device's characteristics; superior camera and the introduction of the S Pen to S22 Ultra.
Approach: We designed a library of images capturing the characteristics and beauty of Galaxy S22 Series. Each visual can work effectively as a standalone Key Visual and tell an even more extensive product story in combination. Along with lifestyle images, the campaign is rich with content, providing the flexibility to generate new varieties that can be refreshed throughout the campaign lifespan.
Results: The campaign resulted in a complete product story, spoke to the consumer, and fulfilled practical marketing needs. Furthermore, the S22 campaign delivered Samsung Galaxy's brand personality; "serious tech, playfully told."; and continues to elevate its brand perception to consumers. As of date, the Galaxy S22 is seeing the highest sales figures since 2019 and has maintained initial sales momentum since its launch.

51 ADM PROSPECTUS 21/22 | Design Firm: FACTORY | Designer: Chrystal Lim
Client: Nanyang Technological University: School of Art, Design and Media
Creative Director: Roy Wang | Main Contributor: Nanyang Technological University: School of Art, Design, and Media
Assignment: The Fourth industrial revolution is characterized by a fusion of technologies that is blurring the lines between the physical, digital, and biological spheres. It also brings renewed focus on how arts and culture are critical in formulating the advancement of society and mankind. Tasked with designing the ADM Undergraduates Prospectus 2021/2022, a yearly print material published by the NTU School of Art, Design and Media introducing their Design Art and Media Art programs, we wanted to echo the college's position in grooming the next generation with the powerful tools to enact meaningful change in this new world.
Approach: This issue features an expressive computer-generated module we designed that represents the diversity of ways in which art and design can impact technology and society. A quadrant is 3D printed onto every cover; juxtaposing how each student has the potential to be a part of this movement.
Results: The result is a sophisticated brochure that is emotive and stunning to the eye. It is also incredibly well received by the prospective students, serving as a limited edition collectible.

52 AEVTIUS BROCHURE | Design Firm: Vanderbyl Design
Designers: Michael Vanderbyl, Tori Koch | Client: Aevtius
Creative Director: Michael Vanderbyl | Main Contributor: Michael Vanderbyl
Assignment: Aevitus advances the legacy of the traditional cooperage process with a reusable barrel system.

53 EVAN SPENCER BROCHURE | Design Firm: Vanderbyl Design
Designers: Michael Vanderbyl, Tori Koch | Client: Evan Spencer | Photographer: David Peterson
Creative Director: Michael Vanderbyl | Main Contributor: Michael Vanderbyl
Assignment: Brochure for the launch of Los Angeles-based Evan Spencer furniture company with portraits of iconic LA figures (John Van Hamersveld, Tyler Ellis, Chad Muska, and others).

54 GLOW OF LIFE | Design Firm: TOPPAN INC. | Designer: Masahiro Aoyagi [TOPPAN INC.]
Client: Komori Corporation | Art Directors: Masahiro Aoyagi [TOPPAN INC.], Misako Fujiwara [TOPPAN INC.] | Photographer: Magda Indigo | Print Designers: Akihiro Takamoto [TOPPAN INC.], Riichi Yamaguchi [TOPPAN INC.] | Other: OFFICE SQUARE LLC.
Main Contributor: Masahiro Aoyagi [TOPPAN INC.]
Approach: This calendar is based on a photograph by Magda Indigo. The calendar reproduces a wide color gamut by making full use of the seven Smart Colors (CMYK + violet, green, and orange) provided by Komori Corporation's printing presses, and adds texture with a high gloss and a rough texture.

55 ROTOR MAGAZINE COVER | Design Firm: Mike Hughes Creative Direction + Design
Designer: Mike Hughes | Client: ROTOR Magazine | Photographer: Tim Kent
Main Contributor: Mike Hughes
Assignment: To design a magazine cover to represent the spirit of ROTOR magazine. Which is an aspirational fashion+design magazine with a bit of an edge to it.
Approach: I created ROTOR's masthead which contains a seismic wave. I paired that with an exclusive fashion photo from Pam Hogg's fashion shoot.
Results: The cover was successful and attracted people in fashion and design.

56 ONE COOL SUMMER | Design Firm: Wainscot Media
Designers: Trevett McCandliss, Nancy Campbell | Client: Earnshaw's Magazine
Photographer: Zoe Adlersberg | Fashion Director: Mariah Walker
Editor-in-Chief: Michele Silver | Main Contributors: Trevett McCandliss, Nancy Campbell
Assignment: Our goal was to create an opening spread for a fashion story that featured children's summer fashion.

Approach: We created a fun type design that played off the word cool.
Results: People enjoyed this story!

56 BEACHY KEEN | Design Firm: Wainscot Media
Designers: Nancy Campbell, Trevett McCandliss | Client: Footwear Plus Magazine
Photographer: Trevett McCandliss | Hand Lettering: Nancy Campbell
Hair & Makeup: Clelia Bergonzoli | Main Contributors: Nancy Campbell, Trevett McCandliss
Assignment: Create a spread that features summer footwear and fashion.
Approach: We created a hand-done type design that has a loose, carefree feel to it.
Results: Everyone loved it!

57 INTO THE LIGHT | Design Firm: Wainscot Media
Designers: Trevett McCandliss, Nancy Campbell | Client: Footwear Plus Magazine
Photographer: Trevett McCandliss | Hair & Makeup: Shane Monden, Next Artists
Editor-in-Chief: Greg Dutter | Model: Kate Demianova from Supreme Model Mgmt.
Main Contributors: Trevett McCandliss, Nancy Campbell
Assignment: Our goal was to create an opening spread for a fashion story that featured pastel-colored footwear that has airy construction.
Approach: We created a custom type solution that is light and airy.
Results: People enjoyed the story!

57 PRECIOUS METALS | Design Firm: Wainscot Media
Designers: Trevett McCandliss, Nancy Campbell | Client: Footwear Plus Magazine
Photographer: Trevett McCandliss | Hair & Makeup: Clelia Bergonzoli, Ray Brown Pro
Editor-in-Chief: Greg Dutter | Model: Rebecca Henobik from Fenton Model Mgmt.
Main Contributors: Trevett McCandliss, Nancy Campbell
Assignment: This is a spread to a fashion story featuring metallic footwear.
Approach: We created black typography to go with our goth inspired photography.
Results: Everyone enjoyed the story!

58 ORANGE CRUSH | Design Firm: Wainscot Media
Designers: Trevett McCandliss, Nancy Campbell. | Client: Footwear Plus Magazine
Photographer: Trevett McCandliss. | Model: Zoie Zeller from Fenton Model Mgmt.
Editor-in-Chief: Greg Dutter. | Main Contributors: Trevett McCandliss, Nancy Campbell
Assignment: Our goal was to create an opening spread for a fashion story that featured orange-colored footwear.
Approach: We created a customized type solution with floating orange shapes.
Results: People enjoyed the story!

58 THE MAN WHO LOVED SHAKERS | Design Firm: Yankee Publishing Inc.
Designers: Trevett McCandliss, Nancy Campbell. | Client: Yankee Magazine
Art Director: Katherine Van Itallie. | Main Contributors: Trevett McCandliss, Nancy Campbell
Assignment: This is the opening spread to a story about a man who befriends and eventually lives with the Shakers.
Approach: We created a typographic solution that feels like embroidery to invoke the feeling of the handmade, which is a big part of Shaker culture.
Results: Everyone enjoyed the story!

59 HOT STUFF | Design Firm: Wainscot Media
Designers: Trevett McCandliss, Nancy Campbell. | Client: Footwear Plus Magazine
Photographer: Trevett McCandliss. | Hair & Makeup: Shane Monden
Editor-in-Chief: Greg Dutter. | Model: Mary Crimmons from Supreme Model Mgmt.
Main Contributors: Trevett McCandliss, Nancy Campbell
Assignment: To create an opening spread for a fashion story that features footwear inspired by the disco era.
Approach: We created a funky, playful custom type solution.
Results: Everyone enjoyed the story!

59 TRAIL MIX | Design Firm: Wainscot Media
Designers: Trevett McCandliss, Nancy Campbell. | Client: Footwear Plus Magazine
Fashion Director: Annie Loynd Burton. | Model: Chris Flora from Fenton Model Mgmt.
Photographer: Trevett McCandliss | Photographer's Assistant: Tara Campbell.
Editor-in-Chief: Greg Dutter | Main Contributors: Trevett McCandliss, Nancy Campbell
Assignment: This is the opening spread to a story featuring hiking boots.
Approach: This fashion story features a potpourri of hiking boot styles. Playing off the outdoor theme, we designed the headline. Trail Mix, as if it were food packaging. We added the subhead and credits to the design and printed out the label. We than attached it to a bag of trail mix and photographed it.
Results: Everyone enjoyed this story and then ate the trail mix.

60 NORTH KANSAS CITY EARLY EDUCATION CENTER | Design Firm: DLR Group
Designer: Chris Cox | Client: North Kansas City School | Architect: Ian Kilpatrick
Project Manager: Robyn O'Roark | Interior Designer: Stacy Davis | Main Contributor: Chris Cox
Assignment: DLR Group's design of North Kansas City Schools Early Education Center responds to a unique group of early learners. Both the need to consolidate the district's Early Childhood Special Education program in one place, coupled with growing early childhood offerings in general, led the district to reuse an existing Hobby Lobby & Price Chopper. The building is broken down into 7 different learning communities designed around themes in nature, ranging from honeycomb to butterflies. Each community is meant to give learners a small cohort to interact with while also having access to the facility's many amenities: multi-purpose spaces with sensory experiences, expanded outdoor play, pull out spaces for de-escalation and testing, anf expansive discovery zones for additional indoor play. Equally important is the inclusion of teacher equanimity spaces, affording educators a space that is intended for adult interaction and collaboration.
Approach: The 112,000 SF facility houses about 900 early learners ages 3-5, making it one of the largest early childhood facilities in Missouri. Approximately 50% of that population are special needs learners. Interior finishes and planning have been carefully considered to make sure all learners are afforded equitable learning experiences. As part of a completely integrated design process, DLR Group created a storybook based on the environmental graphics from the project. One of the project architects served as the author for the exercise. The hardcover book was shared with the school's teachers and a PDF was created to share with parents. The goal is that on day one, the children are welcomed by their "friends" from the storybook and it will help ease the anxiety of their first day of school.
Results: So far the results have been more than could have been expected. One of the greatest fulfillments of this project has been watching the children's reaction to the graphics. Teachers have also been thrilled by the space. The book that was spun off from the graphics is proudly displayed in all of their classroom windows; available for the next story time with the students.

61 SECOND WORLD WAR GALLERIES | Design Firm: Ralph Appelbaum Associates
Designer: Ralph Appelbaum Associates | Client: Imperial War Museum
Project Director: Patrick Swindell | Graphic Designer: Mat Mason
Exhibition Managers: Sarah Pollard, Caroline Sjöholm | Content Coordinator: Sadie Levy Gale
Others: Charlotte Kingston (Content Developer), Helen Schulte (Content Developer)
Main Contributor: Ralph Appelbaum Associates
Assignment: The redevelopment of the Second World War Galleries at London's Imperial War Museum (IWM) represents a major new update and revision of this pivotal period in history. Developed in parallel with the Museum's new Holocaust Galleries, the design ensures that the connection the Holocaust and WWII are fully understood. The Second World War Galleries broadens the context of the Imperial War Museum's traditional story by emphasizing the global nature of the conflict and reflecting on the impact this moment of history still has on Britain and the twenty-first century. Visitors encounter the Second World War narrative through 6 galleries, beginning in 1930 and ending in 1949. Each Gallery in the is rooted in a thematic question: How did WWII begin? How did war spread across Europe? What did war mean for Britain? How did the war turn global? How was the war won and lost? How did the war change the world?
Approach: With more than 1,500 items and personal stories from over 80 countries, the Galleries bring together untold stories and unheard voices to help visitors understand the most devastating conflict in human history. The combination of international stories with well-known artifacts and a full range of modern display techniques engage a new generation of museum visitors with this complex and formative period of history and help them feel a deep, personal connection with these Galleries. Using color-coded graphic information systems and immersive media, the design goal was to strengthen understanding of complex materials without overwhelming visitors. Interactive elements have been included to facilitate intergenerational learning throughout the exhibition, including full-scale Anderson and Morrison air-raid shelters visitors can go inside, as well as digital elements like a tunable radio and screens. The Imperial War Museum's vast archive of imagery and film is utilized throughout the exhibition experience, edited into numerous narrative film installations.
Results: There were record numbers of visitors in the first week the Galleries opened during October 2021. The Galleries are particularly successful at engaging school groups with the story of WWII. They enable a younger generation to learn about the War from a global perspective, tracing the events as they unfold over time and hearing the perspectives of everyday people.

62 THE ALLISON AND ROBERTO MIGNONE HALLS OF GEMS AND MINERALS
Design Firm: Ralph Appelbaum Associates | Designer: Ralph Appelbaum Associates
Client: American Museum of Natural History | Lighting Design: Renfro Design Group
Interactive Designer: American Museum of Natural History | Research: American Museum of Natural History | Other: Kubik Maltbie (Prime Exhibits Contractor)
Main Contributor: Ralph Appelbaum Associates
Assignment: In 2021, the American Museum of Natural History's world-renowned Allison and Roberto Mignone Halls of Gems and Minerals were reopened with a completely new presentation. Within the renovated halls, state-of-the-art lighting is optimized to highlight color variation and refraction in gems and jewelry. The extraordinary role minerals play in science and culture is highlighted with up-to-date knowledge. The halls' elegant design carefully integrates interpretive graphics and media programs for museum visitors. Curated by George E. Harlow, the halls were designed in collaboration with the architects and the Museum's Exhibition Department under the direction of Lauri Halderman.
Approach: Foremost was showcasing the Museum's vast and diverse mineralogy collection of over 5,000 mineral specimens Rich graphics engage visitors in deepening their understanding of individual specimens and mineral groups. Carefully integrated media produced by the Museum's Exhibition department makes visible the mostly unseen processes that make minerals. The three main divisions are the Gem Hall, the Mineral Hall, and the Melissa and Keith Meister Gallery for temporary exhibitions. The Gem Hall includes a display of nearly 2,500 objects accompanied by digital labels. These include the Star of India sapphire, the Patricia Emerald, the DeLong Star Ruby, the Brazilian Princess topaz, and a carving of the Buddhist deity Guan Yin in lavender jadeite jade. The Mineral Hall is anchored by a selection of large minerals that encourage visitor engagement, including a four-ton slab of garnet-bearing amphibolite, a six-foot tall column of polished labradorite, and a grouping of beryl crystals. The Mineral Hall comprises of four sections: Mineral Forming Environments is dedicated to the environments and processes by which minerals form. Mineral Fundamentals displays explore the overarching concepts of mineral sciences, Systematic Classification contains 659 specimens that represent the chemical classification system that scientists use to organize Earth's more than 5,500 mineral species, as well as an interactive feature in which visitors can explore forming minerals from the elements on the periodic table. Finally, the Minerals & Light room explores the optical properties of minerals. Throughout the Mineral Hall, an expansive, new thematic exhibit structure make the Museum unique among its peers. Clusters of double-sided casework presents a rich array of specimens contextualized with accessible yet scientifically accurate stories, illustrations, diagrams, and images. Enhanced by cultural and technological detail, these stories connect minerals to visitors' everyday lives.

Animations further help demystify the age-long processes that create minerals and crystals. A layer of inquiry-based interpretation helps to engage visitors more deeply through Next Generation Science Standards (NGSS) tools for investigating and understanding science practices and concepts as they relate to mineralogy.
Results: The new Mignone Halls of Gems and Minerals at AMNH has been transformed and elevated to a "must-see" for New Yorkers and will be a signature destination for national and international visitors.

63 STATE ETHNOLOGICAL MUSEUM AND MUSEUM OF ASIAN ART AT THE HUMBOLDT FORUM | Design Firm: Ralph Appelbaum Associates
Designer: Ralph Appelbaum Associates | Client: Humboldt Forum
Graphic Designers: Kerstin Neumann-Teufel, Monika Malsy (malsyteufel was Partner to RAA), Kristin Braun, Thomas Meyer | Exhibition Designers: Justin Allen, Serena Bartalucci, Markus Blösl, Anna F Castillo, Ning-Yu Chang, Txell Cisa, Lucille Cros, Eva Csonka, Aleksandra Duczmal, Andrea Perez Fu, Inga Gabriel, Antje Heymann, Ilana Hofmann, Teresa Huber, Andrea Jacob, Ryla Jakelsky, Jennnifer Klähn, Karin Knott, Camille Ladan, Rachel Martin, Marta Masternak, Sara Omassi, Maria C. Orizzonte, Umberto Pinoni, Vicky Regehr, Fiete Rohde, Wided Rouin, Marc Llinares Ruiz, Paulina Samardakiewicz, Kamila Sarnecka, Barbara Véve, Katharina Vraga, Franziska Waldemer
Project Managers: Christian Geisser, Constanze Hager, Sebastian Scheller, Wenke Merkel, Berit Shepard, Anita Walter | Project Director: Tim Ventimiglia | Others: Project Deputy Director: Philipp Teufel (malsyteufel Design Partner to RAA), Artifact Mount Designer: Harry Hauck
Main Contributor: Ralph Appelbaum Associates
Assignment: Located in the reconstructed Berlin Palace on Berlin's Museum Island, the newly opened Humboldt Forum is envisioned as an international forum of art, culture, and science. Comprising over 170,000 square feet over two whole floors of the building, the permanent exhibitions of State Ethnological Museum and Museum of Asian Art present Germany's most comprehensive non-European collections — unique artistic and cultural artifacts from Africa, Asia, America, and Oceania. Thematic exhibition modules, family areas, activity rooms, listening spaces, multimedia installations, and visible study collections provide a multifaceted stage to engage in active dialogue with and between the world's cultures, to engage in a proactive dialog about the history and provenance of collections, and to celebrate the diversity of human experience and achievements.
Approach: The collections occupy over half of the Humboldt Forum's entire interior area and form the heart of this new institution. Far more than a display of some 24,000 historic objects, the exhibitions were designed as a dynamic platform for intercultural discourse. While our primary task was to design for the initial installations, our design also deliberately set the stage for change, through the future incorporation of new exhibitions, interventions, and public programs. Thus, the exhibition installation is a framework for an ongoing process. The exhibitions are organized by continents and geographical regions. Within these regions, the exhibitions are thematically curated into 40 distinct exhibitions. The project also required close collaboration and technical coordination with the curators because a wide range of materials and art objects required a deep understanding of their aesthetics and conservation requirements. Discussions with curators allowed for a design that not only helped with the conservation and aesthetic appreciation of the collections, but also flexibility and the ability to change the presentations. For this project, over 530 speciality showcases were designed according to German State Museum Standards. We also designed over 12,000 object mounts which can be adapted to each object's specific presentation requirements. Visible study collections areas are fitted out with large scale flexible showcases for displaying the mass and breadth of collections and media stations for in-depth study.
Results: The project provides a captivating and emotionally engaging immersive stage for flexible and adaptive messaging, able to connect deeply and emotionally with cultural heritages while also addressing contemporary perspectives and topics. Since its second partial opening in September 2021 under restrictive COVID-pandemic conditions with limited timed ticket entry, the Humboldt Forum in the first 3 months had already received over 100,000 visitors.

64 CALL OF DUTY: VANGUARD KEY ART | Design Firm: PETROL Advertising
Designer: PETROL Advertising | Clients: Activision, Sledgehammer
Main Contributor: PETROL Advertising
Assignment: The goal was to give a completely new take on making WWII timeless. It was the first time there had been a cast that was recognizable likeness linked to in-game characters. The strategy was to maximize the brand of Call of Duty as bold and iconic as possible in digital spaces while still being able to tell the story of these four iconic heroes in a battle moment in the pacific theater. The creative should showcase this massive emotional moment that works across all use-cases and placements (small or large).
Approach: A large scale photoshoot was conducted at an abandoned military base in the southwestern United States, in 15-degree weather, to simulate and re-create the conditions of WWII and all the different theaters the game takes place in. Numerous iconic moments were created and ultimately ended building this profile battle that showcases the scale and heroism of our characters in WWI.
Results: The marketing was very successful and helped drive incredibly high pre-order numbers/sales and helped pivot the brand for the next generation.

65 WRITE A CHRISTMAS CARD 2021 | Design Firm: FACTORY | Designer: Sandra Lau
Client: Self-initiated | Creative Director: Roy Wang | Main Contributor: FACTORY
Assignment: #WriteaChristmasCard is our studio's yearly campaign to encourage people to send a note or card to someone they care about for Christmas. Through the joy of receiving, we hope it inspires the recipients to do the same.
Approach: For the seventh edition of our studio's #WriteaChristmasCard series, we created a one-of-a-kind pinball machine card featuring a beautifully illustrated RoboSanta. There's nothing more satisfying than pinball landing exactly where you want it to be. No matter how old you are, you should never stop having fun. Live a little, and have a Merry Christmas! #ToTheMoon
Results: People who received the cards were overjoyed at the nostalgic nature, as well as how it brings an element of tangibility to an increasingly digital world.

66 STRANGE DUCKS | Design Firm: Mark Braught Studios
Designer: Mark Braught | Client: Strange Duck Brewery | Studio: Mark Braught Studios
Illustrator: Mark Braught | Art Director: Kristan Drake | Main Contributor: Mark Braught
Assignment: Created for Strange Duck promoting the unique aspect of their products, for in-store promotion, merchandising, online and print advertising.
Approach: Creative development as a pencil sketch to fully rendered digital image.
Results: This illustration was used widely across various media: direct mail, web/social, fliers, business cards, packaging, apparel, merchandise, limited print advertising, and in-store display. The client was pleased with the illustrations and more images are in the works.

67 SERPENTINE SWAN | Design Firm: Michael Pantuso Design
Designer: Michael Pantuso | Client: LAGO Innovation Fund | Main Contributor: Michael Pantuso
Assignment: Created for the headquarters of LAGO INNOVATION FUND.
Approach: Creative development as a pencil sketch to fully rendered digital image.
Results: Hanging event scheduled in May 2022. NFT release to be determined.

68 LOOP LINE FOOD & WINE LOGO | Design Firm: Vanderbyl Design
Designers: Michael Vanderbyl, Tori Koch | Client: CRU Wine Distributors
Creative Director: Michael Vanderbyl | Main Contributor: Michael Vanderbyl
Assignment: Logo for high end wine shop located on Toronto streetcar loop.

69 NUTECH PAINT IDENTITY | Design Firm: SML Design
Designer: Vanessa Ryan | Client: NuTech Paint | Main Contributor: Vanessa Ryan
Assignment: NuTech Paint is one of Australia's largest independent paint specialists. 2022 is their 50th year anniversary and they saw an opportunity to celebrate with an identity rebrand to showcase their company and how far they have come.
Approach: It was important that the new identity reflected their brand history and where they came from. The 'droplets' are the same shapes as they were in the original mark. We wanted to infuse the new mark with meaning and modernity but also show a distinct evolution of their history. The droplet shapes take on a new form, working together to encapsulate the invisible letter "N" for NuTech as the anchor holding them in place. Each of the droplet colors carefully blends to create a sophisticated transition, representing the full spectrum of paint color, better reflecting the industry they excel in. It also represents the company's growth as an evolution from the original logo, which only used primary colors.
Results: The 50th year celebration and new logo/brand resulted in a range of significant and demonstrable company benefits and opportunities, including: increased customer and staff engagement, wider audience appeal including global market opportunities, consistency of look and feel across all marketing collateral for a stronger brand appeal, and a powerful standout company image in competition with major paint brands internationally.

70 MOUNTAIN GIRLS FARM LOGO | Design Firm: Michael Schwab Studio
Designer: Michael Schwab | Clients: Jane Kleinman, Nancy Minion
Main Contributor: Michael Schwab
Assignment: Create an icon that graphically evoked 'Rural. Local. Healthy. Farm.'
Approach: We didn't want visually commit to specific vegetables or flowers - so we we agreed upon portraying an old vintage farm tractor along with a rugged, hand-hewn font. Simple. However, at the last minute, the client wanted to communicate the fact that they were also raising chickens. So we quickly placed a hen up on the hood of the tractor.
Results: The hen actually brought the logo to life. The Farm Girls, Jane and Nancy, are very happy with it.

70 BIODIVERSITY | Design Firm: H. Tuncay Design | Designer: Haluk Tuncay
Client: TEMA Foundation | Main Contributor: Haluk Tuncay
Assignment: With reference to meetings annually held by TEMA Foundation under different headings, the topic of the year of 2022 was "Biodiversity". This logo was designed to be utilized in various materials relating to subject meeting.

70 VINTAGE WINE FUND | Design Firm: Michael Schwab Studio
Designer: Michael Schwab | Client: Lawrence D. Dutra | Main Contributor: Michael Schwab
Assignment: To create a graphic icon that evoked several attributes: Vintage. Wine. Sonoma County. Delivery. Fun.
Approach: I have always wanted to portray a relatively small object as overly huge - surreal - in the back of an old, classic pickup - not unlike the old travel postcards from the 1940s and 50s. This was one of those rare occasions where it worked! We kept the image simple, quiet, confident, and comfortable to look at.
Results: A happy, proud client.

71 GARY'S WINE & MARKETPLACE LOGO | Design Firm: Vanderbyl Design
Designers: Michael Vanderbyl, Alex Kinoshita | Client: Gary's Wine & Marketplace
Creative Director: Michael Vanderbyl | Main Contributor: Michael Vanderbyl
Assignment: High end Napa Valley wine purveyor.

71 DK | Design Firm: Annie Chen Design | Designer: Annie Chen
Client: Sigma Intégrale | Main Contributor: Annie Chen
Assignment: An identity for a motion actuator, DK. Coincidentally, the project name is also the acronym for Donkey Kong (video game) and the client felt that gorilla is perfect representation of the product.
Approach: The angular lines were based from the shape of lightning (energy) symbol which speaks to what 'kong' (the product) indicates as strong, robust, and agility.
Results: This was the second identity we have designed for this client.

71 NALINI SCARFE LOGO | Design Firm: Roger Archbold
Designer: Roger Archbold | Client: Nalini Scarfe | Main Contributor: Roger Archbold

Assignment: A wildlife photographer, who specialises in photographing birds, needed a brand mark for use as a watermark and to apply to her merchandise.
Approach: After visiting my client, who also runs a wildlife shelter, I was introduced to a rather cheeky Red Wattlebird (a type of Australian honeyeater) which made quite an impression. We thought it fitting that this bird should feature prominently - serving as one of the counters in the letterform of the logotype.
Results: In the words of my client: "It's fabulous and perfect for me!"

72 WAUSAUKEE CLUB FOUNDATION LOGOMARK
Design Firm: Resource Branding | Designer: Rick Grimsley | Client: The Wausaukee Club
Designer Director: Rick Grimsley | Account Supervisor: Sarah Krausen
Main Contributor: Resource Branding
Assignment: Create a logomark for the Wausaukee Club Foundation. The Wausaukee Club is a 117 year-old rustic cabin retreat on 2,400 pristine forested acres in the remote area of Athelstane, Wisconsin. Club members and their families have summered there for generations. In 2016 they came together to create the Foundation in order to raise money each year and give back to the community by supporting local area high school students in their education by providing textbooks, resources and scholarships.
Approach: Design a logomark that complements the rustic, national park style signage in the area and also ties in the forested setting and educational aspects of the Foundation's primary mission.
Results: The client was very pleased and is using the logomark at the club, on social media and in local onsite promotions.

72 REVIVAL ANALYTICS LOGO | Design Firm: Goodall Integrated Design
Designer: Derwyn Goodall | Client: Revival Analytics | Main Contributor: Derwyn Goodall
Assignment: To create an effective, memorable logo for Revival Analytics.
Approach: Revival Analytics makes remote monitoring systems for legacy oil wells in remote locations in midwestern Canada. Revival's battery-powered, wireless system monitors and reports critical data and delivers alerts on motor function, fluids flow and leaks. The logo represents the collection and processing of cloud based data for analysis and monitoring. This is not the chosen logo but one I feel was a more successful representation of Revival's business.
Results: Excellent results across the board.

72 MYTHOLOGY DISTILLERY | Design Firm: Moxie Sozo | Designer: Nate Dyer
Client: Mythology Distillery | Main Contributor: Nate Dyer
Assignment: Mythology Distillery was founded in 2017 in Denver, Colorado, inspired by the adventures, stories, and spirits three friends shared on a ski trip to Alaska. The distillery offers traditional whiskey, gin, and rum, as well as a rye vodka and more experimental limited release spirits at the Mythology Bar. To stand out in a crowded (and rapidly growing) category, Moxie Sozo was tasked with developing a visually evocative, story-driven brand for the distillery, as well as packaging for its first four spirits: American whiskey, rye vodka, silver rum, and gin.
Approach: The brand began with a name, Mythology, which set the stage for rich, immersive storytelling and the creation of an expansive brand world. Each of Mythology's four core spirits brought that "mythology" to life with playful names and stories. Hell Bear American Whiskey, for example, tells the story of a weary prospector who's led from death's door by his spirit animal, the "Hell Bear"—known also by his common name, the wolverine. The labels lend further color to these stories, depicting the hero or heroine alongside their spirit animal—"brought together by fate"—and tasting notes that tie the liquid and story together.
Results: The brand and liquid were well received by the Denver community and the spirits industry, winning Westword's "Best Colorado Distillery 2019" and taking medals at spirits competitions. In its first year following launch, Mythology became the largest independently distributed distillery in Colorado. The brand quickly found its way into consumers' hearts, with several fans sharing pictures of their favorite spirit animals tattooed onto their bodies. With the success of the Mythology's core line, the brand has continued to launch experimental, limited edition, small batch releases, like a Hell Bear whiskey finished in syrah barrels.

72 THREE LITTLE PIGS | Design Firm: Moxie Sozo | Designer: Nate Dyer
Client: Three Little Pigs | Main Contributor: Nate Dyer
Assignment: Objective: To transform The Three Little Pigs into a mass-market (but not mainstream) brand. Mission: To create more enjoyable, everyday moments through casual charcuterie.
Approach: We exist to spread joie de vivre — the joy of living! We're shining a new light on charcuterie, so we can define what it means. For us, charcuterie includes everything from pâté to egg bites — new use occasions, new presentations, & new products to expand what charcuterie can be.

72 THE LOGO OF TENKODO INC. | Design Firm: USADesign
Designer: Yoshinori Shimousa | Client: Tenkodo Inc. | President: Daisuke Kawajiri
Art Director: Yoshinori Shimousa | Main Contributor: Yoshinori Shimousa
Assignment: TENKODO, the company that commissioned me to create the logo, has as its mission to transform the time people spend worrying and anxious into time that is positive. The company's mission is to contribute to society through the development of products that provide the same attention to detail as Japanese hospitality, and to become a company that achieves world-class results. The project's goal was to create a symbol mark that would be seen by all as a symbol of Japan, based on the concept of the importance of being from Japan.
Approach: TENKODO has the thought and meaning of "a company that will be able to act in a way that shimmers in the heavens". This led us to the idea of what would be recognized by people around the world and "the best in Japan" to create this product. Against this context, I designed the kanji character for "heaven," the first letter of the company name, in the motif of the silhouette of the world-class Mt. Fuji, the highest mountain in Japan.
Results: Since the company's establishment, TENKODO has developed many unique products through crowdfunding and continues to release them to the world one after another, all with high achievement rates. The symbol is now seen by many users and has become a very valuable branding keystone for the company.

73 ST. JEROME | Design Firm: Stjepko Rošin | Designer: Stjepko Rošin
Client: Museum of Croatian Archaeological Monuments
Assignment: St. Jerome (born in Dalmatia, Croatia), a Christian saint, philosopher, translator, and writer, is best known for translating the Bible into Latin (Vulgate). With his authority, he indirectly enabled Glagolitic to become a national alphabet in Croatia, but Latin suppressed it over time. Therefore, the design intended to mark the project "St. Jerome ", implemented by the Museum of Croatian Archaeological Monuments, so that the logo communicates the core of the saint's identity: the beginning of literacy, written work, Latin and Glagolitic.
Approach: Considering that the saint is credited with the beginning of literacy and is the originator of the Bible as it is used today, the initial Latin letter "J" (Jerome) was taken as the basis for the visual: the letter is the basic element of a written work, and so singled out, it is associated with the initials of old books. Also, the initial in the meaning of the word, and within the books, represents the beginning. Furthermore, the "J" visualizes the abstract figure of a saint with the most basic attributes. The position of the serif of "J" was used for unobtrusive visualization of the recognizable red cardinal's hat. The Glagolitic letter "J", below the serif, integrated within the axis of the letter, alluded to the saint's beard, retaining the recognizability of the narrow shape of the Latin letter "J". The narrow Latin letter "J" is also important because of the narrow ascetic saint's structure. Then, the bottom of the letter alludes to the writing pen and the tip of the fountain pen. And the overall impression of the visual, due to the shape of the letter, is spiritual because, with its letter stroke, it leaves the impression that the saint is floating in space.
Results: The logo, to the satisfaction of the client, showed how a typographic solution, with minimal interventions within one letter, can create a simple and complex attribute sign. The logo also affirmed the old, somewhat forgotten Old Croatian Glagolitic alphabet, integrating the Glagolitic alphabet within the Latin alphabet uniquely, retaining the emphasis on the Latin alphabet. Considering that this is a complex museum project of St. Jerome, who was not such a simple person, the necessary technical simplicity and logical complex content of identity are optimal for what we were looking for.

74 MAXWELL FIREPLACES LOGO | Design Firm: AG Creative Group
Designer: Stewart Jung | Client: Maxwell Fireplaces | Main Contributor: Stewart Jung
Assignment: The client Maxwell Fireplaces approached us in helping them rebrand. They have been in business for over 35 years and realize their brand was outdated and needed to be reinvigorated.
Approach: The client didn't want to venture too far from their existing look which was a outdated typeface logo. We proposed a logo to complement the existing font yet retains the history and sentimental attachment of the old brand.
Results: The client was extremely happy with the end result as we were able to connect the sentiment of the old logo with a new one thus giving the brand a fresh look.

74 ENCORE BURGERS LOGO | Design Firm: Islam Hassan
Designer: Islam Hassan | Client: Encore Burgers | Main Contributor: Islam Hassan
Assignment: Encore is a young, fun, and funky burger shop in Paris with a brand persona that is all about the experience being vocal, loud, vibrant, and full of life. Hence the name, which means shouting with excitement to demand a repetition.
Approach: The brand mark draws on capturing that moment and imagining what it looks like in a fun and engaging way, characterizing a happy boy shouting with excitement, his wide open mouth subtly resembles a burger sandwich. Evoking an image of happiness, enjoyment, and satisfaction.
Results: The brand had a successful launch with great reception on experience and appearance. With the brand mark and visual assets, creating engagement through various mediums and touch points, helping the brand to expand its voice, and maintain relevance to consumer lifestyle.

74 HEART HAUS LOGO | Design Firm: Heart Haus at CVS Health
Designers: Ferenc Gaspar, Matt Rayel, Kelsey DeGenaro, Evan Boisvert, Joshua Wiedenroth
Client: Self-initiated | Creative Director: Christopher Lehmann
Executive Creative Director: Brett Gerstenblatt | Main Contributor: Heart Haus at CVS Health
Assignment: Heart Haus is the newly defined in-house creative team at CVS Health. We built this identity to represent our expertise through strategic and creative partnership across our enterprise, as well as to the broader creative community outside of CVS Health. At Heart Haus, we are inspired by the CVS Health purpose and grounded in what makes us distinct: human-centered creativity. With capabilities in branding, ideation and experience design, and supported by account services, creative strategy and planning, and creative operations, Heart Haus helps persuade, empower and inspire consumers, members and patients to achieve healthier lives through the communications and activations we imagine and bring to life.
Approach: Aligning around the Heart Haus name, we conducted a two-week design sprint. Our objectives were to develop a bold visual expression using elements of the CVS Health visual identity that reinforced the new group's name, and that would be visually compelling and distinct in the broader landscape. We also looked for opportunities to leverage a unique symbol as a portal for other visual expressions that reflect the work we do every day, the tools we use and the things that inspire us.
Results: The logo was the starting point for a rich identity that can inform the Heart Haus colleague experience, spanning materials and communications.

74 COLE RANCH LOGO | Design Firm: Spire Agency | Designer: Jason James
Client: Cole Ranch | Creative Director: Kimberly Tyner | Main Contributor: Jason James
Assignment: Cole Ranch is a 3,196-acre master-planned community in rural Denton County, Texas. The once-thriving cattle ranch and picturesque Texas coun-

tryside will soon become the homestead of tens of thousands of North Texans. Rancher, oilman and civil servant M.T. Cole originally settled his family here in 1932. Located along Hickory Creek in the Upper Trinity Basin, Cole Ranch is a place of wildflowers and wildlife, as well as oak, elm and family trees. In addition to a 50-acre city park, two five-acre neighborhood parks and an array of outdoor and nature-oriented amenities, the community will boast one of the most extensive nature trail systems in North Texas.
Approach: Texas is home to four species of quail, a claim only three other states can make. The Cole Ranch logo is a throwback-style of illustration based on the native Northern Bobwhite Quail. A place where family life, wildlife and the good life come together, the tagline for the new piece of Texas tranquility is Settle In to Nature and Nostalgia™. The inviting logo visually develops this line.
Results: As you can imagine, it takes some time to develop a master planned community that will eventually house 30,000+ residents. The community is currently having quiet conversations with select Texas builders before ever putting shovel in the dirt. Groundbreaking is set for February 2023, so there are currently no results other than enthusiasm from the Denton City Council and Denton Independent School District who will both benefit from this new community.

74 SOUND CHRISTIAN ACADEMY LOGO | Design Firm: Peterson Ray & Company
Designer: Scott Ray | Client: Sound Christian Academy | Art Director: Scott Ray
Main Contributor: Scott Ray
Assignment: To create a new logo for Sound Christian Academy.
Approach: The academy wanted an identity that focused on the Christian aspect of the school. Incorporating the cross into the S/C letter forms was a natural making it a simple, powerful image.
Results: The new logo was very well received by the administration, faculty and parents. The logo has made for a unique and powerful brand as it was applied to vehicles, signage and publications for the school.

75 MERMAID, INC. LOGOMARK | Design Firm: Mermaid, Inc.
Designer: Sharon Lloyd McLaughlin | Client: Self-initiated | Developer: Bart McLaughlin
Creative Director: Sharon Lloyd McLaughlin | Main Contributor: Sharon Lloyd McLaughlin
Assignment: We are a graphic design & branding company. This was one of our hardest assignments ever - to redesign our company's logo & brand story :)
Approach: The name of our company is Mermaid, Inc. We believe that creativity isn't a solid thing. It's a fluid process. For us, the fluid world mermaids inhabit is an excellent metaphor for the fluid-state-of-mind philosophy needed to thrive in today's rapidly evolving business environment. Hence Mermaid, Inc.'s tagline, "Fluid Creativity." To showcase this, a fluid, water-esque background creates the tail of our mermaid icon. The stroke of the lowercase "m" acts as a ballast to the tail, creating a harmonious balance.
Results: Simply put, we love it. We believe it showcases our out-of-the-box thinking & let-your-freak-flag-fly philosophy!

75 BORTHWICK MAINS FARM APIARY | Design Firm: Haas Design
Designer: Oliver Haas | Clients: John Young, Borthwick Mains Farm Apiary
Main Contributor: Haas Design
Assignment: John Young runs a small apiary producing Scottish honey on Borthwick Mains Farm near Borthwick Castle, a beautifully restored Scottish 15th-century fortification. John asked me to produce a logo for his apiary that could be used on honey jar labels and promotional material.
Approach: Most apiaries feature a bee in their logos. But I wanted to stay clear of bees, as did John who often gets stung during his work. He was open to the idea of being represented as a hapless knight (from Borthwick Castle), insufficiently protected in his armour from the swarming bees in a Pythonesque take on the iconic Tate&Lyle syrup logo, which shows a lion surrounded by a swarm of bees.
Results: The logo differentiates Borthwick Mains Farm's honey from that of other producers and has become a talking point, giving him attention beyond what could have been expected. He sold his annual produce within days.

75 THE CORSAIR LOGO | Design Firm: Mermaid, Inc.
Designer: Sharon Lloyd McLaughlin | Client: National Resources
Creative Director: Sharon Lloyd McLaughlin | Marketing Manager: Lauren Calabria
Developer: Bart McLaughlin | Main Contributor: Sharon Lloyd McLaughlin
Assignment: This boutique condominium building, located on Greenwich Harbor, was inspired by the luxurious flagship yacht The Corsair, owned by J.P. Morgan. We were commissioned to create a timeless brand that connects the ultra-luxury craftsmanship of its namesake yacht with today's modern amenities.
Approach: These limited edition residences were built with attention to detail, and with natural materials that would be passed down & cherished by future generations. With this top-of-mind, we created the Corsair Crest, combining a modern nautical feel with historical ties to its famous namesake yacht.
Results: This timeless logo has captured the luxurious feeling of its namesake flagship yacht, enabling it to stand out in a crowded market.

76 THE AMON CARTER MUSEUM OF AMERICAN ART BRAND IDENTITY
Design Firm: *TraceElement | Designer: Jeff Barfoot | Client: The Amon Carter Museum of American Art | Chief Creative Officer: Jeff Barfoot | Strategy: Lindsey Phaup
Illustrator: Jeff Barfoot | Account Manager: Lindsey Phaup | Main Contributor: Jeff Barfoot
Assignment: The Amon Carter Museum of American Art in Fort Worth, Texas, needed to update their identity, quite literally. What had begun as a personal collection of western art in the 1930s by businessman Amon Carter, had become a modern and vibrant collection of American artists, including housing the largest collection of photography in the United States. Although they had the reputation they wanted in the museum community, the public still largely saw them as a museum full of western landscapes and horse statuettes. They needed a new brand identity that reflected who they were now: a modern, active institution with a contemporary, vibrant collection.
Approach: Beginning with an inherited logotype that the Texas institution wanted to keep intact, we approached a rebrand knowing that a logo with more presence and connectivity would help guide a flexible and powerful new identity. The façade of the museum itself, a beautiful 1958 mid-century modern design by Pritzker Prize-winning architect Philip Johnson, inspired us. The "window," derived from the iconic entryway, gave the logotype substance and us an extensible element to build a new identity with.
Results: Coinciding with a renovation of the museum itself, the new identity was an immediate signal to the public that the Carter had transformed. In addition, the identity was loved by museum staff, from the curatorial staff who put on exhibitions to the education staff who plan events for adults and toddlers alike. The window gave the in-house team a simple device and toolkit that could tie a plethora of museum communications together, but was flexible enough to allow all of those communications to have some expression and personality of their own.

77 THE TRINITY RIVER BLUES PROJECT | Design Firm: May & Co.
Designer: Douglas May | Client: The Trinity River Blues Society | Main Contributor: Douglas May
Assignment: This series is a self-initiated project that honors 9 of the most influential Texas blues guitarists. All are native Texans except Robert Johnson, who made his only known recordings in San Antonio and Dallas.
Approach: Each icon is an interpretation of each personality into a distinctive reductive form: Blind Lemon Jefferson (1893-1929), Robert Johnson (1911-1938), T-Bone Walker (1910-1975), Lightnin' Hopkins (1912-1982), Gatemouth Brown (1924-2005), Freddie King (1934-1976), Albert "Iceman" Collins (1932-1993), Jimmie Vaughan (1951-), Stevie Ray Vaughan (1954-1990)
Results: The artwork is being considered for a series of limited edition prints collectible digital prints.

78 DORITOS TWISTED LIME HALLOWEEN | Design Firm: PepsiCo Design & Innovation
Designer: PepsiCo Design & Innovation | Client: Self-initiated
Main Contributor: PepsiCo Design & Innovation
Assignment: Doritos® Twisted Lime has long been a fan favorite limited-edition flavor, and the Doritos brand decided to re-release it for Halloween 2021. Halloween was a natural holiday for the brand to play off of, so the Design Team conceptualized an exclusive Halloween-inspired kit featuring a unique pyramid-shaped bag. With only 2,000 available, consumers flocked to snacks.com to purchase their product and participate in a giveaway for the full Doritos Twisted Lime Kit.
Approach: Leaning into the Halloween occasion, the Design Team wanted this packaging to go beyond the typically recognizable holiday motifs and symbols such as ghosts and pumpkins. Instead, we built a narrative around secret societies to feel exclusive and match the edginess of the Doritos brand. We played heavily off the triangle theme that permeates both the Doritos Visual Identity System, even going so far as to transform the bag itself into a pyramid-shaped structure. We leveraged the usual technology used for Doritos bags, but folded it in a unique way for a different tactile experience. We also incorporated secret society symbolism, adding foreboding design elements like the Eye of Providence. The packaging also features artfully illustrated skeletons, spiders, and spiderwebs more typically synonymous with Halloween.
Results: The Design Team developed a consumer experience that would surprise and delight at every touchpoint, from the moment of holding and opening the Doritos Twisted Lime box, to picking up the pyramid-shaped bag, and we created a feeling of exclusivity with Doritos branded pins. With the re-release of Doritos Twisted Lime, we were able to deliver to consumers an innovative and memorable experience with a Doritos flavor they love.

79 CLIO | Design Firm: Sol Benito | Designer: Vishal Vora
Client: Emper | Main Contributor: Sol Benito
Assignment: Brief was to create a Feminine perfume product that is unconventional in term of look and feel. Meant for Middle East Market.
Approach: The challenge was to break the notion of how we perceive perfume bottles. The entire design exercise was to create a visual language for effective packaging that can build a powerful story. Solution: CLIO is enigmatic poetry crafted in a bottle that tells the story of feminity, elegance, and beauty. It's a depiction of Arabian ethos, infinite love, and serenity. We took inspiration from lattice from Islamic architecture and used the flower as a mnemonic and crafted a cylindrical product with floral pattern lattice in aluminum as an oversized cap. The concept emphasized rich with modern charm and would make an intriguing object. Manifestation of craftsmanship, modern-day-elegance, simplicity, sophistication and transcend the ordinary are the elements that gone into making this design.

80 MI BUDS 3T PRO | Design Firm: Xiaomi | Designers: Ecosystem Packaging Design Team, Lei Zhao | Client: Self-initiated | Structural Engineering: Zhizhuang Song
Creative Director: Lu Chen | Main Contributors: Lu Chen, Lei Zhao, Zhizhuang Song
Assignment: Its shape resembles cobblestone and its sound creates ripples. Via the visual effect on the box of this cool high-tech product, we bring the consumers to experience a mood of Zen, a mystical feeling that can establish a close tie between consumers and the product starting at first glance, and the core function of this product is perfectly reflected and echoed. We may be bold to say that we are nowadays paying more attention to the human sensibility when designing the products. The key feature for this product is noise cancellation combined with the outstanding and clear sound quality. The "ripple" idea is generated in the light of the appearance of the product, which resembles a cobblestone lying in river.
Approach: The box's outer surface is designed and regarded as the water surface, and the product is centered with ripples surrounding it. These ripples, implied as sound waves, spread out in circles, just like the extraordinary auditory experienc that this product brings you. We use embossed printing to realize the ripple effect, so that you can have a full view of lines and shadow changing under lights. In addition, the embossed printing technology can also ensure you an unique tactile experience.

What we persistently pursue is the excited and fantastic unboxing experience for the user, and all the efforts made on the product box is naturally to manifest the effect of the inner design. Guided by this philosophy, we surely implement the identical concept on this product. The custom inserts are designed to fit the cobblestone-like product perfectly in the box. The centered cobblestone is emerging from the "sparkling" ripples, allowing plays of light and shadows that give the product a shimmering, animated appearance, which reflects the excellent interaction between the design and the product. Being Eco and environmental-friendly, the inner and outer materials of the box are all paper materials that can be recycled.

81 GOLD LABEL MOONCAKE | Design Firm: Box Brand Design Limited
Designer: Crystal Hu | Client: Xiang Yuen | Art Director: Yvonne Chung
Creative Director: Joey Lo | Main Contributor: Joey Lo
Assignment: This project misson is redesign their high-end mooncake series packaging for XINYUAN, a premium traditional food brand with over 50 years. Client looking forward to get rid of the conservative and traditional packaging image, to enhance market competitiveness. Mooncake is one of the most important product for client. To achieve client's goal, we try to found another angle to present this traditional festival food. Consider mooncake is a gift away during Mid-Autumn Festival and this is the top series of the brand, we decided to create a elegant image for this series in modern tradition way.
Approach: Moonlight is the most iconic icon of Mid-Autumn Festival, also represent reunion with family and friends. Starlight in moon with poetic imagery of mid-autumn storys combine with traditional elements to emphasise the nature of the traditional Mid-Autumn festival atmosphere. Western style patterns infused into the design, so as to convey a sense of product quality, as well as modernize this traditional product image. Its beautiful graphic design makes it the perfect gift, serving as an emotional bond between the brand and the consumers.
Results: Client feedback the new packaging design is popular with consumers, successfully to enhance brand image to premium from old fashioned.

82 QUINTA DO PILOTO'S MOSCATÉIS | Design Firm: Omdesign
Designer: Diogo Gama Rocha | Client: Quinta do Piloto | Main Contributor: Omdesign
Assignment: Quinta do Piloto Moscatel de Setúbal Family Collection and Quinta do Piloto Moscatel Roxo Family Collection are two rare Moscatéis from Quinta do Piloto, both signed and produced by the hands of Omdesign. They are very exclusive wines that carry the legacy of four generations of Cardoso family in a chest that transports us on an authentic "journey through time". This edition of only 25 bottles of each Moscatel is presented in two luxurious packaging and each one of them enhances the uniqueness of these "jewels" of Quinta do Piloto. They are a true ode to the past and a tribute to Humberto da Silva Cardoso, founder of this historic house on the Setúbal Peninsula, known throughout the world for its production of superior quality nectars and unparalleled Moscatéis.
Approach: The entire project was conceived in detail and carefully worked, where each piece was specially designed and produced with distinctive shapes and materials. From the silver spoon, created to calmly enjoy these rarities, to the designed decanter, from the Cherry wood to the Alcantara for these packages, all pieces were designed to give a unique aspect to this edition, honoring the singularity of this special Family Collection. The colors chosen are distinct yet identifying of the Quinta and of the region. Omdesign was inspired by an original bottle of Moscatel de Setúbal to create the exclusive decanter that is adorned with a collar and has several elements that refer to the cinema theatre in Palmela, built at the behest of Humberto da Silva Cardoso. We also used the monogram present on the gate of the cinema with the initials of the founder, we merged all the elements and we took the detail we have on the packaging and on the decanters to the original plaster ceiling of this emblematic room. These exclusive pieces were also completed with details of some tiles of the reception and the bartop has an interlacing which represents the tradition and the art of well-making these Moscatéis. This edition is, without a doubt, a homage to Quinta do Piloto and its founder, as well as to the region and to the Moscatel de Setúbal category.
Results: These special editions offer to taste a century of passion and dedication of a Palmela's historic family and carry inside, in addition to a 50cl decanter and an exclusive spoon, two glasses, a booklet and a certificate. All of this is locked in a chest with a unique key, made of gold and silver, which highlights the rarity of these Moscatéis de Setúbal.

83 COPPER & CASK WHISKEY | Design Firm: Pavement | Designer: Michael Hester
Client: Latitude Beverage Co. | Illustrator: Raphael Montoliu | Main Contributor: Michael Hester
Assignment: Copper & Cask Spirits is a single barrel project curating superior hand-selected whiskeys that are always rare and never ordinary. As an independent bottler dedicated to single barrel selections and unique cask strength releases, a brand and package design was created that captured the distinctiveness and extremely limited nature of their product. Everything Copper & Cask does is built upon a deep respect and unbridled passion for whiskey and aged spirits from around the world. A patriotic eagle and hand drawn typography highlight the classic whiskey aesthetic that adorns each label. As part of the solution, a modular label system was created to capture the bespoke details of each individual single barrel selection. The resulting brand feels established, overtly masculine and undeniably targeted towards the discerning whiskey aficionado.
Approach: To create a vintage-inspired whiskey bottle for today's market.
Results: It was so well received, customers have began collecting bottles.

84 HUNDRED KNOT KHOAI WINES | Design Firm: CF Napa Brand Design
Designer: CF Napa Brand Design | Client: RD Winery | Main Contributor: CF Napa Brand Design
Assignment: After engaging CF Napa to develop the name, logo and packaging design for their new wine brand – Hundred Knot – RD Winery tasked CF Napa with creating the brand's higher tier Khoai Wines.
Approach: The name Hundred Knot drew inspiration from the owner's heritage and was based on a Vietnamese parable that teaches the importance of hard work and perseverance. These tasting room exclusive wines needed to continue to tell this legendary tale while taking on a more luxurious feel.
Results: A hand-painted brush stroke created an abstract illustration of a bamboo stalk to form the main graphic. The brush stroke was embossed and the RDW icon was debossed, providing the final textural touches to the exceptional wine.

85 FOX & ODEN | Design Firm: CF Napa Brand Design | Designer: CF Napa Brand Design
Client: Fox & Oden | Main Contributor: CF Napa Brand Design
Assignment: Michigan craft distillery Fox & Oden came to CF Napa with the task of creating the custom bottle and packaging for their new super-premium North American whiskey. The name "Fox & Oden" was inspired by Michigan's notoriously cunning red foxes, and the island of Oden, a majestic retreat off the Up North portion of the state.
Approach: The packaging needed to embody the rugged beauty of northern Michigan while maintaining a sense of luxury.
Results: The wordmark's hand drawn type gave the whiskey a bespoke sensibility and the delicate gold foil accents reinforced the whiskey's premium positioning. CF Napa commissioned an illustrator to capture our vision of the namesake fox emerging through the tall pines. A dark wood closure and top strip label provided the final touches to this new craft American whiskey.

86 BIRD CREEK DISTILLERY | Design Firm: CF Napa Brand Design
Designer: CF Napa Brand Design | Client: Bird Creek Distillery
Main Contributor: CF Napa Brand Design
Assignment: Portland-based Bird Creek Distillery came to CF Napa to design their new brand packaging, custom bottle, and custom tasting glasses to celebrate nature and the beauty of the Pacific Northwest.
Approach: Inspired by the majestic Mt. Adams, CF Napa created a custom glass bottle and matching tasting glasses with a punt in the shape of the mountain.
Results: A minimalistic screenprint and paper neck label contained the informative whiskey data, allowing the bottle design to stand out. CF Napa designed 6 collectible T-tops with working compasses and images inspired by the fauna found on Mt. Adams. The tops were engraved with the geographic coordinates to the Bird Creek Meadows, further emphasizing the brand's adventurous spirit.

87 OLDE RALEIGH DISTILLERY | Design Firm: CF Napa Brand Design
Designer: CF Napa Brand Design | Client: Olde Raleigh Distillery
Main Contributor: CF Napa Brand Design
Assignment: Olde Raleigh Distillery engaged CF Napa to design the logo, packaging and custom bottle for their new distillery and flagship line of whiskies.
Approach: The packaging would need to reflect the exceptional quality and scarcity of their hand-crafted, small-batch expression, luxury whiskies and evoke the sensibilities of an old school whiskey club.
Results: CF Napa created a bespoke bottle inspired by antique crystal decanters. The intricate seal for the distillery and their Whiskey Society membership, modeled after the seals of historic private clubs and secret societies, was embossed both into the metal coin atop the closure and into the base of the bottle. The label's minty hue and gold foil band formed the quirky final touches.

88 LOOSE TOQUE WHISKEY BOTTLE PACKAGING | Design Firm: Vanderbyl Design
Designer: Michael Vanderbyl | Client: Loose Toque | Creative Director: Michael Vanderbyl
Main Contributor: Michael Vanderbyl
Assignment: Packaging for irreverent Canadian whiskey distillery ("toque" is the Canadian term for a wool beanie hat).

89 ZHUOZHOU (SHANLAN RICE WINE) PACKAGE | Design Firm: Grantz Jansword
Designer: Grantz Zhu | Client: ZHUOZHOU | Models: Chen Ziping, Kong Xiangyi
Main Contributors: Sola Wang, Huang Dacheng
Assignment: "ZHUOZHOU" is a brand of Hainan Shanlan Rice wine, and the winery is located in the middle area of Hainan island, China. Shanlan Rice wine is brewed by the ancestors of the "Li" ethnic group using the unique wild upland rice in Hainan, Shanlan purple rice.
Approach: The design was inspired by the culture of the "Li" Ethnic group whom were the owners of Hainan Island. The bottle design lay on the two core cultural elements; the "fore thatched cottage(cottage with an outline of the fore of boat)" and "Li Brocade". The bottle shoulder uses the characteristic fore outline also the wood box with a fore-outline gate too. The bottle designed to be three-sided which makes it more symbolic. The cap and the side of the bottle adopts the unique pattern from "Li brocade", the traditional of textile of "Li". The cross form in the pattern deprived from the unique "Frogman/Hercules" totem of the Li ethic group. Since the color of Shanlan Rice wine is relatively dark, thick bottom and orange glass were designed to light up the wine color and emphasized its transparency. In the selection of the visual hammer, we chose the Hainan black crested gibbon (Nomascus hainanus) to represent "ZHUOZHOU". Together with Nomascus hainanus, the whole species of Nomascus has been deemed "the most critically endangered ape species in the world". While spreading the wine culture of Hainan, the ZHUOZHOU brand also invested in the establishment of the Hainan Black Crested Gibbon Conservation Association, calling for attention to the protection of Hainan's natural ecology. For the label, The calligraphy is remade by algorithm with the source of calligraphy by Su'Shi(苏轼/蘇軾), who has been the local official in Hainan island. While he is also a famous poet and scholar in Song Dynasty, whom still popular in China. The shape of Hainan island are also adopted in the label.
Results: The successful establishment of a name card of Hainan island.

90 DALVA PURE VINTAGE | Design Firm: Omdesign | Designer: Diogo Gama Rocha
Client: C. da Silva | Main Contributor: Omdesign
Assignment: The renowned Portuguese company C. da Silva, which has a century-old tradition in the production of unique Port wines, launches Dalva Vintage

Pure with an image signed by Omdesign, affirming its commitment to the production of sustainable wines. In line with the environmental concerns that the company has always defended, Omdesign was inspired by the preservation of local biodiversity and carried to this Vintage the sustainability values associated with this product and the brand, whose production methods comply with the cycles of Nature and rely on with as little intervention as possible.
Approach: With a minimalist design, which adopts earth and nature tones, the agency created for this project an exclusive illustration of a branch of a vine, which occupies a prominent position, as a sign of the respect for the environment that the Dalva brand defends, especially in this Port wine, whose grapes are preserved through the Organic Production Method.
Results: Reinforced by the sustainable and recyclable materials and selected finishes, such as fine paper and relief, Dalva Vintage Pure expresses all the purity and character of the Douro region. The exterior packaging was developed in line with the labeling and shares the same finishes, and was produced in Kraft cardboard, highlighting the most natural, ecological, and sustainable aspect of this edition.

91 PRAKRISHI HONEY | Design Firm: Sol Benito | Designer: Vishal Vora
Client: Prakrishi Organic | Main Contributor: Sol Benito
Assignment: A product extension for the mother brand Prakrushi, this range of 6 distinct flavored honey faced a challenge to maintain the fine balance. on one hand, it should have a distinguished identity as product segment but without being too away from the flagship brand's visual grammar.
Approach: The transliteration of bee wings into an aesthetic manner as a visual device that not just creates an eye-catching graphic but also delivers sufficient visual information to the consumer to make an informed decision at the shelf. As we can see, the design parameters of the flagship brand have lots of white space and minimal approach to it. so we carried forward the same principles and used only the necessary part of the graphic to convey the whole story without moving away from the packaging and design guidelines. What makes it more interesting is the fact that the motif of a bee is turned into an interesting, engaging and informative visual that is quite different from the usual lot where we see the insect in its so-called natural (and well, a boring) avatar. But here, the same bee turns into a heart-warming messenger!

92 SHINER HERITAGE | Design Firm: *TraceElement | Designers: Yvette Sierra, Cristina Moore, Dana Nixon | Clients: Shiner Beer, Gambrinus Company | Creative Director: Dana Nixon
Chief Creative Officer: Jeff Barfoot | Production: Eric Flandorfer | Illustrators: Yvette Sierra, Cristina Moore | Account Manager: Anna Mertz | Main Contributor: Jeff Barfoot
Assignment: To commemorate the 108-year history, endurance, and Texas heritage of Shiner Bock, Shiner Beer asked that we create "Shiner Heritage Edition." The limited-edition product series included a commemorative can, 12-pack can wrap, 12-pack bottle wrap, and four "throwback" bottle labels that recreated designs from four different eras of Shiner Bock's past.
Approach: While this was a new and limited-edition release, the packaging still needed to convey that it was a Shiner Bock product. The outer wraps utilized Shiner Bock's signature name, color palette, and textural dot patterning. Because Spoetzl Brewery is the oldest independent brewery in Texas, we also created a Texas-shaped lockup that featured the Heritage Edition product name in a vintage-style script. A particular challenge was that the original Shiner Bock labels were not saved or kept in the brewery's design archive. The four labels were entirely recreated from scratch, utilizing old photographs and Shiner archives as reference. The two oldest Bock rams in the series were hand-illustrated by a designer in Procreate, while the other two were recreated digitally in Adobe Illustrator. All labels were then distressed to give the "new" series a worn and vintage feel, as if you were holding the original historic labels in your hand.
Results: The anniversary product surprised customers. The limited-edition product garnered attention to Shiner's most awarded brew and reminded customers that Shiner Bock is a historic Texas icon.

92 GLORIOUS CANNABIS CO. | Design Firm: Pavement | Designer: Michael Hester
Client: Glorious Cannabis Co. | Main Contributor: Michael Hester
Assignment: Based in the Greater Detroit area, Glorious Cannabis Company seized the opportunity to create a distinctive cannabis brand that embraces the renaissance spirit of Detroit. The city has long been an epicenter of grit, determination and craftsmanship - qualities that exemplified Detroit's past and sparked the city's rise from the ashes in recent years. Amidst this, Glorious dedicated themselves to creating the most superior cannabis products within Michigan created by the best cultivators in the industry. Seeking to attract the modern millennials of the city who identify with the hard work, ingenuity and artistry of the city's roots, an uncomplicated yet bold identity was created. Highlighted by utilitarian typography, a distinctive color palette and a unique envelope-style package, the brand has an earnest appeal that personifies blue collar pride and industriousness.
Approach: Strategically create a brand that separated itself to appeal to the modern millennial cannabis consumer.
Results: It has been very well received by the client and the market in Michigan.

93 1895 SINGLE ORIGIN COFFEE | Design Firm: *TraceElement
Designers: Dana Nixon, Yvette Sierra, Cristina Moore | Client: Lavazza
Chief Creative Director: Jeff Barfoot | Production: Eric Flandorfer
Account Manager: Anna Mertz | Main Contributor: Jeff Barfoot
Assignment: Lavazza approached us four years ago to develop the branding for a premium diffusion line of coffee that would marry their heritage of artistry and excellence with a forward-thinking, technologically advanced approach to sourcing and production. This line, 1895 by Lavazza, needed to emphasize expertise in sourcing — highlighting hyperlocal beans from across the globe — stand out from the competition, and wrap everything up in premium, best-in-class package design.
Approach: We helped design the identity for 1895 by Lavazza, and with that foundation designed the packaging. The single-origin coffee line draws inspiration from the ecology of the country of origin. Illustrations of the coffee's flavor notes are intertwined in a geometric but fluid illustration style that compliments the 1895 logo and brand aroma pattern.
Results: 1895 by Lavazza has been an outstanding success for Lavazza, and we've gone on to execute many other pieces of creative for the brand, from equipment to additional coffee packaging copy, to brand partnerships and even interior design guidance for a factory and cafés.

93 BIC GAMBLING SERIES | Design Firm: Wallace Church & Co. | Designer: Brian Casscles
Client: BIC | Executive Creative Director: John Bruno | Chief Creative Officer: Stan Church
Associate Creative Director: Jodi Lubrich | Senior Designer: Brian Casscles
Account Director: Maureen McKenna | Main Contributor: Brian Casscles
Assignment: Bring the excitement of gambling to a series of BIC lighters.
Approach: After a visual survey of the world of gambling, it was determined that the games at a casino could be called out on the lighters via words. Small icons, Craps, Roulette and Cards, support the words while a bold 'face-of-the-game' graphic exudes a confidence that one associates with gamblers.
Results: WC&Co.'s designs for BIC lighter casino series absolutely hit the jackpot. Using contemporary abstraction and a cohesive color palate, these designs bring to life the spirit of gambling and the excitement of the casino environment. Featuring symbols of luck and invigorating gambling phrases, the graphics and copy are strong, striking, and sure to bring in a winning hand. The thrill of gaming is also conveyed through the texture and tactile nature of the design with the central imagery incorporating a golden halo-foil. For the gambler and casino-lover, these lighters are a must have-- sure to be a lucky charm.

94 PEACE | Design Firm: Goodall Integrated Design | Designer: Derwyn Goodall
Client: Self-initiated | Main Contributor: Derwyn Goodall
Assignment: The Russian incursion into Ukraine shocked the world. How could a peaceful country be experiencing a military takeover in 2022? My poster was a reaction to this hideous, immoral act.
Approach: The poster's message is direct and aspirational — the overarching desire for people to live in peace and harmony. The dove and olive branch image was used because of its iconic meaning; a symbol of peace that originated with the early Christians who portrayed the act of baptism accompanied by a dove holding an olive branch in its beak. Graphically, I was inspired by a 1960's/1970's European modernist sensibility, where clean lines and simple shapes echo the peaceful essence of the message. Ukrainian blue and Ukrainian yellow are the only two colors used.
Results: Overwhelming response from colleagues and clients alike.

95 VIRTUAL IS REAL | Design Firm: Dankook University | Designer: Hoon-Dong Chung
Client: Self-initiated | Main Contributor: Hoon-Dong Chung
Assignment: This work is symbolic that Virtual is Real and Real is Virtual. I conveyed the intertwined relationship with 3D Typography.
Approach: Contrast and Harmony.
Results: The latest work.

96 AU JAZZ WITH HERB SCOTT | Design Firm: Chemi Montes | Designer: Chemi Montes
Client: American University Department of Performing Arts | Main Contributor: Chemi Montes

97 CONTACT | Design Firm: Tsushima Design | Designer: Hajime Tsushima
Client: OSAKA POSTER FEST | Main Contributor: Hajime Tsushima
Assignment: This is a poster for the Cyber Poster Exhibition held by OSAKA POSTER FEST. It has been open to the public at the Cyber Exhibition since October 22, 2021. The poster theme is contact.
Approach: Since last year, the whole world has been affected by the coronavirus infection, which has completely changed our lifestyle. Under the current situation, while "contact" is discouraged, the times are keeping changing. In the midst of such circumstances, people are adapting to the next age by looking at and thinking about things from a different perspective and exploring various ways. In this context, "contact" is also changing. I expressed this situation on a poster.
Results: This cyber exhibition is still going on. Since it is an exhibition on the Internet, it is open to the public until the site is closed. It was also released on youtube videos and digital books.

98 SAY NO TO SINGLE USE | Design Firm: Namseoul University
Designer: Mi-Jung Lee | Client: Ministry of Environment | Main Contributor: Mi-Jung Lee
Assignment: This is a poster that warns of plastic waste chaos. Every year, 1 million sea birds died and microplastics were detected in 47 institutions that were taken from human bodies. The study also showed that by 2100, the concentration of microplastics would increase about 100 times. Plastic is a poster that calls for attention to the practice of the current plastic problem as a problem for all mankind.
Approach: It was intended that avoiding the use of plastics would be a solution to protecting us from a lot of waste and improving the environment.
Results: As the Korean Ministry of Environment continues to launch campaign issues on plastics, the interest of citizens is expanding. Of course, the use of posters is also increasing.

99 64TH MONTEREY JAZZ FESTIVAL POSTER SERIES | Design Firm: *TraceElement
Designer: Jeff Rogers | Client: Monterey Jazz Festival | Chief Creative Officer: Jeff Barfoot
Creative Director: Jeff Rogers | Main Contributor: Jeff Rogers
Assignment: The Monterey Jazz Festival is the longest continuously running jazz festival in the world and has presented nearly every major jazz artist over the last 60-plus years. In 2021, the live festival was back after a virtual festival the year before due to COVID, so the lively and colorful artwork expressed the excitement of fans and artists to get back to Monterey for more memorable live performances.
Approach: We used a design style for the letterforms and imagery inspired by colorful cut paper. Each piece subtly represented a diverse range of individual artists and fans that make up the festival. The pieces were rearranged to use for letters and

imagery across the series. We also used the shapes across many other applications.
Results: The festival sold out days after tickets went on sale. The artwork was featured on festival merch, which also sold out quickly.

100 BEAUTY | Design Firm: Randy Clark | Designer: Randy Clark
Client: Wenzhou-Kean University | Main Contributor: Randy Clark
Assignment: This is a poster/promo piece for Michael Graves College of Architecture and Design as part of the opening of Ge Hekai Hall.
Approach: Since we are a Sino-American Cooperative University, I have attempted to marry both the Chinese character for the word, "beauty" and the visual of things that represent some notion of design that represents beauty.
Results: This has been accepted well overall.

101 TEST THE WATER | Design Firm: Bailey Lauerman | Designer: Caitlin Viar
Client: Special Olympics Nebraska | Creative Director: Casey Stokes | Copywriter: Brad Londy
Chief Creative Officer: Carter Weitz | Account Management: Jessica Jarosh
Production Manager: Gayle Adams | Main Contributor: Carter Weitz
Assignment: Increase participation in the Polar Plunge fundraiser event for Special Olympics Nebraska.
Approach: This poster serves as an invitation to support the cause and to "Test The Water," and provide a heightened sense of anticipation—especially since the event was held virtually during the COVID-19 outbreak.
Results: The poster concept and design was so well received, that the client requested all sorts of swag materials to support the event.

102, 103 MADE IN STL | Design Firm: Rodgers Townsend | Designer: Luke Partridge
Client: B&C Machine Co. | Main Contributor: Michael McCormick
Assignment: To honor the craft of American metalworking and pay tribute to the man who ran B&C Machine Co.
Approach: Shot on a digital Leica with available light, we let the machines, workbenches and warehouse tell their own stories.
Results: The posters became forever keepsakes for friends and family, even leading to another run of postcard-sized replicas.

104 FRANKIMPACT | Design Firm: Traction Factory | Designer: Kristina Karlen
Client: Snap-on Tools | Creative Director: Steve Drifka | Copywriter: Tom Dixon
Project Coordinator: Danny Yadgir | Production Artist: Jenni Wierzba
Print Producer: Krista Dercola | Photographer: Jimmy McDonald
Digital Artist: Jimmy McDonald | Account Director: Shannon Egan
Main Contributor: Kristina Karlen
Assignment: Building on the past "It's Alive" campaign materials, the objective of this work was to bring personality to the CT9010 and support Franchisees with compelling product information in a mobile retail environment.
Approach: We chose to illustrate the power associated with this tool by borrowing from Frankenstein. We transformed the lead product designer on the project into a mad scientist and digitally created his laboratory to add visual interest and quickly communicate the power inherent in this tool.
Results: The fun, visual concept was used in all campaign launch materials: poster, on-van merchandising, social media and monthly sales collateral shared with every technician customer during the launch.

105 TOLERANCE | Design Firm: Carmit Design Studio | Designer: Carmit Makler Haller
Clients: Tolerance—6th International Poster Exhibition, Graphic Stories 2022
Photographer: Adobe Stock | Digital Artists: Jorge Gamboa, Mal De Ojo
Main Contributor: Carmit Makler Haller
Assignment: An entry done for the 6th International Tolerance Competition held by Graphic Stories, Cyprus.
Approach: A photo of hands and feet is portraying our vital yet most battered parts of the body, while defending ourselves from violence. The original photo was in black and white and I altered it into colors—each hand/foot has a different color tone, representing the diversity of human race.

106 RIVETED - THE HISTORY OF JEANS | Design Firm: SJI Associates
Designer: Adam Selbst | Clients: Chika Offurum, American Experience Films
Art Director: David O'Hanlon | President: Suzy Jurist | Main Contributor: SJI Associates
Assignment: Bring the history of denim to life, with art that references its utilitarian roots and its rise to become one of the world's most ubiquitous cultural touchstones.
Approach: A graphic western-themed title treatment against a riveted jean pocket sets the tone for a look back at denim's humble beginnings and unlikely success.
Results: The key art drove interest for the new documentary, and was repurposed for social, digital, and on-air graphics, driving tune-in and streaming views.

107 ESPECTACULAR | Design Firm: Randy Clark | Designer: Randy Clark
Clients: 10 x 10 Exhibition, China Art Museum | Main Contributor: Randy Clark
Assignment: The 10 x 10 show in Shanghai, China was an invitational exhibition open to a select group of graphic and poster designers selected from an international pool. I was privileged to be among those chosen.
Approach: Although, I am an American citizen, I have for the last six years, lived and worked in Eastern China teaching at one of this country's premier universities. The assignment was to celebrate and showcase one of the world's greatest cities, Shanghai. I have been here several times and marvel at its majesty and beauty. The poster is a celebration of the culture, history, and modernity of this great city.
Results: The China Art Museum (the largest in Asia) received my submission with gratitude and excitement. Unfortunately, because of Covid-19 travel restrictions, I was unable to attend the exhibition.

108 YOU WON'T BE ALONE | Design Firm: ARSONAL | Designer: ARSONAL
Clients: Focus Features, Blair Green (SVP Creative Advertising and Head of Brand Design), Marcus Kaye (Director Creative Advertising) | Creative Director: ARSONAL
Assignment: Set in an isolated mountain village in 19th century Macedonia, the movie follows a young girl who is kidnapped and then transformed into a witch by an ancient spirit. After learning she can shape shift, she wields this power in order to understand what it means to be human. Given the extreme and unorthodox nature of this story, it was important to convey the beauty and poetry of its themes that alluded to the eerie creepiness of the story, without going to horror.
Approach: The line between drama and horror was a thin line to walk considering the dark tones, themes and supernatural occurrences in the story. It was important to us to not cross over into horror, but we were able to establish an unsettling feeling through specific cropping, obscuring of facial features and a pallete of darker earthy tones. The witch's claw was also another visual element that helped us allude to the supernatural without falling into predictable or overused tropes.
Results: We ultimately arrived at a striking piece that conveyed a sense of internal conflict that the client was very pleased with. The art ultimately made its appearance at Sundance where the film was met with critical acclaim.

109 VIGNELLI 90 POSTER | Design Firm: Underline Studio
Designer: Fidel Peña | Client: Vignelli 90 | Creative Directors: Claire Dawson, Fidel Peña
Printer: Flash Reproductions | Main Contributor: Underline Studio
Assignment: Más Massimo ("More Massimo") is our entry to a poster exhibition organized by Vignelli 90 celebrating 90 years of Massimo Vignelli's influence.
Approach: Our poster celebrates the desire to always have more, and never enough of Vignelli's work in our lives.
Results: The poster will be part of an exhibition in April 2022.

110, 111 UKRAINE DOVE | Design Firm: Randy Clark
Designer: Randy Clark | Client: Self-initiated | Main Contributor: Randy Clark
Assignment: I was shocked at Russia's unprovoked attack and sustained hostilities in Ukraine. Like most people, I have felt helpless. My contribution is this poster, promoting peace. I pray it comes soon.
Approach: I've sketched a number of ideas but finally decided on a clean modernist composition to succinctly promote peace in the region.
Results: I posted this on social media and have received positive feedback.

112 THOROUGHBRED HORSE OIL—APRIL FOOL'S POSTER
Design Firm: Bailey Lauerman | Designer: Jared Brdicko | Client: Kendall Motor Oil
Creative Director: Sean Faden | Copywriter: Joey Googe
Social Channel Manager: Brenna Doherty | Production Manager: Gayle Adams
Account Director: Brook Dore | Main Contributor: Jared Brdicko
Assignment: We wanted to create an April Fools Day post for social media that would generate conversation among our Kendall Motor Oil followers.
Approach: Since our audience historically responds well to Kendall history posts, we decided to create a poster for a fictional product "Throroughbred Horse Oil". We offered our social media fans a limited edition of real posters for commenting on the social post.
Results: The responses were a fun mix of people that immediately recognized the prank and a few from loyal fans who offered up some constructive criticism along with an insightful history lesson on the brand.

113 MYSTERY ROAD: ORIGIN | Design Firm: ABC Made | Designer: Peter Renigeris
Client: Bunya Productions | Creative Director: Diana Costantini | Retouching: Nicholas Mueller
Producer: Marina Younger | Photographer: David Dare Parker | Main Contributor: Peter Renigeris
Assignment: Mystery Road: Origin takes viewers back to the beginning of one of Australia's most popular drama series. The six-part series explores how a tragic death, an epic love, and the brutal reality of life as a police officer straddling two worlds, form the indelible mould out of which will emerge an iconic character. Alongside a new cast, an exciting new generation of Indigenous filmmakers is charged with bringing a new lens to the world of a young Detective Jay Swan. This poster series introduces the exciting new young cast taking over the roles of longtime beloved characters.
Approach: The portrait series leveraged the iconic typography from the series to reintroduce established characters being played by new cast members. The photography reflected the Western Australian location and highlighted the diverse representation across the ensemble cast.
Results: The show premiered at the Sydney Film Festival and on ABC iview.

114 CT9080 PRODUCT LAUNCH | Design Firm: Traction Factory | Designer: Mike Lyons
Client: Snap-on Tools | Creative Director: Steve Drifka | Copywriter: Tom Dixon
Retouching: Hac Job | Project Coordinator: Danny Yadgir | Production Artist: Jenni Wierzba
Account Director: Shannon Egan | Main Contributor: Mike Lyons
Assignment: Support the launch of the new CT9080 18 V Brushless Impact Wrench, creating excitement in the sales channel and with customers requiring a level of toughness and dependability in the tools they use. These customers cannot compromise with their go-to, high-performance, heavy-duty impact wrench.
Approach: The CT9080 was designed to be the industry's most powerful and durable impact wrench. Built tough inside and out, it delivers unwavering performance under the demanding conditions of a technician's shop. In a category leaning heavily on product features, we chose to create compelling, disruptive, conceptual communications that the male-dominated target audience would certainly appreciate while relating to the unflinching personality of this tool.
Results: Communications supported the product launch and were met with great enthusiasm from the field sales staff and franchisees. That momentum carried through to a successful launch to customers. Communications also extended beyond the trade show environment to point-of-sale, social, collateral, and other tactics.

115 LIFE WELL-CRAFTED | Design Firm: Rodgers Townsend | Designer: Kris Wright
Client: House of Rohl | Chief Creative Officer: Michael McCormick
Account Director: Sherley Moran | Main Contributor: Kris Wright
Assignment: Design a branding campaign that can elevate the House of Rohl within the world of luxury plumbing.

Approach: In the tradition of old Hollywood, our products became supporting characters in a B&W love story —complete with movie posters and a longform film trailer. Directed by Gia Coppola.
Results: Just breaking in May 2022, the photography will extend into the retail environment and product look-books for interior designers.

116 FIXED | Design Firm: Carmit Design Studio
Designer: Carmit Makler Haller | Client: Self-initiated | Photographer: Adobe Stock
Digital Artists: Jorge Gamboa, Mal De Ojo | Main Contributor: Carmit Makler Haller
Assignment: The fragility and dependency when the body is broken and fixed.
Approach: The photo depicts a frail woman—conveying fragility, dependency and weakness. Her body is broken. The red thread (symbolizing life and energy) is stitching her back again, but at what cost? The thread was photographed separately and was digitally edited. Typography was treated in the same manner of threading the letters into the background.

117 KAN MATSUBARA AND 100 YEARS OF NICHIGEI | Design Firm: Noriyuki Kasai
Designer: Noriyuki Kasai | Client: Nihon University College of Art
Copywriter: Kiyomi SOKOLOVA-YAMASHITA | Main Contributor: Noriyuki Kasai
Assignment: Kan Matsubara was a philosopher who played an important role in the establishment of Nihon University College of Art. An exhibition titled "Kan Matsubara and 100 Years of Nichigei" was held in 2021.
Approach: One of his representative photos, with his eyes full of hopes and passions looking to the future. In contact to the eight representative colors of the different departments of art, his black and white photo depicted the connection between the past and the presence. To accentuate the title, the fonts were in dot design, symbolizing each contributor to Nichigei.
Results: This exhibition was successful, because of just timing of 100year of Nichigei anniversary. Many people like Kan Matsubara, children nowadays are provided more opportunities to pursue what they want to study, students in Nichigei are ones of the lucky ones.

118 THE MUSE COLLECTION BY V STARR FOR WOLF-GORDON
Design Firm: Ahoy Studios | Designers: Connie Koch, Denise Sommer
Client: Wolf-Gordon | Photographer: Eva Mueller | Main Contributor: Wolf-Gordon
Assignment: United by the common qualities of excellent design and dependable performance, Wolf-Gordon's product line includes commercial wall-coverings, wall protection, upholstery textiles, Scuffmaster® specialty paints, and Wink® dry-erase products. Through collaborations with leading international designers and in their design studio, Wolf-Gordon develops new work that is provocative, inspiring, and of our time. A new textile collection by Venus Williams for Wolf-Gordon inspired a print advertising campaign celebrating strong women of diverse backgrounds: 'totems' of the collection sculpted by our models are set against dreamy landscapes evoking women's connection to nature.
Approach: In times where human connection was rare, we wanted to bring the textiles to life by making human sculptures. Creating sculptural compositions with the materials was challenging and laborious but absolute fun. Our goal to show case the collection and keep the human element in focus was achieved.
Results: Wolf-Gordon and V Starr's collaboration was a great success and the campaign was able to highlight the beautiful collaboration in a meaningful way.

119 INTERTWINED | Design Firm: Carmit Design Studio
Designer: Carmit Makler Haller | Client: Self-initiated | Digital Artist: Carmit Makler Haller
Photographer: Adobe Stock | Main Contributor: Carmit Makler Haller
Assignment: Two or more human figures are merged together to such extent—that one cannot tell where they start and end. Inspired by Flora Borsi.

120 THE CORONA NUMBERS | Design Firm: UP-Ideas
Designer: Roger Sawhill | Client: Self-initiated | Main Contributor: Roger Sawhill
Assignment: The pandemic was a good time to do design explorations. I spent 9 days building a graphic number for each: 1 - The loneliest number (it's lonely in space), 2 - When you gotta go, 3 - The original trilogy, 4 - The 4th dimension, 5 - Riding in style, 1935 style, 6 - Six days of creation, 7 - Have a 7 and a smile, 8 - Are these the days of our lives?, 9 - Shave a little off the top.

121 LAVAZZA FLAGSHIP STORE LONDON | Design Firm: Ralph Appelbaum Associates
Designer: Ralph Appelbaum Associates | Client: Lavazza Coffee | Project Director: Mirko Cerami
Graphic Designers: Mat Mason, Gareth Edwards | Content Strategist: Tracey Taylor
Content Coordinator: Charlotte Stevens | Main Contributor: Ralph Appelbaum Associates
Assignment: Situated in a Grade II listed building in London's west end on the corner of Great Marlborough and Argyll Street, the Lavazza Flagship Store is the second such store in the world and the only one outside Italy. The project's main objective was to bring Lavazza's unique concept of coffee design, along with its distinctive Italian spirit, to a new London destination and audience. The Lavazza Flagship Store also needed to create an extraordinary experience for a wide range of customers: tourists, shoppers, commuters, and coffee aficionados alike.
Approach: Our communication design is embedded throughout the store. It has a playfulness that invites exploration and promotes a deeper understanding of Lavazza's impressive 120-year history. The brand's dedication to sustainability and the environment is conveyed through real green planting that unfolds from the walls, culminating in a vertical garden. Infused with Italianità spirit, the communication design approach drew inspiration from a blend of playfulness and rich heritage. Fresco-style murals vividly blend Lavazza's iconic imagery, past and present, with dynamic illustrations. Individual, Italian-designed contemporary furniture invites customers to relax and enjoy their coffee in style. The Store also rose to the challenges brought about by the COVID-19 pandemic. The design for Lavazza's Flagship Store enables visitors to enjoy the ultimate Lavazza experience in a safe and socially distanced way. Cutting-edge counter design features advanced anti-viral technology that disinfects itself with ultraviolet light.

122 LOVE 2021 | Design Firm: Bailey Sullivan
Designer: Bailey Sullivan | Client: U.S. Postal Service | Artist: Bailey Sullivan
Art Director: Greg Breeding | Main Contributor: U.S. Postal Service
Assignment: The assignment was to create a stamp design for the U.S. Postal Service's series of Love stamps with an appeal appropriate to a wide constituency sending mail for a variety of occasions and celebrations.
Approach: The design team decided on a lighthearted approach to this year's Love stamp, with the word "LOVE" and various shapes featured in a bold graphic style. An unconventional palette of color duos are strikingly set against a dark background.
Results: In a little over a year more than 156 million stamps have sold.

122 SUN SCIENCE | Design Firm: Studio A | Designer: Antonio Alcalá
Client: U.S. Postal Service | Art Director: Antonio Alcalá
Image Source: NASA/Solar Dynamics Observatory | Main Contributor: U.S. Postal Service
Assignment: Develop U.S. postage stamps that would celebrate the science behind the ongoing exploration of the Sun, the only star that humans are able to observe in great detail. It is a vital source of information about the universe.
Approach: The art director/designer was intrigued by the images generated by NASA's Solar Dynamics Observatory (SDO), a spacecraft launched in February 2010 to keep a constant watch on the Sun. SDO lets us see the Sun in wavelengths of ultraviolet light that would otherwise be invisible to our eyes. Each image is colorized by NASA according to different wavelengths that reveal or highlight specific features of the Sun's activity. The art director chose images based both on their beauty and for the variety of solar activity they represent including coronal holes, coronal loops, solar flares, plasma blasts, sunspots, and an active sun image. Understanding the sun's dynamic environment helps us better understand its effects near Earth and predict its impact on sensitive technology, such as communications systems and satellite electronics.
Results: These stamps were extremely popular. Since the stamps were issued in June, 90% of the stamps produced have been sold.

123 HERITAGE BREEDS | Design Firm: Journey Group
Designer: Zack Bryant | Client: U.S. Postal Service | Art Director: Greg Breeding
Photographer: Aliza Eliazarov | Main Contributor: U.S. Postal Service
Assignment: The USPS stamp development team was tasked with devising postage stamps to pay tribute to heritage breeds, pre-industrial farm animals that take us back to our agricultural roots—and show the way to a more sustainable future.
Approach: The stamp designer, whose family raises heritage breed livestock, and the art director decided that photography would be better than illustration. They came across the work of a photographer who centers her work on sustainability, farming and food issues in the U.S., and seemed to connect with farm animals in uncommon ways. After consulting with subject experts they selected animals that would be good representations of the pre-industrial traditional of raising diverse livestock to thrive in local environments under certain conditions. In addition, they concentrated on visual variety to make a compelling collection. They chose to focus on the heads of the animals to better reveal their unusual appearance. The art director devised a checkerboard pattern with black and white backgrounds to create a grid structure, giving shape and movement to the stamps as a pane.
Results: The stamps were well received by the public. In the nine months since they were issued, the Postal Service has already sold over 83% of the stamps produced.

124 A VISIT FROM ST. NICK | Design Firm: Greg Breeding
Designer: Greg Breeding | Client: U.S. Postal Service | Art Director: Greg Breeding
Illustrator: Brad Woodard | Main Contributor: U.S. Postal Service
Assignment: The task was to create contemporary Christmas stamps for the U.S. Postal Service's annual issuance.
Approach: The art director/designer decided on a fun graphic approach to tell the story of Santa's visit on Christmas Eve. The illustrator created his images by first sketching and then digitizing them. He worked in a palette of original colors of dark blue, red, green, pink, and gold/brown to create unique and fun illustrations of this iconic holiday story.
Results: The stamps flew out of Post Offices over the holidays. On sale only since October, the Postal Service has sold almost 260 million stamps.

125 TRUST | Design Firm: UP-Ideas | Designer: Roger Sawhill
Client: Self-initiated | Main Contributor: Roger Sawhill
Assignment: Trust seems to be harder to find these days. We pine to go back to the days of handshake deals, when one's word was one's bond. This design goes back to those days to imagine this creed in back painted, gilt glass - but the creed is showing the wear of the ages.

126 KRESS FOUNDATION WEBSITE | Design Firm: C&G Partners
Designers: (UX) Bartek Lewandowski, Maya Kopytman, Glenn Jeon | Producer: Shuyler Nazareth
Client: Samuel H. Kress Foundation | Marketing: Sehba Mohammad
Developers: (Front-end) Red de Leon, (Back-end) BMM Art and Computer
Main Contributor: Maya Kopytman, Partner-in-Charge
Assignment: C&G Partners was taked with designing a rich new website for the Kress Foundation, an organization dedicated to "advancing the study, conservation, and enjoyment of the vast heritage of European art, architecture, and archaeology from antiquity to the early 19th century." The new online resource had to bring over 3,000 works of art from the Kress collection into the public view in a single place, and allows extremely close up views of the entire set. Because the Collection is widely distributed, this digital experience is the only way to see it all at once.
Approach: C&G Partners worked with the Kress Foundation to ensure that the site redesign serves those they support. With this mission in mind, art historians and enthusiasts alike can now explore the Collection using a highly visual tool. Site search offers different views including visual gallery and comprehensive list layouts. A powerful digital viewer allows users to zoom to levels that expose brushstrokes, paint textures, and the evidence of time in extreme detail. Search filters

have highly detailed capacity, enabling search by a long list of data fields. The site also showcases the prestigious grant programs The Kress Foundation offers, and hosts an interactive timeline of the organization's history. The reimagined website offers a unique opportunity for visitors to appreciate precious works from museums across the country from their own desktops and devices, advancing the Foundation's core mission to share the art and architecture of Europe. The Collection cannot be seen together anywhere IRL — nor this close up.
Results: L. W. Schermerhorn, Deputy Director of the Samuel H. Kress Foundation called the website, "A stunner with incredible utility."

SILVER WINNERS:
128 CITRIX CSR | Design Firm: Addison | Designer: Jessica Natasha
Client: Citrix | Art Buyer: Anne Crosson | Creative Director: Kevin Barclay
Strategy: Leslie Lammers | Senior Design Director: Nick Schmitz
Production Manager: Joe Kester | Managing Director: Judy Sandford
Main Contributor: Jessica Natasha

128 AGCO AR / SUSTAINABILITY REPORT | Design Firm: Addison
Designer: James Taylor | Client: AGCO | Strategy: Leslie Lammers
Creative Director: Kevin Barclay | Copywriter: David Freedman | Production Manager: Joe Kester
Managing Director: Judy Sandford | Art Buyer: Anne Crosson
Senior Account Director: Susie Kang Poteet | Main Contributor: James Taylor

129 HARBOR GROUP INTERNATIONAL FUND BOOK | Design Firm: Addison
Designer: Kin Yuen | Client: Harbor Group International | Creative Director: Kevin Barclay
Senior Account Director: Malaika Minters | Production Manager: Joe Kester
Main Contributor: Kin Yuen

129 BESSEMER TRUST AR 2021 | Design Firm: Addison | Designer: Kin Yuen
Client: Bessemer Trust | Strategy Director: Rhonda Nichtenhauser
Executive Creative Director: Richard Colbourne | Senior Producer: Anne Crosson
Senior Account Director: Heather Lucania | Production Manager: Joe Kester
Photographers: Ben Baker, Gentl & Hyers | Main Contributor: Kin Yuen

129 ADCB AR | Design Firm: Addison | Designer: Grant Currie | Client: ADCB
Senior Producer: Anne Crosson | Printer: Emirates Printing Press
Photographer: Khalid Al Hammadi | Executive Creative Director: Richard Colbourne
Account Management: Charlotte Greene | Main Contributor: Grant Currie

129 MERALCO 2020 ANNUAL REPORTS: POWER, LIFE, HOPE
Design Firm: Studio 5 Designs Inc. (Manila) | Designer: Studio 5 Designs Inc. (Manila)
Client: Meralco Company | Creative Director: BG Hernandez
Art Directors: Rogel Vidallo, Ermil Carranza, Ice De Leon
Account Supervisor: Marily Y. Orosa | Account Manager: Raffy Ortega
Main Contributor: Studio 5 Designs Inc. (Manila)

129 YSLETA DEL SUR PUEBLO 2020 YEAR-END REPORT
Design Firm: Anne M. Giangiulio Design | Designer: Anne M. Giangiulio
Clients: Ysleta del Sur Pueblo, Helix Solutions | Photographer: John Money
Printer: Tovar Printing, El Paso, TX, USA | Main Contributor: Drone shots and photos by Tigua tribal member John Money

129 L3HARRIS CSR | Design Firm: Addison | Designer: Anna Celine Kaarling Khan
Client: L3Harris | Creative Director: Kevin Barclay | Project Manager: Joe Kester
Managing Director: Judy Sandford | Main Contributor: Anna Celine Kaarling Khan

129 RAINBOWZ | Design Firm: M Books | Designer: Michael Arndt
Client: Andrews McMeel Publishing | Production Manager: Chuck Harper
Production Artist: Holly Swayne | Editor: Patty Rice | Main Contributor: Michael Arndt

130 OGGETTO LIBRO (CATALOGO) / BOOK OBJECT (CATALOGUE)
Design Firm: ESSEBLU | Designer: Susanna Vallebona | Client: SBLU_spazioalbello
Editor: Edizioni ESSEBLU | Printer: Fontegrafica | Video: Davide Cusano
Additional Augmented Reality App Owner (Aria the AR Platform): Alkanoids
Main Contributor: ESSEBLU

130 CRY OF THE HIGH TIDE BOOK, EXHIBITION OF CRISTINA RODRIGES
Design Firm: Duas Faces Design | Designer: Patrícia Machado | Client: Cristina Rodrigues
Creative Director: Sérgio Duarte | Writer: Cristina Rodrigues Studio
Printer: Mania da Cor | Project Manager: Ana Monteiro | Project Director: Sérgio Duarte
PrePress: Mania da Cor | Photographer: Marco Coutinho Longo | Paper: Inapa
Main Contributor: Cristina Rodrigues Studio

130 THE IBM POSTER PROGRAM: VISUAL MEMORANDA | Design Firm: Robert Finkel
Designer: Robert Finkel | Client: Lund Humphries | Author: Shea Tillman
Illustrator: Greer Miceli | Main Contributor: Robert Finkel

130 DOUBLE TRIO | Design Firm: Boyang Xia | Designer: Boyang Xia
Client: New Directions Publishing | Creative Director: Rodrigo Corral
Main Contributor: Boyang Xia

130 CONTRAST II - A FOTOGRAFIA NO ENSINO SUPERIOR | Design Firm: Né S. Design
Designers: Artur Leão, Né Santelmo | Client: Cityscopio – Scopio Editions
Main Contributors: Pedro Leão Neto, Olívia Marques da Silva

131 SESTRY (SISTERS) | Design Firm: Code Switch | Designer: Jan Šabach
Client: Paseka Publishing House | Art Director: Vojta Sedláček | Main Contributor: Jan Šabach

131 PHANTOM MONEY | Design Firm: Greenleaf Book Group
Designer: Neil Gonzalez | Client: S. Alexander O'Keefe | Main Contributor: Neil Gonzalez

131 THE MOMENTS BETWEEN DREAMS | Design Firm: Greenleaf Book Group
Designer: Cameron Stein | Client: Judith F. Brenner | Main Contributor: Cameron Stein

131 SOUNDTRACKS | Design Firm: Faceout Studio | Designer: Jeff Miller
Client: Baker Books | Main Contributor: Jeff Miller

132 IMMORTAL AXES | Design Firms: Nick Steinhardt, 23in
Designers: Nick Steinhardt, 23in | Client: Rock Stars Worldwide | Writer: Lisa S. Johnson
Creative Director: Lisa S. Johnson | Publisher: Princeton Architectural Press
Photographer: Lisa S. Johnson | Equipment: Nikon D810, 35-70mm 2.8f Macro
Editor: Brad Tolinski | Contributor: Lonn M. Friend

132 MOTHERS DON'T | Design Firm: Anna Jordan | Designer: Anna Jordan
Client: Open Letter Books | Art Director: Chad Post | Main Contributor: Anna Jordan

132 DRILLER | Design Firm: Texas Tech University Press
Designer: Hannah Gaskamp | Client: Self-initiated | Main Contributor: Hannah Gaskamp

133 A STORY THAT HAPPENS: ON PLAYWRITING, CHILDHOOD, AND OTHER TRAUMAS | Design Firm: Anna Jordan | Designer: Anna Jordan
Client: Dalkey Archive Press | Art Director: Chad Post | Main Contributor: Anna Jordan

133 LOVECRAFT COCKTAILS: ELIXIRS & LIBATIONS FROM THE LORE OF H. P. LOVECRAFT | Design Firm: Faceout Studio | Designers: Jeff Miller, Paul Nielsen
Client: Countryman Press | Main Contributors: Jeff Miller (cover), Paul Nielsen (interior)

133 VICIOUS CREATURES | Design Firm: Faceout Studio | Designer: Amanda Hudson
Client: Scarlet Publishing | Hand Lettering: Amanda Hudson | Image Source: Shutterstock
Main Contributor: Amanda Hudson

133 LOVE, NORM | Design Firm: Texas Tech University Press
Designer: Hannah Gaskamp | Client: Self-initiated | Main Contributor: Hannah Gaskamp

133 THE STARLESS CROWN | Design Firm: Faceout Studio | Designer: Tim Green
Client: Tor Books | Image Sources: Photo illustrated using imagery from Arcangel, iStock Photo and Shutterstock | Main Contributor: Tim Green

133 STAY SAFE | Design Firm: Alban Fischer Design | Designer: Alban Fischer
Client: Sarabande Books | Author: Emma Hine | Main Contributor: Alban Fischer

133 EXTREME NORTH | Design Firm: Richard Ljoenes Design LLC
Designer: Richard Ljoenes | Client: W. W. Norton | Author: Bernd Brunner
Art Director: Ingsu Liu | Illustrators: Jacket art: viking helmet by Achmad fandhy akhbar / Alamy; traditional Norwegian rose painting by Edwin Remsberg / Alamy; blood stain by Carlos Amarillo / Shutterstock | Main Contributor: Richard Ljoenes Design LLC

133 THE ESSENTIAL WALT MCDONALD | Design Firm: Texas Tech University Press
Designer: Hannah Gaskamp | Client: Self-initiated | Main Contributor: Hannah Gaskamp

133 IN SHAKESPEARE'S SHADOW | Design Firm: Richard Ljoenes Design LLC
Designer: Richard Ljoenes | Client: Hachette Books | Creative Director: Amanda Kain
Author: Michael Blanding | Photographer: Skull by Nick N A / Shutterstock
Main Contributor: Richard Ljoenes Design LLC

134 1.5 KG DE OCUPA! | Design Firm: 1/4 Studio | Designers: Ana Mota, Jorge Araújo
Client: Galeria Ocupa! | Art Directors: Jorge Araújo, Ana Mota | Editor: Galeria Ocupa!
Drawing: Ana Mota | Printer: Serviços Gráficos ESE | Text: Maria de Fátima Lambert, Joana Mendonça, António Fernando Silva, João Terras

134 THAT NIGHT AT MASSEY HALL | Design Firm: Underline Studio
Designer: Brittany Waldner | Client: David Binks | Creative Directors: Claire Dawson, Fidel Peña
Editor: David Binks | Production Manager: Natalia Botti | Printer: Andora Graphics Inc.
Photographer: Paul Weeks | Main Contributor: Underline Studio

134 SNAILS & MONKEY TAILS: A VISUAL GUIDE TO PUNCTUATION & SYMBOLS
Design Firm: M Books | Designer: Michael Arndt | Client: Harper Design
Editor: Elizabeth Viscott Sullivan | Production Designer: Lynne Yeamans
Main Contributor: Michael Arndt

134 MACAU DESIGN AWARD 2021 | Design Firm: Loksophy Design Ltd.
Designer: Hong Ka Lok | Client: Macau Designers Association | Art Director: Hong Ka Lok
Photographer: Bob Wong | Graphic Designer: Rong Rong Chao
Printer: Hung Heng Macau Printing Co. Ltd. | Main Contributor: Hong Ka Lok

134 ANDREA BOWERS | Design Firm: Still Room | Designer: Jessica Fleischmann
Client: MCA Chicago | Content Strategist: Kelsey Campbell-Dollaghan
Writers: Michael Darling, Connie Butler | Editor: Tyler Laminack | Publisher: DelMonico
Main Contributor: Jessica Fleischmann

134 BEAUTY BY DESIGN | Design Firm: Faceout Studio | Designers: Tim Green, Paul Nielsen
Client: Ten Peaks Press | Main Contributors: Tim Green (cover), Paul Nielsen (interior)

134 STRIPE E | Design Firm: Randy Clark | Designer: Randy Clark
Client: Wenzhou-Kean University | Main Contributor: Randy Clark

135 BAD NEWS | Design Firm: Faceout Studio | Designer: Molly von Borstel
Client: Encounter Books | Main Contributor: Molly von Borstel

135 WHY DESIGN MATTERS: CONVERSATIONS WITH THE WORLD'S MOST CREATIVE PEOPLE | Design Firm: What Studio | Designers: Alex Kalman, Debbie Millman
Client: Harper Collins | Main Contributors: Alex Kalman, Debbie Millman

136 PGH STYLE GUIDE CAMPAIGN | Design Firm: Nexus Designs
Designers: Myra Murtagh, Sally Evans, Emily Morant, Nexus Designs
Client: PGH Bricks & Pavers | Art Director: Sally Evans | Stylist: Marsha Golemac
Photographer: Tomas Friml | Main Contributor: Nexus Designs

136 MAKER'S MARK VISUAL IDENTITY | Design Firm: Turner Duckworth: London, San Francisco & New York | Designer: Loren Schott | Client: Maker's Mark
Implementation Directors: Liisa Turan-Walters, Sara Scanlan | Creative Director: Jared Britton
Executive Creative Director: Jamie McCathie | Director of Client Services: Wyeth Whiting
Typography Design: Dalton Maag, Jeremy Mickel | Photographer: Sophia Sinclair
Ad Agency: Doe Anderson - Zach Anderson, Director of Design | Main Contributor: Loren Schott

137 ARCHIVE 81 | Design Firm: Lafayette American | Designer: Lafayette American
Client: Netflix | Chief Creative Officer: Toby Barlow | Project Manager: Vu Nguyen
President: Emily Siegel | Design Director: Meg Jannott | Photographer: Erik Carter
Lead Designer: Asha Cook | Logo Designer: Jon Wolfer | Account Director: Allison Piper
Main Contributor: Lafayette American

137 CELEBRATING PRIDE WITH AN INCLUSIVE BRAND IDENTITY
Design Firm: Lippincott | Designers: Eva Hoffman, Brendán Murphy, Senior Partner
Client: Heritage of Pride | Design Directors: Christal Sih, Kaito Gengo, Coco Han
Senior Design Directors: Thom Finn, Dimitri Theodoropoulos | Production: Jeanine Colgan, Design Production Manager, Gladys Fabara, Presentation Manager, Andrew McCarthy, Director, Design Production | Brand Strategy: Jennifer Rosenbloom, Partner, Brand Strategy, Ben Le, Partner, Brand Strategy, Meredith Brandt, Senior Strategy Consultant, Jordan Steiner, Senior Consultant, Enoch Wong, Consultant, Innovation, Pascale Tam, Partner, Peter Chun, Partner | Brand Creatives: Wesley Tibbs, Brand Voice Associate, Dan Ran, Interaction and Motion Designer, Kishen Pujura, Jenifer Lehker, Partner, Travis DeShong, Consultant, Brand Voice | Main Contributor: Brendán Murphy, Senior Partner

138 DETROIT OPERA | Design Firm: Lafayette American | Designers: Lafayette American, Asha Cook, Alex Rybarczyk | Client: Detroit Opera | Chief Creative Officer: Toby Barlow
Brand Strategy: Bre Alexander | Project Manager: Vu Nguyen | Design Director: Meg Jannott
Creative Strategist: Doug James | Lead Designer: Paolo Catalla
Account Director: Stephanie McMillan | Main Contributor: Lafayette American

138 THE VIRGINIAN LODGE BRAND REFRESH | Design Firm: Fellow Inc.
Designer: Jack Lewin | Client: Outbound | Creative Director: Michael Seitz
Senior Designer: Keelan Campbell | Main Contributor: Fellow Inc.

139 IMNATIV. BORN FOR NATURE. | Design Firm: Andrea Castelletti Studio
Designer: Andrea Flemma | Client: Aurim | Executive Creative Director: Andrea Castelletti
Director: Andrea Pugiotto | Graphic Designer: Andrea Flemma | Website: Parco Studio
Strategy Director: Mila Ligugnana | Production Company: Ippocampostudio
Photographer: Andrea Pugiotto | Marketing Manager: Ersilia Auriemma
Advertising Agency: HOBO | Main Contributor: Andrea Castelletti

139 CREATE PROPERTIES REBRAND | Design Firm: Coastlines Creative Group
Designer: Byron Dowler | Client: Create Properties | Developer: Devon Dowler
Main Contributor: Coastlines

139 THE YOUNG TENT : BRAND IDENTITY DESIGN | Design Firm: Jang Won Lee
Designer: Jang Won Lee | Client: The Young Tent | Main Contributor: Jang Won Lee

139 WEARFOREVER BRAND IDENTITY | Design Firm: Natasha Mozz
Designer: Natasha Mozz | Client: WearForever | Main Contributor: Natasha Mozz

139 THE AWAKENING OF COMMUNICATION | Design Firm: Univisual
Designer: Gaetano Grizzanti | Client: MAX GALLI Comminication | Main Contributor: Univisual

139 X CAMPAIGN | Design Firm: Conjure
Designers: Chelsea Leasure, Braden Nauman, Chris Froeter | Client: United States Steel
Chief Creative Officer: Chris Froeter | Writer: Ted Stoik | Main Contributor: Various

140 ENCOMPASS BRUSH | Design Firm: Cue | Designer: Nate Killam
Client: Ryca | Creative Director: Alan Colvin | Main Contributor: Nate Killam

140 KEH CAMERA | Design Firm: Goods & Services | Designer: Staci Janik
Client: KEH Camera | Chief Creative Officer: Scott Jennings | Writer: Molly Dickinson
Executive Creative Directors: Jason Nitti, Sean Metcalf | Brand Creative: Staci Janik
User Experience: Philip Spradley | Strategy: David Hewitt | Brand Strategy: David Choe
Vice President Brand Creative: Mike Williams | Account Director: Nicole Gregory
Main Contributor: Goods & Services

140 LAUNCHING A GLOBAL LEADER IN LOGISTICS | Design Firm: Lippincott
Designer: Rodney Abbot | Client: GXO | Production: Andrew McCarthy, Director, Design Production, Lippincott, Guan-Huei Wu, Senior Production Specialist, Lippincott
Brand Strategy: Allen Luo, Brand Strategy Consultant, Lippincott, Valerie Garral, Senior Associate, Strategy, Lippincott, Emily Guilmette, Partner, Strategy, Lippincott, Julius Roberge, Partner, Strategy, Lippincott, Jenna Moss, Brand Strategy Associate, Lippincott, Laura Dawson, Senior Associate, Lippincott, Laura Schroeder, Brand Strategy Associate, Lippincott
Brand Creatives: Michael Guerin, Partner, Design, Lippincott, Aline Kim, Partner, Design, Lippincott, Bo Hwang, Designer, Lippincott, Dimitri Theodoropoulous, Senior Design Director, Lippincott, Emiko Osaka, Senior Designer, Lippincott, Rui Maekawa, Senior Design Director, Lippincott, Chet Purtilar, Senior Design Director, Lippincott, Wesley Tibbs, Brand Voice Associate, Lippincott, Nic Adenau, Senior Design Director, Lippincott
Main Contributor: Michael D'Esopo, Senior Partner, Director of Brand Strategy, Lippincott

140 TMI | Design Firm: Balloon Inc. | Designer: Ryo Shimizu
Client: TMI-Nagoya University | Main Contributor: Ryo Shimizu

140 HEART HAUS IDENTITY | Design Firm: Heart Haus at CVS Health
Designers: Jane Wongjirad, Evan Boisvert, Karen David | Client: Self-initiated
Creative Director: Christopher Lehmann | Executive Creative Director: Brett Gerstenblatt
Main Contributor: Heart Haus at CVS Health

140 LAUREN & COLIN ARE GETTING MARRIED BRANDING | Design Firm: Mermaid, Inc.
Designer: Sharon Lloyd McLaughlin | Client: Lauren & Colin | Developer: Bart McLaughlin
Main Contributor: Sharon Lloyd McLaughlin

141 YUE | Design Firm: Loksophy Design Ltd. | Designer: Hong Ka Lok
Client: Yue - Beijing | Photographer: Hu Xue Man | Artist: Hou Zi Chao
Art Director: Hong Ka Lok | Interior Designer: Golucci Interior Architects
Graphic Designer: Loksophy Design | Creative Director: Hong Ka Lok
Advisor: Adj. Project & Consultant | Main Contributor: Hong Ka Lok

141 1895 BY LAVAZZA IDENTITY | Design Firm: *TraceElement
Designers: Dana Nixon, Yvette Sierra | Client: Lavazza | Chief Creative Officer: Jeff Barfoot
Account Manager: Anna Mertz | Main Contributor: Jeff Barfoot

142 PLANET FWD BRAND | Design Firm: SIREN SF | Designer: SIREN SF
Client: Planet FWD | Main Contributor: SIREN SF

142 CORTERRA PROPERTY BRANDING | Design Firm: Compass
Designer: Jared Sawdey | Client: Corterra | Main Contributor: Compass

143 TX CANN MD BRAND IDENTITY | Design Firm: Test Monki | Designer: Test Monki
Client: TX Cann MD | Main Contributors: Suzy Simmons, Gaby Quintana

143 FIRST EAGLE INVESTMENTS | Design Firm: Sequel Studio
Designer: Dana Gonsalves | Client: First Eagle Investments | Project Director: Sybil Rodgers
Creative Director: Dana Gonsalves | Chief Creative Directors: John Nishimoto, Wendy Blattner
Managing Director: Brian Crooks | Interactive Designer: Daniela al-Saleh
Interactive Design Director: Ninja von Oertzen | Photographers: Walter Smith, Bob Coscarelli
Main Contributors: Dana Gonsalves, Daniela al-Saleh, Ninja von Oertzen

143 TRUSTED ADVOCATE BRANDING | Design Firm: Mermaid, Inc.
Designer: Sharon Lloyd McLaughlin | Client: Trusted Advocate | Developer: Bart McLaughlin
Creative Director: Sharon Lloyd McLaughlin | Main Contributor: Sharon Lloyd McLaughlin

143 NATURALLY ITALIAN | Design Firm: Univisual | Designers: Gaetano Grizzanti, Giancarlo Tosoni | Client: Lapitec Group | Main Contributor: Univisual

143 CREATING A FINTECH BRAND THAT EMPOWERS SUSTAINABLE TRADE
Design Firm: Lippincott | Designer: Dan Vasconcelos, Partner | Client: Olea
Brand Strategy: Jessica Lee, Senior Associate, Katrin Krieger, Consultant
Brand Creative: Sean Yoon, Senior Digital Designer | Senior Designer: YK Lam
Designer Directors: Michelle Kwan, Jan Van Wezemael | Main Contributor: Graham Harvey, Senior Partner, Brand Strategy

143 BENETTI SHELL COVE RESIDENTIAL BRANDING | Design Firm: The Property Agency
Designer: Costa Popolizio | Client: Colliers and Oscars Hotels | Art Director: Costa Popolizio
Photographer: Rob Walsh | Other: Studio Modus (CGI Renders)
Main Contributor: Costa Popolizio

144 GEMINI LEAVES IDENTITY | Design Firm: *TraceElement | Designer: Dana Nixon
Client: Gemini Leaves | Chief Creative Officer: Jeff Barfoot | Account Manager: Lindsey Phaup
Main Contributor: Jeff Barfoot

144 CULTURAL BOX | Design Firm: Polygon | Designer: Qixin Wu
Client: Cultural Box | Main Contributor: Qixin Wu

144 SYNEREX | Design Firm: Balloon Inc. | Designer: Ryo Shimizu
Client: Nagoya University - Synerex Project | Main Contributor: Ryo Shimizu

144 HULAGRINS BRAND IDENTITY | Design Firm: Test Monki | Designer: Test Monki
Client: HulaGrins Pediatric Dentistry | Main Contributors: Suzy Simmons, Gaby Quintana

144 DRISCOLL CHILDREN'S HOSPITAL BRAND IDENTITY
Design Firm: *TraceElement | Designer: Cristina Moore | Client: Driscoll Children's Hospital
Chief Creative Officer: Jeff Barfoot | Illustrator: Cristina Moore
Account Manager: Jenna Snyder | Main Contributor: Jeff Barfoot

144 SIGNAL REBRAND | Design Firm: Matchstic | Designers: Brit Blankenship, Gray Hauser
Client: Signal Security | Art Director: Brit Blankenship | Writer: Pamela Henman
Creative Director: Blake Howard | Strategy: Sarah Gail Hughes | Project Manager: Melissa Kruse
Producer: Natalie Hales | Photographer: Jason Hales | Main Contributor: Matchstic

145 COMTE DE GRASSE 06 VODKA | Design Firm: Force MAJEURE
Designer: Pierre Delebois | Client: Comte de Grasse | Main Contributor: Pierre Delebois

145 MAIN STREET LOFTS BRAND IDENTITY | Design Firm: Resource Branding
Designers: Mandy Rahiya, Juliana Bone | Client: Realty Capital Partners
Design Director: Rick Grimsley | Copywriter: Gary Thompson | Strategy: Gary Thompson
Account Management: Lindsey Lane, Cat Touliatous | Main Contributor: Resource Branding

145 MAQI - LAVA COOKIES | Design Firm: Loksophy Design Ltd.
Designer: Hong Ka Lok | Client: Maqi - Lava Cookies | Creative Director: Hong Ka Lok
Graphic Designers: Fearless Lei, Skylar Tai | Photographer: Bob Wong
Main Contributor: Hong Ka Lok

146 REVEL STOKE WHISKY | Design Firm: Cue | Designer: Matt Erickson
Client: Phillips Distilling Co. | Creative Director: Alan Colvin
Main Contributor: Matt Erickson

146 MAUNA LOA | Design Firm: Moxie Sozo | Designers: Silvia Skinner, Moxie Sozo, Jennifer Birdsell | Client: Mauna Loa | Illustrators: Madeleine Veneziano, Qian Liu
Creative Director: Derek Springston | Main Contributor: Derek Springston

146 AMPLIFYING HOW A BRAND ENGINEERS THE EXTRAORDINARY
Design Firm: Lippincott | Designer: Brendán Murphy, Senior Partner | Client: Medtronic
Strategy: Allen Gove, Senior Partner | Production: Brendan deVallance, Senior Production Manager, Andrew McCarthy, Director, Design Production, Luis Vieira, Design Production Manager, Gladys Fabara, Presentation Manager | Brand Strategy: Helen Chow, Partner, Alex Tarnoff, Senior Associate, Kaitlin Leung, Senior Associate, Robert Ferguson, Senior Associate, Tyler Young, Brand Strategy Associate, Harry Parsons, Senior Consultant, Brand Strategy | Brand Creatives: Aurelio Saiz, Partner, Jung Kwon, Senior Design Director, Wen-Chi Huang, Motion Designer, Jenifer Lehker, Partner, Emily Seitz, Senior Consultant, Brand Voice, Travis DeShong, Consultant, Brand Voice, Adam Stringer, Partner
Main Contributor: Brendán Murphy, Senior Partner

146 VIÑA ALMIRANTE BRANDING | Design Firm: Roberto Núñez Studio
Designer: Roberto Núñez | Client: Viña Almirante | Brand Strategy: Roberto Núñez
Creative Director: Roberto Núñez | Copywriter: Roberto Núñez | Web Developer: Rubén Aja
Art Director: Roberto Núñez | Product Photographer: Roberto Treviño
Photographer: Mariano Herrera | Printers: Grafiko, Coreti | Photo Illustrator: Gael Lendoiro
Engraving: Alex Ferreiro | Main Contributor: Roberto Núñez

146 FUNKY BUDDHA | Design Firm: Moxie Sozo | Designer: Charles Bloom
Client: Funky Buddha | Illustrator: Charles Bloom | Main Contributor: Charles Bloom

147 AQUAROO BRAND SYSTEM | Design Firm: Noise 13 | Designer: Zili Ma
Client: Aquaroo | Printer: Andresen | Photographer: GammaNine | Creative Director: Peter Judd
Illustrator: Alexa Pleiko-Izik | Main Contributor: Zili Ma

147 ENSO GROUP BRANDING | Design Firm: Coastlines Creative Group
Designer: Byron Dowler | Client: Enso Group | Brand Strategy: Byron Dowler
Developer: Derek Lam | Main Contributor: Tim Loo

147 PEELER FARMS BRANDING | Design Firm: Doris Palmeros Studio
Designers: Sydney Solomon, Doris Palmeros | Client: Peeler Farms
Assistant Designer: Sydney Solomon | Main Contributor: Doris Palmeros

147 REBRANDING | Design Firm: BUNTIN | Designer: Dan Ferro
Client: Self-initiated | Executive Creative Directors: Jonatan Maldonado, Aron Cleary
Chief Creative Officer: Dave Damman | Main Contributor: BUNTIN

147 SALE REBRANDING | Design Firm: Fellow Inc. | Designer: Jack Lewin
Client: Salo | Creative Director: Michael Seitz | Senior Designer: Keelan Campbell
Main Contributor: Fellow Inc.

147 ELECTRIC OWL STUDIOS BRAND IDENTITY | Design Firm: Resource Branding
Designer: Liz Northcutt | Client: Electric Owl Studios | Design Director: Rick Grimsley
Copywriter: Jessica Childers | Web Developer: Erik Rühling | Strategy: Jessica Childers
Account Management: Cat Touliatos, Sarah Krausen | Main Contributor: Resource Branding

148 RED ATLAS BRANDING | Design Firm: Paolo Catalla
Designer: Paolo Catalla | Client: Red Atlas | Main Contributor: Paolo Catalla

148 HUMAN RIGHTS FIRST REBRAND | Design Firm: Matchstic
Designers: Brian Nelson, Brit Blankenship, John Bowles, Malique Faulks
Client: Human Rights First | Design Director: Brit Blankenship | Creative Director: Blake Howard
Writer: Danielle Wilson | Strategy: Sarah Melnyk, Justin Carr | Project Manager: Melissa Kruse
Main Contributor: Matchstic

149 SOLV ENERGY BRAND IDENTITY | Design Firm: PH Studio
Designers: Richard Patterson, Amy Hershman | Client: SOLV Energy
Main Contributor: Richard Patterson

149 &BARR BUSINESS CARD REDESIGN | Design Firm: &Barr | Designer: McKenzie Estes
Client: Self-inititated | Associate Creative Director: Jacqui Garcia | Art Director: McKenzie Estes
Ad Agency: &Barr | Creative Director: Christian Wojciechowski | Copywriter: Megan Rosenoff
Producer: Lynn Whitney-Smith | Account Executive: Kimberly Blaylock | Main Contributor: &Barr

149 WDGIT - WOMEN AND DIVERSE GENDERS IN TECH | Design Firm: Compass
Designers: Kelly Jung (Designer), Claire Eckstrom (Designer) | Client: Self-initiated
Others: Sophine Lim (Design Director), Roxy Torres (Associate Design Director)
Main Contributor: IN-HOUSE: Compass Design Studio

149 CHOREO | Design Firm: Sequel Studio | Designer: Dana Gonsalves
Client: Choreo Advisors | Chief Creative Director: John Nishimoto | Design Director: Carla Miller
Creative Director: Dana Gonsalves | Interactive Director: Daniela al-Saleh
Project Director: Sybil Rodgers | Managing Director: Brian Crooks
Main Contributors: Carla Miller, Daniela al-Saleh, Dana Gonsalves

149 EXPERIENCE DESIGN CERTIFICATE PROGRAM: IDENTITY SYSTEM
Design Firm: Erica Holeman | Designer: Erica Holeman | Client: Odyssey Works
Main Contributor: Erica Holeman

149 THE GRACEFUL ORDINARY BRANDING | Design Firm: Conjure
Designer: Chelsea Leasure | Client: The Graceful Ordinary | Creative Director: Chris Froeter
Main Contributor: Various

150 COMPASS FALL RETREAT 2021 AUSTIN | Design Firm: Compass
Designers: Chris Ganz (Designer), Alix DeBroux (Designer), Lauren Thawley (Designer),
Emily Critz (Designer) | Client: Self-initiated | Design Director: Benjamin Garner (Design Director)
Others: Roxy Torres (Associate Design Director), Sabrina Evans (Regional Marketing Director),
Paul Vlachou (Senior Creative Director), Stephanie Mathews (Lead, Growth Product Marketing +
National Events), Matt Spangler (Chief Marketing Officer), John LoPresto (Senior Marketing
Manager, National Events), Jordy Addeo (Marketing Advisor), Lauren Griffin (Marketing Advisor),
Keren Landy (Events & Partnerships Associate), Miranda Shaw (Associate Designer),
Samantha Beja (Growth Product Marketing Manager), Nicole Riverso (Sr. Creative Producer),
Juan Pantoja (Associate Designer) | Main Contributor: IN-HOUSE: Compass Design Studio

150 THE FINANCIAL PUBLISHING BRAND | Design Firm: Univisual
Designers: Gaetano Grizzanti, Giancarlo Tosoni | Client: LeFonti Group
Main Contributor: Univisual

150 CREATING A PEOPLE-FIRST HEALTHCARE BRAND | Design Firm: Lippincott
Designer: Aline Kim, Partner, Lippincott | Client: Lyn Health | Brand Strategy: Haley Picone,
Senior Associate, Lippincott, Sarah Koe, Senior Consultant, Lippincott
Brand Creatives: Peter Chun, Partner, Lippincott, Emiko Osaka, Senior Designer, Lippincott,
Sudiksha Krishnan, Senior Designer, Lippincott, Bo Hwang, Senior Designer, Lippincott
Main Contributor: Dylan Stuart, Senior Partner, Lippincott

150 THE RATIONAL IDENTITY | Design Firm: Univisual
Designers: Gaetano Grizzanti, Giancarlo Tosoni | Client: Breton Industry
Main Contributor: Univisual

150 SOVA SCIENCE DISTRICT | Design Firm: MiresBall | Designer: David Alderman
Client: Longfellow Real Estate Partners | Creative Director: John Ball
Main Contributors: John Ball, David Alderman

150 IDEON REBRAND | Design Firm: Coastlines Creative Group | Designer: Byron Dowler
Client: Ideon | Developer: Derek Lam | Main Contributor: Ideon.ai

151 CMARKET | Design Firm: Loksophy Design Ltd.
Designer: Hong Ka Lok | Client: cCentre | Art Director: Hong Ka Lok
Photographer: Bob Wong | Interior Designer: Iman Ng
Graphic Designer: Fearless Lei | Main Contributor: Hong Ka Lok

151 ERIC GELMAN AGENT REBRAND | Design Firm: Compass
Designer: Stacy Zou (Senior Designer) | Client: Eric Gelman
Other: Troy Taylor (Motion Designer) | Main Contributor: IN-HOUSE: Compass Design Studio

152 SASLONG | Design Firm: Onrepeat Studio | Designer: Joao Oliveira
Client: Funivie Saslong S.p.a. | Copywriter: Janak Jani | Main Contributor: Joao Oliveira

152 COPPER BANKING BRAND IDENTITY | Design Firm: SIREN SF
Designer: SIREN SF | Client: Copper Banking | Main Contributor: SIREN SF

153 GALAXY FLIP ECOSYSTEM LAUNCH POSTER | Design Firm: Turner Duckworth:
London, San Francisco & New York | Designer: Cinthia Wen | Client: Samsung
Creative Director: Carolyn Ashburn | Senior Designer: Thom Pastrano
Account Director: Marco Vaschetto | Other: Josh Michels
Main Contributor: Cinthia Wen, Head of Creative

153 SPECIAL OLYMPICS WISCONSIN PROGRAM | Design Firm: Traction Factory
Designer: Brandon Tushkowski | Client: Milwaukee Admirals
Design Director: David Brown | Copywriter: Tom Dixon | Project Coordinator: Danny Yadgir
Production Artist: Jenni Wierzba | Print Producer: Brett Waterhouse
Account Director: Scott Bucher | Main Contributor: Brandon Tushkowski

153 DOLLAR SHAVE CLUB VISUAL IDENTITY | Design Firm: Turner Duckworth: London,
San Francisco & New York | Designers: Michael Bagnardi, Hollis Callas
Client: Dollar Shave Club | Typographer: Jeremy Mickel | Digital Artist: Mike Winston
Executive Creative Director: Chris Garvey | Design Director: Ian Conklin
Production: Craig Snelgrove, Liisa Turan-Walters, Sara Scanlan, Jeff Jones
Photographers: Jeff Vallee, Zach & Buj from Apostrophe | Account Managment: Michael Hope
Account Director: Janice McManemy | Main Contributor: Nicole Jordan

153 REFLECTION POINT REBRANDING | Design Firm: Conjure | Designer: Chelsea Leasure
Client: Books at Work | Chief Creative Director: Chris Froeter | Main Contributor: Various

153 OAK STREET HEALTH BRANDING | Design Firm: Coley Porter Bell
Designers: Linda Becker, Josh Payne | Client: Oak Street Health
Creative Director: Dean Field | Strategy: Ron Allen | Account Manager: Eleanor Potter
Main Contributors: Coley Porter Bell, Oak Street Health

154 VSA PARTNERS: SPACIAL | Design Firm: VSA Partners
Designers: Leslie Carol, Heather Stickney, VSA Partners | Client: Innovatus Capital Partners
Associate Creative Director: Sarah Trent | Executive Creative Director: Thom Wolfe
Writers: Janelle Blasdel, Bill Maday | Website: Nick Lo Bue | Project Manager: Kristin Cella
Strategy: Marisa Rondinelli, Joseph McConellogue | Architect: CAZA Architects
Account Director: Jeff Walker | Main Contributor: VSA Partners

154 MANUKORA LEGACY | Design Firm: Pendo
Designers: Peter Ladd, Timothy King, Miya McGrew | Client: Manukora
Copywriter: Ryan Leeson | Photographer: Makito Inomata
Main Contributors: Peter Ladd, Don Cleland

154 GARNICHE | Design Firm: Creative Energy | Designer: Jacy Embray
Client: Sugar Foods | Creative Director: Greg Nobles | Copywriter: Taylor Waisanka
President: Tony Treadway | Main Contributor: Jacy Embray

154 MYSIMPLEPETLAB | Design Firm: Cue | Designer: Katelyn McVey
Client: MySimplePetLab | Creative Director: Alan Colvin | Main Contributor: Katelyn McVey

154 MANUKORA BOTANICALS | Design Firm: Pendo
Designers: Peter Ladd, Timothy King, Twoo Nguyen | Client: Manukora
Photographer: Makito Inomata | Copywriter: Ryan Leeson
Main Contributors: Peter Ladd, Don Cleland

154 THE WATTS AT HAMPTON COVE BRAND IDENTITY | Design Firm: Resource Branding
Designers: Shaina Patel, Juliana Bone | Client: Daniel Corporation
Design Director: Rick Grimsley | Copywriter: Gary Thompson | Strategy: Gary Thompson
Account Management: Cat Touliatous, Sarah Krausen | Main Contributor: Resource Branding

155 CAN YOU SEE THE MUSIC? | Design Firm: Brand Bar Communications
Designer: László Herbszt | Client: Franz Liszt Chamber Orchestra (LFKZ)
Creative Directors: Gyula Halász, Attila Simon | Senior Designer: Bianka Földi
Music & Sound: Dániel Zelenák | Developer: Péter Fülöp | Account Manager: Izsáki Boglárka
Main Contributor: Brand Bar Communications

155 WEO BRAND IDENTITY | Design Firm: Matchstic
Designers: Meghan Murray, Malique Faulks | Client: Weo | Art Director: Meghan Murray
Creative Director: Blake Howard | Writer: Pamela Henman | Strategy: Pamela Henman
Project Managers: Cody Goshert, Melissa Kruse | Photographer: Gray Hauser
Main Contributor: Matchstic

155 CENTRO DE MEMÓRIAS DA INDÚSTRIA | Design Firm: PMDESIGN
Designer: Paulo Marcelo | Client: Município de S. João da Madeira
Main Contributor: Paulo Marcelo

156 TEKNION BOW TIE BROCHURE | Design Firm: Vanderbyl Design
Designers: Michael Vanderbyl, Tori Koch | Client: Teknion
Creative Director: Michael Vanderbyl | Photographer: David Peterson
Main Contributor: Michael Vanderbyl

156 TEKNION ROUTES BROCHURE | Design Firm: Vanderbyl Design
Designers: Michael Vanderbyl, Tori Koch | Client: Teknion
Creative Director: Michael Vanderbyl | Photographer: David Peterson
Main Contributor: Michael Vanderbyl

156 10TWELVE | Design Firm: House of Current | Designer: Koble Delmer Client: Jones Lang LaSalle | Copywriter: Kate Beck | Creative Director: Wendy Lowden Production Manager: Scott Brannon | Photographer: Scott Lowden Photography Account Management: Stefanie Demoff | Account Director: Lisa Maloof Main Contributor: Wendy Lowden, Creative Director

157 3RD PARTY BROCHURE | Design Firm: House of Current Designer: Koble Delmer | Client: M&J Wilkow | Creative Director: Wendy Lowden Copywriter: Kate Beck | Production Manager: Scott Brannon Account Manager: Stefanie Demoff | Account Director: Lisa Maloof Main Contributor: Wendy Lowden, Creative Director

157 CITYSCAPES -SILENCE- | Design Firm: TOPPAN INC. Designer: MASAHIRO AOYAGI [TOPPAN INC.] | Client: OBAYASHI CORPORATION Photographers: YASUTAKA KOJIMA, TOMOKI HIROKAWA | Print Designer: Kazuya Tanaka [TOPPAN INC.] | Main Contributor: MASAHIRO AOYAGI [TOPPAN INC.]

158 PLANET OF LIFE | Design Firm: TOPPAN INC. Designers: SATORU YAMAMOTO [TOPPAN INC.], MASAHIRO OGAWA [TOPPAN INC.] Client: Mitsubishi Electric Corporation | Print Designer: KAZUYA TANAKA [TOPPAN INC.] Creative Director: MASAHIRO AOYAGI [TOPPAN INC.] | Art Director: KATSUMI ASABA Photographer: JUNJI TAKASAGO | Main Contributor: MASAHIRO AOYAGI [TOPPAN INC.]

158 2022 TOYO INK GROUP CALENDAR SYMBIOSIS | Design Firm: TOPPAN INC. Designers: MASAHIRO AOYAGI [TOPPAN INC.], MASAHIRO OGAWA [TOPPAN INC.] Client: TOYO INK SC HOLDINGS CO., LTD. | Illustrator: KEN MATSUDA Main Contributor: MASAHIRO AOYAGI [TOPPAN INC.]

159 GRATEFUL — TYPOGRAPHY CARD | Design Firm: The Rare Form Designer: Kyle R. Thompson | Client: Self-initiated | Artist: Masa Sasaki Ceramics Creative Director: Christina Thompson | Main Contributor: Kyle R. Thompson

159 HAPPY RAINBOW BIRTHDAY CARD | Design Firm: Legis Design Designer: Mayumi Kato | Client: Self-initiated | Main Contributor: Legis Design

160 SCAD RECRUITMENT / COURSE CATALOG
Design Firm: Savannah College of Art and Design | Designers: Anna-Lea Jenkins-Ferrelle, Senior Designer, Alaina Colleen | Client: Self-initiated | Executive Creative Director: Chris Miller Art Directors: Rosa Triolo, Jen Young-Hammer | Senior Art Director: Jennifer McCarn Main Contributor: Anna-Lea Jenkins-Ferrelle

160 REPRESENT: ACM GRAPHIC DESIGN 2020 BFA PRINTED EXHIBITION
Design Firm: REPRESENT Designers | Designers: Nadya Andrianova, Joseph Ciani, Emily Corson, Kevin Cristancho, Ivelise N. Cruz, Tahiry Cumbicus, Diana Diaz, Ayah Elgendy, Cindy Guzman, Jason Hamilton, Antoinette Lacy, Joseph Labib, Kelly Llumiquinga, Emily Longobardi, Patrick Liu, Brandon Marshall, Nolan Mendoza, Gisela Ochoa, Jose Paredes, Roshani Pise, Evelyne Rendon, Andrea Sanchez, Ronald Solano, Abraam Tawfik, Arely Velasco, Natalia Ziarno | Clients: Rutgers University-Newark, Graphic Design Program, Department of Arts, Culture & Media, School of Arts & Sciences–Newark | Printer: Oddi Creative Directors: Jennifer Bernstein, Rebecca Jampol | Advisors: Chantal Fischzang, Ned Drew | Main Contributors: Jennifer Bernstein, Rebecca Jampol

160 WEST CHESTER UNIVERSITY 2021 BFA CATALOG
Design Firm: Karen Watkins Design | Designer: Karen Watkins | Client: West Chester University Creative Director: Karen Watkins | Printer: Cornerstone Graphic Technologies, LLC Photographers: David Johanson, Karen Watkins | Editor: Heather Sharpe Main Contributor: Karen Watkins

161 PRS IN VIVO | Design Firm: Elmwood | Designers: Richard Hood, Matt Churchill Client: PRS IN VIVO | Animator: Oli Minchin | Senior Designer: Matt Churchill Executive Creative Director: Andrew Lawrence | Senior Account Director: Charlotte Fountain Other: Greg Taylor (Chief Provocation Officer) | Main Contributor: Andrew Lawrence

161 POSTER JJ CHICOLINO | Design Firm: Teiga, Studio Designer: Maria Toucedo Cal | Client: J.J. Chicolino | Creative Director: Xose Teiga Art Directors: Maria Toucedo Cal, Xose Teiga | Graphic Designer: Maria Toucedo Cal Copywriters: Maria Toucedo Cal, Xose Teiga | Main Contributor: Teiga, Studio

161 NIHON UNIVERSITY COLLEGE OF ART 100 YEARBOOK
Design Firm: Noriyuki Kasai | Designer: Noriyuki Kasai Client: Nihon University College of Art | Main Contributor: Noriyuki Kasai

162 A SHORE THING | Design Firm: Wainscot Media Designers: Trevett McCandliss, Nancy Campbell | Client: Earnshaw's Magazine Photographer: Trevett McCandliss | Main Contributors: Trevett McCandliss, Nancy Campbell

162 CULTURE CLUB | Design Firm: Wainscot Media | Designers: Trevett McCandliss, Nancy Campbell | Client: Earnshaw's Magazine | Hair & Makeup: Clelia Bergonzoli Fashion Director: Mariah Walker | Editor-in-Chief: Michele Silver | Photographer: Zoe Adlersberg Main Contributors: Trevett McCandliss, Nancy Campbell

163 COOL FOR COZY | Design Firm: Wainscot Media | Designers: Trevett McCandliss, Nancy Campbell | Client: Footwear Plus Magazine | Editor-in-Chief: Greg Dutter Photographer: Trevett McCandliss | Main Contributors: Trevett McCandliss, Nancy Campbell

163 GROW | Design Firm: Ginkgo Bioworks Designer: Chloe Scheffe | Client: Self-initiated | Creative Director: Grace Chuang Art Directors: Alexa Garcia, Jazsalyn, Livia Foldes, Grace Chuang Illustrators: Ina Jang, Debora Cheyenne Cruchon, Maria Medem, Bernice Liu, Chogiseok Main Contributors: Grace Chuang, Leon Dische Becker, Alexa Garcia, Christina Agapakis

164 AS MOTHER NATURE INTENDED | Design Firm: Aegis Dental Network Designer: Jennifer Barlow | Client: Inside Dentistry | Main Contributor: Jennifer Barlow, Designer

164 THE RIGHT FLUFF | Design Firm: Wainscot Media Designers: Trevett McCandliss, Nancy Campbell | Client: Footwear Plus Magazine Hair & Makeup: Clelia Bergonzoli, Ray Brown Pro | Photographer: Trevett McCandliss Editor-in-Chief: Greg Dutter | Model: Cameron Newbill from Supreme Model Mgmt. Main Contributors: Trevett McCandliss, Nancy Campbell

165 LEX 2021 – THE MAGAZINE OF DREXEL UNIVERSITY THOMAS R. KLINE SCHOOL OF LAW | Design Firm: Ahoy Studios | Designers: Connie Koch, Denis Kuchta, Denise Sommer | Client: Drexel University Thomas R. Kline School of Law Art Director: Brian Crooks | Editor: Nancy Waters Main Contributor: Drexel University Thomas R. Kline School of Law

165 R MAGAZINE FALL 2021 | Design Firm: House of Current | Designer: Wendy Lowden Client: Royal Hawaiian Center | Creative Director: Wendy Lowden | Copywriter: Kate Beck Production Manager: Scott Brannon | Photographer: Scott Lowden Photography Account Services: Stefanie Demoff | Account Director: Lisa Maloof Main Contributor: Wendy Lowden, Creative Director

165 LEQ MAGAZINE COVER HATE | Design Firm: Freaner Creative & Design Designer: Ariel Freaner | Client: San Diego County District Attorneys Office Main Contributor: Ariel Freaner

165 PROJECT DEBATER / NATURE COVER DESIGN | Design Firm: IBM Research Designer: Yijia Xie | Client: Nature | Main Contributor: Yijia Xie

166 ONE HUNDRED AND ONE | Design Firm: Hundredweight Designer: Stephen Robertson | Clients: AXA Investment Managers, Amy Elliot, Tanya Lambert Writer: Camilla Belton - Writing for Design | Senior Account Executive: Charlie Chhay Managing Director: Craig Devitt | Main Contributor: Hundredweight

166 2021 MODERN LUXURY COMPASS HAWAII TAKEOVER | Design Firm: Compass Designer: Stacy Zou | Client: Self-inititated | Senior Designer: Stacy Zou (Senior Designer) Other: Justin Truong (Designer) | Main Contributor: IN-HOUSE: Compass Design Studio

166 REP | MAGAZINE | Design Firm: Daniel Frumhoff Design | Designer: Erica Holeman Client: Stanford d.school | Artist: David Alabo | Photographer: Patrick Beaudouin Illustrator: Yifan Wu | Main Contributor: Daniel Frumhoff

167 AUBURN UNIVERSITY RURAL STUDIO STYLE GUIDE
Design Firms: Courtney Windham, Margaret Fletcher Designers: Graphic Designer—Courtney Windham; Information Designer—Margaret Fletcher Client: Auburn University Rural Studio | Directors: Andrew Freear—Director of Rural Studio, Rusty Smith—Associate Director of Rural Studio | Managing Director: Natalie Butts-Ball—Communications Manager | Writers: Susan A. Youngblood—Coordinator of Technical Communications, Michelle Sidler—Director of Technical Communications Other: Ed Youngblood—Usability Testing | Main Contributors: Courtney Windham, Margaret Fletcher—Designers and Project Managers

167 CSU NANCY RICHARDSON DESIGN CENTER | Design Firm: ArtHouse Design Designers: Marty Gregg (Principal & Founder), Beth Rosa (Design Director) Zach Kotel (Associate Design Director), Abby Knab (Senior Designer), Anaïs Mares (Senior Designer) Client: Colorado State University (CSU) | Fabricator: Concept Signs & Graphics Main Contributor: ArtHouse Design

168 TO LIVE REBRAND | Design Firm: Underline Studio | Designers: Laura Rojas, Fidel Peña Client: TO Live | Creative Directors: Fidel Peña, Claire Dawson | Copywriter: Clive Veroni, Leap Consulting Strategy: Clive Veroni, Leap Consulting | Main Contributor: Underline Studio

168 ROSE | Design Firm: Randy Clark | Designer: Randy Clark Client: Wenzhou-Kean University | Main Contributor: Randy Clark

168 TALL TYPE | Design Firm: Randy Clark | Designer: Randy Clark Client: Wenzhou-Kean University | Main Contributor: Randy Clark

169 SCHINE STUDENT CENTER WAYFINDING | Design Firm: Entro Designers: Rachel Wallace, Donna Liu, Shehrbano Akhtar, John Pereira, Entro Client: Syracuse University | Creative Director: Edmund Li Project Manager: Nima Gopalakrishnan | Main Contributor: Entro Design Team

169 NATIONAL VETERANS RESOURCE CENTER WAYFINDING, DONOR RECOGNITION, AND EXHIBIT | Design Firm: Entro | Designers: Shehrbano Akhtar, Paolo Emili, James Smirlies, John Pereira, Raymond Cheung, Entro | Client: Syracuse University Creative Director: Edmund Li | Project Manager: Nima Gopalakrishnan Other: John Maker, Interpretive Planner | Main Contributor: Entro Design Team

170 PEARL MEISTER GREENGARD PRIZE WALL | Design Firm: C&G Partners Designers: (Graphic Design) Joao Miranda, (Graphic Design) Calista Bohling, Jonathan Alger, (3D) Daniel Fouad, (3D) Greg Mullholland, (Graphic Design) Bruce Chao Client: Rockefeller University | Producers: (Lead) Laura Grady, Alex Kelly, Scott Shaw Main Contributor: Jonathan Alger, Partner in Charge

170 INGENIUM CENTRE SIGNAGE AND WAYFINDING | Design Firm: Entro Designer: Entro | Client: Ingenium Centre | Creative Director: Udo Schliemann Main Contributor: Entro Design Team

171 SIGNAGE AND WAYFINDING AT U OF T OISE | Design Firm: Entro Designers: David Wilkinson, Entro | Client: University of Toronto Ontario Institute for Studies in Education (OISE) | Partner, Creative Director: Rae Lam Fox Other: Aleks Bozovic, Technical Lead | Main Contributor: Entro

171 T-MOBILE YEAR OF THE TIGER | Design Firm: WONGDOODY Designers: Sophia Kim, Drew Jasperse | Client: T-Mobile Main Contributor: Monyee Chau, Artist

171 MEUFIT | Design Firm: Teiga, Studio | Designer: Maria Toucedo Cal | Client: Meufit Art Directors: Xose Teiga, Maria Toucedo Cal | Creative Director: Xose Teiga Graphic Designers: Maria Toucedo Cal, Xose Teiga, Cristina Gonzalez Community Manager: Merce Anleo | Copywriters: Maria Toucedo Cal, Xose Teiga Web Designers: Maria Toucedo Cal, Cristina Gonzalez | Video: Laura Santos Main Contributor: Teiga, Studio

171 ORACLE GLOBAL HEADQUARTERS | Design Firm: Asterisk
Designers: Asterisk, Pam Caperton, Oscar Morris, Callie Gabbert | Client: Oracle
Copywriter: Content & Context | Architect: STG Design | Fabricator: Moss, Inc.
Partners, Creative Directors: Susanne Harrington, Shawn Harrington | Main Contributor: Asterisk

171 COVENANT HOUSE NEW YORK WAYFINDING AND DONOR RECOGNITION
Design Firm: Entro | Designers: Vanessa Tarasio, Jessica Schrader, Lauren Kuzyk, Cristina Paik
Client: Covenant House | Partner, Creative Director: Anna Crider
Project Manager: Jessica Schrader | Additional Title: David Vanden-Eynden, Principal Emeritus
Main Contributor: Entro Design Team

172 FEEEEL MACAU 2021 | Design Firm: Loksophy Design Ltd.
Designer: Hong Ka Lok | Client: Macau Poster Design Association
Art Director: Hong Ka Lok | Photographer: Bob Wong | Main Contributor: Hong Ka Lok

172 PHILIP ROTH PERSONAL LIBRARY | Design Firm: C&G Partners
Designers: Jonathan Alger, Chris Mills | Client: Newark Public Library
Design Director: Daniel Fouad | Architect: Ann Beha Architects | Fabricator: Hadley Exhibits
Other: (Project Managers) Shawmut Design and Construction
Main Contributor: Jonathan Alger, Partner-in-Charge

173 UNIVERSITY OF ARIZONA ALFIE NORVILLE GEM AND MINERAL MUSEUM AT THE HISTORIC PIMA COUNTY COURTHOUSE | Design Firm: Ralph Appelbaum Associates
Designer: Ralph Appelbaum Associates | Client: Pima County
Graphis Designers: Jesen Tanadi, Kelsey Mitchell | Content Coordinator: Kirsten Amundsen
Project Manager: Büke Kumyol | Project Director: Rick Sobel
Other: Content Developer/Script Writer: Karen de Seve
Main Contributor: Ralph Appelbaum Associates

173 EXHIBITION PROJECT: GALLERY MÀROÙ, NAGAOKA INSTITUTE OF DESIGN EXHIBITION HALL | Design Firm: Tetsuro Minorikawa | Designer: Tetsuro Minorikawa
Client: Nagaoka Institute of Design | Main Contributor: Tetsuro Minorikawa

173 VISION ID | Design Firm: Goods & Services | Designer: Sean Metcalf
Client: ZEISS | Executive Creative Directors: Sean Metcalf, Jason Nitti
Chief Creative Officer: Scott Jennings | Project Manager: Betsy Spain
Senior Account Director: Erica Ortmann | Main Contributor: Goods & Services

173 "MY MECHANICAL SKETCHBOOK"—BARKLEY L. HENDRICKS & PHOTOGRAPHY
Design Firm: Siena Scarff Design | Designer: Siena Scarff | Client: The Rose Art Museum
Main Contributor: Siena Scarff

173 PEOPLE OF COLOR: HUE+MAN EXHIBITION | Design Firm: Joba Studio
Designer: Patrick Finley | Clients: Art Basil, USM Modular Furniture
Account Manager: Robyn Jones | Main Contributor: Kevin Jones

174 CRASTO ALTITUDE 430 | Design Firm: Omdesign | Designer: Diogo Gama Rocha
Client: Quinta do Crasto | Main Contributor: Omdesign

174 BELLA OAKS WINE LABEL | Design Firm: Vanderbyl Design
Designers: Michael Vanderbyl, Tori Koch | Client: Bella Oaks Vineyard
Creative Director: Michael Vanderbyl | Main Contributor: Michael Vanderbyl

175 SUPER BOCK COLLECTOR'S EDITION | Design Firm: Omdesign
Designer: Diogo Gama Rocha | Client: Super Bock Group | Main Contributor: Omdesign

175 IMPETUOUS WINE LABEL | Design Firm: Vanderbyl Design
Designers: Michael Vanderbyl, Alex Kinoshita | Client: Checkerboard Vineyards
Creative Director: Michael Vanderbyl | Main Contributor: Michael Vanderbyl

175 REMEDIUM WINE LABEL | Design Firm: Vanderbyl Design
Designers: Michael Vanderbyl, Alex Kinoshita | Client: Remedium Wine
Creative Director: Michael Vanderbyl | Main Contributor: Michael Vanderbyl

176 MOONSHOT | Design Firm: Hatch Design | Designer: Sasha Dusky
Client: Planet FWD | Creative Director: Nicole Flores | Photographer: Vincent Castonguay
Main Contributor: Hatch Design

176 L'APERO LES TROIS LABEL SERIES | Design Firm: Carolyn Gibbs Design
Designer: Carolyn Gibbs | Client: L'Apero les Trois | Art Director: Georgeanne Brennan
Photographer: Craig Lee | Main Contributor: Carolyn Gibbs

177 PARTILHA | Design Firm: Omdesign | Designer: Diogo Gama Rocha
Client: Quinta do Outeiro | Main Contributor: Omdesign

177 OMARÃO PACKAGING – "BEYOND THE MOUNTAINS OF MARÃO, COMMAND THOSE WHO ARE THERE!" | Design Firm: Omdesign | Designer: Diogo Gama Rocha
Client: Self-initiated | Main Contributor: Omdesign

177 HONEY MAMA'S | Design Firm: Hatch Design | Designers: Kristen McGriff, Yijing Yang
Client: Honey Mama's | Creative Director: Nicole Flores | Photo Director: Tanner Deming
Photographers: Vincent Castonguay, Leesa Morales | Main Contributor: Hatch Design

178 PEPSI KICK REDESIGN – MEXICO 2021 | Design Firm: PepsiCo Design & Innovation
Designer: PepsiCo Design & Innovation | Client: Self-initiated
Main Contributor: PepsiCo Design & Innovation

178 NEON ZEBRA BRAND LAUNCH | Design Firm: PepsiCo Design & Innovation
Designer: PepsiCo Design & Innovation | Client: Self-initiated
Main Contributor: PepsiCo Design & Innovation

178 AQUA MINERALE REDESIGN | Design Firm: PepsiCo Design & Innovation
Designer: PepsiCo Design & Innovation | Client: Self-initiated
Main Contributor: PepsiCo Design & Innovation

179 EXTRA REBRAND | Design Firm: Elmwood | Designers: Sam Povey, Rob Dyer,
David Walsh, Mark Laws, Jack Bannerman, Mike Preston, Emily Morris | Client: Mars Wrigley
Executive Creative Director: Andrew Lawrence | Typographer: Rob Clarke
Animator: Doug Brown | Account Manager: Hanni Etherington | Account Director: Beth Stanford
Other: Chief Provocation Officer - Greg Taylor | Main Contributor: Craig Barnes

179 EVERVESS REDESIGN | Design Firm: PepsiCo Design & Innovation
Designer: PepsiCo Design & Innovation | Client: Self-initiated
Main Contributor: PepsiCo Design & Innovation

179 CENTRAL MARKET BRAND BAG | Design Firms: *TraceElement, Plot Twist Creativity
Designer: Jeff Barfoot | Client: Central Market | Chief Creative Officer: Jeff Barfoot
Writer: Chris Smith | Main Contributor: Jeff Barfoot

179 LOGO AND PACKAGING DESIGN FOR CURRY HOUSE HANA-BAN
Design Firm: Legis Design | Designer: Mayumi Kato | Client: Curry House HANA-BAN
Art Director: Mayumi Kato | Main Contributor: Mayumi Kato

179 OPOLIE | Design Firm: PepsiCo Design & Innovation
Designer: PepsiCo Design & Innovation | Client: Self-initiated
Main Contributor: PepsiCo Design & Innovation

180 CALL OF DUTY: VANGUARD X WARZONE KEY ART
Design Firm: PETROL Advertising | Designer: PETROL Advertising
Clients: Activision, Sledgehammer | Main Contributor: PETROL Advertising

180 *TRACEELEMENT 2021 HOLIDAY CARD | Design Firm: *TraceElement
Designers: Cristina Moore, Dana Nixon, Jeff Rogers, Yvette Sierra, Jeff Barfoot, Jocelyn Yun
Client: Self-initiated | Chief Creative Officer: Jeff Barfoot | Account Director: Lindsey Phaup
Account Managers: Anna Mertz, Katherine Scoggin, Jenna Snyder
Main Contributor: Jeff Barfoot

181 NEW YEAR CARD | Design Firm: DesigNV [design + envy]
Designer: Neeta Verma | Client: Self-initiated | Main Contributor: Neeta Verma

181 NUDE WITH OCTOPUS | Design Firm: Michael Pantuso Design
Designer: Michael Pantuso | Client: Gallery and Exhibition
Main Contributor: Michael Pantuso

181 STOCKING STUFFERS | Design Firm: The Refinery
Designer: Elena Worley | Client: Self-initiated | Main Contributor: The Refinery

181 SUMMER READING, BOOK REVIEW, NYT, 2022 | Design Firm: HyunJung Yi
Designer: HyunJung Yi | Client: Self-initiated | Main Contributors: Paul Rogers, Brian Rea

182 CENTRAL MARKET HATCH 2021 | Design Firms: *TraceElement, Plot Twist Creativity
Designer: Cristina Moore | Client: Central Market | Chief Creative Officer: Jeff Barfoot
Creative Director: Dana Nixon | Writers: Chris Smith, Wendy Mayes | Illustrator: Cristina Moore
Account Manager: Anna Mertz | Main Contributor: Jeff Barfoot

182 THE CROWD | Design Firm: Feixue Mei | Designer: Feixue Mei
Client: Self-initiated | Main Contributor: Feixue Mei

183 THE ROAD TO ADVENTURE | Design Firm: 9Rooftops | Designer: Dena Mosti
Client: The Pennsylvania Turnpike Commission | Chief Creative Officer: Scott Seymore
Group Creative Director: Josh Blasingame | Illustrator: Jeff Lavezoli
Main Contributor: Adam Cicco

183 CENTRAL MARKET CHRISTMAS | Design Firms: *TraceElement, Plot Twist Creativity
Designers: Yvette Sierra, Cristina Moore | Client: Central Market | Writer: Plot Twist Creativity
Chief Creative Director: Jeff Barfoot | Illustrators: Yvette Sierra, Cristina Moore
Account Manager: Anna Mertz | Main Contributor: Jeff Barfoot

183 JOURNEY THROUGH SANTA CRUZ | Design Firm: INNOCEAN USA
Designer: Jimbo Phillips | Client: Hyundai Motor America | Creative Director: Lori Martin
Art Directors: Anne Krisl, Ebby St. Pierre | Group Creative Director: Barney Goldberg
Group Account Director: Michelle Sapanaro | Strategy Director: Cindy Scott
Strategy: Erin Burns-Bohlender | Ad Agency: INNOCEAN USA | Account Services: Katie Gordon
Account Manager: Stephanie Yetter | Account Director: Alix Harrison
Main Contributor: Jimbo Phillips

184 ANDREW'S DISTRIBUTING COLORING WALLS | Design Firm: *TraceElement
Designer: Cristina Moore | Client: Andrews Distributing | Chief Creative Officer: Jeff Barfoot
Illustrator: Cristina Moore | Main Contributor: Jeff Barfoot

184 DALLAS PETS ALIVE! APPAREL SERIES | Design Firm: *TraceElement
Designer: Cristina Moore | Client: Dallas Pets Alive! | Chief Creative Officer: Jeff Barfoot
Illustrator: Cristina Moore | Main Contributor: Jeff Barfoot

184 ZETA FREE AS THE WIND | Design Firm: Freaner Creative & Design
Designer: Ariel Freaner | Client: ZETA | Illustrator: Ariel Freaner
Main Contributor: Ariel Freaner

184 THINKPAD SOLUTIONS LETTERHEAD/STATIONERY
Design Firm: Peterson Ray & Company | Designer: Scott Ray | Client: Thinkpad Solutions
Art Director: Scott Ray | Main Contributor: Scott Ray

184 IT IS IN YOUR GENES | Design Firm: Brand Bar Communications
Designer: Bianka Földi | Client: Genecontact | Creative Director: Attila Simon
Main Contributor: Brand Bar Communications

184 CITY CENTER LIVE ART LOGO | Design Firm: Vanderbyl Design
Designers: Michael Vanderbyl, Tori Koch | Client: City Center Bishop Ranch
Creative Director: Michael Vanderbyl | Main Contributor: Michael Vanderbyl

185 WOLF SPIRIT DISTILLERY | Design Firm: Moxie Sozo | Designer: Nate Dyer
Client: Wolf Spirit Distillery | Main Contributor: Nate Dyer

185 AEVTIUS LOGO | Design Firm: Vanderbyl Design
Designers: Michael Vanderbyl, Tori Koch | Client: Aevtius
Creative Director: Michael Vanderbyl | Main Contributor: Michael Vanderbyl

185 SAN ANSELMO COMMUNITY FOUNDATION LOGO
Design Firm: Michael Schwab Studio | Designer: Michael Schwab
Client: San Anselmo Community Foundation | Main Contributor: Michael Schwab

185 GARDEN CITY PLACEMAKING FUND | Design Firm: Rhodes Creative
Designer: Alex Rhodes | Client: Surel's Place | Creative Production Partner: Visionkit Studio
Main Contributor: Alex Rhodes

185 &BARR 65TH ANNIVERSARY LOGO | Design Firm: &Barr
Designer: McKenzie Estes | Client: Self-initiated | Creative Director: Christian Wojciechowski
Art Director: McKenzie Estes | Associate Creative Director: Jacqui Garcia
Copywriter: Megan Rosenoff | Ad Agency: &Barr | Account Executive: Kimberly Blaylock
Main Contributor: &Barr

185 MASK UP IDENTITY | Design Firm: Open Door Design Studio (ODDS)
Designer: Shantanu Suman | Clients: United Way of Delaware, Henry and Randolph Counties
Main Contributor: Shantanu Suman

185 LOOSE TOQUE LOGO | Design Firm: Vanderbyl Design | Designer: Michael Vanderbyl
Client: Loose Toque | Creative Director: Michael Vanderbyl | Main Contributor: Michael Vanderbyl

185 BRIDGEPOINT LOGO | Design Firm: Level Group | Designers: Sydney Saneun Hwang,
Eva Beckendorf | Client: Bridge Point Capital | Art Director: Eva Beckendorf
Creative Directors: Nick Hubbard, Jennifer Bernstein | Main Contributor: Level Group

185 MY HOME REAL ESTATE SERVICES LOGO | Design Firm: Tielemans Design
Designer: Anton Tielemans | Client: My Home Real Estate Services
Main Contributor: Anton Tielemans

185 PALATE DINING SERIES | Design Firm: &Barr | Designer: Jordan Stewart
Client: Rosen Hotels & Resorts | Creative Director: Christian Wojciechowski
Associate Creative Director: Jacqui Garcia | Art Director: Jordan Stewart | Copywriter: Jack Polly
Account Executive: Kim Blaylock | Account Director: Rebekah Bouch | Main Contributor: &Barr

185 WENDY + SAM | Design Firm: Annie Chen Design | Designer: Annie Chen
Client: Wendy + Sam | Main Contributor: Annie Chen

185 FERMENT LAB | Design Firm: Annie Chen Design | Designer: Annie Chen
Client: The Ferment Lab | Main Contributor: Annie Chen

186 GREEN ASPHALT BRAND MARK | Design Firm: Romeo and Company International
Designer: Vincent Romeo | Client: Green Asphalt Co. | Main Contributor: Green Asphalt Team

186 RBD IDENTITY | Design Firm: SML Design | Designer: Vanessa Ryan
Client: Renovate Build Design | Digital Arts & Multimedia: Gerson Mena Murcia
Main Contributor: Vanessa Ryan

186 PROFOUND TALENT LOGO | Design Firm: AG Creative Group
Designer: Stewart Jung | Client: Profound Talent | Main Contributor: Stewart Jung

186 VOICE IN THE AMERICAN WEST | Design Firm: Texas Tech University Press
Designer: Hannah Gaskamp | Client: Self-initiated | Main Contributor: Hannah Gaskamp

186 JENIK ART CONSULTANTS IDENTITY | Design Firm: Goodall Integrated Design
Designer: Derwyn Goodall | Client: Jenik Art Consultants | Main Contributor: Derwyn Goodall

186 WANDER + IVY | Design Firm: Moxie Sozo | Designer: Nate Dyer
Client: Wander + Ivy | Main Contributor: Nate Dyer

186 TALKINGVETS | Design Firm: El Paso, Galería de Comunicación
Designer: Álvaro Pérez | Client: IDEAVET | Creative Team: Álvaro Pérez, Curra Medina
Main Contributor: El Paso, Galería de Comunicación

186 WHY NOT WORKSHOP | Design Firm: Joba Studio
Designer: Patrick Finley | Client: Why Not Workshop | Web Designer: Kelly Wiegand
Account Executive: Robyn Jones | Main Contributor: Kevin Jones

186 TADDLEWOOD HERITAGE ASSOCIATION IDENTITY
Design Firm: Goodall Integrated Design | Designer: Derwyn Goodall
Client: Taddlewood Heritage Association | Main Contributor: Derwyn Goodall

186 RUEFF SCHOOL OF DESIGN, ART, AND PERFORMANCE
Design Firm: HyungjooKimDesignLab | Designer: Hyungjoo A. Kim | Client: Patti and Rusty Rueff
School of Design, Art, and Performance | Main Contributor: Hyungjoo A. Kim

186 LAUREN & COLIN ARE GETTING MARRIED LOGO | Design Firm: Mermaid, Inc.
Designer: Sharon Lloyd McLaughlin | Client: Lauren & Colin | Developer: Bart McLaughlin
Creative Director: Sharon Lloyd McLaughlin | Main Contributor: Sharon Lloyd McLaughlin

186 SUPERIOR CONCRETE LOGO | Design Firm: Level Group | Designers: Eva Beckendorf,
Nicole Kupferman, Sydney Saneun Hwang | Client: Superior Concrete
Creative Directors: Nick Hubbard, Jennifer Bernstein | Art Director: Eva Beckendorf
Main Contributor: Level Group

187 BRANGEA LOGO | Design Firm: Legacy79 | Designer: Genaro Solis Rivero
Client: Brangea | Art Director: Juan Barrera | Main Contributor: Legacy79

187 ANDRÉS LÓPEZ, CHEF | Design Firm: El Paso, Galería de Comunicación
Designer: Álvaro Pérez | Client: Andrés López | Creative Team: Álvaro Pérez, Curra Medina
Main Contributor: El Paso, Galería de Comunicación

187 S'LIGHTLY IDENTITY | Design Firm: MiresBall
Designers: John Ball, David Alderman | Client: S'lightly
Creative Director: John Ball | Main Contributors: John Ball, David Alderman

187 THE OPENING LOGO | Design Firm: Level Group | Designers: Sydney Saneun Hwang,
Eva Beckendorf | Client: The Opening | Creative Directors: Nick Hubbard, Jennifer Bernstein
Art Director: Eva Beckendorf | Main Contributor: Level Group

187 LAKE MURRAY MARINA LOGO | Design Firm: Peterson Ray & Company
Designer: Scott Ray | Client: Lake Murray Marina | Main Contributor: Scott Ray

187 PUBLIC WORX LOGO | Design Firm: Mermaid, Inc. | Designer: Sharon Lloyd McLaughlin
Client: Public WorX | Creative Director: Sharon Lloyd McLaughlin | Developer: Bart McLaughlin
Main Contributor: Sharon Lloyd McLaughlin

187 PROJECT METEOR | Design Firm: Annie Chen Design | Designer: Annie Chen
Client: Sigma Intégrale | Main Contributor: Annie Chen

187 COMMUNITY CROSS | Design Firm: DeVito/Verdi
Designer: Graham Clifford | Client: MetroHealth | Creative Director: Vinny Tulley
Executive Creative Director: Eric Schutte | Main Contributor: Graham Clifford

187 DANA FINKELSTEIN LPGA GOLFER | Design Firm: Tielemans Design
Designer: Anton Tielemans | Client: Dana Finkelstein | Main Contributor: Anton Tielemans

187 COMMODORE FARM & VINEYARD | Design Firm: Holohan Design
Designers: Kelly Holohan, Bryan Satalino | Client: Commodore Farm & Vineyard
Main Contributors: Kelly Holohan, Bryan Satalino

187 BL YINGYANG | Design Firm: Bailey Lauerman | Designer: Jim Ma
Client: Self-initiated | Chief Creative Officer: Carter Weitz | Main Contributor: Jim Ma

187 MABELLE ARTS LOGO | Design Firm: Goodall Integrated Design
Designer: Derwyn Goodall | Client: Mabelle Arts | Main Contributor: Derwyn Goodall

188 MCMASTER MUSEUM OF ART IDENTITY | Design Firm: Underline Studio
Designers: Laura Rojas, Fidel Peña | Client: McMaster Museum of Art
Creative Directors: Claire Dawson, Fidel Peña | Main Contributor: Underline Studio

188 KEEP THE MOUNTAIN CLEAN | Design Firm: Creative Energy
Designer: Jacy Embray | Client: Beech Mountain Resort | Creative Director: Hannah Howard
Copywriter: Theo Harris | Account Executive: Teresa Treadway
Main Contributor: Jacy Embray

188 TARNI BRAND | Design Firm: Dessein | Designer: Leanne Balen
Client: Shark Bay Seafoods Pty Ltd. | Photographer: Geoff Bickford
Director: Geoff Bickford | Main Contributor: Leanne Balen

188 SPIRE B2BBQ | Design Firm: Spire Agency
Designer: Alex Flores | Client: Self-initiated | Creative Director: Kimberly Tyner
Associate Creative Director: Jason James | Main Contributor: Alex Flores

188 OMIH HABANA CANDLES | Design Firm: Our Man In Havana
Designers: Andrew Golomb, Sylve Rosen-Bernstein, Taylor Whitlock | Client: Self-initiated
Executive Producer: Aisling Bodkin | Executive Creative Director: Andrew Golomb
Creative Director: Sylve Rosen-Bernstein | Associate Creative Director: Lisa Alban
Senior Designer: Nick DiPillo | Production Company: Underdog Candles
Printer: Coeur Noir Printers | Account Manager: Francisco De La Cruz
Account Executive: Violet Herzfeld | Account Director: Lacey Gardner
Main Contributor: Our Man In Havana

189 HOLA IPANEMA CACHAÇA | Design Firm: Harcus Design | Designer: Annette Harcus
Client: Spicers | Printer: MultiColor Australasia | Photographer: Stephen Clarke
Paper: Spicers Manter Ipanema Embossed UltraWS | Manufacturer: Bottle: Saverglass
Main Contributor: Harcus Design

189 ISLE OF RAASAY SCOTCH WHISKY | Design Firm: Stranger & Stranger
Designer: Stranger & Stranger | Client: R&B Distillers Ltd.
Main Contributor: Stranger & Stranger

189 SUPERBLOOM | Design Firm: Hatch Design | Designer: Dany Vo
Client: Grove Collaborative | Creative Director: Nicole Flores | Art Director: Grove Collaborative
Photographer Studio: L'ÉLOI | Photographers: Nik Mirus, Vincent Castonguay
Main Contributor: Hatch Design

190 KÁSTRA ELIÓN VODKA | Design Firm: Stranger & Stranger
Designer: Stranger & Stranger | Client: CMC Wine & Spirits
Main Contributor: Stranger & Stranger

190 SAVOIA AMERICANO | Design Firm: Stranger & Stranger | Designer: Stranger & Stranger
Client: Giuseppe Gallo | Main Contributor: Stranger & Stranger

190 AZALINE VERMOUTH | Design Firm: Stranger & Stranger
Designer: Stranger & Stranger | Client: Kanlaon Ltd. (Bleeding Heart Rum)
Main Contributor: Stranger & Stranger

190 ESPOLÒN CRISTALINO | Design Firm: Force MAJEURE | Designer: Kei Hayashi
Client: Campari Group | Main Contributor: Pierre Delebois

191 PEPSI COLA CHINA SERIES - BAMBOO & POMELO FLAVOR
Design Firm: PepsiCo Design & Innovation | Designer: PepsiCo Design & Innovation
Client: Self-initiated | Main Contributor: PepsiCo Design & Innovation

191 GRADIENT VODKA SODA | Design Firm: Trill
Designer: Mark Rowe | Client: Gradient Vodka Soda | Creative Director: John Eresman
Copywriter: John Eresman | Art Director: Mark Rowe | Design Director: Mark Rowe
Main Contributors: John Eresman, Mark Rowe

191 CAMPBELL'S RED & WHITE CONDENSED SOUP PACKAGING
Design Firm: Turner Duckworth: London, San Francisco & New York
Designers: Naomie Ross, Michael Bagnardi, Karen Song | Client: Campbell's
Executive Creative Director: Andy Baron | Design Director: Drew Stocker
Illustrator: Filip Yip | Typographer: Ian Brignell | Production: Craig Snelgrove, Jeff Ennslen
Photographer: Hone Studio | Implementation Director: Jeff Jones
Director of Client Services: Bailey James | Account Director: Kate Wierman
Other: Fakery | Main Contributors: Naomie Ross, Michael Bagnardi, Karen Song

192 NIEPOORT BIOMA – "A VINTAGE WITH THE KNIFE IN TEETH"
Design Firm: Omdesign | Designer: Diogo Gama Rocha
Client: Niepoort | Main Contributor: Omdesign

192 COMTE DE GRASSE 06 VODKA | Design Firm: Force MAJEURE
Designer: Pierre Delebois | Client: Comte de Grasse | Main Contributor: Pierre Delebois

192 HANGAR 1 VODKA SMOKE POINT | Design Firm: Stranger & Stranger
Designer: Stranger & Stranger | Client: Proximo Spirits Inc.
Main Contributor: Stranger & Stranger

192 YAMAGATA | Design Firm: Tsushima Design
Designer: Hajime Tsushima | Client: Sake-Show Yamada | Art Director: Hajime Tsushima
Creative Director: Yukiko Tsushima | Main Contributor: Hajime Tsushima

193 XIAOMI MID-AUTUMN MOONCAKE | Design Firm: Xiaomi
Designers: Ecosystem Packaging Design Team, Lei Zhao | Client: Self-initiated
Creative Director: Lu Chen | Structural Engineering: Zhizhuang Song
Main Contributors: Lu Chen, Lei Zhao, Zhizhuang Song

193 PEPSI NEW YEAR 2022 LTO | Design Firm: PepsiCo Design & Innovation
Designer: PepsiCo Design & Innovation | Client: Self-initiated
Main Contributor: PepsiCo Design & Innovation

193 KR8OM RESERVE | Design Firm: Spire Agency | Designer: Brendan Callahan
Client: Kr8om | Creative Director: Kimberly Tyner | Main Contributor: Brendan Callahan

193 MARMALADE PACKAGING | Design Firm: Box Brand Design Limited
Designers: Joey Lo, Yvonne Chung | Client: KDV Group | Art Director: Yvonne Chung
Creative Director: Joey Lo | Main Contributor: Joey Lo

193 DORITOS SOLID BLACK | Design Firm: PepsiCo Design & Innovation
Designer: PepsiCo Design & Innovation | Client: Self-initiated
Main Contributor: PepsiCo Design & Innovation

193 BLACK GARLIC & CO. | Design Firm: Dessein
Designer: Leanne Balen | Client: Black Garlic & Co. | Art Director: Tracy Kenworthy
Photographer: Geoff Bickford | Main Contributor: Leanne Balen

194 PRAKRISHI DRYFRUITS | Design Firm: Sol Benito
Designer: Vishal Vora | Client: Prakrishi Organic | Main Contributor: Sol Benito

194 VIETNAM TET 2022 LTO | Design Firm: PepsiCo Design & Innovation
Designer: PepsiCo Design & Innovation | Client: Self-initiated
Main Contributor: PepsiCo Design & Innovation

195 AGUARDENTE ESPÍRITO | Design Firm: Omdesign | Designer: Diogo Gama Rocha
Client: José Maria da Fonseca | Main Contributor: Omdesign

195 HOT SAUCE | Design Firm: Rhodes Creative | Designer: Alex Rhodes | Client: Vintage 86
Creative Production Partner: Jonathan Israel Reyes | Main Contributor: Alex Rhodes

195 JERSEY WINE COLLECTION | Design Firm: CF Napa Brand Design
Designer: CF Napa Brand Design | Client: William Heritage Winery
Main Contributor: CF Napa Brand Design

195 THE BIG PINK ROSÉ | Design Firm: CF Napa Brand Design
Designer: CF Napa Brand Design | Client: West Coast Wine Group
Main Contributor: CF Napa Brand Design

195 QUINTA VALE D. MARIA VINHA DO MOINHO | Design Firm: Omdesign
Designer: Diogo Gama Rocha | Client: Aveleda | Main Contributor: Omdesign

195 TICK TOCK TEA COLD BREW | Design Firm: Turner Duckworth: London, San Francisco & New York | Designer: Adam Cartwright | Client: Tick Tock Teas Ltd.
Executive Creative Director: Christian Eager | Production: James Norris, James Chilvers
Account Manager: Jessica Clark | Main Contributor: Adam Cartwright

195 AMY'S BLEND | Design Firm: Cue | Designer: Katelyn McVey
Client: Caribou Coffee | Creative Director: Alan Colvin | Main Contributor: Katelyn McVey

195 CANBEE COCKTAILS | Design Firm: Partners + Napier
Designer: Nate Phelps | Client: Black Button Distilling | Creative Group Head: Sarah Antao
Copywriter: Jocelyn Porter | Proofreaders: Rowan Collins, Maureen McDaniels
Project Manager: Bess Johnson | Main Contributor: Nate Phelps

195 PEPSI CULTURE CANS X PEOPLE'S DAILY
Design Firm: PepsiCo Design & Innovation | Designer: PepsiCo Design & Innovation
Client: Self-initiated | Main Contributor: PepsiCo Design & Innovation

196 BIC VACATION SERIES | Design Firm: Wallace Church & Co. | Designer: Diana Luistro
Client: BIC | Chief Creative Officer: Stan Church | Executive Creative Director: John Bruno
Associate Creative Director: Jodi Lubrich | Senior Designer: Diana Luistro
Senior Account Director: Maureen McKenna | Main Contributor: Diana Luistro

196 DILWORTH COFFEE | Design Firm: The Republik
Designer: Matt Shapiro | Client: Dilworth Coffee | Writer: Neil Hinson
Executive Creative Director: Robert Shaw West | Creative Director: Matt Shapiro
Art Director: Luke Rayson | Main Contributor: Matt Shapiro

196 HEIRLOOM COFFEE ROASTER | Design Firm: Pavement
Designer: Michael Hester | Client: America's Best Coffee Roasters
Main Contributor: Michael Hester

196 SOCKEYE PACKAGING | Design Firm: Duft Watterson | Designer: Alex Rhodes
Client: Sockeye Brewing | Creative Director: Tony Hart | Photographer: Visionkit Studio
Managing Partners: Ward Duft, Jill Watterson | Director of Client Services: Hanna Wenter
Main Contributor: Duft Watterson

196 LOVE ME | Design Firm: Box Brand Design Limited
Designer: Joey Lo | Client: Green Home | Creative Director: Joey Lo
Art Director: Yvonne Chung | Main Contributor: Joey Lo

197 ICELANDIC PROVISIONS | Design Firm: Turner Duckworth: London, San Francisco & New York | Designers: Rosie Hellier, Matt Knight, Sam Jepson | Client: Icelandic Provisions
Illustrators: Rob Clarke, Adam Cartwright | Executive Creative Director: Christian Eager
Strategy: Tim Owen, Charlie Rogers | Production: James Norris, James Chilvers, Alex Man
Account Manager: Shaz Beshirian | Other: Mick Connor | Main Contributor: Matt Lurcock

197 JOHNNY ROTTEN PUZZLE EXPERIENCE PACKAGING
Design Firm: Truth Collective | Designer: Justyn Iannucci | Client: Punkzles
Copywriter: Louis Wittig | Producer: Devon Higby | Photographer: Nue Chanthavongsay
Account Director: Kaitlyn Nolan | Main Contributor: Jeremy Schwartz, Founder

197 TRUE BOTANICALS SKINCARE – SUSTAINABLE GIFT SETS PACKAGING
Design Firm: The Rare Form | Designer: Kyle R. Thompson | Client: True Botanicals
Creative Directors: Christina Thompson, Kyle R. Thompson
Main Contributor: Kyle R. Thompson

197 XY LAVA MOONCAKE | Design Firm: Box Brand Design Limited
Designers: Joey Lo, Bobby Bao | Client: XinYuan | Creative Director: Joey Lo
Art Director: Yvonne Chung | Main Contributor: Joey Lo

197 FLASH FUEL | Design Firm: Trill | Designer: Mark Rowe
Client: Calgary Heritage Roasting Co. | Copywriter: John Eresman
Creative Directors: Mark Rowe, John Eresman | Main Contributor: Mark Rowe

197 ADAMUS SIGNATURE EDITION 2021 | Design Firm: Omdesign
Designer: Diogo Gama Rocha | Client: Destilaria Levira | Main Contributor: Omdesign

197 LA MINITA PEABERRY | Design Firm: Cue | Designers: Katelyn McVey, Matt Erickson
Client: Caribou Coffee | Creative Director: Alan Colvin | Main Contributor: Katelyn McVey

198 READ MORE 2021 | Design Firm: Underline Studio | Designer: Fidel Peña
Client: Self-initiated | Creative Directors: Fidel Peña, Claire Dawson
Printer: Flash Reproductions | Main Contributor: Underline Studio

198 60 YEARS ADG FAD | Design Firm: Teiga, Studio.
Designer: Maria Toucedo Cal | Client: ADG FAD | Creative Director: Xose Teiga
Art Directors: Maria Toucedo Cal, Xose Teiga | Copywriter: Maria Toucedo Cal
Graphic Designer: Maria Toucedo Cal | Main Contributor: Teiga, Studio.

198 HELLS' KITCHEN YOUNG GUNS | Design Firm: ARSONAL | Designer: ARSONAL
Clients: FOX, Michael Bassett – Sr Creative Director at FOX Alexia Pahl – Associate Director at FOX Ian MacRitchie – VP of Visual Innovation Studio at FOX | Main Contributor: ARSONAL

198 LIGATURA | Design Firm: 1/4 Studio | Designers: Jorge Araújo, Ana Mota
Client: Galeria Ocupa! | Art Directors: Jorge Araújo, Ana Mota

199 RE_: RESTART, REVIVE, RECOVER | Design Firm: Braley Design
Designer: Michael Braley | Client: Self-initiated | Creative Director: Michael Braley
Main Contributor: Michael Braley

199 PROHIBIDO OLVIDAR POSTER | Design Firm: Underline Studio
Designer: Fidel Peña | Client: Self-initiated | Creative Directors: Fidel Peña, Claire Dawson
Printer: Flash Reproductions | Main Contributor: Underline Studio

199 EL LISSITZKY 130 YEARS | Design Firm: Braley Design | Designer: Michael Braley
Client: UNOVIS. 21st Century. #EL130 | Creative Director: Michael Braley
Main Contributor: Michael Braley

199 ENGINE 489 | Design Firm: UP-Ideas | Designer: Roger Sawhill
Client: Self-initiated | Main Contributor: Roger Sawhill

200 RAGDOLL S1 KEY ART | Design Firm: ARSONAL | Designer: ARSONAL
Clients: AMC+, Ed Sherman, VP Brand & Design, Kevin Vitale, SVP Creative & Campaign Marketing, Nancy Hennings, VP Production Brand & Design | Copywriter: AMC+
Art Director: ARSONAL | Creative Director: ARSONAL | Photographer: Nadav Kander
Title: Matt Wiley (Title Treatment) | Main Contributor: ARSONAL

200 RUN | Design Firm: Bailey Lauerman | Designer: Jim Ma | Client: Lincoln Track Club
Creative Director: Casey Stokes | Production Manager: Gayle Adams
Account Supervisor: Natalie Hudson | Main Contributor: Carter Weitz

200 EXECUTIVE SEARCH. MADE HUMAN. | Design Firm: Curious | Designer: Alice Munday
Client: Pascoe and Tew | Main Contributors: Senior Copywriter: Becky Rae, Executive Creative Director: Peter Rae, Associate Design Director: Alice Munday

200 WINTER '22 | Design Firm: John Sposato Design & Illustration
Designer: John Sposato | Client: Self-initiated | Main Contributor: John Sposato

200 FOG OF WAR | Design Firm: Steiner Graphics | Designer: Rene V. Steiner
Client: Self-initiated | Main Contributor: Rene V. Steiner

200 TEXAS FANDANGO 3 | Design Firm: May & Co. | Designer: Douglas May
Client: Texas Fandango | Main Contributor: Douglas May

200 MY LUNGS HATE ME NO.1 | Design Firm: Warren Eakins Inc.
Designer: Warren Eakins | Client: ROT$ WORLDWIDE
Chief Creative Officer: Rabhy Ortega | Creative Director: Warren Eakins
Art Director: Warren Eakins | Writer & Content Developer: Warren Eakins
Cheif Marketing Officer: Tiffany Swiney | Main Contributor: Warren Eakins

200 BECOME A HEALTH CARE HERO. | Design Firm: Good Communication Marketing
Designer: Beata Stolarska | Client: Stenberg College | Assistant: Jenny Bernardo
Creative Director: Les Merson | Copywriter: Pam Charach | Model: Nelofar Rahimi
Makeup: Linda Lee | Main Contributor: Ken Villeneuve

200 THE NATIONAL STUDENT SHOW & CONFERENCE 16 POSTER
Design Firm: *TraceElement | Designer: Jeff Barfoot | Client: The Dallas Society of Visual Communications Foundation | Writer: Jeff Barfoot | Chief Creative Director: Jeff Barfoot Illustrator: Jeff Barfoot | Photographer: Dick Patrick Studios Account Management: Lindsey Phaup | Main Contributor: Jeff Barfoot

201 SEEK NEW CINEMA POSTER | Design Firm: WONGDOODY Designers: Reese Murakami, Lauren Beauchemin | Client: Seattle International Film Festival Studios: Scott Engelhardt, Jason Hall | Senior Producers: Laura Haithcock, Paul Morgan Senior Designer: Drew Jasperse | Junior Designer: Ben Gross | Copywriter: Lauren Jones Group Creative Director: Monkey Watson | Executive Producer: Matteo Mosterts Retoucher: Charlie Rakatansky | Proofreader: Coby Jackson | Marketing Manager: Ariel Smith Main Contributors: Lauren Beauchemin, Monkey Watson, Drew Jasperse

201 SEA MONSTER | Design Firm: HyungjooKimDesignLab | Designer: Hyungjoo A. Kim Client: Self-initiated | Photographer Studio: Pics Five | Main Contributor: Hyungjoo A. Kim

201 EXPLORER — THE LAST TEPUI | Design Firm: SJI Associates Designer: Andrew Zimmerman | Clients: National Geographic, EVP Creative - Chris Spencer, VP Design - Brian Everett, Design Director - Carla Daeninckx, Project Manager - Maricruz Merlo Art Director: David O'Hanlon | Copywriter: Katrina Day | President: Suzy Jurist Main Contributor: SJI Associates

201 AMERICAN CRIME STORY: IMPEACHMENT | Design Firm: ARSONAL Designer: ARSONAL | Clients: FX, Stephanie Gibbons, President, Strategy, Creative, and Digital Multiplatform Marketing, Todd Heughens, SVP, Print Design, Michael Brittain, VP, Print Design, Laura Handy, Project Director, Print Design, Lisa Lejeune, Production Director, Print Design Art Director: ARSONAL | Photographer: Kurt Iswarienko | Main Contributor: ARSONAL

201 STAGS LEAP WINERY DECISION TREE | Design Firms: Partners + Napier, Annex88 Designer: Ellie Peters | Client: Treasury Wine Estates | Creative Director: Katy Collar Illustrators: Nico Puertollano, Nick Liefhebber, Katwo Puertollano, Joanna Lisowiec Copywriter: Justin Lahue | Main Contributor: Ellie Peters

201 PERSPECTIVES OF RESILIENCE | Design Firm: Rodgers Townsend Designer: David Illig | Client: The Black Rep | Chief Creative Officer: Michael McCormick Associate Creative Director: Jeremy Hagen | Account Director: Tracy Sykes-Long Main Contributor: David Illig

201 NEVER FORGET | Design Firm: Bailey Lauerman | Designer: Carter Weitz Client: Self-initiated | Art Director: Aaron Jarosh | Production Manager: Gayle Adams Main Contributor: Carter Weitz

201 INVOLUTION | Design Firm: Polygon | Designer: Wu Qixin Client: Human Beings | Main Contributor: Wu Qixin

201 SPIDER-MAN: NO WAY HOME FAN ART SERIES | Design Firm: INNOCEAN USA Designer: Berlin Burkhart | Client: Hyundai Motor America | Creative Director: Joe Reynoso Copywriters: Jeff Tune, Andrew Boyer | Group Creative Director: Cary Ruby Executive Creative Director: Barney Goldberg | Senior Art Director: Nicole Macey Advertising Agency: INNOCEAN USA | Main Contributor: Berlin Burkhart

202 LOVE | Design Firm: Tsushima Design | Designer: Hajime Tsushima Client: Kaohsiung Creators Association | Main Contributor: Hajime Tsushima

202 METAVERSE | Design Firm: Tsushima Design | Designer: Hajime Tsushima Client: Korea Institute of Cultural Product & Design | Main Contributor: Hajime Tsushima

202 ARCHI-NEERING | Design Firm: T9 Brand Designers: Hui Pan, Dawang Sun | Client: Tongji University | Photographer: Fei Wei Model: Xingyi Wang | Main Contributor: Chuguo Communication

203 THE HUNT FOR PLANET B | Design Firm: ARSONAL Designer: ARSONAL | Client: CNN | Main Contributor: ARSONAL

203 SUMMER '21 | Design Firm: John Sposato Design & Illustration Designer: John Sposato | Client: Self-initiated | Main Contributor: John Sposato

203 FLOOD IN THE DESERT DOCUMENTARY FILM POSTER | Design Firm: SJI Associates Designer: David O'Hanlon | Clients: Chika Offurum, American Experience Films Art Director: David O'Hanlon | President: Suzy Jurist | Main Contributor: SJI Associates

203 봄 PEACE | Design Firm: Keith Kitz Design | Designer: Keith Kitz Client: Visual Information Design Association of Korea | Main Contributor: Keith Kitz

203 BELFAST | Design Firm: ARSONAL | Designer: ARSONAL | Clients: Marcus Kaye, Director Creative Advertising, Focus Features, Blair Green, SVP Creative Advertising and Head of Brand Design | Creative Director: ARSONAL | Main Contributor: ARSONAL

203 MAYANS S4 | Design Firm: ARSONAL | Designer: ARSONAL | Clients: FX, Stephanie Gibbons: President, Creative, Strategy & Digital, Multi-Platform Marketing Todd Heughens: SVP, Print Design Michael Brittain: SVP, Print Design Rob Wilson: VP, Print Design, Laura Handy: Project Director, Print Design Lisa Lejeune: Production Director Main Contributor: ARSONAL

203 INTRODUCING, SELMA BLAIR | Design Firm: ARSONAL | Designer: ARSONAL Client: LD Entertainment | Copywriter: LD Entertainment | Photographer: Joseph Yakob Art Director: ARSONAL | Main Contributor: ARSONAL

203 PUT OUT | Design Firm: Keith Kitz Design | Designer: Keith Kitz Client: The 4th Block Graphic Designers Association | Main Contributor: Keith Kitz

203 THE PURPLE MANIFESTO PROJECT | Design Firm: Goodall Integrated Design Designer: Derwyn Goodall | Client: John Van Dyke | Main Contributor: Derwyn Goodall

204 A IS FOR ADVENTURE ARCADE ALIENS | Design Firm: Braley Design Designer: Michael Braley | Client: Poster Stellars | Creative Director: Michael Braley Main Contributor: Michael Braley

204 VIGNELLI 90 POSTER | Design Firm: Osborne Ross Designers: Deborah Osborne, Andrew Ross | Client: Vignelli 90 Project Coordinators: Gabriel Amijai Benderski Perez, Juan Martin Lusiardo, Santiago Ternande Main Contributor: Osborne Ross

204 "WHAT DOES CHICAGO MEAN TO YOU?" POSTER FOR THE CHICAGO GRAPHIC DESIGN CLUB. | Design Firm: The Narrative | Designer: Dan McManus | Client: The Chicago Graphic Design Club | Assistants: Derrick McCormick, Isabela Viazzi | Advisor: Sofya Karash Design Assistant: Mae Mae | Photographer: Nathanael Filbert | Main Contributor: Dan McManus

204 THE 100TH ANNIVERSARY OF JANOME | Design Firm: Nikkeisha, Inc. Designers: Hiroyuki Nakamura, Hikari Maesaka | Client: JANOME Corporation Creative Director: Hiroyuki Nakamura | Art Director: Hiroyuki Nakamura Copywriter: Shu Morihira | Photographer: Tetsuro Ikejima | Producer: Masaki Suzuki Main Contributor: Nikkeisha, Inc.

204 BURNING | Design Firm: Cul-Box | Designer: Wu Qixin Client: Burning | Main Contributor: Wu Qixin

204 W FRAME | Design Firm: Randy Clark | Designer: Randy Clark Client: Wenzhou-Kean University | Main Contributor: Randy Clark

204 UNDER THE BANNER OF HEAVEN | Design Firm: ARSONAL | Designer: ARSONAL Clients: FX, Stephanie Gibbons: President, Creative, Strategy & Digital, Multi-Platform Marketing Todd Heughens: SVP, Print Design Michael Brittain: SVP, Print Design Laura Handy: Project Director, Print Design Lisa Lejeune: Production Director, Print Design Sarin Ma Creative Directors: Todd Heughens: SVP, Print Design, Michael Brittain: SVP, Print Design Photographer: Matthias Clamer | Main Contributor: ARSONAL

204 EXPLORER - THE LAST TEPUI | ALTERNATIVE POSTER Design Firm: SJI Associates | Designer: David O'Hanlon | Clients: National Geographic , EVP Creative - Chris Spencer, VP Design - Brian Everett, Design Director - Carla Daeninckx, Project Manager - Maricruz Merlo | Art Director: David O'Hanlon | President: Suzy Jurist Main Contributor: SJI Associates

204 FAKE NEWS | Design Firm: Noriyuki Kasai | Designer: Noriyuki Kasai Client: Graphic Communication Laboratory | Main Contributor: Noriyuki Kasai

205 CENTRAL MARKET VALENTINE'S DAY 2022 Design Firms: *TraceElement, Plot Twist Creativity | Designers: Jocelyn Yun, Jeff Rogers Client: Central Market | Chief Creative Officer: Jeff Barfoot | Creative Director: Dana Nixon Writers: Chris Smith, Wendy Mayes | Illustrator: Robert Rodriguez Account Manager: Anna Mertz | Main Contributor: Jeff Barfoot

205 CREATIVE NEBRASKA | Design Firm: Bailey Lauerman Designer: Jim Ma | Client: AAF Nebraska | Chief Creative Officer: Carter Weitz Creative Directors: Aaron Jarosh, Sean Faden | Associate Creative Director: Casey Stokes Copywriter: Joey Googe | Editor: Chris Reilly | Digital Artist: Jared Brdicko Production Manager: Gayle Adams | Production Manager: Ryan Faden Account Management: Lauren Schuster | Main Contributor: Sean Faden

205 MODERN LEOPARD | Design Firm: Carolyn Gibbs Design Designer: Carolyn Gibbs | Client: Self-initiated | Main Contributor: Carolyn Gibbs

205 RESIST | Design Firm: Bailey Lauerman | Designer: Carter Weitz Client: Self-initiated | Production Manager: Gayle Adams | Main Contributor: Carter Weitz

205 MAKE 2022... | Design Firm: Goodall Integrated Design | Designer: Derwyn Goodall Client: Self-initiated | Main Contributor: Derwyn Goodall

205 HELLCATS USA VACUUM FORM POSTER | Design Firm: Kimberly Elam Design Designer: Kimberly Elam | Client: Ringling College of Art & Design Main Contributor: Kimberly Elam

205 GEOMETRIA | Design Firm: Luca Pontarelli | Designer: Luca Pontarelli Client: Self-initiated | Main Contributor: Luca Pontarelli

206 GALAXY BUDS2 LAUNCH POSTER Design Firm: Turner Duckworth: London, San Francisco & New York | Designer: Cinthia Wen Client: Samsung | Creative Director: Carolyn Ashburn | Senior Designers: Thom Pastrano, Janice Bonner | Others: Josh Michels, Sara Scanlan | Account Director: Marco Vaschetto Main Contributor: Cinthia Wen, Head of Creative

206 GALAXY A EVENT INVITE POSTER SERIES 2022 Design Firm: Turner Duckworth: London, San Francisco & New York Designers: Jack Powell, Chun Chun Chang, Nick Clemens Zenghui Lin | Client: Samsung Design Directors: Glenn Chan, Akira Yasuda, Alice Koswara | Creative Director: Carolyn Ashburn Senior Designers: Tanawat Pisasuwongse, Janice Bonner | Others: Sara Scanlan, Christy Kim, Craig Snelgrove | Account Directors: Marco Vaschetto, Gabi Lovelace Main Contributor: Cinthia Wen, Head of Creative

206 LYFT POSTERS DESIGN | Design Firm: Lyft Internal Creative Team Designer: John Olson | Client: Self-initiated | Executive Creative Director: Karin Onsager Birch Creative Director: Gianmaria Schonlieb | Copywriter: Nancy Strange Producer: Ellen Black | Photographer: Mark Leibowitz Main Contributors: Lyft Creative Team - John Olson, Gianmaria Schonlieb, Karin Onsager Birch

207 DLR GROUP - LINCOLN OFFICE POSTERS | Design Firm: DLR Group Designer: Jovaney Hollingsworth | Client: Self-initiated Main Contributor: Jovaney Hollingsworth

207 HER MAJESTY THE QUEEN'S PLATINUM JUBILEE COIN Design Firm: Osborne Ross | Designers: Deborah Osborne, Andrew Ross Client: Royal Mint | Design Manager: Lee Jones | Production Artist: Daniel Thorne Main Contributor: Osborne Ross

207 LIVERY DESIGN OF ZQ SERIES ROCKET Design Firm: Dalian Cones Papa Technology Co., Ltd. | Designer: Sui Xin

Client: Land Space Technology Corporation Ltd. | Model: Han Yulong
Chief Creative Director: Sui Xin | Graphic Designer: Wang Lu | Main Contributor: Sui Xin

208 SHE* | Design Firm: Rex C | Designers: Michael Dabbs, Todd Houser, ML Tokyo
Client: Self-initiated | Creative Director: Todd Houser | Writer & Content Developer: Todd Houser
Translator: Jennifer Anderson | Producer: Anthony Reynolds | Printer: Rex 3
Artists: Richard Borge, Johnathan Baez, Rob Priester, Noelle Gunn | Photographer: Todd Houser
Model: Sydney Beauchene | Makeup: Sarah Harris | Hair: Laura Mangin
Illustrator: Brian Stauffer | Main Contributor: Todd Houser

208 BLACK FRIDAY MQA | Design Firm: Teiga, Studio. | Designer: Maria Toucedo Cal
Client: Mais que Auga | Art Directors: Maria Toucedo Cal, Xose Teiga
Copywriters: Maria Toucedo Cal, Xose Teiga | Community Manager: Merce Anleo
Main Contributor: Teiga, Studio.

208 PREVENTION OF VALVULAR DISEASE OF THE HEART | Design Firm: Legis Design
Designer: Mayumi Kato | Client: Self-initiated | Main Contributor: Legis Design

209 LAFAYETTE AMERICAN PUZZLE | Design Firm: Lafayette American
Designer: Lafayette American | Client: Self-initiated | Main Contributor: Lafayette American

209 RE-ENTRY | Design Firm: Bailey Lauerman | Designer: Kelli Meyer | Client: Self-initiated
Chief Creative Officer: Carter Weitz | Creative Directors: Sean Faden, Aaron Jarosh
Copywriter: Lacey Rouse | Production Manager: Gayle Adams | Production Artist: Ryan Faden
Illustrator: Joe McDermott | Main Contributor: Sean Faden

209 POSTER MAIS QUE AUGA | Design Firm: Teiga, Studio. | Designer: Cristina Gonzalez
Client: Mais que Auga | Art Director: Maria Toucedo Cal | Creative Director: Xose Teiga
Community Manager: Merce Anleo | Graphic Designer: Cristina Gonzalez
Main Contributor: Teiga, Studio.

210 SPIRE B2BBQ | Design Firm: Spire Agency | Designer: Alex Flores
Client: Self-initiated | Creative Director: Kimberly Tyner
Associate Creative Director: Jason James | Main Contributor: Alex Flores

210 COVID FEELINGS PACKAGED | Design Firm: Code Switch
Designer: Jan Šabach | Client: Self-initiated | Main Contributor: Jan Šabach

210 HOWDY, LEGACY79 BREW | Design Firm: Legacy79
Designer: Genaro Solis Rivero | Client: Self-initiated | Art Director: Genaro Solis Rivero
Creative Director: Juan Barrera | Main Contributor: Legacy79

210 WIENERISMS | Design Firm: INNOCEAN USA | Designer: Oscar Bastidas
Client: Wienerschnitzel | Advertising Agency: INNOCEAN USA | Creative Director: Joe Reynoso
Art Directors: Kathryn Izquerido-Gallegos, Ryan Owens, Allison Inouye, Sumner Mahaffey
Executive Creative Director: Barney Goldberg | Main Contributor: INNOCEAN USA

210 LOVESKI DELI | Design Firm: Pavement | Designer: Michael Hester
Client: Loveski Deli | Illustrator: Kinga Offert-Ploszaj | Main Contributor: Michael Hester

211 IMAGIN CAFÉ RETAIL PROJECT | Design Firm: Caldas Naya
Designers: Martin Díaz Colodrero, Pol Vilella | Clients: Imagin, CaixaBank, Manel García Puig,
David Urbano | Chief Creative Director: Gustavo Caldas | Account Manager: Fabiana Casañas
Account Executive: Aketz Zubia | Main Contributor: Caldas Naya

211 WILDLIKE IDENTITY | Design Firm: *TraceElement
Designer: Jeff Barfoot | Client: Wildlike | Chief Creative Director: Jeff Barfoot
Environmental Designer: Swoon the Studio | Strategy: Lindsey Phaup
Account Manager: Lindsey Phaup | Main Contributor: Jeff Barfoot

212 PRO PATRIA STAMPS | Design Firm: Res Eichenberger Design
Designer: Res Eichenberger | Client: Swiss Post | Main Contributor: Res Eichenberger

212 MYSTERY MESSAGE | Design Firm: Studio A | Designer: Antonio Alcalá
Client: U.S. Postal Service | Typographer: Antonio Alcalá
Art Director: Antonio Alcalá | Main Contributor: U.S. Postal Service

212 LUNAR NEW YEAR • YEAR OF THE TIGER | Design Firm: Studio A
Designer: Antonio Alcalá | Client: U.S. Postal Service | Art Director: Antonio Alcalá
Artist: Camille Chew | Main Contributor: U.S. Postal Service

212 ESPRESSO DRINKS | Design Firm: Journey Group
Designer: Greg Breeding | Client: U.S. Postal Service | Typographer: Greg Breeding
Artist: Terry Allen | Art Director: Greg Breeding | Main Contributor: U.S. Postal Service

212 HAPPY BIRTHDAY | Design Firm: Catalone Design
Designers: Lisa Catalone Castro, Rodolfo Castro | Client: U.S. Postal Service
Artist: Rodolfo Castro | Art Director: Ethel Kessler | Main Contributor: U.S. Postal Service

213 DAY OF THE DEAD | Design Firm: Studio A | Designer: Antonio Alcalá
Client: U.S. Postal Service | Artist: Luis Fitch | Art Director: Antonio Alcalá
Main Contributor: U.S. Postal Service

213 LET PARENTS STAY (HAN EMBROIDERY TYPEFACE) | Design Firm: Yu Chen Design
Designer: Yu Chen | Client: Hubei Han Embroidery Association | Main Contributor: Yu Chen

214 CAMPBELL'S RED & WHITE CONDENSED SOUP LOGO
Design Firm: Turner Duckworth: London, San Francisco & New York
Designers: Naomie Ross, Michael Bagnardi, Karen Song | Client: Campbell's
Executive Creative Director: Andy Baron | Director of Client Services: Bailey James
Design Director: Drew Stocker | Illustrator: Filip Yip | Typographer: Ian Brignell
Production: Craig Snelgrove, Jess Ennslen | Photographer: Hone Studio
Implementation Director: Jeff Jones | Account Director: Kate Wierman
Other: Fakery | Main Contributors: Naomie Ross, Michael Bagnardi, Karen Song

214 CAMPBELL'S RED & WHITE CONDENSED SOUP TYPE
Design Firm: Turner Duckworth: London, San Francisco & New York | Designers: Naomie Ross,
Michael Bagnardi, Karen Song | Client: Campbell's | Executive Creative Director: Andy Baron
Design Director: Drew Stocker | Production: Craig Snelgrove, Jeff Ennslen | Illustrator: Filip Yip
Typographer: Ian Brignell | Photographer: Hone Studio | Implementation Director: Jeff Jones
Director of Client Services: Bailey James | Account Director: Kate Wierman | Other: Fakery
Main Contributors: Naomie Ross, Michael Bagnardi, Karen Song

214 THE LETTERPRESS QUILT PROJECT | Design Firm: BRED
Designers: Brenda McManus, Ned Drew | Client: Self-initiated | Medium: Letterpress
Printers: Brenda McManus, Ned Drew | Creative Directors: Brenda McManus, Ned Drew
Main Contributors: Brenda McManus, Ned Drew

215 VIRTUAL NURSERY, HUNDREDS + THOUSANDS (MULTI-CITY)
Design Firm: FACTORY | Designers: Sandra Lau, Tan Xaun Yun | Clients: Daniel Kok (Singapore),
Luke George (Melbourne) | Creative Director: Roy Wang | Main Contributors: Daniel Kok
(Singapore), Luke George (Melbourne), Nicholas Tee (Singapore); Hundreds + Thousands was
originally commissioned by National Gallery Singapore for Performing Spaces 2021

215 VIÑA ALMIRANTE. WEBSITE. | Design Firm: Roberto Núñez Studio
Designer: Roberto Núñez | Client: Viña Almirante | Copywriter: Roberto Núñez
Creative Director: Roberto Núñez | Art Director: Roberto Núñez | Photographer: Mariano Herrera
Website: www.vinaalmirante.com | Web Developer: Rubén Aja | Engraving: Alex Ferreiro
Brand Strategy: Roberto Núñez | Product Photographer: Roberto Treviño
Photo Illustrator: Gael Lendoiro | Main Contributor: Roberto Núñez

216 CIRCUIT #1 | Design Firm: FACTORY | Designers: Sandra Lau, Tamelia Lim
Client: Dance Nucleus | Creative Director: Roy Wang | Developer: Wong Huiwen
Main Contributor: The online exhibition is curated by Dance Nucleus and supported by the
National Arts Council (Singapore) through the Digital Presentation Grant.

216 MERMAID, INC. FLUID CREATIVITY WEBSITE | Design Firm: Mermaid, Inc.
Designer: Sharon Lloyd McLaughlin | Client: Self-initiated | Developer: Bart McLaughlin
Main Contributor: Sharon Lloyd McLaughlin

217 AGCO WEBSITE | Design Firm: Addison | Designer: Rachel Pigott
Client: AGCO | Creative Director: Kevin Barclay | Copywriter: David Freedman
Strategy: Leslie Lammers | Managing Director: Judy Sandford | Senior Producer: Anne Crosson
Production Manager: Joe Kester | Senior Account Director: Susie Kang Poteet
Main Contributor: Rachel Pigott

217 VETERANS MUSEUM WEBSITE DESIGN | Design Firm: Freaner Creative & Design
Designer: Ariel Freaner | Client: Veterans Memorial Museum | Creative Director: Ariel Freaner
Main Contributor: Ariel Freaner

FILM/VIDEO PLATINUM WINNERS:
219 GENESIS GV70 "WANT WINS" ARTIST SERIES
Design Firm: INNOCEAN USA | Client: Genesis Motor America | Ad Agency: INNOCEAN USA
Artists: Zachary Darren, Roman Bratschi, Peter Lauridsen, Bloo Woods, Mark Parris,
Roman Laurent, Philip Leuck, Giorgia Ascolani, Blunt Action | Copywriter: Erica Henderson
Creative Director: Erica Henderson | Art Directors: Miranda Lee, Johnny Nguyen
Group Creative Director: Lori Martin | Producers: Rachel Crain, Rob Beckon
Strategy: David McMichael

Assignment: As part of the social launch of our first-ever Genesis GV70 performance SUV, we asked a group of eight buzzworthy digital artists to interpret our "Want Wins" campaign in dazzling, thumb-stopping, never-before-seen ways. Together, their pieces make up the GV70 "Want Wins" Artist Series. Inspired by the GV70's heart-pounding performance and indulgent styling, each piece is made to spark desire. Fans are invited to explore the gallery and imagine all the pleasures of driving a GV70. Our main goal was to create a library of unique, motion-based Instagram content that ladders up to the GV70 "Want Wins" brand campaign, while always making sure the GV70 is the hero. Our secondary goal was to increase brand awareness and position Genesis as a design-led brand.
Approach: We partnered with in-demand, Instagram-based artists to create unique reimaginings of the GV70. Each piece was crafted to maximize feelings of want for our new SUV, and select motion pieces were accompanied by custom composed scoring to set the tone. The artists shared their work for maximum reach, we posted their art to our owned-and-operated Instagram page, and we featured behind the scenes process footage for IG Reels and Stories showing how the pieces were made. We created an Instagram Guide that functions as a gallery tour with highlights from each artist's series on display to be viewed and enjoyed any time. To maximize reach, we repurposed all of the video artwork into three distinct half-hour "mood" mixes to provide background visuals and music for viewers wanting to "Focus", "Create" or who were looking to be "Inspired."
Results: Our GV70 Artist Series saw the most engaged comments of any campaign on our owned-and-operated Instagram. Comments were overwhelmingly positive (with users tagging friends) and fans were quick to save and share the digital art, all of which helped to spread awareness around our new SUV. Here's a snapshot of how the campaign performed on IG: Impressions: 1.1M (from owned channels only), Reach: 982K, Engagements: 38K, ER (on reach): 3.9% (Q2 Avg. 2.3%), Clicks to GV70 VLP: 370K, Video Views: 745,653, IG Saves: 2,481, IG Shares: 1,508

219 COLWELL & CUYLER BRAND IDENTITY
Design Firms: Clinton Carlson Design, University of Notre Dame | Designer: Clinton Carlson
Client: Colwell & Cuyler | Video: Library of Congress: Andrew Simpson Music, Kinograms
Publishing Corp, and Educational Pictures | Music & Sound: Father Son by MusicDog
Typeface: Mr. Eaves, Mrs. Eaves | Image Source: Library of Congress: Bain News Service
Font Designers: Zuzana Licko, Clinton Carlson | Main Contributor: Clinton Carlson

Assignment: This archival brand wanted to capture the wonder of baseball—prior to the industrial sports complex of today. Harkening back to when baseball was king and the "national pastime", Colwell & Cuyler publishes scorebooks and materials for baseball aficionados that reference a past printed tradition of ledgers, calendars, and almanacs.
Approach: The brand utilized ornamental elements found in early- to mid-20th century farm ledgers and materials. The typography utilizes a customized amper-

sand as a central element in the industrial seal-inspired design. Archival images and footage from the Library of Congress give life to the brand message and mission of documenting baseball.
Results: The brand has been well received in initial product offerings and is being implemented into web and additional materials.

FILM/VIDEO GOLD WINNERS:

220 FONT FABRIC TYPOGRAPHIC SERIES | Design Firm: Jennifer Sterling Design
Designer: Jennifer Sterling | Client: Font Fabric | Animator: Jennifer Sterling
Main Contributor: Jennifer Sterling
Assignment: Part of an advertising campaign developed for Font Fabric, a type foundry house, to showcase their various fonts.

220 CALIMAX CRAZY CART - CALIMAX CARRITO LOCO
Design Firm: Freaner Creative & Design | Designer: Ariel Freaner | Client: Calimax
Creative Director: Ariel Freaner | Editor: Fernanda Freaner | Main Contributor: Ariel Freaner
Assignment: The Crazy Cart went from being a seasonal promotional to steady yearly promotion and becoming the spokesperson for Calimax and their official mascot. Our consumer now identify with the Crazy Cart to bring them discounts, promotions and general information with a fun and friendly face, thus increasing the customers flow in all stores as well as online. While the Crazy Cart speaks on the universal language of sound bits, it's also in a way bilingual! Due to its location, Calimax serves both sides of the border so our character celebrates Mexico and United States holidays, special dates and unique events that happens o the border between Baja California and San Diego, focusing mostly in Tijuana, San Diego and Southern California. For some the Crazy Cart has become a figure of friendship between the two countries. Some of our key performance indicator shows an increase of consumers extended time at our stores, increase online presence, online shopping and request for additional services such as home and office delivery, online sales and ecommerce. Nevertheless, the awareness of our stroes and brand positioning has increased in a 5% to 15% depending on the location.
Approach: The Crazy Cart is a Calimax's shopping cart bring back to life. The Cart was reimagined with hight tech futuristic and racing car elements to make it impressive and high tech. His wheels are powerful and its line is sleek. He alos has a source of energy, knowledge, and other surprising things coming from the center of its body with the Calimax symbol, giving him a but of a superhero appearance. On the other hand our character alos have cartoon-like characteristics such as his big eyes, movements and physical abilities like stretching his wheels to act like hands. These characteristics makes our character fun, cute, lovable, funny, friendly, and you can say bit cuddly. We choose a realistic look and feel on the shopping cart going from a 2D design to a 3D design. The materials use to render the cart come from real scanned materials.
Results: Calimax need it to bring back their 1998 Crazy Cart promotional campaign. The objective was to provide a fresh new look for the Crazy Cart promotional campaign and find a spoke person to communicate and get messages across to the public. We work for several months on a very limited budget of $15,000 dollars. Calimax had a growth of a 3% to 5% depending on their area but an increase of 35% on its market position.

220 LIGHT | Design Firm: Tsushima Design | Designer: Hajime Tsushima
Client: Taichung Advertising Association | Main Contributor: Hajime Tsushima
Assignment: I was invited to a poster exhibition to be held in Taiwan. The theme is light. The exhibition will be held in Taiwan from May 21st. This is an exhibition celebrating the 30th anniversary of the Taiwan Advertising Association. This time, I exhibited a printed poster at the exhibition. This is an animated version of the poster.
Approach: The shining light is represented as the light of peace. The shape of light changes with the time it flows. Sometimes people's activities are wrapped in light. There is the light of the war that was born from the conflict. I hope that light will exist as a light that is happy and watches over people's lives.
Results: The exhibition is about to begin. I hope it succeeds.

221 HARMONIOUS CO-EXISTENCE | Design Firm: Tsushima Design
Designer: Hajime Tsushima | Client: Organizing Committee of "Harmonious Co-Existence" 2022
Main Contributor: Hajime Tsushima
Assignment: This is a poster for the exhibition.The theme is Harmonious Co-Existence. I think the world must go toward harmonious coexistence. We must respect each other's cultures, customs and human rights. We want to live in peace with people all over the world in a world without conflict.
Approach: I expressed the flow of harmony between culture, customs and people in this form. It expresses a well-balanced world that respects each other and does not collapse while interacting moderately.
Results: About 300 posters are scheduled to be exhibited in China in May.

221 LOVE | Design Firm: Tsushima Design | Designer: Hajime Tsushima
Client: Kaohsiung Creators Association | Main Contributor: Hajime Tsushima
Assignment: This is a poster for the 2021 Taiwan International Graphic Design Exhibition. 30 graphic designers, including me, were invited for KCA's 30th Anniversary Poster Exhibition. The theme of the exhibition is love.
Approach: I made this poster with the theme of love. The rose flower language is love. I expressed it with a graphic like a rose flower.
Results: The exhibition was held in Taiwan from November 13th to 21st, 2021.

221 REVOLUTION TITLE SEQUENCE | Design Firm: Paolo Catalla
Designer: Paolo Catalla | Client: General Motors | Editor: Shane Patrick Ford
Director: Sean King O'Grady | Director of Photography: Richie Trimble
Music & Sound: David Chapdelaine | Executive Producers: Jesse Ford, Susan Rued Anderson, Sean King O'Grady, Shane Patrick Ford, Laura Hochthanner | Producer: Jesse Ford
Production Companies: WETHEPEOPLE, Hiatus, Atlas Industries
Main Contributor: Paolo Catalla
Assignment: Paolo Catalla was brought in to conceptualize, design, and animate the title sequence for Revolution – a documentary showcasing the groundbreaking development of the all-new GMC Hummer EV. The documentary – produced by WETHEPEOPLE, Hiatus, and Atlas Industries – has been featured on the History Channel along with other major viewing platforms.
Approach: Not your typical, polished intro for an all-new vehicle. The title sequence embraces the transparency of the vehicle's design and development process seen throughout the film. An electrifying aesthetic is weaved throughout the sequence, highlighting the vehicle's design details and capabilities.
Results: The title sequence successfully set the stage for the film and helped create a brand image for the new, electrifying GMC Hummer EV.

FILM/VIDEO SILVER WINNERS:

222 FONT FABRIC TYPOGRAPHIC CAMPAIGN | Design Firm: Jennifer Sterling Design
Designer: Jennifer Sterling | Client: Font Fabric | Animator: Jennifer Sterling
Main Contributor: Jennifer Sterling

222 HYUNDAI SÁBADO FUTBOLERO 'BECAUSE FUTBOL' LOTERIA CARDS
Design Firm: INNOCEAN USA | Client: Hyundai Motor America
Executive Creative Director: Barney Goldberg | Art Directors: Pakko De La Torre, Nicole Macey
Group Creative Directors: Lori Martin, Cary Ruby | Copywriter: Cesar Sanchez
Illustrator: Gerardo Guillen | Art Producer: Christy Borgatta Liuzzi | Producer: Charlles Osorio
Strategy Director: Jose Gonzalez | Group Account Director: Mike Braue
Advertising Agency: INNOCEAN USA | Account Manager: Jose Gonzalez
Account Director: Bryan DiBiagio

222 PEACE | Design Firm: Jennifer Sterling Design | Designer: Jennifer Sterling
Client: Self-initiated | Animator: Jennifer Sterling | Main Contributor: Jennifer Sterling

222 SAKE MIYOSHI FLOWER | Design Firm: OUWN
Designer: Atsushi Ishiguro | Client: Abunotsuru | Art Director: Atsushi Ishiguro
Animator: Mami Kawashima | Main Contributor: Atsushi Ishiguro

222 OCTAGON HAUS BRAND ANIMATION | Design Firm: Paolo Catalla
Designer: Paolo Catalla | Client: Octagon Haus | Main Contributor: Paolo Catalla

222 'AKSHARASADHANA' LETTERPRESS PRINTING IN DEVANAGARI SCRIPT - DOCUMENTARY FILM | Design Firm: Sir J.J. Institute of Applied Art
Designer: Sonali Suresh Mestri | Client: Self-initiated | Editor: Shyam Lagad
Instructor: Prof. Shubhanand Jog | Research: Sonali Suresh Mestri
Copywriter: Sonali Suresh Mestri | Photographer: Swapnil Mali | Source Credits: Mudran Parva, Marathi Viswakosh, Devanagri Mudraksharlekhan Kala, Dean Dr. Santosh Kshirsagar
Main Contributor: Sonali Mestri

223 SCHOOL OF THE ART INSTITUTE OF CHICAGO - ARTBASH 2022
Design Firm: School of the Art Institute of Chicago | Designer: Yu Chen
Client: Self-initiated | Main Contributor: Yu Chen

223 WORLD HEALTH ORGANIZATION AFRICA – PUT YOURSELF FIRST
Design Firm: Ahoy Studios | Designers: Connie Koch, Denise Sommer
Client: World Health Organization Africa | Illustrator: Sonia Pulido
Main Contributor: World Health Organization Africa

223 SIGNAGE & GRAPHICS FOR A FLOATING PARK | Design Firm: C&G Partners
Designers: Bruce Chao, Chris Mills, Jonathan Alger, Amy Siegel, Rachel Lu, Kris Li
Client: Little Island | Lighting Design: Fisher Marantz | Video: Lucas Lind
Marketing: Sehba Mohammad | Construction: Hunter Roberts | Others: (Architect of Record) Standard Architects, (Designer/Fabricator, Timber Seating) SITU, (Owner's Representative) Gardiner & Theobald, (Associate Partner) Alin Tocmacov, (Structural, Civil and MEP Engineer) Arup, (Landscape Architect) Mathews Nielsen Landscape Architects, (Design Architect) Heatherwick Studio, (Theatre Design Consultant) Charcoal Blue
Main Contributors: Jonathan Alger, Amy Siegel

223 NATIVE NEW YORK | Design Firm: C&G Partners
Designers: (Media) Rui Li, (3D) Daniel Steps, (3D) Kris Li, (Lead Experience) Daniel Rodriguez, (Lead Exhibit) Kevin Sayama, (Lead 3D) Dan Fouad, Jonathan Alger | Client: Smithsonian Institution's National Museum of the American Indian | Producers: (Senior) Alex Kelly, (Technical) Shuyler Nazareth, (Lead) Laura Grady | Graphic Designers: (Senior) Christian Montoro, (Graphic and Media) Calista Bohling, (Graphic and Media) Bruce Chao | Lighting Design: Available Light, Jeff Nash Lighting | Fabricator: Hadley Exhibits, Inc. | Marketing: Sehba Mohammad
Architect: Ewing Cole | Others: AV Media Consultants: Phase Shift, Security Consultants: GHD, AV Integrator: Diversified | Main Contributor: Jonathan Alger

223 NEXT-LEVEL RECYCLING | Design Firm: Conjure | Designer: Chelsea Leasure
Client: U.S. Steel | Writer: Ted Stoik | Chief Creative Director: Chris Froeter
Art Director: Chris Froeter | Mani Contributor: Jeff Sciortino

223 SEEK NEW CINEMA FESTIVAL TRAILER | Design Firm: WONGDOODY
Designers: Lauren Beauchemin, Reese Murakami | Client: Seattle International Film Festival
Studios: Jason Hall, Scott Engelhardt | Copywriter: Lauren Jones
Animators: Chris Davies, Lukas Weyandt | Executive Producer: Matteo Mosterts
Senior Producers: Laura Haithcock, Paul Morgan | Senior Designer: Drew Jasperse
Junior Designer: Ben Gross | Group Creative Director: Monkey Watson
Editor: James Whittington | Digital Artist: Jeremiah Dapkey | Retoucher: Charlie Rakatansky
Proofreader: Coby Jackson | Music & Sound: HearBY, Original music by SOUTH
Marketing Manager: Ariel Smith | Main Contributors: Lauren Beauchemin, Lauren Jones, Lukas Weyandt, Chris Davies, James Whittington, Laura Haithcock, Monkey Watson

224 AIGA GET OUT THE VOTE / NATIONAL CAMPAIGN
Design Firm: Jennifer Sterling Design | Designer: Jennifer Sterling | Client: AIGA
Creative Director: Jennifer Sterling | Animator: Jennifer Sterling
Main Contributor: Jennifer Sterling Design

224 2020 IN 4 IMAGES | Design Firm: Jennifer Sterling Design
Designer: Jennifer Sterling | Client: Self-initiated | Creative Director: Jennifer Sterling
Animator: Jennifer Sterling | Main Contributor: Jennifer Sterling Design

Index

DESIGN FIRMS

CLIENTS

DESIGNERS/GRAPHIC DESIGNERS/LEAD DESIGNERS/SENIOR DESIGNERS/JUNIOR DESIGNERS

CREATIVE DIRECTORS, SERVICES, TEAMS, & RELATED POSITIONS

ART DIRECTORS/SENIOR ART DIRECTORS

COMPUTER GRAPHICS/ANIMATORS/DIGITAL ARTISTS/DIGITAL ARTS & MULTIMEDIA/ARTISTS/ILLUSTRATORS/ART BUYERS/ENGRAVING

PHOTOGRAPHERS/PHOTO RETOUCHERS/DIRECTORS OF PHOTOGRAPHY/PHOTO ASSISTANTS/PHOTO ILLUSTRATORS/PHOTO STUDIOS

TYPOGRAPHERS/TYPEFACE/TYPOGRAPHY/TYPOGRAPHY DESIGN/HAND LETTERING

WEB DEVELOPERS, CONTENT DEVELOPERS, INTERACTIVE DEVELOPERS, & RELATED POSITIONS

PRODUCTION, PRODUCERS, & RELATED POSITIONS

CEOS/PRESIDENTS/MANAGING PARTNERS/PARTNERS/ASSOCIATE PARTNERS

PLATINUM

ARSONAL
www.arsonal.com
3524 Hayden Ave.
Culver City, CA 90232
United States
Tel +1 310 815 8824
info@arsonal.com

Bailey Lauerman
www.baileylauerman.com
1299 Farnam St., Ninth Floor
Omaha, NE 68102
United States
Tel +1 402 514 9400
rsack@baileylauerman.com

Carmit Design Studio
www.creativehotlist.com/challer
2208 Bettina Ave.
Belmont, CA 94002
United States
Tel +1 650 283 1308
carmit@carmitdesign.com

Clinton Carlson Design
www.clintoncarlson.com
1244 Garland Road
South Bend, IN 46614
United States
Tel +1 970 402 2599
ccarlso6@nd.edu

Dankook University
www.dankook.ac.kr
Room 317, College of Arts, 126
Jukjeon Suji
Yongin, Gyeonggi, 448-701
South Korea
Tel +82 318 005 3106
finvox3@naver.com

INNOCEAN USA
www.innoceanusa.com
180 Fifth St., Suite 200
Huntington Beach, CA 92648
United States
Tel +1 714 861 5371
awardshows@innoceanusa.com

McCandliss and Campbell/ Wainscot Media
www.mccandlissandcampbell.com
433 N. Windsor Ave.
Brightwaters, NY 11718
United States
Tel +1 631 252 3527
mcandcstudio@gmail.com

Mike Hughs Creative Direction + Design
www.hughescreativework.com
Canada
hughescreative@me.com

PepsiCo Design & Innovation
www.design.pepsico.com
350 Hudson St., 2nd Floor
New York, NY 10014
United States
Tel +1 646 681 5095
emily.ford.contractor@pepsico.com

Sol Benito
www.solbenito.com
1515-16 Ghanshyam Enclave, Link Road
Kandivali West, Mumbai, Maharashtra 400067
India
Tel +91 9967 864 864
solbenitoinfo@gmail.com

Stranger & Stranger
www.strangerandstranger.com
68 Greenpoint Ave., Suite 3
Brooklyn, NY 11222
United States
Tel +1 212 625 2441
nyc@strangerandstranger.com

Studio A
www.studioa.com
1019 Queen St.
Alexandria, VA 22314
United States
Tel +1 703 684 7729
info@studioA.com

GOLD

***TraceElement**
www.traceelement.com
Dallas, TX
United States
Tel +1 469 644 1023
yvette.sierra@traceelement.com

ABC Made
www.peterrenigeris.com
44 Churchill Ave.
Strathfield, NSW 2135
Australia
Tel +6 140 998 0699
renigeris@me.com

Addison
www.addison.com
48 Wall St.
New York, NY 10005
United States
Tel +1 212 229 5038
mlee@addison.com

AG Creative Group
www.agcreative.ca
100 - 2250 Boundary Road
Burnaby, BC V5M 3Z3
Canada
Tel +1 604 559 1411
stew@agcreative.ca

AHOY Studios
www.ahoystudios.com
456 Broadway
New York, NY 10013
United States
Tel +1 212 645 0565
denise@ahoystudios.com

Annie Chen Design
www.iyingchen.com
Toronto, ON
Canada
studio@iyingchen.com

ARSONAL
www.arsonal.com
3524 Hayden Ave.
Culver City, CA 90232
United States
Tel +1 310 815 8824
info@arsonal.com

Bailey Lauerman
www.baileylauerman.com
1299 Farnam St., 9th Floor
Omaha, NE 68102
United States
Tel +1 402 514 9400
rsack@baileylauerman.com

Bailey Sullivan
www.baileysullivan.com
Pennsylvania
United States
hi@baileysullivan.com

Box Brand Design Limited
www.boxbranddesign.com
Room 3208, Central Plaza
18 Harbour Road, Wan Chai
Hong Kong
Tel +852 2830 9976
info@boxbranddesign.com

C&G Partners
www.cgpartnersllc.com
116 E. 16th St., 10th Floor
New York, NY 10003
United States
Tel +1 212 532 4460
sehba@cgpartnersllc.com

Carmit Design Studio
www.carmitdesign.com
2208 Bettina Ave.
Belmont, CA 94002
United States
Tel +1 650 283 1308
carmit@carmitdesign.com

CF Napa Brand Design
www.cfnapa.com
2787 Napa Valley Corporate Drive
Napa, CA 94558
United States
Tel +1 707 265 1891
cfnapa@cfnapa.com

Chemi Montes
www.american.edu/cas/faculty/cmontes.cfm
American University—Katzen Arts Center
4400 Massachusetts Ave. NW
Washington D.C. 20016
United States
Tel +1 703 864 8767
cmontes@american.edu

Dankook University
www.dankook.ac.kr
Room 317, College of Arts, 126
Jukjeon Suji
Yongin, Gyeonggi, 448-701
South Korea
Tel +82 318 005 3106
finvox3@naver.com

DLR Group
www.dlrgroup.com
8611 Winchester St., #8302
Lenexa, KS 66219
United States
Tel +1 402 975 9510
awells@dlrgroup.com

Faceout Studio
www.faceoutstudio.com
414 W. Washington Ave., Suite B
Sisters, OR 97759
United States
Tel +1 541 323 3220
torrey@faceoutstudio.com

FACTORY
www.factory1611.com
Henderson Industrial Park
203A Henderson Road, #10-04
159546
Singapore
Tel +65 9369 1342
workbyfactory@gmail.com

Freaner Creative & Design
www.freaner.com
113 W. G St., No. 650
San Diego, CA 92101
United States
Tel +1 619 870 4699
arielfreaner@freaner.com

Goodall Integrated Design
www.goodallintegrated.com
35 Tyrrel Ave.
Toronto, ON M6G 2G1
Canada
Tel +1 416 435 3653
derwyn@goodallintegrated.com

Grantz Jansword
www.janswordzhu.com
6834 Park Mill Drive
Dublin, OH 43016
United States
Tel +1 740 776 8135
jansword.zhu@gmail.com

Greg Breeding
www.team.journeygroup.com/gregb
418 4th St. NE
Charlottesville, VA 22902
United States
Tel +1 434 961 2500
gregb@journeygroup.com

H. Tuncay Design
www.haluktuncay.com
Omer Rustu Pasa Sokak, Birlik Apt. 26/8
Besiktas Istanbul 34357
Turkey
Tel +90 532 588 3747
haltuncay@gmail.com

Haas Design
www.haasdesign.co.uk
The Gardens
Mavisbank Lasswade Midlothian, EH18 1HY
United Kingdom
Tel +44 131 454 9417
info@haasdesign.co.uk

Heart Haus at CVS Health
www.cvshealth.com
1026 Park East Drive
Woonsocket, RI 02895
United States
Tel +1 401 477 2621
evan.boisvert@cvshealth.com

Islam Hassan
9 Hassan Assem St.,
5th Floor, Apt. 9
Cairo, Zamalek, 4271020
Egypt
Tel +2010 1556 6733
iislam.hassan@gmail.com

Jennifer Sterling Design
www.jennifersterlingdesign.com
80 Varick St.
New York, NY 10013
United States
Tel +1 415 310 5083
info@jennifersterlingdesign.com

Journey Group
www.journeygroup.com
418 4th St. NE
Charlottesville, VA 22902
United States
Tel +1 434 961 2500
info@journeygroup.com

Mark Braught Studios
www.up-ideas.com
740 Ashley Laine Walk
Lawrenceville, GA 30043
United States
Tel +1 770 912 3120
hello@up-ideas.com

May & Co.
www.mayandco.com
6316 Berwyn Lane
Dallas, TX 75214
United States
Tel +1 214 536 0599
dougm@mayandco.com

Mermaid, Inc.
www.mermaidnyc.com
479 W. 152nd St., Studio 1B
New York, NY 10031
United States
Tel +1 646 510 3343
sharon@mermaidnyc.com

Michael Pantuso Design
www.pantusodesign.com
820 S. Thurlow St.
Hinsdale, IL 60521
United States
Tel +1 312 318 1800
michaelpantuso@me.com

Michael Schwab Studio
www.michaelschwab.com
108 Tamalpais Ave.
San Anselmo, CA 94960
United States
Tel +1 415 257 5792
michael@michaelschwab.com

Mike Hughes Creative Direction + Design
www.hughescreativework.com
Canada
hughescreative@me.com

MiresBall
www.miresball.com
2605 State St.
San Diego, CA 92103
United States
Tel +1 619 234 6631
marketing@miresball.com

Moxie Sozo
www.moxiesozo.com
1140 Pearl St., Suite 200
Boulder, CO 80302
United States
Tel +1 314 996 9119
branding@moxiesozo.com

Namseoul University
www.nsu.ac.kr
91 Daehak-ro, Seonghwan-eup, Seobuk-gu
Cheonan-si,
Chungcheongnam-do
South Korea
Tel +82 41 580 2000
mijung6@nate.com

Noriyuki Kasai
www.nihon-u.ac.jp
2-42-1 Asahigaoka
Nerima-ku Tokyo 176-8525
Japan
Tel +81 3 5995 8691
kasai.noriyuki@nihon-u.ac.jp

Omdesign
www.omdesign.pt
Rua de Vila Franca, 54 - Leça da Palmeira
Matosinhos 4450-802
Portugal
Tel +351 229 982 960
comunicacao@omdesign.pt

Onrepeat Studio
www.onrepeat.studio
London, SE8 5ES
United Kingdom
joao@onrepeat.net

Paolo Catalla
www.pao.works
28750 Bella Vista Drive
Farmington Hills, MI 48334
United States
Tel +1 734 578 4946
paolo@paolocatalla.com

Pavement
www.pavementsf.com
420 3rd St., Suite 240
Oakland, CA 94607
United States
Tel +1 917 558 3985
mike@pavementsf.com

PepsiCo Design & Innovation
www.design.pepsico.com
350 Hudson St., 2nd Floor
New York, NY 10014
United States
Tel +1 646 681 5095
emily.ford.contractor@pepsi
co.com

Peterson Ray & Company
www.peterson.com
2220 S. Harwood St., Unit #105
Dallas, TX 75215
United States
Tel +1 214 954 0522
scott@peterson.com

PETROL Advertising
www.petrolad.com
443 N. Varney St.
Burbank, CA 91502
United States
Tel +1 323 644 3720
bnessan@petrolad.com

PH Studio
www.ph-studio.com
530 Miller Ave.
Mill Valley, CA 94941
United States
richard@ph-studio.com

Ralph Appelbaum Associates
www.raai.com
88 Pine St.
New York, NY 10005
United States
Tel +1 212 334 8200
caseylynn@raai.com

Randy Clark
www.randyclark.myportfolio.com
88 Daxue Road, Ouhai District
Wenzhou, Zhejiang
China
Tel +86 5775 5870 000
randyclarkmfa@icloud.com

Resource Branding
www.resourceatlanta.com
3453 Pierce Drive, No.140
Chamblee, GA 30341
United States
Tel +1 404 625 8856
rick@resourceatlanta.com

Richard Ljoenes Design LLC
www.richardljoenes.com
Boulder, CO 80303
United States
Tel +1 917 407 2400
richard.ljoenes@gmail.com

Rodgers Townsend
www.rodgerstownsend.com
200 N. Broadway, Floor 12
St. Louis, MO 63102
United States
Tel +1 314 435 1146
alyson.shead@rodgerstownsend.
com

Roger Archbold
www.rogerarchbold.com
607/42A Nelson St.
Ringwood, VIC 3134
Australia
Tel +61 404 806 354
roger@rogerarchbold.com

SJI Associates
www.sjiassociates.com
127 W. 24th St., 2nd Floor
New York, NY 10011
United States
Tel +1 212 391 4140
david@sjiassociates.com

Sol Benito
www.solbenito.com
1515-16 Ghanshyam Enclave,
Link Road
Kandivali West, Mumbai, Maharashtra 400067
India
Tel +91 9967 864 864
solbenitoinfo@gmail.com

Spire Agency
www.spireagency.com
5055 Keller Springs Road,
Suite 510
Addison, TX 75001
United States
Tel +1 214 393 5200
kimberly.tyner@spireagency.com

Still Room
www.still-room.com
2169 Lemoyne St.
Los Angeles CA 90026
United States
Tel +1 213 453 0370
studio@still-room.com

Stjepko Rošin
www.stjepko.com
Marina Držića 12
Split 21000 HR
Croatia
Tel +385 915210151
stjepko.rosin@gmail.com

Studio A
www.studioa.com
1019 Queen St.
Alexandria, VA 22314
United States
Tel +1 703 684 7729
info@studioA.com

Toben
www.toben.com.au
1 Dank St., Unit 8
Waterloo, NSW 2017
Australia
Tel +61 280 601 136
thorsten@toben.com.au

Toppan Inc.
www.toppan.com/en
9F, 1-3-3, Suido Bunkyo-ku
Tokyo 112-8531
Japan
Tel +81 3 5840 2192
mescal@mac.com

Traction Factory
www.tractionfactory.com
247 S. Water St.
Milwaukee, WI 53204
United States
Tel +1 414 944 0900
tf_awards@tractionfactory.com

Tsushima Design
www.tsushima-design.com
1-17-204, 1-17, Matsukawa-cho,
Minami-ku
Hiroshima 7320826
Japan
Tel +81 82 567 5586
info@tsushima-design.com

Turner Duckworth: London, San Francisco & New York
www.turnerduckworth.com
375 Hudson St., 16th Floor
New York, NY
United States
Tel +1 212 463 2400
kate.bracero@turnerduckworth.
com

Underline Studio
www.underlinestudio.com
247 Wallace Ave., 2nd Floor
Toronto, ON M6H 1V5
Canada
Tel +1 416 341 0475
kristin@underlinestudio.com

UP-Ideas
www.up-ideas.com
740 Ashley Laine Walk
Lawrenceville, GA 30043
United States
Tel +1 770 912 3120
roger.sawhill@gmail.com

USADesign
www.usadesign.jp
5-2-15 #101 Todoroki Se-
tagaya-ku
Tokyo 1580082
Japan
Tel +81 80 5474 3144
shimousa@usadesign.jp

Vanderbyl Design
www.vanderbyl.com
511 Tokay Lane
St. Helena, CA 94574
United States
Tel +1 415 543 8447
michael@vanderbyl.com

Wainscot Media
www.mccandlissandcampbell.
com
433 N. Windsor Ave.
Brightwaters, NY 11718
United States
Tel +1 631 252 3527
mcandcstudio@gmail.com

Wallace Church & Co.
www.wallacechurch.com
330 E. 48th St., 3rd Floor
New York, NY 10017
United States
Tel +1 212 755 2903
rich@wallacechurch.com

Xiaomi
www.mi.com
Anningzhuang Road
Haidian District, Beijing 100085
China
Tel +86 10 606 06666
chenlu@xiaomi.com

Xuecheng Xiong
www.tedxiong.works
Brooklyn, NY 11201
United States
Tel +1 929 310 0413
tedxiongxuecheng@gmail.com

Yankee Publishing Inc.
www.mccandlissandcampbell.
com
433 N. Windsor Ave.
Brightwaters, NY 11718
United States
Tel +1 631 252 3527
mcandcstudio@gmail.com

SILVER

***TraceElement**
www.traceelement.com
Dallas, TX
United States
Tel +1 469 644 1023
yvette.sierra@traceelement.com

&Barr
www.andbarr.co
600 E. Washington St.
Orlando, FL 32801
United States
Tel +1 407 849 0100
hello@andbarr.co

1/4 Studio
Estrada da Circunvalação 12119
Cave Porto Porto 4250-155
Portugal
Tel +351 223166278
quarterstudio.info@gmail.com

23in
www.23in.com
Los Angeles, CA
United States
info@23in.com

9Rooftops
www.9rooftops.com
225 W. Station Square Drive,
Suite 500
Pittsburgh, PA 15219
United States
Tel +1 412 562 2146
dena_mosti@yahoo.com

Addison
www.addison.com
48 Wall St.
New York, NY 10005
United States
Tel +1 212 229 5038
mlee@addison.com

Aegis Dental Network
www.aegisdentalnetwork.com
140 Terry Drive, Suite 103
Newtown, PA 18940
United States
Tel +1 215 504 1275
jbarlow@aegiscomm.com

AG Creative Group
www.agcreative.ca
100 - 2250 Boundary Road
Burnaby, BC V5M 3Z3
Canada
Tel +1 604 559 1411
stew@agcreative.ca

Ahoy Studios
www.ahoystudios.com
456 Broadway
New York, NY 10013
United States
Tel +1 212 645 0565
denise@ahoystudios.com

Alban Fischer Design
www.albanfischerdesign.com
Grand Rapids, MI
United States
albanfischer78@gmail.com

Andrea Castelletti Studio
www.acastelletti.com
Via Breno 2
Milano Milano 20139
Italy
Tel +39 393 627 4111
info@daltraparte.com

Anna Jordan
www.annatype.com
Rochester Institute of
Technology
55 Lomb Memorial Drive
Rochester, NY 14623
United States
Tel +1 401 688 0123
annatype@gmail.com

Anne M. Giangiulio Design
www.annegiangiulio.com
UTEP Department of Art
500 West University Ave.
El Paso, TX 79968
United States
Tel +1 915 222 1134
annegiangiulio@gmail.com

Annex88
www.annex88.com
200 Hudson St.
New York, NY 10013
United States
hello@annex88.com

Annie Chen Design
www.iyingchen.com
Toronto, ON
Canada
studio@iyingchen.com

ARSONAL
www.arsonal.com
3524 Hayden Ave.
Culver City, CA 90232
United States
Tel +1 310 815 8824
info@arsonal.com

ArtHouse Design
www.arthousedenver.com
2373 Central Park Blvd., #204
Denver, CO 80238
United States
Tel +1 303 892 9816
marty@arthousedenver.com

Bailey Lauerman
www.baileylauerman.com
1299 Farnam St., 9th Floor
Omaha, NE 68102
United States
Tel +1 402 514 9400
rsack@baileylauerman.com

Balloon Inc.
www.lloon.jp
Knowledge Capital 8F,
Grand Front Osaka
3-1 Ofuka-cho Kita-ku, Osaka
City, Osaka 530-0011
Japan
Tel +81 6 7167 6109
b@lloon.jp

Box Brand Design Limited
www.boxbranddesign.com
Room 3208, Central Plaza
18 Harbour Road, Wan Chai
Hong Kong
Tel +852 2830 9976
info@boxbranddesign.com

Boyang Xia
14-22 Astoria Park S., Apt. 2
Long Island City, NY 11102
United States
Tel +1 401 489 3478
boyangxia@outlook.com

Braley Design
www.braleydesign.com
3469 Lannette Lane
Lexington, KY 40503
United States
Tel +1 415 706 2700
braley@braleydesign.com

Brand Bar Communications
www.brandbar.eu
Naphegy Utca 21.
Budapest Pest 1016
Hungary
Tel +36 70 380 9419
kapcsolat@brandbar.hu

BRED
www.pace.edu
Pace University
1 Pace Plaza
New York, NY 10038
United States
Tel +1 866 722 3338
bmcmanus@pace.edu

BUNTIN
www.buntingroup.com
230 Willow St.
Nashville, TN 37210
United States
Tel +1 615 244 5720
jmaldonado@buntingroup.com

C&G Partners
www.cgpartnersllc.com
116 E. 16th St., 10th Floor
New York, NY 10003
United States
Tel +1 212 532 4460
sehba@cgpartnersllc.com

Caldas Naya
www.caldasnaya.com
Taulat 93
Barcelona 08005
Spain
Tel +34 6869 88571
info@caldasnaya.com

Carolyn Gibbs Design
www.carolyngibbsdesign.com
738 1st St. W.
Sonoma, CA 95476
United States
Tel +1 707 696 8479
cg@carolyngibbsdesign.com

Catalone Design
www.catalonedesign.com
5929 Onondaga Road
Bethesda, MD 20816
United States
Tel +1 301 263 9673
workwithus@catalonedesign.com

CF Napa Brand Design
www.cfnapa.com
2787 Napa Valley Corporate Drive
Napa, CA 94558
United States
Tel +1 707 265 1891
cfnapa@cfnapa.com

Coastlines Creative Group
www.coastlinescreative.com
77 Walter Hardwick Ave., #412
Vancouver, BC V5Y 0C6
Canada
Tel +1 604 785 1017
byron@coastlinescreative.com

Code Switch
www.codeswitchdesign.com
262 Crescent St.
Northampton, MA 01060
United States
jansabach@mac.com

Coley Porter Bell
www.coleyporterbell.com
636 11th Ave.
New York, NY 10036
United States
Tel +1 212 237 4628
jenn.szekely@coleyporterbell.com

Compass
www.compass.com
90 5th Ave., 3rd Floor
New York NY 10011
United States
Tel +1 212 913 9058
dallas.franklin@compass.com

Conjure
www.conjureinc.com
1828 W. Hubbard St.
Chicago, IL 60622
United States
Tel +1 312 733 8895
cfroeter@conjureinc.com

Courtney Windham
www.courtneywindhamdesign.com
Auburn University
Auburn, AL 36830
United States
Tel +1 334 844 4000
courtney.windham@auburn.edu

Creative Energy
www.cenergy.com
3206 Hanover Road
Johnson City, TN 37604
United States
Tel +1 423 926 9494
wgriffith@cenergy.com

Cue
www.designcue.com
520 Nicollet Mall, Suite 500
Minneapolis, MN 55402
United States
Tel +1 612 465 0030
info@designcue.com

Cul-Box
China
art008.hi@163.com

Curious
www.curiouslondon.com
126 Marina St.,
Leonards On Sea
East Sussex, TN38 0BN
United Kingdom
Tel +44 798 071 5445
gary@curiouslondon.com

Dalian Cones Papa Technology Co., Ltd.
High-Tech Industrial Park, Room 702, West Side, 7th Floor
No.1 Gaoxin St., Dalian Liaoning
116023
China
Tel +86 1554 230 6005
wanglueva@gmail.com

Daniel Frumhoff Design
www.ericaholeman.com
University of North Texas
1155 Union Circle
Denton, TX 76203
United States
Tel +1 940 565 2000
erica.holeman@unt.edu

DesigNV [Design + Envy]
www.designv.us
14624 Heatherton Drive
Granger, IN 46530
United States
Tel +1 505 977 2292
nverma@designv.us

Dessein
www.dessein.com.au
130 Aberdeen St. Northbridge
Perth, WA 6003
Australia
Tel +61 892 280 661
geoff@dessein.com.au

DeVito/Verdi
www.devitoverdi.com
330 Hudson St., 16th Floor
New York, NY 10011
United States
Tel +1 212 431 4694
nryan@devitoverdi.com

DLR Group
www.dlrgroup.com
8611 Winchester St., #8302
Lenexa, KS 66219
United States
Tel +1 402 975 9510
awells@dlrgroup.com

Doris Palmeros Studio
www.dorispalmeros.com
1001 W. Mulberry Ave.
San Antonio, TX 78201
United States
Tel +1 210 865 0988
kdmlmc@gmail.com

Duas Faces Design
www.duasfaces.net
Rua Barata Feyo, 140 - 2º Andar, Escritório 2.5
Porto Porto 4250-076
Portugal
Tel +351 912 452 123
duasfaces.design@gmail.com

Duft Watterson
www.duftwatterson.com
176 S. Capitol Blvd.
Boise, ID 83702
United States
Tel +1 208 917 2181
talia@duftwatterson.com

Elmwood
www.elmwood.com
27 Gee St.
London, EC1V 3RD
United Kingdom
Tel +44 020 7637 0884
alex.ehrensperger@elmwood.com

El Paso, Galería de Comunicación
www.elpasocomunicacion.com
C. Sagunto, 13
Madrid 28010
Spain
Tel +349 1594 2248
elpaso@elpasocomunicacion.com

Entro
www.entro.com
33 Harbour Square, Suite 202
Toronto, ON M5J 2G2
Canada
Tel +1 416 368 7988
cristina@entro.com

Erica Holeman
www.ericaholeman.com
University of North Texas
1155 Union Circle
Denton, TX 76203
United States
Tel +1 940 565 2000
erica.holeman@unt.edu

Esseblu
www.esseblu.it
Via Antonio Cecchi 8
Milano 20146
Italy
Tel +02 4800 0291
info@esseblu.it

Faceout Studio
www.faceoutstudio.com
414 W. Washington Ave., Suite B
Sisters, OR 97759
United States
Tel +1 541 323 3220
Torrey@faceoutstudio.com

FACTORY
www.factory1611.com
Henderson Industrial Park
203A Henderson Road, #10-04
159546
Singapore
Tel +65 9369 1342
workbyfactory@gmail.com

Fellow Inc.
www.fellowinc.com
718 W. 34th St.
Minneapolis, MN 55408
United States
Tel +1 612 670 7336
nknutson@fellowinc.com

Feixue Mei
www.feixuemei.info
United States
feixuefeixuemei@gmail.com

Force MAJEURE
www.forcemajeure.design
219 36th St., 5th Floor
Brooklyn, NY 11232
United States
Tel +1 646 460 5765
lhainaut@forcemajeure.design

Freaner Creative & Design
www.freaner.com
113 W. G St., No. 650
San Diego, CA 92101
United States
Tel +1 619 870 4699
arielfreaner@freaner.com

Ginkgo Bioworks
www.ginkgobioworks.com
27 Drydock Ave., 8th Floor
Boston, MA 02210
United States
Tel +1 877 422 5362
grace@ginkgobioworks.com

Goodall Integrated Design
www.goodallintegrated.com
35 Tyrrel Ave.
Toronto, ON M6G 2G1
Canada
Tel +1 416 435 3653
derwyn@goodallintegrated.com

Good Communication Marketing
www.instagram.com/bigvbc/
#505-1763 Nelson St.
Vancouver, BC V6G 1M6
Canada
Tel +1 778 885 4978
bigvbc@me.com

Goods & Services
www.goods.services
905 Bernina Ave., Suite D
Atlanta, GA 30307
United States
zmian@goods.services

Greenleaf Book Group
www.greenleafbookgroup.com
P.O. Box 91869
Austin, TX 78709
United States
Tel +1 512 891 6100
lmacqueen@greenleafbookgroup.com

Harcus Design
www.harcus.com.au
3/46 Foster St.
Surry Hills, Sydney, NSW 2010
Australia
Tel +61 29212 2755
annette@harcus.com.au

Hatch Design
www.hatchsf.com
1600 Bryant St., #411633
San Francisco, CA 94141
United States
Tel +1 628 895 0067
inquiries@hatchsf.com

Heart Haus at CVS Health
www.cvshealth.com
1026 Park East Drive
Woonsocket, RI 02895
United States
Tel +1 401 477 2621
evan.boisvert@cvshealth.com

Holohan Design
www.tyler.temple.edu/programs/graphic-interactive-design
Tyler School of Art & Architecture
2001 N. 13th St.
Philadelphia, PA 19122
United States
Tel +1 215 621 6559
kholohan@temple.edu

House of Current
www.houseofcurrent.com
154 Krog St., Suite 160
Atlanta, GA 30307
United States
Tel +1 404 816 0094
sbrannon@houseofcurrent.com

Hundredweight
www.hundredweight.com.au
The Commons,
20-40 Meagher St.
Sydney, NSW 2008
Australia
Tel +0422 984 205
craig@hundredweight.com.au

HyungjooKimDesignLab
www.cla.purdue.edu/academic/rueffschool/ad/vcd/Faculty.html
Rueff School of Design, Art, and Performance
552 West Wood St. W
Lafayette, IN 47907
United States
Tel +1 765 494 3071
hakim@purdue.edu

HyunJung Yi
275 E. Green St., Apt. 1438
Pasadena, CA 91101
United States
hyunjung.work@gmail.com

IBM Research
www.research.ibm.com
1 New Orchard Road
Armonk, NY 10504
United States
Tel +1 800 426 4968
aquaxie828@gmail.com

INNOCEAN USA
www.innoceanusa.com
180 5th St., Suite 200
Huntington Beach, CA 92648
United States
Tel +1 714 861 5371
awardshows@innoceanusa.com

Jang Won Lee
South Korea
teaandpine@gmail.com

Jennifer Sterling Design
www.jennifersterlingdesign.com
80 Varick St.
New York, NY 10013
United States
Tel +1 415 310 5083
info@jennifersterlingdesign.com

Joba Studio
www.behance.net/pfinley
2385 Lake Vista Drive
Christiansburg, VA 24073
United States
Tel +1 608 235 9273
pfinley05@gmail.com

John Sposato Design & Illustration
www.johnsposato.carbonmade.com
179 Hudson Terrace
Piermont, NY 10968
United States
Tel +1 845 300 7591
johnsposatodesign@gmail.com

Journey Group
www.journeygroup.com
418 4th St. NE
Charlottesville, VA 22902
United States
Tel +1 434 961 2500
info@journeygroup.com

Karen Watkins Design
www.karenwatkinsdesign.com
704 Dean Court
West Chester, PA 19382
United States
Tel +1 610 420 5851
kwatkins704@gmail.com

Keith Kitz Design
www.keithkitz.com
1945 Commonwealth Ave., Unit 2
Boston, MA 02135
United States
Tel +1 857 321 0957
keith.kitz@gmail.com

Kimberly Elam Design
www.ringling.edu
Ringling College of Art + Design
2700 N. Tamiami Trail
Sarasota, FL 34234
United States
Tel +1 941 351 5100
kelam@c.ringling.edu

Lafayette American
www.lafayetteamerican.com
5000 Grand River Ave.
Detroit, MI
United States
Tel +1 313 757 2720
meg@lafayetteamerican.com

Legacy79
www.legacy79.com
816 Camaron St., Ste. 2.02
San Antonio, TX 78212
United States
Tel +1 210 508 0225
genaro@legacy79.com

Legis Design
273 Ramona Ave.
Sierra Madre, CA 91024
United States
legis@pa2.so-net.ne.jp

Level Group
www.levelnyc.com
270 Jay St., Suite 11-I
Brooklyn, NY 11201
United States
Tel +1 212 594 2522
hello@levelnyc.com

Lippincott
www.lippincott.com
499 Park Ave.
New York, NY 10022
United States
Tel +1 212 521 0000
kate.conrad@lippincott.com

Loksophy Design Ltd.
www.loksophy.design
Rua de Pequim No.202A-246,
Macau Finance Centre, 1
6 Andar H, Macau S.A.R.
999078
Macau
Tel +853 6612 4863
info.loksophy@gmail.com

Luca Pontarelli
www.lucapontarelli.com
Chicago, IL
United States
hello@lucapontarelli.com

Lyft Internal Creative Team
www.lyft.com
185 Berry St., Suite 5000
San Francisco, CA 94107
United States
gianmaria.schonlieb@gmail.com

Margaret Fletcher
www.margaretfletcher.com
Auburn University
Auburn, AL 36830
United States
Tel +1 334 844 4000
mfletcher@auburn.edu

Matchstic
www.matchstic.com
437 Memorial Drive SE, Unit A7
Atlanta, GA 30312
United States
Tel +1 404 446 1511
accounting@matchstic.com

May & Co.
www.mayandco.com
6316 Berwyn Lane
Dallas, TX 75214
United States
Tel +1 214 536 0599
dougm@mayandco.com

M Books
www.michaelparndt.com
148 W. 70th St., #16
New York, NY 10023
United States
Tel +1 212 501 9592
mpa@michaelparndt.com

Mermaid, Inc.
www.mermaidnyc.com
479 W. 152nd St., Studio 1B
New York, NY 10031
United States
Tel +1 646 510 3343
sharon@mermaidnyc.com

Michael Pantuso Design
www.pantusodesign.com
820 S. Thurlow St.
Hinsdale, IL 60521
United States
Tel +1 312 318 1800
michaelpantuso@me.com

Michael Schwab Studio
www.michaelschwab.com
108 Tamalpais Ave.
San Anselmo, CA 94960
United States
Tel +1 415 257 5792
michael@michaelschwab.com

MiresBall
www.miresball.com
2605 State St.
San Diego, CA 92103
United States
Tel +1 619 234 6631
marketing@miresball.com

Moxie Sozo
www.moxiesozo.com
1140 Pearl St., Suite 200
Boulder, CO 80302
United States
Tel +1 314 996 9119
branding@moxiesozo.com

Natasha Mozz
www.natashamozz.com
New York, NY
United States
natasha.mozz@gmail.com

Né S. Design
R. Cidreira, 291
4465-076 Matosinhos
Portugal
Tel +229 015 349
nesantelmo.design@gmail.com

Nexus Designs
www.nexusdesigns.com.au
260 Park St.
South Melbourne, VIC 3205
Australia
Tel +61 3 9690 2277
sallye@nexusdesigns.com.au

Nick Steinhardt
www.23in.com
Los Angeles, CA
United States
info@23in.com

Nikkeisha, Inc.
7-13-20 Ginza Chuo-ku
Tokyo 1048176
Japan
Tel +81 90 1121 5422
nakamu02@gmail.com

Noise 13
www.noise13.com
1616 16th St., Suite 370
San Francisco, CA 94103
United States
Tel +1 415 957 1313
info@noise13.com

Noriyuki Kasai
www.nihon-u.ac.jp
2-42-1 Asahigaoka
Nerima-ku Tokyo 176-8525
Japan
Tel +81 3 5995 8691
kasai.noriyuki@nihon-u.ac.jp

Omdesign
www.omdesign.pt
Rua de Vila Franca, 54 - Leça da Palmeira
Matosinhos 4450-802
Portugal
Tel +351 229 982 960
comunicacao@omdesign.pt

Onrepeat Studio
www.onrepeat.studio
London, SE8 5ES
United Kingdom
joao@onrepeat.net

Open Door Design Studio
www.shantanusuman.com
3401 N. Tillotson Ave.,
AJ 401 Art & Journalism Building
Muncie, IN 47306
United States
Tel +1 352 792 5100
sumanshantanu@gmail.com

Osborne Ross
www.osborneross.com
62a Linden Gardens
Chiswick, London W4 2EW
United Kingdom
Tel +44 20 8742 7227
andrew@osborneross.com

Our Man In Havana
www.omihnyc.com
55 Washington St., 4th Floor
Brooklyn, NY 11201
United States
production@omihnyc.com

OUWN
www.ouwn.jp
Kubo Building 501 1-7-4
Ohashi Meguro-ku Tokyo
153-0044
Japan
info@ouwn.jp

Paolo Catalla
www.pao.works
28750 Bella Vista Drive
Farmington Hills, MI 48334
United States
Tel +1 734 578 4946
paolo@paolocatalla.com

Partners + Napier
www.partnersandnapier.com
1 S. Clinton Ave., Suite 400
Rochester, NY 14604
United States
Tel +1 585 414 1080
melissa.smith@partnersandnapier.com

Pavement
www.pavementsf.com
420 3rd St., Suite 240
Oakland, CA 94607
United States
Tel +1 917 558 3985
mike@pavementsf.com

Pendo
www.pendo.ca
711-402 W. Pender St.
Vancouver, BC V6B 1T6
Canada
Tel +1 604 398 8822
peter@pendo.ca

PepsiCo Design & Innovation
www.design.pepsico.com
350 Hudson St., 2nd Floor
New York, NY10014
United States
Tel +1 646 681 5095
emily.ford.contractor@pepsico.com

Peterson Ray & Company
www.peterson.com
2220 S. Harwood St., Unit #105
Dallas, TX 75215
United States
Tel +1 214 954 0522
scott@peterson.com

PETROL Advertising
www.petrolad.com
443 N. Varney St.
Burbank, CA 91502
United States
Tel +1 323 644 3720
bnessan@petrolad.com

PH Studio
www.ph-studio.com
530 Miller Ave.
Mill Valley, CA 94941
United States
richard@ph-studio.com

Plot Twist Creativity
www.plottwist.com
4849 Greenville Ave., Suite #121
Dallas, TX 75206
United States
hello@plottwistcreativity.com

PMDesign
www.pmdesign.pt
R. Travanca Cima, 570
Santa Maria DA Feira 4520-819
Portugal
Tel +351 914 066 898
mail@pmdesign.pt

Polygon
China
art008.hi@163.com

Ralph Appelbaum Associates
www.raai.com
88 Pine St.
New York, NY 10005
United States
Tel +1 212 334 8200
caseylynn@raai.com

Randy Clark
www.randyclark.myportfolio.com
88 Daxue Road, Ouhai District
Wenzhou, Zhejiang
China
Tel +86 5775 5870 000
randyclarkmfa@icloud.com

REPRESENT Designers
www.levelnyc.com
270 Jay St., Suite 11-I
Brooklyn NY 11201
United States
Tel +1 212 594 2522
hello@levelnyc.com

Res Eichenberger Design
www.reseichenberger.ch
Neptunstrasse 25
Zurich 8032
Switzerland
Tel +41 434 998 336
studio@reseichenberger.ch

Resource Branding
www.resourceatlanta.com
3453 Pierce Drive, No. 140
Chamblee, GA 30341
United States
Tel +1 404 625 8856
rick@resourceatlanta.com

Rex C
www.houserphoto.com
5610 Grandhaven Drive
Durham, NC 27713
United States
Tel +1 919 924 6263
todd@houserphoto.com

Rhodes Creative
www.alexrhodes.net
6906 W. Parapet Court
Boise, ID 83714
United States
Tel +1 208 570 0895
alex@alexrhodes.net

Richard Ljoenes Design LLC
www.richardljoenes.com
Boulder, CO 80303
United States
Tel +1 917 407 2400
richard.ljoenes@gmail.com

Robert Finkel
www.robertfinkel.com
Auburn University
Auburn, AL 36830
United States
Tel +1 334 844 4000
rjfinkel@auburn.edu

Roberto Núñez Studio
www.robertonunez.com
Zamora 40 Int, B7
Barcelona 08005
Spain
Tel +34 655 213 261
robertonunez@robertonunez.com

Rodgers Townsend
www.rodgerstownsend.com
200 N. Broadway, Floor 12
St. Louis, MO 63102
United States
Tel +1 314 435 1146
alyson.shead@rodgerstownsend.com

Romeo and Company International
www.romeoco.com
Florida
United States
Tel +1 212 747 0016
vin@romeoco.com

Savannah College of Art and Design
www.scad.edu
P.O. Box 3146
Savannah, GA 31402
United States
Tel +1 912 525 6830
awards@scad.edu

School of the Art Institute of Chicago
www.saic.edu
36 S. Wabash Ave.
Chicago, IL 60603
United States
Tel +1 800 232 7242
ychen129@artic.edu

Sequel Studio
www.sequelstudio.com
12 W. 27th St., 15th Floor
New York, NY 10001
United States
Tel +1 212 994 4320
business@sequelstudio.com

Siena Scarff Design
www.sienascarff.com
302 Harvard St.
Cambridge, MA 02139
United States
Tel +1 857 756 8372
siena@sienascarff.com

Sir J.J. Institute of Applied Art
www.jjiaa.org
WRVM+48F, Dr. Dadabhai Naoroji Road Fort
Mumbai, Maharashtra 400001
India
Tel +91 22 2262 0231
smestr20@student.scad.edu

SIREN SF
www.sirensf.com
3323 W. Laurelhurst Drive NE
Seattle, WA 98105
United States
Tel +1 415 596 3005
jeff@sirensf.com

SJI Associates
www.sjiassociates.com
127 W. 24th St., 2nd Floor
New York, NY 10011
United States
Tel +1 212 391 4140
david@sjiassociates.com

SML Design
www.smldesign.com.au
1 Kent Lane
Prahran, VIC 3181
Australia
Tel +61 403 814 001
vanessa@smldesign.com.au

Sol Benito
www.solbenito.com
1515-16 Ghanshyam Enclave, Link Road
Kandivali West, Mumbai, Maharashtra 400067
India
Tel +91 9967 864 864
solbenitoinfo@gmail.com

Spire Agency
www.spireagency.com
5055 Keller Springs Road, Suite 510
Addison, TX 75001
United States
Tel +1 214 393 5200
kimberly.tyner@spireagency.com

Steiner Graphics
www.renesteiner.com
155 Dalhousie St., Suite 1062
Toronto, ON M5B 2P7
Canada
Tel +1 416 792 6969
rene@steinergraphics.com

Still Room
www.still-room.com
2169 Lemoyne St.
Los Angeles, CA 90026
United States
Tel +1 213 453 0370
studio@still-room.com

Stranger & Stranger
www.strangerandstranger.com
68 Greenpoint Ave., Suite 3
Brooklyn, NY 11222
United States
Tel +1 212 625 2441
nyc@strangerandstranger.com

Studio 5 Designs Inc. (Manila)
www.studio5designsph.com
Unit 3022, Beacon Residences, Tower 3
Chino Roces Ave., Legaspi Village Makati City 1229
The Philippines
Tel +63 917 885 5507
marilyo@yahoo.com

Studio A
www.studioa.com
1019 Queen St.
Alexandria, VA 22314
United States
Tel +1 703 684 7729
info@studioA.com

T9 Brand
www.t9branding.com
379 S. Pleasant Ave.
Ridgewood, NJ 07450
United States
Tel +1 929 522 9088
dawangsun@hotmail.com

Teiga, Studio.
www.xoseteiga.com
Avd. da Barca 18 Bajo Poio
Pontevedra 36163
Spain
Tel +34 607 155 211
xoseteiga@gmail.com

Test Monki
www.testmonki.com
10800 Gosling Road, #131898
Spring, TX 77393
United States
Tel +1 281 323 4903
suzy@testmonki.com

Tetsuro Minorikawa
www.minorikawa.net
Nagaoka Institute of Design
4-197 Senshu
Nagaoka Niigata 940-2088
Japan
Tel +81 90 5441 9646
info@minorikawa.net

Texas Tech University Press
www.ttupress.org
2310 70th St., Apt 244
Lubbock, TX 79412
United States
Tel +1 512 470 6235
hdgaskamp@gmail.com

The Narrative
www.thenarrative.design
4541 N Ravenswood, #101A
Chicago, IL 60640
United States
hello@thenarrative.design

The Property Agency
www.costadesign.net
Surry Hills, NSW
Australia
Tel +61 0401 511 383
costa.popolizio@gmail.com

The Rare Form
www.therareform.com
1683 Flat Shoals Road SE
Atlanta, GA 30316
United States
k@therareform.com

The Refinery
www.therefinerycreative.com
Sherman Oaks Galleria
15301 Ventura Blvd., Bldg D, Suite 300
Sherman Oaks, CA 91403
United States
Tel +1 818 843 0004
claire.delouraille@therefinercreative.com

The Republik
www.therepublik.net
1700 Glenwood Ave., Suite 200
Raleigh, NC 27608
United States
Tel +1 919 956 9400
mshapiro@therepublik.net

Tielemans Design
www.tielemansdesign.com
1535 Roughrider Circle
Henderson, NV 89014
United States
Tel +1 702.946.5511
anton@tielemansdesign.com

Toppan Inc.
www.toppan.com/en
9F, 1-3-3, Suido Bunkyo-ku
Tokyo 112-8531
Japan
Tel +81 3 5840 2192
mescal@mac.com

Traction Factory
www.tractionfactory.com
247 S. Water St.
Milwaukee, WI 53204
United States
Tel +1 414 944 0900
tf_awards@tractionfactory.com

Trill
www.markkrrowe.com
812 8th St. SE, Suite 208
Calgary, AB T2G 2Z2
Canada
mark@thevalleyyards.com

Truth Collective
www.truthcollective.com
25 Russell St.
Rochester, NY 14607
United States
Tel +1 585 685 8503
jeremy@truthcollective.com

Tsushima Design
www.tsushima-design.com
1-17-204, 1-17, Matsukawa-cho, Minami-ku
Hiroshima 7320826
Japan
Tel +81 82 567 5586
info@tsushima-design.com

Turner Duckworth: London, San Francisco & New York
www.turnerduckworth.com
375 Hudson St., 16th Floor
New York, NY
United States
Tel +1 212 463 2400
kate.bracero@turnerduckworth.com

Underline Studio
www.underlinestudio.com
247 Wallace Ave., 2nd Floor
Toronto, ON M6H 1V5
Canada
Tel +1 416 341 0475
kristin@underlinestudio.com

Univisual
www.identitymarks.it
Lombardia 20125
Milan
Italy
Tel +084 5467 0962
info@identitymarks.it

UP-Ideas
www.up-ideas.com
740 Ashley Laine Walk
Lawrenceville, GA 30043
United States
Tel +1 770 912 3120
roger.sawhill@gmail.com

Vanderbyl Design
www.vanderbyl.com
511 Tokay Lane
St. Helena, CA 94574
United States
Tel +1 415 543 8447
michael@vanderbyl.com

VSA Partners
www.vsapartners.com
600 W. Chicago Ave., Suite 250
Chicago, IL 60654
United States
Tel +1 312 427 6413
mward@vsapartners.com

Wainscot Media
www.mccandlissandcampbell.com
433 N. Windsor Ave.
Brightwaters, NY 11718
United States
Tel +1 631 252 3527
mcandcstudio@gmail.com

Wallace Church & Co.
www.wallacechurch.com
330 E. 48th St., 3rd Floor
New York, NY 10017
United States
Tel +1 212 755 2903
rich@wallacechurch.com

Warren Eakins Inc
www.warreneakins.com
107 University Place, #4F
New York, NY 10003
United States
Tel +1 646 321 3298
warren.eakins@gmail.com

What Studio
www.debbiemillman.com
New York, NY
United States
debbiemillman@gmail.com

WONGDOODY
www.wongdoody.com
1011 Western Ave., Suite 900
Seattle, WA 98104
United States
Tel +1 206 624 5325
awards@wongdoody.com

Xiaomi
www.mi.com
Anningzhuang Road
Haidian District, Beijing 100085
China
Tel +86 10 606 06666
chenlu@xiaomi.com

Yu Chen Design
www.saic.edu
School of the Art Institute of Chicago
36 S. Wabash Ave.
Chicago, IL 60603
United States
Tel +1 800 232 7242
ychen129@artic.edu

BEST IN THE AMERICAS

CANADA

UNITED STATES

BEST IN EUROPE/AFRICA

CROATIA

EGYPT

HUNGARY

ITALY

PORTUGAL

SPAIN

SWITZERLAND

UNITED KINGDOM

BEST IN ASIA/OCEANIA

AUSTRALIA

CHINA

HONG KONG

INDIA

JAPAN

MACAO

PHILIPPINES

SINGAPORE

SOUTH KOREA

TURKEY

Graphis Titles

Poster Annual 2023

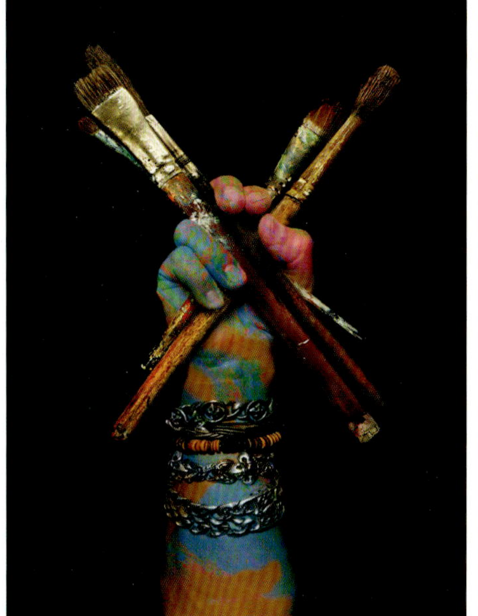

2022
Hardcover: 240 pages
200-plus color illustrations
Trim: 8.5 x 11.75"
ISBN: 978-1-954632-13-4
US $ 90

Awards: Graphis presents 14 Platinum, 88 Gold, and 226 Silver awards, along with 116 Honorable Mentions, to numerous poster designers from around the world who pushed what poster design can be with innovative, creative works.
Platinum Winners: Atelier Bundi AG, Carmit Design Studio, Dankook University, Fons Hickmann m23, João Machado Design, Ken-Tsai Lee Design Lab, LOGAN, Marcos Minini Design, Ron Taft Design, Ryan Slone Design, THERE IS Studio, Tsushima Design, Woosuk University, and Yossi Lemel.
Content: This book features international Platinum, Gold, and Silver-winning work. Honorable Mentions are also presented. Award-winning work from the judges and A Decade of Posters, featuring Platinum-winning works from 2013, is also included.

Packaging 10

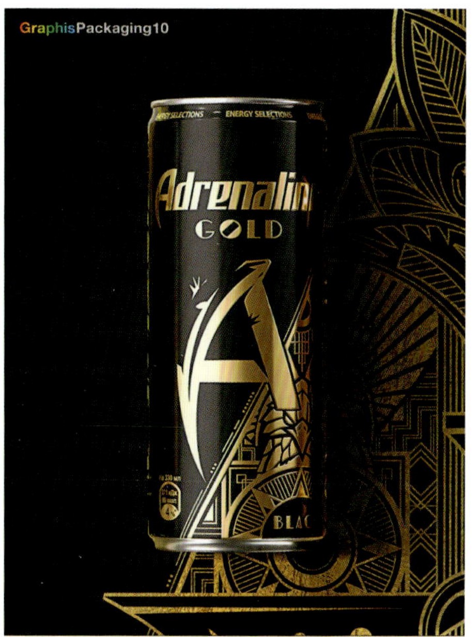

2022
Hardcover: 240 pages
200-plus color illustrations
Trim: 8.5 x 11.75"
ISBN: 978-1-954632-12-7
US $ 90

Awards: Graphis presents 12 Platinum, 100 Gold, 204 Silver, and 249 Honorable Mentions for innovative work in product packaging.
Platinum Winners: Michele Gomes Bush (Next), Chad Roberts (Chad Roberts Design Ltd.), XiongBo Deng (Shenzhen Lingyun Creative Packaging Design Co., Ltd.) and Lu Chen (Xiaomi), Vishal Vora (Sol Benito), Mattia Conconi (Gottschalk+Ash Int'l), and Frank Anselmo (New York Mets), Ivan Bell (Stranger & Stranger), Brian Steele (SLATE), and the team at PepsiCo Design & Innovation.
Content: This book contains award-winning packaging from the judges, as well as international Platinum, Gold, and Silver-winning packaging designs from designers and design firms from around the world. Honorable Mentions are presented, and a feature of award-winning work from our Packaging 9 Annual is also included.

New Talent Annual 2022

GraphisNewTalentAnnual2022

The talent is real. There is genuine gold in this work, and it is exciting to see the seeds of so many future careers.

2022
Hardcover: 272 pages
200-plus color illustrations
Trim: 8.5 x 11.75"
ISBN: 978-1-954632-08-0
US $ 90

Awards: Graphis presents 12 Platinum, 169 Gold, and 344 Silver awards to students who, with help from their professors, produced polished, highly professional works.
Platinum Winners: Platinum-winning instructors include Advertising: Rich Levy, Kevin O'Neill, and Mel White. Design: Elaine Alderette, Brad Bartlett, Eduard Čehovin, Elaine Cunfer, Annie Huang Luck, Theron Moore, Taylor Shipton, and Nancy Skolos and others listed in the book.
Content: This book contains award-winning entries in Advertising, Design, Photography, and Film/Video. We also present A Decade of New Talent, featuring Platinum-winning works from 2012. All entries are organized by discipline like our professional annuals.

Photography Annual 2022

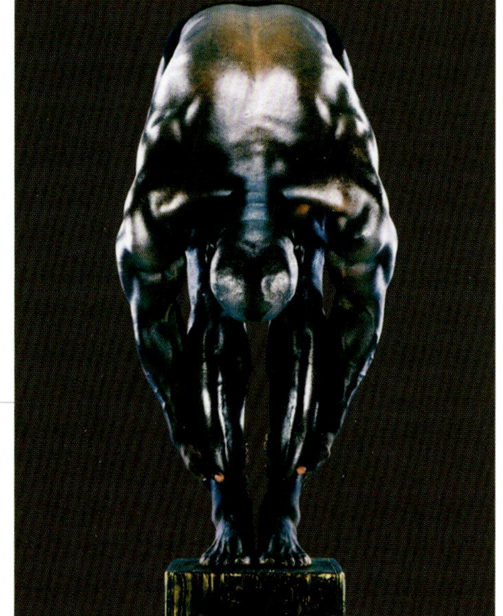

2021
Hardcover: 256 pages
200-plus color illustrations
Trim: 8.5 x 11.75"
ISBN: 978-1-954632-06-6
US $ 90

Awards: Graphis presents 11 Platinum, 103 Gold, 178 Silver awards, and 85 Honorable Mentions for outstanding talent in photography.
Platinum Winners: Stacey Brandford, Laurie Frankel, Beth Galton, Colin Douglas Gray, Takahiro Igarashi, Jonathan Knowles, Darnell McCown, Joseph Saraceno, Howard Schatz, Michael Schoenfeld, and Hadley Stambaugh.
Judges: Laurie Frankel, Beth Galton, Klaus Kampert, Henry Leutwyler, and John Madere.
Content: This year's Annual features exceptional work by our talented judges, our award winners, and our Honorable Mentions. Also included are a retrospective on our Platinum 2012 Photography winners, a list of international photography museums, and our In Memoriam list of talent that has left us over the past year.

Advertising Annual 2022

GraphisAdvertisingAnnual2022

This annual contains a fresh round of inspiration, and continues to set a high standard for creative excellence in advertising.

2021
Hardcover: 224 pages
200-plus color illustrations
Trim: 8.5 x 11.75"
ISBN: 978-1-954632-02-8
US $ 90

Awards: Graphis presents 15 Platinum, 111 Gold, 69 Silver, and 30 Honorable Mentions in this annual.
Platinum Winners: Presenting Platinum winners 360i, 72andSunny Los Angeles, ABC Made, AMPAS Creative, ARSONAL, Judd Brand Media, Lewis Communications, PETROL Advertising, Rhubarb, Ron Taft Design, teiga studio, Vanderbyl Design.
Judges: Kathy Delaney, Gary Mueller, Allen Oke, Xavier Rivera, Mitch Strausberg, and Carter Weitz.
Content: This Annual presents outstanding Platinum, Gold, and Silver Award-winning advertisements, as well as Honorable Mentions. Also featured is a selection of award-winning judge's work and our annual In Memoriam for the advertising talent we've lost the last year.

Protest Posters 2

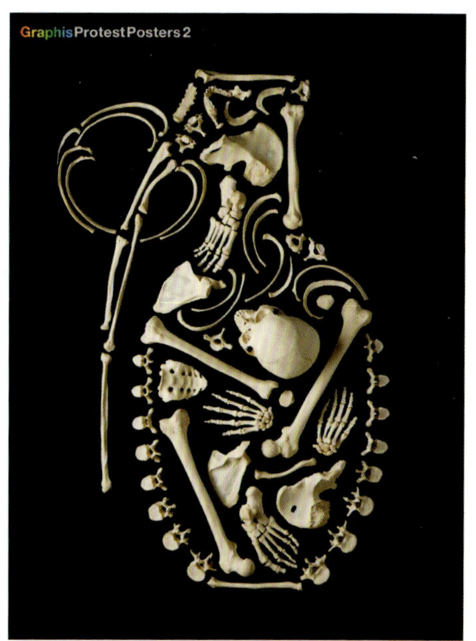

2021
Hardcover: 256 pages
200-plus color illustrations
Trim: 8.5 x 11.75"
ISBN: 978-1-954632-04-2
US $ 90

Awards: Graphis presents 12 Platinum, 137 Gold, 176 Silver awards, and 94 Honorable Mentions for outstanding talent in photography.
Platinum Winners: Presenting Platinum winners Alireza Nosrati Studio, Andrew Sloan, Dogan Arslan Design, IF Studio, Katarzyna Zapart, Marlena Buczek Smith, Randy Clark, Scott Laserow Posters, Wesam Haddad, and Yossi Lemel.
Judges: Andrea Castelletti, Paul Garbett, Wesam Mazhar Haddad, Woody Pirtle, and Marlena Buczek Smith, and Chikako Oguma.
Content: T his book is a source of inspiration with work from talented poster designers that addresses a diverse series of international issues going on in the world today.

Books are available at graphis.com/store

www.Graphis.com